BY THE EDITORS OF CONSUMER GUIDE®

Favorite Brand Name Recipe Cookbook

BEEKMAN HOUSE
New York

Copyright © 1981 by Publications International, Ltd.
All rights reserved. This book may not be reproduced or
quoted in whole or in part by mimeograph or any other
printed means or for presentation on radio or television
without written permission from:

Louis Weber, President
Publications International, Ltd.
3841 West Oakton Street
Skokie, Illinois 60076

Permission is never granted for commercial purposes.

Manufactured in the United States of America
1 2 3 4 5 6 7 8 9 10

Library of Congress Catalog Card Number: 81-82230
ISBN: 0-517-346966

This edition published by:
Beekman House
Distributed by Crown Publishers, Inc.
One Park Avenue
New York, New York 10016

Cover Design: Frank E. Peiler
Cover Photography: Dave Jordano Photography Inc.

Introduction

You, the American consumer, made this great big *FAVORITE BRAND NAME RECIPE COOKBOOK* possible. How? You made it possible by taking certain recipes that first appeared on food product labels and making them part of the American cooking culture. This book is the largest compilation ever of brand name recipes. It contains twenty chapters with over 2,000 separate recipes and dozens of gorgeous color food photographs to tempt the taste buds. Look under chocolate chip cookies and you'll find not one but six different recipes: The Original Nestlé's Toll House® Cookies, Chocolatetown Cookies, Jumbo Oatmeal Chip Cookies, Chocolatey Chocolate Chip, Two-Tone Bites and Chocolate-Almond Honeys.

Clipping recipes from food labels has become a uniquely American cooking tradition. Over the years many recipes have been passed from one generation to another, often with the origin clouded in memory. One food editor working on this project was surprised to discover her mother's delicious Deviled Spread appetizer included in a file of King Oscar Sardine recipes. Her mother admitted she didn't know where she had gotten the recipe—she had been making it for so many years! Quality recipes that become family cooking treasures are the ones we have collected.

Leafing through these pages will bring back delicious memories. Some recipes date as far back as 1934, so lots of well-loved dishes are bound to be rediscovered in this collection. Never again will clipped recipes become lost, grease-splotched, or faded from frequent use. This volume will be a permanent reference for classic favorites like Traditional Chex® Party Mix, Underwood® Deviled Ham Stuffed Tomatoes, Campbell's Condensed Cream of Mushroom Best Ever Meatloaf, Pepperidge Farm® Old Fashioned Stuffing, Hellmann's® Chocolate Mayonnaise Cake and hundreds and hundreds more.

Selecting the Favorites

Choosing the recipes for this book was far from an easy task—in fact, it was a rather monumental one! Our editors, working closely with home economists from the major food companies, spent a year screening hundreds of thousands of recipes. Only by limiting the choices to the true favorites of the consumers could this huge list be whittled down to just over 2,000.

Because the food companies keep close tabs on consumer correspondence, the home economists were able to pinpoint the most popular, all-time favorites by the mail they received. Those are the recipes that have stood the test of time—the Brand Name favorites.

The recipes range in scope from gourmet style dishes such as Caviar-Stuffed Celery, Filet of Sole Veronique, and Chicken Cordon Bleu to family favorites like Lasagne, Tempting Tuna Bake, and Pot-Of-Luck Main Dish Soup.

Regional American favorites like Pennsylvania Dutch Pot Roast, Vermont Turkey Pie, and Creole Seafood Gumbo are included as well as International specialties such as Veal Parmigiana and Ginger Beef Stir-Fry.

Virtually every recipe category is represented: Soups, casseroles, salads, egg dishes, meats, fish and seafood, all types of desserts, and much, much more. You may be surprised to know that many of these same recipes have appeared, with only minor variations, in some very well-known cookbooks.

The recipes are reprinted exactly as they appeared on the labels so unless otherwise stated in the instructions, all indicated temperatures refer to Fahrenheit degrees.

How to Use This Cookbook
The Table of Contents

The book is divided into twenty chapters—from Appetizers and Dips to Alcoholic and Nonalcoholic Beverages. Most of the chapters have subheadings for easy reference: for example, the Poultry Chapter is divided into "Chicken," "Cornish Hens," "Turkey," and "Duck." All recipes of a type will be grouped together, such as Barbecued Chicken recipes, Fried Chicken recipes, etc.

The Index

In our research we found that consumers tend to remember the brand name or the main food ingredient of their "favorites" rather than the exact title of the recipe as it appeared on the label. So, recipes are listed in the index by brand name or under major food categories such as "Beef." Several of the chapters, like casseroles, meat, and the huge salad chapter, present a wealth of ideas for using up leftovers deliciously. So next year when you're stuck with the same old holiday turkey leftovers, just turn to Turkey and Chicken in the index and your problems will be solved with dozens of tempting recipe suggestions.

We didn't want to exclude anyone from the cooking fun, so for individuals with special dietary restrictions, we have included recipes that are low-calorie, low-cholesterol, and low-sodium. Microwave recipes are also featured.

Directory of Food Manufacturers

For the convenience of our readers we have included an address directory of all food manufacturers listed in the book (see Acknowledgments). Any questions or comments should be directed to the individual manufacturers for prompt attention.

CONSUMER GUIDE® wishes to thank all of the participating food companies for their excellent contributions; we believe this collection contains the best and most popular brand name recipes. Of course, by printing these recipes, CONSUMER GUIDE® is not endorsing particular brand name foods.

So there you have it—an easy-to-use, giant reference book of favorite brand name recipes—chosen by you, the consumer, over many years of fine cooking. We hope this book will keep you cooking for many more.

Appetizers

ANTIPASTO

1 small head cauliflower,
   separated into flowerets
1 green pepper, cut into strips
1 large carrot, cut into sticks
4 stalks celery, sliced
2 tomatoes, cut into eighths
1 jar (8 ounces) HEINZ Spiced
   Onions, drained
2 cloves garlic, minced
½ pound small button mushrooms
1 cup olive or salad oil
1¾ cups HEINZ Apple Cider or
   Wine Vinegar
⅓ cup granulated sugar
2 tablespoons HEINZ Mild Mustard
2 teaspoons salt
1 teaspoon oregano leaves
Anchovies
Olives

Combine first 6 ingredients in large
bowl. Sauté garlic and mushrooms
in oil until mushrooms are tender.
Add vinegar and next 4 ingredients;
pour over vegetables. Cover; chill
overnight, stirring occasionally.
Drain well; serve on lettuce-lined
platter. Garnish with anchovies,
ripe or stuffed olives.
Makes 10-12 servings (8 cups)

CAVIAR-STUFFED
CELERY

1 bunch celery
1 pkg. (8 oz.) cream cheese,
   softened
2 Tbsp. milk
1 Tbsp. chopped chives
2 Tbsp. chopped parsley
2 Tbsp. (1 oz.) ROMANOFF®
   Caviar*
Additional caviar for garnish

Trim and wash celery stalks. Cut to
make sixteen 2½ inch pieces. Mix
cheese with milk until smooth. Stir
in chives, parsley and caviar.
Spoon onto celery pieces. Cover.
Chill. Just before serving, garnish
with additional caviar.
Makes 16 pieces

*ROMANOFF® Red Lumpfish or
Salmon Caviar suggested.

YOGURT STUFFED
CELERY

1 bunch celery
2 cups DANNON® Plain Yogurt
½ cup mashed blue cheese
½ cup finely chopped chives
1 Tbsp. brandy
Salt to taste

Wash celery and cut into 2″
pieces. Combine yogurt, blue
cheese, chives and brandy. Chill
until hardened to spreading
consistency. Fill celery pieces and
serve cold.
*Makes filling for approximately 20
pieces*

VARIATION:

Put 2 cups of DANNON® Plain
Yogurt through a cheese cloth.
Drain for 24 hours. Mix "yogurt
cheese" remaining in cloth with
blue cheese, chives, brandy and
salt. Fill celery pieces and serve
cold.
*Makes filling for approximately 12
pieces*

CHEESEY CELERY
SNACK

Combine: ½ lb. grated CHEEZ-
OLA,® ¼ cup finely chopped ripe
olives, 2 tablespoons chopped
green pepper, dash of garlic
powder, ½ cup safflower
mayonnaise. Stuff celery stalks or
serve on crackers or bread.

EGG-AND-CAVIAR
SPREAD

8 hard-cooked eggs, chopped
¼ cup softened butter
2 tsp. prepared mustard
½ cup (4 oz.) ROMANOFF®
   Caviar*
3 Tbsp. lemon juice
1½ Tbsp. Worcestershire
4 Tbsp. mayonnaise for garnish
Rye bread slices

Combine eggs, butter, mustard and
two-thirds (about five tablespoons)
of the caviar with lemon juice and
Worcestershire, blending well.
Spoon into serving dish; cover and
keep cold at least one hour. Just
before serving, spread mayonnaise
over top. Garnish with remaining
caviar. Provide servers, so guest
may spread on rye bread slices.
Enough for 8

*ROMANOFF® Red Salmon Caviar
suggested.

YOGURT ANCHOVY EGG
SPREAD

6 hard boiled eggs, chopped
2 cups DANNON® Plain Yogurt
2 Tbsp. anchovy paste
¼ cup chopped scallions
12 olives, chopped
1 small dill pickle, chopped
Pepper to taste

In a bowl, mix eggs, yogurt,
anchovy paste and scallions, olives
and pickles. Season with pepper.
Chill until ready to serve. Garnish
with chopped chives. Serve spread
on brown bread or crackers.

THE FOOLER

2 cans KING OSCAR Sardines
1 medium onion, grated
½ apple, peeled and grated
2 Tbsp. vinegar
½ tsp. sugar
2 hard-cooked eggs, chopped

Combine all ingredients and mix thoroughly. Let stand in refrigerator until chilled. Use as hors d'oeuvre or in sandwiches.

BERTOLLI® MARINATED SHRIMP

1½ pounds cooked shrimp in shells
½ cup BERTOLLI® Olive Oil
¼ cup BERTOLLI® Red Wine Vinegar
2 tablespoons BERTOLLI® Spaghetti Sauce
2 tablespoons horseradish mustard
½ cup celery, minced
½ cup green onions, minced
½ cup drained capers
1 clove garlic, minced
1½ teaspoons paprika
½ teaspoon salt
Dash cayenne pepper
Shredded lettuce
Lemon wedges

Peel shrimp, leaving tails on. Mix remaining ingredients, except lettuce and lemon in medium bowl; stir in shrimp. Refrigerate covered 12 hours, stirring 2 or 3 times. Spoon onto lettuce-lined plate; garnish with lemon.
Makes 6-8 servings

MARINATED SHRIMP

1 can (4½ ounces) LOUISIANA BRAND Shrimp
½ cup any favorite oil and vinegar type dressing

Drain shrimp. Cover with dressing. Marinate in the refrigerator 2 hours or longer.

HOW TO SERVE THEM

1. As an appetizer before dinner . . . on shredded lettuce . . . atop tomato, cucumber, or avocado slices . . . with grapefruit sections, a little marinade drizzled over.

2. As party food with picks and plenty of crackers . . . on the plate with assorted fresh vegetable relishes . . . dotted on pizza snacks . . . broiled on bread rounds or crackers *under* dabs of melting cheese, especially blue . . . as "dunks" for cheese fondue right along *with* the bread cubes.

3. Tossed in mixed green salad . . . chef's salad with cheese, ham, or chicken . . . potato salad.

4. For family snacks . . . refrigerated. They keep *and* keep.

LIVERWURST SMORREBROD

1 can (4¾ ounces) UNDERWOOD® Liverwurst Spread
2 tablespoons mayonnaise
12 slices party rye bread
24 slices cherry tomato
12 slices cucumber
2 tablespoons chopped scallion

In a bowl, mix liverwurst spread and mayonnaise. Spread on party rye slices. Top with slices of cherry tomato, cucumber and chopped scallion.
Makes 12 snacks

(PARTY) TUNA MOLD

2 6½ oz. cans tuna
1 8 oz. package cream cheese, softened
2 Tbsp. minced onion
2 Tbsp. chopped parsley
1½ Tbsp. BALTIMORE SPICE OLD BAY Seasoning
1½ Tbsp. catsup
½ Tbsp. prepared horseradish

Drain tuna. Mix together remaining ingredients. Add tuna and beat until well blended. Pack into 4 cup mold or small bowl; chill thoroughly. To serve, unmold onto a plate, garnish with parsley and/or olives and serve with crackers.

BRAUNSCHWEIGER RING

1 package (3 oz.) lemon gelatin
¾ cup boiling water
1 can (8 oz.) tomato sauce
1 tablespoon vinegar
½ teaspoon salt
1 package (1 lb.) OSCAR MAYER Braunschweiger Liver Sausage

Add gelatin to boiling water; stir until dissolved. Mix in tomato sauce, vinegar and salt. Chill until slightly thickened. Gradually add to liver sausage and blend well. Pour into lightly oiled 1 quart mold. Chill thoroughly. Unmold on serving plate. Garnish with hard-boiled egg (finely chop egg white and sieve egg yolk). Serve as a spread with crackers.

KASHA TABBOULI

1 cup cooked WOLFF'S® Kasha* (buckwheat groats) (whole, coarse, or medium)
⅓ cup chopped green onions
About 15 fresh mint leaves, chopped
¼ cup chopped parsley
1 large tomato, seeded and chopped
Salt to taste
1 Tbsp. lemon juice
Red wine vinegar & oil dressing
Romaine leaves

Tabbouli is best prepared with kasha that has been cooked in chicken broth. Combine all ingredients, using sufficient salad dressing to moisten kasha (about 3-4 Tbsp.). Chill for at least 2 hours before serving. Place tabbouli in center of plate, surround it with romaine leaves to be used as "scoops" to eat this tangy appetizer. (If available, a food processor speeds preparation).
Serves 4-5 as hors d'oeuvre or 2-3 as salad course

*To cook WOLFF'S® Kasha:

1 cup uncooked WOLFF'S® Kasha
1 egg, slightly beaten
2 cups boiling liquid (water is O.K., but broth, consomme or bouillon is better)
1 tsp. salt**
¼ tsp. pepper
2 Tbsp. butter or margarine (optional)

In two-quart saucepan or skillet, combine kasha, egg, and seasonings. Stir constantly over medium heat for about two minutes or until the egg is "set" and each grain is separate and dry. Add boiling liquid, cover pan tightly, and cook gently over low heat for 15 minutes or until kasha grains are tender. If desired, stir in butter or margarine.
Makes about 3 cups

**Use less if broth is highly seasoned.

CHERRY HAM CANAPÉS

1 package (3 oz.) cream cheese, softened
1 tablespoon orange juice
½ teaspoon grated orange peel
2 tablespoons finely chopped walnuts
16 slices party rye bread
4 slices (4 oz.) thinly sliced ham
16 Northwest fresh sweet cherries, pitted

Combine cream cheese, orange juice and peel, and walnuts. Spread about ½ tablespoon of the cheese mixture on each slice of bread. Cut each slice of ham into 4 triangles; place one triangle on top of cream cheese mixture. Top each canapé with a pitted cherry, secured with a toothpick.
Makes 16 canapés

Recipe from Northwest Cherry Growers

STUFFED EGGS
(Uova Torino)

10 hardboiled eggs, shelled
½ cup mayonnaise
1 teaspoon prepared hot mustard
Dash TABASCO® Sauce
1 tablespoon LIQUORE GALLIANO®
Red caviar
Green pepper strips

Halve eggs lengthwise and remove yolks. Mash or sieve yolks, mix in mayonnaise, mustard, TABASCO® and LIQUORE GALLIANO®. Blend until very smooth. Press yolk mixture through pastry bag into egg white halves. Garnish with red caviar and pepper strips. Chill.
Makes 20

Lea & Perrins
THE ORIGINAL WORCESTERSHIRE

DEVILISH EGGS*

6 hard-cooked eggs, halved
3 tablespoons mayonnaise
1 tablespoon LEA & PERRINS Worcestershire Sauce
½ teaspoon onion powder
Dash TABASCO® Sauce
2 tablespoons finely chopped nuts

Remove yolks from whites, being careful not to break egg whites; set whites aside. In a small bowl mash egg yolks. Add mayonnaise, LEA & PERRINS, onion powder and TABASCO®; mix well. Mound mixture into egg whites using a spoon or pastry bag fitted with a tube. Garnish with chopped nuts.
Yield: 12 stuffed egg halves

*May be prepared in advance of serving.

TUNA STUFFED TOMATOES
(Low Calorie)

1 can (6½ oz.) BUMBLE BEE® Chunk Light Tuna in Water
½ cup chopped celery
⅓ cup imitation or low calorie mayonnaise
¼ cup chopped parsley
2 tablespoons minced green onion
¼ teaspoon black pepper
36 cherry tomatoes
Parsley sprigs for garnish

Drain tuna. Combine tuna, celery, mayonnaise, chopped parsley, green onion and pepper. Cut tops off tomatoes and scoop out seeds; turn upside down to drain. Fill with tuna salad. Serve chilled on parsley lined plate.
Makes 36 appetizers
21 calories per appetizer

MARINATED VEGETABLE HORS D'OEUVRES

1 small cauliflower, broken into flowerets
2 green peppers, cut into ½-inch strips
½ pound small mushroom caps
5¼ ounce can black pitted olives, drained
4½ ounce jar white cocktail onions, drained
¾ cup olive oil
¼ cup salad oil
¼ cup MINUTE MAID® 100% Pure Lemon Juice
1¼ cups white wine vinegar
¼ cup sugar
2 teaspoons salt
¾ teaspoon ground pepper
1 clove garlic, minced

Mix vegetables together in a shallow dish. Bring remaining ingredients to a boil, cook five minutes and pour over vegetables. Cover and marinate for 24 hours in the refrigerator. Drain and serve with toothpicks.

AYRSHIRE CHEDDAR SPREAD

½ lb. Cheddar cheese (or other medium-sharp, firm cheese)
3 oz. cream cheese, softened
3 tablespoons JOHNNIE WALKER Red
⅛ teaspoon salt
⅛ teaspoon pepper
2 teaspoons chopped chives

Grate cheese and mix with other ingredients until well combined. Refrigerate several hours to mellow. Serve with tray of assorted crackers, rye-crisp and dark bread, as a cocktail accompaniment.
About 1½ cups

Note: Mixture spreads more easily at room temperature.

SMOKY CHEESE SPREAD

4 oz. Cheddar cheese, grated
1 8 oz. pkg. cream cheese
1 3 oz. wedge Roquefort cheese (optional)
1 teaspoon WRIGHT'S Natural Hickory Liquid Smoke
Chopped parsley or chopped pecans

Bring cheeses to room temperature. Mix all ingredients, except parsley or pecans, in electric mixer or food processor. Shape into ball if desired, roll in parsley or pecans. Chill. Serve with assorted crackers.

COTTAGE CHEESE NUT RING

2 pounds cottage cheese
½ cup PLANTERS® Dry Roasted Mixed Nuts
1 teaspoon curry powder

Combine cottage cheese, PLANTERS® Dry Roasted Mixed Nuts and curry powder; beat until thoroughly blended. Place cheese mixture in a greased 9-inch ring mold. Chill until firm (about 2 hours). Unmold and serve with sliced fresh fruit.
Makes 6 servings

HAM AND CHEESE-CHIP PINWHEEL

3-ounce package cream cheese
2 tablespoons mayonnaise
½ teaspoon prepared mustard
2 teaspoons horseradish
⅓ cup chopped stuffed olives
¼ teaspoon paprika
1 teaspoon grated onion
⅔ cup finely crushed JAYS Potato Chips
6 thin slices boiled ham

Combine and blend all ingredients except ham. Spread mixture on ham slices. Roll each edge lengthwise and fasten with small wooden picks. Chill. Cut rolled ham crosswise into thin slices. Serve with potato chips.

ALMOND CHEESE PINECONE

2 packages (8 ounces *each*) cream cheese, softened
2 jars (5 ounces *each*) pasteurized process cheese spread with pimiento
½ pound blue cheese, crumbled
¼ cup minced green onion
½ teaspoon Worcestershire sauce
2 cups BLUE DIAMOND® Blanched Whole Almonds, toasted
Pine sprigs for garnish
Crackers

In large bowl with mixer at medium speed, beat cream cheese, cheese spread with pimiento and blue cheese until smooth. With spoon, stir in green onions and Worcestershire sauce. Cover and refrigerate about one hour. On work surface, with hands, shape cheese mixture into shape of large pinecone. Arrange on wooden board. Beginning at narrow end of cone, carefully press almonds about ¼ inch deep into cheese mixture in rows, making sure that pointed end of each almond extends at a slight angle. Continue pressing almonds into cheese mixture in rows, with rows slightly overlapping, until all cheese is covered. Garnish pinecone with pine sprigs. Serve with crackers.

Makes about 25 servings

COCKTAIL PARTY BALL

1 pound shredded FINLANDIA Swiss
¼ pound Roquefort or Blue cheese, crumbled
1 package (8 ounces) cream cheese
1 tablespoon grated onion
2 teaspoons Worcestershire sauce
Dash cayenne pepper
½ cup chopped toasted pecans
½ cup finely chopped parsley

Bring cheeses to room temperature. Place in electric mixer and blend well. Add onion, Worcestershire sauce and cayenne pepper. Shape into ball, wrap in waxed paper or plastic wrap. Chill several hours. Just before serving combine pecans and parsley. Roll ball in mixture. Serve with crackers.

Makes 8 to 10 servings

CHEESY CORN SPREAD

12 oz. (3 cups) shredded sharp Cheddar cheese
½ cup dairy sour cream
½ cup salad dressing or mayonnaise
¼ cup finely chopped onion
½ teaspoon salt
12-oz. can GREEN GIANT® MEXICORN® Golden Whole Kernel Corn with Sweet Peppers, drained

Bring cheese to room temperature. In large bowl, crumble cheese with fork or blend with mixer to form small bits. Mix in remaining ingredients, except corn, until well blended. Stir in corn. Cover; chill several hours or overnight. Can be stored in the refrigerator up to 1 week. Serve with raw vegetables or crackers.   *3½ cups*

High Altitude—Above 3500 Feet: No change.

NUTRITIONAL INFORMATION PER SERVING

SERVING SIZE: 1 Tablespoon		PERCENT U.S. RDA PER SERVING	
Calories	40	Protein	3
Protein	2 g	Vitamin A	2
Carbohydrate	2 g	Vitamin C	*
Fat	3 g	Thiamine	*
Sodium	95 mg	Riboflavin	2
Potassium	15 mg	Niacin	*
		Calcium	5
		Iron	*

*Contains less than 2% of the U.S. RDA of this nutrient.

CHIP CHEESE BALLS

3-ounce package cream cheese
½ cup grated raw carrot
½ cup finely crushed JAYS Potato Chips
Chopped parsley

Soften cream cheese and mix with carrot and potato chips. Shape into balls about an inch in diameter. Roll in parsley. Chill and serve.

FRUIT CHEESE LOG

½ cup DEL MONTE Dried Apricots
1 cup water
1 lb. Monterey Jack cheese, shredded
1 pkg. (8 oz.) cream cheese, softened
⅓ cup milk*
1 tsp. poppy seed
½ tsp. seasoned salt
⅓ cup DEL MONTE Golden Seedless Raisins
¼ cup pitted dates, snipped
¾ cup chopped walnuts
Crackers

Soak apricots in water two hours; drain and chop. Blend cheeses. Add milk, poppy seed and salt; mix well. Fold in fruit; mix well. Turn out on foil; shape into log-type roll. Wrap securely in foil; chill until firm. Roll in nuts before serving. Serve with crackers.

1 log (approximately 2 lbs.)

*VARIATION:

Substitute ⅓ cup sherry for milk.

ARNOLD SORENSIN SPRATT SPREAD

2 cans of ARNOLD SORENSIN Spratts
8 oz. of cream cheese, softened

Just drain the oil from the Spratts and blend the two ingredients together in a food processor or with a fork. Refrigerate for a few hours. Serve with melba toast, crackers or on bread of your choice.

"PHILLY" CHEESE BELL

1 8-oz. pkg. CRACKER BARREL Brand Sharp Cheddar Flavor Cold Pack Cheese Food
1 8-oz. pkg. PHILADELPHIA BRAND Cream Cheese
PARKAY Margarine
2 teaspoons chopped pimiento
2 teaspoons chopped green pepper
2 teaspoons chopped onion
1 teaspoon Worcestershire sauce
½ teaspoon lemon juice

Combine cold pack cheese food, softened cream cheese and 2 tablespoons margarine; mix until well blended. Add remaining ingredients; mix well. Mold into bell shapes, using the cold pack container coated with margarine or lined with plastic wrap. Chill until firm; unmold. Garnish with chopped parsley and pimiento strips, if desired.   *2 bells*

OLIVE LOAF CORNUCOPIA

Cut slices of ECKRICH® Olive Loaf in half. Spread with Mustard Spread.* Roll to form small cornucopias. Fill opening with additional Mustard Spread. Place cornucopias on slices of buttered cocktail rye bread.
Makes 16 servings

*MUSTARD SPREAD

¼ cup butter, softened
6 ounces cream cheese, softened
3 Tbsp. mayonnaise
2½ tsp. prepared mustard
1 tsp. sugar

In electric mixer, cream butter and cheese until light and fluffy. Blend in remaining ingredients.
Makes one cup

SMOKY PIMIENTO CHEESE BALL

One 8-oz. container WISPRIDE Hickory Smoked Cold Pack Cheese Food, softened
One 8-oz. package cream cheese, softened
¼ cup bacon crumbs (4 strips, cooked and crumbled)
1 tablespoon chopped pimiento
1 teaspoon Worcestershire sauce
½ teaspoon lemon juice
½ cup finely chopped pecans

In small bowl, combine WISPRIDE and cream cheese; beat until smooth and creamy. Add bacon, pimiento, Worcestershire sauce and lemon juice; mix well. Chill in refrigerator until pliable (about 1 hour). With spatula or wooden spoon, shape into a ball. Roll in pecans.   *Makes one cheese ball*

CAVIAR "PIE"

6 hard-cooked eggs, chopped
3 Tbsp. mayonnaise
1 large sweet onion, finely chopped (1½ cups)
1 pkg. (8 oz.) cream cheese, softened
⅔ cup sour cream
7 Tbsp. (3½ oz.) ROMANOFF® Caviar*
Lemon wedges and parsley sprigs for garnish

Grease bottom and side of eight-inch springform pan. In a bowl, combine eggs and mayonnaise until well blended. Spread in bottom of pan to make an even layer. Sprinkle with onion. Combine cream cheese and sour cream; beat until smooth. By the spoonful, drop onto onion. With a wet table knife, spread gently to smooth. Cover. Chill three hours or overnight. At party time, top with a layer of caviar, distributing it to the edges of the pan. Run knife around sides of pan; loosen and lift off sides. Arrange lemon wedges in open pinwheel. Fill center with parsley sprigs. Serve with small pieces of pumpernickel bread.
Makes 10 to 12 servings

*ROMANOFF® Black Lumpfish or Whitefish Caviar suggested.

LIVER SPREAD

1 package (3 oz.) cream cheese
1 tablespoon melted butter
1 jar (3½ oz.) GERBER® Strained Beef Liver
1 jar (3½ oz.) GERBER® Strained Chicken
1 teaspoon wine vinegar
½ teaspoon onion powder
¼ teaspoon ground mace
¼ teaspoon celery salt
⅛ teaspoon powdered basil leaves
⅛ teaspoon ground allspice
¼ teaspoon salt

Soften cream cheese with melted butter. Add other ingredients and blend well. Pack into small containers. Cover and chill well before serving.
Yield: Approximately 1 cup

CHAMPIGNON CHICKEN PÂTÉ

1 can (5 ounces) SWANSON Chunk Chicken
1 can (about 2 ounces) mushrooms, drained and chopped
2 tablespoons mayonnaise
2 tablespoons finely chopped onion
1 tablespoon finely chopped parsley
2 teaspoons Worcestershire

Combine ingredients; chill. Serve on crackers.
Makes about 1 cup

CHICKEN LIVER PÂTÉ

½ pound butter (2 sticks)
1 small yellow onion, thinly sliced
1 teaspoon curry powder
1 teaspoon salt
⅛ teaspoon paprika
Pepper
1 pound chicken livers
2 tablespoons JACQUIN'S Brandy

Melt half the butter (1 stick) in a heavy skillet. Add the onion and cook over low heat until onion is soft but not brown, about 10 minutes. With a slotted spoon, remove onion and put in blender jar. Stir curry powder, salt, paprika and a dash of pepper into the butter. Add chicken livers, a single layer at a time, and brown lightly on both sides. Remove from skillet and set aside. Add remaining butter (1 stick) to skillet, stirring as it melts to dissolve any glaze. Add brandy. Pour part of the butter into the blender jar with the onion, add a few of the livers, and blend until smooth. Gradually add remaining livers and butter, blending until smooth. (If you don't have a blender, the ingredients can be pushed through a sieve, but it's difficult and the pâté will be less smooth.) Pack the mixture into a 3-cup mold or loaf pan that has been rinsed in cold water. Chill until firm, about 2 or 3 hours. To serve, unmold on a platter and surround with crisp crackers.

PICNIC PÂTÉ

¼ cup butter
1½ lb. chicken livers
1 tsp. garlic salt
1 small onion, finely chopped
¾ cup THE CHRISTIAN BROTHERS® Riesling
1 Tbsp. Worcestershire sauce
2 hard-cooked eggs
4 drops TABASCO® Sauce
½ cup soft butter

Sauté livers, garlic salt, and onion in ¼ cup butter for 5 minutes; add wine and Worcestershire sauce; simmer 5 minutes longer. Cool, then whirl smooth in blender or food processor with eggs. Blend in TABASCO® and butter. Turn into serving dish; cover and chill overnight.   *4 cups*

NATURALLY NUTTY PÂTÉ
(Low Sodium/Low Calorie)

⅓ cup uncooked brown rice
Boiling water
2 tablespoons FLEISCHMANN'S® Unsalted Margarine
2 cups sliced fresh mushrooms
1 cup grated zucchini
½ cup chopped onion
½ teaspoon crushed fresh garlic
1 egg
1¾ cups ground PLANTERS® Dry Roasted Unsalted Mixed Nuts
½ cup minced fresh parsley
¼ cup wheat germ
1 teaspoon sage
1 teaspoon basil
½ teaspoon thyme
½ teaspoon tarragon
⅛ teaspoon ground black pepper

Prepare rice in boiling water according to package directions eliminating salt.

Melt FLEISCHMANN'S® Unsalted Margarine in a large skillet over medium heat. Add mushrooms, zucchini, onion and garlic; sauté until tender but not browned. Puree sautéed vegetables in blender or food processor; transfer to a mixing bowl. Place prepared rice and egg in blender or processor and blend until smooth. Add to vegetable mixture with remaining ingredients. Mix thoroughly. Spread into a greased 9 × 5 × 3-inch loaf pan. Bake at 375°F. for 25 to 30 minutes, or until golden around edges. Cool 30 minutes. Loosen edges with knife. Remove and cool

on wire rack. Wrap and refrigerate until ready to serve.
Makes 1 loaf (9 × 5 × 2-inches)

Per serving (¼ inch slice): 50 calories, 4 mg. sodium

TERIYAKI TIDBITS

14 COOKIN' GOOD Chicken Wings (about 3 lbs.)

Marinade:
1 cup teriyaki sauce
½ cup molasses
½ cup lemon or lime juice
¼ cup honey
1 teaspoon of garlic powder or 1 clove fresh garlic crushed
¼ cup instant onions minced
1 cup vegetable oil
1 cup white wine
1 teaspoon paprika
Dipping sauce*

Disjoint wings, reserve tips for stock. In a large glass bowl, combine marinade ingredients. Add wing pieces and marinate at least four hours (preferably overnight).

Conventional oven instructions:
Preheat oven to 400 degrees. Drain marinade and reserve for basting and sauce recipe. Place wing pieces in a single layer in a shallow baking dish. Roast 35-45 minutes, basting often with marinade, until crisp and brown.

Microwave instructions: Same as above except use a microwave baking dish. Microwave 12-15 minutes. Baste and stir pieces often. Crisp under browning unit or conventional broiler.

Conventional oven: bake at 400 degrees; 35-40 minutes

Microwave oven: 12-15 minutes, full power, 650 watts

*DIPPING SAUCE

2 teaspoons of cornstarch
1 cup of Marinade

Blend marinade and cornstarch together in a saucepan (without heat). Stirring constantly, bring the mixture to a boil over a medium heat until thick and bubbly. Serve this sauce with the Teriyaki Tidbits.

HOT ORIENTAL CHICKEN WING APPETIZERS

1 package (27 oz.) BANQUET® Heat and Serve Frozen Fully Cooked Fried Chicken Wing Portions
¼ cup soy sauce
¼ teaspoon cayenne pepper

1. Place frozen chicken wing portions on cookie sheet.

2. Combine soy sauce and cayenne. Brush over chicken wing portions.

3. Bake in 375°F oven for 25 minutes. Serve hot.
Makes about 25 appetizers

ZING WINGS

2½ pounds chicken wings
6 tablespoons DURKEE RedHot! Sauce
¼ cup butter or margarine, melted

Split chicken wings at each joint and discard tips; pat dry. Deep fry at 400° (high) for 12 minutes or until crispy. Remove and drain well. (Can also be baked on a rack in a 400° oven for 25 minutes.) Combine hot sauce and butter. Dip chicken wings in sauce.
Makes 6 to 8 appetizer servings

CURRIED ALMOND CHICKEN BALLS

½ cup BLUE DIAMOND® Chopped Natural Almonds, toasted
1 can (6½ ounces) boned chicken
1 package (3 ounces) cream cheese, softened
2 tablespoons chutney, chopped
1 teaspoon curry powder
Salt and pepper
Minced parsley

Finely chop almonds; set aside. In small bowl, mix together chicken and cream cheese, breaking up any large chunks of chicken. Add chutney, curry powder and almonds; mix until well-blended; salt and pepper to taste. Chill until mixture is firm, about one hour. Shape into 1-inch balls and roll in minced parsley. Chill until ready to serve.
Makes about 24 (1-inch) balls

BACON CHEESE NIBBLES

3 tablespoons FRENCH'S®
   Sesame Seed
1 envelope (5 servings) FRENCH'S®
   Idaho Mashed Potato Granules
1 egg, slightly beaten
¼ cup mayonnaise
½ cup shredded Cheddar cheese
5 to 6 slices bacon, crisply cooked
   and crumbled
FRENCH'S® Paprika

Spread sesame seed in shallow pan. Toast in 350° oven 5 to 8 minutes, stirring occasionally, until golden brown. Prepare mashed potatoes following directions on package, except decrease water to ⅔ cup. (Potatoes will be very stiff.) Stir in egg, mayonnaise, cheese, and the crumbled bacon. Shape into small balls, using a rounded teaspoonful for each. Roll in toasted sesame seed; sprinkle with paprika. Arrange on greased baking sheet. Bake in 400° oven 10 to 15 minutes, until golden brown. Serve hot as hors d'oeuvres.

4 to 5 dozen

Crunchy Ham Nibbles: Omit bacon and cheese. Stir in 1 cup very finely diced ham, ¼ cup each very finely diced celery and pickle. Shape, roll in sesame seed, and bake as directed above.

PERNOD®
DANGEROUSLY DELICIOUS
OYSTERS ROCKEFELLER

Rock salt
¾ cup butter (1½ sticks)
3 tablespoons minced green onion
3 tablespoons minced parsley
½ cup bread crumbs
1½ cups chopped raw spinach
2 tablespoons PERNOD
1 teaspoon celery powder
2 teaspoons lemon juice
¼ teaspoon cayenne
24 bacon pieces (1 inch)
24 oysters on the half shell

Preheat oven to 425°F. Fill 6 pie plates (8 inch) with rock salt. Place oysters in shell on rock salt. Heat ¼ cup butter in heavy skillet until foaming; add minced onion and cook slowly until soft. Stir in parsley, bread crumbs, spinach, PERNOD, celery powder, lemon juice, and cayenne. Add remaining

butter and mix thoroughly. Spoon mixture onto oysters by ½ teaspoonfuls, distributing evenly. Top each oyster with bacon piece. Place pans in oven and bake 8-10 minutes or until bacon is crisp-tender. Remove from oven and serve directly from pans (rock salt keeps oyster shells from tipping).

To serve canapés without shells or forks: Remove oysters from shells and place on crisp toast rounds, or in individual, oven-proof butter crocks; process as directed above.

Makes 24

OYSTERS BROCHETTE

1 can (8-oz.) HIGH SEA Oysters
6 slices of bacon
1 box round toothpicks

Drain can of oysters, discarding liquid. Cut bacon into smaller slices, sufficient to just wrap whole oysters, skewering with toothpicks. Place under broiler with a medium flame (about 350°) until bacon is cooked. Serve as hors d'oeuvre.

BAKED CLAMS ITALIANO

1 (10½ ounce) can minced clams
2 tablespoons olive oil
1 tablespoon grated onion
1 tablespoon minced parsley
⅛ teaspoon oregano
¼ cup plus 2 tablespoons
   crumbled HI HO® Crackers
1 teaspoon garlic salt
2 tablespoons grated Parmesan
   cheese

Drain clams and reserve 3 tablespoons broth. Heat olive oil in small frying pan. Sauté onion, parsley, oregano and ¼ cup crumbled crackers for 2 minutes, or until onion is golden. Remove from heat and mix with clams, 3 tablespoons broth, and garlic salt. Spoon into a dozen clam or aluminum shells. Sprinkle lightly with a mixture made of 2 tablespoons Parmesan cheese and 2 tablespoons cracker crumbs. On baking sheet, bake in 375°F. oven for 25 minutes, or until crusty on top. *Yield: 6 servings*

EASY DANISH CHEESE FONDUE

1½ cups dry white wine, or
   1 can (12 ounce) beer
1 clove garlic
4 cups shredded Danish Cheese*
   (combine 2 varieties)
2 Tbsp. cornstarch
1 Tbsp. brandy or akvavit
Dash of white pepper and nutmeg
¼ teaspoon baking soda

Pour wine or beer into a 2-quart saucepan. Add garlic. Heat gently until bubbles start to rise. Discard garlic. Toss cheese with cornstarch. Add the cheese by thirds to saucepan, stirring gently until all cheese is melted. Add brandy and spices. Just before serving, stir in baking soda.

Makes four to six servings

Along with chunks of French bread, offer fresh mushrooms, celery chunks, partly cooked zucchini, broccoli or asparagus, apple wedges, bites of cooked chicken, ham or shrimp for dipping into the savory cheese fondue.

*Mild Danish Cheeses: Tybo, Danbo, Samsoe, Svenbo, Creamy Havarti (Havarti Mild) or Danish Fontina
*Full Flavored Danish Cheeses: Esrom or Havarti

Favorite recipe from Denmark Cheese Association

BLUE CHEESE FONDUE

4-ounce package TREASURE
   CAVE® Blue Cheese, crumbled
½ cup dry white wine
8 ounces cream cheese, cubed
8 ounces Monterey Jack cheese,
   cubed
1 tablespoon kirsch (cherry brandy)

Heat wine and cream cheese, stirring, until cheese melts. Add Monterey Jack cheese, a little at a time, stirring constantly. Blend in blue cheese. When smooth, add kirsch. Serve with dippers of French bread, fresh fruit or vegetables. *Yield: 5 cups*

SWISS FONDUE

1 Tbsp. flour
1½ cups VIRGINIA DARE White Cooking Wine
Half clove garlic
¾ lb. grated Swiss Cheese
Dash of pepper
Loaf of French bread

Stir flour vigorously into about ¼ cup cold VIRGINIA DARE White Cooking Wine; then add to remainder of wine in a fondue cooker or double boiler which has been rubbed with a cut clove of garlic. Heat to just below boiling. Slowly add cheese, stirring constantly. Continue stirring to a smooth consistency and add pepper to taste. Using long handled forks, spear bite-size pieces of French bread and dip into the fondue coating the bread chunk completely. If the fondue becomes too thick through prolonged cooking, it may be thinned with the addition of a little more cooking wine.

Yield: 4 servings

CHEESE 'N MUSHROOM BALLS

4 ounce package TREASURE CAVE® Blue Cheese, crumbled
Shortening for frying
3 cups fresh bread crumbs*
2½ ounce jar mushrooms, drained and chopped
2 tablespoons chopped green onion
½ teaspoon savory
¼ teaspoon pepper
2 eggs, slightly beaten

Heat shortening to 350°F. Combine cheese, 2 cups crumbs, mushrooms, onion, savory and pepper. Fold in eggs. Let stand 10 minutes. Shape into balls, using rounded teaspoon for each. Roll in remaining crumbs. Deep-fat fry about 1½ minutes or until golden brown.

Yield: About 2½ dozen

*To make bread crumbs, put day-old bread in blender or rub bread with spoon through strainer.

Tip: The balls may be frozen before frying. When ready to serve, deep-fat fry 5 minutes.

DEEPFRIED DANISH CAMEMBERT CHEESE

Danish Camembert Cheese (fresh or canned)
Flour
Eggs
Bread crumbs
Oil

The cheese must be cold. Cut Camembert into small wedges. Lightly coat wedges in flour. Dip each wedge in slightly beaten eggs and coat in fine bread crumbs, then refrigerate. You can prepare the Camembert cheese several hours before frying. Fry cheese until golden in 1½ inches very hot salad oil about 1½ minutes; drain briefly on paper towels. Serve hot with toast and your favorite jam.

Favorite recipe from Denmark Cheese Association

MINI SWISS QUICHES

1 11 oz. pkg. piecrust mix
4 slices bacon, diced
½ cup chopped green onion
3 large eggs
½ tsp. salt
⅛ tsp. each pepper and nutmeg
⅔ cup THE CHRISTIAN BROTHERS® Chablis or Chenin Blanc
1½ cups shredded Swiss cheese, tossed with 1 Tbsp. flour

Prepare piecrust mix according to package directions. Roll out pastry, half at a time, to about ¹⁄₁₆ inch thick; cut into 3 inch rounds and line muffin cups. Cook bacon until crisp; drain. Reserve 1 Tbsp. drippings. Cook onion in bacon drippings until soft. Beat eggs; mix in seasonings, wine, onion and bacon. Divide cheese mixture among lined pans and spoon egg mixture into each. Bake at 450 degrees, 10 minutes. Reduce temperature to 350 degrees and continue baking about 12 minutes until quiches are puffed and golden brown. Cool on a rack.

16 quiches

ALMOND-SAUSAGE CHEESE TARTS

Pastry:
1 cup butter or margarine, softened
1 package (8 ounces) cream cheese, softened
1 tablespoon chopped chives
1 teaspoon salt
3 cups sifted all-purpose flour

In medium-size bowl cream butter, cream cheese, chives and salt. Work in flour with a fork or pastry blender. Divide dough in half; shape into balls, wrap in waxed paper and refrigerate one hour. Roll each ball on sheet of aluminum foil into 12 × 15-inch rectangle, about ⅛-inch thick. Cut pastry and foil together with scissors into 1½ × 3-inch rectangles. Moisten ends with water; pinch together; spread out slightly into canoe-shape. Prick pastry well with fork to keep its shape. Place on cookie sheet. Bake in 400 degree F. oven 12 to 15 minutes or until golden. Remove foil. Prepare Almond-Sausage Filling*. Baked pastries may be wrapped and frozen, unfilled, up to 2 weeks. *Makes about 7 dozen*

Food Processor Directions: Place metal blade in processor bowl; add chilled butter (do not soften) and cream cheese (each cut into pieces); process until blended. Remove cover and add chives, salt and flour; mix until well blended. Remove dough from bowl, wrap in waxed paper, chill one hour. Proceed as directed above. (Depending on your processor, it may be easiest to do in two batches.)

*Almond-Sausage Filling:
1½ pounds medium-spiced pork sausage
⅓ cup BLUE DIAMOND® Whole Blanched Almonds, finely chopped
½ cup sliced green onion
Salt, pepper and garlic powder
2 tablespoons hot mustard
1 egg

In large skillet, brown meat, almonds and onion; season with salt, pepper and garlic powder to taste; remove from heat. Beat together mustard and egg and stir into meat mixture. Spoon into baked pastries. Bake in 375 degree F. oven for 10 minutes. Serve warm or at room temperature.

MINI-QUICHES

1 can (8 oz.) refrigerated
    butterflake dinner rolls
1 pkg. (8 oz.) OSCAR MAYER Ham
    and Cheese Spread
2 eggs
2 green onions with tops, chopped

Separate dinner rolls into twelve
pieces. Divide each piece into
three sections. Press dough
sections in 1¾-inch diameter tart
or muffin cups, stretching dough
slightly to form shell. Combine
cheese spread, eggs and onion;
mix well. Divide mixture evenly
among shells. Bake in 375°F oven
for 15 min. or until golden brown.
Freeze extras; reheat on baking
sheet in 350°F oven for 15 min.
Makes 36

HOT CHICKEN AND CHEESE CANAPÉS

1 can (5 ounces) SWANSON
    Chunk Chicken
¼ cup shredded Cheddar cheese
¼ cup chopped celery
3 tablespoons mayonnaise
1 tablespoon chopped parsley
⅛ teaspoon hot pepper sauce

Combine ingredients; spread on
crackers or toast squares. Broil 4"
from heat until cheese melts.
Makes about 1 cup

CHEESE PUFFS LINDSAY®

2 egg whites
⅛ teaspoon salt
1 (7½ oz.) can LINDSAY®
    Chopped Ripe Olives
¼ cup mayonnaise
2 tablespoons crisp bacon bits
2 tablespoons finely chopped
    onion
2 to 3 drops liquid red pepper
    seasoning
36 small toast rounds
Grated Parmesan cheese

Beat egg whites with salt until
stiff. Fold in chopped ripe olives,
mayonnaise, bacon bits, onion and
pepper seasoning. Pile onto toast
rounds and sprinkle with cheese.
Bake in hot oven (400 degrees F.)
about 10 to 12 minutes until puffed
and lightly browned. Serve hot.
Makes about 3 dozen

FINNTASTIC CHEESE BLISTERS

1 cup flour
¼ teaspoon salt
Generous dash cayenne pepper
½ cup butter or margarine
1 cup grated FINLANDIA Swiss
    Cheese
3 tablespoons ice water

In large mixing bowl, combine
flour, salt and pepper. Using pastry
blender or 2 knives, cut butter and
cheese into flour until mixture
resembles coarse meal. Gradually
add cold water, mixing well with
fork after each addition. On lightly
floured board, roll pastry very thin.
Using sharp knife, cut into 3 by
½-inch strips. Place on ungreased
baking sheets. Bake at 425°F.
about 10 minutes, until golden
brown. *Makes about 5 dozen*

CHEDDAR CHICKEN PUFFS WITH TARRAGON SOUR CREAM

1 can (11 ounces) CAMPBELL'S
    Condensed Cheddar Cheese
    Soup
1 can (5 ounces) SWANSON Chunk
    Style Mixin' Chicken
1 egg, slightly beaten
½ cup Italian flavored fine dry
    bread crumbs
2 tablespoons finely chopped
    green pepper
2 tablespoons finely chopped
    green onions
¼ teaspoon hot pepper sauce
Salad oil
¼ cup sour cream
Generous dash crushed tarragon
    leaves

In bowl, mix *thoroughly* ¼ cup
soup, chicken, egg, bread crumbs,
green pepper, green onions and
hot pepper sauce. Shape into 40
small chicken meatballs (½ inch).
Roll in additional bread crumbs.
Half-fill deep fat fryer or large
saucepan with oil; preheat to
350°F. Fry meatballs, a few at a
time, in hot oil until browned.
Drain; keep warm. Meanwhile, in
saucepan, combine remaining
soup, sour cream and tarragon.
Heat; stir occasionally. Serve with
meatballs.
Makes 40 appetizers

CHEESE STRAWS

2 cups (8 ozs.) shredded CRACKER
    BARREL Brand Sharp Natural
    Cheddar Cheese
⅓ cup PARKAY Margarine
1 teaspoon Worcestershire sauce
¼ teaspoon salt
1 cup flour

Heat oven to 375°. Thoroughly
blend cheese and margarine; stir in
Worcestershire sauce and salt.
Add flour; mix well. Roll dough
between two sheets of waxed
paper to ⅛-inch thickness; cut into
3 × 1-inch strips. Place on lightly
greased cookie sheets. Bake at
375°, 12 minutes. *3 dozen*

CHEESY PEANUT STRIPS

1 (8-ounce) package DROMEDARY
    Corn Muffin Mix
1 egg
⅓ cup milk
½ cup chopped salted peanuts
6 ounces Cheddar cheese,
    shredded (about 1½ cups)
1 (2-ounce) jar DROMEDARY Diced
    Pimientos, drained

Prepare corn muffin mix according
to package directions, using egg
and milk. Reserve 2 tablespoons
peanuts; stir remainder into
batter. Spread into a greased
13 × 9 × 2-inch baking pan. Sprinkle
with combined cheese and
pimientos and then reserved
peanuts. Bake in preheated
moderate oven (375°F.) about 20
minutes or until done. Cut into
strips and serve warm.
*Makes 24 (about 3 × 1¼-inch)
strips*

JAYS CHEESE PUFFS

1½ cups grated Cheddar cheese
2 egg yolks
1 teaspoon Worcestershire sauce
2 egg whites
½ cup finely crushed JAYS
    Potato Chips
Whole JAYS Potato Chips

Add beaten egg yolks and
Worcestershire sauce to cheese.
Combine with beaten egg whites
and fold in crushed potato chips.
Place small amount of mixture on
whole potato chips and bake in 400
degree oven until puffed and brown
(5 to 6 minutes). Serve at once.

STRUDEL A LA SUOMI

1 package (10 ounces) frozen puff
  pastry
2 tablespoons butter or margarine,
  softened
1½ cups shredded FINLANDIA
  Swiss Cheese
1½ cups dairy sour cream
1 can (4½ ounces) devilled ham
1 egg, well beaten

Defrost pastry in refrigerator
overnight. Place 3 shells side by
side on floured board. Place 2
shells side by side on top of center
patty shell. Cut remaining shell in
half and place one half on either
side of the 2 rounds on top. Roll
out to 8 x 14 inch rectangle. Brush
with butter. Combine cheese, sour
cream and ham. Add ½ beaten
egg. Pile mixture along 14 inch
side. Roll up, jelly roll fashion.
Pinch ends to seal. Place on
greased cookie sheet. Brush with
remaining egg. Bake at 400°F. for
35 minutes. Cool.

Makes 28 ½-inch slices

CHIPPY CHEESE STRAWS

1 package pie crust mix
⅔ cup grated sharp Cheddar
  cheese
1 cup finely crushed JAYS Potato
  Chips
1 egg white
Salt and cayenne

Prepare pie crust according to
package directions, roll very thin
and in square shape if possible.
Combine cheese with potato chips
and sprinkle half of dough with
half of mixture. Fold over. Sprinkle
remaining mixture on one-half of
folded dough. Fold again. Roll out
to one-quarter inch thickness.
Brush with egg white and sprinkle
with salt and cayenne. Cut in
strips ½-inch by 6 inches. Bake at
450 degrees until crisp and golden
brown.

CHEESE STICKS

1 pkg. refrigerator crescent rolls
1 egg, beaten
1½ cups shredded FINLANDIA
  Swiss Cheese

Place perforated strips of
refrigerator dough side by side and
seal edges to form a large
rectangle. Brush egg over surface
of dough and sprinkle generously
with cheese. Cut into sticks about
4 x 1 in. Place sticks on baking
sheet and bake at 400 deg. 15 min.
or until cheese is puffy and golden.

Note: Puff pastry or pie pastry
  dough may be substituted
  for the rolls.

GRUYERE DELIGHTS

2 packages (6 ounces each)
  VALIO Gruyere wedges
Flour
1 egg, slightly beaten
Fine dry bread crumbs
⅓ cup butter or margarine
Dark pumpernickel bread

Remove foil from wedges of
cheese. Dredge in flour, then egg,
then bread crumbs. Heat butter
until very hot in skillet. Sauté
cheese wedges, turning only once.
(Cheese must be crisp on the
outside and melted on inside.)
Total cooking time is not more
than 5 minutes. Serve with
pumpernickel bread.

Makes 6 to 8 servings

CRUNCHY TOAST STICKS

4 slices white bread, toasted
⅓ cup crumbled CHEEZ-IT®
  Crackers
¼ cup grated Romano cheese
½ teaspoon onion salt
⅓ cup butter, softened
  at room temperature

Remove crust from toast slices.
Cut each slice into 4 long sticks.
Combine cracker crumbs with
cheese. Mix onion salt with butter.
Roll each toast stick first in the
butter and then in the cracker-
cheese mixture. Bake on
ungreased cookie sheet in 400°F.
oven for 5 minutes or until crisp.
Serve immediately.

Yield: 16 sticks

SURPRISE SAUSAGE BARBECUE

8 ounce package SWIFT
  PREMIUM® BROWN 'N SERVE®
  Sausage Links, cut into thirds
½ cup grape jelly
½ teaspoon cornstarch
½ cup catsup

Brown sausage according to
package directions. Drain. In a
small saucepan mix together a
small amount of grape jelly with
the cornstarch. Blend well. Add
remaining jelly and catsup. Cook
over medium heat, stirring
constantly, until mixture thickens
slightly and begins to boil.
Continue to cook and stir 1 minute.
Pour mixture into a chafing dish or
into a heatproof dish on a hot tray.
Add sausages and stir to coat.
Serve with wooden picks.

Yield: 30 appetizers

WILD WIENERS

In large skillet combine 1 bottle (14
oz.) catsup and 1 cup WILD
TURKEY Liqueur. Simmer
uncovered 15 minutes. Add 2 lbs.
miniature cocktail frankfurters or 4
cans (9 oz.) Vienna sausages.
Continue simmering 15 minutes.
Serve in chafing dish with picks.
Makes an easy yet delicious
appetizer.

LITTLE WIENERS WELLINGTON

1 pkg. (4 oz.) OSCAR MAYER
  Braunschweiger
1 9-inch frozen pie shell
1 pkg. (5½ oz.) OSCAR MAYER
  Brand Little Wieners

Allow braunschweiger to soften at
room temperature, about 30 min.
Thaw pie shell about 10 min.;
remove from pan, flatten and repair
any cracks. Spread with
braunschweiger. Cut into five
strips; cut the two end strips in
half; cut three center strips into
fourths. Roll each piece of dough
around little wiener, pinching seam
to seal. Place seam side down on
baking sheet. Bake in 375°F oven
for 20 min. until lightly browned.

Makes 16

HIBACHI APPETIZER KABOBS

1 pkg. (5 oz.) OSCAR MAYER
   Brand Little Wieners
1 pkg. (5½ oz.) OSCAR MAYER
   Brand Little Smokies Sausage
1 can (8 oz.) pineapple chunks,
   reserve liquid
1 lemon, sliced
2 oranges, cut into wedges
6-inch metal skewers

Thread skewers alternating Little Wieners, Little Smokies and fruits. Grill on hibachi. Brush with Honey Sauce;* turn occasionally until heated through.   *Makes 8*

*HONEY SAUCE

⅓ cup pineapple liquid (reserved
   from canned pineapple chunks)
¼ cup honey
1 Tbsp. lemon juice
2 tsp. cornstarch
½ tsp. celery seed
¼ tsp. paprika

Combine all ingredients in saucepan; heat to boiling, stirring constantly. Cook until thickened. Use to brush on kabobs.

Makes ½ cup

PORK SAUSAGE WONTONS

1 pkg. (1 lb.) OSCAR MAYER
   Ground Pork Sausage
1 can (8 oz.) water chestnuts,
   drained, finely chopped
2 green onions, finely chopped
30 wonton skins, 3½-inch square
Peanut or vegetable oil for frying

In skillet cook sausage over medium heat about 12 min., stirring and separating sausage as it cooks; drain on absorbent paper. Combine sausage, water chestnuts and onion. Place 1 Tbsp. sausage mixture on center of wonton skin. Moisten corners of wonton skin with water and fold up over sausage mixture like an envelope. Pinch to seal.* Heat at least 1-inch oil in heavy skillet, wok or deep fat fryer to 375°F. Fry wontons until golden brown, turning once. Drain on absorbent paper. Serve with sweet and sour sauce and Chinese hot mustard.   *Makes 30*

*Wontons and skins should be covered with moist towel when

they are not being handled; they have a tendency to dry out and become brittle.

SESAME PORK TIDBITS WITH SWEET & SOUR SAUCE

1½ pounds boneless pork loin
½ cup cornstarch
¼ cup KIKKOMAN Teriyaki Sauce
3 tablespoons sesame seed,
   lightly toasted
3 cups vegetable oil

Sweet & Sour Sauce:
¼ cup sugar
¼ cup vinegar
¼ cup catsup
¼ cup water
1 tablespoon KIKKOMAN Teriyaki
   Sauce
1½ teaspoons cornstarch

Trim excess fat from pork; cut into 1-inch cubes and set aside. Thoroughly combine cornstarch, teriyaki sauce and sesame seed in medium-size bowl (mixture will be very stiff). Stir in pork cubes and let stand 30 minutes. Meanwhile, combine all ingredients for Sweet & Sour Sauce in saucepan. Cook over high heat, stirring constantly, until thickened; set aside and keep warm. Heat oil in medium-size saucepan over medium-high heat to 300°F. Add ⅓ of the pork pieces and cook, stirring occasionally, until golden brown (approximately 2 minutes). Remove and drain thoroughly on paper towels. Repeat with remaining pork. Serve immediately with warm Sweet & Sour Sauce.

Makes approximately 3 dozen appetizers

LITTLE WIENERS IN ORANGE SAUCE

1 cup sugar
3 tablespoons cornstarch
8 whole cloves
¼ teaspoon cinnamon
1½ cups orange juice
¼ cup vinegar
2 packages (5 oz. each) OSCAR
   MAYER Brand Little Smokies
   Sausage
2 packages (5½ oz. each) OSCAR
   MAYER Brand Little Wieners

Mix sugar, cornstarch, cloves and cinnamon in saucepan or chafing

dish. Add orange juice and vinegar. Cook over medium heat, stirring constantly, until thick. Add little links and cook slowly 5 minutes longer, or until heated through. Keep warm over low heat in chafing dish. Use picks for serving.

Makes 64 appetizers

GINGER PORK BALLS IN SHERRY-ORANGE SAUCE

1 large slice white bread, crumbled
   (about 1 cup crumbs)
¼ cup THE CHRISTIAN
   BROTHERS® Golden Sherry
1½ pounds lean ground pork
½ cup minced water chestnuts
2 tablespoons soy sauce
1 egg yolk
2 teaspoons ground ginger
1 large clove garlic, crushed
Sherry-Orange Sauce (recipe
   follows)

In large bowl combine bread and sherry; set aside 10 minutes. Add remaining ingredients except Sherry-Orange Sauce. Mix to blend thoroughly. Cover and chill at least 30 minutes. Form into 1-inch balls. Place slightly apart on baking sheet. Bake in 400 degree oven about 20 minutes until cooked through and lightly browned. Meanwhile prepare Sherry-Orange Sauce. Add drained pork balls to sauce. Cook over medium heat until hot through, stirring gently. Remove from heat; gently stir in orange segments (reserved in Sherry-Orange Sauce recipe). Serve hot with cocktail picks for spearing.

Makes about 5 dozen

SHERRY-ORANGE SAUCE

2 cans (11 ounces *each*) mandarin
   orange segments
¾ cup chicken broth or bouillon
⅓ cup THE CHRISTIAN
   BROTHERS® Golden Sherry
2 tablespoons *each* cornstarch and
   soy sauce

Drain liquid from orange segments into 2-cup measure; reserve segments. Add broth to orange liquid to make 2 cups. Pour into 2-quart saucepan. Mix sherry, cornstarch and soy sauce; add to saucepan. Cook and stir over medium heat until smooth and thickened. Simmer 1 minute.

First Prize winner THE CHRISTIAN BROTHERS® contest

TURKEY RUMAKI SPANISH STYLE

36 half inch chunks roast BUTTERBALL® SWIFT'S PREMIUM® Turkey
18 slices SWIFT SIZZLEAN®
36 small pimiento stuffed olives

Follow directions on package for cooking SIZZLEAN® , frying only 2 minutes on each side. Drain. Cut each slice in halves crosswise. Place an olive on each turkey chunk, wrap with a half slice of SIZZLEAN® . Place on skewer. Place on outdoor grill 2 to 3 minutes or until SIZZLEAN® is cooked.   *Yield: 36 appetizers*

Broiling directions: Place appetizers on rack in shallow pan and broil 4 to 5 minutes. Serve hot.

FRUIT 'N' TURKEY RUMAKI

36 half inch chunks roast BUTTERBALL® SWIFT'S PREMIUM® Turkey
18 slices SWIFT PREMIUM® Bacon, cut in half crosswise
36 chunks pineapple
Sweet Sour Sauce*

Partially cook bacon. Drain. Top each chunk of turkey with pineapple, wrap with a half slice of bacon and place on skewer. Place on outdoor grill 2 to 3 minutes until bacon is crisp. Dip into Sweet Sour Sauce before serving.
Yield: 36 appetizers

Broiling directions: Place appetizers on rack in shallow pan and broil 4 to 5 minutes.

*SWEET SOUR SAUCE

1 cup brown sugar
2 tablespoons cornstarch
¼ teaspoon salt
¼ teaspoon ground cinnamon
Dash ground cloves
6 ounce can pineapple juice
½ cup white wine vinegar
¼ cup lime juice

Combine sugar, cornstarch, salt and spices in a small saucepan. Gradually stir in pineapple juice, vinegar and lime juice. Cook over medium-low heat, stirring constantly until thick and clear.
Yield: 1¾ cups

HOT BEEF 'N FRANK TIDBITS*

1 pound ground lean beef
1 egg, lightly beaten
¼ cup soft bread crumbs
3 tablespoons LEA & PERRINS Worcestershire Sauce, divided
2 tablespoons catsup, divided
¼ teaspoon salt
⅟₁₆ teaspoon TABASCO® Sauce
2 tablespoons oil
½ cup red currant jelly
1 jar (6 oz.) cocktail frankfurters, drained

In a mixing bowl combine beef, egg, bread crumbs, 1 tablespoon each of the LEA & PERRINS and catsup, salt and TABASCO® . Mix well, but do not overmix. Shape into 1-inch balls. In a large skillet heat oil. Add meatballs and brown well on all sides. Remove and drain on paper towels. Discard fat from skillet. In same skillet combine jelly, remaining 2 tablespoons LEA & PERRINS and 1 tablespoon catsup. Heat and stir until jelly melts. Add meatballs and frankfurters. Cover and cook 10 minutes, stirring occasionally, until mixture bubbles.
Yield: about 35 meatballs and 12 frankfurters
*May be prepared in advance of serving.

HAM CORDON BLEU

1 pkg. (6 oz.) OSCAR MAYER Smoked Cooked Ham (square)
2 Tbsp. bottled horseradish sauce
1 pkg. (6 oz.) OSCAR MAYER Sliced Turkey Breast Meat
8 slices natural Swiss cheese, each 4-inches square
¼ cup butter, melted
½ cup crushed herb seasoned stuffing mix

Spread each slice of ham with horseradish sauce; top with turkey slice and cheese. Roll and secure with picks. Brush with melted butter and roll in seasoned crumbs. Place on baking sheet and heat in 350°F oven for 12 min. until cheese just begins to melt. Remove picks; cut into ½-inch slices. Serve warm.

Microwave in 12 × 7-inch glass baking dish covered with plastic wrap (turning back corner to vent) for 3½-4 minutes.   *Makes 64*

PEPPERIDGE FARM® PATTY SHELL HORS D'OEUVRES

Roll each thawed PEPPERIDGE FARM® Patty Shell to ⅛ inch thickness. Cut with a sharp knife into diamonds, squares, triangles and long narrow strips. Bake at 400°F. for 10 to 15 minutes or until puffed and brown. Cool and then top with desired filling. Use deviled ham topped with red caviar, chicken spread topped with olive slices, liver spread topped with crumbled crisp bacon, tartar sauce spread topped with tiny shrimp, melted butter sprinkled with celery salt, garlic salt and onion salt. Or spoon on a little canned cherry pie filling, topped with whipped cream and slices of strawberries.

Cut 2 inch squares of the ⅛ inch thick puff pastry and top with a whole mushroom (canned), or a whole olive, or a cube of Cheddar, or cooked shrimp, or a piece of chicken liver or cube of ham. Brush edge with egg and fold over into a triangle. Bake at 400°F. for 15 to 20 minutes or until puffed and brown. Serve hot.

SHRIMP TOAST

1 can (4½ ounces) LOUISIANA BRAND Shrimp
2 eggs
1 tablespoon cornstarch
1 teaspoon sugar
2 teaspoons dry sherry (optional)
⅓ cup finely chopped celery
6 slices bread, slightly stale
Salad oil

Drain and chop shrimp. Whisk together eggs, cornstarch, sugar, wine. Add celery and shrimp. Spread mixture on bread, pressing and smoothing with the back of a spoon until it clings. Fill deep-fry pan with salad oil to a depth of 2 inches or enough to float slices and brown without turning. Heat oil to 375 degrees or until it will brown a bread cube almost instantly. Fry slices *one at a time* about 15 seconds, shrimp side *down*. Drain on absorbent paper. Cut in triangles.

Makes 12 or 24 hot appetizers

SARDINE SPIRALS

2 cans KING OSCAR Sardines, drained
4 tsp. lemon juice
¾ tsp. prepared horseradish
Bread, sliced ¼″ thick
Melted butter
Grated Parmesan cheese

Mash sardines with lemon juice and horseradish. Trim crusts from bread. Spread mixture on bread slices. Roll bread up, cut in half crosswise, fasten with picks. Brush with melted butter, sprinkle with Parmesan. Place on shallow pan; toast quickly in hot oven (475°).

HOT BACON SPREAD

1 package (8 oz.) OSCAR MAYER Bacon
2 packages (3 oz. each) cream cheese
2 tablespoons milk
2 tablespoons finely chopped onion
½ teaspoon horseradish

Preheat oven to 375°. Cook bacon until crisp; drain and crumble. Blend cream cheese with milk. Stir in onion, horseradish and crumbled bacon*. Spread in individual casserole or small ovenproof platter. Bake 15 minutes. Serve with crackers or fresh vegetable relishes. *Makes 1 cup*

*A few tablespoons of bacon may be reserved to sprinkle on top of mixture before baking.

DEVILED SPREAD

2 cans KING OSCAR Sardines, drained
8 slices whole wheat bread
2 tsp. prepared mustard with horseradish
2 Tbsp. finely minced Bermuda or sweet onion
1 Tbsp. mayonnaise
1 tsp. Worcestershire sauce
1 tsp. lemon juice
½ tsp. grated lemon peel
¾ cup grated Cheddar cheese

Mash sardines and mix with all remaining ingredients except cheese and bread. Remove crusts from bread and toast both sides. Spread toast with sardine mixture, then cut each slice into 3 pieces. Place closely together on baking sheet; sprinkle grated cheese on each piece. Put into broiler until cheese melts. Serve hot.
Makes 24

PICKLE POCKETS

2 cups finely grated American cheese
½ cup softened butter or margarine
1 cup all-purpose flour
Dash cayenne
HEINZ Dill or Sweet Pickles

Mix cheese and butter well. Using pastry blender, cut in flour and cayenne. Divide into 2 balls; chill. Cut 36 strips (2″ × ½″) from Pickles. Roll each ball to ⅛″ thickness on floured board; cut in rectangles (2½″ × 2″). Wrap each Pickle strip in dough; seal ends well. Place on ungreased baking sheets. Bake in 425°F. oven, 12-15 minutes. *Makes 3 dozen*

THE KING IN A BLANKET

1 can KING OSCAR Sardines
1 can refrigerated crescent rolls
¼ tsp. dry mustard
¼ tsp. onion powder
2 Tbsp. lemon juice

Drain sardines and reserve oil in small dish. Open crescent rolls, unroll crescents and cut each one in half. Mix mustard, onion powder, lemon juice into sardine oil. Spread mixture on each crescent, not quite to edge. Lay 2 whole sardines on each crescent half, roll up, pinch edges together lightly. Place on cookie sheet, bake at 400° about 10 to 12 minutes, until brown. If desired, spear a green pimiento-stuffed olive on a toothpick and place on top of each sardine roll. Serve piping hot.

NALLEY®'S NACHOS

NALLEY®'S Tortilla Chips
2 to 4 tablespoons diced NALLEY®'S Jalapeno Peppers or NALLEY®'S Hot Chili Peppers
1 4-ounce can sliced or chopped olives
½ pound shredded or sliced Muenster or Jack cheese
Guacamole, sour cream and picante sauce or salsa

Spread single layer of tortilla chips on baking sheet. Sprinkle evenly with peppers, olives and cheese. Broil about 4-inches from heat until cheese is melted, about 1½ to 2 minutes. Serve hot with guacamole, sour cream and picante sauce or salsa.

JIMMY DEAN® NACHOS

1 lb. JIMMY DEAN® Seasoned Taco Filling
2 Tbsp. tomato paste
1 bag tortilla chips
1 cup cheddar cheese
Jalapeños to taste

Sauté JIMMY DEAN® Seasoned Taco Filling until brown and crumbly. Add 2 Tbsp. tomato paste. Spread on tortilla chips. Top with grated cheese. Broil till melted. Garnish with jalapeño. Optional: Top with 1 tsp. guacamole.

Hunt's®

CHILIES CON QUESO

½ lb. process American cheese, cut into ½-inch cubes
1 (6 oz.) can HUNT'S Tomato Paste
1 cup water
1 (4-oz.) can diced green chilies
½ cup minced onion
¼ cup diced green pepper
2 tsp. lemon juice
¼ tsp. TABASCO®
Tortilla or corn chips

In a saucepan, melt cheese over low heat. Meanwhile, combine remaining ingredients *except* tortilla chips in a small bowl; stir into melted cheese. Serve in fondue pot or chafing dish with tortilla chips. *Makes 1 quart*

OLD EL PASO® NACHOS

1 box (7½ oz.) OLD EL PASO®
 NACHIPS Tortilla Chips
1 can (16 oz.) OLD EL PASO®
 Refried Beans or OLD EL
 PASO® Refried Beans with
 Green Chilies or OLD EL PASO®
 Refried Beans with Sausage
1 can (4 oz.) OLD EL PASO®
 Chopped Green Chilies or 1 jar
 (11½ oz.) OLD EL PASO®
 Jalapeno Strips
2½ cups (10 oz.) shredded Cheddar
 or Monterey Jack cheese

Spread tortilla chips on a large
baking sheet. Top each with beans
and a few green chilies or a slice
of jalapeno pepper. Sprinkle each
with a tablespoon of cheese. Place
under broiler until cheese melts,
about 2 to 3 minutes. Serve
immediately.

Microwave instructions: Microcook
on full power until cheese is
melted, about 2-3 minutes. Time
will vary with the number of
nachos prepared.

PEANUT CHICKEN
PICK-ME-UPS
(Low Sodium/Low Calorie)

2½ cups ground cooked chicken
½ cup grated carrots
½ cup minced fresh parsley
½ cup finely chopped onion
¾ cup low-sodium mayonnaise
1½ cups ground PLANTERS® Dry
 Roasted Unsalted Peanuts
¼ cup FLEISCHMANN'S®
 Unsalted Margarine, melted

Toss together chicken, carrots,
parsley and onion. Add
mayonnaise; mix well. Roll into
1-inch balls. Roll each ball in
PLANTERS® Dry Roasted Unsalted
Peanuts. Dip one side of ball in
FLEISCHMANN'S® Unsalted
Margarine and place on ungreased
baking sheets, margarine side up.

Bake at 400°F. for 15 minutes, or
until golden. Cool 5 minutes before
serving.

Makes 36 1-inch pieces

Per piece: 95 calories, 8 mg.
sodium

CHEEZ-IT®
STUFFED MUSHROOMS

1 cup fine CHEEZ-IT® Crackers
 crumbs (about half a 6¼ ounce
 package)
½ teaspoon salt
¹⁄₁₆ teaspoon pepper
1 pound large mushrooms
⅓ cup minced onion
⅓ cup minced celery
⅓ cup butter
3 tablespoons minced parsley

Prepare crumbs, a little at a time,
in an electric blender or crush with
rolling pin between two pieces of
waxed paper. Mix with salt and
pepper and set aside. Clean
mushrooms and save stems for
later use in soups or sauces. Sauté
onion and celery in butter over
moderate heat until soft; do not
brown. Remove from heat; stir in
parsley and crumbs. Stuff into
mushroom caps. Place caps,
stuffed side up, in shallow pan.
Pour enough water in bottom of
pan to come up about one-quarter
the depth of the mushroom caps.
Bake in very hot oven (450°F.) for
25 to 30 minutes, or until
mushrooms are tender but not
mushy. *Yield: 4 servings*

STUFFED MUSHROOMS

1 pound medium mushrooms
 (about 18)
¼ cup butter or margarine, melted
¼ cup green onions, finely
 chopped
¼ cup water, white wine or sherry
1 cup PEPPERIDGE FARM® Herb
 Seasoned Stuffing

Wash mushrooms and remove
stems. Dip caps in melted butter
and place upside down in a
shallow baking pan. Finely chop ¼
cup of the mushroom stems and
sauté with green onions in
remaining butter, adding more
butter if necessary. Add water or
wine. Lightly stir in stuffing. Spoon
mixture into mushroom caps. Bake
at 350°F. until hot, about 10
minutes.

Makes about 18 hors d'oeuvres

BACON-STUFFED
MUSHROOMS

1 lb. fresh mushrooms
2 Tbsp. chopped onion
2 Tbsp. butter
1 slice bread, torn into small
 pieces
1 cup (4 oz.) shredded Cheddar
 cheese
1 can (3 oz.) OSCAR MAYER Real
 Bacon Bits

Remove stems from mushrooms
and set aside caps; chop stems.
Cook onions and chopped
mushroom stems in butter until
tender; add bread pieces. Remove
from heat; stir in bacon bits and
cheese. Mound filling in caps;
place in shallow baking pan. Bake
in 400°F oven 15 min. until cheese
is melted. Serve warm.

Makes 15-20 appetizers

BROCCOLI PUFFS

10-oz. pkg. GREEN GIANT® Cut
 Broccoli Frozen in Cheese Sauce
1½ cups yellow cornmeal
½ cup flour
2 tablespoons sugar
1½ teaspoons garlic salt
1¼ teaspoons baking powder
1 teaspoon salt
¾ cup milk
1 egg
Oil for deep frying

Cook broccoli according to
package directions. Empty
contents into small bowl and cut
broccoli, using 2 knives, into
½-inch pieces. Lightly spoon flour
into measuring cup; level off. In
medium bowl, combine cornmeal,
flour, sugar, garlic salt, baking
powder and salt. Stir in broccoli
with cheese sauce, milk and egg;
batter should be fairly thick. Allow
batter to set 5 to 10 minutes. In
deep fat fryer or heavy saucepan
drop batter by teaspoonfuls into 1
to 1½-inches hot fat (375°F.). Fry
until golden brown, turning once.
Drain on paper towel.

48 appetizers

BERTOLLI® STUFFED ARTICHOKES

4 medium artichokes
Juice of 1 lemon
1 rib celery, thinly sliced
½ red pepper, cut into strips
¼ cup finely chopped onion
1 tablespoon BERTOLLI® Olive Oil
1 cup cooked peas
2 tablespoons walnut pieces
¼ cup BERTOLLI® Olive Oil
1 tablespoon BERTOLLI® Red Wine Vinegar
1 teaspoon sugar
Dash each salt and pepper

Cut stem and 1-inch top from artichokes; cut tips off leaves. Rub artichokes with lemon juice; heat to boiling in 2-inches water in saucepan. Reduce heat; simmer covered until tender, about 30 minutes. Drain; cool. Separate top leaves; remove chokes with spoon. Sauté celery, pepper and onion in 1 tablespoon oil in skillet 4 minutes. Stir in peas and walnuts. Mix remaining ingredients; stir into vegetables. Spoon vegetables into center of artichokes. Serve hot or refrigerate and serve cold.
Makes 4 servings

CITRUS SCOOP-OUTS
(Low Sodium)

2 medium grapefruit
2 medium oranges
⅓ cup honey
2 tablespoons FLEISCHMANN'S® Unsalted Margarine, melted
Pinch curry powder
½ cup chopped PLANTERS® Dry Roasted Unsalted Mixed Nuts

Cut grapefruit in half; remove sections and reserve. Remove and discard membrane from grapefruit shells; set shells aside. Peel and section oranges.

In a medium bowl mix honey, FLEISCHMANN'S® Unsalted Margarine and curry powder; fold in grapefruit, orange sections and PLANTERS® Dry Roasted Unsalted Mixed Nuts. Spoon fruit mixture into grapefruit shells and place in a shallow baking dish.

Bake at 450°F. for 15 minutes, or until hot. Serve warm, garnished with fresh mint leaves if desired.
4 servings

Per serving: 310 calories, 5 mg. sodium

BROILED RUBY REDS

2 Texas Ruby Red Grapefruit, halved
¼ cup IMPERIAL Brown Sugar
¼ teaspoon cinnamon
¼ cup shredded coconut
Maraschino cherries

Cut around each section with grapefruit knife. Combine IMPERIAL Brown Sugar and cinnamon and spread over grapefruit. Broil until juice is bubbling. Sprinkle with shredded coconut and broil until coconut is toasted. Add cherries to centers of grapefruit.
Makes 4 servings

NOR'EAST NIBBLES

16 frozen BOOTH Fish Sticks
½ cup grated Parmesan cheese
2 tablespoons butter or margarine
Sea Sauce*

Preheat oven to 450°. Cut frozen fish sticks into thirds. Roll each piece in cheese. Melt butter in a baking pan, 15" × 10" × 1". Place fish in pan. Bake 8 to 10 minutes. Turn carefully. Bake 8 to 10 minutes longer or until crisp and brown. Drain on absorbent paper. Serve with hot Sea Sauce.
Makes 48 hors d'oeuvres

*SEA SAUCE

1 can (8 ounces) tomato sauce
¼ cup chili sauce
¼ teaspoon garlic powder
¼ teaspoon oregano
¼ teaspoon liquid hot pepper sauce
¼ teaspoon thyme
⅛ teaspoon sugar
Dash basil

Combine all ingredients. Simmer 10 to 12 minutes, stirring occasionally.
Makes 1 cup sauce

Quickie Appetizers

SAVORY DEVILED CHEESE SPREAD

Juicy Bartlett wedges "pear" with this savory deviled cheese spread for a refreshing appetizer. Blend together 1 package (3 oz.) softened cream cheese, 2 tablespoons crumbled blue cheese and 1 can (2¼ oz.) deviled ham. Chill several hours to blend flavors.
Makes about ½ cup spread

Favorite recipe from Pacific Bartlett Growers, Inc.

PIGGY WRAPS

Cut HILLSHIRE FARM® Sausage into desired shapes. Wrap in refrigerated crescent dough. Bake at 400° for 5 minutes or until golden brown. May be frozen. To reheat in microwave, microwave uncovered, HIGH 1½ minutes or MEDIUM HIGH 2 minutes. When reheated in microwave, pastry will not be crisp.

CHEESE STUFFED CELERY

Pipe 1 (4¾-ounce) can SNACK MATE Pasteurized Process Cheese Spread Cheddar onto 4 stalks celery. Cut into 1½-inch pieces. Stand a CORN DIGGERS Snack in end of each. Sprinkle with paprika, if desired.
Makes 24 (about 1½-inch) pieces

DATE CARROT CURLS

Using vegetable parer, cut about 36 thin lengthwise strips from raw carrots (about 6). Roll each strip into a curl and fasten with a wooden pick. Chill in ice water several hours. Drain; remove picks and stuff each with a date using 1 (8-ounce) package DROMEDARY Pitted Dates; re-insert picks through dates. To serve: Remove picks; sprinkle lightly with salt.
Makes about 3 dozen

ITALIAN NACHOS

Place thinly sliced HILLSHIRE FARM® Italian Smoked Sausage on tortilla chips. Top with Monterey Jack or taco flavored cheese. Broil until cheese melts or arrange in circle and microwave uncovered, HIGH 15 seconds or MEDIUM HIGH 20 seconds. If desired, garnish with sour cream.

GRECIAN TOUCH

Marinate chunks from 1 lb. HILLSHIRE FARM® Sausage in juice of 1 fresh lemon and 1 tsp. crushed oregano for at least 30 minutes. Bake, covered at 350° for 30 minutes or microwave, covered, HIGH 6-8 minutes, stirring once. Serve with toothpicks.

SWEET & SAUCY

Heat equal parts of currant jelly and catsup in saucepan, or microwave, uncovered, HIGH 1-2 minutes until mixture can be blended smooth. Add bite size pieces of HILLSHIRE FARM® Sausage and heat until sausage is hot. Serve with toothpicks.

FIRESIDE SNACK

Top PREMIUM Saltine Crackers with American cheese and miniature frankfurters. Toast in toaster-oven until cheese is melted.

SMOKEY TIDBITS

Tuck slivers of smoked salmon inside big shiny black LINDSAY® Pitted Ripe Olives, add a tassle of parsley and serve on picks.

Lindsay.

LINDSAY® RIPE OLIVE "FILLERS"

A quick and easy appetizer to spread on crackers or melba toast is prepared by combining 1 (3 oz.) package of cream cheese, ¼ cup LINDSAY® Chopped Ripe Olives, 1 (2¼ oz.) can deviled ham and ½ to 1 teaspoon horseradish.

PIMIENTO DEVILED EGGS

Drain 1 (2-ounce) jar DROMEDARY Sliced Pimientos. Finely chop enough to make 1 tablespoon chopped. Cut 6 hard-cooked eggs in half lengthwise. Remove yolks and mash. Combine with 2 tablespoons mayonnaise, the chopped pimiento, 2 teaspoons cider vinegar and ⅛ teaspoon salt. Stuff egg whites and garnish with remaining sliced pimientos.
Makes 12

SAUCY SUGGESTIONS

Add OSCAR MAYER Brand Little Wieners or Little Smokies Sausage to one of the sauces below. Prepare sauce; add little links and heat about 5 min. longer, stirring occasionally. Serve in chafing dish with picks.
Four pkg. makes 64 appetizers

Little Rubies: Heat together 1 can (21 oz.) cherry pie filling and ¼ cup rosé wine.

Orange Nutmeg: Combine ½ cup sugar with 2 Tbsp. cornstarch and ½ tsp. nutmeg. Stir in 1¼ cups orange juice. Cook over medium heat, stirring constantly until mixture boils and is thickened. Stir in 1 can (11 oz.) mandarin orange segments, drained.

Barbecue: Heat 1 bottle (18 oz.) barbecue sauce.

Currant: Heat 2 jars (10 oz. each) currant jelly.

SAUSAGE BALLS

In large bowl combine 1 pkg. (1 lb.) OSCAR MAYER Ground Pork Sausage, 3 cups buttermilk baking mix and 1 lb. shredded Cheddar cheese. Knead ingredients together to form soft dough. Shape into 1-inch balls. Place on ungreased baking sheet. Bake 20 min. in 350°F oven until golden brown. Serve hot. Reheat cooked frozen sausage balls 10 min. in 350°F oven.
Makes 72

NACHOS

Arrange tortilla chips on baking sheet. Top each with 1 tsp. OSCAR MAYER Cheese and Bacon Spread and a slice of olive, mild banana pepper or jalapeña pepper. Bake in 400°F oven 5 min.

Microwave 12 chips for 30 seconds.

BRAUNSCHWEIGER PARTY LOG

Remove plastic film from 1 pkg. (8 oz.) OSCAR MAYER Braunschweiger, taking care to retain meat in its log shape. Frost log with 1 pkg. (3 oz.) whipped cream cheese and roll in 1 can (3 oz.) OSCAR MAYER Real Bacon Bits. Chill. Serve with crackers.

RIBBON CUBES

Spread 1 pkg. (8 oz.) OSCAR MAYER Chopped Ham and 2 slices very thin square pumpernickel bread with 1 pkg. (3 oz.) cream cheese and chives. Stack in following order: 3 slices ham, one slice bread, 2 slices ham, one slice bread, 3 slices ham. Wrap tightly and chill. Cut into cubes. Use picks to serve. *Makes 16*

WRAP-UPS

Cut OSCAR MAYER Bologna or other sliced cold meats into thirds and wrap around bite-size pieces of dill pickle, cheese, fruit or fresh vegetables. Fasten with a pick. Chill until ready to serve.

BELLS

Cut round sliced meats like OSCAR MAYER Cotto Salami or Bologna in half. Form into cones; insert cherry tomato, radish, olive or cocktail onion in each and fasten with pick.

BACON TIDBITS

Cut OSCAR MAYER Bacon slices in half and wrap around olives, mushrooms or water chestnuts. Fasten with picks. Bake in 400°F oven about 15 min., until bacon is crisp.

STUFFED PICKLES

Core center of CLAUSSEN Kosher Pickles and stuff with OSCAR MAYER Braunschweiger. Chill several hours. Slice stuffed pickles and serve with picks.

FAMOUS CHEESE SIZZLERS

¼ cup DURKEE Imitation Bacon Bits
1½ cups shredded Swiss cheese
¼ cup DURKEE Famous Sauce
¼ cup DURKEE Stuffed Olives, chopped
1 tablespoon DURKEE Freeze-Dried Chives
24 slices party rye

Combine all ingredients except bread. Spread mixture on bread and cut into halves. Broil 4 inches from heat until cheese melts and is lightly brown. *Makes 48 servings*

PRESTO PARTY FRANKS

Slice ECKRICH® Franks into a mixture of one cup currant jelly and ¾ cup prepared mustard. Heat and serve.

Makes about four cups

CELERY LOGS VIRGINIENNE

Blend thoroughly 4 cups softened cream cheese with 1 cup AMBER BRAND Deviled SMITHFIELD Ham. Fill hollows of celery stalks with ham and cheese mixture; top with thin strips of pimiento. Cut into 3-4" lengths. Chill before service.

FAMOUS ECKRICH® SLENDER SLICED PINWHEELS

Stack three slices of your favorite ECKRICH® Slender Sliced Meat. Spread softened cream cheese on the top slice and roll, jelly-roll fashion. Chill until cheese is firm. Then place five toothpicks along loose edge of each roll and cut between the picks with a very sharp knife.

Makes about 15 pinwheels

LUNCHEON MEAT PINWHEELS

1 package (8 oz.) OSCAR MAYER Luncheon Meat
1 package (3 oz.) cream cheese, softened

Spread all meat slices with cream cheese. Roll first slice; join meat edges to start second slice and continue to roll slices, one over another, to make a log. Wrap and chill thoroughly. Cut into slices ¼ inch thick and serve on rye bread or crackers.

Makes 16 appetizers

SAUSAGE AND MUSHROOM APPETIZER

Remove the stems from fresh mushrooms and wash mushroom caps. Cut SWIFT PREMIUM® BROWN 'N SERVE® Sausage Links into thirds. Place mushroom caps in a shallow pan or on a broiler rack, smooth side up. Brush each with melted butter. Broil about 5 inches from the heat source for 3 minutes. Turn and brush with melted butter. Place ⅓ sausage link in center of each mushroom cap. Broil 2 minutes. Insert a pick in each, making sure to secure sausage and mushroom. Serve hot.

PICKLE KABOBS

Alternate cubes of OSCAR MAYER Cooked Ham and Cheddar cheese with pickle pieces on small skewers.

Dips

SOUTH OF THE BORDER DIP

1 cup SEALTEST® Cottage Cheese
¼ cup medium sharp process cheese spread
3 tablespoons chili sauce
½ teaspoon garlic salt

Combine all ingredients, blend well. Refrigerate in container with cover. *1⅓ cups*

LIPTON® CALIFORNIA DIP

In small bowl, blend 1 envelope LIPTON® Onion Soup Mix with 2 cups (16 oz.) sour cream; chill.
Makes about 2 cups

VARIATIONS:

California Vegetable Dip. Add 1 cup each finely chopped green pepper and tomato and 2 teaspoons chili powder.

California Blue Cheese Dip. Add ¼ pound crumbled blue cheese and ¼ cup finely chopped walnuts.

California Seafood Dip. Add 1 cup finely chopped cooked shrimp, clams or crab meat, ¼ cup chili sauce and 1 tablespoon horseradish.

"THE LITTLE MERMAID" DIP

¼ cup mayonnaise
½ cup sour cream
1 can (6½ oz.) tuna, drained & cut in tiny pieces
¼ teaspoon curry
¼ teaspoon tarragon
¼ teaspoon salt
½ cup Danish cheese, shredded (Havarti, Esrom, or Tybo)

In medium bowl, blend mayonnaise & sour cream together. Add tuna, curry, tarragon & salt. Then add Danish cheese & blend well. Refrigerate 1 hour.
Makes about 2 cups dip

Favorite recipe from Denmark Cheese Association

SPICY SEAFOOD DIP

1 cup (8 oz.) BREYERS® Plain Yogurt
¼ cup mayonnaise
1¼ teaspoons curry powder
1 tablespoon finely chopped onion
2 teaspoons lemon juice
½ teaspoon salt
Dash of pepper
1 can (6½ oz.) crab, tuna fish, or shrimp; drained, flaked, or chopped

Combine all ingredients; mix well. Chill several hours. Serve with raw vegetables or crackers.

Makes 1½ cups

DANABLU DIP WITH NUTS

¼ cup Danish Blue cheese, at room temperature
⅔ cup sour cream
⅓ cup mayonnaise
½ teaspoon salt
½ teaspoon chives
¼ teaspoon Worcestershire sauce
1 clove garlic, mashed
¼ cup chopped walnuts

In medium bowl, mash Danish Blue cheese with fork. Add ⅓ cup sour cream & blend thoroughly. Then fold in remaining ingredients & refrigerate 1 hour.
Makes about 1½ cups dip

Favorite recipe from Denmark Cheese Association

GREEN AND WHITE DIP FOR JAYS POTATO CHIPS

3 ounces cream cheese (room temperature)
1 tablespoon horseradish
¼ teaspoon onion juice or grated onion

Cream ingredients until thoroughly mixed and soft. Use a fork or electric mixer. Add cream to make a "dunking" consistency (serve so that chips can be easily "dunked" in the spread). Add onion and horseradish (more or less may be added to suit the taste). Sprinkle the top of spread with chopped chives or parsley flakes as a garnish. Place the bowl of spread in the center of a large attractive platter and surround with JAYS Potato Chips.

MEXICALI DIP

1 lb. VELVEETA Pasteurized Process Cheese Spread, cubed
1 16-oz. can tomatoes, drained, chopped
1 4-oz. can green chilies, drained, chopped
1 tablespoon instant minced onion
Corn or tortilla chips

Combine process cheese spread, tomatoes, chilies and onion in saucepan; cook over low heat until process cheese spread melts. Serve hot with corn chips.
3 cups

GUACAMOLE

Mash 2 CALAVO® Avocados. Blend in a chopped tomato, ¼ cup grated onion, ½ teaspoon seasoned salt, 1 tablespoon fresh CALAVO® Lime Juice. Spread generously on hamburgers. Or serve as dip with corn chips. (For convenience, try CALAVO® Frozen Fresh Guacamole in flavors.)
Makes 2½ cups

GREEN GODDESS DIP FOR JAYS POTATO CHIPS

1 clove garlic, grated
2 tablespoons anchovy paste
3 tablespoons finely chopped chives
1 tablespoon lemon juice
1 tablespoon tarragon wine vinegar
½ cup heavy sour cream
1 cup mayonnaise
⅓ cup finely chopped parsley
Coarse salt
Coarsely ground black pepper

Combine ingredients in order given. Pour in serving bowl and chill. Canned whole anchovies may be chopped fine and substituted for the anchovy paste. Coarse salt may be purchased in pound containers. Lacking a pepper grinder use a pestle to mash the peppercorns in a mortar. Serve with JAYS Potato Chips.

DUBONNET DIP

1 can tuna, mashed
3 3 oz. pkgs. cream cheese
¼ cup DUBONNET Blonde
1 Tbsp. mayonnaise
¼ cup sweet pickle relish, well drained
2 tsp. parsley, finely chopped
1 tsp. grated onion
½ tsp. salt
¼ tsp. garlic salt

Soften cream cheese in DUBONNET. Blend in drained and mashed tuna. Add remaining ingredients and mix well. Refrigerate in covered container.

CURRIED APPLE AND CHICKEN DIP

1 can (5 ounces) SWANSON Chunk Style Mixin' Chicken
½ cup chopped apple
¼ cup chopped almonds
⅓ cup mayonnaise
2 tablespoons chopped raisins
1 tablespoon orange juice
½ teaspoon curry powder

Combine ingredients; chill. Serve on crackers or as a dip with assorted vegetables.
Makes about 1 cup

SUNNY PEANUT BUTTER DIP

½ cup SKIPPY® Creamy or Super Chunk Peanut Butter
½ cup finely shredded carrot
¼ cup orange juice

In small bowl stir together peanut butter, carrot and orange juice until well mixed. Serve as dip for fresh fruits and vegetables.
Makes about 1 cup

CREAMY CLAM CHEESE DIP

1 cup SEALTEST® Cottage Cheese
2 tablespoons minced, drained canned clams
1 teaspoon finely snipped chives
Dash liquid hot-pepper sauce

Blend all ingredients well. Refrigerate in container with cover.
1 cup

CALIFORNIA SPREAD

1 can KING OSCAR Sardines
1 ripe California avocado
2 Tbsp. grated onion
2 Tbsp. lemon juice
½ cup sour cream
Dash TABASCO®
Salt
Parsley

Mash sardines and avocado. Add remaining ingredients, except parsley. Blend thoroughly. Sprinkle with chopped fresh parsley. Serve with crackers or toast fingers.

CONFETTI DIP

5 Tbsp. milk
1 pkg. (8 oz.) cream cheese, softened
1 Tbsp. chives
2 Tbsp. chopped parsley
2 Tbsp. (1 oz.) ROMANOFF® Caviar*

Blend milk with cream cheese until mixture is easy to dip. Gently stir in remaining ingredients. Garnish with additional caviar if desired. Serve with raw vegetable relishes (below) or unsalted crackers.

Makes 1¼ cups dip

*ROMANOFF® Red Salmon Caviar suggested.

RAW VEGETABLE RELISHES

1 bunch celery
1 cucumber
¼ pound very young green beans
4 carrots
½ head cauliflower
1 bunch radishes

Trim celery, wash and separate out small pieces. Cut large ribs into three-inch lengths. Peel cucumber and cut in half crosswise, then into half-inch thick strips. Remove ends from beans. Peel carrots, cut into half-inch thick strips. Cut cauliflower into flowerets. Pare radishes. Place vegetables in ice water at least one hour. Drain, and serve with caviar dip. *Serves 10*

DOUBLE CHEESE BACON DIP

1 cup creamed cottage cheese
1 package (6 ounces) VALIO Gruyere Cheese—grated
4 slices bacon, cooked and crumbled
2 tablespoons salad dressing
1 teaspoon lemon juice
1 small clove garlic, minced
½ teaspoon red pepper, crushed
2 tablespoons minced green pepper
2 tablespoons chopped radishes

Combine cheeses, bacon, salad dressing, lemon juice, garlic and red pepper. Stir in green pepper and radishes. Chill until ready to serve. Serve as dip for assorted raw vegetables.

Makes about 2 cups

ZURICH DIP

1 pkg. (8 oz.) cream cheese
1 pkg. (8 oz.) sour cream
1 tsp. instant minced onion
⅛ tsp. garlic powder
1 can (3 oz.) OSCAR MAYER Real Bacon Bits
Paprika

Combine cream cheese, sour cream, onion and garlic; blend well. Stir in bacon bits, reserving some for garnish. Spoon into shallow 1-quart glass casserole. Bake in 350°F oven for 20 min.* Sprinkle with paprika and reserved bacon bits. Serve warm with fresh vegetables and crackers.

Makes 2 cups

*Microwave 5 min., stirring once, halfway through heating. Stir; garnish as above.

CURRIED LOW CAL DIP
(Low Calorie/Low Cholesterol)

4 packets BUTTER BUDS®
1 cup non-fat dry milk
8 tablespoons warm water
4 egg whites
1 teaspoon salt
2 tablespoons dry mustard
½ teaspoon SWEET 'N LOW,® or equivalent sugar substitute
4 tablespoons vinegar
16 tablespoons oil
16 tablespoons hot water
8 teaspoons lemon juice
1 tablespoon curry powder (or, to taste)
1 tablespoon cayenne pepper (or, to taste)
"Dippers"*

Combine BUTTER BUDS® dry milk, water. In second bowl, beat egg whites till foamy. Blend in salt, mustard, sugar substitute and vinegar. While beating, slowly add oil, then contents of first bowl. Stir thoroughly, then stir in hot water, lemon juice and curry powder and cayenne pepper as desired.

Makes about 4 cups

Calories: 35 (per ½ oz.)
Cholesterol: .18 mg.

*"DIPPERS"

1 2-pound flank steak
1 pound fresh mushrooms
1 pound string beans
1 large broccoli
1 large cauliflower

Brush steak with vegetable oil, sprinkle with salt and pepper and broil. Cut into very thin strips. Steam string beans, broccoli and cauliflower five minutes. Serve mushrooms raw. Arrange on serving platter surrounding bowl of curried dip. Use fondue forks for spearing and dipping.

GARDEN VARIETY DIP
(Low Sodium/Low Calorie)

1½ cups plain yogurt
½ cup finely chopped PLANTERS® Dry Roasted Unsalted Peanuts
¼ cup minced fresh parsley
¼ cup finely chopped, peeled and seeded cucumber
2 tablespoons chopped green onion
¼ teaspoon dill weed
⅛ teaspoon ground white pepper

Thoroughly combine yogurt, PLANTERS® Dry Roasted Unsalted Peanuts, parsley, cucumber, onion, dill weed and white pepper. Chill 2 to 3 hours.

Serve with assorted fresh vegetables such as carrots, celery, cauliflower, mushrooms or broccoli. *Makes 2 cups*

Per tablespoon: 25 calories, 6 mg. sodium

HOT CHILI-CHEESE DIP

1 15-oz. can ARMOUR® STAR Chili without Beans
1 4-oz. can chopped green chilies
1 lb. process American cheese, shredded
1 tablespoon Worcestershire sauce
Corn chips

Combine all ingredients, except chips; heat, stirring occasionally, over low heat until cheese melts. Serve as a dip with corn chips.

4 cups

Microwave instructions: Combine all ingredients, except chips, in 1½-qt. casserole. Cook, covered, 6 minutes, stirring occasionally. Serve as a dip with corn chips.

TUNA DUNK
(Low Calorie/Low Cholesterol)

1 can (8 oz.) PET® Imitation Sour Cream
1 can (7 oz.) tuna, water-packed (drained and flaked)
1 can (4 oz.) mushroom pieces and stems, drained and chopped
2 teaspoons instant minced onions
1 teaspoon Worcestershire sauce
1 tablespoon Sauterne (optional)

Mix all ingredients thoroughly in a medium saucepan or chafing dish. Heat until steaming. Serve warm with crackers, potato chips, pretzels, or French bread.
Makes about 2 cups

ORIENTAL DIP

1 cup mayonnaise or salad dressing
1 (8-ounce) container sour cream
1 (8-ounce) can water chestnuts, drained and finely chopped
2 tablespoons chopped pimiento
1 tablespoon sliced or chopped green onion
2 teaspoons WYLER'S® Beef-Flavor Instant Bouillon
½ teaspoon Worcestershire sauce
¼ teaspoon garlic powder
Potato chips or fresh vegetables

In medium bowl, combine all ingredients except potato chips; mix well. Cover; chill. Stir before serving. Serve with chips. Refrigerate leftovers.
Makes 2½ cups

OLD EL PASO® GUACAMOLE

2 large ripe avocados, peeled, pitted and sliced
1 jar (8 oz.) OLD EL PASO® Taco Sauce
½ cup chopped onion
2 tablespoons lemon or lime juice
1 teaspoon salt
½ teaspoon garlic powder
1 box (7½ oz.) OLD EL PASO® NACHIPS Tortilla Chips

Blend avocado slices, taco sauce, onion, juice, salt and garlic powder in blender or food processor. Chill. Serve with NACHIPS.

KILBIRNIE CLAM DIP

1 can (7½ oz.) minced clams, undrained
⅓ cup JOHNNIE WALKER Red
8 oz. cream cheese, softened
1 envelope onion soup mix
1 cup sour cream

Combine clams with remaining ingredients; mix well. Chill. Serve with potato or corn chips, or crackers.   *About 2½ cups*

ZESTY BEAN DIP

1 can (15 oz.) S&W Chili Beans, undrained
¼ tsp. chili powder (or more if desired)
1 can (4½ oz.) deviled ham
3 Tbsp. S&W Sweet Relish

Blend all ingredients till smooth in electric blender or mixer. To taste, add crumbled bacon bits, chopped onion or S&W Pimiento Slices, chopped.   *Yield: 2 cups*

VARIATIONS:

Blend with medium size ripe avocado, or with a can (2 oz.) S&W Peeled Chili Peppers—or, blend in both.

VEGETABLE DIP
(Low Calorie/Low Cholesterol)

1 can (8 oz.) PET® Imitation Sour Cream
2 teaspoons instant minced onion
½ teaspoon garlic salt
¼ cup minced radishes
¼ cup minced green pepper
3 drops hot sauce

Combine all ingredients. Chill to blend the flavors. Serve with crackers, chips, or fresh crisp vegetables.
Makes about 1¼ cups dip

SAVORY YOGURT DIP
(Low Calorie)

1 packet HERB-OX Instant Onion Broth and Seasoning
1 cup plain yogurt
1½ tablespoons dried chopped chives
1½ tablespoons dried parsley

Combine all ingredients, mix well. Serve as a dip with raw celery, carrots, cauliflowerets, radishes, cucumber slices. Or use as a dressing for vegetable salads.

SNAPPY BEAN DIP

1 10-ounce can tomatoes and green chilies
1 pound sharp American cheese, grated
1 10½-ounce can FRITOS® Brand Jalapeño Bean Dip

Heat tomatoes and chilies with the cheese until cheese is melted. Add FRITOS® Brand Jalapeño Bean Dip and mix well. Serve hot with FRITOS® Brand Corn Chips, DORITOS® Brand Tortilla Chips, and RUFFLES® Brand Potato Chips.

CRUDITES, WITH PERNOD DIP

1 cauliflower, crisp and unmarked
1 bunch radishes, cut and opened
1 head of celery, cut in sticks
6 medium carrots, cut into matchsticks
2 cucumbers, each cut into 8 pieces

Dip:
1 pint sour cream
1 packet dried onion soup
5 soup spoons PERNOD

Split the cauliflower's florets into small pieces, wash and drain. Having cleaned all the vegetables, arrange them on a large dish leaving space for the dip bowl. Combine the sour cream, onion soup and PERNOD and pour into the bowl to be placed in the center of the serving dish.

KIWIFRUIT WINE CREAM DIP

¾ cup GIBSON Kiwifruit Wine
¼ teaspoon grated lemon rind
1 tablespoon cornstarch
¼ cup sugar
1 carton (9 oz.) of prepared whipped cream

Combine all ingredients in a saucepan. Cook and stir over high heat to a rolling boil; continue cooking mixture until it thickens. Cool mixture slightly; fold in whipped cream. Cover and chill 2 hours.
Makes approximately 2½ cups

Tip: Chill and serve as a dip with fruit kabobs, sliced pound cake, or gingersnaps.

Soups

ASPARAGUS SOUP AMERICANA

1 can (10¾ ounces) CAMPBELL'S Chicken Broth
1 package (10 ounces) frozen cut asparagus
¼ cup sliced green onions
⅛ teaspoon ground mace
Dash pepper
1 cup water
Sieved hard-cooked egg

In saucepan, combine broth, asparagus, onions, mace and pepper; bring to boil. Cover; cook over low heat 5 minutes or until asparagus is tender. In blender, blend asparagus mixture until smooth; return to saucepan. Add water. Heat; stir occasionally. Garnish with egg.
Makes about 3 cups, 4 servings

CREAM OF ASPARAGUS SOUP

1 can (14½ oz.) DEL MONTE All-Green Asparagus (Cut Spears—Tips Included)
⅓ cup chopped onion
2 Tbsp. margarine or butter
1 can (10½ oz.) condensed cream of mushroom soup
Dash pepper
1 cup milk
Chopped chives
Thinly sliced lemon

Drain asparagus, reserving liquid. Sauté onion in margarine until tender. Add reserved liquid. Pour into blender; add asparagus, soup and pepper. Blend until smooth; stir in milk. Chill and serve topped with chopped chives or serve hot with thin slice of lemon.
4 servings (approx. 1 cup each)

BASIC LENTIL SOUP

½ pound lentils
4 cups cold water
1 ham hock *or* meaty ham bone
⅓ cup *each* chopped onion, celery and carrots
1 small bay leaf
½ teaspoon salt
1 small garlic clove, if desired

Wash and drain lentils. Combine all ingredients in kettle with tight-fitting lid. Bring to boil. Reduce heat and simmer, covered, 2 hours; stir occasionally. Remove ham hock or bone; cool slightly. Cut ham off bone; dice. Add to soup and heat thoroughly. Remove bay leaf before serving.
Makes about 6 servings

Tip: Lentils require no soaking.
Note: Lentil soups are very thick and may need thinning. To thin lentil soup, heat slowly and stir in chicken broth or water.

Favorite recipe from Idaho-Washington Dry Pea & Lentil Commissions

SOUTHERN BEAN DIP SOUP

3 10½-ounce cans FRITOS® Brand Jalapeño Bean Dip
1 can beef broth
1 broth can water
3 medium potatoes, peeled and cut in 1-inch cubes
1 cup chopped onion
1 cup chopped celery
1 can whole kernel corn
½ cup chopped green pepper

Mix in a kettle the FRITOS® Brand Jalapeño Bean Dip, broth and water. Simmer uncovered for 30 minutes. Add onion, celery, corn and pepper. Simmer for 1 hour. Serve hot.
Makes 8 to 10 servings

BUTTER BEAN SOUP

1 can (15 oz.) VAN CAMP'S® Butter Beans
1 can (1 lb.) STOKELY'S FINEST® Stewed Tomatoes
3 Tablespoons butter or margarine
1 Tablespoon instant minced onion
1½ teaspoons sugar
¼ teaspoon seasoned salt
Dash pepper

Combine all ingredients in a saucepan and simmer for 30 minutes. *Makes 3 to 4 servings*

GOLDEN CAULIFLOWER SOUP

2 (10-ounce) packages frozen cauliflower *or* 1 small head fresh cauliflower, separated into small flowerets
2 cups water
½ cup chopped onion
⅓ cup margarine or butter
½ cup unsifted flour
2 cups milk
2 tablespoons WYLER'S® Chicken-Flavor Instant Bouillon *or* 6 Chicken-Flavor Bouillon Cubes
2 cups (8 ounces) shredded mild Cheddar cheese
⅛ to ¼ teaspoon ground nutmeg
Chopped green onion or parsley

In medium saucepan, cook cauliflower in *1 cup* water until tender. Reserve 1 cup cooked flowerets. In blender or food processor, blend remaining cauliflower and liquid; set aside. In large heavy saucepan, cook onion in margarine until tender; stir in flour. Gradually add remaining *1 cup* water, milk and bouillon, stirring until well blended and thickened. Add cheese, pureed cauliflower, reserved flowerets and nutmeg; cook and stir until cheese melts and mixture is hot (do not boil). Serve garnished with green onion. Refrigerate leftovers.
Makes about 1½ to 2 quarts

FRESH MUSHROOM SOUP

½ lb. fresh mushrooms, thinly sliced
¼ cup butter
3 Tbsp. chopped parsley
¼ tsp. salt
Dash of pepper
1¼ cup THE CHRISTIAN BROTHERS® Chablis
1 cup heavy cream
3 egg yolks
2 cups sour cream

Sauté mushrooms in butter for 5 minutes, or until lightly browned. Stir in parsley and seasonings. Add chablis and ¾ cup heavy cream; stir and simmer about 5 minutes. Beat egg yolks with 1¾ cups sour cream, stir in some of the hot soup. Return all to pan; keep hot. Whip remaining ¼ cup heavy cream; stir in ¼ cup sour cream. Pour soup into individual heat-proof bowls. Spoon whipped cream mixture onto soup. Place under broiler until topping browns. Serve at once. *Serves 6*

MUSHROOM-CHEESE COMBO

2 cans (10¾ ounces *each*) CAMPBELL'S Condensed Cream of Mushroom Soup
2 soup cans milk
1 cup shredded sharp Cheddar cheese
1 can (about 8 ounces) tomatoes, cut up
½ cup sliced celery
2 tablespoons chopped parsley
1 teaspoon prepared mustard
1 teaspoon Worcestershire
2 hard-cooked eggs, coarsely chopped

In large saucepan, combine all ingredients except eggs. Heat until cheese melts; stir occasionally. Add eggs; heat.
Makes about 7 cups

MUSHROOM SOUP

2 pounds mushrooms, chopped fine
6 cups water
¾ teaspoon beef extract or 2 beef bouillon cubes
Freshly ground black pepper
¼ cup HOLLAND HOUSE® Marsala Cooking Wine

Cook mushrooms with water in covered saucepan for 2½ to 3 hours. Strain over a large pan with a collander pressing all liquid out of mushrooms with a large spoon. Discard mushroom pulp. Over medium heat add beef extract to liquid and blend in. Season to taste with pepper. Correct seasoning and stir in Marsala. As soon as wine has had a chance to heat up, serve.
Makes 6 servings

BULLY-HI ONION SOUP

Sauté 2 oz. package dried onion in 2 tablespoons melted butter. Stir until golden brown. Add 2 cups MR. & MRS. "T"® Bully-Hi Mix and one cup water. Heat. *Do not boil.* Pour into heatproof bowls and top with slice of French bread and grated Swiss cheese. Put under broiler until cheese melts. Serve immediately. *Serves 2*

Wyler's®
WYLER'S® FRENCH ONION SOUP

4 cups thinly sliced sweet onions
1 clove garlic, finely chopped
¼ cup margarine or butter
5½ cups water
½ cup dry sherry or white wine, optional
8 teaspoons WYLER'S® Beef-Flavor Instant Bouillon OR 8 Beef-Flavor Bouillon Cubes
6 slices French bread, ¾-inch thick, buttered and toasted
6 slices natural Swiss cheese, cut in half crosswise

In large saucepan, cook onion and garlic in margarine until onions are golden brown. Add water, sherry, if desired, and bouillon; bring to a boil; reduce heat and simmer 30 minutes to blend flavors. Place soup in 6 oven-proof bowls. Top each serving with a bread slice and cheese. Broil until cheese melts. Serve immediately. Refrigerate leftovers.

TIP: If sherry is omitted, substitute ½ cup water.

FRENCH ONION SOUP

4 large onions, thinly sliced
¼ pound butter or margarine
4 tablespoons butter
4 tablespoons all-purpose flour
2 cups beef broth
2 quarts water
1 tablespoon soy sauce
1½ teaspoons salt
1½ teaspoons TABASCO® Pepper Sauce
1 teaspoon KITCHEN BOUQUET®
½ teaspoon Worcestershire sauce
2 beef bouillon cubes
6 slices French bread
1 8-ounce package shredded Mozzarella cheese

Sauté onions in ¼ pound hot butter or margarine until clear. In large saucepan, melt 4 tablespoons butter. Blend in flour and cook over low heat, stirring constantly, until dark brown. Gradually stir in beef broth. Bring to a boil. Boil for 1 minute, stirring constantly. Add sautéed onions in butter, water, soy sauce, salt, TABASCO® Sauce, KITCHEN BOUQUET®, Worcestershire sauce and bouillon cubes. Mix well. Bring to a boil. Then cover and simmer over low heat 30 minutes. Pour into 6 individual soup servers and place slice of bread on top of each. Cover each with shredded cheese. Heat under broiler until cheese is golden and bubbly. Serve at once.
Serves 6

Lea & Perrins
THE ORIGINAL WORCESTERSHIRE

"SPLIT SECOND" PEA SOUP*

1 can (11¼ oz.) condensed green pea soup
1 soup can milk or water
1 tablespoon LEA & PERRINS Worcestershire Sauce
1 teaspoon onion powder
½ cup diced cooked ham or crumbled crisp bacon

In a medium saucepan combine all ingredients; mix well. Heat thoroughly, stirring occasionally. Serve with assorted crackers, if desired.
Yield: 3 portions

*May be prepared in advance of serving.

SPLIT PEA SOUP

½ pound green or yellow split
   peas
4 cups water
1 ham hock or meaty ham bone
⅓ cup *each* chopped onion,
   celery and carrots
1 small bay leaf
½ teaspoon salt
1 small garlic clove, if desired

Wash and drain split peas.
Combine all ingredients in kettle
with tight-fitting lid. Bring to boil.
Reduce heat and simmer, covered,
2 hours; stir occasionally. Remove
ham hock or bone; cool slightly.
Cut ham off bone; dice. Add to
soup and heat thoroughly. Remove
bay leaf before serving.
Makes 4 or 5 servings

TIP: Split peas require no soaking.
Note: Split pea soups are very
   thick and may need thinning.
   To thin split pea soup, heat
   slowly and stir in small
   amount stock, water, light
   cream or undiluted
   evaporated milk.
*Favorite recipe from Idaho-Washington Dry
Pea & Lentil Commissions*

SPLIT PEA 'N' TURKEY SOUP

½ pound green *or* yellow split
   peas
4 cups chicken *or* turkey broth
⅓ cup *each* chopped onion, celery
   and carrots
1 small bay leaf
½ teaspoon salt
1 small garlic clove, if desired
1 cup diced cooked turkey

Wash and drain split peas.
Combine all ingredients except
turkey in kettle with tight-fitting lid.
Bring to boil. Reduce heat and
simmer, covered, 2 hours; stir
occasionally. Add turkey during
last 15 minutes of cooking.
Remove bay leaf before serving.
Makes 4 or 5 servings

TIP: Split peas require no soaking.
Note: Split pea soups are very
   thick and may need thinning.
   To thin split pea soup, heat
   slowly and stir in small
   amount chicken or turkey
   broth, water, light cream or
   undiluted evaporated milk.
*Favorite recipe from Idaho-Washington Dry
Pea & Lentil Commissions*

PLANTATION HAM AND PEA MAIN DISH SOUP

1 cup cooked ham cut in strips
¼ cup chopped onion
2 tablespoons butter or margarine
2 cans (11½ ounces *each*)
   CAMPBELL'S Condensed Green
   Pea Soup
1½ soup cans water
2 cups cooked mixed vegetables
¼ teaspoon ground nutmeg

In saucepan, brown ham and cook
onion in butter until tender. Add
soup; gradually blend in water. Add
vegetables and nutmeg. Heat; stir
occasionally. Recipe may be
doubled.
Makes about 5½ cups

CREAM OF POTATO SOUP

4 slices bacon, diced
1 cup ORE-IDA® fresh frozen
   Chopped Onions
1½ cups hot water
3½ cups frozen ORE-IDA®
   Southern Style Hash Browns*
1½ teaspoons salt
2 cups milk
⅛ teaspoon pepper
Minced parsley (optional)

In large skillet over medium-high
heat, cook bacon until crisp;
remove from skillet and drain on
paper towels. Spoon off excess fat,
reserving two tablespoons. Cook
onions in reserved drippings until
golden and tender. Add water,
frozen Southern Style Hash
Browns and salt; bring to a boil,
stirring occasionally to separate
potatoes. Reduce heat, cover,
simmer 10 minutes or until
potatoes are tender. Lightly mash
potatoes if desired. Stir in milk,
pepper and bacon; heat, but do not
boil. Serve topped with minced
parsley, if desired.
Yield: 5 servings

VARIATION:

Hearty Chowder: Follow basic
recipe omitting bacon dices.
Sauté onions in 3 tablespoons
butter or margarine. Add with the
water, potatoes and salt:

1 carton (10 ounces) frozen mixed
   vegetables, broken apart
8 weiners, cut ¼ " circles
Additional ½ teaspoon salt

Proceed as above.
Yield: 4-6 servings

*May also be prepared with ORE-
IDA® Shredded Hash Browns

POTATO AVOCADO SOUP

2 CALAVO® Avocados peeled,
   seeded, and cubed (reserve ¼ of
   1 avocado)
5 slices of bacon, cut into small
   pieces
1 cup minced onion
2 medium potatoes pared and
   cubed
3 cups chicken broth
½ cup dairy sour cream
Ground pepper
Salt

Fry bacon until crisp. Remove
bacon and add minced onion to
hot fat; sauté until tender,
approximately 5 minutes. Add
potatoes and chicken broth. Heat
to boiling, reduce heat and simmer
until potatoes are tender,
approximately 15 minutes. Remove
from heat and add avocado. Puree
mixture in blender or food
processor. Return puree to pan and
heat to boiling. Remove from heat
and stir in sour cream. Salt and
pepper to taste. Garnish with
bacon and avocado. *Serves 4*

HOT YOGURT SOUP

1 cup semolina
1 cup medium barley
10 cups beef or chicken broth
3 cups finely chopped onion
2 tablespoons finely chopped mint
½ lb. butter or margarine
4 cups DANNON® Plain Yogurt
Salt and pepper to taste

Soak barley for 2 hours, cook in
broth for 1 hour. Soak semolina in
water for ½ an hour. Add semolina
to barley mixture. Simmer on low
heat. In a separate pan, fry onions
golden brown in butter. Add
onions, mint, salt and pepper to
soup. Stir yogurt well and add it
very slowly. Heat until just before
it comes to a boil. Serve hot.
Serves about 6

ALPHABET CHICKEN SOUP

3 to 4 lbs. stewing chicken,
  cut into pieces
3 quarts (12 cups) water
1 tablespoon salt
6 peppercorns
¼ teaspoon poultry seasoning, if
  desired
1⅔ cups AMERICAN BEAUTY®
  Alphabets
1⅓ cups sliced carrots
1 cup finely chopped celery
¼ cup chopped onion
Salt
Pepper

In 6 to 8-quart Dutch oven,
combine chicken, water, 1
tablespoon salt, peppercorns and
poultry seasoning. Bring to boil.
Cover and cook over low heat 1
hour or until chicken is tender.
Remove chicken and peppercorns.
Skim off fat. Cut meat from bone
and return to soup. Add alphabets,
carrots, celery and onion; cook,
covered, 20 to 30 minutes or until
alphabets are tender. Season with
salt and pepper.

16 (1-cup) servings

High Altitude—Above 3500 Feet: No change.

NUTRITIONAL INFORMATION PER SERVING

SERVING SIZE: ⅟₁₆ OF RECIPE		PERCENT U.S. RDA PER SERVING	
Calories	160	Protein	23
Protein	15 g	Vitamin A	25
Carbohydrate	15 g	Vitamin C	3
Fat	4 g	Thiamine	7
Sodium	450 mg	Riboflavin	7
Potassium	215 mg	Niacin	24
		Calcium	2
		Iron	7

SIMPLE TURKEY SOUP

BUTTERBALL® Turkey carcass
3 stalks celery with tops,
  coarsely chopped
1 onion, sliced
1 tablespoon salt
1 bay leaf
12 cups water
1¾ ounce package dry chicken
  noodle soup mix

Simmer turkey carcass, celery,
onion, salt and bay leaf in water
about 2 hours. Turn turkey if
necessary during cooking. Remove
carcass. Strip meat from bones

and add to broth. Bring soup to a
boil and add soup mix. Simmer
about 10 minutes. This soup is
even better if made the day before
it is served.

Note: Small amounts of cooked
  vegetables such as peas,
  corn or carrots may be added
  with the soup mix.

Yield: 13 cups

TURKEY VEGETABLE SOUP

BUTTERBALL® Turkey carcass
Large onion, sliced
3 stalks celery, coarsely chopped
2 teaspoons salt
1 teaspoon ground rosemary
½ teaspoon white pepper
2 bay leaves
6 sprigs parsley
3 quarts water
3 chicken bouillon cubes
2 cups sliced carrots
½ cup rice
10 ounce package frozen peas

Simmer turkey carcass, onion,
celery, salt, rosemary, pepper, bay
leaves and parsley in water 2½ to
3 hours. Turn carcass if necessary
during cooking. Remove carcass,
cool slightly and strip meat from
bones. Reserve turkey meat. Strain
broth and discard vegetables.
Spoon off excess fat, if desired.
Bring broth to boil; add bouillon
cubes, carrots and rice. Simmer 10
to 12 minutes. Add peas and
reserved turkey meat. Continue to
cook 5 to 10 minutes until
vegetables and rice are tender.

Yield: 11 cups

SAVORY TURKEY SOUP

1 turkey carcass (from 10 to
  14-pound turkey)*
2 quarts water
1½ cups sliced celery
1½ cups sliced carrots
½ cup chopped fresh onion
¼ cup chopped fresh parsley
1½ cups (16-ounce can) tomatoes,
  with liquid, cut up
2 cups (about 6 ounces) SAN
  GIORGIO Cut Fusilli (Curly Cut
  Spaghetti)
Salt and pepper to taste
Parmesan cheese, if desired

Place carcass of turkey that has
had most of meat trimmed away in
large 4-quart sauce pot or kettle.
Add water, celery, carrots, onion,
parsley and tomatoes to pot; bring
to a boil. Reduce heat and simmer,
uncovered, about 1 hour or until
turkey carcass is falling apart.
Remove carcass bones; return
meat from bones to stock. Bring
stock back to a boil; stir in 2 cups
Cut Fusilli. Cook about 10 minutes
or until Cut Fusilli is tender. Add
salt and pepper to taste.

For a heartier soup, add 2 cups
diced leftover cooked turkey to
broth. Serve, garnished with
Parmesan cheese, if desired.

*Note: For larger turkey, increase
  water to almost cover
  carcass and add extra
  vegetables and Fusilli, if
  desired.

HEARTY BARLEY SOUP
(Beef 'n Barley Vegetable Soup)

2 lb. soup bones
2 tablespoons vegetable oil
2 qt. water
1 16-oz. can tomatoes, undrained
2 tablespoons fresh chopped
  parsley or 2 teaspoons dried
  parsley flakes
2 teaspoons salt
¼ teaspoon pepper
1 cup diced carrots
½ cup chopped celery
¼ cup chopped onion
⅔ cup QUAKER® SCOTCH®
  BRAND Pearled Barley*
1 cup fresh or frozen peas

In large saucepot or Dutch oven,
brown soup bones in hot oil; drain.
Add water, tomatoes, parsley, salt
and pepper. Bring to a boil; reduce
heat. Add remaining ingredients
except peas. Simmer, uncovered,
about 1 hour or until meat and
barley are tender. Remove soup
bones from broth. Remove meat
from bones; return to broth. Add
peas; continue simmering about 10
minutes.   *Makes 8 servings*

*Note: Substitute 1 cup QUAKER®
  SCOTCH® BRAND Quick
  Pearled Barley for regular
  barley, if desired. Add with
  peas; simmer about 10
  minutes or until meat and
  barley are tender.

HAMBURGER VEGETABLE SOUP

1 lb. ground beef
²⁄₃ cup chopped onion
1 can (46 oz.) STOKELY'S FINEST®
   Tomato Juice
2 cans (1 lb. ea.) STOKELY'S
   FINEST® Mixed Vegetables
2 beef bouillon cubes
1 teaspoon seasoned salt
1 teaspoon sugar

In large saucepan, brown ground
beef and onion; drain excess fat.
Add remaining ingredients and
bring soup to a boil. Lower heat
and simmer for 30 minutes.
Makes 6 servings

QUICK BEEFY VEGETABLE SOUP

1 lb. ground beef
1 (16 oz.) package frozen mixed
   vegetables
2 cups or cans MR. & MRS. "T"®
   Bloody Mary Mix
2 cups or cans MR. & MRS. "T"®
   Bully-Hi Mix
2 cups cubed potatoes
½ teaspoon salt
¼ teaspoon pepper

Brown beef in 3 quart saucepan,
stirring to crumble. Drain off fat.
Return beef to saucepan. Add
remaining ingredients. Bring to
boil. Reduce heat and simmer
20/25 minutes or until potatoes are
tender. Serve with French bread.
Serves 4-6

VEGETABLE BEAN SOUP

½ cup chopped onion
2 Tablespoons butter or margarine
½ lb. wieners, sliced
1 can (1 lb.) VAN CAMP'S®
   Pork and Beans
1 can (1 lb.) STOKELY'S FINEST®
   Mixed Vegetables
2 cups STOKELY'S FINEST®
   Tomato Juice
1 cup water
1 teaspoon instant beef bouillon
1 teaspoon sugar

Sauté onions in butter. Add
remaining ingredients and simmer
30 minutes.   *Makes 6 servings*

VEGETABLE CREAM SOUP

1 tablespoon ARGO® /
   KINGSFORD'S® Corn Starch
2 cups milk
2 tablespoons margarine
½ teaspoon salt
¼ teaspoon pepper
1 chicken bouillon cube
1 cup finely chopped cooked
   vegetables, (spinach, asparagus
   or broccoli)

In saucepan mix corn starch and
½ cup of the milk until smooth.
Stir in next 4 ingredients and
remaining milk. Bring to boil over
medium heat, stirring constantly,
and boil 1 minute. Add vegetables.
Makes 3 cups

CHEESE TOPPED VEGETABLE SOUP

1 cup chopped onion
½ cup sliced celery
2 tablespoons butter or margarine
4 cups beef bouillon
2 cups cubed cooked chicken
½ pound frankfurters, sliced
   pennywise
¼ pound hard dry sausage, diced
1 package (6 ounces) VALIO
   Gruyere Cheese, shredded

In saucepan, cook onion and celery
in butter until vegetables are
tender. Add bouillon, chicken,
frankfurters and sausage. Simmer
for 15 minutes. Garnish each
serving generously with VALIO
Gruyere cheese.
Makes 6 to 8 servings

CHUNKY VEGETABLE SOUP

2 pounds hot or sweet Italian
   sausage, cut into ½" slices
1 large onion, chopped
1 clove garlic, minced
2 cans (13¾ oz. each) beef broth
1 jar (15½ oz.) RAGU' Spaghetti
   Sauce, any flavor
1 medium zucchini, cut into ¼"
   slices
4 cups water
1 cup sliced celery
1 cup sliced carrots
1½ teaspoons basil
Salt, to taste
Pepper, to taste
1½ cups uncooked elbow
   macaroni, cooked and drained
Grated Parmesan cheese

In a large Dutch oven, brown
sausage thoroughly on all sides.
Add onion and garlic. Sauté until
onion is translucent; drain fat. Add
remaining ingredients except pasta
and cheese; simmer 30 minutes.
Add pasta; simmer 10 minutes.
Serve soup with Parmesan cheese.
Serves about 6

RAINY DAY PICK-ME-UP

1 can (10½ ounces) CAMPBELL'S
   Condensed Beef Broth
1 can (10½ ounces) CAMPBELL'S
   Condensed Vegetable Soup
2 soup cans water
2 cups cabbage cut in long thin
   shreds
½ lb. frankfurters, sliced
1 can (about 8 ounces) tomatoes,
   cut up
½ cup uncooked small shell
   macaroni
1 medium onion, sliced
2 tablespoons grated Parmesan
   cheese
1 medium clove garlic, minced
½ teaspoon caraway seed

In large saucepan, combine
ingredients. Bring to boil; reduce
heat. Simmer 30 minutes or until
done; stir occasionally.
Makes about 8½ cups

FINNTASTIC SOUP

2 tablespoons butter or margarine
¼ cup chopped onion
¼ cup minced ham
1 can (10½ ounces) condensed
   cream of potato soup
1 soup can milk
⅛ teaspoon dill weed
1 cup shredded FINLANDIA Swiss
   Cheese

In saucepan, melt butter. Add
onion and ham and cook until
onion is tender. Gradually blend in
soup and milk. Heat, stirring
occasionally, until soup is hot. Do
not boil. Add dill. Garnish each
serving with cheese.
Makes 4 servings

PORK 'N' DUMPLINGS SOUP

1 can (about 4 ounces) sliced
  mushrooms, drained
1 cup sliced celery
2 tablespoons butter or margarine
2 cans (10½ ounces *each*)
  CAMPBELL'S Condensed Old
  Fashioned Vegetable Soup
1 soup can water
1 cup cubed cooked pork
1 cup biscuit mix
⅓ cup milk
1 tablespoon chopped parsley
⅛ teaspoon thyme leaves,
  crushed

In large saucepan, brown
mushrooms and cook celery in
butter until tender. Add soups,
water and pork; bring to boil.
Meanwhile, combine biscuit mix,
milk, parsley and thyme. Drop 5 to
6 spoonfuls on boiling soup;
reduce heat. Cook uncovered over
low heat 10 minutes. Cover; cook
10 minutes more.

Makes about 5½ cups

SWISS GALLO® SALAME AND CHEESE SOUP

¾ cup GALLO® Italian Dry
  Salame cut in julienne pieces
1 large onion, finely chopped
1 Tbsp. butter
3 cups chicken broth
1 cup half-and-half
3 eggs
Salt and pepper to taste
¾ cup shredded Gruyère or Swiss
  cheese
½ cup finely chopped parsley
1 red pepper, seeded and diced
  (optional)

In large saucepan sauté onion in
butter until golden. Add broth,
cover and simmer 10 minutes. Turn
into blender and puree. Return half
the mixture to soup pan. Add half-
and-half and eggs to remaining
mixture in blender and puree until
smooth. Pour into pan and stir to
blend with the broth. Cook over
low heat. Stir until thickened. Add
salt and pepper. Serve in soup
bowls and pass condiment bowls
of GALLO® Salame, Gruyère,
parsley, and red peppers. *Serves 6*

Mueller's®

ZUPPA PASTA FAGIOLA

¾ pound dried white kidney
  or lima beans
Water
Ham shank (about 2 pounds) or
  ham bone
2 cloves garlic, minced
4 medium firm tomatoes,
  peeled and chopped
½ teaspoon pepper
¼ teaspoon rubbed sage
¼ teaspoon thyme leaves
6 cups water
¼ cup olive oil
1 cup dry white wine
1 teaspoon salt
¼ teaspoon pepper
2 ounces (1 cup) MUELLER'S®
  Twist Macaroni

Soak beans in water overnight;
drain. Remove skin and excess fat
from ham shank. In large kettle
combine beans, ham shank, garlic,
2 of the chopped tomatoes, ½
teaspoon pepper, sage, thyme and
6 cups of water. Bring to a boil;
cover and simmer gently 2 hours,
or until beans are tender. Remove
shank from kettle; dice meat and
return to kettle. While beans are
cooking, combine olive oil, the
remaining 2 chopped tomatoes,
wine, salt and ¼ teaspoon pepper
in medium saucepan. Simmer,
uncovered, 20 minutes. Pour into
bean mixture. Bring to a boil; add
macaroni and continue to cook 9
to 12 minutes or until macaroni is
tender. Serve in large soup bowls.

8 to 10 servings

TOMATO CHEESE SOUP

1 can (10¾ ounces) condensed
  cream of tomato soup
1⅓ cups SEALTEST® Milk
Dash salt
½ teaspoon celery salt
1½ cups SEALTEST® Cottage
  Cheese, at room temperature
Snipped parsley (optional)

Pour tomato soup into heavy
saucepan. Stir in milk, salt, and
celery salt until blended. Heat
thoroughly, but do not boil, stirring

constantly. Just before serving,
add cottage cheese and beat with
rotary beater just enough to break
up curds. Heat a minute longer (no
more), stirring constantly. (The soft
tender cheese curds make an
interesting new addition to soups,
in a class with egg balls, custard
cubes, etc. Overcooking toughens
them.) Remove soup from heat;
serve *immediately* in heated bowls.
Garnish with parsley. *4 servings*

ITALIAN PASTA POT

½ cup chopped green pepper
1 large clove garlic, minced
¼ teaspoon rosemary leaves,
  crushed
2 tablespoons olive oil
3 cans (10¾ ounces *each*)
  CAMPBELL'S Tomato Soup
3 soup cans water
1 can (about 16 ounces) chick
  peas, drained
1 cup cooked small shell macaroni
2 teaspoons chopped anchovy
  fillets

In large saucepan, cook pepper
with garlic and rosemary in oil
until tender. Stir in soup and water.
Add remaining ingredients. Heat;
stir occasionally. Garnish with
grated Parmesan cheese, if
desired.

*Makes about 9½ cups, 6 to 8
servings*

HEARTY LUNCHEON SOUP

3 strips bacon
1 tablespoon butter or margarine
½ teaspoon grated onion
8 SUNSHINE KRISPY® Crackers
1 (10½ ounce) can condensed
  tomato soup
1 (10½ ounce) can condensed
  pea soup
Water (fill empty soup can)
Milk (fill empty soup can)

Fry bacon until crisp. Drain on
paper towel. Crumble into pieces.
Work butter or margarine until
softened. Mix in onion. Spread on
KRISPY® Crackers. Mix tomato
and pea soup. Gradually stir in the
water and milk. Heat, stirring
constantly, until soup comes to a
boil. Place KRISPY® Crackers
under broiler, and toast until lightly
browned. Pour soup into 4 soup
bowls. Place 2 crackers on top of
each bowl. Sprinkle with crumbled
bacon. *Yield: 4 servings*

TROPICAL SHERRY SOUP

1 large sweet onion, chopped
¼ cup butter
1 Tbsp. flour
1 Tbsp. curry powder
2 Tbsp. flaked coconut
2 quarts chicken broth
1 cup smooth peanut butter
¼ cup THE CHRISTIAN
    BROTHERS® Dry Sherry
½ cup sour cream
Chopped peanuts or macadamia
    nuts

In 3-quart saucepan sauté onion in butter until limp. Stir in flour, curry powder, coconut, and *one* cup of the chicken broth. Bring to boil, stirring constantly. Pour mixture into blender container with peanut butter; whirl smooth. Return mixture to saucepan. Add remaining broth and sherry. Simmer 5 minutes, stirring. Do not boil. Just before serving, whisk in sour cream to blend. Serve dusted with curry and garnished with dollops of additional sour cream and chopped nuts.
Makes 6-8 servings

1st Prize Winner THE CHRISTIAN BROTHERS® Contest

TORTILLA SOUP

2 or 3 OLD EL PASO® Corn
    Tortillas
Oil for frying
2 teaspoons vegetable oil
⅓ cup chopped onion
1 can (4 oz.) OLD EL PASO®
    Chopped Green Chilies
4 cups chicken broth
1 cup shredded, cooked chicken
Salt
1 can (10 oz.) OLD EL PASO®
    Tomatoes and Green Chilies
1 tablespoon lime juice
4 large lime slices

Cut tortillas in 2 × ½-inch strips. Fry tortillas in small amount of hot oil until brown and crisp. Drain on paper towels. Heat 2 teaspoons of vegetable oil in a large saucepan. Add onion and sauté until translucent. Add green chilies, broth, chicken, salt to taste, and tomatoes and green chilies. Cover and simmer 20 minutes. Stir in lime juice. To serve, pour into soup bowls and add tortilla strips. Float a lime slice in the center of each bowl. *Makes 4 servings*

DUTCH COUNTRY SOUP

½ pound frankfurters, cut into
    ½-inch slices
¼ teaspoon basil leaves, crushed
2 tablespoons butter or margarine
1 can (11½ ounces) CAMPBELL'S
    Condensed Split Pea with Ham
    Soup
1 can (10¾ ounces) CAMPBELL'S
    Condensed Cream of Potato
    Soup
1 soup can water
1 can (about 8 ounces) canned
    tomatoes, cut up

In large saucepan, brown frankfurters with basil in butter. Add soups; gradually stir in water. Add remaining ingredients. Heat; stir occasionally.
Makes about 5 cups

OLD HOMESTEADER SOUP

½ pound ground beef
½ cup green pepper strips
½ cup chopped onion
2 tablespoons chili powder
2 cans (11¼ ounces *each*)
    CAMPBELL'S Condensed Chili
    Beef Soup
½ cup water
1 can (16 ounces) tomatoes, cut up
1 can (about 15½ ounces) kidney
    beans, undrained

In large saucepan, brown beef and cook green pepper and onion with chili powder until tender (use shortening if necessary). Stir to separate meat. Add remaining ingredients. Simmer 15 minutes; stir often.
Makes about 7 cups

POT-OF-LUCK MAIN DISH SOUP

½ pound ground beef
1 tablespoon finely chopped onion
⅛ teaspoon salt
Dash pepper
2 tablespoons shortening
1 cup thinly sliced carrots
2 cans (10½ ounces *each*)
    CAMPBELL'S Condensed Beef
    Broth
2 soup cans water
1 small bay leaf
1½ cups medium noodles,
    broken in pieces

Mix *thoroughly* beef, onion, salt and pepper; shape into 18

meatballs. In large heavy pan, brown meatballs in shortening; pour off fat. Add remaining ingredients. Bring to boil; reduce heat. Simmer 10 minutes or until noodles are done. Stir occasionally. Remove bay leaf.
Makes about 6 cups

JAMBOREE HAM BONE SOUP

1 ham bone with meat or
    ½ pound ham steak, cut in
    narrow 2″ strips
2 quarts water
1 cup onion, diced
1 cup celery, diced
1½ cups green beans, ends
    removed and cut in 2″ lengths
1 cup turnip, diced
1 cup black-eyed peas
2 cups potato, diced
1½ cups tomato, peeled and diced
½ cup fresh or frozen green peas
1 cup fresh or frozen corn kernels
1 teaspoon IMPERIAL Granulated
    Sugar
½ teaspoon black pepper
1 teaspoon salt

Add ham bone or ham strips to water and bring to boil. Simmer for 15 minutes. Add onion, celery, green beans, turnip, black-eyed peas and potato. Simmer until vegetables are barely tender. Add remaining ingredients. Simmer 5 minutes. Adjust seasonings to taste. *Serves 8 to 10*

MIDWEST CHOWDER

2 cups boiling water
2 cups chopped potatoes
½ cup carrot slices
½ cup celery slices
¼ cup chopped onion
1½ teaspoons salt
¼ teaspoon pepper
¼ cup PARKAY Margarine
¼ cup flour
2 cups milk
2½ cups (10 ozs.) shredded
    CRACKER BARREL Brand Sharp
    Natural Cheddar Cheese
1 17-oz. can cream style corn

Combine water, vegetables and seasonings. Cover; simmer 10 minutes. Do not drain. Make a white sauce with margarine, flour and milk. Add cheese; stir until melted. Add corn and undrained vegetables. Heat; do not boil.
6 to 8 servings

CORN CHOWDER

2 cups boiling water
2 cups diced potatoes
½ cup sliced carrot
½ cup sliced celery
¼ cup chopped onion
1½ tsp. salt
¼ tsp. white pepper
¼ tsp. thyme
1 cup grated sharp Cheddar
  cheese
1 (17 oz.) can S&W Cream
  Style Corn

White Sauce:
¼ cup margarine
¼ cup flour
2 cups milk

In a large pot, cook potatoes,
carrots, celery, onion, salt, pepper
and thyme in boiling water (about
20 minutes). Do not drain off liquid.
Add Cheddar cheese and cream
style corn to pot and stir well.

Meanwhile, make white sauce by
making a roux with margarine and
flour in a small saucepan. Add all
of the milk at once while stirring
constantly. Cook until sauce
thickens. Add white sauce to
above mixture slowly while stirring.
Simmer to heat through—Do Not
Boil.   *Serves about 6 to 8*

FRESH VEGETABLE AND CHEDDAR CHEESE CHOWDER

¼ cup margarine
1 cup sliced carrots
1 cup cubed potatoes
1 cup sliced green beans
½ cup chopped onion
½ cup sliced celery
¼ cup chopped green pepper
3 tablespoons ARGO® /
  KINGSFORD'S® Corn Starch
1 teaspoon salt
1 teaspoon dry mustard
4 cups cool chicken bouillon
1 tablespoon Worcestershire sauce
1 cup coarsely shredded Cheddar
  cheese

In a large saucepan melt margarine
over medium heat. Add next 6
ingredients. Sauté 5 minutes,
stirring constantly. Mix corn
starch, salt and dry mustard.
Gradually stir in bouillon and
Worcestershire sauce until smooth.
Add to vegetable mixture. Bring to
boil over medium heat, stirring

constantly, and boil 1 minute.
Reduce heat; cover and simmer ½
hour or until vegetables are tender.
Add cheese; stir until melted.
          Makes 6 (1-cup) servings

MIDWESTERN FISH CHOWDER

1 lb. BOOTH Frozen Fillets
¼ cup chopped bacon or salt
  pork
½ cup chopped onion
½ cup chopped green pepper
1 cup chopped celery
2 cups boiling water
1 cup diced potatoes
¼ teaspoon thyme
1 teaspoon salt
Dash cayenne pepper
2 cups tomato juice

Thaw frozen fillets. Skin fillets
and cut into ½ inch pieces. Fry
bacon until lightly browned. Add
onion, green pepper and celery.
Cook until tender. Add water,
potatoes, seasonings and fish.
Cook about 15 minutes or until
potatoes are tender. Add tomato
juice; heat.   *Makes 6 servings*

VARIATION:

For *New England Fish Chowder,*
omit pepper, celery and thyme.
Substitute 2 cups whole milk for
tomato juice and black pepper for
cayenne. Add a little butter and
parsley to each bowl before
serving.

FAST FISH CHOWDER

1 package (10 ounces)
  MRS. PAUL'S® Buttered Fish
  Fillets, partially thawed
2 cans (10½ ounces, each)
  condensed cream of potato soup
2½ cups milk
1 bay leaf
1 teaspoon onion powder
4 slices bacon, crisply fried and
  crumbled

Cut fish fillets into 1 inch pieces.
Combine remaining ingredients
except bacon in a medium size
saucepan. Bring to a boil, stirring
occasionally. Add fish pieces and
simmer approximately 10-15
minutes, or until fish flakes easily.
Serve at once, garnishing with
crumbled bacon.
          Makes 1½ quarts of soup

BOSTON SEAFOOD CHOWDER

1 pound frozen fish fillets, cod or
  perch
1 medium onion, chopped
1-2 tablespoons cooking oil
2 cans (10¾ oz. each) condensed
  cream of potato soup (undiluted)
1 cup milk
2 cans (16 oz. each) VEG-ALL®
  Mixed Vegetables, undrained
½ teaspoon thyme
Pinch ground black pepper

Partially thaw fish fillets at room
temperature 15 to 20 minutes; cut
fish into cubes. In a large
saucepan or Dutch oven, sauté
onion in cooking oil until tender,
but not browned. Add the canned
potato soup and milk; stir together
until smooth. Stir in remaining
ingredients, and the fish cubes.
Cover and cook over low heat 20-30
minutes, or until fish is opaque
and flakes when tested with a fork.
          Serves 6-8

MANHATTAN FISH CHOWDER

1 pound fish fillets or steaks,
  fresh or frozen
¼ cup chopped bacon or salt pork
½ cup chopped onion
2 cups boiling water
1 can (1 pound) tomatoes
1 cup diced potatoes
½ cup diced carrots
½ cup chopped celery
¼ cup catsup
1 tablespoon Worcestershire sauce
1 teaspoon salt
¼ teaspoon pepper
¼ teaspoon thyme
Chopped parsley

Thaw frozen fish. Remove skin and
bones from fish. Cut fish into
1-inch pieces. Fry bacon until
crisp. Add onion and cook until
tender. Add water, tomatoes,
potatoes, carrots, celery, catsup,
and seasonings. Cover and simmer
for 40 to 45 minutes or until
vegetables are tender. Add fish.
Cover and simmer about 10
minutes longer or until fish flake
easily when tested with a fork.
Sprinkle with parsley.
          Makes 6 servings

*Favorite recipe from National Marine
Fisheries Services*

OLD SALT'S SEAFOOD DELIGHT
(Like Cioppino)

2 (8 oz.) cans S&W Tomato Sauce
2 tomato sauce cans of water
1 medium onion, thinly sliced
1 clove garlic, pressed
3 large tomatoes, diced in small
   pieces
Juice of 1 fresh lemon
Juice of ½ fresh lime
1 tsp. salt
1 tsp. pepper
1 bay leaf
½ tsp. each rosemary, sweet basil,
   thyme and cumin
2 Tbsp. parsley flakes
1 (4½ oz.) can S&W Deveined
   Small Size Whole Shrimp,
   drained
2 (4½ oz.) cans S&W Deveined
   Jumbo Size Whole Shrimp,
   drained
1 (10 oz.) can S&W Minced Clams
1 (10 oz.) can S&W Whole Baby
   Chowder Clams

First, rinse the drained shrimp in
cold water and soak to remove
salty flavor. Meanwhile, empty
cans of tomato sauce and water
into large saucepan. Add onion,
garlic, tomatoes, juices of lemon
and lime and seasonings. Bring to
slow boil. Reduce heat and simmer
for 5 to 10 minutes. Add clams
with clam juice and drained
shrimp; blend all together. Simmer
another 5 minutes until mixture is
hot throughout.   *Serves 4 to 6*

NEW ENGLAND CHOWDER
(Low Calorie)

1 can (6½ oz.) BUMBLE BEE®
   Chunk Light Tuna in Water
2 large boiling potatoes (about 1½
   pounds)
Water
1 cup minced green onion
1 cup minced celery
1 cup sliced carrot
3 cans (14½ oz. each) chicken
   broth
Parsley or green onion for garnish

Drain tuna. Cook potatoes in
boiling water until tender; drain.
Cool; peel skins and cut in chunks.
Meanwhile simmer vegetables in
broth until tender about 15

minutes. Strain broth into blender;
reserve vegetables. Add potato
chunks to blender and puree until
very smooth. Pour puree and
vegetables into soup pot. Simmer
15 minutes, stirring occasionally.
Add tuna to soup and cook 5
minutes longer. Top each serving
with minced parsley or sliced
green onion.   *Makes 8 cups*

124 calories per serving

NEW ENGLAND CLAM CHOWDER

2 dozen shell clams or
   2 cans (8 ounces each) minced
   clams
1 cup water
¼ pound salt pork or bacon,
   minced
½ cup finely chopped onion
1½ cups clam liquor, plus water
5 cups diced potatoes
2 cups milk
8 saltine crackers
2 cups half and half
2 tablespoons margarine or butter
Chopped parsley

Wash clam shells thoroughly.
Place clams in a large pot with 1
cup water. Bring to a boil and
simmer for 5 to 8 minutes or until
clams open. Remove clams from
shell and mince. Strain liquid
remaining in pot. (Or: If using
canned clams, drain and reserve
liquor.) Cook salt pork until
browned and crisp. Remove salt
pork from pan, reserving 2
tablespoons drippings. In
saucepan, add onion and cook
until tender. Add clam liquor and
potatoes. Bring to a boil and
simmer until potatoes are tender.
Pour milk over saltines and let
stand until soft. Stir milk, half and
half, reserved salt pork, and
margarine into chowder mixture.
Heat until hot enough to serve.
Garnish with chopped parsley.
     Makes 6 servings

*Favorite recipe from National Marine
Fisheries Services*

HEARTY FISH CHOWDER

2 tablespoons butter or margarine
½ cup sliced onion
1½ teaspoons salt
½ teaspoon basil, crushed
¼ teaspoon pepper
2 cups potatoes, peeled and cubed
28-oz. can whole tomatoes,
   coarsely chopped
1 lb. pkg. frozen cod or haddock
   fillets, thawed
12-oz. can GREEN GIANT®
   NIBLETS® Golden Whole
   Kernel Corn, drained

In large saucepan, sauté onion in
butter until tender. Add remaining
ingredients except corn and fish.
Cover, bring to a boil and simmer
20 minutes, stirring occasionally.
Cut fish into bite-size pieces. Add
fish and corn to tomato mixture.
Bring to a boil; reduce heat, cover
and simmer for 10 minutes or until
fish flakes easily and potatoes are
tender.   *4 (1½ cup) servings*

NUTRITIONAL INFORMATION PER SERVING			
SERVING SIZE: ¼ OF RECIPE		PERCENT U.S. RDA PER SERVING	
Calories	330	Protein	43
Protein	28 g	Vitamin A	47
Carbohydrate	41 g	Vitamin C	60
Fat	7 g	Thiamine	14
Sodium	1335 mg	Riboflavin	14
Potassium	855 mg	Niacin	17
		Calcium	3
		Iron	11

NEW ORLEANS BOUILLABAISSE

1 pound each of 2 kinds of frozen
   fish fillets (red snapper, cod or
   perch)
2 cans (16 oz. each) tomatoes
2 cans (16 oz. each) VEG-ALL®
   Mixed Vegetables
1 teaspoon salt
¼ teaspoon thyme
¼ teaspoon basil
1 bay leaf
Few drops TABASCO® Pepper
   Sauce

Partially thaw fish at room
temperature 15 to 20 minutes; cut
fish into cubes. Combine tomatoes
(including liquid), VEG-ALL® and
seasonings in a large saucepan.
Bring to simmer and add fish fillet
cubes. Cover and cook over low
heat 20 to 30 minutes, or until fish
is opaque and flakes easily when
tested with a fork. Remove bay leaf
before serving.   *Serves 8-10*

SHERRY SHRIMP SOUP

Chicken Rice Homemade SOUP
    STARTER™
4 cups water
1½ cups dairy sour cream
2 cups whole kernel corn
2 packages (6 ounces each) frozen
    cooked shrimp
⅓ cup sherry
Optional: Crumbled bacon,
    chopped parsley or chives

In a large heavy saucepan combine
SOUP STARTER™ ingredients and
water. Cover and simmer 30
minutes. Pour soup mixture into
blender and blend until smooth.
Add enough water to make 6 cups
soup. Blend in sour cream. Pour
soup into a large saucepan. Add
corn, shrimp and sherry. Heat until
hot, but do not allow soup to boil.
Serve hot. If desired, just before
serving sprinkle top of soup with
crumbled bacon, chopped parsley
or chives.
    Yield: 9 cups, 6 to 8 servings

Sherry Cheese Soup—Substitute
1½ cups shredded sharp Cheddar
cheese for shrimp. Heat until
cheese melts; stir well to blend.

Note: Soup is also delicious chilled
    and served cold.

CALEDONIA SHRIMP SOUP

1 can condensed cream of shrimp
    soup
1 cup milk
¼ cup JOHNNIE WALKER Red
6 whole cooked shrimp (optional)

Combine soup and milk in
saucepan. Heat just to boiling
point. Stir in JOHNNIE WALKER
Red; heat until soup returns to
simmer. Garnish each portion with
whole cooked shrimp, if desired.
    2 to 3 servings

HEARTY TUNA SOUP

4 cups water
1 package FRENCH'S® Au Gratin
    Potatoes
1 can (6½-oz.) tuna, drained
1 package (10-oz.) frozen chopped
    broccoli, partially thawed
1½ cups milk
½ teaspoon salt

Combine in saucepan water and
contents of potato package,
including seasoning mix. Cover
and simmer 20 to 25 minutes,
stirring occasionally. Add tuna,
broccoli, milk, and salt; heat 5 to
10 minutes longer, until hot.
    6 to 8 servings

TABASCO®

CREOLE SEAFOOD GUMBO

¼ cup butter or margarine
2 tablespoons all-purpose flour
2 cups liquid (water and a little
    juice from seafood)
2 cups cut okra*
2 cups peeled and cubed
    tomatoes**
1 large onion, chopped
1 small green pepper, chopped
1 teaspoon TABASCO® Pepper
    Sauce
⅛ teaspoon thyme
1 bay leaf
2 cups shrimp, crab meat, oysters,
    or a combination*
3 cups hot cooked rice

Melt butter in saucepan. Blend in
flour and cook over low heat,
stirring constantly, until dark
brown. Add liquid, okra, tomatoes,
onion, pepper, TABASCO® Sauce,
thyme and bay leaf. Bring to a boil.
Then cover and simmer 30 minutes,
stirring occasionally. Add seafood
and cook 10-15 minutes longer.
Remove bay leaf. Serve in soup
bowls with mound of hot rice in
center.
    Serves 6

 *Fresh, frozen or canned may be
    used.
**Fresh or canned may be used.

SAN FRANCISCO BISQUE

1 can (10¾ ounces) CAMPBELL'S
    Cream of Celery Soup
1 soup can water
¼ cup sauterne or other dry
    white wine
1 pound fillet of white fish, cut
    in 1-inch pieces
¼ cup pimiento strips
¼ cup chopped watercress
1 teaspoon chervil leaves, crushed
½ teaspoon garlic salt
Dash pepper

In saucepan, combine all
ingredients; bring to boil. Cover;
cook over low heat 5 minutes or
until fish is done. Stir occasionally.
    Makes about 4 cups, 4 servings

LOBSTER BISQUE

4 tablespoons butter
1 small onion, sliced
1 carrot, sliced
1 stalk celery, sliced
1 live lobster, 1 to 1¼ pounds
2 cups Maison JACQUIN Chablis
1½ cups chicken stock
2 tablespoons flour
1 cup rich milk
1 cup light cream

Melt 2 tablespoons butter in a
heavy saucepan. Add onion, carrot
and celery and cook over low heat
for about 5 minutes—do not let
them brown. Kill the lobster
instantly by cutting across its body
just below the head. Break off the
claws and cut the tail in 3 or 4
pieces; put into saucepan with any
of the green liver. Sauté 5 minutes.
Add Maison JACQUIN Chablis and
chicken stock; bring to a boil,
cover, reduce heat, and simmer for
15 minutes. Remove lobster; when
it's cool enough to handle, take
meat out of shells and cut in small
dice. In another pan, melt
remaining 2 tablespoons butter;
blend in flour and cook, stirring, for
2 minutes. Strain the stock and
add to butter-flour mixture,
whisking vigorously. Bring to a
boil, stirring. Add milk and cream
and bring to a boil again. Taste for
seasoning; reduce heat and
simmer 5 minutes. Add diced
lobster and heat through.
    Makes 10 servings

OYSTER BISQUE

1 small carrot, diced
½ small onion, chopped
1 small celery stalk, chopped
1 sprig parsley, chopped
2 tablespoons butter, melted
1½ pints oysters
½ cup TAYLOR New York State
  Sauterne
1 cup crumbled soft bread
  crumbs*
2 cups chicken broth
1 cup milk
1½ cups heavy cream
Salt
Pepper

Sauté carrot, onion, celery, and parsley in butter until shiny (3 to 4 minutes). Drain 1 pint (2 dozen) oysters. Save liquid. Chop oysters fine; add to vegetables. Stir over low heat 3 minutes. Stir in Sauterne and continue to simmer 3 minutes more. Soak bread crumbs in oyster liquid. Spoon into vegetable-oyster mixture. Add chicken broth, milk and cream. Heat but do not boil. While bisque is heating, sauté remaining oysters in a small amount of butter until edges ruffle. Combine with bisque. Pour into heated tureen or individual bowls. Serve.
Approximately 8-10 servings

Suggestion: TAYLOR New York State Rhine Wine can be substituted for Sauterne.

*French or Italian bread is preferable.

MUSHROOM-YOGURT BISQUE

2 tablespoons butter or margarine
⅓ cup chopped onion
¾ pound sliced mushrooms
¼ cup flour
1 quart chicken broth
1 tablespoon cornstarch
1 tablespoon cold water
1 cup (8 oz.) BREYERS® Plain
  Yogurt
Chopped dill or chives

Sauté onion and mushrooms in butter until moisture disappears. Sprinkle flour over mushrooms; mix. Gradually add chicken broth, stirring constantly. Cover and simmer 10 minutes. Puree in blender, in small amounts. Dissolve cornstarch in water; blend into yogurt. Add 1 cup of hot soup to yogurt; stir yogurt into hot soup; heat. Taste for seasoning, adding salt and pepper if desired. Garnish each serving with chopped dill or chives.
Makes 6 cups (serves 6 to 8)

BASIC CREAM SOUP
(Low Cholesterol)

2 Tbsp. minced onion
¼ cup soft margarine
¼ cup flour
3½ cups POLY PERX® Frozen
  Polyunsaturated Non-Dairy
  Creamer
1½ cups chopped or sieved
  cooked vegetables and
  vegetable liquid
Carrots, cauliflower, beans,
  broccoli

In a heavy saucepan, over low heat, cook onion and margarine until tender, but not brown. Add flour and stir until smooth. Remove from heat and add 3½ cups POLY PERX® . Stir until smooth. Shortly before serving add vegetables of your choice. Adjust seasoning to taste.
Makes 6 servings

PUREE MONGOLE

1 can (11¼ ounces) CAMPBELL'S
  Condensed Green Pea Soup
1 can (10¾ ounces) CAMPBELL'S
  Condensed Tomato Soup
1 cup milk
1 cup water
Dash curry powder

In saucepan, blend soups, milk, water, and curry powder. Heat; stir occasionally.
Makes about 4½ cups

HOT MADRILENE SOUP

¼ cup Butter
¼ cup Chopped Onion
1 32 oz. jar THANK YOU® Brand
  Tomato Juice
2 10½ oz. cans Beef Consomme
½ cup Snipped Parsley
Parmesan Cheese (if desired)

Heat butter, add onions and cook until tender. Add juice and consomme and simmer 5 minutes. Serve with parsley and cheese.

Mazola.

SUPER SOUP

2 tablespoons MAZOLA®/NUCOA®
  Margarine
½ cup finely chopped onion
¼ cup chopped parsley
½ cup SKIPPY® Creamy or Super
  Chunk Peanut Butter
1 can (1 lb.) whole tomatoes
1½ cups water
2 envelopes instant vegetable
  broth

In medium saucepan melt margarine over medium heat. Add onion and parsley; cook until tender. Stir in peanut butter until blended. Add tomatoes, water and vegetable broth. Bring to boil over medium heat, stirring constantly. Reduce heat and simmer 10 minutes.
Makes 4 cups

A ROSY STRAWBERRY SOUP

1½ cups strawberry preserves
1¼ cups sour cream
¾ cup half and half
⅔ cup sherry
1½ tablespoons grenadine
1 pint basket fresh California
  strawberries, stemmed and
  halved

In large bowl whisk together preserves and sour cream. Stir in half and half, sherry and grenadine. Chill several hours. Just before serving mix in berries. Serve with spoons. Garnish with mint sprigs, if desired.
Makes 6 servings

Favorite recipe from California Strawberry Advisory Board

COLD CHERRY SOUP

Blend half a gallon frozen or canned cherries with half a gallon canned cherry liquid and water. Add 4 Tbsp. wine vinegar. Season with salt, pepper, and sugar to taste. Chill and serve, garnished with a dollop of sour cream and zest of orange julienne.

Favorite recipe from National Red Cherry Institute

CHILLED APRICOT MINT SOUP

2 cans (16 or 17 ounces each)
   apricot halves, chilled
1 cup (½ pint) light cream or
   half and half
1 tablespoon lemon juice
¼ teaspoon mint extract
Sour cream
Mint sprigs

In electric blender container, puree apricot halves with their syrup until smooth. Stir in cream until blended. Then stir in lemon juice and mint extract. To serve, pour into individual bowls; garnish with a dollop of sour cream and mint sprigs.

To Make With Fresh Apricots: In large saucepan, combine 1 cup sugar with 1 cup water. Heat to a boil, stirring to dissolve sugar. Add 1¾ pounds fresh California apricots, halved and pitted. Cook just until tender, stirring occasionally. Refrigerate until cold. Puree and proceed with recipe but omit lemon juice.

Makes about 5 cups

Favorite recipe from California Apricot Advisory Board

BLENDER SHRIMP GAZPACHO

1 can (4½ ounces) LOUISIANA
   BRAND Shrimp
1 medium cucumber, *unpeeled,*
   sliced
1 green pepper, sliced
1 medium onion, sliced
1 garlic clove
4 sprigs fresh parsley
2 cans (13½ ounces or about
   2 cups each) tomato juice
Juice of 1 average lemon
½ teaspoon salt
½ teaspoon hot pepper sauce
2 tablespoons olive oil

Have shrimp and other main ingredients chilled. Place cucumber, pepper, onion, garlic, parsley in a blender. Set on "chop" speed, if available, or turn blender quickly on and off for chopping action, stopping before mixture becomes pureed. Combine with tomato juice, lemon juice, seasonings, olive oil, shrimp and shrimp liquid. Serve well chilled.

5 servings

COLD CUCUMBER AND YOGURT SOUP

2 cups DANNON® Plain Yogurt
1 medium size cucumber
1 cup crushed ice cubes
1 Tbsp. chopped parsley
½ tsp. finely chopped garlic
1 Tbsp. cut fresh dill
½ cup nuts chopped
2 Tbsp. oil

Salt to taste, peel the cucumber and slice it lengthwise into halves. Scoop out and discard the seeds. Dice the cucumber into ¼ inch pieces, place in a bowl, and sprinkle with salt. Set aside at room temperature for 2-3 hours. Place the cucumber dices in a sieve, wash under cold running water. Spread cucumbers on paper towels and pat thoroughly dry. Combine yogurt, the diced cucumbers, chopped nuts, dill, garlic until they are thoroughly mixed. Stir in oil by the teaspoon, making sure each addition is well absorbed before adding more. Salt to taste. Refrigerate 1 hour. Drop 1 or 2 ice cubes into each bowl before serving. Garnish with parsley.

CHILLED YOGURT SOUP

1 medium cucumber
2 cups DANNON® Plain Yogurt
1 cup ice water
½ pound cold boiled lean beef,
   cubed
4 finely chopped scallions,
   including 2 inches of the green
   tops
2 hard-cooked eggs, chopped
2 tablespoons finely chopped fresh
   coriander leaves or parsley
¼ cup finely chopped fresh dill
Salt to taste

Peel the cucumber and halve lengthwise. Cut out the seeds if too large and discard. Slice the cucumber crosswise into ¼-inch pieces and set aside. Pour the yogurt into a deep bowl and stir until smooth. Add the ice water and mix until well blended. Add the reserved cucumber pieces and remaining ingredients. Mix gently but thoroughly. Taste for seasoning and serve chilled.

Serves 4

COLD YOGURT SOUP

1 large cucumber
2 cups DANNON® Plain Yogurt
2 Tbsp. vinegar
1 tsp. salt
1 clove garlic pressed, if desired
3 medium tomatoes
½ finely chopped onion or
   scallions

Peel cucumber and cut lengthwise into halves. Discard the seeds. Cut into chunks. Combine in electric blender or food processor: cucumber, yogurt, vinegar, salt, garlic and onion. Blanch tomatoes, peel and chop. Can also substitute canned tomatoes. Stir tomatoes into yogurt mixture. Chill several hours or overnight and serve. Minced cucumber, onions, green pepper and tomatoes can be used as a garnish.

Makes approximately 4 servings

YOGURT SPINACH SOUP

2 cups DANNON® Plain Yogurt
10 oz. package frozen spinach
1½ cups water
1 Tbsp. chicken seasoned stock
½ tsp. salt
½ tsp. pepper
1 Tbsp. chopped dill
1 Tbsp. chopped chive

Put water and stock in blender, add spinach and blend. Add all remaining ingredients and blend thoroughly. Chill for at least 1 hour before serving. Garnish with lemon slices.

Makes approximately 4 servings

COLD YOGURT VICHYSSOISE

2 cups peeled sliced potatoes
2 cups sliced white leek or
   yellow onion
1 sliced carrot
1 quart chicken broth
3 cups DANNON® Plain Yogurt
Salt & pepper to taste

In large saucepan, combine vegetables and broth. Simmer until vegetables are tender, about 45 minutes. Puree in blender or food processor. Add yogurt, blend. Season with salt and pepper. Chill. Garnish with chopped parsley or chives.

Serves about 6

Poultry

Chicken

GOLDEN FRIED CHICKEN

1 whole broiler-fryer chicken, cut
  in parts
1 teaspoon salt
¼ teaspoon pepper
2 eggs
1 tablespoon water
¾ cup ARGO®/KINGSFORD'S®
  Corn Starch
1 pint (about) MAZOLA® Corn Oil

Sprinkle chicken with salt and
pepper. Beat eggs and water until
well mixed. Dip chicken into egg
mixture, then into corn starch,
coating evenly. Dip into egg
mixture again; drain off excess.
Pour corn oil into large deep skillet
or electric fry pan to depth of
¼-inch. Heat over medium heat to
375°F. Carefully put chicken into
hot oil. Cook, turning once, 25 to
30 minutes or until light golden
brown and tender. Drain on
absorbent paper.

Makes 4 servings

NUTTY CHICKEN

3 to 3½ lb. broiler-fryer, cut up
Salt
1 cup biscuit mix
¾ cup water
⅔ cup chopped FISHER®
  Salted, Roasted Sunflower Nuts
Vegetable oil for frying

Lightly salt chicken pieces.
Combine biscuit mix, water and
nuts. Dip chicken in batter. Fry in 2
inches of hot oil in skillet until
golden. Place chicken in shallow
baking dish; bake at 350° for 1
hour or until fork tender.

Makes 4 servings

GOLDEN OATS FRIED CHICKEN

¾ c. 3-MINUTE BRAND® QUICK
  OATS
¼ c. grated Parmesan cheese
¼ c. chopped blanched almonds
2 Tbsp. minced parsley
1 tsp. salt
¼ tsp. ground thyme
⅛ tsp. pepper
½ c. butter
¼ tsp. garlic powder (or 1 clove
  garlic, crushed)
2½ to 3 lb. frying chicken, cut up

Combine oats, cheese, almonds,
parsley, salt, thyme and pepper. In
a 9 × 13 inch baking dish, melt
butter with garlic powder. Dip
chicken pieces in garlic-butter and
then in oats mixture. Place chicken
pieces in baking dish and bake,
uncovered, at 375°F. for 55 to 65
minutes, or until tender. Do not
turn chicken pieces during baking.

AROMATIC SHERRIED CHICKEN

⅓ cup THE CHRISTIAN
  BROTHERS® Golden Sherry
⅓ cup dried apricots
1 medium onion, sliced
2 Tbsp. corn oil
2½-3 pound chicken, quartered
½ tsp. basil
⅛ tsp. cinnamon or 1
  cinnamon stick

Combine sherry and apricots; set
aside. In electric frying pan, sauté
onion in oil until golden; remove
and reserve onion. Brown chicken
in oil remaining in pan. Add onion,
apricots, sherry, basil and
cinnamon. Cover pan. Cook at 200°
about 50 minutes or until chicken
is tender, turning once. Remove
cover last 10 minutes.

Makes 4 servings

*1st Prize Winner THE CHRISTIAN
BROTHERS® Contest*

WESSONALITY FRIED CHICKEN

Combine ¾ cup flour, 1½ tsp. salt,
¾ tsp. paprika and ¼ tsp. pepper
in a bag. Shake 3 lbs. chicken
pieces, a few at a time, in bag. Dip
chicken in 1 egg beaten with 2
Tbsp. water. Shake in flour mixture
again. Fry in 12-inch skillet in 3
cups WESSON Oil heated to 375°
20 to 30 minutes, turning once.

Makes 6 servings

SESAME BAKED CHICKEN*

1 (2½ to 3 lb.) chicken, cut
  into serving-size pieces
⅔ cup evaporated milk
6 teaspoons LEA & PERRINS
  Worcestershire Sauce, divided
1 teaspoon salt
1 teaspoon garlic salt
⅛ teaspoon TABASCO®
¾ cup cornflake crumbs
¼ cup sesame seed
2 tablespoons butter or margarine

Place chicken in tight fitting bowl
or plastic bag. Combine
evaporated milk with 5 teaspoons
of the LEA & PERRINS, salt, garlic
and TABASCO® ; mix well. Pour
over chicken. Cover. Marinate 2
hours or longer. Combine crumbs
with sesame seed. Roll chicken in
crumb mixture, coating well.
Arrange chicken in a shallow
baking pan, skin side up. Melt
butter; stir in remaining 1 teaspoon
LEA & PERRINS. Dribble over
chicken. Bake, uncovered, in
preheated moderate oven (350°F.)
1 hour or until tender. Serve with
lemon wedges, if desired, or
sprinkle with lemon juice.

Yield: 3 to 4 portions

*May be prepared in advance of
serving.

CRUNCHY BAKED CHICKEN VARIATIONS

Wash 3 lbs. frying chicken pieces. Pat dry. For any of the following variations, dip chicken in liquid mixture. Coat evenly with KELLOGG'S® CORN FLAKE CRUMBS mixture. Place in single layer, skin side up, in well-greased or foil-lined shallow baking pan. Drizzle with 3 tablespoons melted margarine or butter, if desired. Bake at 350°F. about 1 hour or until chicken is tender. Do not cover pan or turn chicken while baking.   *Yield: 6 servings*

Corn-Crisped Chicken: Dip in ½ cup evaporated milk. Coat with mixture of 1 cup KELLOGG'S® CORN FLAKE CRUMBS, 1 teaspoon salt and ⅛ teaspoon pepper.

California Crusty Chicken: Dip in mixture of ¼ cup melted margarine or butter, 3 tablespoons lemon juice and 1 teaspoon grated lemon peel. Coat with mixture of 1¼ cups KELLOGG'S® CORN FLAKE CRUMBS, 1 teaspoon salt and ¼ teaspoon pepper.

Baked Chicken Italiano: Dip in ½ cup Italian-style salad dressing. Coat with 1¼ cups KELLOGG'S® CORN FLAKE CRUMBS. If desired, marinate chicken in dressing for at least 1 hour.

Oven Fried Chicken: Dip in mixture of 1 slightly beaten egg and 2 tablespoons milk. Coat with mixture of 1¼ cups KELLOGG'S® CORN FLAKE CRUMBS, 1 teaspoon salt and ¼ teaspoon pepper.

Parmesan Crisped Chicken: Dip in mixture of 1 slightly beaten egg and 2 tablespoons milk. Coat with mixture of ¾ cup KELLOGG'S® CORN FLAKE CRUMBS, 1 teaspoon salt, ¼ teaspoon pepper and ½ cup grated parmesan cheese.

Zesty Crisped Chicken: Dip in mixture of 1 slightly beaten egg and ¼ cup soy sauce. Coat with 1¼ cups KELLOGG'S® CORN FLAKE CRUMBS.

® Kellogg Company

OVEN FRIED CHICKEN AND BANANAS

2 chickens, about 3 lbs. each, cut-up
Salt and pepper
1 cup COCO CASA™ Cream of Coconut
2 Tbsp. lemon juice
6 medium size bananas
2½ cups cornflake crumbs
¾ cup melted butter or margarine

Sprinkle chicken pieces on all sides with salt and pepper. In a bowl, mix cream of coconut and lemon juice. Peel bananas and cut each banana into halves crosswise. Brush chicken and bananas thickly with cream of coconut mixture and roll in crumbs, pressing firmly to make them adhere. Brush a baking pan with some of the butter. Place chicken pieces in a single layer into pan and drizzle with half of the butter. Bake in preheated 350° oven for 45 minutes. Add bananas and drizzle with remaining butter. Bake for another 15 minutes.
Serves 6

BAKED YOGURT CHICKEN

1 cut up frying chicken, 2½ to 3 pounds
Salt, pepper
6 Tbsp. butter or margarine
2 Tbsp. flour
1 Tbsp. paprika
2 cups DANNON® Plain Yogurt
¼ pound fresh mushrooms, cleaned and sliced
2 Tbsp. fresh lemon juice
2 Tbsp. chopped fresh dill or parsley

Wash chicken pieces and wipe dry. Add salt and pepper. In a large pan, melt 4 tablespoons of butter, fry chicken until golden brown. Remove to buttered shallow baking dish. Sprinkle flour and paprika into pan juices and cook, stirring for 1 minute. Stir in yogurt and mix well. Spoon over chicken. Sauté mushrooms in remaining 2 tablespoons of butter and lemon juice for 1 minute and spoon over pan. Sprinkle with the dill. Bake, covered, in preheated moderate oven (325°F.) for about 1¼ hours, or until chicken is tender.
Serves about 4

ARROZ CON POLLO

2½ pounds cut-up chicken
1 envelope SHAKE 'N BAKE® Seasoned Coating Mix for Chicken—Barbecue Style
2 tablespoons butter or margarine
1½ cups MINUTE® Rice
½ cup chopped onion
1 small clove garlic, crushed (optional)
1½ cups water
1 package (10 oz.) BIRDS EYE® 5 Minute Sweet Green Peas, thawed
1 can (4 oz.) sliced mushrooms, drained
2 chicken bouillon cubes
Pinch of ground bay leaves (optional)

Coat chicken with seasoned coating mix as directed on package. Place in 13 x 9-inch pan. Sprinkle evenly with any remaining mix. Bake at 350° for 50 minutes, or until chicken is tender. Meanwhile, melt butter in skillet or saucepan. Add rice, onion and garlic and sauté until rice is lightly browned. Add remaining ingredients. Bring to a boil. Remove from heat; cover and let stand 5 minutes. Serve with the chicken.
Makes 5 cups rice mixture plus chicken or 4 servings

HONEY CURRIED CHICKEN

2 broiler-fryer chickens, 2½-3 pounds, cut into serving pieces
¼ cup butter or margarine, melted
½ cup SUE BEE® Honey
¼ cup prepared mustard
1 teaspoon salt
½ teaspoon curry powder
Hot cooked rice (optional)

Wash and dry chicken. Combine remaining ingredients, except rice, stirring well. Dip chicken in sauce, coating completely; reserve remaining sauce. Place chicken, skin side up, in roasting pan. Bake at 375° for one hour, basting occasionally with remaining sauce. Serve over hot rice, if desired.
Makes six to eight servings

CHICKEN ORIENTAL

1 3-pound frying chicken (undrawn weight), disjointed
8 small onions
Juice 1 lemon
⅓ cup soy sauce
1½ tsps. BELL'S® Seasoning
2 tsp. salt
1¼ tsp. ginger
½ tsp. black pepper
Flour
Fat for frying
1 cup water

Put chicken and onions in bowl. Mix lemon juice, soy sauce, and seasonings; pour over top. Let stand in refrigerator several hours or overnight. Remove chicken and roll in flour. Brown in hot fat. Put chicken, onions, soy sauce mixture and water in large covered casserole. Bake in moderate oven, 350°F., 50 minutes or until chicken is tender. Serve with rice.

4 servings

LO-CAL BAKED CHICKEN

1 frying chicken, cut up
1 can (about 16-oz.) tomatoes
1 envelope FRENCH'S® Au Jus Gravy Mix
¼ cup chopped celery
1 can (3 or 4-oz.) mushrooms, undrained
¼ cup Rhine wine or other dry wine, if desired

Remove skin and excess fat from chicken; arrange, meaty side up, in shallow pan. Break up tomatoes; combine with gravy mix, celery, mushrooms, and wine; spoon over chicken. Bake at 375° for 50 to 60 minutes, until tender.

4 to 5 servings

200 calories per serving

MICROWAVE LO-CAL BAKED CHICKEN

Arrange chicken in single layer in shallow glass baking dish with meatier portions toward outside edges. Cover with wax paper or plastic wrap and microwave on HIGH 10 minutes. Rearrange chicken pieces and microwave 10 minutes longer. Combine celery with 2 to 3 tablespoons of the tomato liquid in 4-cup glass measure. Microwave on HIGH 1 to 1½ minutes. Stir in gravy mix, cut-up tomatoes, drained mushrooms, and wine. Microwave on HIGH 3 to 4 minutes, until thickened, stirring after 2 minutes and at end of cooking. Spoon off excess liquid; pour sauce over chicken. Microwave, covered, 3 to 5 minutes, until sauce is hot and chicken tender.

Micro Tip: When using celery or green pepper in sauces, precook it slightly.

CREAMY CRUNCHY CHICKEN

2 envelopes LIPTON® Cream of Chicken Flavor Cup-a-Soup
1½ cups boiling water
2 to 2½ pound chicken, cut into serving pieces
1½ cups crushed herb seasoned stuffing mix
2 tablespoons melted butter

Preheat oven to 375°. In bowl, blend 1 envelope LIPTON® Cream of Chicken Flavor Cup-a-Soup and ¾ cup water; dip chicken in mixture, then in crumbs. Place in shallow baking dish and drizzle with butter; bake 1 hour. Combine remaining envelope Cream of Chicken Flavor Cup-a-Soup and ¾ cup water for gravy.

Makes about 4 servings

CLUB CHICKEN

1 frying chicken (2½ to 3 pounds) cut up
1 cup fine KEEBLER Club or Town House Cracker crumbs
1 package (0.7 ounce) dry onion or Italian salad dressing mix
3 tablespoons butter, melted

Wash and dry chicken. Combine cracker crumbs and salad dressing mix in large plastic bag. Shake 1 or 2 chicken pieces at a time in crumb mixture. Place chicken, skin side up, in 9 x 13 inch baking pan. Drizzle with melted butter. Bake in preheated 375°F. oven 40 to 50 minutes.

4 to 6 servings

GRECIAN CHICKEN

2 packages (10 oz. each) frozen chopped spinach
1 teaspoon dried dill weed
1 cup (4 oz.) grated mozzarella cheese
1 package (32 oz.) BANQUET® Heat and Serve Frozen Fully Cooked Fried Chicken
½ cup (4 oz.) crumbled feta cheese

Cook spinach as directed on package. Drain well. Stir in dill weed. Spread spinach on bottom of buttered 12 x 8-inch baking dish. Spread grated mozzarella cheese evenly on top of spinach. Place single layer of frozen chicken on top of mozzarella cheese. Sprinkle feta cheese on chicken. Heat in 375°F. oven for 35 to 40 minutes, until chicken is golden brown and heated through.

Makes 5 servings

ROAST CHICKEN IN KIKKO-WINE SAUCE

3-pound frying chicken
6 tablespoons KIKKOMAN Soy Sauce, divided
1 teaspoon garlic powder, divided
3 carrots, peeled and cut diagonally crosswise into quarters
1 cup water
6 tablespoons white wine
1 teaspoon brown sugar, packed
10-ounce package frozen broccoli spears, thawed and drained

Rinse chicken and pat dry. Combine 2 tablespoons soy sauce and ½ teaspoon garlic powder; rub chicken, including cavities, with mixture. Place in large, shallow baking pan. Roast in 325°F. oven 30 minutes. Meanwhile, cook carrots in boiling, salted water about 10 minutes or until tender yet crisp; remove and reserve. Combine remaining soy sauce and garlic powder, water, wine and brown sugar; pour mixture evenly over chicken. Roast 30 minutes, basting chicken with sauce twice. Add carrots and broccoli. Roast 15 minutes longer, or until chicken is thoroughly cooked. Remove chicken to serving platter; surround with vegetables and serve with pan drippings.

Makes 4 to 6 servings

ARGO

ORANGE ROASTED CHICKEN

1 (5 lb.) roasting chicken
¼ cup margarine, melted
Salt and pepper
½ teaspoon dried rosemary
2 oranges, cut in half
¼ cup ARGO® /KINGSFORD'S®
   Corn Starch
2 cups orange juice
1 cup chicken bouillon
1 tablespoon brown sugar

Brush chicken with margarine;
season with salt, pepper and
rosemary. Place oranges in
chicken cavity. Roast in 325°F.
oven about 2½ hours. Remove
chicken from pan. Sprinkle corn
starch into pan. Stir and cook over
medium heat just until smooth;
remove from heat. Gradually stir in
remaining ingredients until
smooth. Bring to boil over medium
heat, stirring constantly, and boil 2
minutes.   *Makes 6 servings*

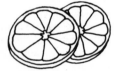

CHICKEN FRICASSE
(Low Cholesterol)

4 cups water
1 5½-6½ lb. chicken portioned
1 tsp. salt
2 bay leaves
2½ cups POLY PERX® Frozen
   Polyunsaturated Non-Dairy
   Creamer
7 Tbsp. flour
1½ tsp. salt
Pinch of ground thyme
2 cups cooked whole kernel corn

Simmer water, chicken, salt and
bay leaves in a heavy pot until
chicken is tender, about 1½ hours.
Remove from heat. Discard bay
leaves. Remove chicken and keep
warm. Skim off fat. Simmer to
reduce broth to 2 cups. Mix
together ¾ cup POLY PERX® and
flour, add to broth, stirring
vigorously, add 1¾ cups POLY
PERX® Stir over moderate heat and
continue to cook until thickened.
Season with salt and thyme. Add
corn. Serve chicken with gravy.
     Makes 8 servings

HEINZ CHICKEN FRICASSEE

Coat 2½ to 3 pounds chicken
pieces with mixture of ¼ cup flour,
½ teaspoon salt, ½ teaspoon
paprika, ⅛ teaspoon pepper; brown
well in 2 tablespoons shortening.
Stir in 1 jar HEINZ Homestyle
Chicken Gravy and ¼ teaspoon
ground nutmeg. Cover; simmer
50-60 minutes; baste occasionally.
     Makes 4-6 servings

FINGER-LICKIN' FRICASSEE

3 lb. chicken
½ cup flour
½ cup shortening
1 onion, sliced
1 green pepper, chopped
2 cloves garlic
4 tablespoons catsup
1½ cups water
1 teaspoon GEBHARDT Chili
   Powder
2 teaspoons salt
4 tablespoons raisins (optional)
8 ripe olives, chopped (optional)

Cut chicken into serving pieces,
dip in flour, brown in hot
shortening. Remove to larger pan.
Fry onion, green pepper and garlic
until brown in remaining hot
shortening; add catsup, water,
GEBHARDT Chili Powder; boil 5
minutes. Pour over chicken. Salt,
adding water as needed; cover,
allow to simmer until chicken is
tender; about 1½ hours. 15
minutes before serving, add raisins
and ripe olives.   *4 to 6 servings*

SARA'S COUNTRY CHICKEN

3 pounds chicken, cut in eighths
¼ cup flour
¼ cup olive oil
1 cup diced onion
1 garlic clove, crushed
½ pound fresh mushrooms, sliced
1½ cups HOLLAND HOUSE®
   White Cooking Wine
½ cup pitted black olives
⅓ cup capers
1 pound can plum tomatoes,
   drained and cut up
1 teaspoon lemon juice
⅛ teaspoon each: pepper, basil,
   oregano, ground sage

Coat chicken parts with flour.
Brown in olive oil. Remove chicken.

Sauté onion and garlic until
golden. Add mushrooms. Cook 2
minutes. Add HOLLAND HOUSE®
White Cooking Wine. Cook 10
minutes. Add remaining
ingredients including chicken;
cover, simmer 30 minutes.
     Serves 4 to 6

BRONTE
CHICKEN IN SHERRY WINE

1 chicken, or breasts and legs
2 Tablespoons flour
2 teaspoons paprika
Salt & Pepper
¾ cup chicken stock
⅓ cup BRONTE Sherry Wine
½ cup heavy cream

Disjoint chicken, wipe each piece
with a damp cloth and dip them in
mixture of flour, paprika, salt &
pepper. Brown quickly in butter,
place in a heavy casserole. Pour
over chicken stock and BRONTE
Sherry Wine. Cover tightly, simmer
gently, 1 hour. Remove chicken to
a heated platter, keep hot. To
juices in pan, add cream and a
scant teaspoon of leftover flour—
paprika mixture. Stir until sauce
thickens without letting it boil.
Strain and serve separately.

HOME STYLE CHICKEN IN MUSTARD SAUCE

5 packets G. WASHINGTON'S®
   Golden Seasoning and Broth Mix
½ cup flour
1 chicken, cut in pieces
¼ cup butter or margarine
1 cup water
1 tablespoon chopped scallions
1 teaspoon tarragon
3 tablespoons GULDEN'S® Spicy
   Brown Mustard
1 cup half and half

Combine 3 packets of seasoning
and broth with flour; coat chicken
pieces. Brown chicken pieces in
butter until golden. Dissolve
remaining 2 packets of seasoning
and broth in 1 cup water. Add to
skillet along with scallions and
tarragon. Cover; continue cooking
over low heat until sauce begins to
thicken and chicken is fork tender.
Mix mustard with half and half.
Pour over simmered chicken; stir
gently; cover. Allow to simmer 10
more minutes.   *Serves 4*

CHICKEN AND RICE DUBONNET

2 young broilers cut for frying
  (approx. 1½ lbs. ea.)
2 limes
Salt
4 large tomatoes
1 green pepper
1 sweet red pepper
Parsley
Freshly ground pepper
⅓ cup olive oil
¼ lb. lean, raw ham
8 small green onions
2 bay leaves
Saffron (powdered)
3 chicken bouillon cubes
3 cups long grain rice
3 oz. DUBONNET Red

Sprinkle chicken pieces with lime juice, then season with salt and pepper and put in refrigerator for 2 hours. Heat ⅓ cup olive oil in oven until it's smoking hot. Add chicken pieces and brown lightly on all sides. Then add diced raw ham and chopped green onions (stems included). When the onions begin to brown, add the tomatoes peeled and quartered; chopped peppers; 3 tablespoons chopped parsley; 2 crumbled bay leaves; ½ teaspoon saffron and salt and pepper to taste. Mix well and simmer covered, for about 5 minutes. Dissolve the chicken bouillon cubes in 2 cups boiling water and add. Cover and simmer 25 minutes. Now add 3 cups of rice. Cover and simmer another 25 minutes (until rice has absorbed most of the liquid). Before serving, add 3 oz. DUBONNET Red.

Makes 6 servings

ITALIAN CHICKEN

3½ pounds chicken pieces
Salt and pepper
¼ cup BERTOLLI® Olive Oil
1 medium onion, thinly sliced
8 ounces mushrooms, sliced
2 cloves garlic, minced
1 teaspoon dried basil leaves
½ teaspoon dried oregano leaves
¼ teaspoon salt
2 cups BERTOLLI® Spaghetti
  Sauce
½ cup sliced ripe olives
½ cup BERTOLLI® Soave Wine
1 jar (6 ounces) marinated
  artichoke hearts, drained

Sprinkle chicken with salt and pepper; sauté in oil in Dutch oven until brown; remove. Sauté onion, mushrooms, garlic, basil, oregano and ¼ teaspoon salt 3 minutes. Stir in sauce, olives and wine. Add chicken, spooning sauce over. Heat to boiling. Reduce heat; simmer covered until chicken is tender, about 45 minutes. Stir in artichokes; cook 3 minutes.

Makes 6 servings

CHICKEN NORMANDY

2 COOKIN' GOOD Chickens cut
  into parts or 6 lbs. of your
  favorite COOKIN' GOOD Parts
4 tablespoons butter
¼ cup brandy or cognac
1 medium onion sliced
1 teaspoon salt
¼ teaspoon pepper
¼ teaspoon basil
1 clove garlic, pressed
2 medium apples, cored and sliced
¼ cup apple juice
1 tablespoon flour
½ cup heavy cream
¼ cup fresh snipped parsley

Crock pot instructions: Melt butter in a skillet and brown onion, garlic and chicken. Pour brandy over chicken and set aflame. When flames die down, remove chicken, onions and garlic to crock pot. Add remaining ingredients except flour, cream and parsley. Cover and cook on high, 3-4 hours or low, 5 hours. Before serving remove chicken to a warmed platter. Blend flour and cream together. Stir into the remaining juice in the crock pot until sauce thickens. Serve over rice or buttered noodles, garnish with fresh parsley.

Crock pot cooking time: 3-4 hours (high) or 5 hours (low)

Range top instructions: Follow the above instructions for browning and flaming. Add remaining ingredients as above to skillet. Cover and cook for 1-1½ hours until tender. Remove chicken to a warmed serving platter. Blend together flour and cream. Stir into remaining pan juices. Bring to a boil, stirring constantly. Serve as above.

GLORIFIED CHICKEN

2 pounds chicken parts
2 tablespoons shortening
1 can (10¾ ounces) CAMPBELL'S
  Condensed Cheddar Cheese,
  Cream of Celery, Chicken, or
  Mushroom Soup

In skillet, brown chicken in shortening; pour off fat. Stir in soup. Cover; cook over low heat 45 minutes or until tender. Stir occasionally.

Makes 4 servings

Oven Method: In shallow baking dish (12 × 8 × 2″), arrange chicken skin-side down. Pour 2 tablespoons melted butter over chicken. Bake at 400°F. for 20 minutes. Turn chicken; bake 20 minutes more. Stir soup; pour over chicken. Bake 20 minutes more or until done. Stir sauce before serving.

POULET FLAMBÉ

1 (3-pound) frying chicken, cut up
2 teaspoons salt
¼ teaspoon pepper
¼ teaspoon paprika
¼ cup PLANTERS® Peanut Oil
2 medium onions, thinly sliced
2 chicken bouillon cubes
½ cup water
⅓ cup brandy, heated
1 cup heavy cream
1 tablespoon lemon juice
1 tablespoon cornstarch
Hot cooked rice

Sprinkle chicken pieces with salt, pepper and paprika. In a large skillet or Dutch oven, brown chicken in peanut oil, a few pieces at a time. Remove chicken. Add onions and sauté over medium-high heat, until tender, about 5 minutes. Return chicken to pan, add bouillon cubes and water; bring to a boil. Reduce heat to low; cover and cook about 45 minutes or until chicken is tender.

Pour the warm brandy over the chicken and ignite it. When the flame dies, transfer chicken to a warm serving platter. Stir in cream to liquid remaining in skillet; bring to a boil and cook for 1 minute. Blend lemon juice into cornstarch. Stir into sauce and cook on medium-high heat until sauce thickens. Pour over chicken. Serve with rice. *Makes 4 servings*

CRISP SKILLET CHICKEN WITH GRAVY

2 pounds chicken parts
Seasoned flour
¼ cup butter or margarine
¼ cup water
1 can (10½ ounces) FRANCO-AMERICAN Chicken Gravy
Lemon slices
Parsley

Dust chicken with flour. In skillet, brown chicken in butter. Add water. Cover; cook over low heat 45 minutes or until done. Uncover the last 10 minutes to crisp chicken. Remove chicken to warm platter. Add gravy. Heat, stirring to loosen browned bits. Serve with chicken. Garnish with lemon slices and parsley. *Makes 4 servings*

MRS. COOKIN' GOOD'S CHICKEN 'N DUMPLINGS

Chicken Recipe:
1—3½-4 pound COOKIN' GOOD Chicken
1 cup celery, chopped (3-4 ribs)
1 large onion, diced
1 carrot, sliced thin
2 teaspoons salt
½ teaspoon pepper
2 tablespoons parsley flakes
4 large potatoes, quartered
4-6 cups of water

Dumpling Recipe:
2 cups all-purpose flour, sifted
1 teaspoon salt
4 tablespoons CRISCO Shortening
¾-1 cup cooled chicken broth

Chicken Recipe: In a large covered Dutch oven, combine all ingredients except potatoes. Bring to a boil then simmer, covered 1-1½ hours or until chicken is fork tender. Remove chicken and one cup of broth to cool for dumpling recipe. Add potatoes. Cook in broth 20 minutes. Prepare dumplings while potatoes are cooking using recipe below. Drop dumplings into rapid boiling chicken broth and cover. Cook 20 minutes or until dumplings are firm. Shake pot often so dumplings will not stick together. While dumplings are cooking, remove chicken from bones. Discard skin and bones. To serve, pour broth, dumplings and potatoes over cooked chicken.

Dumpling Recipe: Sift dry ingredients together. Cut in shortening using two knives or a pastry blender until the mixture resembles coarse corn meal. Gradually with a fork stir in enough cooled chicken broth to make a soft dough. Knead two minutes or until all of the flour is mixed into dough. Turn dough onto a floured surface. With a floured rolling pin, roll dough to about ⅛″ thickness. Cut into 4″ × 4″ squares. Continue with recipe above.
Makes 4-6 servings

CHICKEN TAM O'SHANTER

2 tablespoons each oil and butter
1 broiler-fryer chicken, cut up
1 small onion, finely chopped
¼ lb. mushrooms, sliced
¼ cup JOHNNIE WALKER Red, warmed
½ cup chicken broth or bouillon
1 cup sour cream, at room temperature
Salt and pepper, to taste

Heat oil and butter in large skillet. Add chicken pieces; sauté over medium heat, turning often until golden brown on both sides. Add onion and mushrooms, cook until softened. Pour JOHNNIE WALKER Red into pan, ignite. When flames go out, add broth; cover pan and reduce heat. Simmer until chicken is tender, about 25 minutes. Remove chicken pieces and keep warm. Reduce heat to very low, stir in sour cream. Heat through. Add salt and pepper to taste. Spoon over chicken. *4 servings*

QUICK CHICKEN JUBILEE

1 3½-pound chicken, cut into serving size pieces
2 tablespoons butter or margarine
Salt and pepper
1 jar (10 ounces) plus ¼ cup WELCH'S® Grape Preserves
1 can (1 pound) pitted dark sweet cherries
¼ cup lemon juice
2 tablespoons cornstarch
¼ cup water
2 teaspoons slivered lime peel

Brown chicken in butter at 350°F. in electric skillet. Season with salt and pepper. Blend in grape preserves. Drain cherries and set fruit aside. Add liquid to sauce; stir in lemon juice. Reduce heat to 212°F. Cover and simmer until chicken is tender; stir now and then. Blend cornstarch into water; stir into sauce and cook, stirring, until sauce is thickened and smooth. Add cherries and lime peel. Heat. Serve over hot cooked rice. *Makes 4 servings*

CHICKEN MARSEILLES

1 2½ to 3-lb. broiler-fryer, cut up
CATALINA French Dressing
1 16-oz. can tomatoes
8 onion slices, ¼-inch thick
1 teaspoon salt
½ teaspoon celery seed
¼ teaspoon pepper
¼ cup wine or water
2 tablespoons flour

Brown chicken in ⅓ cup dressing over low heat. Add ¼ cup dressing, tomatoes, onion and seasonings. Cover; simmer 45 minutes. Remove chicken and vegetables to serving platter. Gradually add wine to flour, stirring until well blended. Gradually add flour mixture to hot liquid in pan; cook stirring constantly until mixture boils and thickens. Simmer 3 minutes, stirring constantly. Serve with chicken and vegetables.
4 servings

CHICKEN MARENGO

1 broiler-fryer (2 to 2½ lbs.), cut-up
1 teaspoon LAWRY'S® Seasoned Salt
1 package (1½ oz.) LAWRY'S® Spaghetti Sauce Mix with Imported Mushrooms
½ cup bread crumbs
¼ cup salad oil
½ cup sauterne
3 tomatoes, peeled and quartered
2 cups sliced fresh mushrooms

Sprinkle chicken pieces with Seasoned Salt. Blend Spaghetti Sauce Mix and crumbs. Roll chicken in seasoned crumb mixture. Fry in hot oil in skillet. Add wine, tomatoes, mushrooms and remaining crumb mixture. Cover and simmer about 45 minutes or until chicken is tender.
Makes 4 servings

San Giorgio

CHICKEN CACCIATORE

4 slices bacon, cut in small pieces
⅓ cup chopped onions
1 clove garlic, minced
½ cup (4-ounce can) sliced
    mushrooms
4 cups spaghetti sauce
1 teaspoon salt
1 teaspoon oregano
¼ teaspoon pepper
1—2½ to 3 pound chicken, cut-up
½ cup vegetable oil
1 pound SAN GIORGIO Cappellini
    or Thin Spaghetti

Sauté bacon in large saucepan
until browned. Add onions, garlic
and mushrooms; cook until onions
are tender. Stir in spaghetti sauce,
salt, oregano and pepper; simmer
about 10 minutes. Sauté chicken in
oil in large skillet until browned on
all sides. Add chicken to sauce;
cover and simmer 45 minutes or
until chicken is tender. Cook
Cappellini or Spaghetti according
to package directions; drain.
Arrange chicken over Spaghetti in
large serving dish.   *6 servings*

CHICKEN MADEIRA

½ cup butter
4 cups DOLE® Fresh Mushrooms,
    sliced
One 3-pound chicken, cut up
1 teaspoon garlic salt
¼ cup brandy
¾ cup Madeira
½ teaspoon fines herbes,
    crumbled
½ cup half & half
½ cup chopped green onion

Melt butter in a large frying pan
until bubbly. Sauté mushrooms
until browned; remove and reserve.
Brown chicken in pan. Sprinkle
with garlic salt during browning.
Carefully pour brandy over chicken
and flame. Add Madeira and fines
herbes. Cover lightly and cook 20
minutes until almost all liquid has
cooked off. Remove chicken to
serving platter. Add half & half,
green onion and mushrooms to
pan. Cook, stirring constantly until
thickened. Serve over chicken.
            Makes 4 servings

POACHED CHICKEN WITH LEMONS AND ORANGES

4 ripe lemons
3½ lb. broiling chicken, cut in
    pieces
⅛-¼ teaspoon salt
2 tablespoons melted butter or
    margarine
1 cup chicken bouillon
2 oranges, freshly squeezed
¼ teaspoon black pepper
1 cup CANADA DRY® Club Soda

Rub chicken pieces with ½ lemon
and salt. Place in lidded sauté pan,
add butter and cook over medium
heat for 5 minutes until pieces are
golden. Turn heat to simmer; add
chicken bouillon and poach for
about 30 minutes. Remove chicken
to warming dish. Add orange juice
and pepper to sauté pan and cook
for about 5 minutes. Add CANADA
DRY® Club Soda (at room
temperature). Heat 15 seconds and
serve in large soup dishes. Garnish
with parsley and lemon slices.
            Makes 4 servings

CELESTIAL GOLD CHICKEN

4 large chicken breasts, split,
    skinned and boned
Salt and pepper
Flour
2 eggs, slightly beaten
1 tablespoon water
Fine dry bread crumbs
⅓ cup butter

Filling:
2 cups finely shredded cabbage
¼ cup finely chopped green
    onions
¼ cup (½ stick) butter
1 cup chopped, drained, rinsed
    LA CHOY® Bean Sprouts
1 cup finely chopped LA CHOY®
    Water Chestnuts
1½ tablespoons chopped pimiento
½ teaspoon salt
2 teaspoons sugar
¼ teaspoon dried basil leaves
Dash allspice

Sauce:
¼ cup chopped onion
1 clove garlic, minced
2 tablespoons butter
¾ cup chicken broth
1 cup whipping cream
2 teaspoons LA CHOY® Soy Sauce
3 tablespoons flour
LA CHOY® Chow Mein Noodles

For Filling: Cook cabbage and
green onions in butter until tender,
about five minutes. Add remaining
ingredients for filling; heat until
hot. Cool.

Cover each chicken breast with
plastic wrap; flatten with flat side
of meat pounder or rolling pin to
⅛-inch thickness, taking care not to
tear chicken. Peel off plastic wrap.
Sprinkle chicken with salt and
pepper. Place ¼ cup filling in
center of each piece of chicken.
Roll up tightly, folding in the ends.
Dip chicken in flour, shaking off
excess. Next dip in eggs and water
which have been blended together;
then in bread crumbs, coating well.
Brown in butter in skillet. Arrange
in greased baking pan.

For Sauce: Cook onion and garlic
in butter until onion is golden,
about 3 minutes. Blend in ½ cup
broth, cream and soy sauce. Pour
sauce over chicken. Cover and
bake at 350 degrees for 45
minutes. Remove cover and bake
15 minutes more or until tender.
Remove chicken to serving dish;
keep warm. Combine remaining ¼
cup chicken broth and flour; mix
until smooth. Blend into pan
juices. Cook over medium heat,
stirring constantly, until thickened.
Pour over chicken. Garnish with
chow mein noodles.
            Yield: 8 servings

CHICKEN CORDON BLEU

3 chicken breasts (about 2½
    pounds), split, skinned, and
    boned
3 slices (4 ounces) Swiss cheese,
    cut in half
3 slices (4 ounces) boiled ham,
    cut in half
2 tablespoons butter or margarine
1 can (10¾ ounces) CAMPBELL'S
    Condensed Cream of Chicken
    Soup
¼ cup milk or light cream
Chopped parsley

Flatten chicken breasts with flat
side of knife. Top each with ½
slice cheese, then ham; secure
with toothpicks. In skillet, brown
chicken-side down in butter. Stir in
soup and milk. Cover; cook over
low heat for 20 minutes or until
tender. Stir occasionally. Garnish
with parsley.
            Makes 6 servings

GOLD CHIP CHICK CHESTS

5 whole chicken breasts, boned
1½ cups pineapple juice
⅓ cup sour cream
⅓ cup milk
⅔ cup cream of celery soup, canned
2 3-ounce cans deviled ham
¼ cup finely cut green pepper
2½ cups crushed JAYS Potato Chips
⅓ cup melted butter

Marinate boneless chicken breasts in pineapple juice 1 hour at room temperature, or overnight in refrigerator. Reserve ½ cup of the juice for basting later. Preheat oven to 375°F. Mix sour cream, milk, undiluted celery soup and 1 can deviled ham. Stir in green pepper and crushed potato chips. Pat inside of chicken breasts dry and spread with second can of deviled ham. Divide potato chip filling into five parts and spoon on chicken. Roll up; fasten with skewers. Combine melted butter with ½ cup pineapple juice and warm over low heat. Place Chick Chests upright in flat bottomed baking dish and baste. Bake at 375°F. for 50 minutes, basting at 15 minute intervals. Serve on a platter garnished with slices of fresh green pepper and tomato.

DELICIOUS CHICKEN COCONUT
(Ono moa niu)

1 fryer & 2 chicken breasts
6 Tbsp. butter
½ cup flour
1 cup heavy cream
2 cups hot chicken broth
3 tsp. salt
1 tsp. monosodium glutamate
1 13½ oz. can pineapple tidbits
3 large fresh CALAVO® Coconuts

Cook chicken in water. Bone meat, sprinkle with 1 tsp. of salt. Strain, measure 2 cups broth. Melt butter, add flour, hot cream, and chicken broth to make medium thick sauce. Season with 2 tsp. salt and monosodium glutamate. Fold in chicken pieces and pineapple tidbits. Use saw to cut off each

end of coconut for a standing surface. Saw nuts in half. Drain milk once cut is made. Rinse shells. Fill coconut halves with chicken mixture. Cover each with foil. Place shells in ½ inch water in baking pan. Bake in 350° oven for 45 minutes. Remove foil last 5 minutes. Serve with grapefruit spoons so coconut meat can be eaten with chicken.   *Serves 6*

TERIYAKI SALAD
(Low Calorie)

1 large head iceberg lettuce
Teriyaki Salad Dressing (recipe follows)
4 half-breasts of chicken
8 diagonal slices zucchini, 1 inch thick
4 squares (1-inch) green pepper
8 cherry tomatoes
4 mushrooms, halved

Core, rinse and thoroughly drain lettuce; refrigerate in disposable plastic bag or plastic crisper. Prepare Teriyaki Salad Dressing. Remove skin and bones from chicken and cut each breast into thirds lengthwise. Ripple three strips onto each of 4 bamboo skewers. Parboil zucchini and green pepper 1 minute; drain. Arrange on 4 skewers, along with tomatoes and mushrooms. Broil chicken skewers 5 inches from heat 10 minutes, basting well with Teriyaki Dressing and turning often. Add vegetable skewers last 5 minutes chicken cooks; turn and baste with dressing often. Cut lettuce into bite-size chunks to measure 2 quarts. Arrange 1 chicken and 1 vegetable skewer on a bed of lettuce for each serving. Pass remaining dressing.
Makes 4 servings

TERIYAKI SALAD DRESSING

Combine ½ cup beef consomme, ¼ cup salad oil, 2 tablespoons *each* naturally brewed soy sauce, dry sherry and white wine vinegar, 1 small clove garlic, minced, and ¼ teaspoon ground ginger in a small jar. Cover jar and shake well to blend. Shake again just before serving.

Makes 1 cup dressing

Calories: Total salad: 1475 calories
Per serving: 369 calories

Favorite recipe from California Iceberg Lettuce Commission

APPLE CHICKEN BAKE

2 cups LUCKY LEAF® Apple Sauce
½ tsp. allspice
1 tsp. salt
1 Tbsp. flour
1 Tbsp. catsup
½ cup diced celery
¼ cup diced onion
4 medium size chicken breasts (split in half)
½ cup evaporated milk
1½ cups fine cheese cracker crumbs
½ tsp. paprika
½ tsp. salt

Blend apple sauce with allspice, 1 teaspoon salt, flour, and catsup; stir in celery and onion. Pour mixture into baking dish 13¼" × 8½" × 1¾". Dip chicken in evaporated milk and roll in crumbs seasoned with paprika and ½ teaspoon salt. Arrange on top of apple sauce. Bake 350° for about 45 minutes or until chicken is tender.

FINLANDIA
IMPORTED
SWISS CHEESE

CHICKEN SIBELIUS

2 whole chicken breasts, boned and cut into 3-inch pieces
1 teaspoon salt
⅛ teaspoon poultry seasoning
¼ cup butter or margarine
2 packages (10 ounces each) frozen asparagus spears, cooked and drained
1 can (10½ ounces) condensed cream of chicken soup
½ cup light cream
½ teaspoon curry powder
1 cup shredded FINLANDIA Swiss Cheese

Season chicken with salt and poultry seasoning. Melt butter in large skillet; add chicken and sauté until lightly browned. Arrange asparagus in bottom of greased 1½-quart shallow baking dish. Top with chicken. Combine soup, cream and curry powder. Pour over chicken and asparagus. Top with cheese. Bake at 350°F. for 30 minutes or until done.
Makes 4 servings

HUNTER-STYLE CHICKEN WITH RISSOTTO

4 chicken breasts, boned
Salt, pepper
2 tablespoons olive oil
½ cup chopped onion
1 garlic clove, minced
1 can (14½ oz.) whole tomatoes
1 cup sliced fresh mushrooms
¼ cup white wine
¼ teaspoon each basil, oregano
    leaves, and sugar
1 bag SUCCESS® Rice
2 tablespoons grated Parmesan
    cheese
1 teaspoon parsley flakes

Season chicken breasts to taste with salt and pepper. In 10″ skillet, brown chicken on both sides in hot oil. Remove chicken from skillet. Stir in onion and garlic. Sauté 2-3 minutes. Drain tomatoes, reserving ¾ cup liquid. Chop tomatoes. Return chicken to skillet along with the tomato liquid, tomatoes, mushrooms, wine, and seasonings. Cover and simmer over moderately low heat for 15-20 minutes. Cook bag of rice according to package directions. Drain. Empty rice into saucepan and stir in the Parmesan cheese and parsley. To serve, spoon rice onto platter. Arrange chicken on the rice and pour the tomato-mushroom sauce over.
Makes 4 servings (1 chicken breast and ⅔ cup rice-tomato mixture)

STUFFED CHICKEN BREASTS

2 chicken breasts, skinned, boned
    and halved
1 cup dry white wine
¾ pound mushrooms, thinly sliced
    (about 3 cups)
¼ cup butter or margarine
1 large clove garlic, minced or
    pressed
3 tablespoons finely chopped
    parsley
1 tablespoon lemon juice
⅓ cup BLUE DIAMOND®
    Blanched Slivered Almonds,
    toasted
Salt and pepper
Flour
1 egg, beaten
½ cup BLUE DIAMOND®
    Blanched Slivered Almonds,
    ground
¼ cup butter or margarine, melted

Pound breasts between waxed paper to flatten to about ¼-inch thickness. In shallow glass baking dish marinate in wine 8 hours or overnight. In skillet sauté mushrooms in butter over moderately high heat 3 to 4 minutes. Add garlic, parsley and lemon juice and continue sautéing another 3 minutes; stir in the ⅓ cup toasted almonds. Pat breasts dry with paper towel. Lightly sprinkle with salt and pepper. With slotted spoon place about ⅓ cup of mushroom mixture on unskinned side of each chicken breast; fold in sides, roll and secure with toothpicks. Refrigerate 1 hour. Dredge in flour, dip in egg, roll in ground almonds. Drizzle with melted butter. Bake in 425 degree F. oven about 20 minutes in buttered casserole dish. If coating is not crispy brown, place under broiler until golden brown.
Makes 4 servings

FLORENTINE CHICKEN

3 whole chicken breasts, split
    (about 3 lb.)
¼ teaspoon salt
Dash of paprika
2 tablespoons butter or margarine
1 package (10 oz.) BIRDS EYE®
    5 Minute Chopped Spinach
1½ cups very hot water
¼ cup softened butter or
    margarine
1 package (6 oz.) STOVE TOP®
    Chicken Flavor Stuffing Mix
1 tablespoon lemon juice
½ cup sour cream

Place chicken, skin side up, in 3-quart shallow baking dish. Sprinkle with salt and paprika; dot with 2 tablespoons butter. Bake at 400° for 30 minutes. Meanwhile, prepare spinach as directed on package; drain well, squeezing out all liquid. Combine hot water, ¼ cup butter and contents of Vegetable/Seasoning Packet in a bowl, stirring until butter is melted. Add Stuffing Crumbs, lemon juice, sour cream and the spinach; stir just to moisten. Move chicken to one side of dish; baste with pan drippings. Mound stuffing on other side and bake 15 minutes longer.
Makes 4 cups stuffing plus chicken or 6 servings

CHICKEN BREASTS EL GRECO

4 whole chicken breasts, boned
    and skinned
¼ cup chopped parsley
Salt and pepper
3 cups chicken broth
¼ cup butter
¼ cup flour
¾ cup milk
¼ cup dry vermouth
2 tablespoons grated Parmesan
    cheese
Juice of ½ lemon (1 tablespoon)
2 drops TABASCO®
2 cups California grapes, halved
    and seeded

Sprinkle inside of chicken breasts with parsley, salt and pepper. Roll chicken breasts up, skewer or tie with string. Bring broth to a boil; simmer chicken breasts 25 to 30 minutes. Remove chicken (reserve broth) and keep warm, while making sauce. Melt butter, stir in flour, then gradually add milk. Stirring constantly, add 1½ cups broth. Stir in vermouth, cheese, lemon juice and TABASCO®, stirring until cheese melts; add grapes. Remove skewers; arrange chicken on serving dish. Spoon sauce over all. Serve with steamed rice. *Makes 4 servings*

Favorite recipe from California Table Grape Commission

LEMON CHICKEN CRUZAN®

3 whole chicken breasts, split
¼ cup CRUZAN® Gold Rum
¼ cup lemon juice
¼ cup melted butter
1 tablespoon honey
¼ teaspoon garlic powder
¼ teaspoon dried tarragon
Salt and pepper, to taste

Remove skin from each chicken breast half. Combine remaining ingredients and brush on both sides of each piece. Arrange chicken in a lightly greased shallow baking pan. Bake in preheated 400°F. oven 45-50 minutes. *6 servings*

QUICK CHICKEN CHASSEUR

1 pound boneless and skinless chicken breasts, cut in strips
⅓ cup corn starch
¼ cup vegetable oil
½ teaspoon *each* tarragon and ground thyme
¼ teaspoon pepper
1 cup sliced scallions
2 cups chicken broth
¾ cup HOLLAND HOUSE® Sherry Cooking Wine
1 cup sliced mushrooms, fresh or canned
3 tomatoes, cut in eighths
3 to 4 cups hot cooked rice

Dredge chicken in corn starch. In large skillet, brown coated chicken in oil. Stir in seasonings and scallions. Cook 2 minutes longer. Add broth and HOLLAND HOUSE® Sherry Cooking Wine. Cover; simmer 10 minutes. Gently stir in mushrooms and tomatoes. Cover; simmer 5 minutes longer. Serve over rice. Sauce may be served separately. *Makes 6 servings*

DRAMBUIE® POULET

4 skinned, boned chicken breasts, cut in half
Salt and pepper
1½ cups (8 ounces) diced, cooked ham
¼ cup DRAMBUIE®
¼ cup white wine
1 lb. small mushrooms or two 4½ oz. cans, drained
2-3 tablespoons butter
1 10½ oz. can cream of mushroom soup
1 cup sour cream
4 slices each, Cheddar and Swiss cheese, cut in half

Season chicken breasts with salt and pepper. Sprinkle ham in bottom of 13 x 9 x 2 inch baking dish; arrange chicken breasts over ham. Pour DRAMBUIE® and wine over chicken. Bake in a 350° oven for 30 minutes. Sauté mushrooms in butter; stir in mushroom soup and sour cream. Top each chicken breast with a piece of each cheese; spoon mushroom mixture over all. Bake an additional 30 minutes or until chicken is done. May be served over rice.

Four to six servings

CHICKEN WITH ARTICHOKES

2 whole boned chicken breasts
½ lb. sliced mushrooms
1 can artichoke hearts (water pack)
1 lemon, thinly sliced
3 Tbsp. clarified butter
1 Tbsp. capers
1½ oz. HIRAM WALKER Apricot Flavored Brandy
Parsley, salt and pepper

Cut chicken into bite-size pieces and sauté with mushrooms in clarified butter. Add artichoke hearts. Season and add lemon slices and capers. Pour Apricot Flavored Brandy over mixture. Flambé, if desired. Garnish with parsley. *Serves 4*

CHEESE-BAKED CHICKEN BREASTS

1 cup fine CHEEZ-IT® Cracker crumbs, about ½ of 6¼ ounce package
½ teaspoon salt
½ teaspoon garlic salt
¼ teaspoon marjoram, well rubbed
1 egg
1 tablespoon water
4 chicken breasts, about 12 ounces each, split, boned and skinned
⅓ cup melted butter

Between waxed paper, crush CHEEZ-ITS® into very fine crumbs with rolling pin; there should be about 1 cup. Mix well with salt, garlic salt and marjoram; place in a shallow dish. Beat egg and water well together in another shallow dish. Dip pieces of chicken in egg mixture, drain a bit and coat well in the crumb mixture. Let sit on waxed paper for about 15 minutes to set the crumbs. Place in lightly buttered, shallow pan about an inch apart. Drizzle with remaining butter. Bake in preheated moderate oven (350°F.) for about 30 to 35 minutes, or until golden brown and done through. Garnish with parsley and a wedge of lemon. (If desired you can buy canned chicken gravy to serve on the side. The 10¾ ounce can is suggested.)

Yield: 4 servings

SUN·MAID® RAISINS

GOLDEN GATE CHICKEN, CANTONESE

⅓ cup SUN-MAID® Golden Seedless Raisins
1 (13¾ oz.) can chicken broth
1 tablespoon chopped fresh ginger (or ¾ teaspoon powdered ginger)
2½ teaspoons soy sauce
2 tablespoons cornstarch
¼ cup dry sherry
2 teaspoons sugar
3 tablespoons vinegar
2 lbs. boned, skinned chicken breasts
Batter (recipe follows)
½ cup cooking oil

Bring first 4 ingredients to simmer. Blend cornstarch, sherry and sugar; stir into sauce and cook clear. Add vinegar; keep warm. Cut chicken in 1½ inch chunks. Dip in Batter, drain and fry until golden in heated oil. Cook single layer at a time. Combine with hot sauce. *Makes 6 servings*

BATTER

Heat together ½ cup each sifted flour and water, 1 egg, 1 teaspoon onion powder, ¾ teaspoon salt.

BLUE RIBBON®

CHINATOWN ALMOND CHICKEN

Skin, bone and cut 1½ pounds chicken breast in ½ inch cubes. In bowl mix 1 tsp. ginger, 2 tsp. sugar, 1 Tbsp. cornstarch; blend in 3 Tbsp. *each* water and soy sauce, and ⅓ cup sherry. Thaw 2 (6-oz.) pkgs. Chinese pea pods. In wok (or skillet) heat ¼ cup oil over medium heat. Add 1 cup BLUE RIBBON® Natural (or Blanched) Whole Almonds; stir and cook about 3 minutes. Add chicken and cook just till meat turns white. Pour in sherry mixture; cook till sauce thickens. Add pea pods; stir-fry till hot and glazed. Serve at once. *Serves 4*

CHICKEN A LA BLUE

4-ounce package TREASURE CAVE® Blue Cheese, crumbled
3 large chicken breasts, skinned, boned and halved lengthwise
2 tablespoons finely chopped onion
½ stick (¼ cup) butter or margarine
10 ounce package frozen chopped spinach, thawed and drained
½ cup soft bread crumbs
2 teaspoons lemon juice
3 tablespoons flour
¾ cup chicken broth or bouillon
¼ cup dry white wine
¼ teaspoon salt
Paprika

Pound chicken to ¼ inch thickness. Sauté onion in 2 tablespoons butter until tender. Add spinach; cook just to remove moisture. Add crumbs, cheese and lemon juice. Put ¼ cup of mixture on each chicken piece. Fold in sides, roll, and skewer or tie. Coat in flour and brown in remaining butter. Place in an 11 by 7 by 1½ inch baking dish. Add broth, wine and salt to drippings in skillet. Heat; pour over chicken. Cover; bake in a 350°F. oven 35 minutes. Uncover, sprinkle with paprika. Bake 10 to 15 minutes. Stir juice in pan to blend. Thicken, if necessary, with 1 teaspoon flour mixed with 1 tablespoon water. Serve over chicken. *Yield: 6 servings*

RIPPLED CHICKEN SKEWERS
(Low Calorie)

4 half breasts of chicken (about 1¼ lbs.), boned and skinned
2 tablespoons soy sauce
2 tablespoons lemon juice
2 tablespoons white table wine
½ teaspoon dry mustard
½ teaspoon tarragon, crumbled
½ teaspoon salt
⅛ teaspoon crushed garlic
3 medium green-tipped DOLE® Bananas
12 cherry tomatoes

Pull out small inner filet from chicken breasts and cut outer portion in halves lengthwise, making a total of 12 pieces. Combine all remaining ingredients except bananas and tomatoes. Peel bananas and cut into quarters. Pour 2 tablespoons soy mixture over bananas to marinate. On each of 6 (10-inch) skewers, ripple two pieces of chicken, spreading chicken toward ends of skewers. Place on broiler pan. Broil 5 inches from heat 4 minutes each side, basting often with soy mixture. Remove skewers from broiler, push chicken pieces together and add 2 pieces of banana and 2 cherry tomatoes to each skewer. Broil 1 minute on each side, basting twice. Serve at once. *Makes 6 servings*

1,005 calories per recipe, or 297 calories per serving.

CURRIED CHICKEN WITH ALMOND RICE

1 bag SUCCESS® Rice
4 chicken breast halves, boned
¼ cup flour
2 teaspoons curry powder
¾ teaspoon salt
¼ teaspoon ground ginger
¼ cup butter or margarine, divided
1 cup light cream
¼ cup slivered almonds
¼ cup sliced green onions
¼ cup raisins

Cook bag of rice according to package directions. While rice is cooking, remove skin from chicken and cut into strips. On waxed paper, coat chicken in mixture of flour, curry, salt, and ginger. In 10" skillet, melt 2 tablespoons butter over medium heat. Add the chicken pieces, a few pieces at a time, and brown on all sides, removing them as they brown. After all pieces are browned, melt 1 tablespoon butter in skillet. Stir in 1 tablespoon of remaining flour mixture. Add the cream and heat and stir until thickened. Return chicken to skillet, cover, and simmer on low heat 10 minutes. Drain rice and pour out water. Melt remaining butter in saucepan; add almonds and sauté lightly. Stir in the rice, green onion and raisins. Heat gently. To serve, pour rice onto platter and pour chicken and sauce over it.
Makes 4 servings (about ⅔ cup chicken and sauce with ⅔ cup rice)

CHICKEN PARISIENNE

2-4 whole chicken breasts, halved
Salt and pepper to taste
3 Tablespoons butter or margarine
1 small onion, sliced
1 cup sour cream
1 cup fresh mushrooms, sliced
1 10¾ oz. can, Cream of Chicken soup
½-¾ cup HOLLAND HOUSE® Sherry Cooking Wine

Season breasts with salt and pepper. Melt butter or margarine in a skillet or frying pan; brown chicken on both sides. Arrange chicken, onion and mushrooms in a casserole or baking pan. Mix remaining ingredients together in a separate bowl; pour over chicken. Bake in 400° oven for 40 to 50 minutes. *Serves 4*

AMARETTO ORANGE CHICKEN

¼ cup flour
¾ teaspoon salt
½ teaspoon white pepper
¼ teaspoon sage
8 skinless and boneless chicken breast halves (about 2 lbs.)
2 tablespoons butter (or margarine)
1 tablespoon oil
1 cup heavy cream
½ cup HEREFORD'S Amaretto Cows
½ teaspoon finely grated fresh orange rind
⅛ teaspoon sage
2 tablespoons toasted sliced almonds

Combine flour, salt, white pepper and ¼ teaspoon sage in plastic bag. Shake chicken to coat. Brown chicken in butter and oil. Reduce heat. Continue cooking just until tender. Remove to heated platter. Add cream, Cows, orange rind, and ⅛ teaspoon sage to pan drippings. Cook, stirring until slightly thickened. Spoon sauce over chicken. Sprinkle with toasted sliced almonds. Garnish with orange slices and parsley, if desired. *Serves 6*

SHANGHAI CHICKEN AND VEGETABLES

2 whole chicken breasts, split, skinned, boned, and cut in 2-inch pieces (1 pound boneless)
2 tablespoons salad oil
2 cans (10¾ ounces each) CAMPBELL'S Condensed Chicken Broth
½ cup raw regular rice
½ cup sherry
2 tablespoons soy sauce
1 large clove garlic, minced
¼ teaspoon ground ginger
2 cups diagonally sliced carrots
1 cup diagonally sliced green onions
1 can (about 8 ounces) bamboo shoots, drained
1 package (6 ounces) frozen pea pods
½ cup water
3 to 4 tablespoons cornstarch

In skillet, lightly brown chicken in oil. Add broth, rice, sherry, soy, garlic, and ginger. Bring to boil; reduce heat. Cover; simmer 15 minutes. Add carrots, onions, and bamboo shoots. Simmer 5 minutes more or until done. Stir occasionally. Add pea pods. Blend water into cornstarch until smooth; slowly stir into stew. Cook, stirring until thickened.

Makes about 7 cups

MEXICAN DRUMSTICKS

8 chicken drumsticks
Salt
Pepper
¼ cup butter or margarine
1 15½-oz. can ARMOUR® STAR Chili with Beans
Sliced pitted ripe olives
2 cups hot cooked rice
2 tablespoons chopped green chilies

Heat oven to 350°. Season chicken with salt and pepper; brown in butter or margarine in oven-proof fry pan. Spoon chili over chicken; top with olives. Bake, covered, at 350°, 45 minutes. Combine rice and green chilies; serve chicken over rice mixture.

4 servings

Microwave Instructions: Season chicken with salt and pepper. Melt butter or margarine in 3-qt. casserole. Arrange chicken in dish, turning to coat with butter or margarine. Cook, covered, 14 minutes; turning chicken occasionally. Spoon chili over chicken; top with olives. Cook, covered, 14 minutes. Combine rice and green chilies; serve chicken over rice mixture.

EAST-WEST CHICKEN DRUMSTICKS
(Microwave Recipe)

2 pounds COUNTRY PRIDE® Broiler-Fryer Chicken Drumsticks
1 cup corn flake crumbs
1 teaspoon salt
⅛ teaspoon pepper
½ cup evaporated milk
1 tablespoon soy sauce
Mustard Sauce (recipe follows)

Mix corn flake crumbs with salt and pepper in shallow dish. Mix evaporated milk and soy sauce in another shallow dish. Dip chicken drumsticks in evaporated milk, then roll immediately in seasoned corn flake crumbs. Place drumsticks in lightly greased 12 × 7½ × 2-inch glass baking dish. Cover with waxed paper and cook in microwave oven 10 minutes, turn dish, cook 8 to 10 minutes longer. Let stand 3 to 5 minutes. Serve with Mustard Sauce if desired. Total cooking time: 20 minutes.

Yield: 4 to 6 servings

MUSTARD SAUCE

¼ cup prepared mustard
1 teaspoon sugar
½ teaspoon salt
⅛ teaspoon TABASCO® Pepper Sauce
½ cup evaporated milk
1 teaspoon lemon juice

In small glass bowl or 2-cup glass measuring cup mix all ingredients except lemon juice. Cover with waxed paper and cook in microwave oven 2 minutes. Stir in lemon juice. Serve with chicken drumsticks. Cooking time: 2 minutes.

Yield: ¾ cup

Note: 2 pounds COUNTRY PRIDE® Chicken Wings may be substituted for drumsticks.

PILAF WITH CHICKEN WINGS

2 pounds chicken wings (without tips)
3 tablespoons oil
1 onion, chopped
1 cup rice
3 HERB-OX Chicken Bouillon Cubes or 1 tablespoon HERB-OX Instant Chicken Style Bouillon
2½ cups boiling water

Brown chicken wings in oil, turning often; move to one side of pan. Add rice and onions to center of pan, stir until rice is golden. Add water and bouillon cubes, or instant bouillon, stir to dissolve. Arrange chicken over rice, cover, cook 25 minutes, until rice is tender and water absorbed.

Makes 6 servings

BARBECUED CHICKEN WINGS

2 to 3 pounds chicken wings
2 tablespoons shortening
1 can (10¼ ounces) FRANCO-AMERICAN Beef Gravy
¼ cup ketchup
1½ teaspoons hot pepper sauce
1 teaspoon brown sugar
½ teaspoon vinegar
Cooked rice

In skillet, brown chicken in shortening; pour off fat. Stir in remaining ingredients except rice. Cover; cook over low heat 30 minutes or until done. Stir occasionally. Serve with rice.

Makes 4 servings

BARBECUE CHICKEN, SOUTHERN STYLE

1 cup HEINZ Tomato Ketchup
2-3 tablespoons honey
1 tablespoon lemon juice
Dash hot pepper sauce
2 to 2½ pounds broiler-fryer pieces
Salt and pepper

Combine ketchup, honey, lemon juice and hot pepper sauce. Brush on chicken during last 5 to 10 minutes of grilling or broiling time. Season wth salt and pepper.

Makes 4-6 servings
(about 1¼ cups sauce)

BARBECUED CHICKEN— APRICOT SAUCE

2 lbs. chicken
½ cup SIMON FISCHER Apricot Butter
¼ cup light molasses
½ cup catsup
1 medium onion, chopped
4 whole cloves
Dash garlic salt
1 tablespoon lemon juice
1 Tbsp. salad oil
1 Tbsp. vinegar
½ tsp. prepared mustard
¼ tsp. salt
¼ tsp. pepper
½ tsp. Worcestershire sauce
1 Tbsp. butter
¼ tsp. TABASCO®

Combine ingredients except chicken and boil for 5 minutes—heat oven to 325 degrees—cover chicken with aluminum foil in shallow pan and roast 1 hour, pouring off excess grease occasionally—remove foil—pour off excess fat and pour sauce over chicken. Roast chicken at 400 degrees, uncovered, until glazed and tender.

BARBECUED ROSÉ CHICKEN

¼ cup butter
1 tsp. cornstarch
½ tsp. garlic salt
¼ tsp. marjoram
¾ cup THE CHRISTIAN BROTHERS® Napa Rosé Wine
3 broiling chickens, cut in half

Melt butter; blend in cornstarch and seasonings, add wine, cook, stirring until mixture thickens slightly. Place chicken halves over glowing coals; turn and baste frequently with sauce until chicken is done. (Chickens may be broiled in oven, if desired.)   *Serves 6*

BARBECUED CHICKEN

Barbecue Sauce:
½ cup tomato sauce
½ cup COCO CASA™ Cream of Coconut
4 Tbsp. white vinegar
½ tsp. onion powder
½ tsp. ground ginger
2 cloves garlic, crushed
3 Tbsp. oil
1 tsp. salt

Mix all ingredients and keep refrigerated.   *Yield: 1½ cups*

Barbecued Chicken: Use chicken wings for appetizer, use fryer, cut into serving pieces, for a main course. Marinate chicken in sauce for one to two hours. Broil under preheated broiler, at bottom third of oven, for 20 minutes on each side. Baste frequently. Chicken is ready when skin is crisp and golden brown.

LEMON BARBECUED CHICKEN

One 2½ to 3 pound broiler-fryer, split in half
1 cup salad oil
¾ cup lemon juice
1 tablespoon DURKEE Garlic Salt
1 tablespoon DURKEE Parsley Flakes
2 teaspoons DURKEE Onion Powder
2 teaspoons DURKEE Sweet Basil
2 teaspoons DURKEE Thyme
1 teaspoon DURKEE Monosodium Glutamate

Place chicken in a shallow pan. Combine remaining ingredients; pour over chicken and cover tightly. Marinate several hours or overnight in refrigerator, turning chicken occasionally. Barbecue chicken over hot coals for 15 to 20 minutes on each side, basting often with the marinade.
Makes 2 servings

BARBECUED CHICKEN WITH SHERRY MARINADE

¼ cup POMPEIAN Olive Oil
2 Tbsp. soy sauce
1 chicken, about 3 lbs., whole or cut up
1 cup dry sherry
½ tsp. oregano

Combine olive oil, soy sauce, sherry, and oregano; pour over chicken and refrigerate 6 to 12 hours, turning several times. Remove chicken from marinade. Place whole chicken on rotisserie spit and cook, basting frequently with marinade for 1 to 1¼ hours

over medium-hot fire, until leg moves very easily. Place cut-up chicken on flat grill; turn and baste frequently until pieces are well-browned on both sides. If roasted on electric rotisserie or broiled save drippings and serve as unthickened gravy with the chicken.   *Makes 4 servings*

CHICKEN CREOLE

2 cups chicken broth
2½ cups canned tomatoes and juice
½ cup chopped green pepper
½ cup chopped onion
½ cup chopped celery
1 tsp. salt
1 tsp. sugar
¼ tsp. pepper
1¼ cups uncooked rice
2 5-oz. cans BANQUET® Boned Chicken, drained and cubed
2 bay leaves

Combine all ingredients in saucepan; cover. Bring to boil. Reduce heat and simmer 20 minutes, or until rice is tender and most of liquid is absorbed. Remove bay leaves before serving.
6 servings

BROILED CHICKEN PATTIES

6 double SUNSHINE KRISPY® Crackers
¼ teaspoon salt
¼ teaspoon pepper
2 cups ground or finely minced cooked chicken
½ cup light cream
1 egg yolk, beaten
1 teaspoon lemon juice
1 tablespoon minced parsley
¼ cup melted butter (approximately)

Crush crackers into fine crumbs between two sheets of waxed paper. Mix with salt and pepper and set aside. Blend remaining ingredients, except butter, together and work in prepared crumbs. Shape into four patties about ½ to ¾-inch thick. Place on broiler rack and brush edges with butter. Brown about 3 inches from the sides and finish browning. Serve with asparagus and a tossed salad.   *Yield: 4 servings*

Note: If canned chicken is used, buy 2 cans solid pack, each weight 5½ ounces.

SAN FRANCISCO CHICKEN

1 package (10 oz.) BIRDS EYE®
   AMERICANA RECIPE®
   Vegetables, San Francisco Style
½ to ¾ pound raw chicken, cut
   in strips
2 tablespoons oil
2 tablespoons water
1 tablespoon white wine (optional)
1 teaspoon soy sauce
1 teaspoon toasted sesame seed
   (optional)
½ teaspoon salt

Set aside packet of topping. Sauté
chicken in oil in skillet just until
tender, about 5 minutes. Add
vegetables, water, wine, soy sauce,
sesame seed and salt. Bring to a
full boil over medium heat,
separating vegetables with a fork
and stirring occasionally. Reduce
heat; cover and simmer 5 minutes.
Sprinkle with topping just before
serving.
Makes 2½ cups or 3 servings

CHICKEN AND BROCCOLI AU GRATIN

¼ cup butter or margarine
¼ cup chopped onion
¼ cup flour
1 teaspoon salt
½ teaspoon curry powder
Dash pepper
1 can (4 oz.) sliced mushrooms
1 tall can (13 fl. oz.) PET®
   Evaporated Milk
1 package (10 oz.) frozen broccoli
   spears, cooked and drained
1 chicken, cooked and cut in large
   cubes
1 cup (4 oz.) shredded Monterey
   Jack Cheese

Melt butter in skillet. Sauté onions
until transparent. Remove from
heat. Stir in flour, salt, curry
powder, and pepper. Drain
mushrooms, reserving liquid. Add
water to make ½ cup liquid.
Gradually stir into flour mixture in
skillet. Blend in evaporated milk
until smooth. Add mushrooms.
Cook and stir over medium heat
until sauce begins to thicken.
Arrange broccoli spears and
chicken on bottom of a 13 × 9-inch
baking dish. Pour sauce over. Top
with cheese. Bake at 375°F. for 20
minutes, or until bubbly around
edges. Cool 15 minutes before
serving.   *Makes 6 servings*

CHICKEN DIVAN

1 bunch broccoli or 2 packages
   (10 ounces each) frozen spears
¼ cup butter
¼ cup flour
2 cups milk
2 teaspoons HERB-OX Instant
   Chicken Style Bouillon or 2
   HERB-OX Chicken Bouillon
   Cubes
1½ pounds sliced cooked chicken
   or turkey
¼ cup grated Parmesan cheese

Cook broccoli until just tender,
drain, arrange on flat flameproof
dish. Melt butter, stir in flour. Add
milk and cook, stirring, until the
sauce is thickened and smooth.
Add instant bouillon or bouillon
cubes, stir to dissolve. Pour half
the sauce over the broccoli, top
with the sliced chicken, and cover
with remaining sauce. Sprinkle
with grated cheese, put dish under
broiler until cheese is melted and
sauce bubbling hot.
Makes 6 servings

TOMATO CHICKEN PILAF

1 can (3 oz.) sliced mushrooms,
   drained, reserving liquid
½ cup chopped onions
1 small clove garlic, chopped
2 tablespoons vegetable oil
¾ cup KELLOGG'S® ALL-BRAN®
   Cereal or KELLOGG'S® BRAN
   BUDS® Cereal
2 cups cut-up cooked chicken
⅓ cup uncooked regular rice
½ teaspoon salt
Dash pepper
¼ teaspoon leaf thyme
1 can (28 oz.) whole peeled
   tomatoes

In large frypan, cook drained
mushrooms, onions and garlic in
oil until lightly browned. Stir in
reserved mushroom liquid and
remaining ingredients, cutting
tomatoes into pieces. Bring to boil.
Reduce heat, cover tightly and
simmer about 30 minutes or until
rice is tender.
Yield: 5 servings

® Kellogg Company

EASY CHICKEN PAPRIKASH

3 5-oz. cans BANQUET® Boned
   Chicken, drained
¼ tsp. salt
¼ tsp. pepper
¼ tsp. paprika
2 Tbsp. butter
1 onion, chopped
2 Tbsp. tomato paste
1 cup chicken broth
½ cup sifted all-purpose flour
1 cup sour cream
½ tsp. salt
Rice, cooked according to
   package directions

Melt butter in saucepan. Sauté
onion; add chicken. Combine
chicken broth, tomato paste, ¼
tsp. salt, pepper and paprika. Pour
over chicken and bring to boil.
Drain off liquid. Combine flour,
sour cream, and ½ tsp. salt. Add
hot liquid slowly to sour cream
mixture, stirring well. Pour over
chicken and heat. (Caution: Sour
cream will curdle if cooked too
long, or at too high a temperature.)
Serve over rice.   *6-8 servings*

BEST CHICKEN CROQUETTES

1 can (10¾ ounces) CAMPBELL'S
   Condensed Cream of Chicken
   Soup
1½ cups finely chopped cooked
   chicken
¼ cup fine dry bread crumbs
2 tablespoons finely chopped
   celery
1 tablespoon finely chopped onion
¼ teaspoon poultry seasoning
Shortening
½ cup milk

To make croquettes, combine ⅓
cup soup, chicken, bread crumbs,
celery, onion and ⅛ teaspoon
poultry seasoning. Mix well; shape
into 6 croquettes or patties (if
mixture is difficult to handle, chill
before shaping). Roll in additional
bread crumbs. In skillet, brown
croquettes in shortening.
Meanwhile, in saucepan, combine
remaining soup, ⅛ teaspoon
poultry seasoning and milk. Heat;
stir occasionally. Serve with
croquettes.   *Makes 3 servings*

PETTENGILL SCHOOLHOUSE CHICKEN PIE

2 tablespoons margarine
1 cup sliced mushrooms
1 clove garlic, minced
2 tablespoons ARGO® / KINGSFORD'S® Corn Starch
1½ cups milk
2½ cups cooked chicken, cut in bite-size pieces
2 cups fresh peas, cooked
1 whole pimiento, chopped
½ teaspoon dried thyme leaves
1 teaspoon salt
¼ teaspoon pepper
1 recipe double crust pastry

In skillet melt margarine. Add mushrooms and garlic. Sauté over medium heat until lightly browned. In saucepan stir together corn starch and milk until smooth. Mix in mushrooms, garlic and pan drippings. Bring to a boil over medium heat, stirring constantly, and boil 1 minute. Stir in next 6 ingredients. Pour into pastry-lined 9-inch pie plate. Cover pie with pastry; seal and flute edge. Cut slits in top. Bake in 375°F. oven 35 minutes or until crust is golden brown.   *Serves 6 to 8*

MILE-HIGH CHICKEN PIE

½ lb. sweetbreads
6 cups cold water
1 Tbsp. lemon juice
1 clove garlic, slivered
1 sprig parsley
½ tsp. salt
½ tsp. thyme
2 (10-oz.) cans chicken à la king
1 (8¼-oz.) can sliced carrots, drained
¼ cup dry sherry
1 (10-oz.) pkg. PEPPERIDGE FARM® Frozen Patty Shells, thawed
1 egg yolk
2 Tbsp. water

Soak sweetbreads in 2 cups water. Meanwhile combine 1 quart cold water, lemon juice, slivered garlic, parsley, salt and thyme. Simmer, covered, for 5 minutes. Add sweetbreads, drained. Simmer, covered, for 5 minutes or until tender (do not overcook). Drain, rinse in cold water. Cut into 1-inch pieces discarding any gristle or tough skin. Blend sweetbreads with chicken à la king, carrots (drained) and sherry. Place in 1½ quart casserole. Cover with foil. Set aside. Preheat oven to 450°.

Press 6 thawed Patty Shells together. On lightly floured surface roll out to fit top of casserole. Place pastry on cookie sheet. Decorate with fanciful motifs cut from surplus pastry. Brush lightly with beaten egg yolk and water mixture. Bake 10-15 minutes or until risen and deep golden brown. At the same time place casserole on shelf under pastry, to heat through. To serve: remove foil from casserole, and set pastry lid on top.   *Serves 6*

ROAST CAPON WITH RICE STUFFING AND PEACH-GREEN GRAPE GARNISH

1 frozen capon (5½ to 6 pounds) defrosted
½ cup butter or margarine
1 cup diced celery
⅓ cup sliced green onion
4 cups well-drained cooked seasoned rice
½ cup seedless grape halves
2 tablespoons dry sherry, optional
Salt
Small canned peach halves, drained, for garnish
Green grape clusters, for garnish
Watercress or favorite washed greens, for garnish

Wash, drain and dry Capon with paper toweling. Sprinkle body and neck cavities with salt. Prepare stuffing. Melt butter or margarine in large skillet. Add celery and onions; cook over low heat until vegetables are tender, stirring often. Fold in rice, grape halves, sherry and salt, if needed. Fill cavities of Capon loosely with stuffing. Skewer neck skin to back. Return legs and tail to tucked position. Place breast side up on rack in open roasting pan. (use no water in pan.) Brush skin with melted butter or margarine. Cover Capon loosely with aluminum foil, crimping it to edges of pan. Place in slow oven (325°F.) for about 40 minutes per pound. Remove foil 45 minutes before end of roasting time. Brush Capon with melted butter or margarine and continue roasting until leg joint moves easily. To serve place Capon on platter and garnish with peach halves, green grape clusters and favorite garnishing greens.
Makes 6 servings

Favorite recipe from National Capon Council

ROAST CAPON WITH ORANGE PECAN STUFFING

1 frozen capon (5-6 pounds), defrosted
¼ cup butter or margarine
1 cup thinly sliced celery
¼ cup chopped onion
¾ cup water
5 cups toasted crust-free bread cubes (½-inch)
¾ cup drained, sectioned, diced oranges
⅓ cup coarsely chopped pecans
1 teaspoon grated orange rind
1 teaspoon salt
½ teaspoon curry powder, optional
Orange slices for garnish
Watercress for garnish

Wash, drain and dry capon. Prepare stuffing. Melt butter or margarine in skillet. Add celery, onion and water; cook over moderate heat until vegetables are tender. Combine bread cubes, orange pieces, pecans, orange rind, ½ teaspoon salt and curry powder, if used; mix. Add vegetables and mix carefully. Sprinkle remaining salt over neck and body cavities. Stuff neck and body cavities loosely with bread mixture. Skewer neck skin to back. Return legs and tail to tucked position. Place capon, breast side up, on rack in open roasting pan. (Don't add water to pan.) Brush skin with melted butter or margarine. Cover capon loosely with aluminum foil, crimping it to edges of pan. Foil should not touch capon. Place in slow oven (325°F.) 3 to 3¾ hours. Remove foil 45 minutes before end of roasting time. Brush capon with melted butter or margarine and continue roasting until leg joint moves easily. To serve, place capon on platter and garnish with orange slices and watercress.
Makes 6 to 8 servings

Favorite recipe from National Capon Council

Cornish Hens

CORNISH WITH CRABMEAT STUFFING

4 TYSON Cornish Game Hens
Salt, pepper, garlic powder and
   paprika to taste
Oil
Stuffing (recipe follows)

Rinse hens lightly and pat dry.
Season (inside and out) with salt,
pepper, garlic and paprika—rub
lightly with oil. Divide Stuffing
among hens. Tie legs together and
place on rack in roasting pan.
Preheat oven to 350°F. and roast
hens 1 hour.   *Serves 4*

STUFFING

1 stick butter (about)
⅓ C. half & half
¼ C. green onions (chopped fine)
¼ C. celery (chopped fine)
1 clove garlic (chopped fine)
⅛ C. parsley
1 C. crabmeat (6½ oz. can)
1 C. fine breadcrumbs
½ tsp. salt
Dash pepper

Melt butter, add garlic, parsley,
green onion, and celery; sauté
vegetables until soft. Add
crabmeat. Salt and pepper. Stir
gently not to break up crabmeat,
simmer. Add breadcrumbs and half
& half, a little at a time so mixture
is not too dry.

TEXAS-STYLE GAME HENS ON THE GRILL

4 TYSON Cornish Game Hens

Seasoning:
½ tsp. salt
½ tsp. garlic powder
½ tsp. chili powder

Sauce:
½ C. apple jelly
½ C. catsup
1 Tbsp. vinegar
½ tsp. chili powder

Rub cornish inside and out with
seasonings and place on grill.
Cook 1 hour, or until tender,
basting frequently during last ½
hour with sauce.   *Serves 4*

CHRISTMAS CORNISH WITH WALNUT-APPLE STUFFING

6 TYSON Cornish Game Hens
Paprika, salt, pepper
Oil
3 C. cooked wild rice (6 oz.
   package)
¼ C. finely chopped celery
¼ C. finely chopped onion
3 oz. walnut pieces
2 apples, cored and chopped
⅓ C. port
½ tsp. salt
Pepper
1 Tbsp. parsley flakes

Wash hens and pat dry, season
with salt, paprika, and pepper. Rub
lightly with oil. Add remaining
ingredients for stuffing and toss
lightly. Divide stuffing among hens
and truss. Place in roasting pan
and roast 1 hour or until tender in
preheated 350°F. oven.
                            Serves 6

ROCK CORNISH HENS ELEGANTÉ

6-8 Rock Cornish Hens
Salt and pepper

Stuffing:
2 Tbsp. butter
1 onion, chopped
2 cups sliced celery
2 tsp. fines herbes
6 cups cooked brown rice
¼ cup chopped almonds
⅓ cup HIRAM WALKER Amaretto
   or Apricot Flavored Brandy
½ cup golden raisins

Glaze:
¼ cup melted butter
½ cup HIRAM WALKER Amaretto
   or Apricot Flavored Brandy

Sauce:
¼ cup flour
2 cups orange juice
Strips of orange peel

Season hens inside and out with
salt and pepper.

Heat butter in sauce pan and sauté
onion until golden brown. Add
herbes and celery and sauté for 5
minutes. Stir in brown rice,
almonds, raisins and Amaretto or
Apricot Flavored Brandy. Stuff
hens. Sew or skewer openings.
Preheat oven to 350°. Bake for 1½
to 2 hours until hens are tender,
basting occasionally with glaze.

Place hens on warm platter and
place roasting pan on top of range
(low heat). Gradually stir flour and
orange juice into pan juices.
Season to taste with salt and
pepper. Spoon over hens and
garnish with orange peel and
watercress.   *Serves 6 to 8*

COUNTRY CORNISH

3 TYSON Cornish Hens (halved)
2 C. sour cream
¼ C. lemon juice
2 Tbsp. Worcestershire
2 Tbsp. celery salt
1 Tbsp. paprika
1 Tbsp. salt
½ tsp. pepper
2 C. dry bread crumbs

In large bowl, combine sour cream,
lemon juice, Worcestershire, celery
salt, paprika, salt and pepper. Dip
each cornish half in mixture. Coat
with bread crumbs. Arrange in
single layer in large shallow baking
pan. Bake uncovered in preheated
350°F. oven for 45 minutes or until
tender.   *Serves 6*

APRICOT CORNISH WITH PECAN STUFFING

6 TYSON Cornish Game Hens
Salt
2 6-oz. pkgs. stuffing mix
1 C. pecans
1 C. apricot preserves
3 tsp. cornstarch
⅓ C. dry white wine
¼ C. butter

Rinse hens and pat dry; sprinkle
inside and out with salt. Prepare
stuffing mix according to package
directions and stir in pecans. Fill
hens loosely with stuffing,
spooning remainder into baking
dish. Truss hens securely. Arrange
in roasting pan. Combine
remaining four ingredients in
saucepan cooking over medium
heat until glaze thickens (about 5
minutes). Brush each hen
generously with some of the
apricot sauce. Bake hens in
preheated oven at 350°F., basting
frequently until done. Spoon
remaining stuffing onto serving
platter and arrange hens on top.
Garnish with watercress. *Serves 6*

APPLE/RAISIN STUFFED CORNISH GAME HENS

4 Cornish game hens
1 (6 oz.) bag Melba Toasted Dressing
½ cup chopped celery
⅓ cup chopped onion
½ cup butter
1 large or 2 small apple(s) peeled and sliced
½ cup S&W Apple Juice
1 cup S&W Apple Sauce
¾ cup chopped S&W Walnuts
⅔ cup S&W Seedless Raisins
Salt and pepper

Sauté celery and onions in butter until tender. Combine with remaining ingredients except salt and pepper. Wash and pat dry thawed hens—season cavities with salt and pepper. Stuff hens with stuffing mixture and fasten openings with skewers. Place hens breast side up in roaster pan. (Do not cover, a foil tent may be used if excessive browning occurs.) Roast 1½ hours at 325°, basting 4 or 5 times with the following sauce.

SAUCE

1 cup S&W Apple Juice
½ cup firmly packed brown sugar

Heat on stove until well blended or in the microwave for one minute.
Serves 4

CORNISH DINNER DUO
(Microwave Recipe)

2 20-ounce frozen COUNTRY PRIDE® Cornish Game Hens, defrosted
2 tablespoons butter or margarine
¼ cup finely chopped onion
¼ cup chopped celery
¾ cup chicken broth
¼ cup chopped nuts
¼ teaspoon salt
¼ teaspoon dried leaf thyme
⅛ teaspoon pepper
1 teaspoon paprika
¾ cup packaged precooked rice

Remove giblets from Cornish Game Hens, chop and reserve. Melt butter in 12 x 7½ x 2-inch glass baking dish in microwave oven, 1 minute. Add giblets, onion and celery, cover and cook 2 minutes. Stir in chicken broth, nuts, salt, thyme and pepper. Place hens in baking dish, breast side down. Cover with waxed paper and cook 12 minutes. Place hens on backs and sprinkle with paprika. Cover, turn dish and cook an additional 13 to 15 minutes. Remove hens to serving platter. Stir rice into liquid in dish, cover and cook 3 to 4 minutes before serving. Total cooking time: 34 minutes. *Yield: 2 servings*

SUMMER CORNISH ROAST

3 TYSON Cornish Game Hens (halved)
1 pt. buttermilk (2 cups)
1 C. cream of mushroom or cream of celery soup
¼ tsp. garlic
1 tsp. basil
1 tsp. thyme
1 tsp. rosemary
1 tsp. salt
2 dashes pepper
8 oz. grated Cheddar cheese
New (small) potatoes
New (small) onions
3 stalks celery, sliced (save leaves)
Mushrooms

Place cornish in baking dish, skin side up. Mix buttermilk, soup and garlic; set aside. Sprinkle cornish with seasonings and cheese. Spoon sauce over all. Bake at 350°F. (preheated) for 45-60 minutes. Last 30 minutes, add new potatoes, onions, celery, and mushrooms. Arrange on platter and garnish with celery leaves.
Serves 6

LITTLE RED HENS

6 Cornish game hens (about 1 pound *each*)
2 cloves garlic, halved
Salt
Pepper
½ cup plus 2 tablespoons water
1 teaspoon instant chicken bouillon
¼ cup red currant jelly
1 pint basket fresh California strawberries, stemmed
2 tablespoons red wine vinegar
2 teaspoons cornstarch
Parsley sprigs

Rub hens inside and outside with garlic. Sprinkle with salt and pepper. Place on rack, spaced apart, in shallow baking pan. Roast in 350 degree oven 30 minutes. Meanwhile, prepare glaze: In 1-quart saucepan combine ½ cup of the water, the bouillon and jelly. Stir over medium heat to melt jelly. In container of electric blender combine 1 cup of the berries and the vinegar. Blend until smooth, scraping sides of container as needed. Stir berry mixture into bouillon mixture. Mix cornstarch with the remaining 2 tablespoons water. Stir into berry mixture. Cook and stir until mixture comes to a boil and thickens slightly. After hens have roasted for 30 minutes, brush all over with glaze. Continue to roast 30 to 40 minutes, brushing frequently with glaze, until juices run clear when pricked with a fork. Garnish with parsley. Serve hot or chilled with the remaining berries.
Makes 6 servings

Favorite recipe from California Strawberry Advisory Board

GOLDEN HENS WITH HERB RICE
(Microwave Recipe)

4 Rock Cornish hens (1 pound each)
Salt
2 cups packaged pre-cooked rice
1½ cups chicken broth
½ cup chopped onion
1 teaspoon poultry seasoning, divided
HOLLAND HOUSE® Microwave Browning Sauce for Chicken

Remove giblets from hens; reserve giblets for another use. Rinse hens; drain well and pat dry. Sprinkle cavities with salt. Tie the legs of each hen together loosely. Turn wings under. Cover legs with foil; set hens aside. Mix rice, broth, onion and ½ teaspoon poultry seasoning in an 8 x 10-inch microwave oven-proof baking dish. Place hens breast-side-down on rice mixture. Sprinkle with remaining ½ teaspoon poultry seasoning. Brush hens with browning sauce. Pierce skins with fork; cover with wax paper. Microwave on medium power 7 minutes. Turn hens breast-side-up; cover, microwave on medium power 7 minutes longer. Turn hens breast-side-down, reversing outside edges to inside; microwave, uncovered, on medium power 7 minutes. Turn hens breast-side-up, reversing outside edges to inside; microwave, uncovered, on medium power 7 minutes longer or until hens are done.
Yield: 4 servings

ROAST STUFFED CORNISH HENS COCO CASA™

2 Rock Cornish Hens
Salt, pepper, thyme
1 clove garlic, crushed

1 cup mixed dried fruit
1 cup seasoned croutons
½ stick unsalted butter, melted
¼ cup COCO CASA™ Cream of Coconut

½ cup frozen orange concentrate, undiluted
½ cup COCO CASA™ Cream of Coconut
2 Tbsp. HOLLAND HOUSE® Sherry Cooking Wine

Wash and dry hens. Rub lightly with salt, pepper, thyme and garlic. Stuff* and skewer. Brush with Basting Sauce** and roast in preheated 400° oven, basting every ten minutes. Roast hens for 1 to 1½ hours, or until tender when pierced with a fork. Spoon pan juices over hens before serving.

Serves 4

*STUFFING

Cut fruit in small chunks and toss with croutons, butter and ¼ cup cream of coconut.

**BASTING SAUCE

Mix together orange concentrate, ½ cup cream of coconut and sherry.

OUTDOOR CORNISH GOURMET

4 TYSON Cornish Game Hens

Marinade:
½ C. olive oil
⅓ C. orange juice
2 Tbsp. soy sauce
½ C. wine vinegar
2 dashes TABASCO® Sauce
¼ tsp. Worcestershire sauce
¼ tsp. thyme
¼ tsp. coarse black pepper
½ tsp. salt

Combine marinade ingredients. Marinate for 4 to 5 hours turning occasionally. Place on grill spit and broil over coals basting with marinade until done (1 hour).

Serves 4

Turkey

MICROWAVE OVEN TURKEY ROASTING INSTRUCTIONS

LI'L BUTTERBALL™ Turkey, completely thawed according to package directions
1 egg or egg yolk
1 teaspoon KITCHEN BOUQUET®
2 tablespoons oil
1 tablespoon water

1. To estimate total cooking time multiply purchased weight (adding 1 to 1½ pounds if turkey is stuffed) by 9 minutes per pound.
2. Remove LI'L BUTTERBALL™ Turkey from bag. Free legs and tail from tucked position. Do not cut band of skin.
3. Remove packages containing neck and giblets and cook conventionally or if desired, by microwave.*
4. Rinse and drain turkey. Pat dry with paper towels. If desired, stuff body and neck cavities with a favorite stuffing. Return tail and legs to tucked position. Skewer neck skin to back with round wooden picks. Fold wing tips under back side of wing joint.
5. For browning sauce, beat together egg, KITCHEN BOUQUET® oil and water and brush over turkey.
6. Place turkey, breast side down, in large microwave-safe roasting dish, platter or tray. Use small glass casserole lids or custard cups to stabilize bird as necessary.
7. Multiply the weight of the turkey used in step 1 by 3 minutes per pound. Microwave the turkey, uncovered, for half this time on HIGH or COOK (full or 100% power). Multiply the weight of the turkey by 6 minutes per pound. Microwave for half this time on setting #6, MEDIUM OR ROAST (two thirds power). See example.
8. Apply small pieces of foil as necessary to shield wing tips, drumsticks and portions of breast to prevent overbrowning. Rotate dish containing turkey as often as oven manufacturer suggests. Remove juices when they accumulate and reserve for gravy.

9. Turn turkey breast side up; brush with browning sauce.
10. Use the settings and remaining estimated time as described in step 7, basting once or twice with the browning sauce. If microwave oven is equipped with temperature probe or automatic thermometer, insert probe into center of thigh, next to body not touching bone and set temperature for 190°F.
11. When cooking time has been completed, insert thermometer into thickest portion of thigh, breast and stuffing to check internal temperatures: 175° to 180°F. in breast, 185° to 190°F. in thigh, 160° to 165°F. in stuffing. If temperatures have not been reached, remove thermometer and microwave on the same setting for a few more minutes.
12. When temperatures have been reached, cover with foil and let turkey stand for 20 to 30 minutes to finish cooking interior and let juices "set" to make carving easier.

EXAMPLE for a 7 pound unstuffed turkey:
7×9 minutes per pound = 63 minutes.
First half: HIGH or COOK—Breast side down—$7 \times 3 = 21 \div 2 = 11$ minutes
Setting #6, MEDIUM or ROAST—breast side down—$7 \times 6 = 42 \div 2 = 21$ minutes
Second half: HIGH or COOK—breast side up—$7 \times 3 = 21 \div 2 = 11$ minutes
Setting #6, MEDIUM or ROAST—breast side up—$7 \times 6 = 42 \div 2 = 21$ minutes.

*HOW TO MICROWAVE TURKEY GIBLETS

Turkey gizzard, heart, liver and neck
3 cups water
½ teaspoon salt
⅛ teaspoon white pepper
⅛ teaspoon onion powder
¼ teaspoon celery seed
1 bay leaf

Combine all ingredients except liver in a 2 quart glass casserole. Microwave covered, on setting #6, MEDIUM or ROAST, 35 minutes. Add liver, re-cover, and continue cooking on the same setting for 10 minutes. Remove meat, cool slightly, chop finely or grind. Strain broth. Use giblets and broth, as desired, in gravy, stuffing or soup.

ARMOUR®

ROAST TURKEY WITH APPLE-YAM DRESSING

1 3- to 8-lb. ARMOUR® GOLDEN STAR Boneless Young Turkey, thawed
2 cups chopped apples
⅔ cup chopped onion
¾ cup butter or margarine
2 16-oz. cans yams, drained, mashed
2 tablespoons sugar
2 teaspoons salt
½ teaspoon nutmeg
½ teaspoon cinnamon
4 cups soft bread cubes

Heat oven to 350°. Roast turkey in 15 × 11-inch roasting pan according to label instructions. While turkey is roasting, in fry pan, cook apples and onion in butter or margarine 10 minutes; combine with remaining ingredients. Toss lightly; set aside. One hour before turkey is scheduled to be done, remove turkey from oven. Lift turkey and rack from pan. Scrape drippings from pan to use for gravy. Return turkey to pan without rack; turn turkey over. Brush turkey with some of reserved pan drippings. Spoon dressing into pan around turkey. Return turkey and dressing to oven; continue roasting until done.

GLAZED TURKEY ROAST

Turkey roast*
Apricot jam or preserves
1 cup dried apricots
1 cup water
1 tablespoon brown sugar
1 tablespoon lemon juice
½ cup butter or margarine
1 package (8 oz.) PEPPERIDGE FARM® Herb Seasoned Cube Stuffing
½ cup slivered almonds
¼ teaspoon salt

Roast turkey according to package directions. For glaze, brush top of the roast with apricot jam frequently during the last 30 minutes. Meanwhile place the apricots, water, brown sugar and lemon juice in a small saucepan and simmer for 5 minutes. Drain, reserving the liquid. Add water to liquid to make 1 cup. Place in a large saucepan with butter and heat until butter is melted. Stir in stuffing, almonds and salt. Cut apricots in strips and add to mixture. Place in a 1-quart baking dish and bake alongside of turkey for the last 25 minutes. To serve: make a bed of dressing on a hot platter and place roast on top.

*Turkey roasts vary from 2 to 4½ pounds in size. They can be all white meat or a combination of white and dark. Some come with prepared gravy. For best results use a meat thermometer and roast to 185°F. Let stand 10 minutes before slicing. Allow ⅓ pound meat for each serving.

ROAST TURKEY SOUTHERN STYLE

1 cup shredded carrots
1 cup chopped onion
1 teaspoon rubbed sage
½ teaspoon pepper
½ teaspoon thyme leaves, crushed
¼ cup butter or margarine
6 cups packaged cornbread stuffing mix
1 can (14½ fl. oz.) chicken broth
4 cups cubed zucchini squash, cooked and well drained
12-pound turkey
2 cans (10½ ounces *each*) FRANCO-AMERICAN Turkey or Chicken Gravy

In saucepan, cook carrots and onion with sage, pepper and thyme in butter until tender. Toss lightly with stuffing mix, broth and zucchini. Fill body and neck cavities of turkey loosely with stuffing; truss. Place on rack in roasting pan. Cover loosely with aluminum foil. Roast at 325°F. for about 4 hours (18 to 22 minutes per pound or until internal temperature reaches 185°F. and leg moves easily). Uncover last hour to brown. Baste occasionally. Remove turkey to serving platter. Spoon off fat, reserving 6 tablespoons drippings. On top of range, in roasting pan, stir gravy into reserved drippings. Heat, stirring to loosen browned bits. Serve with turkey and stuffing.

Makes 10 to 12 servings

SLOW COOKED TURKEY BREAST WITH MUSHROOM SAUCE
(Slow Cooker Recipe)

BUTTERBALL® Breast of Turkey, completely thawed
2 tablespoons melted butter or margarine
2 tablespoons finely chopped parsley
¼ teaspoon tarragon leaves, crumbled
Paprika
¼ cup sherry or dry white wine
½ teaspoon salt
⅛ teaspoon white pepper
Mushroom Sauce (recipe follows)

Rinse turkey breast, drain well and pat dry with paper towel. Place, skin side up, in slow cooker. Brush with butter. Sprinkle with parsley, tarragon and paprika. Add wine, salt and pepper. Cover and cook on HIGH setting for 1 hour, then turn to LOW setting for 6 to 7 hours. Internal temperature of breast should reach 170°F. when done. Slice and serve with Mushroom Sauce.

MUSHROOM SAUCE

Drippings
2½ ounce jar sliced mushrooms, undrained
2 tablespoons cornstarch
¼ cup water or sherry wine
¼ teaspoon tarragon leaves
Salt and pepper

Strain drippings from slow cooker into large liquid measure. Spoon off fat. Add mushrooms to drippings and enough water to make 1¾ cupfuls. Dissolve cornstarch in water or wine and stir into drippings. Pour into saucepan, add tarragon and season to taste with salt and pepper. Cook over medium to low heat, stirring constantly, until thickened and clear.

Yield: 2 cups

Wright's

EASY SMOKED TURKEY

1 small to medium size turkey,
    fresh or thawed
2 quarts water
1 bottle WRIGHT'S Natural
    Hickory Liquid Smoke

Mix water and liquid smoke for
marinade. Place bird and marinade
in large plastic bag. Leave for 24
hours. Remove turkey, roast your
favorite way.

HOT TURKEY SALAD

2 cups cubed roast BUTTERBALL®
    Turkey
2 cups chopped celery
½ cup chopped blanched almonds
⅓ cup chopped green pepper
2 tablespoons chopped pimiento
2 tablespoons finely chopped
    onion
1 teaspoon salt
2 tablespoons lemon juice
½ cup mayonnaise
Sliced Swiss cheese
½ stick (¼ cup) butter, melted
1 cup cracker crumbs

Combine turkey, celery, almonds,
green pepper, pimiento, onion, salt,
lemon juice and mayonnaise.
Spoon into buttered 1½ quart
casserole or baking dish. Top with
slices of cheese. Combine butter
and cracker crumbs and sprinkle
on top of casserole. Bake in a
350°F. oven for about 30 minutes.
Yield: 6 servings

VERMONT TURKEY PIE

2 cups diced, roast BUTTERBALL®
    SWIFT'S PREMIUM® Turkey
1 to 1½ cups cooked vegetables
    (peas, carrots or green beans)
1 cup diced cooked potatoes
½ stick (¼ cup) butter or
    margarine
⅓ cup flour
½ teaspoon salt
½ teaspoon ground poultry
    seasoning or sage
3 cups milk
1 package (10 biscuits) refrigerator
    biscuits

Combine turkey and vegetables in
a 9 by 9 inch baking dish. To make
white sauce melt butter in a
saucepan. Blend in flour, salt and
seasoning. Remove from heat and
add milk gradually. Stir and cook
until mixture thickens. Combine
with turkey and vegetables. Place
in 425°F. oven for 10 minutes.
Place biscuits on baking sheet and
put in oven with biscuits. Continue
to bake 10 to 12 minutes. Remove
turkey and biscuits from oven.
Place biscuits on hot turkey and
serve.   *Yield: 5 to 6 servings*

LAND O' LAKES®
TURKEY TACO BAKE

6-oz. pkg. (3 c.) corn chips
15-oz. can chili type beans in
    chili gravy
10-oz. can enchilada sauce
2 c. LAND O LAKES® Butter
    Moist Turkey Roast, cut into
    strips (2½ × ¼ × ¼")
½ c. sliced (⅛") ripe olives
½ c. chopped onion
½ c. catsup
1 Tbsp. Worcestershire sauce
1 c. (4 oz.) shredded LAND O
    LAKES® Process American
    Cheese

Preheat Oven: 375°. In 12 × 8 × 2"
greased baking dish sprinkle 1 c.
corn chips. Reserve remaining corn
chips for topping. In 1-qt. bowl
combine remaining ingredients
except cheese; mix well. Pour
turkey mixture over corn chips in
baking dish. Sprinkle with cheese.
Top with remaining chips. Bake
near center of 375° oven 30 to 40
min. or until bubbling vigorously
around edges and heated in center.
Yield: 8 (¾ c.) servings

TURKEY CANTONESE
(Low Calorie)

½ cup chicken or turkey broth
    (fat skimmed)
1 clove grated garlic
½ cup pineapple juice
1 pound julienned LOUIS RICH
    Turkey Breast Slices
2 medium Spanish onions, halved
    and sliced
2 chopped green bell peppers
2 chopped red bell peppers
4 tablespoons soy sauce
Pinch of anise seed or fennel seed

Combine the broth, garlic and
pineapple juice in a wok or large
frying pan and bring to a boil. Boil
for 10 to 15 minutes to reduce
liquid. Julienne LOUIS RICH Turkey
Breast Slices and place in the wok;
stir fry for 10 minutes. Add the
sliced onions, peppers, soy sauce
and anise seed. Stir and cook for
an additional 4 minutes. (Serve on
a bed of rice, if desired.)
Makes 5 servings

About 160 calories each

San Giorgio

TURKEY FLORENTINE

8 oz. (about 4 cups) SAN GIORGIO
    Egg Noodles*
8 slices bacon, cooked crisp and
    crumbled
1 cup chopped onion
1 10 oz. pkg. frozen chopped
    spinach, cooked and drained
½ cup thinly sliced celery
¼ cup chopped pimiento
2 10¾ oz. cans condensed cream
    of mushroom soup
1 cup sour cream
1½ tsp. salt
4 cups cubed cooked turkey*
1 cup bread crumbs
3 Tbsp. melted margarine or butter
Slivered almonds

Cook noodles as directed on
package. Drain. Cook onion in
bacon drippings. Combine bacon
pieces, onion, noodles, spinach,
celery and pimiento. Combine soup
with sour cream and salt and stir
half into noodle mixture. Pour into
a greased 13 × 9 × 2 inch baking
dish. Arrange turkey pieces on top
and pour remaining soup mixture
over turkey. Top with crumbs,
melted margarine and slivered
almonds. Bake at 350° for about 35
to 40 minutes.
Makes 12 to 14 servings

*You may use any SAN GIORGIO
Pasta instead of noodles, and
substitute chicken for turkey.
Microwave cooking requires about
6 minutes covered with plastic
wrap. Cook 3 minutes, rotate half
a turn and cook 3 minutes more.
Test to see if hot enough.

TURKEY CREOLE

1 cup cubed cooked Butter Basted SWIFT'S PREMIUM® Turkey Roast
1 tablespoon butter or margarine
2 tablespoons chopped celery
2 tablespoons chopped green pepper
1 tablespoon chopped onions
16 ounce can whole tomatoes, chopped
¼ teaspoon garlic salt

Melt butter in an 8 inch skillet. Add celery, green pepper and onion. Sauté 5 minutes, stirring constantly. Add tomatoes and garlic salt. Simmer 10 minutes, stirring frequently. Add turkey and continue to simmer 15 minutes longer. Serve hot over rice.

Yield: 2 servings, one cup each

TURKEY PAPRIKA

2 cups sliced, roasted BUTTERBALL® SWIFT'S PREMIUM® Turkey
½ stick (¼ cup) butter
1 medium onion, sliced
¼ cup flour
1 teaspoon salt
2 cups milk
2 egg yolks, beaten
4 teaspoons paprika
4-ounce can mushroom stems and pieces, drained
1 cup dairy sour cream
1 tablespoon poppy seed
2 tablespoons butter
7-ounce package noodles, cooked

Melt ½ stick butter in skillet. Add onion and cook until tender. Blend in flour and salt. Remove from heat. Gradually add milk. Stirring constantly, cook until mixture thickens. Stir ¼ cup white sauce into egg yolks; return to hot mixture. Bring to boil stirring constantly. Reduce heat to low and stir in paprika. Add mushrooms and turkey slices. Simmer 5 minutes. Stir in sour cream and heat just until sauce is hot. Serve on Poppy Seed Noodles. To make Poppy Seed Noodles: Add poppy seed and butter to drained, cooked noodles. Toss together lightly.

Yield: 6 servings

TURKEY A LA QUEEN

2 cups diced, roast BUTTERBALL® Turkey
½ stick (¼ cup) butter or margarine
¼ cup flour
1 teaspoon salt
2 cups milk
1 egg yolk, beaten
8 ounce can chunk pineapple drained, reserving ¼ cup juice
1 red skinned apple, cored and chopped
6 slices toast
¼ cup slivered almonds
1 tablespoon butter

Melt butter in saucepan. Blend in flour and salt. Remove from heat. Gradually add milk. Stirring constantly, cook until mixture thickens. Pour a little over the egg yolk; return to hot mixture. Bring to boil, stirring constantly. Reduce heat to low and stir in turkey. Simmer 5 minutes. Add pineapple, pineapple juice and apple just before serving. Serve on hot toast or in toast cups. Top with almonds browned lightly in 1 tablespoon butter.

Yield: 5 to 6 servings (5 cups)

TURKEY PARMIGIANA
(Low Calorie)

1 egg or 2 egg whites or ¼ cup defrosted no-cholesterol substitute
2 tablespoons salad oil
1 pound LOUIS RICH Turkey Breast Slices
⅓ cup seasoned dry bread crumbs
½ teaspoon salt
Dash pepper
3 ounces tomato paste
¾ cup fat-skimmed turkey or chicken broth
1 clove minced garlic
1 teaspoon oregano
4 ounces part-skimmed Mozzarella cheese
Shredded parsley

Fork-blend the egg and the oil. Dip the LOUIS RICH Turkey Breast Slices into egg mixture, then coat both sides lightly with the bread crumbs. Arrange the turkey in a single layer on a cookie sheet prepared with non-stick spray. Bake 8 to 10 minutes at 450 degrees until golden and crisp. Do not turn. Transfer to an oven-proof platter. Combine the salt, pepper,

tomato paste, broth, garlic and oregano. Simmer uncovered over moderate heat until thickened, then spoon over the turkey. Top with cheese, then broil until cheese bubbles. Garnish with parsley. *Makes four servings*

About 275 calories each
(10 calories less per serving with egg whites or substitute)

CANTONESE TURKEY STIR-FRY

1 cup diagonally-sliced celery
1 cup sliced onion
2 tablespoons oil
2 cups cubed cooked turkey or chicken
2 cups fresh bean sprouts or 1 can (16-oz.) bean sprouts, drained
1 carrot, coarsely shredded
1¼ cups water
2 tablespoons soy sauce
1 envelope FRENCH'S® Mushroom Gravy Mix
Cooked rice

Using a medium-size skillet, stir-fry celery and onion in hot oil 1 minute, or until tender-crisp. Add remaining ingredients, except rice, and bring to a boil, stirring constantly. Cover and simmer 2 minutes. Serve with rice.

4 to 5 servings

TURKEY CHOW MEIN

8 onion slices, separated into rings
2 cups sliced celery
2 tablespoons vegetable oil
1 16-oz. can bean sprouts, drained
2 cups chopped cooked ARMOUR® GOLDEN STAR Boneless Young Turkey
2 chicken bouillon cubes dissolved in 1½ cups boiling water
2 tablespoons soy sauce
¼ teaspoon salt
Dash of pepper
2 tablespoons cornstarch
¼ cup cold water
Hot cooked rice
Chow mein noodles

In large fry pan, cook onion and celery in oil 10 minutes. Add bean sprouts, turkey and bouillon to fry pan; simmer 5 minutes. Add soy sauce, salt and pepper. Combine cornstarch with water; stir into mixture. Cook, stirring until thickened. Serve over rice. Garnish with noodles. *4 to 6 servings*

JENNIE-O TURKEY CHOW MEIN

2 tablespoons butter or margarine
1 medium green pepper, cut in strips
1 cup sliced celery
2 tablespoons cornstarch
¼ cup cold water
2 tablespoons soy sauce
1¾ cup strong chicken bouillon
½ envelope (¼ cup) dry onion soup mix
2 to 3 cups diced cooked JENNIE-O Turkey
16 oz. can bean sprouts, drained
8 oz. can water chestnuts, drained and sliced
3 oz. can mushrooms, drained
Chow mein noodles

In large skillet, stir fry green pepper and celery in butter until tender-crisp. Combine cornstarch, water, and soy sauce; blend into green pepper mixture. Stir in bouillon; cook and stir until thickened. Stir in remaining ingredients except chow mein noodles; heat thoroughly. Serve over chow mein noodles.

About 6 servings

BREADED TURKEY ROAST SLICES PARMESAN

6 slices cooked Butter Basted SWIFT'S PREMIUM® Turkey Roast, cut ½ inch thick
¼ cup flour
⅛ teaspoon garlic powder
¼ teaspoon pepper
2 eggs
¼ cup milk
¼ cup Parmesan cheese
¼ cup fine bread crumbs
2 tablespoons butter or margarine

Combine flour, garlic powder and pepper. Beat eggs and milk together. Combine Parmesan and bread crumbs. Melt butter in skillet over medium heat. Coat turkey slices with flour mixture, then with egg mixture and then with cheese mixture. Brown on both sides in butter, about 5 minutes. Serve immediately.

Yield: 2 to 3 servings

TURKEY DIVAN
(also Chicken Divan)

1 package (10 ounces) frozen broccoli or asparagus spears, cooked and drained
4 servings sliced cooked turkey or chicken
1 can (10¾ ounces) CAMPBELL'S Condensed Cream of Celery, Chicken, or Mushroom Soup
⅓ cup milk
½ cup shredded Cheddar cheese

Arrange broccoli in shallow baking dish (10 × 6 × 2″). Top with turkey slices. Blend soup and milk; pour over turkey; sprinkle with cheese. Bake at 450°F. until sauce is slightly browned, about 15 minutes.

Makes 4 servings

CHILI CON TURKEY
(Low Calorie)

½ pound ground LOUIS RICH Turkey
2 peeled, chopped onions
1 seeded, chopped green bell pepper
1 minced clove garlic
1 16-ounce can tomatoes
3 cups canned, drained kidney beans
2 teaspoons chili powder (or more, to taste)
1 teaspoon cumin seeds, (optional)
Salt to taste

Brown LOUIS RICH Turkey lightly in a nonstick skillet with no fat added. Stir in all remaining ingredients. Cover and simmer 25 minutes. Uncover and continue cooking until thickened.

Makes six servings

About 210 calories each

HERBED SAUSAGE PATTIES
(Low Sodium)

1 pound ground turkey
1 egg
¾ teaspoon DURKEE Ground Sage
½ teaspoon DURKEE Rosemary Leaves, crushed
½ teaspoon DURKEE Ground Black Pepper
¼ teaspoon DURKEE Marjoram
¼ teaspoon DURKEE Leaf Thyme, crushed

Combine all ingredients and mix thoroughly. Shape into 4 patties. Chill 1 hour. Bake or fry as desired.

Makes 4 patties

Duck

ROAST DUCKLING FRANGELICO®

1 4-5 lb. duckling
Salt as needed
Pepper as needed
¼ tsp. rosemary
¼ tsp. thyme
1 wedge orange (⅛ of orange)
1 wedge apple (⅛ of apple)
1 wedge onion (⅛ of onion)
Sauce FRANGELICO® (recipe follows)

Trim and wash out cavity of duck and drain well. Season cavity with salt, pepper and orange wedges, apple and onion, also rosemary and thyme. Roast on wire rack in pre-heated (375°-400°) oven in a roasting pan, approximately 1 hour-1 hour 15 minutes. When done, remove duck from pan and allow to cool. When duck is still warm, split and quarter. Place on platter and into 375°-400° oven to heat and crisp skin. Ladle Sauce FRANGELICO® on warm serving platter. Place crisp duckling on sauce and serve immediately.

Yield: 2-4 servings (depending on size of portion)

SAUCE FRANGELICO®

½ cup sugar, granulated
½ cup cider vinegar
½ cup Soave white wine
1 lemon (juice of 1 lemon)
1 lime (juice of 1 lime)
4 Tbsp. currant jelly
4 Tbsp. lingonberries
1 oz. orange juice concentrate
16 oz./1 pt. brown sauce or demi-glace
2 oz. hazelnuts, chopped
1½ oz. butter, sweet (solid)
4 oz. FRANGELICO® Liqueur

Combine sugar, vinegar, Soave, lemon and lime juice. Reduce and evaporate moisture completely and allow sugar to carmelize to light brown color (amber). Add currant jelly, lingonberries and orange juice. Bring to a boil. Add brown sauce or demi-glace. Bring to a boil and simmer for 10 minutes. Add chopped hazelnuts and swirl in butter. Whip in the FRANGELICO.® This sauce may be served with roast pork, roast chicken or venison.

NAPA ROSÉ DUCKLING

1 duckling (about 5 lbs.), quartered
Salt, pepper, ground ginger
1 Tbsp. grated onion
1 cup THE CHRISTIAN
 BROTHERS® Napa Rosé Wine
½ cup brown sugar
1 Tbsp. cornstarch
1 tsp. grated orange peel

Place quarters in baking pan. Roast at 400 degrees, 30 minutes; drain off fat. Sprinkle quarters with salt, pepper, ginger and onion. Pour ¼ cup wine into pan; cover tightly. Bake 45 minutes or until tender. Combine brown sugar, cornstarch, orange peel and remaining wine in saucepan. Cook, stirring, until thickened. Pour over duckling and roast, uncovered, 10 minutes, basting frequently.

Serves 4

ROAST DUCKLING MANDARINE

4½-5 lb. duckling
Salt, pepper, garlic powder
Juice of 1 large orange
8 tablespoons MANDARINE
 NAPOLEON
1 small onion, halved
1 cup chicken or duck broth

Remove excess duck fat. Prick skin with a fork. Sprinkle inside and out with seasonings. Combine orange juice with 3 tablespoons MANDARINE NAPOLEON. Tuck orange rinds and onion in duck cavity. Set duck on rack in roasting pan; place in preheated 425°F. oven. Roast 30 minutes, then drain fat from pan. Reduce heat to 375°F., roast 1½ to 2 hours longer. Start basting with Mandarine-orange juice mixture 20 minutes after reducing heat, and then every 15 minutes, until done. Remove duck from oven and discard orange rinds and onion. Place duck on heated platter and keep warm. Skim fat from pan drippings. Add broth, 2 tablespoons MANDARINE NAPOLEON and any remaining

basting mixture to pan. Bring to boil, stirring to loosen crusty brown bits, and simmer 5 minutes. Taste for seasoning and thicken if desired. Strain into heated sauceboat. Warm remaining 3 tablespoons MANDARINE NAPOLEON, ignite and pour flaming over duck. Allow flames to burn out. Then carve and serve with sauce.

4 servings

GOURMET DUCK

2 large (4½ pounds each) ducks,
 skin and fat removed, cut into
 serving pieces
1 quart water
1 small, whole onion
1 cup flour
1 teaspoon salt
Dash curry
Dash basil
Dash marjoram
½ cup cooking oil
½ cup minced onion
1 small can frozen orange juice
 concentrate, undiluted
⅓ cup OLD VIRGINIA® Currant
 Jelly
1 teaspoon salt
1 teaspoon KITCHEN BOUQUET®

Preparation and cooking time—2½ hours. Simmer the duck giblets and necks in 1 quart of water with the onion for 1 hour. Strain and add enough water to bring back to a quart. Reserve liquid. Coat the pieces of duck with a mixture of the flour, salt, curry, basil, and marjoram, and brown them in the oil. Remove the duck pieces and sauté the minced onion in the same pan. Stir in the flour left over from coating the duck. Add the duck broth and stir over medium heat until the gravy is thick and smooth. Add the frozen orange juice (defrosted but undiluted), the currant jelly, salt, and KITCHEN BOUQUET® Pour the sauce over the browned duck pieces in a 5-quart casserole and bake at 325 for 1½ hours, uncovered.

Serves 8

GLAZED DUCK

1 jar orange marmalade
1 cup NOILLY PRAT Dry Vermouth

Combine marmalade and NOILLY PRAT until well blended. Spoon over duck and baste continuously while baking. Add more NOILLY PRAT as needed. Follow cooking directions for the weight of duck you are using. When roast duck is finished, drain fat, add more NOILLY PRAT, and spoon drippings over duck before serving. Garnish with fresh orange slices and black olives. This glaze is also especially good with ham, cornish hens and pork roasts.

CURRANT GLAZED DUCKLING WITH GOURMET STUFFING

2 (12 ounce) packages long grain
 white and wild rice frozen in
 pouch
2 (2½ ounces) jars or 1 (4½ ounce)
 jar whole mushrooms, drained
1½ cups chopped celery
⅓ cup chopped green pepper
¼ cup minced onion
½ cup herb seasoned stuffing mix
1 teaspoon (1 cube) instant
 chicken bouillon
½ cup boiling water
2 tablespoons butter, melted

Cook rice according to package directions only until thawed. Combine rice with mushrooms, celery, green pepper, onion and stuffing mix. Dissolve bouillon in boiling water. Stir bouillon and butter into rice mixture to moisten.

Makes about 6 to 7 cups stuffing or enough to stuff two ducklings.

CURRANT GLAZE

1 jar (10 ounce) currant jelly
¼ cup red wine vinegar
4 whole cloves
1 (3 inch) stick cinnamon

Combine and mix jelly, vinegar and spices in saucepan. Place over moderate heat; bring to a boil and simmer gently 3 minutes. Brush duckling with glaze several times during last 30 minutes of roasting.

Makes 4 servings

Favorite recipe from the National Duckling Council

Meat

Beef

BEEF EN BROCHETTE

1 can (13¼ ounces) pineapple chunks
½ cup HEINZ 57 Sauce
2 tablespoons dry white wine
1 tablespoon salad oil
½ teaspoon salt
Dash pepper
2 pounds beef sirloin tip or top round, cut into 1-inch cubes
Salt and pepper

Drain pineapple, reserving ½ cup liquid. Cover and refrigerate pineapple chunks. Combine the ½ cup pineapple liquid with 57 Sauce and next 4 ingredients; pour over meat. Marinate 2 to 3 hours in refrigerator, turning occasionally. Thread meat and pineapple chunks alternately on six (12-inch) skewers, allowing 4-5 pieces of meat and 5-6 pieces of pineapple for each skewer. Brush with marinade; season lightly with salt and pepper. Grill or broil 3 inches from heat source 5 minutes on each side for medium rare.

Makes 6 servings

TERIYAKI SHISH KABOBS

1 (3-pound) round steak (about 1½-inches thick), cut into cubes
1 (15¼-ounce) can pineapple chunks, drained
8 ounces (about 2 cups) small whole fresh mushrooms, cleaned
3 medium onions, quartered and separated into bite-size pieces
2 medium green peppers, cut into bite-size pieces
1 pint cherry tomatoes
Teriyaki Marinade*
Hot cooked rice

Prepare vegetables and meat; place all but tomatoes in large shallow baking dish. Pour Teriyaki Marinade on top. Marinate overnight; stir occasionally. Skewer marinated ingredients with tomatoes. Grill or broil to desired doneness; brush with marinade during cooking. Serve over rice. Refrigerate leftovers.

Makes 8 servings

*TERIYAKI MARINADE

1 cup firmly-packed COLONIAL® Light Golden Brown Sugar
⅔ cup catsup
⅔ cup vinegar
½ cup soy sauce
½ cup vegetable oil
5 to 6 cloves garlic, finely chopped
2 teaspoons ground ginger

In medium bowl, combine ingredients; mix well.

TIP: Teriyaki Marinade is also delicious when used to marinate pork chops or chicken.

TERIYAKI BEEF KABOBS

1 can (1 lb. 4 oz.) DOLE® Chunk Pineapple in Juice
1½ pounds sirloin steak
½ cup soy sauce
½ cup pale dry sherry
1 tablespoon honey
½ teaspoon ground ginger
¼ teaspoon garlic powder
1 teaspoon cornstarch
Wooden skewers
16 small DOLE® Fresh Mushrooms
16 cherry tomatoes
4 green onions, cut into 4 (2-inch long) pieces

Drain pineapple reserving 1 tablespoon juice.* Cut steak into 16 cubes. Arrange in shallow glass dish. Combine reserved juice, soy sauce, sherry, honey, ginger and garlic powder. Pour over beef.

Cover and marinate 5 hours, turning 2 to 3 times. Drain marinade in a small saucepan. Stir in cornstarch. Cook until sauce boils and thickens. Skewer 4 cubes of beef onto each of 4 skewers. Brush with sauce. Broil 4 inches from heat 5 minutes. Keep warm. Skewer each of 16 skewers as follows: a pineapple chunk, a mushroom, a pineapple chunk, a cherry tomato, pineapple chunk, green onion. Brush with sauce; broil 2 to 3 minutes. Place a meat skewer and 2 pineapple skewers onto each of 4 serving plates to serve. Brush with more sauce, if desired.

Makes 4 servings

*Reserve remaining juice for beverage.

PET.

QUICKIE BEEF STROGANOFF

1 package (8 oz.) fresh mushrooms, sliced
2 tablespoons butter
2 pounds chuck steak, cut into ¼-inch thick strips
1 teaspoon paprika
1 envelope (1¼ oz.) dry onion soup mix
2 cups water
1 can (8 oz.) PET® Imitation Sour Cream
1 tablespoon flour

Cook mushrooms in butter in 10-inch skillet until limp. Remove from skillet. Sprinkle beef strips with paprika. Brown well in skillet. Stir in mushrooms, soup mix, and water. Heat to boiling. Lower heat. Cover. Simmer 30 minutes or until meat is tender. Just before serving, combine imitation sour cream and flour. Stir into meat mixture. Heat until steaming. Serve immediately over hot buttered noodles.

Makes 8 servings, ⅔ cup each

BRONTE

BEEF STROGANOFF

2 Pounds boneless Chuck, cut
½″ thick
½ Teaspoon each Salt & Pepper
1 Stick Butter (¼ pound)
4 Sliced Green Onions, white part
only
4 Tablespoons Flour
1 Can Condensed Beef Broth
1 Teaspoon prepared Mustard
1 6 ounce can sliced Mushrooms
⅓ Cup Dairy Sour Cream
⅓ Cup BRONTE Rhine Wine
Steamed Rice

Remove fat and gristle from meat
and cut meat across the grain in
strips 2″ long. Sprinkle with salt
and pepper. Heat skillet, add
butter, sauté meat quickly, brown
evenly. Push meat to one side. Add
onions, cook slowly a few minutes;
push aside. Stir flour into drippings
and add beef broth, bring to a boil,
stirring all the while. Turn heat
down, stir in mustard. Cover pan,
simmer 1 hour or until meat is
tender. Five minutes before
serving, (THIS POINT IS
IMPORTANT), add mushrooms,
dairy sour cream and BRONTE
Rhine Wine. Heat briefly, salt to
taste and serve with rice.

RAGOUT OF BEEF DUBONNET

2 lbs. cubed round steak
1 teaspoon salt
½ teaspoon pepper
2 medium onions, sliced
¼ teaspoon powdered cloves
½ cup chopped parsley
¼ cup flour
1½ oz. butter
2 bay leaves
½ cup sour cream
½ cup DUBONNET Red

Place round steak, flour, salt and
pepper in a paper bag. Shake until
meat is well dredged. Melt butter
in heavy skillet, add beef and
brown on all sides. Add onions,
bay leaves, cloves, parsley and
DUBONNET Red. Cover and
simmer for ½ hour or until meat is
tender. If liquid cooks down add
more DUBONNET Red. Just before
serving correct seasoning and stir
in sour cream. Serve over rice or
Kasha (buckwheat groats).

Makes 4 servings

BEEF RAGOUT

2 pounds beef cubes (1½ inch)
2 tablespoons shortening
2 cans (10¾ ounces *each*)
CAMPBELL'S Condensed Cream
of Mushroom Soup
½ cup water
1 tablespoon Worcestershire
6 medium carrots (about ¾ pound),
cut in 2-inch pieces
8 small whole white onions (about
½ pound)
1 package (10 ounces) frozen whole
green beans
Cooked noodles

In large heavy pan, brown beef in
shortening; pour off fat. Add soup,
water, and Worcestershire. Cover;
cook over low heat 1 hour 30
minutes. Add carrots and onions.
Cook 45 minutes. Add beans. Cook
15 minutes more or until done. Stir
occasionally. Thicken sauce if
desired. Serve over noodles.

Makes about 7 cups

CHINESE-STYLE BEEF

1½ pounds lean chuck steak
3 tablespoons oil
1 large onion, sliced
1½ cups thin diagonally-sliced
carrots
1½ cups water
2 cups fresh bean sprouts or
1 can (16-oz.) bean sprouts,
drained
½ cup thawed frozen peas
1 envelope FRENCH'S® Au Jus
Gravy Mix
1 tablespoon soy sauce
¼ teaspoon instant minced garlic
Cooked rice

Cut meat into very thin slices. In
skillet or wok, brown meat quickly
in 2 tablespoons oil; remove from
pan. Add remaining tablespoon oil;
stir-fry onion and carrots 3 minutes
over medium-high heat. Add water,
bean sprouts, peas, gravy mix, soy
sauce, and garlic. Simmer, covered,
4 minutes or just until carrots and
bean sprouts are tender-crisp. Add
meat and heat through. Serve over
rice.

4 to 5 servings

Hint: To cut super-thin slices of
meat for Chinese-style beef,
first firm up the meat in the
freezer. The thinner the
slices, the more servings you
will make.

TERIYAKI ROUNDSTEAK WITH RICE

1 bag SUCCESS® Rice
1 lb. round steak, trimmed and
thinly sliced
2 tablespoons vegetable oil
1 onion, thinly sliced
1 garlic clove, minced
¼ cup water
2 tablespoons soy sauce
2 tablespoons sherry or water
1 tablespoon brown sugar
1 tablespoon lemon juice
½ teaspoon ground ginger
½ teaspoon corn starch

Cook bag of rice according to
package directions. Drain and keep
warm. While rice is cooking, sauté
steak strips in 10″ skillet in oil, a
few pieces at a time, until all are
browned. Return all strips to
skillet, along with the remaining
ingredients, except corn starch.
Mix well. Cover and simmer over
moderately low heat for 20
minutes. Dissolve corn starch in
small amount of water and stir into
the meat mixture. Serve the
teriyaki over the hot rice.

Makes 4 servings
(about 1 cup each)

BEEF AND PEPPER RICE SKILLET

1½ pounds round steak, cut into
thin strips
1 tablespoon cooking oil
1 cup sliced onion
1 cup UNCLE BEN'S®
CONVERTED® Brand Rice
1 can (10½ ounces) beef broth
Water
2 tablespoons soy sauce, or to
taste
2 green peppers, coarsely chopped
1 jar (2 ounces) sliced pimiento,
drained

Brown beef in oil in 10-inch skillet.
Add onion, rice, beef broth, one
soup can of water and soy sauce
to beef; stir. Bring to boil. Reduce
heat, cover and cook over low heat
until liquid is absorbed, about 25
minutes. Stir in green pepper and
pimiento. Serve hot.

Makes 4 to 6 servings

PEPPER STEAK

1 pound round steak (cut in thin strips)
1 cup sliced green pepper
1 cup sliced onion
½ cup coarsely chopped celery
1 cup sliced mushrooms
2 Tbsp. butter or margarine
1 tsp. salt
2 Tbsp. soy sauce
1 Tbsp. corn starch
1 cup water
1-1½ tsp. BALTIMORE SPICE OLD BAY Seasoning

In skillet, brown round steak slightly in butter or margarine. Add vegetables, salt and BALTIMORE SPICE OLD BAY Seasoning. Stir fry about 5 minutes. Mix corn starch with water and soy sauce. Pour over vegetables. Stir until sauce is thick and slightly transparent. Serve over rice.   *6 servings*

GINGER BEEF STIR-FRY

1 pound top sirloin
1 can (8 oz.) water chestnuts, drained
2 tablespoons vegetable oil
3 medium carrots, cut in 2-inch sticks
1 medium onion, sliced
1 clove garlic, pressed
1 tablespoon chopped fresh ginger root
1 large green bell pepper, chunked
1 quart BUD OF CALIFORNIA® Salad Lettuce
¼ cup orange marmalade
2 tablespoons soy sauce

Thinly slice sirloin against grain in 1-inch wide strips. Cut each water chestnut in half. In a large skillet or wok, quickly brown sirloin in hot oil. Stir in chestnuts, carrots, onion, garlic and ginger until onion is soft. Stir in pepper and lettuce for one minute. Stir in marmalade and soy sauce. Cook, stirring about 2 minutes. Serve at once.
Makes 4 servings

CAMPBELL'S BEEF BOURGUIGNONNE

2 slices bacon
1½ pounds beef cubes (about 1½ inches)
1 can (10¾ ounces) CAMPBELL'S Condensed Golden Mushroom Soup
⅓ cup Burgundy or other dry red wine
1 large clove garlic, minced
1 medium bay leaf
2 tablespoons chopped parsley
¼ teaspoon thyme leaves, crushed
1 pound small whole white onions (about 16)
Cooked noodles

In skillet, cook bacon until crisp; remove and crumble. Brown beef in drippings. Add soup, wine, garlic, bay, parsley, thyme, and bacon. Cover; cook over low heat 1 hour. Add onions; cook 1 hour more or until done. Stir occasionally. Remove bay leaf. Serve over noodles.

Makes about 4½ cups

BEEF BOURGUIGNON FLAMBÉ

2 slices bacon, cut into ½-inch pieces
2 tablespoons flour
1 teaspoon LAWRY'S® Seasoned Salt
2 pounds sirloin tip steak, cut in bite-size strips
Burgundy
Water
1 package LAWRY'S® Beef Stew Seasoning Mix
12 small boiling onions
¼ pound fresh mushrooms, sliced
16 cherry tomatoes, stems removed
¼ cup flaming brandy (100 proof), optional

CONVENTIONAL METHOD: Fry bacon in a Dutch oven. Combine flour and Seasoned Salt. Coat meat strips with seasoned flour. Add meat to bacon. Brown thoroughly. Add 1 cup Burgundy, 1 cup water and Beef Stew Seasoning Mix. Cover and simmer gently for 45 minutes. Peel onions and pierce each end with a fork so they will retain their shape when cooked. Add onions to beef mixture and simmer 40 minutes longer or until meat and onions are tender. Then add mushrooms and

cherry tomatoes and simmer another 5 minutes. Heat brandy quickly and gently over hot water. Pour beef mixture into shallow serving dish. Pour brandy over the top. Set aflame at the table. Stir gently and serve immediately.

MICROWAVE OVEN METHOD: In 3-quart glass casserole, place bacon with one paper towel over top. Microwave on HIGH for 2 to 2½ minutes, stirring after 1 minute. Combine flour and Seasoned Salt. Coat meat strips with seasoned flour. Add meat to bacon. Mix in ¾ cup Burgundy, ½ cup water and Beef Stew Seasoning Mix. Cover with lid or plastic wrap, venting one corner. Microwave on HIGH for 12 minutes; stir. Microwave at 50% power for 30 minutes. Peel onions and pierce each end with a fork so they will retain their shape when cooked. Add onions to beef mixture; cover. Microwave at 50% power for 20 minutes or until meat and onions are tender. Add mushrooms and cherry tomatoes; microwave on HIGH for 2 minutes. Heat brandy on conventional range and serve as directed above.
Makes 6 servings

TERIYAKI

1½ pounds boneless sirloin steak (1-inch thick)
1 can (10½ ounces) CAMPBELL'S Condensed Beef Broth
¼ cup soy sauce
¼ cup diagonally sliced green onions
1 large clove garlic, minced
1 tablespoon brown sugar
¼ teaspoon ground ginger
Cooked rice

Freeze meat 1 hour to firm (makes slicing easier); slice into *very* thin strips. Combine remaining ingredients except rice; pour over steak. Marinate 2 hours. Thread meat on 4 skewers. Broil about 4 inches from heat until desired doneness (5 to 10 minutes), brushing with marinade and turning once. Heat remaining marinade; thicken if desired. Serve with meat and rice.   *4 servings*

BOEUF BOURGUIGNONNE

2½ pounds beef chuck, in cubes
½ cup flour
2 teaspoons HERB-OX Instant Beef
  Style Bouillon
3 slices bacon, in squares
2 cloves garlic
1 bay leaf
½ teaspoon thyme
2 cups dry red wine

Toss beef with flour seasoned with instant bouillon. Brown with bacon and garlic. Add herbs, red wine and water to cover. Simmer, covered, about 2 hours, until meat is tender. Adjust seasoning of gravy with more HERB-OX. (If desired, add cooked carrots and onions, and mushrooms, browned in butter, to the stew.)

Makes 6 or more servings

QUICK SUKIYAKI

1 pound round steak (¾-inch thick)
1½ cups sliced fresh mushrooms
  (about ¼ pound)
1 cup diagonally sliced carrots
1 cup diagonally sliced celery
½ cup green onions cut in 2-inch
  pieces
2 tablespoons salad oil
1 can (10¼ ounces) FRANCO-
  AMERICAN Beef Gravy
½ pound fresh spinach torn in
  bite-size pieces (about 6 cups)
2 tablespoons soy sauce
½ cup sliced radishes
Cooked rice

Freeze meat 1 hour to firm (makes slicing easier); slice into very thin strips. In skillet, brown mushrooms and cook carrots, celery and onions in oil until *just* tender; push to one side. Add meat; cook until color changes. Add gravy, spinach and soy. Heat; stir occasionally. Stir in radishes. Serve with rice.

Makes about 6 cups, 6 servings

GRILLED DILL STEAK

¾ cup POMPEIAN Olive Oil
¾ cup dill pickle liquid
⅓ cup sliced dill pickles
1 clove garlic, minced
3 lbs. beef top round (about 1½ to
  2 in. thick)
Salt and pepper

Combine olive oil, pickle liquid, sliced pickles and garlic in large shallow dish. Add meat and turn until coated. Cover and marinate overnight, turning meat once. Remove meat to grill or broiler rack reserving marinade. Cook 6 inches from source of heat for about 14 to 17 minutes per side for medium doneness. Brush meat with additional marinade during grilling and sprinkle each side with salt and pepper after grilling. (If cooked in broiler, catch pan juices and pour over meat before serving.) Cut meat diagonally across grain into thin slices.
Makes 8 servings

STEAK DIANE

2 boneless sirloin steaks, ¾-inch
  thick
¼ cup butter or margarine
2 teaspoons dry mustard
½ teaspoon onion salt
2 tablespoons olive oil
1 teaspoon freshly cracked pepper
3 tablespoons butter or margarine
1 teaspoon Worcestershire sauce
¼ cup COLONIAL CLUB
  Blackberry Liqueur
2 tablespoons chopped parsley

Cut each steak in half to make 4 pieces. Place steaks between 2 sheets of wax paper; pound with flat of knife or wooden mallet until ½ inch thick. Melt ¼ cup butter or margarine on large griddle (or use two skillets); stir in mustard and salt. Drizzle 1 tablespoon olive oil over steaks. Sprinkle with half the pepper; rub pepper and oil into steaks with bowl of spoon. Cook steaks with oil-pepper side down for 2 minutes; spoon pan juices over steaks occasionally. Rub remaining oil and pepper on unseasoned side of steaks; turn over; cook 2 minutes longer. Steaks will be pink inside. Remove from pan; keep warm. Remove pan from heat; add 3 tablespoons butter or margarine and Worcestershire sauce. Add ¼ cup COLONIAL CLUB Blackberry Liqueur into skillet; blend all juices; add parsley; pour over steak; serve at once.

Makes 4 servings

CORDON BLEU

4 lean sirloin steaks, ⅓ lb. (150 g)
  each
1 teaspoon Dijon mustard
4 thin slices Danish ham
4 thin slices Svenbo or Danbo
  cheese
⅓ cup (50 g) flour
1 teaspoon salt
½ teaspoon pepper
1 egg, lightly beaten
⅔ cup (90 g) bread crumbs
⅓ cup (90 g) butter
Lemon and parsley for garnish

Pound steaks until approx. 4″ × 7″ (10 × 18 cm). Spread with mustard. Top each with slice of ham and of cheese. (Both slices smaller than steaks.) Fold steaks over, secure with skewers. Mix flour with spices. Dip each steak in flour on both sides, then in egg, finally in bread crumbs. Fry in butter for 4 minutes on each side until golden brown. Garnish. Serve with vegetables. *Makes 4 servings*

Favorite recipe from Denmark Cheese Association

OUR SECRET SIRLOIN STEAK

¼ cup plus 1 teaspoon LEA &
  PERRINS Worcestershire Sauce,
  divided
2 tablespoons lemon or lime juice
2 tablespoons olive oil
¼ cup instant minced onion
¾ teaspoon salt
½ teaspoon instant minced garlic
3 pound sirloin steak
2 tablespoons butter or margarine
1 tablespoon chopped parsley

Combine ¼ cup of the LEA & PERRINS, lemon juice, oil, minced onion, salt and minced garlic; mix well and set aside. Place steak in tight-fitting bowl or plastic bag. Pour LEA & PERRINS mixture over steak. Marinate 2 hours. Remove steak from marinade. Place on rack. Grill over hot charcoal or broil under preheated hot broiler for 7 to 10 minutes on each side or until done as desired, brushing occasionally with leftover marinade. Remove steak to serving plate. In a small saucepan melt butter. Stir in parsley and remaining 1 teaspoon LEA & PERRINS. Pour over steak. Slice and serve.

Yield: 4 to 6 portions

BUSHMILLS FLAMED STEAK

1½ lb. boneless steak (sirloin strip) ¾" thick
4 Tbsp. butter
2 c. sliced fresh mushrooms
½ c. thinly sliced onions
¼ c. OLD BUSHMILLS Irish Whiskey
¾ c. cream
2 tsp. flour
¼ tsp. tarragon
⅛ tsp. sugar
Salt and pepper
Parsley to garnish

Heat skillet very hot. Melt butter 'til golden and add steak. Sear on both sides and cook to your taste. Remove steak to heated platter. Quickly sauté onions and mushrooms in pan drippings. Put steak back into skillet and drizzle with ¼ cup OLD BUSHMILLS Irish Whiskey and flame. Remove steak only back to platter. Reduce heat to medium and sprinkle sugar, flour and tarragon on mushrooms and onions. Cook, stirring, 1 minute. Stir in cream and cook 'til reduced by half. Season to taste. Pour over steak and garnish with parsley.

Lea & Perrins
THE ORIGINAL WORCESTERSHIRE

ROUND STEAK SIZZLER

¾ cup catsup
½ cup LEA & PERRINS Worcestershire Sauce
⅓ cup oil
1 teaspoon salt
3-pound boneless beef round steak

In a small bowl combine catsup, LEA & PERRINS, oil, and salt. Place steak in a snug-fitting bowl or doubled plastic bag. Pour catsup mixture over steak. Cover or fasten and refrigerate for 24 hours. Remove steak from marinade. Place on a rack over hot charcoal. Grill until done as desired, about 12 minutes on each side for medium, brushing with marinade occasionally. Or, if desired, place on a rack in a broiler pan. Place under a preheated hot broiler; follow preceding directions for cooking. *8 servings*

CATTLEMAN'S CHUCK STEAK

½ cup KIKKOMAN Teriyaki Sauce
¼ cup water or white wine
½ teaspoon black pepper
½ teaspoon onion powder
2½-pound beef chuck steak, about 1 inch thick
Instant meat tenderizer

Mix together first 4 ingredients. Place steak and sauce in large plastic bag; press air out and close top securely. Refrigerate 4 to 5 hours; turn over occasionally. Remove steak; reserve marinade. Sprinkle with meat tenderizer; pierce surfaces with fork to allow tenderizer to penetrate. Let stand 15 minutes. Grill 5 to 6 inches from coals 6 minutes on each side or to desired doneness; turn and brush with marinade.

Makes 4 to 5 servings

STUFFED SOUTH AMERICAN FLANK STEAK

3 pounds flank steak
2¼ teaspoons salt
½ teaspoon black pepper
6 tablespoons instant minced onion
½ cup bottled oil and vinegar dressing
½ cup mixed vegetable flakes
½ cup water
½ cup BELL'S® Ready-mixed Stuffing
½ cup cooked chopped spinach
½ cup cooked corn
1 hard cooked egg, chopped
3 crisp bacon slices, crumbled
2 tablespoons shortening
2 cups beef bouillon

Score one side of steak in diamond pattern. Sprinkle both sides with 1½ teaspoons salt, ¼ teaspoon pepper. Place in bowl. Combine 4 tablespoons onion with oil and vinegar dressing; pour over meat. Cover. Refrigerate 6 hours. Mix 2 tablespoons onion, vegetable flakes, ½ cup water. Let stand 8 min. Add stuffing, spinach, corn, egg, bacon, ¾ teaspoon salt, ¼ teaspoon pepper. Remove meat from marinade; reserve marinade. Spoon filling onto scored side of steak spreading almost to edge. Roll; tie with string. Heat shortening in large skillet. Brown steak on all sides, 15 to 20 min.

Pour reserved marinade and bouillon over steak. Cover; simmer about 1 hour or until fork tender. Serve with strained skimmed gravy.
6 servings

MARINATED FLANK STEAK
(Low Cholesterol)

1 (2 lb) beef flank steak
¼ cup sesame seeds
¼ cup MAZOLA® Corn Oil
¼ cup soy sauce
¼ cup KARO® Dark Corn Syrup
1 small onion, sliced
1 clove garlic, crushed
¼ teaspoon pepper
¼ teaspoon ground ginger

Remove excess fat and membrane from steak; score both sides. In shallow dish stir together remaining ingredients. Add steak; cover and marinate in refrigerator, turning once, several hours or overnight. Broil 6 inches from heat, turning once, 8 minutes or until cooked to desired doneness.
Makes 6 servings

105 mg cholesterol per serving

Gebhardt®

TAMALE FLANK STEAKS

2 beef flank steaks (about a pound each)
1 can (15 oz.) GEBHARDT Tamales
¼ cup cooking oil
1 can (8 oz.) tomato sauce
1 can (10 oz.) GEBHARDT Chili Hot Dog Sauce
¾ teaspoon salt
⅛ teaspoon garlic salt
⅛ teaspoon pepper
¼ cup strong beef broth
1 tablespoon GEBHARDT Chili-Quik
1 teaspoon GEBHARDT Hot Sauce

Pound meat on both sides until meat is about ¼ inch thick; sprinkle with salt, garlic salt and pepper. Unwrap tamales; place in bowl. Break up with fork. Spread tamales over seasoned steaks. Roll up each steak, starting with the narrow end as for jelly roll. Tie and brown on all sides in oil. Place in shallow baking pan. Combine remaining ingredients and pour over meat. Bake at 350° for 1½ hours, or until tender, basting occasionally with sauce. Top each slice with sauce.

Ginger Pork Balls in Sherry-Orange
Sauce (**The Christian Brothers®**)

Jimmy Dean® Nachos

Stuffed Pickles (**Claussen/Oscar Mayer**)

Olive Loaf Cornucopia (**Eckrich®**)

Bertolli® Stuffed Artichokes

Lipton® California Dip

Teriyaki Tidbits (Cookin' Good)

Bertolli® Marinated Shrimp

Golden Cauliflower Soup **(Wyler's®)**

Butter Bean Soup, Quick Chilee Weenee Tacos **(Stokely's Finest®/Van Camp's®)**

Plantation Ham and Pea Main Dish Soup **(Campbell's)**

Cold Yogurt Soup **(Dannon®)**

Creole Seafood Gumbo **(Tabasco®)**

Wyler's® French Onion Soup

Cream of Potato Soup **(Ore-Ida®)**

Italian Chicken **(Bertolli®)**

Microwave Oven Turkey and Stuffing for **Li'l Butterball™**

Currant Glazed Duckling with Gourmet Stuffing **(National Duckling Council)**

Apricot Cornish with Pecan Stuffing **(Tyson)**

Baked Yogurt Chicken **(Dannon®)**

Turkey Cantonese **(Louis Rich)**

Sesame Baked Chicken **(Lea & Perrins)**

Roast Turkey Southern Style **(Franco-American)**

Amaretto Orange Chicken **(Hereford's)**

Delicious Chicken Coconut **(Calavo®)**

Roast Capon with Orange Pecan Stuffing
(National Capon Council)

Chicken Fricasse **(Poly Perx®)**

Orange Roasted Chicken **(Argo®/Kingsford's®)**

Arroz con Pollo **(Shake 'N Bake®/Minute® Rice/Birds Eye®)**

Zesty Saltine Meatloaf **(Keebler)**

Round Steak Sizzler **(Lea & Perrins)**

Gift Wrapped Ham Dinner **(Oscar Mayer)**

Kikko Lamb Kabobs **(Kikkoman)**

Veal Paprika **(Delft Blue®-Provimi®)**

Country Comfort Ribs **(Southern Comfort®)**

Cherry Glazed Pork Roast
(Thank You® Brand)

Pot Roast Caribe **(Blue Ribbon®)**

Danish Surprise Hamburgers
(Denmark Cheese Association)

Ham Slices in Champagne Sauce
(John Morrell®)

Scotch Glazed Ham Steak
(Johnnie Walker Red)

Beef Wellington (**Pepperidge Farm®**)

Baked Ham Gourmet (**Southern Comfort®**)

Spicy Barbecued Spareribs
(**Hunt-Wesson**)

Cattleman's Chuck Steak (**Kikkoman**)

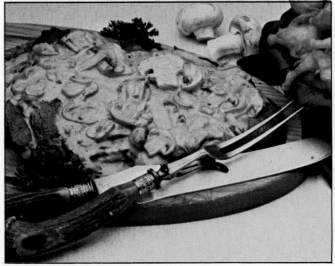

Bushmills Flamed Steak (**Old Bushmills**)

Pork Chops in Plum Sauce (**Taylor Wine**)

Meat Loaf Under Wraps **(Hunt·Wesson)**

Saucy Meatloaf **(Wyler's®)**

California Golden Sherry Pork Roast
(The Christian Brothers®)

Sun Country Smoked Pork **(Argo®/Kingsford's®)**

Snow Crab Mornay with Broccoli
(Alaska Crab Institute)

Pan-Fried Shrimp Medallions with
Chinese Cabbage **(La Choy®)**

Deviled Seafood **(Pepperidge Farm®)**

Finnegan's Flounder **(Irish Mist®)**

Broiled Salmon Auld Angus
(Johnnie Walker Red)

Perch Turbans a la Newburg **(National Marine Fisheries Service)**

Hawaiian Kabobs Teriyaki **(National Marine Fisheries Service)**

The Laird's Shrimp **(Johnnie Walker Red)**

Broiled Hawaiian Fish Fillets **(Kikkoman)**

Shrimp **Pernod**

FLANK STEAK CREOLE

1½ to 2½ pound flank steak
⅓ cup butter or margarine
2 tablespoons chopped onion
2 tablespoons chopped green
  pepper
1 tablespoon tomato paste
½ teaspoon horseradish
¼ teaspoon salt
¼ teaspoon sugar
½ cup water
2 cups PEPPERIDGE FARM®
  Herb Seasoned Stuffing
1 can (10½ oz.) condensed beef
  broth
1 tablespoon tomato paste
1½ tablespoons cornstarch

Preheat oven to 500°F. Score one
side of steak in a diamond pattern
and rub with salt and pepper. Melt
butter in a saucepan and sauté
onion and green pepper until
tender. Stir in 1 tablespoon tomato
paste, horseradish, salt, sugar,
water and stuffing. Place mixture
down center on unscored side of
steak, but not quite to the ends.
Fold ends over stuffing, then bring
together and overlap long sides.
Skewer together. Place in a
shallow baking pan and roast for
15 minutes. Reduce heat to 350°F.
and continue baking 40 to 50
minutes. Meanwhile, combine beef
broth, remaining tomato paste and
cornstarch in a saucepan. Bring to
a boil, stirring, and boil 1 minute
until shiny and thickened. Pass
with the sliced steak.

Serves 4 to 6

STUFFED FLANK STEAK

1 flank steak
Salt, pepper, flour
4 cups bread cubes
1 medium onion, chopped
¾ cup chopped celery
½ cup LINDSAY® Chopped Ripe
  Olives
1½ teaspoons sage
3 tablespoons butter

Have flank steak scored lightly
crosswise. Sprinkle with salt and
pepper, dredge with flour and
pound well with potato masher.
Combine bread cubes, onions,
celery, chopped olives, sage and
butter. Moisten with water and
season with salt and pepper.
Spread stuffing over flank steak,
roll meat and tie or fasten edge
with toothpicks. Brown in fat, add

½ cup water, cover pan and cook
in moderate oven (350 degrees F.)
about 1½ hours or until tender.
Baste meat occasionally.

Makes 6 servings

BEEF WELLINGTON

1 4-lb. eye round of beef
¼ cup softened butter or
  margarine
1 tsp. unseasoned tenderizer
1 (4-oz.) can chopped mushrooms,
  drained
2 (4¾-oz.) cans liver pâté
¼ tsp. rosemary
2 (10-oz.) pkgs. PEPPERIDGE
  FARM® Frozen Patty Shells,
  thawed
1 egg
1 tsp. milk

Spread top of eye round with
softened butter or margarine. Prick
with a fork at ½-inch intervals.
Sprinkle with unseasoned
tenderizer. Roast in a hot (450°)
oven 60 minutes (medium rare),
then cool completely. Meanwhile,
combine chopped mushrooms, liver
pâté and rosemary. When beef is
cool, spread liver-mushroom
mixture over entire surface. Roll
out 2 (10-oz.) pkgs. thawed Patty
Shells (12 shells) about ¼ inch
thick making one long piece of
pastry. Wrap it around the beef.
Trim edges of pastry, moistening
edges with water and seal by
pressing together. Brush crust with
egg beaten with milk. Prick crust in
a few places to allow steam to
escape. Roll out trimmed pastry
and cut into narrow strips. Lay
across dough-wrapped beef in
lattice pattern. Brush these also
with beaten egg and milk. Bake in
hot (425°) oven 20 minutes, or until
pastry is golden brown.

Serves 8 to 10

GOOD AND EASY
SAUERBRATEN

3 pounds lean, boneless shoulder
  roast
1 cup water
1 cup wine vinegar
Freshly ground black pepper
1 medium onion, sliced
2 bay leaves
16 SUNSHINE® Gingersnaps,
  crushed to fine crumbs

Season roast with pepper; place in
a Dutch oven and roast, uncovered,
in a 475°F. oven until both sides
are browned, turning once—about
4 or 5 minutes on each side.
Remove from the oven, pour
vinegar and water over roast.
Arrange onion slices on top, add
bay leaves to the pot liquid. Cover
and return to the oven. Reduce
heat to 350°F. and cook 1½ hours,
or until tender. Add Gingersnaps,
replace cover, and cook ½ hour
longer. Additional water may be
added to thin the gravy. Remove
meat from gravy and slice as thin
as possible. Serve with sour red
cabbage and applesauce.

Yield: 8 servings

MARINATED
SAUERBRATEN

3 to 4 pound 7-bone roast*
1 package LAWRY'S® Tenderizing
  Beef Marinade, prepared
  according to package directions
½ cup red wine vinegar
½ cup water
1 can (6 oz.) tomato paste
½ teaspoon LAWRY'S® Seasoned
  Salt
¼ teaspoon EACH: LAWRY'S®
  Seasoned Pepper and allspice
2 bay leaves
1 large onion, thickly sliced
12 gingersnap cookies, crushed
2 teaspoons sugar
1 small head cabbage

Pierce roast thoroughly with fork.
In large Dutch oven, add roast,
prepared marinade, vinegar, water
and tomato paste; marinate 15
minutes. Mix in spices and onion
slices. Bring to boil, reduce heat,
cover and simmer for 1 to 1½
hours. Remove bay leaves. Stir in
gingersnaps and sugar. Cut
cabbage into 8 wedges; place in
sauce with meat. Cover and
simmer 15 minutes or until
cabbage is tender.

Makes 6 to 8 servings

*May use 3 lbs. boneless chuck or
 rump roast. May use 2 to 3 lbs.
 beef stew meat, cut into 1½-inch
 cubes.

65

SAN FERNANDO RANCH ROAST

1 (12 oz.) package SUNSWEET® Pitted Prunes
1 (12 oz.) package SUNSWEET® Dried Peaches
3 cups water
1 cup Sauterne
½ teaspoon ground allspice
1 stick cinnamon
⅓ cup vinegar
¼ cup brown sugar (packed)
3 pounds boneless lean beef
2 teaspoons salt
¼ teaspoon pepper
2 tablespoons oil
1 large onion, sliced
1 bay leaf
3 tablespoons catsup
2 teaspoons cornstarch

Simmer fruits, water, wine and spices 10 minutes. Add vinegar and sugar; cook 5 minutes. Cut beef into 6 serving pieces. Sprinkle with salt and pepper. Brown slowly in oil. Add onion, bay leaf, catsup and 1½ cups liquid from fruits. Cover tightly, cook slowly until tender, about 2 hours. Stir in cornstarch blended with a tablespoon water, and 2 cups fruit. Heat a few minutes longer. Serve remaining spiced fruit on the side.

Makes 6 servings

POT ROAST CARIBE

2 to 3 lbs. beef chuck
1 clove garlic, minced
½ cup chopped onion
1 teaspoon salt
2 to 3 tablespoons diced green chiles
1 can (about 1 lb.) tomato sauce
½ cup dry red wine
1 tablespoon cocoa
1 teaspoon chili powder
1 teaspoon grated orange rind
¼ teaspoon each cinnamon, nutmeg and allspice
½ teaspoon oregano, crushed
½ cup BLUE RIBBON® Ground Almonds
6 to 8 small onions
1 to 1½ lbs. Hubbard or butternut squash
BLUE RIBBON® Slivered Almonds, toasted
Parsley and cherry tomatoes for garnish

Trim a small amount of fat from pot roast and render in a heavy frying pan or top-of-stove casserole. Brown meat well in drippings; pour off any excess. Add garlic to meat along with onion. Sprinkle with salt, turning meat and onions. When onions are lightly browned, stir in chiles.

Combine tomato sauce and wine. Stir in cocoa, chili powder, orange rind and spices. Stir oregano into sauce with ground almonds; pour over meat. Cook, covered, over low heat about 2 hours or until meat is tender. About half an hour before serving, peel onions and pare squash. Cut squash into 4 to 6 chunks. Add onions and squash to sauce around meat; cover and continue to cook about ½ hour or until onions and squash are fork-tender.

To serve, place meat in center of platter; spoon sauce over. Arrange vegetables around. Sprinkle slivered almonds over meat. Garnish with parsley and cherry tomatoes.

Makes 4 to 6 servings

SPICY POT ROAST

4 teaspoons salt
2 teaspoons ground mace
1 teaspoon minced garlic
½ teaspoon pepper
4 pounds rolled rump roast
½ cup HEINZ Apple Cider Vinegar
1 tablespoon salad oil
¾ cup HEINZ Tomato Ketchup
¼ cup water
1 cup chopped green pepper
1 cup chopped onions

Combine first 4 ingredients, rub thoroughly into meat on all sides. Place meat in bowl; pour vinegar over meat. Cover; marinate in refrigerator overnight, turning meat occasionally. Drain meat well; discard marinade. Brown meat on all sides in oil in Dutch oven. Combine ketchup and remaining ingredients; spoon over meat. Cover; bake in 350°F. oven, 2½ to 3 hours or until meat is tender, basting occasionally. Skim excess fat from sauce; thicken sauce, if desired. *Makes 8-10 servings*

PENNSYLVANIA DUTCH POT ROAST

3½ to 4-pound 7-bone beef pot roast*
1 package LAWRY'S® Pot Roast Seasoning Mix
1 medium onion, thinly sliced in rings
2 green apples, peeled and sliced about ½-inch thick
¼ cup water

Place meat on a piece of aluminum foil large enough to wrap the meat; sprinkle with Pot Roast Seasoning Mix. Add a layer of onion rings and apples on the meat. Pour water over meat; wrap securely and place in a roasting pan. Bake in 350°F. oven for 3 hours.

Makes 6 to 8 servings

*Or similar cut such as chuck or rump roast

MEXICAN POT ROAST

4 to 5 lb. pot roast, sprinkled with salt and pepper (shoulder roast is good)
1 Tbsp. cooking oil
1 clove garlic chopped or put through press
1 medium onion, chopped
1 (1 lb.) can S&W Peeled Whole Tomatoes, chopped
2 (4 oz.) cans S&W Green Chilies, chopped
½ tsp. oregano
1 tsp. salt
½ tsp. pepper
¼ tsp. crushed red pepper
2 (15½ oz.) cans S&W Chili Beans or S&W Dark Red Kidney Beans, undrained
1 (3½ oz.) can S&W Pitted Ripe Olives, chopped (optional)

In Dutch oven, heat cooking oil. Sprinkle roast with salt and pepper, then brown quickly on both sides. Remove meat temporarily. To drippings, add onion and garlic and cook over medium heat till onion is tender but not brown. Then add tomatoes, green chilies, oregano, salt, peppers and beans. Heat to boiling, then reduce heat to simmer. Return meat to Dutch oven; add olives. Cover tightly; put in 350° oven and cook till tender (about 2½ hrs.) Serve with hot, steamy rice and a tossed green salad. *Serves 4 to 6*

SPANISH POT ROAST

3 to 4-lb. pot roast
1 8-oz. bottle CATALINA French
　Dressing
¾ cup water
8 small onions
8 small potatoes
1 cup stuffed green olive slices
2 tablespoons flour

Brown meat in ¼ cup dressing.
Add remaining dressing and ½ cup
water. Cover; simmer 2 hours and
15 minutes. Add onions, potatoes
and olives; continue simmering 45
minutes or until meat and
vegetables are tender. Remove
meat and vegetables to serving
platter. Gradually add remaining
water to flour, stirring until well
blended. Gradually add flour
mixture to hot liquid in pan; cook,
stirring constantly, until mixture
boils and thickens. Simmer 3
minutes, stirring constantly. Serve
with meat and vegetables.

6 to 8 servings

IRISH-STYLE CHUCK
ROAST

3½-pound boneless chuck roast
　(about 2-inches thick)
2 tablespoons shortening
2 cans (10¾ ounces *each*)
　CAMPBELL'S Condensed Golden
　Mushroom Soup
½ cup chopped canned tomatoes
1 tablespoon prepared horseradish
½ teaspoon celery seed
6 small potatoes (about 1½
　pounds), cut in half
1 medium head cabbage (about 2
　pounds), cut in 6 wedges

In large heavy pan, brown beef in
shortening; pour off fat. Add soup,
tomatoes, horseradish and celery
seed. Cover; cook over low heat 2
hours. Add potatoes; cook 30
minutes. Stir occasionally. Place
cabbage on top; cook 30 minutes
more or until done. Spoon off fat;
thicken sauce if desired.

Makes 6 servings

EASY POT ROAST

3 to 4-pound boneless beef pot
　roast
1 can (10½ ounces) CAMPBELL'S
　Condensed Onion, Golden
　Mushroom, or Cream of
　Mushroom Soup

In large heavy pan, brown meat on
all sides (use shortening if
necessary); pour off fat. Stir in
soup. Cover; cook over low heat
2½ to 3 hours. Stir occasionally.
Remove meat. To thicken,
gradually blend ¼ cup water into 2
to 4 tablespoons flour until
smooth; slowly stir into soup.
Cook, stirring until thickened.
Serve with meat.

Makes 6 to 8 servings

SAVORY POT ROAST

3 to 3½ pound boneless pot
　roast (rump, chuck or round)
1 envelope LIPTON® Beef Flavor
　Mushroom Soup Mix
2¼ cups water
2 tablespoons flour

In Dutch oven, brown roast. Add
LIPTON® Beef Flavor Mushroom
Soup Mix blended with 2 cups
water. Simmer covered, turning
occasionally, 2½ hours or until
tender. Blend remaining water with
flour; stir into gravy. Bring to a
boil, then simmer, stirring
constantly, until thickened, about 5
minutes.

Makes about 6 servings

Microwave Directions: In 3-quart
casserole, blend soup mix with ½
cup water; heat at HIGH (600 to
700 watts) 5 minutes. Add roast
and heat at HIGH 10 minutes,
turning once. Heat at DEFROST
(30% of HIGH power) 60 minutes
or until roast is tender, turning
occasionally. Remove ¼ cup
liquid; blend with flour. Stir into
gravy and heat at HIGH 2 minutes
or until thickened, stirring twice.

SWEET AND SOUR
POT ROAST

3½ lbs. of beef
Salt and pepper
1 quart canned tomatoes
6 medium onions (onions may be
　eliminated)
2 tablespoons ROKEACH Kosher
　Nyafat
½ cup ROKEACH Pure Honey
Lemon juice (optional)
2 sweet potatoes

Fry the onions, cut small, until a
golden brown and set aside. Salt
and pepper the meat, brown on all
sides in ROKEACH Kosher Nyafat,
cover kettle tightly and let simmer
for 1½ hours or until nearly tender.

Add hot water only if necessary.
Add fried onions, tomatoes, honey,
and lemon juice if not sour
enough. Finish cooking in oven
until gravy is thick and meat well
browned. Add 2 sweet potatoes,
cut up fine, 15 or 20 minutes
before meat is done.

Favorite ROKEACH Kosher recipe from 1932

NORMANDY POT ROAST

4-pound boneless beef pot roast
1 can (10¼ ounces) FRANCO-
　AMERICAN Beef Gravy
¼ teaspoon salt
Generous dash pepper
1 medium bay leaf
4 medium potatoes (about 1
　pound), halved
4 medium carrots (about ½ pound),
　halved
8 small whole white onions
　(about ½ pound)
Parsley

In large heavy pan, brown meat
(use shortening if necessary); pour
off fat. Add gravy, salt, pepper and
bay leaf. Cover; cook over low heat
2 hours. Add vegetables; cook 1
hour more or until tender. Stir
occasionally. Uncover; cook to
desired consistency. Spoon off fat.
Remove bay leaf. Garnish with
parsley. *Makes 8 servings*

MUSTARD-ONION CHUCK
ROAST IN FOIL

2 tablespoons dry mustard
1½ teaspoons water
3-pound beef chuck pot roast,
　2 inches thick
2 medium onions, chunked
½ cup KIKKOMAN Soy Sauce

Blend mustard with water to make
a smooth paste; cover and let
stand 5 minutes. Meanwhile, place
large enough piece of heavy-duty
foil to cover meat in shallow
baking pan; place meat on foil.
Sprinkle onion pieces over meat.
Stir 1 tablespoon soy sauce into
mustard mixture, blending until
smooth; stir in remaining soy
sauce. Pour mixture evenly over
beef and onions. Fold foil over
meat; seal securely. Roast in
325°F. oven 3 hours. Remove from
oven and spoon off excess fat. Cut
across grain into thin slices and
serve with meat juices.

Makes 6 to 8 servings

HICKORY SMOKED BRISKET

Take a medium size brisket and pierce a number of holes in it with a large kitchen fork. Place the brisket in a zip lock or tie bag along with approximately 12 ounces of FIGARO Liquid Barbecue Smoke. Close bag and check for leaks. Allow the brisket to soak at room temperature a minimum of 12 hours. Turn the brisket over at least twice during this soaking period. When ready to cook, remove brisket from the bag and place in a shallow pan on the middle rack in your oven. Cook for six hours at 275°. Serve hot with our brisket sauce.*

*OUTWEST BARBECUE SAUCE

3 parts catsup
1 part FIGARO Liquid Barbecue Smoke

Mix ingredients in sauce pan and heat. Don't boil. Serve hot on Brisket.

CORNED BEEF WITH VEGETABLES

SWIFT PREMIUM® Corned Beef for Oven Roasting
1 cup water
1 medium head cabbage, cut into 6 wedges
3 medium carrots, pared
3 onions, peeled
3 potatoes, pared and cut into halves
½ cup water

Place meat on a rack in a large Dutch oven. Add 1 cup water. Cover. Place in a 325°F. oven for 2½ hours. Arrange vegetables around meat. Add ½ cup water. Cover and continue cooking 30 minutes or until meat and vegetables are tender.

Yield: 6 servings

CORNED BEEF WITH ZESTY HORSERADISH SAUCE

3 to 4 pound corned beef brisket
4 to 6 carrots, cut in quarters
4 to 6 wedges of cabbage
1 envelope FRENCH'S® Gravy Mix for Chicken
1 to 3 tablespoons prepared horseradish

Cover corned beef with water in large pan; simmer, covered, 2½ hours or until almost tender. Add carrots; simmer 20 minutes. Add cabbage; simmer 10 minutes longer, until meat and vegetables are tender. Arrange on platter. Measure 1½ cups cooking liquid; stir in gravy mix and horseradish. Bring to a boil, stirring frequently. Serve meat and vegetables with sauce.
6 to 8 servings

CRISPY BARBECUED SHORT RIBS

4 pounds beef short ribs
⅔ cup KIKKOMAN Teriyaki Sauce
¼ cup orange marmalade
1 teaspoon garlic salt
½ teaspoon lemon & pepper seasoning (optional)

Score meaty side of ribs, opposite bone, ½ inch apart, ½ inch deep, lengthwise and crosswise. Combine remaining ingredients; set aside. Place ribs and sauce in large plastic bag; press air out and close top securely. Marinate in refrigerator 8 hours or overnight; turn bag over occasionally. Remove ribs from marinade. Broil 2 to 3 inches from heat 15 minutes, or until crispy brown on all sides.
Makes 4 servings

PEACHY SHORT RIBS

4 pounds beef short ribs
1 tablespoon vegetable oil
1 can (29 oz.) cling peach halves
⅓ cup KIKKOMAN Soy Sauce
¼ cup tomato catsup
1 clove garlic, crushed

Brown ribs slowly in hot oil in Dutch oven with heat-proof handles. Drain peaches; reserve ¾ cup syrup. Mix syrup with remaining ingredients; add to ribs. Cover; place in 350°F. oven. Bake about 2 hours, or until tender. Add peaches to ribs, return to oven 10 minutes.
Makes 4 to 6 servings

OVEN BAKED SHORT RIBS WITH GARDEN VEGETABLES

3 pounds beef short ribs
1 teaspoon salt
¼ teaspoon pepper
1 pound carrots, cleaned and halved
1 pound potatoes, pared and halved
½ pound fresh green beans
4 small white onions
1 can (13¾ oz.) beef broth
2 tablespoons horseradish
2 teaspoons prepared mustard
2 tablespoons ARGO® / KINGSFORD'S® Corn Starch
¼ cup water

Trim excess fat from meat. Place in 13 × 9 × 2-inch baking pan; sprinkle with salt and pepper. Bake uncovered in 350°F. oven 2 hours; drain fat. Add next 4 ingredients. Mix broth, horseradish and mustard; pour over meat and vegetables. Cover with foil; bake 1 to 1½ hours longer or until tender. Arrange meat and vegetables on serving platter; keep warm. Strain broth; remove excess fat. Add water, if necessary, to make 2 cups and return to baking pan. Mix corn starch and ¼ cup cool water; stir into pan. Bring to boil over medium heat, stirring constantly, and boil 1 minute. Serve gravy with meat and vegetables.
Makes 4 servings

MARY MEATLOAF

2 lbs. ground beef
1 package onion soup mix
2 tablespoons finely chopped onion
1½ cups MR. & MRS. "T"® Bloody Mary Mix
Bacon slices

Mix meat, onion soup mix, onion and one cup MR. & MRS. "T"® Bloody Mary Mix. Shape into loaf shape. Place in baking pan. Top with bacon slices. Bake in preheated 350° oven for 45 minutes. Drain off fat. Add remaining MR. & MRS. "T"® Mix to pan. Baste loaf. Thicken pan juices slightly with a little cornstarch mixed with water. Serve meatloaf with green salad.
Serves 4-6

SNOW PEAKED MEAT LOAF

1 can (10¾ ounces) CAMPBELL'S Condensed Golden Mushroom Soup
2 pounds ground beef
½ cup fine dry bread crumbs
⅓ cup finely chopped onion
1 egg, slightly beaten
1 teaspoon salt
4 cups mashed potatoes
Shredded Cheddar cheese
¼ cup water

Mix *thoroughly* ½ cup soup, beef, bread crumbs, onion, egg and salt. Shape *firmly* into loaf (8 × 4-inch); place in shallow baking pan. Bake at 375°F. for 1 hour. Frost with potatoes; sprinkle with cheese. Bake 15 minutes more. Blend remaining soup, water and 2 tablespoons drippings. Heat; stir occasionally. Serve with loaf.

Makes 6 to 8 servings

BEST EVER MEAT LOAF

1 can (10¾ ounces) CAMPBELL'S Condensed Cream of Mushroom or Golden Mushroom Soup
2 pounds ground beef
½ cup fine dry bread crumbs
1 egg, slightly beaten
⅓ cup finely chopped onion
1 teaspoon salt
⅓ cup water

Mix thoroughly ½ cup soup, beef, bread crumbs, egg, onion, and salt. Shape *firmly* into loaf (8 × 4"); place in shallow baking pan. Bake at 375°F. for 1 hour 15 minutes. In saucepan, blend remaining soup, water, and 2 to 3 tablespoons drippings. Heat; stir occasionally. Serve with loaf.

Makes 6 to 8 servings

Frosted Meat Loaf: Prepare loaf as above; bake for 1 hour. Frost loaf with 4 cups mashed potatoes; sprinkle with shredded Cheddar cheese. Bake 15 minutes more.

Swedish Meat Loaf: Add ½ teaspoon nutmeg to loaf. Blend remaining soup with ⅓ cup sour cream; omit drippings and water. Serve over loaf; sprinkle with additional nutmeg. Garnish with thinly sliced cucumber.

Meat Loaf Wellington: Crescent Rolls (Refrigerated): Prepare loaf as above. Bake at 375°F. for 1 hour. Spoon off fat. Separate 1 package (8 ounces) refrigerated crescent dinner rolls; place crosswise over top and down sides of meat loaf, overlapping slightly. Bake 15 minutes more.

Patty Shells: Thaw 1 package (10 ounces) frozen patty shells. Prepare loaf as above. Bake at 375°F. for 30 minutes. Spoon off fat. Increase oven temperature to 400°F. On floured board, roll 5 patty shells into rectangle (12 × 8"); prick several times with fork. Cover top and sides of loaf with pastry. Decorate top with remaining patty shell, rolled and cut into fancy shapes. Bake 45 minutes more or until golden brown. Serve with sauce.

FINNISH FRUIT STUFFED MEAT LOAF/ORIENTAL-STYLE MEAT LOAF

Prepare 1 package LAWRY'S® Meat Loaf Seasoning Mix using two pounds ground beef according to package directions; divide uncooked meat mixture in half.

Finnish Fruit Stuffed Meat Loaf
½ recipe Meat Loaf Mixture
½ cup chopped apple
½ cup chopped, pitted prunes
½ cup chopped pecans or walnuts
1 teaspoon LAWRY'S® Lemon Pepper Marinade

Divide meat in half again and press one portion into a 1½-quart loaf pan. Combine remaining ingredients and spread on meat not quite to edges. Place remaining meat on top of fruit and press down along edges to seal in fruit. Bake in 375°F oven 1 hour.

Makes 6 servings

Oriental-Style Meat Loaf
½ recipe Meat Loaf Mixture
2 eggs, separated
1 can (1 lb.) chow mein vegetables, well drained
¼ cup soy sauce
1 can (5 oz.) chow mein noodles

Combine meat mixture and egg yolks and divide in half again. Press one portion into 8 × 4-inch rectangle on baking sheet. Combine vegetables and 2 tablespoons soy sauce and spread over meat not quite to edges. Place remaining meat on top of vegetables and press along edges to seal. Brush meat with remaining soy sauce. Beat egg whites until stiff but not dry; fold in noodles and press into top and sides of meat. Bake in 375°F. oven 45 minutes. To slice, turn loaf over so noodles are on bottom.

Makes 6 servings

HI HO® MEAT LOAF

1½ cups crushed HI HO® Crackers
¼ cup minced onion
¼ cup minced green pepper
2 eggs, slightly beaten
1½ pounds ground lean beef
½ pound pork sausage
2 tablespoons grated horseradish
1 tablespoon salt
¼ cup milk
½ cup catsup

Preheat oven to 350°F. (moderate oven). Grease a 9 × 5 × 3-inch pan. Crush HI HO® Crackers medium-fine by rolling on sheet of waxed paper with rolling pin. In medium-sized bowl, combine cracker crumbs, onion, green pepper, eggs, beef, sausage, horseradish, salt, milk and ¼ cup catsup. Mix well and press into greased loaf pan. Spread top with remaining ¼ cup catsup. Bake at 350°F. for 1 hour. Remove to heated platter, slice and serve hot; or chill, slice and serve cold.

Yield: 6 to 8 servings

CHILI MEAT LOAF

1 can (15-oz.) NALLEY®'S Chili With Beans
2 eggs, slightly beaten
1 medium onion, minced
½ cup diced green pepper
1 tsp. salt
2 pounds lean ground beef

Pour Chili into large mixing bowl. Stir in eggs. Add onion, pepper, salt, and meat broken into pieces. Tip bowl and cut through mixture with fork until blended. (Tender mixing makes tender meat loaf.) Shape into loaf. Turn out on greased shallow pan; smooth into shape. Bake in 400° oven 1 hour.

Makes 6 servings

MIGHTY MINI MEAT MUFFINS

2 eggs beaten
1 cup rolled crumbs of
  BROWNBERRY® Natural Wheat
  Bread
1 lb. ground beef
2 Tbsp. steak sauce
1 tsp. salt
¾ cup milk

Preheat oven to 450°. Mix
ingredients in order given and pack
mixture level or slightly rounded
into greased muffin tins. Bake 15
minutes.   *Makes 6 servings*

Hunt's.

MEAT LOAF UNDER WRAPS

1 (6-oz.) can HUNT'S Tomato Paste
1½ cups water
1½ lb. lean ground beef
1 cup fine cracker crumbs
½ cup *each:* finely chopped
  onion and green pepper
2 eggs, separated
½ tsp. salt
¼ tsp. pepper
3 cups hot prepared mashed
  potatoes
¼ cup shredded Cheddar cheese
1 Tbsp. butter
2 Tbsp. brown sugar, packed
2 Tbsp. Worcestershire
2 Tbsp. mushroom stems and
  pieces

Blend together HUNT'S Tomato
Paste and water in small
saucepan. set aside. Combine in a
bowl ½ *cup* tomato paste mixture,
ground beef, cracker crumbs,
onion, green pepper, *egg whites*,
salt and pepper; mix well. Shape
mixture into a loaf in a shallow
baking dish. Bake at 350°F. 45
minutes. Meanwhile, in a
saucepan, combine hot prepared
mashed potatoes, cheese, butter
and *egg yolks.* Stir and heat 2 to 5
minutes to melt cheese. Drain fat
from meat loaf; frost with potato
mixture. Bake 15 to 20 minutes
longer. Add brown sugar,
Worcestershire and mushrooms to
saucepan of remaining tomato
paste mixture; heat 3 to 5 minutes.
Serve over slices of meat loaf.
          Makes 6 to 8 servings

GLAZED MEAT LOAF

Meat Loaf:
1½ pounds ground beef chuck
1 cup NABISCO® 100% Bran
  Cereal
½ cup chopped onion
⅓ cup ketchup
¼ cup water
2 eggs
1½ teaspoons Worcestershire
  sauce
1¼ teaspoons salt
¼ teaspoon ground black pepper

Glaze:
1 tablespoon ketchup
1 tablespoon dark corn syrup
¼ teaspoon Worcestershire sauce

Make meat loaf. Combine ground
chuck, NABISCO® 100% Bran
Cereal, onion, ketchup, water,
eggs, Worcestershire sauce, salt
and pepper; mix lightly until well
blended. Shape into a loaf. Place
in an aluminum foil-lined
13 × 9 × 2-inch baking pan. Bake at
375°F. for 50 minutes.

Make glaze. In small bowl, blend
ketchup, corn syrup and
Worcestershire sauce. Brush over
top of meat loaf; bake 10 minutes
longer or until done.

Garnish meat loaf with parsley
sprigs and surround with sautéed
carrots, onions and mushrooms,
which have been tossed with
chopped parsley.   *Serves 6*

WHEATENA® MEAT LOAF

½ cup *cooked* WHEATENA®
1½ pounds ground beef*
1 egg, slightly beaten
2 tablespoons minced onion
1 tablespoon minced parsley
1½ teaspoons salt
⅛ teaspoon pepper
4 teaspoons chili sauce

Prepare WHEATENA® according
to package directions. Combine
cooked WHEATENA® and all other
ingredients. Pack into lightly
greased 9 × 5 × 3-inch loaf pan.
Bake in preheated 350°F. oven
about 1½ hours, or until tests
done.
          Makes about 6 servings

*Use half ground beef and half
 ground pork or veal if desired.

WHEAT GERM MEAT LOAF

2 pounds ground beef chuck or
  round
½ cup ELAM'S® Natural Wheat
  Germ
½ cup cooked ELAM'S® Cracked
  Wheat Cereal
⅓ cup finely chopped onion
1½ teaspoons salt
¼ teaspoon pepper
1 cup tomato juice
2 eggs, beaten
1 tablespoon Worcestershire
  sauce, optional

Combine ingredients in bowl; mix
well. Pack into greased loaf pan
(9 × 5 × 3-inches). Bake in moderate
oven (350°F.) until done, about 70
minutes. Cool 10 minutes before
removing from pan and slicing.
Serve hot or cold, plain or with
favorite cheese, cream or tomato
sauce.   *Yield: 8 servings*

MEATLOAF À LA RUSSE

1½ pounds ground beef
1½ pounds ground sausage
1 cup crumb-style herbed
  stuffing mix
1 egg
1 teaspoon dillweed, crumbled
½ teaspcon rosemary, crumbled
⅛ teaspoon garlic powder
8 large DOLE® Fresh Mushrooms
1 tablespoon vegetable oil
1 cup dairy sour cream
1 tablespoon horseradish
¼ teaspoon salt

Combine beef and sausage in a
large bowl with stuffing mix, egg,
dillweed, rosemary and garlic
powder. Blend well. Place ½
mixture in a 9-inch square baking
pan forming into an oval. Wipe
mushrooms with a damp towel and
trim ends. Stand mushrooms in
meat mixture stem down. Press
remaining meat mixture over all
pressing firmly to shape into an
oval loaf. Brush with oil. Bake in a
350°F. oven 1½ hours. Remove to
serving plate. Blend sour cream,
horseradish and salt; serve over
meatloaf as sauce.
          Makes 6 to 8 serv

ZESTY SALTINE MEATLOAF

1½ pounds ground beef
1 cup coarse KEEBLER Zesta
  Saltine Crackers
⅓ cup chopped onion
¼ cup milk
1 egg
¼ cup ketchup
1 teaspoon Worcestershire sauce
1 teaspoon salt
¼ teaspoon pepper
1 cup shredded Cheddar cheese

In large mixing bowl, combine
ground beef, ½ cup cracker
crumbs, onion, milk, egg, ¼ cup
ketchup, Worcestershire sauce,
salt and pepper; blend thoroughly.
Place mixture on large piece of
waxed paper. Cover with another
piece of waxed paper and roll out
to rectangle about 9 × 15 inches.
Remove top sheet of paper.
Combine remaining cracker
crumbs and cheese. Sprinkle over
meat mixture. Beginning with
9-inch side, roll up jelly roll
fashion, using waxed paper to help
roll. Place in 9 × 5 inch loaf pan.
Spread additional ketchup over
top. Bake in preheated 350°F. oven
1-1¼ hours.   *5 to 6 servings*

MEATLOAF PIE ITALIANO

1 envelope FRENCH'S® Ground
  Beef Seasoning Mix with Onions
1 pound ground beef
¼ cup water
1 can (8-oz.) tomato sauce
½ teaspoon herb seasoning
¼ teaspoon garlic powder
1 cup shredded mozzarella cheese
¼ cup grated Parmesan cheese
¼ cup pitted ripe olives, cut in half

Combine seasoning mix, ground
beef, and water; form a meat
"shell" in 9-inch pie pan. Combine
tomato sauce, herb seasoning, and
garlic powder; pour into shell.
Sprinkle with mozzarella and
Parmesan cheese; garnish with
olives. Bake at 350° for 45 minutes.
Pour off excess fat before serving.
                    5 to 6 servings

Microwave Meatloaf Pie Italiano:
Microwave on HIGH 10 minutes,
rotating dish two or three times.

SAVORY CHIPPER LOAF

2 pounds ground beef
1 egg slightly beaten
¼ cup minced onion
¼ teaspoon pepper
1 can condensed vegetable soup
2 cups crushed JAYS Potato Chips

Combine all ingredients in a bowl.
Blend together. Shape into a loaf
and bake in a shallow pan,
uncovered, in a 350° oven for 1½
hours.   *Makes 6-8 servings*

SAUCY MEAT LOAF

1½ pounds lean ground beef
1 tablespoon WYLER'S® Beef-
  Flavor Instant Bouillon *or* 3 Beef-
  Flavor Bouillon Cubes
¼ cup water
1½ cups soft bread crumbs
½ cup catsup
½ cup chopped green pepper,
  optional
¼ cup chopped onion
2 eggs
1 (8-ounce) can tomato sauce
Parsley or green pepper rings

Preheat oven to 350°. In small
saucepan, over low heat, dissolve
bouillon in water. In large bowl,
combine all ingredients except
tomato sauce and parsley; mix
well. Shape into loaf in shallow
baking pan. Bake 1 hour. Remove
from oven; pour off fat. Pour
tomato sauce over loaf; bake 15
minutes longer. Garnish with
parsley. Refrigerate leftovers.
                   Makes 6 servings

PRIZE WINNING MEAT LOAF

1½ lb. ground beef
1 cup tomato juice
¾ cup QUAKER® Oats (Quick or
  Old Fashioned, uncooked)
1 egg, beaten
¼ cup chopped onion
1 teaspoon salt
¼ teaspoon pepper

Heat oven to 350°F. Combine all
ingredients; mix well. Press firmly
into ungreased 8 × 4-inch loaf pan.
Bake about 1 hour. Let stand 5
minutes before slicing.
                   Makes 8 servings

FRUIT STUFFED MEAT LOAF

2 pounds ground round
2 eggs, slightly beaten
1 cup soft bread crumbs
1½ teaspoons salt
¼ teaspoon thyme, crushed
⅛ teaspoon pepper
½ cup finely chopped apple
¼ cup chopped dried apricots
¼ cup raisins
¼ cup chopped parsley
¼ teaspoon all spice
½ cup WELCH'S® Grape
  Preserves

In bowl, combine ground beef,
eggs, bread crumbs, salt, thyme
and pepper; blend well. Spread
mixture into a rectangle about ½
inch thick on large piece of heavy
duty aluminum foil. Combine
remaining ingredients and blend
thoroughly. Spread over meat loaf
mixture. Roll up meat and filling
jellyroll fashion. Bring foil up
around meat loaf and seal it
securely. Place package in shallow
roasting pan and bake at 350°F.
for 1 hour. Open foil to allow
surface to brown and bake 30
minutes longer.
                Makes 6 to 8 servings

MEAT LOAF ITALIANO

¼ cup finely chopped onion
2 tablespoons butter or margarine
½ cup PEPPERIDGE FARM® Herb
  Seasoned Stuffing
½ cup beef bouillon
1 pound ground chuck
1 tablespoon chopped parsley
3 tablespoons grated Parmesan
  cheese
1 egg, slightly beaten
1 teaspoon salt
¼ teaspoon pepper
1 can (8 oz.) tomato sauce
1 teaspoon oregano

Sauté onion in butter until tender.
In a large bowl, combine stuffing
and beef bouillon. Add all but the
last two ingredients. Mix lightly
until well blended. Shape into a
loaf and place in a shallow baking
pan. Bake at 375°F. for 30 minutes.
Pour tomato sauce over top and
sprinkle with oregano. Continue
baking 30 minutes longer.
                     Serves 4 to 6

Wright's

BAKED SECRET GARDEN

8 oz. lean ground beef
½ teaspoon WRIGHT'S Natural
  Hickory Liquid Smoke
Salt-pepper
¼" slice of large tomato
Dried chives
Chopped parsley
1-2 tablespoons diced celery

Add WRIGHT'S Natural Hickory Liquid Smoke, salt and pepper to ground beef and work in with hands. Form seasoned meat into two large patties making them as flat and thin as possible; about 5 inch diameter. Place the first pattie on rack in baking pan and top with tomato slice. Sprinkle tomato with chives, parsley, celery, salt and pepper. Cover with remaining beef pattie and seal carefully around edges. Bake at 450° until done to desired degree. About 15 minutes for medium. *Serves 1*

GRAND BRAN BURGERS

1 pound ground beef chuck
1 pound ground veal*
2 eggs, slightly beaten
¼ cup water
¼ cup milk
1 cup NABISCO® 100% Bran
  Cereal
½ cup finely chopped onion
¼ cup chopped parsley
1½ teaspoons salt
1 teaspoon caraway seeds
¼ teaspoon ground black pepper

In large bowl, combine meat, eggs, water and milk. Blend in NABISCO® 100% Bran Cereal, onion, parsley, salt, caraway seeds and black pepper. Shape into 12 even patties, ½-inch thick. Or make 6 large dinner-size patties. Broil 3 inches from heat or pan fry for 3 to 5 minutes each side for rare. *Serves 6*

*Or substitute 1 pound ground beef chuck for veal. Beef chuck is best for flavor and has a good proportion of fat to marbled meat. For a touch of luxury, ground beef sirloin can be used. Additional cooking information: Broil 6 to 7 minutes each side for medium, and 8 to 9 minutes each side for well done.

FIESTA BEEF MEDLEY

1 pound ground beef
1 medium onion, chopped
1 clove garlic, crushed
1 can (1 lb.) tomatoes
½ cup water
¼ cup KIKKOMAN Soy Sauce
¼ teaspoon pepper
1 package (9 oz.) frozen green
  beans
½ cup uncooked rice, washed and
  drained

Brown beef with onions and garlic in large frying pan with cover. Stir in tomatoes, water, soy sauce and pepper; bring to boil. Mix in green beans and rice. Cover, reduce heat, and simmer 30 minutes, or until rice is tender.
Makes about 6 servings

LATIN BURGERS

Combine lean ground beef with BLUE RIBBON® Slivered Almonds, raisins, beaten egg, dry bread crumbs, salt and pepper to taste; form into burgers. Grind more BLUE RIBBON® Almonds in blender and coat burgers. Fry over medium heat in pre-heated, buttered skillet. Serve with a quick and easy Mexican sauce made with 1 can (7 oz.) green chile salsa, 2 teaspoons cocoa, 1 teaspoon sugar, ¼ teaspoon salt, 2 medium cloves garlic, minced, and ⅛ teaspoon each ground cinnamon and cloves.

SALISBURY STEAK

1 can (10¾ ounces) CAMPBELL'S
  Condensed Golden Mushroom
  Soup
1½ pounds ground beef
½ cup fine dry bread crumbs
¼ cup finely chopped onion
1 egg, slightly beaten
⅓ cup water

Mix *thoroughly* ¼ cup soup, beef, bread crumbs, onion, and egg; shape *firmly* into 6 patties. In skillet, brown patties (use shortening if necessary); pour off fat. Blend in remaining soup and water. Cover; cook over low heat 20 minutes or until done. Stir occasionally.
Makes 6 servings

DANISH SURPRISE HAMBURGERS

2 medium-size onions, sliced
1 Tbsp. butter
2 pounds lean ground beef
5 tomato slices, ¼-inch thick
10 slices Danish Cheese, ¼-inch
  thick*
1 Tbsp. spicy mustard
Salt and pepper

Sauté onions in butter until tender, not browned. Form ground beef into ten patties, about four inches wide. Divide sautéed onions evenly between five patties, spooning them on centers. Place a slice of tomato and a slice of cheese on top of onions. Spread mustard on remaining five patties. Sprinkle with salt and pepper. Place the mustard patties on top of the patties with other ingredients and pinch edges together to enclose all ingredients. It is very important to seal the edges securely. Sprinkle tops with salt and pepper. Broil or grill, six inches from heat about 12 minutes, turning carefully once. Just before serving, place remaining cheese on top of burgers and cook until cheese melts. *Makes five servings*

*Danish Blue Cheese, Samsoe, Tybo, Danbo, Creamy Havarti (Havarti Mild) or Danish Fontina

Favorite recipe from Denmark Cheese Association

CHILI MEAT ROLL

2 pounds ground chuck
½ cup fine dry bread crumbs
2 eggs
1 cup finely-minced onion
1 can (15-oz.) NALLEY®'S Big
  Chunk Chili
1 cup crushed NALLEY®'S Corn
  Chips

Preheat oven to 350°. Combine ground chuck, crumbs, eggs and onion; mix well. On waxed paper, pat meat mixture to 8 x 14-inch rectangle. Spread with Chili and Corn Chips. Roll up meat jelly-roll fashion. Place in shallow baking dish. Bake 1 hour; drain off excess fat. Bake 15 minutes more, or until done. *Makes 6 to 8 servings*

ITALIAN BEEF AND CHEESE ROLL

1½ pounds lean ground beef
1 egg
¾ cup Italian style bread crumbs
½ cup finely chopped onion
1 can (15 oz.) tomato sauce
1 teaspoon salt
½ teaspoon pepper
2 cups (8 oz.) SARGENTO Shredded Cheese with Spices for Pizza

Combine beef, egg, bread crumbs, onion, ⅓ cup tomato sauce, salt and pepper. Mix well and shape into a flat rectangle about 10″ × 12″ on a piece of wax paper. Sprinkle SARGENTO Shredded Cheese with Spices for Pizza evenly over meat mixture. Starting with shortest end, roll up jelly roll fashion and press ends of roll to seal. Bake in a shallow baking pan for 1 hour at 350°. Drain off excess fat. Pour remaining sauce over roll. Garnish with SARGENTO Cheese and green pepper rings. Bake an additional 5 minutes, or just until cheese starts to melt.

Yield: 4-6 servings

BEEF TACOS

1 pound ground beef
1 medium onion, chopped
1 clove garlic, minced
1 envelope (1¼ oz.) OLD EL PASO® Taco Seasoning Mix
¾ cup water
12 OLD EL PASO® Taco Shells
2 tomatoes, chopped
1 cup (4 oz.) shredded sharp Cheddar cheese
Shredded lettuce
OLD EL PASO® Taco Sauce

Brown ground beef, onion and garlic in medium skillet. Drain fat. Stir in seasoning mix and water. Heat to boiling. Reduce heat and simmer, uncovered, 15 to 20 minutes, stirring occasionally. Preheat oven to 350°F. Arrange taco shells on baking sheet. Warm in oven for 5 to 7 minutes. Fill each of the taco shells with some of the meat mixture, tomatoes, cheese and lettuce. Serve with taco sauce.

Makes 12 tacos

NEW ENGLAND STYLE GROUND BEEF

¾ pound ground beef
1 package (10 oz.) BIRDS EYE® AMERICANA RECIPE® Vegetables, New England Style
¼ cup water
2 teaspoons soy sauce or Worcestershire sauce

Brown beef in skillet, adding a small amount of oil, if necessary, and leaving meat in large chunks. (Or, shape meat into small oval patties.) Set aside packet of topping. Add vegetables, water and soy sauce to skillet. Bring to a *full* boil over medium heat, separating vegetables with a fork and stirring occasionally. Reduce heat; cover and simmer 5 minutes. Sprinkle with topping.

Makes about 3½ cups or 3 servings

GREEN CHILI STEAKS

½ pound lean ground beef
½ teaspoon LAWRY'S® Seasoned Salt
¼ teaspoon LAWRY'S® Seasoned Pepper
Dash LAWRY'S® Garlic Powder with Parsley
1 fresh green chili, seeded and minced
3 tablespoons chopped green onion

In medium bowl, thoroughly combine all ingredients. Form into 2 oval steak patties or 4 hamburger patties. Cook in skillet, broiler or on barbecue until done.

Makes 2 steak patties or 4 hamburger patties

UNSTUFFED CABBAGE FOR TWO

½ pound ground beef
½ small head cabbage, coarsely chopped (about 3 cups)*
3 envelopes LIPTON® Tomato Cup-a-Soup
2 envelopes LIPTON® Onion Cup-a-Soup
1¾ cups water
½ cup instant rice

In large saucepan, brown ground beef with cabbage. Add instant tomato and onion soups and water;

cook covered 10 minutes or until cabbage is almost tender. Add rice; cook covered an additional 5 minutes or until rice is tender.

Makes 2 servings

*VARIATION:

For *Unstuffed Peppers*, use 2 small green peppers, cut into strips.

MEMORABLE MEATBALLS

1 pound ground beef
¼ cup fine dry bread crumbs
1 egg, slightly beaten
¼ cup finely chopped onion
2 teaspoons prepared horseradish
1 tablespoon prepared mustard
1 tablespoon Worcestershire
2 tablespoons shortening
1 can (10¾ ounces) CAMPBELL'S Condensed Cream of Mushroom Soup
½ cup water

Mix *thoroughly* all ingredients except shortening, soup, and water. Shape firmly into 16 meatballs. In skillet, brown meatballs in shortening; pour off fat. Stir in soup and water. Cover; cook over low heat 20 minutes or until done. Stir occasionally.

Makes about 3½ cups

SWEET-AND-SOUR MEATBALLS

1 cup fresh bread cubes
1 cup milk
2 pounds ground beef
⅓ cup finely chopped onion
1 egg
1 teaspoon salt
¼ teaspoon pepper
2 (12-ounce) bottles chili sauce
1 cup SMUCKER'S Grape Jelly
½ cup water
1 cup dairy sour cream
Hot cooked noodles

Soak bread cubes in milk. Combine with ground beef, onion, egg, salt, and pepper. Shape mixture into balls about 1 inch in diameter. In large saucepan, combine chili sauce, Grape Jelly, and water; heat to simmering. Drop meatballs into hot sauce and simmer gently about 1 hour. Skim off excess fat. Just before serving, add sour cream to sauce and heat, but do not boil. Serve on a bed of hot cooked noodles.

6 to 8 servings

MANY WAY MEATBALLS

1 pound ground beef
¼ cup fine dry bread crumbs
¼ cup finely chopped onion
1 egg, slightly beaten
¼ teaspoon salt
1 can (11 ounces) CAMPBELL'S Condensed Cheddar Cheese, Cream of Celery or Mushroom, Golden Mushroom, Tomato or Vegetable Soup
2 to 4 tablespoons water
2 tablespoons chopped parsley

Mix beef, bread crumbs, onion, egg, and salt; shape into 16 meatballs. In skillet, brown meatballs; pour off fat. Stir in soup, water, and parsley. Cover; cook over low heat 20 minutes or until done. Stir occasionally.

Makes about 3½ cups

BEEF PORCUPINES

1 pkg. (8 oz.) GOLDEN GRAIN® Beef Flavor RICE-A-RONI®
1 lb. ground beef
1 egg, beaten
2½ cups water

Combine rice and vermicelli with ground beef and egg. Shape into polpette or small meatballs (approximately 20). Brown on all sides in skillet. Combine contents of flavor packet with water. Pour over meatballs. Cover and simmer 30 minutes. Thicken gravy if desired.

Makes approximately 20 meatballs

OVEN EASY MEATBALLS

1½ lb. ground beef
½ cup soft bread crumbs
1 egg
½ tsp. salt
1 can HUNT'S Manwich Sauce
¼ cup water

Combine first 4 ingredients with ⅓ cup Manwich; form into 1-inch balls. Arrange in shallow baking pan; bake at 450° for 15 minutes. Drain excess fat. Pour remaining Manwich mixed with water over meatballs; bake 15 minutes longer. Turn and baste often.

Makes 6 servings

BURGUNDY BEEF PATTIES

1½ pounds lean ground beef
¾ cup soft bread crumbs
1 can (4 ounces) mushrooms, drained, finely chopped
¼ cup HEINZ Tomato Ketchup
2 tablespoons dry red wine
1 teaspoon onion salt
1 teaspoon HEINZ Worcestershire Sauce
Dash pepper

Combine all ingredients. Form into 6 oval patties, about ¾-inch thick. Broil or grill 6 inches from heat source to desired doneness, turning once.

Makes 6 servings

EASY BEEF HASH

1 cup chopped celery
1 cup chopped onion
¼ cup butter
3 cups cooked diced potatoes
1½ cups cooked diced beef
1 package LAWRY'S® Brown Gravy Mix, prepared according to package directions

Conventional Method: Sauté celery and onions in butter until tender. Add potatoes and beef; mix together thoroughly. Place mixture in a shallow baking dish and pour prepared Brown Gravy over top. Bake in a 350°F. oven 30 minutes.

Microwave Oven Method: In 2-quart glass casserole dish or 8 × 8 × 2-inch glass baking dish, place butter. Microwave on HIGH for about 45 seconds to melt butter. Stir in celery and onions; cover with plastic wrap, venting one corner. Microwave on HIGH for 4 to 5 minutes. Add potatoes and beef; mix together thoroughly. Pour prepared Brown Gravy over top. Cover and microwave on HIGH for 15 minutes, turning dish after first 8 minutes. *Makes 4 servings*

BEEF SAVOY

2 cups leftover roast beef slices
½ cup butter
½ lb. mushrooms
2 cups thick gravy
½ cup orange juice
1 cup THE CHRISTIAN BROTHERS® Pinot Noir
Steamed rice

Sauté beef slices lightly in butter; remove. Sauté mushrooms lightly, add gravy, orange juice and wine. Simmer 5 minutes; stir in beef. Serve over rice. *Serves 4-6*

QUICK BEEF ROULADES

2 cups seasoned mashed potatoes
1 tablespoon chopped parsley
1 teaspoon finely chopped onion
8 thin slices (about 8 ounces) cooked beef
1 can (10¼ ounces) FRANCO-AMERICAN Beef Gravy

In bowl, combine potatoes, parsley and onion. Place about 2 tablespoons potato mixture near center of each piece of meat. Roll up; tuck in ends and fasten with toothpicks. In skillet, arrange roll-ups in gravy. Heat; stir occasionally. *Makes 4 servings*

HEARTY BEEFY ENCHILADAS

1½ cups cooked shredded beef
2 cups (8 oz.) shredded sharp Cheddar cheese, divided usage
¾ cup chopped onion
1 can (4 oz.) OLD EL PASO® Chopped Green Chilies
1 can (10¾ oz.) cream of mushroom soup
1 can (10¾ oz.) tomato soup
1 can (10 oz.) OLD EL PASO® Hot Enchilada Sauce
12 OLD EL PASO® Corn Tortillas

Combine beef, ½ cup cheese, onion and green chilies; set aside. Combine soups and enchilada sauce. Fry tortillas in hot oil to soften, a few seconds on each side. Drain on paper towels. Preheat oven to 350°F. Top each tortilla with one heaping tablespoon of meat mixture. Roll and place seam-side down in a 13 × 9-inch baking dish. Pour sauce over and top with remaining cheese. Bake for 25 to 30 minutes.

Makes 6 servings

Microcook enchiladas on 70% power for 14 to 16 minutes or until heated through. Turn twice during cooking time.

Pork

ORANGE HONEY BAKED HAM

1 ham, 6 to 10 pounds
Whole cloves
1 can (6-oz.) frozen orange
concentrate, thawed
1¾ cups water
½ cup SUE BEE® Honey
1 teaspoon dry mustard
½ teaspoon salt
1 cinnamon stick
⅛ teaspoon nutmeg
3 tablespoons corn starch
2 oranges, sectioned

Score ham and stud with cloves. Bake at 350° ten to fifteen minutes per pound (or per directions on wrapper). While ham is baking, combine orange juice concentrate, water, honey, dry mustard, salt, cinnamon stick and nutmeg in saucepan. Blend corn starch with ¼ cup of mixture; return to saucepan. Cook over medium heat, stirring constantly, until mixture thickens and comes to a boil. Boil one minute. Remove from heat and cool. Brush ham with small amount of sauce two or three times during last 30 minutes of baking time. Add orange slices to remaining sauce, reheat, and serve with ham.

GIFT WRAPPED HAM WITH RAISIN WINE SAUCE

1 can (3 lb.) OSCAR MAYER
Jubilee Ham (oblong)

Pastry:
1 package (9½ oz.) pie crust mix
1 teaspoon dry mustard
½ teaspoon sage
1 egg, beaten
Paprika

Preheat oven to 400°. Remove ham from can. Add mustard and sage to dry pie crust mix; then prepare according to package directions. Roll pastry out to a 17-inch square. Place ham in center. Wrap as you would a package. Moisten edges with cold water and press together firmly to seal. Place seam-side down on baking sheet. Cut strips for ribbon and bow with leftover pastry. Put on ham. Brush pastry with egg. Sprinkle paprika on ribbon and bow. Bake 1 hour. Serve with Raisin Wine Sauce.*

Makes 12 servings

*RAISIN WINE SAUCE

¼ cup sugar
3 tablespoons cornstarch
1 teaspoon dry mustard
1 cup dry red wine
½ cup water
¼ cup seedless raisins
1 jar (10 oz.) currant jelly

In a saucepan, stir together sugar, cornstarch and mustard. Add wine, water and raisins. Cook over low heat 5 minutes, stirring occasionally. Add currant jelly and heat until jelly melts.

Makes 2 cups

POLISH HAM EN CROUTE WITH BURGUNDY

10 pounds fully cooked KRAKUS/
ATALANTA/POLKA Polish Ham
¾ cup Burgundy
3 tablespoons honey
6 cups unsifted flour
¼ teaspoon powdered juniper
berries
4 teaspoons baking powder
¼ teaspoon ground sage
1¾ teaspoons salt
¾ teaspoons dry mustard
1 cup lard
1½ cups cold milk

Place ham in deep roasting pan, pour wine over ham. Bake at 350°F. for 2½ hours, basting frequently with wine in pan. Lay ham on wooden board and carefully slice into thin slices. Replace slices to reshape ham. Combine honey and 3 tablespoons wine from pan; brush over ham.

In large bowl, combine flour, berries, baking powder, sage, salt and mustard. Cut in lard using pastry blender or two knives until mixture resembles coarse meal. Stir in enough milk to make soft but not sticky dough. Roll out on lightly floured board to ¼-inch thickness. Fold over reshaped ham covering it completely. Use scraps to make leaves or other designs to decorate top of ham.

Bake on cookie sheet at 425°F. for 10 minutes to set pastry. Reduce heat to 350°F. and bake 15 minutes longer, or until crust is delicately browned, brushing the crust twice with cold milk.

Serve ham hot or cold, with sauce, like wine sauce from pan if hot; or chilled cranberry sauce or jelly with applesauce flavored with a little grated horseradish, if served cold.

BONELESS SMOKED HAM—CUMBERLAND FRUIT SAUCE

7 to 10-pound boneless "fully-cooked" smoked ham
1 can (30 ounces) fruit cocktail
¼ cup frozen orange juice
concentrate
¼ cup currant jelly
2 tablespoons sherry or port wine
¼ teaspoon ground ginger
2 tablespoons cornstarch
2 tablespoons lemon juice

Insert rotisserie rod lengthwise through center of ham.* Balance ham and tighten spit forks so ham turns with rod. Insert meat thermometer at an angle so tip is in center of ham, but not resting in fat or on rod. Place on rotisserie and cook at low to moderate temperature.

To prepare Cumberland Fruit Sauce, drain fruit cocktail, reserve 1½ cups syrup and combine with orange juice concentrate, jelly, wine and ginger in saucepan. Heat until jelly melts, stirring occasionally. Blend cornstarch and lemon juice until smooth and combine with jelly mixture. Cook, stirring constantly, until mixture thickens. Brush ham with sauce during last 15 minutes cooking time. Cook ham to 140°F. (Allow 15 to 18 minutes per pound.) Add fruit cocktail to remaining sauce, heat 1 to 2 minutes and serve hot with ham.

*To cook ham on covered grill, follow manufacturer's instructions.

Favorite recipe from Pork Industry Group National Live Stock & Meat Board

HAM BAKED IN CHAMPAGNE

1 whole ready-to-bake ham
Whole cloves
1 bottle Maison JACQUIN'S Champagne
1 cup brown sugar
½ cup Dijon mustard
¼ cup JACQUIN'S Apricot, Peach or Cherry Brandy

Remove rind from ham and trim away excess fat. Score remaining fat in diamond shapes and dot the diamonds with whole cloves. Place ham in a roasting pan and pour Maison JACQUIN'S Champagne over it. Put in a 300° oven to bake for 15 minutes per pound; baste occasionally while baking. Meanwhile, make glaze by mixing brown sugar, mustard and JACQUIN'S fruit flavored brandy. When ham is done, remove it from the oven and apply glaze; return ham to oven, increase heat to 425° and bake 20 to 25 minutes longer to set the glaze.

BEER BAKED HAM

1 thirteen-pound canned KRAKUS/ATALANTA/POLKA Polish Ham
Whole cloves
2 teaspoons dry mustard
½ cup molasses
2 cups beer
2½ tablespoons cornstarch
2 tablespoons wine vinegar
¼ cup ground ginger
¾ cup plumped raisins
Peach slices

Remove top from can and heat ham in 350°F. oven until gelatin softens. Invert can on rack in baking pan. Punch holes in bottom of can and remove; pour off liquid. Score ham into diamond pattern and stud with cloves. Combine mustard and molasses and spread over ham. Bake one hour, basting with beer. Remove ham and keep warm.

Cook juices till reduced to 1½ cups. Blend cornstarch into ½ cup water. Stir into pan juices and cook, stirring until thickened and smooth. Add wine vinegar and ginger and simmer several minutes. Stir in raisins. Serve sauce over ham. Garnish with peach slices.

Makes 24 servings

HAM WITH FRUIT STUFFING

1 5-pound smoked picnic ham
1 cup seedless raisins
2 cups pitted prunes
2 cups dried apricots
2 cups HOLLAND HOUSE® Red Cooking Wine

Have the butcher bone ham. Combine fruit and wine in a large mixing bowl; soak at least 4 hours or overnight, stirring occasionally. Fill the cavity of the boned ham with stuffing. Bake in 350° oven 2½ hours. *Serves about 8*

HAM 'N YAM GLAZIN' RECIPE

1 can (5 lb.) RATH® Hickory Smoked Boneless Ham
Whole cloves
1½ cups light brown sugar, firmly packed
3 tablespoons cornstarch
1 can (6 oz.) frozen orange juice concentrate, thawed
1¼ cups water
¼ cup golden seedless raisins
3 cans (17 oz. each) small whole yams, drained
1 can (11 oz.) mandarin oranges, drained
Spicy Pecans*

To Prepare Ham: Heat ham on wire rack as directed on can. Last ½ hour of heating time, remove ham from oven; score fat surface in diamond pattern. Pour over ¾ cup of glaze (see below); stud with whole cloves. Heat 30 minutes more.

Makes 14/4-oz. servings

To Prepare Glaze: In small saucepan, blend brown sugar and cornstarch. Stir in thawed orange juice concentrate and water. Bring to boiling, stirring constantly; boil 2 minutes, stirring, or until glaze is thickened and clear. Measure ¾ cup of glaze for ham. Add raisins to remaining 1¾ cups and set aside for yams.

Makes 2½ cups

To Prepare Yams: Place yams and mandarin oranges in shallow 2-qt.

casserole. Pour over glaze with raisins; arrange Spicy Pecans atop. Bake with RATH® Ham at 325°F. for 30 minutes.

Makes 6 to 8 servings

*Spicy Pecans: In small fry pan, melt 2 teaspoons butter or margarine; stir in ⅓ cup pecan halves. Drop into small bag containing mixture of 2 teaspoons granulated sugar and ¾ teaspoon cinnamon. Close bag; shake until pecans are coated.

APRICOT COCONUT GLAZED HAM

1 whole smoked ham, about 10 lbs.
Whole cloves
1 can (12 ozs.) apricot nectar
½ cup COCO CASA™ Cream of Coconut
Grated rind of 1 orange
Dash cloves

Remove heavy rind from ham and score fat with a sharp knife into diamonds. Press a whole clove into each diamond. Roast ham in a preheated 350° oven for 1 hour. In a bowl, mix remaining ingredients. Spoon some of the mixture over ham and continue roasting for another hour. Continue spooning cream of coconut mixture over ham every 15 minutes.

Serves 10 to 12

GLAZED HAM AND RAISIN SAUCE

2 cans (10¼ ounces *each*) FRANCO-AMERICAN Beef Gravy
¼ cup packed brown sugar
1 teaspoon grated orange rind
5-pound canned ham
½ cup raisins
1 tablespoon lemon juice

In bowl, combine gravy, brown sugar and orange rind. In shallow baking pan, bake ham at 325°F. for 1 hour. Brush ham with gravy mixture; bake 30 minutes more (18 minutes per pound or until internal temperature reaches 140°F.). Remove ham to serving platter. Add remaining gravy mixture, raisins and lemon juice to roasting pan. Cook over low heat 10 minutes, stirring to loosen browned bits. Serve with ham.

Makes 8 to 10 servings

BAKED HAM GOURMET

10-12 lb. smoked ham
¾ cup SOUTHERN COMFORT®
Cloves
1 cup brown sugar
2 Tbsp. dry mustard

Cook ham according to directions. 30 minutes before ham is done, remove rind and score fat. Cover with mixture of ¼ cup SOUTHERN COMFORT® and brown sugar; stud with cloves. Add mustard to remaining SOUTHERN COMFORT® , pour over ham and continue baking, basting occasionally.

HOSTESS® HAM WITH LEMON SAUCE

4 pound can SWIFT PREMIUM®
HOSTESS® Ham
1 cup brown sugar
¼ cup fresh lemon juice
1 teaspoon dry mustard
1 teaspoon Worcestershire sauce

Place ham on rack in a shallow open pan. Add ½ cup water. Heat in a 325°F. oven for 1 hour. Turn ham over and continue to heat 1½ hours. In a small saucepan combine remaining ingredients. Heat just to boiling. Spoon over ham during last 30 minutes cooking time. Serve remaining sauce with ham. Garnish with candied lemon peel.

MANDARINE BAKED HAM

6-8 lb. canned boneless ham
1 can (11 oz.) mandarin oranges
¼ cup MANDARINE NAPOLEON
¼ cup brown sugar, packed
1 tablespoon lemon juice
1 tablespoon mustard (preferably Dijon)
1 teaspoon Worcestershire sauce

Trim excess fat from ham and heat in oven according to directions on can. About 40 minutes before ham is done, drain syrup from mandarin oranges. Set oranges aside. Combine ¼ cup syrup with remaining ingredients. Baste ham

with mixture, repeat after 15 minutes. Bake 10 minutes longer, then arrange oranges on top of ham and baste with remaining mixture. Bake about 15 minutes more or until well glazed.

12 to 15 servings

APPLE STUFFED HAM SLICES

2 KRAKUS/ATALANTA/POLKA
Polish Ham slices, ½ inch thick
¼ cup chopped onion
¼ cup chopped green pepper
3 tablespoons butter or margarine
2 cups croutons
1 cup finely diced unpared apple
¼ teaspoon poultry seasoning
¼ teaspoon salt
⅛ teaspoon pepper
2 tablespoons orange juice
Apple rings

In saucepan, cook onion and green pepper in 2 tablespoons butter until tender. Add croutons, apple, poultry seasoning, salt and pepper. Slash edges of ham slices at 2 inch intervals. Place one slice in greased shallow baking dish. Top with stuffing and remaining ham slice. Bake at 350°F. for 45 minutes, basting several times with orange juice and remaining 1 tablespoon butter. Garnish with apple rings.

Makes 6 servings

SWISS HAM KABOBS

Drain a 20-oz. can of pineapple chunks, reserving 2 tablespoons of juice. Cut 1-lb. RATH® Hickory Smoked Boneless Ham into ¼ inch slices and then into 3½ × 1½ inch strips. Cut ½-lb. of Swiss cheese into 1½ × ½ × ½ inch sticks. Roll the ham strips around a cheese stick. Alternate ham rolls, pineapple chunks, and green pepper chunks on skewer. For marinade, combine ½ cup orange marmalade, 1 teaspoon prepared mustard, 2 tablespoons reserved pineapple juice, and ¼ teaspoon cloves. Broil kabobs, brushing frequently with marinade. Cook, turning occasionally, until ham is light brown and cheese melted.

Makes 4 servings

♥ JOHN MORRELL ®

HAM SLICES IN CHAMPAGNE SAUCE

6 to 8 slices JOHN MORRELL®
Fully Cooked Ham, cut ⅜-inch thick
2 cans (11 oz. each) mandarin orange sections, drained
2 cups orange juice
3 tablespoons cornstarch
3 tablespoons sugar
1 cup champagne
2 tablespoons orange Curacao liqueur (optional)
½ cup pecan halves

In a saucepan, combine orange juice with sugar and cornstarch until well blended. Cook over medium-low heat, stirring constantly, until mixture thickens and begins to boil. Remove from heat, blend in champagne and orange liqueur. Add oranges and pecans. Arrange ham slices in chafing dish or skillet. Pour thickened sauce over ham; baste several times while warming over low heat.

Yield: 6 to 8 servings

HAM HAWAIIAN

Chicken Vegetable Homemade
SOUP STARTER™
4 cups water
2½ cups thin strips (1½ inches long) fully cooked or canned ham
½ cup uncooked converted rice
2 tablespoons brown sugar
1½ teaspoons vinegar
½ teaspoon dry mustard
⅛ teaspoon ginger
1½ cups water
8¼ ounce can pineapple chunks, drained and reserve liquid
½ green pepper cut into ½ inch squares

In large skillet combine SOUP STARTER™ ingredients and 4 cups water. Cover and simmer 30 minutes. Drain off liquid. Stir in ham and rice. Combine sugar, vinegar, seasonings, 1½ cups water and reserved pineapple juice. Cover and simmer 20 minutes. During last 5 minutes add pineapple and green pepper.

Yield: 6 cups

SCOTCH GLAZED HAM STEAK

1 fully-cooked ham steak, 1 inch thick
2 tablespoons brown sugar
2 teaspoons prepared mustard
⅛ teaspoon ginger
3 tablespoons JOHNNIE WALKER Red

Slash outside fat of ham steak to prevent curling. Combine sugar, mustard, ginger and enough JOHNNIE WALKER Red to make a paste. Warm remaining Scotch. Broil ham steak about 5 minutes until browned. Turn, broil second side about 4 minutes. Spread with brown sugar mixture, broil 1-2 minutes longer, until glazed. Place ham on heated serving plate. Ignite warmed Scotch, pour flaming over ham. Serve when flames go out, spooning sauce on each portion.

2 to 3 servings

BEANS AND HAM ALOHA

1 28 ounce can B&M® Brick Oven Baked Beans
1 1½ pound fully cooked ham steak, cut into bite-size pieces
2 pineapple rings, cut in halves
2 tablespoons brown sugar

In a large bowl, combine beans and ham. Pour into a 2 quart casserole. Top with pineapple slices and sprinkle with brown sugar. Bake at 350°F. for 30 minutes.

Makes 6 servings

THE ORIGINAL WORCESTERSHIRE

CRANBERRY HAM

1 cup packaged herb seasoned bread stuffing
½ cup canned whole cranberry sauce
¼ cup finely chopped celery
5 teaspoons LEA & PERRINS Worcestershire Sauce, divided
½ teaspoon salt
2 ready-to-eat ham steaks, ½-inch thick

In a small mixing bowl combine bread stuffing with cranberry sauce, celery, 3 teaspoons of the LEA & PERRINS and salt; mix well. Brush both sides of each steak

with the remaining 2 teaspoons LEA & PERRINS. Place one steak in a greased baking dish. Spread the stuffing evenly over steak and top with the second steak. Bake uncovered in a preheated moderate oven (350°F.) 1 hour or until lightly browned.

Yield: 6 portions

HAM EN CROUTE

2 pounds ground smoked ham
2 tablespoons minced onions
1 egg
1 cup drained crushed pineapple
¼ teaspoon ground cloves
1 package (10 ounces) PEPPERIDGE FARM® Frozen Patty Shells
1 egg, well beaten

In a bowl mix ham, onion, egg, pineapple and cloves. Shape mixture into 6 ham patties, 1 inch thick. Thaw Patty Shells. Roll out on a floured surface making dough large enough to cover sides and top of each ham patty. Place ham patties on a greased shallow baking pan. Place pieces of rolled dough over ham patties fitting dough over top and down the sides but not the bottom of the ham patties. Brush with egg. Bake in a preheated hot oven (400°F.) for 30 to 35 minutes or until pastry is richly browned and puffed. Serve hot, garnished with thick sautéed mushroom slices and your favorite mushroom sauce, if desired.

Serves 6

PORK CHOPS WITH APPLE RAISIN SAUCE

1 bag SUCCESS® Rice
4 lean pork chops
Salt, pepper
1 tablespoon vegetable oil
4 slices onion
1¼ cups apple juice
¼ cup catsup
1 tablespoon prepared mustard
2 packets instant beef broth or bouillon cubes
½ cup raisins
1 tablespoon cornstarch

Cook bag of rice according to package directions. Drain and keep warm. While rice is cooking, season pork chops to taste with salt and pepper. In 10 inch skillet, brown pork chops in oil on both sides. Remove pork chops. Stir in

onion and sauté until transparent; add 1 cup of the apple juice, catsup, mustard and beef broth. Mix well. Return the pork chops to skillet and add the raisins. Cover and simmer 20 minutes. To serve, empty rice onto platter and arrange pork chops over it. Combine remaining apple juice with the cornstarch and stir into sauce in skillet. Bring to boil, then pour over pork chops.

Makes 4 servings (1 pork chop and ½ cup rice)

JOHNNY APPLE CHOPS

4 large pork chops
Salt and pepper
1 cup apple juice or cider
1 cup water
¼ cup raisins
4 slices lemon
1 envelope FRENCH'S® Brown Gravy Mix

Brown chops in medium-size skillet; season with salt and pepper. Pour off excess fat. Add apple juice and water; cover and simmer 30 minutes. Add raisins; place a lemon slice on each chop. Simmer, covered, 15 minutes longer or until tender. Remove chops and add gravy mix to skillet. Bring to a boil, stirring occasionally. Spoon gravy over pork chops.

4 servings

Microwave Johnny Apple Chops: Arrange chops in single layer in shallow baking dish with meatiest portions toward outside edges. Top with lemon slices. Add ⅔ cup apple juice and ⅓ cup water. Cover with plastic wrap and microwave on HIGH 5 minutes. Reduce power to MEDIUM; microwave 15 to 18 minutes. Let stand, covered, while preparing gravy. Pour 1 cup pan juices into 2-cup glass measure; discard remaining juices. Stir in raisins and gravy mix. Microwave on HIGH 1 to 1½ minutes, or until thickened, stirring after 45 seconds and at end of cooking. Season chops with salt and pepper; serve with gravy.

Micro Tip: For moist and tender pork, cook minimum time. Check for doneness after standing time.

PORK CHOPS IN PLUM SAUCE

4 loin pork chops, 1½" thick
Salt
Pepper
Sage
Flour
Butter

1 jar (7¾-oz.) plums with tapioca (junior food)
1 teaspoon grated lemon rind
¼ teaspoon cinnamon
⅛ teaspoon cloves
½ cup TAYLOR New York State Tawny Port

Trim fat from chops. Season both sides with salt, pepper, and sage; coat well with flour. Brown in butter in skillet over medium heat.

While chops are browning, combine plums, grated lemon rind, cinnamon, cloves, and Tawny Port. Pour sauce over chops. Reduce heat to simmer; cover. Continue cooking until tender, 1½ to 2 hours; baste occasionally. Remove cover. Increase heat, if necessary, 5 to 10 minutes to thicken sauce. Transfer chops to platter or individual plates. Spoon sauce over chops. Garnish with fresh parsley and whole spiced crabapples.

4 servings

BAKED PORK CHOPS

4 lean pork chops about 1¼ inches thick
½ cup flour
Salt and pepper
2 tablespoons butter
MR. & MRS. "T"® Bloody Mary Mix to cover

Trim off all fat from pork chops. Put flour, salt and pepper into plastic bag. Add chops and shake until well coated. Lightly brown chops in melted butter. Remove from pan and place chops close together in shallow baking dish. Barely cover chops with MR. & MRS. "T"® Bloody Mary Mix. Cover baking dish with foil and bake for 45 minutes in moderate oven. Remove foil and cook for 15 minutes longer. Serve chops with sauce from dish and sprinkle with chopped parsley. This dish needs no extra seasoning. *Serves 4*

NO-FUSS PORK CHOPS

1 cup applesauce
¼ cup KIKKOMAN Soy Sauce
⅛ teaspoon onion powder
6 pork chops, cut ¾ to 1-inch thick

Brown pork chops on both sides over medium-high heat. Place in shallow baking pan (not glass), side by side. Combine remaining ingredients; spoon evenly over chops. Cover pan well with foil. Place in oven; turn heat control to 350°F. Bake 45 minutes; remove foil and bake 15 minutes longer, or until chops are tender.

Makes 6 servings

SATURDAY NIGHT SUPPER

4 center cut pork chops, thinly sliced
1 tablespoon oil
1 28 ounce can B&M® Brick Oven Baked Beans
2 tablespoons apple jelly
2 teaspoons water
8 apple slices
Cinnamon

In a skillet, brown chops evenly in oil, about 10 minutes each side. Drain chops on paper towels. Pour beans into a 2 quart casserole and place chops on top of beans. Bake at 350°F. for 45 minutes. In a small bowl, combine jelly and water. Baste chops with this mixture and arrange apple slices on top. Sprinkle with cinnamon. Return to oven and continue baking for another 15 minutes.

Makes 4 servings

FANTASTIC PORK CHOPS

In skillet, brown 4 (¾-inch thick) loin or rib pork chops in 1 tablespoon shortening. Drain excess fat. Season chops lightly with salt and pepper. Pour 1 jar (12 ounces) HEINZ Homestyle Pork Gravy over chops. Cover; simmer 40 to 45 minutes or until pork chops are tender; baste occasionally. *Makes 4 servings* *(about 1⅓ cups gravy)*

TANGY BAKED STUFFED PORK CHOPS

1½ to 2 cups favorite prepared stuffing
6 double pork chops, slit for stuffing
1 tablespoon shortening
Salt and pepper
½ cup HEINZ 57 Sauce
⅓ cup water

Place stuffing in pockets of chops; secure with toothpicks or string. Brown in shortening; sprinkle with salt and pepper. Place chops in shallow baking pan. Combine 57 Sauce and water; pour over chops. Cover pan with foil. Bake in 350°F. oven, 1 hour 15 minutes or until chops are tender. Remove toothpicks from chops before serving. Skim excess fat from sauce; thicken sauce with flour/water mixture, if desired.

Makes 6 servings
(about 1½ cups sauce)

ORANGE GLAZED PORK CHOPS

4 double cut loin pork chops
2 tablespoons chopped onion
¼ cup butter or margarine
⅓ cup orange juice
½ teaspoon orange rind
1 tablespoon chopped pecans
¼ teaspoon salt
2 cups PEPPERIDGE FARM® Corn Bread Stuffing
¼ cup corn syrup
½ teaspoon orange rind

Have butcher make a slit or pocket in side of each pork chop. Sauté onions in butter until tender. Stir in orange juice and rind, pecans, salt and stuffing. Season pork chops with salt and pepper and fill pockets with stuffing mixture. Skewer. Place in a shallow baking pan, cover with foil and bake at 375°F. for 1 hour. Uncover, and continue baking 30 minutes, while brushing frequently with orange glaze. Make glaze by combining the last two ingredients.

Serves 4

STUFFED DOUBLE PORK CHOPS
(Microwave Recipe)

⅓ cup water
¼ cup seedless dark raisins
3 tablespoons butter or margarine
1 cup packaged stuffing mix
8 rib pork chops (about 1¾ pounds) cut ½-inch thick
Dried leaf sage
HOLLAND HOUSE® Microwave Browning Sauce for Pork

Combine water, raisins and butter in an 8 × 10-inch microwave oven-proof baking dish. Microwave on medium power 1 minute. Remove. Place stuffing in small bowl; stir in raisin mixture. Place 4 pork chops in baking dish, arranging chops with bones in the center of the dish. Place ¼ cup stuffing on each chop; top with remaining chops. Lightly sprinkle with sage. Brush with browning sauce. Cover dish with plastic wrap, turning back 2 inches at one edge for vent. Microwave on medium power 7 minutes. Turn dish. Microwave on medium 7 minutes longer. Remove dish from oven. Remove plastic wrap. Turn chops over and change positions, keeping meaty areas to edge and bones to center. Brush with browning sauce. Microwave on medium, uncovered, 7 minutes. Turn dish. Microwave on medium, uncovered, 7 minutes longer or until chops are done.

Yield: 4 servings

CALIFORNIA GOLDEN SHERRY PORK ROAST

12 to 14 pitted prunes (about 4 ounces)
¾ cup THE CHRISTIAN BROTHERS® Golden Sherry
3 pounds lean boned pork loin
¼ cup honey
3 tablespoons soy sauce
1 small onion, grated
1½ tablespoons finely chopped crystallized ginger
½ teaspoon salt
¼ teaspoon pepper
Water
1 tablespoon cornstarch

In small bowl combine prunes with enough sherry to cover. Set aside 1 to 2 hours. Make a slit lengthwise about 2½ inches deep in boned side of pork; fill with drained prunes, reserving sherry. Tie pork around in several places to make a firm roll. In stainless steel pan or glass dish large enough to hold pork, combine reserved sherry (there should be about ½ cup), honey, soy sauce, onion, ginger, salt and pepper; blend thoroughly. Add pork; marinate, covered, 2 to 4 hours, turning occasionally.

Place pork slit-side-down on rack in roasting pan containing 1 cup water; reserve marinade. Roast in 350 degree oven basting frequently with reserved marinade, 1½ to 2 hours until meat thermometer inserted in center of pork registers 160 degrees. (As pork roasts, add water to moisten pan as needed; cover pork lightly with aluminum foil if necessary to prevent overbrowning.) Remove pork to serving platter; cover lightly and keep warm.

Remove rack from roasting pan and place pan over low heat. Combine cornstarch with 2 tablespoons water; add to contents of roasting pan with any remaining marinade, stirring, to thicken sauce and loosen brown particles. Stir in enough additional water to make a syrupy sauce. Strain and serve hot with sliced pork.

Makes 8 servings

First Prize Winner THE CHRISTIAN BROTHERS® contest

PORK LOIN ROAST—CRAB APPLE GLAZE AND GARNISH

4 to 6-pound pork loin roast
Crab Apple Glaze* and Garnish

Have the meat retailer loosen the chine (back) bone by sawing across the rib bones. Place roast, fat side up, on rack in open roasting pan. Insert roast meat thermometer so the bulb is centered in the thickest part. Make certain bulb does not rest in fat or on bone. Do not add water. Do not cover. Roast in a slow oven (325°F.) until the meat thermometer registers 170°F. Allow 2½ to 3 hours (30 to 40 minutes per pound) for roasting. During last 20 to 30 minutes cooking time, brush roast occasionally with Crab Apple Glaze. When roasting is finished, the back bone can be removed easily by running the carving knife along the edge of the roast before meat is carved.

Garnish with crab apples, heated if desired.

*CRAB APPLE GLAZE

1 jar (16 ounces) crab apples
⅓ cup brown sugar
1 tablespoon lemon juice

Drain crab apples and combine liquid with brown sugar and lemon juice in a saucepan. Bring to boil, stirring to dissolve sugar, and cook slowly 5 to 8 minutes.

Favorite recipe from Pork Industry Group National Live Stock & Meat Board

CHERRY GLAZED PORK ROAST

4 pounds pork loin roast, bone in
1 can (21 oz.) THANK YOU® Brand Cherry Pie Filling
1 Tbsp. lemon juice
2 Tbsp. rum (optional)
Pinch of ginger, clove
⅛ tsp. garlic salt, cinnamon

Place pork roast on rack in roasting pan. Roast, uncovered, at 325°F. until meat thermometer registers 170°F., about 2½ hours. Meanwhile, combine remaining ingredients and baste roast several times during last 20 minutes cooking time. Heat the remaining sauce on range or in microwave. Serve with roast.

Makes 6 servings

BRAISED PORK SHOULDER

1 boned, rolled pork shoulder, about 4 pounds
¼ cup flour
1 tablespoon HERB-OX Instant Vegetarian Style Bouillon
1½ cups water
6 potatoes, peeled and quartered
6 carrots, peeled and quartered
½ teaspoon thyme

Trim fat from pork, lightly grease stew pan. Sprinkle meat with flour mixed with instant bouillon, brown on all sides. Add water, bring to boil, reduce heat. Simmer, covered, about 2½ hours, until meat is tender. Add more water if necessary. Add potatoes, carrots and thyme, simmer ½ hour longer, until vegetables are tender. Adjust seasoning of sauce with more instant bouillon.

Makes 6 servings

SUN COUNTRY SMOKED PORK

½ cup firmly packed brown sugar
2 tablespoons ARGO® / KINGSFORD'S® Corn Starch
¼ teaspoon ground cinnamon
¼ teaspoon ground cloves
3 cups orange juice
6 small sweet potatoes, pared and halved
2 cups or 1 package (11 oz.) dried mixed fruit
1 (2 lb.) smoked pork shoulder roll (butt)

In saucepan mix first 4 ingredients. Gradually stir in orange juice until smooth. Bring to boil over medium heat, stirring constantly, and boil 1 minute. In 13 × 9 × 2-inch baking pan place potatoes and fruit around meat; pour orange sauce over all. Bake in 325°F. oven, basting occasionally, 2 hours or until meat thermometer reaches 170°F. and potatoes are tender.

Makes 6 servings

WELCH'S® SWEET AND SOUR PORK

1½ pounds lean pork, cut into 1-inch cubes
1 tablespoon oil
1¾ cups water
⅓ cup soy sauce
1 teaspoon salt
⅛ teaspoon pepper
1 clove garlic, minced
1 can (6 ounces) Frozen WELCHADE Grape Drink Concentrate
¼ cup cider vinegar
¼ cup sugar
¼ cup cornstarch
1 can (8 ounces) pineapple chunks, undrained
½ cup coarsely chopped green pepper
½ cup green onions, cut into 1-inch pieces
2 tablespoons sherry (optional)

In large skillet, brown pork in oil. Add water, soy sauce, salt, pepper and garlic. Cover and cook over low heat until meat is tender, about 45 minutes. Add Frozen WELCHADE Grape Drink Concentrate, vinegar and sugar. Stir in cornstarch. Bring to a boil, stirring, until mixture is thickened and smooth. Add remaining ingredients; simmer 5 minutes longer. Serve over cooked rice.

Makes 6 servings

S&W
ITALIAN BEAN AND PORK CASSEROLE

2 lbs. lean pork, thinly sliced
4 Italian style sausages, quartered
4 Tbsp. olive oil
1 onion, thinly sliced
2 stalks celery, chopped
2 carrots, chopped
2 cloves garlic, minced (optional)
2 sprigs parsley, minced
1 tsp. oregano
½ cup red or white wine, or water
1 can (15 oz.) S&W White Kidney Beans, drained and rinsed, salt and pepper to taste

Brown pork and sausages in hot oil; set aside. In same oil, gently sauté onion for 5 minutes, then add celery, carrots, garlic, and parsley. Continue cooking for 5 minutes. Return pork to casserole, and add wine and spices. Bring to boil and cook over moderate heat for 45 minutes, or until pork is tender. Add beans and simmer 10 minutes longer. Serve with buttered noodles, or mashed potatoes. *Yield: 6-8 servings*

PORK 'N' POTATO SKILLET

1½ pounds pork shoulder steaks
1 tablespoon oil
1 cup chopped celery
1 package FRENCH'S® Scalloped Potatoes
2 cups water
½ cup milk
½ cup mayonnaise
1 tomato, cut in wedges
1 green pepper, sliced

Cut pork into small cubes; cook in oil in large skillet until well browned and cooked. Add celery; continue to cook, stirring frequently, until celery is tender but not brown. Pour off excess fat. Add contents of potato package, including seasoning mix, water, milk, and mayonnaise, stirring until well mixed. Cover and simmer 15 to 20 minutes, stirring occasionally, or until potatoes are tender and pork is thoroughly cooked. Arrange tomato and pepper around edge of skillet; cook 5 minutes longer.

5 to 6 servings

CARIBBEAN PORK

1 can (1 lb. 4 oz.) DOLE® Sliced Pineapple in Syrup
1 pound boneless pork loin, cubed
2 tablespoons vegetable oil
1 large onion, chopped
1 clove garlic, pressed
1½ cups water
½ teaspoon grated lime peel
1 tablespoon lime juice
1 teaspoon thyme, crumbled
1 teaspoon salt
⅛ teaspoon cayenne pepper
2 teaspoons cornstarch
1 medium green bell pepper, julienne-cut
1 medium red bell pepper, julienne-cut
6 cups BUD OF CALIFORNIA® Salad Lettuce

Drain pineapple, reserving syrup. Brown pork in hot oil. Add onion and garlic. Sauté until onion is soft. Stir in reserved syrup, water, lime peel and juice, thyme, salt and cayenne. Cover, simmer 20 minutes. Mix small amount of pan juices with cornstarch. Pour back into pan. Add bell peppers and pineapple; cook until sauce boils and thickens. Arrange lettuce on serving platter. Spoon pork mixture over all. *Makes 4 servings*

MAN-STYLE PORK ROAST

7-oz. package CREAMETTES® Macaroni (2 cups uncooked)
2 large onions, sliced
1 cup celery, chopped
2 tablespoons butter or margarine
2½ pounds pork shoulder, cut in strips, OR 2 cups cooked pork
Salt and pepper
1 can (1-lb. or 2 cups) whole tomatoes, cut up
1 can (1-lb. or 2 cups) lima beans, drained
2 cans (4-oz. each) mushrooms with liquid

Prepare CREAMETTES® according to package directions. Drain. Sauté onions and celery in butter. Remove from pan. Season pork with salt and pepper; brown slowly until tender, about 30 minutes. Drain excess fat. Combine all ingredients in 3-quart casserole and bake, covered, at 325° for 30-40 minutes.

8 to 10 servings

BARBECUED SPARE RIBS

Barbecue Sauce:
½ cup tomato sauce
½ cup COCO CASA™ Cream of Coconut
4 Tbsp. white vinegar
½ tsp. onion powder
½ tsp. ground ginger
2 cloves garlic, crushed
3 Tbsp. oil
1 tsp. salt

Mix all ingredients and keep refrigerated.

Yields: 1½ cups

Barbecued Spare Ribs: Place whole ribs in baking pan. Cover with hot water, bake in preheated 400° oven for ½ hour. Drain, brush with barbecue sauce and cut into individual ribs. Let marinate for 1 or 2 hours. Broil ribs under preheated broiler, at bottom third of oven, for 10 minutes on each side. Baste frequently with sauce.

COUNTRY COMFORT® RIBS

3-5 lbs. spare ribs (1 to 1½ lbs. per serving)
Barbecue Sauce (recipe follows)

The secret to our savory barbecued ribs: skin 'em first. Remove breast bone. Turn ribs over and remove skirt. Save skirt and cook as appetizer. Slip paring knife under skin at end of rib and separate from bone. Grip skin with paper towel and peel back from complete slab. Scrape off fat between bones with spoon. Cook in charcoal-water smoker or on grill, following manufacturer's instructions.

BARBECUE SAUCE

1 med. onion, finely chopped
4 Tbsp. bacon grease or
   3 slices finely chopped bacon
½ cup SOUTHERN COMFORT®
1 pint spicy catsup
Juice 1 lemon
⅓ cup brown sugar
1 tsp. salt
½ tsp. chili powder

Lightly brown onion in bacon grease or cook with chopped bacon. Remove from heat. Add catsup and SOUTHERN COMFORT, stir. Add remaining ingredients and simmer slowly for 10 minutes.

COUNTRY-STYLE RIBS AND KRAUT

3 to 4 pounds country-style ribs, cut in 1 to 6-rib pieces
1 teaspoon salt
⅛ teaspoon pepper
1 can (27 ounces) sauerkraut, drained
1 can (16 ounces) tomatoes
3 medium-sized potatoes, coarsely grated
3 tablespoons instant minced onion
1 teaspoon salt

Place ribs, meaty side up, in large roasting pan. Cover tightly and bake in moderate oven (350°F.) 45 minutes. Remove ribs to absorbent paper and season with 1 teaspoon salt and pepper. Pour off drippings and thoroughly combine in pan the sauerkraut, tomatoes, grated potatoes, onion and 1 teaspoon salt. Place ribs on top of kraut mixture, meaty side down. Cover tightly, return to oven and bake 45 minutes. Uncover and bake 20 minutes or until meat is done. Arrange ribs and kraut mixture on platter. *6 to 8 servings*

Favorite recipe from Pork Industry Group National Live Stock & Meat Board

MR. & MRS. "T"® BAKED RIBS

1½ lbs. meaty back ribs
Salt
1 cup MR. & MRS. "T"® Barbeque Sauce

Sprinkle ribs lightly with salt and place in shallow baking pan. Cover with foil and bake in moderate oven (350°) for about an hour. Brush MR. & MRS. "T"® Barbeque Sauce generously over the ribs. Uncover the pan and continue to bake for another half-hour, basting frequently until ribs are brown and crisp. *Serves 2*

TAHITIAN SPARERIBS

3 to 4 pounds pork spareribs
½ cup apricot-pineapple preserves
⅓ cup KIKKOMAN Teriyaki Sauce
¼ cup tomato catsup
1 teaspoon ground ginger

Cut ribs into serving-size pieces. Place on rack in roasting pan and bake, uncovered, in 300°F. oven 1 hour. Meanwhile, combine remaining ingredients. Remove ribs from rack; drain off excess fat and place ribs on bottom of pan. Pour sauce mixture over ribs; bake 1 hour longer, basting every 15 minutes with sauce.

Makes 4 servings

BARBECUED COUNTRY RIBS

3 pounds country-style ribs, cut into individual ribs
ADOLPH'S 100% Natural Tenderizer Unseasoned*
1 bottle barbecue sauce (any brand)

Moisten meat with water; sprinkle evenly with tenderizer and pierce deeply with a fork. Repeat on other side. (Use no salt.) Basting and turning occasionally, broil ribs 4-5" from heat 35 minutes or until done.

Serves 4

*Use approximately 1 teaspoon per pound of meat

To barbecue: Broil ribs 3" from heat about 35-45 minutes, basting and turning occasionally.

SPICY BARBECUED SPARERIBS

2 strips (about 5½ to 6 lbs. each) pork spareribs, cracked
1½ cups minced onion
2 large cloves garlic, minced
2 Tbsp. WESSON Oil
1 cup *each*: HUNT'S Tomato Ketchup and wine vinegar
⅓ cup lemon juice
¼ cup Worcestershire
¼ cup brown sugar, packed
4 tsp. chili powder
2 tsp. ground celery seed
1 tsp. ground cumin

Place spareribs on hot grill approximately 5 inches from coals or source of heat. Cook 45 minutes to 1 hour, turning frequently. Meanwhile, in a small pan, sauté onion and garlic in oil until onion is transparent. Add remaining ingredients. Heat to boiling. Reduce heat; simmer, uncovered, 25 to 30 minutes. Use to baste spareribs last 10 to 15 minutes of grilling; turn and baste often.

Makes 10 to 12 servings

POMPEIAN BARBECUED SPARERIBS

4 lbs. pork spareribs
3 cans (8 oz. each) tomato sauce
⅓ cup dark brown sugar
3 Tbsp. chopped onion
1 clove garlic, crushed
Juice of 2 lemons
⅓ cup POMPEIAN Olive Oil
½ tsp. ground white pepper
2 Tbsp. aromatic bitters

Have butcher crack spareribs so they can be cut easily after cooking. Wash spareribs and pat dry. Trim excess fat. Combine remaining ingredients and simmer in a saucepan for 10 minutes. Brush spareribs with the sauce and place ribs 8-10 inches above gray coals. Broil turning frequently and brushing every few minutes with sauce for 1 hour or until ribs are brown and done. *Makes 4 servings*

HARVEST MOON PORK

1 cup Oriental short grain rice (available in supermarkets)
1 pound lean ground pork
1 can (8 oz.) LA CHOY® Water Chestnuts, drained, chopped fine
¼ cup grated carrot
1½ tablespoons minced green onion
1 tablespoon minced fresh ginger
2 tablespoons cornstarch
4 tablespoons LA CHOY® Soy Sauce
1 tablespoon sherry
1 teaspoon Oriental sesame oil or cooking oil
Salt and pepper to taste

Rinse rice in sieve under cold running water until water runs clear. Place rice in bowl; cover with cold water and let soak 1 hour. Drain thoroughly. Combine pork with water chestnuts, carrot, green onion and ginger, mixing well. Combine cornstarch, soy sauce, sherry and sesame oil; add to pork mixture and blend thoroughly.

Spread drained rice on a plate. Make balls about ¾-inch in diameter from pork mixture; roll each ball in rice until well coated. Arrange balls about ¼-inch apart on bamboo steamer trays lined with waxed paper. Steam, covered, 45 minutes. Serve Harvest Moon

Pork with LA CHOY® Chinese Hot Mustard and Sweet and Sour Sauce for dipping. *4 servings*

Note: A vegetable steamer may also be used to cook Harvest Moon Pork; or a steamer can be improvised by placing a greased plate on a metal rack or inverted custard cups over about 1-inch of simmering water in a large, covered saucepan.

HAWAIIAN HAM LOAF

3 Tbsp. butter
½ c. brown sugar
8¾ oz. can crushed pineapple
1 lb. lean ground ham
2 eggs, slightly beaten
1 c. 3-MINUTE BRAND® Quick Oats
½ c. milk
¼ c. juice from pineapple
¼ tsp. pepper
¼ tsp. ginger

Melt butter in a 9 × 5-inch loaf pan. Sprinkle with brown sugar. Drain pineapple, reserving juice. Spread pineapple over the brown sugar layer. Combine remaining ingredients and press this mixture on top of the pineapple layer. Bake at 350°F. for 50 minutes. Invert loaf for serving.

Lamb

BUTTERFLIED LEG OF LAMB

1 leg of lamb, boned and butterflied
2 cups THE CHRISTIAN BROTHERS® Claret
2 tsp. poultry seasoning
2 tsp. salt
3 cloves garlic, peeled
2 Tbsp. grated onion

Place lamb, spread flat, in glass or porcelain dish; pour over combined wine and seasonings. Marinate 12 to 24 hours, turning occasionally. Grill over hot coals 20 minutes on each side; baste with marinade. Transfer to heated serving platter; slice across grain to serve.
Serves 6

TIME-HONORED GREEK LAMB LEG COOKED IN PAPER

Leg of lamb, 6 to 9 pounds
2 cloves garlic, slivered
2 to 3 lemons, cut in half
Salt
Pepper
2 teaspoons dried oregano
1 to 2 tablespoons olive oil
2 large brown paper bags*

Trim fat from leg of lamb. With point of sharp knife, make slits in lamb surface, including underside. Press garlic slivers into slits. Insert one large brown bag inside the other. Slip lamb leg into paper bags and place in roasting pan. Working with hands inside the paper bag, squeeze juice from lemons over the lamb and rub entire surface of lamb with face of cut lemons. Sprinkle generously with salt and pepper. Rub oregano between fingers in the process of sprinkling evenly over lamb. Rub olive oil over seasoned lamb. Carefully seal end of bag by folding and stapling closed or tying tightly with string or long twist ties used for closing plastic bags. Roast in 325°F. oven for 15 to 20 minutes per pound for rare, 20 to 25 minutes per pound for medium, or 25 to 30 minutes per pound for well done. Let stand in bag for 20 minutes before carving. If a richer brown finish on lamb is desired, run under broiler for a few minutes.

6 to 10 servings (depending upon size of lamb leg)

*A three-foot, six-inch by one-foot, six-inch sheet of aluminum foil or parchment may be substituted for paper bags. Place lamb in center. Fold ends to middle and seal, then tightly seal sides together.

Favorite recipe from American Lamb Council

ROAST LAMB CAFÉ, MADE WITH STOCK COFFEE ESPRESSO LIQUEUR

Five-seven lb. leg of lamb
Four tablespoons STOCK Coffee Espresso Liqueur
Two cloves garlic, crushed
⅛ teaspoon pepper

Combine STOCK Coffee Espresso Liqueur, garlic and pepper and brush over meat. Let stand two hours before roasting. Preheat oven to 325°F. Roast 30 to 35 minutes per lb. for medium rare, or until meat thermometer registers 170°F. Do not overcook.

SWEET AND SOUR BAKED LAMB

1 8-ounce can crushed pineapple
½ cup honey
½ cup HOLLAND HOUSE® White Cooking Wine
¼ cup soy sauce
1 teaspoon ginger
½ teaspoon thyme
Salt and pepper to taste
¼ teaspoon rosemary
1 rib rack of lamb, cut into about 12-16 chops

Drain 2 tablespoons pineapple syrup to mix with ¼ cup of honey; set aside for glaze. Combine pineapple, remaining honey and other ingredients except meat, in a small mixing bowl. Arrange ribs in large pan or bowl. Pour marinade over meat; refrigerate 3 hours or overnight, turning meat several times. Drain off marinade and reserve. Arrange meat on rack in roasting pan; bake in 350° oven for about 30 minutes, basting with marinade several times. When meat is tender but pink, heat glaze mixture and brush over chops. Broil for 3 minutes, watching carefully to avoid burning.

Serves 6 to 8

BARBECUED LAMB STEAKS

6 lamb steaks, about 1 inch thick
½ cup POMPEIAN Olive Oil
¼ cup red wine vinegar
1 Tbsp. grated onion
¼ tsp. oregano
½ tsp. freshly ground black pepper
Salt

Make slashes about one inch apart in fat around steaks to prevent curling. Make marinade of olive oil, vinegar, onion, oregano and pepper. Pour over steaks and let stand several hours or overnight in refrigerator. Bring to room temperature and drain, reserving marinade. Grill steaks over hot coals about 25 minutes, or to desired degree of doneness, turning and basting several times with marinade. When done, salt to taste. *Makes 6 servings*

MID-EASTERN LAMB SHOULDER CHOPS

6 shoulder blade or arm chops or lamb shanks
Salt
Pepper
2 tablespoons cooking oil
1 teaspoon dried dill weed
2 teaspoons dried parsley
¼ teaspoon ground cloves
1 tablespoon diced orange peel
2 teaspoons brown sugar
½ cup raisins
¼ cup catsup
¼ cup water
¼ cup dry white wine
Cooked rice

Arrange chops on aluminum foil in baking or broiler pan. Sprinkle with salt and pepper. Broil about 7 minutes, turn, sprinkle with salt and pepper and broil again for 7 minutes. Pour cooking oil in small pan and add dill weed, parsley and cloves. Simmer for a few minutes; add remaining ingredients except rice. Arrange chops or shanks in crockpot or casserole with tight-fitting cover. Cover. Cook at low heat for 6 to 8 hours or cook in oven heated to 350° for 2 to 3 hours, or until tender. Serve lamb and sauce over cooked rice.

6 servings

Favorite recipe from American Lamb Council

PLANKED LAMB CHOPS

4 lamb sirloin chops, cut 1½ inches thick
Salt
Pepper
2 medium-size tomatoes, sliced in half
3 to 4 cups seasoned mashed potatoes
¼ cup melted butter or margarine
¼ cup Parmesan cheese

Set regulator for broiling. Place chops on broiler rack. Insert broiler rack and pan in broiler so the top of steaks is 2 to 3 inches from the heat. Broil until steaks are browned on one side, approximately 10 minutes. Season. Remove steaks and place, broiled side down, on heated plank or fireproof platter. Place tomato halves around lamb chops. Make a border of mashed potatoes around food on plank. Brush tomatoes and potatoes with melted butter or margarine. Sprinkle tomatoes with Parmesan cheese. Broil 8 minutes or until meat is done and vegetables are browned.

4 servings

Favorite recipe from Lamb Committee of National Live Stock & Meat Board

LAMB CHIP CHOPS

1½ pounds shoulder lamb chops (1 thick chop apiece)
2 tablespoons margarine
2 medium onions (chopped fine)
1 clove garlic
1 bouillon cube
5-ounce bag JAYS Potato Chips
4 canned whole tomatoes (well drained)
½ cup hot water
1 tablespoon parsley (chopped)
Freshly ground pepper

Brown chops on both sides in margarine in heavy casserole. Add onions, garlic, Turn chops in the onions and put a tomato on each. Dust with freshly ground pepper. Cover with 5 ounces potato chips to make a thick layer. Dissolve bouillon cube in hot water. Pour this stock over food in casserole, cover closely, and cook in 350° oven for 1 hour. Remove to top of stove; uncover and cook on medium flame 10 minutes to reduce sauce. Sprinkle with parsley. Serve with French bread and salad.

VIRGINIA BARBECUED LAMB RIBLETS WITH RICE

3 to 4 pounds lamb riblets
Water
1 can (16 ounces) tomato sauce
½ cup molasses
¼ cup vinegar
1 teaspoon salt
½ teaspoon thyme
½ teaspoon liquid smoke
¼ teaspoon crushed bay leaf
¼ teaspoon pepper
1 cup brown rice
2 tablespoons butter
½ cup grated cheddar cheese
¼ cup grated parmesan cheese
¼ cup grated mozzarella cheese

Simmer lamb riblets in water to cover for 1 hour, or until tender. Drain riblets and place in large casserole that has a lid to fit. Mix together tomato sauce, molasses, vinegar, salt, thyme, liquid smoke, bay leaf and pepper; then pour over riblets. Cover lamb and bake at 350 degrees for another hour, or until hot and bubbly. While in the oven, baste the lamb occasionally with the sauce. Meanwhile, cook rice in water according to package directions. When tender, gently stir in the butter, cheddar, parmesan and mozzarella cheeses. Keep warm and serve with riblets spooned over top of rice.

4 servings

Favorite recipe from American Lamb Council

GINGERED LAMB AND VEGETABLES ORIENTALE

1 pound lean lamb, trimmed of fat and cut into thin strips
2 tablespoons safflower oil
1 cup green onions, sliced lengthwise
1 can (4 ounces) whole mushrooms
½ cup sliced water chestnuts
1 can (5 ounces) bamboo shoots, drained
3 tablespoons soy sauce
1 tablespoon shredded whole ginger root or 1 teaspoon ground ginger
1 tablespoon cornstarch
Water
Cooked rice or Chinese noodles

In skillet or wok, quickly brown lamb in hot oil, stirring constantly. Remove lamb and add onions, cooking until brown. Drain mushrooms, reserving liquid. Add mushrooms, lamb, water chestnuts, bamboo shoots, soy sauce and ginger to onions in skillet. Heat through, stirring constantly. Dissolve cornstarch in ¼ cup cold water. Add mushroom liquid and enough water to measure 1 cup. Blend with lamb mixture. Cover, cook over medium heat, stirring constantly, until thickened and clear. Serve with cooked rice or Chinese noodles.

2 to 4 servings

Flavorful Additions or Substitutes:
Diagonally sliced carrots and celery, snow pea pods, zucchini, broccoli, asparagus, Chinese cabbage, green beans, green peppers and quartered tomatoes.

Favorite recipe from American Lamb Council

BAKED LAMB SHANKS IN FRUIT SAUCE

4 lamb shanks
Salt
Pepper
Flour
1 cup SUNSWEET® Dried Apricots, cooked and drained
1 cup SUNSWEET® Prunes, cooked and drained
2 tablespoons each vinegar, lemon juice, and light corn syrup
⅓ cup brown sugar, firmly packed
½ teaspoon *each* ground cinnamon and allspice
¼ teaspoon ground cloves
1 cup water

Season lamb with salt and pepper; dust with flour. Place in greased baking pan. Cover and bake in a moderate oven (350°) for about 1 hour, 45 minutes or until meat is tender. Combine in a saucepan apricots, prunes, vinegar, lemon juice, syrup, brown sugar, spices, and water. Bring to a boil, reduce heat, and simmer for 5 minutes. When meat is tender, drain off fat. Pour fruit sauce over meat. Cover again and bake in a hot oven (400°) for 30 minutes more. Serve lamb shanks with fruit sauce and pan juices spooned over top.

Makes 4 servings

LAMBROSIAN SHANKS

4 fresh lamb shanks (about ¾ lb. each)
2 tablespoons vegetable oil
½ cup KIKKOMAN Teriyaki Sauce
1 tablespoon grated orange rind
½ cup orange juice
2 cloves garlic, crushed
2 teaspoons curry powder

Slowly brown lamb on all sides in oil; drain off excess fat. Combine remaining ingredients; pour over lamb. Cover and simmer 2 hours or until lamb is tender, turning over occasionally. *Makes 4 servings*

THE BROTHERS' LAMB SHANKS

1½ tsp. salt
½ tsp. freshly ground pepper
½ tsp. dried rosemary leaves
4 lamb shanks (¾-1 pound *each*)
1 Tbsp. tomato paste
¾ cup THE CHRISTIAN BROTHERS® Golden Sherry
1 eggplant (¾-1 pound), cut in chunks
2 large green peppers, cored, seeded, and cut in chunks
3 medium onions, cut in wedges
3 medium tomatoes, cut in wedges
2 Tbsp. chopped parsley
1 tsp. garlic, minced

Combine salt, pepper and rosemary. Sprinkle lamb shanks with half the seasoning mixture. Place in 13" x 9" baking pan; broil until golden, about 5 minutes on each side. Remove from oven. Combine tomato paste and sherry. Pour over lamb shanks; set aside to marinate, turning occasionally. Meanwhile, in large bowl combine eggplant, peppers, onions, tomatoes, parsley and garlic. Toss with remaining seasoning mixture. Turn into roasting pan, surrounding lamb shanks. Cover tightly with aluminum foil. Bake in 300° oven 30 minutes. Remove pan from oven, uncover and turn lamb and vegetables. If mixture seems dry, add additional sherry diluted with water as needed. Cover and continue baking 30 minutes longer or until lamb is fork tender and vegetables thoroughly cooked. Serve with steamed rice and crusty chunks of garlic bread, if desired.

Makes 4 servings

Grand Prize Winner THE CHRISTIAN BROTHERS® contest

BAKED LAMB SHANKS WITH TOMATO SAUCE

4 to 6 lamb shanks, about ¾
   pounds each, trimmed of fat
Olive oil
2 medium-size onions, cut into
   ¼-inch slices
1 teaspoon ground allspice
½ teaspoon ground nutmeg
1 teaspoon salt
½ teaspoon pepper
3 cups chopped, canned tomatoes

Preheat oven to 450°F. Lightly coat
lamb shanks with oil. Arrange in
13 x 2 x 9-inch baking dish. Bake
lamb for 30 minutes, turning once.
Reduce oven temperature to 350°F.
Remove lamb from oven. Place
onion slices over lamb. Sprinkle
with allspice, nutmeg, salt and
pepper. Pour tomatoes evenly over
all. Return lamb to oven. Bake for 2
hours, or until lamb is tender,
basting frequently.

4 to 6 servings

Favorite recipe from American Lamb Council

LAMB CURRY

2 pounds boneless lamb stew
   meat, cut into 1-inch cubes
2 tablespoons butter or margarine
2 cups chopped onion
2 cloves garlic, minced or pressed
2 teaspoons tumeric
¾ teaspoon salt
¼ teaspoon *each* ground ginger,
   ground cumin, ground coriander
   and chili powder
½ cup plain yogurt
1 tablespoon all-purpose flour
½ cup BLUE DIAMOND®
   Blanched Slivered Almonds,
   toasted

Trim excess fat from lamb. In
heavy skillet melt butter; sauté
onions and garlic until lightly
browned; remove with slotted
spoon and reserve. Add lamb to
hot skillet and cook, stirring, until
well browned. Reduce heat and
return onion mixture to skillet; add
tumeric, salt, ginger, cumin,
coriander and chili powder.
Simmer, covered, over low heat
until lamb is tender, about an hour.
(Add water if sauce becomes dry.)
Stir together yogurt and flour; add
to meat; bring to boil. Stir in
almonds and serve immediately.

Makes 4 servings

CALCUTTA LAMB CURRY
(Pressure Cooker Recipe)

2 tablespoons oil
2 pounds lamb, cut into 1-inch
   cubes
1 can (10½ ounces) condensed
   chicken broth, undiluted
1 cup WELCH'S® Grape Jelly
1 cup chopped onion
2 teaspoons curry powder
1 teaspoon sugar
½ teaspoon dried mint leaves
1 medium ripe melon, cut into
   1-inch pieces (cantaloupe or
   honeydew)
1 large ripe mangoe, cut into bite-
   size pieces
½ cup lime juice
½ cup heavy cream
PLANTERS® Peanuts

Heat pressure cooker. Add oil;
brown lamb. Add chicken broth,
WELCH'S® Grape Jelly, onion,
curry, sugar and mint. Close cover
securely. Place pressure regulator
on vent pipe. Cook 10 minutes.
Cool pressure cooker at once. Add
fruit and simmer 5 minutes. Stir in
lime juice and cream. Do not allow
sauce to boil. Serve curry with rice
if desired, garnish with chopped
PLANTERS® Peanuts.

Makes 6 to 8 servings

LUAU LAMB GRILL

Cut 2 pounds boneless lamb
shoulder into 1½-inch cubes.
Arrange meat, pineapple chunks,
green pepper slices, and
mushrooms on skewers.

½ cup SUE BEE® Honey
1 cup pineapple juice
¼ cup lemon juice
3 tablespoons butter or margarine
1 teaspoon Worcestershire sauce
1 teaspoon prepared mustard
1 teaspoon garlic salt
¼ teaspoon ginger
2 tablespoons chopped mint
   leaves (optional)

Combine all ingredients and
simmer in a saucepan for 10
minutes. Brush marinade
generously over kabobs. Grill for
15-20 minutes, or until tender,

turning often and basting with
marinade. Serve over fluffy
seasoned rice.

Makes 6-8 servings

TERIYAKI LAMB KABOBS

1½ pounds boneless lamb, cut
   into 1-inch cubes
⅓ cup soy sauce
⅓ cup cooking oil
Juice of 1 lemon
½ teaspoon ground ginger
¼ teaspoon ground pepper
1 clove garlic, crushed
2 zucchini, washed and cut into
   6 pieces each
12 cherry tomatoes
12 green pimiento-stuffed olives
Salt

Place lamb cubes in 2-quart bowl.
In measuring cup, combine soy
sauce, oil, lemon juice, ginger,
pepper and garlic. Pour over lamb.
Cover and refrigerate several
hours, or overnight. Pour off
marinade and set aside. Assemble
kabobs by alternating lamb cubes,
zucchini, tomatoes and olives on
skewers or bamboo sticks. Grill
lamb kabobs 3 to 4 inches from
source of heat for about 8 minutes
on each side, or until desired
degree of doneness, brushing
frequently with marinade. Sprinkle
with salt before serving.

Preparation time: 20 to 30 minutes
Cooking time: 13 minutes
6 servings

Note: Mushrooms and small,
   parboiled onions may be
   added or substituted for
   other vegetables.

Favorite recipe from American Lamb Council

KIKKO LAMB KABOBS

½ cup wine vinegar
¼ cup KIKKOMAN Soy Sauce
2 tablespoons vegetable oil
2 teaspoons instant minced onion
1 clove garlic, crushed
¼ teaspoon pepper
1½ pounds fresh lamb shoulder,
   cut into 2-inch cubes

Combine vinegar, soy sauce, oil,
onion, garlic and pepper in
saucepan; bring to boil. Cool
thoroughly; stir in lamb and
marinate 2 to 3 hours. Arrange
lamb on skewers; brush with
marinade. Broil or grill to desired
doneness, brushing with marinade.

Makes 4 servings

DEEP DISH LAMB & BISCUITS

2 lbs. boneless lamb shoulder, cubed
2 tablespoons salad oil
1 cup chopped onion
1 clove garlic, crushed
2 cups chicken broth
1 teaspoon caraway seeds
½ teaspoon salt
⅛ teaspoon pepper
1 cup sliced celery
1 pkg. (10 oz.) frozen peas and carrots, defrosted
2 tablespoons cornstarch
1 tablespoon cold water
1 cup (8 oz.) BREYERS® Plain Yogurt
1 cup biscuit mix
1 tablespoon chopped parsley
⅓ cup BREYERS® Plain Yogurt

Brown lamb in oil; add onion and garlic, sauté 5 minutes. Add broth, caraway seeds, salt and pepper. Cover and simmer 45 minutes. Add celery; simmer 15 minutes or until meat is tender. Stir in peas and carrots. Dissolve cornstarch in water, blend into yogurt. Stir yogurt into stew; heat. Turn stew into 2-quart casserole. Combine biscuit mix, parsley, and ⅓ cup yogurt. Spoon 6 biscuits on top of stew. Bake at 425°F 20 minutes until biscuits are browned.

Makes 6 servings

SHEPHERD'S PIE

4 carrots, cut in 1-inch pieces
1 pound ground lamb
1 envelope FRENCH'S® Brown Gravy Mix
1 cup water
½ teaspoon celery seed
1 can (16-oz.) whole onions, drained
2 to 3 cups mashed potatoes
Melted butter
Paprika

Cook carrots in salted boiling water until tender; drain. Brown lamb in large skillet, stirring to crumble; pour off excess fat. Add gravy mix, water, and celery seed, stirring to blend. Combine with carrots and onions; spoon into 2-quart casserole. Spoon potatoes around edge of casserole. Drizzle with melted butter and sprinkle with paprika. Bake at 350° for 30 minutes, until bubbling hot.

4 to 6 servings

Veal

VEAL ROAST WITH ANCHOVIES AND GARLIC

6 lb. rump, boned, rolled and tied
3 garlic cloves
5 anchovy filets
Chopped basil
2½ cups NOILLY PRAT Dry Vermouth

Cut garlic cloves into thin slivers. Roll anchovy filets in chopped basil. Insert both in folds of veal roast. Put veal in deep dish; cover with NOILLY PRAT. Marinate for 24 hours in refrigerator. Roast in moderately slow oven (325 degrees) 2 hours, basting with NOILLY PRAT.

VEAL CUTLET CORDON BLEU

12 thin slices DELFT BLUE®-PROVIMI® Veal
Salt
Black pepper
6 thin slices Swiss cheese
6 thin slices ham
Flour
3 eggs, beaten
¾ cup bread crumbs
¾ cup butter

Flatten the veal slices with a cleaver; sprinkle with salt and pepper. Put 1 slice of cheese and 1 slice of ham on each of 6 veal slices; cover with remaining veal slices. Pound edges together. Dip in flour, then eggs, then in crumbs. Fry in butter for 8 minutes.

Yield: 6 servings

VEAL SCALOPPINE AL MARSALA

4 veal scallops (cut from leg—about 1 pound)
Salt
Freshly ground pepper
Flour
3 tablespoons butter or margarine
1 garlic clove, crushed
1 tablespoon butter or margarine
½ cup HOLLAND HOUSE® Marsala Cooking Wine
½ pound sliced mushrooms
Chopped fresh parsley

Place scallops between waxed paper or foil and pound with side of cleaver until they are about ⅛ inch thick. Salt and pepper to taste and dredge in flour. Melt butter or margarine in skillet and brown garlic. Add veal, cooking over medium heat until brown. Remove veal to shallow baking pan. Add butter or margarine to skillet and brown mushrooms. Add Marsala and bring to a boil. Simmer approximately 2 minutes to blend flavors. Pour wine-mushroom sauce over veal. Cover pan and bake approximately 20 minutes at 350°. Garnish with parsley.

Serves 2 to 3

WIENER SCHNITZEL

4-8 DELFT BLUE®-PROVIMI® Veal Escalopes (about 1½ pounds)
6 tablespoons clarified butter, or oil and butter, mixed (for frying)
2 lemons, halved (for garnish)
Sautéed or château potatoes (for serving)

For coating:
¼ cup seasoned flour (made with ¼ teaspoon salt and pinch of pepper)
1 egg (beaten with seasoning and 1 teaspoon oil)
½ cup dry white breadcrumbs

Coat escalopes with seasoned flour, patting it in thoroughly. Brush with beaten egg and coat with breadcrumbs, pressing them on well. Heat butter, or oil and butter in a large skillet and fry escalopes over medium heat for 3-4 minutes on each side until golden brown and tender. To obtain a crisp, even coating, do not let escalopes touch each other in pan and do not move them for the first 2-3 minutes of cooking so a coating can form. Drain escalopes thoroughly on paper towels, arrange on a platter with the sautéed or château potatoes, garnish with lemon halves and serve at once while escalopes are still crisp. The classic wiener schnitzel is garnished only with lemon, but many chefs like to add the following garnish: On each escalope place a lemon slice, and top the slices with crossed anchovy fillets.

VIENNA SCHNITZEL

2 pounds filet of veal
Flour
Salt and pepper
2 beaten eggs
HI HO® Cracker crumbs
½ cup oil
3 hard-boiled eggs
5-6 anchovy filets
5-6 stoned olives
1 peeled lemon, sliced

Cut veal into scallops, flatten to make them very thin. Put a little flour in a paper bag, season with salt and pepper, and shake to mix well. Dip veal in seasoned flour, then in beaten egg, and finally in cracker crumbs, pressing well to make them adhere. Heat oil and fry scallops until golden on both sides. Shell eggs and chop the white and the yolks separately. Arrange schnitzels on a heated serving dish, top each with an olive wrapped in anchovy filet. Garnish with egg whites and yolks in separate groups. Serve with lemon slices around the dish.

Yield: 5 to 6 servings

SWISS VEAL CHIP DELIGHT

1 pound veal round, ½ inch thick
6 thin slices prosciutto ham
(Danish ham can be substituted)
6 thin slices imported Swiss Cheese
1 cup all-purpose flour
2 large eggs slightly beaten
½ cup milk
2 cups finely crushed JAYS Potato Chips
½ cup butter or margarine
Sauce (recipe follows)

Have butcher cut veal into 6 equal portions; pound very thin, about ⅛ inch thick. Place 1 slice of ham and cheese on each slice of veal. Roll meat as for a jelly roll, tucking in the sides, and pressing ends to seal well. Roll each portion of meat in flour, then dip in the beaten egg and milk. Carefully roll each piece in the finely crushed potato chips. Heat shortening in heavy skillet and sauté veal until

golden brown, about 10 to 15 minutes, turning once.

SAUCE

½ cup butter or margarine
1 cup finely crushed JAYS Potato Chips
1 teaspoon dehydrated onion chips
1 teaspoon salt
1 teaspoon MSG (monosodium glutamate)
¼ teaspoon white pepper
2 cups commercial sour cream
2 tablespoons finely minced chives

Melt butter or margarine in heavy skillet, carefully stir in finely crushed potato chips, onion, salt, MSG and white pepper. Cook over low heat about five minutes, stir in sour cream and continue to cook over low heat about 10 minutes, stirring gently. Place veal rolls on warm large platter. Spoon sauce over the rolls, sprinkle the minced chives over the top and serve. Serve with white or wild rice.

VEAL PROVENCALE

1 small onion, chopped
1 carrot, peeled, chopped
1 stalk celery, chopped
1 Tbsp. butter
¼ oz. dried mushrooms, covered with hot water, soaked 30 minutes, drained, chopped
⅓ cup dry white wine
⅔ cup water
4 canned plum tomatoes, drained, chopped
1 tsp. chicken stock base
1 tsp. cornstarch dissolved in 1 Tbsp. water
Salt and pepper to taste
1 Tbsp. chopped parsley
1 small clove garlic, minced
½ tsp. grated lemon rind
1 pkg. (12 oz.) DELFT BLUE®-PROVIMI® Fancy Veal Cube Steaks

Sauté onion, carrot and celery in butter until onion is limp. Add chopped mushrooms and wine. Boil until liquid is almost evaporated. Add water, tomatoes and stock base. Bring to a boil; reduce heat and simmer 10 minutes. Stir in cornstarch; cook until bubbly. Adjust seasonings. Combine parsley, garlic, lemon rind. Cook cube steaks according to BASIC DIRECTIONS.* Spoon sauce over cube steaks; sprinkle with parsley mixture.

Makes 4 servings

*BASIC DIRECTIONS: Thaw 30 minutes. Remove from package; sprinkle each cube steak with salt, pepper and flour. Heat 2 Tbsp. butter in a large skillet. Cook over medium high heat 2½ to 3 minutes per side.

VEAL PAPRIKA

1 pkg. (12 oz.) DELFT BLUE®-PROVIMI® Fancy Veal Slices thawed but cold
3 Tbsp. butter
2 Tbsp. oil
2 medium onions, sliced
1 red pepper, seeded, chopped
2 Tbsp. flour
1⅔ cup whipping cream
1 tsp. chicken stock base
½ tsp. sweet paprika
⅓ cup grated Gruyére or Swiss cheese
3 Tbsp. grated Parmesan cheese
1½ cup frozen peas, cooked, drained
⅓ cup dairy sour cream
Salt and white pepper to taste
6 oz. medium noodles, cooked, drained

Prepare veal slices according to BASIC DIRECTIONS.* Remove from pan; keep warm. In drippings, sauté onion and pepper until onion is limp over medium heat. Stir in flour; cook until bubbly. Gradually add cream, cooking and stirring until thickened and bubbly. Stir in stock base, paprika, cheeses and peas. Stir until cheeses are melted. Stir in sour cream; taste and adjust seasonings. Combine half of sauce with noodles in serving dish; arrange veal on top. Serve with remaining sauce.

Makes 4 to 6 servings

*BASIC DIRECTIONS: Thaw slices 30 minutes. Remove from package; place each slice between 2 sheets of waxed paper. Pound with flat side of mallet to about 1/16" thickness. Sprinkle both sides of meat with salt, pepper and flour. Heat 3 Tbsp. butter and 2 Tbsp. oil in large skillet. Sauté over medium high heat 1½ to 2 minutes per side.

CHIP VEAL PARMIGIANA

**1 can (16 ounces) tomatoes,
  undrained, coarsely blended
1 can (8 ounces) tomato sauce
¼ cup chopped onion
1 teaspoon basil
½ teaspoon sugar
Salt and pepper, to taste
1½ cups crushed potato chips
¾ cup grated Parmesan cheese
1½ pounds boneless veal,
  pounded thin
2 eggs, beaten**

In saucepan combine tomatoes, sauce, onion and seasonings. Simmer 5 minutes; set aside. Combine chips and cheese. Dip veal slices in egg, then chip mixture to coat. Fry in lightly oiled skillet over medium-high heat until golden and just cooked through, about 1 minute per side. Serve with hot sauce.

Makes 6 servings

Favorite recipe from Potato Chip Information Bureau

VEAL PARMIGIANA

**2 pounds veal round steak, cut
  ½ inch thick (or 6 cutlets)
2 tablespoons flour
1 egg
2 tablespoons water
½ cup fine dry bread crumbs
½ cup grated Parmesan cheese
½ teaspoon basil leaves
½ teaspoon salt
⅛ teaspoon pepper
3 tablespoons cooking oil
1 can (15 ounces) tomato sauce
1 clove garlic, crushed
1 tablespoon sugar
½ teaspoon leaf oregano
¼ cup grated Parmesan cheese
6 slices (1 ounce each) mozzarella
  cheese
Leaf oregano, if desired**

Cut steaks in 6 serving-size pieces and dredge in flour. Beat egg and water. Combine bread

crumbs, ½ cup Parmesan cheese, basil leaves, salt and pepper. Dip veal in egg mixture and then in crumb mixture, coating evenly. Measure oil into large roasting pan and place in oven; preheat oven to 400°F. (5 to 10 minutes). Place breaded veal in pan and bake, uncovered, in hot oven (400°F.) 30 to 40 minutes, until golden brown. Pour off drippings. Combine tomato sauce, garlic, sugar and ½ teaspoon leaf oregano and pour over meat. Sprinkle with ¼ cup Parmesan cheese. Cover securely with foil and bake 15 minutes. Place a slice of mozzarella cheese on each piece of veal. Crush leaf oregano and sprinkle on cheese, if desired. Bake, uncovered, 3 to 5 minutes, until cheese is melted.

6 servings

Favorite recipe from Beef Industry Council National Live Stock & Meat Board

VEAL FLORENTINE STYLE
(Vitello alla Fiorentina)

**1 small onion, sliced
¼ cup olive oil
2 pound veal rump, cubed
1 clove garlic
1 cup canned tomato puree
Pinch of rosemary
¼ cup SAMBUCA di GALLIANO™
Salt and pepper to taste**

Fry onion in oil for 2 minutes. Add garlic and brown 1 minute longer. Add meat and brown well on all sides over medium heat. Add remaining ingredients, cover pan, and cook over low heat until meat is tender, about 30 minutes. Stir occasionally. Serve hot over rice or polenta.

Serves 4

VEAL CUBES WITH GREEN BEANS

**1 pound veal steak or veal shoulder
  cut into 1 inch cubes
2 tablespoons oil
1 teaspoon salt
¼ teaspoon pepper
1 pound fresh or canned green
  beans
1 cup water
1 cup ENRICO'S Spaghetti Sauce**

Brown the meat in the oil in a deep kettle. Add the salt and pepper and

2 tablespoons of the ENRICO'S Spaghetti Sauce. Combine and cook for two minutes. Add the water and bring to boil, then add the fresh green beans and allow to cook until meat is tender. If canned beans are used, do not add until meat is tender. When meat and beans are cooked, add the ENRICO'S Spaghetti Sauce and simmer for five minutes more.

SAUTÉ OF VEAL MARENGO

**2 lbs. of DELFT BLUE® -PROVIMI®
  Veal cubed
2 Tbsp. oil
2 medium onions, finely chopped
1 Tbsp. flour
2 tsp. tomato paste
½ cup white wine
1½-2 cups stock
2 cloves of garlic, crushed
Bouquet garni
2 tomatoes, peeled, seeded and
  coarsely chopped
Salt and pepper
1 cup (¼ lb.) mushrooms, thickly
  sliced**

For Garnish:
**1 tsp. chopped parsley
Triangular croûtes of fried bread**

METHOD: Heat oil in a sauté pan and brown the meat a few pieces at a time. Remove from the pan, add onions and cook slowly until golden brown, then sprinkle with the flour and continue cooking until a deep brown. Remove pan from heat, stir in the tomato paste, the wine and 1½ cups stock and blend until smooth. Bring slowly to a boil, stirring; add the meat, crushed garlic, bouquet garni and tomatoes. Season, cover and simmer on top of the stove or cook in a moderate oven (350°F.) for 45-60 minutes or until meat is tender. Stir occasionally, adding reserved stock if the sauce reduces too much. Add the mushrooms to the pan for the last 10 minutes of cooking. Transfer the sauté to a hot deep platter, sprinkle with parsley and surround with croûtes. Remove bouquet garni.

VEAL STEW MARSALA

½ lb. mushrooms, halved
3 Tbsp. minced shallots
2 cloves garlic, crushed
6 Tbsp. butter, divided
1 cup HOLLAND HOUSE®
   Marsala Cooking Wine
2 lbs. veal, cubed
¼ cup flour for dredging
3 tomatoes, quartered
2 green peppers, cubed
2 large potatoes, pared and cubed
1 large yellow onion, chopped
1 tsp. grated orange peel
2 Tbsp. flour
1½ cups beef broth
1 bay leaf

In 12-inch skillet, sauté first 3 ingredients in 4 Tbsp. butter. Over high heat, add wine; cook until reduced to half. Pour mixture into 3-quart casserole. Toss veal lightly in flour. Sauté in remaining 2 Tbsp. butter. Add next 4 ingredients; sauté 5 minutes, stirring frequently. Add grated orange peel. Stir in flour. Add beef broth. Cook, stirring constantly, until mixture thickens. Boil 1 minute. Stir mixture into casserole; add bay leaf. Cover; bake 1¼ hrs. in 350° oven, or until meat and vegetables are tender. Remove bay leaf and serve or freeze.   *Serves 6-8*

BARBECUED VEAL RIBLETS

1 veal breast, cut into riblets
3 tablespoons cooking fat
1 medium onion, chopped
⅓ cup water
¾ cup catsup
¼ cup lemon juice
2 tablespoons brown sugar
1 tablespoon Worcestershire
   sauce
1½ teaspoons salt
Dash red pepper
Cooked rice, if desired

Brown riblets in cooking fat in large frying-pan. Pour off drippings. Add onion and water, cover tightly and cook slowly for 1 hour. Combine catsup, lemon juice, brown sugar, Worcestershire sauce, salt and red pepper. Add to riblets and continue cooking, covered, 30 minutes or until meat is done. Serve with hot cooked rice, if desired.   *4 to 6 servings*

Favorite recipe from Beef Industry Council National Live Stock & Meat Board

DORMAN'S HUNGARIAN VEAL RIBS

1 tablespoon paprika
⅛ teaspoon cayenne pepper
2 tablespoons butter, melted
2 medium onions, sliced
½ teaspoon salt
1 pint dairy sour cream, warmed to
   room temperature
4 rib veal chops cut 1-inch thick
   with rib bones cut short
2 tablespoons rosemary
4 DORMAN'S Dorelle Wedges
1 medium cooking apple, peeled
   and cut in ¼-inch wedges

In skillet, add paprika and cayenne to butter. Add onions and sprinkle with salt. Cover and cook until onions brown, about 15 minutes, stirring as necessary. Gradually stir in enough sour cream to reach a depth of ¼-inch in pan.

Have deep pocket in veal chops. Roll cheese wedges in rosemary and stuff pocket. Then insert narrow edge of apple wedge and press pocket together, or secure with wooden toothpick.

Place chops on onion slices. Cover pan and cook gently until chops are tender, about 25 minutes. Remove to warm platter. Thicken pan liquid with flour if desired and spoon over chops.

Makes 4 servings

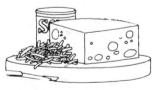

SWISS VEAL DORMANDIA

1 slice white bread, crust removed
¼ cup white wine
1 lb. ground veal
1½ teaspoons salt
¼ cup chopped onion
1 egg
1 package (6 oz.) DORMAN'S Swiss
5 or 6 midget sweet gherkins
2 tablespoons vegetable oil
1 cup water
1 tablespoon flour
¼ cup cold milk

Soak bread in wine until completely absorbed. Combine veal, soaked bread, 1 teaspoon salt, 1 tablespoon chopped onion and egg; mix well. Spread mixture

onto large sheet of waxed paper into a rectangle ½-inch thick. Cover with cheese slices. Place gherkins along narrow edge of meat. Starting at this end, roll meat layer up, jelly-roll fashion. If necessary, use waxed paper to help roll meat. Gently slice roll into 5 equal pieces. Coat rolls with flour. In a medium-size skillet, heat oil. Sauté remaining 3 tablespoons chopped onion until tender. Add water and ½ teaspoon salt; bring to a boil. Add veal rolls; bring to a boil. Lower heat; cover and steam for 15 minutes. Remove rolls; keep warm. Dissolve flour in cold milk. Add to skillet, stirring constantly. Bring to a boil. Grate remaining cheese in electric blender. Add to sauce; continue stirring until cheese melts. Serve sauce with warm veal rolls.

Makes 5 servings

GALLO® SALAME MEAT ROLL

18 GALLO® Italian Dry Salame
   slices
2 eggs
2 slices French bread
½ cup milk
2 Tbsp. toasted onion flakes
2 cloves garlic, minced
1½ tsp. grated fresh lemon peel
¼ tsp. ground nutmeg
1½ tsp. salt
Freshly ground pepper
2 pounds ground veal
¼ cup each chopped parsley,
   grated Parmesan cheese, and
   pine nuts

Place in blender container eggs, bread, milk, onion flakes, garlic, lemon peel, nutmeg, salt, freshly ground pepper to taste, and blend. Place meat and blended mixture in mixing bowl and mix. Pat out meat mixture onto sheet of waxed paper, making a 10″ by 12″ rectangle. Lay GALLO® Italian Dry Salame slices on meat, covering evenly, and sprinkle with parsley, cheese, and pine nuts. Roll up from the longer side and place seam side down on a buttered baking pan. Bake 45 minutes at 375° or until cooked through. Place on a serving platter and slice ¾ inch thick.   *Serves 8*

Note: If desired, accompany with a
   sauce composed of ½ cup
   each yogurt and sour cream
   and 2 tablespoons each
   chopped chives and parsley.

Fish and Seafood

CRUNCHY FISH DILLY

1 pound fish fillets
2 tablespoons lemon juice
½ cup water
1 cup fine KEEBLER Town House
   or Club Cracker crumbs
1 teaspoon salt
1 teaspoon grated lemon peel
1 teaspoon dried dill weed
¼ teaspoon pepper
1 egg, beaten
Oil for frying

Soak fish fillets in lemon juice and water. In large plastic bag, combine cracker crumbs with salt, lemon peel, dill and pepper. Drain fish and pat dry. Dip in beaten egg and then cracker crumb mixture. Fry in ¼ to ½ inch hot oil 3 to 4 minutes on each side.

3 to 4 Servings

BREADED HERBED FISH FILLETS
(Low Cholesterol)

½ cup fine dry bread crumbs
¼ cup flour
2 teaspoons chicken-flavored
   instant bouillon
1 teaspoon paprika
1 teaspoon dried minced onion
1 teaspoon dried parsley flakes
½ teaspoon salt
½ teaspoon dried dill weed
½ teaspoon dried thyme leaves
¼ teaspoon garlic powder
1 pound fish fillets
3 tablespoons MAZOLA® Corn
   Oil

In plastic bag mix together all dry ingredients. Brush fish with corn oil. Place, one at a time, in bag and shake to coat evenly. Place on greased cookie sheet. Bake in 400°F oven 20 minutes or until fish flakes easily.

Makes 4 servings

55 mg cholesterol per serving

LAYERED FILLETS SURPRISE

4 fish fillets (about 1 lb.—sole or
   cod)
Salt and pepper
¼ teaspoon tarragon
4 teaspoons instant minced onion
6 Tablespoons shredded process
   sharp cheese
1 can (8 oz.) STOKELY'S FINEST®
   Tomato Sauce
⅓ cup fresh bread cubes

Place 2 fillets in bottom of a 9 × 5 × 3-inch pan. Sprinkle next 4 ingredients over fish. Top with remaining fillets, Tomato Sauce and bread cubes. Bake at 375°F. for 25 minutes. *Makes 3 servings*

GOLDEN FISH FILLETS

1 egg, slightly beaten
2 tablespoons FRENCH'S®
   Prepared Mustard
½ teaspoon FRENCH'S® Seafood
   Seasoning or salt
1½ to 2 pounds fish fillets
FRENCH'S® Big Tate Mashed
   Potato Flakes
Oil or melted shortening
FRENCH'S® Parsley Flakes

Lightly beat together egg, mustard, and seafood seasoning. Dip fish in mustard mixture; roll in potato flakes until well coated. Fry in hot oil or shortening 3 to 4 minutes on each side, until fish flakes easily when pierced with a fork and is golden brown. Garnish with parsley flakes. *4 to 5 servings*

FISH 'N SPINACH ROLL-UPS

10-oz. pkg. GREEN GIANT® Cut
   Leaf Spinach Frozen in Butter
   Sauce
1 lb. frozen fish fillets, thawed
3 eggs, beaten
1½ cups herb seasoned stuffing
   mix
½ cup grated parmesan cheese
10¾-oz. can condensed cream of
   shrimp soup
½ cup dairy sour cream
1 teaspoon lemon juice
¼ teaspoon salt

Heat oven to 350°F. Cook spinach according to package directions. Divide fish fillets into 6 or 7 thin serving pieces.

In medium bowl, combine eggs, stuffing mix, cheese and spinach. Wrap each fillet around evenly divided portions of the stuffing mixture. Place seam-side-down in 12 × 8-inch (2-quart) baking dish.

In small bowl, combine remaining ingredients; pour half of sauce over fish. Bake at 350°F. for 30 to 35 minutes or until fish flakes easily and stuffing is firm. Heat remaining sauce and serve over baked fillets. *4 to 6 servings*

Microwave Directions: Assemble roll-ups as directed above. Microwave on HIGH for 15 to 20 minutes or until fish flakes easily. Microwave remaining sauce on HIGH for 2 to 3 minutes or until heated through, stirring every minute. Serve over baked fillets.

NUTRITIONAL INFORMATION PER SERVING

SERVING SIZE: ⅙ OF RECIPE		PERCENT U.S. RDA PER SERVING	
Calories	451	Protein	53%
Protein	34g	Vitamin A	47%
Carbohydrate	18g	Vitamin C	14%
Fat	27g	Thiamine	10%
Sodium	1280mg	Riboflavin	20%
Potassium	675mg	Niacin	13%
		Calcium	21%
		Iron	16%
		Phosphorus	45%

CIOPPINO

1 lb. firm fleshed fish (cod, turbot, haddock, etc.) and/or seafood (raw shrimp, scallops, steamed clams)
2 Tbsp. butter or margarine
1 large onion, 1″ diced
1 large green pepper, 1″ diced
2 cloves garlic, finely chopped
1 cup water
1 1 lb. can tomatoes, chopped, plus their juice
1 Tbsp. BALTIMORE SPICE OLD BAY Seasoning
¼ tsp. basil
¼ tsp. marjoram
¾ cup red wine
6 or more mushrooms, halved

Cut deboned fish in large bite-size pieces. Sauté vegetables in butter until crisp tender. Add water, tomatoes with juice, and seasonings; heat to boiling. Reduce heat, cover and simmer 10 minutes. Add wine and mushrooms; bring to boiling. Reduce heat, cover and simmer 10 minutes. Add fish, shrimp and/or scallops, cover and simmer until done, about 8 minutes. Clams (if used) should be added during last 3 minutes.

BROILED FISH WITH FRESH TOMATOES
(Low Cholesterol)

2 medium tomatoes, coarsely chopped
2 tablespoons finely chopped onion
½ teaspoon dried basil leaves, crushed
½ teaspoon salt
Dash pepper
1 pound fish fillets
2 tablespoons NUCOA® or MAZOLA® Margarine, melted

Stir together first 5 ingredients. Brush both sides of fish with margarine. Arrange fish on rack in broiler pan. Top with tomato mixture. Broil 4 inches from heat 4 to 6 minutes or until fish flakes easily.   *Makes 4 servings*

55 mg cholesterol per serving

FISH FILLET CORDON BLEU

1 package (8 ounces) MRS. PAUL'S® Fried Fish Fillets
4 slices boiled ham
4 slices Swiss cheese
1 can (10¾ ounces) cream of mushroom or cream of celery soup
¼ cup milk
Parsley, chopped

Prepare fish fillets according to package directions. Top each cooked fillet with a slice of ham and cheese. Return to oven for 2-3 minutes or until cheese is partially melted. Meanwhile, heat soup and milk together in a small saucepan. Pour over fish fillets and serve at once. Garnish with parsley.
Serves 4

JAPANTOWN TEMPURA

Oil for deep frying
1 pound thick fish fillets, cut in 2-inch squares (halibut, haddock, cod, red snapper)
1 quart raw vegetables (sliced zucchini, mushrooms, snow peas, parsley sprigs)
Tempura Batter (recipe follows)
2 cups crushed potato chips
Ginger Dipping Sauce (recipe follows)

In deep saucepan, heat 3 inches oil to 350 degrees. Dip fish and vegetable pieces in Tempura Batter, drain, then coat lightly with chips. Deep fry fish and vegetables a few pieces at a time about 3 minutes until golden and crisp. Drain on paper toweling. Serve hot with individual bowls of Ginger Dipping Sauce.

TEMPURA BATTER

In bowl combine 1 cup flour, ¼ cup cornstarch, and 1¼ cups water. Fold in 1 stiffly beaten egg white.

GINGER DIPPING SAUCE

In bowl combine 1 cup chicken bouillon, 3 tablespoons *each* soy sauce and dry sherry, 1 teaspoon sugar and 2 teaspoons grated fresh ginger *or* ¼ teaspoon ground ginger.

Favorite recipe from Potato Chip Information Bureau

FRIED FILETS OF FISH

1½ pounds fish filets (sole, halibut, cod, haddock)
1 egg
1 tablespoon milk
Salt and pepper
Pinch mace
SUNSHINE KRISPY® Cracker crumbs
Oil

Wash and dry the filets carefully. Mix egg with milk, season with salt, pepper and mace. Dip filets in egg, then in KRISPY® Cracker crumbs. Pat down to coat all over, then shake lightly to shed surplus crumbs. Use enough oil to submerge the filets. Heat oil until a haze begins to rise. Put filets in a few at a time, to prevent sudden cooling of oil temperature; this would make the filets soggy. Fry until brown all over, drain on paper, garnish with parsley and serve piping hot.   *Yield: 4 servings*

IMPORTED
SWISS CHEESE

FILLETS FINLANDIA

½ cup (1 stick) butter or margarine
¼ cup flour
2 cups hot milk
3 whole eggs, separated
1 teaspoon salt
½ pound FINLANDIA Swiss Cheese, cubed
1 pound fresh fish fillets (or frozen, thawed)
⅓ cup grated FINLANDIA Swiss Cheese
Snipped dill

In saucepan, melt butter and add flour; cook, stirring, until hot and bubbly. Add milk all at once and cook, stirring, until thickened and smooth. Remove from heat and gradually blend in egg yolks, salt and cubed cheese. Fold in stiffly beaten egg whites. Place fillets in greased shallow baking dish. Pour sauce over. Bake at 400°F. for 40 minutes. Top with shredded cheese. Bake 5 minutes longer. Garnish with dill.

Makes 4 servings

DIVINE FISH DIVAN

**6 pieces frozen VAN DE KAMP'S®
Batter-Dipped Fish Fillets,
Haddock, Perch or Halibut**
**10 ounce package frozen broccoli
spears**
½ cup (1 stick) butter or margarine
3 egg yolks
2 tablespoons lemon juice
Dash of white pepper
¼ teaspoon dry mustard

Prepare fish fillets according to package directions; cook broccoli according to package directions. Meanwhile, prepare hollandaise sauce by heating butter in small saucepan until bubbly but not browned. Put egg yolks, lemon juice, white pepper and dry mustard in blender container; cover and blend at low speed about 5 seconds. With blender still running, add ½ of butter in a slow, steady stream; turn to high speed and add remaining butter slowly. Drain broccoli; place down center of oblong serving platter with flowerettes on outside and stems in center. Arrange fish fillets down center of broccoli stems. Drizzle hollandaise sauce over center of fish fillets.

Makes 6 servings

INSTANT HINT: Prepare fish fillets and broccoli as directed, but use packaged hollandaise sauce mix or commercially prepared hollandaise sauce.

SEA TOASTIES

**1 package (9 ounces)
MRS. PAUL'S® Fish Sticks**
**1 package (8 ounces) refrigerated
crescent rolls**
1 cup Cheddar cheese, grated
1 teaspoon dry mustard
2 teaspoons Worcestershire sauce
**6 slices bacon, crisply fried and
crumbled**

Prepare fish sticks according to package directions. Separate crescent roll dough into individual pieces at perforations. In a medium size bowl, combine remaining ingredients and spread approximately 1½ tablespoons of mixture onto each crescent roll dough piece. Place 1½ cooked fish sticks on each dough piece and roll up as for crescent rolls. Bake according to directions on roll package. *Serves 8*

FISH ITALIANO

**6 pieces frozen VAN DE KAMP'S®
Batter-Dipped Fish Fillets,
Haddock, Perch or Halibut**
8 ounce can tomato sauce
2 teaspoons oregano, crushed
**4 ounce can sliced mushrooms,
drained**
2 tablespoons chopped parsley
1 cup shredded Mozzarella cheese
Grated Parmesan cheese

Place fish fillets in shallow, foil-lined baking pan. Pour tomato sauce over. Sprinkle oregano over and top with mushrooms, parsley and Mozzarella cheese. Sprinkle grated Parmesan cheese over as desired. Heat according to fish fillet package directions, or until sauce is bubbly.

Makes 6 servings

INSTANT HINT: Place fish in shallow, foil-lined pan. Top with 15½ ounce jar extra thick spaghetti sauce with mushrooms and 4 ounce package shredded Mozzarella cheese. Heat as directed.

DILL STUFFED SEA BASS

3 to 4 pound striped sea bass
¼ cup butter or margarine
½ cup chopped onion
¼ cup chopped celery
**1 tablespoon chopped fresh dill or
1 teaspoon dried dill**
1 tablespoon capers
½ teaspoon salt
⅓ cup water
**2 cups PEPPERIDGE FARM®
Herb Seasoned Cube Stuffing**

Prepare fish for stuffing by removing head, tail and backbone. Rub inside with salt and pepper. Place ¼ cup butter in a medium saucepan and sauté onion and celery until tender. Stir in the dill, capers, salt, water and stuffing cubes. Place stuffing on one-half of fish, fold over the other half and secure with skewers and string. Grease a shallow baking pan, place fish in pan and brush with soft butter. Bake at 375°F. 12 to 15 minutes per pound, or until fish is easily flaked with a fork. Carefully

remove to a hot platter and serve with sauce made by combining the ingredients below.

Serves 4 to 6

FOR SAUCE

¼ cup melted butter or margarine
2 tablespoons lemon juice
¼ cup chopped parsley

FRIED CATFISH

**2 pounds catfish, cleaned and
skinned**
½ cup flour
Salt and pepper to taste
½ cup yellow cornmeal
Pinch IMPERIAL Granulated Sugar
**3 tablespoons shortening or bacon
fat**

Dry fish with cloth or paper towel. Combine dry ingredients. Dip fish in the cornmeal mixture and fry in hot shortening until golden brown on each side.

Makes about 4 servings

TENNESSEE FRIED CATFISH

**6 skinned, pan-dressed catfish or
other fish, fresh or frozen**
2 teaspoons salt
¼ teaspoon pepper
2 eggs
2 tablespoons milk
2 cups cornmeal

Thaw frozen fish. Sprinkle both sides with salt and pepper. Beat eggs slightly and blend in the milk. Dip fish in the eggs and roll in cornmeal. Place fish in a heavy fry pan which contains about ⅛ inch melted fat, hot but not smoking. Fry at a moderate heat. When fish is brown on one side, turn carefully and brown the other side. Cooking time is about 10 minutes, depending on the thickness of the fish. Drain on absorbent paper. Serve immediately on a hot platter, plain or with a sauce. *Serves 6*

*Favorite recipe from National Marine
Fisheries Services*

CRISPY FISH 'N CHIPS

2 pounds frozen cod or haddock
  fillets
½ cup evaporated milk
1 teaspoon *each* lemon juice and
  salt
½ cup crushed potato chips
1 tablespoon butter

Allow frozen fish to stand at room
temperature 15 minutes. Cut each
block into three equal portions.
Combine milk, lemon juice and
salt. Drain fish; dip in milk mixture;
roll in chips to coat. Place in
greased shallow pan; dot with
butter. Bake in 450 degree oven
until fish flakes, about 25 minutes
per inch thickness.

Makes 6 servings

*Favorite recipe from Potato Chip Information
Bureau*

HAWAIIAN KABOBS TERIYAKI

2 pounds cod fillets or other
  thick fillets, fresh or frozen
1 can (16 ounces) pineapple
  chunks
¼ cup reserved pineapple juice
½ cup soy sauce
¼ cup sherry, optional
2 tablespoons brown sugar
1 tablespoon fresh-grated
  ginger root or 1 teaspoon
  ground ginger
1 teaspoon dry mustard
1 clove garlic, crushed
1 green pepper, cut into 1-inch
  squares
3 cups cooked rice, optional

Thaw fish if frozen. Cut into one-
inch cubes. Drain pineapple;
reserve ¼ cup of liquid. Combine
pineapple juice, soy sauce, sherry,
brown sugar, ginger, mustard, and
garlic. Pour marinade over fish;
cover and refrigerate for at least
one hour. Drain fish and reserve
marinade. Thread fish, pineapple
chunks, and green pepper
alternately on skewers. Cook over
hot coals or under broiler, 4 to 5
inches from source of heat, for 4 to
5 minutes. Baste with marinade.
Turn and cook for 4 to 5 minutes
longer or until fish flakes easily

when tested with a fork. Serve as
an entree on a bed of rice or alone
as an appetizer. For an extra
festive touch, place a flower on the
end of each skewer after cooking.

*Makes 6 entree servings or
18 to 20 appetizers*

*Favorite recipe from National Marine
Fisheries Services*

FLOUNDER FLORENTINE

¼ cup chopped onion
⅛ teaspoon rosemary, crushed
2 tablespoons butter or margarine
1 package (9½ ounces) frozen
  chopped spinach, cooked and
  well-drained
½ cup cooked rice
¼ cup chopped toasted almonds
1 tablespoon lemon juice
6 fresh fillets of flounder
  (about 1½ pounds)
1 can (10¾ ounces) CAMPBELL'S
  Condensed Cream of Mushroom
  Soup
¼ cup water
Paprika

In saucepan, cook onion with
rosemary in butter until tender.
Add spinach, rice, almonds,
and lemon juice. Heat; stir
occasionally. Place ¼ cup mixture
on each fish fillet. Roll; secure with
toothpicks. Arrange in shallow
baking dish (12 × 8 × 2 inches).
Bake at 350°F. for 20 minutes.
Meanwhile, blend soup and water;
pour over fish, stirring around
sides. Bake 15 minutes more or
until done. Stir sauce before
serving. Sprinkle with paprika.

6 servings

Irish Mist®

FINNEGAN'S FLOUNDER

2 lb. flounder fillets
1 small onion, chopped
1 teaspoon salt
Freshly ground pepper
¾ cup apple juice
¼ cup IRISH MIST®
¼ cup lemon juice
2 tablespoons butter (or margarine)
2 tablespoons flour
¼ cup heavy cream
¼ cup (2 oz.) freshly shredded
  Parmesan cheese
Finely minced parsley
Boiled new potatoes

In large buttered baking dish,
arrange fish. Sprinkle with onion,
salt and pepper. Combine apple
juice, IRISH MIST® and lemon
juice. Pour over fish. Cover. Bake
in preheated 350°F. oven 15
minutes. Strain liquid. Reserve.
Keep fish warm. In small
saucepan, melt butter. Mix in flour.
Cook 2 minutes. Stir in fish liquid
and cream. Cook until thickened.
Pour over fish. Sprinkle with
cheese. Place under broiler until
browned. Sprinkle with parsley.
Serve with potatoes.   *Serves 4-6*

PERCH TURBANS A LA NEWBURG

2 pounds ocean perch or other
  fish fillets, fresh or frozen
1 teaspoon salt
¼ teaspoon pepper
¼ cup melted margarine or butter
2 cups cooked rice
Paprika

Thaw fish if frozen. Skin fillets and
cut into serving size portions.
Sprinkle with salt and pepper. Roll
fillets into a turban and secure
with a toothpick. Place turbans on
end in a well-greased baking dish,
8 × 8 × 2 inches. Brush with melted
margarine. Bake in a moderate
oven, 350°F., for 15 to 20 minutes
or until fish flakes easily when
tested with a fork. To serve,
remove toothpicks from turbans
and place on a bed of rice. Spoon
Newburg Sauce* over turbans.
Garnish with paprika.

Makes 6 servings

*NEWBURG SAUCE

½ cup margarine or butter
¼ cup all-purpose flour
½ teaspoon salt
⅛ teaspoon cayenne pepper
3 cups half and half
6 egg yolks, beaten
⅓ cup sherry

In a saucepan melt margarine. Stir
in flour, salt, and cayenne. Add
half and half gradually and cook
until thick and smooth, stirring
constantly. Stir a little of the hot
sauce into the egg yolks; add to
remaining sauce, stirring
constantly. Remove from heat and
slowly stir in sherry.

*Favorite recipe from National Marine
Fisheries Services*

LIME BAKED HALIBUT WITH FRESH GRAPES

4 halibut steaks or other white
   fish fillets
2 tablespoons butter
Salt and pepper
1 small onion, carrot and
   cucumber, each very thinly
   sliced
1 can (7½ ounces) minced clams
2 cups California seedless grapes
1 fresh lime, sliced
½ cup white wine
Chopped parsley

Put fish in shallow casserole. Dot
with butter, sprinkle with salt and
pepper. Cover with vegetables,
then clams (and liquid), grapes and
lime. Pour wine over all. Bake in
400 degree oven 10 minutes, or
until the fish flakes easily with a
fork (vegetables will be crisp).
Garnish with parsley.

Makes 4 servings

*Favorite recipe from California Table Grape
Commission*

BARBECUED HALIBUT STEAKS

⅓ cup California Brandy
⅓ cup lemon juice
¼ teaspoon dill weed
1 bay leaf
4 halibut steaks (about 1½ pounds)
1 medium red onion, thinly sliced
½ lemon, thinly sliced
⅓ cup chili sauce
2 tablespoons melted butter
Salt

Combine brandy, lemon juice, dill
weed and bay leaf. Place steaks in
shallow pan in a single layer. Top
with onion and lemon slices. Pour
brandy mixture over. Refrigerate
and let stand an hour or longer
before cooking. Drain steaks,
reserving marinade. Place steaks
on grill over hot coals. Combine
chili sauce and butter with
reserved marinade. Baste steaks
often with mixture as they broil.
Cook about 5 minutes each side,
just until fish is cooked through
and flakes easily. Sprinkle with
salt to taste.

Makes 4 servings

*Favorite recipe from California Brandy
Advisory Board*

BROILED SALMON AULD ANGUS

1 salmon steak, about 1 inch thick
2 tablespoons melted butter
¼ teaspoon salt
⅛ teaspoon pepper
⅛ teaspoon garlic powder
2 tablespoons JOHNNIE WALKER
   Red
¼ cup bread crumbs

Oil broiler pan lightly. Brush both
sides of salmon with a little melted
butter and place in pan. Combine
rest of butter, seasonings, and
JOHNNIE WALKER Red with bread
crumbs. Pat half of crumb mixture
on top of salmon. Broil about 2
inches from heat, for 3 minutes.
Carefully turn salmon. Pat on rest
of crumb mixture and broil 5
minutes longer. *2 servings*

BAKED CHIPPED SNAPPER

2 cups crushed JAYS Potato Chips
1 3 pound red snapper
1 cup chopped onions
1 clove garlic, minced
½ cup vegetable oil
1 No. 2 can tomatoes (2½ cups)
1 cup diced celery
½ cup white raisins
½ cup chopped parsley
1 teaspoon salt
¼ teaspoon pepper
1 cup dry white wine
½ cup lemon juice
1 teaspoon oregano
1 thinly sliced lemon

Sprinkle one cup potato chips in a
3 quart baking dish. Place fish in
center. Brown onions and garlic in
the vegetable oil. Add tomatoes,
celery, raisins, parsley, salt and
pepper and arrange around the
fish. Sprinkle remaining potato
chips over the vegetables. Mix
wine and lemon juice; pour over
the fish. Sprinkle with oregano.
Arrange lemon slices around sides
of fish. Bake in moderate oven
350°F. about 45 minutes.

Serves 6

POACHED RED SNAPPER WITH LEMONS AND GRAPES

1 13 ounce Red Snapper (Cleaned
   and scaled with head/tail left on)
Lemons, peeled, pitted and thinly
   sliced
Grapes (Red or white, seedless)
¼ cup olive oil
⅛-¼ teaspoon salt
⅛-¼ teaspoon pepper
½ cup CANADA DRY® Club Soda

Preheat oven to 400°F. Place large
pan, half filled with boiling water
and grill rack in center of oven.
Rub Snapper with oil and set
aside. Combine lemons and grapes
in medium-size bowl. Lightly salt
and pepper Snapper. Place on grill
and bake about 30 minutes. Add
remaining oil and CANADA DRY®
Club Soda to pan and simmer. Add
lemons and grapes and heat to
warm. Serve on a platter. Pour
lemon/grape sauce over fish and
garnish with parsley or dill.

Makes 2 Servings

STUFFED FILLET OF SOLE

4 Tablespoons melted butter
½ cup crushed rye crackers
8 to 10 scallions, minced
2 Tablespoons chopped fresh
   parsley
½ cup celery, chopped fine
1 cup chopped apples
½ pound sea scallops, chopped
½ teaspoon poultry seasoning
6 fillet of sole fillets
Mushroom-n-Wine Sauce

Combine crumbs, scallions,
parsley, celery, apples, scallops,
and poultry seasoning. Melt butter
and combine well with above
mixture. Spread on fillets; roll up.
Place close together in a lightly
greased baking pan. Bake at 375°
for 30 minutes. Brush with butter;
run under broiler to brown. Serve
with Mushroom-n-Wine Sauce
below. *Yield: 6 servings*

MUSHROOM-N-WINE SAUCE

Combine 1 can (10½ ounces)
condensed mushroom soup with ¼
to ⅓ cup white wine and 2
tablespoons chopped fine parsley.
Heat through. *Makes 6 servings*

*Favorite recipe from Western New York
Apple Growers*

FILET OF SOLE VERONIQUE

Butter
2 tablespoons green onions, chopped
8 sole filets
White pepper
¾ cup HOLLAND HOUSE® White Cooking Wine
Water
2 tablespoons butter
2 tablespoons flour
1 cup milk
1 egg yolk slightly beaten
1 cup seedless white grapes (canned or fresh)
2 tablespoons whipped cream

Coat the bottom of a saucepan with butter, add chopped green onions and sole filets that have been rolled and secured with toothpicks. Sprinkle filets with a little white pepper and add ¾ cup white wine and ½ cup water. Cover the top of the pan with butcher's paper in which you have punched a hole in the center about the size of a dime. Place pan over medium heat and when it reaches the boiling point, cover, simmer gently for 8 to 10 minutes or until filets are fork tender. Remove filets to warm heat-proof platter and discard toothpicks.

Reduce liquid in which fish was cooked until about ½ cup remains. In another saucepan melt 2 tablespoons of butter, blend in 2 tablespoons flour, remove pan from heat and very gradually add 1 cup milk, blending it in carefully until sauce is smooth. Return to heat and cook slowly stirring constantly until sauce begins to thicken. Add a few tablespoons of the hot sauce to a dish containing a lightly beaten egg yolk and mix well. Add egg mixture to saucepan and stir until sauce is smooth and thick. Add this cream sauce to mixture in which fish was cooked and fold 2 tablespoons whipped cream into sauce and pour it over fish on platter. Place white grapes around fish (if grapes are fresh, simmer in water for a few minutes) and put platter under the broiler flame for several minutes until top is browned. *Makes 4 servings*

SOLE IN ALMOND SHRIMP SAUCE

1 to 1½ pounds sole filets
1 cup dry white wine
3 ounces baby shrimp
4 tablespoons butter or margarine
2 tablespoons all-purpose flour
½ cup half and half
¼ teaspoon salt
Dash pepper
⅓ cup BLUE DIAMOND® Blanched Slivered Almonds, toasted

Place sole filets in 13 × 9 × 2-inch baking dish; pour wine over fish and bake in 350 degree F. oven 15 to 20 minutes, or until fish flakes easily with fork, but is still moist. *Do not overcook.* While fish bakes set aside ¼ cup of the shrimp; mash remaining shrimp with 2 tablespoons of the butter; set aside. When fish is cooked remove to heated platter; measure ½ cup of the cooking liquid; reserve.

In a small saucepan heat remaining 2 tablespoons butter; add flour and cook, stirring, 2 to 3 minutes. Gradually add half and half, stirring constantly to blend well. Continue cooking and stirring over medium heat until sauce begins to thicken; add reserved fish liquid and continue cooking, stirring constantly, until sauce comes to a boil. Reduce heat, add reserved shrimp butter, salt and pepper; stir until butter is melted. Stir in ¼ cup of the almonds. Drain liquid from fish; pour sauce over and garnish with reserved baby shrimp and remaining almonds. *Makes 4 servings*

FILET DE SOLE AU PERNOD

8 sole filets
1½ oz. flour
1 large egg
¼ teaspoon tarragon
Ground salt and pepper
4½ oz. breadcrumbs
3 oz. butter
2 tablespoons cooking oil
Juice of a lemon
2-3 tablespoons PERNOD
Fresh chopped parsley

Coat the fish with flour. Beat the egg with the tarragon and the

ground salt and pepper. Dip each filet in this mixture and then coat with breadcrumbs. Heat the butter and oil in a fry pan and grill the fish for about 3 minutes each side. When the fish is cooked, put it on a hot serving platter and keep hot. Pour the lemon juice and PERNOD in the fry pan and heat. Cover the fish with the sauce and garnish with chopped parsley.
Serves 4

SPINACH STUFFED SOLE

1½ lbs. fillet of sole (6 fillets)
1 (15 oz.) can S&W Chopped Spinach, drained
Salt
Paprika
Lemon peel
¼ tsp. nutmeg
1 (4½ oz.) can S&W Deveined Small Size Whole Shrimp, drained and chopped
3 Tbsp. melted butter
6 fresh mushroom caps

Rinse fillets and pat dry with paper toweling. Place the fillets of sole on a kitchen counter and sprinkle each one with salt, paprika, lemon peel. To the drained chopped spinach, add the nutmeg and chopped shrimp. Divide this mixture evenly and spread each fillet of sole with the mixture. Roll and secure with toothpicks. Place in a greased shallow casserole and drizzle with melted butter. Bake at 350° for 15 to 20 minutes or until fish flakes easily with a fork. Top with Sherry Cheese Sauce* and garnish each fillet with a mushroom cap. Place under the broiler to lightly brown the cheese sauce (2 to 4 minutes).
Serves 4-6

*SHERRY CHEESE SAUCE

2 Tbsp. butter
2 Tbsp. flour
½ tsp. salt
¼ tsp. white pepper
1½ cups milk
Dash of TABASCO® Sauce
1½ cups grated Cheddar cheese
2 Tbsp. dry sherry

In a saucepan melt butter, add flour, salt, pepper, milk and TABASCO® Sauce. Cook until slightly thickened and smooth. Stir in cheese and sherry. Cook over low heat until cheese has melted. Pour over Spinach Stuffed Sole.

SEVICHE CON TWO FINGERS®

½ cup lemon juice
½ cup lime juice
½ cup TWO FINGERS® Tequila
2 small dried red chili peppers
1 clove garlic, pressed or diced
1 teaspoon salt
Dash dill weed
1 pound sole, halibut or any white flesh fish
1 sweet red onion, sliced
Lettuce

Combine lemon and lime juice with tequila. Seed peppers, and finely grind. Add to first mixture, along with garlic, salt and dill. Cut fish in 1-inch pieces, and pour the mixture over. Top with onion slices. Cover and refrigerate for at least 3 hours, until fish is opaque. Serve as an appetizer or as a salad on lettuce.

Makes about 2⅔ cups

Note: The citrus juices have much the same effect on the white fish meat that boiling the meat does, so it is essentially "cooked."

BAKED SOLE ROLLUPS
(Low Calorie)

1 can (6½ oz.) BUMBLE BEE® Chunk Light Tuna in Water
1 large carrot, thinly sliced
1 medium zucchini, thinly sliced
4 sole fillets
Salt
Pepper
⅓ cup green apple, cored & diced
⅓ cup minced green onions
1 egg
2 tablespoons fresh lemon juice
¼ teaspoon thyme, crumbled
¼ teaspoon celery seed
¼ teaspoon salt
Paprika for garnish

Drain tuna. Steam carrots for 5 minutes, then add zucchini and steam additional 5 minutes. Arrange vegetables in 1-quart casserole dish. Rinse fillets with water, pat dry. Sprinkle with salt and pepper. In small mixing bowl, combine tuna, apple, green onions, egg, 1 tablespoon lemon juice and seasonings. Spread mixture evenly on fillets, then roll up. Place fillets

seam side down on vegetable slices. Drizzle remaining lemon juice over fillets. Sprinkle with paprika. Cover and bake in 350°F. oven for 25 minutes or until fish flakes with a fork.

Makes 4 servings

213 calories per serving

RAINBOW TROUT WITH MUSHROOM-HERB STUFFING

6 pan-dressed rainbow trout or other pan-dressed trout, fresh or frozen
2 teaspoons salt
4 cups (½-inch) soft bread cubes
⅔ cup butter or margarine
1 cup sliced fresh mushrooms
⅔ cup sliced green onions
¼ cup chopped parsley
2 teaspoons chopped pimiento
4 teaspoons lemon juice
½ teaspoon marjoram

Thaw frozen fish. Sprinkle 1½ teaspoons salt evenly over trout fillets. Sauté bread cubes in ½ cup butter or margarine until lightly browned, stirring frequently. Add mushrooms and onion; cook until mushrooms are tender. Stir in remaining salt, parsley, pimiento, lemon juice, and marjoram; toss lightly. Stuff the inside of each dressed fish and secure with a skewer or toothpick. Arrange in single layer in a well-greased baking pan. Brush with remaining melted butter or margarine. Bake in a moderate oven, 350°F., 25 to 30 minutes or until fish flakes easily when tested with a fork. Serve plain or with favorite fish sauce.

Makes 6 servings

Favorite recipe from North Carolina Department of Natural Resources

ROASTED TROUT IN BACON

⅓ cup LEA & PERRINS Worcestershire Sauce
2 tablespoons onion powder
1 tablespoon lemon juice
2 teaspoons salt
¾ teaspoon garlic powder
3 (1½ lb. each) dressed trout or other firm-fleshed fish
9 strips bacon

Combine all ingredients except fish and bacon; mix well. Brush LEA & PERRINS mixture inside and out of fish. Place fish in a buttered baking pan. Score skin in two or three places and strip with bacon. Bake in a preheated moderate oven (350°F.) 40 to 45 minutes or until fish flakes easily when tested with a fork. Baste often with pan juices during baking.

Yield: 6 portions

STUFFED TROUT COCO ALMONDINE

4 small trout, ¾ pound each
½ cup COCO CASA™ Cream of Coconut
2 Tbsp. olive oil
4 Tbsp. lemon juice
4 Tbsp. sliced almonds, lightly toasted
4 boiled shrimp for garnish (Optional)

Rinse trout and pat dry. Sprinkle with salt and brush thoroughly with cream of coconut and olive oil. Sprinkle with lemon juice. Fill cavity with stuffing* and place fish side by side in ovenproof dish. Slide any leftover stuffing under fish. Broil at 450° on middle shelf of oven for 10 minutes, basting occasionally with cream of coconut. Turn fish over, baste again, and cook ten minutes more. Sprinkle with almonds.

Serves 4

*STUFFING FOR TROUT

2 carrots
2 stalks celery
1 small onion
3 sprigs parsley
3 Tbsp. butter
¼ lb. shrimp, chopped
¼ cup COCO CASA™ Cream of Coconut
4 Tbsp. breadcrumbs
2 Tbsp. sliced almonds, toasted
2 Tbsp. coconut flakes
½ tsp. salt

Finely chop carrots, celery, onion and parsley. Cook mixture gently in butter for 4 minutes. Remove from heat and stir in remaining ingredients.

PLANKED LAKE TROUT

3 or 4 pounds dressed trout or other dressed fish, fresh or frozen
1½ teaspoons salt
Dash pepper
2 tablespoons melted fat or oil
Seasoned hot mashed potatoes
Seasoned hot cooked vegetables (broccoli, carrots, cauliflower, onions, or tomatoes)

Thaw frozen fish. Clean, wash, and dry fish. Sprinkle inside and out with salt and pepper. Place fish on a plank or well-greased bake and serve platter, 16 × 10 inches. Brush with fat. Bake in a moderate oven, 350°F., for 40 to 60 minutes or until fish flakes easily when tested with a fork. Remove from oven and arrange border of hot mashed potatoes around fish. Broil about 8 inches from source of heat for 6 to 8 minutes or until potatoes are lightly browned. Remove from broiler and arrange two or more hot vegetables around fish.

Serves 6

Favorite recipe from North Carolina Department of Natural Resources

TROUT AMANDINE
(Low Calorie/Low Cholesterol)

2 (about 12 oz. each) trout, dressed and boned
⅓ cup (1 oz.) slivered almonds
1 packet (½ oz.) BUTTER BUDS®
⅛ tsp. black pepper
½ tsp. chopped parsley
¼ tsp. almond extract (optional)

Preheat oven to 350°F. Arrange almonds single layer on ungreased cookie sheet. Bake for 3-4 minutes or until golden brown. Set aside. Place fish in ungreased baking dish. Mix BUTTER BUDS® with ½ cup (4 fluid ounces) hot tap water, pepper, parsley and almond extract. Add almonds and pour mixture over fish. Bake, covered, at 350°F for 20-25 minutes or until fish flakes easily when touched with a fork. *Makes 4 servings*

Calories:
w/BUTTER BUDS® —252
w/Butter —440
Cholesterol:
w/BUTTER BUDS® — 93 mg.
w/Butter —134 mg.

BROILED HAWAIIAN FISH FILLETS

⅓ cup KIKKOMAN Soy Sauce
1 tablespoon brown sugar, packed
2 tablespoons vegetable oil
1 tablespoon cider vinegar
½ teaspoon ground ginger
1 clove garlic, crushed
1½ pounds white fish fillets
1 tablespoon minced fresh parsley

Combine first 6 ingredients; marinate fish in sauce 20 minutes, turning once. Reserve sauce; broil fish 5 inches from heat 4 minutes. Turn, baste with sauce and broil 4 minutes longer. Just before serving, sprinkle with parsley.

Makes 4 servings

DOOR COUNTY FISH BOIL

2 pounds whitefish or other fish fillets, fresh or frozen
10 cups water
⅓ cup salt
12 small red potatoes
6 medium onions, peeled
6 wedges cabbage
1 can (1 pound) small whole beets
Horseradish Sauce*
Chopped parsley

Thaw fish if frozen. Cut into serving size portions. In a large pot heat water and salt to boiling. Remove a ½ inch strip of peeling around middle of potatoes. Add potatoes and onion to water; simmer 30 minutes or until fork tender. Add cabbage wedges; simmer about 10 minutes until tender. Add fish and simmer 3 to 4 minutes or until fish flakes easily when tested with a fork. Remove vegetables and fish to a serving platter and keep warm. Add beets to water and heat. Remove beets to platter with other vegetables and fish. Pour Horseradish Sauce over vegetables and fish. Garnish with finely chopped parsley.

Makes 6 servings

*HORSERADISH SAUCE

½ cup prepared horseradish
1 tablespoon all-purpose flour
¼ teaspoon paprika
½ teaspoon salt
1 cup half and half

In a small saucepan combine horseradish, flour, paprika, and salt. Stir in half and half. Cook until thickened, stirring constantly.

Makes approximately 1½ cups sauce

Favorite recipes from National Marine Fisheries Services

PARSLEYED FISH STEAKS

2 pounds white fish steaks
2 tablespoons fresh minced parsley
½ cup KIKKOMAN Teriyaki Sauce
¼ teaspoon TABASCO® Pepper Sauce

Place fish steaks in single layer in shallow pan. Combine 1 tablespoon parsley with remaining ingredients; pour over fish. Marinate 5 to 10 minutes; turn fish over once. Remove fish; reserve marinade. Broil 3 to 4 minutes on each side, or until fish flakes easily with fork; brush with reserved marinade after turning. Just before serving, sprinkle remaining parsley over fish.

Makes 4 to 6 servings

DEVILED SCROD

1½ to 2 lbs. scrod (small cod)
¼ cup chopped green pepper
¼ cup minced onion
1 Tbsp. prepared mustard
1 tsp. Worcestershire sauce
⅛ tsp. TABASCO®
3½ Tbsp. lemon juice
½ cup butter or margarine
2 cups fine, soft bread crumbs
2 Tbsp. grated Parmesan cheese

Wipe scrod with a damp cloth; cut into 4 portions. Combine green pepper, onion, mustard, Worcestershire sauce, TABASCO® and lemon juice. Melt butter or margarine, stir in bread crumbs; add to vegetable mixture, blending well. Season scrod with salt and pepper; dot with additional butter or margarine. Place on foil-lined broiler rack with surface about 4 inches below source of heat. Broil 5 minutes. Remove from broiler. Turn scrod; top with bread mixture. Return to broiler. Broil 5 to 7 minutes, or until fish will flake easily with a fork. Sprinkle with Parmesan cheese. Broil 1 minute longer. *Makes 4 servings*

Favorite recipe from New Bedford Seafood Council, Inc.

FROSTED TUNA PARTY LOAF

Savory Tuna Sandwich Filling*
Egg Salad Sandwich Filling**

1 cucumber, sliced paper thin
  (25 to 30 slices)
1 loaf white bread, unsliced
2 tablespoons butter or margarine,
  softened to room temperature
2 packages (8 ounces each) cream
  cheese, softened to room
  temperature
⅓ cup chopped parsley

Prepare fillings. Place cucumber slices on paper towel to absorb excess moisture. Cut all crusts from bread with sharp knife. Place loaf on its side; cut into 5 even lengthwise slices. Spread first slice with soft butter; cover with overlapping cucumber slices; spread second slice with half of the Savory Tuna Sandwich Filling; spread third slice with Egg Salad Sandwich Filling; spread fourth slice with remaining tuna filling. Stack slices; top with fifth slice of bread. Beat cream cheese until smooth; spread on top and sides of loaf. Gently press chopped parsley on sides of loaf. To make flower garnish on top, use strips of green pepper or cucumber skin for flower stems, and circles of carrots, radishes, black or green olives for flowers.

Yield: 8 to 10 servings

*SAVORY TUNA SANDWICH FILLING

1 can (6½ or 7 ounces) tuna,
  drained and flaked
¼ cup chopped celery
¼ cup mayonnaise
2 tablespoons pickle relish
2 tablespoons capers, chopped

In medium bowl, combine all ingredients; mix well.

**EGG SALAD SANDWICH FILLING

2 hard cooked eggs, chopped
¼ cup chopped green or red
  pepper
2 tablespoons mayonnaise
⅛ teaspoon salt
Dash of pepper and dry mustard

In small bowl, combine all ingredients; mix well.

Favorite recipe from Tuna Research Foundation, Inc.

SAVORY TUNA LOAF

2 eggs
½ cup milk
2 cups soft bread crumbs
¼ cup frozen minced onion
1 tablespoon dehydrated parsley
  flakes
¼ teaspoon thyme
1 teaspoon salt
¼ teaspoon pepper
3 cans (6½ or 7 ounces each)
  CHICKEN OF THE SEA Tuna

Combine eggs, milk, bread crumbs and seasonings in mixing bowl; blend together. Add tuna; mix thoroughly. Turn into foil-lined loaf pan 8½ × 4½ × 2¾-inches. Bake in a 375°F. oven 1 hour. Turn loaf onto platter; remove foil. (Turn right side up onto another platter.) Garnish with lemon slices.

Yield: 6 servings

TUNA MEDLEY PILAF

2 cans (7 oz. each) tuna, drained
1 package (10 oz.) frozen mixed
  vegetables
1 medium onion, chopped
1 cup uncooked long-grain rice
2 tablespoons vegetable oil
1⅔ cups water
¼ cup KIKKOMAN Soy Sauce

Combine tuna with vegetables in 1½-quart casserole. Sauté rice in oil over medium heat until golden brown, stirring constantly. Slowly stir in water and soy sauce; bring to boil. Remove from heat and add to tuna mixture, stirring to combine. Cover and bake in 350°F. oven 45 minutes, or until rice is tender, stirring occasionally.

Makes 6 servings

CRISPY PEPPER PLATE
(Low Calorie)

1 can (6½ oz.) BUMBLE BEE®
  Chunk Light Tuna in Water
¼ cup dairy sour cream
¼ cup diced cucumber
½ cup shredded carrot
¼ teaspoon dill weed, crumbled
Dash freshly ground black pepper
Dash garlic salt
1 large green bell pepper
For garnish: carrot sticks,
  radishes, fresh fruit

Drain tuna; combine with sour cream, cucumber, carrot and seasonings. Cut pepper in half lengthwise; remove seeds. Fill each half with tuna mixture. Sprinkle with additional dill weed. Serve on luncheon plates garnished with carrot sticks, radishes and fresh fruit.

Makes 2 servings

206 calories per serving

TUNA STUFFED PEPPERS

6 large green peppers
2 cans (7 oz. each) light tuna in
  olive oil (tonno)
PROGRESSO Olive Oil
¾ cup drained salad olives,
  finely chopped
¾ cup PROGRESSO Italian Style
  Bread Crumbs, divided
¼ teaspoon salt
⅛ teaspoon ground black pepper
Herbed Tomato Sauce*

Preheat oven to 375°F. Cut a ½-inch crosswise slice from the top of each pepper; remove membrane and seeds. Drop peppers into boiling water to cover; parboil for 5 minutes; drain. Place peppers upright in an oiled shallow baking pan. Drain tuna, reserving both oil and tuna separately. To oil from tuna add sufficient olive oil to make 7 tablespoons; set aside. In a large bowl combine tuna, olives and ½ cup of the bread crumbs. Add salt, black pepper and 5 tablespoons of the oil; mix well. Spoon into green peppers. Mix remaining oil and bread crumbs. Spoon crumbs on top of each pepper. Cover with foil. Bake until peppers are fork-tender, about 25 minutes. Serve with Herbed Tomato Sauce. Garnish with olive halves, if desired.

Yield: 6 portions

*HERBED TOMATO SAUCE

1 can (8 oz.) tomato sauce
¼ teaspoon oregano leaves,
  crushed
⅛ teaspoon salt
1/16 teaspoon ground black pepper

In medium saucepan combine all ingredients. Reduce heat and simmer, covered, for 5 minutes.

SASSY SEAFOOD TART
(Low Calorie)

1 can (6½ oz.) BUMBLE BEE®
 Chunk Light Tuna in Water
Poppy Seed Crust*
1 cup shredded zucchini
1 cup sliced green onion
2 tablespoons water
4 eggs, lightly beaten
1 cup nonfat milk
¼ cup diced green chiles
½ teaspoon salt
½ teaspoon thyme, crumbled
1 cup shredded Swiss cheese

Drain tuna. Arrange tuna in Poppy
Seed Crust. Simmer zucchini and
onion in water 1 minute; combine
with eggs, milk, chiles, salt and
thyme. Pour into crust. Top with
cheese. Bake in 350°F. oven 35 to
40 minutes until knife inserted
comes out clean. Cool 10 minutes
before serving.

Makes 6 servings

*POPPY SEED CRUST

1½ cups flour
1 tablespoon poppy seed
½ teaspoon salt
½ cup vegetable shortening
3 to 4 tablespoons cold water

Combine flour, poppy seed and
salt. Cut in shortening until
mixture resembles peas. Stir in
enough water to form a ball. Roll
out to fit 9-inch pie plate. Prick
crust. Bake in 375°F. oven 10
minutes until crust begins to
brown.

462 calories per serving

TUNA RAMEKINS
(Low Calorie)

1 can (6½ oz.) BUMBLE BEE®
 Chunk Light Tuna in Water
1 clove garlic, pressed
2 cups diced DOLE® Fresh
 Mushrooms
½ cup diced yellow onion
2 tablespoons butter
1 chicken bouillon cube, crumbled
½ cup unseasoned bread crumbs
½ cup warm water
½ cup chopped parsley
¼ teaspoon thyme, crumbled
2 tablespoons grated Parmesan
 cheese
Chopped parsley for garnish

Drain tuna. Lightly sauté garlic,
mushrooms and onion in butter.
Stir in bouillon cube, bread
crumbs, water, parsley and thyme.
Cook 1 to 2 minutes. Fold in tuna.
Spoon into 2 (7-inch) gratin dishes.
Sprinkle each with cheese. Place
under broiler until cheese browns.
Garnish with chopped parsley.

Makes 2 servings

316 calories per serving

TEMPTING TUNA CAKES

2 cans (6½ oz. each) BUMBLE
 BEE® Chunk Light Tuna in Water
3 eggs, lightly beaten
1 clove garlic, pressed
1 cup chopped parsley
½ cup grated Parmesan cheese
¼ cup diced green onion
1 teaspoon dill, crumbled
½ cup bread crumbs
¼ to ⅓ cup vegetable oil for
 frying
Lemon wedges

Drain tuna. Flake tuna and
combine with eggs, garlic, parsley,
cheese, onion and dill. Mix well.
Form mixture into 6 equal patties.
Coat patties with bread crumbs.
Sauté in hot oil until golden.
Gently turn patties and cook until
golden on other side. Serve with
lemon. *Makes 6 tuna cakes*

TUNA PATTIES

1 envelope (5 servings) FRENCH'S®
 Idaho Mashed Potato Granules
1 egg, slightly beaten
1 tablespoon FRENCH'S®
 Minced Onions
1 can (6½-oz.) tuna, drained
2 tablespoons oil
Sliced American cheese or tartar
 sauce, if desired

Prepare mashed potatoes following
directions on package, except
decrease water to 1 cup; cool
slightly. Stir in egg, onion, and
tuna. Shape 6 patties. Heat oil in
large skillet; cook tuna patties,
turning to brown both sides. If
desired, top each with half slice of
cheese or tartar sauce.

6 servings

TUNA TACOS

2 (6½ oz.) cans S&W Chunk Light
 Tuna, drained
1 (3½ oz.) can S&W Pitted Large
 Ripe Olives, chopped
1 (4 oz.) can S&W Green Chili
 Peppers, diced
3 green onions, chopped
3 rounded Tbsp. mayonnaise
1 (17¼ oz.) jar S&W Mixed Bean
 Salad
1 (14 oz.) can S&W Small Artichoke
 Hearts, chopped
2 medium tomatoes, chopped
12 corn tortillas
Oil for frying tortillas

Mix first five ingredients in bowl.
Set aside. Drain bean salad,
artichoke hearts and set those and
the chopped tomatoes in separate
serving bowls. To assemble and
serve: Fry tortillas in oil till lightly
crisp. Place layer of tuna mixture,
followed by layers of other
ingredients, topping off with a
generous helping of mixed bean
salad. *Serves 6*

COUNTDOWN TUNA
STIR-FRY
(Low Calorie)

1 tablespoon butter or margarine
¼ cup chopped onion
½ clove garlic, minced
2 cups shredded Chinese cabbage
1 chopped peeled tomato or red
 pepper
1 can (6½ or 7 ounces) tuna in
 water, drained
2 scallions, cut in 1-inch lengths
2 cups cooked fine noodles
½ teaspoon salt

In large skillet, melt butter; cook
onion and garlic until tender. Add
cabbage, cook over medium heat 5
minutes, stirring frequently. Stir in
tomato, tuna and remaining
ingredients, cook 5 to 10 minutes
longer. *Yield: 4 servings*

203 calories per serving

*Favorite recipe from Tuna Research
Foundation, Inc.*

DEEP DISH PIE

Filling:
2 cans (6½ oz. each) BUMBLE BEE® Chunk Light Tuna in Water
1 large onion, chopped
2 cups sliced DOLE® Fresh Mushrooms
1 cup sliced celery
2 tablespoons butter
¼ cup flour
1 can (14½ oz.) chicken broth
1 package (10 oz.) frozen cut green beans, partially thawed
1 cup diced carrots, cooked
1 teaspoon thyme, crumbled
¼ teaspoon salt

Pastry*
1 egg, beaten

Drain tuna. Sauté onion, mushrooms and celery in butter. Blend in flour. Gradually stir in chicken broth; simmer until sauce thickens (3 to 5 minutes). Add green beans, carrots, thyme and salt; fold in tuna. Spoon into 2½-quart casserole dish. Cover with pastry. Make 6 slits in pastry. Brush with beaten egg. Bake in 400°F. oven 30 to 40 minutes until bubbly and brown.

Makes 4 to 6 servings

*For pastry, use standard recipe for a one crust pie. Substitute ½ cup grated Parmesan cheese for ½ cup flour. Add 2 tablespoons chopped parsley to flour mixture. Roll dough to cover top of 2½-quart casserole dish.

TUNA PIE

2 tablespoons butter or margarine
½ cup slivered almonds
2 cans (6½ ounces each) tuna, drained
1 can (16 ounces) cut green beans, drained
1 can (6 ounces) sliced mushrooms, drained
2 cans (10½ ounces each) condensed cream of mushroom soup, undiluted
⅓ cup sherry
1 package (10 ounces) PEPPERIDGE FARM® Frozen Patty Shells
1 egg, well beaten

Thaw package of Patty Shells in refrigerator overnight or on a kitchen counter until workable, always keeping them cold to the touch. In a skillet, heat butter and sauté almonds until golden. Stir in

tuna, green beans, mushrooms, soup and sherry. Pour mixture into a shallow 1½ quart casserole. Stack 3 Patty Shells one atop the other. On a lightly floured surface roll out to about 4 x 9 inches. With a cookie cutter cut pastry into 2 inch rounds. Repeat with remaining Patty Shells. Place rounds on a cookie sheet and brush tops with beaten egg. Bake casserole and pastry rounds in 400°F. oven for 15 to 20 minutes or until rounds are puffed and brown. Place puff pastry rounds over the top of the tuna casserole. Serve at once.

Serves 6

FISHERMAN'S WHARF JAMBALAYA

1 pkg. (8 oz.) GOLDEN GRAIN® Chicken Flavor RICE-A-RONI®
2 Tbsp. butter or margarine
2¾ cups hot water
¼ tsp. pepper
Dash TABASCO® Sauce
1 Tbsp. instant minced onions
¼ cup diced celery
¼ cup diced green pepper
2 cups diced cooked ham
1 can (6 oz.) tuna or shrimp

Lightly brown rice-vermicelli mixture in butter. Stir in water and contents of flavor packet. Add remaining ingredients. Cover and simmer 15 minutes.

Makes 5 (1⅓ cup) servings

STEAMED SESAME TUNA

1 can (12½ oz.) BUMBLE BEE® Chunk Light Tuna*
Water
1 teaspoon sesame seeds, toasted
1 stalk green onion, chopped
2 tablespoons soy sauce
2 tablespoons vegetable oil or sesame oil
Chinese parsley for garnish

Drain tuna. Turn tuna into a heat-proof shallow dish set over a rack in a skillet filled with about ½ inch of water. Cover and steam tuna about 5 minutes. Toss in sesame seeds, green onion and soy sauce. Heat oil and carefully pour over tuna. Garnish with parsley.

Makes 4 servings

*or use 2 cans (6½ oz. each) BUMBLE BEE® Chunk Light Tuna

SALMON MOUSSE A LA CANADA DRY®

2 cups canned salmon, drained and flaked
Lemon Juice to taste
⅛-¼ teaspoon salt
⅛-¼ teaspoon pepper
1 envelope unflavored gelatin
½ cup CANADA DRY® Club Soda
3 tablespoons mayonnaise
3 tablespoons whipped cream

Place salmon flakes in electric blender or food processor; whirl about 60 seconds. Season with lemon juice, salt and pepper. Soften gelatin in CANADA DRY® Club Soda. Dissolve it in a double boiler. Add dissolved gelatin to the salmon mixture and stir thoroughly. Fold in mayonnaise and whipped cream. Chill slightly. Put mousse in large or individual molds and chill until set.

Makes 6-8 Servings

TUESDAY'S SPECIAL

1 can (15½ oz.) BUMBLE BEE® Pink Salmon
3 cups egg noodles
5 cups boiling water
2 cups sliced DOLE® Fresh Mushrooms
¼ cup butter
3 medium zucchini, sliced
2 cups sliced carrots
2 tablespoons flour
1 teaspoon dill weed, crumbled
1 teaspoon salt
Dash ground nutmeg
1¾ cups milk
2 tablespoons pale dry sherry
½ cup grated Parmesan cheese

Drain salmon. Remove skin, if desired. Mash bones. Cook noodles in boiling water 6 to 7 minutes. Drain. Sauté mushrooms in 2 tablespoons butter. Remove mushrooms and combine with salmon, mashed bones, noodles, zucchini and carrots. Melt remaining butter in same skillet. Stir in flour, dill, salt and nutmeg until blended. Gradually stir in milk, stirring constantly, until mixture boils and thickens. Remove from heat. Stir in sherry. Stir into salmon and vegetable mixture. Pour into 2-quart shallow casserole. Sprinkle with Parmesan cheese. Bake in 350°F. oven 25 to 30 minutes.

Makes 4 to 6 servings

GRANDMA'S SALMON LOAF

1 can (15½ oz.) BUMBLE BEE®
  Keta Salmon
1 clove garlic, pressed
1 cup diced celery
½ cup diced onion
1 tablespoon vegetable oil
2 eggs, lightly beaten
1 cup cooked bulgur wheat
½ cup grated Parmesan cheese
1 teaspoon thyme, crumbled
Parsley for garnish
Sour Cream Dill Sauce*

Drain salmon. Sauté garlic, celery
and onion in vegetable oil. Mash
salmon in a bowl. Add sautéed
vegetables, eggs, bulgur, cheese
and thyme. Mix until blended. Turn
into 8 × 4½ × 2½-inch loaf pan.
Bake in 350°F. oven 40 minutes.
Cool 10 minutes. Turn onto serving
plate. Garnish with parsley. Serve
with Sour Cream Dill Sauce.
Makes 4 servings

*SOUR CREAM DILL SAUCE

2 tablespoons butter
2 tablespoons flour
1¼ cups milk
½ cup dairy sour cream
1 cup frozen peas, thawed
1 teaspoon dill weed, crumbled
½ teaspoon salt
¼ teaspoon onion powder

Cook butter and flour 2 minutes.
Add milk and sour cream. Simmer,
stirring, 5 minutes. Add remaining
ingredients and cook until heated
through.

WESTERN SALMON LOAF

1 can (15½ oz.) BUMBLE BEE®
  Pink Salmon
1 egg, lightly beaten
1½ cups shredded Monterey Jack
  cheese
3 tablespoons wheat germ
1 cup cooked spinach noodles
1 cup cooked chopped broccoli
¼ cup dairy sour cream
¾ teaspoon oregano, crumbled
1 medium onion, diced
1 clove garlic, minced
½ cup diced celery
1 tablespoon vegetable oil
1 can (15 oz.) tomato sauce

Drain salmon. Remove skin, if
desired. Mash bones. Combine
salmon and bones with egg, 1 cup

cheese and wheat germ. Combine
noodles, broccoli, sour cream,
remaining ½ cup cheese and ¼
teaspoon oregano. Sauté onion,
garlic and celery in oil until onion
is soft. Stir in tomato sauce and
remaining ½ teaspoon oregano.
Simmer 15 minutes. Combine one-
half with salmon mixture. Spoon
one-half salmon mixture in well
greased square *1-quart casserole
dish.* Spoon broccoli mixture on
top. Top with remaining salmon
mixture. Bake in a 375°F. oven 35
to 40 minutes. Let stand 10
minutes before serving. Warm
remaining tomato sauce mixture
and spoon over each serving.
Makes 4 servings

CURRIED SALMON CROQUETTES

¼ c. butter
¼ c. flour
½ tsp. salt
⅛ tsp. pepper
¾ c. milk
1 c. 3-MINUTE BRAND® Oats
1 lb. canned salmon, drained
1 egg, beaten
1½ c. dry bread crumbs
Oil for deep fat frying

Sauce:
10½ oz. can cream of mushroom
  soup
1 c. light cream
1 Tbsp. lemon juice
½ tsp. curry powder

Melt butter in saucepan. Stir in
flour, salt and pepper. Slowly add
milk, stirring constantly. Cook over
medium heat until mixture has
thickened. Remove from heat and
stir in oats and salmon. Cool
thoroughly. Shape into eight
croquettes. Roll each croquette in
flour, then dip in egg and finally
into bread crumbs. Heat frying oil
to 375°F. Fry the croquettes until
they are golden brown (about 2½
to 3 minutes). Turn the croquettes
during frying. Drain on paper
towels to remove excess oil.

Combine all of the ingredients for
the sauce. Heat to boiling. Remove
from heat and serve over the hot
croquettes.

RICE PARMESAN

1 can (15½ oz.) BUMBLE BEE®
  Keta Salmon
1 large onion, chopped
1 clove garlic, pressed
2 cups sliced DOLE® Fresh
  Mushrooms
½ cup diced carrots
2 tablespoons butter
1 cup brown rice
1 can (14½ oz.) chicken broth
½ cup water
1 teaspoon Italian herbs, crumbled
½ teaspoon salt
1 medium zucchini, shredded
½ cup grated Parmesan cheese

Drain salmon. Sauté onion, garlic,
mushrooms and carrots in butter
until onion is soft. Stir in rice,
chicken broth, water, herbs and
salt. Cover; simmer 35 minutes.
Fold in zucchini and cheese. Break
salmon into bite-size pieces; fold
into rice. Simmer until salmon is
heated through.
Makes 4 to 6 servings

SALMON STUFFED POTATOES

1 can (7¾ oz.) BUMBLE BEE®
  Pink Salmon
4 baking potatoes (about 2½ lbs.)
Vegetable oil
¾ cup milk
¼ cup butter, softened
½ cup grated Parmesan cheese
½ cup chopped parsley
1 teaspoon thyme, crumbled
¼ teaspoon salt

Drain salmon. Wash potatoes. Oil
skins. Bake in 400°F. oven 1 hour
until done. Cool enough to handle.
Slice top off each potato
lengthwise. Scoop out potato being
careful not to prick hole in skin. In
a mixer bowl, mash potatoes. Beat
in milk and butter until fluffy. Beat
in cheese, parsley, thyme and salt
until blended. Stir in salmon.
Spoon mixture into each potato
skin, mounding tops. Bake in
350°F. oven 40 minutes.
Makes 4 servings

Shellfish

SHRIMP WITH CASHEW NUTS

2 tablespoons PLANTERS® Peanut Oil
2 pounds raw shrimp, shelled and deveined
¼ cup finely sliced green onions
2 cups (10-ounce package) frozen peas
1 cup chicken bouillon
½ cup sliced water chestnuts
1 teaspoon salt
½ teaspoon ground ginger
¼ cup soy sauce
4 teaspoons cornstarch
½ cup PLANTERS® Dry Roasted Cashew Nuts (salted or unsalted)

Heat PLANTERS® Peanut Oil in a skillet. Add shrimp and sliced green onions. Cook, stirring constantly, until shrimp turn pink and onions are tender. Add peas, chicken bouillon, water chestnuts, salt and ginger. Cover; bring to a boil and simmer for 5 minutes or until peas and shrimp are tender. Blend soy sauce and cornstarch. Stir into shrimp mixture and cook until sauce is clear and slightly thickened. Stir in PLANTERS® Dry Roasted Cashew Nuts. Serve immediately with hot rice and fried noodles. *Makes 6 servings*

SWEET AND SOUR SHRIMP

5 tablespoons butter
1½ pounds shrimp*, shelled and cleaned
1 cup pineapple chunks, fresh or canned
¼ cup JACQUIN'S Triple Sec
2 tablespoons soy sauce
½ cup seeded and chopped green pepper
½ cup wine vinegar
¼ cup sugar
1 cup pineapple juice
Salt and pepper
1 teaspoon cornstarch dissolved in ½ cup water

Melt the butter in a heavy skillet and sauté the shrimp for about 5 minutes. Add pineapple chunks, JACQUIN'S Triple Sec liqueur and soy sauce; simmer 1 minute. Add green pepper, vinegar, sugar, and pineapple juice and simmer another 3 minutes. Season to taste with salt and pepper. Add cornstarch and water mixture and cook, stirring until sauce barely thickens, about 3 minutes longer. Do not overcook. Serve over hot rice or Chinese noodles. *Serves 4*

*Lobster chunks may be substituted for the shrimp.

SOUTH COAST BUTTERFLY SHRIMP

1 pound large shrimp, shelled and deveined (leave tail on shrimp)
1 beaten egg
¼ cup cornstarch
¼ cup flour
¼ cup chicken broth
½ teaspoon salt
Oil for deep frying
1 large green pepper, diced
1 cup thinly sliced carrot
1 clove garlic, minced
2 tablespoons cooking oil
1 cup chicken broth, fresh or canned
½ cup IMPERIAL Granulated Sugar
⅓ cup cider vinegar
2 teaspoons soy sauce
¼ cup water
2 tablespoons cornstarch
Freshly cooked rice

Shell and devein shrimp, leaving tails on. Combine egg, cornstarch, flour, chicken broth, and salt; beat until smooth. Dip shrimp in batter and fry in deep hot fat (375°) until golden brown, about 5 minutes. Drain and keep warm. In skillet, sauté green pepper, carrot, and garlic in cooking oil until tender but still crisp. Add to vegetables, broth, sugar, vinegar and soy sauce. Bring to boil and boil 1 minute. Blend water slowly into cornstarch and stir into vegetables. Cook and stir until thickened and bubbling. To serve, arrange hot shrimp over rice and pour sauce over shrimp and rice. *Serves 4*

CARIBBEAN BUTTERFLY SHRIMP

1 pound large shrimp
1 tablespoon butter
1 tablespoon oil
⅔ cup chopped onion
⅔ cup chopped celery
¾ teaspoon dill weed
2 cups sliced green DOLE® Bananas
1 teaspoon paprika
1 cup dry white wine
1 cup water
4 chicken bouillon cubes, crumbled
1 tablespoon cornstarch
2 tablespoons chopped parsley
2 teaspoons lemon juice
Hot cooked rice

Shell and butterfly shrimp, removing vein. Heat butter and oil in 10-inch skillet. Add onion, celery and dill and sauté until tender, about 3 minutes. Add shrimp and bananas, and sauté 5 minutes. Stir in paprika. Combine wine, water, bouillon cubes and cornstarch and add to skillet. Cook, stirring gently, until mixture boils and thickens. Stir in parsley and lemon juice. Serve at once over hot cooked rice. *Makes 4 servings*

SHRIMP CURRY
(Microwave Preparation)

¼ cup (½ stick) butter
1 medium green pepper, cut into ½ inch squares
½ cup thinly sliced celery
2 tablespoons sliced green onion
¼ cup cornstarch
2 teaspoons curry powder
½ teaspoon salt
2 cups chicken broth
1 can (8 ounces) LA CHOY® Sliced Water Chestnuts, drained
1½ cups cooked shrimp
2 tablespoons chopped pimento
LA CHOY® Chow Mein Noodles

Place butter, green pepper, celery and onion in 2-quart glass baking dish. Cover loosely. Microwave 4 minutes at HIGH (100% power), stirring once. Blend cornstarch with seasonings; stir into vegetable mixture. Add chicken broth, water chestnuts and shrimp; mix well. Cover loosely. Microwave 9 to 10 minutes, or until thickened, at HIGH. Stir every 2 to 3 minutes. Stir in pimiento. Serve over noodles. *4 to 6 servings*

FAR EAST SHRIMP

1 cup LINDSAY® Sliced Ripe
  Olives
1 pound shelled, deveined shrimp
1 clove garlic, minced
¼ teaspoon powdered ginger
2 tablespoons cooking oil
½ cup green pepper (cut in large
  pieces)
½ pound lean ground pork
½ cup sliced celery
1 (10½ oz.) can chicken broth
2 tablespoons cornstarch
2 tablespoons soy sauce
¼ cup chopped onion

Sauté shrimp with garlic and
ginger in oil for 1 minute. Shape
ground pork into little balls, add to
shrimp and cook for 2 or 3
minutes. Add celery, green pepper,
and 1 cup chicken broth. Bring to a
boil. Cover and simmer 10 minutes
over low heat. Blend cornstarch
with remaining broth and soy
sauce. Stir into shrimp mixture.
Add ripe olives and onion. Cook,
stirring, until sauce thickens. Serve
with steamed rice.

Makes 4 servings

SHRIMPOREE CREOLE

1 pound cooked shrimp, shelled,
  deveined
3 tablespoons butter or margarine
½ cup chopped onion
½ cup chopped green pepper
¼ cup minced celery
2 cloves garlic, minced
1 tablespoon flour
1 (1 pound) can sliced stewed
  tomatoes
⅛ teaspoon dried thyme
1 bay leaf
½ teaspoon IMPERIAL Granulated
  Sugar
Dash hot pepper sauce
1 teaspoon Worcestershire sauce
Several whole allspice
Salt and pepper
Minced parsley
Hot, freshly cooked rice

Cook shrimp. Remove shells. To
make creole sauce, sauté onion,
green pepper, garlic and celery in
butter or margarine until limp; add
flour and cook and stir until flour
is light tan. Add all other
ingredients except parsley and rice
and cook until sauce is thickened.
Taste for salt and pepper and add
more if needed. Stir in parsley.
Serve over hot, freshly cooked rice.

Serves 4

SHRIMP PERNOD

24-30 shrimp (according to size)
2 oz. butter
1 small, finely chopped onion
2 lbs. tomatoes skinned and
  chopped
1 pinch sugar
1 clove garlic
½ teaspoon chopped parsley
Salt and pepper
1 tablespoon PERNOD, diluted
  with 1 tablespoon water
A little tomato paste

Poach the shrimp in salted water
for 3-5 minutes (allow 5 minutes
more if they are not shelled. Shell
after they are poached.) Drain. Melt
the butter in a large saucepan,
then fry the onion slowly, without
browning, for about 3 minutes. Add
the tomatoes and other ingredients
except the tomato paste and leave
to simmer for about 30 minutes,
stirring from time to time. Check
the seasoning, and add tomato
paste according to taste. Reheat
the shrimp in the sauce and serve
with rice.

Serves 4

BEER FRIED SHRIMP

1½ lbs. ATALANTA Frozen Shrimp,
  raw, shelled, leaving tail, and
  deveined
4 Tbsp. Lemon Juice
1½ cups Flour
12 oz. Beer
1 Tbsp. Paprika
1 tsp. Salt
Frying Oil as needed
Lemon Wedges from 2 lemons
Parsley as needed

Beer batter: Pour beer in bowl. Sift
together 1 cup flour, paprika and
salt and beat into beer. Dry shrimp
and sprinkle with lemon juice.
Dredge shrimp in remaining flour
and dip in beer batter. Coat the
shrimps well. Deep fat fry at 375°
until golden brown about 5
minutes. Drain and serve with
lemon wedges and parsley.

Yield: 4 servings

THE LAIRD'S SHRIMP

¼ lb. butter
2 cloves garlic, crushed
1 tablespoon finely minced onion
1 lb. raw shrimp, peeled and
  deveined
3 tablespoons JOHNNIE WALKER
  Red
2 teaspoons lemon juice
¼ teaspoon dried basil
Salt and pepper

Heat butter in skillet. Add garlic
and onion and cook over low heat
until translucent. Add shrimp,
JOHNNIE WALKER Red, lemon
juice and basil. Sauté shrimp just
until pink, stirring often. Be careful
not to overcook. Add salt and
pepper to taste.

2 to 3 servings

CREOLE SHRIMP

2 packages (6 ounces)
  MRS. PAUL'S® Fried Shrimp*
1 tablespoon cooking oil
2 tablespoons butter
1 medium onion, thinly sliced
1 small green pepper, diced
½ cup celery, chopped
1 small clove garlic, minced or
  ½ teaspoon garlic powder
1 can (16 ounces) tomatoes, cut
  into small pieces
1 bay leaf
¼ teaspoon thyme leaves
Dash of cayenne pepper
½ teaspoon chili powder
2 teaspoons sugar
1 teaspoon salt
⅛ teaspoon black pepper
1 tablespoon flour

In large skillet sauté onion, green
pepper, celery and garlic in butter
and oil for approximately 5
minutes. Drain tomatoes and
reserve ¼ cup juice. Stir in
remaining ingredients except flour,
shrimp and reserved tomato juice,
bring to boil. In a small bowl, blend
together the reserved tomato juice
and flour. Add to mixture in skillet
and simmer over low heat for 15-20
minutes. Meanwhile, prepare
shrimp according to package
directions. Serve over rice and
cooked shrimp.   *Serves 7*

*Note: Scallops, fish fillets, fish
  sticks, chicken patties or
  chicken sticks may be
  substituted for shrimp as a
  variation.

JADE AND CORAL ALMOND

¾ pound shrimp, peeled and deveined
Marinade (recipe follows)
2 tablespoons vegetable oil
½ cup BLUE DIAMOND® Whole Natural Almonds
1 cup ¼-inch diagonal slices celery
½ cup ¼-inch diagonal slices green onion
2 tablespoons water
1 package (10 ounces) frozen peas, thawed

Combine shrimp and marinade; let stand at least 10 minutes while assembling other ingredients, stirring occasionally. Heat heavy skillet or wok over high heat; add 1 tablespoon of the oil. When oil is hot, add almonds and stir-fry about 2 minutes or until crisp; remove from pan. Add celery and stir-fry 1 minute, then add green onions and stir-fry 1 minute more; remove from pan. Add remaining tablespoon oil and heat. With slotted spoon remove shrimp from marinade and add to skillet; stir-fry 2 to 3 minutes, or until shrimp turns pink. Add reserved marinade, water, peas, celery, green onions and almonds; stir until peas are heated through and sauce is thickened, about 2 minutes more.

Makes 4 servings

MARINADE

Combine 2 tablespoons dry sherry or rice wine, 1 tablespoon *each* soy sauce and cornstarch, ½ teaspoon granulated sugar, ¼ teaspoon ground ginger or fresh, minced, and 1 clove garlic, minced or pressed.

BOOTH

SHRIMP DE JONGHE

1 lb. BOOTH Peeled and Deveined Shrimp, frozen
½ cup butter or margarine
2 tablespoons instant minced onions
1 clove garlic, minced
½ teaspoon salt
Dash pepper
¼ teaspoon Worcestershire sauce
¾ cup bread crumbs

Melt butter in large skillet. Add garlic clove and instant minced onions. Sauté over medium heat for 3 to 5 minutes; do not let onions turn brown. Add salt, pepper and Worcestershire sauce; blend to distribute seasonings. Carefully add frozen shrimp and sauté over medium-high heat until shrimp lose their translucency, about 5 to 8 minutes. Add bread crumbs and stir until all ingredients are well blended. Serve immediately.

JAPANESE TEMPURA

3 cups PLANTERS® Peanut Oil
1½ cups cold water
1 egg yolk
1½ cups unsifted flour
½ cup cornstarch
4 tablespoons sugar
1 teaspoon salt
1 teaspoon ground ginger
1 egg white, stiffly beaten
1 pound raw shrimp, shelled and deveined
¼ pound fresh mushrooms, cleaned and halved
¼ pound fresh green beans, cut into diagonal slices
4 carrots, peeled and cut into thin strips
1 large sweet potato, peeled, halved and cut in ¼-inch slices
1 green pepper, seeded and cut into rings
1 large Bermuda onion, sliced and separated into rings

Heat peanut oil in a large saucepan to 375°F. Combine water, egg yolk, flour, cornstarch, sugar, salt and ginger in a blender container. Cover and blend on high speed until smooth, using a rubber spatula to keep mixture flowing to blades. Fold mixture into beaten egg white. Dip shrimp and assorted vegetables into batter, shaking off excess. Fry in hot peanut oil until golden and tender. Drain on paper towels. Serve hot with Dipping Sauce (recipe follows). *Makes 4 to 6 servings*

DIPPING SAUCE

Dissolve 1 beef bouillon cube in 1 cup boiling water. Stir in ¼ cup DRY SACK Sherry and ¼ cup soy sauce. Serve warm.

SARA'S SHERRY SHRIMP

½ stick butter
5 garlic cloves, crushed
1½ pounds shrimp, shelled and deveined
¼ cup fresh lemon juice
¼ teaspoon pepper
1 cup HOLLAND HOUSE® Sherry Cooking Wine
2 tablespoons chopped parsley
2 tablespoons chopped chives
Salt to taste

Melt butter in skillet over medium heat. Add garlic, shrimp, lemon juice and pepper. Cook, stirring until shrimp turns pink (about 5 minutes). Add HOLLAND HOUSE® Sherry Cooking Wine, parsley and chives. Bring just to a boil. Serve immediately over cooked rice. Garnish with lemon and parsley.

Serves 4

THE LUXURY LINER

2 Tbsp. butter
½ cup onion, finely chopped
1 cup zucchini, finely diced
½ cup HOLLAND HOUSE® Sherry Cooking Wine
½ cup water
2 Tbsp. tomato sauce, or 1 ripe tomato, chopped
1 Chicken flavor bouillon cube
½ lb. medium-size fresh or frozen shrimp,* shelled and deveined
1 Tbsp. cornstarch, dissolved in 2 Tbsp. cold water
1 Tbsp. breadcrumbs
3 California Avocados, halved, pitted and peeled

Melt butter in saucepan. Add onion and zucchini and cook 5 minutes over medium heat. Stir in sherry, water, bouillon cube and tomato. Cook 3 minutes over high heat. Add shrimp and cook, stirring, about 1 minute until shrimp turn pink. Add cornstarch mixture and cook, stirring, until mixture comes to boil. Remove from heat. Place Avocado halves on baking dish. Fill each half with shrimp mixture, spooning remainder of sauce around them. Sprinkle with crumbs and broil 1-2 minutes until crumbs brown. Serve immediately.

Appetizer for 6 or luncheon entree for 3

*Chicken breast cut into ¼ inch cubes may be substituted.

PAN-FRIED SHRIMP MEDALLIONS WITH CHINESE CABBAGE

1 lb. Chinese cabbage (bok choy) or celery cabbage
1 lb. shrimp, shelled, deveined and minced
⅓ cup LA CHOY® Water Chestnuts, minced
1 green onion, minced
1 slice fresh ginger root, minced
1 egg, beaten
1 teaspoon cornstarch
½ teaspoon salt
Dash pepper
¼ cup cooking oil
2 tablespoons cooking oil

Cut cabbage stems into ½ inch sections and blanch. Tear leaves into bite size pieces. Combine shrimp, water chestnuts, green onion and ginger root. Mix in beaten egg. Add cornstarch, salt and pepper. Form mixture into small cakes, about ½-inch thick and 1½ inches in diameter. Chill, covered, about one hour. Heat ¼ cup oil in large skillet. Fry shrimp cakes over medium heat until golden brown on both sides. Remove and drain on paper towels; keep warm. Add remaining oil to skillet and heat. Add cabbage stems and leaves and cook, stirring, until leaves are wilted and stems are tender-crisp. Serve at once with shrimp medallions.

8-10 servings

SHRIMP JAMBALAYA

2 lbs. ATALANTA Frozen Shrimp, raw, shelled, deveined
5 Tbsp. Butter
2 Tbsp. Flour
1½ cups Onions, chopped
1 cup Green Pepper, diced
½ cup Cooked Ham, cubed
2 cups Canned Tomatoes
1 tsp. Dried Basil
⅛ tsp. Salt
Pepper as needed
2 cups Rice, raw, white
3 cups Chicken Stock

Sauté onions and green pepper in butter until onions are transparent. Blend in flour. Add ham and tomatoes. Simmer for 5 minutes until thickened. Add basil, salt and pepper. Stir in rice and cover with chicken stock. Cover pan and simmer slowly for about 20

minutes. Stir in shrimp and cook 10 minutes. If mixture is dry add additional stock.

Yield: 6 servings

MINUTE MAID® SHRIMP JAMBALAYA

4 slices bacon
½ cup chopped onion
½ cup chopped green pepper
½ cup uncooked long grain rice
1½ cups MINUTE MAID® Orange Juice, reconstituted
1 teaspoon salt
1 tablespoon Worcestershire sauce
1 can (1 lb.) tomatoes, undrained
1 can (8 oz.) tomato sauce
2 cloves garlic, minced
2 cups frozen shrimp
1 package (10 oz.) frozen okra, partially thawed and sliced
¼ cup sherry, if desired

In large fry pan, or Dutch oven, fry bacon until crisp; remove bacon and crumble. In bacon drippings, sauté onion and green pepper until tender crisp. Add remaining ingredients except shrimp, okra, sherry and crumbled bacon; cover and simmer for 30 minutes until rice is tender. Add remaining ingredients. Simmer, uncovered, for about 15 minutes until okra is tender.

Makes 6 to 8 servings

JIFFY SHRIMP JAMBALAYA

1 can (4½ ounces) LOUISIANA BRAND Shrimp
3 tablespoons cooking oil
¾ cup (about ¼ pound) cubed lean ham
1¼ cups uncooked rice
1 can (14½ ounces) stewed tomatoes
1 bay leaf
¼ teaspoon thyme
1 garlic clove, sliced
Dash or two cayenne pepper

Have shrimp chilled in the can. Heat oil in a heavy pan or Dutch oven and sauté ham about 2 minutes. Add rice, tomatoes (solid pieces chopped), seasonings, and 1½ cups water. Cook rapidly *uncovered* 5 minutes and turn heat to lowest point. Add shrimp and shrimp liquid; toss lightly with a fork to mix. Cover closely; steam *without stirring* 15 minutes or until rice is tender and liquid absorbed.

5 servings

DEVILED SEAFOOD

¼ cup finely chopped green pepper
¼ cup finely chopped onion
1 cup finely chopped celery
1 teaspoon Worcestershire sauce
½ teaspoon salt
1 can (6 to 7 oz.) shrimp, drained
1 can (6 to 7 oz.) crab meat, flaked
2 cups PEPPERIDGE FARM® Herb Seasoned Stuffing, crushed
1 cup mayonnaise

Stir together all ingredients until blended. Spoon into a 1-quart shallow casserole or 8 ovenproof shells. Bake at 350°F. for 30 minutes or until lightly browned.

Serves 6 to 8

PACIFIC NEWBURG

6 Tbsp. butter
½ cup THE CHRISTIAN BROTHERS® Dry Sherry
1½ cups heavy cream
¾ tsp. salt
⅛ tsp. cayenne
1 tsp. lemon juice
5 egg yolks
3 cups cooked shrimp or crab, in bite size pieces
3 cups steamed rice

Melt butter over moderate heat; stir in sherry, 1 cup cream and seasonings. Simmer 2 minutes. In small bowl, beat egg yolks into remaining ½ cup cream. Beat in ¼ cup hot sherry sauce. Slowly pour egg mixture into sherry sauce, stirring constantly. Cook over low heat until thickened; stir in seafood. Serve at once over rice.

Serves 6

CRAB MEAT LUGENBUHL

1 onion, chopped
2 cans mushroom soup
2 pkgs. chopped broccoli
½ stick butter
2 cans HIGH SEA Crab Meat
1 Tbsp. Worcestershire sauce
6 oz. garlic cheese
Dash of TABASCO®

Sauté onion in butter, add mushroom soup, cheese and seasoning, mixing well. Add crab meat and drained cooked broccoli to mixture and stir. Heat and serve.

Serves 8

CRABMEAT FLORENTINE

1 package (6 oz.) frozen crabmeat*
1 package (10 oz.) frozen chopped
  spinach
1 cup sliced DOLE® Fresh
  Mushrooms
2 tablespoons butter
2 tablespoons flour
1 teaspoon garlic salt
¼ teaspoon freshly ground black
  pepper
¼ cup dry sherry
½ cup milk
1 cup dairy sour cream
1 cup grated Swiss cheese

Thaw crabmeat in refrigerator
overnight. Thaw and drain spinach.
Sauté mushrooms in butter in a
large skillet until golden. Blend in
flour, garlic salt, pepper, sherry
and milk. Stir in sour cream,
spinach and crabmeat with all
liquid. Cook, stirring constantly
until mixture boils and thickens.
Spoon into 4 large baking shells or
individual ramekins. Sprinkle with
cheese. Place under broiler about 5
inches from heat until cheese is
bubbly and browned. Serve at
once.   *Makes 4 servings*

*Or use fresh crabmeat.

Mrs. Paul's

DEVILED CRAB
FLORENTINE

1 package (15 ounces)
  MRS. PAUL'S® Deviled Crabs
1 package (10 ounces) frozen
  chopped spinach
2 tablespoons butter
2 tablespoons flour
1 cup milk
2 wedges (1 ounce, each) of
  Gruyère or 2 slices of Swiss
  cheese, grated
Salt and pepper to taste
Parmesan cheese, grated

Prepare deviled crabs and
spinach according to package
directions. Meanwhile, melt butter
in a medium saucepan. Add flour
and stir constantly over low heat
for about 2 minutes. Gradually add
milk, stirring constantly, and

continue to cook until mixture
comes to a boil. Add cheese and
stir over low heat until cheese
melts. Place spinach in bottom of
a buttered 1½ quart casserole.
Add crab cakes and spoon cheese
sauce over casserole. Sprinkle
lightly with Parmesan cheese.
Place briefly under broiler to
brown.   *Serves 5*

SNOW CRAB MORNAY
WITH BROCCOLI

6 to 8 oz. Alaska Snow crab meat,
  frozen or canned
⅓ cup chopped celery
¼ cup chopped green onion
1 clove garlic, minced
1 tablespoon butter or margarine
1½ tablespoons flour
¼ teaspoon salt
Dash cayenne pepper
Milk
1 tablespoon sherry wine
¼ cup shredded Swiss cheese
1 tablespoon snipped chives
Cooked broccoli spears

Thaw crab if frozen. Drain and
slice, reserving liquid. Sauté celery,
green onion, and garlic in butter
until tender. Blend in flour, salt
and cayenne. Add milk to reserved
crab liquid to equal 1¼ cups. Add
to skillet with sherry wine. Cook
and stir until mixture thickens and
bubbles. Add cheese and stir until
melted. Fold in crab and chives.
Serve over cooked broccoli spears.
            Makes 2 or 3 servings

Favorite recipe from Alaska Crab Institute

KING CRAB KRUNCH

1 pound king crab meat, fresh or
  frozen
1 can (8¾ ounces) crushed
  pineapple
3 tablespoons butter or margarine
½ cup thinly sliced celery
2 tablespoons cornstarch
2 cups chicken broth
½ cup toasted blanched
  slivered almonds
1 tablespoon lemon juice
1 can (5 ounces) chow mein
  noodles

Thaw frozen crab meat. Drain crab
meat. Remove any remaining shell
or cartilage. Drain pineapple,
reserving liquid. Melt butter in a
10-inch fry pan. Add celery,
pineapple, and crab meat. Cook
over low heat for 5 minutes,
stirring frequently. Dissolve
cornstarch in pineapple juice. Stir
into crab mixture. Add chicken
broth gradually and cook until
thick, stirring constantly. Add
almonds and lemon juice. Serve
over noodles.   *Makes 6 servings*

*Favorite recipe from National Marine
Fisheries Services*

1-2-3 CRAB

1 pound lump blue crab meat,
  fresh, frozen, or pasteurized
½ cup butter or margarine, melted
1 tablespoon tarragon vinegar

Thaw frozen crab meat. Drain crab
meat. Remove any remaining shell
or cartilage. Place crab meat in a
shallow 1-quart casserole.
Combine butter and vinegar. Pour
over crab meat. Mix lightly. Broil
about 4 inches from source of heat
for 12 to 15 minutes or until lightly
browned.   *Makes 6 servings*

*Favorite recipe from National Marine
Fisheries Services*

SCALLOPS EN
BROCHETTE

1-2 lbs. sea scallops
½ to 1 lb. mushrooms
Squares of bacon
French dressing

Skewer whole scallops, medium
size mushrooms and squares of
bacon. Grill over charcoal or in
broiler about 10 minutes, turning
often and brushing with highly
seasoned French dressing
throughout the cooking.
            4-6 servings

*Favorite recipe from New Bedford Seafood
Council, Inc.*

LOBSTER FRA DIAVOLO

2 lbs. ATALANTA Frozen Lobster
  Tails, thawed
½ cup Olive Oil
4 Tbsp. Parsley, chopped
1 tsp. Oregano, dried
½ tsp. Basil, dried
⅛ tsp. Salt
Pepper as needed
1 cup Onion, chopped
1 clove Garlic, minced
2 cups Canned Tomatoes
2 Tbsp. Cognac

Heat the olive oil and add lobster.
(Remove membrane and cut tails in
sections.) Toss well until shells are
red. Add parsley, oregano, basil,
salt and pepper and simmer for ten
minutes. Then add onion, garlic
and tomatoes. Stir and cover. Cook
for 20 minutes. Add cognac. Serve
over rice.   *Yield: 6 servings*

BOILED STATE OF MAINE LOBSTER

Place live Maine lobsters in a
kettle of briskly boiling salted
water. Boil rapidly for twenty
minutes for 1¼ pound lobsters,
longer for larger sized ones.
Remove from the water and wipe
dry. Then place each lobster on its
back, split lengthwise with a heavy
knife and crack the large claws.
Serve whole lobster with a side
dish of melted butter.

*Favorite recipe from Maine Department of
Marine Resources*

BOOTH LOBSTER-PINEAPPLE CURRY

1 8 oz. package BOOTH Rock
  Lobster Tails
2 tablespoons butter or margarine
2 tablespoons chopped green
  pepper
2 tablespoons flour
¾ cup chicken broth
¼ teaspoon curry powder
1 8 oz. can pineapple chunks,
  drained
¼ cup diced water chestnuts
¼ cup cashew nuts

Boil lobster tails according to
package directions. Cut away
underside membrane and remove
meat from shells. Reserve shells

for serving. Cut meat into ½″ thick
slices. Melt butter in saucepan.
Sauté green pepper in butter until
tender—about 5 minutes. Stir in
flour. Gradually stir in broth and
curry powder. Cook over low heat,
stirring constantly until mixture
thickens. Stir in pineapple chunks,
water chestnuts, cashew nuts and
lobster pieces. Heat thoroughly.
Spoon mixture into shells, serve
with seasoned rice.

"BEST-EVER" FRIED CLAMS

1 egg yolk, beaten
½ cup milk
1 tablespoon melted butter
¼ teaspoon salt
½ cup flour
1 egg white, beaten stiff
24 clams, cleaned

Combine beaten egg yolk and half
the milk. Add butter. Add salt to
flour, sift together and beat into
egg-milk mixture until smooth. Add
rest of milk, then fold in stiffly
beaten egg white. Drain clams. Dip
each clam into batter and fry in
deep fat (375°) until golden brown,
turning frequently. Drain on
absorbent paper. Serve with
ketchup.   *Makes 4 servings*

*Favorite recipe from Maine Department of
Marine Resources*

HANGTOWN FRY

1 can (12 ounces) medium Pacific
  oysters, fresh or frozen
3 slices bacon, cut in 1-inch
  pieces
8 eggs
¼ cup water
½ teaspoon salt
Dash of pepper
½ cup dry bread or cracker
  crumbs
⅓ cup flour
¼ cup milk
2 tablespoons melted margarine or
  cooking oil
2 teaspoons minced parsley
Lemon wedges

Thaw oysters if frozen; drain. Fry
bacon in 10-inch frypan until crisp.
Drain on absorbent paper. Reserve
bacon drippings. Combine eggs,
water, salt, and pepper; beat
slightly, set aside. Combine and
mix crumbs and flour. Dip oysters
in milk; roll in crumb mixture. Heat
margarine and reserved bacon

drippings in frypan. Fry oysters in
hot fat over moderate heat for 2 or
3 minutes or until lightly browned.
Sprinkle crisp bacon pieces over
oysters. Pour egg mixture over
bacon and oysters. Cook over low
heat. Gently lift edge of omelet
with spatula to allow uncooked
egg to flow to bottom of pan. Cook
just until eggs are set. Sprinkle
with parsley before serving. If
preferred, loosen omelet around
edge of pan; fold and roll onto
heated platter and sprinkle with
parsley. Serve with lemon wedges.
          Makes 6 servings

*Favorite recipe from National Marine
Fisheries Services*

OYSTER VEGETABLE SAUTÉ

1 can (3¾ oz.) BUMBLE BEE®
  Smoked Oysters
1 cup celery chunks
1 cup broccoli flowerettes
½ cup butter
2 tablespoons heavy cream
1½ teaspoons prepared
  horseradish
½ teaspoon dill weed

Drain oysters. Sauté celery and
broccoli in 2 tablespoons butter
until tender-crisp about 4 minutes.
Remove from pan. Melt remaining
6 tablespoons butter. Stir in cream,
horseradish and dill with wire
whisk until slightly thickened. Add
vegetables and oysters to sauce.
Stir gently to coat and heat
through. Serve warm with picks.
          Makes 4 to 6 servings

OYSTERS GRAND ISLE

3 cans (8-oz. each) HIGH SEA
  Oysters
1 onion, minced
½ tsp. garlic
1 Tbsp. flour
3 Tbsp. Worcestershire sauce
¼ lb. butter
2 stalks of celery, minced
1 small can mushrooms
1 8-oz. can tomato sauce

Melt the butter, then add onion,
celery, garlic, and flour. Cook until
soft. Add tomato sauce,
Worcestershire sauce, mushrooms,
and season to taste. Cook 5
minutes. Drain oysters then add to
mixture, stirring gently until
heated. Serve in individual ramekin
dishes.   *Serves 6*

Hearty Main Dishes

CHILI

1 lb. ground beef
½ cup chopped onion
½ cup chopped celery
1 can (46 oz.) STOKELY'S
 FINEST® Tomato Juice
1 can (1 lb.) STOKELY'S FINEST®
 Stewed Tomatoes
1 can (15½ oz.) VAN CAMP'S®
 Mexican Style Chili Beans
⅓ cup uncooked macaroni
1 teaspoon chili powder

In large saucepan, brown first 3 ingredients; drain excess fat. Stir in remaining ingredients and simmer 30 minutes, stirring occasionally.   *Makes 6 servings*

SAUSAGE CHILI

2 lbs. BOB EVANS FARMS® Roll
 Sausage (Original Recipe or
 Zesty Hot)
1 lb., 14 oz. can red kidney beans
1½ c. tomato puree
12 oz. can tomato paste
2 tsp. chili powder
1 tsp. salt
2 Tbsp. sugar
2 medium onions, diced
3 c. water

Crumble BOB EVANS FARMS® Sausage in a skillet, cook until tender and lightly browned. Add remaining ingredients to a large pot and bring to a full boil. To enhance the flavor, let cook. Refrigerate overnight; reheat the next day. This chili will keep refrigerated for several days or it may be frozen.
 Yield: 14 8-oz. servings

REAL TEXAS CHILI

½ lb. chorizo
½ lb. ground beef
1½ cups chopped onion
2 cloves garlic, minced
1 (15-oz./425 g) can HUNT'S Tomato
 Sauce with Tomato Bits
1 (15½-oz./439 g) can small red
 beans, undrained
1 (8-oz./226 g) can refried beans
3 to 4 Tbsp. chili powder
1 tsp. ground cumin
1 tsp. oregano
½ tsp. salt

In 3-quart (3 liter) saucepan, cook chorizo, beef, 1 cup (250 mL) onion and garlic until onion is soft; spoon off excess fat. Add HUNT'S Sauce, red beans, refried beans and seasonings; mix thoroughly. Cover, simmer 10 minutes; stir once or twice. To serve, spoon chili into individual serving bowls and top with equal amounts of remaining chopped onion.
 Makes 5 (1-cup/250 mL) servings

San Giorgio

CHILI SKILLET SUPPER

8 ounces (about 2 cups)
 SAN GIORGIO Short Cut Elbow
 Macaroni, uncooked
1 clove garlic, minced
¼ cup chopped green pepper
½ cup chopped onion
1 lb. ground beef
1 (28 ounce) can tomatoes, cut up
1 (21 ounce) jar Italian cooking
 sauce
2 teaspoons salt
2 teaspoons chili powder
⅛ teaspoon pepper

In a large saucepan add garlic, green pepper, onion and ground beef. Brown lightly. Drain off fat. Add tomatoes, Italian cooking sauce and seasonings, mixing well. Bring to boiling. Gradually stir in macaroni. Reduce heat and simmer, stirring occasionally, about 20 minutes or until macaroni reaches desired tenderness.
 Makes about 4 to 6 servings

ONE DISH RONI-MAC® CHILI

1 lb. ground beef
½ cup chopped onion
28-oz. can tomatoes, undrained
15-oz. can kidney beans, undrained
 and cut up
1 cup water
6-oz. can tomato paste
1½ cups AMERICAN BEAUTY®
 RONI-MAC®
1 tablespoon chili powder
1 teaspoon salt
½ teaspoon oregano

In Dutch oven, brown ground beef with onion; drain. Add remaining ingredients. Stirring frequently, bring to a boil over high heat. Cover and cook over low heat, stirring occasionally, for 25 to 30 minutes or until RONI-MAC® is tender.

 8 servings

High Altitude—Above 3500 Feet: no change.

NUTRITIONAL INFORMATION PER SERVING

SERVING SIZE: ⅛ OF RECIPE		PERCENT U.S. RDA PER SERVING	
Calories	273	Protein	26
Protein	17 g	Vitamin A	32
Carbohydrate	31 g	Vitamin C	47
Fat	9 g	Thiamine	16
Sodium	430 mg	Riboflavin	12
Potassium	707 mg	Niacin	23
		Calcium	4
		Iron	22

FIERY POT TEXAS CHILI

2 pounds chili meat*
½ cup cooking oil
1½ cups water (or beer)
1 (8-ounce) can tomato sauce
2 small onions, chopped
1 medium green pepper, finely chopped
5-6 cloves garlic, minced
1 teaspoon oregano
1 teaspoon ground cumin
4 tablespoons chili powder
1 teaspoon salt
½ teaspoon IMPERIAL Granulated Sugar
Cayenne pepper
4-5 medium jalapeño peppers, chopped

In large skillet, braise meat in ¼ cup oil until brown. Transfer meat to large kettle or electric slow-cooker, leaving liquid in skillet. Add water and tomato sauce to meat, cook over low heat. Sauté onion, green pepper and garlic in remaining ¼ cup oil and liquid in skillet. Add remaining dry ingredients and chopped jalapeño peppers with seeds removed. Simmer about 30 minutes then transfer to kettle. Simmer about 2 hours. Dip off grease that settles on top. (Cayenne and jalapeño peppers are the "zingers" in this recipe. Add both with caution.)

Serves 8

*Chili meat is coarsely ground round steak or well-trimmed chuck steak.

TEXAS-STYLE CHILI

3 lbs. beef (stew beef, round steak, etc.)
2 garlic buds, quartered
2 fresh tomatoes, chopped
1 (8 oz.) can S&W Tomato Sauce
1 Tbsp. oregano
1 tsp. salt
1 tsp. cumin
1½ tsp. powdered cayenne pepper
5 Tbsp. chili powder
2 small (15¼ oz.) cans or 1 large (27 oz.) can S&W Dark Red Kidney Beans, undrained
3 Tbsp. yellow corn meal

Cut meat into bite size pieces, about ½ inch in diameter, trim fat-suet and save. Render suet in a 3 to 4 quart pan. Add the garlic and cook until brown. Discard excess suet pieces and garlic. Add the meat to fat and cook until all liquid has evaporated. Add the remaining ingredients except the corn meal and the kidney beans. Simmer at least 1½ hours adding water if necessary to keep from burning. At the end of this time, adjust seasoning to taste. Add water to the corn meal (consistency of pancake batter) and stir into the chili. Stir in the beans, including liquid; simmer 30 minutes longer.

Makes about 2 quarts

NALLEY®'S TOSTADAS

6 corn tortillas, Oil for frying
⅓ to ½ pound chorizo sausage
1 can (15-oz) NALLEY®'S Thick Chili With Beans
1 head lettuce, shredded
Avocado slices and tomato wedges
1 cup shredded cheddar cheese
6 pitted ripe olives for garnish

Fry tortillas in oil until crisp. Remove chorizo from casing and fry; strain off fat. Sauté and mash Chili beans with fork until thick. At serving time, spread tortillas with Chili, then with chorizo. Pre-heat oven to 450°; bake 15 minutes or until crisp. Heap lettuce on tostadas; arrange avocado and tomato. Spoon on dressing* and top with cheese. Garnish and serve immediately.

Makes 6 servings

*DRESSING

Combine ½ cup salad oil, ¼ cup red wine vinegar, ½ tsp. crushed oregano, ½ tsp. salt, coarse pepper.

SAVORY PORK-STUFFED PEPPERS

1½ pounds ground pork
1 teaspoon salt
⅛ teaspoon pepper
1 can (10¾ ounces) cream of celery soup
1 can (7 ounces) whole kernel corn, drained
1 medium onion, finely chopped
3 large green peppers
6 tomato slices, cut ¼ inch thick
Salt
Parmesan cheese

Lightly brown ground pork in large frying-pan; pour off drippings. Sprinkle salt and pepper over meat. Add celery soup, corn and onion and cook slowly 10 to 12 minutes, stirring occasionally. Cut green peppers in half lengthwise and remove membrane and seeds; cook in boiling salted water for 2 minutes; invert and drain thoroughly. Fill pepper halves with meat mixture and place on rack in roasting pan. Bake in a moderate oven (350°F.) for 15 minutes. Sprinkle salt on both sides of tomato slices and place on top of stuffed peppers. Sprinkle with Parmesan cheese and bake 15 minutes longer. *6 servings*

Favorite recipe from Pork Industry Group National Live Stock & Meat Board

TUNA-STUFFED BAKED PEPPERS
(Low Calorie)

1 teaspoon olive or salad oil
2 tablespoons finely chopped onion
1 small tomato, peeled, seeded and chopped
1 anchovy fillet, rinsed and chopped
1 tablespoon capers
1 tablespoon currants
2 teaspoons pine nuts
1 can (3½ ounces) tuna in water, drained
Salt
Pepper
1 small red pepper, top cut off and seeded
1 small green pepper, top cut off and seeded

In a small skillet, heat oil; cook onion until tender. Add the tomato and stir over moderate heat 8 to 10 minutes, until most of the liquid has evaporated. Stir in anchovy, capers, currants and pine nuts. Add the tuna and season to taste with salt and pepper. Spoon tuna mixture into the peppers. Place peppers in a small, lightly oiled baking dish. Bake, uncovered, in a 350°F. oven 35 minutes, or until peppers are tender. Chill slightly. Serve at room temperature.

Yield: 1 serving

260 calories per serving

Favorite recipe from Tuna Research Foundation, Inc.

SUMPTUOUS STUFFED PEPPERS

4 large green peppers
¼ cup thinly sliced celery
¼ cup sliced green onion
2 tablespoons butter or margarine
2 cups corn cut from the cob
1½ cups cooked rice
1 medium tomato, chopped
1 teaspoon salt
½ teaspoon chopped fresh dill
Generous dash pepper
1¼ cups grated FINLANDIA Swiss
1 can (15 ounces) tomato sauce

Cut thin slice from stem end of each pepper. Remove all seeds and membrane. Wash thoroughly. Cook in boiling salted water 5 minutes; drain. Cook celery and onion in butter until tender. Add corn, rice, tomato, salt, dill and pepper. Heat, stirring. Remove from heat and stir in ¾ cup cheese and ½ cup tomato sauce. Stuff mixture into peppers and place them upright in 8-inch ungreased baking dish. Pour remaining tomato sauce over peppers. Bake at 350°F. for 20 minutes. Sprinkle remaining ½ cup cheese on top of peppers; bake 10 minutes longer, until cheese is melted and peppers are done.

Makes 4 servings

SPANISH STUFFED PEPPERS

3 green peppers
1 lb. ground beef
3 Tablespoons chopped onion
1 can (15 oz.) VAN CAMP'S® Spanish Rice
2 Tablespoons STOKELY'S FINEST® Tomato Catsup
Parmesan cheese

Cut green peppers in half lengthwise. Steam peppers with 1-inch water in pan for 5 minutes. Cool quickly. Meanwhile, brown ground beef and onion; drain excess fat. Stir in Spanish Rice and Catsup. Spoon ingredients into green pepper halves. Place peppers in baking pan. Bake at 350°F. for 20 to 25 minutes. Sprinkle with Parmesan cheese.

Fills 6 pepper halves

SAUSAGE STUFFED PEPPERS

4 medium green peppers
1 lb. BOB EVANS FARMS® Roll Sausage
1 medium tart apple, peeled and diced
¼ c. fine dry bread crumbs
1 egg
8 oz. can tomato sauce with mushrooms

Cut top off peppers and scoop out seeds and membranes; cook in boiling salted water until almost tender. Drain and place in 1½-quart casserole. Meanwhile, pan fry pork sausage, drain. Stir in apple, bread crumbs and egg. Fill peppers with sausage mixture; top with tomato sauce. Cover and bake at 350° for 30 minutes.

CABBAGE ROLLS

1½ pounds ground beef chuck or round
¾ cup finely chopped onion
½ cup ELAM'S® Steel Cut Oatmeal
1 egg
1¼ teaspoons salt
½ teaspoon dry mustard
¼ teaspoon pepper
2 cans (8 ounce each) tomato sauce
8 large cabbage leaves
3 tablespoons ELAM'S® Unbleached White Flour with Wheat Germ
2 tablespoons (packed) brown sugar
1½ teaspoons lemon juice
1 can (8 ounce) tomatoes

Combine first 7 ingredients and 1 can tomato sauce; mix well. Divide into 8 equal portions. Cut out the stiff back ridge from each cabbage leaf. Dip 2 cabbage leaves at a time into boiling water. Cook until cabbage is limp; drain and chill in cold water. Drain 1 cabbage leaf at a time; dry and place a portion of meat mixture to one end of leaf. Roll up, folding the sides in over meat mixture. Fasten securely with toothpicks or small skewers. Repeat 7 times. Arrange rolls in shallow 2-quart baking dish. Combine remaining 1 can of tomato sauce, flour, sugar and lemon juice; mix until smooth. Add tomatoes; stir and break tomatoes up with spoon. Pour over cabbage

rolls. Cover dish with aluminum foil, crimping it securely to edge of dish. Bake in moderate oven (350°F.) 1 hour and 15 minutes. Uncover; spoon sauce over rolls. Bake uncovered until meat is tender and sauce thickens slightly, about 10 minutes. Baste with sauce two times during baking.

Yield: 8 servings

DILL BRAISED CABBAGE ROLLS*

1 head (3 lb.) green cabbage
1 pound ground lean pork
1 pound ground lean beef, divided
1½ cups cooked rice
⅔ cup finely chopped onion, divided
4 tablespoons LEA & PERRINS Worcestershire Sauce, divided
1 tablespoon chopped parsley
1¼ teaspoon salt, divided
¼ teaspoon TABASCO® Sauce
1 can (1 lb.) tomatoes, broken up
1 can (8 oz.) tomato sauce
1 teaspoon dill seed
½ teaspoon sugar

Core cabbage. Place in a large saucepan filled with boiling water. Cover and cook until leaves separate from head, removing them as this occurs. Drain leaves. Trim thick center vein from cabbage leaves, being careful not to tear leaves; set leaves aside. In a mixing bowl combine pork, ½ pound of the beef, rice, ⅓ cup of the onion, 2 tablespoons of the LEA & PERRINS, parsley, 1 teaspoon of the salt and TABASCO® Mix well, but do not overmix. Place a heaping tablespoon of filling in center of each cabbage leaf. Fold two sides over filling; roll up. Fasten with toothpick, if needed. In a Dutch oven or large saucepan place leftover cabbage. Arrange cabbage rolls over leftover leaves, seam-side down. Brown remaining ½ pound ground beef in heavy skillet, stirring often. Combine browned meat with tomatoes, tomato sauce, dill, sugar and remaining ⅓ cup onion, 2 tablespoons LEA & PERRINS and ¼ teaspoon salt; mix well. Pour over cabbage rolls. Cover; bring to boiling point. Reduce heat and simmer 2 to 2½ hours.

Yield: approximately 26 stuffed cabbage rolls

*May be prepared in advance of serving

TABASCO®

STUFFED CABBAGE

1 head cabbage (approx.
   1 kilogramm) (2 pounds)
500 gramms (1 pound) ground pork
1 teaspoon TABASCO® Sauce
½ teaspoon salt
1 egg
1 medium-sized onion
500 gramms (1 pound) tomatoes
100 gramms (¼ pound) leeks
2 cloves garlic
50 gramms (¼ cup) butter
1 heaped teaspoon oregano
½ liter (1 pint) meat broth
¼ liter (1 cup) tomato juice

Remove the outside leaves from cabbage. Press open carefully and cut out the kernel with a pointed knife. Chop half of this very finely. Mix the ground pork, TABASCO® Sauce, salt, egg and finely chopped cabbage together in a bowl and fill this mixture into cabbage. Spread out a large cotton cloth and place the filled cabbage in the center. Cross and knot the cloth corners. Bring salted water to a boil in a large pan. Hang the cabbage on the handle of a wooden spoon and suspend in the water, allowing to simmer for 45 minutes. Remove and allow to drain while still in the cloth. Cut the onion, tomatoes, leeks and garlic finely. Heat the butter in a pan and fry the vegetables briefly. Sprinkle the oregano on and then add the meat broth. Allow to boil until half of the fluid has evaporated. Pass the sauce through a fine sieve, add the tomato juice and boil lightly for a further 15 minutes. Add salt to taste. Divide the cabbage into segments and serve with the tomato sauce. Serve with boiled potatoes.   *Serves 4-6*

STUFFED CABBAGE ROLLS

8 large cabbage leaves
1 can (10¾ ounces) CAMPBELL'S
   Condensed Tomato Soup
1 pound ground beef
1 cup cooked rice
¼ cup chopped onion
1 egg, slightly beaten
1 teaspoon salt
¼ teaspoon pepper

Cook cabbage in salted water a few minutes to soften; drain. Mix 2 tablespoons soup with remaining ingredients. Divide meat mixture among cabbage leaves; fold in sides and roll up (secure with toothpicks, if necessary). In skillet, place rolls seam side down; pour remaining soup over. Cover; cook over low heat for 40 minutes. Stir occasionally, spooning sauce over rolls.   *4 servings*

CALIFORNIA TAMALE PIE

1 cup yellow cornmeal
2 cups milk
1 egg, beaten
1 pound ground beef
1 package LAWRY'S® Chili
   Seasoning Mix*
2 teaspoons LAWRY'S® Seasoned
   Salt
1 can (1 lb.) whole tomatoes, cut
   into pieces
1 can (17 oz.) whole kernel corn,
   drained
1 can (2¼ oz.) sliced ripe olives,
   drained
1 cup grated Cheddar cheese

CONVENTIONAL METHOD: In 2½-quart casserole dish, blend together cornmeal, milk and egg; set aside. Brown beef in skillet until crumbly; drain fat. Add remaining ingredients, except cheese. Stir into cornmeal mixture. Bake in 350°F. oven for 1 hour and 15 minutes. Sprinkle cheese on top and bake until cheese melts, about 5 minutes longer. Let stand 10 minutes before serving.

MICROWAVE OVEN METHOD: In 2½-quart glass casserole dish, microwave beef on HIGH for 5 to 6 minutes; drain fat and crumble beef. Mix in cornmeal, milk and eggs; blend thoroughly. Add remaining ingredients, except cheese. Cover with plastic wrap, venting one corner. Microwave on HIGH for 15 minutes, stirring after 8 minutes. Sprinkle cheese over top and microwave on HIGH for 2 minutes longer. Let stand 10 minutes before serving.
              Makes 6 to 8 servings

*Or may use 1 package (1¼ oz.) LAWRY'S® Taco Seasoning Mix

Elam's®

TAMALE PIE

1½ cups cold water
1½ cups ELAM'S® Stone Ground
   100% Whole Yellow Corn Meal
1½ teaspoons salt
2 cups boiling water
1 pound ground beef chuck or
   round
½ cup chopped onion
2 tablespoons flour
1 teaspoon chili powder
1 can (1 pound) tomatoes
1 can (8 ounce) tomato sauce
1 can (8¾ ounce) whole kernel
   corn, drained (1 cup)

Combine and mix cold water and corn meal. Add ½ teaspoon salt to boiling water. Add corn meal mixture, stirring constantly, bring to a boil. Partially cover pan; cook slowly 7 minutes, stirring often. Line bottom and sides of greased 2-quart casserole with cooked mush. Cook beef and onion in fry pan until beef is grey and crumbly. Stir in flour, remaining 1 teaspoon salt and chili powder. Add tomatoes, breaking them up into chunks with spoon. Stir in tomato sauce and corn. Spoon into mush-lined casserole. Bake in moderate oven (350°F.) until hot and bubbly, 40 to 45 minutes.
              Yield: 6 servings

EASY STROGANOFF

1 pound ground beef
1 can (4 oz.) sliced mushrooms,
   drained
½ cup chopped onion
1 teaspoon salt
2 cups water
1 beef bouillon cube
1½ cups MINUTE® Rice
½ cup sour cream

Brown ground beef quickly with mushrooms, onion and salt in large skillet, stirring frequently. Stir in water and bouillon cube. Bring to a full boil. Stir in rice. Reduce heat; cover and simmer 5 minutes. Remove from heat. Stir in sour cream. Garnish with chopped parsley, if desired.
              Makes about 5 cups or 4 servings

IMPERIAL HAMBURGER

¼ cup blanched slivered almonds
1 tablespoon butter or margarine
¾ pound ground beef
1 cup water
¼ teaspoon salt
1 cup fine noodles
1 package (10 oz.) BIRDS EYE®
  Japanese Style Vegetables with
  a Seasoned Sauce
1 tablespoon soy sauce

Sauté almonds in butter in skillet
until lightly browned. Remove
almonds from pan; set aside.
Brown ground beef well in butter
remaining in skillet, leaving meat
in chunks. Stir in water and salt;
bring to a boil. Stir in noodles;
cover and simmer for 2 minutes.
Add vegetables. Bring to a *full* boil
over medium heat, separating
vegetables with a fork and stirring
frequently. Cover and simmer for 3
minutes. Stir in soy sauce. Sprinkle
with almonds.
Makes 4 cups or 4 servings

CHINESE BEEF WITH BROCCOLI

2 packages (10 oz. each) frozen
  broccoli spears, partially thawed,
  or 1 bunch fresh broccoli*
½ pound flank steak, thinly sliced
  across grain
2 teaspoons cornstarch
1 teaspoon sugar
¼ teaspoon ground ginger
1 tablespoon soy sauce
Water
1 clove garlic, crushed
5 tablespoons PLANTERS®
  Peanut Oil
1 can (8 oz.) sliced bamboo shoots,
  drained
½ cup sliced fresh mushrooms
1 teaspoon salt

Cut broccoli flowerets and stems
into 1½-inch length about ½-inch
thick; set aside. Cut steak slices
into 2-inch lengths. In a small
bowl, combine 1 teaspoon
cornstarch, ¼ teaspoon sugar,
ginger, soy sauce, 1½ teaspoons
water and garlic; blend well. Mix
beef with marinade; set aside.
(Meat will absorb marinade.)

Preheat wok or large skillet; add 2
tablespoons peanut oil and heat 30
seconds. Add beef and brown until
just slightly pink. Return beef to
bowl. Heat remaining 3
tablespoons peanut oil in wok or

skillet. Stir in broccoli, bamboo
shoots and mushrooms; stir-fry
until broccoli is tender, 2–5
minutes. Add salt, remaining
sugar, 3 tablespoons water and
remaining cornstarch; mix well.
Bring to a boil; stirring constantly
until slightly thickened. Return
meat and heat 1 minute. Serve
immediately.   *Makes 4 servings*

*If using fresh broccoli, break
 flowerets with stems from large
 stems. Peel skin from large and
 small stems.

SUPPER NACHOS

1 pound lean ground beef
1 large onion, chopped
1 teaspoon LAWRY'S® Seasoned
  Salt
½ teaspoon ground cumin
2 cans (1 lb. each) refried beans
1 package (1¼ oz.) LAWRY'S®
  Taco Seasoning Mix
2 cups grated Monterey Jack
  cheese
1 can (4 oz.) chopped green chiles
1 cup grated Cheddar cheese
¾ cup LAWRY'S® Chunky Taco
  Sauce
Fried tortilla chips

Garnish with any or all of the
following:
1 cup guacamole
½ cup dairy sour cream
¼ cup chopped green onions
1 cup sliced ripe olives

Brown meat and onions; drain well
and season with Seasoned Salt
and cumin. Combine beans and
Taco Seasoning Mix; blend well.
Add grated Monterey Jack cheese;
mix together. Spread beans in a
shallow, oval (10 x 15-inch) baking
dish. Cover with browned meat and
onions. Sprinkle chiles over meat;
top with Cheddar cheese. Pour
Chunky Taco Sauce over cheese.
(May be made ahead and
refrigerated at this point—do not
freeze.) Bake, uncovered, in a
400°F. oven 20 to 25 minutes or
until thoroughly heated. Tuck
tortilla chips around edge of
platter and garnish as desired.
*Makes 4 to 6 main dish servings or
10 to 12 appetizer servings*

Mueller's®
BUSY DAY BEEF BAKE
(Low Calorie)

1 pound lean ground beef (10%
  fat)
1 small eggplant, cubed (about
  3 cups)
1 cup finely chopped onion
2 medium cloves garlic, mashed
1 can (16 ounces) tomatoes,
  chopped (with liquid)
1 cup beef broth
1 teaspoon salt
½ teaspoon ground cinnamon
¼ teaspoon pepper
8 ounces (3½ to 4 cups)
  MUELLER'S® Sea-Shell
  Macaroni
1 package (about 1 ounce)
  hollandaise sauce mix,
  prepared according to package
  directions

In large saucepan brown beef and
cook eggplant, onion and garlic
until crisp-tender; pour off fat.
Add all remaining ingredients
except macaroni and hollandaise.
Simmer 10 minutes. Meanwhile,
cook macaroni as directed on
package; drain. Combine
macaroni with meat mixture; pour
into a 2½-quart casserole. Top
with hollandaise sauce. Bake at
325°F. for 15 minutes or until
bubbling.
*Makes about 10 cups;
six generous servings*

Approximately 2110 calories;
about 355 calories each

SORRENTO SUPPER

1 cup sliced zucchini squash
1 cup cubed eggplant
¼ teaspoon basil leaves, crushed
2 tablespoons butter or margarine
1 can (19 ounces) CAMPBELL'S
  Chunky Sirloin Burger Soup
1 medium tomato, cut in wedges
Cooked spaghetti

In skillet, cook zucchini and
eggplant with basil in butter until
tender. Add soup. Heat; stir
occasionally. Add tomato; heat.
Serve over spaghetti.
Makes about 4 cups

FRANKS WITH RICE, NEW ORLEANS

¼ cup each chopped green pepper, onion, celery
1 small clove garlic, minced
2 tablespoons margarine
1 can (8¼ ounces) whole, peeled tomatoes
1¼ cups water
½ cup uncooked rice
¼ cup plus 1 tablespoon tomato paste
½ teaspoon each sugar, salt
½ teaspoon each Worcestershire sauce, hot pepper sauce
8 ECKRICH® Franks, any variety, sliced

In medium saucepan, cook green pepper, onion, celery and garlic in margarine until tender, about 5 minutes. Stir in remaining ingredients except franks; cover. Simmer, stirring occasionally for 20 minutes, or until rice is cooked. Stir in franks; heat through.

6 servings

Microwave directions: Measure all ingredients except franks into 2-quart casserole. Mix well, cover. Microwave 16 to 18 minutes, until rice is tender, on HIGH (100% power). Stir often. Stir in franks, cover. Microwave 2 minutes longer or until hot.

SPEEDY BAKED BEANS WITH WIENERS

1 package (16 oz.) OSCAR MAYER Bacon
3 cans (1 lb. each) baked beans in molasses sauce
½ cup chopped onion
¼ cup firmly packed brown sugar
1 tablespoon molasses
2 teaspoons Worcestershire sauce
½ teaspoon dry mustard
1 package (1 lb.) OSCAR MAYER Wieners

Cut bacon into one-inch pieces; cook in skillet until crisp. Add onion to bacon; cook until tender. Stir in remaining ingredients except wieners. Place wieners on top of beans. Heat 15 minutes.

Makes 5 servings

WESTERN STYLE BARBECUE

4 frankfurters, cut in 1-inch pieces
2 tablespoons butter or margarine
1 can (19¼ ounces) CAMPBELL'S Chunky Old Fashioned Bean with Ham Soup
1 can (12 ounces) whole kernel golden corn with sweet peppers, drained
1 can (about 8 ounces) lima beans, drained
½ cup barbecue sauce

In saucepan, brown frankfurters in butter. Add remaining ingredients. Heat; stir occasionally. Garnish with green pepper rings.

Makes about 5 cups

VIENNA BEEF® FRANKS HAWAIIAN

1 12 oz. pkg. VIENNA BEEF® Franks
2 Tbsp. brown sugar
4 Tbsp. butter or margarine
1 cup chopped onion
1 green pepper, sliced
1 8¾ oz. can pineapple tidbits, drained
1 cup peeled and chopped tomatoes
2 Tbsp. cornstarch
½ cup pineapple juice
1 Tbsp. vinegar
Salt and pepper
Hot cooked rice

In skillet melt butter or margarine; add onion, green pepper, pineapple and tomatoes; cook over low heat until heated through. Combine cornstarch, pineapple juice and vinegar; stir in tomato mixture. Add franks, brown sugar, salt and pepper. Simmer covered 10 minutes, stirring occasionally. If necessary, add hot water to mixture if too thick. Serve over rice.

Makes 4 servings

CORNY DOGS

Frankfurters, heated, split
Crushed corn chips
KRAFT Jalapeno Pepper Pasteurized Process Cheese Spread, cubed
WOLF® Brand Chili, heated

For each serving, fill hot frankfurter with corn chips and process cheese spread cubes. Broil until process cheese spread melts. Top with hot chili.

KNOCKWURST 'N CABBAGE

4 knockwurst sausage
1 tablespoon vegetable oil
2 quarts BUD OF CALIFORNIA® Shredded Cabbage
1 large onion, sliced
1 clove garlic, pressed
1 cup thinly sliced carrots
1 pound small new potatoes, peeled and sliced
¾ cup dry white wine
¾ cup water
1 teaspoon chicken stock base
1 teaspoon pickling spice
½ teaspoon salt

Make three slits in each knockwurst. In a large skillet, brown knockwurst in hot oil. Remove from skillet. In same skillet, sauté cabbage, onion, garlic and carrots until onion is soft. Stir in potatoes, wine, water, chicken stock base, pickling spice and salt. Cover and simmer 20 minutes. Add knockwurst; cover and simmer 10 minutes longer.

Makes 4 servings

VIENNA BEEF® POLISH SAUSAGE POLONAISE

1 12 oz. pkg. VIENNA BEEF® Polish Sausage
1 1 lb., 11 oz. can sauerkraut, drained
Large onion, chopped
1 unpeeled apple, chopped
1 Tbsp. brown sugar
1 Tbsp. caraway
1 bay leaf
¼ tsp. ground cloves
Salt and pepper

Combine sauerkraut, onion, apple and seasonings in heavy pot. Barely cover with water. Cook slowly ½ hour. Add sausage and cook for additional ½ hour, until water is almost gone.

Variation:

For a Russian touch, stir in 1 cup sour cream. Turn into casserole and bake at 425° until hot.

Makes 4 servings

CHOUCROUTE GARNI

4 slices OSCAR MAYER Bacon
3 onions, chopped
4 carrots, scraped and diced
1½ jars (32 oz. each) CLAUSSEN Sauerkraut, drained
12 whole black peppercorns
10 juniper berries, optional
1 can (13¾ oz.) chicken broth
¾ cup dry white wine
1 package (16 oz.) OSCAR MAYER Wieners
1 pkg. (12 oz.) OSCAR MAYER Ring Bologna
1 package (12 oz.) OSCAR MAYER Chubbies Knackwurst
1 package (5 oz.) OSCAR MAYER Brand Little Smokies
1 package (6 oz.) OSCAR MAYER Sliced Canadian Bacon

Cut bacon in pieces and partially cook in large kettle. Add onions, carrots and sauerkraut. Add all remaining ingredients, cover and simmer for 2 hours. To serve, mound sauerkraut in center of platter and surround with sausage.
Makes 8 servings

MAMA'S FAVORITE

¾ pound mild Italian sausage, cut into 1-inch pieces
2 to 3 tablespoons butter or margarine
1 medium onion, chopped
½ cup diagonally sliced celery
3 zucchini, diagonally sliced
1 cup broccoli flowerettes
1 cup diagonally sliced carrots
1 can (1 lb. 12 oz.) tomatoes, cut up
2 teaspoons LAWRY'S® Garlic Salt*
1 teaspoon EACH: LAWRY'S® Seasoned Pepper, sugar and basil
2 tablespoons butter or margarine
1 EACH: green and red bell pepper, thinly sliced
¼ pound fresh mushrooms, sliced
Chopped parsley

In a Dutch oven or large skillet, brown sausage; remove and drain fat. Melt butter or margarine and sauté onion, celery, zucchini, broccoli and carrots until just tender. Add canned tomatoes, Garlic Salt, Seasoned Pepper, sugar and basil; blend well. Add browned sausage and heat thoroughly over low heat about 10 minutes. Meanwhile, sauté green and red bell pepper and

mushrooms. Just before serving add peppers and mushrooms; serve over buttered egg noodles and sprinkle chopped parsley over top.
Makes 4 servings

Note: Any type of sausage or meatball may be substituted for Italian sausage.

*May use ½ teaspoon LAWRY'S® Garlic Powder with Parsley and 1 teaspoon LAWRY'S® Seasoned Salt in place of 2 teaspoons LAWRY'S® Garlic Salt.

SAUSAGE N' RICE SKILLET SUPPER

1 lb. HILLSHIRE FARM® Smoked Sausage
¾ cup raw rice*
1 can (10¾ oz.) condensed cream of celery soup
¾ cup water
1 Tbsp. butter or margarine
¼ tsp. salt
1 package (10 oz.) frozen peas, separated
1 can (3 oz.) sliced mushrooms, drained
1 cup shredded Swiss cheese
Sprig of parsley (optional)

Cut sausage into bite size chunks. Combine with rice, soup, water, butter, and salt in an electric skillet set at 350° or a heavy skillet on medium heat. Cover and bring mixture to boil; reduce heat and simmer 5 minutes. Stir in frozen peas and mushrooms. Sprinkle with cheese. Simmer, covered, for 15 minutes or until rice is done. Garnish with parsley.

MICROWAVE:

Combine 1 cup *instant* rice, soup, water, butter and salt in a 2 qt. microwave safe casserole. Microwave, covered, HIGH 5 minutes. Cut sausage into bite size chunks. Combine with rice mixture, peas and mushrooms. Microwave, covered, HIGH 6–8 minutes or until hot and bubbly. Stir in cheese, reserving a little for garnish. Let stand, covered, 2–3 minutes. Garnish with reserved cheese and parsley.
Yield: 4 servings

*For microwave, substitute 1 cup instant rice.

CASSOULET

2 packages (1 lb. each) OSCAR MAYER Ground Pork Sausage
1 can (1 lb.) kidney beans, drained
1 can (1 lb.) white beans, drained*
1 can (1 lb.) sliced carrots, drained
1 can (1 lb.) stewed tomatoes
⅛ teaspoon garlic powder OR 1 garlic clove, minced
1 tablespoon dried parsley flakes
4 slices OSCAR MAYER Bacon

Preheat oven to 350°F. Cook pork sausage in skillet over medium heat, stirring with fork as it browns. When browned throughout, remove sausage with slotted spoon and drain on absorbent paper. Combine sausage with remaining ingredients except bacon in 2-quart crock or bean pot. Top with bacon slices and bake 45 minutes.
Makes 8 servings

*May use canned or cooked Great Northern beans, marrow beans, navy beans or pea beans.

Skillet Method: Cook bacon slices in large skillet or Dutch oven until crisp; remove and drain on absorbent paper. Add sausage to skillet and cook over medium heat, stirring with fork as it browns. Pour off drippings. Add remaining ingredients and cook over low heat 15 minutes longer, until flavors blend. Top with bacon slices for garnish. Serve in soup bowls.
Makes 8 one-cup servings

SANTA CLARA SAUSAGE SUPPER

1 (12 oz.) package brown 'n serve sausage links
1½ cups SUNSWEET® Pitted Prunes
1 (12 oz.) can apricot nectar
1½ teaspoons cornstarch
¼ teaspoon salt
½ teaspoon dry mustard
1 tablespoon vinegar

Brown sausage and drain off fat. Combine all remaining ingredients and pour over sausage. Simmer, uncovered, 10 minutes.
Makes 4 servings

CONFETTI SMOKIE SKILLET

1 package (12 oz.) OSCAR MAYER Smokie Links Sausage
1 can (1 lb. 1 oz.) cream style corn
1 can (1 lb.) mixed vegetables, drained
½ teaspoon salt
¼ teaspoon thyme, optional

Cut Smokie Links into bite-size pieces. Combine with remaining ingredients in skillet or saucepan. Cook slowly 5 minutes or until heated through, stirring occasionally.   *Makes 4 servings*

BRATWURST A LA VERN

6 onions, sliced and simmered
USINGER'S Grilled Bratwurst
12 ounces beer

Sauce:
1 cup chili sauce
1 tablespoon Worcestershire sauce
1 cup catsup
2 tablespoons vinegar
½ teaspoon salt
2 tablespoons brown sugar
½ teaspoon paprika

Put onions and sauce ingredients in saucepan. Add beer and sausage and heat. Serve hot.

POLISH SAUSAGE SKILLET

1 pound USINGER'S Smoked Polish Sausage, cut in ¼-inch slices
¼ cup sliced green onions
⅔ cup sliced celery
1 (4-ounce) can mushroom stems and pieces
1½ cups boiling water
¼ teaspoon salt
¼ teaspoon pepper
2 envelopes individual tomato soup mix
1 tablespoon Worcestershire sauce
1½ cups instant rice

Combine USINGER Smoked Polish Sausage, onion and celery in large skillet. Cook over low heat until vegetables are tender-crisp. Add mushrooms, water, salt, pepper, soup mix and Worcestershire sauce. Heat until bubbling, add rice, stir and cover. Remove from heat and let stand 10 to 15 minutes.   *Serves six*

PORK SAUSAGE AND VEGETABLE HOT DISH

10 USINGER'S Pork Sausage Links
6 large potatoes
1 can whole corn, drained
1 can green beans, drained
½ stick butter
Salt and pepper

Fry USINGER'S Pork Sausage. When done, cut in 2-inch pieces. Set aside. Slice potatoes and fry in butter. Salt. Warm corn and beans in pan. Mix all ingredients together. Serve hot. Add pepper to taste.

APPLE SAUSAGE SKILLET

1 pkg. (10 oz.) brown and serve sausages, chunked
1 medium apple, cored and chunked
2 Tablespoons butter or margarine
¼ cup brown sugar
1 can (15 oz.) VAN CAMP'S® New Orleans Style Kidney Beans, drained

Brown sausage and apple in butter until apple is tender. Stir in remaining ingredients and heat to serving temperature.
    Makes 4 servings

INDIAN CHICKEN CURRY

⅓ cup butter or margarine
1 large onion, chopped
1 cup chopped celery
2 tart apples, peeled and chopped
1 Tbsp. curry powder
6 Tbsp. flour
1 cup chicken broth
½ cup COCO CASA™ Cream of Coconut
2 cups (1 pint) half and half
3 cups diced cooked chicken, turkey or lamb
Salt and pepper

In a large saucepan, melt butter and sauté onion, celery and apples for 5 minutes. Stir in curry and flour. Gradually stir in chicken broth, cream of coconut and half and half. Stir over moderate heat until sauce bubbles and thickens. Stir in chicken and season to taste with salt and pepper. Serve spooned over rice.   *Serves 6 to 8*

CHICKEN DIVAN ROLL-UP

1 package (10 ounces) buttermilk flaky biscuits
2 cans (4¾ ounces each) UNDERWOOD® Chunky Chicken Spread
1 package (10 ounces) frozen broccoli spears, cooked according to package directions
1 can (11 ounces) condensed Cheddar cheese soup
⅓ cup milk

Preheat oven to 375°F. On a floured surface, roll each biscuit into an oval shape 4 by 3 inches. Spread a scant 2 tablespoons chunky chicken spread over center of each biscuit. Arrange 2 broccoli spears on each biscuit so that flower ends extend beyond edge of roll. Fold ends of dough over broccoli so that they overlap; pinch to seal together. Place biscuits on ungreased baking sheet and bake 15 minutes, until golden brown. Meanwhile, in a small saucepan mix soup and milk. Heat to boiling; simmer 2 minutes, stirring almost constantly. Serve sauce over biscuits.   *Makes 10 roll-ups*

POLYNESIAN CHICKEN

1 can (16 ounces) unpeeled apricot halves
2 tablespoons cornstarch
2 cans (19 ounces *each*) CAMPBELL'S Chunky Chicken with Rice Soup
½ cup diagonally sliced green onions
¼ teaspoon ground ginger
⅛ teaspoon ground mace
1 package (about 7 ounces) frozen Chinese pea pods
1 medium banana, sliced (about ½ cup)
Chow mein noodles

Drain apricots, reserving ¼ cup juice; gradually blend in cornstarch until smooth. In saucepan, combine soup, onion, ginger, mace and cornstarch mixture. Heat, stirring until thickened; bring to boil. Add apricots, pea pods and banana. Cover; cook over low heat 5 minutes or until pea pods are just tender. Serve over chow mein noodles.   *Makes about 6 cups*

CHICKEN À LA CHINOIS

1 cup sliced mushrooms
⅛ teaspoon ground ginger
2 tablespoons butter or margarine
1 can (14½ fl. oz.) SWANSON Chicken Broth
1 package (6 ounces) frozen snow peas
1 can (about 8 ounces) pineapple chunks
3 tablespoons cornstarch
1 tablespoon soy sauce
2 cans (5 ounces *each*) SWANSON Chunk White or Thigh Chicken
1 small tomato, cut in wedges
Cooked rice

In skillet, brown mushrooms with ginger in butter. Add remaining ingredients except chicken, tomatoes and rice. Cook, stirring until thickened. Add chicken and tomatoes; heat. Serve over rice.

Makes about 5 cups, 4 servings

3-WAY A LA KING

2 tablespoons chopped green pepper
¼ cup chopped onion
2 tablespoons butter or margarine
1 can (10¾ ounces) CAMPBELL'S Condensed Cream of Chicken or Mushroom Soup
⅓ to ½ cup milk
1½ cups cubed cooked chicken, ham, or turkey
2 tablespoons diced pimiento
Patty shells, toast, or rice

In saucepan, cook green pepper and onion in butter until tender. Blend in soup and milk; add chicken and pimiento. Heat; stir occasionally. Serve in patty shells.

Makes about 2½ cups

CHICKEN WITH CREOLE SAUCE

1 package (25 oz.) BANQUET® Heat and Serve Frozen Fully Cooked Fried Chicken Thighs With Back Portion and Drumsticks
2 tablespoons butter or margarine
1 large onion, sliced
½ cup sliced mushrooms
1 large green pepper, cut into ¼-inch strips
1 teaspoon garlic powder
Pinch cinnamon
1 can (15 oz.) tomato sauce with tomato bits

Place frozen chicken on cookie sheet or in shallow aluminum pan. Heat on center rack of 375°F. oven for 30 minutes. Meanwhile, melt butter in large saucepan. Add onion, mushrooms, green pepper, garlic powder, and cinnamon. Cook over medium heat until vegetables are tender. Add tomato sauce to vegetable mixture and heat to boiling. Keep warm. To serve, pour sauce over hot chicken.

Makes 5 servings

CHICKEN LIVER VOL-AU-VENT

2 cups sliced DOLE® Fresh Mushrooms
3 tablespoons butter
1 pound chicken livers
½ cup chopped green onion
½ teaspoon salt
½ teaspoon garlic salt
¼ cup brandy
1 tablespoon flour
1 cup dairy sour cream
¼ teaspoon fines herbes
6 patty shells, baked

In a large skillet, sauté mushrooms in 2 tablespoons butter until just tender; remove from pan. Add remaining butter; sauté chicken livers and green onion. Add salt and garlic salt; cook over medium-high heat until most liquid is absorbed. Add brandy and flame, gently stirring until flame expires. Blend flour into sour cream, then stir into chicken liver mixture. Add mushrooms and fines herbes; bring to simmer over low heat. Spoon into and around baked patty shells to serve.   *Makes 6 servings*

SMITHFIELD BARBEQUED TURKEY TURNOVER WITH POTATOES

2 cups freshly baked potatoes scooped out of shell
2 oz. butter
½ teaspoon salt
2 whole eggs
Pinch grated nutmeg
12 oz. JAMES RIVER SMITHFIELD Turkey Barbeque

In saucepan, heat butter. Into it, add the scooped out baked potatoes and beat well with wooden spoon until they are well mashed and blended. Add seasonings. Stir in the two well beaten eggs and continue to cook until the potato mix will readily leave the sides of the saucepan. Turn this mixture into bowl and allow to cool.

When cold, roll potato mix onto floured board. Roll as you would pastry dough to one-quarter inch thickness, cut with a round 4-inch cutter. Into center of round potato base, place 2 ounces of JAMES RIVER SMITHFIELD Turkey Barbeque, moisten the edges with egg, wash and fold over, sealing the edges carefully with the tines of fork. Bake in oven at 350° for 25 minutes or until well browned.

Serve 6

STIR FRY TURKEY AND VEGETABLES

2 cups thin strips roast BUTTERBALL® SWIFT'S PREMIUM® Turkey
½ stick (¼ cup) butter
½ pound fresh mushrooms, thinly sliced
1 cup sliced celery, cut on an angle into ½ inch slices
About ¾ pound fresh spinach, washed and torn into large pieces*
1 large onion, sliced
Soy sauce
Cooked rice

Melt butter in wok pan or large skillet. Stir in mushrooms and celery and cook about 2 minutes. Push to side. Add spinach and onion. Stir to coat with butter. Cover and steam 2 minutes. Remove vegetables from pan to keep from overcooking. Add turkey, cover and cook 3 minutes. Return vegetables to wok or skillet, arranging attractively. Sprinkle with soy sauce and toss just before serving with lightly seasoned cooked rice.

Yield: 4 servings

*If fresh spinach is not available, use a 10 ounce package frozen leaf spinach, cooking and stirring only enough to heat through.

Carl Buddig

BUDDIG TURKEY BONNETS

2 packages (2.5 oz. ea.) BUDDIG
  Smoked Sliced Turkey
1 can CAMPBELL'S Cream of
  Chicken Soup
½ cup milk
Pimento, chopped (optional)
1 package (5 oz.) PILLSBURYS
  HUNGRY JACK® Refrigerator
  Biscuits
Paprika
Cranberry sauce

Conventional directions: Arrange
BUDDIG Turkey slices in five
servings in a baking dish. Combine
soup, milk and pimento and pour
over meat. Heat in 400°F. oven
until warm. Place an unbaked
HUNGRY JACK® biscuit on top of
each pile, sprinkle with paprika.
Bake 15 minutes longer. Serve with
slices of cranberry sauce.
Makes 5 servings

Microwave directions: Prepare
recipe as above in 9-inch round
glass dish. Cook on high for 2 to 3
minutes or until warm and bubbly.
Top with biscuits arranged in circle
over 5 overlapping servings.
Sprinkle with paprika. Cook on
high for 2 to 3 minutes or until no
longer doughy. Let stand 5 minutes
before serving. Serve with slices of
cranberry sauce.

BUDDIG CORNED BEEF HASH

1 package (4 oz.) BUDDIG Sliced
  Corned Beef or Pastrami
3 tablespoons cooking oil
1 package frozen, diced, O'Brien-
  style potatoes
Salt and pepper to taste
4 poached eggs (optional)

Cut BUDDIG meat into slices and
separate. Heat cooking oil in large
skillet over medium heat. Carefully
add potatoes; cover and cook
stirring now and then until slightly
brown. Then stir in BUDDIG meat;
continue cooking until thoroughly
heated. Salt and pepper to taste.
(Optional: top with 4 poached
eggs.)
Ample serving for four hearty
appetites

HASH 'N SQUASH

2 acorn squash
Salt
Pepper
2 15-oz. cans ARMOUR® STAR
  Corned Beef Hash
½ cup (2 oz.) shredded Cheddar
  cheese
4 green pepper strips

Heat oven to 350°. Rinse squash;
cut in half, remove seeds. Place
cut side down in shallow baking
dish. Bake at 350°, 30 minutes.
Turn squash cut side up; season
with salt and pepper. Divide hash
evenly into squash halves; heat 20
minutes. Sprinkle with cheese;
continue heating until cheese
melts, about 5 minutes. Garnish
with green pepper strips.
4 servings

Microwave instructions: Rinse
squash; leave whole. Cook 10 to 12
minutes or until tender; let stand 5
minutes. Cut in half and remove
seeds. Place cut side up in shallow
baking dish; season with salt and
pepper. Divide hash evenly into
squash halves. Cook, covered with
wax paper, 4 to 5 minutes. Sprinkle
with cheese; garnish with green
pepper strips.

TURKEY AND SAUSAGE HASH

2 cups chopped roast
  BUTTERBALL® SWIFT'S
  PREMIUM® Turkey
4 or 5 SWIFT PREMIUM® BROWN
  'N SERVE® Sausage Links,
  cut into bite-size pieces
2 tablespoons butter or margarine
¼ cup chopped onion
¼ cup chopped green pepper
2 tablespoons flour
1 cup milk
2 tablespoons chopped parsley
½ teaspoon salt
½ teaspoon poultry seasoning
1 cup toasted unseasoned bread
  cubes

Brown sausage as directed on
package. Add butter, onion and
green pepper and cook about 5
minutes. Stir in flour, then milk.
Cook and stir until mixture
thickens. Add turkey, parsley,
seasonings and bread cubes. Cook
over very low heat about 25
minutes to blend flavors. Serve hot.
Yield: 4 servings

CURRIED HAM ROLL-UPS
(Low Calorie)

1 package (6 ounces) ECKRICH®
  Sliced Cooked Ham
1 package (10 ounces) frozen
  broccoli spears
1 tablespoon butter
2 tablespoons all-purpose flour
½ teaspoon salt
¼ teaspoon curry powder
¼ teaspoon onion powder
Dash white pepper
1 cup skim milk
Paprika

Separate ham slices; set aside.
Cook broccoli according to
package directions, just until
barely tender; drain well and divide
evenly between ham slices. Roll
ham around broccoli. Place rolls,
seam side down, in shallow baking
dish; set aside. Melt butter in small
saucepan. Remove from heat and
stir in flour and seasonings. When
smooth, stir in skim milk. Cook
over medium heat, stirring
constantly, until sauce is bubbly.
Pour sauce over ham rolls. Bake,
uncovered, at 350°F. for 25
minutes. Sprinkle with paprika
before serving.
6 servings; 1 serving = 1 slice
ham, 2 broccoli spears,
3½ tablespoons sauce

105 calories per serving

WESTMINSTER HAM AND CHEESE

¼ cup chopped onion
2 tablespoons butter or margarine
1 can (10½ ounces) FRANCO-
  AMERICAN Mushroom Gravy
¼ cup water
½ cup shredded sharp Cheddar
  cheese
¼ cup grated Parmesan cheese
2 tablespoons dry sherry
1 cup cooked ham cut in strips
2 tablespoons chopped parsley
2 tablespoons chopped pimiento
Cooked noodles

In saucepan, cook onion in butter
until tender. Blend in gravy, water,
cheeses and sherry. Heat until
cheese melts; stir often. Add ham,
parsley and pimiento. Heat; stir
occasionally. Serve over noodles.
Makes about 3 cups, 4 servings

SAUCY SALISBURY SKILLET

1 pound ground beef
¼ cup finely chopped onion
½ teaspoon salt
Generous dash pepper
1 can (10¾ ounces) CAMPBELL'S Condensed Golden Mushroom Soup
¼ cup water
1 teaspoon Worcestershire
1 cup thinly sliced carrot
1 package (9 ounces) frozen cut green beans

Mix *thoroughly* beef, onion, salt and pepper; shape firmly into 4 oval patties. In skillet, brown patties (use shortening if necessary); pour off fat. Stir in remaining ingredients. Cover; cook over low heat 20 minutes or until done. Stir occasionally.

Makes 4 servings

CREAMED SIZZLEAN® ON TOAST OR POPOVERS

12 ounce package SWIFT SIZZLEAN® cut into 1 inch pieces
2 tablespoons finely minced onion
2 tablespoons flour
1 cup milk
1 cup sour cream
1 cup shredded Cheddar cheese
4½ ounce can mushroom slices
2 tablespoons finely minced parsley
Popovers, crisp buttered toast triangles, rice, cornbread or baked potatoes

In a skillet over medium heat, panfry SIZZLEAN® until lightly browned. Remove from skillet; drain on paper towels. Pour off all but 1 tablespoon drippings. Add onion; cook until transparent. Stir in flour and milk to make white sauce. Add remaining ingredients; blend. Stir in SIZZLEAN® and heat through. Serve over popovers, toast, cooked rice, cornbread or baked potatoes.

Yield: 5 servings

ORIENTAL KEBABS

1 pound medium shrimp, shelled and deveined (about 18)
1 pound boneless pork in 1-inch cubes
2 cups Oriental Barbecue Glaze*
1 cup rice
2 cups water
2 teaspoons HERB-OX Instant Chicken Style Bouillon or 2 HERB-OX Chicken Bouillon Cubes

Marinate shrimp and pork cubes in Oriental Barbecue Glaze for 30 minutes. Meanwhile, bring water, rice and instant bouillon or bouillon cubes to a boil. Simmer, covered, until liquid is absorbed and rice tender, to make 6 servings. Thread shrimp on 6 skewers, pork on 6 skewers. Broil pork kebabs until no trace of pink remains, brushing often with glaze. Broil shrimp for last five minutes, turning often. Arrange one pork kebab, one shrimp kebab on each serving of rice.

Makes 6 servings

*ORIENTAL BARBECUE GLAZE

2 HERB-OX Beef Flavor Bouillon Cubes (or Chicken, or Vegetarian Style) or 2 teaspoons any HERB-OX Instant Bouillon
1 cup boiling water
⅓ cup honey
⅓ cup vinegar
¼ cup soy sauce
½ teaspoon ginger
¼ teaspoon garlic powder
2 tablespoons sherry (optional)

Add bouillon cubes or instant bouillon to boiling water, stir to dissolve. Add remaining ingredients. Use to marinate and baste chicken parts, pork, beef or ribs for grilling over charcoal or in the oven.

Makes 2 cups

"T"ERRIFIC KABOBS

¼ cup water
¼ cup vinegar
1 teaspoon salt
½ teaspoon pepper
1 can or cup MR. & MRS. "T"® Bloody Mary Mix
2 tablespoons olive oil
1 to 1¼ lbs. cubed beef or lamb
Tiny whole onions
Green pepper pieces about 2" square
Tomato wedges
Fresh mushrooms

Combine first six ingredients in a jar and shake well. Place meat in a shallow dish single layer and pour marinade over. Refrigerate for several hours or overnight. Cook onions in boiling water for about 3 minutes. Arrange meat on skewers, alternating with onions, green pepper, tomato, and mushrooms. Grill over medium heat about 8 to 12 minutes. Turn frequently and baste all the while with leftover marinade. Serve with rice and green salad.

Serves 4-6

NEW ORLEANS JAMBALAYA

¼ cup chopped onion
2 tablespoons butter or margarine
1 cup cubed ARMOUR®'S Pork Shoulder Picnic
1 4½-oz. can shrimp, drained, rinsed
1½ cups cooked rice
1 cup hot water
3 tablespoons tomato paste
2 tablespoons chopped parsley
1½ teaspoons flour
¼ teaspoon garlic powder

Cook onion in butter or margarine 5 minutes. Stir in remaining ingredients. Cook over low heat 10 minutes or until thoroughly heated.

4 servings

SMITHFIELD BARBEQUE PORK WITH RED KIDNEY BEANS AND BOILED RICE

½ lb. Red Kidney Beans, soaked overnight
1 Medium onion chopped very fine
½ tsp. salt
1 Pound can of JAMES RIVER SMITHFIELD Barbeque Pork

In sauce pan, place well drained soaked red kidney beans, add the finely chopped onion, one-half teaspoon salt and cover with cold water. Top sauce pan with cover. Bring to a boil, cook slowly until beans are tender. When beans are done, stir in the JAMES RIVER SMITHFIELD Barbeque Pork and continue to cook slowly for ten to fifteen minutes. Serve on bed of freshly cooked well drained rice.

Serves 4

BUDDIG MEAT 'N' POTATOES AU GRATIN

2 packages (2.5 oz. ea.) BUDDIG Beef or Pastrami
1 box (5.5 oz.) BETTY CROCKER® Au Gratin or Scalloped Potatoes
2¼ cups boiling water
⅔ cup milk
2 tablespoons margarine

Conventional directions: Heat oven to 400°F. Cut BUDDIG Beef or Pastrami into squares and separate. Mix BUDDIG, potato slices, water, milk and margarine in ungreased 2-quart round casserole. Bake uncovered 30 to 35 minutes. Let stand a few minutes before serving.

Makes 6 servings

Microwave directions: Mix ingredients same as above in 2-quart casserole. Cook on high for 6 minutes. Stir and cook on medium (50%) for 10 minutes longer. Let stand 5 minutes before serving.

CHINESE PORK AND VEGETABLE STIR-FRY

1 lb. JOHN MORRELL® TABLE TRIM® boneless fresh pork loin end, cut into thin bite-sized strips
1 Tbsp. cornstarch
½ tsp. ground ginger
2 tsp. sugar
2 Tbsp. dry sherry
2 Tbsp. soy sauce
½ cup chicken broth
4 Tbsp. cooking oil
6 oz. frozen package pea pods, partially thawed
1 lb. can mixed Chinese vegetables, drained
1 sweet red pepper, cut into ¼″ strips (or tomato)
Hot cooked rice

In a small bowl, combine cornstarch, ginger, sugar, sherry, soy sauce, and chicken broth. Set aside. Heat 2 Tbsp. oil in 12 in. skillet or wok pan. Add vegetables, and stir-fry 2 to 3 minutes. Remove vegetables, set aside. Add remaining oil, and pork strips. Stir-fry until pork is well browned, 4 to 5 minutes. Add vegetables, and soy sauce mixture to pork. Stir to blend. Heat until sauce is bubbly. Serve at once over hot, fluffy rice.

Serves 4

LAWRY'S® ENCHILADAS—BEEF, CHICKEN, TURKEY AND RANCHERO

Sauce:
Prepare LAWRY'S® Enchilada Sauce Mix according to package directions, using tomato paste and 3 cups water.

Each recipe uses 8 corn tortillas.

Filling:
Each of the following filling recipes makes enough for 8 enchiladas. Combine all ingredients except ¾ cup cheese (for topping).

Beef:
1 pound ground beef, browned, fat drained
1 teaspoon LAWRY'S® Seasoned Salt
2½ cups grated Monterey Jack or mild Cheddar cheese
1 can (2¼ oz.) sliced ripe olives

Chicken:
3 cups diced, cooked chicken
1½ teaspoons LAWRY'S® Seasoned Salt
2½ cups grated Monterey Jack cheese

Turkey:
1 pound ground turkey, browned
1½ teaspoons LAWRY'S® Seasoned Salt
2½ cups grated Cheddar cheese
1 can (2½ oz.) chopped ripe olives

Ranchero:
1 can (7 oz.) diced green chiles*
4 cups grated Monterey Jack or mild Cheddar cheese

To Assemble:
Pour ½ cup prepared enchilada sauce into a 12 × 8 × 2-inch baking dish. Dip each tortilla into enchilada sauce. Place about ½ cup filling in center of each tortilla. Fold sides over filling; place in dish, seam side down. Pour remaining sauce over enchiladas. Top with reserved cheese. Bake in 350°F. oven 20 minutes. Sour cream and olives may also be used as garnish.

Each filling recipe above makes 4 servings of 2 enchiladas each

*Or use 8 fresh chiles, peeled, seeded and diced

QUESADILLAS

1 lb. JIMMY DEAN® Seasoned Taco Filling
8 eight-inch flour tortillas
4 cups grated Cheddar cheese (1 cup for each quesadilla)
2 Tbsp. butter
Black olives
Guacamole, sour cream
Hot sauce, jalapeños (optional)

Sauté JIMMY DEAN® Seasoned Taco Filling until brown and crumbly. Sprinkle 4 eight-inch flour tortillas with about ½ cup grated Cheddar cheese and spoon over about ¼ of the filling. Then sprinkle the remaining ½ cup over the meat. Cover with a second tortilla. Melt 2 Tbsp. butter in a large frying pan over medium heat. Lay in filled tortillas and cook until golden brown underneath. Turn and brown other side. Serve at once or place in a baking pan uncovered and keep warm in a 250° oven until all are fried. To serve as an appetizer, cut in 8 wedges. Serve in larger portions for main course. Garnish with guacamole, sour cream, black olives. Hot sauce and jalapeños, optional. *Serves 4*

NORWEGIAN STRATA

3 cans KING OSCAR Sardines
8 slices white bread
Butter
1 lb. sharp Cheddar cheese, thinly sliced
3 eggs, beaten
2 cups milk
1 small minced onion
2 tsp. prepared mustard
¼ tsp. TABASCO®
Pepper

Drain sardines and set aside. Butter both sides of the bread thickly. Place 2 slices side by side in greased loaf pan. Cover each piece of bread with cheese slices. Top with sardines. Repeat until all bread is used, making 4 layers. Beat together remaining ingredients and pour over the layered sardines and cheese and bread. Let stand in refrigerator for at least 1 hour, or longer. Remove from refrigerator and place in pan of water. Bake in 325° oven until puffy and brown (about 1 hour).

Serves 6

OSCAR'S TOMATO BROIL

3 medium tomatoes, halved
2 cans KING OSCAR Sardines, drained
1 Tbsp. lemon juice
2 Tbsp. grated Cheddar cheese
6 slices toast

In a bowl, mash one can of sardines with lemon juice. Spread mixture over tomato halves. Top each with 4 or 5 whole sardines from second can. Sprinkle with grated cheese. Place in shallow baking pan and broil at 450° until tomatoes are tender and cheese is melted. Serve on hot buttered toast.   *Serves 3 as main dish*

LAYERED WHEAT GERM SUPPER PIE

2 frozen patty shells, thawed
6 Tbsp. KRETSCHMER Regular Wheat Germ, divided
3 cups sliced zucchini (3 medium)
½ cup chopped onion
1 small clove garlic, minced
½ tsp. dill weed
¼ tsp. salt
⅛ tsp. pepper
1 Tbsp. butter or margarine
1¼ cups grated Monterey Jack cheese
2 Tbsp. minced parsley

Press patty shells together. Roll patty shells into an 8-inch circle on cloth-covered board sprinkled with 2 tablespoons wheat germ. Turn often to coat evenly. Press pastry into a 7-inch petite pie plate. Sauté zucchini, onion, garlic and seasonings in butter for 5 minutes until vegetables are tender-crisp. Place half the vegetable mixture in pastry shell. Cover with half the cheese. Sprinkle with remaining ¼ cup wheat germ. Repeat layers of vegetable and cheese. Bake at 425° for 15–18 minutes. Sprinkle with parsley and bake 5 minutes longer. Cut into wedges.
         Makes 2-3 servings

NOTE: To make 4–6 servings follow recipe above *except* double ingredients. Press pastry onto bottom and sides of 9-inch springform pan. Bake 20–22 minutes. Top with parsley and bake 5 minutes longer.

LUNCH IN SKILLET

½ cup chopped onions
½ cup sliced celery
1 cup sliced carrots
¼ cup chopped green pepper
1 package (10 oz.) frozen peas, thawed
¼ cup butter or margarine
2 cans (15 oz.) CHEF BOY-AR-DEE® ABC's & 123's with Mini Meat Balls
½ cup milk
¼ cup shredded Cheddar cheese

In a large skillet sauté onions, celery, carrots, pepper and thawed green peas in butter. Add ABC's & 123's with Mini Meat Balls and milk; cover. Simmer 5 minutes, stirring constantly. Add shredded Cheddar cheese and stir.
         Serves 4 to 6

Stews

HONEST AND TRUE IRISH STEW

6 medium potatoes (about 2 pounds) peeled and thinly sliced
2 pounds lean, bone-in lamb or 1½ pounds boneless lamb, cut into 1½-inch pieces
2 medium onions, peeled and sliced
1 teaspoon salt
¼ teaspoon pepper
¼ teaspoon thyme
1 teaspoon dried summer savory
2 tablespoons minced fresh parsley, or 1½ teaspoons dried
1½ cups water

In Dutch oven layer half the potatoes, and then all the lamb and onions. Combine salt, pepper, thyme and summer savory. Sprinkle half of salt mixture and 1 tablespoon of the parsley over onions. Layer remaining potatoes; sprinkle with remaining salt mixture. Pour water over all. Bring to boil; cover, reduce heat and simmer gently 2 to 2½ hours until lamb is tender. Add water as needed to maintain level about 1 inch in bottom of pan. Just before serving sprinkle with remaining parsley.   *6 servings*

Favorite recipe from American Lamb Council

MRS. O'LEARY'S IRISH STEW

2 pounds lamb or beef, cut into 1 inch cubes
¼ cup flour
1 teaspoon salt
Dash ground black pepper
Cooking oil
1 medium onion, sliced
1 can (16 oz.) VEG-ALL®, Mixed Vegetables, undrained
1 can (16 oz.) tomatoes, undrained
1 can (8 oz.) baking powder biscuits

Coat lamb cubes with a mixture of the flour, salt and pepper. Brown in cooking oil in a Dutch oven. Stir in sliced onion; cook until translucent. Add VEG-ALL® and tomatoes and cover. Bake in a preheated 325°F. oven for 1½ hours. Skim off excess fat. Place biscuits over stew. Cook, uncovered for 30 minutes, or until biscuits are browned and meat is tender.   *Serves 8*

IRISH STEW CHICKEN

2 medium carrots, cut into ¼-inch dices
2 medium onions, sliced
2 tablespoons flour
3 cups chicken broth, divided usage
2 medium potatoes, peeled and sliced ⅛-inch thick
½ teaspoon salt
⅛ teaspoon pepper
2 medium tomatoes, sliced
1 package (32 oz.) BANQUET® Heat and Serve Frozen Fully Cooked Fried Chicken
5 slices bacon, cut in half

Place carrots and onions in saucepan. Toss with flour. Stir in 2 cups broth. Heat to boiling. Boil 1 minute. Set aside. In 13 x 9-inch baking dish, layer potato slices. Sprinkle with salt and pepper. Spread carrot-onion mixture evenly over potatoes. Layer with tomato slices. Place frozen chicken parts on top of tomatoes. Top with bacon strips. Pour remaining 1 cup broth over chicken, being sure to moisten each piece. Heat in 375°F. oven 45 to 50 minutes, until vegetables are tender.
         Makes 6 servings

ITALIAN VEAL STEW
(Low Calorie)

8 pieces of veal shank, well-trimmed
1 tablespoon olive oil
1 medium onion, diced
1 clove garlic, minced
½ cup white wine
2 tablespoons ketchup
1 tablespoon lemon juice
2 chicken bouillon cubes
1 teaspoon oregano
½ teaspoon rosemary
1 cup water
4 medium potatoes, peeled and quartered
8 small white onions, peeled
4 medium carrots, peeled and chopped
2 medium stalks celery, chopped
1 tablespoon chopped parsley

In large, heavy, non-stick Dutch oven, brown veal in olive oil. Add chopped onion and garlic; cook five minutes. Stir in wine, ketchup, lemon juice, bouillon cubes, oregano, rosemary and 1 cup water. Cover and simmer one hour or until meat is almost tender. Add remaining ingredients; simmer, covered, 30 minutes longer or until meat and vegetables are tender.

Makes 8 servings

About 235 calories each

Favorite recipe from The Potato Board

BUTTERMILK VEAL STEW

2 pounds veal for stew, cut in 1-inch pieces
⅓ cup flour
2 teaspoons salt
⅛ teaspoon pepper
⅛ teaspoon thyme
¼ cup cooking fat
3 medium onions, quartered
1 cup sliced celery
1 cup water
1 medium head cauliflower, broken in pieces
1 cup buttermilk
1 package (10 ounces) frozen peas, cooked and drained
2 tablespoons diced pimiento
Hot biscuits

Combine flour, salt, pepper and thyme; dredge meat. Reserve excess flour. Brown meat in cooking fat. Pour off drippings. Add onions, celery and water. Cover tightly and cook slowly 1¼ hours. Add cauliflower and continue cooking, covered, 30 to 40 minutes or until meat and vegetables are done. Stir buttermilk into reserved flour, add to meat and cook, stirring constantly until thickened. Stir in peas and pimiento and cook slowly 2 minutes. Serve with hot biscuits.

6 to 8 servings

Favorite recipe from Beef Industry Council National Live Stock & Meat Board

VEAL STEW WITH PERNOD
(Blanquette de Veau Pernodine)

1 lb. veal cut into 1 inch cubes
2 chopped onions
1 sachet bouquet garni
1 chicken stock cube

Sauce:
3 oz. butter
2 oz. cornstarch
1 pint milk
2 beaten egg yolks
1 tablespoon PERNOD
Salt and pepper

Garnish:
4 bacon slices, grilled crisp
Lemon slices
Parsley

Put the veal in a casserole with the onions and bouquet garni. Cover with chicken stock (made from cube) and leave to simmer slowly for about 1½ hours or until the meat is tender. Pour off the juices, reserve; keep the meat hot. Melt the butter, add cooking juices and mix in the cornstarch blended with a little water. Cook gently for about 2 minutes. Add the milk and bring to the boil, while stirring. When the sauce begins to thicken, remove from heat and blend in the egg yolks and PERNOD. Season to taste and reheat without boiling. Pour over the veal on a hot serving dish. Garnish with bacon, lemon slices and parsley.

SPANISH VEAL STEW

2 pounds veal for stew, cut in 1-inch pieces
¼ cup flour
1 teaspoon salt
¼ cup cooking fat
1 jar (16 ounces) onions
1 can (8 ounces) tomato sauce
½ cup sherry
1 teaspoon parsley flakes
½ teaspoon thyme
⅛ teaspoon garlic powder
¼ cup water
2 cups sliced fresh mushrooms
1 jar (2 to 3 ounces) stuffed green olives, drained
¼ cup grated Parmesan cheese, if desired

Combine flour and salt; dredge meat. Reserve any excess flour. Brown meat in cooking fat. Pour off drippings. Drain onions; reserve liquid and combine ½ cup liquid with tomato sauce, sherry, parsley flakes, thyme and garlic powder. Add to meat and mix. Cover tightly and cook slowly 1½ hours or until meat is tender. Dissolve any reserved flour in remaining onion liquid or water and use to thicken gravy, if desired. Stir in onions, mushrooms and olives. Continue cooking slowly, covered, 15 minutes. Sprinkle with Parmesan cheese, if desired.

6 to 8 servings

Favorite recipe from Beef Industry Council National Live Stock & Meat Board

VINTNER'S BEEF STEW

1 lb. stew meat, cubed and floured
2 Tbsp. oil
½ onion, studded with 3 cloves
2 cups THE CHRISTIAN BROTHERS® Burgundy
1 cup beef broth
1 tsp. each thyme, basil, salt and pepper
1 bay leaf
5 potatoes, peeled and diced
6 carrots, peeled and cut into sticks

Brown meat in hot oil; add onion, wine, broth and seasonings. Simmer over low heat 1½ hours, or until meat is tender. Add potatoes and carrots; continue cooking 30 minutes.

Serves 4

SWEET 'N SOUR STEW

2 pounds beef chuck, cut into
  1½-inch cubes
3 tablespoons flour
1 tablespoon salad oil
1 can (1 pound) tomatoes
2 medium onions, sliced
1 teaspoon celery salt
1 teaspoon salt
¼ teaspoon pepper
⅓ cup vinegar
⅓ cup GRANDMA'S® Molasses
  (Unsulphured)
1 cup water
3 large or 4 medium carrots,
  pared and cut into 1-inch pieces
½ cup raisins
½ teaspoon ginger

Coat beef with the flour. Brown in
oil in heavy saucepan; add
tomatoes, onions, celery salt, salt
and pepper. Mix vinegar, molasses
and water; add to meat. Cover and
simmer until meat is almost
tender, about 2 hours. Add carrots,
raisins and ginger. Cook until
carrots and meat are tender, 30 to
40 minutes. Serve over hot cooked
rice.   *Yield: 6 servings*

HERBED STEW

3 lbs. stew meat
½ cup flour
Salt & pepper
2 tablespoons butter
2 onions
1½ cups MR. & MRS. "T"®
  Bloody Mary Mix
1½ cups water
1 tablespoon vinegar
1 clove garlic
½ teaspoon rosemary
½ teaspoon oregano
2 cups fresh mushrooms

Place flour and seasoning in
plastic bag. Add cubed meat and
shake well until coated. Brown
meat in butter. Chop onions into
large pieces and add to meat. Add
remaining ingredients except
mushrooms. Cover and simmer two
hours over low heat. *Do not boil.*
After two hours, add mushrooms
whole. Simmer further 30 minutes.
                        Serves 6

BEEF STEW

3 tablespoons MAZOLA® Corn Oil
2 pounds stewing beef, cut in
  2-inch cubes*
1 beef bouillon cube
2 teaspoons salt
1 bay leaf
¼ teaspoon crushed dried thyme
  leaves
4½ cups water
6 carrots, cut in 3-inch strips
12 small white onions
¼ cup ARGO® /KINGSFORD'S®
  Corn Starch

In skillet heat corn oil over medium
heat. Add beef; brown on all sides.
Add next 4 ingredients and 4 cups
of the water. Cover; bring to boil.
Reduce heat; simmer 1½ hours.
Add carrots and onions. Simmer ½
hour or until tender. Mix corn
starch and ½ cup water. Stir into
beef mixture. Bring to boil, stirring
constantly; boil 1 minute.
                    Makes 6 servings

*Note: Lamb may be substituted
  for beef.

BAVARIAN STEW WITH POTATO DUMPLINGS

1½ to 2 pounds stewing beef or
  chuck steak, cut in cubes
1 tablespoon oil or melted
  shortening
2 cups water
1 envelope FRENCH'S® Onion
  Gravy Mix
¼ cup vinegar
2 tablespoons brown sugar
½ cup raisins
4 gingersnaps, crushed into
  crumbs
Potato Dumplings (recipe below)

Brown beef in oil in large skillet or
pan. Add water, contents of gravy
mix envelope, vinegar, and brown
sugar. Cover; simmer 1½ to 2
hours, or until tender, stirring
occasionally. Stir in raisins and
gingersnap crumbs. Prepare Potato
Dumplings following directions
below; drop by spoonfuls on top of
simmering stew. Cover; simmer 15
minutes longer, until dumplings are
firm.   *4 to 6 servings*

POTATO DUMPLINGS

Lightly beat together 1 egg, ½ cup
water, and 1 tablespoon melted
butter. Add 1 envelope
FRENCH'S® Potato Pancake Mix
and ¼ cup finely chopped green
pepper; stir until blended. Let
stand 10 minutes.

*Microwave directions for Potato
Dumplings:* Heat any prepared
stew to boiling in microwave oven.
Add dumplings. Cover; cook on
HIGH 4 to 5 minutes, until firm.

ALL-AMERICAN SAUSAGE STEW

1 can (10½ ounces) condensed
  beef broth
1 cup water
⅛ teaspoon pepper
1 bay leaf
2 medium onions, quartered
6 carrots, pared, cut in julienne
  pieces
1½ cups diced celery
2 potatoes, pared, diced
2 tablespoons water
1 tablespoon all-purpose flour
1 pound ECKRICH® Smoked
  Sausage, cut in ½" pieces
Salt to taste
Grated Parmesan cheese

Combine broth, 1 cup water,
pepper, bay leaf, and vegetables
except potatoes in a 4-quart
saucepot. Simmer, covered, 10
minutes. Add potatoes; cook until
vegetables are tender. Remove bay
leaf. Mix 2 tablespoons water with
flour; stir into vegetables. Add
sausage; heat. Add salt. Top each
serving with cheese.
                    6 to 8 servings

Microwave oven directions:
Combine broth, 1 cup water,
pepper, bay leaf, and vegetables
except potatoes in a 3-quart glass
baking dish. Cook, covered, 14
minutes, stirring twice. Add
potatoes; cook 12 minutes, stirring
twice. Remove bay leaf. Mix 2
tablespoons water with flour; stir
in vegetables. Add sausage; cook,
uncovered, 6 minutes, stirring
once. Add salt. Let stand 5
minutes before serving.

Casseroles

ARGO®

TUNA CASSEROLE

⅓ cup margarine
3 tablespoons ARGO® /
  KINGSFORD'S® Corn Starch
½ teaspoon salt
⅛ teaspoon pepper
3 cups milk
1 onion, chopped
2 cans (7 oz. each) tuna, drained
  and flaked
1 package (8 oz.) elbow macaroni,
  cooked and drained
1 package (10 oz.) frozen peas,
  thawed
1 cup shredded Cheddar cheese

In saucepan melt margarine over
medium heat. Stir in corn starch,
salt and pepper until smooth.
Remove from heat; gradually stir in
milk until smooth. Bring to boil
over medium heat, stirring
constantly, and boil 1 minute; add
onion. Place remaining ingredients
in greased 2-quart casserole. Stir
in corn starch mixture. Bake in
350°F. oven 25 minutes or until
heated.   *Makes 6 servings*

PERFECT TUNA CASSEROLE

1 can (10¾ ounces) CAMPBELL'S
  Condensed Cream of Celery or
  Mushroom Soup
¼ cup milk
1 can (about 7 ounces) tuna,
  drained and flaked
2 hard-cooked eggs, sliced
1 cup cooked peas
½ cup slightly crumbled potato
  chips

In 1-quart casserole, blend soup
and milk; stir in tuna, eggs, and
peas. Bake at 350°F. for 25
minutes or until hot; stir. Top with
chips; bake 5 minutes more.
          Makes about 4 cups

TUNA STROGANOFF

1 8-oz. package medium noodles
2 (6½ oz.) cans tuna (chunk)
1 cup yogurt (plain)
1 cup cottage cheese (farmer style)
1 tablespoon Worcestershire
  sauce
1 tablespoon minced onion
2 teaspoons salt
⅛ teaspoon pepper
1 (2¼ oz.) can LINDSAY® Sliced
  Olives
½ pound bacon

Bring 2 quarts water to a boil. Add
1 teaspoon salt and package of
noodles. Boil 8 minutes and drain.
Line bottom of casserole with
noodles. Add tuna, cottage cheese,
yogurt, Worcestershire, onions,
salt, pepper and mix gently.
Sprinkle olives on top. Fry ½
pound bacon in strips. Cut with
sharp knife or scissors over the
top. Cover with foil. Bake at 350
degrees F. for 30-40 minutes.
          Serves 6-8

HURRY-UP CASSEROLE

7-oz. package CREAMETTES®
  Macaroni (2 cups uncooked)
1 can condensed cream of
  mushroom soup
1 cup milk
1 can (7-oz.) tuna, drained and
  flaked

Prepare CREAMETTES® according
to package directions. Drain. Mix
macaroni, soup, milk and tuna.
Pour into 1½-quart casserole.
Bake, covered, at 350°F. for 25-30
minutes.   *4 servings*

VARIATIONS:

Luncheon meat, ham, franks or
chicken may be substituted for
tuna.

COTTAGE TUNA NOODLE

6 oz. uncooked noodles (4 cups
  cooked)
¼ cup chopped onion
1 teaspoon salt
⅛ teaspoon pepper
1 cup cottage cheese
1 can (8 oz.) PET® Imitation Sour
  Cream
¼ cup water
1 can (6½ oz.) tuna
¼ cup grated Romano cheese

Cook noodles according to
package directions, until tender.
Drain. Add onion, salt, pepper,
cottage cheese, imitation sour
cream, water, and tuna. Mix well.
Pour into 1½-quart casserole dish.
Top with cheese. Bake in 400°F.
oven for 20 minutes or until bubbly.
Serve hot.
          Makes 6-8 servings, ¾ cup each

TUNA FLORENTINE

4 ounces egg noodles
1 package frozen chopped spinach
1 (9¼ ounce) can tuna
1 can cream of mushroom soup
1 tablespoon WRIGHT'S Natural
  Hickory Liquid Smoke
1 onion, chopped
½ cup celery, chopped
½ cup green pepper, chopped
½ cup butter
1 cup Swiss cheese, grated

Cook noodles and spinach
according to package directions.
Spread drained noodles over
bottom of greased casserole dish.
Cover with tuna and drained
spinach. Sauté onion, celery and
green pepper in butter, stir in
mushroom soup and WRIGHT'S
Natural Hickory Liquid Smoke.
Pour sauce over casserole and
bake in 325° oven for 20 minutes,
top with Swiss cheese and bake
additional 3 minutes.   *Serves 6*

CORNY TUNA CASSEROLE

2 cups chopped onion
¼ cup butter or margarine
2 (6½ oz.) cans S&W Chunk Light Tuna, drained
½ cup snipped parsley
2 Tbsp. snipped chives or scallions
2 S&W Pimientos, diced
1½ cups corn muffin mix
1 egg
⅛ tsp. salt
½ cup milk
1 (8½ oz.) can S&W Cream Style Corn
2 cups dairy sour cream
1½ cups shredded sharp Cheddar cheese

Brown onions in the butter or margarine and cook until soft, stir occasionally. Add tuna, parsley, chives or scallions and pimientos. Heat and mix well. In a bowl combine muffin mix, salt, egg, milk and cream style corn. Stir until well-moistened but still lumpy. Pour into well-greased 3 qt. baking dish, spread evenly to edges. Spoon hot tuna mixture over batter and spread sour cream over all. Sprinkle with the grated cheese and bake at 400° for 30 to 35 minutes. If desired, garnish top with chopped parsley, chopped fresh dill or chopped watercress.

Serves 8

TEMPTING TUNA BAKE

8 slices white bread
1 cup shredded FINLANDIA Swiss
1 can (7 ounces) tuna, drained and flaked
¼ cup chopped green onion
¼ cup chopped celery
2 tablespoons butter or margarine
2 cups milk
2 eggs, slightly beaten
½ teaspoon salt

Alternate layers of bread and cheese in well buttered 9-inch square baking dish. Begin with bread and end with cheese. Sprinkle tuna over all. In small saucepan, cook onion and celery in butter until vegetables are tender. Remove from heat. Blend with milk, eggs and salt. Pour mixture over tuna in baking dish. Bake at 350° until puffy and lightly browned.

Makes 4 to 6 servings

SUPERB SWISS TUNA BAKE

2 cans (6½ or 7 ounces each) tuna, drained
¼ cup chopped scallions
¼ pound mushrooms, chopped
½ teaspoon dried dillweed
1 teaspoon salt, divided
2 cups (8 ounces) shredded Swiss cheese, divided
6 slices bread, crusts trimmed
6 eggs
2 cups milk
1 teaspoon Worcestershire sauce
⅛ teaspoon TABASCO® sauce

Flake tuna in large bowl. Add scallions, mushrooms, dill, ½ teaspoon salt and 1 cup cheese. Mix well. Butter a shallow 2-quart baking dish. Arrange bread in baking dish. Spoon tuna mixture over bread. Beat eggs with milk, Worcestershire, TABASCO® Sauce and remaining ½ teaspoon salt; pour over tuna. Sprinkle top with remaining 1 cup cheese. Cover; chill 2 hours. Leave at room temperature ½ hour before baking. Bake in a 325°F. oven 1 to 1¼ hours, until tip of knife inserted in center comes out clean. (May be reheated.)

Yield: 6 servings

Favorite recipe from Tuna Research Foundation, Inc.

TUNA SUNFLOWER CASSEROLE

2 cans (7 oz. each) tuna fish, flaked
2 cans (10½ oz. each) cream of mushroom soup
⅔ cup milk
1 jar (4½ oz.) sliced mushrooms, drained
¾ cup FISHER® Salted, Roasted Sunflower Nuts
¼ cup chopped pimiento
½ cup crushed potato chips

Combine first 6 ingredients. Spoon into buttered 1½ quart casserole. Sprinkle with potato chips. Bake at 350° for 30 minutes.

Makes 4 to 5 servings

JAYS TUNA CASSEROLE

3 tablespoons chopped onions
3 tablespoons chopped green pepper
1 tablespoon melted butter or margarine
2 tablespoons diced pimiento
1 can cream of chicken soup
1 can cream of celery soup*
⅔ cup milk
1 tablespoon lemon juice
2 cans (7-ounces each) tuna, drained and flaked
2 cups coarsely crushed JAYS Potato Chips

Sauté onion and green pepper in butter or margarine 3 minutes, or until tender; remove from heat. Combine sautéed onion and green pepper, pimiento, soups, milk, lemon juice, and tuna; mix well. Place 1 cup crushed potato chips in bottom of lightly buttered 1½-quart casserole; add tuna mixture. Sprinkle remaining 1 cup potato chips on top. Bake in moderate oven 350°F. for 30 minutes. *Makes 6 servings*

*Or use 1 can cream of spinach or asparagus soup.

TUNA 'N RICE NAPOLI

1 bag SUCCESS® Rice
1 can (7 oz.) tuna
¼ cup chopped green pepper
¼ cup chopped onion
¾ teaspoon salt, divided
1 cup shredded Mozzarella cheese, divided
1 cup milk
1 egg, slightly beaten
½ teaspoon oregano leaves

Cook bag of rice according to package directions. While rice is cooking, combine the tuna, green pepper, onion, and ¼ teaspoon salt, and ½ cup of the cheese. Drain rice and empty into buttered 1 quart casserole. Spread tuna mixture over the rice. Combine the milk, egg, remaining cheese, salt, and oregano. Pour over the tuna. Bake, uncovered at 375°F. for 15 minutes.

Makes 4 servings (about 1 cup each)

TUNA CURRY CASSEROLE

4 strips bacon, cut in 1-inch pieces
3 tablespoons butter
2 cups sliced DOLE® Fresh Mushrooms
3 tablespoons chopped green onion
1 tablespoon curry powder
1 can (14½ oz.) whole tomatoes
2 cans (7 oz. each) BUMBLE BEE® Solid White Albacore Tuna
1 tablespoon lime juice
3 cups fluffy buttered rice
¼ cup water

Fry bacon pieces until crisp; remove and drain. Pour off all but 1 tablespoon bacon fat. Add 2 tablespoons butter to skillet. Sauté mushrooms and onion until just tender; remove from pan. Add remaining butter and curry to pan. Cook and stir about 1 minute. Add tomatoes with all liquid, breaking up tomatoes with a spoon. Simmer about 5 minutes. Drain tuna; add to curry sauce along with lime juice. Remove from heat. Combine fluffy rice with bacon and sautéed vegetables. Turn rice mixture into a 2-quart casserole dish. Spoon tuna-curry sauce over rice. Pour water over all. Cover and bake in a 350°F. oven until bubbly and hot, about 20 minutes.

Makes 8 servings

FRENCH'S® TUNA FLORENTINE

8 ounces egg noodles
1 envelope FRENCH'S® Italian Style Spaghetti Sauce Mix
1 can (6½-oz.) tuna, drained and flaked
1 package (10-oz.) frozen chopped spinach, thawed
¼ cup grated Parmesan cheese

Cook and drain noodles. Prepare spaghetti sauce; combine with noodles and tuna in 2-quart casserole. Spoon spinach around edge of casserole; sprinkle with cheese. Bake at 375°F. for 20 to 25 minutes, until hot.

4 to 5 servings

Microwave Tuna Florentine: Cook noodles conventionally; drain. Prepare sauce mix in small glass bowl; microwave on HIGH 6 minutes, stirring every 2 minutes. Combine with noodles and tuna in 2-quart casserole. Place frozen spinach in small bowl, cover with plastic wrap, and microwave on HIGH 4 to 5 minutes; drain well. Spoon around edge of casserole. Sprinkle with cheese, cover with wax paper, and microwave on HIGH 4 to 6 minutes, or until hot.

SUNSHINE® TUNA BAKE

1 cup sliced celery
1 cup green pepper
½ cup chopped onion
4 tablespoons butter or margarine
1 (10½ ounce) can condensed cream of chicken or celery soup
½ soup can milk
2 cups cooked shell macaroni
1 cup chopped tomato
1 can (9½ ounce) tuna, drained and flaked
1½ cups SUNSHINE® Oyster Crackers
2 tablespoons melted butter or margarine
¼ cup grated Parmesan cheese

In a saucepan, cook vegetables in butter until tender. Combine with soup, milk, macaroni, tomato and tuna in 1½-quart buttered baking dish. Bake at 350°F. for 20 minutes. Meanwhile, combine crackers, melted butter and cheese; sprinkle around edge of casserole. Bake 10 minutes until hot and bubbly.

Yield: 4 to 5 servings

Lea & Perrins
THE ORIGINAL WORCESTERSHIRE

SALMON CASSEROLE

1 pound elbow macaroni
2 cans (10¾ oz. each) condensed Cheddar cheese soup
1½ cups milk
2 tablespoons instant minced onion
4 teaspoons LEA & PERRINS Worcestershire Sauce
⅛ teaspoon ground red pepper
1 can (1 lb.) salmon, drained and chunked
1 small tomato, diced
½ cup buttered soft bread crumbs

Cook macaroni until tender; drain well. In a saucepan combine soup with milk; stir in onion, LEA & PERRINS and red pepper. Heat, but do not boil. In an ovenproof casserole combine drained macaroni, salmon and tomato. Pour soup mixture over all. Top with buttered bread crumbs. Bake, uncovered in a preheated oven (375°F.) 30 minutes.

Yield: 8 portions

Note: Mixture may be baked in individual baking dishes.

SEAFARER'S CASSEROLE

⅓ cup butter or margarine
1 cup rice
2 vegetable bouillon cubes
Boiling water
½ cup white wine (optional)
4 ounce can sliced mushrooms, drained
1 cup frozen green peas
6 pieces frozen VAN DE KAMP'S® Batter-Dipped Fish Fillets, Haddock, Perch or Halibut

Melt butter in skillet over medium heat. Add rice; cook until lightly browned, stirring constantly. If using wine, dissolve bouillon cubes in 1¼ cups boiling water; add with wine to rice. (Or, omit wine and dissolve bouillon cubes in 1¾ cups boiling water.) Add mushrooms and frozen peas. Transfer mixture to rectangular 2 quart casserole and bake, covered, at 400 degrees F. 30 to 45 minutes. Prepare fish according to package directions in oven with rice. To serve, arrange fish fillets on top of rice.

Makes 6 servings

INSTANT HINT: Prepare fish fillets according to package directions. Prepare 2 packages, 11 ounces each, frozen seasoned rice with peas and mushrooms, also according to package directions. Serve as directed.

SHRIMP NOODLE DINNER CASSEROLE

¾ pound peeled, cleaned, and deveined shrimp, fresh or frozen or 3 cans (4½ ounces each) shrimp
1 package (8 ounces) medium noodles
2 cans (10¾ ounces each) condensed cream of mushroom soup
1 cup dairy sour cream
⅓ cup sliced green onion
½ teaspoon dried dill weed
½ cup shredded Cheddar cheese
1 medium size tomato, sliced
Fresh dill sprigs for garnish, optional

Cook shrimp as directed on package; drain. If canned shrimp is used, drain and rinse with cold water. Cook noodles as directed on package; drain well. Combine and mix soup, sour cream, onion and dill weed; stir in noodles. Cut ¼ of the shrimp into thirds and fold cut shrimp and cheese into noodle mixture. Spoon into a shallow 2-quart baking dish. Cover dish with aluminum foil, crimping it to edges of dish. Bake in moderate oven, 350°F., 20 minutes. Remove from oven; remove foil. Arrange remaining shrimp in rows on top of casserole. Return to oven and continue baking 10 to 15 minutes or until hot and bubbly. Garnish with half tomato slices and fresh dill weed sprigs, if desired.

Makes 6 servings

Favorite recipe from National Marine Fisheries Service

SAVANNAH SCALLOP

3 tablespoons butter or margarine
½ cup frozen ORE-IDA® Chopped Onions
½ cup sliced celery
½ cup diced green pepper
3 tablespoons flour
1 teaspoon salt
⅛ teaspoon pepper
½ teaspoon dry mustard
1½ cups milk
¾ cup shredded Cheddar cheese
4 cups frozen ORE-IDA® GOLDEN FRIES® *
1½ cups cubed cooked ham

Preheat oven to 400°F. Grease a shallow 2-quart baking dish. In large skillet, in melted butter, sauté onion, celery and green pepper until golden. Reduce heat to medium; blend in flour and seasonings. Add milk, cook while stirring until smooth and thickened. Add ½ cup shredded Cheddar cheese and stir until melted. Arrange a layer of potatoes, then ham cubes in baking dish; pour cheese-vegetable sauce over the top. Cover tightly with foil. Bake for 30 minutes. Uncover; top with remaining ¼ cup cheese. Return to oven 15 minutes or until bubbly.

Yield: 5 servings

*May also be prepared with ORE-IDA® GOLDEN CRINKLES®

BAKED SEAFOOD SALAD

2 cans HIGH SEA Crab Meat
1 can 4½-oz. LOUISIANA BRAND Shrimp
¾ cup chopped green pepper
1 cup diced celery
2 Tbsp. chopped onions
¾ cup mayonnaise
1 cup cooked peas, drained
1 small jar pimento, chopped
⅛ tsp. pepper
1 Tbsp. lemon juice
¼ cup finely crushed potato chips
1 cup grated sharp cheese

Combine all ingredients - *except* potato chips and cheese. Mix thoroughly. Place in greased baking dish and top with potato chips and cheese. Bake in preheated 350°F oven for 30 minutes.

Serves 8

CRAB AND RICE SUPREME

1 bag SUCCESS® Rice
1 can (6-oz.) white crab meat
1 pkg. (3-oz.) cream cheese, softened
⅓ cup milk
¼ cup sliced green onion
2 tablespoons lemon juice
¼ cup butter or margarine, divided
2 garlic cloves, minced
1 teaspoon parsley flakes
½ teaspoon salt
¼ teaspoon hot pepper sauce
¼ cup dry bread crumbs

Cook bag of rice according to package directions. Drain. Combine rice with the crab meat, cream cheese, milk, onion, lemon juice, 2 tablespoons of the butter, garlic, parsley, salt, and hot pepper sauce. Mix well. Pour into 1-quart casserole. Sprinkle with mixture of bread crumbs and remaining butter (melted). Bake at 425°F. for 10 minutes.

Makes 4 servings (about 1 cup each)

SCALLOPED OYSTERS

2 cans (8-oz. each) HIGH SEA Oysters
¾ cup dry bread crumbs
¾ cup unsalted cracker crumbs
½ cup butter
¼ tsp. Worcestershire sauce
1 cup milk
Dash of pepper

Drain the cans of oysters, discarding the liquid. Melt butter in a saucepan over a low heat, then add crumbs and pepper, mixing well. Place about ⅓ of mixture into well-greased 8-in. round baking dish covering bottom. Add a layer of oysters then repeat with crumb-mixture, making two more layers. Add the Worcestershire sauce to the milk and pour over top layer of oysters. Sprinkle remaining crumbs on top and bake in hot oven (400°F.) for 20-25 minutes or until brown.

Serves 6

SWISS CHICKEN SCALLOP

2 packages (10 ounces *each*) frozen whole green beans, cooked and drained
2 cans (10¾ ounces *each*) CAMPBELL'S Condensed Cream of Chicken Soup
⅓ cup Chablis or other white wine
2 cans (5 ounces *each*) SWANSON Chunk Chicken
½ cup shredded Swiss cheese
1 can (1½ ounces) potato sticks

In 2-quart shallow baking dish (12 x 8 x 2"), arrange beans. Combine soup, wine, chicken and cheese; pour over beans. Bake at 350°F. for 25 minutes or until hot; stir. Top with potato sticks; bake 5 minutes more.

Makes 6 servings

CHICKEN RAVIOLI CASSEROLE

¼ cup cooking oil
2 tablespoons butter or margarine
2 broiler/fryer chickens, cut into serving parts
¼ cup chopped onion
¼ cup chopped green pepper
2 cans (15 oz.) CHEF BOY-AR-DEE® Mini Ravioli in Tomato and Meat Sauce
1 cup table cream
Dash hot pepper sauce
1 package (10 oz.) frozen peas, cooked and drained
2 tablespoons toasted almonds

Combine cooking oil and butter; heat in large skillet. Drain chicken parts. Remove browned parts to warm platter. Sauté onion and pepper in remaining fat. Add Mini Ravioli, table cream, hot pepper sauce, and frozen peas; cover, simmer for 5 minutes. Place layer of chicken on bottom of baking dish. Pour Mini Ravioli mixture over. Arrange remaining chicken on top; cover. Bake for 40 minutes in 350°F. oven. Garnish with toasted almonds.

GREAT CHICKEN CASSEROLE

7-oz. package CREAMETTES® Macaroni (2 cups uncooked)
1½ cups celery, chopped
½ cup green pepper, chopped
¼ cup onion, chopped
¼ cup butter or margarine
2 cans condensed cream of chicken soup
⅔ cup milk
2 cups Cheddar cheese, shredded
1½ cups diced cooked chicken or turkey
1 jar (4-oz.) pimiento, drained and diced
½ teaspoon salt
¼ teaspoon nutmeg
½ cup toasted almonds, slivered or whole

Prepare CREAMETTES® according to package directions. Drain. Sauté celery, green pepper and onion in butter until tender. Add soup, milk and cheese. Stir until cheese melts. Combine macaroni, cheese mixture, chicken, pimiento, salt and nutmeg. Pour into 2½-quart casserole. Top with almonds. Bake at 350°F. for 30-35 minutes.
6 to 8 servings

Uncle Ben's®

WILD RICE-CHICKEN SUPREME

1 package (6 ounces) UNCLE BEN'S® Long Grain & Wild Rice
¼ cup butter or margarine
⅓ cup chopped onion
⅓ cup flour
1 teaspoon salt
Dash black pepper
1 cup half and half
1 cup chicken broth
2 cups cubed cooked chicken
⅓ cup chopped pimiento
⅓ cup chopped parsley
¼ cup chopped almonds

Prepare contents of rice and seasoning packets according to package directions. Meanwhile, melt butter in large saucepan. Add onion and cook over low heat until tender. Stir in flour, salt and pepper. Gradually stir in half and half and chicken broth. Cook, stirring constantly, until thickened. Stir in chicken, pimiento, parsley, almonds and cooked rice. Place in 2-quart casserole. Bake, uncovered, in 425°F. oven for 30 minutes.
Makes 6 to 8 servings

GREEN BEAN DIVAN

6 Tablespoons butter or margarine, melted
6 Tablespoons flour
1½ cups chicken broth
½ cup milk
3 Tablespoons sherry
½ teaspoon salt
Dash pepper
⅔ cup Parmesan cheese, divided
2 cans (1 lb. ea.) STOKELY'S FINEST® Cut Green Beans, well drained
2 cups cooked cubed chicken breast

Blend butter and flour in saucepan. Stir in broth and milk. Cook and stir over medium heat until mixture bubbles and thickens. Remove from heat and stir in sherry, salt, pepper and ⅓ cup cheese. Place half the Beans in a 2 quart casserole. Top with half the sauce, all the chicken, the remaining Beans and remaining sauce. Sprinkle with remaining ⅓ cup cheese and bake at 375°F. for 15 minutes.
Makes 5 to 6 servings

ALPINE CHICKEN CASSEROLE

4 cups chopped cooked chicken
2 cups celery slices
2 cups toasted bread cubes
1 cup KRAFT Real Mayonnaise
½ cup milk
¼ cup chopped onion
1 teaspoon salt
Dash of pepper
1 8-oz. pkg. KRAFT Natural Swiss Cheese Slices, cut into cubes
¼ cup slivered almonds, toasted

Combine ingredients except nuts; mix well. Pour into 2-quart casserole; sprinkle with nuts. Bake at 350°, 40 minutes.
6 servings

To Make Ahead: Prepare the recipe as directed. Cover; refrigerate several hours. Bake at 350°, 50 minutes. Uncover; continue baking 10 minutes.

FIESTA CASSEROLE

1 can (10¾ oz.) cream of chicken soup
1 jar (8 oz.) pasteurized process cheese spread
2 cups chopped, cooked or canned chicken
1 can (4 oz.) OLD EL PASO® Chopped Green Chilies, drained
12 OLD EL PASO® Corn Tortillas
1 can (10 oz.) OLD EL PASO® Mild Enchilada Sauce
1-2 cups shredded lettuce
½ cup chopped tomato

Preheat oven to 350°F. Combine soup and process cheese spread, mixing until well blended. Add chicken and green chilies. Spread ½ cup of chicken mixture over bottom of a 2-quart rectangular baking dish. Layer four of the tortillas, dipping each in enchilada sauce, and one third of the remaining chicken mixture; repeat layers two more times. Cover with foil; bake 20 minutes. Remove foil, continue baking 15 minutes. Top with lettuce and tomato.
Makes 6 servings

Microwave instructions: Microcook uncovered on 70% power for 24 to 27 minutes or until heated through. Turn twice during cooking time.

EASY CHICKEN CASSEROLE
(Low Calorie)

1 can (8 oz.) FEATHERWEIGHT Chicken Noodle Soup
1 can (5 oz.) FEATHERWEIGHT Boned Chicken
1 can (8 oz.) FEATHERWEIGHT Cream of Mushroom Soup
1 cup cooked noodles
½ cup FEATHERWEIGHT Colby or Cheddar Cheese, grated
1 Tbsp. unsalted butter
⅓ cup celery, chopped
⅓ cup onion, chopped

Melt butter in a saucepan, add celery and onion. Sauté a few minutes. Combine all remaining ingredients with sautéed vegetables. Pour into a casserole dish. Bake at 350°F. for 30 minutes. Just before serving, add 1 Tbsp. of Cheese to top of casserole. Serve when Cheese is melted.
Serves 4-5

EASY BAR-B-QUE CHICKEN CASSEROLE

1 can (1 lb.) VAN CAMP'S® Pork and Beans
4 pieces of chicken (thighs, breasts or legs)
¼ cup STOKELY'S FINEST® Tomato Catsup
2 Tablespoons peach preserves
2 teaspoons instant minced onion
¼ teaspoon soy sauce
¼ cup brown sugar

Place Pork and Beans in a 2-quart casserole. Top with chicken. Mix together the remaining ingredients and pour over chicken and Beans. Cover and bake at 325°F. for 1 hour and 45 minutes.
Makes 4 servings

INSIDE-OUT CHICKEN AND STUFFING

½ cup chopped onion
½ cup sliced celery
2 tablespoons butter or margarine
2 cans (5 ounces *each*) SWANSON Chunk Style Mixin' Chicken
1 can (7¾ ounces) CAMPBELL'S Semi-Condensed Savory Cream of Mushroom Soup
2 tablespoons water
1 cup herb-seasoned stuffing mix
¼ cup chopped pecans
2 tablespoons chopped parsley

In saucepan, cook onion and celery in butter until tender. Mix in chicken and soup. Add remaining ingredients. Pour into 1½-quart casserole; bake at 400°F. for 25 minutes or until hot.
Makes about 4 cups, 4 servings

CRUNCHY BISCUIT CHICKEN CASSEROLE

2 (5-oz.) cans boned chicken or 2 cups cooked, cubed chicken
10¾-oz. can condensed cream of chicken soup
8½-oz. can GREEN GIANT® KITCHEN SLICED® Green Beans, drained
2½-oz. jar GREEN GIANT® Brand Sliced Mushrooms, undrained
4 oz. (1 cup) shredded Cheddar or American cheese
½ cup mayonnaise or salad dressing
1 teaspoon lemon juice
10-oz. can PILLSBURY'S HUNGRY JACK® Refrigerated Big Flaky Biscuits
1 to 2 tablespoons margarine or butter, melted
¼ to ½ cup crushed Cheddar cheese or seasoned croutons

Heat oven to 375°F. In medium saucepan, combine chicken, chicken soup, green beans, mushrooms, cheese, mayonnaise and lemon juice. Heat until hot and bubbly. Pour hot chicken mixture into ungreased shallow 2-quart casserole or 12 × 8-inch (2-quart) baking dish. Separate biscuit dough into 10 biscuits. Arrange biscuits over hot chicken mixture. Brush each biscuit with margarine; sprinkle with crushed croutons. Bake at 375°F. for 25 to 30 minutes or until deep golden brown. Serve immediately.
4 to 6 servings

TIP: To reheat, cover loosely with foil; heat at 375°F. for 15 to 20 minutes.

High Altitude—Above 3500 Feet: No change.

NUTRITIONAL INFORMATION PER SERVING
SERVING SIZE: ⅙ OF RECIPE

⅙ OF RECIPE		PERCENT U.S. RDA PER SERVING	
Calories	530	Protein	35%
Protein	22 g	Vitamin A	15%
Carbohydrate	28 g	Vitamin C	5%
Fat	37 g	Thiamine	15%
Sodium	1275 mg	Riboflavin	20%
Potassium	215 mg	Niacin	20%
		Calcium	20%
		Iron	15%

PILLSBURY BAKE-OFF® recipe

BAKED CHICKEN SALAD

3 cups chopped cooked chicken
1½ cups celery slices
1 cup (4 ozs.) shredded KRAFT Sharp Cheddar Cheese
1 tablespoon chopped onion
1 tablespoon lemon juice
1½ teaspoons salt
Dash of pepper
MIRACLE WHIP Salad Dressing
Tomato slices
1½ cups crushed potato chips

Combine chicken, celery, ½ cup cheese, onion, lemon juice, seasonings and enough salad dressing to moisten; mix lightly. Spoon into 1½-quart casserole; top with tomatoes. Bake at 350°, 35 minutes. Top with combined remaining cheese and chips; continue baking until cheese is melted.
6 servings

HOT CHICKEN SALAD

4 cups cooked chicken*
4 cups celery, chopped
2 teaspoons salt
½ teaspoon tarragon, optional
¼ cup grated onion
1 tablespoon lemon juice
2 cups mayonnaise
¼ cup TAYLOR Extra Dry Vermouth
1 cup sliced, blanched, toasted almonds
1 cup crushed corn flakes
½ cup freshly grated Parmesan or Romano cheese

Remove chicken from bones, skin and cut into ¾″ cubes. (Cut dark meat slightly smaller.) Thoroughly combine chicken and celery with salt, tarragon, grated onion, lemon juice, mayonnaise, Dry Vermouth and toasted almonds. Allow to stand at least 1 hour; taste. Add additional salt if desired. Spoon into a buttered shallow PYREX® brand 2-quart oblong baking dish.** Top with crushed corn flakes and freshly grated Parmesan or Romano cheese. Place in a 350°F. oven for 25 to 30 minutes or until heated through and lightly browned.
Approximately 12 to 15 servings

*4 to 5 pounds chicken parts—breasts and thighs. 4 breasts and 4 or 5 thighs, depending upon size.

**Casserole can be refrigerated at this point until baking time.

TURKEY AND WILD RICE CASSEROLE

1 cup SHOAL LAKE Pure Canadian Wild Rice
¼ teaspoon salt
3 cups water
2 cups diced cooked turkey or chicken
½ pound sliced mushrooms (about 3 cups) sautéed in 2 tablespoons butter
½ pint heavy cream (35%)
1½ cups turkey stock or chicken stock or 2 chicken bouillon cubes dissolved in 1½ cups boiling water
2 tablespoons finely chopped chives or green onion
2 tablespoons diced pimiento
1 teaspoon salt
¼ teaspoon pepper
2 tablespoons grated Parmesan cheese
1 tablespoon butter

Follow the "quick-soak method"* to prepare wild rice for cooking. Cook rice in boiling and salted water until kernels are tender—30 minutes. Drain the rice if necessary and put it in a mixing bowl. Toss the rice with turkey and sautéed mushrooms. Add cream and stock or dissolved cubes. Add chives, pimiento, salt and pepper. Turn the turkey mixture into a well-buttered casserole (1½ quart); cover, and bake for 1 hour at 350°F. Sprinkle the casserole with Parmesan, dot with butter; brown the topping lightly under the broiler.

Makes 4 servings

Quick-soak method for preparing wild rice: Wash required amount of SHOAL LAKE Pure Canadian Wild Rice under cold, flowing water. Stir rice into 3 times the amount of boiling water (1 cup rice requires 3 cups water). Parboil for 5 minutes only. Remove from heat. Let soak in the same water (covered) for 1 hour. Drain, wash, and cook as directed in recipe.

Note: One cup of SHOAL LAKE Pure Canadian Wild Rice (8 oz.) swells to about four times its size when cooked.

WILD RICE TURKEY CASSEROLE

6 oz. pkg. long grain and wild rice mix, cooked according to package directions
3½ cups cubed cooked JENNIE-O Turkey
1½ cups chopped celery
½ cup chopped onion
10¾ oz. can condensed cream of mushroom soup
8 oz. can water chestnuts, drained and sliced (reserve liquid)
4 oz. can mushrooms, drained (reserve liquid)
¼ cup soy sauce
¾ cup soft bread crumbs
2 tablespoons melted butter or margarine

Preheat oven to 350°. Add water to reserved liquids to make 1 cup. Combine all ingredients except bread crumbs and butter. Spoon into a 3-quart baking dish. Sprinkle with mixture of crumbs and butter. Bake, uncovered, about 1 hour.

About 8 servings

TURKEY PILAF

2 cups chopped, roast BUTTERBALL® SWIFT'S PREMIUM® Turkey
1 stick (½ cup) butter or margarine
1 medium onion, thinly sliced
1 cup rice
½ teaspoon salt
⅛ teaspoon pepper
2 cups chicken bouillon
¼ cup water
½ cup shredded sharp cheese
¼ cup thinly sliced green pepper

Melt butter in a heavy pan. Add onion and cook 1 minute. Add rice, salt and pepper and cook slowly for 3 minutes, stirring constantly. Add bouillon and water to rice mixture and bring to a boil. Add turkey. Cover and cook over low heat or bake in 375°F. oven for about 25 minutes or until rice is tender. Remove and stir in cheese and green pepper.

Yield: 5 to 6 servings (5 cups)

PLAN-OVER TURKEY CASSEROLE

⅓ cup chopped celery
1 Tablespoon butter or margarine
1 can (1 lb. 1 oz.) STOKELY'S FINEST® Whole Kernel Golden Corn
⅓ cup mayonnaise
⅓ cup sour cream
2 cups cooked diced turkey
1 teaspoon parsley flakes

Sauté celery in butter until tender. Drain Corn reserving 2 Tablespoons Corn liquid; add Corn to celery and warm until heated through. Stir together mayonnaise, sour cream, and reserved Corn liquid. Fold sauce into Corn mixture. Place turkey in a greased 1½ quart casserole and top with Corn mixture. Sprinkle with parsley. Bake at 350°F. for 15 minutes.
Makes 4 servings

ALL-IN-ONE TURKEY CASSEROLE

1½ cups cubed roasted BUTTERBALL® SWIFT'S PREMIUM® Turkey
3 cups leftover seasoned rice casserole, or cooked rice
1 cup sliced cooked asparagus, or other vegetable
1 cup turkey gravy
½ cup dairy sour cream

In a large bowl mix together turkey, rice and asparagus. Combine gravy and sour cream. Pour over turkey mixture and mix well. Turn into a greased 1½ quart casserole. Bake in a 350°F. oven for 30 to 40 minutes.
Yield: 4 servings

BIG BIRD PUFF

2 eggs
1 cup milk
1 cup biscuit mix
¼ teaspoon McCORMICK/SCHILLING Sage
1 package McCORMICK/SCHILLING Chicken Gravy Mix
2 cups chopped, cooked turkey
½ cup shredded Swiss cheese

Beat eggs, milk, biscuit mix, sage and gravy mix together. Stir in turkey and cheese. Pour into 1-quart casserole. Bake in 350°F. oven 45 minutes or until knife inserted near center comes out clean.
Makes 4 servings

GERMAN REUBEN CASSEROLE

3 medium potatoes, cooked
1 can (16 ounces) sauerkraut, drained
½ lb. ECKRICH® Smoked Sausage, or Polska Kielbasa, thinly sliced
½ cup Thousand Island dressing
2 tablespoons chopped parsley
¾ cup (3 ounces) shredded Swiss cheese
½ green pepper, cut into strips (about ⅓ cup)

Pare and cube potatoes; set aside. Combine sauerkraut, potatoes (about 2 cups), sausage, dressing and parsley. Spoon into greased 10 × 6 × 1¾-inch oven-proof glass baking dish. Bake at 350°F. for 25 to 30 minutes. Sprinkle cheese and green pepper strips over top. Bake 5 minutes more.   *5 servings*

Microwave directions: Combine sauerkraut, potatoes (about 2 cups), sausage, dressing, and parsley in a 10 × 6 × 1¾-inch glass baking dish. Cover and microwave on HIGH, 6 to 8 minutes. Sprinkle cheese and green pepper strips over top and microwave on HIGH, 1½ minutes.

CHEDDAR-BAKED ZUCCHINI AND TURKEY HAM
(Low Calorie)

3 medium sliced zucchini (or 2 10-ounce packages, defrosted)
3 ounces diced extra-sharp Cheddar cheese broken up
1 16-ounce can chopped tomatoes
1 pound cubed LOUIS RICH Turkey Ham
3 tablespoons Italian-seasoned bread crumbs

Put a layer of zucchini in the bottom of a casserole or baking dish. Add layers of cheese, tomatoes, and LOUIS RICH Turkey Ham. Continue layering zucchini, cheese, tomatoes and LOUIS RICH Turkey Ham; then sprinkle with crumbs. Bake in preheated 350-degree oven 20 to 30 minutes until tender, brown, and bubbly.
Makes six servings

About 205 calories each

VIENNA BEEF® KNOCKWURST PAELLA

1 12 oz. pkg. VIENNA BEEF® Knockwurst
1 onion, chopped
1 clove garlic, crushed
2 Tbsp. butter or margarine
¼ lb. fresh mushrooms, sliced
1 1 lb. can tomatoes, drained
1 cup uncooked rice
Salt and pepper to taste
2 cups bouillon
1 10 oz. pkg. frozen peas, cooked and drained

Melt butter in large casserole. Sauté onion and garlic. Add mushrooms and sausages cut in ½″ chunks. Heat through. Add tomatoes and rice, stir. Add hot stock and seasonings. Stir and bring to a boil. Cover and place in 425° oven for ½ hour. Uncover. Stir and cook until rice is cooked. Stir in peas.   *Makes 4 servings*

FRANKLY MEXICAN CASSEROLE

1 package FRENCH'S® Scalloped Potatoes
½ pound frankfurters, sliced
1 can (15-oz.) kidney beans, drained and rinsed
1 tablespoon butter or margarine
¼ cup fine dry bread crumbs
½ teaspoon FRENCH'S® Chili Powder

Prepare potatoes as directed on package, except use 2-quart casserole and increase boiling water to 2⅔ cups. Stir in frankfurters and beans. Bake in 400° oven 35 minutes; stir casserole. Melt butter in small pan; stir in bread crumbs and chili powder. Sprinkle over casserole and bake 10 to 15 minutes longer, until potatoes are tender.
6 servings

Microwave directions: Combine potato slices with 3 cups hot tap water in 2-quart casserole. Cover; cook on HIGH 14 minutes. Stir in ⅔ cup milk, seasoning mix, kidney beans, and frankfurters. Cook covered 7 minutes. Sprinkle with crumb mixture; cook 2 minutes.

BEANS AND SAUSAGES

½ pound pork sausage links (6 links)
1 28 ounce can B&M® Brick Oven Baked Beans
1 medium onion, sliced

Place sausages in a skillet with 2 tablespoons water. Cover and cook over medium heat for 4 minutes. Uncover and continue cooking until lightly browned or about 5 minutes, turning often. Place beans in a 2 quart casserole and arrange sausages on top. Cover with onion slices and bake at 350°F. for 30 minutes.   *Makes 4 servings*

BROWN 'N SERVE® SAUSAGE-POTATO CASSEROLE

8-ounce package SWIFT PREMIUM® BROWN 'N SERVE® Sausage Links, Original or Kountry Kure Flavor
1 tablespoon butter or margarine
½ cup finely chopped onion
10½ ounce can condensed cream of celery soup
¼ cup milk
3 cups cooked, sliced potatoes (about 6 small)*
½ cup shredded Cheddar cheese
16-ounce can sauerkraut, drained
1 teaspoon caraway seeds

Brown 6 sausage links in a skillet; remove. Add butter to drippings and sauté onion until tender. Stir in soup and milk; heat through. Place potatoes in a 2 quart casserole. Pour in soup mixture. Top with cheese then sauerkraut. Bury the browned links in the sauerkraut. Place remaining sausage in a pinwheel design on top of casserole. Sprinkle with caraway seeds. Bake uncovered in a 350°F. oven for 30 minutes
Yield: 4 to 5 servings

*Note: A 5.5 ounce package of scalloped potato mix may be substituted for the cooked potatoes, celery soup, milk and Cheddar cheese. Follow package instructions for potato preparation. Bake uncovered in a 350°F. oven for 50 minutes.

HOT DOG MACARONI

7-oz. package CREAMETTES®
 Macaroni (2 cups uncooked)
½ cup onion, chopped
¼ cup green pepper, chopped
2 tablespoons butter or margarine
2 tablespoons flour
1½ cups milk
1 cup carrots, grated
½ cup sour cream
½ teaspoon salt
¼ teaspoon dillweed
10 frankfurters, split lengthwise

Prepare CREAMETTES® according
to package directions. Drain. Sauté
onion and green pepper in butter
until tender. Add flour and cook,
stirring constantly, for 2 minutes.
Do not brown. Stir in milk and cook
until smooth and thickened.
Remove from heat, add macaroni,
carrots, sour cream, salt and
dillweed. Arrange frankfurters
vertically around a deep 1½-quart
casserole, pour macaroni mixture
in center. Bake at 350°F. for 25-30
minutes.   *6 servings*

SAUSAGE HASH

32 oz. package JIMMY DEAN®
 Sausage
3 Tablespoons margarine
2 large onions chopped
½ cup diced celery
½ cup green pepper, chopped
1 (16 oz.) can peeled tomatoes,
 mashed
½ cup uncooked rice or 1 cup
 uncooked macaroni
1 teaspoon chili powder
½ teaspoon salt
¼ teaspoon pepper

Brown, crumble and drain JIMMY
DEAN® Sausage. Add sautéed
onions, celery and green pepper.
Mix well. Add tomatoes, rice, and
seasonings. Pour into 9 x 13
casserole. Bake, covered at 375°
for 45 minutes.   *Serves 6*

APPLE, SAUSAGE, SWEET POTATO "MEDLEY"

2 large sweet potatoes cooked
 (or one 17-oz. can of sweet
 potatoes)
½ pound seasoned sausage (link
 or bulk)
2 Tablespoons brown sugar
2 Tablespoons butter or margarine
1 can (21 oz.) THANK YOU® Brand
 Apple Pie Filling
¼ cup chopped nuts (optional)

In 8-inch square baking dish, slice
sweet potatoes; arrange sausage
over top (make 8 or 10 small balls
of the bulk sausage). Sprinkle
sugar over top and dot with butter.
Spread apple pie filling over all.
Sprinkle with nuts. Bake at 350°
for 1 hour or until sausage is done.
          Serves 5-6

CRUNCHY BEANS AND WIENER CASSEROLE

1 can (1 lb. 5 oz.) VAN CAMP'S®
 Pork and Beans
½ lb. wieners, sliced
2 Tablespoons molasses
2 Tablespoons STOKELY'S
 FINEST® Tomato Catsup
1 can (3 oz.) French fried onion
 rings

Combine first 4 ingredients in
greased 1½ quart casserole. Bake
uncovered at 350°F. for 30
minutes. Top with onion rings and
bake an additional 30 minutes.
          Makes 4 servings

ARMOUR®

GARDEN SAUSAGE BAKE

1 lb. ARMOUR® STAR Polish
 Sausage, cut in 1-inch pieces
3 cups shredded cabbage
1 cup sliced celery
¼ cup chopped green onions
2 10¾-oz. cans cream of
 mushroom soup

Heat oven to 350°F. Combine all
ingredients; place in 2-qt.
casserole. Bake, covered, at 350°F.
50 minutes.   *6 servings*

BEEF & BISCUIT CASSEROLE

2 cans (16 ounces each) mixed
 vegetables, drained
2 cans (4¾ ounces each)
 UNDERWOOD® Roast Beef
 Spread
1 can (10¾ ounces) condensed
 golden mushroom soup
1 cup buttermilk biscuit mix
¼ cup cold water

Preheat oven to 350°F. In a large
bowl, mix together vegetables,
roast beef spread and soup. Spoon
mixture into a 2 quart baking dish.
Bake 15 minutes. Meanwhile, in a
small bowl, mix biscuit mix and
water with a fork to make a soft
dough. Increase oven temperature
to 425°F. Remove casserole from
oven and top with spoonfuls of
dough. Return to oven and
continue baking for 10 minutes.
          Makes 4 servings

MEAL-IN-A-PIE CASSEROLE

Filling:
1 16 oz. can VEG-ALL® Mixed
 Vegetables
1 deep-dish pie crust
1 lb. ground beef
1 cup grated cheddar cheese
1 egg
2 Tbsp. milk
½ tsp. salt

Brown Sauce:
2 Tbsp. butter
2 Tbsp. flour
1 cup beef broth
¼ tsp. TABASCO® Pepper Sauce

Prepare brown sauce base by
browning flour in melted butter,
stirring constantly. Stir in broth
and TABASCO® Sauce. Simmer,
stirring constantly until sauce
thickens and comes to a boil. Add
VEG-ALL® (drained), browned
ground beef (drained) and salt to
brown sauce. Mix well. Pierce
deep-dish pie crust with fork in
several places and bake at 400° for
5 minutes. Pour meat mixture into
pie crust. Mix together grated
cheddar cheese, egg and milk.
Pour over meat mixture in pie
plate. Bake 15 minutes at 400°, or
until cheese topping is lightly
browned.   *Serves 6-8*

HAMBURGER BRAN CASSEROLE

1 lb. ground beef
¼ cup butter
1 cup celery, minced
1 onion, chopped
8 oz. can sliced mushrooms, drained
¼ teaspoon pepper
½ cup ELAM'S® Bran
2 cups tomato juice
14½ oz. can stewed tomatoes, drained

Melt butter in skillet. Add celery, onion, mushrooms and pepper. Cook until onions and celery are soft. Add ground beef and cook until brown. Drain any excess fat. In a casserole combine cooked mixture with bran, tomato juice and stewed tomatoes. Bake at 400°F. for 45 minutes. *Serves 4*

GEBHARDT'S CASSEROLE

3 cups cooked rice
1 cup tomato sauce
½ cup stuffed olives
½ teaspoon salt
⅛ teaspoon pepper
2 teaspoons GEBHARDT Chili Powder
¼ teaspoon ground cumin
2 cups chopped cooked meat
1 cup meat broth or 1 cup water plus bouillon cube
3 or 4 ripe olives, sliced (optional)
1 can refrigerated biscuit dough or homemade equivalent

Combine rice, tomato sauce, olives, seasonings, cooked meat and broth. Pour into well-greased, two-quart casserole or baking dish and bake in moderate oven (350°F.) for about 30 minutes. Place biscuits on top of casserole dish, return to oven and bake at 400° until biscuits are done, about 10 minutes. Garnish with sliced olives, if desired. *6 servings*

BEEF ZUCCHINI CASSEROLE

4 cups sliced zucchini (about 3 medium)
1 medium onion, sliced
2 tablespoons butter or margarine
¼ cup grated Parmesan cheese
1½ pounds lean ground beef
1 tablespoon flour
1 teaspoon salt
⅛ teaspoon pepper
⅔ cup HEINZ Tomato Ketchup
¼ cup grated Parmesan cheese

In large skillet, sauté zucchini and onion in butter until onion is tender. Pour into baking dish (10″×6″×1½″); sprinkle with ¼ cup Parmesan cheese; set aside. In same skillet, brown ground beef; drain excess fat. Stir flour, salt, pepper, then ketchup into meat. Spoon meat mixture evenly over zucchini. Cover; bake in 350°F. oven, 20 minutes. Remove cover; top with ¼ cup Parmesan cheese; bake, uncovered, an additional 5 minutes or until cheese is lightly browned. Cut into squares to serve. *Makes 6 servings*

TWISTY BEEF BAKE

2 cups corkscrew macaroni, uncooked
1 pound ground beef
1 can (10¾ oz.) condensed cream of mushroom soup
1 can (14½ oz.) whole tomatoes, cut up
¾ cup (3 oz.) shredded Cheddar cheese
¼ cup chopped green pepper
¾ teaspoon DURKEE Seasoned Salt
1 can (3 oz.) DURKEE French Fried Onions

Cook macaroni as directed on package; drain. Brown ground beef; drain fat. Combine all ingredients except French fried onions. Pour half the mixture into a greased 2 quart casserole. Top with ½ can onions. Pour remaining macaroni mixture over onions. Cover and bake at 350°F. for 30 minutes. Uncover, top with remaining onions and bake 5 minutes longer. *Makes 4 to 6 servings*

HASHED BROWN BARBEQUED BEEF DELUXE

1 cup finely chopped onions
2 lbs. boiled potatoes, cold, peeled and cut in very small pieces
2 bay leaves
½ cup MAZOLA® Corn Oil
1 #2 can JAMES RIVER SMITHFIELD Barbeque Beef

In saucepan, heat oil, slowly smother chopped onions until lightly browned. Stir in the potatoes and the Barbeque Beef. Season to taste, add the two bay leaves, place mixture in well buttered baking pan, cover with aluminum foil and bake in preheated oven at 350°F. for 30 minutes. Spoon out or brown individually for one service. Serve hot with JAMES RIVER SMITHFIELD Special Barbeque Sauce. *Serves 8*

TURKU LAYERED CASSEROLE

½ pound ground beef
1 cup finely chopped onion
1 medium clove garlic, crushed
2 cans (15 ounces each) tomato sauce
1 teaspoon basil, crushed
½ teaspoon oregano, crushed
½ teaspoon salt
1 package (10 ounces) frozen chopped spinach, thawed and well drained
1 pint small curd cottage cheese
¼ cup grated Parmesan cheese
1 egg, slightly beaten
4 cups cooked elbow macaroni
½ pound grated FINLANDIA Swiss Cheese

In skillet, brown beef and cook onion with garlic until tender. Add tomato sauce and seasonings; simmer 5 minutes. Combine spinach and cottage cheese, Parmesan cheese, and egg. In 2-quart greased shallow baking dish, layer half each macaroni, grated FINLANDIA cheese, and meat sauce. Cover with spinach mixture; then add remaining macaroni, grated cheese and meat sauce. Bake at 375°F. for 40 minutes, until hot and bubbly. Let stand several minutes before serving. *Makes 6 to 8 servings*

TACO TWIST

1 pound ground beef
1 package (1⅛ oz.) DURKEE Taco
  Seasoning Mix
1 can (15 oz.) tomato sauce
¼ cup chopped green pepper
3 cups (8 oz.) corkscrew macaroni,
  cooked and drained
1 cup (4 oz.) shredded Cheddar
  cheese
½ cup sour cream

Brown ground beef; drain. Stir in
seasoning mix, tomato sauce, and
green pepper. Bring to a boil and
remove from heat. Combine cooked
macaroni, ½ cup cheese and sour
cream; place on bottom of
6 × 10-inch baking dish. Top with
meat mixture and remaining
cheese. Bake at 350° for 30
minutes.   *Makes 6 servings*

MEXICAN CASSEROLE

1¼ cups biscuit mix
¼ cup sour cream
1 egg
1 lb. ground beef
1 teaspoon salt
½ cup chopped onion
1 can (15½ oz.) VAN CAMP'S®
  Mexican Style Chili Beans
½ cup shredded lettuce
1 cup diced fresh tomato
¾ cup grated Monterey Jack
  cheese

Blend first 3 ingredients to form
soft dough. With lightly floured
hands, spread dough on bottom
and up sides of a 10 × 6 × 1¾ inch
pan. Brown ground beef; drain
excess fat. Add next 3 ingredients
and spoon into crust. Bake at
425°F. for 20-30 minutes or until
crust is browned. Top with
remaining ingredients. Let stand 5
minutes before cutting.
          Makes 6 servings

GREEK MOUSSAKA

2 medium size eggplants (about
  2½ pounds)
Salt
¾ cup PLANTER'S® Peanut Oil
  (about)
¾ cup chopped onion
1 pound ground beef
¼ cup dry red wine
3 tablespoons tomato paste
3 tablespoons chopped parsley
2 tablespoons water
Few grains ground cinnamon
Ground black pepper
1 egg, beaten
½ cup fine dry bread crumbs
¼ cup grated Parmesan cheese
3 tablespoons flour
1½ cups milk
2 egg yolks, beaten

Peel eggplant and cut into ½-inch
thick crosswise slices; sprinkle
lightly with salt on both sides.
Stack several slices together and
top with a heavy weight to press
out water. Let stand 1 hour.

Heat 2 tablespoons peanut oil in a
skillet over medium heat. Add
onion; sauté until tender. Add beef
and cook until lightly browned. Stir
in wine, tomato paste, parsley,
water, cinnamon and ⅛ teaspoon
pepper. Cook over low heat 5
minutes to blend flavors. Stir in
egg, ¼ cup bread crumbs and 2
tablespoons Parmesan cheese.
Remove from heat and set aside.

Heat 2 tablespoons peanut oil in a
large skillet and cook eggplant
slices until lightly browned on both
sides. Add additional peanut oil as
needed to skillet to prevent
sticking. Grease a 13 × 9 × 2-inch
baking dish and sprinkle bottom
with remaining ¼ cup bread
crumbs. Arrange a layer of
eggplant slices in bottom of
baking dish. Spread meat mixture
over slices; arrange remaining
eggplant over meat.

Pour 3 tablespoons oil in a
saucepan. Stir in flour and a few
grains pepper. Gradually add milk
and cook over medium heat until
thickened. Mix ½ cup of the sauce
into egg yolks. Return yolk mixture
to sauce and cook about 1 minute.
Pour over top layer of eggplant and
sprinkle with remaining Parmesan
cheese. Bake at 350°F. for 35
minutes. Let stand 10 minutes
before serving.

          Makes 6 servings

SHERRY LAMB
CASSEROLE

2 lbs. lean lamb, cubed
4 Tbsp. butter, divided
3 Tbsp. brandy
1 lb. small white onions
¼ lb. *each* carrots, turnips,
  mushrooms and green beans,
  cut up
2 Tbsp. flour
2 Tbsp. tomato paste
1½ cups beef broth
¾ cup HOLLAND HOUSE® Sherry
  Cooking Wine
2 Tbsp. chopped fresh dill weed

In 12-inch skillet, sauté lamb in 2
Tbsp. butter. Heat brandy; ignite
over meat. Place meat in 3-quart
casserole. Sauté vegetables in
remaining 2 Tbsp. butter. Stir in
tomato paste and flour; add broth
and wine. Cook, stirring constantly,
until mixture thickens. Cook 5
minutes. Combine with lamb in
casserole. Sprinkle with chopped
dill. Cover; bake 1¼ hrs. in 350°
oven, or until meat and vegetables
are tender. Serve or freeze.
          Serves 6

CORNY BAKED BEANS

1 cup whole kernel corn, fresh or
  canned
1 (16 ounce) can baked beans
1 tablespoon IMPERIAL Brown
  Sugar
1 teaspoon fresh minced onion
1 tablespoon grated Parmesan
  cheese
1 tablespoon crumbled crisp bacon
1 tablespoon butter or margarine
1 tablespoon catsup

Combine all ingredients in baking
dish and heat in oven until
bubbling.

Microwave: Heat in oven on full
power for about 6 minutes.
          Serves 6 to 8

EARLY AMERICAN BEAN
BAKE

Combine in casserole 16-ounce can
pork-and-beans, 1 cup chopped
celery, 1 chopped apple, ¼ cup
water, and contents of
FRENCH'S® Brown Gravy Mix
envelope. Top with brown-and-serve
sausage links. Bake at 400°F. for
30 minutes.   *4 servings*

NEW DIMENSION BAKED BEANS

4 slices bacon, cooked and
  crumbled
1 (28-ounce) can pork and beans
  in tomato sauce
½ cup firmly-packed COLONIAL®
  Dark Brown Sugar
1 tablespoon soy sauce
1 tablespoon vinegar
1 teaspoon instant minced onion
¼ teaspoon ground ginger

Preheat oven to 350°. In 1-quart
casserole, combine all ingredients
except bacon. Top with bacon.
Bake, uncovered, 45 minutes or
until hot and bubbly. Refrigerate
leftovers.　　*Makes about 4 cups*

MOM'S BAKED BEANS

1 Tablespoon chopped onion
1 Tablespoon butter or margarine
1 can (1 lb. 5 oz.) VAN CAMP'S®
  Pork and Beans
¼ cup brown sugar
2 Tablespoons STOKELY'S
  FINEST® Tomato Catsup

Sauté onion in butter until tender.
Combine onion with remaining
ingredients in a greased 1½ quart
casserole. Bake, uncovered, at
350°F. for 1 hour 15 minutes.
　　　　　　Makes 4 servings

BAYOU BAKED BEANS

4 slices bacon
1 onion, chopped
2 cups prepared pork and beans
3 tablespoons catsup
3 tablespoons brown sugar
½ teaspoon TABASCO® Pepper
  Sauce
¼ teaspoon prepared mustard

Heat oven to 350°. Fry bacon;
remove and drain. Sauté onion in
bacon drippings. Pour beans into
1½-quart casserole. Stir bacon and
onion into beans. Add remaining
ingredients. Mix well. Bake 45
minutes.　　　　*Serves 4*

CHILI BEANS

1 tablespoon butter or margarine
1 tablespoon chopped onion
1 teaspoon chili powder
½ pound frankfurts, cut into 1"
  pieces
1 28 ounce can B&M® Brick Oven
  Baked Beans

In a skillet, melt butter or
margarine and add onions, chili
powder and frankfurts. Sauté
frankfurts until lightly browned. In
a 2 quart casserole, combine
frankfurts and beans; bake at
350°F. for 30 minutes.
　　　　　　Makes 4 servings

CHILI PIE CASSEROLE

3 cups FRITOS® Brand Corn Chips
1 large onion, chopped
1 19-ounce can chili
1 cup grated American cheese

Spread 2 cups of FRITOS® Brand
Corn Chips in a baking dish.
Arrange chopped onion and half of
cheese on the FRITOS® Brand Corn
Chips. Pour chili over onion and
cheese. Top with remaining
FRITOS® Brand Corn Chips and
cheese. Bake at 350°F. for 15 to 20
minutes until hot and bubbly.
　　　　　Makes 4 to 6 servings

NEXT-DAY NOODLE BAKE

1 can (4 ounces) sliced
  mushrooms, drained, reserving
  liquid
⅓ cup chopped onion
¼ cup butter or margarine
3 tablespoons flour
¾ teaspoon salt
Dash pepper
Dash cayenne
3 cups milk and mushroom
  liquid
2 cups cubed cooked pork, beef,
  ham, chicken, turkey, or other
  meat
8 ounces (6 to 6½ cups)
  MUELLER'S® Wide Egg Noodles
Grated Parmesan cheese
Paprika

Sauté mushrooms and onion in
butter until crisp-tender. Blend in
flour and seasonings; add milk and
mushroom liquid. Cook, stirring
constantly, until sauce thickens.
Add cooked meat. Meanwhile, cook
noodles as directed on package;

drain. Combine noodles with sauce
in 2-quart casserole; top with
Parmesan cheese and paprika.
Bake at 400°F. about 20 to 25
minutes or until bubbling and
browned.　　　　*4 to 6 servings*

ENCHILADAS AZTECAS

1½ lbs. pork loin chops
1 tablespoon vegetable oil
1 small onion, chopped
¾ cup slivered BLUE RIBBON®
  Almonds
½ cup bottled chili sauce
½ oz. unsweetened chocolate
1 can (8 oz.) tomato sauce
TABASCO® Sauce
4 corn tortillas
1 cup dairy sour cream

Trim bone and fat from chops. Cut
meat into ½-inch cubes. In skillet,
heat oil; fry pork over high heat,
turning, until browned; lower heat
to medium. Add onion and ½ cup
almonds; cook, stirring, until onion
is tender. Add chili sauce,
chocolate and ½ of the tomato
sauce; heat, stirring, until
chocolate melts. Add TABASCO®
to taste. Fry tortillas in oiled skillet
until they *begin* to crisp. Remove
to paper towels. Spoon pork
mixture onto tortillas; roll up and
place in baking dish, seam sides
down. Bake 15 minutes at 400
degrees. Stir sour cream; spoon in
strips over tortillas. Dollop
remaining tomato sauce over sour
cream strips. Sprinkle with
almonds. Bake 5 minutes longer or
until hot through.
　　　　　　Makes 4 servings

BAKED BEANS AND BARBEQUE PORK

In earthenware casserole, place 2
oz. of JAMES RIVER SMITHFIELD
Barbeque Pork. Over it, place 4 oz.
of canned baked beans and over
the beans, spread 2 oz. of JAMES
RIVER SMITHFIELD Barbeque
Pork. Over the Barbeque Pork,
spread one good tablespoon of
fresh bread crumbs and over the
bread crumbs, sprinkle one
tablespoon melted butter. Place
casserole in a pre-heated oven at
350° for 25 minutes or until the top
is well browned. Serve hot.

CASSEROLE SUPPER

4 pork chops
1 can (1 lb. 1 oz.) STOKELY'S FINEST® Peas
1 can (10¾ oz.) cream of mushroom soup
¼ cup chopped onion

Arrange chops in a 9 × 9 × 2-inch dish. Combine Peas, ¼ cup Pea liquid, soup and onion; pour over chops. Cover, bake at 350°F. for 50 minutes. Uncover and bake 10 minutes more.

Makes 4 servings

HAM BAKE

1 7¼-oz. pkg. KRAFT Macaroni and Cheese Dinner
1 cup ham cubes
2 tablespoons chopped green pepper
Salt and pepper
1 cup milk
2 eggs, beaten

Prepare Dinner as directed on package. Add ham and green pepper; season to taste. Place in 10 × 6-inch baking dish. Combine milk and eggs; pour over dinner mixture. Bake at 350°, 25 to 30 minutes. *4 to 6 servings*

REGAL HAM AND BROCCOLI

3 cups cooked rice
2 packages (10 ounces, each) frozen broccoli spears, cooked and drained
¼ cup butter or margarine
½ cup chopped onion
¼ teaspoon thyme, crushed
3 tablespoons flour
3 cups milk
4 cups cubed cooked KRAKUS/ ATALANTA/POLKA Polish Ham
1 package (8 ounces) Swiss cheese
½ cup buttered bread crumbs

Spoon rice into buttered 3-quart casserole. Layer broccoli over rice. Melt butter in saucepan, add onion and thyme and cook until onion is tender. Stir in flour and cook, stirring, until hot and bubbly. Bring milk to a boil and add all at once to flour. Cook, stirring, until thickened and smooth. Stir in ham. Pour over broccoli. Layer cheese on top. Sprinkle with bread crumbs. Bake at 350°F. for 45 minutes, until golden brown on top.

Makes 8 servings

CREAMETTES® & HAM CASSEROLE

7-oz. package CREAMETTES® Macaroni (2 cups uncooked)
1½ cups cubed cooked ham, or luncheon meat
1 can condensed cream of chicken soup
½ cup milk
½ cup dairy sour cream
1 package (10-oz.) frozen broccoli spears, cooked and drained
½ cup Cheddar cheese, shredded

Prepare CREAMETTES® according to package directions. Drain. Combine macaroni and ham. Pour into 13 × 9 × 2" pan (or 3-quart casserole). Blend soup, sour cream and milk, pouring half this mixture over ham and macaroni. Arrange broccoli on top. Pour remaining sauce atop broccoli and sprinkle with cheese. Bake at 350°F. for 20 minutes. *6 servings*

HAM 'N YAM CASSEROLE

2 tablespoons butter or margarine
3 tablespoons flour
Dash pepper
1 cup water
1 tall can (13 fl. oz.) PET® Evaporated Milk, divided usage
3 cups (1 pound) diced cooked ham
2 cans (23 oz. each) sweet potatoes, drained and mashed (about 3 cups mashed)
1¼ teaspoons salt

Melt butter in saucepan. Blend in flour and pepper. Stir in water until smooth. Boil for 1 minute stirring constantly. Stir in 1 cup evaporated milk and ham. Pour into greased 2-quart round casserole. Beat together potatoes, ⅔ cup evaporated milk, and salt. Drop by tablespoonfuls over creamed ham. Bake at 400°F. for 20 minutes or until sweet potatoes are browned and creamed mixture is bubbly. Serve hot.

Makes 6 servings

BUDDIG HAM, CHEESE & MACARONI CASSEROLE

1 package (7¼ oz.) KRAFT Macaroni and Cheese Dinner
2 packages (2.5 oz. ea.) BUDDIG Smoked Sliced Ham
Bread crumbs (optional)

Conventional directions: Prepare Macaroni and Cheese Sauce as directed on package. Pour into 1½-quart round glass casserole. Cut BUDDIG Smoked Sliced Ham into ½-inch squares. Stir into macaroni and cheese. Sprinkle with bread crumbs. Heat in 300°F. oven for 5 minutes.

Makes 4 to 6 servings

Microwave directions: Prepare recipe as above. Cook on high for 2 to 3 minutes or until hot and bubbly.

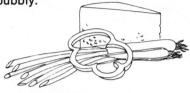

BACON AND EGG CASSEROLE

¼ cup margarine or butter
⅛ teaspoon onion salt
½ teaspoon freeze-dried chives or parsley flakes
1 cup KELLOGG'S® RICE KRISPIES® Cereal, crushed to measure ¾ cup
2 tablespoons all-purpose flour
½ teaspoon dry mustard
¾ cup milk
2 hard-cooked eggs, sliced
4 slices bacon, fried crisp and crumbled

Melt 2 tablespoons of the margarine. Stir in salt and chives. Combine with crushed RICE KRISPIES® Cereal. Set aside.

Melt the remaining 2 tablespoons margarine in small saucepan over low heat. Stir in flour and mustard. Add milk gradually, stirring until smooth. Cook until mixture thickens and boils, stirring constantly. Set aside.

In two greased 9-oz. custard cups or individual casseroles, layer half the sliced eggs, half the crumbled bacon, half the sauce and half the cereal mixture. Repeat layers. Bake at 350°F. about 15 minutes or until thoroughly heated.

Yield: 2 servings

Note: To prepare in advance, assemble casseroles omitting top layer of cereal mixture. Store in refrigerator. Sprinkle on topping just before baking.

® *Kellogg Company*

ZUCCHINI AND CHEESE CASSEROLE

1 cup dry bread crumbs
1 cup grated Parmesan cheese
1 clove garlic
1 teaspoon dried basil leaves
½ teaspoon dried oregano leaves
¼ teaspoon pepper
3 large zucchini, sliced
1 egg, beaten
½ to ¾ cup BERTOLLI® Olive Oil
3 cups ricotta cheese
3 eggs
¼ cup minced parsley
½ teaspoon salt
2½ cups BERTOLLI® Spaghetti Sauce
2 cups shredded mozzarella cheese

Process crumbs, Parmesan, garlic, basil, oregano and pepper in blender 20 seconds; reserve ⅔ cup crumbs. Dip zucchini in beaten egg; coat with crumbs. Sauté in oil in large skillet until golden; drain. Mix ricotta, eggs, parsley and salt. Spread ½ the spaghetti sauce in a 13 x 9-inch baking pan. Layer with ⅓ the zucchini, ½ the ricotta mixture and ⅓ the mozzarella. Repeat the layers, ending with the other ½ of the spaghetti sauce and mozzarella; sprinkle with reserved crumbs. Bake at 350°F. for 1 hour; let stand 10 minutes before cutting into squares.
Makes 6-8 servings

SQUASH CASSEROLE

6 medium summer squash (yellow or white)
1 package FRITO-LAY® Brand Toasted Onion Dip Mix
1½ cups boiling water
½ teaspoon salt
¼ teaspoon pepper
3 tablespoons bacon drippings
½ cup grated American cheese
½ cup lightly crushed RUFFLES® Brand Potato Chips

Cut squash into medium slices. Place in boiling water to which the FRITO-LAY® Brand Roasted Onion Dip Mix and salt have been added. Cook until tender. Add pepper and bacon drippings. Pour into baking dish. Top with cheese and RUFFLES® Brand Potato Chips. Bake at 350°F. for 20 minutes.
Makes 6 to 8 servings

CREAMED CAULIFLOWER CASSEROLE

1 medium head cauliflower
3 tablespoons butter or margarine
¼ cup flour
2 cups milk
¾ teaspoon salt
⅛ teaspoon pepper
1 package (8 oz.) PEPPERIDGE FARM® Herb Seasoned Stuffing
1 cup water
½ cup butter or margarine, melted

Break cauliflower into small pieces and cook until just tender. Drain and place in a shallow 2-quart casserole. Melt butter in a medium saucepan. Stir in flour and cook together a few minutes, while stirring. Remove from heat and blend in milk. Bring to a boil, stirring constantly, and simmer until thickened. Pour over cauliflower in casserole. Combine the last three ingredients and spoon on top, pressing down if necessary. Bake at 350°F. for 30 minutes.
Serves 8 to 10

Note: Broccoli used in place of cauliflower makes a delicious change.

CARROT CASSEROLE

2 cans (1 lb. ea.) STOKELY'S FINEST® Sliced Carrots, well drained
1 can (10¾ oz.) cream of celery soup
1 cup grated American cheese
½ cup dry bread crumbs
2 Tablespoons butter or margarine, melted

Combine Carrots, soup and cheese in a 1½ quart casserole. Mix bread crumbs and butter together; sprinkle over top of casserole. Bake at 350°F. for 25 to 30 minutes.
Makes 8 servings

ASPARAGUS CASSEROLE
(Low Calorie)

1 can (14½ oz.) FEATHERWEIGHT Cut Asparagus, drained
1½ Tbsp. unsalted butter, melted
1 Tbsp. flour
¾ cup skim milk
⅓ cup grated FEATHERWEIGHT Colby or Cheddar Cheese
⅛ tsp. FEATHERWEIGHT K-Salt
¼ cup cracker crumbs (crushed FEATHERWEIGHT Unsalted Crackers)
½ Tbsp. unsalted butter

Place Asparagus in casserole. Blend butter and flour, add milk gradually and cook slowly until thickened, stirring constantly. Add Cheese and K-Salt. Pour sauce over Asparagus, sprinkle with Cracker Crumbs and dot with butter. Bake at 325°F. for 30 minutes.
4-6 servings

GREEN VEGETABLE CASSEROLE

½ lb. fresh spinach
1 cup chopped iceberg lettuce
1 cup chopped green onions
1 cup chopped fresh parsley
1 cup (4 oz.) SARGENTO Shredded Monterey Jack
1 Tbsp. monosodium glutamate
4 eggs, beaten
4 Tbsp. butter, melted
Plain yogurt

Preheat oven to 325 degrees. Mix together first six ingredients. Add eggs and mix well. Coat 2-quart casserole or baking dish with melted butter. Add vegetable mixture and bake for 1 hour until top is brown and crisp. Serve hot with dollop of yogurt.
Yield: 5-6 servings

CRUNCHY GARDEN CASSEROLE

2 (10-ounce) packages frozen
   broccoli spears, thawed*
1 (10¾-ounce) can cream of
   mushroom soup
⅔ cup milk
¼ cup finely chopped onion
½ teaspoon curry powder
⅛ teaspoon ground black pepper
6 hard-cooked eggs, halved
   lengthwise
1 cup NABISCO® 100% Bran
   Cereal
1 cup sharp cheddar cheese,
   grated (about 4 ounces)

Slit broccoli stalks to depth of
several inches; arrange half in
2-quart shallow baking dish.
Combine mushroom soup, milk,
onion, curry powder and black
pepper; pour half over broccoli.
Add remaining broccoli in second
layer. Place egg halves between
each stalk around edge of
casserole. Spoon over remaining
sauce. Cover casserole with
aluminum foil. Bake at 375°F. for
35 to 40 minutes. Combine
NABISCO® 100% Bran Cereal and
cheese. Remove foil; sprinkle bran
mixture over center of casserole.
Bake uncovered 15 minutes longer.
Serves 6

*Or 2 (10-ounce) packages frozen
  cut asparagus, which have been
  thawed.

GOURMET SPINACH CASSEROLE

3 eggs
2 cups creamed cottage cheese
1 cup coarsely grated Monterey
   Jack cheese
1 (15 oz.) can S & W Chopped
   Spinach, drained
3 Tbsp. flour
1 tsp. nutmeg
½ tsp. salt
¼ cup melted butter or margarine

In medium size mixing bowl, beat
eggs until frothy. Add cottage
cheese, Monterey Jack cheese,
flour and seasonings. Beat well.
Fold spinach into cheese mixture;
pour into a well greased 1½ quart
casserole. Drizzle melted butter or
margarine over top. Bake at 350°
for about 1 hour or until set and
bubbly.   *Serves 4 to 6*

CREAMED SPINACH CASSEROLE

2 packages (10 oz. each) frozen
   chopped spinach
5 slices bacon
1 can (8 oz.) PET® Imitation Sour
   Cream
½ teaspoon salt
½ cup shredded mozzarella
   cheese

Cook spinach according to
package directions. Drain. Fry
bacon until crisp. Crumble. Add to
spinach. Stir imitation sour cream
and salt into spinach. Pour into
1½-quart casserole dish. Top with
cheese. Bake in 350°F. oven for 15
minutes or until cheese has
melted. Serve hot.
Makes 7 servings, ½ cup each

CHEF'S DELIGHT POTATO CASSEROLE

4-5 medium sized potatoes, sliced
2 tablespoons flour
1 teaspoon salt
Dash of pepper
¾ lb. CHEF'S DELIGHT (cubed)
¾ cup milk
¼ cup green pepper (diced)
¼ cup onion (diced)

Heat oven to 350°. Coat potatoes
with flour, salt and pepper. Heat
milk, add cubed CHEF'S DELIGHT.
Stir over low heat until CHEF'S
DELIGHT melts. Add green pepper
and onion. Make layers with
potatoes and sauce, top with
sauce. Cook 1 hour or until
potatoes are done.
4-6 servings

ALPINE POTATO CASSEROLE
(Low Calorie)

4 cups cooked cubed potatoes
1 cup plain yogurt
1 cup low-fat cottage cheese
¼ cup chopped chives
1 teaspoon salt
Dash garlic powder

In non-stick 9-inch square baking
pan, combine all ingredients. Bake
at 350 degrees for 30 minutes or
until hot and bubbly.
Makes 8 servings

About 105 calories each

Favorite recipe from The Potato Board

YAM COCONUT CASSEROLE

1 pound yams, or sweet potatoes
1 stick unsalted butter
½ cup COCO CASA™ Cream of
   Coconut
¼ cup heavy cream
3 egg yolks
½ tsp. cinnamon
½ tsp. nutmeg
¼ tsp. salt
2 dozen large marshmallows

Boil yams until tender and peel
while hot. Place them in mixing
bowl with butter, cream of
coconut, heavy cream, egg yolks,
and spices. Whip until smooth.
Place in casserole. Press
marshmallows into mixture so they
are half submerged. Sprinkle
lightly with cinnamon. Bake in
preheated 350° oven for 30
minutes or until marshmallows are
melted.   *Serves 6*

TAMALE CASSEROLE

Combine 15 oz. can NALLEY®'S
Big Chunk Chili, 1 sm. can whole
kernel corn, drained and ½ cup
sliced ripe olives in baking dish.
Remove parchment from can of
NALLEY®'S Beef Tamales and
place tamales on top. Top with
sauce and ⅓ cup grated American
cheese. Bake at 350° for 20-25
minutes.   *Serves 3-4*

BAKED CHEESE GARLIC GRITS

1 cup QUAKER® or AUNT
   JEMIMA® Enriched Hominy
   Quick Grits
1 teaspoon salt
4 cups boiling water
1½ cups (6 oz.) shredded sharp
   Cheddar cheese
½ cup butter or margarine
½ cup milk
2 eggs, beaten
1 small garlic clove, minced

Heat oven to 350°F. Grease 2-qt.
casserole or baking dish. Prepare
grits in salted boiling water as
directed on package. Stir in
cheese, butter, milk, eggs and
garlic; continue cooking over low
heat until cheese is melted. Pour
into prepared baking dish; bake
about 1 hour.
Makes 6 servings

Egg Dishes

SAVORY SCRAMBLED EGGS

2 tablespoons PARKAY Margarine
6 eggs, beaten
⅓ cup milk
Salt and pepper
1 3-oz. pkg. PHILADELPHIA BRAND Cream Cheese, cubed

Melt margarine in skillet over low heat; add combined eggs, milk and seasonings. Cook slowly, stirring until eggs begin to thicken. Add cream cheese; continue cooking, stirring occasionally, until cream cheese is melted and eggs are cooked. Serve with toast and sprinkle with paprika if desired.
4 servings

COMPANY SCRAMBLED EGGS

1 2½ oz. jar ARMOUR® STAR Sliced Dried Beef, rinsed, chopped
1 cup sliced mushrooms
4 tablespoons butter or margarine
6 eggs
⅓ cup milk
Dash of salt
Dash of pepper
1 tablespoon chopped parsley

In fry pan, cook dried beef and mushrooms in 3 tablespoons butter or margarine 10 minutes. Remove mixture, keeping warm. Add remaining butter or margarine to pan. Combine eggs, milk, salt and pepper; pour into pan. Cook slowly, stirring until eggs are thickened but moist; remove to serving platter. Top with dried beef mixture; sprinkle with parsley.
4 servings

FRITTATA

1 jar (6 oz.) marinated artichoke hearts
2 tablespoons butter
1 cup DOLE® Fresh Mushrooms, sliced
¼ cup chopped green onion
6 eggs
1½ teaspoons garlic salt
2 tablespoons white wine
2 tablespoons grated Parmesan cheese

Drain artichoke marinade into a 10-inch oven-proof skillet. Add butter and melt. Sauté mushrooms until golden. Add artichoke hearts and green onion tossing until heated through. Turn heat to medium. Beat eggs with garlic salt and wine until blended. Pour over mushroom mixture. *DO NOT STIR.* Cook slowly until sides are bubbly. Sprinkle with cheese and place under broiler until cheese is browned and eggs are set. Serve directly from skillet.
Makes 4 servings

DORMAN'S CHEESE FRITTATA

Lightly beat 1 to 2 eggs with 1 to 2 tablespoons water. Season with salt and pepper. Pour into heated, buttered 6- to 8-inch skillet and top with any DORMAN'S Sliced Natural Cheese. Fry at low temperature until set.
One serving

POACHED EGGS WITH TARRAGON & YOGURT

6 poached eggs
2 cups DANNON® Plain Yogurt
1 tsp. paprika
2 tsp. chopped tarragon-½ tsp. dried
Salt and pepper to taste

Arrange eggs on hot serving dish. In saucepan, mix yogurt, paprika and tarragon. Salt to taste. Stir over low heat until warm. Spoon over eggs. Garnish with parsley.
Makes 3 servings

EGGS AU GRATIN

6 hard-cooked eggs
Salt and pepper
Grated cheese
Buttered crumbs
2 cups ENRICO'S Spaghetti Sauce

Remove the shells from the eggs and slice them. Arrange the slices in a greased baking dish. Season with salt and pepper and pour the ENRICO'S Spaghetti Sauce over the top. Sprinkle with grated cheese and cover with buttered crumbs. Bake in a moderate oven (350°F.) until the sauce bubbles and the crumbs are brown.

SUPER SPECIAL EGGS BENEDICT

Top toasted English muffins with slices of grilled ham and eggs poached in HOLLAND HOUSE® White Cooking Wine, cover with Hollandaise Sauce (see recipe below).

BASIC HOLLANDAISE SAUCE

Combine 4 egg yolks, 2 Tbsp. lemon juice and 1 Tbsp. HOLLAND HOUSE® White Cooking Wine in blender. Turn on blender and add ½ lb. of melted butter in a thin stream. As soon as all butter has been added, turn off blender. Makes about 1¼ cups. Perfect over asparagus, broccoli and other vegetables.

EGGS BENEDICT
(Low Calorie/Low Cholesterol)

BUTTER BUDS® "Hollandaise"
  Sauce (see recipe below)
4 eggs, egg substitute, or egg
  whites
2 English muffins, split, toasted
4 slices turkey breast
Parsley flakes

Prepare BUTTER BUDS®
"Hollandaise" Sauce as directed
below. Poach eggs. Cover each
English muffin half with a turkey
slice; top with poached egg. Spoon
2 tablespoons "Hollandaise"
Sauce over each egg. Garnish with
chopped parsley.

Makes 2 servings

BUTTER BUDS®
"HOLLANDAISE" SAUCE

2 packets (1 oz.) BUTTER BUDS®
¼ cup non-fat dry milk
2 Tbsp. hot tap water
1 egg white
¼ tsp. salt
½ tsp. dry mustard
⅛ tsp. SWEET 'N LOW® (sugar
  substitute)
1 Tbsp. vinegar
4 Tbsp. vegetable oil
4 Tbsp. hot water
2 tsp. lemon juice

Combine BUTTER BUDS,® dry milk,
2 tablespoons hot tap water. In
second bowl, beat egg white until
foamy. Blend in salt, mustard,
SWEET 'N LOW® and vinegar.
While beating, slowly add oil, then
contents of first bowl. Stir in 4
tablespoons hot water and lemon
juice.

Makes approximately 1 cup sauce

Calories: w/Butter Buds® — 514
         w/Butter   —1066
Cholesterol:
         w/Butter Buds® —548 mg.
         w/Butter   —688 mg.

Using an egg substitute:
Calories: w/Butter Buds® —434
         w/Butter   —986
Cholesterol:
         w/Butter Buds® — 0 mg.
         w/Butter   —140 mg.

EGGS A LA BENEDICT

Circular pieces of toast
AMBER BRAND Deviled
  SMITHFIELD Ham
Poached eggs
Hollandaise Sauce

Spread toast with Deviled
SMITHFIELD Ham; place poached
egg on each piece; serve with
Hollandaise sauce.

BAYS® BENEDICT

6 BAYS® English Muffins,
  lightly toasted
12 eggs, poached
12 slices Canadian bacon or ham,
  cooked
Black olive slices (optional)
Minced parsley (optional)

Toast muffins and keep warm.
Poach eggs. Prepare Easy Blender
Hollandaise Sauce.* Top each
toasted muffin with a slice of
bacon or ham, then a poached egg.
Cover with about 2 tablespoons of
Hollandaise Sauce. Garnish with a
slice of olive or minced parsley.

Serves 6

*EASY BLENDER
HOLLANDAISE SAUCE

½ pound butter
4 egg yolks
Dash white pepper or 2-3 drops
  TABASCO® Sauce
1 tablespoon lemon juice
1 tablespoon water

Melt butter until bubbling. Remove
from heat. Place egg yolks, lemon
juice, water, and seasoning in
blender; blend at high speed for 30
seconds. Open top of blender and
slowly pour in hot butter in a thin
stream. Hollandaise will be thick
and creamy.

EGGS BENJAMIN

Spread half a LENDER'S Bagel
with butter, a layer of sautéed
mushrooms. Top with poached egg
and slice of cheese. Broil until
cheese melts. Serve open-face.

OLIVE DEVILED EGGS

2 dozen eggs, hard-cooked
⅔ cup mayonnaise
¼ cup minced pimiento-stuffed
  green olives
1 teaspoon oregano
½ teaspoon MORTON Table Salt
¼ teaspoon black pepper
¼ teaspoon garlic powder
Lettuce leaves

Day before serving or early in day:
Cut hard-cooked eggs in half
lengthwise. Remove yolks to small
mixing bowl; mash. Add remaining
ingredients; mix well. Fill whites
with yolk mixture. Cover and
refrigerate.

Just before serving: Place eggs on
lettuce-lined platter. *Makes 48*

DEVILED EGGS AU
POULET
(Low Calorie)

6 hard-cooked eggs
1 can (5 ounces) SWANSON Chunk
  Style Mixin' Chicken
3 tablespoons imitation
  mayonnaise
1 tablespoon finely chopped celery
1 tablespoon finely chopped onion
1 tablespoon Dijon mustard
1 tablespoon sweet pickle relish

Cut eggs in half lengthwise. Scoop
out yolks; mash. Stir in remaining
ingredients. Stuff into egg whites;
sprinkle with paprika. Chill.

Makes 12 deviled eggs

About 70 calories each.

CAVIAR DEVILED EGGS

12 eggs, hard-cooked and shelled
6 Tbsp. regular or low-calorie
  mayonnaise
1 tsp. prepared spicy mustard
¼ tsp. TABASCO®
2 Tbsp. (1 oz.) ROMANOFF®
  Caviar*
Additional caviar for garnish

Cut eggs in half, lengthwise. With
tip of spoon, remove yolk. Mash
with mayonnaise, mustard and
TABASCO® . Fold in caviar. Spoon
into whites. Garnish with
additional caviar.

Makes 24 halves

*ROMANOFF® Red Salmon Caviar
 suggested.

CALIFORNIA-STYLE EGGS

1 can (8 oz.) tomato sauce
1 can (4 oz.) diced green chiles, divided
½ cup KRETSCHMER Regular Wheat Germ, divided
2 Tbsp. chopped green onion
1 Tbsp. cooking oil
4 eggs
¼ tsp. oregano leaves, crushed
⅛ tsp. salt
½ cup grated Monterey Jack cheese, divided
2 flour or corn tortillas
Dairy sour cream
Chopped green onion
Avocado slices

Combine tomato sauce, half the chiles, 2 tablespoons wheat germ and 2 tablespoons green onion. Mix well. Heat oil in skillet. Add eggs, remaining chiles and wheat germ, oregano and salt. Stir to combine, breaking up eggs. Cook over medium-low heat 2-2½ minutes until eggs are softly set. Stir in ¼ cup cheese. Remove from heat. Spread ¼ cup sauce on one side of each tortilla. Divide egg mixture onto tortillas. Roll up. Place seam-side down in oven-proof baking dish. Top with remaining sauce and cheese. Bake at 450° for 10-12 minutes until thoroughly heated. Garnish with last three ingredients.
Makes 2 servings

GOLDEN EGGS IN A NEST

6 hard-cooked eggs, cut in half
½ cup finely chopped cooked ham
¼ cup mayonnaise
4 teaspoons FRENCH'S® Prepared Mustard
1 package (10-oz.) frozen chopped spinach, thawed and well drained
3 cups cooked rice
1 tablespoon lemon juice
2 tablespoons butter or margarine, melted
1 envelope FRENCH'S® Cheese Sauce Mix
1 cup milk

Remove yolks from eggs; mash. Combine with ham, mayonnaise, and 3 teaspoons of the mustard. Stuff egg whites. Combine spinach, rice, lemon juice, and butter; spoon into a shallow 1½-quart casserole or six individual casseroles. Top with stuffed eggs. Prepare sauce mix using milk and stirring in 1 teaspoon mustard; spoon over casserole. Bake at 350°F. for 20 minutes, until hot. *6 servings*

NEST EGGS

6 NABISCO® Shredded Wheat Biscuits, finely rolled (about 1¾ cups crumbs)
3 tablespoons butter or margarine, melted
3 ounces pasteurized process American cheese, grated (about ¾ cup)
6 eggs
6 tablespoons milk
Salt
Ground black pepper
Paprika

Toss shredded wheat crumbs and butter or margarine until well blended. Place ¼ cup of mixture in each of 6 greased (6-ounce) custard cups, pressing mixture against bottom and sides with the back of a spoon to within ½ inch of top. Spoon half of cheese into cups. Top with 1 egg and 1 tablespoon milk per cup; sprinkle with salt and pepper. Cover with remaining cheese and spoon remaining shredded wheat mixture around edges. Sprinkle with paprika. Place on cookie sheet. Bake in a preheated moderate oven (350°F.) 15 to 20 minutes, or until eggs are baked to desired firmness.
Makes 6 (about 4-ounce) servings

CREAMY SHRIMP 'N EGGS IN TOAST CUPS

1 can (4½ ounces) LOUISIANA BRAND Shrimp
6 eggs
½ cup milk
½ teaspoon *each* salt and pepper
1 teaspoon Worcestershire Sauce
1 package (3 ounces) cream cheese, cubed
1 tablespoon chopped chives
2 tablespoons butter

Drain shrimp. Whisk together eggs, milk, salt, pepper, Worcestershire. Add shrimp, cheese, chives. Melt butter in a large skillet and scramble egg mixture until set. Fill toast cups.

TOAST CUPS

Preheat oven to 350 degrees. Cut crusts from 12 slices soft, fresh bread. Press into standard muffin tins, leaving corners perked up. Toast about 10 minutes.
6 servings

TURKEY OMELET WITH SOUR CREAM SAUCE

Roast BUTTERBALL® SWIFT'S PREMIUM® Turkey, sliced or cubed
2 tablespoons butter or margarine
6 eggs
¼ cup milk
½ teaspoon salt
Sour Cream Bacon Sauce*

Add butter to skillet and place over medium heat until bubbly. Combine eggs, milk and salt. Beat until well blended. Pour into skillet and cook over medium heat until egg is slightly set and some liquid remains on the surface. Tilting the pan, lift the edge of the egg opposite handle with spatula. This allows uncooked egg to run under the edge of cooked mixture. Cover with lid for about ½ minute to allow surface to become creamy. Top with turkey. Tilt pan and roll omelet onto hot platter. Serve with Sour Cream Bacon Sauce.
Yield: 4 servings

*SOUR CREAM BACON SAUCE

4 slices SWIFT PREMIUM® Bacon
1 cup sliced fresh mushrooms
¼ cup grated Parmesan cheese
1 cup dairy sour cream
2 teaspoons lemon juice

Cook bacon and drain on paper towel. Crumble into mixing bowl. Remove all except 2 tablespoons of bacon drippings from pan. Sauté mushroom slices in bacon drippings until tender. Spoon into bowl with bacon. Add remaining ingredients and blend.
Yield: 2 cups

SPANISH OMELET

½ cup LINDSAY® Pitted Ripe
 Olives
⅓ cup sliced onion
⅓ cup sliced green pepper
¼ cup finely chopped celery
2 teaspoons cooking oil
1 (1 lb.) can tomatoes
¼ teaspoon salt
Dash pepper
Dash basil
8 eggs
½ cup milk
½ teaspoon salt
2 tablespoons butter OR margarine

Quarter olives. Heat oil. Sauté
onion, green pepper, and celery
until tender. Add tomatoes, salt,
pepper and basil. Cook over low
heat, uncovered, 15 to 20 minutes,
until thickened. Add ripe olives and
heat a few minutes longer. Beat
eggs lightly. Add milk and salt.
Melt 1 tablespoon butter or
margarine in 8-inch skillet; add half
the egg mixture. Cook over
moderate heat until set, lifting
edges as mixture cooks to allow
uncooked portion to run
underneath. Spoon about ¼ of the
tomato mixture over half the
omelet and fold other half over.
Slip from pan onto heated platter
and keep warm in very low oven
while cooking second omelet.
Spoon remaining sauce over tops
of omelets just before serving. Cut
each omelet in half to serve.

Makes 4 servings

EASY DOES IT
PUFF OMELET

2 tablespoons butter
1 can (8 oz.) BUMBLE BEE®
 Whole Oysters
6 eggs, separated
½ teaspoon tarragon, crumbled
¼ teaspoon salt
Dash pepper
⅓ cup chopped green onion

Melt butter in a 6-inch cast iron
skillet or oven-proof omelet pan.
Drain oysters. Beat egg yolks with
tarragon, salt and pepper until
lemon color. Stir in oysters and
green onion. Beat egg whites until
stiff but not dry. Fold into oyster
mixture. Pour into skillet. Bake in
350°F. oven 20 minutes. Serve
immediately.

Makes 4 servings

SAN PEDRO TUNA
OMELET

2 cans (6½ or 7 ounces each)
 tuna, drained and flaked
2 cups half-and-half
2 tablespoons sliced green onion
½ teaspoon leaf thyme
½ teaspoon salt
6 or 8 drops liquid hot pepper
 sauce
2 tablespoons flour
¼ cup water
¼ cup margarine or butter
12 eggs
1½ teaspoons salt
Dash pepper
1½ cups shredded Cheddar cheese

In a saucepan, heat tuna, half-and-
half, onion, thyme, salt, and liquid
hot pepper sauce until hot. Blend
flour and water together. Add to
sauce, stirring constantly, and
cook until thick. For each omelet
beat 2 eggs, ¼ teaspoon salt, and
a dash of pepper together. To a
small omelet pan add 2 teaspoons
margarine and heat until margarine
sizzles. Pour egg mixture into
omelet pan. When eggs are
partially cooked, run a spatula
around the edge, lifting slightly to
allow uncooked egg to flow
underneath. When omelet is almost
done, sprinkle ¼ cup cheese on
top and continue to cook until
cheese melts. Remove omelet to a
hot platter. Repeat omelet
procedure until 6 omelets are
made. Place ½ cup tuna mixture
on 1 side of each omelet. Fold
omelets in half.

Makes 6 servings

*Favorite recipe from National Marine
Fisheries Services*

WHOLE MEAL
BREAKFAST OMELET

5 large eggs
¼ cup dairy sour cream
½ teaspoon salt
¹⁄₁₆ teaspoon white pepper
2 tablespoons butter
½ cup slivered cooked ham
1 large firm-ripe DOLE® Banana,
 sliced

Beat eggs with sour cream, salt
and pepper. Melt butter in a
10-inch skillet. Add ham and sauté
lightly a minute. Add banana, stir
gently to mix with ham. Pour in
egg mixture. Cook over moderate
heat, lifting edges as mixture sets,
to allow uncooked portion to run
underneath. When eggs are set,
turn out onto serving plate folding
omelet in half.

Makes 3 to 4 servings

CAVIAR OMELET

3 eggs
¼ tsp. salt
Dash of pepper
1 Tbsp. water
2 Tbsp. butter or margarine
2 Tbsp. sour cream
2 Tbsp. (1 oz.) ROMANOFF®
 Caviar*
Additional sour cream and caviar
 for garnish

Beat together eggs, salt, pepper
and water. Heat butter in nine-inch
skillet. When it sizzles, pour in
eggs. Cook over medium heat,
lifting cooked portion at edge with
spatula to allow uncooked egg to
flow underneath. When egg is
nearly dry on top, spoon sour
cream and caviar across one-third
of omelet. Loosen edge with
spatula, fold in thirds and slide
onto plate. Garnish with more sour
cream and caviar.

Serves 1 generously

*ROMANOFF® Red Lumpfish or
Salmon Caviar suggested.

CHEEZ-OLA® OMELET
(Low Cholesterol)

4 egg whites
2 tablespoons skim milk
1 tablespoon safflower oil
Dash of pepper
4 or 5 drops yellow food coloring
1 oz. CHEEZ-OLA® sliced

Beat egg whites until slightly
thickened. Add milk, oil, pepper
and food coloring. Pour into skillet
with small amount of oil. Cook
slowly, keeping heat low. When
eggs start to set, add CHEEZ-
OLA® slices. Cover skillet with a
lid. *Turn off heat.* As soon as
cheese melts, serve immediately.
Tomato wedges make a nice
garnish.

BAKED SPICY SAUSAGE OMELET

12 oz. JIMMY DEAN® Sausage
1 tablespoon flour
½ cup milk
½ teaspoon salt
Dash pepper
¼ teaspoon oregano
4 eggs, well beaten
2 slices American Cheese, diced
¼ cup green pepper, finely
   chopped
1 small tomato, diced

Brown sausage in skillet. Drain off
excess fat. Line a 9-inch pie plate
with the cooked sausage. Mix
flour, milk, and seasonings. Beat
until smooth. Add beaten eggs,
cheese, green pepper, and tomato.
Mix well. Pour over the layer of
sausage. Bake at 425° for 5
minutes. Reduce heat to 350° and
continue baking 15 to 20 minutes
or until firm. Cut omelet into 6
wedges and serve hot.

Serves 6

GARDEN PATCH OMELET

6 eggs
¼ cup water
¾ teaspoon salt
⅛ teaspoon FRENCH'S® Pepper
1 cup FRENCH'S® Big Tate
   Mashed Potato Flakes
4 tablespoons butter or margarine
¼ to ½ cup chopped green
   pepper
6 slices American cheese, diced
¼ cup milk
1 medium-size tomato, diced

Lightly beat together eggs, water,
salt, and pepper; stir in potato
flakes. Melt 3 tablespoons of the
butter in large skillet; add egg
mixture and cook over medium
heat until bottom begins to set.
Lift edges of omelet with spatula
and tilt pan, letting uncooked egg
mixture flow to bottom of pan.
Continue to cook until bottom is
browned and top is set. Meanwhile,
cook green pepper in remaining 1
tablespoon butter in small
saucepan about 5 minutes, until
tender-crisp. Add cheese and milk;
cook over low heat, stirring
frequently, until cheese melts. Stir
in tomato. Spoon half the sauce
onto omelet; fold omelet in half
and turn out on serving platter.
Spoon remaining sauce on top of
omelet. *4 to 6 servings*

FLUFFY SAUSAGE OMELET

8 ounce package SWIFT
   PREMIUM® Bacon 'N Sausage
   or Smoke Flavored BROWN
   'N SERVE® Sausage Links,
   cut into fourths
6 eggs, separated
¼ cup water
¼ teaspoon cream of tartar
½ teaspoon salt

In large bowl, beat egg whites and
water at high speed until foamy.
Add cream of tartar and continue
beating just until stiff peaks form.
In small bowl, beat egg yolks and
salt until thick and lemon colored.
Gently fold yolk mixture into
beaten whites. In ovenproof 10-inch
skillet lightly brown sausage. Add
egg mixture and cook on low heat
about 3 minutes. Bake in 350°F.
oven 15 to 20 minutes or until
golden brown.

Yield: 5 to 6 servings

GOURMET FRENCH OMELET

2 2½-oz. jars sliced mushrooms,
   drained
3 tablespoons PARKAY Margarine
6 eggs, beaten
⅓ cup milk
Salt and pepper
¾ cup (3 ozs.) shredded CRACKER
   BARREL Brand Sharp Natural
   Cheddar Cheese
1 teaspoon finely chopped chives

Sauté mushrooms in 1 tablespoon
margarine. Melt remaining
margarine in 10-inch skillet over
low heat. Combine eggs, milk and
seasonings; pour into skillet. Cook
slowly. As egg mixture sets, lift
slightly with a spatula to allow
uncooked portion to flow
underneath. Cover omelet with ½
cup cheese, mushrooms and
chives; fold in half and sprinkle
with remaining cheese.

3 to 4 servings

OMELET EN CROUTE

12 eggs
12 Tbsp. cream or milk
1 7 oz. pkg. BROWNBERRY®
   Seasoned Croutons
Salt and white pepper to taste

Break eggs into small bowl.
Combine in large bowl with cream
or milk (if milk is used, about 1 tsp.
more shortening should be used on
the griddle). Beat with fork only
enough to absorb the cream or
milk. Ladle the equivalent of 3
eggs onto the griddle, keeping as
round a circle as possible. As the
eggs are just about set, place ½
cup croutons in the center, fold the
left end of the egg round over the
croutons, then fold the right end
over, and carefully lift from griddle.
Place omelet on serving plate and
cut almost through the mid-section
allowing croutons to tumble out.
Add chopped ham or bacon in
cream sauce as a topping.

Serves 6

CRAB MEAT OMELETTE

4 eggs
2 Tbsp. milk
1 tsp. salt
¼ tsp. pepper
Dash of TABASCO®
2 Tbsp. chopped green onions
2 tsp. chopped parsley
2 Tbsp. butter
1 can HIGH SEA Crab Meat
1 tsp. lemon juice

Prepare a basic omelette by mixing
eggs, milk, salt, pepper, and
TABASCO®. Cook in an omelette
pan after melting 1 Tbsp. butter.
Sauté green onions and parsley in
remaining butter until soft, being
careful not to let butter brown. Add
crab meat and lemon juice, mixing
lightly. As eggs begin to set, lower
heat, add crab meat mixture, cook
until almost set. Fold and finish
cooking. Garnish with parsley
sprigs. *Serves 2*

PUFFY OMELET WEDGES

4 eggs, separated
¼ to ½ teaspoon salt
⅛ teaspoon pepper
1 cup SEALTEST® Cottage Cheese
1½ tablespoons butter

Preheat oven to 350°. Beat egg whites with egg beater until stiff but not dry. Beat yolks until thick and lemon-colored. Add salt, pepper, and cottage cheese. Continue beating with beater until smooth and blended. Fold in egg whites. Heat butter slowly in 9-inch skillet until just moderately hot but not brown. Add egg mixture; cook over low heat about 3 minutes or until puffed up and delicately browned on bottom. Bake 15 minutes or until top is dry. Cut in wedges. Serve at once.

4 to 5 servings

RICE-A-RONI® EGG FU YUNG

1 pkg. (6¼ oz.) GOLDEN GRAIN® Fried RICE-A-RONI®
6 eggs
1 Tbsp. soy sauce
½ tsp. salt
Dash pepper
1 can (16 oz.) bean sprouts, drained
¼ cup sliced green onion

Sauce:
2 Tbsp. cornstarch
2 Tbsp. soy sauce
2 cups water

Prepare Fried RICE-A-RONI® according to package directions; cool. Beat eggs with 1 Tbsp. soy sauce, salt and pepper. Stir in cooked RICE-A-RONI®, bean sprouts and green onion. Drop mixture by ½ cupfuls onto greased griddle. Brown on each side.

Sauce: combine cornstarch, 2 Tbsp. soy sauce and water; cook until thick. Serve over Egg Fu Yung. *Serves 4*

EGG FOO YUNG

2 Tbsp. vegetable oil
3 eggs
½ cup well-drained mixed Chinese vegetables
¾ tsp. salt
1 5-oz. can BANQUET® Boned Chicken, drained and cubed
Soy sauce

Heat oil in skillet. Break eggs into mixing bowl. Beat until yolks and whites are well blended. Add Chinese vegetables, chicken, and salt. Using a tablespoon, pour one portion of the mixture at a time into skillet or on preheated griddle. Brown each side about 1 minute. Serve with soy sauce. *16 patties*

Quiches

CHICKEN FLORENTINE QUICHE

9-inch unbaked prepared pie shell, thawed
1 can (10¾ ounces) CAMPBELL'S Chunky Chicken Soup
3 eggs, slightly beaten
1 cup dry curd cottage cheese
½ cup grated Parmesan cheese
½ cup *well-drained* cooked chopped spinach
¼ cup finely chopped onion
½ teaspoon oregano leaves, crushed

Prick pie shell with fork; bake at 350°F. for 10 minutes. Meanwhile, combine remaining ingredients, pour into pie shell. Bake at 350°F. for 1 hour or until knife inserted in center comes out clean. Let stand 15 minutes before serving.

Makes 6 servings

Gerber.

HAM 'N CHEESE PIE

1 8-inch baked pie shell
1 jar (3½ oz.) GERBER® Junior Ham
1 small can (5.33 fl. oz.) evaporated milk (⅔ cup)
2 eggs, beaten
4 oz. grated Cheddar cheese (approx. 1 cup)
1 tablespoon dried minced onion
1 teaspoon minced parsley
⅛ teaspoon salt

Preheat oven to 325°F. Combine ingredients and mix well. Pour into pie shell. Bake in 325°F. oven for 30-40 minutes, or until set.

SUNSHINE BACON PIE

14 slices JOHN MORRELL® Bacon
¼ cup chopped onion
¼ cup chopped green pepper
1 tablespoon butter or margarine
¾ cup grated Swiss cheese
4 oz. can mushrooms
3 eggs
2 cups milk
1 tablespoon and 1 teaspoon flour
1 teaspoon salt
½ teaspoon Worcestershire sauce
¼ teaspoon sweet basil
2 (9-inch) unbaked pie crust shells

Place bacon slices in cold skillet over low heat and cook until crisp. Drain and crumble 10 slices. Set aside 4 slices for garnish. In a skillet, sauté onion and green pepper in butter over moderate heat until soft. Alternately layer cheese, crumbled bacon, onion-pepper mixture and mushrooms in each pie crust. In a small bowl, blend together lightly eggs, milk, flour, salt, Worcestershire sauce and basil. Pour half over filling in each crust. Bake in preheated 375°F. oven 35 to 40 minutes or until set. Custard is done when knife inserted in center comes out clean. Arrange remaining bacon slices on top of each pie and serve. *Yield: 8 servings*

MUSHROOM-ONION TART

2 large onions, sliced
3 tablespoons butter
9-inch unbaked pastry shell
2 cups sliced DOLE® Fresh Mushrooms
4 eggs
⅔ cup milk
½ teaspoon salt
½ teaspoon fines herbes
⅛ teaspoon pepper

In a large skillet, sauté onions in 2 tablespoons butter, until just tender. Place onions in bottom of pastry shell. Add remaining butter to skillet; sauté mushrooms lightly; arrange on top of onions. Beat eggs well; beat in milk, salt, herbes and pepper. Pour over mushrooms. Bake in a 400°F. oven for 30 minutes, until set.

Makes 6 servings

POTATO CHIP QUICHE LORRAINE

1½ cups finely crushed potato chips
1 teaspoon paprika
1 cup *each* half and half and whipping cream
3 eggs, beaten
¼ pound bacon, cooked crisp and crumbled
2 tablespoons sliced green onions
¼ teaspoon salt
Dash *each* pepper and nutmeg
2 cups grated Swiss cheese

Combine chips and paprika; gently press into bottom and 1½ inches up sides of 8-inch springform pan. In saucepan warm half and half and cream; beat into eggs to blend. Stir in remaining ingredients. Pour into crust. Bake in 375 degree oven 30 to 35 minutes, until custard is set and golden.

Makes 6 servings

Recipe from Potato Chip Information Bureau

PET.

QUICHE LORRAINE

1 PET-RITZ® Regular Pie Crust Shell
6 slices bacon, fried and crumbled
1 can (4 ounces) sliced mushrooms, drained
1 cup (4 ounces) Swiss cheese, shredded
½ cup onion, finely chopped
1 Tablespoon flour
½ teaspoon salt
¼ teaspoon garlic powder
2 eggs, beaten
1 small can (5.33 fl. oz.) PET® Evaporated Milk

Preheat oven and cookie sheet to 450°F. Partially bake pie shell, about 6 minutes. Remove from oven. Reduce oven temperature to 325°F. In mixing bowl combine bacon, mushrooms, cheese, onion, flour, salt and garlic powder. Mix until well blended. Spoon into pie shell. Beat together eggs and evaporated milk. Slowly pour over bacon mixture. Bake on preheated cookie sheet until knife inserted in center comes out clean, about 55 to 60 minutes. Cool 10 to 15 minutes before serving.

SALMON QUICHE

1 10-inch unbaked pie shell
1 can (15½ oz.) BUMBLE BEE® Pink Salmon
1 package (9 oz.) frozen chopped spinach
1½ cups shredded Monterey Jack cheese
1 package (3 oz.) cream cheese, softened
½ teaspoon salt
½ teaspoon thyme, crumbled
4 eggs, lightly beaten
1 cup milk

Preheat oven to 375°F. Bake pie shell 10 minutes until partially set. Drain salmon. Remove skin, if desired. Mash bones. Cook spinach according to package directions. Drain well. Combine spinach, Monterey Jack cheese, cream cheese, salt and thyme. Arrange salmon and mashed bones in pie shell. Spoon spinach mixture on top. Combine eggs and milk. Pour over salmon and spinach. Bake in preheated oven 40 to 45 minutes. Let stand 10 minutes before serving.

Makes 6 to 8 servings

DOWN HOME SAUSAGE AND CHEESE PIE

1 unbaked deep dish pie shell (9″)
¾ lb. HILLSHIRE FARM® Smoked Sausage, chopped
2 eggs, beaten
1 cup evaporated milk
1 tsp. Worcestershire sauce
1 cup shredded Swiss cheese
¼ cup shredded cheddar cheese
½ cup chopped onion

Preheat oven to 400°. Prick bottom and sides of prepared pie crust with fork. Bake 8 minutes. Remove from oven and reduce heat to 350° Sprinkle ½ of sausage over partially baked crust. Combine remaining ingredients (except sausage) and pour into pie shell. Sprinkle with remaining sausage. Bake at 350° for 45–50 minutes or until set. Allow to cool 10 minutes before serving.

MICROWAVE:

Place unbaked pie crust in a 9″ glass (or ceramic) pie or quiche

dish. Prick bottom and sides of crust with fork. Brush top edge of crust with a little Worcestershire sauce. Microwave, uncovered, HIGH 4–5 minutes or until dry and opaque. Sprinkle crust with cheeses and onion and top with sausage. Pour milk into a glass bowl and microwave, uncovered, HIGH 2 minutes. Beat eggs and 1 tsp. Worcestershire sauce together and carefully whisk in the hot milk. Pour into shell. Microwave, uncovered, MEDIUM 15–18 minutes or HIGH 9–11 minutes, rotating the dish every three minutes. Custard should be slightly set in the center when done. Allow to stand 10 minutes before serving.

Yield: 6 regular servings or 16 snacks

HAM AND EGG PUFF
(Quiche au Jambon)

1 (10-oz.) pkg. PEPPERIDGE FARM® Frozen Patty Shells, thawed
1½ cups diced cooked ham
6 eggs beaten
¾ cup milk
1 tsp. dry mustard
½ tsp. hot-pepper sauce
¼ tsp. mace

Parsley Caper Sauce
1 (1-oz.) pkg. white sauce mix
¼ cup chopped parsley
1 Tbsp. drained capers
½ tsp. salt

Heat oven to 450°. Press 6 thawed patty shells together. Roll out on lightly floured surface to a 12-inch circle. Fit into a 10-inch pie plate. Scatter ham over bottom of unbaked shell. Lightly beat eggs with milk, mustard, hot-pepper sauce, and mace. Pour into pie shell. Place in oven and immediately reduce heat to 400° Bake 30 to 40 minutes or until puffed and brown.

Serve hot with Parsley Caper Sauce. Prepare the white sauce mix according to label directions, increasing water to 1½ cups. Just before serving, stir in chopped parsley, drained capers and salt. Makes 1½ cups.

Serves 6 to 8

Note: When pressing patty shells together, place one on top of another; do not roll in a ball. This helps assure high rising pastry.

PET® SALMON QUICHE

1 PET-RITZ® Regular Pie Crust
  Shell
1 can (8 oz.) salmon, drained
1 small can (5.33 fl. oz.) PET®
  Evaporated Milk
1 cup (4 oz.) Cheddar cheese,
  shredded
½ cup finely chopped onion
2 eggs, separated
1 Tablespoon dried parsley flakes
1 Tablespoon lemon juice
1 teaspoon seasoned salt
¼ teaspoon pepper

Preheat oven and cookie sheet to
450°F. Partially bake pie shell,
about 6 minutes. Reduce oven
temperature to 375°F. Remove the
bone and skin from salmon. Flake
salmon and mix with evaporated
milk, cheese, onion, egg yolk,
parsley, lemon juice and
seasoning. Beat egg whites until
stiff. Fold egg whites into salmon
mixture. Spoon into partially baked
pie shell. Bake on preheated
cookie sheet, until filling puffs and
is golden brown, about 30 to 35
minutes. Cool 10 minutes before
serving.

BUDDIG REUBEN QUICHE

1 package (4 oz.) BUDDIG Sliced
  Corned Beef or Pastrami
1 cup sauerkraut, drained
1 PET-RITZ® Deep Dish Pie Crust
  Shell
1 cup (4 oz.) Swiss cheese, grated
5 eggs
¾ cup milk

Conventional directions: Preheat
oven and cookie sheet to 425°F.
Cut BUDDIG Corned Beef or
Pastrami into ½-inch squares.
Squeeze excess moisture from
sauerkraut. Line pie crust with
sauerkraut, meat and cheese. Beat
together eggs and milk. Pour over
meat mixture. Bake on preheated
cookie sheet 15 minutes. Reduce
oven temperature to 300°F. and
continue baking an additional 40 to
45 minutes or until knife inserted
in center comes out clean. Let
stand 10 minutes before cutting.

Microwave directions: Slip pie
crust from metal tin into 9-inch
glass pie plate. Prick crust
generously and cook on high 4 to 5
minutes. Set aside to cool. Prepare
quiche filling as above. Pour in

baked crust and cook on high 9 to
12 minutes or until set in center.
Rotate dish every 3 minutes. Let
stand 10 minutes and serve.
Six main dish servings

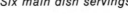

SAUSAGE QUICHE

½ lb. BOB EVANS FARMS® Roll
  Sausage
1 unbaked 9-in. pie crust
1 tsp. butter
1 medium onion, chopped
½ c. grated Swiss cheese
4 eggs
1 c. milk
1 c. heavy cream
½ tsp. salt
¼ tsp. pepper

Crumble sausage and cook until
brown. Remove sausage and add
butter and onions to drippings.
Cook for five minutes. Cover
bottom of pie crust with sausage,
onions and ¼ cup cheese. In
mixing bowl combine remaining
cheese, eggs, milk, cream, salt and
pepper. Mix well and pour over
sausage mixture. Bake at 425° for
15 minutes. Reduce heat to 350°
and continue baking until brown
and well set (approximately 20
minutes longer). *Serves 6*

LINDSAY® QUICHE & TELL

1½ cups whipping cream
½ cup buttermilk
4 eggs, lightly beaten
¼ teaspoon salt
Dash pepper
¼ pound bacon, cooked and
  crumbled
¼ pound Swiss cheese, shredded
  (about 2 cups)
2 tablespoons sliced green onions
1 can (6 ounces) LINDSAY® Large
  Pitted, Ripe Olives, drained
1 pastry-lined 9-inch pie plate or
  quiche dish (unbaked)

Heat cream and buttermilk; whisk
in eggs and seasonings. Stir in
cheese, bacon, onions and
LINDSAY® Olives. Pour into pastry
shell. Bake in 375° oven 30 to 35
minutes, until custard is set and
golden. Garnish with chopped
parsley, if desired.
Makes 6 servings

SHRIMP CHILIE QUICHE

1 PET-RITZ® Regular Pie Crust
  Shell, thawed
2 eggs
1 small can (5.33 fl. oz.) PET®
  Evaporated Milk
2 Tablespoons flour
¾ teaspoon garlic salt
½ cup (2 oz.) shredded Cheddar
  cheese
½ cup (2 oz.) shredded Monterey
  Jack cheese
½ cup chopped onion
1 can (4 oz.) OLD EL PASO®
  Chopped Green Chilies
1 can (4½ oz.) ORLEANS®
  Deveined Medium Shrimp,
  drained

Preheat oven and cookie sheet to
450°F. Partially bake pie shell
about 6 minutes. Remove from
oven. Reduce oven temperature to
350°F. Beat together eggs,
evaporated milk, flour and garlic
salt. (Mixture need not be smooth.)
Stir in cheese, onion and chilies.
Pour into pie shell. Spread shrimp
on top of custard mixture. Bake on
preheated cookie sheet, until knife
inserted in center comes out clean,
about 35 to 40 minutes. Cool 15
minutes before serving.

Soufflés

EASY SOUFFLE

1 can (10¾ ounces) CAMPBELL'S
  Condensed Cream of Celery
  Soup
1 cup shredded sharp process
  cheese
6 eggs, separated

In saucepan, combine soup and
cheese. Heat slowly until cheese
melts. Stir occasionally. Remove
from heat. Beat egg yolks until
thick and lemon-colored; gradually
stir in soup mixture. In large bowl,
using clean beater, beat egg
whites until stiff peaks form; fold
in soup mixture. Pour into
ungreased 2-quart casserole. Bake
at 300°F. for 1 to 1 hour 15
minutes or until soufflé is brown.
Serve immediately.
Makes 4 to 6 servings

CHEESE 'N CRACKER SOUFFLÉ

1 cup fine KEEBLER TUC Cracker
   crumbs
4 eggs, separated
2 cups milk
1 teaspoon salt
⅛ teaspoon pepper
¾ cup grated Parmesan Cheese
¼ cup chopped green onion
2 tablespoons of cracker crumbs
   to dust soufflé dish

Butter a 1-quart soufflé dish; dust
with 2 tablespoons of cracker
crumbs. In a medium saucepan,
combine egg yolks, milk, salt and
pepper over medium heat. Cook,
stirring constantly, until mixture
thickens, about 8 to 10 minutes.
Stir in cheese and onions. Add
cracker crumbs. Beat egg whites
until stiff, but not dry, forming
peaks. Fold into crumb mixture.
Pour into soufflé dish. Bake in
preheated 375°F. oven 35 to 40
minutes or until top is lightly
browned. Serve immediately.
4 Servings

WORLD'S EASIEST SOUFFLÉ

Butter
Grated Parmesan cheese
4 eggs
4 ounces sharp Cheddar cheese,
   cubed
1 package (3 oz.) cream cheese,
   cubed
⅓ cup milk, light cream or half
   and half
¼ cup grated Parmesan cheese
½ teaspoon onion salt
½ teaspoon dry mustard

Butter bottom and sides of 1-quart
soufflé dish or casserole. Dust
with Parmesan cheese. Set aside.
Combine remaining ingredients in
blender container. Cover and blend
at medium speed until smooth,
about 30 seconds. Blend at high
speed another 10 to 15 seconds.
Carefully pour into prepared dish.
Bake in preheated 350°F. oven 25
to 30 minutes or until puffy and
delicately browned. Serve
immediately.　　　　*4 servings*

American Egg Board favorite recipe

A SORT OF SOUFFLÉ

1 loaf BROWNBERRY® White Bread
4 eggs
¾ cup grated Cheddar cheese
2½ cups milk
1 Tbsp. prepared mustard
4 tsp. salt, dash of pepper, or to
   taste
4 Tbsp. coarsely chopped onion
2-3 Tbsp. grated or crumbled
   cheese (optional)

Place bread in greased 9 x 5 bread
pan. Beat eggs, blend milk, cheese,
mustard, salt, pepper and 3 Tbsp.
chopped onion. Pour mixture over
bread. Sprinkle top with remaining
Tbsp. chopped onion and crumbled
cheese. Cover dish with foil and let
stand overnight or 3-4 hours in the
refrigerator. Mixture will absorb
into bread and form a two-inch
custard base when baked. Bake at
325° for one hour or until topping
is crusty brown. Let stand 5
minutes before serving.
Makes 8 generous servings

SOUFFLÉ MEDLEY

10-oz. pkg. GREEN GIANT® Rice
   Originals Frozen Rice Medley
2 tablespoons margarine or butter
3 tablespoons flour
¾ cup milk
4 oz. (1 cup) shredded Cheddar
   cheese
½ teaspoon salt
¼ teaspoon pepper
Dash cayenne
4 eggs, separated

Heat oven to 325°F. Butter and
flour 1½-quart soufflé dish. Cook
rice according to package
directions. In small saucepan, melt
margarine; stir in flour until
smooth. Gradually stir in milk.
Heat, stirring constantly, until
thickened. Add cheese, salt,
pepper and cayenne; stir until
cheese is melted. Remove from
heat.

In large bowl, beat egg whites until
stiff peaks form. In medium bowl,
beat egg yolks; stir in small
amount of cheese sauce. Slowly
add remaining cheese sauce,
stirring briskly to prevent lumping.
Stir in rice. Gently fold cheese-rice
mixture into beaten egg whites.
Pour into prepared soufflé dish.
Bake at 325°F. for 45 to 50 minutes
or until puffy and golden brown.
4 servings

ONION CHEESE STRATA

1 package (16 ounces)
   MRS. PAUL'S® Onion Rings
4 eggs, slightly beaten
⅛ teaspoon black pepper
½ teaspoon salt
1 cup Swiss cheese, grated
2 cups milk
4-6 slices white bread, quartered

Preheat oven to 350°F. Combine all
ingredients except onion rings and
bread in a large bowl. Mix
thoroughly. Butter a shallow 9 inch
square baking dish. Place ½ the
bread and onion rings in dish and
cover with ½ egg mixture. Let
stand 3-4 minutes. Repeat layers
ending with onion rings. Bake 45
minutes or until puffy and browned
and all egg has set.　　*Serves 6-8*

SOUFFLÉ ITALIAN

3 tablespoons butter
3 tablespoons grated Parmesan
   cheese
1 can (15 oz.) BUMBLE BEE®
   Pink Salmon
1 clove garlic, minced
1 cup chopped green onion
1 cup shredded zucchini
4 eggs, separated
1 carton (8 oz.) ricotta cheese
¼ cup dairy sour cream
½ teaspoon tarragon, crumbled
½ teaspoon salt
¼ teaspoon ground nutmeg
¼ teaspoon cream of tartar

Preheat oven to 350°F. Coat
bottom and sides of a 1-quart
soufflé dish with 1 tablespoon
butter. Sprinkle with grated
Parmesan cheese. Drain salmon.
Remove skin, if desired. Mash
bones. Sauté garlic, onion and
zucchini in 2 tablespoons butter.
Remove vegetables from pan.
Combine egg yolks, ricotta cheese,
sour cream, tarragon, salt and
nutmeg. Cook in same pan over
low flame, stirring constantly until
sauce thickens. Remove from heat.
Stir in sautéed vegetables. Fold in
salmon and bones. Beat egg
whites until foamy. Beat in cream
of tartar until egg whites are stiff
but not dry. Fold one-fourth of egg
whites into salmon mixture. Gently
fold in remaining egg whites.
Spoon into prepared soufflé dish.
Bake in preheated oven 45
minutes. Serve immediately.
Makes 4 servings

FRESH APRICOT SOUFFLÉ

1 pound fresh California apricots,
  peeled and pitted
Sugar
¼ cup water
1 envelope plus 1 teaspoon
  unflavored gelatin
5 eggs, separated
1 or 2 tablespoons apricot brandy
⅛ teaspoon salt
1 cup heavy cream, whipped

Puree apricots in electric blender.
(There should be about 1½ cups
puree.) Add ½ cup sugar. Combine
water and ½ cup sweetened puree;
sprinkle gelatin over puree to
soften. Set aside. Beat egg yolks
with ½ cup sugar in top of double
boiler. Cook over boiling water,
stirring frequently, for 10 minutes
or until thickened. Add brandy and
gelatin mixture; stir until gelatin
dissolves. Cook, then combine with
remaining puree in large bowl; chill
until mixture mounds slightly. Beat
egg whites with salt until soft
peaks form. Gradually add ¼ cup
sugar and continue beating until
stiff and shiny. Fold egg whites
into gelatin mixture; then fold in
whipped cream. Turn into 1-quart
soufflé dish with collar. (See note.)
Chill several hours, until set.
Remove collar before serving.
Makes 10 servings

To Make with Canned Apricots: If
desired, use 1 can (30 ounces)
apricot halves instead of fresh
apricots. Puree fruit in electric
blender, do not sweeten. Sprinkle
gelatin over puree to soften. Set
aside. Proceed with recipe.
Makes 1½ cups

Note: Cut a strip of wax paper
  about 4 inches deep and
  long enough to extend
  around the outside of a
  1-quart soufflé dish; fasten
  with string.

*California Apricot Advisory Board favorite
recipe*

COLD CHERRY SOUFFLÉ

Prepare base for chilled fruit
soufflé. Add 1 cup kirsch and ¼
cup syrup from defrosted frozen
cherries. Chill until slightly
thickened. Combine with stiffly
beaten egg whites, whipped heavy
cream, and 2 cups drained,
defrosted frozen red tart cherries.

Turn into 1½ qt. soufflé dish. Use
foil to form collar. Chill 4 hours, or
until firm. Garnish with red tart
cherries.

*Favorite recipe from National Red Cherry
Institute*

COLD LEMON SOUFFLÉ

1 tablespoon unflavored gelatin
¼ cup JACQUIN'S Rum
3 eggs, separated
1 cup sugar
Grated rind and juice of 2 lemons
1½ cups heavy cream
Candied violets, optional

Sprinkle gelatin over JACQUIN'S
Rum in a Pyrex® cup and let soften
5 minutes; then put the cup in a
small pan of simmering water and
stir until gelatin is dissolved.
Meanwhile, beat egg yolks and
sugar until very thick and light.
Beat in grated lemon rind and
juice. With clean beaters, beat egg
whites until stiff but not dry. Whip
1 cup of the heavy cream. Stir the
dissolved gelatin into the lemon
mixture; then fold in beaten egg
whites and whipped cream. Pour
into a 1½ quart soufflé dish and
refrigerate for at least 2 hours. (It
can be made the day before
serving.) When ready to serve, whip
remaining ½ cup heavy cream and
garnish soufflé with rosettes of
whipped cream. Decorate with
candied violets if you have them.
Serves 6 to 8

PURPLE PLUM SOUFFLÉ

1 package (3-ounce) ROYAL
  Lemon Gelatin
1 cup boiling water
1 cup pureed purple plums
¼ teaspoon ground cinnamon
½ cup heavy cream, whipped
½ cup chopped PLANTERS® or
  SOUTHERN BELLE Pecans
1 egg white, stiffly beaten

Dissolve ROYAL Lemon Gelatin in
boiling water. Stir in pureed plums
and cinnamon. Chill until
thickened. Set bowl of thickened
gelatin mixture firmly in a bowl of

ice. Beat until light and fluffy. Fold
in whipped cream and chopped
PLANTERS® or SOUTHERN
BELLE Pecans, then fold in beaten
egg white. Let stand over ice until
mixture is of mounding
consistency. Pile mixture into a
1-quart soufflé dish. Chill until
firm. If desired, garnish with
whipped cream rosettes sprinkled
lightly with cinnamon.

WALNUT PRUNE SOUFFLÉ

4 egg whites
⅛ teaspoon cream of tartar
¼ teaspoon salt
¼ cup sugar
2 jars (4¾ oz. each) GERBER®
  Strained Prunes
½ teaspoon vanilla
½ teaspoon cinnamon
⅔ cup walnuts, chopped

Beat egg whites until foamy, add
cream of tartar and salt, and
continue beating to form soft
peaks. Gradually add sugar beating
until stiff peaks form. Gently fold
in prunes, vanilla, cinnamon and
walnuts. Turn into a buttered 1½
quart soufflé dish. Set dish in pan
of warm water and bake in
preheated 325°F oven for 40-50
minutes or until firm. Garnish with
sweetened whipped cream. Serve
at once.

SOUFFLÉ AU DUBOUCHETT
(Low Calorie)

2 egg yolks
¼ cup powdered sugar
1 Tbsp. DUBOUCHETT Peach
  Brandy
4 egg whites
¼ tsp. Cream of Tartar
Few grains salt
⅓ cup DUBOUCHETT Apricot
  Brandy

Beat the yolks until light yellow.
Add the powdered sugar, tartar and
the salt. Stir in the DUBOUCHETT
Peach Brandy. Beat the egg whites
till stiff and dry. Fold delicately
into the yolk mixture. Butter an
omelet pan and pour in ½ the
mixture; brown lightly, fold over
and place on a hot serving dish.
Repeat the process with the
remaining mixture. Heat ⅓ cup of
the DUBOUCHETT Apricot Brandy
and pour around the soufflés and
set in flames.

Pasta, Rice and Dumplings

HURRY-UP SPAGHETTI 'N HAM

½ cup thinly sliced onion
¼ cup cooking oil
¼ pound boiled ham, cut into strips*
¼ cup butter or margarine
½ cup chicken broth
8 ounces MUELLER'S® Thin Spaghetti
2 egg yolks, slightly beaten
½ cup chopped parsley
½ cup grated Parmesan cheese

Cook onion in oil until soft but not browned. Add ham, butter, and chicken broth; heat. Meanwhile, cook spaghetti as directed on package; drain. Quickly stir spaghetti and egg yolks; then add ham mixture, parsley and cheese; toss and serve immediately.

4 servings

*Note: Prosciutto may be used in place of ham.

SPAGHETTI WITH ITALIAN MEATBALLS

2 lbs. ground beef
1⅓ cups dry bread crumbs
½ cup grated parmesan cheese
2 teaspoons oregano leaves
1 teaspoon garlic salt
½ teaspoon pepper
2 eggs
3 tablespoons oil
2 quarts prepared spaghetti sauce
16 oz. pkg. AMERICAN BEAUTY® Long Spaghetti
4 quarts water
4 teaspoons salt
1 tablespoon oil
Grated parmesan cheese, if desired

In medium bowl, combine ground beef, bread crumbs, ½ cup cheese, oregano, garlic salt, pepper and eggs. Shape into 1½-inch balls. In Dutch oven, heat 3 tablespoons oil. Brown one-third of meatballs over high heat, turning to prevent sticking. Remove from pan. Repeat with remaining meatballs; drain. Return browned meatballs to Dutch oven; add spaghetti sauce. Cover and simmer 30 minutes.

Boil water in large deep pot with salt and 1 tablespoon oil (to prevent boiling over). Add spaghetti; stir to separate. Cook uncovered after water returns to a full rolling boil for 9 to 10 minutes (al dente—firm) or 11 to 12 minutes (tender). Stir occasionally. Drain and rinse under hot water.

Serve meatballs and sauce over long spaghetti. Sprinkle with additional parmesan cheese, if desired. *8 servings*

High Altitude—Above 3500 Feet: Cooking times may need to be increased slightly for spaghetti; no additional changes.

NUTRITIONAL INFORMATION PER SERVING
SERVING SIZE: ⅛ OF RECIPE

		PERCENT U.S. RDA PER SERVING	
Calories	815	Protein	60
Protein	39 g	Vitamin A	5
Carbohydrate	89 g	Vitamin C	—
Fat	32 g	Thiamine	26
Sodium	2222 mg	Riboflavin	26
Potassium	532 mg	Niacin	35
		Calcium	22
		Iron	39

SPEEDY SKILLET SPAGHETTI WITH TURKEY SAUSAGE
(Low Calorie)

1 pound LOUIS RICH Turkey Sausage
1¼ cups fat-skimmed turkey broth
3½ cups water
1 6-ounce can tomato paste
Garlic salt to taste
3 tablespoons minced onion (or 1 tablespoon dried onion flakes)
1 teaspoon dried oregano
6 ounces (dry) very thin spaghetti, broken

Spread the sausage in a large, heavy nonstick skillet. Over moderate heat, brown slowly without adding fat, stirring constantly to avoid sticking. (Add a little water, if needed.) Add all remaining ingredients except spaghetti; heat to boiling. Add spaghetti, a little at a time. Cover and cook, stirring occasionally, until spaghetti is tender, about 10 minutes. Uncover and continue to simmer until sauce is thick. (Sprinkle with 6 teaspoons grated Parmesan cheese, if desired.)
Makes six servings

About 285 calories each; about 295 calories with cheese added.

FAMILY SPAGHETTI

1 pound mild Italian sausage
3 cups sliced DOLE® Fresh Mushrooms
1 cup sliced celery
1 medium onion, chopped
1 clove garlic, pressed
1 can (15 oz.) tomato sauce
1 can (14½ oz.) Italian-style tomatoes
¾ cup water
1 teaspoon oregano, crumbled
1 teaspoon sugar
¼ teaspoon rosemary, crumbled
¼ teaspoon salt
¼ teaspoon pepper
8 ounces (or ½ 16-oz. package) spaghetti
Grated Parmesan cheese

Cut sausage in bite-size chunks and brown in large skillet. Drain pan drippings, leaving 2 tablespoons. Add mushrooms, celery, onion and garlic; sauté until onion is soft. Stir in tomato sauce, Italian tomatoes, water, oregano, sugar, rosemary, salt and pepper. Simmer, uncovered, 20 minutes. Cook spaghetti according to package directions. Drain and arrange on serving platter. Spoon sauce over spaghetti. Serve with grated Parmesan cheese.
Makes 4 servings

SPRING GARDEN SPAGHETTI

1 bunch fresh broccoli
2 small zucchini, cut in 1″ lengths
1½ cups green beans, cut in 1″ lengths
½ cup frozen peas
¾ cup fresh or frozen pea pods (optional)
3 or 4 asparagus spears (optional)
2 cups thinly sliced mushrooms
⅓ cup pine nuts (optional)
1 tablespoon cooking oil
2 packages (19.5 oz. each) CHEF BOY-AR-DEE® Complete Spaghetti Dinner with Meat Sauce
¼ cup butter or margarine
1 packet G. WASHINGTON'S® Golden Seasoning and Broth Mix
¾ cup heavy cream
¼ cup finely chopped parsley

Clean broccoli and break into bite-sized pieces. Blanch or steam broccoli, zucchini, beans, peas, pea pods and asparagus in boiling water until just tender (about 5 minutes); drain. Sauté mushrooms and pine nuts in cooking oil, drain. Cook spaghetti from package according to package directions; drain. Use spaghetti pot to melt butter. Reduce heat, add seasoning and broth mix, heavy cream and grated cheese from package; stir until sauce thickens. Add vegetables and parsley and toss; add drained spaghetti and toss. Heat canned sauce from package; serve over vegetable-spaghetti mixture.   *Serves 8 to 10*

Mueller's®

SPAGHETTI WITH ZUCCHINI SAUCE

1 medium onion, sliced
¼ cup olive oil
2 medium zucchini, sliced (about 6 cups)
3 cups diced tomatoes
½ teaspoon salt
1 bay leaf
¼ teaspoon pepper
¼ teaspoon basil leaves
¼ teaspoon oregano leaves
8 ounces MUELLER'S® Spaghetti
Grated Parmesan cheese

In large skillet or pot, sauté onion in hot oil until crisp-tender. Add zucchini, tomatoes, salt, bay leaf, pepper, basil, and oregano. Simmer covered for 15 minutes; uncover and simmer 10 minutes longer. Discard bay leaf. Meanwhile, cook spaghetti as directed on package; drain. Serve spaghetti topped with zucchini sauce and grated Parmesan cheese.   *4 to 6 servings*

MARINARA SAUCE & SPAGHETTI

½ cup POMPEIAN Olive Oil
2 cloves garlic, crushed
2 cans (28 oz. each) Italian plum tomatoes, drained and crushed
½ tsp. basil
6 anchovy fillets (optional)
6 eggs
1 lb. spaghetti, cooked and drained
Parsley

Heat olive oil in heavy pan and brown garlic. Add tomatoes, basil and anchovies and simmer 45 minutes. Slip one egg per person into sauce; cover pan and poach eggs until slightly firm. Pour sauce over cooked spaghetti. Garnish with poached egg and parsley.
Makes 6 servings

LEMON CLAM SPAGHETTI

½ cup butter
3 Tbsp. POMPEIAN Olive Oil
⅓ cup finely chopped onion
2 cloves garlic, crushed
2 cans (8 oz. each) minced clams, drained (save liquid)
3 Tbsp. lemon juice
1 Tbsp. chopped parsley
2 tsp. grated lemon peel
¼ tsp. pepper
1 bay leaf
1 lb. spaghetti, cooked and drained
1 cup grated Parmesan cheese
6 lemon wedges

Heat 3 Tbsp. butter and olive oil in heavy pan. Sauté onion and garlic until tender. Add liquid from clams, lemon juice, parsley, lemon peel, pepper and bay leaf; simmer until liquid is reduced to about 1 cup. Remove bay leaf. Stir in clams and heat thoroughly. Add remaining butter; stir until melted. Pour sauce over spaghetti, sprinkle with cheese and serve with lemon wedges.   *Makes 8 servings*

SHRIMP PASTA

1 lb. Spaghetti, cooked, drained
¼ cup Olive Oil
2 Tbsp. Parmesan cheese, grated
Pepper as needed
2 drops TABASCO®
¼ cup Heavy Cream
½ lb. ATALANTA Frozen Shrimp, raw, shelled & deveined
3 Tbsp. Butter
3 Tbsp. Parsley, chopped

Sauté shrimp in butter for 5 minutes. Cut into chunks. Set aside. Heat olive oil and toss in spaghetti, pepper, cheese and TABASCO® Add cream and simmer. Add sautéed shrimp. Sprinkle with parsley and serve.
Yield: 4 servings

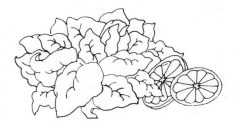

IDEAL LINGUINE WITH CLAMS AND SPINACH

1 lb. IDEAL Linguine
¼ cup butter, melted hot
1 lb. fresh spinach leaves, washed, drained well and chopped
2 Tbsp. chopped fresh parsley
4 green onions, chopped
¼ cup oil
1 tsp. salt
⅛ tsp. pepper
2 cans (8-oz. can) minced clams
Parmesan cheese

Cook IDEAL Linguine according to package directions. Drain well. Return Linguine to cooking pot and toss with hot melted butter. Meanwhile, sauté onions in oil until transparent (5 min.) Add drained minced clams with ¼ cup reserved clam juice. Add salt and pepper and continue to sauté for 5 minutes longer. Add spinach and parsley and toss a few times lightly. Cook 5 minutes longer. Serve hot IDEAL Linguine topped with spinach-clam mixture and sprinkle with Parmesan cheese.
Serves 4-6

LASAGNE

1 pound ground beef
6 cups spaghetti sauce
1 package (16 ounces) rippled edge
  SAN GIORGIO Lasagne
4 cups (2 pounds) Ricotta cheese
2 cups (8 ounces) shredded
  Mozzarella cheese
¼ cup grated parmesan cheese
4 eggs
1 tablespoon parsley
1 teaspoon salt
¼ teaspoon pepper

Brown meat in 3-quart saucepan; add sauce and simmer about 10 minutes. Cook Lasagne according to package directions for about 10 minutes; drain well. (Separate Lasagne and lay out flat on wax paper or aluminum foil to keep them from sticking together as they cool.) Mix together Ricotta, Mozzarella, Parmesan, eggs, parsley, salt and pepper for filling. Pour about ½ cup sauce on bottom of 13 x 9 x 2-inch pan; arrange layer of Lasagne over sauce. Spread ⅓ of the cheese filling over Lasagne and cover with about 1 cup meat sauce. Repeat layers of Lasagne, cheese, and meat sauce twice. Top with a layer of Lasagne and 1 cup meat sauce; sprinkle with additional Parmesan cheese, if desired. Bake, covered with aluminum foil, at 350° for about 30 minutes or until hot and bubbly. Remove foil; bake about 10 minutes longer until lightly browned. Allow to stand about 10 minutes before cutting for easier handling. Serve with additional sauce if desired.

Hunt's®
HUNT'S LASAGNA

2 lbs. ground beef or half ground
  beef and half Italian sausage
1 onion, chopped
1 (48-oz.) jar HUNT'S Prima Salsa
1 cup water
1 lb. mozzarella cheese
1 qt. small curd cottage cheese
1 egg, slightly beaten
2 Tbsp. chopped parsley
1½ tsp. seasoned salt
¼ tsp. pepper
1 lb. lasagna noodles, cooked and
  drained
½ cup grated Parmesan cheese

Cook beef and onion in a large skillet until beef loses redness and onion begins to soften; drain excess fat. Stir in Prima Salsa and water and bring to a boil, stirring often; simmer 5 minutes. Cut *12 thin slices* of mozzarella and set aside for topping. Shred *remainder* of mozzarella and combine in a bowl with cottage cheese, egg, parsley, salt and pepper. Spread several spoons of meat sauce over bottom of each of 2 (2-quart) baking dishes.* Arrange 3 cooked noodles lengthwise in each. Next add a layer of about 1½ cups cottage cheese mixture, then a layer of about 1½ cups meat sauce. Repeat layers of noodles, cheese mixture and meat sauce until all used up. Sprinkle *half* the Parmesan over each and top with reserved sliced mozzarella.

   For 8 servings, bake one *pan at 350° 30 to 35 minutes until bubbly.*

*Prepare it in two baking dishes, each large enough to serve 8 people. Bake and serve one. Cover and freeze the other to bake and serve on a night you don't have time to make Lasagna from scratch. Remove from freezer at least 1 hour before baking. Bake, lightly covered with foil, at 375° 1 hour and 15 minutes.

CARBONARA LASAGNA

1 package CHEF BOY-AR-DEE®
  Complete Lasagna Dinner
10 slices bacon
4 hard cooked eggs
1 lb. Mozzarella cheese

Cook lasagna macaroni according to package directions; drain. Cook bacon until crisp; drain; crumble. Slice hard cooked eggs. Cut cheese into thin slices. Grease 6" x 10" baking dish or 10" PYREX® pie plate. Place 2 tablespoons of lasagna sauce from package on bottom of dish. Place a layer (4 or 5) cooked lasagna macaroni on bottom of dish. Arrange a layer of cheese slices, then sliced egg, then crumbled bacon. Spoon 3 tablespoons of lasagna sauce over bacon. Repeat layers to use all of the lasagna macaroni. Top with lasagna sauce and grated cheese from package. Bake 20 minutes in 425°F. oven.
Serves 4-6

SanGiorgio

TURKEY LASAGNE FLORENTINE

8 ounces (9 pieces) SAN GIORGIO
  Rippled Edge Lasagne
1 cup (9-ounce package) frozen
  chopped spinach
2 to 3 cups diced cooked turkey or
  chicken
2 cups shredded American or
  Cheddar cheese
1 can (10¾ ounces) cream of
  mushroom soup
1 cup dairy sour cream
½ cup (4-ounce can) sliced
  mushrooms, drained
⅓ cup minced fresh onion
½ teaspoon salt
¼ teaspoon pepper
½ cup grated Parmesan cheese

Cook Lasagne according to package directions for 10 minutes; drain well. Separate Lasagne pieces and lay flat on wax paper or aluminum foil to keep from sticking together as they cool. Cook spinach according to package directions; drain well.

Combine diced turkey or chicken, 1½ cups shredded cheese, cream of mushroom soup, sour cream, sliced mushrooms, minced onion, salt, pepper and well-drained spinach in large bowl; toss until mixture is well blended.

Butter bottom and sides of an 11½ x 7½ x 1½-inch baking dish; arrange layer of Lasagne (3 pieces) lengthwise in bottom of pan. Spread half the turkey mixture over Lasagne; sprinkle with 2 tablespoons Parmesan cheese. Arrange another layer of Lasagne (3 pieces) lengthwise over turkey mixture. Spread remaining turkey mixture over Lasagne; sprinkle with 2 tablespoons Parmesan cheese. Top with layer of Lasagne; sprinkle with remaining ½ cup shredded cheese and ¼ cup Parmesan cheese. Cover with aluminum foil. Bake at 350°F for 30 minutes. Remove foil; bake 10 minutes longer or until lightly browned and bubbly. Allow to stand 15 minutes before cutting. Garnish with fresh parsley and pimento, if desired.
6 to 8 servings

151

CAMPBELL'S LASAGNA

½ pound ground beef
1 cup chopped onion
2 large cloves garlic, minced
2 teaspoons oregano, crushed
2 cans (10¾ ounces each)
  CAMPBELL'S Condensed
  Tomato Soup
½ cup water
2 teaspoons vinegar
9 lasagna noodles (about
  ½ pound), cooked and drained
1 pint small or large curd cottage
  cheese or ricotta cheese
1½ cups shredded Mozzarella
  cheese
Grated Parmesan cheese

In saucepan, brown beef and cook
onion, garlic, and oregano until
onion is tender. Add soup, water,
and vinegar. Cook over low heat 30
minutes; stir occasionally. In
shallow baking dish (12 × 8 × 2
inches), arrange 3 alternate layers
of noodles, cottage cheese, meat
sauce, and Mozzarella cheese.
Sprinkle with Parmesan cheese.
Bake at 350°F. for 30 minutes. Let
stand 15 minutes before serving.
6 servings

SMOKED SAUSAGE
LASAGNA

6 ounces lasagna noodles, cooked,
  drained
1½ cups ricotta cheese
3 cups spaghetti sauce
1 pound ECKRICH® Smoked
  Sausage, thinly sliced
16-ounce pkg. sliced mozzarella
  cheese
1 tablespoon oregano
⅓ cup Parmesan cheese
Salt to taste

Place ½ cup sauce in the bottom
of a 2-quart oblong casserole.
Alternate layers of noodles, ricotta
cheese (dropped by spoonfuls),
spaghetti sauce, Smoked Sausage,
and mozzarella cheese. Sprinkle
top with oregano, Parmesan
cheese, and salt. Cover. Bake in a
preheated 350°F. oven 45 minutes
until heated through.
6 servings

MICROWAVE OVEN DIRECTIONS:
Prepare as directed, using a glass
baking dish. Cover with fitted
casserole lid or plastic wrap.
Microwave 15 minutes.

CLASSIC LASAGNE

1 pound ground beef
¾ cup chopped onion
2 tablespoons salad or olive oil
1 can (1 pound) tomatoes
2 cans (6 ounces each) tomato
  paste
2 cups water
1 tablespoon chopped parsley
2 teaspoons salt
1 teaspoon sugar
1 teaspoon garlic powder
½ teaspoon pepper
½ teaspoon oregano leaves
8 ounces MUELLER'S® Lasagne
1 pound ricotta cheese
8 ounces Mozzarella cheese,
  shredded or thinly sliced
1 cup grated Parmesan cheese

In large heavy pan, lightly brown
beef and onion in oil. Add
tomatoes (put through blender or
cut with edge of spoon), tomato
paste, water, parsley, salt, sugar,
garlic powder, pepper, and
oregano; simmer uncovered,
stirring occasionally, about 30
minutes. Meanwhile, cook lasagne
as directed on package; drain. In
13 × 9 × 2″ baking pan, spread
about 1 cup sauce. Then alternate
layers of lasagne, sauce, ricotta,
Mozzarella, and Parmesan cheese,
ending with sauce, Mozzarella, and
Parmesan. Bake at 350°F. for 40 to
50 minutes until lightly browned
and bubbling. Allow to stand for 15
minutes; cut in squares to serve.
8 servings

MEATLESS LASAGNE

8 ounces lasagne noodles
1 tablespoon salad oil
⅛ teaspoon McCORMICK/
  SCHILLING Garlic Powder
1 1½-ounce package McCORMICK/
  SCHILLING Spaghetti Sauce Mix
1 8-ounce can tomato sauce
1½ cups water
2 cups ricotta or cottage cheese
¾ cup grated Parmesan cheese
1 8-ounce package sliced
  Mozzarella cheese

Cook noodles as directed on
package, adding oil and garlic
powder to the boiling water. Drain,

then rinse in cold water; drain
again. Combine spaghetti sauce
mix, tomato sauce and water;
simmer 20 minutes. In a buttered
2-quart baking dish, make layers of
noodles, sauce and ricotta,
Parmesan and Mozzarella cheeses,
using one-half of each. Repeat.
Bake in 350°F. oven 30 minutes or
until bubbly. *Serves 6*

UP-SIDE DOWN
VEGETABLE LASAGNA

1 package (23⅞ oz.) CHEF BOY-
  AR-DEE® Complete Lasagna
  Dinner
5 or 6 asparagus stalks, fresh,
  frozen, or canned
1 carrot, sliced
2 tablespoons butter or margarine
2 cups Ricotta cheese
1 egg, beaten
Dash nutmeg
6 mushrooms, sliced
½ cup chopped onions
¼ teaspoon salt
¼ teaspoon basil
¼ teaspoon oregano
4 oz. shredded Mozzarella cheese

Prepare lasagna macaroni
according to package directions;
drain. Meanwhile, blanch fresh or
frozen asparagus and carrot slices
in boiling water for 1 to 3 minutes;
drain. If using canned asparagus,
drain. Butter 6″ × 10″ × 2″ baking
pan. Arrange several asparagus
spears and carrot slices in floral
design on bottom of dish. Spoon
about three teaspoons of lasagna
sauce from package over
asparagus arrangement.

Place one layer of drained lasagna
macaroni on top. Combine Ricotta
cheese, egg, nutmeg and cheese
from package; spread one-half of
mixture on lasagna. Place another
lasagna layer on cheese mixture.
Sauté mushrooms and onions; add
salt, basil and oregano. Arrange on
top. Add another lasagna layer and
spread with remaining Ricotta
mixture. Place final lasagna layer
on top; pour remaining sauce from
package over; sprinkle with
shredded Mozzarella cheese. Bake
in 425°F. oven for 20 to 25
minutes. Allow to stand for 5
minutes. Go around edge with
knife or spatula to loosen any
baked-on cheese. Place large flat
platter on top of baking dish and
turn upside down.
Serves 4 to 6

EASY LASAGNE CASSEROLE

3 cups uncooked egg noodles
1 pound ground beef
½ cup chopped onion
1 can (15 oz.) tomato sauce
1 package (1½ oz.) spaghetti sauce mix
1 package (3 oz.) cream cheese, softened
1 cup PET® Evaporated Milk
½ teaspoon garlic salt
1 cup (4 oz.) shredded mozzarella cheese

Cook noodles in boiling salted water until tender. Cook ground beef and onion in skillet until ground beef is browned. Drain. Stir in tomato sauce and spaghetti sauce mix. Cook until thickened. Drain noodles. Combine cream cheese and evaporated milk in warm saucepan until smooth. Stir in noodles and garlic salt. Pour into 9-inch square baking dish. Spread meat mixture over top. Top with shredded cheese. Bake at 350°F. for 20 minutes or until bubbly.   *Makes 6 servings*

Mueller's®

LIGHT'NING LASAGNE
(Low Calorie)

Sauce:
½ pound lean ground beef (10% fat)
1 can (29 ounces) tomato sauce
1 cup beef broth
2 large cloves garlic, mashed
2 tablespoons instant minced onion
1 teaspoon oregano leaves, crushed
1 medium bay leaf

Filling:
3 cups low fat cottage cheese
½ cup grated Parmesan cheese
2 tablespoons sliced green onion
⅛ teaspoon pepper
8 ounces MUELLER'S® Lasagne
2 ounces part skim milk Mozzarella cheese, shredded or thinly sliced

To make sauce: In saucepan brown beef; pour off fat. Add tomato sauce, broth, garlic, minced onion, oregano and bay leaf; simmer 30 minutes, stirring occasionally. Remove bay leaf. *To make filling:* In bowl combine cottage and Parmesan cheeses, green onion

and pepper; set aside. Meanwhile, cook lasagne as directed on package; drain. In 13 × 9 × 2″ baking dish, spread about 1 cup sauce. Then alternate layers of lasagne, sauce, cheese filling and Mozzarella, ending with sauce and Mozzarella. (Make sure lasagne edges are covered with sauce.) Bake at 350°F. for 45 minutes or until bubbling. Allow to stand 15 minutes; cut in squares to serve.
Makes 8 servings

Approximately 2590 calories; eight servings of about 325 calories each.

LAWRY'S® LASAGNA ROLL-UPS

1 pound ground beef
2 teaspoons LAWRY'S® Seasoned Salt
2 cloves garlic, crushed
½ teaspoon LAWRY'S® Seasoned Pepper
1 can (1 lb. 12 oz.) tomatoes
1 can (6 oz.) tomato paste
1 package (1½ oz.) LAWRY'S® Spaghetti Sauce Mix with Imported Mushrooms
½ pound lasagna (broad noodles), about 6 to 8 long noodles
Salad oil
½ pound ricotta cheese*
½ pound Mozzarella cheese, grated
½ cup grated Parmesan cheese

Brown the meat in a Dutch oven or deep kettle. Add Seasoned Salt, crushed garlic and Seasoned Pepper. Simmer slowly for about 10 minutes. Add canned tomatoes, tomato paste, and Spaghetti Sauce Mix with Imported Mushrooms. Stir thoroughly; cover and simmer for 30 minutes. Meanwhile, boil lasagna noodles in salted water until they are almost tender; drain, rinse and toss gently in oil. Lay two noodles side by side, just overlapping about ½-inch. Spread with ¼ of ricotta. Then spread ½ cup of meat mixture and ¼ of Mozzarella and Parmesan cheeses. Roll-up noodles, place seam side down in oblong baking dish. Prepare remaining 3 roll-ups the same. Top lasagna roll-ups with remaining meat sauce.
Makes 6 to 8 servings

*Cottage cheese may be substituted for ricotta; however, drain thoroughly. To freeze: Prepare as above, except for

baking. Cover securely and seal with freezer tape. When ready to use, thaw, remove cover, and bake as directed.

LASAGNE ROLL-UPS

4 quarts water
4 teaspoons salt
1 tablespoon oil
8 pieces AMERICAN BEAUTY® Lasagne
1 quart prepared spaghetti sauce
1 lb. Italian sausage or ground beef
¼ cup chopped onion
½ cup dry bread crumbs
1 teaspoon salt
½ teaspoon basil leaves
¼ teaspoon pepper
2 cups (8 oz.) shredded mozzarella cheese
12-oz. carton cottage cheese
1 egg, beaten
Grated parmesan cheese, if desired

Heat oven to 350°F. Boil water in large deep pot with 4 teaspoons salt and oil (to prevent boiling over). Add lasagne; stir. Cook uncovered after water returns to a full rolling boil for 10 to 12 minutes. Stir occasionally. Drain and rinse under cold water.

Spread 2 cups of spaghetti sauce over bottom of 13 × 9-inch baking dish. In large skillet, brown sausage with onion over medium heat; drain. Add bread crumbs, 1 teaspoon salt, basil, pepper, mozzarella cheese, cottage cheese and egg. Cut each lasagne noodle in half crosswise; spread about 3 tablespoons of sausage mixture evenly on each half. Roll up from shorter side and place seam down in pan. Pour remaining sauce over top.

Cover and bake at 350°F. for 1 hour. Serve rolls with sauce. Serve with parmesan cheese, if desired.
8 servings

High Altitude—Above 3500 Feet: Cooking times may need to be increased slightly for lasagne; no additional changes.

NUTRITIONAL INFORMATION PER SERVING			
SERVING SIZE:		PERCENT U.S. RDA	
⅛ OF RECIPE		PER SERVING	
Calories	536	Protein	39
Protein	25 g	Vitamin A	6
Carbohydrate	37 g	Vitamin C	—
Fat	32 g	Thiamine	22
Sodium	1429 mg	Riboflavin	30
Potassium	113 mg	Niacin	13
		Calcium	32
		Iron	20

BAKED MANICOTTI

1 pound ricotta cheese
½ pound shredded mozzarella
cheese
¾ cup grated Parmesan cheese
(reserve ¼ cup)
2 eggs
1 teaspoon parsley flakes
Salt, to taste
Pepper, to taste
1 jar (15½ oz.) RAGU' Spaghetti
Sauce, any flavor
1 package (5½ oz.) manicotti,
cooked and drained

Preheat oven to 350°F. Combine
ricotta, mozzarella and Parmesan
cheese, eggs, parsley, salt and
pepper, mix well. Pour ½ cup
spaghetti sauce into an 11"×7"
baking dish. Fill manicotti with
about 3 tablespoons cheese
mixture and arrange over sauce.
Pour remaining sauce over top and
sprinkle with reserved Parmesan
cheese. Bake 45 minutes or until
bubbly.   *Serves 4*

CHEESE-FILLED
MANICOTTI

1 package (8 oz.) manicotti shells
(approximately 14), cooked
1 package (10 oz.) frozen chopped
spinach, cooked
1 pound (2 cups) ricotta cheese
½ cup grated Parmesan cheese
1 package (1½ oz.) DURKEE
Roastin' Bag Italian Style
Chicken Sauce Mix
1 can (6 oz.) tomato paste
2 cups water

Preheat oven to 350°. Stir together
cooked spinach and cheeses; stuff
mixture into prepared manicotti
shells. Place shells, in single layer,
in oven cooking bag. Combine
sauce mix, tomato paste, and
water; pour over filled shells. Close
open end of bag with twist-tie.
Place in a baking dish 1½ to 2
inches deep and large enough to
contain entire bag. Punch 4 small
holes along top of bag. Place on
rack in lower half of oven, leaving
at least 10 inches between rack
positions to allow for expansion of
bag. Roast in preheated 350° oven
for 30 minutes. Cut top of bag;
remove manicotti to serving dish
and pour sauce over all.
                     6 to 8 servings

MANICOTTI
MAGNIFICENT

1 can (15½ oz.) BUMBLE BEE®
Pink Salmon
12 manicotti shells
1 pkg. (10 oz.) frozen broccoli
flowerettes
1 carton (8 oz.) ricotta cheese
1 egg, slightly beaten
Lemony Cream Sauce*
½ cup grated Parmesan cheese

Drain salmon. Remove skin, if
desired. Mash bones. Cook
manicotti according to package
directions. Cook broccoli
according to package directions.
Drain well, and chop. Combine
ricotta cheese and egg until
blended. Stir in salmon and
broccoli until blended. Fill
manicotti with salmon mixture.
Spoon small amount of Lemony
Cream Sauce in 2-quart shallow
casserole. Arrange stuffed
manicotti over sauce. Pour
remaining sauce over and sprinkle
with Parmesan cheese. Bake in
350°F. oven 30 to 35 minutes.
                  Makes 6 servings

*LEMONY CREAM SAUCE

2 tablespoons butter
2½ tablespoons flour
½ teaspoon dillweed, crumbled
½ teaspoon salt
Dash ground nutmeg
2 cups milk
2 tablespoons lemon juice

Melt butter in saucepan. Stir in
flour, dill, salt and nutmeg. Heat
until bubbly. Gradually stir in milk,
stirring constantly, until mixture
boils and thickens. Remove from
heat. Stir in lemon juice.

MANICOTTI SUPREME

8 manicotti shells
8 oz. mozzarella cheese, diced
¼ cup grated Parmesan cheese
1 Tbsp. chopped parsley
1 tsp. seasoned salt
¼ tsp. pepper
¼ tsp. garlic powder
1½ cups HUNT'S Prima Salsa
½ cup *each:* water and burgundy
wine

Place manicotti shells in
7½ × 12 × 1½-inch baking dish,
cover with boiling water, let stand
5 to 10 minutes; rinse in cold
water, drain thoroughly. Combine

next 6 ingredients in a small bowl;
mix well. Fill drained manicotti
shells with mixture. Return filled
shells to baking dish. Combine
HUNT'S Prima Salsa, water and
wine; blend well. Pour over filled
manicotti shells. Bake, covered, at
375° 45 to 50 minutes. Serve with
additional Parmesan if desired.
                  Makes 4 servings

MANICOTTI WITH
CHEESE FILLING

4 quarts water
4 teaspoons salt
1 tablespoon oil
14 AMERICAN BEAUTY®
Manicotti Shells
2 cups (8 oz.) shredded mozzarella
cheese
2 (12-oz.) cartons cottage cheese
2 eggs, beaten
½ cup dry bread crumbs
½ cup grated parmesan cheese
2 tablespoons chopped parsley
1 teaspoon sugar
½ teaspoon salt
¼ teaspoon pepper
1 quart prepared spaghetti sauce
¼ cup grated parmesan cheese

Heat oven to 350°F. Boil water in
large deep pot with 4 teaspoons
salt and oil (to prevent boiling
over). Add manicotti shells; stir to
separate. Cook uncovered after
water returns to a full rolling boil
for 10 to 12 minutes. Stir
occasionally. Drain and rinse under
cold water.

In medium bowl, combine
remaining ingredients except
spaghetti sauce and ¼ cup
parmesan cheese. Stuff each
cooked shell with ⅓ cup filling.
Spread 2 cups spaghetti sauce on
bottom of 13 × 9-inch baking dish.
Place filled shells in a single layer
over sauce. Pour remaining sauce
over top. Cover and bake at 350°F.
for 40 to 45 minutes. Let stand 5 to
10 minutes before serving. Sprinkle
¼ cup parmesan cheese over top.
                       7 servings

High Altitude—Above 3500 Feet: Cooking
times may need to be increased slightly for
manicotti shells; no additional changes.

NUTRITIONAL INFORMATION PER SERVING
SERVING SIZE: PERCENT U.S. RDA
⅐ OF RECIPE   PER SERVING

Calories	705	Protein	43
Protein	28 g	Vitamin A	11
Carbohydrate	49 g	Vitamin C	3
Fat	43 g	Thiamine	16
Sodium	1546 mg	Riboflavin	28
Potassium	194 mg	Niacin	8
		Calcium	29
		Iron	17

CHEESE FILLED JUMBO SHELLS

1 box (12 ounces) SAN GIORGIO Jumbo Shells
4 cups (2 pounds) Ricotta cheese
2 cups (8 ounces) shredded Mozzarella cheese
¾ cup grated Parmesan cheese
3 eggs
1 tablespoon chopped parsley
¾ teaspoon crushed oregano
½ teaspoon salt
¼ teaspoon pepper
4 cups spaghetti sauce

Cook Jumbo Shells according to package directions for about 10 minutes; drain well. (Cool in a single layer on wax paper or aluminum foil to prevent sticking together.) Mix together cheeses, eggs, parsley, oregano, salt and pepper. Fill each Shell with about 2 tablespoons cheese mixture. Spread a thin layer of sauce on bottom of 13 × 9 × 2-inch baking pan. Place the Shells, open side down, in a single layer in the pan; cover with about 2 cups sauce. Sprinkle with additional Parmesan cheese, if desired. Bake, covered with aluminum foil, at 350° for about 35 minutes or until hot and bubbly. Heat remaining sauce and serve with Shells.

Fills about 36 Shells

RAVIOLI WITH TOMATO SAUCES

¼ cup (½ stick) butter
½ package JENO'S® Meat or Cheese Ravioli (25 by count)
3 cups canned whole tomatoes, stewed tomatoes, or a combination of tomatoes and canned tomato sauce
Salt and pepper to taste
Herbs (oregano, basil, thyme, marjoram, etc.) to taste
½ to 1 cup Parmesan cheese to fold into sauce and serve with ravioli

Melt butter in wide frying pan. Add frozen ravioli, turn over with spatula until ravioli are coated with butter. Pour canned tomatoes over top of ravioli and bring to a boil; add salt, pepper and herbs to taste and simmer for 5 to 10 minutes or until ravioli is cooked through and sauce has thickened slightly. To further thicken sauce, add Parmesan cheese and serve.

Makes about 4 or more servings

VARIATIONS:

Ravioli Provençal: Add ½ cup each chopped onion and green pepper to butter, then add ravioli and proceed as directed above.

Ravioli Marinara: Fold in 1 to 2 cups cooked tiny shrimp at the same time as Parmesan is added to the sauce; heat just until shrimp are hot.

Mushroom Ravioli Sauce: Add 1 cup sliced fresh or canned mushrooms to butter, then add ravioli and proceed as directed above.

Cooking time about 10 minutes.

RAVIOLI PRIMA

¼ cup (½ stick) butter
½ package (25 by count) JENO'S® Meat or Cheese Ravioli, still frozen
1 cup water
1 jar (2 cups) 15 to 16 oz. prepared spaghetti sauce, marinara sauce, or any favorite prepared pasta sauce
1 cup grated Parmesan cheese
Additional cheese for serving

Melt butter in frying pan; spread in the ravioli, still frozen, heat over high heat until butter coats ravioli completely; add water, bring to a boil. Pour sauce over ravioli evenly, bring to a boil and boil for 5 to 10 minutes or until ravioli is done to your liking. Fold in the Parmesan cheese. Serve with additional Parmesan cheese.

Makes about 4 or more servings

VARIATIONS:

Ravioli with Tomato Mushroom Sauce: Add 1 cup sliced fresh mushrooms to the butter and immediately add the ravioli. Continue as directed above.

Ravioli in Clam Sauce: Drain 1 can (6½ oz.) clams, and add water to equal 1 cup liquid, follow directions above and replace water with the clam-water mixture. Add reserved clams at the same time as the Parmesan cheese.

Ravioli with Shrimp Sauce: Follow directions above. Just before addition of the Parmesan cheese, fold in 1 package (6 to 8 oz.) baby frozen shrimp. Cook until shrimp is thawed. Add Parmesan cheese.

Cooking time about 10 minutes.

RAVIOLI IN SUPREME SAUCE

¼ cup (½ stick) butter
½ package (25 by count) JENO'S® Meat or Cheese Ravioli, still frozen
1½ cups heavy cream
¾ cup grated Parmesan cheese

Melt butter in wide frying pan. Add ravioli; spread in even, single layer. Pour cream over. Bring to a boil. Boil 5-10 minutes or until ravioli is heated through and cooked to your liking; stir occasionally. Add Parmesan and serve.

Makes about 4 or more servings

VARIATIONS:

Ravioli in Mushroom Supreme Sauce: Add 2 cups sliced fresh or canned mushrooms in butter.

Ravioli in Supreme Sauce with Ham: Add 1 cup diced ham to butter before adding ravioli.

Ravioli with Shrimp Sauce Supreme: Add ½ cup each diced green onions and green pepper to butter before adding ravioli. Add about 2 cups cooked shrimp along with the Parmesan cheese.

Ravioli in Spinach Supreme Sauce: Add 1 package (10 oz.) thawed, drained, chopped spinach to butter before adding ravioli.

Cooking time about 10 minutes.

SPINACH CANNELLONI

1 cup chopped onion
1 cup diced celery
2 tablespoons butter or margarine
2 packages (10 oz. each) frozen chopped spinach, cooked & drained
¾ cup fresh bread crumbs
¼ cup shredded Cheddar Cheese
2 tablespoons light cream
2 cans (15 oz. each) CHEF BOY-AR-DEE® Cannelloni (beef filled macaroni product in meat sauce)

Sauté onion and celery in butter. Add cooked, drained spinach, bread crumbs and cheese; stir. Spread spinach mixture on bottom of baking dish. Save some spinach mixture for garnish. Add light cream to Cannelloni and arrange on top of spinach. Garnish with remaining spinach mixture. Bake in 350°F. oven for 20 minutes.

Serves 4

CREAMY TUNA FETTUCINI

1 can (9¼ oz.) BUMBLE BEE®
  Chunk Light Tuna*
8 ounces spinach noodles
Boiling water
4 tablespoons butter
2 tablespoons olive oil
2 cloves garlic, pressed
1½ cups sliced DOLE® Fresh
  Mushrooms
1 to 1½ cups dairy sour cream
⅓ cup grated Romano cheese
1 tablespoon chopped parsley

Drain tuna. Cook noodles in boiling
water according to package
directions until just tender. Drain.
Heat butter and oil in saucepan
and sauté garlic and mushrooms.
Blend in sour cream and cheese.
Fold in tuna and heat through.
Serve noodles on hot platter and
top with sauce. Sprinkle parsley
over sauce. Toss before serving.
Makes 4 to 6 servings

*Or use 2 cans (6½ oz. each)
BUMBLE BEE® Chunk Light Tuna.

IDEAL FETTUCCINI A L' IPPOLITO

½ cup butter or margarine,
  softened
½ lb. prosciutto or cooked ham
  cut in strips
½ cup whipping cream (room
  temp.)
½ cup grated Parmesan cheese
1 6-oz. can whole mushrooms,
  drained
1 lb. IDEAL Fettuccini
2 Tbsp. butter

Cream butter or margarine. Beat in
whipping cream, a little at a time,
till well mixed. Beat in Parmesan
cheese. Set aside at room
temperature. Sauté cooked ham in
2 Tbsp. butter for 5 minutes. Stir in
mushrooms; season to taste. Cook
IDEAL Fettuccini according to
package directions, stirring
occasionally; drain. Put drained
fettuccini in a warm bowl. Add the
creamed mixture and toss very well
till all fettuccini is coated. Stir in
mushrooms and ham. Serve with
extra Parmesan cheese.
Makes 4-6 servings

BUTTERBALL® TURKEY TETRAZZINI

2 cups chopped, roast
  BUTTERBALL® SWIFT'S
  PREMIUM® Turkey
½ stick (¼ cup) butter or
  margarine
½ cup sliced onions
¼ cup flour
1 teaspoon salt
¼ teaspoon white pepper
½ teaspoon poultry seasoning
⅛ teaspoon dry mustard
2 cups milk
½ cup shredded aged Cheddar
  cheese
2 tablespoons chopped pimiento,
  optional
¼ cup sherry wine, optional
4 ounce can mushroom stems and
  pieces
7 ounce package spaghetti,
  cooked, drained
⅓ cup shredded aged Cheddar
  cheese

Melt butter in saucepan. Sauté
onions in butter until tender. Blend
in flour and seasonings. Remove
from heat. Gradually add milk.
Stirring constantly, cook until
mixture thickens. Add ½ cup
cheese and pimiento, stirring until
cheese melts. Add sherry and
mushrooms and liquid to white
sauce. Place a layer of spaghetti in
a 2 quart casserole. Cover with a
layer of turkey and a layer of
sauce. Repeat and finish with a
layer of spaghetti. Sprinkle ⅓ cup
cheese over top. Cover and bake in
a 400°F. oven about 20 minutes.
Yield: 6 servings

FETTUCCINE ALFREDO

1 package RONZONI® Extra Long
  Fettuccine
½ cup grated Parmesan cheese
⅔ cup light cream (sour cream
  may be substituted)
¼ lb. butter (preferably sweet)
1 egg yolk

Cook noodles according to
directions on the panel. While
noodles are cooking, beat egg yolk
lightly with fork and add to cream.
Melt butter. Place drained, hot
noodles in warm serving bowl or
platter. Pour over the noodles egg
and cream mixture, melted butter
and about half of the grated
cheese. Toss noodles with fork and

spoon until well blended, adding
balance of cheese a little at a time
while tossing. Top with additional
grated cheese, if desired, and
serve immediately.

CHICKEN TETRAZZINI

¼ cup chopped onion
2 tablespoons butter or margarine
1 can (10¾ ounces) CAMPBELL'S
  Condensed Cream of Chicken
  Soup
½ cup water
½ cup shredded sharp Cheddar
  cheese
1 tablespoon dry sherry
2 cups cooked spaghetti
1 can (5 ounces) SWANSON Chunk
  White or Thigh Chicken
2 tablespoons chopped parsley
2 tablespoons chopped pimiento
Grated Parmesan cheese

In saucepan, cook onion in butter
until tender. Blend in soup, water,
Cheddar cheese and sherry. Heat
until cheese melts; stir
occasionally. Add spaghetti,
chicken, parsley and pimiento;
heat. Serve with Parmesan.
Makes about 4 cups, 4 servings

LAND O' LAKES® TURKEY TETRAZZINI

4 oz. spaghetti, broken in thirds
2 c. cubed (½″) LAND O LAKES®
  Butter Moist Turkey Roast
1 c. (4 oz.) shredded process
  American cheese
10¾-oz. can condensed cream of
  chicken soup, undiluted
4-oz. can mushroom stems and
  pieces, drained
2-oz. jar chopped pimiento, drained
½ c. half and half
1 Tbsp. instant minced onion
¼ tsp. salt
1 Tbsp. Worcestershire sauce
¼ c. grated Parmesan cheese

Heat oven to 350°. In 3-qt.
saucepan cook spaghetti
according to pkg. directions, drain
well. Set aside. In same pan, stir
together remaining ingredients
except Parmesan cheese. Stir in
cooked spaghetti. Turn into
greased 2-qt. round baking dish;
sprinkle top with Parmesan
cheese. Bake for 35 to 40 min. or
until mixture bubbles around
edges. *Yield: 6 (¾ c.) servings*

ROTINI TETRAZZINI

6 tablespoons butter
6 tablespoons unsifted all-purpose flour
1¾ cups chicken broth
½ cup heavy cream
2 egg yolks, slightly beaten
2 cups cooked chicken, cubed
1 cup sautéed mushrooms
¼ cup chopped pimentos
¼ cup chopped fresh parsley
¼ cup dry white wine
Salt and pepper to taste
2 tablespoons grated Parmesan cheese
½ package (8 ounces) SAN GIORGIO Rotini

Melt butter; stir in flour. Gradually add chicken broth and heavy cream. Cook and stir constantly over medium heat until mixture begins to boil; boil and stir 1 minute. Remove from heat. Add small amount of sauce to egg yolks; blend well. Return egg mixture to sauce; stir until smooth. Add chicken, mushrooms, pimentos, parsley, wine, salt and pepper to sauce; keep warm over low heat. Cook Rotini according to package directions; drain. Toss immediately with sauce mixture; top with Parmesan cheese.

4 to 6 servings

MUELLER'S® CHICKEN TETRAZZINI

1 can (4 ounces) sliced mushrooms, drained, reserving liquid
⅓ cup chopped onion
4 tablespoons butter or margarine
3 tablespoons flour
1½ cups chicken broth
½ cup light cream
½ teaspoon salt
Dash pepper
½ cup dry vermouth or chicken broth
¾ cup grated Parmesan cheese
8 ounces MUELLER'S® Thin Spaghetti
2 cups diced cooked chicken

In saucepan, cook mushrooms and onion in butter until soft; stir in flour. Gradually add 1½ cups broth, cream and reserved mushroom liquid; cook, stirring, until sauce thickens. Remove from heat. Add salt, pepper, vermouth and ¼ cup of the cheese; set aside. Meanwhile, cook spaghetti

as directed on package; drain. Combine spaghetti and chicken in 2-quart casserole; pour sauce over and mix lightly. Sprinkle with remaining cheese. Bake at 375°F. for 20 minutes or until bubbling.

4 to 6 servings

BANQUET® CHICKEN TETRAZZINI

¼ cup butter
¼ cup minced green pepper
½ lb. fresh mushrooms, sliced
1 Tbsp. minced onion
1 cup chopped celery
¼ cup all-purpose flour
2 tsp. salt
2 cups chicken or turkey broth
1 cup light cream
2 Tbsp. sherry
2 5-oz. cans BANQUET® Boned Chicken, drained and cubed
2 Tbsp. chopped pimiento
½ lb. spaghetti, cooked
⅓ cup grated Parmesan cheese
Parsley
Pimiento strips

Sauté green pepper, mushrooms, onion, and celery in butter for 5 minutes. Remove vegetables. Add flour and salt; mix well. Stir in broth, cream, and sherry. Cook, stirring constantly, until thickened. Add vegetables, chicken, and chopped pimiento; heat thoroughly. Serve over hot spaghetti; sprinkle with cheese. Garnish with parsley and pimiento strips.

6-8 servings

BAKED MACARONI AND CHEESE

2 cups (8 ounces) SAN GIORGIO Elbow Macaroni
1¼ cups milk
1 egg
1 teaspoon salt
½ teaspoon dry mustard
⅛ teaspoon pepper
2 cups (8 ounces) shredded cheddar cheese
Dash paprika

Cook Macaroni according to package directions for 5 minutes; drain well. Combine milk, egg, salt, dry mustard and pepper in buttered 2-quart casserole; stir in cooked Macaroni and 1¾ cups cheese. Top with remaining cheese and paprika. Bake at 350° for 30 to 35 minutes or until top is golden brown.

4 to 6 servings

MACARONI LOAF

7-oz. package CREAMETTES® Macaroni (2 cups uncooked)
2 pimientos, chopped
1 cup soft bread crumbs
1 cup Swiss cheese, grated
¼ cup onion, grated
2 eggs, beaten
1 cup light cream
2 tablespoons parsley, chopped
1 teaspoon salt
⅛ teaspoon pepper
½ cup melted butter or margarine

Prepare CREAMETTES® according to package directions. Drain. Combine macaroni and pimientos. Pour into an 11 × 7 × 1½ ″ pan. Top with bread crumbs and cheese. Mix onion, eggs, cream, parsley, salt and pepper. Pour over macaroni mixture. Drizzle with butter. Bake at 350°F. for 30 minutes, or until set.

6 servings

SEASHELLS AND TUNA

¼ cup minced onion
¼ cup butter or margarine
⅓ cup unsifted all-purpose flour
3 cups milk
1 cup shredded sharp cheese
1 teaspoon salt
Dash each pepper and nutmeg
1 can (7 ounces) tuna, drained and flaked
¼ cup chopped fresh parsley
2 tablespoons chopped pimento
½ package (8 ounces) SAN GIORGIO Large Shells
⅓ cup bread crumbs (optional)

Sauté onion in butter or margarine until soft, but not brown; blend in flour. Gradually add milk. Cook and stir constantly over medium heat until mixture begins to boil; boil and stir 1 minute. Remove from heat. Add sharp cheese, salt, pepper and nutmeg; blend well until cheese is melted. Stir in tuna, parsley and pimento; keep warm over low heat. Cook Large Shells according to package directions; drain. Toss with warm sauce mixture; serve immediately. **OR** turn shell mixture into a buttered 2-quart casserole. Sprinkle with bread crumbs; bake at 350° for 25 minutes.

4 to 6 servings

IDEAL SHELL—TUNA SURPRISE RING

1 lb. IDEAL Small Shells
1 can whole green beans
Water
¼ cup butter or margarine
⅓ cup flour
1 tsp. salt
Parsley
½ cup pimientos, chopped
4 eggs, slightly beaten
1 cup process American cheese, grated
1 can (6½ to 7 oz.) tuna, drained and flaked
⅓ tsp. salt
¼ cup butter or margarine
Pepper

Cook IDEAL Small Shells according to package directions. Drain liquid from beans and reserve. Add enough water to make 2 cups liquid. Heat ¼ cup butter over low heat. Add flour and blend. Gradually add 2 cups reserved liquid and cook until thickened, stirring constantly. Add 1 tsp. salt, parsley, pimientos, eggs, cheese and tuna. Mix thoroughly. Add macaroni and mix lightly. Turn into greased 3 qt. ring mold. Place in pan of hot water and bake in 350° oven for 45 minutes, or until done. Meanwhile, combine beans, remaining ¼ cup butter, ⅓ tsp. salt and pepper. Cover; cook over low heat until thoroughly heated. Unmold shell macaroni-tuna ring and turn green beans into center.
Makes 6-8 servings

PIZZERIA MACARONI

7-oz. package CREAMETTES® Macaroni (2 cups uncooked)
1 lb. ground beef
1 medium onion, finely chopped
2 cans (8-oz. each) tomato sauce, or 2 cans condensed tomato soup
1 teaspoon salt
½ teaspoon Italian seasoning
½ teaspoon oregano
¼ teaspoon pepper
⅛ teaspoon garlic powder
½ cup milk
1 egg
¼ to ½ lb. Mozzarella or Cheddar cheese, grated or thin sliced

Prepare CREAMETTES® according to package directions. Drain. Brown ground beef and onion.

Drain excess fat. Add tomato sauce, ½ teaspoon salt, Italian seasoning, oregano, pepper, garlic powder. Simmer for 5 to 10 minutes. Beat milk, egg and ½ teaspoon salt together. Blend into macaroni and spread on a greased 10 x 15-inch jellyroll pan. Cover with meat mixture. Top with cheese. Bake at 350° for 20 minutes. Let stand 5-10 minutes before cutting.
6 servings

VARIATION:

Substitute a combination of 2 cups left-over meats such as roast beef, luncheon meat, frankfurters, bacon or sausage for the ground beef in the recipe.

TUNA-MACARONI MINGLE

1 can (10¾ ounces) CAMPBELL'S Condensed Cream of Chicken Soup
½ teaspoon salt
¼ teaspoon dried dill weed, crushed
⅛ teaspoon hot pepper sauce
3 cups cooked elbow macaroni
2 cans (about 7 ounces *each*) tuna, drained and flaked
2 hard-cooked eggs, chopped
½ cup diagonally sliced celery
¼ cup sliced ripe olives
Salad greens
Cherry tomatoes, cut in half
Sliced cucumber

In bowl, blend soup, salt, dill and hot pepper sauce. Lightly toss with macaroni, tuna, eggs, celery, and olives. Chill. Serve on salad greens. Garnish with tomatoes and cucumbers.
Makes about 7 cups, 4 servings

BUDGET-STRETCHING DINNER

1 pound ground beef
1 large onion, chopped
1 clove garlic, minced
1 can (1 lb.) tomatoes
Water
⅓ cup KIKKOMAN Soy Sauce
1½ teaspoons chili powder
2 cups elbow macaroni, uncooked
4 ounces shredded Cheddar cheese

Brown beef. Stir in onions and garlic; cook until onions are translucent. Cut up tomatoes, reserving liquid. Combine liquid with enough water to measure 3 cups; stir liquid into beef mixture with tomatoes, soy sauce and chili powder. Bring to boil. Place macaroni and cheese in shallow baking pan; add hot meat mixture and stir to combine. Bake in 350°F. oven 15 minutes. Gently stir mixture and bake 15 minutes longer or until macaroni is tender, yet firm. Stir again before serving.
Makes 6 servings

NOODLES ROMANOFF

4 chicken or beef bouillon cubes
4 cups boiling water
8 ounces fine noodles
1½ cups SEALTEST® Cottage Cheese
1 cup SEALTEST® Sour Cream
1 small onion, minced
½ teaspoon salt
¼ teaspoon thyme
¼ teaspoon garlic salt
½ cup bread crumbs

Dissolve chicken or beef bouillon cubes in boiling water. Cook noodles in broth until tender. Do not drain. Stir cottage cheese, sour cream, onion and seasonings into hot cooked undrained noodles. Mix until blended. Turn into a shallow 10-cup baking dish. Top with crumbs. Bake, uncovered, in a preheated 350° oven for 25 minutes. Serve hot. *6 servings*

PARMESAN NOODLES

1 can (10¾ ounces) CAMPBELL'S Condensed Cream of Mushroom Soup
¾ cup milk
½ cup grated Parmesan cheese
3 cups hot cooked noodles
¼ cup butter or margarine

In large saucepan, stir soup until smooth; blend in milk and cheese. Heat; stir occasionally. Just before serving, toss hot noodles with butter; combine with soup mixture. Serve with additional cheese.
Makes about 3½ cups

Rice

MUSHROOM SKILLET RICE

¾ cup chopped onion
¾ cup long-grain white rice
2 tablespoons butter
1 cup sliced DOLE® Fresh Mushrooms
1 can (10¾ oz.) condensed chicken broth
1 cup water
1 medium tomato, peeled and diced
1½ teaspoons chili powder
¾ teaspoon salt
½ teaspoon marjoram, crumbled
1 cup diced cooked ham
¼ cup chopped parsley

Sauté onion and rice in butter 5 minutes. Add mushrooms, broth, water, tomato, chili powder, salt, marjoram and ham. Heat to boiling. Cover tightly and simmer 20 minutes. Stir in parsley. Let stand covered 5 minutes before serving.   *Makes 4 servings*

RICE WITH ZUCCHINI

1 pound small zucchini, cut into ½″ slices
½ cup BERTOLLI® Olive Oil
1 clove garlic, minced
¼ teaspoon dried basil leaves
¼ cup finely chopped onion
1½ cups Italian or long grain converted rice
4½ to 5 cups chicken broth
⅓ cup grated Parmesan cheese
2 tablespoons diced pimento
Freshly ground pepper

Sauté zucchini in oil in Dutch oven until lightly browned. Remove zucchini from pan. Sauté onion, garlic, basil, and rice in remaining oil for one minute. Stir in ½ cup broth; cook on medium-high heat, stirring constantly, until broth is absorbed. Continue the process of adding broth and letting it absorb until rice is *al dente*, about 30 minutes. Stir in cheese, pimento, zucchini and pepper to taste.
          Makes 4-6 servings

GRECIAN RICE

3 tablespoons butter or margarine
½ cup finely chopped onion
½ cup finely chopped green pepper
2 cloves garlic, minced or pressed
1 cup long grain rice
2 cups beef bouillon
1 teaspoon cinnamon
½ teaspoon salt
⅔ cup BLUE DIAMOND® Chopped Natural Almonds
½ cup dark, seedless raisins

In large skillet melt butter; sauté onion, green pepper and garlic until barely tender. Add rice and cook, stirring often, until lightly toasted, about 4 to 6 minutes. Stir in bouillon, cinnamon and salt; cover and simmer 10 minutes. Stir in almonds and raisins; continue cooking, covered, another 5 minutes or until all liquid is absorbed.   *Makes 4 servings*

DORMAN'S ALMOND CRUNCH RICE

½ cup diced almonds
¼ cup butter, melted
3 cups cooked rice (1 cup raw)
8 DORMAN'S Dorelle Wedges, shredded

Add almonds to butter and cook until butter is slightly browned. Drain rice after cooking, if necessary, and toss immediately with cheese. Add almonds and butter and toss again. Season to taste and serve hot.
          Makes 4 servings

ITALIAN SAUSAGE RICE & CEREAL DRESSING

½ pound Italian sausage
½ cup chopped onion
½ cup chopped celery
½ cup uncooked rice
1½ cups water
½ teaspoon salt
1½ cups HEARTLAND® Natural Cereal, Plain Variety

Brown sausage with onion and celery. Add rice, water and salt. Heat to boiling. Cover and reduce heat. Simmer 15 to 20 minutes or until done. Gently toss in cereal. Cover. Let steam 5 minutes. Serve warm with hamburgers.
          Makes 1 quart

RICE MEDLEY

1 bag SUCCESS® Rice
1 jar (2½ oz.) sliced mushrooms, drained
2 tablespoons sliced green onion
2 tablespoons butter or margarine
1 pkg. (10 oz.) frozen sweet peas
½ cup water
1 packet instant chicken flavored broth
1 teaspoon cornstarch

Cook bag of rice according to package directions. While rice is cooking, sauté mushrooms and onion in butter. Stir in peas, water, and chicken broth. Bring to a boil, cover, lower heat and simmer 10 minutes. Combine cornstarch with 2 teaspoons water. Stir into pea mixture. Heat until thickened. Add to hot, cooked rice; stir well.
          Makes 6 servings (½ cup each)

OYSTER BEEF RICE

1 can (8 oz.) BUMBLE BEE® Whole Oysters
1 pound boneless chuck steak
1 tablespoon diced gingerroot
2 tablespoons oil
¾ cup water
2 tablespoons soy sauce
1 teaspoon cornstarch
4 stalks green onion, cut in 2-inch strips
Hot fluffy rice

Drain oysters, reserving liquid. Cut steak into thin strips. Brown steak with gingerroot in oil. Combine reserved oyster liquid, water, soy sauce and cornstarch. Pour into beef and cook until sauce is clear and thickened. Remove from heat. Stir in oysters and onion. Cover and steam to heat through. Serve with hot fluffy rice.
          Makes 4 servings

LINDSAY® PARMESAN RICE

Cook 1½ cups rice and ½ cup chopped onion slowly in ½ cup butter, stirring until lightly browned. Add 3 cups hot broth. Cover; cook slowly 10 minutes. Add 1 cup white wine (or broth), 3 tomatoes, chopped, 1½ teaspoons salt, dash pepper. Cook 12 minutes. Stir in ¾ cup grated Parmesan and 1 cup LINDSAY® Pitted Ripe Olives cut into wedges. Heat thoroughly.
          Makes 6-8 servings

Uncle Ben's®
FRIED RICE

1 cup UNCLE BEN'S®
   CONVERTED® Brand Rice
2 cups chopped cooked pork*
¼ cup cooking oil
2 eggs, lightly beaten
¼ teaspoon black pepper
2 tablespoons soy sauce
½ cup chopped green onions

Cook UNCLE BEN'S®
CONVERTED® Brand Rice
according to package directions.
Fry pork in oil until coated and
heated, about 1 minute, stirring
constantly. Add eggs and pepper
and fry over medium heat for 5
minutes, stirring constantly. Add
cooked rice and soy sauce. Fry,
stirring frequently, about 5
minutes. Sprinkle green onions
over top and serve.   *Serves 5-6*

*Diced cooked shrimp, ham or
chicken may be used in place of
pork.

CALICO RICE

6 slices bacon
1½ cups sliced fresh mushrooms
   (about ¼ pound)
1 cup diagonally sliced celery
½ cup sliced green onions
2 cans (10½ ounces *each*)
   FRANCO-AMERICAN Au Jus or
   Chicken Giblet Gravy
2½ cups quick-cooking rice,
   uncooked
½ cup shredded carrot
½ teaspoon poultry seasoning
Carrot curls
Parsley

In skillet, cook bacon until crisp;
remove and crumble. Pour off all
but 2 tablespoons drippings. Brown
mushrooms and cook celery and
onions in drippings until tender.
Add remaining ingredients; cover.
Bring to boil; reduce heat. Simmer
10 minutes or until done; stir
occasionally. Garnish with carrot
curls and parsley.

Makes about 5 cups, 10 servings

RICE CASSEROLE NOIR

2 cans peeled green chilies
3 cups sour cream
1 cup LINDSAY® Sliced Ripe
   Olives
3 cups cooked rice
Salt and pepper to taste
½ pound mild cheese (Monterey
   type)
1 cup grated Cheddar cheese
Paprika

Chop chilies and mix with sour
cream and 1 cup sliced ripe olives.
Cut cheese in 1-inch strips. Season
rice with salt and pepper and place
a layer in a 2-quart casserole
slathered with butter. Next a layer
of the sour cream mixture, a layer
of cheese strips . . . and repeat.
Top layer must be rice. Bake 25
minutes in 350 degree F. oven.
Cover top with grated cheese,
sprinkle with paprika and dot with
whole pitted ripe olives. Bake
another five minutes to allow the
cheese to melt.   *Serves six*

RICE WITH SPINACH
AND WATER CHESTNUTS

¼ cup chopped onion
3 tablespoons butter
1½ cups cooked ELAM'S®
   Organically Grown Short Grain
   Brown Rice*
¼ cup liquid from rice or water
½ cup sliced water chestnuts
¼ teaspoon salt
1 package (10 ounce) frozen
   chopped spinach, cooked and
   drained
2 tablespoons grated or shredded
   Parmesan cheese

Cook onion in butter until tender,
not brown. Stir in rice and reserved
rice liquid or water, water
chestnuts and salt; mix. Fold in
spinach; heat. Spoon into serving
dish. Sprinkle cheese over top.
Yield: 4 servings

*To cook ELAM'S® Organically
Grown Short Grain Brown Rice
rinse ½ cup rice in cold water.
Place in saucepan; add ½
teaspoon salt and 2 cups cold
water and bring to a boil. Reduce
heat; cover and simmer until rice
is tender, about 1 hour. Drain,
saving any liquid.
Yield: 1½ cups cooked rice

BROWN RICE
POTPOURRI

¾ cup SUNSWEET® Pitted
   Prunes
¾ cup chopped onion
2 tablespoons butter or margarine
1 cup uncooked quick-cooking
   brown rice
1 can (8 ounces) stewed tomatoes
¼ cup diced green pepper
1 cup water
2 teaspoons lemon juice
2 chicken bouillon cubes, crumbled
¼ teaspoon salt
¼ teaspoon dill weed
½ small bay leaf
⅛ teaspoon pepper

Cut prunes into quarters. In a
2-quart saucepan, sauté onion in
butter until soft but not brown. Stir
in remaining ingredients. Bring
mixture to a boil, turn heat low,
cover and simmer 15 minutes or
just until rice is tender and most of
the liquid absorbed.

Makes 4 servings (3⅔ cups)

WILD RICE BROCCOLI
BAKE

1 package (6 ounces) UNCLE
   BEN'S® Long Grain & Wild Rice
1 cup sliced celery
2 packages (10 ounces each)
   frozen broccoli spears, cooked
   and drained
3 tablespoons butter or margarine
3 tablespoons flour
¼ teaspoon salt
2 cups milk
1 chicken bouillon cube, crushed
½ cup grated Parmesan cheese
1 tablespoon lemon juice

Cook contents of rice and
seasoning packets according to
package directions. Stir in celery.
Spoon into shallow 2-quart
casserole; arrange broccoli spears
over top. Melt butter in saucepan;
stir in flour and salt. Gradually add
milk and bouillon. Cook, stirring
constantly, until thickened and
smooth. Stir in ¼ cup cheese and
lemon juice. Pour over broccoli.
Sprinkle with remaining cheese.
Bake in 375°F. oven until hot and
bubbly, about 20 minutes.

Makes 6 to 8 servings

Stuffed Cabbage **(Tabasco®)**

Corny Dogs **(Wolf® Brand)**

Beef Ragout, Stuffed Cabbage Rolls, Shanghai Chicken and Vegetables **(Campbell's)**

Chinese Pork and Vegetable Stir-Fry **(John Morrell®)**

All-American Sausage Stew **(Eckrich®)**

One Dish **Roni-Mac®** Chili

Buddig Turkey Bonnets

Confetti Smokie Skillet **(Oscar Mayer)**

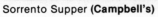

Sorrento Supper **(Campbell's)**

Sausage N' Rice Skillet Supper **(Hillshire Farm®)**

Speedy Baked Beans with Wieners **(Oscar Mayer)**

Chicken Divan Roll-Up **(Underwood®)**

Buddig Meat 'N' Potatoes Au Gratin

Vienna Beef® Polish Sausage Polonaise, Knockwurst Paella, Franks Hawaiian

Turkey and Wild Rice Casserole **(Shoal Lake)**

Sausage Hash **(Jimmy Dean®)**

Buddig Ham, Cheese & Macaroni Casserole

Chili Pie Casserole **(Fritos®)**

Frankly Mexican Casserole **(French's®)**

Turku Layered Casserole **(Finlandia Cheese)**

Shrimp Noodle Dinner Casserole **(National Marine Fisheries Service)**

Bacon and Egg Casserole **(Kellogg's®)**

Twisty Beef Bake **(Durkee)**

Zucchini and Cheese Casserole **(Bertolli®)**

Hot Chicken Salad **(Taylor Wine)**

Rice-A-Roni® Egg Fu Yung

Golden Eggs in a Nest **(French's®)**

Baked Spicy Sausage Omelet **(Jimmy Dean®)**

Ham 'N Cheese Pie **(Gerber®)**

Down Home Sausage and Cheese Pie **(Hillshire Farm®)**

Salmon Quiche **(Bumble Bee®)**

Eggs Benjamin **(Lender's)**

Buddig Reuben Quiche

Walnut Prune Soufflé **(Gerber®)**

Lasagne Roll-Ups **(American Beauty®)**

Baked Manicotti **(Ragu')**

Ravioli with Shrimp Sauce Supreme (**Jeno's®**)

Cool and Green Rice Salad (**Success®**)

Rotini Tetrazzini (**San Giorgio**)

Ideal Shell-Tuna Surprise Ring

Hurry-Up Spaghetti 'N Ham (**Mueller's®**)

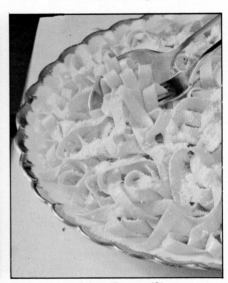

Fettuccine Alfredo (**Ronzoni®**)

Calico Rice (**Franco-American**)

Seashells and Tuna (**San Giorgio**)

Rice with Zucchini **(Bertolli®)**

Manicotti Supreme **(Hunt·Wesson)**

Summer Chef Salad **(Durkee)**

Chicken Salad Ambrosia **(Swanson)**

Italian Salad **(Brownberry®)**

California Fruit Salad Rosé **(Knox®)**

Cucumber Parsley Dressing **(Dannon®)**

Free-Style, Herb, and Italian Dressings
(Mazola®)

Caesar Salad **(Leafy Greens Council)**

Taco Salad **(Wyler's®)**

Sun World® Summer Salad

Health-Kick Pear Salad **(Libby's)**

South Pacific Seafood Bowl
(California Iceberg Lettuce Comm.)

Wikiwiki Yumiyumi **(Calavo®)**

Big Burger Slaw **(Heinz)**

Sauerkraut Salad **(Claussen)**

Lemon-Ginger Chicken Salad
(Hellmann's®/Best Foods®)

Elam's®

GREEN PEPPERS WITH BROWN RICE STUFFING

4 medium size green peppers
½ pound ground beef chuck or round
⅓ cup finely chopped onion
⅓ cup finely chopped celery
1 tablespoon shortening
1½ cups cooked ELAM'S® Organically Grown Short Grain Brown Rice*
1 can (8 ounce) tomato sauce
¼ cup liquid from rice or water
¾ teaspoon salt
½ teaspoon chili powder
Dash of pepper

Cut green peppers in half lengthwise. Remove seeds and membranes; wash. Blanch in boiling water to soften slightly, about 4 minutes; drain. Cook beef, onion and celery in shortening until beef is crumbly and grey in color. Add remaining ingredients; mix well. Spoon an equal amount of mixture into green pepper shells. Arrange in shallow baking dish. Bake in moderate oven (350°F.) until rice mixture is hot and pepper shells tender, 20 to 25 minutes. *Yield: 4 servings*

*To cook ELAM'S® Organically Grown Short Grain Brown Rice rinse ½ cup rice in cold water. Place in saucepan; add ½ teaspoon salt and 2 cups cold water and bring to a boil. Reduce heat; cover and simmer until rice is tender, about 1 hour. Drain, saving any liquid.
Yield: 1½ cups cooked rice

PILAF EXTRAORDINAIRE

¼ cup butter or margarine
1½ cups uncooked rice
½ teaspoon salt
⅛ teaspoon saffron, crumbled
Dash of pepper
2 cans (10½ oz. each) condensed beef consommé
¼ cup water
1 medium onion
¾ cup raisins

Melt 2 tablespoons of the butter in heavy skillet. Add rice; cook over medium heat, stirring occasionally, until golden brown. Add seasonings, consommé and water. Cover and simmer 20 to 25 minutes, or until rice is tender. Meanwhile, thinly slice onion and sauté in remaining 2 tablespoons butter until soft and tender; set aside. Stir raisins into cooked rice; let stand 5 minutes before serving. Mound rice on serving platter and garnish with sautéed onions.
Makes 6 to 8 servings

Favorite recipe from California Raisin Advisory Board

APRICOT PILAFF
(Low Cholesterol)

1½ tablespoons margarine (made with liquid corn or safflower oil)
1 medium onion, chopped
1 cup converted rice
1 teaspoon salt
2½ cups water
1 can (17 ounces) apricot halves, drained & quartered
¼ cup chopped parsley

Melt margarine in heavy, medium saucepan. Add onion; sauté over medium heat, stirring constantly, until shiny. Add rice and sauté until rice is golden. Stir in salt and water; bring to a boil. Cover and cook over low heat until liquid is absorbed. Gently fold in apricots and parsley; heat to serving temperature.
Makes 6 servings

Favorite recipe from California Apricot Advisory Board

PILAF

½ cup fine noodles, broken in pieces
2 tablespoons butter or margarine
1 can (10¾ ounces) CAMPBELL'S Condensed Chicken Broth
⅓ cup water
½ cup raw regular rice

In saucepan, brown noodles in butter; stir often. Add remaining ingredients. Bring to a boil; reduce heat. Cover; cook over low heat 20 minutes or until liquid is absorbed. Stir occasionally.
Makes about 2 cups

GOLDEN RICE SALAD
(Low Calorie)

1 bag SUCCESS® Rice
2 hard-cooked eggs, diced
1 cup diced celery
¼ cup sliced green onion
¼ cup diced dill pickle
½ cup mayonnaise
¾ teaspoon salt

Cook bag of rice according to package directions. Drain, empty into mixing bowl and cool. Add remaining ingredients and toss lightly. Serve on lettuce and garnish with green olives, tomato wedges or radish roses. Stuffed olives may be used instead of pickle. *Makes 6 servings (about ½ cup each)*

227 calories per serving

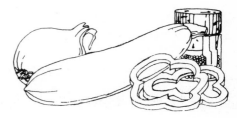

TWICE AS NICE RICE SALAD

½ cup WISH-BONE® Italian Dressing
½ cup mayonnaise
Suggested Fresh Vegetables*
2 tablespoons finely chopped fresh parsley, basil or dill
2 tablespoons finely chopped onion
3 cups cooked rice

In large bowl, blend Italian dressing with mayonnaise; stir in vegetables, parsley and onion. Add rice and toss well; pack into 5½ cup ring mold or bowl; chill. Garnish center, if desired, with vegetables tossed with Italian dressing.
Makes 6 to 8 servings

*Use any combination of the following chopped or shredded to equal 1½ cups: carrots, cucumbers, green pepper, mushrooms, radishes, tomato or zucchini.

Uncle Ben's®

BETTER-THAN-POTATO SALAD

1 cup UNCLE BEN'S®
  CONVERTED® Brand Rice
2 cups mayonnaise or salad
  dressing
2 cups sliced celery
1 medium onion, finely chopped
4 teaspoons prepared mustard
½ teaspoon salt
4 hard-cooked eggs, chopped
8 radishes, sliced
1 cucumber, pared and diced

Cook rice according to package
directions. Chill. Add mayonnaise
or salad dressing, celery, onion,
mustard and salt; mix well. Chill.
Stir in eggs, radishes and
cucumber before serving.

Makes 6 to 8 servings

COOL AND GREEN RICE SALAD
(Low Calorie)

1 bag SUCCESS® Rice
2 small or 1 large zucchini
1 or 2 green onions, sliced
3 tablespoons bottled creamy
  Italian dressing
¼ teaspoon black pepper
1 avocado
1 tablespoon lemon juice

Cook bag of rice according to
cooking directions; but cook 20
minutes. During last five minutes,
gently place the zucchini on top of
the bag and let steam. With tongs,
remove zucchini to cutting board.
Cut off ends and slice zucchini
into ¼" pieces. Drain bag and
empty rice into mixing bowl. Add
the zucchini, green onion, dressing,
and black pepper. Chill. Just
before serving, peel the avocado,
slice and dip in the lemon juice.
Arrange around the salad or gently
toss with it.

*Makes 6 servings
(about ½ cup each)*

174 calories per serving

Dumplings

SOUP 'N DUMPLINGS

¾ cup milk
¼ teaspoon salt
¼ cup CREAM OF WHEAT®
  Cereal, Regular, Quick or Instant
  (Uncooked)
1 tablespoon butter or margarine
1 egg
½ teaspoon parsley flakes
3 cups hot soup*

Bring milk and salt to a boil in a
small saucepan; slowly sprinkle in
CREAM OF WHEAT® Cereal,
stirring constantly. Return to a
boil, then lower heat and cook until
very thick, a few minutes. Remove
from heat and beat in butter or
margarine and egg until well
mixed. Stir in parsley. Drop the
mixture by heaping teaspoonfuls
into hot soup in medium saucepan.
Simmer, covered, 8 to 10 minutes.
Makes 12 (1½-inch) dumplings.

Makes 4 (about 1 cup) servings

*Note: 3 cups water and 4 bouillon
cubes may be used or any soup
of your choice.

GRAPE DUMPLINGS

2 cups flour
4 teaspoons baking powder
¼ teaspoon salt
⅓ cup sugar
⅓ cup butter
¾ cup milk
4 cups WELCH'S® Grape Juice
1 jar (10 ounces) WELCH'S®
  Grape Jam
2 tablespoons lemon juice

Sift flour, baking powder, salt and
1 tablespoon sugar. Cut in butter
using pastry blender or two knives
until mixture resembles coarse
meal. Stir in milk until mixture
leaves sides of bowl. Roll out on
lightly floured board and cut into
2-inch squares. In large heavy
saucepan, heat WELCH'S® Grape
Juice, WELCH'S® Grape Jam,
remaining sugar and lemon juice to
boiling. Add dumplings. Cover and
simmer 20 minutes or until tender.
Serve hot.   *Makes 4 servings*

ALMOND DUMPLINGS

1½ cups fine HI HO® Cracker
  crumbs (36 crackers)
¼ cup finely chopped or ground
  blanched almonds
½ cup milk
1 egg, beaten
3 tablespoons melted butter or
  margarine
½ teaspoon salt
⅛ teaspoon white pepper
⅛ teaspoon ground nutmeg

Prepare crumbs, a little at a time,
in an electric blender or crush with
a rolling pin between two sheets of
waxed paper. Combine with
remaining ingredients in order
given. Mix well.
Yield: about one dozen dumplings

BUCKWHEAT DUMPLINGS FOR TOPPING STEW

2 cups ELAM'S® Pure Buckwheat
  Flour
4 teaspoons baking powder
1 teaspoon salt
¼ teaspoon pepper
¾ cup milk
1 egg
3 tablespoons cooking oil or
  melted shortening

Combine first 4 ingredients; sift
into bowl. Combine milk, egg and
oil or melted shortening; beat. Add
to dry ingredients; stir just until dry
ingredients are moistened. Drop
tablespoonfuls of mixture into
simmering stew. Cover pan tightly;
cook until done, about 15 minutes,
without lifting cover.
Yield: 12 dumplings

DUMPLINGS FOR CHICKEN OR MEAT STEW

2 cups sifted E-Z-BAKE Flour
1 teaspoon salt (scant)
5 teaspoons baking powder
¾ cup milk

Combine dry ingredients and mix
thoroughly. Stir in milk. Drop
mixture from spoon into broth.
Cover closely. Boil slowly 12
minutes *without lifting cover.* Serve
immediately.

Salads and Salad Dressings

Main Dish Salads

CHICKEN POTATO SALAD

1½ pounds small new potatoes, pared
1 can (10¾ ounces) condensed chicken broth, undiluted
Mustard Dressing (recipe follows)
1 cup diced cooked chicken
1 cup sliced celery
½ cup sliced pimiento-stuffed green olives
½ cup chopped toasted DIAMOND® Walnuts
¼ cup sliced green onion
1 tablespoon chopped parsley
Crisp lettuce leaves

Cook potatoes, covered, in chicken broth until tender. Drain potatoes, reserving broth. Prepare Mustard Dressing. Slice potatoes and combine with chicken, celery, olives, walnuts, onion and parsley. Add cooled Mustard Dressing and toss lightly. Chill. Serve on lettuce.
Makes 6 servings (about 6¼ cups)

MUSTARD DRESSING

Mix together in small saucepan, 2 tablespoons oil, 1 tablespoon flour, ¾ teaspoon salt and ⅛ teaspoon *each* pepper and paprika. Measure broth reserved from cooking potatoes; add water if needed to measure ½ cup. Add to saucepan, along with 3 tablespoons tarragon-flavored wine vinegar and 1 teaspoon Dijon mustard. Cook, stirring constantly, until mixture boils and thickens. Stir into one lightly beaten egg yolk. Return to low heat and cook about a half minute longer, stirring briskly. Cool.

CRUNCHY CHICKEN SALAD

½ cup chopped, toasted peanuts
½ cup toasted sesame seeds
2 generous cups cooked chicken, cubed
¼ cup finely chopped onion
2 tablespoons soy sauce
2 tablespoons HOLLAND HOUSE® Red Cooking Wine
⅔ cup mayonnaise

To toast nuts and sesame seeds, spread in shallow pan, place in 350° oven for 8 to 10 minutes, stirring often. When cooled, combine with chicken and chopped onion. In a separate bowl, blend soy sauce, wine and mayonnaise. Pour over chicken mixture, tossing thoroughly. Serve chilled on lettuce leaves. *Serves 4*

Lindsay®
CHICKEN SALAD AMANDINE

2 cups cooked chicken, cubed
½ cup celery, thinly sliced
¼ cup LINDSAY® Chopped Ripe Olives
2 tablespoons sweet pickles, diced
3 tablespoons toasted almonds, slivered
½ cup mayonnaise
½ teaspoon salt
1 teaspoon tarragon
2 tablespoons garlic wine vinegar

Combine chicken, celery, chopped olives, pickles, almonds, mayonnaise, salt, garlic wine vinegar and tarragon in a large bowl—toss until completely mixed. Chill thoroughly. Serve garnished with slivered almonds and parsley.
Makes two luncheon salads

CHICKEN SALAD SUPREME

3 5-oz. cans BANQUET® Boned Chicken, drained and cubed
1½ cups thinly sliced celery
3 Tbsp. lemon juice
1 cup seedless grapes
4 ripe olives, sliced
2 Tbsp. sliced pimiento
½ tsp. dry mustard
1 tsp. salt
¼ tsp. pepper
Dash ground allspice
2 tsp. capers
½ cup mayonnaise
½ cup toasted slivered almonds or nut meats
Endive
Black olives
Pimiento strips

Combine chicken, celery and lemon juice. Chill. Add grapes, olives and pimiento. Combine mustard, salt, pepper, allspice, capers and mayonnaise; add to chicken mixture. Toss lightly. Add almonds; toss again. Serve on beds of endive, garnished with olives and pimiento.

6-8 servings

LEMON-GINGER CHICKEN SALAD
(Low Cholesterol)

¾ cup HELLMANN'S® or BEST
  FOODS® Real Mayonnaise
1 tablespoon sugar
½ teaspoon grated lemon rind
1 tablespoon lemon juice
½ teaspoon ground ginger
¼ teaspoon salt
2 cups cooked cubed chicken
1 cup seedless green grapes
1 cup sliced celery

In large bowl stir together first
6 ingredients. Add chicken, grapes
and celery; toss to coat well.
Cover; chill at least 2 hours. If
desired, serve in lettuce cups and
garnish with toasted almonds.

Makes 4 servings

80 mg cholesterol per serving.

SERENDIPITY SALAD
(Low Calorie)

1 can (5 ounces) SWANSON Chunk
  White or Thigh Chicken
2 cups salad greens torn in bite-
  size pieces
1 cup cauliflowerets
½ cup cherry tomatoes cut in half
1 small onion, sliced
⅓ cup bottled low-calorie Italian
  dressing

In bowl, combine all ingredients
except dressing. Toss lightly with
dressing.

Makes about 5 cups, 3 servings

About 115 calories per serving.

GARDEN STYLE CHICKEN SALAD

1 cup broccoli flowerets
1 cup cauliflowerets
½ cup diagonally sliced carrot
½ cup cherry tomatoes cut in half
1 can (5 ounces) SWANSON Chunk
  White or Thigh Chicken
⅔ cup salad oil
⅓ cup wine vinegar
2 teaspoons honey
1 teaspoon salt
¼ teaspoon pepper

To make salad, in saucepan, cook
broccoli, cauliflowerets and carrot
in boiling water 3 minutes; drain. In
shallow dish, arrange cooked
vegetables, tomatoes and chicken.

To make marinade, combine
remaining ingredients; pour over

salad. Chill 6 hours or more. Stir
occasionally. Serve with slotted
spoon.

Makes about 3 cups, 2 servings

CHICKEN SALAD AMBROSIA

¼ cup bottled Italian dressing
¼ cup orange juice
1 teaspoon honey
1 tablespoon toasted sesame seed
⅛ teaspoon grated orange rind
2 cans (5 ounces *each*) SWANSON
  Chunk Chicken
6 cups salad greens torn in bite-
  size pieces
1 cup sliced cucumber
½ cup sliced radishes
½ cup green pepper strips
½ cup orange sections cut-up
1 small red onion sliced

To make salad dressing, in bowl,
combine bottled dressing, orange
juice, honey, sesame seed and
orange rind; chill. In large bowl,
combine remaining ingredients.
Serve with salad dressing.

Makes about 9 cups, 6 servings

CHINESE CHICKEN ON A RAFT

1 head iceberg lettuce
Soy-Anise Dressing*
2 boned, skinned half breasts of
  chicken
1 tablespoon flour
1/16 teaspoon paprika
1 tablespoon oil
½ cup blanched pea pods
  (3 ounces)
½ cup sliced water chestnuts
½ cup sliced fresh mushrooms
½ cup halved cherry tomatoes
¼ cup alfalfa sprouts
2 tablespoons sliced green onion

Core, rinse and drain lettuce; chill
in disposable plastic bag or plastic
crisper. Prepare Soy-Anise
Dressing. Cut chicken into 1-inch
strips. Dust with mixture of flour
and paprika. Heat oil in skillet, add
chicken and sauté until browned,
stirring frequently. Remove from
heat and combine chicken with ½
cup dressing. Marinate in
refrigerator an hour or longer.
Shortly before serving, add pea
pods, water chestnuts,
mushrooms, tomatoes, alfalfa
sprouts and green onion to
chicken. Slice lettuce crosswise
into 4 "rafts," each about 1 inch

thick. Place each on an individual
salad plate. Top "rafts" with
chicken mixture and serve at once,
passing remaining Soy-Anise
Dressing.

Makes 4 servings

*SOY-ANISE DRESSING

Measure ½ cup oil, ⅓ cup rice
vinegar, 1 tablespoon *each* soy
sauce and brown sugar, ¼
teaspoon ground ginger and 1/16
teaspoon anise seed, crushed, into
a jar. Cover tightly and shake well
to blend. Shake again just before
serving.

Makes 1 cup dressing

*Favorite recipe from California Iceberg
Lettuce Commission*

CHICKEN COCKTAIL SALAD

½ cup mayonnaise or salad
  dressing
1 Tablespoon cream or milk
1 teaspoon lemon juice
¼ teaspoon nutmeg
⅛ teaspoon curry powder
2 whole cooked chicken breasts,
  diced
1 can (1 lb. 14 oz.) STOKELY'S
  FINEST® Fruit Cocktail, drained
  and chilled
¼ cup slivered toasted almonds

Combine first 5 ingredients. Fold in
chicken and chill 30 minutes. Add
Fruit Cocktail and almonds. Serve
on lettuce leaves.

Makes 5 servings

PLANTERS® CHICKEN SALAD

4 cups cubed cooked chicken
1 cup chopped celery
1 cup halved seedless green
  grapes
1 teaspoon salt
¼ teaspoon pepper
¾ cup mayonnaise
¼ cup sour cream
1 cup coarsely chopped
  PLANTERS® Mixed Nuts (salted
  or unsalted)
Crisp lettuce

Combine chicken, celery and
grapes in a large bowl. Sprinkle
with salt and pepper. Add
mayonnaise and sour cream; mix
thoroughly. Chill. Toss nuts lightly
with chicken. Serve on lettuce.

Makes about 8 servings

GREEN 'N GOLD CHICKEN SALAD WITH ORANGE POPPY SEED DRESSING

6 to 8 cups assorted salad greens (iceberg, romaine, Bibb)
1½ to 2 cups cooked chicken cut in strips
3 to 4 SUNKIST® Oranges, peeled, sliced in half-cartwheels
3 to 4 hard-cooked eggs, cut in wedges
1 avocado, sliced
1 cup diagonally sliced celery
⅓ cup thinly sliced green onion
Orange Poppy Seed Dressing (recipe follows)

In large bowl, combine salad greens, chicken, oranges, eggs, avocado, celery and onion. Serve with Orange Poppy Seed Dressing.
Makes 6 servings (about 12 cups)

ORANGE POPPY SEED DRESSING

⅔ cup salad oil
2 tsp. fresh grated SUNKIST® Orange peel
¼ cup fresh squeezed SUNKIST® Orange juice
3 Tbsp. vinegar
1 Tbsp. poppy seed
1 Tbsp. sugar
½ tsp. onion salt
½ tsp. salt

In jar with lid, combine all ingredients; chill. Shake well before using.
Makes about 1 cup

TATRA HAM AND CHICKEN SALAD

3 cups cut-up KRAKUS/ ATALANTA/POLKA Polish Ham
2 cups cut-up cooked chicken
1 cup diagonally sliced celery
1 cup cubed fresh or canned pineapple
½ cup finely chopped green pepper
½ cup halved green grapes
¼ cup light cream
2 teaspoons grated onion
⅔ cup mayonnaise
1 teaspoon salt
Generous dash pepper
2 tablespoons lemon juice
Salad greens
Toasted slivered almonds

Combine ham, chicken, celery, pineapple, green pepper, grapes and onion. Blend cream into mayonnaise; stir in salt, pepper and lemon juice. Toss dressing with ham mixture. Refrigerate until ready to serve. To serve, arrange salad on greens and garnish with almonds.   *Makes 6 to 8 servings*

MARINATED TURKEY BEAN SALAD

2 cups chopped roast BUTTERBALL® Turkey
8-ounce can wax beans, drained
8-ounce can kidney beans, drained
8-ounce can or 1 cup cooked lima beans
1 cup sliced celery
1 small red onion, sliced and separated into rings
¼ cup chopped green pepper
¼ teaspoon salt
½ cup sugar
½ cup vinegar
2 tablespoons oil

Toss together turkey and all vegetables. Combine remaining ingredients and pour over turkey-bean mixture, stirring only enough to moisten all. Cover and refrigerate several hours. Serve on lettuce with hot rolls or French bread.   *Yield: 4 servings*

TURKEY SALAD HAWAIIAN

1½ to 2 cups thin strips roast BUTTERBALL® Turkey
13-ounce can pineapple chunks, drained
1 red skinned apple, cored and chopped
½ cup sliced sweet pickles
6-ounce can water chestnuts, drained and sliced
1 teaspoon salt
½ cup mayonnaise
Lettuce
Shredded coconut

Combine all ingredients except the lettuce and coconut. Chill about 1 hour. Spoon into lettuce cups for individual servings. Top with shredded coconut.
Yield: 6 servings (6 cups)

ICEBERG TACO SALAD

1 head iceberg lettuce
1 pound lean ground beef
Vegetable oil
½ cup chopped onion (1 small onion)
1 can (8 ounce) tomato sauce
1 tablespoon chili powder
¾ teaspoon cumin powder
½ teaspoon salt
2 medium tomatoes, cut into wedges
1 small green pepper, cut into rings
⅓ cup pitted ripe olives
16 tortilla chips
1 small red onion, thinly sliced into rings
¼ cup grated Cheddar cheese
1 small avocado, cubed
Sour Cream Dressing*

Core, rinse and thoroughly drain lettuce; refrigerate in disposable plastic bag or plastic crisper. Shortly before serving, tear into bite-sized pieces enough lettuce to equal 2 quarts; set aside. Crumble ground beef into hot, lightly oiled large skillet. Add onion and sauté over high heat for 7 minutes or until beef is browned and the juices have evaporated. Stir in tomato sauce, chili powder, cumin and salt. Continue cooking over high heat for 2 minutes, stirring often. To arrange salads, place about 2 cups lettuce each on 4 salad plates. Spoon beef mixture onto lettuce. Top with tomato wedges, green pepper, ripe olives, tortilla chips, onion, cheese and avocado. Serve with Sour Cream Dressing.
Makes 4 servings

*SOUR CREAM DRESSING

Combine 1 cup dairy sour cream with ½ cup buttermilk, 1½ teaspoons oregano, ¼ teaspoon salt and ⅛ teaspoon pepper.
Makes 1½ cups

Favorite recipe from California Iceberg Lettuce Commission

TACO SALAD

1 pound lean ground beef
1 (16-ounce) can stewed tomatoes
1 (4-ounce) can chopped green
   chilies, drained
2 teaspoons WYLER'S® Beef-
   Flavor Instant Bouillon OR
   2 Beef-Flavor Bouillon Cubes
¼ teaspoon hot pepper sauce
⅛ teaspoon garlic powder
Dash pepper
1 quart shredded lettuce (1 medium
   head)
1 to 1½ cups corn chips
1 medium tomato, chopped (about
   1 cup)
1 cup (4 ounces) shredded Cheddar
   cheese

In large skillet, brown meat; pour
off fat. Add remaining ingredients
except lettuce, corn chips,
chopped tomato and cheese.
Simmer uncovered 30 minutes. In
large bowl or platter, arrange all
ingredients; toss to serve.
Refrigerate leftovers.
Makes 4 servings

STUFFED TOMATO
SALAD

1 package (10 ounces) frozen
   Italian-style vegetables (2 cups)
½ cup salted boiling water
½ cup mayonnaise
1 teaspoon lemon juice
½ teaspoon Italian herb seasoning
¼ teaspoon garlic salt
½ cup BLUE DIAMOND®
   Blanched Slivered Almonds,
   toasted
Salt and pepper
4 large tomatoes
Lettuce leaves

Cook vegetables in ½ cup salted
boiling water 2 to 3 minutes, until
just tender-crisp. Drain; refresh
under cold water; pat dry with
paper towels. In a bowl combine
mayonnaise, lemon juice, Italian
herb seasoning, and garlic salt;
add vegetables and almonds; salt
and pepper to taste. Refrigerate at
least half an hour. Core tomatoes
and remove seeds. Sprinkle
cavities lightly with salt and invert
on paper towels to drain. Just
before serving, spoon about ½ cup
vegetable mixture into each tomato
cavity. Arrange tomatoes on
lettuce leaves.
Makes 4 servings

WALNUT TUNA STUFFED
TOMATO

4 large or 6 medium tomatoes
1 can (6½ or 7 ounces) tuna
2 hard-cooked eggs, diced
2 thinly-sliced green onions
1 cup sliced celery
2 tablespoons chopped pickle
1 tablespoon chopped pimiento or
   green pepper
1 tablespoon capers
2 teaspoons lemon juice
1 teaspoon prepared mustard
¼ teaspoon salt
¼ cup mayonnaise
¾ cup chopped, toasted
   DIAMOND® Walnuts, divided

Peel tomatoes, sprinkle lightly with
salt and pepper; chill about two
hours. Mix tuna with next 9
ingredients; chill. At serving time,
add mayonnaise and ½ cup of the
walnuts; toss until blended. Turn
tomatoes stem-end down; cut each
one not-quite-through into 6 or 8
sections; spread apart. Fill with
salad mixture and top with
additional mayonnaise and
remaining walnuts.
Makes 4 to 6 stuffed tomatoes

DEVILED HAM STUFFED
TOMATOES

2 cans (4½ ounces each)
   UNDERWOOD® Deviled Ham
1 cup (4 ounces) shredded Swiss
   cheese
½ cup chopped pimento-stuffed
   olives
2 tablespoons chopped onion
4 medium tomatoes, cut into
   quarters, to within ¼ inch of
   bottom

In a bowl, mix together deviled
ham, cheese, olives and onion.
Spoon mixture into center of
tomatoes. Chill.   *Makes 4 servings*

TROPICANA SALAD

2 quarts torn salad greens
2 medium DOLE® Bananas, sliced
2 cups melon balls
2 cups ham strips
1 cup sliced strawberries
Curry Yogurt Dressing (recipe
   follows)

Toss salad greens, bananas, melon
balls, ham and strawberries in a
large bowl. Serve with Curry Yogurt
Dressing.
Makes 4 to 6 servings

CURRY YOGURT DRESSING

1 cup plain yogurt
2 tablespoons honey
1 tablespoon lime juice
1 teaspoon curry powder

Combine all ingredients.
Makes 1 cup dressing

HAM WALDORF SALAD

4 medium apples, quartered, cored,
   cubed
2 tablespoons lemon juice
2 cups cubed ARMOUR® STAR
   Ham
½ cup chopped celery
¼ cup chopped walnuts
¼ cup mayonnaise
¼ cup dairy sour cream
Dash of salt
Dash of pepper

In a large bowl, toss apples with
lemon juice. Add remaining
ingredients; mix well. Chill.
Preparation time: 15 minutes.
6 servings

SALMON TOSS

1 tart apple
3 teaspoons lemon juice
½ cup mayonnaise
⅛ teaspoon *each* chili powder,
   curry powder and ground
   coriander
1 can (7¾ ounces) salmon, drained
   and flaked
½ cup BLUE DIAMOND® Chopped
   Natural Almonds
½ cup coarsely chopped green or
   red pepper
¼ cup sliced green onion
Spinach leaves

Pare and coarsely grate apple; toss
with 2 teaspoons of the lemon
juice. In medium-size bowl blend
mayonnaise, the remaining
1 teaspoon lemon juice, chili
powder, curry powder and ground
coriander. Add salmon, apple,
almonds, green pepper and onion;
toss lightly. Serve on spinach
leaves.   *Makes 2 servings*

SHRIMP MANDARIN SALAD

1 can (4½ ounces) LOUISIANA BRAND Shrimp
1 can (11 ounces) mandarin orange segments
½ cup sour cream
1 tablespoon oil and vinegar dressing
1 cup sliced celery
1 cup chopped onion
½ cup cashew nuts (optional)

Have shrimp and mandarin segments chilled in the cans. Drain. Rinse shrimp in *cold* water; blot dry. Soften sour cream with dressing; combine with shrimp, fruit, celery, onion, cashews. Serve on shredded lettuce. *4 servings*

SOUTH PACIFIC SEAFOOD BOWL

1 head iceberg lettuce
Green Goddess Dressing*
8 ounces cooked prawns or shrimp
1 papaya
2 kiwi fruit
½ fresh pineapple
8 whole strawberries
4 sprigs fresh mint

Core, rinse and drain lettuce; chill in disposable plastic bag or plastic crisper. Prepare Green Goddess Dressing. Shortly before serving, cut lettuce in bite-size chunks to measure 1½ quarts. Place in 4 individual serving bowls. Cut prawns in halves lengthwise. Peel papaya, kiwi and pineapple. Seed papaya and cut into wedges. Slice kiwi, and cut pineapple into spears. Arrange shrimp and fruits on lettuce. Garnish with mint sprigs. Serve with Green Goddess Dressing. *Makes 4 servings*

*GREEN GODDESS DRESSING

Combine ¾ cup mayonnaise, 2 tablespoons chopped green onion, 1½ tablespoons tarragon flavor white wine vinegar, 1 tablespoon chopped parsley, ½ teaspoon *each* tarragon, crumbled, and anchovy paste, and ⅛ teaspoon pressed fresh garlic.

Makes 1 cup dressing

Favorite recipe from California Iceberg Lettuce Commission

ATLANTIC BANKS SALAD

2 cans (4 oz. ea.) MAINE Sardines
2 quarts greens, mixed
Onion rings
Tomato wedges
¼ cup grated Parmesan cheese
½ cup grated sharp Cheddar cheese
1 raw egg
¾ cup lemon French dressing
3 hard-cooked eggs
1 cup potato chips, coarsely broken (optional)

Drain MAINE Sardines. Place greens, onion rings, and tomato wedges in shallow bowl and sprinkle with grated cheese. Add raw egg and French dressing. Toss thoroughly. Add sardines, hard-cooked eggs cut in wedges, and potato chips. Toss again, gently.
Yield: 4 servings

HELSINKI HERRING SALAD

6 herring fillets
3 tart large apples
2 cups finely diced FINLANDIA Swiss
2 cups diced boiled new potatoes, peeled
1 cup sour cream
1 cup mayonnaise
1 tablespoon vinegar
3 tablespoons minced dill
Salt, pepper

Soak herring in cold water for two hours, drain, bone and dice. Peel, core and dice apples. Combine herring, apples, cheese and potatoes in large bowl. Combine next four ingredients, season to taste and mix carefully with salad. Serve with Finncrisp and Rye Bread.

LATIN TUNA SALAD

1 can (12½ oz.) BUMBLE BEE® Chunk Light Tuna*
½ cup seeded chopped tomatoes
⅓ cup dairy sour cream
¼ cup diced green chiles
¼ cup diced celery
¼ cup chopped green onion
½ teaspoon ground cumin
½ teaspoon garlic salt
Crisp salad greens
Tortilla chips

Drain tuna. Combine tomatoes, sour cream, chiles, celery, onion, cumin and garlic salt. Fold in tuna. Mound onto each of 4 salad plates lined with crisp salad greens. Serve with tortilla chips.
Makes 4 servings

*or use 2 cans (6½ oz. each) BUMBLE BEE® Chunk Light Tuna

FINNISH TUNA SALAD

2 cans (6½ ounces each) tuna, drained, flaked
1 cup julienne strips FINLANDIA Swiss
1 cup mayonnaise
2 tablespoons chopped green onions
1 tablespoon lemon juice
1 cup sliced celery
2 cups halved green grapes
2 cups fresh pineapple chunks
1 can (11 ounces) mandarin oranges, drained
Leaf lettuce

Combine all ingredients, except lettuce. Chill several hours. When ready to serve, line salad bowl with greens. Spoon in salad. If desired, garnish with sliced almonds.
Makes 6 to 8 servings

PACIFIC TUNA SALAD

1 can (12½ oz.) BUMBLE BEE® Chunk Light Tuna*
3 tablespoons vegetable oil
2 tablespoons red wine vinegar
1 tablespoon toasted sesame seeds
1 teaspoon Dijon mustard
1 teaspoon sugar
½ teaspoon onion powder
½ teaspoon garlic powder
⅓ cup chopped green onion
⅓ cup diced celery
2 tomatoes
Crisp salad greens
¼ cup mayonnaise

Drain tuna. Combine oil, vinegar, 2 teaspoons sesame seeds, mustard, sugar, onion and garlic powders until well blended. Stir in onion and celery. Fold in tuna. Slice tomatoes in half. Place on salad greens. Mound tomatoes with tuna mixture. Top each with a dollop of mayonnaise and sprinkle with remaining sesame seeds to serve.

Makes 4 servings

*or use 2 cans (6½ oz. each) BUMBLE BEE® Chunk Light Tuna

CURRIED TUNA SALAD

2 cans (6½ oz. each) BUMBLE
  BEE® Chunk Light Tuna in
  Water
1 small DOLE® Fresh Pineapple
1 small red apple
½ cup mayonnaise
½ cup sliced celery
½ cup peanuts
⅓ cup diced green onion
½ teaspoon curry
¼ teaspoon salt
Crisp salad greens

Drain tuna. Twist off crown from
pineapple; trim off shell. Cut
pineapple crosswise into 4 one-
inch rounds. Refrigerate any
remaining pineapple for later use.
Core and dice apple. Toss tuna,
apple, mayonnaise, celery,
peanuts, onion, curry and salt
together. Place a pineapple slice
on each of 4 salad plates lined
with crisp salad greens. Spoon
tuna mixture on top of each.

Makes 4 servings

LINDSAY® SALAD Á LA NICOISE

1 green pepper
¼ cup cubed celery
1 can (4 oz.) pimientos
4 hard-cooked eggs
1 can (2 oz.) rolled anchovies
1 can (6½ or 7 oz.) tuna
Olive OR salad oil
1 cup LINDSAY® Large Pitted, Ripe
  Olives
½ cup blanched whole almonds
1 clove garlic
3 to 4 tablespoons red wine
  vinegar
½ teaspoon salt
Freshly ground black pepper
1 head butter lettuce
1 bunch chicory or romaine

Sliver green pepper, celery, and
pimientos; slice eggs. Drain oil
from anchovies and tuna into
measuring cup; add olive oil to
make ½ cup. Flake tuna. Stuff
olives with almonds. Crush garlic
in salad bowl. Pour in combined
oils and vinegar; let stand at least
30 minutes. Remove garlic; add
salt and pepper. Tear greens into
bowl, saving some frilly leaves to
line sides. Add remaining
ingredients; toss lightly to coat
with dressing.

Makes 6 servings

CRISP AND CRUNCHY TUNA

1 can (1 lb. 4 oz.) DOLE® Sliced
  Pineapple in Juice
1 can (7 oz.) BUMBLE BEE® Solid
  White Albacore Tuna, drained
1 can (11 oz.) mandarin orange
  segments, drained
1 medium cucumber, scored and
  sliced
¼ cup chopped green onion
Crisp salad greens
1 cup mayonnaise
1 tablespoon lemon juice
¼ teaspoon curry powder

Drain pineapple reserving
2 tablespoons juice.* Break large
chunks of tuna with a spoon. Toss
tuna, oranges, cucumber and green
onion. Spoon onto each of 5 salad
plates lined with crisp salad
greens. Arrange 2 slices pineapple
over each. Combine reserved juice,
mayonnaise, lemon juice and curry.
Spoon over each salad to serve.

Makes 5 servings

*Reserve remaining juice for
beverage.

CALIFORNIA GALLO® SALAME SALAD

12 GALLO® Italian Dry Salame
  slices, cut in half
1 head romaine, washed and
  chilled
2 oranges, thinly sliced
1 small red onion, sliced
1 jar (6 oz.) marinated artichoke
  hearts
⅓ cup toasted slivered almonds
Tarragon Dressing (recipe follows)

Tear romaine into bite-size pieces.
Place in salad bowl. Arrange
orange slices in a circle on top and
cover with GALLO® Salame slices.
Scatter over onion. Cut artichokes
in half (save dressing) and place in
the center. Scatter over almonds.
At table pour over dressing and
mix lightly.   *Serves 4*

TARRAGON DRESSING

Combine artichoke dressing with
2 Tbsp. olive oil, 1 Tbsp. white
wine vinegar, 1 tsp. grated fresh
orange peel, ¼ tsp. crumbled dried
tarragon, 1 clove minced garlic,
and ½ tsp. Dijon-style mustard.

MEAL-IN-A-BOWL SALAD

2 5-oz. cans ARMOUR® STAR
  Vienna Sausage in Beef Stock,
  drained, sliced
2 cups cooked, diced potatoes
2 cups shredded lettuce
1 cup sliced carrots
½ cup sliced celery
½ cup (2 oz.) shredded Cheddar
  cheese
⅓ cup chopped onion
4 hard-cooked eggs, chopped
½ cup mayonnaise
1 teaspoon dry mustard
½ teaspoon salt
Dash of pepper
Lettuce cups
Dash of paprika

Combine sausages, potatoes,
lettuce, carrots, celery, cheese,
onion and eggs. Combine
mayonnaise, mustard, salt and
pepper; pour over salad mixture.
Mix lightly; chill. Serve in lettuce
cups; garnish with paprika.

6 servings

MEXICAN COBB SALAD

1 head iceberg lettuce
Mexicali Dressing*
2 hard-cooked eggs, chopped
1 medium tomato, chopped
1 small avocado, peeled and
  chopped
4 slices crisp-cooked bacon,
  crumbled
½ cup shredded Cheddar cheese

Core, rinse and drain lettuce; chill
in disposable plastic bag or plastic
crisper. Prepare Mexicali Dressing.
Shortly before serving, shred
lettuce to measure 1½ quarts and
turn into serving bowl. Arrange
egg, tomato, avocado, bacon and
cheese on top to create stripes of
color. Serve with Mexicali
Dressing.

Makes 5 servings (2 quarts)

*MEXICALI DRESSING

Measure ⅓ cup oil, ¼ cup red
wine vinegar, 2 tablespoons
catsup, 1 tablespoon sliced green
onion, ½ teaspoon *each* bottled
Mexican seasoning and salt, ¹⁄₁₆
teaspoon pressed fresh garlic and
4 drops TABASCO® Sauce in a jar.
Cover tightly and shake well to
blend. Shake again just before
serving.   *Makes ¾ cup dressing*

*Favorite recipe from California Iceberg
Lettuce Commission*

SUMMER CHEF SALAD

6 cups bite-size pieces mixed
  salad greens
1½ cups (approx. 6 oz.) turkey
  ham or ham cut in julienne
  strips
1 can (11 oz.) DURKEE Granadaisa
  Mandarin Orange Segments,
  drained
1 cup green seedless grapes
1 can (3 oz.) DURKEE French
  Fried Onions

In a large salad bowl, combine all
ingredients except ½ can French
fried onions. Drizzle with Wine
Vinaigrette Dressing* and toss
gently. Serve immediately,
garnished with remaining onions.
Makes 6 servings

*WINE VINAIGRETTE DRESSING

¾ cup salad oil
½ cup red wine vinegar
2 teaspoons sugar
½ teaspoon salt
½ teaspoon DURKEE Tarragon
¼ teaspoon DURKEE RedHot!
  Sauce

Thoroughly combine all
ingredients.

MANDARIN BACON SALAD

½ head lettuce, bite size pieces
¼ head romaine, bite size pieces
6 slices RATH® BLACK HAWK
  Bacon, fried and crumbled
2 green onions, thinly sliced
1 small zucchini
1 11-oz. can mandarin orange
  segments, drained
¼ cup sliced almonds

Toss together; mix with dressing*
Just before serving, add one 11-oz.
can mandarin orange segments,
drained. Top with ¼ cup sliced
almonds, slightly toasted.

*DRESSING

¼ cup vegetable oil
2 Tbsp. sugar
2 Tbsp. vinegar
½ tsp. salt
Dash red pepper sauce

Mix well, add to greens as desired.

CRESCENT CITY SALAD

⅔ cup salad oil
⅓ cup HEINZ Wine Vinegar
2 tablespoons chopped parsley
1 clove garlic, minced
½ teaspoon caraway seeds
½ teaspoon salt
½ pound fresh mushrooms, sliced
6 cups torn salad greens, chilled
½ pound cooked shrimp
1 cup tomato chunks
½ cup chopped onion

Combine first 6 ingredients in jar.
Cover; shake vigorously. Add
mushrooms; chill to blend flavors.
Shake again before tossing with
salad greens, shrimp, tomatoes
and onion.
Makes 8 servings (about 8 cups)

ANTIPASTO SALAD BOWL

2 or 3 heads iceberg lettuce
1 cup garbanzos, cooked, drained
1 cup artichoke hearts, cooked
1 cup sliced mushrooms
1 cup coarse-cut celery
2 cups Italian dressing
1 cup cherry tomatoes, halved
1 large onion, cut into rings
¾ cup pitted ripe olives
3 ounces salami, julienne cut
  (about 1 cup)
½ cup crumbled Fontinella or
  white Cheddar cheese
½ cup pepperoncini, drained
¼ cup chopped parsley

Core, rinse and thoroughly drain
lettuce; chill in disposable plastic
bag or plastic crisper. Marinate
garbanzos, artichokes, mushrooms
and celery in 1 cup dressing. Cut
lettuce into 12 wedges; arrange in
big serving bowl. Top with
marinated vegetables and
remaining ingredients. Pour on
remaining dressing or serve on the
side.   *Makes 12 servings*

*Favorite recipe from California Iceberg
Lettuce Commission*

NORWEGIAN CHEF'S SALAD

4-6 cups torn salad greens
3 hard-cooked eggs, sliced
3 green onions (with tops),
  chopped
½ cup radishes, sliced
1 medium cucumber, sliced
2 tomatoes, cut in wedges
¼ lb. Swiss cheese, shredded
3 cans KING OSCAR Sardines,
  drained
French dressing

Place ingredients in cold salad
bowl. Toss with favorite French
dressing, and serve on cold salad
plates.   *Serves 6*

BRAN PILAF SALAD WITH COLD CUTS AND FRUIT

½ cup uncooked long-grain rice
1 cup NABISCO® 100% Bran
  Cereal
½ cup thinly sliced celery
¼ cup sliced scallions
¾ cup oil and vinegar dressing
2 navel oranges, peeled and sliced
1 large yellow grapefruit, peeled
  and sliced
Boston or Iceberg lettuce
8 ounces liverwurst, cubed
6 ounces sliced salami, cut in
  strips
3 ounces sliced bologna, cut in
  strips
¼ cup thinly sliced pitted black
  olives

At least 2 hours before serving
cook rice according to package
directions; chill. Just before
serving toss rice with NABISCO®
100% Bran Cereal, celery,
scallions and ½ cup salad
dressing. Sprinkle remaining
¼ cup salad dressing over orange
and grapefruit slices; set aside.
Line large oval platter with lettuce
leaves. Arrange pilaf in wide strip
in center. Toss liverwurst, salami
and bologna; arrange in two strips
either side of pilaf. Place orange
and grapefruit slices alternately in
two strips at side of meat. Garnish
with black olive slices, arranged on
either side of center of pilaf.
Serves 6

HEARTY MACARONI SALAD

4 cups cooked elbow macaroni
½ cup sliced celery
1 cup shredded Cheddar cheese
1 cup mayonnaise
1 teaspoon McCORMICK/
    SCHILLING Instant Minced
    Onion
2 teaspoons McCORMICK/
    SCHILLING SEASON-ALL®
    Seasoned Salt
¼ teaspoon McCORMICK/
    SCHILLING Black Pepper
¼ teaspoon McCORMICK/
    SCHILLING Dry Mustard
¼ cup McCORMICK/SCHILLING
    Imitation Bacon Chips

Combine macaroni, celery and cheese. Mix mayonnaise with onion, SEASON-ALL® pepper and dry mustard. Pour over salad and toss to mix well. Chill. Mix in bacon chips before serving.
Makes 6 servings

MACARONI PEANUT SALAD

3 cups broccoli flowerettes
3 cups sliced unpeeled yellow
    squash
Cold water
⅓ cup PLANTERS® Oil
1 cup diagonally sliced celery
1 cup chopped tomato
½ cup minced green onion
½ teaspoon crushed garlic
1 teaspoon salt
1 teaspoon basil leaves
1 teaspoon oregano leaves
⅛ teaspoon ground black pepper
½ pound bowtie macaroni, cooked,
    drained and cooled
1 cup chopped PLANTERS®
    Salted Peanuts
1 cup freshly grated Parmesan
    cheese

Steam broccoli and squash for 5 minutes. Rinse with cold water to cool. Drain well. Heat PLANTERS® Oil in large skillet over medium heat. Add celery, tomato, green onion and garlic. Sauté 5 minutes stirring occasionally, until celery is tender crisp. Stir in salt, basil, oregano and pepper. In a large bowl combine steamed vegetables, cooked macaroni, sautéed vegetables, PLANTERS® Salted Peanuts and Parmesan cheese. Toss well. Chill before serving.
Makes 8 to 10 servings

ITALIAN GARDEN SALAD

3 quarts water
3 teaspoons salt
1 tablespoon oil
3⅓ cups AMERICAN BEAUTY®
    Mostaccioli or 3 cups RONI-
    MAC®
⅓ cup tarragon vinegar
¼ cup oil
2 teaspoons dill weed
1½ teaspoons salt
½ teaspoon dry mustard
¼ teaspoon pepper
1 garlic clove, minced
2 cups (4 small) chopped tomatoes
2 cups (2 to 3 medium) sliced
    zucchini
2 cups pitted ripe olives

Boil water in large deep pot with 3 teaspoons salt and 1 tablespoon oil (to prevent boiling over). Add mostaccioli; stir to separate. Cook uncovered after water returns to a full rolling boil for 11 to 12 minutes. Stir occasionally. Drain and rinse under cold water.

In small bowl, combine vinegar, ¼ cup oil, dill weed, 1½ teaspoons salt, mustard, pepper and garlic. In large bowl, combine cooked mostaccioli, tomatoes, zucchini and olives. Pour dressing over salad mixture; toss well to combine ingredients. Chill for at least 1 hour to blend flavors.
22 (½-cup) servings

High Altitude—Above 3500 Feet: Cooking times may need to be increased slightly for mostaccioli; no additional changes.

NUTRITIONAL INFORMATION PER SERVING
SERVING SIZE:
½₂ OF RECIPE

		PERCENT U.S. RDA PER SERVING	
Calories	90	Protein	3
Protein	2 g	Vitamin A	4
Carbohydrate	11 g	Vitamin C	10
Fat	4 g	Thiamine	5
Sodium	220 mg	Riboflavin	3
Potassium	96 mg	Niacin	3
		Calcium	—
		Iron	3

MACARONI SALAD SUPREME

4 cups cooked elbow macaroni,
    drained and rinsed
½ cup each chopped celery and
    green pepper
¼ cup each finely chopped
    scallions and parsley
3 Tbsp. wine vinegar
¾ cup mayonnaise
4 Tbsp. (2 oz.) ROMANOFF®
    Caviar*
Crisp salad greens

Combine macaroni with vegetables. Stir vinegar into mayonnaise along with caviar. Add to macaroni; mix well. Chill. Serve on salad greens.
Makes 8 servings

*ROMANOFF® Red Salmon Caviar suggested.

MACARONI FRUIT SALAD

7-oz. package CREAMETTES®
    Macaroni (2 cups uncooked)
1 can (13¼-oz.) pineapple tidbits,
    drain and reserve liquid
1 can (11-oz.) mandarin oranges,
    drained
1 can (8-oz.) seedless green
    grapes, drained
1 cup celery, finely chopped
1 cup miniature marshmallows
1 apple, diced and dipped in
    lemon juice
½ cup dairy sour cream
½ cup mayonnaise
2 Tbsp. reserved pineapple juice
Lettuce
½ cup chopped nuts

Prepare CREAMETTES® according to package directions for salad use. Drain. Combine macaroni, pineapple, oranges, grapes, celery, marshmallows and apple. Blend sour cream, mayonnaise and pineapple juice until smooth. Toss macaroni mixture with sour cream dressing. Chill. Serve in lettuce lined bowl. Garnish with nuts.
6 to 8 servings

MACARONI SALAD TIVOLI

4 cups cooked elbow macaroni
2 cans (5 ounces *each*) SWANSON
    Chunk White or Thigh Chicken
½ cup diced Cheddar cheese
1 cup coarsely chopped cucumber
½ cup quartered radishes
¼ cup diagonally sliced green
    onions
2 tablespoons chopped green
    pepper
1 cup mayonnaise
½ cup bottled Italian dressing
½ teaspoon salt
¼ teaspoon pepper

In large bowl, combine ingredients; toss lightly. Chill 6 hours or more.
Makes about 8 cups, 4 servings

FIESTA MAC SALAD

1 7¼-oz. pkg. KRAFT Macaroni
  and Cheese Dinner
1 cup chopped tomato
½ cup chopped cucumber
½ cup shredded carrot
½ cup MIRACLE WHIP Salad
  Dressing
¼ teaspoon salt

Prepare Dinner as directed on package. Add remaining ingredients; mix lightly. Chill. Add additional salad dressing before serving, if desired.

4 to 6 servings

Vegetable Salads

BLUE DIAMOND® HOT GERMAN POTATO SALAD

1¾ pounds red waxy potatoes
  (about 5 to 6 medium)
Salted water
1 large tart apple
1 cup BLUE DIAMOND®
  Blanched Slivered Almonds,
  toasted
½ cup sliced green onion
¼ pound salami, diced
½ cup water
¼ cup cider vinegar
1 tablespoon all-purpose flour
2 tablespoons granulated sugar
1 teaspoon salt
¼ teaspoon pepper
1 tablespoon butter
½ cup dairy sour cream

In large saucepan cook potatoes, covered, in salted water 35 to 40 minutes or until fork-tender; drain, peel and slice. Cube unpared apple and place in bottom of large bowl; add potatoes, almonds and onion. Set aside. In large skillet brown salami. With slotted spoon remove meat from drippings; discard drippings. Add water and vinegar to skillet; gradually stir in flour. Add sugar, salt and pepper and butter; bring to boil, stirring constantly. Remove from heat, add sour cream and mix thoroughly.

Add potato mixture and salami to skillet; over low heat, stir until blended and heated through. Serve warm.   *Makes 5 to 6 servings*

Microwave Directions: Pierce each potato all the way through with large fork; arrange in oven on paper towel at least 1-inch apart. Bake 14 to 16 minutes, turning halfway through time. Cool, peel and slice. Combine with cubed apple, almonds and onion as directed above. Cook salami in 11 × 7-inch baking dish for 1½ minutes. Remove salami; wipe out dish. In same dish combine water and vinegar; stir in flour, sugar, salt, pepper and butter. Cook 3 to 4 minutes, stirring once. Remove from oven, stir in sour cream; add potato mixture and salami, stirring to coat; cook 4 minutes or until heated through, stirring once.

HOT GERMAN POTATO SALAD
(Low Calorie)

1 can (10¾ ounces) condensed
  cream of celery soup
2 tablespoons lemon juice
¼ cup water
4 medium potatoes, peeled, cooked
  and cubed
½ cup sliced celery
¼ cup chopped parsley
2 teaspoons salt
½ teaspoon sugar
Dash pepper
1 tablespoon bacon-flavored bits

In large saucepan, combine soup, lemon juice and ¼ cup water. Heat, stirring occasionally. Stir in remaining ingredients except bacon bits. Cook just until heated through, stirring constantly and gently. Serve immediately topped with bacon bits.

Makes 8 servings

About 75 calories each
Favorite recipe from The Potato Board

QUICK POTATO SALAD

1 package FRENCH'S® Scalloped
  Potatoes
1 cup chopped celery
½ cup chopped green pepper
3 hard-cooked eggs, chopped
1 cup mayonnaise
¼ cup milk
1 tablespoon FRENCH'S® Prepared
  Mustard
Lettuce

Simmer potato slices from package in about 3 cups water 15 minutes, until tender. Drain and chill. Combine with celery, pepper, and eggs. Stir together mayonnaise, milk, mustard, and seasoning mix from package of potatoes; gently stir into potato mixture. Chill. Serve on lettuce.

6 servings

Note: If desired, add 6½-oz. can tuna, drained and flaked.

LINDSAY® PARTY POTATO SALAD

1 cup LINDSAY® Chopped Ripe
  Olives
1 cup chopped onion
¼ cup chopped green pepper
⅓ cup butter
½ to ⅔ cup vinegar
½ to 1 teaspoon salt
½ teaspoon celery seed
¼ teaspoon pepper
1 teaspoon dill weed
5 cups diced, cooked potatoes
½ cup whipping cream
LINDSAY® Pitted Ripe Olives

Cook onion and green pepper in butter until tender-crisp. Add vinegar, salt, pepper and dill. Combine with potatoes. Mix in cream and olives. Pack into 5 or 6-cup ring mold; chill. Unmold; garnish with LINDSAY® Pitted Ripe Olives.

Makes 8-10 servings

HELLMANN'S. Best Foods.

YOGURT POTATO SALAD
(Low Cholesterol)

½ cup HELLMANN'S®/BEST
  FOODS® Real Mayonnaise
½ cup plain low-fat yogurt
3 Tbsp. lemon juice or cider
  vinegar
2 Tbsp. sugar
1 tsp. salt (optional)
2 lb. potatoes, cooked, peeled,
  sliced (4 cups)
½ cup sliced green onions

In large bowl stir together first 5 ingredients. Add potatoes and onions; toss to coat well. Cover; chill at least 4 hours.

Makes 8 (½-cup) servings

10 mg. cholesterol per serving

OLD-FASHIONED POTATO SALAD

3-4 cups frozen ORE-IDA®
Southern Style Hash Browns
1 quart water
1 tablespoon salt
¼ cup mayonnaise
¼ cup dairy sour cream
1 tablespoon sweet pickle juice
½ tablespoon HEINZ Mustard
½ teaspoon salt
⅛ teaspoon pepper
¼ cup chopped celery
3 tablespoons diced HEINZ Sweet Pickles
2 tablespoons frozen ORE-IDA® Chopped Onions
2 hard-cooked eggs, coarsely chopped

In boiling water, in covered saucepan, cook frozen potatoes with salt until fork tender—about 2 minutes after return of boil. Drain well. In serving bowl, combine mayonnaise, sour cream, pickle juice, mustard, salt and pepper; mix until smooth and well blended. Add celery, pickles, onions, eggs and warm potatoes; lightly toss; adjust seasonings. Cover salad, then refrigerate several hours. At serving time, garnish with tomato or hard-cooked egg wedges, if desired.　　*Yield: 4-6 servings*

Note: For a large salad use one bag (32 ounces) and double all ingredients.
　　　　Yield: 8-12 servings

WINTER POTATO SALAD

1 can (16 oz.) VEG-ALL® Mixed Vegetables
2 cups diced cooked potatoes
¼ cup thinly sliced green pepper
¼ cup diced sweet pickle
1 small bunch green onions (cut into ¾″ pieces, include tops)
6 salami slices, cut into ⅛″ strips
3 hard cooked eggs, sliced
1¼ teaspoons salt
¾ cup mayonnaise or salad dressing
2 teaspoons prepared horseradish
1 dash TABASCO® Pepper Sauce

Drain VEG-ALL® thoroughly. Combine with potatoes, green pepper, sweet pickle, green onion, two thirds of the salami strips, and two of the sliced hard cooked eggs. Sprinkle mixture with the salt; chill thoroughly. Mix together mayonnaise, horseradish and TABASCO® pepper sauce. Add to chilled VEG-ALL® mixture; toss together lightly. Line a chilled salad bowl with crisp greens. Fill with chilled salad. Garnish with remaining salami strips and hard cooked egg slices.　　*Serves 4-6*

POTATO BEAN SALAD

6 med. size potatoes, cooked and diced
1 cup S&W Fresh Whole Dill Pickles, coarsely chopped
½ cup chopped onion
½ cup mayonnaise or salad dressing
1 can (15 oz.) S&W Barbecue Beans
Salt

Toss potatoes, pickles and onions together in large bowl. Mix beans with mayonnaise or salad dressing and pour over potato mixture. Toss gently until all ingredients are well blended. Taste for seasoning and add salt if necessary. Chill well; overnight if desired. Before serving, garnish with pickles or chopped parsley.　　*Yield: 8 servings*

BEAN AND BACON SLAW

1 (15¼ oz.) can S&W Dark Red Kidney Beans, drained
1½ cups shredded cabbage
½ cup diced celery
⅓ cup finely chopped onion
2 Tbsp. finely chopped parsley
5 strips bacon, cooked and crumbled
1 tsp. salt
½ tsp. pepper
2 Tbsp. vinegar
1 Tbsp. sugar
½ cup mayonnaise

Combine beans with cabbage, celery, parsley, onion and bacon. Add salt and pepper. Stir vinegar and sugar into mayonnaise; pour over salad mixture. Toss lightly, chill.　　*Serves 6*

QUICK COLESLAW

4 cups (½ medium head) shredded cabbage
½ medium cucumber, chopped
¼ cup chopped onion
½ teaspoon celery seed
½ teaspoon salt
1 cup mayonnaise or salad dressing
¼ cup frozen MINUTE MAID® Orange Juice Concentrate, thawed and undiluted

In large mixing bowl, combine cabbage, cucumber, onion, celery seed and salt; toss lightly. Combine mayonnaise and orange juice concentrate; pour over cabbage mixture. Toss lightly. Serve immediately.
　　　　Makes 4 to 6 servings

HONEY-LEMON SLAW
(Low Cholesterol)

½ cup HELLMANN'S® or BEST FOODS® Real Mayonnaise
2 Tbsp. honey
½ tsp. grated lemon rind
2 Tbsp. lemon juice
¼ tsp. ground ginger
4 cups shredded cabbage
½ cup raisins

Stir together first 5 ingredients. Add cabbage and raisins; toss. Cover; chill.
　　Makes 8 (about ½-cup) servings

10 mg cholesterol per serving

LUCKY LEAF® STYLE COLESLAW

4 cups shredded cabbage
½ cup grated carrot
1 Tbsp. finely chopped onion
1 cup diced celery
1 cup LUCKY LEAF® Apple Sauce
¾ cup sour cream
1 tsp. salt
2 Tbsp. lemon juice
Lettuce
Paprika

Combine cabbage, carrot, onion, celery and apple sauce. Stir in sour cream, salt and lemon juice. Mix well. Serve on lettuce leaves. Sprinkle with paprika.
　　　　　　Serves 6-8

PINEAPPLE-CABBAGE SLAW*

4 cups shredded cabbage
1 cup shredded carrots
½ cup peanuts or walnuts
1 can (8¼ oz.) crushed pineapple
3 tablespoons mayonnaise
1½ teaspoons LEA & PERRINS Worcestershire Sauce
¾ teaspoon salt
½ teaspoon sugar

In a large bowl combine cabbage, carrots and nuts; set aside. Drain pineapple, reserving 2 tablespoons of the liquid. Add crushed pineapple to cabbage mixture. In a small bowl combine reserved pineapple liquid with remaining ingredients; mix well. Pour over cabbage mixture. Toss thoroughly.
Yield: 8 portions

*May be prepared in advance of serving.

HALF MOON BAY SLAW

1 can (8¼ oz.) DOLE® Crushed Pineapple in Syrup
1 quart BUD OF CALIFORNIA® Shredded Cabbage
1 medium red apple, cored and chunked
1 cup shredded carrots
1 cup sliced celery
½ cup chopped green onions
½ cup salted peanuts
Tangy Blender Mayonnaise (recipe follows)

Drain pineapple well, reserving ¼ cup syrup. Combine pineapple, reserved syrup, cabbage, apple, carrots, celery, onion and peanuts. Toss with Tangy Blender Mayonnaise. Cover; refrigerate at least 1 hour.
Makes 6 servings

TANGY BLENDER MAYONNAISE

1 egg yolk
2 teaspoons lemon juice
1 teaspoon Dijon mustard
½ teaspoon salt
½ teaspoon Worcestershire sauce
Dash cayenne pepper
½ cup vegetable oil

Combine egg yolk, lemon juice, mustard, salt, Worcestershire and cayenne in blender. With blender turned on, add oil a few drops at a time. Oil may be added in a continuous drizzle until mayonnaise has thickened. It is best to add oil a few drops at a time at the beginning and end of procedure.
Makes about ¾ cup

YOGURT CALICO SLAW

1 cup (8 oz.) BREYERS® Plain Yogurt
1 tablespoon prepared mustard
2 tablespoons tarragon vinegar
1 teaspoon salt
Dash of pepper
2 teaspoons sugar
1½ quarts finely shredded cabbage
1 cup shredded carrots
½ cup each thinly sliced radishes, celery, green pepper, and scallions

Combine yogurt, mustard, vinegar, salt, pepper, and sugar. Chill. Combine vegetables. Chill. Mix dressing thoroughly with cabbage mixture. Serve at once.
Makes 7 cups or 6 to 8 servings

LOW-CAL COLESLAW
(Low Calorie)

8 cups finely shredded cabbage (2½ pound medium head)
1 cup finely sliced celery
½ cup shredded carrot (1 medium carrot)
½ cup sliced green onion
¼ cup chopped parsley
2 tablespoons salad oil
¾ teaspoon salt
½ teaspoon celery salt
¼ teaspoon pepper
¼ teaspoon monosodium glutamate
¼ cup wine vinegar, vinegar, lemon juice or combination thereof

Combine cabbage, celery, carrot, green onion and parsley. Pour on salad oil and toss till slaw is evenly coated. Sprinkle on and toss in the seasonings—salt, pepper, celery salt, and monosodium glutamate—which will now stick to the oil coated slaw. Finally add wine vinegar and toss. *Makes 8 cups*

Favorite recipe from Leafy Greens Council

BIG BURGER SLAW

In large bowl, grate 1 small head cabbage. Chop 2 stalks celery, 1 green pepper, 1 medium onion. Combine ¾ cup HEINZ Tomato Ketchup, ¼ cup HEINZ Apple Cider Vinegar, 2 tablespoons sugar, 1 tablespoon *each* HEINZ Worcestershire Sauce and prepared mustard, 1 teaspoon salt, dash cayenne pepper; toss with vegetables. Cover; chill.
Makes about 1 quart

QUEEN CITY SALAD

½ cup mayonnaise or salad dressing
¼ cup HEINZ Sweet Relish
3 tablespoons HEINZ Wine Vinegar
¼ teaspoon salt
⅛ teaspoon pepper
4 cups shredded cabbage
1½ cups diced red-skinned apples
½ cup coarsely grated New York State Cheddar cheese
Lettuce
Apple wedges

Combine first 5 ingredients; toss with cabbage, apples and cheese. Cover; chill to blend flavors. Serve on lettuce; garnish with apple wedges.
Makes 4-6 servings (about 4 cups)

LAYERED BUFFET SALAD

6 cups torn iceberg lettuce
1 cup chopped celery
1 (16-oz.) can GREEN GIANT® KITCHEN SLICED® Green Beans, drained
4 hard cooked eggs, sliced
1 cup chopped green pepper
⅓ cup thinly sliced onion rings
1 (17-oz.) can LE SUEUR® Early Peas, drained
2 cups real mayonnaise
1 cup coarsely grated Cheddar cheese

In a large salad bowl layer the lettuce, celery, green beans, eggs, green pepper, onion and peas in order given. Spread the mayonnaise over the top of the salad; sprinkle with grated cheese. Cover well and let stand for 8 hours or overnight.
Serves 8 to 10

HELLMANN'S Best Foods.

LAYERED SUMMER SALAD

4 cups torn lettuce
1 medium red onion, sliced
2 cups sliced green pepper
1 cup shredded Cheddar cheese
1 pint cherry tomatoes, halved
4 cups sliced summer squash
¾ cup HELLMANN'S® or BEST
  FOODS® Real Mayonnaise
3 tablespoons horseradish
2 tablespoons lemon juice
1 tablespoon Worcestershire sauce
⅛ teaspoon hot pepper sauce
¼ teaspoon garlic salt

In large, deep bowl layer lettuce, onion, green pepper and cheese. Add a ring of tomatoes; top with a ring of squash. In medium bowl stir together real mayonnaise, horseradish, lemon juice, Worcestershire, hot pepper sauce and garlic salt until smooth. Spoon dressing into center; surround with remaining tomatoes. Cover and refrigerate 4 to 6 hours or overnight.

Makes 10 to 12 servings

CAESAR SALAD

2 medium heads romaine lettuce
3 to 4 anchovy fillets
6 tablespoons salad oil
1 egg
1 tablespoon Worcestershire sauce
¼ teaspoon salt
Dash freshly ground pepper
¼ cup grated Parmesan cheese
Juice from 2 lemons
  (4 tablespoons)
2 cups garlic croutons

Tear romaine into medium-sized pieces and put into large salad bowl. Mash anchovies in small bowl. Pour in 3 tablespoons of the salad oil; add egg, Worcestershire sauce, salt and pepper. Whip together with fork. Toss greens with remaining 3 tablespoons salad oil and Parmesan cheese. Add egg-anchovy mixture and lightly toss again. Sprinkle with lemon juice, toss lightly. Add croutons, toss lightly. Serve salad immediately while croutons are still crisp.

Favorite recipe from Leafy Greens Council

BROWNBERRY® CAESAR SALAD

1 head romaine lettuce
1 egg boiled 1 minute
4 Tbsp. olive oil
½ clove garlic
½ large lemon
4 anchovies (optional)
¼ cup Parmesan cheese, grated
Salt and pepper
1 cup BROWNBERRY® Caesar
  Salad Croutons

Break romaine into wooden salad bowl. Sprinkle with ¼ tsp. salt and plenty of freshly ground pepper. Crush the garlic and add to olive oil. Pour over greens and toss until every piece is coated with oil. Then break in the 1-minute egg, squeeze in the juice of ½ lemon, add the 4 anchovies cut in small pieces. Toss again. Last of all, add grated Parmesan cheese and Seasoned Croutons.

ROQUEFORT SALAD

¼ teaspoon chervil
¼ pound Roquefort or Blue cheese
¾ cup light cream
5 tablespoons lemon juice
½ teaspoon freshly ground black
  pepper
2 heads Romaine lettuce
BROWNBERRY® Onion and Garlic
  Croutons

Soak the chervil (if dried) in warm water 10 minutes. Drain. If fresh chervil is available, use 2 teaspoons. Mash the cheese and blend in the cream, lemon juice, pepper and chervil, very smooth. Tear the lettuce into bite-sized pieces and pour the dressing over it. Add croutons at the last minute and toss until well coated.

PARISIAN SALAD

Romaine lettuce (or any other fresh
  greens)
6 Tbsp. olive oil
1 Tbsp. lemon juice
2 Tbsp. tarragon vinegar
1 clove garlic
Paprika
Salt
Pepper
1 tsp. DUBONNET Red

In shallow bowl rubbed with garlic put lemon juice, tarragon vinegar and 1 teaspoon DUBONNET Red. Add olive oil slowly, hand beating mixture with whisk until dressing is of a smooth consistency. Add salt, pepper, and paprika to taste. Chill until ready to serve. Pour over greens, and toss.

WILTED CUCUMBER SALAD

2 large cucumbers (about 1 pound
  each), pared
2 teaspoons salt
½ cup HEINZ Salad Vinegar
3 tablespoons sugar
⅓ cup onion rings
Pimiento strips

Score cucumbers with fork; thinly slice. Arrange cucumbers in layers in bowl, sprinkling each layer with salt. Weigh cucumbers down with smaller bowl; refrigerate several hours. Drain cucumbers well, squeezing out any excess liquid. Stir sugar into vinegar until dissolved; pour over cucumbers and onion rings. Cover; refrigerate at least 1 hour, turning occasionally. Serve as a salad or meat accompaniment. Garnish with pimiento strips.

Makes 4-6 servings (about 3 cups)

CUCUMBERS AND RADISHES IN SOUR CREAM
(Low Calorie/Low Cholesterol)

1 cucumber, peeled and thinly
  sliced
1 package (6 oz.) radishes, sliced
  (about 2 cups sliced)
1 medium onion, thinly sliced
1 can (8 oz.) PET® Imitation
  Sour Cream
2 tablespoons vinegar
1½ teaspoons salt

Place cucumber, radishes, and onion in a large bowl. Cover with ice water. Combine imitation sour cream, vinegar, and salt. Chill. To serve, drain vegetables. Stir in sour cream mixture until vegetables are well coated. Serve immediately.

Makes about 6 servings

TOMATOES WITH AVOCADO DRESSING

1 ripe CALAVO® Avocado
⅓ cup mayonnaise
1 tablespoon lemon or lime juice
1 tablespoon onion juice
Dash of Worcestershire
3 large tomatoes
Lettuce leaves
Salt to taste
Chopped chives

Put avocado in blender or food processor. Mix with mayonnaise, add lemon or lime juice, onion juice, Worcestershire and salt. Peel 3 large tomatoes, slice and arrange on lettuce leaves. Pour dressing over tomatoes and sprinkle with chopped chives. *Serves 4*

FRESH SPINACH SLAW

1⅔ cups LINDSAY® Pitted Ripe Olives
4 cups shredded fresh spinach
1 thinly shredded carrot
½ cup thinly sliced radishes
2 tablespoons thinly sliced green onion
¼ cup thinly sliced celery
1 cup cottage cheese
2 tablespoons salad oil
2 tablespoons cider vinegar
1 teaspoon salt
¼ teaspoon dry mustard
Dash liquid red pepper seasoning

Quarter olives. Combine olives, spinach, carrot, radishes, onion, and celery. Blend remaining ingredients and toss with spinach mixture. *Makes 6 servings*

CRUNCHY FRISCO SALAD

2 quarts bite-size pieces fresh spinach
1 cup sliced fresh mushrooms
1 can (11 oz.) DURKEE Mandarin Oranges, drained and chilled
1 can (3 oz.) DURKEE French Fried Onions
½ cup Italian salad dressing

Toss spinach, mushrooms and mandarin oranges. Just before serving, add French fried onions and dressing; toss gently. Serve immediately.
Makes 6 to 8 servings

FRESH SPINACH SALAD

2 bunches fresh spinach
½ pound mushrooms, sliced
½ cup BLUE DIAMOND® Blanched Slivered Almonds, toasted
¼ cup vegetable oil
2 tablespoons olive oil
2 tablespoons wine vinegar
1 tablespoon white wine
½ teaspoon crushed tarragon
¼ teaspoon salt
⅛ teaspoon nutmeg

Wash and dry spinach; remove stems and tear leaves into pieces to measure 8 cups, loosely packed. Place spinach in a bowl with mushrooms and almonds. In small saucepan combine remaining ingredients and heat just to boiling. Pour hot dressing over and toss. Serve immediately.
Makes 6 to 8 servings

SPINACH AND EGG SALAD WITH YOGURT

4 cups spinach leaves
2 to 6 scallions, finely chopped, including 2 inches of the green tops
1 cup DANNON® Plain Yogurt
½ cup olive oil
Salt and freshly ground black pepper to taste
4 hard-cooked eggs, chopped
12 black olives

Wash the spinach thoroughly. Drain. Dry with paper towels. Shred and combine with the scallions in a salad bowl. Beat the yogurt, olive oil, and salt and pepper with a fork until well blended. Add the eggs. Pour the mixture over the spinach. Mix gently but thoroughly, taking care not to mash the eggs. Taste for seasoning. Garnish with the olives. Serve chilled. *Serves 4*

WINTER TOSSED SALAD

⅔ cup oil
⅓ cup THE CHRISTIAN BROTHERS® Riesling
2 Tbsp. wine vinegar
1 Tbsp. soy sauce
1 tsp. each sugar, dry mustard, garlic salt and pepper
½ tsp. curry powder
½ lb. bacon, diced
3 hard-cooked eggs, chopped
2 bunches torn fresh spinach

Combine oil, wine, vinegar, soy sauce and seasonings in covered jar. Shake well and chill. Fry bacon until crisp; drain. Toss spinach, eggs and bacon with dressing.
Serves 8

SPINACH-ORANGE TOSS
(Low Calorie)

1 can (10½ oz.) FEATHERWEIGHT Mandarin Oranges, drained
6 cups spinach or other greens, torn into bite size pieces
1 small cucumber, thinly sliced
1 avocado, peeled and sliced (optional)
2 Tbsp. green onions, sliced

Dressing:
½ tsp. grated orange peel
¼ cup orange juice
¼ cup oil
2 Tbsp. sugar (or FEATHERWEIGHT Liquid Sweetening)
2 Tbsp. wine vinegar
1 Tbsp. lemon juice
¼ tsp. salt

Combine ingredients for dressing in a covered container and shake. Combine remaining ingredients in a bowl, add dressing, toss lightly.
Serves 8

MID-EAST SPINACH SALAD

1½ quarts (6 cups) tender young spinach leaves
½ cup chopped toasted DIAMOND® Walnuts
Yogurt Dressing (recipe follows)

Remove stems from spinach; rinse, drain and chill. Tear leaves into bite-size pieces. Just before serving, add walnuts and Yogurt Dressing. Toss well. Serve at once.
Makes 4 servings

YOGURT DRESSING

Combine ½ cup plain yogurt, 3 tablespoons red wine vinegar, 2 tablespoons *each* olive oil and honey, ¾ teaspoon salt, ½ teaspoon *each* onion powder, and mint flakes, crumbled, ¼ teaspoon basil, crumbled, and ⅛ teaspoon paprika. Stir together until well blended.
Makes ⅞ cup dressing

SPINACH SALAD WITH YOGURT-SESAME DRESSING

1 cup (8 oz.) BREYERS® Plain Yogurt
2 tablespoons lemon juice
2 tablespoons grated onion
1 clove garlic, crushed
1 tablespoon chopped chives
½ teaspoon salt
Dash of cayenne
2 quarts crisp raw spinach (omit stems)
2 cucumbers, peeled and thinly sliced
½ cup thinly sliced celery
½ cup thinly sliced water chestnuts
2 tablespoons toasted sesame seeds

Combine yogurt, lemon juice, onion, garlic, chives, salt, and cayenne. Chill for at least an hour. In large salad bowl combine spinach, cucumbers, celery, and water chestnuts. Add yogurt dressing and toss. Sprinkle sesame seeds over each serving.

Makes 6 to 8 servings

WILTED SPINACH SALAD

6 slices bacon
1 can (1 lb. 4 oz.) DOLE® Chunk Pineapple in Syrup
1 bunch fresh spinach
2 teaspoons cornstarch
3 tablespoons cider vinegar
½ teaspoon Worcestershire sauce
¼ teaspoon dry mustard
1 can (3 oz.) French fried onions
Freshly ground pepper

Chop bacon. Fry in wok until crisp. Drain and reserve. Discard all but 2 tablespoons pan drippings. Drain pineapple reserving syrup. Wash spinach. Dry and remove stems. Mix cornstarch, vinegar, Worcestershire, mustard and pineapple syrup. Stir into hot bacon drippings. Cook, stirring, about 2 minutes until sauce thickens slightly. Add pineapple chunks and heat through. Remove from heat. Stir in spinach, onions, reserved chopped bacon and a few grinds of fresh pepper. Toss until spinach is coated with dressing. Serve immediately.

Makes 4 to 6 servings

MIXED BEAN SALAD

1 15 oz. can STAR Garbanzo Beans, drained
1 15 oz. can STAR Dark Red Kidney Beans, drained
1 16 oz. can wax beans, drained
1 16 oz. can cut green beans, drained
1 cup sliced celery
1 small red onion, thinly sliced into rings
1 red or green bell pepper, cut into strips
¾ cup STAR Italian Kitchen Olive Oil
¾ cup STAR Italian Kitchen Red Wine Vinegar
¼-½ cup granulated sugar, to taste
1 tsp. crushed oregano
¼ tsp. garlic powder
⅛ tsp. ground black pepper
Salt to taste

Combine all ingredients, and gently toss. Marinate in refrigerator overnight for maximum flavor.

Serves 6-8

BEANS-BEANS-BEANS

1 can drained wax beans (or frozen, cooked)
1 can drained cut green beans (or frozen, cooked)
15 oz. can kidney beans drained and rinsed
1 Tbsp. Worcestershire sauce
8 oz. jar Italian-style salad dressing (or*)
¾ cup sweet pickle relish
½ cup sliced sweet onion, preferably red
1 qt. crisp salad greens
1 cup BROWNBERRY® Seasoned or Cheddar Cheese Croutons

Mix all the beans with Worcestershire sauce and the Italian dressing. Cover, chill several hours. When ready to serve, stir in pickle relish and onion, add greens, and toss lightly. Add croutons at the last minute, or serve separately to be added while eating.

*FRENCH DRESSING II

¼ cup olive oil
¼ cup peanut oil
¼ cup wine vinegar
1 tsp. paprika
1 tsp. salt
Garlic clove

Combine ingredients in glass jar and shake well. This is enough for a large tossed salad, but any remaining may be stored in refrigerator.

ARTICHOKE, BEAN AND OLIVE SALAD

1 (14 oz.) can S&W Small Artichoke Hearts, drained and halved
1 (15½ oz.) can S&W Garbanzos (Ceci Beans), drained and rinsed
1 (5 oz.) jar S&W Stuffed Queen Olives, drained and sliced
1 bunch green onions, sliced
¼ cup chopped green pepper
¼ cup chopped celery
⅓ cup olive oil
¼ cup lemon juice
2 tsp. parsley flakes
Grated peel from one whole lemon
Dash cayenne pepper (be careful not to use too much!)

Mix artichokes, beans, olives, onion, green pepper and celery in a large salad bowl. Mix together olive oil, lemon juice, parsley flakes, lemon peel and cayenne pepper. Pour over salad ingredients. Mix well, cover and refrigerate for at least 2 hours or as long as 24 hours. Serve in salad bowls lined with iceberg lettuce.

Serves 4 to 6

TREASURE CITY SALAD

1 can (20 ounces) garbanzos or chick peas, drained
1 cup chopped celery
⅓ cup sliced pitted ripe olives
¼ cup chopped green pepper
2 tablespoons chopped onion
¾ cup mayonnaise or salad dressing
¼ cup HEINZ Wine Vinegar
½ teaspoon sugar
½ teaspoon chili powder
¼ teaspoon salt
6 cups torn salad greens, chilled
1 cup broken tortilla chips

Combine first 5 ingredients in bowl. Blend mayonnaise and next 4 ingredients. Pour dressing over vegetables, mixing well. Cover; chill to blend flavors. Toss with salad greens and chips just before serving. Garnish with additional chips, if desired.

Makes 6-8 servings (about 8 cups)

ITALIAN SALAD

1 medium can tiny whole green
  beans or French-cut cooked
  fresh beans
8-10 cherry tomatoes, halved
4 fresh green onions, sliced
½ cup French Dressing II*
BROWNBERRY® Seasoned
  Croutons

Drain the chilled green beans and
gently mix together all ingredients
except croutons. Chill at least one
hour, or longer if more convenient.
Toss in the croutons at serving
time, and serve in an ice-cold
lettuce lined bowl.

*FRENCH DRESSING II

¼ cup olive oil
¼ cup peanut oil
¼ cup wine vinegar
1 tsp. paprika
1 tsp. salt
Garlic clove

Combine ingredients in glass jar
and shake well. This is enough for
a large tossed salad, but any
remaining may be stored in
refrigerator.

S (SPICY) AND
W (WONDERFUL) SALAD

1 clove garlic, minced
1 tsp. salt
1 Tbsp. Worcestershire sauce
1 tsp. TABASCO® Sauce
1 lemon, juice of
6 Tbsp. olive oil (or vegetable oil)
3 ripe tomatoes, diced
2 ripe avocados, peeled, seeded
  and diced
3 Tbsp. diced S&W Green Chili
  Peppers
1 (1 lb.) can S&W Cut Green
  Beans, drained
1 (8¾ oz.) can S&W Garbanzos
  (Ceci Beans), drained
½ cup diced Monterey Jack
  cheese
½ cup crisp bacon bits
3 heaping Tbsp. minced onions

With the back of a spoon, or
mortar and pestle, cream the garlic
with salt to a fine paste. Transfer
garlic mixture to a small bowl and
add the Worcestershire,
TABASCO® , lemon juice and olive
oil. Beat briskly with a fork. In a

large bowl, mix together all the
other ingredients. Pour on the
dressing. Toss to distribute
dressing evenly. Allow to marinate
in the refrigerator 30 minutes.
Serve on a bed of chilled shredded
lettuce. *Serves 6*

GREEN BEAN SALAD
(Insalata di Fagiolini Verde)

⅓ cup PROGRESSO Olive Oil
1¼ teaspoons oregano leaves,
  crushed
½ teaspoon garlic powder
1½ teaspoons salt, divided
PROGRESSO Wine Vinegar
4 cups water
1 pound fresh green beans,
  trimmed or 1 package (9 oz.)
  frozen whole green beans
½ cup sliced small onion rings

In a small bowl combine oil,
oregano, garlic powder and 1
teaspoon of the salt; set aside for
10 minutes for flavors to blend. Mix
in 2 tablespoons red wine vinegar.
In a large skillet combine ½ cup
red wine vinegar, water, and
remaining ½ teaspoon salt; bring
to a boil. Add green beans and
onions; reduce heat and simmer,
covered, until beans are crisp-
tender, about 8 minutes. Drain and
place in a bowl. Pour seasoned
vinegar mixture over beans and
onions; toss well to coat. Cover
and refrigerate at least 2 hours or
overnight. Serve with cold meats,
as a luncheon salad, garnished
with roasted red peppers, if
desired.
*Yield: About 4½ cups; 4 to 6
portions*

CHICK PEA SALAD

1 can (20 oz.) chick peas, drained
¼ teaspoon salt
¾ cup thinly sliced celery
1 small onion, thinly sliced
¼ cup chopped green pepper
¼ cup chopped dill pickle
½ cup prepared GOOD SEASONS®
  Italian or Mild Italian Salad
  Dressing
Dash of pepper

Sprinkle chick peas with salt; let
stand about 5 minutes. Add
remaining ingredients; mix well.
Marinate in refrigerator at least 3
hours. Serve on salad greens, if
desired.
Makes 3½ cups or 4 servings

DORMAN'S
MATTERHORN SALAD

1 cup canned chick peas
2 slices DORMAN'S Swiss, cut into
  julienne strips
3 tablespoons finely chopped
  parsley
2 tablespoons finely chopped
  red onion
3 tablespoons vegetable oil
1 tablespoon vinegar or lemon
  juice
½ teaspoon garlic salt

Combine all ingredients except oil,
vinegar and garlic salt; gently toss
until well mixed. Combine
remaining ingredients until well
blended. Toss with salad. Chill in
refrigerator 1 hour. *Serves 6*

CARROT RAISIN SALAD

½ cup SUN-MAID® Raisins
2 cups grated carrot
1 (8¾ ounce) can pineapple tidbits
⅓ cup mayonnaise
1 tablespoon lemon juice
¼ teaspoon salt
Salad greens

Combine SUN-MAID® Raisins,
carrot and drained pineapple.
Blend in mayonnaise, lemon juice
and salt. Serve on crisp salad
greens.
Makes 4 to 6 servings

FAVORITE CARROT
SALAD

1½ cups grated carrots
1 cup raisins
½ cup finely sliced celery
½ cup chopped nuts
⅓ cup mayonnaise
¼ teaspoon salt

Combine carrots, raisins, celery
and nuts. Blend mayonnaise and
salt; mix lightly with carrot
mixture. Chill.
Makes 6 to 8 servings

*Favorite recipe from California Raisin
Advisory Board*

GOLDEN CARROT SALAD

Refreshing and nutritious describe this colorful apple salad. Core and finely chop Golden Delicious apples to measure 1½ cups. Toss with 1½ cups grated carrots, ½ cup raisins and ¼ cup salted peanuts. Blend ½ cup mayonnaise with 1 tablespoon lemon juice; toss with salad.

Makes 6 servings

Favorite recipe from Washington State Apple Commission

Lindsay®
MANDARIN RIPE OLIVE SALAD

1 (11 oz.) can Mandarin Oranges, drained
1 large avocado, peeled and sliced
2 green onions, thinly sliced
½ cup LINDSAY® Sliced Ripe Olives
Romaine or other lettuce
French dressing

Arrange oranges, avocado slices, onions and olives on lettuce on individual salad plates. Pour French dressing over all just before serving. Garnish with LINDSAY® Pitted Ripe Olives.

Makes 6 servings

MARINATED OLIVE SALAD

1 clove garlic, cut in half
2 teaspoons chili powder
1 bay leaf
¼ teaspoon cracked pepper
1 tablespoon salad oil
1 can LINDSAY® Pitted Ripe Olives
1 jar (small) sliced pimiento
1 jar (3½ oz.) LINDSAY® Cocktail Onions
1 jar (medium size) button mushrooms

Mix together the garlic, chili powder, bay leaf, pepper and salad oil. Drain liquid from can of olives. Add seasoning mixture to liquid. Stir well. Combine remaining ingredients. Pour liquid over olive mixture. Cover tightly and let stand in refrigerator for 2 to 3 days.

Makes approximately 2⅓ cups

SAUERKRAUT SALAD

1 jar (2 lb.) CLAUSSEN Sauerkraut, drained
1 cup sugar*
1 cup white vinegar
3 ribs celery, chopped
2 medium green peppers, chopped
1 medium onion, chopped
½ (1 can, 1 lb.) pitted ripe olives, sliced

In large bowl combine all ingredients. Cover and chill several hours or overnight.

Makes 10 (½ cup) servings

*To further reduce calories, an artificial sugar replacement can be substituted. Use as package directs for equivalency to granulated sugar or to taste.

SWEET AND SAUERKRAUT SALAD

¾ cup IMPERIAL Granulated Sugar
¾ teaspoon salt
½ cup cider vinegar
¼ cup vegetable oil
½ cup onion, chopped
½ cup green pepper, chopped
½ cup celery, chopped
1 (4 ounce) jar diced pimento
1 cup unpeeled apple, diced
2 cups (1 pound can) sauerkraut, rinsed and drained

Combine IMPERIAL Granulated Sugar, salt, vinegar and oil to make dressing. Combine remaining ingredients and toss well with dressing. Chill thoroughly and drain before serving. Dressing may be saved and used again.

Serves 8

SALAD VALENCIANA

2 cups DOLE® Fresh Mushrooms, sliced
½ cup olive oil
½ cup dry white wine
2 teaspoons snipped chives
1 teaspoon sweet basil, crumbled
1 teaspoon garlic salt
2 cans (4 oz. each) whole pimientos
Crisp lettuce

Combine mushrooms, oil, wine, chives, basil and garlic salt in a large bowl. Drain pimiento and cut into ¼-inch strips. Fold into mushroom mixture. Cover and marinate 2 hours. Spoon onto large lettuce-lined tray to serve.

Makes 6 to 8 servings

CALIFORNIA MUSHROOM SALAD

2 cups sliced DOLE® Fresh Mushrooms
½ cup Italian-style dressing
1 large tomato
1 cup julienne-cut green pepper
1½ quarts torn crisp salad greens
2 oz. Greek feta cheese, crumbled

In a large salad bowl, toss sliced mushrooms with Italian-style dressing. Coarsely chop tomato and toss with green pepper and mushrooms. Let stand 5 minutes. Add salad greens to vegetables, mixing well. Sprinkle feta cheese on top to serve.

Makes 6 to 8 servings

SPECIAL TOUCHES:

Marinate sliced DOLE® Fresh Mushrooms, artichoke hearts and ripe olives in an olive oil and lemon juice marinade with garlic and oregano. Drain marinade, toss vegetables and spoon them onto individual salad plates. Sprinkle with Greek Feta cheese.

Tear Romaine lettuce into bite size pieces; combine with sliced DOLE® Fresh Mushrooms and chopped green onions. Toss with Italian dressing and sprinkle with grated Parmesan cheese.

Marinate sliced DOLE® Fresh Mushrooms and sliced cauliflowerettes in white wine vinegar, salad oil, garlic salt, rosemary and black pepper. Drain marinade. Arrange vegetables on salad plates lined with crisp salad greens. Top with chopped green onions.

MARINATED VEGETABLE SALAD

1½ cups MAZOLA® Corn Oil
1 cup wine vinegar
1 clove garlic, cut in half
2 tablespoons lemon juice
1 tablespoon sugar
1 tablespoon minced onion
1 tablespoon Worcestershire sauce
½ teaspoon salt
½ teaspoon dried dill weed
½ teaspoon paprika
¼ teaspoon pepper

1 bunch (about 2½ pounds)
  broccoli, broken into flowerets
1 head cauliflower, broken into
  flowerets
1 pound green beans, trimmed
1 pound carrots, sliced
Lettuce leaves
Cherry tomatoes

In jar with tight fitting lid place corn oil, vinegar, garlic, lemon juice, sugar, onion, Worcestershire sauce, salt, dill weed, paprika and pepper. Cover; shake well. Refrigerate about 1 hour.

Cook broccoli, cauliflower, green beans and carrots until tender-crisp. *(Do not overcook.)* Drain vegetables, reserving ¼ cup bean liquid. Add liquid to corn oil mixture and shake well. Arrange vegetables in large shallow dish. Pour corn oil mixture over vegetables. Refrigerate at least 3 hours, basting frequently with corn oil mixture. To serve, drain vegetables and arrange on lettuce-lined serving platter. Garnish with tomatoes.   *Makes 6 servings*

INDONESIAN VEGETABLE SALAD WITH PEANUT DRESSING

5 cups coarsely chopped cabbage
1 package (10-ounce) frozen
  French-style green beans

1½ cups PLANTERS® Peanuts
2 tablespoons firmly packed light
  brown sugar
1 teaspoon onion salt
½ teaspoon salt
2 tablespoons lemon juice
1 can (1-pound) bean sprouts,
  drained
1 cucumber, peeled and sliced
½ cup sliced radishes
2 hard-cooked eggs
Hot cherry peppers

Cook cabbage in boiling salted water until tender crisp; drain and remove water. Cook green beans half as long as package directs after coming to a boil; drain and reserve water. Chill vegetables. Combine vegetable waters and set aside 1 cup.

In blender container combine peanuts, light brown sugar, onion salt, salt, lemon juice and reserved vegetable water. Blend until fairly smooth. Chill. To serve, layer cabbage, green beans, bean sprouts, cucumber and radishes on a large platter. Garnish platter with wedged or sliced hard-cooked eggs and hot peppers. Serve with prepared dressing.
      Makes 8 servings

Lea & Perrins
THE ORIGINAL WORCESTERSHIRE

CALIFORNIA SLICED VEGETABLE SALAD

2 ripe avocados, peeled, pitted,
  and sliced
2 ripe tomatoes, sliced
1 red onion, thinly sliced
⅓ cup oil
1 tablespoon LEA & PERRINS
  Worcestershire Sauce
1 tablespoon lemon juice
1 teaspoon basil leaves, crumbled
1 teaspoon salt
½ teaspoon sugar
2 tablespoons chopped parsley

On a shallow platter alternately arrange avocado, tomato, and onion slices, one slice overlapping the next. In a small container combine remaining ingredients except parsley. Mix well. Pour over vegetables. Cover and refrigerate for 1 hour. Sprinkle with parsley and serve.   *6 servings*

SALAD SKEWERS

1 box cherry tomatoes
½ lb. fresh mushrooms
½ head cauliflower, broken into
  flowerets
2 green peppers, cut into squares
1 cup ripe olives
⅔ cup oil
½ cup THE CHRISTIAN
  BROTHERS® Riesling
3 Tbsp. lemon juice
½ tsp. salt
1 clove garlic, crushed
¼ tsp. pepper

Put vegetables in container with tight fitting lid. Combine oil, wine, lemon juice, salt, garlic and pepper; pour over vegetables. Marinate until serving time. For each serving, place assorted marinated vegetables on wooden skewer.   *Serves 6*

Fruit Salads

ORANGE ONION AND AVOCADO SALAD

1 CALAVO® Avocado cubed
2 oranges peeled and sliced
1 large red onion peeled and
  sliced
French dressing (optional)
Salad greens

Arrange orange and onion slices alternately on salad greens around the outside of a salad plate. Place the avocado cubes in the center extending out onto the orange and onion slices. Add French dressing if desired.

SLIM JANE SALAD
(Low Calorie)

1 cup fresh bean sprouts
1 tablespoon lemon juice
1 tablespoon oil
1 teaspoon soy sauce
1 teaspoon sugar
1 medium DOLE® Banana, sliced
½ cup thinly sliced celery
½ cup thinly sliced pared
  cucumber
¼ cup thinly sliced radishes
2 tablespoons sliced green onion

Crisp bean sprouts in ice water 5 minutes. Blend lemon juice, oil, soy sauce and sugar together. Mix with sliced banana. Drain bean sprouts well and toss with bananas. Toss in remaining ingredients and serve at once.
      Makes 2 servings

321 calories per recipe, or
161 calories per serving

WALNUT TOSSED SALAD

¾ cup large pieces DIAMOND® Walnuts
2 tablespoons butter
¼ teaspoon minced or crushed garlic
Orange Vinaigrette Dressing (recipe follows)
1 large or 2 small heads chilled butter lettuce
½ cup thinly sliced red onion rings
1 can (11 ounces) mandarin orange sections, drained

Sauté walnuts in small skillet with butter and garlic over moderately low heat about 5 minutes, until very lightly browned, stirring constantly. Cool. Prepare Orange Vinaigrette Dressing. At serving time, tear lettuce into bite-size pieces to measure 1½ quarts; turn into chilled salad bowl. Top with onion rings, drained orange sections and garlic toasted walnuts. Pour dressing over salad and toss lightly.

Makes 6 servings

ORANGE VINAIGRETTE DRESSING

Combine ½ cup oil, 3 tablespoons red wine vinegar, ¾ teaspoon salt and 1 teaspoon *each* grated orange peel and basil, crumbled, in a small jar. Cover and shake well to blend. Shake again just before using. *Makes ¾ cup dressing*

ASIAN GARDEN SALAD

2 quarts torn spinach
1 cup bean sprouts
1 large orange, peeled and sectioned
1 can (8 oz.) water chestnuts
2 medium DOLE® Bananas, sliced
Honey Soy Dressing (recipe follows)

Toss together spinach, bean sprouts and oranges. Drain water chestnuts and slice. Toss with spinach mixture. Just before serving, add bananas and toss with Honey Soy Dressing.

Makes 4 to 6 servings

HONEY SOY DRESSING

½ cup salad oil
3 tablespoons white wine vinegar
2 tablespoons honey
1 tablespoon soy sauce
2 teaspoons toasted sesame seeds
⅛ teaspoon garlic powder

Combine all ingredients in a screw-top jar. Shake well. Toss with salad.

Makes 1 scant cup dressing

GOLD COAST SALAD

⅔ cup salad oil
⅓ cup HEINZ Wine Vinegar
3 tablespoons honey
1 teaspoon poppy seeds
½ teaspoon salt
6 cups torn salad greens, chilled
2 cups orange sections, chilled
1½ cups grated raw carrots, chilled
½ cup seedless raisins, plumped

Combine first 5 ingredients in jar. Cover; shake vigorously. Chill to blend flavors. Shake again before tossing with salad greens and sections, carrots and raisins.

Makes 6-8 servings (about 8 cups)

GATEWAY SALAD

⅔ cup salad oil
⅓ cup HEINZ Wine Vinegar
3 tablespoons honey
2 teaspoons dry mint leaves
½ teaspoon salt
8 cups torn salad greens, chilled
1½ cups cantaloupe balls
2 fresh pears, sliced
1 avocado, peeled, sliced
1 cup grated sharp cheese

Combine first 5 ingredients in jar. Cover; shake vigorously. Chill to blend flavors. Shake again before tossing with salad greens and remaining ingredients.

Makes 8 servings (about 9 cups)

CREAM CHEESE AND AVOCADO SALAD

2 CALAVO® Avocados cut in half
1 (3 oz.) package cream cheese
1 tablespoon black olives sliced
2 tablespoons pimento chopped
3 tablespoons Italian salad peppers chopped
Lemon juice

Add 1 teaspoon vinegar from Italian peppers to cream cheese and mix well in a food processor or blender. Add pimentos, peppers and black olives. Peel, seed and cut the avocados in half. Coat with lemon juice. Fill the cavity with cream cheese mixture. Refrigerate for 1 hour. Serve on lettuce leaves.

Serves 4

SUNSWEET® SURPRISE SALAD

20 cooked SUNSWEET® Prunes
2 large oranges
1½ quarts shredded or torn lettuce
½ cup sweet red onion rings
½ cup cucumber slices
½ cup crumbled Feta or blue cheese
French dressing

Pit prunes. Pare oranges, removing all white membrane, and cut into slices. For each serving, place 1½ cups lettuce on individual plates. Arrange 5 prunes and 2 or 3 orange slices on lettuce; top with onion rings and cucumber slices. Sprinkle with crumbled cheese. Serve with French dressing.

Makes 4 servings

STUFFED FRUIT SALAD

Combine ½ cup cottage cheese with ⅓ cup LINDSAY® Chopped Ripe Olives, ⅓ cup chopped nuts and 1 tablespoon lemon juice. Put 8 canned pear or cling peach halves together in pairs with cheese mixture. Serve on garnished salad plates. *Serves 4*

HELLMANN'S.
Best Foods.

HEARTY FRUIT SALAD
(Low Cholesterol)

1 cup low-fat cottage cheese (8 oz.)
½ cup HELLMANN'S® or BEST FOODS® Real Mayonnaise
2 Tbsp. honey
1 Tbsp. grated lemon rind
2 Tbsp. lemon juice
1 small cantaloupe, peeled, cut in chunks
1 small honeydew, cut in balls
1 pint blueberries
1 pint strawberries, halved

Place first 5 ingredients in blender container; cover. Blend on high speed until smooth. Cover; chill. Arrange fruit in bowl. Cover; chill. Serve with dressing.

Makes 6 servings

10 mg cholesterol per serving

BERRIED WALDORF

Combine thoroughly and refrigerate for 2-3 hours:

1 cup GIBSON Cherry Wine (or GIBSON Concord Wine)
8-oz. jar orange marmalade (one cup)

Mix in salad bowl:

1 cup large pineapple chunks
1 cup apple cubes (Delicious)
1 cup celery chunks
¾ cup walnut halves

Cover salad with refrigerated dressing, tossing gently. Serve immediately on finely shredded lettuce or cabbage. *Serves 4*

WALDORF GRAPE SALAD

¾ cup California seedless green grapes
¾ cup diced apples
½ cup each sliced celery and broken walnuts
¼ cup mayonnaise
1½ teaspoons milk
1 teaspoon lemon juice
Salt and pepper to taste
Lettuce

Gently toss together grapes, apples, celery, and walnuts. Thin mayonnaise with milk; stir in lemon juice. Add to grape mixture and toss. Add salt and pepper to taste. Serve on lettuce leaves. *Makes 3 to 4 servings*

Favorite recipe from California Table Grape Commission

PICTURE-PRETTY WALDORF

2 medium-size Golden Delicious apples
2 medium-size Red Delicious apples
Lemon Water (recipe follows)
⅔ cup coarsely chopped DIAMOND® Walnuts
½ cup thinly sliced celery
Crisp lettuce leaves
Mayonnaise

Core apples. Cut one of each color into 16 wedges; dip in lemon water. Dice remaining apples; dip in lemon water; drain well; mix with walnuts and celery. Spoon onto 4 lettuce-lined salad plates. Arrange 8 apple wedges of alternating colors around each serving. Top each with a dollop of mayonnaise. Decorate with a walnut piece. *Makes 4 servings*

LEMON WATER

Combine 1 tablespoon lemon juice with ½ cup cold water.

Note: If preferred, toss salad mixture with ½ cup mayonnaise. Decorate as above.

PET®

OVERNIGHT FRUIT SALAD

1½ cups miniature marshmallows
1 can (20 oz.) pineapple chunks, drained
1 can (11 oz.) mandarin oranges, drained
1 cup shredded coconut
1 can (8 oz.) PET® Imitation Sour Cream

Toss all ingredients together. Refrigerate overnight for best flavor. Serve on lettuce as a salad or top with melted orange marmalade for a dessert. *Makes 9 servings, ½ cup each*

FRUIT IN THE SUN AT MIDNIGHT

4 medium size ripe cantaloupes
1 pint raspberries
1 pint blueberries
½ pound green grapes, halved
½ cup kirschwasser or sauterne
1 package (6 ounces) VALIO Gruyere Cheese
Fresh mint sprigs

Using pencil, mark a line completely around outside of cantaloupe. Cut in half carefully being sure to cut through to center. Remove seeds. Scoop out melon in balls, leaving ½-inch shell. Refrigerate shells. Combine fruits and liqueur. Refrigerate at least 1 hour. Meanwhile, cut cheese into strips or small cubes. Just before serving, combine cheese and marinated fruit. Spoon into cantaloupe shells. Garnish with mint. *Makes 8 servings*

AVOCADO CITRUS SALAD

1 large grapefruit or 1 cup drained canned grapefruit sections
2 oranges
3 cups mixed salad greens
1 cup green grapes or canned, sliced pears
2 California avocados
¼ cup walnuts
1 cup sour cream or yogurt
½ teaspoon dill weed

Section grapefruit and oranges. Place salad greens in bottom of large salad bowl. Add grapefruit and orange sections and grapes. Halve, peel and slice avocados. Arrange avocado slices over top of salad in spin wheel fashion. Mound walnuts in center of bowl. Blend sour cream with dill weed, serve with salad. *Makes 6 to 8 servings*

Favorite recipe from California Avocado Commission

APRICOT-PINEAPPLE SALAD
(Low Calorie)

1 can (20 oz.) FEATHERWEIGHT Pineapple Chunks
1 can (16 oz.) FEATHERWEIGHT Apricot Halves
2 envelopes FEATHERWEIGHT Orange Gelatin
2 cups boiling water
1 cup fruit juice
½ cup cold water

Sauce:
2 Tbsp. sugar (or FEATHERWEIGHT Liquid Sweetening)
3 Tbsp. flour
1 egg yolk
1 cup fruit juice
1 cup FEATHERWEIGHT Whipped Topping
2 Tbsp. cheddar cheese, grated

Dissolve Gelatin in hot water. Add fruit juice (from canned fruit), water and chill until partially set. Then add fruit and chill until set.

For sauce, mix all of the ingredients, except Whipped Topping and cheese, and cook until thick, stirring constantly. Cool, then blend with Whipped Topping. Spread over Gelatin, garnish with grated cheddar cheese. *Serves 8*

WIKIWIKI YUMIYUMI

1½ cups sliced mango
1 cup sliced banana
1 cup sliced grapefruit
1 cup sliced strawberries
6 lettuce leaves
Juice of 1 CALAVO® Fresh Lime
2 Tbsp. honey
¼ cup salad oil
⅛ tsp. salt

Chill fruit. Blend lime juice and honey. Add salad oil and salt. Place fruit in mixing bowl (except strawberries). Pour lime juice and honey over fruit. Mix gently. Arrange fruit on lettuce leaves in individual salad bowls. Add strawberries. *8 servings*

CHERRY SALAD (WITH HONEY-LIME DRESSING)

2 cups pitted Northwest fresh
   sweet cherries
½ honeydew melon or cantaloupe,
   cut in wedges
8 fresh apricot halves
1 banana, cut in ½-inch slices
Lettuce
½ teaspoon grated lime peel
2 tablespoons lime juice
2 tablespoons honey
¼ teaspoon salt
½ cup mayonnaise

Arrange fruits on lettuce-lined platter or individual salad plates. Combine remaining ingredients and serve with salad.

Makes 4 servings

Favorite recipe from Northwest Cherry Growers

Libby's
Libby's
Libby's®

HEALTH-KICK PEAR SALAD

1 cup plain yogurt
1 tablespoon honey
½ teaspoon grated lemon rind
2 cups shredded carrots
⅓ cup seedless raisins
⅓ cup chopped salted peanuts
1 can (16 oz.) LIBBY'S Juice
   Pack Pear Halves, chilled
Crisp salad greens

In a small bowl, combine yogurt, honey and lemon rind; stir to mix well. In medium bowl, combine carrots, raisins and peanuts; add ⅓ cup of the yogurt dressing and toss lightly to mix. Drain pear halves and cut each in half lengthwise. For each salad, mound about ⅓ cup carrot mixture in a strip down the center of a lettuce lined salad plate; arrange a pear piece on each side of carrot mixture. Serve with remaining yogurt dressing.

Yields 6 servings

SUN WORLD® SUMMER SALAD

5 Tbsp. honey
Juice of 1 lemon
½ cup water
2 cantaloupes
2 oranges, peeled and cut into
   segments
½ honeydew melon
8 SUN WORLD® Dates, pitted and
   quartered
1 dessert apple, cored and diced
   in large pieces
1 cup black grapes, halved and
   seeded

Mix the honey, lemon juice and water and boil for 2 minutes. Halve the melons, remove the seeds and scoop out the flesh with a ball scoop. Mix with the other fruits. Pour the cooled honey syrup over the fruit salad and pile into the 4 cantaloupe shells.

RAINBOW SALAD WITH PINK CLOUD DRESSING

1 whole pineapple, quartered with
   fruit removed, reserve shell
1 pint strawberries, hulled and
   sliced, reserve several whole
   berries for garnish
½ cup seedless Thompson grapes
1 kiwi fruit, pared and sliced
1 medium banana, peeled and
   sliced

Cut the pineapple fruit into chunks. Combine the fruits gently. Fill the quartered pineapple shells with the mixed fruit and serve with Pink Cloud Dressing.*

*PINK CLOUD DRESSING

½ cup soy oil mayonnaise
1 (8 oz.) container red raspberry
   yogurt
½ of (6 oz.) can frozen lemonade
   concentrate

In a small bowl, blend the mayonnaise, yogurt and lemonade. Spoon over quartered pineapple shells filled with fruit salad. Garnish with whole strawberries.

Makes 4 to 6 servings

Favorite recipe from American Soybean Association

MELON MOSAIC

1 small watermelon
1 small cantaloupe
1 small honeydew melon
1 cup blueberries, raspberries or
   grapes
⅔ cup sugar
1 cup THE CHRISTIAN
   BROTHERS® Chateau La Salle
   Light Wine
1 lime

With sharp knife, cut watermelon into scalloped basket. With a melon scooper, form melons into balls. Combine sugar and wine in small saucepan; heat to boiling. Add 1 tsp. grated lime rind and squeezed lime juice; cool. Pour over melon balls and blueberries. Chill, covered, several hours. Serve in watermelon basket. Garnish with mint, if desired. *Serves 8*

A SALAD FOR PASSOVER OR EASTER

24 SUN WORLD® Whole Pitted
   Dates
3 sticks celery, sliced
Butter lettuce leaves

Dressing:
½ cup plain yogurt
Juice of ½ lemon
1 Tbsp. honey
2 red-skinned apples, cored and
   sliced
½ cup walnuts, halved

Mix the dressing ingredients together and chill. Quarter the dates and add to the dressing, together with the apples, celery and walnuts. Spoon onto a bed of lettuce and serve. *Serves 4*

SPEEDY SALAD SUGGESTIONS

Top peach slices with cranberry-orange relish or pecan-stuffed dates. Serve on greens with an easy fruit dressing: Blend a small amount of grated orange rind and juice from LIBBY'S Juice Pack Peaches into mayonnaise to make a pouring consistency.

Blend cream cheese with just enough juice from LIBBY'S Juice Pack Fruit Cocktail to make it light and fluffy. Spoon over fruit on bed of greens; sprinkle with chopped walnuts.

Gelatin Salads

LEMONY WALNUT-VEGETABLE MOLD

1 package (6 ounces) lemon-flavored gelatin
2 cups boiling water
1½ cups cold water
¼ cup tarragon-flavored vinegar
1 tablespoon lemon juice
½ teaspoon salt
½ teaspoon onion juice
½ cup coarsely chopped toasted DIAMOND® Walnuts
½ cup thinly-sliced raw cauliflower
½ cup thinly-sliced unpeeled cucumber
¼ cup thinly-sliced radishes
¼ cup cooked peas
Crisp lettuce leaves

Dissolve gelatin in boiling water. Stir in cold water, vinegar, lemon juice, salt and onion juice. Chill until syrupy. Stir the walnuts and vegetables into the chilled gelatin. Pour into a 1½-quart mold; chill until firm. Unmold on lettuce. Serve with sour cream dressing.

Makes 8 servings

Note: If desired, garnish the salad with cream cheese balls rolled in finely chopped walnuts.

FRESH ASPARAGUS CHICKEN SALAD

3 envelopes KNOX® Unflavored Gelatine
4 cups chicken broth, divided
12 fresh asparagus spears (about 1 pound)
4 to 5 fresh mushrooms thinly sliced
3 cups cooked chicken, chopped
1½ cups chopped celery
¼ cup chopped onion
½ cup bottled Italian dressing
2 tablespoons fresh lemon juice
Salad greens
Lemon slices

In medium bowl, mix unflavored gelatine with 1½ cups cold chicken broth. Heat remaining 2½ cups broth to boiling; add to gelatine mixture and stir until gelatine is completely dissolved. Chill until mixture is the consistency of unbeaten egg whites. Meanwhile, cut asparagus spears into 8-inch lengths; wash and trim. Cook asparagus in 1-inch boiling salted water in covered skillet, 8 minutes or until crisp-tender. Arrange asparagus and mushrooms on bottom of 8 × 12 × 2-inch (2-quart) baking dish. Pour 2 cups gelatine mixture over vegetables; chill until almost set. Combine chicken, celery, onion, Italian dressing and lemon juice; mix well. Spread chicken salad over gelatine. Pour remaining 2 cups gelatine over chicken salad. Refrigerate at least 4 hours, or overnight. Unmold onto serving plate. Garnish with salad greens and lemon slices.

Makes 6 servings

PINEAPPLE CHEESE SALAD

1 package (3 ounces) lemon flavored gelatin
1 cup boiling water
1 cup cold water
3 bananas, peeled and sliced
1 cup miniature marshmallows
¼ cup sugar
1½ tablespoons cornstarch
1 can (8¼ ounces) crushed pineapple
½ cup heavy cream
1 package (6 ounces) VALIO Gruyere Cheese, shredded

Dissolve gelatin in boiling water. Add cold water and chill until slightly thickened. Fold in bananas and marshmallows. Pour into 8-inch square baking pan. Chill until firm. Combine sugar and cornstarch and stir into undrained pineapple. Cook over medium heat, stirring, until thickened and smooth. Cool. Whip cream and fold into pineapple mixture. Fold in half of cheese. Spread on chilled gelatin. Sprinkle remaining cheese on top. Chill overnight. To serve, cut into squares.

Makes 6 to 8 servings

MOLDED ORANGE SALAD

3 envelopes unflavored gelatin
3 cups orange juice
½ cup lemon juice
⅔ cup orange marmalade
2 cups LINDSAY® Pitted Ripe Olives
Mandarin Orange sections

Sprinkle gelatin on 1 cup orange juice to soften. Stir over low heat until dissolved. Remove from heat and add remaining 2 cups orange juice, lemon juice and marmalade. Chill until mixture starts to set. Arrange about 10 ripe olives cut in halves and orange sections in pattern on bottom of 1½-quart mold. Fold remaining ripe olives into gelatin and spoon carefully into mold. Chill firm.

Makes 6 servings

JAMAICAN FROST

2 cans (16 ounces each) DIET DELIGHT Fruit Cocktail
4 cups DANNON® Plain or Strawberry Yogurt
1 large package (6 ounces) gelatin

Drain fruit cocktail well. In saucepan combine 1 cup yogurt and gelatin. Cook over low heat, stirring constantly until gelatin is dissolved. Stir in remaining yogurt. Chill until almost set. Whip gelatin until smooth and frothy. Place ⅓ cup fruit in a 8-cup mold; fold remainder into gelatin. Pour into mold. Chill until set. Unmold gelatin onto platter. *Serves 6-8*

Mousse variations: Follow same directions through whipped gelatin, (except reserve ½ cup fruit for garnish). Then puree and fold into whipped gelatin. Pour into stemmed glasses; chill. Garnish with reserved fruit.

HAM AND PINEAPPLE MOLD ALMONDINE

2 packages (3-ounces each) ROYAL
  Pineapple Gelatin
2 cups boiling water
1 can (8-ounce) crushed pineapple
1 cup mayonnaise
1 package (0.7-ounce) bleu cheese
  salad dressing mix
1½ cups (8-ounces) coarsely
  chopped cooked ham
½ cup coarsely chopped celery
¼ cup finely chopped green
  pepper
2 tablespoons chopped, toasted
  PLANTERS® Slivered Almonds
1 tablespoon chopped pimiento
Salad greens

Dissolve ROYAL Pineapple Gelatin
in boiling water. Add undrained
pineapple, mayonnaise and salad
dressing mix. Beat with rotary
beater until thoroughly blended.
Chill until slightly thickened. Fold
in ham, celery, green pepper,
chopped PLANTERS® Slivered
Almonds and pimiento. Turn into a
6-cup mold and chill until firm.
Unmold on greens.

Makes 6 servings

DOUBLE DECKER
CHICKEN LIME MOLD

2 packages (3 ounces *each*) lime-
  flavored gelatin
2 cups boiling water
½ cup cold water
2 teaspoons lemon juice
¼ teaspoon salt
2 cans (5 ounces *each*) SWANSON
  Chunk White or Thigh Chicken
2 tablespoons cut-up pimiento
2 packages (3 ounces *each*) cream
  cheese, softened
⅓ cup mayonnaise
1½ cups chopped cucumber
½ cup chopped celery
⅓ cup chopped green onions

Dissolve 1 package gelatin in 1 cup
boiling water; add ½ cup cold
water, lemon juice and salt. Chill
until slightly thickened. *First layer:*
Gently fold chicken and pimiento
into gelatin mixture; pour into
6-cup mold. Chill until slightly firm.

Second layer: Meanwhile, dissolve
remaining package gelatin in
remaining 1 cup boiling water; chill
until slightly thickened. Beat with
rotary beater or electric mixer until
fluffy and about double in volume.
Beat cream cheese and
mayonnaise until smooth; add
cucumber, celery and green
onions. Fold into whipped gelatin.
Pour onto chicken layer; chill until
firm. Unmold on salad greens;
garnish with carrot curls if desired.

Makes 6 servings

ASPIC RING A LA
MR. AND MRS. "T"®

2 cups or cans MR. & MRS. "T"®
  Bloody Mary Mix
1 cup or can MR. & MRS. "T"®
  Bully-Hi Mix
3 envelopes unflavored gelatin
1 small package cooked shrimp
1 avocado
⅓ cup chopped celery
⅓ cup chopped cucumber
⅓ cup chopped onion

Heat MR. & MRS. "T"® Bloody
Mary Mix, Bully-Hi Mix and gelatin
to boiling point. *Do not boil.* Cool
to room temperature. Paint sides
of 3½ cup mold with gelatin
mixture. Place shrimp and avocado
fancifully about the mold. Place
mold in freezer for a few minutes
to set. Meanwhile, add chopped
celery, cucumber and onion to the
remainder of the gelatin mixture.
Pour into the mold. Chill in
refrigerator for about 2 hours.

Serves 4

CALIFORNIA FRUIT
SALAD ROSÉ

1 envelope KNOX® Unflavored
  Gelatine
2 tablespoons sugar
¾ cup boiling water
1¼ cups rosé wine
1 cup thinly sliced peaches
½ cup sliced banana
½ cup sliced strawberries

In medium bowl, mix unflavored
gelatine with sugar; add boiling
water and stir until gelatine is
completely dissolved. Stir in wine.
Chill, stirring occasionally, until
mixture is consistency of unbeaten
egg whites. Fold in peaches,
banana and strawberries. Turn into
4-cup mold or bowl and chill until
firm. *Makes about 6 servings*

FRESH 'N NATURAL
GAZPACHO SALAD

3 envelopes KNOX® Unflavored
  Gelatine
1½ cups beef broth
¼ cup wine vinegar
2 tablespoons fresh lemon juice
2 teaspoons Worcestershire sauce
1 teaspoon salt
⅛ teaspoon hot pepper sauce
3 cups chopped fresh tomatoes
1 cup finely chopped green pepper
½ cup finely chopped celery
¼ cup finely chopped onion
1 clove garlic, minced

In medium saucepan, mix
unflavored gelatine with cold broth;
let stand 1 minute. Stir over
medium heat until gelatine is
completely dissolved, about 2
minutes. Remove from heat; stir in
vinegar, lemon juice,
Worcestershire sauce, salt and hot
pepper sauce. Chill, until mixture
is the consistency of unbeaten egg
whites. Fold in remaining
ingredients. Turn into individual
cups or molds or a 6-cup ring mold.
Chill until firm. Unmold on lettuce
leaves, if desired.

Makes 8 servings

GAZPACHO SALAD

2 envelopes unflavored gelatin
1 (1 pint, 2 oz.) can tomato juice
¼ cup red wine vinegar
1 teaspoon salt
Dash liquid red pepper seasoning
1 (6-inch) cucumber
¼ cup celery, thinly sliced
1⅔ cups LINDSAY® Pitted Ripe
  Olives (medium size)
2 medium-sized tomatoes, peeled
  and diced
1 small green pepper, diced
¼ cup thinly sliced green onion

Sprinkle gelatin on tomato juice to
soften. Place over low heat and stir
until gelatin is dissolved; remove
from heat. Stir in vinegar, salt and
liquid red pepper seasoning. Cool
until slightly thickened. Pare
cucumber and slice thinly. Drain
ripe olives; leave whole. Add olives,
tomatoes, green pepper, onion,
celery and cucumber slices to
gelatin. Pour mixture into 6-cup
ring mold. Chill several hours or
overnight. Unmold and garnish
with LINDSAY® Pitted Ripe Olives
stuffed with cocktail onions or
cheese. *Makes 8 servings*

GELATIN SHRIMP MOLD

1½ cups THANK YOU® Brand
    Tomato Juice
1 3 oz. package Lemon Gelatin
2 8 oz. packages Cream Cheese
    softened
1 cup Mayonnaise
2 tablespoons Chopped Onion
2 cups finely Chopped Celery
½ cup chopped Green Pepper
½ cup sliced Pimiento Stuffed
    Green Olives
1 6½ oz. can of Shrimp drained

Heat tomato juice, add gelatin to
dissolve. Cool, add cream cheese
and blend well. Add mayonnaise
and continue to blend. Electric
mixer may be used if desired. Fold
in remaining ingredients. Mix well.
Pour into a mold and refrigerate
until set. Unmold and serve with
crackers.

MOLDED CRAB SALAD

1 pkg. JELL-O® Brand Lemon
    Flavor Gelatin
1 cup hot water
1 cup mayonnaise
Juice of ½ lemon
1 cup chopped pecans
1 cup chopped celery
Small jar stuffed olives
2 or 3 small sweet pickles
2 hard boiled eggs
Dash of onion juice
1 can HIGH SEA Crab Meat

Dissolve JELL-O® in hot water.
Chill but *do not set*. Slice olives,
chop pickles and eggs then
combine all remaining ingredients
to JELL-O® mix. Chill until set and
serve on bed of lettuce.

Serves 6

UNDER-THE-SEA SALAD

1 can (16 oz.) pear halves
1 package (3 oz.) JELL-O® Brand
    Lime Flavor Gelatin
¼ teaspoon salt
1 cup boiling water
1 tablespoon lemon juice
2 packages (3 oz. each) cream
    cheese
⅛ teaspoon cinnamon

Drain pears, reserving ¾ cup of
the syrup. Dice pears and set
aside. Dissolve gelatin and salt in
boiling water. Add reserved syrup
and lemon juice. Pour 1¼ cups
into 8 × 4-inch loaf pan or 4-cup
mold. Chill until set, but not firm,
about 1 hour. Meanwhile, soften
cheese until creamy. Very slowly
blend in remaining gelatin, beating
until smooth. Add cinnamon and
pears and spoon into pan. Chill
until firm, about 4 hours. Unmold.
*Makes about 3½ cups or 6
servings*

MOLDED RUBY SALAD

1 6 oz. pkg. raspberry gelatin
1½ cups cranberry juice cocktail
1½ cups THE CHRISTIAN
    BROTHERS® Ruby Port
1 8 oz. can crushed pineapple,
    undrained
½ cup finely chopped celery
2 Tbsp. finely chopped green onion
1 cup diced apple

Heat cranberry juice to boiling.
Add gelatin; stir until dissolved.
Stir in port, pineapple tidbits and
juice. Chill until slightly thickened;
fold in celery, onions and apple.
Pour into 5 cup mold; chill until
firm.
Serves 8

TART CRANBERRY MOLD

1 package (3 ounces) lemon flavor
    gelatin
1½ cups boiling water
1½ cups raw cranberries
½ medium orange, seeded,
    unpeeled
⅓ cup chopped HEINZ Sweet
    Pickles
3 tablespoons sugar
2 cups prepared whipped topping
    mix

Dissolve gelatin in boiling water;
chill until slightly thickened.
Meanwhile, put cranberries and
orange through food chopper using
fine blade. Stir in pickles and
sugar. Fold cranberry mixture into
thickened gelatin; then gently fold
in whipped topping mix. Pour into
a 1-quart or 8 (½ cup) molds. Chill
until firm. Unmold on lettuce or
endive as a salad or serve as a
dessert topped with additional
whipped topping, if desired.
Makes 8 servings

MILNOT®'S WALDORF SALAD
(molded)

1 3-ounce package lemon flavored
    gelatin
1 cup boiling water
½ cup mayonnaise—or salad
    dressing
1½ to 2 cups chopped apples
    (approx. 2 medium size)
3 tablespoons lemon juice
1 cup chopped celery (approx.
    3 ribs)
½ cup chopped nuts
⅔ cups chilled MILNOT®,
    whipped

Dissolve gelatin in boiling water,
cool. Blend in the mayonnaise and
chill until slightly thickened—
about like unbeaten egg whites.
Meanwhile, chop apples (no need
to peel) and toss in the lemon juice
(prevents darkening); add the celery
and nuts. Whip MILNOT® until it
holds stiff peaks, whip in the
gelatin mixture; fold in the apple
mixture and pour into desired
mold—or flat dish (approx. 9 × 12).
Chill well, unmold (or cut in
squares) serve on salad greens;
additional salad dressing may be
desirable for topping.
Yield: approx. 6-8 cups

Note: This keeps well for several
    days covered and
    refrigerated.

CALIFORNIA SOUFFLÉ SALAD

3 packages (3 ounces *each*) lemon
    flavor gelatin
2 cups boiling water
2½ cups cold water
1 cup dairy sour cream
1½ cups California grapes, halved
    and seeded
1 orange, peeled and sectioned
1 apple, cored and diced
1 cup coarsely chopped walnuts

Dissolve gelatin in boiling water.
Add cold water; chill until partially
set. Pour ¾ cup gelatin into
1½-quart mold. Chill. Add sour
cream to remaining gelatin; whip
with electric mixer until fluffy. Chill
until slightly thickened; fold in fruit
and nuts; pour into mold. Chill
until firm.

Makes 8 servings

*Favorite recipe from California Table Grape
Commission*

CARIBBEAN FIESTA MOLD

1 package (3 ounce) orange flavor gelatin
1 cup boiling water
1 can (11 ounce) mandarin orange segments
½ cup (about) orange juice or dry sherry wine
¼ cup chopped nuts
2 ripe CHIQUITA® Brand Bananas, peeled and sliced

Dissolve gelatin in boiling water. Drain juice from orange segments into measuring cup. Reserve oranges. Add enough orange juice or sherry to juice to measure 1 cup. Stir into dissolved gelatin. Chill until mixture begins to thicken. Fold in orange segments, nuts and sliced bananas. Spoon into 4-5 cup mold. Chill until firm.

Makes 4 to 6 servings

CREAM CHEESE SURPRISE SALAD

1 can (16-ounce) pears
1 can (16-ounce) pitted dark sweet cherries in water syrup
1 package (3-ounce) ROYAL Blackberry Gelatin
1 package (3-ounce) cream cheese
½ cup chopped PLANTERS® Pecans
Salad greens
Mayonnaise

Drain pears and cherries reserving syrups. Dice pears. Add water to syrups to make 1¾ cups liquid. Heat to boiling and add to ROYAL Blackberry Gelatin. Stir until gelatin is dissolved. Chill until thick and syrupy. Make tiny balls from cream cheese; fold into thickened gelatin mixture. Fold in PLANTERS® Pecans, diced pears and cherries. Spoon mixture into a 5-cup ring mold. Chill until firm. To serve, unmold onto platter; fill center with mayonnaise.

Makes 8 servings

LEMONY SNOW

½ cup KOOL-AID® Sugar-Sweetened Lemonade Mix
⅓ cup sugar
1 envelope unflavored gelatin
¼ teaspoon salt
1¼ cups boiling water
2 egg whites

Combine soft drink mix, sugar, gelatin and salt in a bowl. Add boiling water and stir until gelatin is dissolved. Chill until thickened. Add egg whites and beat with electric mixer until fluffy and thick and double in volume. Pour into a 3- or 4-cup mold, individual molds, individual dessert glasses or a serving bowl. Chill until firm, about 2 hours. Unmold. Serve with custard sauce, or sweetened fruit and garnish with whole fresh strawberries, if desired.

Makes 3 cups or 6 servings

GARLAND SALAD

1 package (3 oz.) orange flavored gelatin
½ cup water
1 jar (4½ oz.) GERBER® Strained Squash
½ cup dairy sour cream
1 cup crushed pineapple (undrained)
½ cup chopped walnuts

Empty gelatin in a bowl and pour boiling water over it; stir until completely dissolved. Add the squash and mix thoroughly. Gradually add gelatin mixture to the sour cream. Chill until the mixture becomes slightly thickened. Stir in pineapple and nuts. Turn into a pint ring mold and chill until firm, approximately 4 hours. Unmold and serve.

Salad Dressings

SWEET AND SOUR DRESSING

1 cup HELLMANN'S®/BEST FOODS® Real Mayonnaise
3 Tbsp. cider vinegar
2 Tbsp. sugar
1 Tbsp. milk
¼ tsp. dry mustard
¼ tsp. salt

Stir ingredients together. Cover; chill. *Makes 1¼ cups*

STAR SWEET AND SOUR DRESSING

⅓ cup STAR Olive Oil
½ cup STAR Red Wine Vinegar
4 Tbsp. sugar
2 Tbsp. minced fresh chives
2 Tbsp. minced celery
1 Tbsp. minced green pepper
1 Tbsp. minced watercress
1 tsp. powdered dry mustard
2 tsp. Worcestershire sauce
1 tsp. salt
Freshly ground black pepper

Combine all ingredients in a jar. Shake well before using.

DANNON® THOUSAND ISLAND DRESSING

⅓ cup mayonnaise
¼ cup chili sauce
2 tablespoons chopped pimiento-stuffed olives
1 tablespoon chopped onion
1 tablespoon chopped green pepper
2 teaspoons chopped parsley
1 cup DANNON® Plain Yogurt

In small bowl, mix mayonnaise with chili sauce, olives, onion, green pepper and parsley. Fold in yogurt. Cover and chill until serving time. Serve as a dressing for salad greens or as a sandwich spread (in place of butter).

Makes about 1⅔ cups

THOUSAND ISLAND DRESSING

1 cup HELLMANN'S®/BEST FOODS® Real Mayonnaise
⅓ cup chili sauce or catchup
3 Tbsp. sweet pickle relish
1 hard-cooked egg, chopped

Stir ingredients together. Cover; chill. *Makes 1½ cups*

FAMILY FRENCH DRESSING

Combine ½ cup HEINZ Tomato Ketchup, ½ cup salad oil, ¼ cup HEINZ Apple Cider Vinegar, 2 teaspoons confectioners' sugar, 1 clove garlic, split, ¼ teaspoon salt and dash pepper; shake vigorously. Chill to blend flavors. Remove garlic; shake again before serving.

Makes 1¼ cups

SUPERB FRENCH-STYLE DRESSING

1 medium onion, quartered
½ cup white vinegar
½ cup STOKELY'S FINEST®
 Tomato Catsup
1½ teaspoons salt
1 cup salad oil
1 cup sugar

Place first 4 ingredients in blender and blend. Gradually add oil and sugar until well blended. Chill. Shake before serving.

Makes 3 cups salad dressing

BASIC FRENCH DRESSING

⅔ cup salad oil
⅓ cup HEINZ Vinegar
1 teaspoon sugar
½ teaspoon salt
¼ teaspoon paprika

Combine ingredients in jar. Cover; shake vigorously. Chill to blend flavors. Shake again before serving over sliced tomatoes, chilled cooked vegetables or tossed salads.

Makes 1 cup

Note: For a tangier dressing, use ½ cup vinegar and ½ cup oil.
For a milder dressing, use ¼ cup vinegar and ¾ cup oil.

VARIATIONS:

Roma French Dressing—Add 2 cloves garlic, split, and ¼ teaspoon oregano leaves to 1 cup Basic French Dressing. Serve over mixed greens or Chef's Salad.

Honey French Dressing—Add 3 tablespoons honey to 1 cup Basic French Dressing. Serve over canned or fresh fruit salads.

Mint French—Add 1 or 2 tablespoons crushed (fresh or dried) mint leaves to 1 cup Basic French Dressing.

Basil French—Add 1 tablespoon crushed basil leaves and 1 clove garlic, split, to 1 cup Basic French Dressing.

MAZOLA® BASIC FRENCH DRESSING

1 cup MAZOLA® Corn Oil
⅓ to ½ cup vinegar (lemon juice may be substituted for all or part of the vinegar)
1 to 3 tablespoons sugar
1½ teaspoons salt
½ teaspoon paprika
½ teaspoon dry mustard
1 clove garlic

Measure all ingredients into a bottle or jar. Cover tightly and shake well. Chill several hours, then remove garlic. Shake thoroughly before serving.

Makes 1⅓ to 1½ cups

Zesty Dressing: Follow recipe for Basic French Dressing. Add 2 tablespoons catchup, 1 tablespoon lemon juice and 1 teaspoon Worcestershire sauce.

CHEF'S TOMATO FRENCH DRESSING

1 cup salad oil
½ cup vinegar
½ cup tomato juice
½ teaspoon sugar
2 teaspoons HERB-OX Instant Vegetarian Style Bouillon
Freshly ground black pepper to taste

Blend ingredients.
Makes 2 cups dressing for green salad, chef's salad

TOMATO FRENCH DRESSING

1 can (10¾ ounces) CAMPBELL'S Condensed Tomato Soup
½ cup salad oil
¼ cup vinegar
½ teaspoon dry mustard

In covered jar or shaker, combine ingredients; shake well before using. (Or mix in an electric blender.)

Makes about 1½ cups

VARIATIONS:

To 1 recipe of Tomato French Dressing add any one of the following:
4 slices bacon, cooked and crumbled
¼ cup crumbled blue cheese
1 medium clove garlic, minced
¼ cup sweet pickle relish

CREAMY FRENCH DRESSING

1 cup HELLMANN'S®/BEST FOODS® Real Mayonnaise
2 Tbsp. sugar
2 Tbsp. cider vinegar
1 Tbsp. milk
1 tsp. paprika
½ tsp. dry mustard
¼ tsp. salt
1 garlic clove, minced (optional)

Stir ingredients together. Cover; chill. *Makes 1¼ cups*

BLEU CHEESE

1 pint BISON Plain Yogurt
½ pint BISON Sour Cream
2 tablespoons honey
2 tablespoons white vinegar
1 cup bleu cheese
Dash salt, pepper, garlic & onion powder

Just combine all ingredients and blend till smooth and creamy. Chill and serve.

CREAMY BLUE CHEESE DRESSING

1 can (10¾ ounces) CAMPBELL'S Cream of Celery Soup
½ cup sour cream
¼ cup crumbled blue cheese
2 tablespoons milk
1 tablespoon lemon juice

Combine ingredients; chill. Serve with chef's salad.
Makes about 2 cups

DANISH BLUE CHEESE HERB DRESSING

½ cup mayonnaise
1 cup dairy sour cream
2 tsp. fresh lemon juice
¼ tsp. tarragon
¼ cup parsley, minced
2 Tbsp. green onion, minced
1 cup Danish blue cheese, crumbled

Combine all ingredients in order given, blending well. Cover and chill to allow flavors to blend.

Favorite recipe from Denmark Cheese Association

STAR BLUE CHEESE DRESSING

1 small clove garlic, sliced
1 Tbsp. minced onion
⅔ cup STAR Olive Oil
⅓ cup STAR Red Wine Vinegar
2 oz. Blue Cheese or Roquefort
1 tsp. paprika
1 tsp. sugar
1½ tsp. salt
Few grains cayenne

Add onion and garlic to oil and allow to stand for ½ hour to 1 hour. Remove from oil and discard. Cream cheese to a smooth paste and add oil gradually, stirring constantly to keep the mixture as smooth as possible. Add the remaining ingredients and beat or shake, in a tightly covered jar, until well blended. Serve on salad greens or vegetable salads.

Makes 1 cup

DANISH BLUE CHEESE CREAMY DRESSING

½ cup Danish blue cheese, crumbled
½ cup mayonnaise
½ cup dairy sour cream
⅓ cup buttermilk
1 tsp. fresh lemon juice
¼ tsp. grated onion
¼ tsp. garlic, pressed
Freshly ground pepper

Combine all ingredients in order given, blending well. Cover and chill to allow flavors to blend.

Favorite recipe from Denmark Cheese Association

DANISH BLUE CHEESE FRENCH MUSTARD

¾ cup olive oil
½ cup red wine vinegar
1½ tsp. Dijon-style mustard
¼ tsp. salt
½ tsp. freshly ground pepper
½ tsp. sugar
1 clove garlic, pressed
Dash cayenne pepper
½ cup Danish blue cheese, crumbled

Combine all ingredients in order given, blending well. Cover and chill to allow flavors to blend.

Favorite recipe from Denmark Cheese Association

BASIC ROQUEFORT DRESSING

1 cup Roquefort
1 tablespoon Worcestershire sauce
1 tablespoon lemon juice
⅔ cup salad oil
2 tablespoons vinegar

Mash cheese with little salad oil. Add Worcestershire sauce, lemon juice, vinegar and balance of oil. Shake well until creamy. Serve on lettuce, cucumbers or endive.

Favorite recipe from Roquefort Association, Inc.

ROQUEFORT CREAM DRESSING

2 tablespoons crumbled Roquefort cheese
½ cup sour cream
1 teaspoon vinegar
½ teaspoon salt
¼ teaspoon pepper
½ teaspoon chopped parsley
½ teaspoon dried tarragon
1 head iceberg lettuce, shredded

Place Roquefort cheese in a bowl. Gradually add sour cream, vinegar, salt, pepper, parsley and tarragon. Stir with a wooden spoon until well blended. Add lettuce. Toss. Serve with rye or pumpernickel bread.

Serves 4

Favorite recipe from Roquefort Association, Inc.

CREAMY GARLIC DRESSING

1 cup HELLMANN'S®/BEST FOODS® Real Mayonnaise
3 Tbsp. milk
2 Tbsp. cider vinegar
1 medium garlic clove, crushed
½ tsp. sugar
¼ tsp. salt
⅛ tsp. pepper

Stir ingredients together. Cover; chill.   *Makes 1 cup*

ITALIAN SALAD DRESSING

⅔ cup POMPEIAN Olive Oil
⅓ cup wine vinegar
½ tsp. salt
Dash pepper
¼ tsp. garlic salt
1 tsp. oregano

Mix all ingredients and blend thoroughly. Chill before using.

Makes 1 cup

HONEYED ITALIAN DRESSING

¾ cup vegetable oil
½ cup REALEMON® Reconstituted Lemon Juice
¼ cup BORDEN® Grated Parmesan and Romano Cheese
¼ cup honey
½ teaspoon oregano leaves
¼ teaspoon salt
Dash pepper

In 1-pint jar with tight-fitting lid, combine ingredients; shake well. Chill to blend flavors. Serve with tossed salad greens. Refrigerate.

Makes 1½ cups

CREAMY ITALIAN

1 pint BISON Plain Yogurt
4 tablespoons BISON Cottage Cheese
½ cup white vinegar
Salt
Pepper
Garlic salt
Oregano
4 tablespoons honey
1 tablespoon prepared mustard
6 tablespoons mayonnaise
1 tablespoon chopped parsley

Just combine all ingredients and blend till smooth and creamy. Chill and serve.

ITALIAN CHEESE DRESSING

1 can (10¾ ounces) CAMPBELL'S Tomato Soup
½ cup salad or olive oil
¼ cup vinegar
¼ cup grated Parmesan cheese
1 teaspoon basil leaves, crushed
1 teaspoon oregano leaves, crushed
⅛ teaspoon garlic salt

In covered jar or shaker, combine ingredients; chill. Shake well before using. Serve with tossed green salad.

Makes about 2 cups

VINAIGRETTE DRESSING

¾ cup BERTOLLI® Olive Oil
¼ cup BERTOLLI® Red Wine
 Vinegar
1 anchovy fillet, mashed (optional)
1 clove garlic, minced
½ teaspoon salt
¼ teaspoon pepper

Shake all ingredients in covered
jar; refrigerate. *Makes 1 cup*

VINAIGRETTE ITALIANO

¾ cup PROGRESSO Olive Oil
1 teaspoon salt
½ teaspoon oregano leaves,
 crushed
½ teaspoon basil leaves, crushed
⅛ teaspoon ground black pepper
1 clove garlic, crushed
¼ cup PROGRESSO Wine Vinegar

Combine olive oil, salt, oregano,
basil, black pepper and garlic; set
aside for 10 minutes. Add vinegar
and mix well. Allow to stand
several hours in a cool place to
develop flavors. Use over greens.
Yield: 1 cup

VARIATIONS:

Olive Vinaigrette: add 2
tablespoons chopped salad olives
to above mixture.

Anchovy Vinaigrette: reduce salt in
above recipe to ½ teaspoon and
add 2 anchovies, minced.

Red Pepper Vinaigrette: add 2
tablespoons each chopped roasted
red peppers and minced onion to
above recipe.

WESSON 2-MINUTE BASIC MAYONNAISE

1 egg
¼ tsp. salt
2 Tbsp. lemon juice
1 cup WESSON Oil

Method: Combine egg, salt, lemon
juice and ¼ cup WESSON in
blender container. Blend together
until mixture begins to thicken.
Blend in *remaining* ¾ cup
WESSON, pouring in a thin stream
until mixture is thick and smooth,

about 2 minutes. Allow slightly
longer beating time for rotary or
electric beater.
Makes about 1 cup

Note: For best results have all
 ingredients at room
 temperature.

LOW-SODIUM MAYONNAISE
(Low Sodium)

2 tablespoons red wine vinegar
2 tablespoons lemon juice
3 egg yolks
1 teaspoon dry mustard
½ teaspoon onion powder
⅛ teaspoon ground red pepper
2 cups PLANTERS® Oil, chilled

Combine vinegar and lemon juice;
set aside. Place yolks, dry mustard,
onion powder and red pepper in
small mixing bowl. Beat at low
speed of electric mixer until
thickened. Pour PLANTERS® Oil
into egg yolk mixture in a slow,
steady stream. Add vinegar and
lemon juice mixture a few
teaspoons at a time while beating
in oil. To store, cover and
refrigerate. *Makes 2½ cups*

Per tablespoon: 110 calories, 1 mg.
sodium

YOGURT FRUIT DRESSING

½ cup HELLMANN'S®/BEST
 FOODS® Real Mayonnaise
1 container (8-oz) fruit-flavored
 yogurt

Fold Real Mayonnaise into yogurt.
Cover; chill.
Makes 1½ cups

YOGURT MUSTARD-HORSERADISH DIP OR DRESSING

2 cups DANNON® Plain Yogurt
1 Tbsp. mustard
1 Tbsp. horseradish
Salt to taste

Mix all ingredients until blended.
Use as a dip for vegetables and/or
a spread with cold meats.

TASTY YOGURT SALAD DRESSING

1 carton (8 ounces) DANNON®
 Lowfat Plain Yogurt
½ cup chopped onion
¾ teaspoon salt
⅛ teaspoon garlic powder
1/16 teaspoon pepper

Combine all ingredients. Chill
several hours before serving.
Makes 1¼ cups

YOGURT MUSTARD DRESSING

2 cups DANNON® Plain Yogurt
2 Tbsp. mustard
2 Tbsp. chopped capers
4 scallions finely chopped
2 tsp. dill chopped
Salt & pepper to taste

In a bowl, blend all ingredients.
Chill.
Makes approximately 2 cups

YOGURT "MAYONNAISE"

1 cup DANNON® Plain Yogurt
2 Tbsp. butter
4 Tbsp. flour
1 cup milk
1 egg yolk
2 Tbsp. lemon juice
½ tsp. dry mustard
½ tsp. salt

Melt the butter in a skillet and stir
in flour. Add milk all at once and
stir over medium heat until thick.
Remove from heat and beat in egg
yolk, lemon juice, mustard and
salt. Stir in yogurt & cool.
Makes approximately 2 cups

YOGURT "THOUSAND ISLAND DRESSING"

2 cups DANNON® Plain Yogurt
2 Tbsp. chili sauce
1 hard boiled egg
2 Tbsp. chopped dill pickle
Salt to taste

Combine all ingredients in a small
bowl. Blend well. Refrigerate about
2 hours in airtight jar before
serving.
Makes approximately 2 cups

ANCHOVY SALAD DRESSING

6 Tbsp. STAR Olive Oil
3 Tbsp. STAR Red Wine Vinegar
1 tsp. prepared mustard
¼ tsp. salt
⅛ tsp. pepper
1 clove garlic
2 STAR Anchovy fillets, chopped
   fine

Combine all ingredients in a covered jar and shake well. Chill in refrigerator. Before serving, shake thoroughly.

HOT DAN'S DRESSING

¼ cup FRENCH'S® Prepared
   Mustard
2 tablespoons sugar
2 tablespoons vinegar
2 tablespoons half-and-half or
   undiluted evaporated milk
¼ teaspoon salt

Combine all ingredients; beat with rotary beater until light and fluffy. Especially good in potato salad, coleslaw, and deviled eggs.
Makes ½ cup

MILNOT®'S BASIC SALAD DRESSING

½ cup MILNOT®
¼ teaspoon salt
⅛ teaspoon pepper
¼ cup vinegar
¼ cup sugar

Blend all ingredients together, allow to stand until thickened; chill well before using.
Yield: approx. ¾ cup

VARIATIONS:

Thousand Island Dressing: add ¼ cup chili sauce.

Blue Cheese Dressing: omit salt and add 1½ oz. blue cheese.

Creamy Cheese Dressing: add 3 oz. cream style cheese.

HOUSE DRESSING

1 pint BISON Plain Yogurt
¼ pint BISON Sour Cream
¼ pint BISON Cottage Cheese
¼ jar Hot-n-Spicy Mustard (to
   taste)
4 teaspoons white vinegar
Dash salt, garlic powder, onion salt

Just combine all ingredients and blend till smooth and creamy. Chill and serve.

TANGY COCONUT SALAD DRESSING FOR FRUIT, HAM OR CHICKEN SALADS

½ cup corn oil
½ cup COCO CASA™ Cream of
   Coconut
1 can (6 ozs.) frozen concentrated
   orange juice, thawed and
   undiluted
¼ tsp. curry powder
½ tsp. salt

In a bowl, combine all ingredients and beat until smooth and thick. Chill until ready to serve. Beat again and toss with salad when ready to serve. *Makes 1¾ cups*

FRUIT SALAD DRESSING

Combine 1 cup sour cream, ¾ cup SOLO® Peach Glaze and ¼ cup orange juice. Combine well and refrigerate until ready to use. Delicious over fresh fruit!

APPLE SAUCE SALAD DRESSING

½ cup POMPEIAN Olive Oil
2 large (or 4 small) cloves garlic,
   quartered
1 medium onion, thinly sliced
½ cup apple sauce
1 tsp. salt
⅛ tsp. pepper
¼ cup vinegar

Combine olive oil with garlic and onion. Let stand at room temperature for 2 to 3 hours. Remove garlic and onion. Stir in remaining ingredients. Store in refrigerator; allow to come to room temperature before using. Good on fruit salads, tossed salads or as a marinade for cooked vegetable salads. *Makes 1¼ cups*

HONEY FRUIT SALAD DRESSING

½ cup SUE BEE® Honey
¼ cup hot water
¼ cup lemon juice
¼ cup salad oil
¼ teaspoon salt
¼ teaspoon ground ginger

Combine all ingredients in small mixing bowl, and beat until well blended. Store in a covered jar in refrigerator. Shake well before using. *Makes 1¼ cups*

BLOODY MARY MIX SALAD DRESSING

6 ounces TABASCO® Bloody Mary
   Mix
5 tablespoons salad oil
2 tablespoons vinegar
1 tablespoon sugar
½ teaspoon salt
¼ teaspoon Worcestershire sauce
Dash garlic powder

Place all ingredients in container. Shake well. Chill before serving.
Makes about 1 cup

LEMON DRESSING

Blend together ½ cup lemon juice, ¼ cup oil, 1½ tablespoons granulated sugar, 1 teaspoon prepared mustard, ¼ teaspoon each salt and mace. Makes 4 servings for 4 cups of assorted fruits mixed with ⅓ cup chopped DIAMOND® Walnuts.

LEMON SESAME DRESSING

⅔ cup salad oil
Juice of 1 SUNKIST® Lemon
2 Tbsp. vinegar
2 Tbsp. toasted sesame seed
1 Tbsp. sugar
½ tsp. onion salt
½ tsp. salt

In jar with lid, combine all ingredients; shake well. Serve over any crisp green, tuna, chicken or fruit salad.
Makes about 1 cup

SALAD DRESSING FINLANDIA

½ cup mayonnaise
¼ cup ketchup
2 tablespoons light cream
2 tablespoons chili sauce
2 teaspoons horseradish
½ teaspoon sugar
¼ teaspoon celery seed
½ cup shredded FINLANDIA Swiss cheese

Blend mayonnaise with ketchup and cream until smooth. Stir in chili sauce, horseradish, sugar and celery seed. Add cheese. Toss with assorted salad greens or chill until ready to use.

Makes about 1½ cups dressing

CAVIAR DRESSING FOR CHEF'S SALAD

½ cup mayonnaise
⅓ cup corn oil
¼ cup chili sauce
2 Tbsp. wine vinegar
2 tsp. lemon juice
3 Tbsp. (1½ oz.) ROMANOFF® Caviar*
1 Tbsp. parsley flakes
Dash of pepper

Combine mayonnaise with next four ingredients. Fold in remaining ingredients. Cover and keep cold. At serving time, combine with foods for salad (see below).

Makes about 1¼ cups, enough for 6 servings

CHEF'S SALAD

A good blend is 6 torn salad greens, 2 cups (8 oz.) julienne ham, 2 cups (8 oz.) julienne cheese, 1½ cups julienne chicken (3 legs) and 4 hard-cooked eggs, quartered.

*ROMANOFF® Red Lumpfish or Salmon suggested.

FROSTY FRUIT DRESSING

1 cup HELLMANN'S® /BEST FOODS® Real Mayonnaise
1 cup orange, lemon, lime or raspberry sherbet, softened

Stir ingredients together. Cover; chill.   *Makes 2 cups*

DRESSING LAMAZE

1 can (10¾ ounces) CAMPBELL'S Condensed Tomato Soup
1 cup mayonnaise
¼ cup India or sweet pickle relish
1 hard-cooked egg, chopped
½ teaspoon grated onion
½ teaspoon prepared mustard
1 tablespoon lemon juice

Blend soup and mayonnaise. Add remaining ingredients; mix well. Chill. Serve with cooked shrimp or salad greens.

Makes about 2½ cups

COLESLAW DRESSING

1 cup HELLMANN'S® /BEST FOODS® Real Mayonnaise
3 Tbsp. sugar
3 Tbsp. cider vinegar
1 Tbsp. milk
1 tsp. salt
¼ tsp. dry mustard
¼ tsp. celery seeds

Stir ingredients together. Cover; chill.

Makes 1¼ cups

SOUR CREAM SLAW DRESSING
(Low Calorie/Low Cholesterol)

1 can (8 oz.) PET® Imitation Sour Cream
3 tablespoons sugar
3 tablespoons vinegar
¼ teaspoon dry mustard
½ teaspoon celery seeds

Combine all ingredients. Let sit at least 2 hours before mixing with shredded cabbage.

Makes 1 cup dressing

RUSSIAN DRESSING

1 cup HELLMANN'S® /BEST FOODS® Real Mayonnaise
⅓ cup chili sauce or catchup
2 tsp. lemon juice
1½ tsp. sugar

Stir ingredients together. Cover; chill.   *Makes 1⅓ cups*

FREE-STYLE DRESSING
(Basic Oil and Vinegar Dressing)

1 cup MAZOLA® Corn Oil
⅓ cup lemon juice or vinegar
½ teaspoon salt
½ teaspoon dry mustard
¼ teaspoon paprika
⅛ teaspoon cayenne pepper

Measure into jar corn oil, lemon juice or vinegar, salt, dry mustard, paprika and cayenne pepper. Cover; shake well. Chill. Shake before serving.

Makes 1⅓ cups dressing

VARIATIONS:

Herb Dressing: Prepare Free-Style Dressing using white wine vinegar. Add ½ teaspoon dried savory leaves, ½ teaspoon dried basil leaves, ¼ teaspoon dried dill weed and ½ clove garlic. Remove garlic before serving.

Makes 1⅓ cups dressing

Italian Dressing: Prepare Free-Style Dressing using red wine vinegar. Add ½ teaspoon dried oregano leaves, ½ teaspoon dried marjoram leaves and ½ clove garlic. Remove garlic before serving.

Makes 1⅓ cups dressing

CUCUMBER PARSLEY DRESSING

1 cup mayonnaise
1 cup pared, seeded, chopped cucumber
2 tablespoons finely chopped parsley
1 clove garlic, minced
½ teaspoon salt
⅛ teaspoon ground black pepper
1 cup DANNON® Plain Yogurt

Stir together first 6 ingredients. Fold in yogurt. Chill.

Makes 2⅔ cups

Sandwiches and Pizza

THE TEAM HERO

1 package (1 lb.) frozen
    pumpernickel or wheat bread
    dough
1 package (1 lb.) frozen white
    bread dough
Butter
Lettuce leaves
4 large tomatoes, thinly sliced
1 large onion, thinly sliced and
    separated into rings
3 packages (6 oz. each) OSCAR
    MAYER Smoked Cooked Ham
3 packages (8 oz. each) OSCAR
    MAYER New England Brand
    Sausage
2 tubes (8 oz. each) OSCAR
    MAYER Cheese and Salami
    Spread

Thaw bread dough according to
package directions. Stretch each
loaf into a 20 to 24-inch rope. Twist
one pumpernickel rope and one
white rope together to form a
braid. Lay braid diagonally across
greased baking sheet. Repeat to
form second braid. Cover dough
and let rise in warm place until
doubled in bulk, about 2 hours.
Bake in 375°F. oven 20 to 25
minutes. Brush with melted butter.
Cool; slice in half lengthwise.
Layer bottom half with half of the
lettuce, tomato, onion rings and
meat. Spread one tube cheese and
salami spread on cut surface of
top half of bread. Place over meat
layer. Repeat with remaining
ingredients to form second hero
sandwich. Cut each hero into 8 to
10 servings.

Makes 20 sandwiches

410 calories each

JOHN'S PARTY LOAF

1 loaf French bread, 12 inches
    in length
6 slices JOHN MORRELL® Salami
6 slices JOHN MORRELL® Bologna
6 slices JOHN MORRELL® P & P
    Loaf
6 oz. pkg. Cheddar cheese slices
6 oz. pkg. Swiss cheese slices
6 oz. pkg. Mozzarella cheese slices
1 Bermuda onion, cut into ⅛-inch
    slices
1 green pepper, cut into thin rings
1 tomato, cut into ⅛-inch slices
Sweet and Sour Mustard Sauce
    (recipe follows)

Split bread in half lengthwise. On
the bottom of the loaf, place
overlapping layers of salami,
Cheddar cheese, onion, bologna,
Swiss cheese, tomato, P & P loaf,
Mozzarella cheese slices and green
pepper rings. Wrap in foil, sealing
securely; bake in preheated 350°F.
oven 20 to 30 minutes. Prepare
mustard sauce; set aside. Place
top half of loaf on broiler pan 6
inches from unit; toast 3 to 4
minutes or until lightly browned.
Remove bottom loaf from oven; cut
it and top loaf into serving pieces.
Spoon sauce over each bottom
serving; add tops. Garnish with
olives; serve with warmed
shoestring potatoes or chips. May
be served cold. *Yield: 4 servings*

SWEET AND SOUR MUSTARD
SAUCE

1 cup sugar
2 eggs
½ cup white wine vinegar
2 tablespoons dry mustard
1 tablespoon Worcestershire sauce
Dash salt
2½ tablespoons flour
1 cup milk

Combine sugar, eggs, vinegar,
mustard, Worcestershire sauce and
salt in saucepan. Blend in flour to
form paste. Over low heat, stir in
milk. Heat, stirring constantly, until
thickened. *Yield: 2 cups*

GALLO® SALAME
SOURDOUGH
SANDWICHES

24 slices GALLO® Italian Dry
    Salame
1 small round flat loaf of
    sourdough French bread
¼ cup butter
3 cups shredded Swiss cheese
½ cup GALLO® Italian Dry Salame
    strips (cut in julienne style)
½ cup pimiento-stuffed olives,
    sliced
3 green onions, chopped
½ cup chopped red or green
    pepper
⅓ cup mayonnaise

Slice bread in thirds horizontally
and save middle round for other
use. Spread cut sides of 2 rounds
with butter. Arrange on baking
sheet. Place under broiler until
lightly toasted. Arrange
GALLO® Salame slices on top. Mix
together cheese, GALLO® Salame
strips, olives, onion, pepper, and
mayonnaise. Spread on top of
the GALLO® Salame-covered
bread. Cook at 400° for 10
to 15 min. until bread is hot
through and cheese melted. If
desired, brown lightly under broiler.
Cut into wedges. *Serves 8*

SANDWICH SMORGASBORD

Split 1 large round loaf French bread; hollow out excess bread from both halves and spread with soft butter. Cover bottom half with 12 thin slices of Swiss cheese, 18 slices Italian dry salami, a large green pepper cut into rings, and a large Bermuda onion. Top with 2 cups drained LINDSAY® Sliced Ripe Olives. Cover with top of loaf. Cut into 6 or 8 wedges.

Lindsay®
MIDNIGHT SPECIAL

½ teaspoon grated onion
1 (3¼ oz.) can kippered herring, mashed
18 slices rye bread
6 slices Swiss cheese
2 hard-cooked eggs, mashed
4 tablespoons mayonnaise
1 teaspoon prepared mustard
⅛ teaspoon salt
Dash pepper
¼ cup LINDSAY® Chopped Ripe Olives
6 lettuce leaves
6 slices tomato
6 LINDSAY® Pitted Ripe Olives, sliced

Combine onion with mashed kippered herring and spread on six of the slices of bread. Cover each with one slice of cheese, then with another slice of bread. Combine mashed egg, mayonnaise, mustard, salt, pepper and chopped olives; spread over top of each sandwich. Cover each with lettuce leaf and another slice of bread; on top place tomato slices and cut sandwiches diagonally. Place slices of ripe olives on corners.

Makes 6 sandwiches

CHICKEN TOSTADOS

2 tostados
Shredded lettuce
1 can (5 ounces) SWANSON Chunk Style Mixin' Chicken
2 tablespoons taco sauce
Shredded Cheddar cheese
Chopped onion
Diced green pepper

To make each sandwich, top each tostado with lettuce, half the chicken and 1 tablespoon taco sauce. Garnish with remaining ingredients.

Makes 2 sandwiches

TANGY CHICKEN OPEN-FACE

8 1 inch diagonal slices French bread, toasted
¼ cup cranberry-orange relish
1 can (4¾ ounces) UNDERWOOD® Chunky Chicken Spread
8 slices Swiss cheese

Spread toasted slices of bread with relish. Then spread with chunky chicken spread and top each with a slice of cheese. Broil until cheese is melted and bubbly.

Makes 8 open-faced sandwiches

CHICKEN BARBECUE ON BUNS

2 tablespoons chopped celery
2 tablespoons chopped onion
2 tablespoons chopped green pepper
Dash garlic powder
1 tablespoon butter or margarine
¼ cup prepared barbecue sauce
1 can (5 ounces) SWANSON Chunk White or Thigh Chicken
2 hamburger buns, split and toasted

In saucepan, cook celery, onion and green pepper with garlic powder in butter until tender. Add barbecue sauce and chicken. Heat; stir occasionally. Serve on buns.

Makes 4 open-face sandwiches

Lea & Perrins
THE ORIGINAL WORCESTERSHIRE

THE CHICKEN LUSCIOUS*

2 cups finely chopped, cooked chicken
½ cup finely chopped celery
2 tablespoons finely chopped pitted ripe olives
1 tablespoon finely chopped onion
1 tablespoon chopped pimiento
6 tablespoons dairy sour cream
1 teaspoon lemon juice
½ teaspoon LEA & PERRINS Worcestershire Sauce
½ teaspoon salt

In a medium bowl combine chicken, celery, olives, onion and pimiento; set aside. Mix sour cream, lemon juice, LEA & PERRINS and salt. Stir into chicken mixture, blend well. Spread on soft buns topped with crisp lettuce, if desired, or on buttered toast.

Yield: 2¼ cups filling

*May be prepared in advance of serving.

CHICKEN-IN-THE-SNOW
(Low Calorie)

1 can (5 ounces) SWANSON Chunk Style Mixin' Chicken
½ cup small curd creamed cottage cheese
¼ cup chopped radishes
2 tablespoons chopped green pepper
¼ teaspoon onion salt
3 slices thin white bread

In bowl, combine all ingredients except bread; chill. Serve as a sandwich spread. Garnish with green pepper strips.

Makes 3 open-face sandwiches

About 155 calories per serving

CURRIED CHICKEN FACE-UPS
(Low Sodium)

½ cup (1 stick) FLEISCHMANN'S® Unsalted Margarine, softened
¾ cup ground PLANTERS® Dry Roasted Unsalted Cashews
2 tablespoons minced fresh parsley
2 tablespoons minced green onion
½ teaspoon curry powder
8 slices low-sodium whole wheat bread
16 thin slices cooked chicken (1 pound)
1 large apple, cored and cut into 16 slices
16 cucumber slices

Combine FLEISCHMANN'S® Unsalted Margarine, PLANTERS® Dry Roasted Unsalted Cashews, parsley, green onion and curry powder; blend well. Spread each slice of bread with curry-nut mixture. Top with sliced chicken and garnish with apple and cucumber slices.

Makes 8 servings

Per serving: 385 calories, 42 mg. sodium

CHICKEN AND ASPARAGUS RAREBIT

1 can (10¾ ounces) CAMPBELL'S Condensed Cream of Chicken Soup
¼ cup water
1 cup shredded Cheddar cheese
1 can (5 ounces) SWANSON Chunk Chicken
Cooked asparagus spears
Toast

In saucepan, combine soup, water and cheese. Heat until cheese melts; stir occasionally. Add chicken; heat. Arrange asparagus on toast; pour chicken mixture over asparagus.
Makes about 2½ cups, 3 servings

COPENHAGEN OPEN-FACE

2 slices bread
Lettuce
1 can (5 ounces) SWANSON Chunk Chicken
¼ cup sliced cherry tomatoes
2 teaspoons thinly sliced green onions
Mayonnaise

Top each slice of bread with lettuce. Arrange chicken, tomatoes and green onions on lettuce. Top with mayonnaise.
Makes 2 sandwiches

TOASTED CHICKEN SALAD
(On Buns)

2 5-oz. cans BANQUET® Boned Chicken, drained and diced
1½ cups diced celery
⅓ cup chopped pickle
¼ tsp. salt
¼ tsp. pepper
⅔ cup mayonnaise
4 hamburger buns, halved
½ cup coarsely grated American cheese

Combine chicken, celery, pickle, salt, pepper, and mayonnaise. Toss lightly. Toast each bun half. Spread with chicken salad. Sprinkle with 1 Tbsp. cheese and broil until cheese melts.
Yield: 8

CHICKEN SALAD AND EGG CLUB

1 can (5 ounces) SWANSON Chunk Style Mixin' Chicken
⅓ cup chopped celery
2 tablespoons finely chopped green onions
2 tablespoons bottled thousand island dressing
6 slices whole wheat bread, toasted
Lettuce
Sliced tomatoes
2 hard-cooked eggs, sliced

In bowl, combine chicken, celery, onions and dressing; chill. Arrange lettuce on 2 slices toast; spread with chicken mixture. Top each with slice toast, additional lettuce, tomato and egg slices. Top with remaining toast.
Makes 2 sandwiches

HERBED CHICKEN CRESCENTS

1 can (5 ounces) SWANSON Chunk Style Mixin' Chicken
¼ cup chopped toasted almonds
¼ cup finely chopped celery
¼ cup finely chopped onion
2 tablespoons chopped parsley
⅛ teaspoon salt
⅛ teaspoon rosemary leaves, crushed
⅛ teaspoon rubbed sage
⅛ teaspoon thyme leaves, crushed
1 package (8 ounces) refrigerated crescent dinner rolls
1 egg, slightly beaten

In bowl, combine all ingredients except rolls and egg. Meanwhile, unroll dough; separate into 8 triangles. Flatten triangles. Spread about 1 tablespoon chicken mixture on each triangle. Roll up to point, starting at shortest side of triangle. Place seam-side down on ungreased cookie sheet; curve into crescent shape. Brush with egg. Bake at 375°F. for 20 minutes or until done.
Makes 8 sandwiches

GREEK PITA POCKETS
(Low Calorie)

1 pound ground LOUIS RICH Turkey or LOUIS RICH Turkey Sausage
Pinch of ground cinnamon
Pinch of nutmeg
2 tablespoons lemon juice
1 onion, peeled, halved and thinly sliced
1 clove garlic, finely minced
1 large ripe tomato, peeled and cubed
2 tablespoons chopped fresh mint (or 2 teaspoons dried)
½ teaspoon dried oregano
1 tablespoon chopped parsley
½ cup sliced deli-style pickles
8 ounces plain lowfat yogurt, optional
6 small (or 3 large) pita breads

Shape the meat into tiny meatballs. Brown lightly in a large non-stick skillet which has been sprayed with cooking spray for no-fat frying. Drain and discard fat, if any. Stir in lemon juice, seasonings, onion, pickle and tomato cubes. Cover tightly and simmer 2 to 3 minutes, just until vegetables are heated through but still crisp. Meanwhile, slit pita pockets into half moons. Open to form pockets. Spoon the meat and vegetables into pockets and spoon on yogurt.
Makes six servings

About 300 calories each

12 O'CLOCK WHISTLE SANDWICH

1 can (5 ounces) SWANSON Chunk Style Mixin' Chicken
¼ cup sliced celery
2 tablespoons mayonnaise
1 tablespoon chopped pimiento
¼ teaspoon lemon juice
4 slices bread

In bowl, combine all ingredients except bread; chill. Serve as sandwich spread.
Makes 2 sandwiches

LAND O'LAKES® TURKEY PINE-BERRY SANDWICHES

3-oz. pkg. cream cheese, softened
⅓ c. crushed pineapple, well drained
12 slices raisin bread
6 slices (¼") LAND O LAKES® Butter Moist Turkey Roast
6 Tbsp. cranberry orange relish, drained
6 slices (4½ × 4½ × ⅛") boiled ham luncheon meat

In small bowl combine softened cream cheese and pineapple; blend well. Spread 2 tsp. cream cheese-pineapple mixture on each slice of bread. Top six slices of the bread with one slice of turkey roast; spread ½ Tbsp. relish over each. Place ham slice over relish and top with remaining bread slices. Slice each sandwich in half to serve.

Yield: 6 sandwiches

BROILED TURKEY AND CHEESE SANDWICHES

Sliced roast BUTTERBALL® Turkey
8 slices SWIFT PREMIUM® Bacon
4 tablespoons butter
2 tablespoons flour
½ teaspoon salt
¼ teaspoon ground cumin
⅛ teaspoon turmeric
1 cup milk
4 slices bread, toasted
1 large tomato, sliced ¼ inch thick
Lettuce
4 tablespoons crumbled blue cheese

Cook bacon until crisp and drain on paper towels. Melt butter in saucepan. Blend in flour and seasonings. Remove from heat. Gradually add milk. Stirring constantly, cook until mixture thickens. To assemble sandwiches, arrange in layers on toast: Lettuce, tomato slices, bacon and sliced turkey. Pour ½ cup sauce over turkey on each sandwich. Sprinkle blue cheese over sauce. Broil a few minutes if desired.

Yield: 4 servings

TURKEY BARBECUE ON BUNS

2 cups diced roast SWIFT'S PREMIUM® BUTTERBALL® Turkey
½ cup chopped celery
¼ cup chopped onion
¼ cup chopped green pepper
2 tablespoons butter or margarine
1 cup catsup
3 tablespoons vinegar
2 tablespoons brown sugar
½ teaspoon dry mustard
¼ teaspoon salt
Hamburger buns

Pan fry celery, onion and green pepper in butter until lightly browned. Add remaining ingredients except buns and simmer 10 to 15 minutes. Spoon half of the mixture into a 1 pint freezer container. Cool, label and freeze for a future meal.

Yield: 3 cups

To serve: Spoon turkey barbecue on bottom halves of 4 to 6 hamburger buns. Cover with top halves.

To serve frozen turkey barbecue: Thaw barbecue mixture. Simmer 10 minutes or until hot. Serve as a filling in toasted hamburger buns.

Makes 4 to 6 servings

LEFTOVER-MAGIC TURKEY STACK

2 3-oz. packages cream cheese, softened
¼ cup (1 oz.) blue cheese, crumbled
⅓ cup chopped stuffed green olives
1 teaspoon grated onion
12 whole wheat bread slices
Mayonnaise
6 slices cooked ARMOUR® GOLDEN STAR Boneless Young Turkey
1½ cups leftover poultry stuffing
1 16-oz. can whole berry cranberry sauce, chilled, sliced
Lettuce leaves

Combine cream cheese, blue cheese, olives and onion. Spread six bread slices with mayonnaise; stack each with turkey slice, ¼ cup stuffing, cranberry sauce and lettuce. Spread cheese mixture on each remaining bread slice; invert on top of lettuce. Secure with picks and cut. *6 sandwiches*

ISLANDER'S TURKEY OPEN-FACE
(Low Sodium)

1 green pepper
½ pound (1½ cups) finely chopped cooked turkey
½ cup chopped PLANTERS® Dry Roasted Unsalted Mixed Nuts
⅓ cup low-sodium mayonnaise
Dash ground red pepper
4 slices low-sodium whole wheat bread
1 can (8 oz.) sliced pineapple packed in juice, drained

Slice 4 thin rings from green pepper; set aside for garnish. Finely chop remaining pepper. Combine chopped pepper, turkey, PLANTERS® Dry Roasted Unsalted Mixed Nuts, mayonnaise, and red pepper; mix well. Spread ¼ of turkey mixture on each slice of bread. Garnish each open face sandwich with a green pepper ring and a pineapple slice to serve.

Makes 4 servings

Per serving: 524 calories, 11 mg. sodium

FRENCH'S TURKEY TACOS

1 can (about 16-oz.) tomatoes
1 envelope FRENCH'S® Taco Seasoning Mix
1 to 2 cups finely diced cooked turkey
¼ cup chopped green pepper
1 tablespoon oil
6 to 8 taco shells
Shredded lettuce and Cheddar cheese

Break up tomatoes with fork in saucepan; combine with seasoning mix, turkey, pepper, and oil. Simmer 5 minutes, stirring frequently. Heat taco shells for 3 to 4 minutes in 300° oven. Spoon turkey mixture into shells and garnish with lettuce and cheese.

6 servings

TURKEY TACOS

1½ cups diced, roast SWIFT'S
  PREMIUM® BUTTERBALL® Turkey
7 ounce can taco sauce
6 taco shells
Shredded lettuce
Shredded Cheddar cheese
Tomato bits
Sliced green pepper or chopped
  onion

Mix together the diced turkey and
taco sauce in a saucepan and heat
until hot. Place mixture in taco
shells and top with lettuce, cheese,
tomatoes and green pepper or
chopped onion.
Yield: 6 servings

FAMOUS SAUCED
STACK-UPS

3 English muffins, split and
  toasted
6 slices Canadian bacon, ham, or
  turkey
1 cup shredded Swiss cheese
1 package (10 oz.) frozen asparagus
  spears, cooked
1 package (1 oz.) DURKEE White
  Sauce Mix
1 tablespoon DURKEE Famous
  Sauce
½ teaspoon Worcestershire sauce

On a baking sheet, top each
toasted English muffin half with a
bacon, ham, or turkey slice, some
shredded cheese, 4 or 5 asparagus
spears, and more shredded cheese.
Bake in 425° oven for 15 minutes.
Meanwhile prepare medium White
Sauce according to package
directions. Stir in Famous Sauce
and Worcestershire sauce. Spoon
warm sauce over baked
sandwiches.   *Makes 6 servings*

HAM ROLL-UPS

1 Package (3 ounces) Cream
  Cheese, softened
⅓ cup WELCH'S® Grape Jam or
  Jelly
¼ Cup Crushed Pineapple,
  well drained
¼ Cup Chopped Peanuts
8 Slices Ham
4 Hot Dog Rolls
Butter or Margarine

Blend cream cheese, WELCH'S®
Grape Jam and pineapple. Stir in
nuts. Overlap 2 slices of ham.
Place about ¼ cup pineapple
mixture on one end and roll up.
Repeat with remaining ham and
spread. Spread rolls lightly with
butter; place ham rolls inside.
Makes 4 sandwiches

HAM SALAD HAWAIIAN
SANDWICH

12 ounces ham (diced)
⅓ cup fresh dill pickles (diced)
¾ cup celery (diced)
¼ medium green pepper (diced)
¾ cup mayonnaise
Salt (pinch)
White pepper (pinch)
6 tablespoons butter
⅔ cup Parmesan cheese (grated)
1 cup cheddar cheese (shredded)
12 pineapple slices
⅔ cup thousand island dressing
6 BAYS® English Muffins (split)

Mix together ham, pickles, celery,
green pepper, mayonnaise, salt
and white pepper to make
sandwich. Set aside. Mix together
butter and Parmesan cheese.
Spread butter/Parmesan mixture
over muffin halves; broil until
brown. Spread thousand island
dressing over broiled muffin
halves. Divide ham salad and place
on all muffin halves. Top with ¼
ounce shredded cheddar cheese;
broil until cheese melts. Broil both
sides of pineapples; place one on
each muffin half. Garnish each
plate with a slice of tomato, a
piece of fresh fruit, two pickle
slices and a sprig of parsley.
6 servings

FRENCH TOASTED HAM
AND CHEESE
(The Boulevardier)

4 tablespoons butter or margarine,
  softened
2 teaspoons LEA & PERRINS
  Worcestershire Sauce, divided
8 slices white bread
8 slices American cheese
4 slices boiled ham
2 eggs, lightly beaten
¼ cup milk
¼ teaspoon salt
Butter or margarine

Mix butter with 1 teaspoon of the
LEA & PERRINS until well blended.
Spread on one side of each slice of
bread. Top each of 4 slices bread
with 2 slices cheese and 1 slice
ham. Place remaining bread, butter
side down, over each sandwich.
Mix eggs with milk, salt and
remaining 1 teaspoon LEA &
PERRINS. Dip one sandwich at a
time into egg mixture, turning
once. Fry in a buttered large
skillet. Cook until brown on both
sides, adding more butter as
needed.   *Yield: 4 sandwiches*

BROILED HAM
SANDWICH

1 cup (4-oz.) shredded Cheddar
  cheese
½ cup chopped celery
¼ cup chopped onion
¼ cup chopped green pepper
½ cup mayonnaise
4 ARMOUR® STAR Ham Patties,
  heated
2 hamburger buns, split

Combine cheese, vegetables and
mayonnaise. Place ham pattie and
¼ of mixture on each bun half.
Broil 5 to 6 inches from heat until
mixture is hot and bubbly, about 5
minutes. Preparation time: 15
minutes.   *4 sandwiches*

BREAKFAST ON THE
RUN

4 English muffins
4 slices (about 4 oz.) Monterey
  Jack or other mild cheese
2 SUNKIST® Oranges, peeled,
  sliced in thick cartwheels
4 slices (about 6 oz.) cooked ham
¼ cup orange marmalade

Split muffins; place on baking
sheet. On 4 muffin halves, arrange
cheese, orange cartwheels and
ham. Brush top of ham and
remaining 4 muffin halves with
marmalade. Broil 6 inches from
heat for 5 to 7 minutes until heated
through. Press muffin halves
together.   *Makes 4 sandwiches*

THE ORIGINAL BRUNCH-WICH

1 can (4½ ounces) UNDERWOOD®
  Deviled Ham
2 English muffins, split, toasted
4 eggs, poached
4 slices, your favorite cheese

Spread deviled ham on each muffin
half; top with poached egg. Lay
cheese slice over each muffin.
Broil 3 to 4 minutes until cheese is
melted.   *Makes 4 servings*

GRILLED EGG AND SIZZ-SANDWICH

12 slices SWIFT SIZZLEAN®
8 slices white bread or
  4 hamburger buns
4 eggs
4 slices process cheese
Butter

Cook SIZZLEAN® using package
directions. Remove from pan or
griddle. Drain. Fry eggs, over easy,
being sure to break the yolk. Butter
4 slices of bread and place butter
side down in pan. Place 1 cooked
egg on each slice. Top each egg
with 3 slices SIZZLEAN® and 1
slice cheese. Top with remaining
bread. Butter top of slice. When
bottom slice is toasted, turn
sandwich over and toast second
side. Serve hot. If you prefer the
buns, split and butter hamburger
buns. Toast cut side on grill.
Assemble remaining ingredients as
above and serve hot.
              Yield: 4 servings

BROIL 'EMS

4 NABISCO® Shredded Wheat
  Biscuits, split
1½ teaspoons prepared mustard
¼ cup butter or margarine, melted
1 (12-ounce) can luncheon meat
1 (8-ounce) package pasteurized
  process American cheese
Canned peach halves, drained and
  chilled (optional)
India Relish or jelly (optional)

Place biscuit halves on a baking
sheet, hollow side up. Combine
mustard and butter; drizzle over
biscuits. Cut luncheon meat into 8
slices to fit biscuits. Top with
cheese, sliced to fit luncheon
meat. Broil until cheese melts and
bubbles. If desired, serve with a
peach half filled with India Relish
or jelly.
   *Makes 4 servings of 2 halves of
            shredded wheat*

OPEN FACE SANDWICHES
(Low Calorie)

1 package (8 ounces) ECKRICH®
  Gourmet Loaf
2 English muffins, split, toasted
1 small tomato, chopped
½ small cucumber, diced
¾ cup canned bean sprouts,
  rinsed, drained
¾ cup shredded iceberg lettuce
3 tablespoons low calorie Thousand
  Island dressing
2 tablespoons sliced pitted ripe
  olives (reserve 8 slices)
¼ teaspoon salt
⅛ teaspoon onion powder
Dash pepper
2 slices (2 ounces) Brick cheese,
  cut in half

Fold meat slices into quarters and
place two on each muffin half.
Combine remaining ingredients,
except cheese; divide evenly
between muffin halves. Top each
with a half slice of cheese. Broil
until cheese is melted. Garnish
with reserved olive slices; serve
immediately.   *4 sandwiches*

271 calories per sandwich

BIG BOLOGNA SANDWICH SPREAD

2 pound chunk USINGER'S Big
  Bologna
¾ cup salad dressing
2 large dill or sweet pickles

In meat grinder, combine USINGER
Big Bologna and pickles. Add
salad dressing and mix well.
Optional: Add three finely chopped
hard-cooked eggs.

HEARTY LIVERWURST SANDWICH

1 can (4¾ ounces) UNDERWOOD®
  Liverwurst Spread
2 tablespoons chopped onion
4 teaspoons bacon bits
4 teaspoons mayonnaise
8 slices rye bread
8 slices tomato
2 hard-cooked eggs, sliced

In a small bowl, mix together
liverwurst spread, onion and bacon
bits. Spread mayonnaise on 4
slices rye bread. Then spread with
liverwurst mixture. Top with tomato
slices and egg slices. Close
sandwiches with remaining slices
of bread.   *Makes 4 sandwiches*

SPECIALTY OF THE HOUSE SANDWICH

For each sandwich, place a large
slice of buttered rye bread on
dinner plate. Cover with lettuce
leaf and slice of OSCAR MAYER
Braunschweiger Liver Sausage.
Top with 2 slices cooked OSCAR
MAYER Bacon and a tomato slice.
Spoon thousand island dressing
generously over all. Garnish with
an olive and a cocktail onion if
desired.

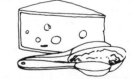

REUBEN SANDWICHES

12 slices rye bread
6 Tablespoons Thousand Island
  dressing
6 slices Swiss cheese
1 can (16 oz.) STOKELY'S FINEST®
  Bavarian Style Sauerkraut,
  drained
1 lb. thinly sliced corned beef
2 eggs, slightly beaten
½ cup milk
Dash salt & sugar
Butter or margarine

Spread 6 slices rye bread with
Thousand Island dressing; top with
Swiss cheese, Sauerkraut, corned
beef and second bread slice. Mix
together eggs, milk, salt and sugar.
Melt butter in skillet. Dip each side
of sandwich into egg mixture and
brown each side in skillet until
golden.   *Makes 6 sandwiches*

THANK YOU, MR. REUBEN

To make six sandwiches, spread 12 slices BROWNBERRY® Rye Bread with thousand island dressing, top each with a thick slice of Swiss cheese, 2 slices corned beef, 2 teaspoons sauerkraut, and ½ slice cheese. Spread outsides of bread with butter and grill in frying pan or on griddle until cheese is melted. Or, if bread is fresh, serve plain without grilling.

FRANKS-SAUERKRAUT SWISS CHEESE

Cut 6 slices RATH® BLACK HAWK Bacon into 1-inch pieces and brown in fry pan. Drain pan, reserving 1-2 tablespoons drippings. Add 1 cup sauerkraut and heat. Split 6 RATH® Wieners horizontally, but not through. Fill wieners with sauerkraut-bacon mixture and wrap each filled wiener in slice of Swiss cheese. Place in frankfurter bun and broil until cheese melts.

Makes 6 servings

FRANKS N' CRESCENTS

8 frankfurters, partially split
CRACKER BARREL Brand Sharp
  Natural Cheddar Cheese, cut
  into strips
1 8-oz. can PILLSBURY
  Refrigerated Quick Crescent
  Dinner Rolls

Heat oven to 375°. Fill each frankfurter with strip of cheese. Separate crescent dough into eight triangles. Place frankfurter on wide end of each triangle; roll up. Place on greased cookie sheet, cheese side up; bake at 375°, 10 to 12 minutes, or until rolls are golden brown.

8 servings

CHEESE HOUNDS

16 oz. (1 pkg.) OSCAR MAYER
  Wieners
4 oz. Cheese
10 slices Bacon

Slit wieners lengthwise to make pocket. Stuff each pocket with a strip of cheese. Wrap each wiener diagonally with a slice of bacon, and fasten ends with pics. Broil four to five inches from heat for five minutes, turning as necessary. Serve in buns.

Makes ten

QUICK CHILEE WEENEE® TACOS

2 cans (7¾ ounces each) VAN
  CAMP'S® CHILEE WEENEE®
6 taco shells
1 cup shredded lettuce
¾ cup shredded Cheddar cheese
Chopped tomato

Heat CHILEE WEENEE® to serving temperature and warm taco shells a few minutes in 300°F. oven. Arrange lettuce in taco shells; spoon on CHILEE WEENEE®. Sprinkle with cheese and chopped tomato. Serve immediately.

6 tacos

VARIATION:

Substitute 3 English muffins, split and toasted, for the taco shells.

BARBECUE BURGERS

1 egg, slightly beaten
1½ teaspoons onion powder
1½ teaspoons prepared
  horseradish
1½ teaspoons Worcestershire
  sauce
¾ teaspoon salt
¾ teaspoon chili powder
2 tablespoons barbecue sauce
1½ cups WHEAT CHEX® Cereal
  crushed to ½ cup
1½ pounds lean ground beef

Combine first seven ingredients. Blend well. Mix in WHEAT CHEX® crumbs and ground beef. Shape into six patties. Broil or grill 8-12 minutes or to desired doneness. Turn midway during cooking. Brush with additional barbecue sauce.

Makes 6 hamburgers

Surprise Burgers: Form into 12 thin patties about 4½ inches in diameter (scant ⅓ cup). Combine one package (3 oz.) cream cheese, ¼ cup chopped green onions with tops and 2 teaspoons barbecue sauce. Place rounded tablespoon in center of six patties. Cover each with second patty. Carefully seal edges. Broil or grill.

LEMON-ZESTY HAMBURGERS

2 pounds ground chuck
2 tablespoons MINUTE MAID®
  100% Pure Lemon Juice
2 teaspoons salt
½ teaspoon monosodium
  glutamate
½ teaspoon pepper
¼ teaspoon nutmeg
¼ pound fresh mushrooms
2 medium tomatoes
3 green onions with tops
6 slices Cheddar, Swiss, or
  American cheese

Mix meat and seasonings together, handling lightly, and shape into six patties. Grill, broil or panfry to desired doneness, and place each patty on a toasted bun. Blanket tops with sliced mushrooms, tomatoes and green onion, top all with slices of cheese.

QUICK BBQ BURGERS

2 pounds ground beef
¼ cup KIKKOMAN Soy Sauce
2 tablespoons instant minced
  onion
3 tablespoons tomato catsup
2 teaspoons prepared mustard
1½ teaspoons chili powder

Thoroughly combine beef with soy sauce, onion, catsup, mustard and chili powder; let stand 15 minutes. Shape into 6 or 8 patties. Broil or grill to desired degree of doneness.

Makes 6 to 8 servings

BEAN BURGERS

1 pound ground beef
¼ cup chopped green pepper
¼ cup chopped onion
1 tablespoon oil
1 28 ounce can B & M® Brick
  Oven Baked Beans
6 hamburger rolls, split and toasted

Fry ground beef, green pepper and onion in oil for 5 minutes. In a saucepan, heat beans and add meat mixture and stir. Spoon over bottoms of hamburger rolls and cover with tops of rolls.

Makes 6 bean burgers

TEXAS HOAGIES

2 pounds ground beef
1 envelope FRENCH'S® Chili-O
   Seasoning Mix
½ cup water
8 crusty rolls
8 slices American cheese
2 tomatoes, sliced
1 onion, sliced

Combine ground beef, seasoning
mix, and water; shape 8 patties.
Broil 10 to 15 minutes, or grill over
hot coals until done. Serve on rolls
topped with cheese, tomatoes, and
onion.   *8 servings*

FIESTA CHEESE BURGERS

1 egg
¼ cup OLD EL PASO® Taco Sauce
¾ cup dry bread crumbs
1 can (4 oz.) OLD EL PASO®
   Chopped Green Chilies
½ teaspoon salt
1½ pounds ground beef
8 slices (8 oz.) American cheese
8 hamburger buns

In a bowl combine egg, taco sauce,
bread crumbs, green chilies and
salt. Add ground beef; mix
thoroughly. Shape into 8 patties.
Grill over medium coals for 8 to 10
minutes. Turn and grill until
desired doneness. Add 1 slice of
cheese to each patty and cook
until melted. Serve on buns.
                    Makes 8 servings

TEXAS BURGERS

3½ lbs. ground beef
½ cup VIRGINIA DARE Red
   Cooking Wine
Pepper
¼ lb. butter
12 hamburger rolls
12 slices Bermuda onion
6 Tbsp. chili sauce

Mix ground beef, red cooking wine
and pepper. Blend thoroughly.
Mold into 12 patties and broil for
3-4 minutes on each side. Butter
hamburger rolls and toast. Serve 1
patty on each roll with a slice of
onion and top with chili sauce.
                    Yield: 12 servings

Lea & Perrins
THE ORIGINAL WORCESTERSHIRE

THE CRAZY! BURGER

1 package (4 oz.) grated Cheddar
   cheese
3 tablespoons LEA & PERRINS
   Worcestershire Sauce, divided
2 tablespoons tomato sauce
2 tablespoons finely chopped
   onion
1 tablespoon finely chopped green
   pepper
2 pounds ground lean beef
1 teaspoon salt
8 frankfurter rolls

Prepare filling by combining in a
small bowl cheese, 1 tablespoon of
LEA & PERRINS, tomato sauce,
onion and green pepper; mix well.
Divide meat into 8 portions,
shaping each portion into a 6-inch
long roll. Make a lengthwise well in
each roll. Spoon approximately 1
tablespoon filling into each well.
Bring meat together to cover
filling. Combine remaining 2
tablespoons LEA & PERRINS with
salt. Brush each hamburger with
LEA & PERRINS mixture. Broil
under preheated hot broiler,
approximately 10 minutes without
turning. Serve on frankfurter rolls.
                    Yield: 8 portions

BIG BEAN BOAT

1 loaf French bread
¼ cup (½ cube) butter, melted
1 cup thinly sliced celery
4 green onions, sliced
2 cans (15 oz. each) NALLEY®'S
   Thick Chili With Beans
½ cup shredded cheddar cheese

Cut top from bread and set aside.
Hollow out loaf, reserving crumbs
and leaving about ½ inch on
bottom and sides. Brush inside
and out with butter. Mix one cup of
reserved crumbs, celery and onions
with Chili. Fill loaf and replace top.
Wrap in foil and heat on cookie
sheet in 375° oven about 50
minutes. Remove top; sprinkle
filling with cheese. Cut loaf into 8
slices; serve hot.   *Serves 8*

VARIATION:

Fill French rolls. Heat in foil about
25 minutes.

SLOPPY JOE—TEXAS STYLE

Beef Barley Homemade
   SOUP STARTER™
1½ pounds ground beef
4 cups water
½ cup barbecue sauce
½ cup catsup
¼ cup chopped onion
2 teaspoons chili powder
2 cups shredded cabbage
Toasted buns

Brown meat in Dutch oven. Drain.
Add SOUP STARTER™ ingredients,
water, barbecue sauce, catsup,
onion and chili powder. Mix well.
Bring to a boil, reduce heat, cover
and simmer for 1 hour. Mix in
cabbage. Cook 5 minutes. Serve on
buns.   *Yield: 7 cups*

Bob Evans FARMS®

SAUSAGE SLOPPY JOES

1 lb. BOB EVANS FARMS® Roll
   Sausage
1 large onion, diced
2 8-oz. cans tomato sauce
½ small green pepper, diced
½ tsp. oregano (optional)
¼ tsp. basil (optional)
1 tsp. chili powder (optional)
1 tomato, diced (optional)

Brown BOB EVANS FARMS®
Sausage. Add onions and green
pepper. Cook a little longer, drain.
Add remaining ingredients and
simmer for 20 minutes. Serve on
hamburger buns or other bread.
Salt and pepper to taste.

SAVORY SLOPPY JOES

1 lb. ground beef
1 cup KRAFT Barbecue Sauce
¼ cup chopped green pepper
¼ cup chopped onion
8 hamburger buns, split
VELVEETA Pasteurized Process
   Cheese Spread, sliced

Brown meat; drain. Add barbecue
sauce, green pepper and onion.
Cover; simmer 5 minutes. For each
sandwich, spoon meat mixture
onto bottom half of bun; top with
process cheese spread. Broil until
process cheese spread melts.
Serve with top half of bun.
                    8 sandwiches

OPEN PIT® SLOPPY JOE

½ cup finely chopped onion
1 tablespoon butter or margarine, melted
1 pound ground beef
½ teaspoon salt
⅔ cup OPEN PIT® Barbecue Sauce, any flavor
4 hamburger buns or English muffins, split, toasted and buttered

Sauté onion in butter in skillet until tender. Add ground beef and salt. Cook and stir about 5 minutes. Pour off any excess fat. Stir in barbecue sauce and heat thoroughly. Serve on buns.
Makes 2 cups or 4 servings

CABBAGE JOES

1 pound lean ground beef
1 tablespoon shortening
1 cup HEINZ Tomato Ketchup
2 tablespoons chopped onion
1 teaspoon HEINZ Mild Mustard
½ teaspoon salt
¼ teaspoon pepper*
2 cups shredded cabbage
8-10 sandwich buns, split, toasted

Brown meat in shortening; drain excess fat. Add ketchup and next 4 ingredients; heat. Quickly stir in cabbage. Spoon filling on buns; serve immediately.
Makes about 3 cups filling

*If a less spicy flavor is desired, decrease pepper to ⅛ teaspoon.

SLOPPY JOES

2 lb. ground beef
1 c. chopped green pepper
1 c. chopped celery
1 c. chopped onion
2 c. barbecue sauce
2 c. water
1 c. 3-MINUTE BRAND® Oats
2 Tbsp. flour
1 tsp. salt

Combine beef, green pepper, celery and onion in skillet and cook until meat is browned. Add remaining ingredients and simmer for 35 minutes. Serve hot on buns.

BARBEQUED BEEF

½ cup chopped onion
1 Tablespoon butter or margarine
1 can (8 oz.) STOKELY'S FINEST® Tomato Sauce
¼ cup brown sugar
3 Tablespoons lemon juice
3 Tablespoons STOKELY'S FINEST® Tomato Catsup
1 Tablespoon Worcestershire sauce
1 teaspoon salt
1 teaspoon dry mustard
⅛ teaspoon garlic powder
3 cups cooked diced roast beef

Sauté onion in butter until tender. Stir in next 8 ingredients and heat until bubbling. Add beef and simmer 30 minutes, stirring occasionally. Serve on buns.
Makes 8 sandwiches

GRILLED TUNA 'N CHEESE SANDWICHES

1 can (6½ oz.) BUMBLE BEE® Chunk Light Tuna in Water
¼ cup diced onion
¼ cup diced celery
1 teaspoon prepared mustard
½ teaspoon marjoram, crumbled
⅓ cup mayonnaise
8 slices rye bread
4 slices Cheddar cheese
2 tablespoons butter, melted

Drain tuna. Combine tuna, onion, celery, mustard and marjoram. Fold in mayonnaise. Spoon mixture equally on 4 slices of bread. Top each with a slice of cheese and remaining bread. Brown sandwiches in butter pressing them down with a pancake turner. Turn and brown other side. Slice each sandwich in half.
Makes 4 servings

BAGEL TUNA ITALIANO, MELTED CHEESE

Spread half a LENDER'S Bagel with mayonnaise. Top with tuna fish salad, seasoned with Italian seasoning and garlic powder. Top with tomato slice and slice of cheese. Broil until cheese melts. Serve open-faced.

HOT TUNA SALAD SANDWICHES

1 can (6½ oz.) chunk light tuna, drained and flaked
2 Tablespoons mayonnaise
1 Tablespoon chopped celery
1 Tablespoon chopped onion
⅛ teaspoon salt
1 can (8½ oz.) STOKELY'S FINEST® Peas, drained
4 slices bread, toasted
4 slices Swiss cheese

Combine first 5 ingredients. Carefully fold in Peas, spread on toast. Broil 3 minutes; top each sandwich with cheese and broil until cheese begins to melt.
Makes 4 sandwiches

CALIFORNIA VEGGIE BURGERS

1 can (12½ oz.) BUMBLE BEE® Chunk Light Tuna*
8 English muffins
½ cup grated zucchini
3 eggs
1 cup minced onion
¾ cup minced DOLE® Fresh Mushrooms
¼ cup bread crumbs
¾ teaspoon Worcestershire sauce
½ teaspoon garlic powder
¼ teaspoon pepper
Vegetable oil for frying
Lettuce leaves
Tomato slices

Drain tuna. Split muffins in half lengthwise. Squeeze zucchini through a sieve to drain out excess water. Combine zucchini with tuna, eggs, onion, mushrooms, bread crumbs, Worcestershire, garlic powder and pepper. Form into 8 patties. Fry in oil on both sides until golden. Toast muffins. Serve burgers and muffins garnished with lettuce and tomato slices.
Makes 8 servings

*Or use 2 cans (6½ oz. each) BUMBLE BEE® Chunk Light Tuna.

BROILED TUNA MUSHROOM SANDWICH

1 can (7 oz.) BUMBLE BEE®
  Solid White Albacore Tuna
2 tablespoons finely chopped
  green onion
2 teaspoons lemon juice
½ teaspoon salt
⅛ teaspoon pepper
1 cup finely chopped DOLE®
  Fresh Mushrooms
1 cup grated Cheddar cheese
2 large eggs, separated
4 slices bread, lightly toasted
Butter

Drain and flake tuna. Mix with
onion, lemon juice, salt and
pepper. Add mushrooms and
cheese. Beat egg whites stiff but
not dry. Beat yolks lightly, and fold
into whites. Fold into tuna mixture.
Spread hot toast with butter. Heap
with tuna mixture, spreading just
to edges. Broil 8 inches from heat
5 to 6 minutes, until puffy and
browned.   *Makes 4 servings*
(Filling makes 2⅓ cups)

TUNA FRENCH ROLLS

1 can (12½ oz.) BUMBLE BEE®
  Chunk Light Tuna*
3 French rolls
1 package (8 oz.) cream cheese,
  softened
1 avocado, seeded, peeled and
  sliced
4 ounces alfalfa sprouts
1 stalk green onion, chopped
6 slices Monterey Jack cheese
1 tablespoon chopped parsley

Drain tuna. Split French rolls in
half lengthwise. Spread 1
tablespoon cream cheese on each
half reserving 2 tablespoons cream
cheese. Divide avocado slices and
alfalfa sprouts among rolls.
Combine tuna, remaining 2
tablespoons cream cheese and
green onion. Divide tuna mixture
among rolls. Top with a slice of
Monterey Jack cheese, tucking
mixture under cheese. Broil
sandwiches until golden. Garnish
with chopped parsley.
              Makes 6 servings

*Or use 2 cans (6½ oz. each)
  BUMBLE BEE® Chunk Light Tuna.

TUNA LORENZO

1 can (6½ oz.) BUMBLE BEE®
  Chunk Light Tuna in Water
¼ cup dairy sour cream
½ teaspoon chervil, crumbled
¼ teaspoon seasoned salt
2 English muffins
4 tomato slices
¼ cup grated Parmesan cheese

Drain tuna. Combine tuna, sour
cream, chervil and salt. Split
English muffins and brown in
broiler 4 inches from heat for 3 to
4 minutes. Top each muffin half
with tuna mixture, tomato slice
and 1 tablespoon cheese. Broil 5
minutes or until heated through.
              Makes 2 servings

377 calories per serving

A GREAT DANE: SMOKED SALMON & MUSHROOM OPEN FACE SANDWICH

Generously butter a slice of
BROWNBERRY® Dark Sandwich
Bread and arrange thin slices of
smoked salmon across it. Having
sautéed a few large mushroom
caps, place three or four of them
diagonally across the salmon.
Slide a small sprig of parsley or a
bit of chicory leaf under each
mushroom. Slice the sandwich
diagonally so that the cut bisects
and runs in the opposite direction
from the diagonally arranged line
of mushroom caps.

TASTE O' THE SEA SANDWICH
(Low Sodium)

1 can (7¾ oz.) unsalted Alaskan
  pink salmon packed in water,
  drained and flaked
¾ cup chopped PLANTERS® Dry
  Roasted Unsalted Peanuts
½ cup finely chopped tomato
¼ cup chopped green onion
¼ cup low-sodium mayonnaise
2 tablespoons lemon juice
2 tablespoons chopped fresh
  parsley
1 teaspoon basil
1 teaspoon marjoram
8 slices low-sodium white bread
8 lettuce leaves

In a medium mixing bowl combine
salmon, PLANTERS® Dry Roasted
Unsalted Peanuts, tomato, green
onion, mayonnaise, lemon juice,
parsley, basil and marjoram; blend
well. Spread ¼ cup salmon
mixture on each of four slices of
bread. Top with lettuce leaves and
remaining bread. Cut into quarters
to serve.
              Makes 4 sandwiches

Per sandwich: 380 calories, 40 mg.
sodium

BAKED SARDINE & CHEESE SANDWICH

¼ lb. Cheddar cheese, grated
4 hard-cooked eggs, chopped
2 cans KING OSCAR Sardines,
  drained
1 Tbsp. chopped celery
2 Tbsp. minced onion
3 Tbsp. green olives, chopped
2 Tbsp. pickle relish
½ cup mayonnaise
6 hamburger buns, split & buttered

Combine all ingredients except
buns. Fill each bun with sardine
mixture. Wrap in foil. Bake at
300°F. in oven for about 20
minutes.   *Serves 6*

SARDINE SUBMARINE

1 loaf French bread, split
  lengthwise and buttered
3 cans KING OSCAR Sardines,
  drained
1 (6 oz.) pkg. Monterey Jack cheese
2 ripe medium-size California
  avocados
3 Tbsp. lemon juice
Salt & pepper
2 cups shredded lettuce
1 (7¾ oz.) can Mexican hot style
  tomato sauce

Cover bottom half of buttered
bread with sardines. Top with
cheese. Mash avocados with
lemon juice, salt and pepper.
Spread mixture on top of cheese.
Sprinkle shredded lettuce over all,
and top with tomato sauce.
Replace top half of bread. Divide
into 6 portions.

MAINE SARDINE SANDWICH

Drain MAINE Sardines, mash and season sharply with lemon juice, TABASCO® and chili sauce. Spread on toast for a quick, high protein sandwich.

SARDINES A LA PARMIGIANA

6 English muffins, split and toasted
1 can (8 oz.) tomato sauce
½ tsp. oregano
⅛ tsp. each salt and pepper
4 Tbsp. Parmesan cheese
3 cans KING OSCAR Sardines, drained
12 oz. Mozzarella or Cheddar cheese, cut in 12 slices
Dash paprika

Stir oregano, salt and pepper into tomato sauce. Spoon a tablespoon of sauce mixture onto each muffin half. Sprinkle 1 teaspoon Parmesan cheese over each. Then place sardines on top, and add 1 slice of Mozzarella or Cheddar cheese to each muffin half. Sprinkle with paprika. Broil at 350° until heated through and cheese is melted. *Serves 6*

SCANDINAVIAN SANDWICH

6 slices rye bread
2 tablespoons butter or margarine
⅓ cup mayonnaise
¼ teaspoon dill weed
¼ teaspoon salt
3 slices FINLANDIA Swiss
1 can (3¾ ounces) sardines
2 green onions, thinly sliced
3 lettuce leaves
3 lemon slices

Spread bread with butter. Blend mayonnaise, dill and salt; spread on 3 slices of buttered bread. Arrange cheese, sardines, onion and lettuce on mayonnaise mixture. Cover with remaining slices of bread. Garnish with lemon slices.

Makes 3 sandwiches

ANTONIO'S SANDWICH

For each sandwich:
1 French roll or hero roll
1 can KING OSCAR Sardines
5 or 6 pepperocini in vinegar
2 or 3 slices Italian red onion
5 or 6 ripe pitted olives
Pepper

Slice roll lengthwise. Place sardines on bottom half, reserving oil. Remove stems from pepperocini, and slice pepperocini and olives and onions over sardines. Pour oil from sardines over all. Pepper to taste, and top with other half of roll.

FAST AND EASY SARDINE SANDWICH

For a quick summer sandwich, peel and chop a cucumber and mix with equal amount of drained MAINE Sardines. Season with horseradish, lemon juice and salt. Spread thickly on dark bread and serve with your favorite summer beverage.

COLE SLAW FISH-WICH

3 cups finely-shredded cabbage
¼ cup grated carrot
¼ cup chopped green pepper
½ cup chopped celery
⅓ cup mayonnaise
4 teaspoons vinegar
1 teaspoon milk
2 teaspoons sugar
½ teaspoon salt
⅛ teaspoon pepper
⅛ teaspoon celery seed
½ teaspoon prepared mustard
8 frozen VAN DE KAMPS® Fish Sticks
8 hot dog buns

Prepare cole slaw by tossing cabbage, carrot, green pepper and celery together in large bowl. Combine mayonnaise, vinegar, milk, sugar, salt, pepper, celery seed and mustard; mix thoroughly and pour over cabbage mixture, tossing to coat. Cover bowl tightly and refrigerate several hours or

overnight to blend flavors. To serve, prepare fish sticks according to package directions. Wrap hot dog buns in foil and heat in oven with fish sticks. Drain cole slaw and place ⅛ of slaw (about ¼ cup) into each heated bun, leaving a "nest" in the center. Place 1 fish stick in each "nest." Serve immediately.
Makes 8 sandwiches

INSTANT HINT: To make cole slaw, use prepared packaged cole slaw vegetables and mix with bottled cole slaw dressing as desired. Prepare fish sticks and hot dog buns and assemble sandwiches as directed.

NEW ORLEANS OYSTER LOAF

1 can (8 oz.) BUMBLE BEE® Whole Oysters
1 egg, beaten
¼ cup milk
½ cup cracker crumbs
Oil for frying
1 medium tomato, sliced
Crisp lettuce leaves
1 sourdough baguette, split and warmed
¼ cup tartar sauce
Dash cayenne pepper

Drain oysters. Combine egg and milk. Spoon in oysters. Roll oysters in cracker crumbs. Fry in hot oil until golden. Drain on paper towels. Arrange tomato slices and lettuce on one half of baguette. Combine tartar and cayenne pepper. Spread over remaining half of baguette. Top with oysters. Cut loaf into four pieces.
Makes 4 servings

CHILE CHEESE SANDWICHES

¼ cup butter, softened
2 teaspoons LAWRY'S® Garlic Spread Concentrate
8 medium size slices French bread
4 thick slices Monterey Jack cheese
Whole green chiles

Blend butter and Garlic Spread Concentrate. Spread mixture evenly on one side of each slice of bread. Place cheese and chile on unbuttered side of four slices, top with remaining four slices, buttered side out. Grill until golden brown. *Makes 4 sandwiches*

BURRITOS

8 flour tortillas
1 lb. JIMMY DEAN® Seasoned Taco Filling
1 can refried beans (heated)
1 cup grated cheddar cheese
1 cup hot sauce
1 cup shredded lettuce
1 cup chopped tomatoes
1 cup guacamole or additional hot sauce

Sauté JIMMY DEAN® Seasoned Taco Filling until brown and crumbly. Put 2 Tbsp. of filling and 1 Tbsp. canned refried beans on hot flour tortilla. Add 1 Tbsp. grated cheese, 1 Tbsp. hot sauce, and fold up. Garnish with lettuce, tomatoes, guacamole, or additional hot sauce. *Serves 8*

PUMPERNICKEL CHEESE DELISH

4 cups shredded FINLANDIA Swiss
3 tablespoons flour
1 teaspoon dry mustard
¾ cup beer
2 teaspoons Worcestershire sauce
1 tablespoon butter or margarine
1 egg, slightly beaten
4 slices pumpernickel bread, toasted
2 tablespoons chopped chives
2 large tomatoes, thickly sliced

Combine cheese, flour and mustard. Toss to coat cheese with flour. Combine in saucepan with beer, Worcestershire sauce and butter. Cook over medium heat, stirring constantly, until sauce is smooth and cheese is melted. Remove from heat and gradually blend in egg. Place bread in shallow baking dish. Top with all but ½ cup cheese sauce. Sprinkle with chives. Top with tomato slices. Spoon remaining cheese sauce over tomatoes. Broil until hot and bubbly.

Makes 4 servings

CLASSIC CHEESE RABBIT

2 cups (8 ozs.) shredded CRACKER BARREL Brand Sharp Natural Cheddar Cheese
½ cup beer or ale
2 tablespoons PARKAY Margarine
½ teaspoon paprika
¼ teaspoon dry mustard
1 egg, slightly beaten
White bread slices, toasted, cut in half diagonally

Heat cheese, beer, margarine and seasonings in double boiler or saucepan over low heat; stir until smooth. Blend in egg; stir until thickened. Serve over toast.

4 servings

VEGETABLE SANDWICH

2 slices bread
Mayonnaise
Tomato slices
Onion slices
Thin slices of jack cheese
CALAVO® Avocado slices

Spread bread with mayonnaise, arrange tomato, onion and cheese slices on bread. Add avocado slices to the top. *Serves 1*

NUTTY CARROT-RAISIN SANDWICH
(Low Sodium)

½ cup ground PLANTERS® Dry Roasted Unsalted Peanuts
½ cup coarsely grated carrot
¼ cup dark seedless raisins
6 tablespoons low-sodium mayonnaise
6 slices low-sodium white bread

In a small bowl mix PLANTERS® Dry Roasted Unsalted Peanuts, carrot, raisins and 4 tablespoons low-sodium mayonnaise. Spread nut mixture over 3 slices of bread. Spread remaining slices of bread with remaining mayonnaise and place over nut mixture. Slice and serve.

Makes 3 sandwiches

Per sandwich: 525 calories, 24 mg. sodium

LAND O'LAKES® VEGETARIAN STACK-UPS

1 c. bean sprouts
1 c. sliced mushrooms (⅛")
¼ c. sliced green onion (⅛")
¾ c. Italian dressing
¼ c. sugar
1 c. sour cream
¼ c. salad dressing or mayonnaise
2 Tbsp. prepared horseradish
2 tsp. *each* sugar and chervil
½ tsp. salt
½ tsp. hot pepper sauce
½ tsp. Worcestershire sauce
4 slices cracked wheat bread, toasted
8 leaves spinach
4 slices (3½ × 3½ × ⅛") LAND O LAKES® Natural Sharp Cheddar Cheese
4 slices (3½ × 3½ × ⅛") LAND O LAKES® Monterey Jack Cheese
1 c. sliced cucumber (⅛")
8 slices tomato (⅛")

In small bowl combine bean sprouts, mushrooms, onion, Italian dressing and sugar; stir to combine. Cover mixture and store in refrigerator for at least 2 hr. In small bowl combine sour cream, salad dressing, horseradish, sugar, chervil, salt, pepper sauce and Worcestershire sauce; stir to combine. For each sandwich, spread bread with 2 Tbsp. sour cream mixture. Layer the following on each sandwich: 2 leaves spinach, 1 slice Cheddar cheese, 1 slice Monterey Jack cheese, ¼ c. cucumber, 2 tomato slices and ¼ c. drained bean sprout mixture. Top each sandwich with 3 to 4 Tbsp. sour cream mixture.

Yield: 4 sandwiches

OPEN FACE VEGETABLE SANDWICH

Mayonnaise
1 slice bread
CALAVO® Avocado slices
CALAVO® Cucumber slices
Alfalfa sprouts
Nuts (walnuts)

Spread mayonnaise on bread, cover with cucumber slices and alfalfa sprouts, sprinkle with nuts and add avocado slices on top.

Serves 1

FROSTED SANDWICH LOAF

6 hard-cooked eggs, finely chopped
1 teaspoon KRAFT Pure Prepared
  Mustard
¼ teaspoon salt
Dash of pepper
MIRACLE WHIP Salad Dressing

2 cups finely chopped ham
¼ cup finely chopped sweet
  pickle
MIRACLE WHIP Salad Dressing

3 8-oz. pkgs. PHILADELPHIA
  BRAND Cream Cheese
¼ cup finely chopped watercress
Dash of salt and pepper

1 unsliced sandwich loaf, 16-inch
  long
Soft PARKAY Margarine
¼ cup milk

Combine eggs, mustard,
seasonings and enough salad
dressing to moisten; mix lightly.

Combine meat, pickle and enough
salad dressing to moisten; mix
lightly.

Combine ½ package softened
cream cheese, watercress and
seasonings, mixing until well
blended.

Trim crust from bread; cut into four
lengthwise slices. Spread bread
slices with margarine. Spread one
bread slice with egg salad, a
second slice with ham salad, and a
third slice with cream cheese
mixture. Stack layers; cover with
fourth bread slice. Combine
remaining cream cheese and milk,
mixing until well blended. Frost
sandwich loaf; chill thoroughly.

VEGETABLE GARDEN SALAD-SANDWICH

1 head iceberg lettuce
½ cup thinly sliced radish
½ cup finely chopped green
  pepper
2 tablespoons finely chopped
  green onion
Good Earth Dressing (recipe
  follows)
1 large avocado
8 large slices whole grain bread
Salt
2 medium tomatoes, sliced

Core, rinse and drain lettuce; chill
in disposable plastic bag or
crisper. Shortly before serving,
shred enough lettuce to measure 1
quart (lightly packed). Toss with
radish, green pepper and onion.
Chill until crisp. Prepare "Good
Earth Dressing." Peel and slice
avocado. Arrange on 4 slices bread
and spread to cover. Sprinkle with
salt and place tomato slices on
top. Toss lettuce mixture with
dressing and pile on each
sandwich. Top with second slice of
bread. Press down lightly and cut
in halves.

Makes 4 large sandwiches

GOOD EARTH DRESSING

Combine ½ cup corn oil, ¼ cup
garlic flavor red wine vinegar, 1½
teaspoons seasoned salt, 1
teaspoon *each* prepared mustard
and horseradish, ½ teaspoon
paprika and ⅛ teaspoon pepper in
a small jar. Cover and shake well.
Shake again just before using.

Makes about ¾ cup dressing

*Favorite recipe from California Iceberg
Lettuce Commission*

Pizza

ITALIAN DEEP DISH PIZZA

1 cup buttermilk biscuit mix
¼ to ⅓ cup milk
¼ cup each: chopped green
  pepper, onion
1 tablespoon vegetable oil
1 can (8 ounces) tomato sauce
½ lb. ECKRICH® Smoked Sausage,
  or Polska Kielbasa, diced
¾ teaspoon oregano
½ teaspoon each: salt, basil
1 package (10 ounces) frozen
  chopped spinach, thawed
½ cup (2 ounces) shredded
  mozzarella cheese

In bowl, combine biscuit mix and
¼ cup milk. Stir with fork until
dough clings together, adding
more milk if necessary. On lightly
floured surface, knead dough 8 to
10 times. Pat onto bottom and
sides of greased 9-inch pie plate;
set aside. Cook green pepper and
onion in oil until tender. Stir in
tomato sauce, sausage and
seasonings; set aside. Squeeze
liquid out of spinach until spinach
is almost dry. Spoon half of sauce
over crust, cover with spinach.
Spoon remaining sauce over
spinach. Sprinkle with cheese.
Bake at 400° for 20 minutes.

4 servings

DEEP DISH PIZZA

1 loaf RHODES Frozen White,
  French, Italian, or Honey Wheat
  Baking Dough, thawed according
  to package directions
1 tablespoon oil
1 cup tomato sauce
1 cup canned tomatoes, chopped
  and well drained
1 pound ground beef
⅓ cup each chopped green
  pepper, onion and mushrooms
8 ounces Mozzarella cheese,
  shredded
¼ cup grated Parmesan cheese
1 teaspoon each oregano and
  garlic powder
Salt and pepper

Shape thawed and softened dough
into a ball. Roll or stretch and pat
out to a 12-inch circle or to fit the
baking dish. Grease dish (12-inch
skillet or pizza pan or 13 × 9-inch
cake pan). Place dough in dish and
pat out to edges. Dough will be
springy. Let rest 15-25 minutes and
pat out to edges again. (Repeat if
necessary). Brown beef in oil. Drain
off excess fat. Add tomato sauce
and chopped tomatoes. When
dough fits pan, make a ridge along
edge so filling will not run over
edge. Spread with tomato/meat
mixture, green peppers, onions,
and mushrooms. Combine
cheeses, oregano, garlic powder,
salt and pepper. Sprinkle over
filling. Bake in a preheated 450°F.
oven for 20 minutes.

LAWRY'S® DEEP-DISH PIZZA

1 loaf frozen bread dough*
1¼ cups LAWRY'S® Extra Rich & Thick Spaghetti Sauce Mix, prepared according to package directions
½ teaspoon leaf oregano, crushed
12 ounces Mozzarella cheese, grated
6 ounces Provolone cheese, grated
2 ounces pepperoni, sliced
1 can (2¼ oz.) sliced ripe olives
1 cup sliced mushrooms
1 green bell pepper, sliced into rings
Optional additions and/or substitutions:
   Sausage   Green chiles
   Anchovies   Canadian bacon

Let dough thaw and rise once; punch down and roll out to fit a 15½ × 11-inch jelly roll pan. Spread sauce over dough; sprinkle with crushed oregano. Cover with grated cheese. Arrange the remaining ingredients (and optional additions and/or substitutions) on cheese. Bake in 400°F. oven (on lowest shelf) for ½ hour.

Makes 6 to 8 servings or approximately 24 appetizer portions

*Or your favorite pizza bread recipe

ITALIAN-STYLE PIZZA

2 packages (8 ounces each) SWIFT PREMIUM® Seasoned Hot or Milano Brand BROWN 'N SERVE® Sausage Links, cut into pennywise slices
Packaged hot roll mix or your favorite pizza dough recipe
¼ teaspoon salt
¼ teaspoon oregano
¼ teaspoon garlic salt
8 ounce can tomato sauce
6 ounce can tomato paste
2 cups (8 ounces) shredded sharp cheese
½ cup minced onion

Prepare pizza dough. Divide in half. Roll each half to fit a 14 inch pizza pan. Place on pans. Combine seasonings with tomato sauce and tomato paste. Spread tomato mixture over dough. Sprinkle cheese and onion over tomato mixture. Top with sausage pieces. Bake in 450°F. oven for 15 to 20 minutes.

Yield: 2 14-inch pizzas

PIZZA RUSTICA

1 package (15⅞ oz.) CHEF BOY-AR-DEE® Complete Cheese Pizza Mix
1 lb. Ricotta cheese
3 eggs
½ teaspoon salt
Dash pepper
Dash nutmeg
¼ lb. sliced salami or ham
¼ lb. sliced Provolone or Mozzarella
1 tablespoon melted butter

Prepare Pizza Flour Mix according to package directions. Let rise five minutes. Roll one-half dough out on floured board to fit 9″ pie pan. Place dough in pan, leaving a small overhang. Combine Ricotta cheese, canned grating cheese from package, eggs, salt, pepper and nutmeg. Layer ingredients in pie shell in this order: meat, Ricotta mixture and sliced cheese. Repeat. Roll out remaining dough. Place over pie. Trim off excess dough; crimp edges. Make four slits in crust and brush with butter. Bake at 350°F. for 40-45 minutes. Cut in wedges. Serve with hot pizza sauce from package.

Serves four to six

PIZZA WITH OATMEAL CRUST

Crust:
1 pkg. active dry yeast
¼ c. warm water (110°F.)
½ c. milk
¼ c. oil
1 tsp. salt
½ c. 3-MINUTE BRAND® Oats
1¾ to 2 c. flour

Topping:
10½ oz. can pizza sauce with cheese
1 lb. ground beef, browned
½ c. chopped green pepper
2 Tbsp. dry parsley flakes
1 tsp. dry oregano leaves
2 Tbsp. instant minced onion
Dash of salt
Dash of garlic salt
8 oz. Mozzarella cheese, grated
¼ c. grated Parmesan cheese

For crust, sprinkle yeast over warm water. Set aside to soften. Scald the milk. Add oil and salt and cool to lukewarm. Stir in the softened yeast and oats. Gradually add flour to form a stiff dough. Cover and let rise until double in size (30 to 40 minutes). Press the dough onto two greased pizza pans.

Divide the ingredients for the topping equally between the two pans. Spread the pizza sauce on the crust. Sprinkle the beef, green pepper and seasonings over the sauce. Top with the two cheeses. Bake at 425°F. for 20 minutes or until crust is brown and crisp.

FIVE CHEESE PIZZA CRESCENT

1 loaf frozen bread dough
1 cup (8 oz.) SARGENTO Shredded Cheese for Pizza
1 cup SARGENTO Shredded Monterey Jack
1 cup SARGENTO Provolone Cheese, grated
1 cup SARGENTO Swiss Cheese, grated
1 cup SARGENTO Shredded Cheddar
1 can mushrooms, bits and pieces, drained (4 oz.)
1 large tomato, diced
1 green pepper, diced
1 medium onion, sliced thin
½ teaspoon oregano
½ teaspoon pepper
½ teaspoon garlic
¼ cup SARGENTO Grated Parmesan Cheese
Olive oil

Defrost and raise bread dough according to package directions. Roll out dough to a thickness of ½ inch.

Spread cheese over dough. Sprinkle mushrooms, tomato and green pepper over cheese. Top with onion rings, seasonings and Parmesan cheese. Roll out dough, as you would a jelly roll. Shape into a crescent and seal the edges firmly.

Brush pizza crescent with olive oil. Puncture 3 or 4 times with a fork to allow steam to escape. Place on an oiled cookie sheet and bake in a preheated oven at 350° for 30-40 minutes or until dough is done and lightly browned.

Yield: 4-6 servings

HEALTH NUT PIZZA
(Low Sodium/Low Calorie)

4 cups unsifted flour (about)
1 package FLEISCHMANN'S®
  Active Dry Yeast
1¼ cups water
3 tablespoons FLEISCHMANN'S®
  Unsalted Margarine
2 tablespoons PLANTERS® Oil
1 cup chopped green pepper
½ cup chopped onion
1 teaspoon minced garlic
2 cans (16 oz. each) low-sodium
  tomatoes, coarsely chopped
1 teaspoon oregano
1 teaspoon basil
1 bay leaf
2 cups sliced mushrooms
1 cup thinly sliced zucchini
2 cups grated low-sodium
  Lorraine Swiss cheese
⅔ cup PLANTERS® Dry Roasted
  Unsalted Cashews

Combine 1¼ cups flour and yeast.
Heat water and margarine until
very warm (120°F.-130°F.). Add to
dry ingredients and beat 2 minutes.
Add ½ cup flour; beat 2 minutes.
Stir in enough additional flour to
make a soft dough. On floured
board knead 6 to 8 minutes. Place
in greased bowl, turning to grease
top. Cover; let rise until doubled,
about 50 minutes.

Heat oil in a large skillet. Add
green pepper, onion, and garlic;
sauté until tender. Add tomatoes,
oregano, basil and bay leaf; bring
to a boil. Reduce heat and simmer
20 minutes. Add mushrooms and
zucchini; simmer 15 minutes.

Punch dough down. Divide in half.
Roll out into 2 12-inch circles.
Press into 2 12-inch pizza pans,
forming rim. Cover; let rise 30
minutes. Sprinkle ¾ cup grated
cheese on each. Spread each with
vegetable mixture. Sprinkle with
remaining cheese and
PLANTERS® Dry Roasted
Unsalted Cashews. Bake at 400°F.
for 30 to 35 minutes. Slice and
serve.

Makes 2 12-inch pizzas (20 slices)

Per slice: 210 calories, 7 mg.
sodium

FIX-A-PIZZA!

4 cups FRITOS® Brand Corn Chips
½ pound Mozzarella cheese,
  sliced thin
1 pound ground beef
1 clove garlic, minced
1 12-ounce can tomato paste
1 teaspoon salt
¼ teaspoon black pepper
1 teaspoon oregano
1 3-ounce can mushrooms,
  drained and sliced
3 eggs, well beaten
½ cup canned tomatoes, drained
  and cut into pieces
1 2-ounce can anchovies
½ cup grated sharp Cheddar
  cheese
¼ cup grated Parmesan cheese

Arrange the FRITOS® Brand Corn
Chips in a 12″ pizza pan. Cover
with Mozzarella cheese slices.
Sauté ground beef with garlic until
light brown. Add tomato paste,
salt, pepper, oregano, mushrooms
and eggs. Mix well. Spread beef
mixture over cheese. Sprinkle with
tomato pieces, Cheddar cheese,
and anchovies. Top with Parmesan
cheese. Bake at 375°F. for 20
minutes. *Makes 1 12″ pizza*

MAINE SARDINE PIZZA

1 package pizza mix
2 cans (4 oz. ea.) MAINE Sardines
3 tablespoons salad oil
1 large clove garlic, minced
1 can (8 oz.) tomato sauce
4 tomatoes, sliced
2 sweet onions, sliced
2 green peppers, sliced
1 tablespoon minced parsley
½ teaspoon salt
⅛ teaspoon pepper
1 teaspoon oregano
4 slices mozzarella cheese
Parmesan cheese, grated

Prepare dough according to
package directions. Pat into 12″
pizza pan. Drain MAINE Sardines
and mash 2 or 3 with 1 tablespoon
salad oil, garlic and tomato sauce.
Spread over pizza dough. Arrange
tomato slices, onion, and green
pepper on sauce and top with
whole sardines. Combine parsley,
seasonings, and remaining oil.

Drizzle over sardines and
vegetables. Dot with mozzarella
cheese. Bake 30-35 minutes in a
hot oven (450°F.) until crust is well
browned. Sprinkle with Parmesan
cheese. *Yield: 6 servings*

HAM 'N CHEESE PIZZA

Crust:
1 (15-ounce) package DROMEDARY
  Corn Bread Mix
¼ cup butter or margarine,
  softened
1 egg
3 tablespoons milk

Topping:
4 slices boiled ham (about
  4 ounces)
4 slices natural Swiss or Cheddar
  cheese (about 4 ounces)
2 eggs
¼ cup milk
Parsley flakes

Empty corn bread mix into medium
mixing bowl. Cut butter or
margarine into mix until coarse
and crumbly. Add egg and milk and
mix until dry ingredients are
moistened. With floured hands
press mixture evenly against
bottom and sides of a well-greased
12-inch pizza pan and forming an
edge about ½ inch above the sides
of the pan.

Line bottom of crust with ham; top
with a layer of cheese. Beat eggs
and milk together and pour over
ham and cheese. Sprinkle with
parsley. Bake in a preheated hot
oven (400°F.) 20 to 25 minutes, or
until eggs are firm and crust is
browned.
  Makes 8 (about 4¾-inch) wedges

CHILI STYLE PIZZA

12 tortillas
1 19 oz. can WOLF® Brand
  Chili (with or without Beans)
1 medium green pepper, cut into
  strips
1 small onion
½ lb. KRAFT Jalapeno Pepper
  Process Cheese Spread, cubed

Cover bottom and sides of lightly
greased 14-inch round pizza pan
with tortillas. Spread chili evenly
over tortillas to edge. Top with
green pepper and onion. Bake at
350°, 20 minutes. Top with process
cheese spread, continue baking 5
minutes. *6 servings*

AFTER-THE-GAME PIZZA

1 loaf Italian bread (about 14"
   long), split and toasted
1 jar (14 oz.) RAGU' Pizza Quick
   Sauce—Traditional or With
   Mushrooms
1½ cups thinly sliced pepperoni
   (about ¾ pound)
2 cans (4 oz. each) sliced
   mushrooms, drained
2 medium green peppers, sliced
   into rings
2 cups shredded mozzarella cheese

Preheat oven to 425°F. Cover each
piece of bread with half a jar of
sauce. Evenly top with pepperoni,
mushrooms, green peppers and
cheese. Bake 20 minutes or until
heated through.
Serves about 6

PIZZA QUICKIES

3 Tablespoons butter or margarine,
   softened
4 English muffins, split
1 can (8 oz.) STOKELY'S FINEST®
   Tomato Sauce
2 Tablespoons finely chopped
   onion
¼ teaspoon garlic salt
¼ teaspoon oregano
1 pkg. (10 oz.) brown and serve
   sausages, sliced (optional)
½ cup shredded mozzarella cheese

Butter each muffin half. Combine
next 4 ingredients and spread on
muffins. Arrange sausage slices on
muffins, if desired. Top each with
cheese; broil until cheese melts.
Makes 8 mini-pizzas

MERRY PIZZA ROUNDS

1 can of your favorite pizza or
   spaghetti sauce
1 pound BORDEN® Mozzarella
   Cheese
1 pound OSCAR MAYER Jumbo
   Franks
5 BAYS® English Muffins, split

Cut 10 deep crosswise slits along
one side of each frankfurter
without cutting completely
through. Broil 2 to 3 minutes or

until lightly browned. Cut 10 round
thin slices of cheese about 1
ounce each and place on muffins.
Broil 2 minutes, or until melted.
Place one hot dog on each muffin
and top with 2 tablespoons sauce.
Fill center with remaining grated
cheese, sprinkle with a pinch of
oregano. Broil 2 minutes more.
Makes 10 servings

*Favorite recipe from International Sausage
Council*

ROAST BEEF MUFFIN PIZZAS

1 can (8 ounces) tomato sauce
2 tablespoons grated onion
Dash of garlic powder
½ teaspoon dried leaf oregano
4 English muffins, split and
   toasted
1 can (4¾ ounces) UNDERWOOD®
   Roast Beef Spread
¼ cup grated Parmesan cheese

In a bowl, mix together tomato
sauce, onion, garlic powder and
oregano. Spread sauce over each
muffin. Top with roast beef spread.
Sprinkle with cheese; place on
baking sheet and broil about 4
inches from heat until hot and
bubbly. *Makes 8 snacks*

MINI FINN PIZZA

½ pound hot Italian sausage
1 small clove garlic, minced
1 can (15 ounces) tomato·sauce
2 tablespoons tomato paste
½ pound shredded FINLANDIA
   Swiss
Crushed oregano
Crushed red peppers, optional
6 English muffins, split and
   toasted
6 tablespoons butter or margarine

Remove skin from sausage and
break into small pieces. Brown in
skillet with garlic. Add tomato
sauce and paste; simmer 5
minutes. Spread muffins with
butter while hot. Top with tomato
sauce mixture. Top with cheese;
sprinkle with oregano and red
peppers. Bake at 400°F. until hot
and bubbly. *Makes 12 servings*

PIZZA SNACKS

2 tablespoons butter, softened
½ teaspoon garlic powder
1 teaspoon sweet basil, crumbled
3 English muffins, split
1 cup sliced DOLE® Fresh
   Mushrooms
⅓ cup pizza sauce with cheese
¾ cup shredded mozzarella cheese

Combine butter, garlic powder and
basil; spread over English muffins.
Broil until toasted. Top with
mushrooms, pizza sauce and
cheese. Broil until cheese melts.
Makes 6 snacks

PIZZA BAGEL

Spread LENDER'S Bagel halves
with grilled onions. Top with
tomato sauce mixed with
parmesan cheese and Italian
seasoning or spaghetti sauce. Add
mozzarella cheese and your
favorite meat or fish topping. Broil
until bubbly.

BAYS® ENGLISH MUFFIN PARTY PIZZAS

¼ lb. ground beef
¼ lb. hot Italian sausage
1 can condensed tomato soup
2 tablespoons water
1 teaspoon crushed oregano
1 clove garlic, minced
Dash pepper
3 BAYS® English Muffins, lightly
   toasted
10 slices mozzarella cheese
Green pepper strips
Stuffed green olives

Sauté ground beef and sausage
until browned. Drain excess fat.
Add soup, water, oregano, garlic
and ground pepper. Cover and
simmer for 5 minutes over low
heat. Place a slice of cheese on
each toasted muffin half. Top with
meat mixture then place an "X" of
cheese strips made from the
remaining slices of mozzarella.
Decorate with pepper strips and
olive slices. Bake at 400° for 5-10
minutes or until the cheese melts
and the pizzas are heated through.
6 servings

Pancakes, Waffles and Crepes

BANANA-SPICE PANCAKES WITH WHIPPED HONEY-BUTTER

Honey-Butter:
½ cup butter or margarine
¼ cup honey

Pancakes:
1 cup AUNT JEMIMA® Buttermilk
   Complete Pancake & Waffle Mix
½ cup water
½ cup mashed ripe banana
2 eggs
½ teaspoon cinnamon

For honey-butter: Beat butter at high speed on electric mixer until light and fluffy. Gradually beat in honey; chill.

For pancakes: Heat lightly greased griddle over medium heat (350°F. for electric griddle). Combine all ingredients, mixing until batter is fairly smooth. For each pancake, pour scant ¼ cup batter onto hot griddle. Turn when pancakes begin to rise and edges look cooked. Turn only once. Serve with Honey-Butter.

Makes 8 to 10 pancakes

PANCAKES CHIQUITA® BANANA STYLE

Make pancake mix according to package directions and to each cup of batter add ½ cup of diced or sliced CHIQUITA® Brand Bananas (about 1 large or 2 small bananas). Cook until golden brown. Serve with Banana Honey Topping.*

*BANANA HONEY TOPPING

2 ripe CHIQUITA® Brand Bananas
2 to 4 tablespoons honey
2 tablespoons whipped butter or margarine (or softened regular butter or margarine)

Peel and mash bananas. Blend in honey and butter.

NUT PANCAKES

1¼ cups sifted all-purpose flour
1 teaspoon baking powder
½ teaspoon soda
1 tablespoon sugar
1 egg, beaten
1½ cups buttermilk
2 tablespoons butter, melted
¼ cup chopped FISHER®
   Salted, Roasted Sunflower Nuts

Sift together flour, baking powder, soda and sugar. Combine egg, buttermilk and butter; add to dry ingredients, stirring just until flour is moistened. Fold in nuts. Using ¼ cup measure, pour batter onto hot griddle. Bake until top is bubbly and edges baked. Turn and bake other side.

Makes 8 cakes

PISTACHIO PANCAKES

2 cups flour
2 cups milk
3 egg yolks
1 Tbsp. butter, melted
2 Tbsp. brandy
⅛ tsp. salt
½ cup ground BLUE RIBBON®
   Pistachios

In large bowl, mix flour and milk. Stir in egg yolks and butter. Blend in brandy, salt and nuts. Batter should be thin, adjust by adding a little milk if necessary. Butter 6 inch skillet and place over medium heat. Pour in enough batter to cover bottom. When pancake is golden on both sides, butter and roll up. Serve with favorite toppings.

BRAN 'N DATE GRIDDLE CAKES

1 cup all-purpose flour
¼ cup granulated sugar
2½ teaspoons baking powder
½ teaspoon salt
½ teaspoon ground cinnamon
1 cup milk
1 egg, beaten
¼ cup vegetable oil
1 cup NABISCO® 100% Bran
   Cereal
1 cup DROMEDARY Chopped
   Dates

Mix together first five ingredients in a medium bowl. Combine next three ingredients; stir into dry ingredients until just blended. Batter will look lumpy. Fold in bran and dates. Preheat greased griddle or skillet on medium-low heat.* For each pancake drop one rounded tablespoonful on griddle. Cook until bubbles appear on the surface and bottom is evenly browned. Turn; brown other side. Serve with whipped cream cheese, butter or margarine.

Makes 18 (about 3-inch) pancakes

About 117 calories per griddle cake.

*If griddle is hot enough, a few drops of water will bounce a second before evaporating.

FEATHERLIGHT YOGURT PANCAKES

2 cups flour
2 teaspoons baking powder
1 teaspoon baking soda
1 tablespoon sugar
1 teaspoon salt
1 cup (8 oz.) BREYERS® Plain Yogurt
1 to 1¼ cups milk
2 eggs, slightly beaten
¼ cup melted butter or margarine

Sift together flour, baking powder, soda, sugar, and salt. Combine yogurt, milk, and eggs. Stir in butter. Pour liquids into flour mixture, mixing just until dampened. Pour ¼ cup batter on hot greased griddle for each pancake.

Makes 16 pancakes, 4½ inches

FLUFFY POLKA-DOT PANCAKES

1 cup raisins
1 teaspoon cinnamon
¼ cup sugar
3 eggs, separated
1¾ cups buttermilk
1 teaspoon soda
1½ cups flour
1 teaspoon baking powder
1 teaspoon salt
3 tablespoons butter or margarine, melted

Plump raisins in hot water for several minutes; drain and dry on paper towels. Mix cinnamon with *2 tablespoons* of the sugar and toss with raisins; set aside. Beat egg whites to soft peaks; add remaining 2 tablespoons sugar, beating until stiff peaks form. In large bowl, beat egg yolks until creamy. Stir in buttermilk and soda. Sift flour, baking powder and salt and blend into buttermilk mixture. Stir in melted butter. Fold in beaten egg whites. Gently fold in cinnamon-coated raisins. Spoon batter onto lightly greased griddle; bake, turning once.

Makes 16 to 18 large pancakes

Favorite recipe from California Raisin Advisory Board

COTTAGE CHEESE PANCAKES

1 cup SEALTEST® Cottage Cheese
6 eggs, well beaten
6 tablespoons all-purpose flour
6 tablespoons melted margarine

Beat the cottage cheese with a whisk or hand beater, until smooth. Add the remaining ingredients and beat until well blended. Drop the batter by spoonfuls on a hot buttered griddle or frying pan and cook as any pancake until brown on both sides, turning only once.

6 servings

APPLE RICE PANCAKES

1 egg
1 cup Dutch apple yogurt
½ cup milk
2 tablespoons oil
1 cup flour
1 tablespoon sugar
1 teaspoon baking powder
½ teaspoon baking soda
½ teaspoon salt
1 cup cooked SUCCESS® Rice*

Heat electric griddle to 375°F. or regular griddle until drops of cold water bounce on the surface. In bowl, mix egg, yogurt, milk and oil. Add remaining ingredients and mix until large lumps disappear. Lightly grease griddle. Pour batter, about ¼ cup at a time, onto griddle. Bake until bubbles form and edges start to dry; turn and bake other side. *Makes 12 4" pancakes*
*Use leftover rice from dinner.

HAWAIIAN PANCAKES

1 can (1 lb. 4 oz.) DOLE® Chunk Pineapple in Juice
1½ cups maple syrup
1 package pancake mix
Honey Butter*

Drain pineapple reserving all juice. Combine juice and maple syrup in a heavy saucepan. Heat. Make pancakes according to package directions. Top pancakes with pineapple chunks. Serve with warm syrup and Honey Butter.

Makes 4 servings

*HONEY BUTTER

Combine equal amounts of honey and softened butter (about ⅓ cup each). Blend well. Store in covered container in refrigerator.

APPLE SAUCE PANCAKES

1 cup sifted flour
½ tsp. salt
1½ tsp. baking powder
1 cup LUCKY LEAF® Apple Sauce
¼ tsp. grated lemon or orange peel
¼ tsp. cinnamon
1 Tbsp. sugar
¼ tsp. vanilla extract
2 eggs, separated
1½ tsp. melted butter (or margarine)

Sift flour, salt and baking powder into mixing bowl. Blend in next 5 ingredients. Beat egg yolks and add with butter. Beat egg whites until stiff and fold in. Pour about ¼ cup batter for each pancake onto hot greased griddle. Turn cakes once.

Makes 10 pancakes

BRAN PANCAKES

½ cup NABISCO® 100% Bran Cereal
½ cup pancake mix
⅔ cup milk
1 egg
1 tablespoon vegetable oil

In medium bowl, combine NABISCO® 100% Bran Cereal and pancake mix. Stir in milk, egg and vegetable oil. Let stand 5 minutes. Using a scant ¼ cup batter for each pancake, cook on lightly greased griddle, browning on both sides.

Makes 10 pancakes

CANADIAN FLAPJACKS

1 pint buttermilk
2 cups E-Z BAKE Flour
2 eggs
2 tablespoons melted butter
1 teaspoon soda
½ teaspoon salt
Strawberries or apple sauce

Gradually beat the buttermilk into the flour. When smooth, cover and let stand several hours. Then add remaining ingredients, beating eggs in well. Bake on greased, hot griddle. Spread with butter and pile in layers with sliced sugared strawberries or sweetened apple sauce for filling.

Second Prize Winner E-Z-BAKE Flour Contest

JEAN ALICE PANCAKES

2 eggs
1¼ cups flour
¾ cup MALT-O-MEAL®
1 tsp. soda
1 tsp. salt
1 Tbsp. baking powder
1 Tbsp. sugar
2 cups buttermilk or sour milk
2 Tbsp. melted shortening

Beat eggs in mixer bowl. Add remaining ingredients; beat until smooth. Bake on hot griddle.* For lighter batter, add more buttermilk.
Makes 8—6-inch pancakes

*Griddle is hot enough when droplets of water "skip" along griddle.

HEARTLAND® PANCAKES

1 cup milk
1 cup HEARTLAND® Natural Cereal, Plain, Raisin, or Coconut
¾ cup all purpose flour
2 teaspoons baking powder
½ teaspoon salt
1 egg
2 tablespoons melted butter or margarine

Pour milk over cereal. Let set 5 minutes. Meanwhile, stir together flour, baking powder and salt. Beat egg and melted butter into cereal mixture. Add flour mixture. Stir until smooth. Pour onto oiled griddle, using about ¼ cup batter for each pancake. Cook until bubbly. Turn. Serve hot with butter and syrup.
Makes 9, 4-inch pancakes

OLD-TIME BUCKWHEAT CAKES

1 cup ELAM'S® Pure Buckwheat Flour
1 teaspoon baking powder
¼ teaspoon salt
1 egg
1¼ cups sour milk* or buttermilk
½ teaspoon baking soda
1 tablespoon cooking oil or melted shortening
1 tablespoon molasses

Combine and mix flour, baking powder and salt in bowl; save. Combine remaining ingredients in bowl in order listed. Add flour mixture; beat just until batter is smooth. For each pancake, pour ¼ cup batter onto hot lightly greased griddle. Bake until top is covered with bubbles and edges look cooked. Turn; brown second side. Batter tends to thicken as it stands; stir well just before using. Serve with butter and syrup.
Yield: 8 to 9 cakes, 4½ to 5 inches in diameter or 4 servings

*To make "sour" milk, measure 3¾ teaspoons vinegar into measuring cup. Add enough sweet milk to make 1¼ cups. Let stand 5 minutes.

MAYPO® PANCAKES

2 cups sifted flour
3 teaspoons baking powder
1 teaspoon salt
½ cup MAYPO® 30-Second Oatmeal
2 cups milk
2 eggs
¼ cup melted shortening

Sift flour, baking powder and salt together. Stir in MAYPO®. Combine milk and eggs; beat well. Add to dry ingredients and mix thoroughly. Stir in melted shortening. Drop by spoonsful onto hot greased griddle. Turn pancakes when covered with bubbles; turn only once. (Batter thickens as it stands; for thinner pancakes, add slightly more milk.)
Makes 12 medium

TINY RICE FLOUR PANCAKES

1 cup ELAM'S® Stone Ground Brown Rice Flour
2 teaspoons baking powder
2 tablespoons honey
¾ cup milk
2 eggs, beaten
2 tablespoons cooking oil

Combine ELAM'S® Stone Ground Brown Rice Flour and baking powder in bowl, mix. Add milk, eggs, oil and honey, stir just until smooth. For each pancake pour 1 tablespoon of batter onto a hot lightly greased griddle. Bake until top is full of bubbles and underside is brown. Turn carefully

with wide spatula and brown second side. Serve with butter and syrup, honey or applesauce.
Yield: About 32 pancakes, 4 to 6 servings

SOY PANCAKES

1 cup milk
2 tablespoons soybean or cooking oil
2 eggs
1 teaspoon vanilla, optional
¾ cup sifted ELAM'S® Soy Flour
¼ cup ELAM'S® 100% Whole Wheat Pastry Flour
1 tablespoon sugar
1 teaspoon baking powder
½ teaspoon salt

Combine milk, oil, eggs and vanilla; beat just until well mixed. Combine dry ingredients in bowl; mix well. Add liquids to dry ingredients and beat just until smooth. For each pancake pour a scant ¼ cup batter onto moderately hot grill (375°F.). Cook until pancake is cooked on underside and top is full of bubbles; turn and cook until done and browned on underside.
Yield: About 1⅞ cups batter, 8 pancakes

GRAHAM CRACKER FLIPS

7 HONEY MAID Graham Crackers, finely rolled (about ½ cup crumbs)
½ cup pancake mix
⅔ cup milk
1 egg
1 tablespoon vegetable oil
Honey or maple syrup

Combine cracker crumbs and pancake mix in a mixing bowl. Add next three ingredients and stir until fairly smooth. Pour batter from ¼-cup measuring cup onto preheated lightly greased griddle (about 400°F.*). Cook first side, leaving about an inch between pancakes, until bubbles appear on the surface and bottom is evenly browned. Flip over and cook second side until golden brown (bottom will not be as evenly browned as first side). Serve with honey or maple syrup.
Makes 8 (about 4-inch) pancakes

*If griddle is hot enough, a few drops of water will bounce a second before evaporating.

CORN FESTIVAL FRITTERS

½ cup sifted flour
¾ teaspoon baking powder
¼ teaspoon salt
2 teaspoons IMPERIAL Granulated Sugar
1 egg
¼ cup water or milk
1 tablespoon cooking oil
1 cup fresh or canned whole kernel corn
Brown Sugar Syrup (recipe follows)

Combine dry ingredients and mix well. Combine remaining ingredients and stir into dry ingredients. Drop by tablespoonfuls into hot oil (375°F.). Fry until golden brown, turning once. Serve with Brown Sugar Syrup.

Makes about 12 (2") fritters

BROWN SUGAR SYRUP

In saucepan, combine 1 pound (2⅓ cups) IMPERIAL Brown Sugar, dash of salt and 1 cup of water; bring to boil. Reduce heat and simmer 10 minutes. Thickens upon cooling.

HOT TURKEY PAN-SANS

Filling:
2 cups chopped cooked turkey or chicken
1 10¾-oz. can condensed cream of mushroom soup
⅓ cup milk

Pancakes:
1 cup AUNT JEMIMA® Original Pancake & Waffle Mix
1 cup milk
1 egg
1 tablespoon vegetable oil

For filling: In medium saucepan, combine all ingredients; heat thoroughly.

For pancakes: Heat lightly greased griddle over medium heat (350°F. for electric griddle). Combine all ingredients, mixing until batter is fairly smooth. For each pancake, pour scant ¼ cup batter onto hot griddle. Turn when tops are covered with bubbles and edges look cooked. Turn only once. For each serving, place 1 pancake on plate; top with filling. Place second pancake over filling. Top with hot cranberry sauce, if desired.

Makes 6 servings

TOAD-IN-THE-HOLE

8 ounce package SWIFT PREMIUM® Original BROWN 'N SERVE® Sausage Links
2 eggs
½ teaspoon salt
1 cup sifted flour
1 cup milk
Maple syrup

Beat eggs and salt until frothy. Add flour and milk. Beat until mixture is smooth and creamy. Refrigerate batter at least 1 hour. Place sausages in a 10-inch heavy skillet. Bake in a 425°F. oven about 5 minutes. Remove skillet from oven. Arrange sausages in spoke-like fashion. Pour batter over sausages. Return skillet to oven. Bake 20 to 25 minutes until puffy and well browned. Serve immediately with maple syrup.

Yield: 4 to 5 servings

HAM GRIDDLE CAKES

1 cup milk
1 cup quick or old-fashioned oats
2 tablespoons vegetable oil
2 eggs
½ cup flour
2 tablespoons sugar
1 tablespoon baking powder
1 cup diced ARMOUR® STAR Ham
Maple syrup, heated

Combine milk and oats; let stand 5 minutes. Add oil and eggs; mix well. Stir in flour, sugar and baking powder only until moistened; stir in ham. Cook on hot lightly greased griddle, using ¼ cup batter for each. Turn when top is bubbly and edges slightly dry. Serve with syrup. Preparation time: 25 minutes.

4 servings

GALLO® SALAME OVEN PANCAKE

½ cup finely diced GALLO® Italian Dry Salame
4 GALLO® Salame Slices, cut in half
3 eggs
½ cup unsifted all-purpose flour
½ teaspoon salt
½ cup milk
2 Tbsp. melted butter
Fresh fruit or apricot jam for garnish
Sour cream

Place eggs in blender container and blend. Add flour, salt, milk. Blend until smooth. Stir in GALLO® Italian Dry Salame and butter. Pour into well-buttered 10-inch pie pan. Lay GALLO® Salame half slices on top. Bake 20 min. at 450°. Reduce to 350°. Bake 5 to 10 minutes longer or until golden brown. Place in a heated plate and serve at once, cut in wedges. Pass fruit and sour cream to spoon over.

Serves 3 to 4

OVEN BAKED APPLE PANCAKES 'N SAUSAGE

8 ounce package SWIFT PREMIUM⌐ Maple Flavored BROWN 'N SERVE® Sausage Links
1 cup pancake mix
¼ teaspoon ground nutmeg
¼ teaspoon ground cinnamon
½ cup milk
1 egg
½ cup chopped apple

Brown sausages according to package directions. In a mixing bowl, combine all ingredients except apple. Mix until batter is smooth. Add apple. Pour into a well-greased 10 by 6 by 2 inch baking dish. Arrange sausages on top. Bake in 450°F. oven for 20 minutes. Serve hot with maple syrup.

Yield: 5 servings

POTATO PANCAKES

Beat one egg well in bowl. Mix in 1¼ cups cold water. (For thicker pancakes less water may be used.) Add one package CARMEL KOSHER® Potato Pancake (and Kugel) Mix and stir until batter is well mixed. Do not add any salt. Heat oil or shortening in pan until very hot (slightly smoking). Pour amount of batter desired with tablespoon and fry on both sides until pancakes are golden brown.

Note: For extra rich potato pancakes use two eggs and 1 cup cold water. Follow same directions for preparation as above.

FRIED MUSH

Pour cooked corn meal mush (recipe follows) into 8 x 4-inch loaf pan. Cool slightly; cover. Refrigerate several hours or overnight. Cut chilled mush into 12 slices. Pan-fry in small amount of butter in large heavy skillet over medium heat, about 10 minutes per side or until golden brown. Serve with AUNT JEMIMA® Syrup.

Makes 6 servings

CORN MEAL MUSH

1 cup QUAKER® or AUNT
   JEMIMA® Enriched Corn Meal
1 teaspoon salt
1 cup cold water
3 cups boiling water

Combine corn meal, salt and cold water. Gradually pour into boiling water in 2-qt. saucepan, stirring constantly. Return to boil, stirring constantly. Reduce heat; cover. Continue cooking over low heat about 5 minutes, stirring frequently.

Makes 6 servings

CHEESE-POTATO PANCAKES

4 medium boiling potatoes, peeled
   and shredded
1 cup (4 oz.) SARGENTO Shredded
   Monterey Jack Cheese
¼ cup coarsely shredded onion
   (1 small)
3 eggs
2 Tbsp. flour
1 tsp. salt
⅛ tsp. pepper
Oil
Applesauce (optional)

In large bowl mix potatoes, cheese, onion, eggs, flour, salt and pepper. In large skillet heat enough oil to coat bottom. With ¼ cup measure drop in potato batter; with back of spoon spread evenly, forming 3 inch pancake. Cook both sides over medium-high heat until golden brown and crisp. Drain on paper towels. Serve at once with applesauce.

Makes about 12

Waffles

BELGIAN WAFFLES

1½ cups flour
2 tablespoons IMPERIAL
   Granulated Sugar
2 teaspoons baking powder
½ teaspoon soda
¼ teaspoon salt
3 egg yolks, beaten
¾ cup sour cream
¾ cup buttermilk
¼ cup shortening, melted and
   cooled
¼ cup butter or margarine, melted
   and cooled
3 egg whites, stiffly beaten

Whisk dry ingredients together. Combine beaten egg yolks, sour cream and buttermilk and add to dry ingredients alternately with cooled fats. Stir gently until no longer lumpy. Fold in stiffly beaten egg whites. Cook in waffle iron. Serve with Cherry Topping.*

Makes 10 waffles

*CHERRY TOPPING

2 cups (1 pound can) red sour
   pitted cherries, drained
½ cup IMPERIAL Granulated
   Sugar
1 tablespoon lemon juice
1 teaspoon cornstarch dissolved
   in a little water

Combine cherries, IMPERIAL Granulated Sugar and lemon juice in saucepan and bring to boil. Stir in dissolved cornstarch (add a few drops red food color if desired) and cook over low heat, stirring, until thickened and translucent. Serve on waffles (kept warm in heated oven) with peaks of whipped cream sweetened with IMPERIAL 10X Powdered Sugar.

Note: These waffles are delicious topped with creamed chicken or used like English muffins for Eggs Benedict.

CHOCOLATE BANANA WAFFLES

½ cup butter
1 square (1 oz.) semi-sweet
   chocolate
1 cup sifted all-purpose flour
3 tablespoons sugar
1¾ teaspoons baking powder
¼ teaspoon baking soda
¼ teaspoon salt
2 large eggs
1 cup buttermilk
1 medium DOLE® Banana
Banana Hard Sauce*

Melt butter with chocolate and let cool while measuring remaining ingredients. Resift flour with sugar, baking powder, soda and salt. Add eggs, buttermilk and butter-chocolate mixture. Beat with rotary beater until smooth. Dice banana to make ½ cup. Fold in banana. Heat waffle iron, setting control to moderately low. Pour in 1 cup batter or enough to cover iron. Cook about 6 minutes, or until waffle stops steaming. Repeat, until all of batter is baked. Serve with Banana Hard Sauce.

Makes 3 (10½ x 6 inch) waffles

*BANANA HARD SAUCE

¼ cup soft butter
1½ cups sifted powdered sugar
2 teaspoons lemon juice
1 small DOLE® Banana, chopped

Beat together butter, sugar and lemon juice until smooth. Stir in banana. *Makes 1 cup*

WHEATENA® BUTTERMILK WAFFLES

1¾ cups sifted flour
2 teaspoons baking powder
1 teaspoon soda
½ teaspoon salt
½ cup WHEATENA®
2 eggs
2 cups buttermilk or sour milk
6 tablespoons melted shortening

Sift together flour, baking powder, soda and salt; add WHEATENA®. Beat eggs thoroughly and add to buttermilk. Combine milk mixture with sifted dry ingredients and mix well. Blend in melted shortening. Bake on preheated waffle iron until golden brown. Serve immediately.

Makes about 8

CRISPY RICE FLOUR WAFFLES

1¾ cups ELAM'S® Organically Grown Stone Ground 100% Whole Brown Rice Flour
2 tablespoons turbinado or brown sugar
3 teaspoons baking powder
¾ teaspoon salt
3 eggs, separated
1¾ cups milk
¼ cup cooking oil or melted shortening

Combine and mix first 4 ingredients in bowl; reserve. Beat egg yolks until thick and lemon colored; stir in milk and oil or melted shortening. Add to flour mixture; beat just until batter is smooth. Beat egg whites until they hold soft peaks. Carefully fold egg whites into batter. For each waffle, pour about 1⅓ cups batter into preheated 9-inch square waffle iron; spread over grid at once. Close iron and bake until done. Serve with butter and syrup or fruit sauce, or if served for dessert, top with fruit sauce.

Yield: 3 nine-inch waffles or 12 four-inch waffle squares

COCOA WAFFLES

¼ cup butter or margarine, melted
1 tablespoon oil
½ cup HERSHEY'S® Cocoa
¾ cup sugar
2 eggs
1 teaspoon vanilla
1 cup unsifted all-purpose flour
½ teaspoon baking soda
½ teaspoon salt
½ cup buttermilk or sour milk*

Melt butter or margarine in small saucepan; remove from heat. Stir in cocoa and oil; blend well. Blend cocoa mixture and sugar in small mixer bowl; add eggs and vanilla. Combine flour, baking soda and salt; add alternately with buttermilk or sour milk to cocoa mixture. Bake according to manufacturer's directions in a waffle iron. Carefully remove waffle from iron. Serve warm with butter, powdered sugar or syrup.

8 to 10 four-inch waffles
*To Sour Milk: Use 1½ teaspoons vinegar plus milk to equal ½ cup.

Crepes

BUTTERMILK BLINTZES
(Crepes)

¾ cup sifted cake flour
¼ teaspoon baking soda
Salt
2 tablespoons sugar
3 eggs
2 tablespoons butter, melted
1½ cups SEALTEST® Buttermilk
1 egg yolk
3 cups SEALTEST® Cottage Cheese
2 tablespoons confectioners sugar
½ teaspoon cinnamon
¾ teaspoon vanilla extract
SEALTEST® Sour Cream
Cherry preserve

Sift together cake flour, soda, ½ teaspoon salt, and granulated sugar. Beat eggs well. Stir in butter and buttermilk. Gradually stir in sifted dry ingredients until smooth. Slowly heat 6-inch skillet. Pour 2 tablespoons batter into buttered skillet. Tip skillet from side to side to spread batter evenly over bottom. Bake blintze on one side only until lightly browned. Loosen edge from pan with spatula; tip pan and slide out blintze. Repeat until all batter is used. Beat egg yolk slightly. Stir in cottage cheese, confectioners sugar, cinnamon, ¾ teaspoon salt, and vanilla. Spoon 2 level tablespoonfuls of filling in center on brown side of each blintze. Fold in 2 opposite sides of blintze together. Before serving, brown blintzes in butter on both sides. Serve topped with sour cream and cherry preserve. *5 to 6 servings*

WOLF® BRAND CHILI CREPE

4 crepes
8 oz. shredded lettuce
1 small diced tomato
1 16 oz. can WOLF® Brand Chili with Beans
¾ cup grated cheddar cheese
¼ cup sour cream
¼ cup chopped green onions

Have crepes ready. Heat chili. Place ¼ cup plus 1 tablespoon chili in center of each crepe. Top

with shredded lettuce and diced tomatoes. Sprinkle grated cheese on filling and fold sides of crepe over center to enclose. Top crepe with 1 tablespoon sour cream, one teaspoon chopped green onion and one teaspoon grated cheese.
Serves four (one crepe per serving)

BEEF STROGANOFF CREPES

1 can (4 ounces) mushrooms
1 pound ground beef
⅓ cup chopped onion
2 tablespoons shortening
1 tablespoon flour
1 teaspoon salt
⅓ cup HEINZ 57 Sauce
¼ cup minced parsley
½ cup dairy sour cream
6 prepared basic crepes*

Drain mushrooms; reserve liquid; add enough water to liquid to measure ½ cup; set aside. Brown mushrooms, beef and onion in shortening until onions are tender. Drain excess fat. Sprinkle flour and salt over meat; mix well. Stir in reserved mushroom liquid, 57 Sauce and parsley. Simmer, uncovered, 5 minutes. Gradually stir in sour cream; cool mixture slightly. Fill each crepe with about ½ cup meat mixture; fold 2 sides over filling. Place crepes, folded side up, in lightly greased baking dish (12" × 7½" × 2"). Bake in 350°F. oven, 20-25 minutes or until hot. Crepes may be topped with additional sour cream seasoned with 57 Sauce, if desired.
Makes 6 crepes

*BASIC CREPE RECIPE

⅔ cup all-purpose flour
⅔ cup milk
1 egg
1 tablespoon melted butter or margarine
½ teaspoon salt

Combine ingredients; beat until smooth. For each crepe, pour about ¼ cup batter in hot, lightly greased, 7 or 8-inch skillet. Tilt skillet to spread batter evenly and thinly. When lightly browned, turn and brown on the other side. Remove; keep crepes separated between pieces of paper towel.
Makes 6 crepes

Note: Crepes may be prepared ahead of time. Fill and bake just before serving.

HAM CREPES MORNAY

2 cups JOHN MORRELL® Fully
  Cooked Ham, cut into ½-inch
  cubes
2 cups sliced fresh mushrooms
2 to 3 tablespoons butter or
  margarine, melted
2 cups corn bread stuffing mix
1 teaspoon parsley flakes
1 teaspoon Worcestershire sauce
5 to 6 tablespoons butter or
  margarine, melted
8 prepared crepes*
Wooden picks
Mornay Sauce**

In a small skillet or electric fry
pan, sauté mushrooms in 2 to 3
tablespoons butter over low heat
until soft; set aside. In a bowl,
combine stuffing mix, parsley,
Worcestershire sauce and 5 to 6
tablespoons butter; toss well with
fork. Fold ham and mushrooms
into mixture. Spoon stuffing onto
crepes; fold, secure with wooden
picks. Place crepes in lightly
buttered 8 x 8-inch baking dish,
cover with foil; heat in preheated
350°F. oven, 25 minutes. Place two
crepes on each plate; spoon sauce
over each serving. *Yield: 4 servings*

*CREPES

1 cup biscuit mix
3 eggs
2⅓ cups milk
1 tablespoon sugar

In medium bowl, blend all
ingredients together; beat lightly
with hand beater or low speed
electric mixer. Pour batter from a
measuring cup to hot, lightly oiled
griddle or fry pan (using about ¼
cup batter per crepe); cook until
browned on one side, turn and
brown other side. Keep crepes in
preheated oven.
        Yield: about 10 crepes

**MORNAY SAUCE

¼ cup butter or margarine, melted
¼ cup flour
½ teaspoon dry mustard
¼ teaspoon salt
⅛ teaspoon black pepper
Dash cayenne pepper
2¼ cups milk
⅓ cup grated Swiss cheese
3 tablespoons grated Parmesan
  cheese

In a saucepan, blend flour and
seasonings into butter to form

smooth paste; gradually add milk,
blending well. Cook over medium-
low heat, stirring constantly until
sauce thickens and begins to boil.
Remove from heat; add cheeses,
stirring until cheeses are melted.
        Yield: 3 cups

CHICKEN VERONA CREPES

2 tablespoons butter or margarine
2 tablespoons flour
1¼ cups milk
3 tablespoons dry sherry
1 teaspoon instant chicken
  bouillon
½ teaspoon salt
¼ cup (about 1 ounce) grated
  Cheddar cheese
2 cups diced cooked chicken
1 cup sour cream
1 can (8 ounces) white grapes,
  drained, or 1 cup seedless grapes
¼ cup chopped parsley
½ cup BLUE RIBBON® Sliced
  Natural (Unblanched) Almonds,
  toasted
6 baked (7-inch) crepes
6 parsley sprigs

In 2-quart saucepan melt butter
over medium heat. Stir in flour;
cook 1 minute. Gradually whisk in
milk and sherry. Cook and stir
about 5 minutes until mixture is
smooth and thickened. Stir in
bouillon, salt and cheese; cook and
stir 2 minutes. Stir in chicken; heat
through. Stir in ½ cup of the sour
cream to blend thoroughly. Stir in
grapes and 2 tablespoons of the
chopped parsley; heat through.
Remove from heat; stir in almonds.
On lightly buttered baking sheet
spoon ½ cup hot chicken mixture
across center of each crepe; fold
over sides to enclose filling. Heat
in 375 degree oven about 10
minutes until edges begin to curl.
With large spatula transfer to
heated individual serving plates.
Dollop with remaining sour cream;
sprinkle with remaining chopped
parsley. Garnish with parsley
sprigs. Serve immediately.
        Makes 6 filled crepes

CHANTILLY CREPES

1 cup apricot preserves
¼ cup packed brown sugar
2 tablespoons lemon juice
½ teaspoon aromatic bitters
6 bananas, sliced
6 baked (7-inch) crepes
1 cup whipping cream, whipped
½ cup BLUE RIBBON® Slivered
  Almonds, toasted
Powdered sugar

In small bowl combine preserves,
brown sugar, lemon juice and
bitters; set aside (or refrigerate,
covered, up to 2 days). Just before
serving, gently toss bananas
(reserving 12 slices for garnish)
with 1 cup of the preserves
mixture. Place crepes on individual
serving plates. Spoon banana
mixture across centers of crepes;
top each with about 3 tablespoons
of the whipped cream. Fold sides
of crepes over to enclose filling.
Dollop remaining whipped cream
across centers of filled crepes;
drizzle with remaining preserves
mixture. Garnish with reserved
banana slices. Sprinkle with
almonds and dust with powdered
sugar. Serve immediately.
        Makes 6 filled crepes

SOLO® GLAZE FILLED CREPES

1 c. plus 2 Tbsp. flour
¼ c. sugar
¼ tsp. salt
3 eggs, beaten
1½ c. milk
2 Tbsp. melted butter or margarine
1 jar (16 ozs.) SOLO® Glaze,
  any flavor

Sift flour, sugar and salt together.
Combine eggs, milk and butter or
margarine; add to flour mixture,
beating until smooth. Cover bowl
and let stand at room temperature
for two hours. Melt ½ to 1 tsp.
butter or margarine in 6 or 7 inch
skillet. Pour in 2 Tbsp. batter into
hot skillet, tilting pan to spread
batter evenly over bottom. Brown
on one side and turn to brown on
the other. Remove crepe from pan
and keep warm. Repeat until all
batter is used. To serve, place
about 2 Tbsp. SOLO® Glaze in
center of crepe. Fold sides of
crepe over filling. Place seam side
down and sprinkle with powdered
sugar.   *Makes 12 crepes*

APPLE COCONUT CREPE DESSERT

8 large dessert crepes

Filling:
4 tart cooking apples (or 1 lb. can, cooked sliced apples)
½ cup COCO CASA™ Cream of Coconut
½ stick unsalted butter

Sauce:
1½ sticks unsalted butter
¾ cup COCO CASA™ Cream of Coconut
1 Tbsp. lemon juice
1 tsp. orange rind, grated

Filling: Peel, core and slice apples. Sauté in hot butter until they start to brown. Stir in cream of coconut.

Sauce: Melt butter. Stir in cream of coconut, lemon juice and orange rind. Warm before using.

Dip each crepe in sauce. Place 2 Tbsp. filling in one corner of crepe. Fold in half, and half again to form a wedge. Place in heatproof serving dish overlapping crepes if desired (do not stick in layers). Pour remainder of sauce over crepes. Bake in a preheated 350° oven for 20 minutes. Sprinkle with sugar and place under broiler for 2-3 minutes until sugar starts to carmelize. Flambé if desired.

Serves 6 to 8

STRAWBERRY ROSÉ CREPES

4 cups strawberries
½ cup THE CHRISTIAN BROTHERS® La Salle Rosé Wine
⅔ cup sugar
2 Tbsp. cornstarch
10 cooked crepes
Sour cream

Crush 1 cup berries; cook gently with La Salle Rosé until soft; puree. Combine sugar and cornstarch; stir into strawberry juice. Cook, stirring until thickened; cool. Slice remaining strawberries and stir into glaze. Fill crepes and fold over. Chill. To serve, top each with a dollop of sour cream. *Makes 10 crepes*

Jams, Jellies, and Syrups

BLUEBERRY-STRAWBERRY JAM

3 pints (about) strawberries
2 pints (about) blueberries
3 cups sugar
1½ cups KARO® Light Corn Syrup
⅓ cup lemon juice

Rinse and stem strawberries; fully crush berries one layer at a time to let juice flow freely. Measure 3 cups. Rinse blueberries; fully crush berries one layer at a time to let juice flow freely. Measure 3 cups. In 6-quart stainless steel or enamel saucepot stir together strawberries, blueberries, sugar, corn syrup and lemon juice. Stirring constantly, bring to hard boil over high heat. Reduce heat; stirring frequently, boil rapidly 40 to 50 minutes or until mixture thickens or sheets from spoon. To test thickness pour small amount of boiling mixture on small cold plate. Place in freezer for a few minutes. If mixture gels it is done. Remove from heat; skim surface. Immediately ladle into clean hot ½-pint jars leaving ¼-inch headspace. With nonmetallic utensil, remove air bubbles. Wipe top edge with damp towel. Seal according to jar manufacturer's directions. Process in boiling water bath 5 minutes. Cool jars on wire rack or folded towel.

Makes 6 to 7 (½-pint) jars

NO-COOK NECTARINE JAM

2¼ lb. ripe fresh nectarines or peaches
5½ cups sugar
1 cup KARO® Light Corn Syrup
1 tsp. ascorbic acid crystals (optional)
2 pouches (3 oz. each) liquid fruit pectin
⅓ cup lemon juice

Pit, peel and fully crush fruit. Measure exactly 2¾ cups. In large bowl stir together fruit, sugar, corn

syrup and ascorbic acid crystals until well blended. Let stand 10 minutes. Mix pectin and lemon juice. Stir into fruit mixture. Continue stirring vigorously 3 minutes (a few sugar crystals will remain). Ladle into clean ½-pt freezer containers leaving ½" headspace. Cover with tight lids. Let stand at room temperature until set. (It may take up to 24 hours.) Jam to be eaten within a week or two may be stored in refrigerator. Store remaining containers in freezer and transfer to refrigerator as needed.

Makes 8 (½-pt) containers

RED ZINGER®/ EMPEROR'S CHOICE™ JELLY

Heat 2 cups apple juice (filtered is best) to a boil in a 2 qt. pan. Add 6-8 CELESTIAL SEASONINGS® RED ZINGER® or EMPEROR'S CHOICE™ Tea Bags, and let steep 20 minutes off the heat. Remove tea bags. Add 3 Tbsp. lemon juice (1 juicy lemon). Add 1¾ oz. package of apple pectin. Bring to a boil while stirring. Add 2 cups honey. Boil until jelly test.* Skim foam off. Bottle. Add paraffin.

*Jelly Test—Dip a large spoon into jelly. Tilt spoon until syrup runs over side. When jelly stage is reached, liquid will stop flowing in a stream and divide into distinct drops that will run together and flake or sheet from the edge of the spoon.

CINNAMON ROSE™ SYRUP

Heat 3 cups apple juice, cider or pear-apple cider to a boil. Add 8 CELESTIAL SEASONINGS® CINNAMON ROSE™ Tea Bags and let steep 20 minutes off the heat. Remove tea bags. Add 3 Tbsp. lemon juice. Add 1¾ oz. package of apple pectin. Bring to a boil while stirring. Add 2 cups honey. Return to boil. Bottle and keep refrigerated. Use on pancakes, waffles, ice cream (as a topping). Drizzle over baked apples. Stir into plain yogurt. Use your imagination.

Vegetables

ATHENIAN ARTICHOKES

1 package (9 ounces) frozen
   artichoke hearts
1 tablespoon salad or olive oil
¼ cup HEINZ Vinegar
¼ cup thinly sliced onion,
   separated into rings
2 tablespoons chopped pimiento
2 tablespoons chopped green
   pepper
1 clove garlic, minced
1 teaspoon salt
Dash pepper
Dash paprika

Cook artichokes following package
directions; drain; chill. Combine
salad oil and remaining ingredients
in jar; shake well. Pour dressing
over chilled hearts. Cover; chill
several hours or overnight, stirring
occasionally. Serve as relish, salad
or appetizer.   *Makes 2 cups*

STUFFED ARTICHOKES

6 medium artichokes
3 tablespoons lemon juice
1¼ teaspoons salt
¼ cup butter or margarine
½ cup water
2 cups PEPPERIDGE FARM®
   Herb Seasoned Stuffing
1 tablespoon finely chopped onion
¼ cup finely chopped parsley
2 tablespoons Parmesan cheese
1 clove garlic, minced
1 tablespoon pine nuts
½ teaspoon oregano

Wash artichokes. Cut off the stem
and top third with a sharp knife.
Remove center young leaves and
choke, scraping until the heart is
exposed and clean. Rub cut
surfaces with lemon juice. Place
close together in a snug-fitting
saucepan. Add remaining lemon
juice, 1 teaspoon salt, and 1-inch
boiling water. Cook uncovered 5
minutes, cover and cook 30 to 35

minutes or until base of stem can
be easily pierced with a fork.
Remove and place upside down to
drain. Prepare stuffing by heating
¼ cup butter and the water in a
saucepan until butter melts. Stir in
remaining ingredients. Spoon
stuffing into artichokes; place
close together in a baking dish.
Add ½-inch boiling water, and
bake at 350°F. for 20 minutes.
Serve with melted butter if desired.
       Serves 6

ALMOND ASPARAGUS

1 pound asparagus
2 tablespoons butter or margarine
1 tablespoon lemon juice
½ cup BLUE DIAMOND®
   Blanched Slivered Almonds,
   toasted
Salt and pepper

Wash asparagus; cut into 1-inch
diagonal slices. Heat butter in
skillet; add asparagus and sauté 3
to 4 minutes. Cover skillet and
steam about 2 minutes or until
tender-crisp. Toss asparagus with
lemon juice and almonds; salt and
pepper to taste.   *Makes 4 servings*

GREEN BEANS WITH BROWN BUTTER

2 pounds green beans, French cut
   (approx. 8 cups)
¼ pound butter or margarine
½ teaspoon TABASCO® Pepper
   Sauce

Place beans in 1-inch boiling
water. Cook 5-10 minutes, or until
beans have reached desired degree
of doneness. Drain off liquid. Melt
butter and brown lightly. Stir in
TABASCO® Sauce. Pour butter
over beans in serving dish. Toss
lightly to cover beans well.

       Serves 4-8

CONFETTI BEANS PARMESAN

2 Tablespoons chopped celery
2 Tablespoons chopped onion
2 Tablespoons butter or margarine,
   melted
1 can (15½ oz.) STOKELY'S
   FINEST® French Style Wax
   Beans, drained
2 Tablespoons chopped STOKELY'S
   FINEST® Pimiento
2 Tablespoons butter or margarine,
   melted
2 Tablespoons Parmesan cheese
2 Tablespoons dry bread crumbs

Sauté celery and onion in butter.
Fold in Wax Beans and Pimiento;
heat to serving temperature. Place
in serving bowl. Combine
remaining ingredients and sprinkle
over Beans.   *Makes 4 servings*

GREEN BEANS WITH BACON DRESSING

5 slices bacon
2 eggs, well beaten
⅓ cup vinegar
½ cup water
3 Tablespoons sugar
¼ teaspoon salt
2 cans (1 lb. ea.) STOKELY'S
   FINEST® Whole Green Beans

Cook bacon until crisp; drain and
crumble, reserving ¼ cup
drippings in skillet. Beat together
eggs, vinegar, water, sugar and
salt. Add egg mixture to drippings;
cook over low heat, stirring
constantly until thickened. Heat
Beans in saucepan; drain and
arrange in serving dish. Pour hot
dressing over Beans. Sprinkle with
crumbled bacon.

       Makes 8 servings

GREEN BEANS REINDEER

2 packages (10 ounces each)
  frozen green beans
1 can (10½ ounces) condensed
  cream of chicken soup
½ cup milk
Generous dash thyme, crushed
1 package (6 ounces) VALIO
  Gruyere Swiss
1 cup French fried onion rings

Cook green beans according to
package directions, drain. Stir in
soup, milk, thyme and cheese.
Pour into 1-quart baking dish. Top
with onions. Bake at 350°F. for 20
minutes or until hot and bubbly.
Makes 4 servings

SWEET-SOUR SHELLIE® BEANS

2 strips bacon, diced
⅓ cup chopped onion
1 can (1 lb.) STOKELY'S FINEST®
  SHELLIE® Beans
1 Tablespoon sugar
⅛ teaspoon salt
Few grains pepper
2 Tablespoons white vinegar

Brown bacon until golden. Add
onion and liquid drained from
SHELLIE® Beans. Cook liquid
down to about ½ cupful. Add
remaining ingredients; gently fold
in Beans. Heat to serving
temperature.   *Makes 4 servings*

GREEN BEAN BAKE

1 can (10¾ ounces) CAMPBELL'S
  Condensed Cream of Mushroom
  Soup
½ cup milk
1 teaspoon soy sauce
Dash pepper
2 packages (9 ounces each) frozen
  green beans, cooked and drained
1 can (3½ ounces) French fried
  onions

In 1½-quart casserole, stir soup,
milk, soy, and pepper until smooth;
mix in green beans and ½ can
onions. Bake at 350°F. for 25
minutes; stir. Top with remaining
onions. Bake 5 minutes more.
Makes about 4 cups

Heinz

QUICKY PICKLED BEETS

1 can (1 pound) sliced beets*
½ cup HEINZ Vinegar
2 tablespoons sugar
½ teaspoon ground ginger
½ teaspoon ground allspice
¼ teaspoon salt
1 medium onion, sliced, separated
  into rings (optional)

Drain beets reserving ¾ cup liquid.
Combine beet liquid with vinegar
and next 4 ingredients in
saucepan. Bring to boil; pour over
beets. Refrigerate overnight in
covered bowl. Onion may be added
just before serving.
Makes 4-6 servings

*1 can (1 pound) small whole beets
may be substituted. Add enough
water to beet liquid to measure ¾
cup.

SPICY ORANGE BEETS

¼ cup granulated sugar
½ cup HEINZ Apple Cider Vinegar
2 bay leaves
½ cup orange juice
1 can (1 pound) sliced beets,
  drained*

Simmer first 3 ingredients in
saucepan 5 minutes. Stir in orange
juice and pour over beets. Cover;
chill overnight to blend flavors.
Makes about 2 cups

*2 cups sliced cooked fresh beets
may be substituted.

ORANGE GLAZED BEETS

1 can (1 lb.) STOKELY'S FINEST®
  Cut Beets
1 Tablespoon butter or margarine
2 teaspoons flour
2 Tablespoons brown sugar
½ cup orange juice

Heat Beets in their own liquid. In
small saucepan, melt butter.
Remove from heat; add flour,
brown sugar and orange juice.
Return to heat, stirring constantly
until thickened. Drain Beets; add
sauce to Beets.
Makes 4 to 5 servings

BROCCOLI AU GRATIN

1 bunch broccoli (about 2 pounds)
  or 1 small head cauliflower
  (or two 10-ounce frozen
  packages of either vegetable)
1 can (11 ounces) CAMPBELL'S
  Condensed Cheddar Cheese
  Soup
¼ cup milk
2 tablespoons buttered bread
  crumbs
4 slices bacon, cooked and
  crumbled

Cook vegetable; drain. Place in
shallow baking dish (10 × 6 × 2
inches). Stir soup; blend in milk;
pour over vegetable. Top with
crumbs. Bake at 350°F. for 20
minutes or until hot. Garnish with
bacon before serving.
4 to 6 servings

Mazola.

10-K BROCCOLI

2 tablespoons MAZOLA® Corn Oil
¾ pound broccoli, cleaned,
  trimmed, cut into flowerets,
  stems sliced
1¼ cups sliced mushrooms
1 large carrot, cut into 2-inch
  strips
1 clove garlic, minced
1 teaspoon grated lemon rind
½ teaspoon salt
¼ teaspoon dried thyme leaves

In large skillet heat corn oil over
medium high heat. Add broccoli,
mushrooms, carrot, garlic, lemon
rind, salt and thyme. Stir-fry 5 to 8
minutes or until vegetables are
tender.
Makes 4 (about ¾ cup) servings

VARIATIONS:

Stir-Fried Zucchini: Follow recipe
for 10-K Broccoli omitting broccoli
and mushrooms. Use ¾ pound
zucchini, sliced (2¾ cups) and 1
cup sliced celery.
Makes 4 (about ¾ cup) servings

Stir-Fried Green Beans: Follow
recipe for 10-K Broccoli omitting
broccoli and mushrooms. Use ¾
pound green beans, cut into 1-inch
pieces (3 cups) and 1 cup sliced
onion.
Makes 4 (about ¾ cup) servings

GOLDEN PUFFED BROCCOLI
(Low Cholesterol)

**2 bunches broccoli, cut into spears
  or 2 pkg (10 oz each) frozen
  broccoli spears, cooked, drained
2 egg whites, at room temperature
¼ tsp salt (optional)
½ cup shredded part-skim Swiss
  cheese (2 oz)
½ cup HELLMANN'S® or BEST
  FOODS® Real Mayonnaise**

Arrange cooked broccoli in shallow
1½-quart pan or broiler-proof
serving dish. In small bowl with
mixer at high speed beat egg
whites and salt until stiff peaks
form. Fold in cheese and Real
Mayonnaise; spoon evenly over
broccoli. Broil 6″ from source of
heat 4 minutes or until golden
brown. Serve immediately.

Makes 8 servings

15 mg cholesterol per serving

CURRIED CARROTS

3 cups sliced carrots

**½ cup THE CHRISTIAN
  BROTHERS® Golden Sherry
½ tsp. grated orange peel
⅓ cup orange juice
1 Tbsp. cornstarch
½ tsp. seasoned salt
2 tsp. sugar
¼ tsp. ground ginger
⅛ tsp. curry powder
2 Tbsp. butter
1 Tbsp. lemon juice**

Cook carrots in boiling water until
just tender. Drain; combine with
sauce. *Sauce:* in small saucepan,
mix sherry, orange peel, juice,
cornstarch, salt, sugar, ginger and
curry powder. Cook, stirring, until
mixture thickens. Stir in butter and
lemon juice.   *Serves 6*

GLAZED CARROTS

**1 bunch carrots, cut in ovals
1 tablespoon butter
2 tablespoons honey
Salt
4 oz. COLONIAL CLUB Peach
  Liqueur**

Cook carrots, barely covered with
water, in shallow saucepan. Add
butter, honey, salt to taste, and
COLONIAL CLUB Peach Liqueur.
Stir and cook slowly until water
has evaporated and carrots are
slightly glazed.

GLAZED CARROTS WITH ONION

**2 cups pared and diagonally sliced
  carrots
1 medium onion, thinly sliced
¼ cup firmly-packed COLONIAL®
  Light Golden Brown Sugar
2 tablespoons butter or margarine
¼ teaspoon ground nutmeg**

In medium skillet or saucepan,
partially cook carrots in water
(about 10 minutes); drain. Stir in
onion, sugar, butter and nutmeg.
Simmer, stirring occasionally, 15
minutes or until tender.

Makes 4 servings

GLAZED CARROTS AND BRUSSELS SPROUTS

**1 pound carrots, cut in 1½-inch
  pieces
2 packages (10 ounces each)
  frozen Brussels sprouts
2 tablespoons chopped onion
2 tablespoons butter or margarine
1 can (10½ ounces) CAMPBELL'S
  Condensed Consomme
⅓ cup apple juice
2 teaspoons lemon juice
2 tablespoons cornstarch
1 tablespoon brown sugar
Generous dash ground clove**

Cook carrots and Brussels sprouts;
drain. Meanwhile, in saucepan,
cook onion in butter until tender.
Add remaining ingredients. Cook,
stirring until thickened. Combine
with hot vegetables.

Makes about 4 cups

BRANDIED CARROTS

**24 small carrots
1 tablespoon butter
3 tablespoons CHAMBORD
Juice of one lemon
¼ cup brandy
¼ cup honey
2 tablespoons finely chopped
  parsley**

Put carrots in saucepan and cover
with cold salted water. Bring to a
boil, reduce heat to simmer and
cover and cook until tender. Drain
and arrange in buttered casserole.
Make syrup of CHAMBORD, lemon
juice, brandy and honey. Pour over
carrots and bake in 350° oven for
15 or 20 minutes. Sprinkle with
chopped parsley.   *Serves 4*

COPPER CARROTS
(a "quickie")

**2 pounds carrots, thinly sliced
1 small green pepper, thinly
  sliced into rings
1 medium onion, thinly sliced
1 teaspoon Worcestershire sauce
1 cup sugar
¾ cup HEINZ White Vinegar
1 teaspoon prepared mustard
1 can tomato soup
½ cup salad oil
Salt and pepper to taste**

Cook carrots in boiling salted
water until fork tender. When cool,
alternate layers of carrots with
pepper and onion slices. Combine
Worcestershire sauce and
remaining ingredients over heat.
Pour sauce mixture over layered
vegetables; cover and refrigerate.
This is best when allowed to set
for a few days. Good with meats or
as an appetizer.

GLAZED CARROTS COCO CASA™

**½ pound carrots
1 Tbsp. butter
2 Tbsp. COCO CASA™ Cream of
  Coconut
1 Tbsp. parsley, finely chopped**

Cut carrots into thin sticks 2″ long.
Boil until just tender. Drain, and
stir in butter and cream of
coconut. Cook over high heat
about 2 minutes until sauce
thickens. Sprinkle with parsley and
serve.

CAULIFLOWER GRATINE

**1 medium head cauliflower
1 can (10½ ounces) condensed
  cream of chicken soup
¼ cup milk
1 cup shredded FINLANDIA Swiss
¼ cup buttered bread crumbs
4 slices bacon, cooked and
  crumbled**

Cook cauliflower in boiling salted
water about 12 minutes, just until
fork tender. Drain and place in
shallow baking dish. Combine
soup and milk; stir in cheese. Pour
over cauliflower. Sprinkle with
crumbs. Bake at 350°F. for 20
minutes, until hot and bubbly.
Garnish with bacon.

Makes 4 servings

FIDDLER'S ROASTING EARS

¼ cup (½ stick) butter or margarine
½ teaspoon salt
¼ teaspoon each marjoram and rosemary
¼ teaspoon black pepper
Pinch IMPERIAL Granulated Sugar
4 ears corn

Melt butter or margarine in saucepan; add salt, herbs, pepper and IMPERIAL Granulated Sugar (or process in glass dish in microwave oven on full power about 30 seconds). Pull back cornhusks, remove silks and roll corn in herb butter. Replace husks and wrap each ear of corn tightly in foil. Roast on grill over hot coals about 15 minutes, turning several times.   *Serves 4*

CORN ON THE COB IN HUSK
(Low Calorie/Low Cholesterol)

4 ears unhusked corn
1 reconstituted packet (½ oz.) BUTTER BUDS®

Peel down husk, remove silk and divide BUTTER BUDS® liquid evenly over each ear of corn. Recover with husk. Heat over coals or grill. Turn one-fourth the way around every 3-5 minutes.

Calories: *Makes 4 servings*
  w/BUTTER BUDS® —212
  w/Butter   —400
Cholesterol:
  w/BUTTER BUDS® — 0 mg.
  w/Butter   —70 mg.

Morton Salt
ROASTED SEASONED CORN

½ cup margarine or butter, softened
2 tablespoons MORTON NATURE'S SEASONS® Seasoning Blend
8 ears corn, husks and silk removed

About 35 Minutes Before Serving: Prepare outdoor grill for barbecuing. Mix margarine and seasoning blend. Spread each ear of corn evenly with 1 tablespoon seasoned margarine. Wrap each

ear tightly in heavy-duty foil. Grill corn over medium coals 30 minutes, turning often.
          Makes 8 servings

Oven Roasting Variation: Prepare corn as above. Bake at 375°F. for 30 minutes, or until tender.

CORN SPOON

3 eggs, separated
¾ cup corn meal
¾ tsp. salt
1¼ cups milk, scalded
2 Tbsp. margarine or butter
1 can (17 oz.) DEL MONTE Golden Cream Style Corn
¾ tsp. baking powder

Beat egg whites (at room temperature) until stiff, but not dry. Beat egg yolks until thick and lemon colored. Gradually add corn meal and salt to scalded milk, beating vigorously. Cook over low heat, stirring constantly, until consistency of thick mush. Add margarine, corn and baking powder. Fold in egg yolks, then egg whites. Pour into greased 11¾ × 7½ inch baking dish. Bake at 350°F. 45 minutes or until tests done. Serve immediately.
          5 to 6 servings

CLASSIC CUCUMBERS

3 or 4 peeled cucumbers (under 7")
2 tablespoons salt
1½ cups sour cream
1 tablespoon sugar
3 tablespoons vinegar
½ teaspoon pepper, fresh ground
1 tablespoon dill or chives
BROWNBERRY® Onion and Garlic Croutons

Slice cucumbers thinner than you thought possible. (Use a potato peeler.) Sprinkle with the salt and let stand in icebox for 2 or 3 hours. Rinse in cold water and squeeze out all the moisture you can. Make dressing from the sour cream, sugar, vinegar, pepper and dill. Fold in cucumbers and return to icebox until served. Garnish with Onion and Garlic croutons.

SAUTÉED CUCUMBERS

Melt ½ cup butter in skillet—add 2 CALAVO® BURNAC EUROPEAN Cucumbers sliced crosswise, 1 tsp. salt and ¼ tsp. pepper. Cook until cucumbers are tender.

FRESH DELI DILLS

3 pounds 3- or 4-inch cucumbers (about 18)
5 cups water
1½ cups white vinegar
½ cup MORTON Cooking, Canning and Pickling Salt
2 garlic cloves, split
1 tablespoon dill weed

Up to 1 Week or at Least 3 Days Before Serving: Scrub cucumbers under cold running water. Place in large heat-proof bowl. Heat water, vinegar and cooking, canning and pickling salt to boiling; pour over cucumbers. Add garlic and dill weed. Place a saucer over top and weight it down with a water-filled jar. The saucer should keep the cucumbers immersed in the brine. Cover with a clean towel. Store at room temperature. *Early in Day:* Transfer cucumbers and enough brine to cover into a clean quart jar. Cover and refrigerate until serving time.
          Makes 18 pickles or about 1 quart

ITALIAN EGGPLANT

12 double SUNSHINE KRISPY® Crackers
2 tablespoons grated Parmesan cheese
1 egg
1 tablespoon water
Salt to taste
½ teaspoon pepper
1 medium eggplant (about 1¼ pounds)
Buttery flavored vegetable oil for frying

With rolling pin, crush crackers into very fine crumbs between waxed paper. There should be about 1 cup. Stir with the cheese and put in a shallow plate. Beat egg well with water, salt and pepper in another shallow plate. Cut unpeeled eggplant into slices about ¼ inch thick. Dip slices into egg mixture, drain a bit and coat well with crumb mixture. Let sit on waxed paper for about 15 minutes to set the crumbs. Put about ¼ inch oil in large skillet and place over moderate heat. Cook the slices on both sides until golden brown. Add more oil as necessary. Drain on paper towels in warm place.   *Yield: 4 to 6 servings*

PEPPER-MUSHROOM SAUTÉ

2 tablespoons butter
2 cups sliced DOLE® Fresh
   Mushrooms
½ cup chopped green onion
½ cup julienne-cut green pepper
½ cup julienne-cut red pepper*
1 teaspoon dried Italian herbs,
   crumbled
¼ cup dry white wine

Melt butter in a large skillet. Sauté
sliced mushrooms and green onion
just until tender; remove from
skillet. Add green and red pepper
strips; sauté lightly. Sprinkle
Italian herbs over peppers; add
wine. Cover and simmer 8 to 10
minutes until peppers are tender.
Add mushrooms and onion back to
skillet. Heat thoroughly.
Makes 4 servings

*Or ¼ cup sliced pimiento.

HERBED MUSHROOM SIZZLE

1 pound DOLE® Fresh
   Mushrooms
¼ cup butter
2 teaspoons garlic salt
¼ teaspoon thyme, crumbled
1 tablespoon chopped parsley

Brush mushrooms lightly and
remove stems by twisting gently.
Carve each cap by placing tip of
paring knife in center of cap and
bringing it to outer edge with a
gentle curving motion. Repeat cut
about 1/16-inch from first cut and
remove small portion of cap.
Continue around entire mushroom.
Melt butter in a large frying pan
until bubbly. Add mushrooms,
garlic salt and thyme. Sauté 3 to 4
minutes until golden brown.
Sprinkle with parsley to serve.
Makes 4 to 6 servings

VALENCIA MUSHROOMS

½ lb. fresh mushrooms, very thinly
   sliced
4 ribs celery very thinly sliced
2 Tbsp. lemon juice
3 Tbsp. HIRAM WALKER Triple
   Sec
Finely chopped parsley

Combine ingredients and chill for
several hours. Serve on bibb lettuce.
Garnish with lemon slices.
Serves 4

MUSHROOMS À LA GRECQUE

1 lemon
Mustard Seed Dressing*
1 cup DOLE® Fresh Mushrooms,
   small whole or halved
⅓ cup ripe olives
1 tablespoon pimiento
1 tablespoon finely
   chopped parsley
2 tablespoons feta cheese
   (optional)

Squeeze juice from half the lemon,
to measure 1 tablespoon. Reserve
for dressing. Thinly slice remaining
half lemon for salad. Prepare
Mustard Seed Dressing. Combine
mushrooms, lemon slices, olives,
pimiento, parsley and dressing.
Chill. Toss with crumbled cheese,
if desired.
Makes 3 to 4 servings

*MUSTARD SEED DRESSING

¼ cup olive oil
3 tablespoons garlic flavored red
   wine vinegar
1 tablespoon reserved lemon juice
½ teaspoon salt
¼ teaspoon mustard seed
1 small bay leaf

Combine ingredients in a covered
jar. Shake well to blend.

MUSHROOMS SAUTÉED IN OLIVE OIL

Lightly sauté 1 chopped onion and
1 minced garlic clove in ¼ cup
STAR Italian Kitchen Olive Oil. Add
1 lb. fresh mushrooms, ½ tsp.
crushed basil, 2 Tbsp. dry white
wine (optional), salt and pepper to
taste. Sauté until tender.
Serves 4-6

HOLIDAY VEGETABLES

1 can (10¾ ounces) CAMPBELL'S
   Condensed Cream of
   Mushroom Soup
¼ cup milk
½ teaspoon curry powder
1 pound (about 16) small whole
   white onions, cooked and
   drained
1 package (10 ounces) frozen
   chopped broccoli, cooked and
   drained
Toasted slivered almonds

In saucepan, combine soup, milk,
and curry; add onions and broccoli.
Heat a few minutes to blend
flavors. Stir occasionally. Garnish
with almonds.
Makes about 4 cups

CREAMLESS CREAMED ONIONS
(Low Calorie/Low Cholesterol)

2 lbs. small white onions
6 whole cloves
1 packet BUTTER BUDS®
2 Tbsp. flour
1½ cups skim milk
Salt and pepper to taste

Cook unpeeled whole onions in
salted water with cloves until
tender, about 25 minutes.
Meanwhile, combine remaining
ingredients and mix until smooth.
Drain onions well and discard
cloves. Trim root ends and slip off
skins. Heat sauce, stirring
constantly, until thickened. Add
cooked onions and heat.
Makes 8-10 servings

1 cup = 1 serving
73 cal./0 mg. cholesterol

CREAMED ONIONS

2 tablespoons butter
2 tablespoons flour
1 cup top milk, or light cream
1 can No. 303 TAYLOR'S Whole
   Onions
Dash pepper
½ teaspoon salt

Melt butter in saucepan, add flour,
blend. Add milk, stirring constantly
until thick and smooth. Season;
add drained onions and cook until
onions are heated through.
Serves 4 to 5

DILLED PEAS HELSINKI

3 pounds fresh green peas or
   2 packages (10 ounces each)
   cooked and drained
2 tablespoons chopped shallots
2 tablespoons butter or margarine
2 tablespoons flour
1½ cups milk
1 cup shredded FINLANDIA Swiss
½ teaspoon dill weed
2 tablespoons chopped pimiento

While peas are cooking sauté shallots in butter until tender. Stir in flour and cook until smooth. Gradually stir in milk and cook, stirring, until thickened and smooth. Stir in cheese, dill and pimiento. Add peas. Heat, stirring, until cheese is melted.

Makes 4 servings

IRISH POTATO BAKE

4 cups CORN CHEX® Cereal
   crushed to 2 cups
4 tablespoons butter or margarine,
   melted
3 cups seasoned, stiff hot
   mashed potatoes
½ cup dairy sour cream
½ teaspoon onion powder
¼ teaspoon seasoned salt
Dash white pepper
1 package (10 oz.) frozen chopped
   broccoli, cooked and drained
   (omit salt)
1 cup (4 oz.) shredded process
   American cheese

Butter 1½-quart shallow baking dish. Thoroughly combine CORN CHEX® crumbs and butter. Set aside. Combine potatoes, sour cream, seasonings and broccoli. Stir gently until well mixed. Turn half of mixture into baking dish. Sprinkle with half of cheese, then with half of crumbs. Repeat. Bake in 350° oven 20-25 minutes or until crumbs are golden.

Makes 8 servings

BAKED POTATOES WITH CAVIAR

4 baking potatoes
¾ cup sour cream
2 Tbsp. (1 oz.) ROMANOFF®
   Caviar*

Prick skin of potatoes. If desired, rub with butter or margarine. Bake at 450°F. (hot oven) one hour or until fork tender. Cut an X in each potato; squeeze gently. Top with a dollop of sour cream and a heaping teaspoonful of caviar.

Gourmet Baked Potatoes: After baking, cut off thin horizontal slice from top. Fluff up potatoes with fork, then mash in one tablespoon butter or margarine, a squeeze of lemon juice and a sprinkling of chopped chives. Top with sour cream and caviar as above.

*ROMANOFF® Black Lumpfish or Whitefish Caviar suggested.

SCALLOPED POTATOES

1 can (10¾ ounces) CAMPBELL'S
   Condensed Cream of Celery or
   Mushroom Soup
⅓ to ½ cup milk
¼ cup chopped parsley
Dash pepper
4 cups thinly sliced potatoes
1 small onion, thinly sliced
1 tablespoon butter or margarine
Dash paprika

Combine soup, milk, parsley, and pepper. In 1½-quart casserole, arrange alternate layers of potatoes, onion, and sauce. Dot top with butter; sprinkle with paprika. Cover; bake at 375°F. for 1 hour. Uncover; bake 15 minutes more or until potatoes are done.

Makes about 3½ cups

SKINNY POTATO SCALLOP
(Low Calorie)

2 cups thinly sliced potatoes
½ cup sliced mushrooms
½ cup sliced onion
4 beef bouillon cubes
1 teaspoon salt
¼ teaspoon thyme leaves
Dash pepper

In non-stick 9-inch square baking pan, combine potatoes, mushrooms and onion. Dissolve bouillon cubes in 1½ cups boiling water. Add salt, thyme and pepper. Pour over vegetables. Cover and bake at 350 degrees for 30 minutes. Uncover and bake 15 minutes more or until vegetables are tender.   *Makes 6 servings*

About 55 calories each

Favorite recipe from The Potato Board

BUTTER BUDS® SCALLOPED POTATOES
(Low Calorie/Low Cholesterol)

6 medium (about 2 lbs.) potatoes
2 packets (½ oz. each) BUTTER
   BUDS®
¼ cup diced onion
Paprika
3 Tbsp. all-purpose flour
⅛ tsp. pepper
2½ cups skim milk

Preheat oven to 350°F. Spray a 2-quart casserole dish using low-calorie non-stick coating agent. Peel potatoes and cut into slices ⅛-¼ inch thick. In a small bowl combine BUTTER BUDS,® onion, flour and pepper. Mix well. In casserole dish arrange potato slices in 4 layers, sprinkling each of first 3 layers with one fourth the BUTTER BUDS®-onion mixture. Add the fourth layer of potatoes and sprinkle top with remaining BUTTER BUDS® mixture. Heat milk to scalding; pour over potatoes. Cover and bake 30 minutes. Uncover, bake 55-60 minutes longer or until potatoes are tender and sauce is thickened. Let stand 5-10 minutes before serving. Sprinkle with paprika.

Makes 6 servings

Calories:
  w/BUTTER BUDS® —157
  w/Butter   —408

Cholesterol:
  w/BUTTER BUDS® — 0 mg.
  w/Butter   —94 mg.

RUS-ETTES AU GRATIN POTATOES

1½ cups of half and half or
   coffee cream
1 package RUS-ETTES Shredded
   Hash Brown Potatoes, defrosted
2 oz. butter
Salt and pepper to taste
1 Tbsp. grated Parmesan cheese

Heat half and half in sauce pan. Add potatoes, butter, salt, and pepper. Simmer slowly until thickened. Pour into baking dish. Sprinkle with Parmesan cheese and a little melted butter. Place under broiler to brown.

CREAMY AU GRATIN POTATOES

½ cup frozen ORE-IDA® Chopped Onions
1 can (10½ ounces) condensed cream of celery or cream of mushroom soup
1 package (3 ounces) cream cheese, cut in cubes
3-4 cups frozen ORE-IDA® Southern Style Hash Browns*
⅓ cup shredded Cheddar cheese

Preheat oven to 400°F. Grease a 1-quart casserole. In 1-quart saucepan, over medium heat, cook frozen onion until tender. Stir in undiluted soup and cream cheese cubes; cook, stirring constantly, until smooth and hot. In casserole, alternately layer frozen potatoes and hot cream sauce ending with a sauce layer. Cover and bake 45 minutes or until sauce is bubbly and potatoes are tender. Remove from oven and sprinkle with shredded cheese.

Yield: 4-5 servings

*May also be prepared with the following ORE-IDA® products: Country Style Dinner Fries,® Potatoes O'Brien or Cottage Fries.

BARBECUE POTATOES
(Low Cholesterol)

6 medium potatoes, unpeeled
⅓ cup NUCOA® or MAZOLA® Margarine, melted
¼ cup catchup
2 teaspoons prepared mustard
½ teaspoon paprika
½ teaspoon salt

Cut each potato into 4 wedges. Cut each wedge crosswise at ¼-inch intervals, to within ¼ inch from bottom of potatoes; place in ice water 1 hour. Dry with paper towels; place in shallow baking pan. Mix together remaining ingredients. Brush potatoes with ½ the margarine mixture. Bake in 425°F. oven, brushing occasionally with remaining mixture, 35 minutes or until tender.

Makes 6 servings

0 mg cholesterol per serving

COUNTRY STYLE POTATOES

2 cans No. 303 TAYLOR'S Whole White Potatoes
¾ teaspoon basil
½ teaspoon salt
Dash pepper
¼ cup butter, or margarine, melted
1 medium size onion, chopped

Cut drained potatoes into small pieces. Add potatoes and seasonings to melted butter in skillet. Cook until potatoes are lightly browned, stirring occasionally. Add chopped onion and cook a few minutes. (Onion should be hot but still crisp.)

Serves 6

MAUDIE'S RUS-ETTES POTATOES

4 or 5 frozen RUS-ETTES Hash Brown Patties

Put in pan and partially thaw. In separate pan combine:

1 can cream of mushroom soup or 1 can cream of chicken soup
¼ cup chopped onions
Salt and pepper to taste
1½ cups shredded cheddar cheese
2 Tbsp. milk
1 cube butter

Cook until thoroughly mixed. Pour over potato patties. Cook 45 minutes at 375°.

POTATO KUGEL
(Pudding)

Peel and grate 6 large potatoes and 1 onion. Add 1 tablespoon ROKEACH Kosher Nyafat, 2 eggs, ⅛ teaspoon pepper, 1 tablespoon salt, 1 tablespoon matzoh flour. Mix well. Melt 2 tablespoons ROKEACH Kosher Nyafat in pudding dish; add mixture and bake in moderate oven until brown (about 45 minutes). Serve hot.

Favorite ROKEACH Kosher recipe from 1932

SHERRIED SWEET POTATO RING

4 tablespoons light brown sugar
10 walnut halves
3 pounds sweet potatoes or yams
3 well-beaten egg yolks
¼ cup soft butter
1 teaspoon salt
⅛ teaspoon freshly ground black pepper
⅓ cup undiluted evaporated milk
⅓ cup TAYLOR New York State Golden Sherry or Cream Sherry
3 well-beaten egg whites

Butter generously a *6-cup* ring mold. Sprinkle with brown sugar. Place walnut halves in sugar, rounded side down. Boil potatoes until tender; peel and mash. Stir in egg yolks, butter, salt, pepper, evaporated milk and Sherry. Fold in egg whites. Spoon carefully into prepared ring mold. Bake in a preheated 350°F. oven 40 to 45 minutes. Remove from oven. Allow to cool 5 minutes. Unmold onto *warm* serving plate.

Approximately 12 servings

Flambé: Heat ⅓ cup Cream Sherry until it almost boils. Ignite with a match. Pour flaming over potato ring. Decorate with watercress, curly endive or parsley and orange sections.

MARSHMALLOW TOPPED SWEET POTATOES

1 17-oz. can sweet potatoes (halves or pieces), drained
2 tablespoons butter or margarine
⅓ cup SUE BEE® Honey
½ cup miniature, or diced, marshmallows

Slice lengthwise, extra thick pieces of potatoes. Arrange in a single layer on bottom of buttered, shallow baking pan. Dot with the butter and drizzle with the honey. Bake 20 minutes at 350°F. Spoon hot honey sauce from bottom of pan over potatoes and sprinkle with marshmallows. Return to oven just long enough to lightly brown marshmallow topping. Before serving, baste potatoes again with the hot honey sauce.

Makes 3-4 servings

CANDIED SWEET POTATOES (LEMON GLAZED)

1 can TAYLOR'S Syrup Sweet Potatoes

Drain off syrup into saucepan, add ½ cup sugar, 1 piece cinnamon stick, ½ lemon, juice and peel, and boil about five minutes. Arrange potatoes in flameproof pan; add 2 tablespoons butter, pour in syrup mixture and cook over slow flame or under broiler about ten minutes.

AMBROSIAL YAMS

1 lemon, sliced
1 orange, sliced
2 (17-ounce) cans yams or sweet potatoes, drained and sliced
¼ cup butter or margarine
½ cup firmly-packed COLONIAL® Light Golden Brown Sugar
1 (8¼-ounce) can crushed pineapple, drained
1 teaspoon ground allspice
½ teaspoon salt
½ cup coconut

Preheat oven to 350°. In 8-inch square baking dish, alternate lemon and orange slices with the yams. In small saucepan, melt butter. Stir in sugar, pineapple, allspice and salt; spoon evenly over yams. Sprinkle with coconut. Bake 25 to 30 minutes.
Makes 6 to 8 servings

CANDIED YAMS

1-1lb. can sweet potatoes, cut into 1-inch slices
1-1lb. can crushed pineapple in its own juice
1 tsp. SWEET 'N LOW® Brown
2 Tbsp. butter
½ tsp. salt

Place half of the sweet potatoes in a 1½-qt. greased casserole. Top with one-half of the pineapple. Repeat layers with remaining sweet potatoes and pineapple. Combine SWEET 'N LOW® Brown, butter and salt. Crumble over top. Bake, covered, at 350° for 45 minutes.
Serves 6-8

THE ORIGINAL WORCESTERSHIRE

YAM-BROSIA

2 cans (1 lb. 1 oz. each) vacuum packed sweet potatoes, sliced
2 bananas, sliced
⅔ cup light corn syrup
¼ cup butter or margarine
3 tablespoons orange juice
1 teaspoon LEA & PERRINS Worcestershire Sauce
¼ teaspoon salt
⅓ cup flaked coconut

In a 2-quart casserole place alternate layers of potatoes and bananas; set aside. In a small saucepan combine remaining ingredients except coconut. Heat until butter is melted. Pour over potato mixture. Cover and bake in a preheated moderate oven (375°F.) 30 minutes. Remove cover; baste with syrup by tilting casserole. Sprinkle coconut over all. Return to oven for 10 minutes longer.
Yield: 8 portions

HONEYED YAMS

1½ cups SUE BEE® Honey
2 tablespoons corn starch
⅛ teaspoon salt
1½ cups water
1 tablespoon melted butter
6 large cooked, sliced yams

Combine all ingredients except yams; cook until clear. Pour over cooked yams. Bake at 400° until brown. (Delicious over baked apples, too.) *Makes six servings*

CANDIED YAMS IN ORANGE CUPS

4 sweet potatoes
3 oranges, halved
3 oz. HIRAM WALKER Orange Curacao
2 Tbsp. butter
½ tsp. powdered cinnamon
Salt and pepper

Bake sweet potatoes in oven until tender. Remove pulp and mash. Add Orange Curacao, butter, cinnamon, salt and pepper. Beat until smooth and fluffy. Remove pulp from oranges and fill shells with mixture. Bake 15 minutes in 400° oven. *Serves 6*

ACORN SQUASH STUFFED WITH ESCALLOPED APPLES

1 package frozen escalloped apples
2 acorn squash, halved lengthwise
Water
½ cup chopped PLANTERS® Walnuts
Chopped walnuts

Thaw package of frozen escalloped apples. Scrape out seeds and stringy pulp of squash. In a deep, large skillet bring ½" of water to boil. Add squash, cut side down. Cover. Turn heat to simmer and cook squash until almost tender, about 20 minutes. Drain well, place cut side up in baking dish. Add ½ cup chopped walnuts to apples and pack mixture into squash cavities. Garnish with chopped walnuts. Bake at 375°F. for 20 to 30 minutes. (Leftover ham, bacon or sausage may be added to the apple/nut filling.)

APPLE-FILLED ACORN SQUASH

2 medium acorn squash
Water
1 can (20 oz.) THANK YOU® Brand Apple Pie Filling
2 Tbsp. sherry (optional)
Onion powder
Seasoned salt
Mace or ginger
2 Tbsp. butter or margarine
¼ cup sliced almonds
4 brown-and-serve sausages (optional)

Halve each squash lengthwise; discard seeds. Place cut side down in large baking dish; add ½ inch water. Bake at 400° for 25 minutes. Turn squash cut side up and sprinkle with onion powder, seasoned salt, mace or ginger and dot with butter. If desired, place one sausage in each squash. Mix apple filling with sherry (optional) and fill squash cavities. Cover pan with foil and bake at 350° for 30 minutes or until squash is tender when pierced. Top with almonds and bake uncovered for 5 minutes more or until almonds are toasted.
Serves 4

GLAZED ACORN SQUASH

3 acorn squash
¼ cup GRANDMA'S®
  Unsulphured Molasses
½ teaspoon salt
¾ cup chopped nuts, optional
1 tablespoon grated orange rind
3 tablespoons butter or margarine,
  melted

Wash squash and halve lengthwise; remove seeds and stringy portion. Place squash, cut side down, in a greased shallow baking pan. Bake in 375°F. oven 30 minutes. While squash is baking, combine remaining ingredients. Remove squash from oven; turn right side up. Divide the molasses mixture among the halves. Return to oven and bake approximately 30 minutes longer, or until squash is tender. *Yield: 6 servings*

NEW ENGLAND BAKED SQUASH

2 medium acorn squash (about 1
  pound *each*)
2 tart apples
½ cup BLUE DIAMOND®
  Blanched Slivered Almonds,
  toasted
½ cup dark, seedless raisins
1½ cups maple syrup
2 tablespoons lemon juice
¼ cup butter or margarine
¼ cup cornstarch
1 teaspoon cinnamon
½ teaspoon ginger
½ teaspoon nutmeg

Halve squash; remove seeds. Place cut-side down in greased shallow baking pan; bake in 350 degree F. oven 30 to 40 minutes or until barely tender. Cool and peel; cut into ½-inch slices. Spread on bottom of 11 x 7 x 2-inch baking dish. Pare and thinly slice apples; arrange over squash. Combine almonds and raisins; sprinkle over apples. In saucepan combine syrup, lemon juice, butter, cornstarch, and spices; cook, stirring, until thickened; pour over squash and apples. Bake in 350 degree F. oven 25 to 30 minutes or until tender.

Makes 6 to 8 servings

SPICED SQUASH

Fresh Acorn Squash:
2 acorn squash
Salt to taste
4 tablespoons butter or margarine
4 tablespoons SUE BEE® Honey
Ground cinnamon

Frozen Squash:
1 12-ounce pkg. frozen squash
½ teaspoon salt
3 tablespoons butter or margarine
3 tablespoons SUE BEE® Honey
⅛ teaspoon ground cinnamon

Fresh Acorn Squash—Cut squash in half and seed. Bake, cut side down, on baking sheet at 350°F., until tender. Allow 30-45 minutes, depending upon size of squash. Turn halves up and sprinkle with salt. Place 1 tablespoon each of butter and honey in seed cavity. Dust with cinnamon. Bake an additional 10 minutes.
Makes 4 servings

Frozen Squash—Cook squash according to package directions with salt and butter. Blend in honey and cinnamon and return to heat a minute or two.
Makes 3-4 servings

SUNNY SQUASH COMBO

1 can (20 oz.) THANK YOU® Brand
  Apple Pie Filling
2 lbs. fresh butternut* squash,
  peeled and cubed
½ tsp. nutmeg
¾ tsp. seasoned salt
1 Tbsp. butter or margarine

Peel squash, cut into 2-inch cubes, and place in an oiled ovenproof casserole. Top with apple pie filling. Sprinkle with nutmeg and salt; dot with butter. Cover (use foil if lid doesn't fit tightly) and bake at 350° for 50-60 minutes or until squash is tender. (Oven temperature and time can vary if other baked items require different temperatures.) Leftovers can be frozen. *Makes 6 generous servings*

*Other winter squash can be substituted.

CHEDDAR ZUCCHINI SUPREME

2 Tablespoons butter or margarine
6 cups thinly sliced fresh zucchini
1 teaspoon salt
⅛ teaspoon pepper
Dash garlic salt
1 can (8 oz.) STOKELY'S FINEST®
  Tomato Sauce
1 cup shredded cheddar cheese

In medium skillet, melt butter; then add next 5 ingredients. Heat for 10 minutes, stirring occasionally. Add half the cheese, heating and stirring until cheese is melted. Pour into a greased 1½ quart casserole dish. Sprinkle on remaining cheese and bake for 20 minutes at 375°.
Makes 6 cheesy servings

BROILED STUFFED ZUCCHINI

6 double SUNSHINE KRISPY®
  Crackers
¼ teaspoon salt
¼ teaspoon pepper
6 zucchini, about 5-6 inches long
1 tablespoon salad oil
¼ cup minced onion
1 egg, beaten
⅓ cup minced ripe olives
½ cup grated Cheddar cheese
Paprika

Crush crackers into very fine crumbs between two sheets waxed paper (there should be about ½ cup). Mix with salt and pepper and set aside. Trim ends of zucchini and slice in halves lengthwise. Boil in salted water until barely tender, about 3 to 4 minutes. Drain on a rack and let cool a bit. In a skillet, heat oil, add onion and sauté until onion is soft but not brown. Mix crumbs and egg, stir in olives and sautéed onion. Scoop seeds from zucchini leaving shells about ¼ inch thick. Chop the scooped-out part and add to the crumb mixture. Spoon into the shells. Sprinkle with cheese and dust with paprika. Place in a shallow pan under broiler, preheated to 450°F. for about 5 minutes to heat through and melt cheese.
Yield: 6 servings

Specialty of the House Sandwich **(Oscar Mayer)**

Chili Style Pizza **(Wolf® Brand)**

Vegetable Sandwich **(Calavo®)**

Open Face Vegetable Sandwich **(Calavo®)**

Reuben Sandwiches **(Stokely's Finest®)**

Barbecue Burgers **(Wheat Chex®)**

Greek Pita Pockets **(Louis Rich)**

John's Party Loaf **(John Morrell®)**

Merry Pizza Rounds **(International Sausage Council)**

Quick BBQ Burgers **(Kikkoman)**

The Team Hero **(Oscar Mayer)**

Ham Crepes Mornay **(John Morrell®)**

Old-Time Buckwheat Cakes **(Elam's®)**

Blueberry-Strawberry Jam **(Karo®)**

Wolf® Brand Chili Crepe

Apple Sauce Pancakes **(Lucky Leaf®)**

Sautéed Cucumbers **(Calavo®)**

Candied Sweet Potatoes **(Taylor's)**

Creamy Au Gratin Potatoes **(Ore-Ida®)**

Nina's Fresh Vegetable Bake
(Argo®/Kingsford's®)

French Style Vegetable Stew **(Heinz)**

Almond Asparagus **(Blue Diamond®)**

Classic Cucumbers **(Brownberry®)**

Dilled Peas Helsinki **(Finlandia Cheese)**

Sweet 'N Spicy Onion Glaze
(Wish-Bone®/Lipton®)

Irish Potato Bake **(Corn Chex®)**

Turkey Gravy **(Argo®/Kingsford's®)**

100% Whole Wheat Flour Bread
(Elam's®)

Land O'Lakes® Zesty Butter Sticks

Potato Chip Stuffing **(Jays)**

Pumpkin Nut Bread **(Libby's)**

German Sweet Bread **(Blue Ribbon®)**

Wheat Chex® Applesauce Nut Bread

Heath® Brunch Coffee Cake

Thanksgiving Date Stuffing **(Sun World®)**

Molasses Brown Bread **(Kellogg's®)**

Orange'y Pumpkin Bread
(Stokely's Finest®)

Anytime Coffee Cake (**Gerber**®)

Chocolate Chip Party Muffins (**Hershey's**®)

Land O'Lakes® Easy Caramel Orange Ring

Date-Bran Bread for Brownbaggers
(**Sun World**®)

Old Fashioned Stuffing
(**Pepperidge Farm**®)

Orange Raisin Nut Bread (**Colonial**®)

Old Fashioned Corn Bread (**Elam's**®)

Ever-So-Easy Fruitcake **(Eagle® Brand)**

Chocolate Mayonnaise Cake
(Hellmann's®/Best Foods®)

Peaches 'N Cream Cheesecake
(3-Minute Brand®)

Pistachio Pudding Cake **(Jell-O® Brand)**

Chocolate Cake Roll with Almond-Plum
Filling **(Blue Diamond®)**

Blender Avocado Cheesecake
(California Avocado Comm.)

Sunlite Carrot Cake

Devils Food Cake **(Hershey's®)**

Comfort® Cake **(Southern Comfort®)**

Father's Day Date Cheesecake
(Sun World®)

Peaches 'N Cream Pudding Cake
(Thank You® Brand)

Praline® Pecan Cake

Sunshine Loaf **(Gerber®)**

Toll House® Deluxe Cake, Crunchy
Fudge Sandwiches **(Nestlé)**

STIR-FRY ZUCCHINI

4 cups sliced zucchini
  (about ¼ inch thick)
¼ cup POMPEIAN Olive Oil
1 to 2 tsp. oregano
2 tsp. sugar
1 tsp. salt

Sauté zucchini in skillet with olive oil and seasonings until tender, about 15 minutes, stirring frequently. *Makes 6 servings*

ZUCCHINI WITH PECAN RICE STUFFING

Dissolve 1 beef bouillon cube in ½ cup boiling water. Mix in 1 tablespoon BLUE BONNET® Margarine and ½ cup packaged precooked rice. Cover and let stand 5 minutes. Trim off ends of 6 small zucchini squash and cut a thin lengthwise slice off one side of each. Scoop out pulp leaving a ¼-inch shell. Place shells in boiling salted water for 5 minutes. Drain. Finely chop zucchini slices and pulp; mix with prepared rice, ½ cup PLANTERS® Pecan Pieces and ¼ cup grated Parmesan cheese. Stuff mixture into shells and arrange in a shallow baking dish. Bake at 400°F. for 15 to 20 minutes, or until lightly browned.
Serves 6

GRILLED TOMATO PUFFS
(Low Calorie)

1 large tomato
2 tablespoons grated Parmesan cheese
½ cup low-fat cottage cheese, drained
1 egg white
1 packet HERB-OX Onion Flavored Instant Broth and Seasoning

Slice tomato in half. Sprinkle each half with 1 tablespoon Parmesan cheese. Top with mixture of remaining ingredients. Broil until browned, 2 to 3 minutes.
Makes 2 servings

TOMATOES STUFFED WITH SPINACH SOUFFLÉ

1 package frozen spinach soufflé
6 medium size tomatoes
½ cup PLANTERS® Slivered Almonds
Parmesan cheese
PLANTERS® Slivered Almonds

Thaw a package of frozen spinach soufflé. Scoop out 6 medium size tomatoes. Add ½ cup PLANTERS® Slivered Almonds to thawed soufflé and spoon into tomatoes. Sprinkle with Parmesan cheese and more slivered almonds. Bake at 350°F. for 20 to 30 minutes.
Serves 6

SAVORY BAKED TOMATOES

4 large tomatoes
⅓ cup POMPEIAN Olive Oil
1 small onion, chopped
1 pimiento, cut into strips
2 Tbsp. minced ham
½ tsp. salt
⅛ tsp. pepper
¼ tsp. marjoram
1 Tbsp. minced parsley
1 cup soft bread crumbs

Cut a 2-inch wide cap from the stem end of the tomatoes. Hollow out tomatoes, removing pulp and discard with the caps. Heat 4 Tbsp. of olive oil in a skillet, add onion, and sauté until tender. Stir in remaining ingredients, browning slightly. Spoon stuffing mixture into tomatoes. Place remaining 2 Tbsp. olive oil into a shallow baking pan, arrange stuffed tomatoes in the pan, brush with a little of the oil. Bake at 350°F. for 40 minutes or until cooked through. *Makes 4 servings*

SKEWERED VEGETABLES DELUXE

8 small new potatoes
2 small zucchini
12 large DOLE® Fresh Mushrooms
2 tablespoons oil
2 tablespoons shredded Parmesan cheese
1 tablespoon lemon juice
½ teaspoon salt
½ teaspoon basil, crumbled
¼ teaspoon paprika

Pare potatoes and cut zucchini in ¾-inch diagonal slices. Parboil potatoes 15 minutes or until almost done. Add zucchini to potatoes and cook 3 minutes longer. Add mushrooms the last few seconds vegetables cook. Drain well. Alternate vegetables on four 8-inch skewers. Place skewers on flat pan. Mix together all remaining ingredients. Brush vegetables with half the sauce. Broil 7 inches from heat 5 minutes. Turn skewers and brush with remaining sauce. Broil 5 minutes longer. *Makes 4 servings*

OVEN CRISPED VEGETABLES

3½ cups WHEAT THINS Crackers, finely rolled (about 2 cups crumbs)
1½ teaspoons onion salt
¼ teaspoon ground black pepper
¾ cup mayonnaise
¼ cup milk
1 pound eggplant, peeled and cut into 1-inch cubes
¼ pound mushrooms
1 large onion, sliced

Combine first three ingredients in a shallow pan. Blend together next two ingredients. Add vegetables to mayonnaise mixture, a few at a time. Remove with a slotted spoon; roll in crumbs. Place on baking sheets. Bake in a preheated hot oven (425°F.) 15 to 20 minutes, or until golden.
Makes 12 (about 1½-ounce) servings

About 285 calories per 1½-ounce serving

ARGO®

NINA'S FRESH VEGETABLE BAKE

6 carrots, cut in strips
3 small zucchini, cut in ¼"
  diagonal slices
1 cup cherry tomatoes
1 cup herb-seasoned croutons
2 tablespoons ARGO®/
  KINGSFORD'S® Corn Starch
1½ cups milk
¼ cup margarine
1 teaspoon salt
¼ teaspoon pepper
1 teaspoon dried basil leaves

Cook carrots in boiling salted
water about 5 minutes or until
tender crisp; drain. In 1-quart
shallow baking dish toss
vegetables and croutons. In
saucepan stir together corn starch
and milk until smooth; add
margarine, salt and pepper. Bring
to boil over medium heat, stirring
constantly, and boil 1 minute; pour
over vegetables. Sprinkle with
basil. Bake in 350°F. oven 25
minutes, or until vegetables are
tender.   *Makes 6 servings*

SAUCY VEGETABLE MEDLEY

1 can (10¾ ounces) CAMPBELL'S
  Condensed Cream of Chicken
  Soup
¾ cup water
1 cup shredded sharp Cheddar
  cheese
¼ cup chopped parsley
1 tablespoon instant minced onion
½ teaspoon salt
1 package (10 ounces) frozen
  sliced carrots, cooked and
  drained
1 package (10 ounces) frozen
  cauliflower, cooked and
  drained
1 package (10 ounces) frozen peas,
  cooked and drained

In saucepan, blend soup, water,
cheese, parsley, onion and salt;
add vegetables. Heat; stir
occasionally.
     Makes about 5 cups, 8 servings

ITALIAN VEGETABLE MEDLEY

2 cups sliced zucchini squash
½ cup chopped onion
½ teaspoon basil leaves, crushed
2 tablespoons butter or margarine
1 can (10½ ounces) FRANCO-
  AMERICAN Mushroom Gravy
1 cup diced green pepper
1 can (20 ounces) white kidney
  beans, drained
1 large tomato, cut in wedges

In saucepan, cook zucchini and
onion with basil in butter until
tender. Add gravy and green
pepper. Cover; cook over low heat
15 minutes. Stir occasionally. Add
remaining ingredients; heat.
     Makes about 5½ cups, 4 servings

FINLANDIA
IMPORTED
SWISS CHEESE

FINN RATATOUILLE

6 tablespoons olive oil
1 medium unpeeled eggplant, cut
  in 1½-inch cubes
3 medium zucchini, sliced
1 teaspoon salt
⅛ teaspoon pepper
2 cups onion rings
2 medium green peppers, cored,
  seeded and cut into strips
2 large cloves garlic, minced
4 medium tomatoes, cut into
  wedges
½ cup chopped fresh parsley
2 teaspoons finely chopped basil
1½ cups coarsely grated
  FINLANDIA Swiss

Heat 3 tablespoons oil in large
skillet. Add eggplant and zucchini;
season with salt and pepper. Cook
over medium heat for 5 minutes,
stirring often. Remove from skillet
and set aside. Pour remaining oil
into skillet; sauté onions and green
pepper with garlic until tender.
Blend with eggplant mixture. Add
tomatoes, parsley and basil; blend
well. Spoon mixture into 1½-quart
casserole; cover and bake at
350°F. for 20 minutes, until
vegetables are almost tender.
Uncover and sprinkle generously
with cheese. Bake 5 minutes
longer or until cheese is melted
and hot.   *Makes 6 servings*

FRENCH STYLE VEGETABLE STEW

1 cup chopped onions
2 cloves garlic, minced
2 small zucchini, thinly sliced
1 medium green pepper, cut into
  thin strips
½ cup olive or salad oil
1 medium eggplant, pared,
  cut into strips (2" × ½")
3 tablespoons flour
4 medium tomatoes, peeled, cut
  into eighths
¼ cup HEINZ Tomato Ketchup
1 tablespoon salt
1 teaspoon HEINZ Apple Cider
  Vinegar
½ teaspoon crushed oregano
  leaves
¼ teaspoon pepper

In Dutch oven, sauté first four
ingredients in oil until onion is
transparent. Coat eggplant with
flour; add with tomatoes to
sautéed vegetables. Combine
ketchup and remaining ingredients;
pour over vegetables. Cover;
simmer 30-35 minutes; stir
occasionally, or until vegetables
are tender.
   Makes 8-10 servings (about 7 cups)

Note: Zucchini may be peeled if
    skin is tough.

FOOLPROOF BATTER FOR DEEP FRIED VEGETABLES

1 cup all purpose flour
1 cup beer (any brand)
Vegetables (see below)
Soy Oil for deep frying

Frying Temperature 375°. Mix beer
and flour together in a covered
container. Refrigerate for 3-4 hours
before using. Dip vegetables in
batter. Deep fry in soy oil. This
batter can be used for coating any
deep fried vegetable like
mushrooms, zucchini, cauliflower,
broccoli, sweet potato slices or
onion rings. Drain on paper towels
or brown paper bags. Serve piping
hot.

*Favorite recipe from American Soybean
Association*

Sauces and Gravies

CHILI SAUCE—CANADA STYLE

1 cup chopped celery
1 cup chopped onion
1 (17 oz.) can S&W Sliced Cling Peaches, drained and chopped
1 (17 oz.) can S&W Bartlett Pears, drained and chopped
4 (16 oz.) cans S&W Stewed Tomatoes
1 rounded Tbsp. whole pickling spice (tied in cheese cloth bag)
1 cup brown sugar
½ cup S&W Garlic Flavored Red Wine Vinegar
1 tsp. seasoned salt
Dash dill weed

Cook first six ingredients together in a saucepan for 15 minutes. Add remaining ingredients and cook until thickened and tender. Remove spice bag. Pour into pint jars and seal according to manufacturer's directions. Serve with meat, poultry or eggs. *Makes 4 to 6 pints*

ALL 'ROUND TOMATO BARBECUE SAUCE

1 can (10¾ ounces) CAMPBELL'S Condensed Tomato Soup
2 to 4 tablespoons sweet pickle relish
¼ cup finely chopped onion
1 tablespoon brown sugar
1 tablespoon vinegar
1 tablespoon Worcestershire

In saucepan, combine ingredients. Cover; cook over low heat 10 minutes. Stir occasionally.
Makes about 1½ cups

TABASCO® BARBECUE SAUCE

2 tablespoons butter or margarine
1 medium onion, chopped
1 clove garlic, chopped
½ cup chopped celery with leaves
¼ cup chopped green pepper
1 can (1 pound, 4 ounces) tomatoes
1 can (6 ounces) tomato paste
1 bay leaf
2 teaspoons TABASCO® Sauce
2 teaspoons dry mustard
⅓ cup vinegar
½ teaspoon cloves
½ teaspoon allspice
2 slices lemon
1½ teaspoons salt
3 tablespoons brown sugar

Melt butter; add onion and garlic; cook until tender but not brown. Add remaining ingredients and simmer 30 minutes. Let stand until cool. Pour into jar; cover and refrigerate. Use for all meats, chicken and turkey parts.
Yield: 2¼ cups

BARBECUE SAUCE

1 tsp. salt
¼ cup vinegar
1 tsp. chili powder
¼ cup Worcestershire sauce
1 tsp. celery seed
2 cups water
1 cup tomato catsup
1 tsp. SWEET 'N LOW® Brown
Few drops TABASCO® Sauce

Mix all the ingredients together. Simmer half an hour.

ALL-PURPOSE SWEET/SOUR SAUCE

½ cup SMUCKER'S Grape Jelly
2 tablespoons soy sauce
1 tablespoon Worcestershire sauce
½ cup wine vinegar

In a saucepan, combine all ingredients and simmer 5 minutes, stirring constantly. Serve hot with roast beef, lamb, or pork chops. Or try it with cauliflower, beets or carrots. *About 1¼ cups*

YOGURT PARSLEY SAUCE

1 cup DANNON® Plain Yogurt
4 Tbsp. chopped parsley
1 Tbsp. white vinegar
½ tsp. salt

Mix all ingredients in a bowl. Serve chilled over salad, cold ham, cold chicken, fish or hot spaghetti with parmesan sprinkled on top.

SAUCE NICOISE

1 cup mayonnaise
1 can (7 oz.) tuna, drained and flaked
¼ cup chili sauce
1 teaspoon Worcestershire sauce
1 teaspoon grated onion
½ teaspoon dry mustard
1 cup DANNON® Plain Yogurt

Stir together first 6 ingredients. Fold in yogurt. Chill.
Makes 2½ cups

Sunkist.

CREAMY CUCUMBER SAUCE

½ cup mayonnaise or salad
  dressing
½ cup coarsely grated peeled
  cucumber
1 teaspoon fresh grated
  SUNKIST® Lemon peel
2 teaspoons fresh squeezed
  SUNKIST® Lemon juice
¼ teaspoon dried dill weed
Salt and pepper

In small bowl, combine,
mayonnaise, cucumber, lemon
peel, juice and dill weed. Salt and
pepper to taste.

Makes about 1 cup

BASIC WHITE SAUCE MIX

2¾ cups nonfat dry milk powder
½ cup ARGO® /
  KINGSFORD'S® Corn Starch
1 teaspoon salt
½ teaspoon pepper

In medium bowl stir together dry
milk, corn starch, salt and pepper.
Store in tightly covered jar at room
temperature. Stir well before each
use.

Makes 2⅔ cups mix

To make white sauce use: 2
tablespoons NUCOA® or MAZOLA®
Margarine. For thin sauce add: ⅓
cup Basic White Sauce Mix and 1
cup cold water. For medium sauce
add: ⅓ cup Basic White Sauce Mix
and ¾ cup cold water. For thick
sauce add: ⅔ cup Basic White
Sauce Mix and 1 cup cold water.

In small saucepan melt margarine
over medium heat. Remove from
heat. Stir in White Sauce Mix and
water. Stirring constantly, bring to
boil over medium heat and boil 1
minute.

Makes about 1 cup

Cream of Asparagus Soup: Prepare
double recipe for thin white sauce.
Add 1 chicken-flavored bouillon
cube to water. Stir in 1 cup finely
chopped cooked asparagus.

Makes 3 cups

Creamed Vegetables: Prepare 1
recipe medium white sauce. Mix in
3 cups cooked vegetables.

Makes about 3 cups

Cheese Soufflé: Prepare 1 recipe
thick white sauce. In saucepan add
½ pound diced Cheddar cheese to
white sauce. Stirring constantly,
cook over medium-low heat until
cheese is melted. Remove from
heat and pour gradually over 4
slightly beaten egg yolks, mixing
well. In large bowl with mixer at
high speed beat 4 egg whites until
stiff peaks form. Gently fold in
cheese mixture. Pour into
ungreased 1½-quart casserole.
Place casserole in baking pan. Fill
baking pan with warm water to
depth of 1 inch. Bake in 350°F
oven 1¼ hours or until knife
inserted halfway between center
and edge comes out clean. Serve
immediately.

Makes 6 servings

MEDIUM WHITE SAUCE

1 cup cold milk
1 Tbsp. ARGO® /
  KINGSFORD'S® Corn Starch
2 Tbsp. margarine
¼ tsp. salt
⅛ tsp. pepper

In saucepan, gradually stir milk
into corn starch. Add margarine,
salt and pepper. Stirring
constantly, bring to boil over
medium heat. Boil 1 minute.

Makes 1 cup

VARIATIONS:

Cheese Sauce: Stir 1 cup shredded
cheese into 1 cup Medium White
Sauce until cheese melts.

Herb Sauce: Add ¼ tsp. dried dill
weed or basil to 1 cup Medium
White Sauce.

MOCK HOLLANDAISE SAUCE
(Low Cholesterol)

1 cup HELLMANN'S® or BEST
  FOODS® Real Mayonnaise
2 egg whites
2 Tbsp. lemon juice
½ tsp. dry mustard
¼ tsp. salt (optional)

In small saucepan with wire whisk
beat all ingredients until smooth.
Stirring constantly, cook over
medium-low heat until thick (do not
boil). Serve over vegetables or fish.

Makes 1½ cups

5 mg cholesterol per tablespoon

CAMPBELL'S MOCK HOLLANDAISE

1 can (10¾ ounces) CAMPBELL'S
  Condensed Cream of Celery,
  Chicken, or Mushroom Soup
½ cup milk
2 tablespoons butter or margarine
2 tablespoons lemon juice
2 egg yolks, slightly beaten

In saucepan, combine all
ingredients. Cook over low heat
just until thickened, stirring
constantly. Do not boil. Serve with
cooked vegetables or fish.

Makes about 1½ cups sauce

BLENDER HOLLANDAISE SAUTERNE

3 eggs, separated
¼ cup THE CHRISTIAN
  BROTHERS® Sauterne
¼ tsp. salt
Pinch cayenne
¾ cup butter

Place egg yolks, wine and
seasonings in blender. Heat butter
to foaming hot. Blend egg yolk
mixture at high speed for 2
seconds; uncover and pour butter
into mixture while still blending at
high speed. Fold in stiffly beaten
egg whites and serve immediately
or keep warm by placing container
in warm water. Serve over cooked
asparagus, broccoli or with Eggs
Benedict.

Approximately 1½ cups

QUICKIE HOLLANDAISE SAUCE

½ cup butter or margarine
Juice of ½ fresh SUNKIST®
  Lemon
⅛ teaspoon salt
3 egg yolks

In small saucepan, heat butter with
lemon juice and salt until bubbly.
Add slowly to egg yolks, beating
constantly.   *Makes about ¾ cup*

BASIC NEWBURG SAUCE

Heat 2 Tbsp. butter in large skillet. Sprinkle 1 Tbsp. flour into butter and blend thoroughly. Gradually add 1 cup heavy cream to butter flour mixture and cook, stirring constantly until thick and smooth (do not boil). Pour mixture over 2 well-beaten egg yolks, stirring constantly with spoon or whisk. Add salt and pepper to taste. Cook over boiling water for 1-2 minutes, stirring constantly. Add 2 Tbsp. HOLLAND HOUSE® Sherry Cooking Wine.

HAPPY AS A CLAM SAUCE

2 tablespoons butter or margarine
1 clove garlic, minced
2 level tablespoons flour
¾ cup half and half (light cream)
1 (6½ ounce) can minced or chopped clams
2 tablespoons chopped parsley
¼ teaspoon oregano, crumbled
¼ teaspoon salt
⅛ teaspoon pepper
3 tablespoons California Brandy

Melt butter with garlic in saucepan over moderate heat. Stir in flour. Slowly blend in half and half, stirring constantly. Cook, stirring, until sauce boils and thickens. Add undrained clams, brandy, and all remaining ingredients. Heat just to boiling. Serve over hot buttered spaghetti.

Makes 1⅔ cups

Favorite recipe from California Brandy Advisory Board

FISHERMAN'S WHARF ALMONDINE

Melt ½ cup butter or margarine. Add ⅓ cup BLUE RIBBON® Sliced Natural California Almonds. Stir over medium heat till golden. Blend in ½ tsp. salt and 3 Tbsp. lemon juice. Spoon over (about) 2 pounds cooked fish.   *6 servings*

LEMON TARTAR SAUCE

½ cup mayonnaise or salad dressing
2 tablespoons finely chopped dill pickle
2 tablespoons finely chopped green onion
1 tablespoon chopped canned pimiento (optional)
1 teaspoon fresh grated SUNKIST® Lemon peel
2 teaspoons fresh squeezed SUNKIST® Lemon juice

In small bowl, combine all ingredients.

Makes about ¾ cup

SAUCE BORDELAISE

⅛ cup diced onions
1 Tbsp. flour
½ cup bouillon
¼ cup VIRGINIA DARE Red Cooking Wine
1½ Tbsp. butter
1 clove garlic crushed
1 Tbsp. chopped parsley

Sauté diced onions in butter until lightly browned, add flour and mix thoroughly. Add bouillon, stir until smooth. Slowly mix in red cooking wine, crushed garlic and chopped parsley.

BASIC BORDELAISE SAUCE

Heat 3 Tbsp. butter in large skillet. Sauté ¼ cup diced onions in butter until golden, add 2 Tbsp. flour and blend thoroughly. Add 1 cup beef bouillon, stir until smooth. Blend in ½ cup HOLLAND HOUSE® Red Cooking Wine, 1 Tbsp. chopped parsley and 1 clove garlic crushed. Delicious on steak, roast beef and chops.

RED WINE SAUCE

In a small saucepan combine 1½ cups CRUSE Beaujolais, ½ cup MARTELL Cognac, and 3 Tbsp. lemon juice. Stir in 1 tsp. potato starch, mixed to a paste with 2 tsp. water, and a pinch each of cinnamon and cloves. Bring the sauce to a boil and remove the pan from the heat. Add sugar to taste and serve the sauce hot.

HERBED LEMON BUTTER FOR VEGETABLES

¼ cup butter or margarine
Grated peel and juice of ½ SUNKIST® Lemon
1 Tbsp. chopped parsley
¼ tsp. oregano or basil leaves, crushed
Cooked vegetables

In small saucepan, melt butter. Add lemon peel, juice, parsley and oregano; heat. Serve over cooked vegetables. Serve over: Cooked cauliflower, lima beans, peas, summer squash (zucchini, yellow, pattypan), spinach.

Makes about ⅓ cup sauce

Variation: In small bowl, combine softened butter, lemon peel, juice, parsley and oregano. Serve over cooked vegetables.

SWEET 'N SPICY ONION GLAZE (MARINADE)

1 bottle (8 oz.) WISH-BONE® Russian Dressing
1 envelope LIPTON® Onion Soup Mix
1 jar (12 oz.) apricot preserves

In small bowl, combine WISH-BONE® Russian Dressing, LIPTON® Onion Soup Mix and preserves. Use as marinade or glaze for chicken, spareribs and other meats.

Makes about 2½ cups

LEMON CHICKEN MARINADE

¾ cup STAR Italian Kitchen Olive Oil
½ cup lemon juice
1 small onion, chopped
1 large clove garlic, finely minced
1 tsp. salt
¾ tsp. ground thyme

Combine all ingredients. Makes enough to marinate one 3-lb. cut up chicken. Marinate chicken parts for 3 to 8 hours and turn often.

ReaLemon

VERSATILE MARINADE

½ cup REALEMON® Reconstituted
  Lemon Juice
½ cup olive or vegetable oil
2 cloves garlic, finely chopped
2 teaspoons salt
¼ teaspoon pepper
Herbs*

In shallow baking dish, combine
ingredients. Use to marinate lamb,
pork or chicken. Refrigerate
overnight or several days; turn
occasionally. Remove meat from
marinade; broil, fry or bake as
desired.

Makes 1 cup

*Use ½ teaspoon rosemary leaves
with lamb *or* ½ teaspoon thyme
leaves with pork *or* ½ teaspoon
tarragon leaves with chicken.

"BUTTER" SAUCE FOR
ITALIAN GARLIC BREAD
(Low Calorie/Low Cholesterol)

1 packet BUTTER BUDS® Natural
  Butter Flavor Granules
½ cup warm water
1 large clove garlic, finely minced

Dissolve BUTTER BUDS® in water.
Add garlic. Brush liberally on
slices of crusty Italian bread.

One ounce serving equals 13
calories, .001 gram cholesterol.

NEAPOLITAN CLAM SAUCE
FOR PASTA
(Low Calorie/Low Cholesterol)

To "Butter" Garlic Sauce, add one
6½ ounce can minced clams
(drained) and one tablespoon finely
chopped fresh parsley. Heat to
simmering.

Five ounce serving equals 125
calories, .08 gram cholesterol.

CHINESE PLUM SAUCE

1 (17 oz.) can S&W Purple Plums,
  undrained
¼ cup minced onion
1 Tbsp. salad oil
2 Tbsp. molasses
1 Tbsp. sugar
2 Tbsp. soy sauce

Remove pits from plums. Puree
plums and syrup in blender. In
saucepan sauté onion in oil until
softened. Add remaining
ingredients including pureed plums
and cook until slightly thickened,
about 20 minutes. Use to glaze
poultry or pork. Store in covered jar
in refrigerator. *Makes 2 cups*

RAISIN HAM SAUCE

½ cup Dark or Golden SUN-MAID®
  Raisins
1¼ cups water
¼ cup brown sugar (packed)
1 tablespoon cornstarch
Few grains salt
2 tablespoons vinegar
1 tablespoon butter or
  margarine

Combine SUN-MAID® Raisins and
water and simmer 5 minutes. Blend
together brown sugar, cornstarch
and salt, and stir into SUN-MAID®
raisins. Cook and stir until clear
and slightly thickened. Blend in
vinegar and butter. Serve hot.
Serves 5 to 6

RAISIN GROWERS'
RAISIN SAUCE

⅓ cup firmly packed brown sugar
1½ tablespoons cornstarch
¼ teaspoon cinnamon
¼ teaspoon cloves
¼ teaspoon dry mustard
¼ teaspoon salt
1¾ cups water
1 cup raisins
1 tablespoon vinegar

In a saucepan combine brown
sugar, cornstarch, spices, mustard
and salt. Stir in water and raisins.
Cook over moderate heat, stirring
constantly, until mixture thickens
and boils. Remove from heat; blend
in vinegar. Serve warm with ham.
Makes 2 cups

*Favorite recipe from California Raisin
Advisory Board*

EASY FRUIT SAUCE

1 package (10 oz.) frozen
  strawberries, raspberries,
  blueberries or peaches, thawed
2 tablespoons sugar
1 tablespoon ARGO®/
  KINGSFORD'S® Corn Starch

Add water to fruit to make 2 cups.
In saucepan stir together all
ingredients. Bring to boil over
medium heat, stirring constantly,
and boil 1 minute. Chill.
Makes 2 cups

SPEEDY LEMON SAUCE

To contents 1 can LUCKY LEAF®
Lemon Pie Filling add 1 cup water.
Mix until well blended. Makes
about 1 qt. sauce. Delicious on
warm gingerbread or spice cake,
apple brown Betty or bread
pudding.

For Cottage Pudding, heat lemon
sauce. Spoon over squares of
yellow cake. Sprinkle nutmeg on
top. Unused portion of sauce may
be stored in covered container in
refrigerator several days.

GRAPE DESSERT SAUCE

2 cups SMUCKER'S Grape Jelly
½ cup SMUCKER'S Apricot Syrup
½ cup orange juice
2 teaspoons lemon juice
¼ teaspoon ground nutmeg

In a saucepan, combine all
ingredients. Cook over low heat,
stirring constantly, until jelly is
melted. Serve warm over ice cream,
cake squares, pancakes, or
waffles. *About 3 cups*

CREAMY-ORANGE
BUTTERSCOTCH SAUCE

¾ cup evaporated milk
½ cup corn syrup
One 6-oz. pkg. (1 cup) NESTLÉ
  Butterscotch Morsels
¼ measuring teaspoon orange
  extract

In medium saucepan, combine
evaporated milk and corn syrup.
Bring to boil, over moderate heat.
Remove from heat. Add NESTLÉ
Butterscotch Morsels; stir until
melted. Stir in orange extract.
Serve warm over ice cream or cake.
Makes 1⅔ cups

Gravies

BASIC GRAVY

2 Tbsp. fat drippings
2 cups liquid (water, broth or
bouillon)
2 Tbsp. ARGO® /
KINGSFORD'S® Corn Starch
¼ cup cold water
Desired seasonings

Measure fat into roasting pan. Stir
in liquid. Cook over medium heat,
stirring to loosen browned
particles. Remove from heat. Mix
corn starch and water. Stir into
pan. Add seasonings. Stirring
constantly, bring to boil over
medium heat. Boil 2 minutes.

Makes 2 cups

VARIATIONS:

Herb Chicken Gravy: Use 2 cups
chicken bouillon. Add 1 tsp.
chopped parsley and ¼ tsp.
poultry seasoning.

Fruited Chicken Gravy: Use 2 cups
chicken bouillon. After boiling 2
minutes, stir in ¼ cup orange
marmalade or apricot preserves
until smooth.

Onion & Mushroom Gravy: Sauté 1
cup chopped onion and ½ cup
chopped mushrooms in 2 Tbsp. fat
in roasting pan for 5 minutes. Then
add 2 cups beef bouillon for liquid.

Hint: Easy Rule of Thumb: 1 Tbsp.
corn starch = 2 Tbsp. flour.
To use ARGO® or
KINGSFORD'S® Corn Starch
for thickening gravies,
sauces, soups and stews
when your recipe calls for
flour, substitute half as much
corn starch for flour.

TURKEY GRAVY

Turkey giblets and neck
7 cups water
2 onions, peeled, halved
2 stalks celery, halved
2 teaspoons salt
1 bay leaf
6 tablespoons turkey pan drippings
¼ cup ARGO® /
KINGSFORD'S® Corn Starch
¼ cup water
3 chicken-flavored bouillon cubes

In large saucepan place turkey
giblets and neck, water, onion,
celery, salt and bay leaf. Bring to
boil; cover and simmer 30 minutes
or until giblets are tender. Drain
broth; reserve. Pour pan drippings
into large measuring cup. Allow to
stand several minutes until fat
separates from turkey juices.
Return 6 tablespoons fat drippings
to pan; discard remaining fat
drippings. Add reserved giblet
broth to turkey juices to equal 6
cups; return to roasting pan. Stir
together corn starch and water
until smooth; add to roasting pan.
Add bouillon cubes. Stirring
constantly, bring to boil over
medium heat, stirring up brown
bits from bottom of pan and boil 1
minute. If desired, chop giblets and
add to gravy. *Makes 6 cups*

Relishes

KRAUT RELISH

1 can (1 lb.) STOKELY'S FINEST®
Chopped Sauerkraut*, drained
½ cup sugar
½ cup finely chopped celery
½ cup finely chopped green
pepper
½ cup finely chopped carrot
¼ cup finely chopped onion

Combine all ingredients; cover and
chill 12 hours before serving.

Makes 8 servings

*Shredded Sauerkraut may be
snipped and substituted for
chopped.

GRAPE-PEAR CHUTNEY

1 can (1 pound) pear slices, well
drained
1 can (11 ounces) mandarin
oranges, well drained
1 jar (10 ounces) WELCH'S® Grape
Preserves
½ cup golden raisins
½ cup coarsely chopped dates
¼ cup lemon juice
1 tablespoon slivered lemon peel

Combine all ingredients and blend
well. Cover and refrigerate several
hours to blend flavors. Serve with
roast veal, baked turkey breast or
ham slices.

Makes about 3½ cups

CALIFORNIA SUMMER
FRUIT CHUTNEY

2 lbs. ripe fresh nectarines, halved,
pitted, diced
1 lb. ripe fresh plums, halved,
pitted, diced
1 lb. ripe fresh peaches, halved,
pitted, peeled, diced
3 cups diced onions
1½ cups KARO® Light Corn Syrup
1½ cups cider vinegar
1 cup firmly packed brown sugar
1 cup raisins
2 tsp. lemon rind
3 Tbsp. lemon juice
1 tsp. uniodized salt
1 tsp. ground ginger
1 tsp. ground allspice

In 8-qt. stainless steel saucepot
stir together all ingredients.
Stirring frequently, bring to boil
over high heat. Reduce heat; boil
gently uncovered, stirring
frequently, 50 to 60 minutes or
until thickened. Immediately ladle
into clean hot ½-pt. jars leaving
¼" headspace. Wipe jar edge. Seal
according to jar manufacturer's
directions. Process in boiling water
bath 5 minutes.

Makes about 10 (½-pt.) jars

Breads, Muffins and Stuffings

SALT FREE WHITE BREAD
(Low Sodium)

5¾ to 6¾ cups unsifted flour
2 tablespoons sugar
1 package FLEISCHMANN'S® Active Dry Yeast
¼ cup FLEISCHMANN'S® Soft Unsalted Margarine
2 cups very warm tap water (120°F.-130°F.)

Mix 2 cups flour, sugar, and undissolved yeast. Add margarine. Add water and beat 2 minutes at medium speed. Add ½ cup flour. Beat at high speed 2 minutes. Stir in enough flour to make a stiff dough. Turn out onto floured board; knead until smooth and elastic, about 8 to 10 minutes. Place in greased bowl, turn to grease top. Cover; let rise in warm place, until doubled, about 1 hour. Punch dough down; turn out onto floured board. Divide in half. Shape each into a loaf. Place in greased 9 × 5 × 3-inch loaf pans. Cover; let rise until doubled, about 1 hour. Bake at 400°F. about 35 minutes, or until done.   *Makes 2 loaves*

ANADAMA BREAD

9 cups CERESOTA or HECKER'S Unbleached Flour, sifted
2 packages active dry yeast, dissolved in ½ cup warm water
1 tablespoon honey or sugar
½ cup molasses
2 cups water, lukewarm
4 teaspoons salt
¼ cup melted and cooled butter (or margarine)
1 cup yellow cornmeal

Sift flour. In a very large mixing bowl, put yeast mixture, honey, molasses, water and salt; mix. Add melted butter and cornmeal and mix well. Add 4 cups flour and mix in. Then add 4 more cups flour and mix thoroughly. Flour board with remaining cup of flour. Turn dough out and knead flour (all if necessary) into the dough to make a slightly sticky dough. Place in a greased bowl, cover, and let rise in a warm (80-85°) place for 1½ hours. Return dough to board. Divide in two, and let rest 10 minutes. Shape into loaves to fit well-greased 9 × 5 × 3″ loaf pans. Return to warm place; let rise about 45 minutes. Bake in preheated 400° oven 35 to 40 minutes.   *Makes 2 loaves*

NO-KNEAD BRAN BREAD

3 cups all-purpose flour
½ cup instant nonfat dry milk (in dry form)
1½ teaspoons salt
2 pkgs. active dry yeast
¼ cup sugar
1½ cups warm water (110° to 115°F.)
2 cups KELLOGG'S® ALL-BRAN® Cereal or KELLOGG'S® BRAN BUDS® Cereal
1 egg
⅓ cup margarine or butter, softened

Stir together flour, dry milk and salt. Combine yeast, sugar, warm water and cereal in large bowl of electric mixer. Let stand 2 minutes. Add egg, margarine and 1 cup of the flour mixture. Beat at medium speed for 2 minutes. Gradually mix in remaining flour mixture by hand to form a stiff, sticky dough. Cover. Let rise in warm place until double in volume (about 1 hour). Stir down dough to original volume. Spoon into greased 9 × 5 × 3-inch loaf pan. Bake at 375°F. about 40 minutes or until browned. Remove from pan. Brush with melted margarine.
Yield: 1 loaf

® Kellogg Company

BRAN SWISS CHEESE BREAD

1 package active dry yeast
¼ cup warm water
½ cup milk
½ cup butter or margarine
3 eggs, beaten
½ teaspoon salt
2½ cups all-purpose flour
1 cup NABISCO® 100% Bran Cereal
1½ cups coarsely grated natural Swiss cheese (about 6 ounces)

In large bowl, combine yeast with warm water; stir until dissolved. Heat milk and butter or margarine until just melted; cool and add to yeast mixture. Stir in eggs and salt. With wooden spoon or electric mixer at low speed, beat in flour and NABISCO® 100% Bran Cereal. Increase speed to medium; beat 2 minutes.

Cover and let rise in warm place until double in bulk, about 1 hour. Stir in grated cheese. Turn into well-greased 9-cup Bundt® pan. Cover and let rise until double in bulk, about 1 hour.

Preheat oven to 375°F. Bake for 35 to 40 minutes or until crisp and brown and sounds hollow when tapped on surface. Cool on wire rack 10 minutes; remove from pan and cool completely.
Makes 18 (1½-inch) wedges

100% WHOLE WHEAT FLOUR BREAD

2 cups milk, scalded
2 tablespoons cooking oil
2 tablespoons molasses
2 tablespoons honey
2 teaspoons salt
1 package (¼ ounce) active dry yeast*
¼ cup warm water (105-115°F.)*
About 5½ cups ELAM'S® Stone Ground 100% Whole Wheat Flour

Combine first 5 ingredients in bowl; mix well and cool to lukewarm. Dissolve yeast in warm water; stir into milk mixture. Gradually stir in flour as needed to make a stiff dough; beat well after each addition. Cover bowl with damp towel. Let rise in warm draftless area until double in size; punch down. Knead dough until smooth and elastic on a board lightly sprinkled with whole wheat flour. Divide dough in half; shape into 2 loaves. Place loaves in greased loaf pans (8½ × 4½ × 2⅝-inch). Brush tops lightly with additional cooking oil or melted butter. Cover; let rise until almost double in size. Bake in moderate oven (375°F.) until done, 40 to 45 minutes. Remove from pans; cool on wire racks.

Yield: 2 loaves

*1 cake (0.6 ounce) compressed yeast can be substituted for dry yeast and dissolved in lukewarm water (about 95°F.).

PUMPERNICKEL-STYLE RYE BREAD

2 cakes (6/10 ounce each) compressed yeast
½ cup lukewarm water
2 cups milk
2 tablespoons butter or shortening
¼ cup molasses
1 egg, beaten slightly
1 tablespoon salt
6 cups ELAM'S® Stone Ground Whole Rye Flour
2 tablespoons caraway seeds

Dissolve yeast in lukewarm water. Scald milk; add butter or shortening. Cool to lukewarm; stir in molasses, egg, salt and yeast.

Add 2 cups ELAM'S® Rye Flour and caraway seeds; beat until smooth. Cover; let rise in warm area 30 minutes, or until bubbly. Stir in 1½ cups ELAM'S® Rye Flour. Cover; let rise 30 minutes. Stir in 1½ cups ELAM'S® Rye Flour. Sprinkle remaining 1 cup ELAM'S® Rye Flour onto bread board gradually and knead dough 10 minutes working in all rye flour. Shape into 2 flat loaves 8 inches long.

Place loaves in 2 well-greased 9 × 5 × 3 inch loaf pans. Cover; let rise in warm draftless area until nearly doubled in size, about 1 hour. Bake in moderate oven (350°F.) 40 minutes or until done. Cool in pans 5 minutes. Turn onto wire rack and finish cooling. Slice *very* thin. Wrap in foil or plastic film. Store in refrigerator. This bread will not resemble light commercial rye breads. It will be flat, compact, moist and have a slightly yeasty flavor very much like pumpernickel. Delicious topped with cheese or spread with butter and topped with sausage or jam.

Makes 2 loaves, 9 × 5 × 1¾ inches high in center

RHODES GARLIC BREAD

1 loaf RHODES Frozen White or Italian Baking Dough, thawed according to package directions
¼ cup (½ stick) melted butter
1 tablespoon finely chopped fresh or dried parsley flakes
¼ teaspoon garlic powder (or more, depending on taste)
1 tablespoon beaten egg

Slice thawed dough into 16 pieces forming each into a ball. Melt butter in small saucepan over low heat. Remove from heat and stir in egg, parsley, and garlic powder. Dip each ball of dough into butter mixture, coating completely. Arrange in single layer in buttered 9 × 5-inch loaf pan. Pour over any remaining butter mixture. Let rise in warm place until dough just reaches top of pan, about 2½ hours. Preheat oven to 375°F. Bake until top is golden brown, about 25 minutes. Let cool slightly in pan before serving.

OATMEAL BREAD

2 pkg. active dry yeast
¾ c. warm water (110°F.)
3 c. milk, scalded
3 Tbsp. shortening
3 Tbsp. sugar
1 Tbsp. salt
1½ c. 3-MINUTE BRAND® Oats
7 to 8 c. flour

Sprinkle yeast over water. Set aside to soften. Combine milk, shortening, sugar and salt. Cool to lukewarm. Stir in the softened yeast, oats and 1 cup of flour. Add enough of the remaining flour to form a soft dough. Knead on a floured board until very smooth and elastic (8 to 10 minutes). Place in a lightly greased bowl, turning once to grease surface. Cover and let rise until double in size (about one hour). Punch down and let rest for 10 minutes. Shape into two loaves and place into greased 9 × 5 inch loaf pans. Cover and let rise for one hour. Bake at 375°F. for 45 minutes or until golden brown.

HERBED BUBBLE BREAD

2 loaves (1 lb. each) frozen bread dough
¼ cup (½ stick) margarine
2 tablespoons Parmesan cheese
1 teaspoon DURKEE Leaf Thyme, crushed
½ teaspoon DURKEE Dill Weed
½ teaspoon DURKEE Sweet Basil, crushed
¼ teaspoon DURKEE Rosemary Leaves, crushed

Thaw bread dough in refrigerator overnight. Allow to rise at room temperature for 1 hour. Melt margarine and add remaining ingredients. Knead both loaves of bread into 1 ball. Roll dough into a 12-inch square; cut into 25 squares. Dip each square of dough into herb mixture and place in greased BUNDT® pan, overlapping each square slightly. Let rise in warm place until doubled in size. Bake at 350°F. for 30-40 minutes. Best served warm.

Makes 8 servings

MY SPECIAL BREAD

**1 package compressed or granular
  yeast**
¼ cup lukewarm water
2 cups sweet milk
2 tablespoons sugar
2 teaspoons salt
2 tablespoons shortening
6 cups sifted E-Z-BAKE Flour

Soften yeast in lukewarm water.
Scald milk; add sugar, salt,
shortening. Cool to lukewarm, then
add 2 cups flour, beat well; add
yeast. Add more flour gradually to
form a moderately stiff dough.
Turn out on board; knead until
smooth—5 to 8 minutes. Place in
greased bowl. Cover. Let rise until
double in bulk. Punch down; let
rise again until doubled. Shape
into loaves. Cover, let rise on board
10 minutes. Place in greased pans.
Let rise until double. Bake in hot
oven (400°F.) 45 to 50 minutes.
Makes two one-pound loaves

First prize winner E-Z-BAKE Flour contest

GREEN BEANS AND
BACON BREAD

½ pound fresh green beans
Boiling salted water
7 slices bacon
**3¼ to 3¾ cups unsifted white
  flour**
**1½ cups unsifted whole wheat
  flour**
2 cups warm water (105°F.-115°F.)
**2 packages FLEISCHMANN'S®
  Active Dry Yeast**
3 tablespoons sugar
2½ teaspoons salt
**1 egg, beaten (at room
  temperature)**

Wash beans and snap off both
ends with a sharp knife. Slice
lengthwise to make French-style
green beans and cut into 1-inch
pieces. Cook in boiling salted
water for 5 minutes, drain well and
cool. Set aside. Cook bacon until
crisp; drain reserving 3
tablespoons drippings. Crumble
bacon into tiny pieces. Set aside.

Mix together 2 cups white flour
and whole wheat flour. Measure
warm water into large warm bowl.
Sprinkle in yeast; stir until
dissolved. Add sugar, salt, bacon
drippings, egg and 3 cups flour
mixture; beat until smooth. Stir in

crumbled bacon, green beans,
remaining flour mixture and
enough additional white flour to
make a stiff batter. Cover; let rise
in a warm place, free from draft,
until doubled in bulk, about 45
minutes.

Stir batter down. Beat vigorously,
about ½ minute. Turn into 2
greased 9 × 9 × 2-inch baking pans.
Cover; let rise in warm place, free
from draft, until doubled in bulk,
about 1 hour. Bake at 400°F. about
35 minutes, or until done. Remove
from pans and cool on wire racks.
Makes 2 loaves

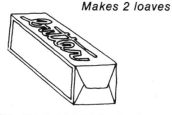

LAND O' LAKES® ZESTY
BUTTER STICKS

**½ loaf French or Italian bread
  (10 × 4")**
**½ c. LAND O LAKES® Sweet
  Cream Butter, softened**
**½ tsp. *each* chervil and basil
  leaves**
**¼ tsp. *each* garlic powder and
  onion powder**

Preheat Oven: 425°. Cut half loaf in
half lengthwise, then cut each half
lengthwise to make 3 wedges. In
small bowl combine remaining
ingredients; blend well. Spread
butter on cut surfaces of bread
wedges. Bake on ungreased
15 × 10" baking sheet near center
of 425° oven for 7 to 9 min. or until
golden brown. Serve warm.
Yield: 6 (10") sticks

HERB SOUR CREAM
RING
(Food Processor Preparation)

2¾ cups unsifted flour
**5 tablespoons FLEISCHMANN'S®
  Margarine**
3 tablespoons sugar
**½ teaspoon dried marjoram
  leaves**
¼ teaspoon dried thyme leaves
**¼ teaspoon dried oregano
  leaves**
**1 package FLEISCHMANN'S®
  Active Dry Yeast**
¼ cup warm water (105°F.-115°F.)
½ cup dairy sour cream
¼ cup milk

Food Processor Preparation:
With metal blade in place
combine flour, 3 tablespoons
margarine, sugar, marjoram,
thyme and oregano in bowl;
process 5-10 seconds to combine.
Dissolve yeast in warm water;
pour through feed tube. Add sour
cream and begin processing. Pour
milk through feed tube in a fast
stream until ball forms, about
10-15 seconds. Continue
processing for 60 seconds to
knead dough.

Carefully remove dough from
processor bowl. Shape into a ball
and place in a greased bowl,
turning to grease top. Cover; let
rise in a warm place, free from
draft, until doubled in bulk, about
1 hour.

Punch dough down. Divide into 10
pieces and shape each into a ball.
Arrange balls in a circle in a
greased 6½ cup ring mold. Cover;
let rise in a warm place, free from
draft, until doubled in bulk, about
1 hour, 10 minutes.

Melt remaining margarine; pour
over dough. Bake at 375°F. for 20
to 25 minutes, or until done.
Remove from pan and cool on
wire rack. *Makes 1 loaf*

FINLANDIA
IMPORTED
SWISS CHEESE

CHEESY CRESCENTS

**1 package refrigerator crescent
  rolls**
**1 package (6 ounces) sliced
  FINLANDIA Swiss Cheese**
Sesame seeds

Open rolls according to package
directions. Cut cheese to fit into
rolls. Roll up and generously
sprinkle top of rolls with sesame
seeds. Bake according to package
directions. *Makes 8 rolls*

ENSAIMADA ROLLS

1 package FLEISCHMANN'S®
  Active Dry Yeast
¼ cup warm water (105°F.-115°F.)
4 cups unsifted flour
1 tablespoon baking powder
½ teaspoon salt
¾ cup sugar
¾ cup (1½ sticks) BLUE BONNET®
  Margarine
6 egg yolks
½ cup evaporated milk
2¼ cups grated sharp Cheddar
  cheese
Melted BLUE BONNET® Margarine
Sugar

Dissolve FLEISCHMANN'S®
Active Dry Yeast in warm water.
Sift flour, baking powder and salt
together twice. Stir ¼ cup sugar
and ½ cup flour mixture into
dissolved yeast. Cover; let rise in
warm place, free from draft, until
doubled in bulk, about 20 minutes.

Cream BLUE BONNET®
Margarine, gradually adding
remaining sugar until well blended.
Add egg yolks, one at a time,
beating well after each addition.
Beat in remaining flour mixture
alternately with evaporated milk.
Stir in yeast mixture; beat until
smooth. Turn dough out onto a
lightly floured board; divide into 12
equal pieces. Roll each piece out
to an 8-inch circle. Sprinkle each
circle with 2 tablespoons cheese.
Roll circles up like a jellyroll and
coil into a snail shape. Place on
ungreased baking sheets. Cover;
let rise in a warm place, free from
draft, until doubled in bulk, about
1 hour. Bake at 400°F. for 15-20
minutes, or until golden brown.
Remove from oven and brush with
melted margarine. Sprinkle with
remaining cheese and sugar. Serve
warm.   *Makes 1 dozen large rolls*

BAGELS

1 cup lukewarm water
2 tablespoons sugar
1¼ teaspoons salt
1 egg (reserve half of egg white for
  wash)
1 package active dry yeast
3½ to 4 cups KING ARTHUR Flour
2 tablespoons sugar

Place first 5 ingredients in a
mixing bowl, add 1 cup of flour and
beat for 2 minutes with electric
beater. Gradually add balance of
flour, stirring by hand until the
dough no longer sticks to the sides
of the bowl. Place dough on a
floured board and knead for 7 to 8
minutes. Then put in an ungreased
bowl, cover and let rise for 30
minutes. Cut dough into 12 pieces,
form each piece into a ball and
with your fingertip punch a hole in
the center. Gradually enlarge the
hole, shaping it to look like a
donut. Place rings on a lightly
floured board, cover and let rise for
20 minutes.

Put 2 inches of water in a large
saucepan or electric frying pan,
add 2 tablespoons of sugar and
bring to a boil. Drop rings into
gently boiling water, making sure
not to crowd them as they will
increase in size. Boil for 3 minutes
on each side and drain on paper
toweling. After draining, place on a
greased cookie sheet, brush with a
mixture of 1 teaspoon of water and
the egg white you reserved, and
bake in a preheated 400 degree
oven for 25 minutes or until golden
brown.

For variations, sprinkle with poppy
seed or onion flakes immediately
after brushing with egg wash.

BRAN BAGELS

1 package active dry yeast
1 cup water
¼ cup butter or margarine
2 tablespoons granulated sugar
2 teaspoons salt
1 egg, beaten
1½ cups NABISCO® 100% Bran
  Cereal
2½ to 2¾ cups all-purpose flour
Sesame or poppy seeds, optional

Sprinkle yeast over ¼ cup warm
water (105° to 115°F.); stir until
dissolved; set aside. Bring
remaining ¾ cup water to a boil;
add butter or margarine, sugar and
salt; stir until butter or margarine
is melted. Cool to lukewarm in
large bowl.

Stir in egg, NABISCO® 100% Bran
Cereal and dissolved yeast
mixture. Gradually stir in 2¼ cups
flour. Form into a ball; then knead
until smooth and elastic, 8 to 10
minutes, using remaining flour.
Place in greased bowl, turning to

grease top. Cover with lightly
dampened towel and let rise in
warm place, about 1 hour. (Dough
will not double in bulk.)

Form into a 12-inch roll; cut into 12
even portions. Form into balls.
With thumb, make a hole in center
of each; spread slightly. Place on
cookie sheet; set in warm place
until they start to rise (about 20
minutes).

Preheat oven to 425°F. Bring water
to a boil in a large skillet. Drop 3
or 4 bagels, one at a time, into
boiling water. Simmer 2 to 3
minutes, turning once. Remove
with slotted spatula and drain on
absorbent paper. Place on lightly
greased cookie sheet. Sprinkle
with sesame or poppy seeds, if
desired. Bake about 17 to 20
minutes, or until lightly browned.
Remove to rack to cool.
Makes 12 (about 3-inch) bagels

GERMAN SWEET BREAD

½ cup butter or margarine
  softened
1⅓ cups sugar
3 eggs
1 teaspoon vanilla
1 cup BLUE RIBBON® Slivered
  Almonds
2 squares (1 oz. each) unsweetened
  chocolate, finely chopped
1 cup vacuum-packed regular
  wheat germ
½ cup dark seedless raisins
½ cup diced mixed glacé fruit
1½ cups flour
1 teaspoon baking powder
½ teaspoon salt
1 cup milk

Cream butter with sugar; beat in
eggs and vanilla. Mix almonds with
chocolate, wheat germ, raisins,
fruit, flour, baking powder and salt;
stir into creamed mixture
alternately with milk. Turn into
well-greased and floured 7 to 9-cup
crown or turban mold with hole in
center. Bake 1 hour at 350 degrees
or until a cake tester or long pick
comes out dry. Cool 20 minutes in
mold; invert and cool on wire rack.
Decorate with powdered sugar
glaze, chocolate curls, whole
blanched almonds and candied
violets, if you like.

Makes 1 loaf

WHOLE WHEAT RAISIN APPLE BREAD

2 cups unbleached flour
2 cups whole wheat flour
2 packages active dry yeast
½ cup warm water (110 to 115 degrees)
1 cup milk
3 tablespoons honey
1 tablespoon salt
1 egg, beaten
½ cup cracked wheat
1 cup raisins
1 cup peeled, chopped tart apple
1 egg *yolk*
1 teaspoon milk

Combine unbleached and whole wheat flour; set aside. Dissolve yeast in warm water. Scald milk. Add honey and salt to warm milk and gradually pour milk mixture into beaten egg. Add dissolved yeast. Stir in cracked wheat, raisins, apple and 3 cups flour. Knead in the remaining flour. Place in greased bowl, turning to grease top. Cover; let rise in warm place for about 1 hour or until doubled. Punch down and form loaf. Put in greased 9 x 5-inch loaf pan; cover, let rise in a warm place until double, about 45 minutes. Beat egg yolk with milk and brush top of loaf. Sprinkle with additional cracked wheat. Bake at 375 degrees for 45 to 50 minutes, or until loaf sounds hollow when lightly tapped. Remove from pan and cool on wire rack.

Makes one loaf

California Raisin Advisory Board's favorite recipe

RAISIN PUMPERNICKEL

2¼ cups cold water
¾ cup cornmeal
2 teaspoons salt
½ cup GRANDMA'S® Molasses (Unsulphured)
2 tablespoons shortening
2 packages active dry yeast
¼ cup warm water
1 teaspoon sugar
3 to 3½ cups whole wheat flour
3 to 3½ cups rye flour
1 cup raisins

Stir water into cornmeal in saucepan and cook over medium heat, stirring frequently, until thickened and just boiling. Remove from heat and stir in salt, molasses and shortening; cool to

lukewarm. Sprinkle yeast into warm water in small cup. Add sugar and stir until yeast dissolves. Add yeast to cornmeal and stir in 2 cups each whole wheat flour and rye flour to form a soft dough. Sprinkle some of the remaining flour on board and knead dough, adding flour as needed to form a dough that does not stick. Continue to knead 10 minutes. Knead in raisins. Form dough into a ball and place in large, well greased bowl, turning so that all sides are greased. Cover and let rise in warm place until double, about 1 hour.

Punch down dough and divide in half. Shape each half into a well-rounded ball and place on a greased baking sheet. Cover and let rise until double, about 45 minutes. Bake in 375°F. oven 45 minutes. Remove from oven and rub surface with butter. Cool on wire rack. *Yield: 2 loaves*

SUN-MAID® RAISINS
SUNLAND VINEYARD LOAF

1 cup SUN-MAID® Seedless Raisins
⅓ cup sherry
1 (13¾ oz.) package hot roll mix
¼ cup warm water
½ cup hot milk
2 tablespoons butter
1 tablespoon sugar
1 egg, beaten
½ cup chopped walnuts
4 bay leaves (optional)
Melted butter

Chop raisins coarsely; add sherry. Let stand an hour or more. Dissolve yeast from mix in warm water. Combine milk, butter, and sugar; when lukewarm, add yeast and egg. Beat in flour mixture from package. Mix in walnuts and drained raisins. Cover, and let rise in warm place until doubled, 1¼ to 1½ hours. Punch down. Divide into 8 portions. Shape each into a slender roll 8 inches long. Twist 2 together for each loaf; fit into greased pans, 5½ x 3 inches, with a bay leaf in bottom of pan. Brush with melted butter. Let rise until doubled, 30 to 40 minutes. Bake on low shelf at 375°F. 30 to 35 minutes. Turn out and cool.

RAISIN BREAD

1½ cups milk
½ cup butter or margarine
½ cup sugar
2 teaspoons salt
2 packages active dry yeast
1 cup warm water (110 to 115 degrees)
2 eggs, beaten
7 to 8 cups flour
3 cups raisins, dusted in flour

Heat milk to scalding; add butter, sugar and salt. Cool to lukewarm. Dissolve yeast in warm water. Add the lukewarm milk mixture. Stir in eggs. By hand or using an electric mixer, gradually beat in 5 cups of flour. Add raisins. By hand, work in remaining flour to make a medium firm dough. Place in deep, greased bowl, turning to grease top. Cover; let rise in warm place until doubled in size, about 1½ to 2 hours. Punch down dough. Turn dough out onto floured surface; knead slightly. Form into three loaves and place in well greased 8 x 4-inch loaf pans. Cover; let rise in warm place until doubled, about 1 hour. Bake at 375 degrees for 30 to 35 minutes or until golden brown. Remove from pans; brush tops with butter and cover with cloth. Cool on wire rack. *Makes 3 loaves*

California Raisin Advisory Board's favorite recipe

APPLE SAUCE NUT BREAD

4 cups sifted flour
4 tsp. baking powder
1 tsp. soda
1½ tsp. salt
1 cup sugar
2 cups chopped nuts
2 beaten eggs
½ cup melted butter (or margarine)
2 cups LUCKY LEAF® Apple Sauce
2 Tbsp. lemon juice
1 tsp. grated lemon rind

Sift all dry ingredients together. Mix in nuts. Combine apple sauce, beaten eggs, lemon juice, rind, butter. Add to dry ingredients. Stir only until no dry flour is visible. Pour into 3 greased loaf pans. Bake at 350° about 45 minutes.

WHEAT CHEX® APPLESAUCE NUT BREAD

1 ¾ cups sifted all-purpose flour
2 teaspoons baking powder
¾ teaspoon salt
½ teaspoon cinnamon
¼ teaspoon nutmeg
1 cup sugar
1 ½ cups WHEAT CHEX® Cereal crushed to ¾ cup
⅓ cup raisins, coarsely chopped
½ cup chopped walnuts
1 egg, slightly beaten
3 tablespoons vegetable oil
1 ½ cups canned applesauce

Preheat oven to 350°. Grease 8½ × 4½ × 2½-inch loaf pan. Sift together flour, baking powder, salt, spices and sugar. Stir in WHEAT CHEX® crumbs, raisins and nuts. Combine egg, oil and applesauce. Add all at once to dry ingredients. Stir just until moistened. Turn into pan. Bake 70-75 minutes or until tester inserted in center comes out clean. Let cool 15 minutes before removing from pan.

Makes 1 loaf

Note: Bread may also be baked in three 5¼ × 3¼ × 2-inch loaf pans (bake about 40 minutes) OR six 4½ × 2½ × 1¼-inch loaf pans (bake about 30 minutes).

TOM'S® APPLE DATE BREAD

1 egg
1 cup canned applesauce
2 tablespoons peanut oil
2 cups sifted flour
¾ cup sugar
3 teaspoons baking powder
½ teaspoon cinnamon
¼ teaspoon allspice
½ teaspoon soda
¾ cup chopped TOM'S® Toasted Peanuts
½ cup chopped dates

Heat oven to 350°F. (moderate). Beat egg lightly in mixing bowl and stir in applesauce and peanut oil. Sift dry ingredients together; mix in chopped peanuts and dates. Add to egg mixture, stirring just enough to blend. Turn into well-greased 9″ × 5″ × 3″ loaf pan (or use a narrow pan). Bake 60 to 70 minutes at 350°F. until done. For a pretty topping, brush hot top crust with egg white and decorate with salted peanut halves. Return to oven for three minutes. Cool in pans 10 minutes; turn out on rack and cool completely. Wrap in foil or wax paper and store overnight before slicing. Slice thinly.

APRICOT BREAD

3 cups flour
5 tsp. baking powder
½ tsp. salt
1 cup finely chopped pecans
1 egg, well beaten
1 cup milk
¾ cup grated orange rind
1 Tbsp. SIMON FISCHER Apricot Butter (or substitute SIMON FISCHER Prune Butter)

Mix and sift flour, baking powder, salt . . . stir in nutmeats. Combine egg, milk, grated orange rind and Apricot Butter, then stir in dry ingredients. Pour into greased 4 × 8 inch loaf pan. Bake at 350 degrees, 1¼ hours. Let the bread cool before slicing.

EVER-FAVORITE APRICOT NUT BREAD

1 can (17 ounces) apricot halves
2 cups sifted all-purpose flour
1 teaspoon baking powder
½ teaspoon baking soda
½ teaspoon salt
½ cup chopped walnuts
⅔ cup sugar
⅓ cup vegetable shortening
2 eggs
3 tablespoons orange juice

Drain apricots, reserving syrup. Puree apricots in electric blender or force through food mill. Add enough apricot syrup to puree to measure 1 cup. Sift together flour, baking powder, soda and salt; mix with nuts. Cream together sugar and shortening in bowl; beat in eggs. Stir in orange juice and apricot puree. Add flour-nut mixture and mix well. Pour batter into greased 9 × 5 × 3-inch loaf pan or six greased 4½ × 2½ × 1¼ inch pans. Bake in 350°F. oven until bread tests done, about 40 to 45 minutes for large loaf and about 25 to 30 minutes for small loaves. Cool 10 minutes; remove from pan, cool on rack.

Makes one 9 × 5-inch loaf or six 4½ × 2½-inch loaves

California Apricot Advisory Board Favorite Recipe

BRANDIED APRICOT LOAVES

1½ cups (8 ounces) coarsely chopped dried apricots
⅔ cup THE CHRISTIAN BROTHERS® Brandy
⅓ cup water
1 cup sugar
2 eggs
⅓ cup vegetable oil
½ teaspoon baking soda
1 tablespoon baking powder
½ teaspoon salt
2¾ cups flour
1 cup chopped nuts
Brandied Cream Cheese (recipe follows)

In 1-quart saucepan combine apricots, brandy and water. Bring just to boil. Remove from heat and set aside 10 minutes. In large bowl combine sugar, eggs, oil, baking soda and liquid drained from apricots. Beat 2 minutes. Mix in baking powder, salt, flour and apricots just to blend. Fold in nuts. Turn equally into 2 greased and floured 8½ × 4½ × 2⅝-inch loaf pans. Bake in 350 degree oven 35 to 45 minutes until tops are browned and loaves are springy to the touch. Cool 5 minutes. Turn out on wire racks. Wrap in aluminum foil while still slightly warm. Store 24 hours before slicing. Serve with Brandied Cream Cheese.

Makes 2 loaves (about 1¼ pounds each)

Note: Brandied Apricot Loaves may be securely wrapped and frozen up to 1 month.

BRANDIED CREAM CHEESE

2 packages (3 ounces each) cream cheese, softened
3 tablespoons powdered sugar
2 tablespoons butter or margarine, softened
3 tablespoons THE CHRISTIAN BROTHERS® Brandy

Combine all ingredients in small bowl. Beat until smooth. Chill. Store in refrigerator 24 hours before serving.

Makes about ¾ cup

CLASSIC BANANA BREAD

2 ripe medium DOLE® Bananas, peeled
¾ cup packed brown sugar
½ cup butter, softened
1 egg
¼ cup dairy sour cream
1 teaspoon vanilla
2¼ cups flour
1 teaspoon baking powder
½ teaspoon baking soda
½ teaspoon salt
½ teaspoon ground cinnamon
1 cup chopped walnuts

Slice bananas into blender; whir until pureed (should have 1 cup). Beat sugar and butter until light and fluffy. Beat in egg. Beat in banana, sour cream and vanilla until blended. Combine flour, baking powder, soda, salt and cinnamon. Add to banana mixture. Beat until blended. Stir in walnuts. Pour into 9 × 5 × 2-inch loaf pan. Bake in 350°F. oven 65 to 70 minutes until toothpick inserted comes out clean. Cool in pan 10 minutes. Invert on wire rack to completely cool.

Makes 1 loaf

BANANA SPICE BREAD

1¾ cups sifted flour
2 teaspoons baking powder
¼ teaspoon soda
½ teaspoon salt
1 teaspoon cinnamon
¼ teaspoon cloves
½ cup SUE BEE® Honey
2 eggs, well beaten
⅓ cup salad oil
1 cup mashed bananas (2 to 3)
½ cup chopped nuts

Sift dry ingredients together. Combine honey, eggs, salad oil and mashed bananas. Add to dry ingredients and beat until smooth. Add nuts. Pour into greased 9 × 5 × 3-inch loaf pan or two small greased 8½ × 4½ × 2½-inch loaf pans. Bake in a 350°F. oven, 50-65 minutes in a large loaf pan or 45-50 minutes in small loaf pans, or until toothpick inserted in center comes out clean. Remove from pan and cool before slicing. Glaze loaf with thin confectioners' sugar icing, if you like, or serve plain.

BANANA BREAD CAKE

125 mL or ½ cup of butter
150 mL or ⅔ cup honey
3 eggs, beaten
250 mL or 1 cup bananas, mashed
75 mL or ⅓ cup of milk
45 mL or 3 tablespoons of TIA MARIA®
5 mL or 1 teaspoon of salt
10 mL or 2 teaspoons of baking powder
5 mL or 1 teaspoon baking soda
500 mL or 2 cups whole wheat flour
250 mL or 1 cup raisins

Preheat the oven to 350°F. (180°C). Butter and flour standard size loaf tin. Mix butter and honey together in a large bowl with beater until light and fluffy. Beat in the eggs, bananas, milk and TIA MARIA®. Sift together the salt, baking powder, baking soda and flour. Add raisins. Gradually mix all dry ingredients into banana batter. Spoon the batter into prepared loaf tin. Bake at 350°F. (180°C) for 1 hour. Cool before removing from tin.

SUN WORLD
DATE-BRAN BREAD FOR BROWNBAGGERS

10 oz. pkg. SUN WORLD® Pitted Dates, diced
2 cups boiling water
2 large eggs, at room temp.
¾ cup sugar
1½ cups whole wheat flour
2 tsp. baking powder
1 tsp. baking soda
2 cups unbleached white flour
1 tsp. vanilla
2 cups whole bran
1 cup chopped nuts
½ tsp. salt

Place the dates in a bowl and pour the boiling water over them. Let cool. Preheat oven to 350 degrees. Beat the eggs until very light and thick. Gradually beat in sugar until mixture makes a rope when dropped from the beaters. Mix together whole wheat flour, baking powder and baking soda. Fold one cup of the whole wheat flour mixture into the egg mixture. Fold

in half the dates, half the soaking water, white flour and vanilla. Stir in the remaining whole wheat flour mixture, remaining dates and water, the bran, nuts and salt. Turn the mixture into a 10-inch tube pan with bottom greased and floured. Bake 50 minutes or until done. Cool in pan 20 minutes before turning onto cooling rack.

Yields 12 to 16 servings of very solid textured bread

PEANUTTY DATE BREAD

⅔ cup PETER PAN® Peanut Butter, Crunchy
¼ cup shortening
1 cup sugar
2 eggs, beaten
1 teaspoon vanilla
2 cups sifted flour
1 teaspoon baking powder
½ teaspoon baking soda
½ teaspoon salt
1 cup milk
1½ cups chopped dates

Preheat oven to 350°F. Cream together peanut butter, shortening and sugar. Add eggs and vanilla. Beat until light and fluffy. Sift together flour, baking powder, soda and salt. Add flour mixture and milk. Stir until just blended. Mix in dates. Spoon into a greased 9 by 5 by 3 inch loaf pan. Bake in 350°F. oven for about 1 hour and 10 minutes until wooden pick inserted in center comes out clean.

Yield: One 9 by 5 by 3 inch loaf

Creamy Orange Spread: Combine 6 ounces cream cheese, softened; 2 tablespoons orange juice and 1⅓ tablespoons grated orange peel. Use as a spread on slices of Peanutty Date Bread.

As a Frosting: Combine 4 ounces cream cheese, softened; 1⅓ tablespoons orange juice and 1 tablespoon grated orange peel.

BRAN DATE-NUT BREAD

½ cup butter or margarine
½ cup dark brown sugar, firmly
   packed
⅓ cup unsulphured molasses
1 (8-ounce) package DROMEDARY
   Chopped Dates
1 cup milk
1 cup NABISCO® 100% Bran
   Cereal
2¼ cups all-purpose flour
½ cup chopped walnuts or pecans
1 teaspoon baking soda
½ teaspoon salt
2 eggs, lightly beaten

Preheat oven to 350°F. In medium
saucepan, combine butter or
margarine, sugar, molasses and
DROMEDARY Chopped Dates.
Heat to melt butter or margarine.
Stir in milk and NABISCO® 100%
Bran. In large bowl, blend flour,
chopped nuts, baking soda and
salt. Make well in center. Stir in
bran mixture and eggs just until
well blended. Turn into well-
greased 9 × 5 × 3-inch loaf pan.
Bake 1 to 1¼ hours or until cake
tester comes out clean. Cool in
pan on wire rack 10 minutes;
remove from pan; cool completely.
Makes 1 (9-inch) loaf

Durkee
FAMOUS FOR FLAVOR

FESTIVE CHERRY BREAD

1 jar (16 oz.) DURKEE Maraschino
   Cherries (1½ cups chopped
   cherries, ⅔ cup cherry juice)
2 cups sugar
4 eggs
1 cup DURKEE Flaked Coconut
1½ cups chopped walnuts, pecans
   or almonds
3 cups flour
1 tablespoon baking powder
½ teaspoon salt

Dice cherries and reserve cherry
juice. Beat sugar and eggs
together. Add cherries, coconut,
and nuts. Combine flour, baking
powder, and salt. Add flour mixture
and cherry juice alternately to the
egg mixture. Bake in 2 greased and
floured 8½ × 4½ × 2½-inch loaf
pans at 350°F. for 60 to 70
minutes. *Makes 2 loaves*

MOLASSES BROWN BREAD

1 cup all-purpose flour
1 teaspoon baking soda
½ teaspoon salt
½ teaspoon ground cinnamon
1 egg
1 cup KELLOGG'S® ALL-BRAN®
   Cereal or BRAN BUDS® Cereal
½ cup seedless raisins
2 tablespoons shortening
⅓ cup molasses
¾ cup very hot water

Stir together flour, soda, salt and
cinnamon. Set aside. In large
mixing bowl, beat egg slightly. Mix
in ALL-BRAN® Cereal, raisins,
shortening and molasses. Add
water, stirring until shortening is
melted. Add flour mixture, stirring
only until combined. Fill 2 greased
metal cans, 4¼ inches deep and 3
inches across, about two-thirds
full. Bake at 350°F. about 45
minutes or until wooden pick
inserted near center comes out
clean. Remove from cans. Let cool
slightly. Slice and serve warm. Or
cool completely on wire rack, wrap
tightly and store overnight.
Yield: 2 loaves, 4¼ × 3 inches
® Kellogg Company

PUMPKIN BREAD

2⅓ cups sugar
⅔ cup cooking oil
4 eggs, beaten
2 cups canned pumpkin (1 lb. can)
⅔ cup water
3⅓ cups CERESOTA or HECKER'S
   Unbleached Flour, sifted
½ teaspoon baking powder
2 teaspoons baking soda
1½ teaspoons salt
½ teaspoon cinnamon
½ teaspoon ground cloves
⅔ cup nuts, finely chopped
⅔ cup raisins (soaked in boiling
   water for 1 minute, drained and
   dried)

Mix the first five ingredients in a
large bowl. Sift dry ingredients
together; add raisins and nuts. Add
to pumpkin mixture and mix until
well blended. Grease and flour four
1-pound coffee cans. Fill halfway
with batter. Bake in preheated 350°
oven for 1¼ hours.
Makes four 1-pound coffee cans

ORANGE'Y PUMPKIN BREAD

⅔ cup shortening
2⅔ cups sugar
4 eggs
1 can (1 lb.) STOKELY'S FINEST®
   Pumpkin
⅔ cup water
3⅓ cups flour
2 teaspoons baking soda
1½ teaspoons salt
1 teaspoon cinnamon
1 teaspoon cloves
½ teaspoon baking powder
1 orange
⅔ cup chopped nuts
⅔ cup chopped raisins or dates

Cream shortening and sugar
thoroughly; add eggs, Pumpkin and
water. Sift together next 6
ingredients and add to Pumpkin
mixture. Remove seeds from
orange. Using blender or grinder,
grind orange, including peel; add to
Pumpkin batter. Stir in nuts and
raisins or dates. Pour into two well
greased 9 × 5 × 3-inch loaf pans or
seven 1-lb. cans and bake at
350°F. for 1 hour.
Makes 7 small or 2 large loaves

PUMPKIN NUT BREAD

2 cups sifted flour
2 teaspoons baking powder
½ teaspoon soda
1 teaspoon salt
1 teaspoon cinnamon
½ teaspoon nutmeg
1 cup LIBBY'S Solid Pack
   Pumpkin
1 cup sugar
½ cup milk
2 eggs
¼ cup softened butter
1 cup chopped pecans

Preheat oven to 350°F. Sift
together first 6 ingredients.
Combine pumpkin, sugar, milk and
eggs in mixing bowl. Add dry
ingredients and butter; mix until
well blended. Stir in nuts. Spread
in well-greased 9 × 5 × 3-inch loaf
pan. Bake at 350°F. for 45 to 55
minutes or until toothpick inserted
in center comes out clean.
Yields 1 loaf

Note: For 2 loaves, use 1 can (16
   oz.) LIBBY'S Solid Pack
   Pumpkin and double
   remaining ingredients. Bread
   may be frozen.

OLD FASHIONED PUMPKIN BREAD

3 cups all-purpose flour
2 cups sugar
½ cup FRENCH'S® Big Tate
  Mashed Potato Flakes
1 teaspoon baking powder
1 teaspoon baking soda
½ teaspoon each FRENCH'S®
  Allspice, Cinnamon, and Nutmeg
¼ teaspoon salt
1 cup chopped walnuts or pecans
3 eggs
1 can (18-oz.) pumpkin pie filling
¾ cup oil
½ cup milk
1 teaspoon FRENCH'S® Vanilla
  Extract

Combine flour, sugar, potato
flakes, baking powder, soda,
spices, salt, and nuts in large
mixing bowl. Lightly beat together
eggs, pie filling, oil, milk, and
vanilla; add to flour mixture,
stirring just until moistened. Spoon
into 2 well-greased 9 × 5-inch loaf
pans. Bake in 350°F. oven 60 to 70
minutes, until food pick inserted in
center comes out clean. Let stand
10 minutes; remove from pans.
Makes 2 loaves

ORANGE RAISIN NUT BREAD

2¼ cups unsifted flour
1 cup firmly-packed COLONIAL®
  Light Golden Brown Sugar
1½ teaspoons baking powder
1 teaspoon baking soda
½ teaspoon salt
1 cup buttermilk
1 egg
¼ cup butter or margarine, melted
1 teaspoon vanilla extract
1 cup raisins
1 cup chopped nuts
1 tablespoon grated orange rind

Preheat oven to 350°. In large
bowl, combine dry ingredients. Add
buttermilk, egg, butter and vanilla.
Mix just until moistened. Stir in
raisins, nuts and rind. Turn into
lightly greased 9 × 5-inch loaf pan.
Bake 45 to 50 minutes or until
toothpick inserted into crack near
center comes out clean. Cool 15
minutes; turn out of pan. Store,
tightly wrapped, in refrigerator.
Makes one 9 × 5-inch loaf

OLD FASHIONED DIAMOND® NUT BREAD

1½ cups DIAMOND® Walnuts
3 cups sifted all-purpose flour
1 cup granulated sugar
4 teaspoons baking powder
1½ teaspoons salt
1 egg, lightly beaten
¼ cup shortening, melted
1½ cups milk
1 teaspoon vanilla

Coarsely chop walnuts. Resift flour
with sugar, baking powder and
salt. Add egg, shortening, milk and
vanilla to dry mixture. Stir just until
all of flour is moistened. Stir in
walnuts. Turn into greased
9 × 5 × 3-inch loaf pan, or divide
batter between 2 greased #2½
cans. Bake at 350 degrees F. about
1 hour 20 minutes for rectangular
loaf or 1 hour 10 minutes for round
loaves.

VARIATIONS:

Streusel Variation. Blend ⅓ cup
brown sugar, packed, 1½
tablespoons flour, 1 teaspoon
cinnamon and 2 tablespoons butter
together in a small mixing bowl.
Prepare the batter as recipe
directs. Turn half of batter into loaf
pan. Sprinkle sugar mixture over
batter and top with remaining
batter. Bake according to recipe
directions.

Candied Fruit Variation. Prepare
the batter as recipe directs, adding
2 teaspoons grated orange peel to
egg and milk mixture. Stir in ¾
cup chopped candied fruit with the
walnuts. Bake according to recipe
directions.

PISTACHIO-DATE NUT BREAD

¾ cup flour
¾ cup sugar
½ tsp. baking powder
3 eggs, beaten
1 tsp. vanilla
1 tsp. grated orange peel
½ cup shelled, chopped BLUE
  RIBBON® Pistachios
1 cup chopped dates

Combine flour, sugar and baking
powder in large bowl. Add beaten
eggs, vanilla, and orange peel; mix
gently. Combine Pistachios and
dates with batter; turn into 6 × 3 × 2
inch loaf baking pans. Bake at 300
degrees for 40 minutes.
Makes two loaves

NUT BREAD

3 cups E-Z-BAKE Flour
3 teaspoons baking powder
1 teaspoon salt
⅔ cup sugar
1 cup chopped nut meats
2 eggs, well beaten
1 cup milk
4 tablespoons melted butter or
  margarine

Sift flour once, measure, add
baking powder, salt and sugar; sift
again. Add nuts. Combine eggs,
milk and shortening; add to flour
mixture and blend. Bake in greased
loaf pan in moderate oven (350°F.)
1 hour, or until done. Store the
bread overnight or for several
hours in order to cut into thin
slices.

First prize winner E-Z-BAKE Flour contest

OLD FASHIONED CORN BREAD

1 cup sifted ELAM'S® Unbleached
  White Flour with Wheat Germ
3 teaspoons baking powder
½ teaspoon salt
1 cup ELAM'S® Stone Ground
  100% Whole Yellow Corn Meal*
1 cup milk
2 eggs, beaten
¼ cup honey or maple syrup
¼ cup melted butter or bacon
  drippings

Combine and sift first 3
ingredients into bowl. Stir in corn
meal. Combine milk, eggs, honey
or syrup and melted butter or
bacon drippings; mix. Add liquids
to dry ingredients; stir just until dry
ingredients are moistened. Pour
into greased 8-inch square baking
pan. Bake in hot oven (425°F.) until
done and lightly browned, about 20
minutes.
*Yield: One 8 × 8 × 1½-inch bread,
12 to 16 pieces*

*ELAM'S® Organically Grown
Stone Ground 100% Whole Yellow
Corn Meal may be substituted, if
desired.

COCO WHEATS BREAD

¾ cup COCO WHEATS
1½ cups milk
2 cups BISQUICK® Baking Mix
½ cup brown sugar
1 cup nutmeats

Soak COCO WHEATS in milk for 3 minutes. Combine BISQUICK, brown sugar and nutmeats; add COCO WHEATS, stirring until mixture is moistened. Bake in a greased loaf pan in 350° oven for 45 minutes or until done.

WHEAT, EGG, MILK FREE BREAD

2½ cups ELAM'S® 100% Whole Rye Flour
2 teaspoons baking powder
1 teaspoon salt
½ cup seedless raisins or chopped figs
½ teaspoon baking soda
1½ cups warm water
¼ cup molasses
2 tablespoons cooking oil or melted shortening

Combine and mix flour, baking powder and salt in bowl. Stir in raisins or figs. Combine soda, warm water, molasses and oil or melted shortening. Add liquids to dry ingredients; stir just until dry ingredients are moistened. Turn into greased loaf pan (9 × 5 × 3-inch). Bake in moderate oven (350°F.) until done, 45 to 50 minutes.

Yield: One loaf, 9 × 5 × 2-inch

OATMEAL HAWAIIAN BREAD

4 eggs
1½ c. sugar
2½ c. flour
2 tsp. salt
2 tsp. soda
1½ c. 3-MINUTE BRAND® Oats
2½ c. (20 oz.) crushed pineapple, undrained
3 c. (10 oz.) flaked coconut

Combine eggs and sugar and beat until light (about 2 minutes). Sift flour, salt and soda. Add to egg mixture and blend until smooth (about 2 minutes longer). Add remaining ingredients and mix very well. Spoon into two greased and floured 9 × 5 inch loaf pans. Bake at 325°F. for one hour. Remove from pan immediately and serve warm or cold.

LAND O' LAKES® BUTTER BATTER BREAD

3 c. whole wheat flour
2 pkg. active dry yeast
2½ c. buttermilk
¼ c. molasses
¼ c. honey
1 Tbsp. salt
⅓ c. LAND O LAKES® Sweet Cream Butter
1½ c. regular rolled oats
2 eggs
2½ to 3 c. all-purpose flour
LAND O LAKES® Sweet Cream Butter, melted

Grease two 1½-qt. round 2½″ deep casseroles. Combine whole wheat flour and yeast. In 2-qt. saucepan heat buttermilk, molasses, honey, salt and butter until warm (105-115°F.). Pour into 3-qt. mixer bowl. Add oats, whole wheat-yeast mixture and eggs. Blend at low speed (with electric mixer) until moistened. Beat 3 min. at high speed. Stir in enough flour to make a stiff dough. Brush with melted butter. Cover; let rise in warm place until doubled, about 1 hr. Punch down; shape into 2 round loaves. Place in casseroles; cover. Let rise until double, about 45 min. Heat oven to 375°. Bake for 25 to 35 min. or until loaf sounds hollow when tapped.

Yield: 2 round loaves

MAGIC MUFFINS

1¼ cups flour
¾ cup MALT-O-MEAL®
½ cup sugar
3 tsp. baking powder
½ tsp. salt
¾ cup milk
¼ cup soft or liquid shortening
1 egg

In mixing bowl combine all ingredients until flour is moistened. Fill greased muffin pans ¾ full. Bake at 400° for 20 minutes. *12 Muffins*

BEST-EVER MUFFINS

1¾ cups unsifted all-purpose flour
2 tablespoons sugar
2½ teaspoons CALUMET® Baking Powder
¾ teaspoon salt
1 egg, well beaten
¾ cup milk
⅓ cup liquid shortening

Mix together flour with sugar, baking powder and salt. Combine egg and milk and add all at once to flour mixture. Add shortening. Then stir *only* until dry ingredients are moistened. (Batter will be lumpy.) Spoon into greased muffin pans, filling each about two-thirds full. Bake at 400°F. for 25 minutes, or until done. *Makes 10 muffins*

COUNTRY-CORN MUFFINS

1 can (8¾ oz.) LIBBY'S Whole Kernel Corn
Milk
1 egg, slightly beaten
4 teaspoons prepared mustard
1 teaspoon instant minced onion
1 package (12 oz.) corn muffin mix

Preheat oven to 400°F. Drain liquid from corn into a measuring cup; add enough milk to liquid to make amount called for on corn muffin mix. Combine with corn, egg, mustard and onion. Add to muffin mix in a medium bowl; stir just until moistened. Spoon batter into greased muffin cups, filling half-full. Bake at 400°F. for 15 to 18 minutes or until tops are golden. Serve warm.

Yields 12 to 14 muffins

Note: To reheat muffins, wrap in foil; place in 350°F. oven for 8 to 10 minutes or until hot.

VARIATIONS:

Stir any of the following into the above recipe before spooning into muffin cups: 2 tablespoons grated Parmesan cheese; 3 tablespoons crisp bacon bits or 1 teaspoon of either chili powder or crumbled rosemary.

241

APPLE BRAN MUFFINS

¾ cup all-purpose flour
⅓ cup granulated sugar
2 teaspoons baking powder
¾ teaspoon ground cinnamon
½ teaspoon baking soda
½ teaspoon salt
1 cup NABISCO® 100% Bran Cereal
½ cup milk
½ cup pared, grated apple
1 egg
3 tablespoons vegetable oil

Preheat oven to 400°F. Combine flour, sugar, baking powder, cinnamon, baking soda and salt; set aside. Stir together NABISCO® 100% Bran Cereal and milk; let stand 5 minutes. Add apple, egg and oil, beating until blended. Add flour mixture, stirring just until combined; do not overmix. Fill greased 2½ × 1¼-inch muffin-pan cups ⅔ full. Bake 18 to 20 minutes or until done.   *Makes 12 muffins*

MOLASSES BRAN MUFFINS

1 egg, beaten
1 cup milk
3 tablespoons vegetable oil
2 tablespoons molasses
1½ cups NABISCO® 100% Bran Cereal
1 cup all-purpose flour
3 teaspoons baking powder
1 teaspoon salt
⅓ cup light brown sugar, firmly packed

Combine first four ingredients. Stir in NABISCO® 100% Bran Cereal; let stand 5 minutes. Combine flour, baking powder and salt; blend in brown sugar. Add bran mixture to dry ingredients, stirring just until combined; do not overmix. Fill greased 2½ × 1¼-inch muffin-pan cups two thirds full. Bake in a preheated hot oven (400°F.) 20 to 25 minutes, or until done.
Makes 12 (about 2½-inch) muffins

BRAN MUFFINS

1¼ cups all-purpose flour
1 tablespoon baking powder
½ teaspoon salt
½ cup sugar
1½ cups KELLOGG'S® ALL-BRAN® Cereal or KELLOGG'S® BRAN BUDS® Cereal
1¼ cups milk
1 egg
⅓ cup shortening or vegetable oil

Stir together flour, baking powder, salt and sugar. Set aside. Measure cereal and milk into large mixing bowl. Stir to combine. Let stand 1 to 2 minutes or until cereal is softened. Add egg and shortening. Beat well. Add flour mixture, stirring only until combined. Portion batter evenly into 12 greased 2½-inch muffin-pan cups. Bake at 400°F. about 25 minutes or until lightly browned.
Yield: 12 muffins

VARIATIONS:

3 cups KELLOGG'S® RAISIN BRAN Cereal or 2½ cups KELLOGG'S® 40% BRAN FLAKES Cereal may be substituted for the ALL-BRAN® Cereal.

® Kellogg Company

QUICK BANANA MUFFINS

1 13¾ or 14 ounce package muffin mix (any flavor)
Egg and milk as specified on package
1 cup diced CHIQUITA® Brand Banana (1½ to 2 bananas)
1½ tablespoons sugar
½ teaspoon cinnamon

Heat oven to 400°. Grease 12 muffin cups or use paper or aluminum cup liners. Use orange, date, apple cinnamon or plain muffin flavor. Follow package directions for mixing. Then with a spoon gently fold in bananas. Fill muffin cups half full. Mix cinnamon and sugar and sprinkle on top of muffin batter in cups. Bake 20 minutes or until golden brown.
Makes 12 medium sized muffins

CHEESE POPOVERS

1½ cups unsifted flour
½ teaspoon dry mustard
1 teaspoon salt
1⅓ cups milk
8 eggs, well beaten
1 package (6 ounces) VALIO Gruyere Cheese, cut into small pieces

Sift together flour, mustard and salt. Add milk and beat with rotary beater until smooth. Add eggs and cheese and beat till well blended. Fill greased popover pans or muffin cups ⅓ to ½ full with batter. Bake at 450°F. for 10 minutes. Reduce heat to 350°F. and bake 20 minutes longer. Popovers will be golden and popped to irregular shapes.
Makes 10 to 12 popovers

OATMEAL MUFFINS

3 cups ELAM'S® Scotch Style Oatmeal
3 tablespoons sugar
3 teaspoons baking powder
¾ teaspoon salt
1½ cups milk
1 egg, beaten
3 tablespoons cooking oil or melted shortening

Combine first 4 ingredients in bowl; mix. Combine milk, egg and oil or melted shortening; beat slightly. Add liquids to dry ingredients; stir just until dry ingredients are moistened. Fill greased muffin cups (2½ × 1¼-inches) about ⅞ full using an equal amount of batter in each cup. Bake in hot oven (425°F.) until done and lightly browned, 20 to 25 minutes.   *Yield: 12 muffins*

WHOLE WHEAT MUFFINS

2 cups ELAM'S® 3 in 1 Mix*
¼ cup honey or sugar
1 cup milk
1 egg
2 tablespoons melted butter

Combine 3 in 1 mix and sugar in bowl; mix well. If honey is used, add it to liquids. Combine milk, egg and melted butter; beat slightly. Add liquids to dry ingredients; stir just until dry ingredients are moistened. Fill greased muffin cups (2½ × 1¼-inches) about ¾ full using an equal amount of batter in each cup. Bake in hot oven (400°F.) until done and lightly browned, about 20 minutes.
Yield: 12 muffins

*To measure, spoon 3 in 1 Mix into measuring cup and level off with knife or spatula; do not pack or shake down.

RALSTON® WHOLE WHEAT MUFFINS

1 cup all-purpose flour*
⅓ cup sugar
½ teaspoon salt
2½ teaspoons baking powder
1 cup Instant RALSTON® OR
¾ cup Regular RALSTON®
1 egg, beaten
¾ cup milk
¼ cup vegetable oil

Preheat oven to 400°. Grease 12 medium-size muffin cups. Stir together flour, sugar, salt, baking powder and RALSTON® Combine egg, milk and oil. Add all at once to dry ingredients. Stir only until moistened. Do not over mix. Fill muffin cups ⅔ full. Bake 20 minutes or until lightly browned. Remove from cups immediately. Serve warm.

Makes 12

*Stir flour; then spoon into measuring cup.

VARIATIONS:

Raisin Muffins: Add ¼ teaspoon cinnamon to dry ingredients and ½ cup raisins to liquid ingredients.
Blueberry Muffins: Gently stir ¾ cup blueberries into batter. Use fresh, frozen (unthawed) or well-drained canned berries.

SOUR CREAM APPLESAUCE BRAN MUFFINS

1¼ cups flour
1 teaspoon baking powder
½ teaspoon soda
½ teaspoon salt
1 teaspoon cinnamon
½ cup sugar
1 cup bran
1 DARIGOLD Egg, beaten
½ cup DARIGOLD Sour Cream
¼ cup DARIGOLD Butter, melted
1 8-oz. can applesauce

Sift dry ingredients except bran, into mixing bowl. Combine bran, beaten egg, DARIGOLD Sour Cream, DARIGOLD Butter and applesauce. Let stand approximately 2 minutes until bran softens. Stir into dry ingredients just until flour is moistened. Spoon into buttered muffin pans, filling ¾ full. Sprinkle with Nut-Crunch Topping* if desired. Bake in 400 degree oven about 25 minutes.

Makes 12 2-in. muffins

*NUT-CRUNCH TOPPING

Mix ⅓ cup brown sugar (packed) ⅓ cup broken nuts and ½ teaspoon cinnamon. Sprinkle on top of muffins before baking.

PEANUT BUTTER AND JELLY MUFFINS

1 (8-ounce) package DROMEDARY Corn Muffin Mix
¼ cup creamy peanut butter
1 egg
½ cup milk
4½ teaspoons jelly or preserves

Grease muffin pan cups or use paper baking cups. Empty corn muffin mix into mixing bowl. Cut peanut butter into mix until coarse and crumbly. Add egg and milk; stir until dry ingredients are just moistened, but batter is still lumpy. Fill muffin cups ⅔ full. Drop ½ teaspoon jelly into center of each cup. Bake in a preheated moderate oven (375°F.) 20 minutes, or until golden brown. Cool slightly on wire rack; serve warm or at room temperature.

Makes 9 (2½-inch) muffins

HONEY PECAN MUFFINS

2 cups sifted E-Z-BAKE Flour
½ cup chopped nuts
¾ cup milk
1 egg, beaten
4 teaspoons baking powder
¾ teaspoon salt
3 tablespoons honey
4 tablespoons margarine, melted

Sift together flour, baking powder, salt; add nuts. Add milk, honey and cooled melted margarine to egg.

Add liquid mixture to dry ingredients, mixing quickly, only enough to dampen flour. Half fill greased muffin tins. If desired, garnish each with a whole nut. Bake in hot oven (400°F.) about 25 minutes.

First prize winner E-Z-BAKE Flour contest

ORANGE STREUSEL MUFFINS

2 cups PILLSBURY'S BEST® All Purpose, Unbleached or Self-Rising Flour*
½ cup chopped pecans
⅓ cup sugar
3 teaspoons baking powder
1 teaspoon salt
½ cup orange juice
½ cup orange marmalade
¼ cup milk
¼ cup oil
1 tablespoon grated orange peel
1 egg, slightly beaten

Topping:
¼ cup sugar
1 tablespoon flour
½ teaspoon cinnamon
¼ teaspoon nutmeg
1 tablespoon margarine or butter, softened

Heat oven to 400°F. Line 12 muffin cups with paper baking cups. Lightly spoon flour into measuring cup; level off. In large bowl, combine 2 cups flour, pecans, ⅓ cup sugar, baking powder and salt. Combine orange juice, marmalade, milk, oil, orange peel and egg; add to flour mixture. Stir just until dry ingredients are moistened. Fill prepared muffin cups ⅔ full. In small bowl, combine all topping ingredients until crumbly; sprinkle evenly over muffins. Bake at 400°F. for 20 to 25 minutes or until golden brown. Serve warm.   *12 muffins*

*If using PILLSBURY'S BEST® Self-Rising Flour, omit baking powder and salt.

High Altitude—Above 3500 Feet: Decrease baking powder to 1½ teaspoons.

NUTRITIONAL INFORMATION PER SERVING			
SERVING SIZE:		PERCENT U.S. RDA	
¹⁄₁₂ OF RECIPE		PER SERVING	
Calories	250	Protein	6
Protein	3 g	Vitamin A	2
Carbohydrate	38 g	Vitamin C	6
Fat	10 g	Thiamine	10
Sodium	280 mg	Riboflavin	6
Potassium	90 mg	Niacin	6
		Calcium	4
		Iron	4

PILLSBURY BAKE-OFF® recipe

CHOCOLATE CHIP PARTY MUFFINS

1½ cups unsifted all-purpose flour
½ cup sugar
2 teaspoons baking powder
½ teaspoon salt
1 egg, slightly beaten
½ cup milk
¼ cup vegetable oil
½ cup HERSHEY'S® Mini Chips
¾ cup crushed pineapple, well-drained
½ cup chopped nuts
¼ cup chopped maraschino cherries, well-drained

Combine flour, sugar, baking powder and salt. Add egg, milk and vegetable oil; stir just until blended. Mix in Mini Chips, crushed pineapple, nuts and cherries. Fill greased or paper-lined muffin cups (2¾-inches in diameter) ⅔ full. Bake at 400° for 25 to 30 minutes.

About 12 muffins

VARIATIONS:

Banana: Substitute ¾ cup mashed ripe bananas (about 1½ medium bananas) for ¾ cup crushed pineapple; bake as above.

Orange: Substitute 2 teaspoons grated orange peel for ¾ cup crushed pineapple. Bake at 400° for 20 to 25 minutes.

Mini-Loaves: Prepare any of the above recipes and pour equal amounts of batter into three well-greased miniature (3¼ × 5¾ × 2¼-inch) loaf pans. Bake at 375° for 30 to 35 minutes.

HUSH PUPPIES

Vegetable oil
1½ cups QUAKER® or AUNT JEMIMA® Enriched Corn Meal
½ cup all-purpose flour
2 teaspoons baking powder
1 teaspoon salt
¾ cup milk
1 egg, beaten
1 small onion, finely chopped

Heat 1-inch deep oil to 375°F. In medium bowl, combine corn meal, flour, baking powder and salt. Add milk, egg and onion; mix well. Drop by rounded teaspoonfuls into hot oil, frying only a few at a time until golden brown. Drain on absorbent paper. *Makes about 2 dozen*

HOMEMADE BISCUIT MIX

8 cups flour
¼ cup baking powder
4 teaspoons salt
1 cup lard for soft wheat flour or 1½ cups lard for hard wheat flour

Sift together flour, baking powder and salt. Cut lard into flour with a fork or pastry blender until the mixture has a fine even crumb. Cover and store in refrigerator until ready to use. This mixture will keep at least a month in refrigerator.

Yield: 10 cups biscuit mix

To make biscuits: Add ½ cup milk to 2 cups Homemade Biscuit Mix. Turn onto a lightly floured surface and knead gently for ½ minute. Pat or roll ½ inch thick and cut with a medium-size cutter, dipped in flour. Bake in a very hot oven (450°F.) 12 to 15 minutes or until brown. *Yield: 10 to 12 biscuits*

Favorite recipe from Pork Industry Group National Live Stock & Meat Board

SEASONED BISCUITS

⅓ cup pre-creamed SWIFT'NING/ JEWEL Shortening
2 cups sifted flour
1 tablespoon baking powder
¾ teaspoon poultry seasoning
½ teaspoon whole celery seeds
½ teaspoon salt
⅔ to ¾ cup milk

Sift together flour, baking powder, poultry seasoning, celery seeds and salt. Cut in shortening until mixture is the consistency of cornmeal. Make well in shortening mixture. Add milk and stir just until moistened. Turn onto lightly floured board. Knead 6 times. Roll or pat to ½ inch thickness. Cut with 2-inch biscuit cutter. Place on cooky sheet. Bake in a 425°F. oven until golden brown, about 12 minutes.

Yield: 12 to 14 two inch biscuits

CHEESE BISCUITS

¼ pound (1 stick) butter or margarine
2 egg yolks, well beaten
5 ounces grated FINLANDIA Swiss Cheese
1½ teaspoons prepared mustard
Dash cayenne pepper
1 cup sifted flour

Cream butter in electric mixer; add egg yolks and mix well. Gradually blend in cheese, mustard and pepper. Beat in flour until thoroughly blended. Mixture will be a stiff dough. Roll dough out on floured board and cut into circles using 2½-inch cutter. Place on ungreased baking sheet. Bake at 350°F. for 20 minutes.

Makes about 1 dozen biscuits

BAKING POWDER BISCUITS

2 cups sifted ELAM'S® Unbleached White Flour with Wheat Germ
3 teaspoons baking powder
¾ teaspoon salt
½ cup soft shortening
¾ cup milk

Combine and sift first 3 ingredients into bowl. Cut in shortening with pastry blender or knives until mixture resembles coarse meal. Add milk; mix lightly and quickly with fork just until dry ingredients are moistened. Turn onto lightly floured board; knead gently 6 to 8 times. Roll dough ½ to ¾-inch thick for fluffy biscuits or ¼-inch thick for crisp crusty biscuits. Cut with floured 2-inch round cutter. Arrange biscuits on ungreased baking sheet. Bake in very hot oven (450°F.) until done and lightly browned, 10 to 15 minutes, depending on thickness.

Yield: About 15 to 20 biscuits, depending on thickness

Whole Wheat Biscuits: Follow above recipe for Baking Powder Biscuits and change as follows. Reduce ELAM'S® Unbleached White Flour with Wheat Germ to 1 cup and stir 1 cup ELAM'S® Stone Ground 100% Whole Wheat Flour into sifted dry ingredients.

MALTEX® BISCUITS

¼ cup MALTEX®
1¾ cups sifted flour
3 teaspoons baking powder
¾ teaspoon salt
6 tablespoons shortening
⅔ cup milk

Combine MALTEX,® flour, baking powder and salt in large bowl. Cut in shortening until mixture resembles coarse meal. Stir in milk to make soft dough. Gather into ball; turn out onto lightly floured board and knead gently a few times. Roll out to about ½-inch thickness. Cut with biscuit cutter and place on ungreased baking sheet. Bake in preheated 450°F. oven 10 to 12 minutes, or until golden brown. Serve hot with butter. *Makes about 10*

SONOMA BUTTER-UPS

1 (8 oz.) package refrigerated biscuits
2 tablespoons melted butter
10 SUNSWEET® Pitted Prunes, cooked
¼ cup chopped walnuts
1 tablespoon sugar
¼ teaspoon cinnamon

Place biscuits in buttered 8-inch layer cake pan. Brush with half the butter. Press a prune in center of each. Sprinkle with walnuts, sugar and cinnamon. Drizzle remaining butter over top. Bake in 425°F. oven 15 to 20 minutes. Serve warm. *Makes 10*

POTATO SPLIT BISCUIT

2 large Irish potatoes
1 tablespoon butter or margarine
1 tablespoon shortening
1 teaspoon salt
2 eggs, well beaten
1 cup milk
½ cake compressed yeast
1 tablespoon sugar
4 cups E-Z-BAKE Flour

Mix one hour before meal time.
Boil and mash the potatoes. Stir in butter, shortening and salt. Cool and add eggs, then add milk in

which the yeast has been dissolved, and sugar. Stir in flour. Cover and set in warm place to rise. Turn out on pastry canvas with enough flour to handle, and roll out. Cut with biscuit cutter. Place biscuits, one on top of another in baking pan; let rise and bake in a hot oven (425°F.) 15 minutes.

Second price winner E-Z-BAKE Flour contest

SWEET POTATO BISCUITS OR BUNS

2 cups flour
6 teaspoons baking powder
2 tablespoons sugar
¾ cup milk
1½ teaspoons salt
3 tablespoons shortening
1½ cups TAYLOR'S Sweet Potatoes, mashed

Mix and sift flour, baking powder, sugar and salt. Cut in shortening with a knife or rub in with the finger tips. Work the Sweet Potatoes into the flour mixture. Add milk and mix to a soft dough. Roll out on a slightly floured board to ½ inch thickness. Cut with a biscuit cutter. Bake in a quick oven, 425°F. 15 to 20 minutes. For Sweet Potato Buns, spread rolled out dough with butter, sprinkle with brown sugar, cut dough in 1½ inch strips and roll up. Place in muffin tins which have a little butter and brown sugar in the bottom. Bake at 350°F. for 30 minutes.

CHEESE CRACKERS

1 cup butter
2 cups cheddar cheese, grated
2 cups CERESOTA or HECKER'S Unbleached Flour, sifted

Topping:
1 egg yolk and 1 tablespoon milk beaten together

Cream the butter and cheese together until light. Blend in the flour. Chill the dough for 1 hour. Roll out on a lightly floured board to about ¼″ thickness. Cut into 2″ squares. Brush egg yolk and milk on top of squares. Place on an ungreased cookie sheet and bake in a preheated 325° oven 15-20 minutes, or until golden brown. *Makes about 3½ dozen*

VITA SNACK CRACKERS
(Low Sodium/Low Calorie)

¾ cup unsifted whole wheat flour
½ cup wheat germ
½ cup old-fashioned oats
½ cup ground PLANTERS® Dry Roasted Unsalted Peanuts
2 tablespoons sugar
⅓ cup FLEISCHMANN'S® Unsalted Margarine, melted
⅓ cup water

Combine whole wheat flour, wheat germ, oats, PLANTERS® Dry Roasted Unsalted Peanuts and sugar. Stir melted FLEISCHMANN'S® Unsalted Margarine and water together. Gradually stir in peanut mixture. Press together into a ball. On a lightly floured board roll out half the dough to an ⅛ inch thickness. Cut into 1¾ inch circles; place on an ungreased baking sheet. Repeat with remaining dough and scraps. Bake at 375°F. for 8 to 10 minutes or until lightly browned. Remove to wire rack to cool.

Makes 4 dozen

Per cracker: 35 calories, 4 mg. sodium

SCOTCH OAT CRACKERS

1 cup ELAM'S® Scotch Style Oatmeal
½ teaspoon salt
¼ teaspoon baking soda
4 to 5 tablespoons cold water
2 tablespoons melted shortening or drippings

Combine first 3 ingredients in bowl; mix. Add 4 tablespoons water and melted shortening or drippings; stir just until dry ingredients are moistened. Add remaining water if needed to make a pliable dough that can be shaped into a ball. Roll dough as thin as possible (about ⅛-inch) on a board sprinkled with ELAM'S® Scotch Style Oatmeal. Cut into 2-inch diamonds or squares using a floured cookie cutter or cut into bars using a sharp knife or pizza wheel. Bake on hot lightly greased griddle (375°F.) until crisp and lightly brown, 4 to 5 minutes, turning once. Cool.

Yield: 2 to 3 dozen crackers depending on size and shape

PEANUT BUTTER WHEAT CRACKER

1 cup unsifted flour
1 cup unsifted whole wheat flour
¼ cup wheat germ
1½ teaspoons caraway seeds
1 teaspoon salt
½ teaspoon baking soda
1 cup SKIPPY® Super Chunk
  Peanut Butter
½ cup (about) water
2 tablespoons cider vinegar
Milk
Coarse salt (optional)

In large bowl mix together flour, whole wheat flour, wheat germ, caraway seeds, salt and baking soda. With pastry blender or two knives, cut in peanut butter until coarse crumbs form. Add water and vinegar; mix until dough holds together (if mixture is too dry additional water may be added 1 tablespoon at a time). Divide dough in half. On lightly floured surface roll half of dough out to ⅛-inch thickness. Cut with 3-inch round cookie cutter. Repeat with scraps and remaining half of dough. Place on ungreased cookie sheet. Brush surface with milk. If desired, sprinkle with coarse salt. Bake in 375°F oven 13 to 15 minutes or until browned and crisp. Remove from pan and cool on wire racks. Store in airtight container.

Makes about 40 crackers

CRISP WHOLE WHEAT CRACKERS

1 cup ELAM'S® Stone Ground 100%
  Whole Wheat Flour
½ teaspoon baking powder
½ teaspoon baking soda
½ teaspoon salt
½ cup cold water
1 tablespoon cooking oil
1 tablespoon melted butter,
  optional
2 teaspoons caraway seeds,
  optional

Combine and mix first 4 ingredients in bowl. Add water and oil; mix well and shape into 2 flat patties of equal size. Cover dough; let stand 10 minutes. Place 1 patty on ungreased baking sheet sprinkled generously with additional ELAM'S® Stone Ground 100% Whole Wheat Flour. Turn patty to coat second side with flour. Roll into 12 by 8-inch rectangle on baking sheet. Cut into 2-inch squares using a floured pizza wheel or sharp knife. If desired, brush lightly with melted butter. Prick each square with tines of fork. If desired, sprinkle with 1 teaspoon caraway seeds. Repeat with second dough patty. Bake in moderate oven (350°F.) until crisp and done, 15 to 20 minutes.   *Yield: 48 crackers*

GLAZED APPLE COFFEE CROWN

4½ to 5 cups PILLSBURY'S BEST®
  All Purpose or Unbleached
  Flour*
⅓ cup sugar
1 teaspoon salt
1 pkg. active dry yeast
1 cup milk
½ cup water
¼ cup margarine or butter
1 egg

Filling:
¾ cup sugar
1 teaspoon cinnamon
¼ cup margarine or butter,
  softened
3-oz. pkg. cream cheese, softened
2 cups (2 medium) peeled, chopped
  apples
⅓ cup firmly packed brown sugar
½ teaspoon cinnamon

Glaze:
1 cup powdered sugar
1 tablespoon milk
1 tablespoon margarine or butter,
  softened
1 teaspoon lemon juice

Grease 12-cup fluted tube pan or 10-inch tube pan.** Lightly spoon flour into measuring cup; level off. In large bowl, combine 2 cups flour, ⅓ cup sugar, salt and yeast. In small saucepan, heat milk, water and ¼ cup margarine until very warm (120° to 130°F.). Add warm liquid and egg to flour mixture. Blend at low speed until moistened; beat 2 minutes at medium speed. By hand, stir in 2 cups flour. On floured surface, knead in ½ to 1 cup flour until smooth and elastic, about 5 to 8 minutes. Place in greased bowl; cover loosely with plastic wrap and cloth towel. Let rise in warm place (80° to 85°F.) until light and doubled in size, about 1 hour.

In small bowl, combine ¾ cup sugar, 1 teaspoon cinnamon, ¼ cup margarine and cream cheese; blend until smooth. In small bowl, combine apples, brown sugar and ½ teaspoon cinnamon. Divide dough in half. On lightly floured surface, roll out half into 18 × 8-inch rectangle. Spread with half of cream cheese mixture to within ½ inch of edges, then spread with half of apples. Starting at longer side, roll up tightly; pinch edges and ends to seal. Repeat with remaining half of dough. Place both rolls in prepared pan. Cover; let rise in warm place until light and doubled in size, about 1 hour.

Heat oven to 350°F. Bake 45 to 55 minutes or until golden brown. Remove from pan immediately. In small bowl, combine all glaze ingredients; drizzle over warm coffee cake.   *16 servings*

  *Self-rising flour not
  recommended.
  **If tube pan has removable tube,
  line pan with foil and grease.
High Altitude—Above 3500 Feet: No change.

NUTRITIONAL INFORMATION PER SERVING
SERVING SIZE: PERCENT U.S. RDA
¹⁄₁₆ OF RECIPE   PER SERVING

Calories	330	Protein	8%
Protein	5 g	Vitamin A	8%
Carbohydrate	54 g	Vitamin C	*
Fat	10 g	Thiamine	15%
Sodium	240 mg	Riboflavin	10%
Potassium	105 mg	Niacin	10%
		Calcium	4%
		Iron	6%

*Contains less than 2% of the U.S. RDA of
  this nutrient.

PILLSBURY BAKE-OFF® recipe

CINNAMON RING

⅓ cup chopped walnuts
½ cup firmly packed brown sugar
1 teaspoon cinnamon
1 can refrigerated biscuits
  (10 biscuit size)
⅓ cup butter or margarine, melted
⅓ cup raisins

Sprinkle chopped walnuts in greased 4½-cup ring mold.* Combine brown sugar and cinnamon. Separate biscuit dough into 10 biscuits. Dip biscuits in butter, then in sugar mixture. Place in mold, overlapping slightly. Tuck raisins in between biscuits. Add any remaining sugar mixture and butter. Bake at 425 degrees for 12 to 15 minutes. Invert pan to remove ring. Serve warm.

Makes 4 to 6 servings

*8 or 9-inch square baking pan
  may be substituted.

*California Raisin Advisory Board's favorite
recipe*

LAND O' LAKES® EASY CARAMEL ORANGE RING

1 Tbsp. LAND O LAKES® Sweet Cream Butter, softened
½ c. orange marmalade
2 Tbsp. chopped nuts
1 c. firmly packed brown sugar
½ tsp. cinnamon
2 (10-oz.) cans refrigerated buttermilk flaky biscuits
½ c. LAND O LAKES® Sweet Cream Butter, melted

Preheat Oven: 350°. Grease 12 c. Bundt® pan with 1 Tbsp. butter. Place teaspoonfuls of orange marmalade in pan; sprinkle with nuts. In small bowl combine brown sugar and cinnamon until blended; set aside. Separate biscuits; dip biscuits in melted butter, then sugar mixture. Stand biscuits on edge in greased pan, spacing evenly. Sprinkle with remaining sugar mixture; drizzle with remaining butter. Bake near center of 350° oven for 30 to 40 min. or until dark golden brown. Cool upright in pan for 5 min. Invert onto serving plate; remove pan. Serve warm or cool.

Yield: 6 to 8 servings (20 biscuits)

TIP: Do *not* use a removable bottom tube pan. A 3-qt. ring mold may be substituted for a 12 c. Bundt® pan.

E-Z-BAKE ICE BOX DOUGH

2 cakes compressed yeast
½ cup lukewarm water
½ cup sugar
2 teaspoons salt
3 tablespoons shortening
1½ cups boiling water
2 eggs
7 cups E-Z-BAKE Flour

Crumble yeast in lukewarm water. Combine sugar, salt, shortening and boiling water. Cook to lukewarm, add yeast and beaten eggs. Stir in E-Z-BAKE Flour until thoroughly mixed. Cover and place in refrigerator. Use at your convenience to make delicious parkerhouse, pocketbook, cloverleaf, pan rolls or breakfast type cakes, such as cinnamon rolls, coffee cake, raisin bread and apple cake. The perfect results and satisfaction will be highly pleasing.

To use the same day, let the dough rise in a warm place until doubled in size (about 2 hours). Knead well and form into rolls or breakfast cake; place in a greased pan and again allow to double in size (about 1 hour). If glazed top is desired, brush with well beaten egg before baking. Bake in moderately hot oven (425°F.) for 15 minutes. Remove and brush top with melted butter.

To use dough at your convenience, take from refrigerator, form into rolls or breakfast cake, place in a greased pan and allow to rise in a warm place for about two hours. Follow baking directions given above. Should dough rise beyond volume of pan while in refrigerator, remove and knead gently for a few seconds.   *4 dozen small rolls*

CREAM FILLED COFFEE CAKE

1 frozen SARA LEE Pecan or Butter Streusel All Butter Coffee Cake
½ cup dairy sour cream or 1 cup shredded Cheddar or Swiss cheese
Water
1 teaspoon lemon juice
1 banana, sliced
1 cup sliced fresh strawberries

Slice frozen Pecan Coffee Cake in half lengthwise to form 2 layers; spread sour cream over bottom layer. Replace cake top. Cut coffee cake into 6 wedges; return to foil pan or place on ovenproof surface. Heat in preheated 350°F. oven 15 minutes. Dip bananas in mixture of water and lemon juice. Arrange bananas and strawberries on top of warm coffee cake.

Makes 6 servings

Microwave instructions: remove coffee cake from foil pan, place on plain side of lid, warm on full power about 1½ minutes. Complete instructions.

VARIATION:

While coffee cake is heating, stir together ¼ cup drained, canned chunk pineapple, ¼ cup sliced fresh strawberries, 1 sliced banana, 1 tablespoon flaked coconut and 1 tablespoon honey. Spoon about 2 tablespoons mixed fruit over each piece of warm coffee cake.

PECAN YOGURT COFFEE CAKE

2 cups flour
1 teaspoon baking powder
1 teaspoon baking soda
¼ teaspoon salt
½ cup butter or margarine
1 cup sugar
3 eggs
1 cup (8 oz.) BREYERS® Plain Yogurt

Sift together flour, baking powder, soda, and salt. Set aside. Cream butter and sugar; add eggs, one at a time, beating well after each. Add flour mixture alternately with yogurt, blending after each addition. Pour batter into greased 9 × 13-inch pan. Sprinkle streusel topping* over batter. Bake at 350°F. 25 to 30 minutes until done.

*STREUSEL TOPPING

Mix together ⅔ cup light brown sugar, 1 tablespoon flour, 1 teaspoon cinnamon, 2 tablespoons melted butter, and ¾ cup chopped pecans.

CHERRY CRUNCH COFFEE CAKE

½ cup brown sugar
2 Tbsp. flour
2 Tbsp. butter
⅓ cup nuts
1½ cups flour
1½ tsp. baking powder
¼ tsp. salt
2 eggs
1 cup granulated sugar
¼ cup melted butter
½ cup milk
1 can LUCKY LEAF® Cherry Pie Filling

Mix first 4 ingredients for topping. Set aside. Sift flour, baking powder and salt. Beat eggs until very light and thick. Gradually add granulated sugar. Beat well after each addition. Stir in melted but not hot butter. Add mixture of flour, baking powder and salt alternately with milk. Beat until smooth. Spread half this batter in greased 9″ square pan. Spoon pie filling over batter. Cover with remaining batter. Sprinkle with topping. Bake at 350° for 45-50 minutes.

STREUSEL COFFEE CAKE

1 can (1 lb. 4 oz.) DOLE®
  Crushed Pineapple in Juice
½ cup packed brown sugar
¼ cup butter, softened
1 egg
1 teaspoon vanilla
1½ cups flour
2½ teaspoons baking powder
½ teaspoon salt
½ teaspoon allspice
1 teaspoon grated orange peel
¼ teaspoon ground nutmeg
Streusel Topping*

Drain pineapple well, pressing out excess juice with back of spoon. Reserve ½ cup juice. Beat sugar and butter until fluffy. Beat in egg, reserved ½ cup juice and vanilla. Combine flour, baking powder, salt, allspice, orange peel and nutmeg. Beat into creamed mixture. Spread batter in a greased 9-inch square baking pan. Top evenly with pineapple. Sprinkle Streusel Topping over pineapple. Bake in 375°F. oven 45 to 50 minutes until cake tests done.
Makes 6 servings

*STREUSEL TOPPING

Combine ½ cup packed brown sugar with 3 tablespoons flour and ¼ teaspoon allspice. Cut in ¼ cup butter. Stir in ½ cup chopped pecans.

BLUEBERRY STREUSEL COFFEE CAKE

Topping:
½ cup (packed) brown sugar
3 tablespoons ELAM'S®
  Unbleached White Flour with
  Wheat Germ
2 teaspoons cinnamon
2 tablespoons butter
¾ cup finely chopped pecans

Batter:
2 cups sifted ELAM'S® Unbleached
  White Flour with Wheat Germ
1 teaspoon baking powder
½ teaspoon baking soda
½ teaspoon salt
½ cup butter
1 cup granulated sugar, turbinado
  or (packed) brown sugar
2 teaspoons grated lemon rind
3 eggs
1 cup (½ pint) dairy sour cream
1 cup fresh or drained canned
  blueberries

Prepare topping. Combine sugar, flour and cinnamon. Cut in butter with pastry blender or knives until mixture resembles fine crumbs. Stir in nuts; reserve.

Prepare batter. Combine first 4 ingredients; sift into bowl and reserve. Cream butter until soft and fluffy. Add sugar and lemon rind; beat well. Add eggs, one at a time; beat well after each addition. Add dry ingredients alternately with sour cream; blend well after each addition. Spread batter evenly over bottom of greased 13 × 9 × 2-inch baking pan. Sprinkle blueberries and ¾ cup of reserved topping over batter. Using a knife, fold berries and topping into batter, marblecake fashion. Sprinkle remaining topping over batter. Bake in moderate oven (350°F.) until done, 30 to 35 minutes. Serve warm or cold.
Yield: One 13 × 9-inch coffee cake

SOUR CREAM COFFEE CAKE

2 cups CERESOTA or HECKER'S
  Unbleached Flour, sifted
1½ teaspoons baking soda
1 teaspoon baking powder
1 teaspoon vanilla
1 cup sour cream
½ cup butter (or margarine)
1 cup sugar
2 eggs

Topping:
½ cup sugar
¼ cup chopped walnuts
1 teaspoon cinnamon
½ cup raisins
1 tablespoon butter, melted

Sift flour, soda and baking powder together. Blend vanilla and sour cream together. Cream butter and sugar; and beat in eggs, one at a time. To this, add the flour alternately with the sour cream, mixing well after each addition.

Combine all topping ingredients and mix well. Pour ½ the batter into a well-greased 9" or 10" tube pan. Sprinkle ½ the topping evenly over the batter. Cover with remaining batter; then remainder of topping. Bake in a preheated 350° oven for about 45 minutes. Cool on rack for 10 minutes before slicing.
Makes one 9" or 10" ring

Gerber®
ANYTIME COFFEE CAKE

½ cup butter or margarine
½ cup sugar
1 egg
¾ cup sour cream
1 teaspoon almond extract
1 cup unsifted flour
½ teaspoon baking powder
½ teaspoon baking soda
½ teaspoon salt
1 jar (7¾ oz.) GERBER® Junior
  Peaches
½ cup sliced almonds

Glaze:
½ cup confectioners sugar
1 tablespoon water
½ teaspoon almond extract

Beat butter or margarine and sugar until fluffy. Add egg and blend well. *Stir* in sour cream and almond extract. Stir together flour, baking powder, baking soda and salt. Gradually add dry ingredients to sour cream mixture. Spread half of batter into greased 8-inch square pan. Spoon peaches over the batter and sprinkle with half of the almonds. Spread remaining batter over the top. Bake in preheated 375°F oven for 30-35 minutes or until a toothpick comes out clean. Cool slightly. Combine glaze ingredients, spread on top of cake and sprinkle with remaining almonds.
Yield: 9-12 servings

HEATH® BRUNCH COFFEE CAKE

½ cup butter
2 cups flour
1 cup brown sugar
½ cup white sugar
1 cup buttermilk
1 teaspoon soda
1 egg
1 teaspoon vanilla
1 bag HEATH® BITS 'O BRICKLE® OR 1 cup finely chopped HEATH® Bars (6 ounces in bar form)
¼ cup chopped pecans

Batter: Blend the flour, butter and sugars. Set aside one-half cup this mixture. To the rest, add the buttermilk, soda, egg and vanilla. Blend well. Stir in one-half of candy bits. Pour into greased and floured 9 x 12 baking pan. **Topping:** Stir together rest of candy bits, pecans and reserved dry mixture. Sprinkle over batter in pan. Bake at 350 for 30 minutes. Freezes well.

Serves 16

Note: Best way to use HEATH® Bars for baking is to freeze the bars first. Unwrap and put in heavy plastic bag. Strike with mallet until broken into small bits. Six ounces candy in bar form equals 1 cup chopped candy.

ORANGE COFFEE CAKE

Batter:
¾ cup sugar
¼ cup soft shortening
¼ cup WHEATENA® , uncooked
1 egg
¼ cup orange juice
¼ cup milk
1¼ cups sifted flour
2 teaspoons baking powder
½ teaspoon salt
2 teaspoons grated orange rind

Topping:
½ cup brown sugar
2 tablespoons flour
2 teaspoons cinnamon
2 tablespoons soft butter
½ cup chopped nuts
2 teaspoons orange rind

Batter: Cream sugar, shortening and WHEATENA® together. Add egg, orange juice and milk; mix until well-blended. Sift together flour, baking powder and salt; stir into creamed mixture. Blend in

orange rind. Spread into lightly greased and floured 9-inch layer cake pan. **Topping:** Mix all Topping Ingredients together; sprinkle over batter. Bake in preheated 375°F. oven 25 to 35 minutes, or until tests done.

Makes one 9-inch cake

HOT CROSS BUNS

1 cup milk
2 tablespoons butter or margarine
1 package active dry yeast
¼ cup warm water (110 to 115 degrees)
4 cups flour
⅓ cup sugar
1 teaspoon salt
1 teaspoon cinnamon
1 cup raisins
½ cup candied fruit
2 eggs, well beaten
1 egg *yolk* diluted with 1 teaspoon water for topping
Lemon Icing*

Scald the milk, stir in the butter and cool to lukewarm. Dissolve yeast in the ¼ cup warm water. Sift flour with the sugar, salt and cinnamon. Combine the flour mixture with raisins and candied fruit; stir in the eggs, cooled milk and yeast; blend well. Turn dough out onto a lightly floured board and knead until smooth and elastic (5 to 8 minutes). Place in a greased bowl, turning to grease top. Cover; let rise in a warm place until doubled in bulk, about 1½ hours.

Stir down dough, pinch off pieces, and form smooth, rounded balls about 1½" in diameter. Place balls of dough on greased baking sheet about 2" apart. Brush each bun lightly with the diluted egg yolk. Snip a ½" deep cross in center of each bun with greased scissors. Let buns rise in a warm place until doubled in bulk, about 30 minutes. Bake at 400 degrees for about 8 to 10 minutes, or until lightly browned. Cool on wire racks about 5 minutes. Then, with a spoon or the tip of a knife, drizzle icing on the cross. *Makes 30*

*LEMON ICING

Combine 1 cup powdered sugar, 2 teaspoons lemon juice, and 1 teaspoon water; beat until smooth.

California Raisin Advisory Board's favorite recipe

PINEAPPLE STICKY BUNS

¾ cup drained crushed pineapple
½ cup butter, softened
½ cup firmly packed brown sugar
1 teaspoon cinnamon
½ cup FISHER® Salted, Roasted Sunflower Nuts
1 can (9½ oz.) refrigerated buttermilk biscuits

Combine pineapple, butter, sugar, cinnamon and nuts. Spoon into 10 greased muffin cups. Place biscuits over mixture. Bake at 350° for 20 minutes. Let cool in pan 5 minutes; invert to remove from pan. Serve warm.

Makes 10

ALL TIME FAVORITE CARAMEL ROLLS OR STICKY BUNS

1 loaf RHODES Frozen White Baking Dough or Sweet Roll Dough, thawed according to package directions
¼ cup firmly packed brown sugar
2 tablespoons butter, melted
2 teaspoons water
2 tablespoons light corn syrup
½ cup chopped or whole pecan halves, if desired
2 tablespoons soft butter
¼ cup brown sugar
1 teaspoon cinnamon

Let dough rise until almost doubled in size. Combine ¼ cup brown sugar, melted butter, water, and corn syrup and spread in a 10 x 8- or 9 x 9-inch pan. Sprinkle nuts over brown sugar mixture. Stretch and roll dough to a 16 x 12-inch (approximate) rectangle. Spread with soft butter, ¼ cup brown sugar and cinnamon. Roll up tightly, jelly roll fashion, starting with long edge. Seal edge by pinching dough together. Cut into 15 or 16 pieces. Place cut rolls on top of brown sugar mixture in pan. Let rise in warm place until doubled in size, about 1 hour. Bake in a 375°F. oven for 25-30 minutes. Cool 1 minute. Loosen edges and turn out onto wire rack lined with waxed paper.

WALNUT HONEY BUNS

5¼ to 6¼ cups unsifted flour
⅓ cup sugar
1 teaspoon salt
½ teaspoon grated lemon peel
2 packages FLEISCHMANN'S®
  Active Dry Yeast
1 cup (2 sticks) softened
  FLEISCHMANN'S® Margarine
1⅓ cups very warm tap water
  (120°F.-130°F.)
2 eggs (at room temperature)
Confectioners' sugar

Prepare Honey Walnut Filling
(below). Set aside until ready to
use. In a large bowl thoroughly mix
1½ cups flour, sugar, salt, lemon
peel and undissolved
FLEISCHMANN'S® Active Dry
Yeast. Add softened
FLEISCHMANN'S® Margarine.

Gradually add very warm tap water
to dry ingredients and beat 2
minutes at medium speed of
electric mixer, scraping bowl
occasionally. Add eggs and ½ cup
flour. Beat at high speed 2
minutes, scraping bowl
occasionally. Stir in enough
additional flour to make a soft
dough. Cover; let dough rest 20
minutes.

Turn dough out onto well-floured
board. Divide into 3 equal pieces.
Roll each piece to an 8-inch
square. Cut each into 8 1-inch
strips. Twist each strip and coil
into a circle, sealing ends
underneath. Place on greased
baking sheets. Make wide
indentations in center of each coil,
pressing to bottom. Spoon
prepared filling into indentations,
using about 1 teaspoon for each
roll. Cover loosely with plastic
wrap. Freeze until firm. Transfer to
plastic bags. Freeze up to 4 weeks.

Remove from freezer; place on
ungreased baking sheets. Cover
loosely with plastic wrap. Let
stand at room temperature until
fully thawed, about 1 hour 45
minutes. Let rise in warm place,
free from draft, until more than
doubled in bulk, about 45 minutes.
Bake at 375°F. 15 to 20 minutes, or
until done. Remove from baking
sheets and cool on wire racks.
Sprinkle with confectioners' sugar.

To bake without freezing: After
shaping, let rise in warm place,
free from draft, until doubled in

bulk (unfrozen dough will rise
faster then frozen dough). Bake
according to above directions.

HONEY WALNUT FILLING

Combine ⅓ cup honey, 1 cup
finely chopped PLANTERS® or
SOUTHERN BELLE English
Walnuts, and ¼ teaspoon salt in
saucepan. Bring to a boil and
simmer over low heat about 3
minutes. Gradually stir in 2 lightly
beaten egg yolks. Cook, stirring,
until slightly thickened. Stir in 1
teaspoon grated lemon peel. Cool.

STICKY PECAN ROLLS

½ cup SUE BEE® Honey
6 tablespoons butter or margarine
¼ teaspoon ground cinnamon
⅓ cup coarsely chopped pecans
1 package (12) brown-and-serve
  dinner rolls

Select a baking pan (8- or 9-inch
cake or pie pan), providing a
"snug" fit for the rolls. Pour honey
into pan. Add 4 tablespoons of the
butter and the cinnamon. Heat in
oven until butter melts. Blend
ingredients. Sprinkle with pecans.
Arrange rolls, tops up, in honey
mixture. Spread roll tops with
reserved butter. Bake at 400°F. for
10-12 minutes, or until rolls are
browned. Cool 5-10 minutes before
inverting pan over serving plate.

Individual Sticky Pecan Rolls may
be baked in muffin pans. Spoon
honey mixture into bottoms of 12
muffin cups. Place a roll in each
cup. Butter tops and bake as
directed above.

RHODES HONEY
YUMMIES

1 loaf RHODES Frozen White or
  Honey Wheat Baking Dough,
  thawed according to package
  directions
½ cup butter or margarine
½ cup sugar
2 tablespoons honey
2 tablespoons cream or milk
½ cup chopped pecans or walnuts
½ cup shredded coconut or
  oatmeal or combination of
  both

Let dough rise until almost
doubled. Cream butter and sugar
together. Blend in honey and milk.
Add nuts and coconut (or oatmeal).
Mixture should be very thick. Roll
or pat out dough to a 15 × 10-inch
rectangle. Spread with one-third of
the filling. Roll up, starting with
the 15-inch side. Seal edges by
pinching dough together. Cut into
12 slices. Place slices, cut side up,
in a greased 9 × 12-inch baking
pan. Let rise until almost doubled.
Heap remaining honey topping in
center of each roll, dividing
equally. Bake in a 350°F. oven for
20 to 25 minutes, or until light,
golden brown. Remove from pan
and cool on wire rack.

PRUNE SWEET ROLLS

1 package (13¾ ounces) hot roll
  mix
⅔ cup warm water
¼ cup granulated sugar
3 tablespoons butter, melted
1 large egg, beaten
1 teaspoon grated orange peel
Prune Filling (recipe follows)

Soften yeast from hot roll mix in
warm water. Let stand 5 minutes.
Add sugar, butter, egg and orange
peel. Gradually blend in flour
mixture from package. Beat well to
make soft dough. Cover and let
rise in warm place until doubled,
about 1 hour. Prepare Prune
Filling. When dough has doubled,
turn out onto floured board and
knead lightly to round up. Roll to a
10 × 20-inch rectangle. Set aside ⅓
cup Prune Filling. Spread
remainder evenly over dough,
leaving a ½-inch margin on all
sides. Roll up as for jelly roll,
starting from long side. Cut into 16
slices; place cut-side down in 2
greased 8-inch, round layer cake
pans. Press slices in even layer so
they barely touch. Let rise until
doubled, about 45 minutes. Bake at
375°F. for 25 minutes. Remove
from oven; spread tops with
reserved filling. Return to oven and
bake 5 minutes.

Makes 16 rolls

PRUNE FILLING

Beat together ¼ cup soft butter,
1½ cups sifted powdered sugar
and ½ teaspoon *each* vanilla and
mace. Stir in 1 cup chopped
cooked SUNSWEET® Prunes.

GLAZED ORANGE ROLLS

4½ to 5½ cups unsifted flour
⅓ cup sugar
1½ teaspoons salt
2 packages FLEISCHMANN'S®
  Active Dry Yeast
¾ cup water
½ cup milk
¼ cup (½ stick)
  FLEISCHMANN'S® Margarine
2 eggs (at room temperature)
¾ cup sugar
1 8-ounce package DROMEDARY
  Pitted Dates
2 tablespoons grated orange peel
Melted FLEISCHMANN'S®
  Margarine
1 cup unsifted confectioners' sugar
2 tablespoons orange juice

In a large bowl thoroughly mix 1½ cups flour, ⅓ cup sugar, salt and undissolved FLEISCHMANN'S® Active Dry Yeast. Combine water, milk and ¼ cup FLEISCHMANN'S® Margarine in a saucepan. Heat over low heat until liquids are very warm (120°F.-130°F.). Margarine does not need to melt. Gradually add to dry ingredients and beat 2 minutes at medium speed of electric mixer, scraping bowl occasionally. Add eggs and ½ cup flour. Beat at high speed 2 minutes, scraping bowl occasionally. Stir in enough additional flour to make a soft dough. Turn out onto lightly floured board; knead until smooth and elastic, about 8 to 10 minutes. Place in greased bowl, turning to grease top. Cover; let rise in warm place, free from draft, until doubled in bulk, about 1 hour. Combine remaining ¾ cup sugar, DROMEDARY Dates and grated orange peel.

Punch dough down, divide in half. Roll each half to an 18 × 9-inch rectangle. Brush each rectangle with melted FLEISCHMANN'S® Margarine. Evenly sprinkle each with ½ date mixture. Roll each rectangle up from long side as for jelly roll. Seal edges firmly. Cut each roll into 1½-inch slices. Place in greased 2½ × 1¼-inch muffin pans. Cover; let rise in warm place, free from draft, until doubled in bulk, about 1 hour. Bake at 375°F. 15 to 20 minutes, or until done. Remove from pans and cool on wire racks. Blend together confectioners' sugar and orange juice. Frost warm rolls with glaze.
Makes 2 dozen

Stuffing

BASIC STUFFING FOR ROAST POULTRY

Sauté ⅓ cup minced onion and ½ cup chopped celery in 4 Tbsp. margarine or butter until golden. Pour sautéed vegetables and ½ cup water or milk over 8 slices of white bread, cubed (plain or toasted) and toss. Add 1½ tsp. BELL'S® Seasoning, ¼ tsp. salt, and a dash of pepper. Toss until mixed.

OLD FASHIONED STUFFING

¾ cup chopped onion
1 cup chopped celery
1 cup butter or margarine
2 cups water
1 package (1 lb.) PEPPERIDGE
  FARM® Herb Seasoned Stuffing

In a large saucepan, sauté the onion and celery in butter until tender but not browned. Stir in water and then stuffing.
Makes enough to fill a 12 to 16 pound turkey

VARIATIONS

Try the following variations with a 1 pound bag of PEPPERIDGE FARM® Herb Seasoned Stuffing, prepared according to package directions.

Parsley: 1 cup chopped parsley, ¾ cup chopped onion and 1 cup chopped celery sautéed in 1 cup butter.

Oriental: ¼ cup chopped onion, ½ cup chopped celery, 1 cup sliced mushrooms and ½ cup sliced water chestnuts sautéed in 1 cup butter.

Nut: 1 cup chopped celery, ½ cup onion and 1 cup nuts sautéed in 1 cup butter. Almonds, Brazil nuts, chestnuts, filberts, pecans or walnuts may be used.

Giblet: Simmer turkey giblets with seasonings 2 to 3 hours. Remove liver after 10 to 20 minutes. Drain, reserving broth; chop coarsely. Sauté ¾ cup chopped onion and 1 cup chopped celery in 1 cup butter. Use reserved broth in place of water in recipe.

OLD-FASHIONED BREAD STUFFING

¾ cup finely chopped onion
¾ cup finely chopped celery
½ stick (¼ cup) butter or
  margarine
¾ teaspoon salt
¼ teaspoon poultry seasoning
¼ teaspoon sage
Pepper
4 cups dry bread cubes
2 tablespoons water

Cook onion and celery in butter until tender. Mix seasonings together and sprinkle over bread cubes. Add onion mixture and water. Combine. Stuff thawed, rinsed turkey and roast immediately.
Yield: 4 cups (enough for 6 pound LI'L BUTTERBALL™ Turkey)

Note: 6 slices white bread = 5 cups soft bread cubes, dried overnight = 4½ cups dry bread cubes.

VARIATIONS:

Oyster Stuffing: Add 1 cup oysters, chopped, uncooked, or heated in butter, to Bread Stuffing.

Corn Bread Stuffing: Replace 4 cups bread cubes in Bread Stuffing with 4 cups crumbled corn bread. Combine as for Bread Stuffing.

Chestnut Stuffing: Add ½ cup chopped, cooked chestnuts.

Giblet Stuffing: Add cooked, cooled, chopped giblets to Bread Stuffing.

NATURALLY EASY DRESSING

1 cup chopped onion
1 cup chopped green pepper
1 cup thin celery slices
⅔ cup butter or margarine
6 cups soft bread cubes
2½ cups QUAKER® 100% Natural Cereal with Raisins & Dates
1 10¾-oz. can condensed chicken broth
4 teaspoons poultry seasoning
Dash of pepper

Heat oven to 350°F. In large skillet, sauté onion, green pepper and celery in butter; combine with remaining ingredients, mixing well. Spoon into 1½-qt. casserole; cover. Bake about 30 minutes. Remove cover; continue baking about 15 minutes. Serve with pork chops, chicken, roast duck, Rock Cornish hen or baked ham.

Makes 6 to 8 servings

QUAKER® COUNTRY CORN BREAD DRESSING

1 cup chopped onion
½ cup butter or margarine
1 pan Corn Bread,** cooled, crumbled
6 cups soft bread cubes
3 cups fresh mushroom slices
2 cups celery slices
2 to 2½ cups chicken broth*
2 eggs, beaten
4 teaspoons poultry seasoning
½ teaspoon salt

Heat oven to 325°F. In small skillet, sauté onion in butter. Combine remaining ingredients; add onion mixture. Toss lightly, mixing well. Place in 3-qt. casserole; cover. Bake about 1 hour. Or, lightly stuff dressing into body cavity and neck region of a 16 to 18-lb. turkey; roast according to standard roasting directions.

Makes about 3 qt. dressing

VARIATION:

Substitute 2 cups coarsely chopped apple and 1 cup raisins for mushrooms.

*Note: When baking dressing in casserole, use 2½ cups broth; when baking dressing in turkey, use 2 cups broth.

**CORN BREAD

1 cup QUAKER® or AUNT JEMIMA® Enriched Corn Meal
1 cup all-purpose flour
1 tablespoon baking powder
½ teaspoon salt
1 cup milk
1 egg
¼ cup vegetable oil

Heat oven to 425°F. Grease 8-inch square baking pan. In medium bowl, combine corn meal, flour, baking powder and salt. Add milk, egg and oil, mixing just until smooth. Pour into prepared pan; bake for 20 to 25 minutes.

Makes 8-inch square corn bread

CORN BREAD STUFFING
(For Chicken, Duck or Pork Chops)

½ cup finely chopped onion
½ cup finely chopped celery
½ cup melted butter or bacon drippings
3 cups coarsely crumbled corn bread*
1 cup small torn soft bread crumbs
¼ teaspoon salt
¼ teaspoon pepper
¼ teaspoon poultry seasoning
⅓ cup hot water

Cook onion and celery in melted butter or bacon drippings until celery is almost tender. Combine with crumbled corn bread, bread crumbs and seasonings; toss lightly to mix. Sprinkle water over mixture; toss lightly. For a dry crumbly stuffing decrease water to ¼ cup, for a more moist stuffing increase water to ½ cup. Use as a stuffing for chicken, duck or pork chops.

Yield: About 4 cups stuffing

*Prepare recipe for Old Fashioned Corn Bread in Bread chapter or use the corn bread recipe on ELAM'S® Stone Ground 100% Whole Yellow Corn Meal package.

BACON SEASONED STUFFING

6 slices SWIFT PREMIUM® Bacon
¾ cup finely chopped onion
½ to ¾ cup chopped green pepper
½ teaspoon thyme
¼ teaspoon salt
Pepper
4 cups dry bread cubes
2 tablespoons water

Panfry bacon in medium-size skillet over low heat until crisp. Drain on paper towel. Crumble. Cook onion and green pepper in bacon drippings until tender. Combine seasonings and sprinkle over bread cubes. Add onion mixture, bacon and water. Toss to combine. Stuff thawed, rinsed turkey and roast immediately.

Yield: 4 cups (enough for 6 pound LI'L BUTTERBALL™ Turkey)

BACON STUFFIN' BALLS

1 cup chopped celery
2 tablespoons margarine
¼ cup McCORMICK/SCHILLING Instant Chopped Onion
½ cup McCORMICK/SCHILLING Imitation Bacon Bits or Chips
2 eggs, beaten
1 10¾-ounce can chicken broth
1 tablespoon McCORMICK/SCHILLING Parsley Flakes
1 teaspoon McCORMICK/SCHILLING Poultry Seasoning
½ teaspoon McCORMICK/SCHILLING SEASON-ALL® Seasoned Salt
¼ teaspoon McCORMICK/SCHILLING Black Pepper
8 cups dry bread cubes

Sauté celery in margarine until soft. Combine with all other ingredients except bread cubes. Gently mix in bread cubes. Portion stuffing into 12 buttered muffin cups. Bake in 325°F. oven 25-30 minutes. Remove from muffin cups; serve hot.

CHILI STUFFING

1 can (15-oz.) NALLEY®'S Big Chunk Chili
4 cups croutons
¾ cup chopped celery
¼ cup chopped onion

Combine all ingredients and mix well. (A good rule for poultry is 1 cup stuffing per pound.) Leftover Chili Stuffing can be baked in a greased casserole.

Makes about 6 cups stuffing

252

CHESTNUT STUFFING FOR FOWL

½ cup butter or margarine
½ cup chopped onion
½ teaspoon sage
½ teaspoon thyme
¾ teaspoon salt
¼ cup chopped parsley
1 cup chopped celery and leaves
1 quart soft, stale bread cubes
1 (1 pound) can RAFFETTO Prepared Chestnuts

Melt butter or margarine in a skillet. Add onion, sage, thyme, salt, parsley and celery. Cook over low heat for a few minutes, just until onion is limp but not browned. Stir in bread cubes. Drain chestnuts and crumble. Add to mixture and toss lightly.

Makes about 5 cups stuffing

PEACH STUFFING FOR CHICKEN

RAFFETTO Brandied Peaches
½ (7 or 8 ounce) package prepared herb stuffing mix

Cut enough peaches to make up 1 cup of pieces. This will take 3 to 4 peaches, depending on size. Toss lightly with stuffing mix. Add 2 tablespoons of the liquid from the brandied peaches. Use mixture to stuff a chicken for roasting. Put any extra stuffing in a piece of foil and bake in pan with chicken. Baste chicken with liquid from brandied peaches during last 15 to 20 minutes of cooking time for a crisp, brown skin. Serve chicken and stuffing with additional chilled brandied peaches.

MUSHROOM & SAUSAGE STUFFING

4 qts. toasted bread crumbs
1 lb. BOB EVANS FARMS® Roll Sausage
½ lb. mushrooms, chopped
½ tsp. salt
½ tsp. sage
¼ c. minced onion
¼ c. minced celery

Cook sausage until brown and crisp, after breaking into pieces. Sauté mushrooms in the drippings. Toss sausage, mushrooms, bread and seasonings together, using part of the sausage drippings, and moisten further with stock if desired.

Stuffing for 12 to 16-lb. turkey

WHEAT CRISP DRESSING FOR BROILERS

1 (7¾ ounce) box SUNSHINE® Wheat Wafers (about 2½ cups) coarsely crushed
½ cup chopped onion
¼ cup butter or margarine
2 (2½ pound) broilers
½ cup water
½ teaspoon salt
⅛ teaspoon pepper
⅓ cup canned applesauce
½ teaspoon nutmeg
¼ teaspoon cinnamon

First, crush Wheat Wafers coarsely between the palms of the hands. Sauté onion in butter or margarine until tender but still crisp (about 2 to 3 minutes). Add onion, together with salt, pepper, applesauce, nutmeg, and cinnamon, to cracker crumbs in bowl. Toss to blend well. Place 2 broiler halves in a shallow roasting pan. Top each half broiler with half of the dressing. Top each mound of dressing with another half broiler. Skewer each set of 2 half broilers together and pour ½ cup water around them in pan. Bake at 325°F. (moderate) for 1 hour or until broilers are tender and lightly browned.

Yield: 4 portions

CRANBERRY-ORANGE-WALNUT STUFFING

¼ cup finely chopped onion
¼ cup finely chopped celery
½ stick (¼ cup) butter or margarine
½ cup cut-up orange sections
½ cup chopped raw cranberries
½ cup chopped walnuts
2 tablespoons sugar
½ teaspoon poultry seasoning
¼ teaspoon salt
4 cups dry bread cubes
1 egg, beaten
2 tablespoons water

Sauté onion and celery in butter until tender. Add orange, cranberries and walnuts. Combine sugar and seasonings and sprinkle over bread cubes. Add cranberry mixture, egg and water. Toss mixture lightly with forks until bread cubes are well moistened. Stuff thawed, rinsed turkey and roast immediately.

Yield: 4½ cups (enough for a 6 to 7 pound LI'L BUTTERBALL™ Turkey)

THANKSGIVING DATE STUFFING

Giblets, boiled and chopped
2 cups giblet broth (use broth from giblets and add water to make two cups)
8 cups toasted bread cubes (approx. 2 slices per cup)
½ cup celery
1 cup chopped pitted SUN WORLD® Dates
1 medium sized apple
1½ Tbsp. sage
2 Tbsp. lemon juice
Salt and pepper to taste

Boil giblets until tender. Drain, saving 2 cups of liquid. While giblets are cooking, toast and cube bread slices. Chop celery, dates and apple. Chop giblets when cooked and cool. Mix all ingredients together, tossing lightly.

Stuffing for 10-15 lb. turkey

POTATO CHIP STUFFING

½ lb. of butter or ½ lb. bacon cut in small pieces
2 cups of onion cut fine
2 cups of celery cut in thin slices crosswise
1 medium size can of mushrooms—optional (stems and pieces or whole)
1 lb. of sliced white bread
1 cup crushed JAYS Potato Chips
2 eggs
About ½ cup parsley chopped medium fine
¼ tsp. of black or white pepper
Salt to taste
About 1 Tbsp. of sage or poultry seasoning

Toast bread in oven at about 400°F., until golden brown and dry, about 20 mins. Turn several times while toasting. Cover this bread with cold water until it swells (about three slices at a time); press the bread until it is of a consistency that can be made fluffy. Sauté the onions, celery, and mushrooms in the butter or bacon and drippings until tender. Pour this mixture over the soaked bread. Add crushed potato chips and season with pepper, sage, salt and parsley. Lastly, add the eggs and mix lightly with two forks. If mixture appears dry, more melted butter may be poured over it. Taste and season further, if necessary.

Enough for a 15 to 18 lb. turkey

Cakes and Frostings

CHOCOLATE SOUR CREAM CAKE

3 squares unsweetened chocolate, melted
¼ cup butter or margarine
1 can (8 oz.) PET® Imitation Sour Cream
3 eggs
2 cups sugar
2 cups all purpose flour
1 teaspoon salt
1 teaspoon baking soda
1 teaspoon baking powder
½ cup water
2 teaspoons vanilla

Combine melted chocolate, butter, and imitation sour cream. Beat in eggs, one at a time. Gradually add sugar. Stir together flour, salt, baking soda, and baking powder. Mix half of flour mixture into chocolate mixture. Stir in water and vanilla. Add remaining flour mixture. Mix well. Pour into two 9-inch greased round layer cake pans. Bake in 350°F. oven for 30 minutes or until center tests done. Cool 10 minutes then turn out onto cooling racks. Cool thoroughly before frosting. Frost with Chocolate Sour Cream Frosting.*
Makes one 2-layer cake

*CHOCOLATE SOUR CREAM FROSTING

3 squares unsweetened chocolate, melted
2 tablespoons butter
1 can (8 oz.) PET® Imitation Sour Cream
4 cups powdered sugar
2 teaspoons vanilla

Combine melted chocolate, butter, and imitation sour cream. Gradually beat in powdered sugar. Add vanilla. Spread on cake. If frosting is too soft, chill slightly before spreading.

DEVILS FOOD CAKE

2 cups sugar
1¾ cups unsifted all-purpose flour
¾ cup HERSHEY'S® Cocoa
1½ teaspoons baking soda
¾ teaspoon salt
1⅔ cups milk
½ cup shortening
3 eggs
1 teaspoon vanilla
Mocha Cream Frosting (recipe below)

Grease and dust with flour two 9-inch layer pans or one 13 x 9 x 2-inch pan. Combine dry ingredients in large mixer bowl. Add milk, shortening, eggs and vanilla. Blend ingredients on low speed 30 seconds; beat on medium speed 3 minutes. Pour into pans. Bake at 350°F. for 30 to 35 minutes for layers; 35 to 40 minutes for large cake or until cake tester inserted in center comes out clean. Cool 10 minutes; remove from pans and cool completely. Frost with Mocha Cream Frosting.

MOCHA CREAM FROSTING

2⅔ cups confectioners' sugar
¼ cup HERSHEY'S® Cocoa
6 tablespoons butter or shortening
2 tablespoons strong coffee
2 to 3 tablespoons milk
1 teaspoon vanilla

Combine confectioners' sugar and cocoa. Cream butter with ½ cup cocoa mixture in small bowl. Add remaining cocoa mixture alternately with strong coffee and milk, beating to spreading consistency. Blend in vanilla.
About 2 cups frosting

BLACK FOREST CAKE

2 15- or 16-ounce cans pitted tart cherries, drained and each cut in half
½ cup kirsch (cherry-flavor brandy)
1 package chocolate-cake mix for 2-layer cake
3 squares semisweet chocolate
2 cups heavy or whipping cream
½ cup confectioners' sugar
14 maraschino cherries, well drained

EARLY IN DAY:
In medium bowl combine tart cherries and ⅓ cup kirsch; set aside, stirring occasionally.

Preheat oven to 350°F. Prepare cake mix as label directs but pour batter into three 9-inch round cake pans. Stagger pans on two oven racks so no pan is directly above another. Bake 20 minutes or until toothpick inserted in center comes out clean. Cool on racks 10 minutes; remove from pans; cool.

Meanwhile, with vegetable peeler, shave few curls from chocolate for garnish; grate remaining chocolate. With fork, prick top of each cake layer. Drain cherries well and slowly spoon the drained liquid from cherries over cake layers. In small bowl with mixer at medium speed, beat cream, sugar and remaining kirsch until stiff.

Place one cake layer on cake platter; spread with one-fourth whipped cream and top with half of cherries; repeat. Top with third layer. Frost side of cake with half of remaining whipped cream. With hand, gently press grated chocolate into cream. Garnish top of cake with dollops of remaining cream; top each dollop with a maraschino cherry. Pile chocolate curls on center of cake. Keep refrigerated. *Makes 14 servings*

Favorite Recipe from National Red Cherry Institute

CHOCOLATE CAKE ROLL WITH ALMOND-PLUM FILLING

4 eggs, separated, at room
   temperature
¾ cup granulated sugar
1 teaspoon vanilla extract
¾ cup sifted cake flour
3 tablespoons unsweetened cocoa
1 tablespoon instant coffee powder
¾ teaspoon baking powder
¼ teaspoon salt
Sifted powdered sugar
Almond-Plum Filling
   (recipe follows)
½ cup BLUE DIAMOND® Sliced
   Natural Almonds, toasted
¼ cup plum jam

Grease 15 × 10 × 1-inch jelly roll pan; line with waxed paper; lightly grease waxed paper. In small bowl beat egg yolks with electric mixer until thick and lemon-colored, 3 to 5 minutes; gradually add ½ cup of the sugar, beating until pale yellow. Blend in vanilla; set aside. In large bowl, beat egg whites to soft peaks; gradually add remaining ¼ cup sugar, beating to stiff peaks. Fold yolk mixture into whites. Sift together flour, cocoa, coffee powder, baking powder and salt; fold into egg mixture. Spread in prepared jelly roll pan.

Bake in a 375 degree F. oven for 12 to 15 minutes or just until surface springs back when gently pressed with fingertip. Immediately turn out onto towel generously dusted with powdered sugar; peel away waxed paper. Roll up starting with narrow end; cool. Unroll; spread with Almond-Plum Filling; sprinkle with almonds and reroll. In small saucepan, melt ¼ cup plum jam. Brush on cake roll. Garnish with additional almonds if desired.
Makes 10 servings

ALMOND-PLUM FILLING

Thoroughly blend 1 to 1⅓ cups almond paste* and ¾ cup plum jam.

*HOME-MADE ALMOND PASTE

1½ cups BLUE DIAMOND®
   Blanched Whole Almonds
1½ cups sifted powdered sugar
1 egg white
1 teaspoon almond extract
¼ teaspoon salt

Grind almonds, a portion at a time, in electric blender or food chopper using fine blade. Combine with remaining ingredients and work to a stiff paste. Store in airtight container or disposable plastic bag.
This makes 13 ounces (1⅓ cups) almond paste

FUDGE RIBBON CAKE

RIBBON LAYER:
1 8-oz. pkg. cream cheese,
   softened
¼ cup sugar
2 measuring tablespoons butter
1 measuring tablespoon cornstarch
1 egg
2 measuring tablespoons milk
½ measuring teaspoon vanilla
   extract

CAKE:
2 cups *unsifted* flour
1 measuring teaspoon baking
   powder
½ measuring teaspoon baking
   soda
½ cup butter, softened
2 cups sugar
1 measuring teaspoon vanilla
   extract
2 eggs
1⅓ cups milk
4 envelopes (4-ozs.) NESTLÉ
   CHOCO-BAKE

CHOCOLATE FROSTING:
¼ cup milk
¼ cup butter
2 envelopes (2-ozs.) NESTLÉ
   CHOCO-BAKE
1 measuring teaspoon vanilla
   extract
2½ cups sifted confectioners'
   sugar

RIBBON LAYER: Preheat oven to 350°F. In small bowl, combine cream cheese, sugar, butter and cornstarch; beat until creamy. Add egg, milk and vanilla extract; beat until well blended and smooth; set aside.

CAKE: In small bowl, combine flour, baking powder and baking soda; set aside. In large bowl, combine butter, sugar and vanilla extract; mix well. Beat in eggs. Alternately add flour mixture with

milk; blend in NESTLÉ CHOCO-BAKE; mix well. Pour half of batter into a greased and floured 13″ × 9″ × 2″ baking pan. Spoon Ribbon Layer mixture over batter; spread to cover. Top with remaining batter. Bake at 350°F. 50-60 minutes. Cool cake in pan. Frost with Chocolate Frosting.

CHOCOLATE FROSTING: In large saucepan, combine milk and butter; bring to a boil; remove from heat. Blend in NESTLÉ CHOCO-BAKE and vanilla extract. Stir in confectioners' sugar; blend until smooth. Thin with a few drops milk, if necessary.
Makes one frosted 13″ × 9″ × 2″ cake

CHOCOLATE CHERRY SURPRISE
(Microwave Recipe)
CHOCOLATE CAKE

1 pkg. (18.5 oz.) double layer
   chocolate cake mix (pudding
   type)
¼ cup oil
¾ cup water
3 eggs
1 tsp. almond extract
1 cup THANK YOU® Brand Cherry
   Pie Filling
Creamy Cherry Frosting (recipe
   follows)

Lightly oil or spray fluted tube pan; sprinkle sides of pan with granulated sugar; shake out excess. Mix together all ingredients; beat according to package directions. Pour batter into pan. Microwave 10 min./50% power, rotating once. Increase power level to HIGH and continue cooking 6-8 minutes more, rotating one more time. Let stand in pan 5 minutes to finish cooking. Turn out of pan. Cool. Frost.

CREAMY CHERRY FROSTING

1 9 oz. carton frozen whipped
   topping, thawed
2 Tbsp. Kirsch or maraschino
   cherry juice
½ tsp. unflavored gelatine
Sliced almonds

Sprinkle gelatine into Kirsch or juice to soften. Heat in microwave 10-15 seconds. Cool a minute or two, then whip mixture into topping with wire whip. Frost cake, garnishing with sliced almonds. Refrigerate.

CHOCOLATE MAYONNAISE CAKE

1 package (18½ oz) devil's food cake mix
3 eggs
1 cup water
½ cup HELLMANN'S® or BEST FOODS® Real Mayonnaise

Grease and flour 2 (9-inch) round cake pans. In large bowl with mixer at low speed beat together cake mix, eggs, water and real mayonnaise until blended. With mixer at medium speed beat 2 minutes. Pour into prepared pans. Bake in 350°F oven 30 to 35 minutes or until cake tester inserted in center comes out clean. Cool in pans 10 minutes. Remove from pans and cool on wire racks. Frost as desired.

Makes 12 to 16 servings

To Make With Chocolate Cake Mix With Pudding In Mix: Follow recipe for Chocolate Mayonnaise Cake increasing real mayonnaise to 1 cup.

To Bake In Other Pans: In 13 × 9 × 2-inch baking pan, bake 35 to 40 minutes. Cool in pan on wire rack. In 12-cup fluted tube pan, bake 40 to 45 minutes. Cool in pan 20 minutes; remove from pan and cool on wire rack.

CHOCOLATE TOFFEE CAKE

½ cup shortening
1 cup firmly-packed COLONIAL® Dark Brown Sugar
2 eggs
1 teaspoon vanilla extract
2 cups unsifted flour
¼ cup cocoa
2 teaspoons instant coffee
1 teaspoon baking soda
1 cup buttermilk
3 (1⅛-ounce) or 5 (¾-ounce) bars chocolate-covered toffee candy, crushed*
Mocha Topping (recipe follows)

Preheat oven to 350° (325° for glass dish). In large mixer bowl, cream together shortening and sugar; blend in eggs and vanilla. Combine flour, cocoa, coffee and baking soda. Add alternately with buttermilk to sugar mixture, beating well after each addition. Pour into lightly greased and floured 13 × 9-inch baking pan.

Sprinkle with about ½ of the candy (reserve remaining candy for topping). Bake 25 to 30 minutes or until cake springs back when lightly touched. Cool. Spread with Mocha Topping; sprinkle with remaining candy. Cover and refrigerate until serving time.

Makes one 13 × 9-inch cake

*TIP: To crush candy, chill bars. Place in small plastic bag; pound until pieces are of desired size.

MOCHA TOPPING

1½ cups whipping cream
¼ teaspoon instant coffee
3 tablespoons COLONIAL® Dark Brown Sugar
1 teaspoon vanilla extract

In medium mixer bowl, beat cream with coffee until slightly thickened. Add sugar and vanilla; continue beating until stiff.   *Makes 3 cups*

TOLL HOUSE® DELUXE CAKE

Cake:
3 cups *unsifted* flour
1 measuring tablespoon baking powder
1 measuring teaspoon salt
1 cup butter, softened
2 cups firmly packed brown sugar
1 measuring tablespoon vanilla extract
4 eggs
1 cup milk
1 12-oz. pkg. (2 cups) NESTLÉ Semi-Sweet Real Chocolate Morsels, divided

Chocolate Glaze:
½ cup (3-oz.) NESTLÉ Semi-Sweet Real Chocolate Morsels, reserved from 12-oz. pkg.
¼ cup boiling water
1 cup sifted confectioners' sugar

Cake: Preheat oven to 350°F. In small bowl, combine flour, baking powder and salt; set aside. In large bowl, combine butter, brown sugar and vanilla extract; beat until creamy. Add eggs, one at a time, beating well after each addition. Alternately blend in flour mixture

with milk. Stir in 1½ cups NESTLÉ Semi-Sweet Real Chocolate Morsels. Spoon batter evenly into well-greased and floured 10" Bundt® pan or tube pan. Bake at 350°F. 60 minutes. Cool 15 minutes. Remove from pan. Cool completely. Pour Chocolate Glaze over top. Let glaze set at room temperature 15 minutes before serving.

Chocolate Glaze: In blender container, combine remaining ½ cup NESTLÉ Semi-Sweet Real Chocolate Morsels and boiling water; process at high speed until smooth. Gradually blend in confectioners' sugar; process until smooth. Refrigerate 20 minutes or until desired consistency.

Makes one 10" Bundt® cake and ¾ cup glaze

CHOCOLATE FUDGE CAKE

1¾ cups sifted E-Z-BAKE Flour
3 teaspoons baking powder
½ teaspoon soda
¼ teaspoon salt
½ cup butter
1 cup sugar
2 eggs, separated
3 squares chocolate, melted
1¼ cups milk
1 teaspoon vanilla

Resift flour with baking powder, soda and salt three times. Cream together butter and sugar until light and fluffy. Add egg yolks and chocolate, then flour and milk alternately; beat after each addition. Add vanilla. Fold in egg whites. Bake in two greased layer pans in moderate oven (350°F.) 30 minutes. Put layers together with a favorite frosting.

IMPORTANT: This recipe gives instructions for *hand mixing only.* To make cakes with an *electric mixer,* follow these directions:

Measure shortening into bowl. Add flour, resifted with sugar, salt, leavening and three-fourths of the milk. Add chocolate at this point. Beat 2 minutes at low to medium speed, frequently scraping down sides of bowl and beater. Add unbeaten eggs, remaining milk and flavoring, and beat another 2 minutes. For best results, have all ingredients at room temperature.

First prize winner E-Z-BAKE Flour contest

SWISS CHOCOLATE SQUARES

1 cup water
½ cup PARKAY Margarine
1½ 1-oz. squares unsweetened chocolate
2 cups flour
2 cups sugar
2 eggs
½ cup dairy sour cream
1 teaspoon baking soda
½ teaspoon salt

Frosting:
½ cup PARKAY Margarine
6 tablespoons milk
1½ 1-oz. squares unsweetened chocolate
4½ cups sifted confectioners' sugar
1 teaspoon vanilla
½ cup chopped nuts

Combine water, margarine and chocolate in saucepan; bring to boil. Remove from heat. Stir in combined flour and sugar. Add eggs, sour cream, baking soda and salt; mix well. Pour into greased and floured 15½ × 10½-inch jelly roll pan. Bake at 375°, 20 to 25 minutes.

Combine margarine, milk and chocolate in saucepan; bring to boil. Remove from heat. Add sugar; beat until smooth. Stir in vanilla. Frost cake while warm; sprinkle with nuts. Cool; cut into squares.

UPSIDE DOWN GERMAN CHOCOLATE CAKE

Frosting:
1¼ cups water
¼ cup margarine or butter
1 cup firmly packed brown sugar
1 cup coconut
2 cups miniature marshmallows
1 cup chopped nuts

Cake:
4-oz. bar German sweet chocolate
½ cup water
2½ cups PILLSBURY'S BEST® All Purpose, Unbleached or Self-Rising Flour*
1½ cups sugar
1 teaspoon soda
½ teaspoon salt
1 cup dairy sour cream
½ cup margarine or butter, softened
1 teaspoon vanilla
3 eggs

Heat oven to 350°F. In small saucepan, heat 1¼ cups water and ¼ cup margarine until margarine melts. Pour into ungreased 13 × 9-inch pan. Stir in brown sugar and coconut; sprinkle marshmallows and nuts over top.

In saucepan over low heat, melt chocolate with ½ cup water. Lightly spoon flour into measuring cup; level off. In large bowl, combine chocolate mixture with remaining cake ingredients. Beat 3 minutes at medium speed. Carefully spoon batter over coconut-marshmallow mixture. (Place pan on foil or cookie sheet during baking to guard against spillage.) Bake at 350°F. for 40 to 50 minutes or until toothpick inserted in center comes out clean. Serve inverted onto serving plates. Refrigerate leftovers. *12 servings*

*If using PILLSBURY'S BEST® Self-Rising Flour, omit baking powder and salt.

High Altitude—Above 3500 Feet: Bake at 375°F. for 40 to 50 minutes.

NUTRITIONAL INFORMATION PER SERVING
SERVING SIZE:
¹⁄₁₂ OF RECIPE		PERCENT U.S. RDA PER SERVING	
Calories	580	Protein	10
Protein	7 g	Vitamin A	10
Carbohydrate	77 g	Vitamin C	*
Fat	27 g	Thiamine	15
Sodium	350 mg	Riboflavin	10
Potassium	220 mg	Niacin	8
		Calcium	4
		Iron	15

*Contains less than 2% of the U.S. RDA of this nutrient.

PILLSBURY BAKE-OFF® recipe

CHOCOLATE VANILLA SWIRL CAKE

1 12-oz. pkg. (2 cups) NESTLÉ Semi-Sweet Real Chocolate Morsels
2½ cups *unsifted* flour
2 measuring teaspoons baking powder
½ measuring teaspoon salt
1 cup butter, softened
1½ cups sugar
4 eggs
1 measuring tablespoon vanilla extract
1 cup milk
1 cup chopped pecans
Confectioners' sugar

Preheat oven to 375°F. Melt over hot (not boiling) water, NESTLÉ Semi-Sweet Real Chocolate Morsels; remove from heat and cool. In small bowl, combine flour, baking powder and salt; set aside. In large bowl, combine butter and sugar; beat until creamy. Add eggs, one at a time, beating well after each addition; beat in vanilla extract. Gradually blend in flour mixture alternately with milk. Divide in half. Stir melted chocolate into half the batter and chopped pecans into other half. Alternately layer batter into greased 10" Bundt® or tube pan. Bake at 375°F. 60-70 minutes. Cool 10 minutes and remove from pan. Dust top with confectioners' sugar, if desired.
Makes one 10" tube cake

MILKY WAY® CAKE

2 tablespoons vegetable shortening
¾ cup finely chopped nuts
12 snack size MILKY WAY® Bars
1 cup buttermilk, plain yogurt, or sour cream
1 cup butter or margarine
1½ cups sugar
½ teaspoon vanilla
4 eggs
2½ cups flour
1 teaspoon salt
¾ teaspoon soda

Generously grease 12-cup BUNDT® pan or 10-inch tube pan with shortening; coat pan with nuts. In heavy saucepan over low heat, melt MILKY WAY® Bars with ¼ cup buttermilk, stirring frequently until smooth. Beat together butter and sugar until light and fluffy; blend in vanilla. Add eggs, one at a time, mixing well after each addition. Add combined flour, salt and soda alternately with remaining ¾ cup buttermilk, mixing just until dry ingredients are moistened. Blend in MILKY WAY® Bar mixture; spoon into prepared pan. Bake at 350°F. for 55 to 60 minutes or until wooden pick inserted in center comes out clean. Cool 10 minutes; invert onto wire rack. Cool completely.
Makes one 12-cup BUNDT® or 10-inch tube pan cake

VARIATION:

Omit nuts; lightly flour greased pan.

BRAZILIAN CHOCOLATE CAKE

1¼ c. hot coffee
1 c. 3-MINUTE BRAND® Oats
½ c. butter
1½ c. sugar
1 tsp. vanilla
2 eggs
3 oz. unsweetened chocolate, melted
1½ c. sifted flour
1 tsp. soda
½ tsp. salt
1 c. (6 oz.) semi-sweet chocolate chips

Icing:
¼ c. butter
2 c. powdered sugar
1 tsp. vanilla
Light cream

Pour hot coffee over the oats. Set aside for 20 minutes. Cream the butter and sugar until light and fluffy. Blend in vanilla, eggs, chocolate and soaked oats. Mix well. Sift together flour, soda and salt. Fold into above mixture. Stir in the chocolate chips. Pour the batter into a greased and floured Bundt® pan. Bake at 350°F. for 50 to 55 minutes or until an inserted toothpick comes out clean. Cool in the pan for 10 minutes. Loosen edges and turn cake out on a rack to finish cooling.

For icing, cream butter. Add powdered sugar and vanilla and beat well. Stir in enough cream to make icing of spreading consistency. Spread on cooled cake.

GERMAN SWEET CHOCOLATE CAKE

1 package (4 oz.) BAKER'S® GERMAN'S® Sweet Chocolate
⅓ cup boiling water
2 cups sifted SWANS DOWN® Cake Flour
¾ teaspoon baking soda
¼ teaspoon salt
¾ cup butter or margarine
1⅓ cups sugar
3 egg yolks
¾ teaspoon vanilla
¾ cup buttermilk
3 egg whites, stiffly beaten
Coconut-Pecan Filling and Frosting (recipe follows)

Melt chocolate in boiling water. Cool. Sift flour with soda and salt. Cream butter. Gradually beat in sugar and continue beating until light and fluffy. Add egg yolks, one at a time, beating after each. Blend in vanilla and chocolate; mix until blended. Add flour mixture alternately with buttermilk, beating after each addition until smooth. Fold in egg whites.

Pour into two 9-inch layer pans which have been lined on bottoms with paper. Bake at 350° for about 30 minutes, or until cake springs back when lightly pressed in center. Cool in pans 15 minutes. Then remove from pans and finish cooling on racks. Spread Coconut-Pecan Filling and Frosting between layers and over top of cake.

COCONUT-PECAN FILLING AND FROSTING

Combine 1 can (5.33 oz.) evaporated milk, ⅔ cup sugar, 2 egg yolks, slightly beaten, ⅓ cup butter or margarine and ¾ teaspoon vanilla in saucepan. Cook and stir over medium heat until mixture thickens, about 10 minutes. Remove from heat; add 1 cup BAKER'S® ANGEL FLAKE® Coconut and ⅔ cup chopped pecans. Beat until cool and of spreading consistency.

Makes about 2 cups

HERSHEY® BAR SWIRL CAKE

1 cup butter or margarine
2 cups sugar
1 teaspoon vanilla
5 eggs
2½ cups unsifted all-purpose flour
¾ teaspoon baking soda
¼ teaspoon salt
1½ cups dairy sour cream
¼ cup honey or light corn syrup
¾ cup chopped pecans
1 HERSHEY'S® Milk Chocolate Bar (½ pound)
½ cup HERSHEY'S® Chocolate Flavored Syrup

Cream butter or margarine, sugar and vanilla until light and fluffy; add eggs and beat well. Combine flour, baking soda and salt; add alternately with sour cream to creamed mixture. Stir honey or corn syrup and pecans into 2 cups of batter; set aside. Melt chocolate

bar in chocolate syrup over warm water; blend into remaining batter. Pour into a greased and floured 10-inch tube pan. Spoon reserved mixture evenly over chocolate batter. Bake on lowest rack of oven at 350°F. for 45 minutes; decrease temperature to 325°F. without opening oven and continue to bake for 50 to 55 minutes or until cake tester inserted comes out clean. Cool cake one hour; remove from pan and cool completely. Glaze with Mini Chip-Marshmallow Glaze.

MINI CHIP-MARSHMALLOW GLAZE

⅓ cup sugar
3 tablespoons water
1 cup HERSHEY'S® Mini Chips
3 tablespoons marshmallow creme
1 to 2 tablespoons hot water

Combine sugar and 3 tablespoons water in small saucepan; bring to boil. Remove from heat; immediately add Mini Chips and stir until melted. Blend in marshmallow creme; add hot water, a teaspoonful at a time, until glaze is desired consistency.

1 cup glaze

Mazola®

COCOA CUP CAKES
(Low Cholesterol)

1½ cups sifted flour
⅓ cup unsweetened cocoa
2 teaspoons baking powder
¾ cup NUCOA® or MAZOLA® Margarine
1 teaspoon vanilla
1 cup sugar
½ cup water
3 egg whites

Place paper liners in 18 (2½-inch) muffin pan cups. Sift together first 3 ingredients. In bowl with mixer at medium speed beat margarine until soft; beat in vanilla. Gradually beat in sugar until blended. At low speed add flour mixture alternately with water. Beat egg whites until stiff peaks form; fold into batter. Spoon into muffin cups. Bake in 350°F oven 30 minutes or until cake tester comes out clean. Cool in pans. Remove; cool.

Makes 18 cup cakes

0 mg cholesterol per serving

CHOCOLATE NUT CAKE

2½ cups sifted SWANS DOWN®
   Cake Flour
1 teaspoon baking soda
1 teaspoon salt
1 cup vegetable shortening*
2 cups sugar
5 eggs
3 squares BAKER'S® Unsweetened
   Chocolate, melted
1⅓ cups buttermilk or sour milk
2 teaspoons vanilla
1 cup finely chopped nuts

Sift flour with soda and salt.
Cream shortening. Gradually add
sugar, beating until light and fluffy.
Add eggs, one at a time, beating
thoroughly after each addition.
Blend in chocolate. Add flour
mixture alternately with buttermilk,
beating after each addition until
smooth. Mix in vanilla and nuts.
Pour into two 9 × 5-inch loaf pans
that have been lined on bottoms
with paper. Bake at 350°F. for
about 60 minutes or until cake
tester inserted into center comes
out clean. Cool cakes in pans 10
minutes. Remove from pans and
finish cooling on racks. Frost or
glaze, if desired.

*Or use butter or margarine and
  decrease buttermilk to 1 cup.

Note: To sour milk, add milk to 1
  tablespoon plus 1 teaspoon
  vinegar to make 1⅓ cups;
  then let stand 5 minutes. For
  1 cup, add milk to 1
  tablespoon vinegar.

CHOCOLATETOWN SPECIAL CAKE

½ cup HERSHEY'S® Cocoa
½ cup boiling water
⅔ cup shortening
1¾ cups sugar
1 teaspoon vanilla
2 eggs
2¼ cups unsifted all-purpose flour
1½ teaspoons baking soda
½ teaspoon salt
1⅓ cups buttermilk or sour milk*

Combine cocoa and boiling water
in small bowl to form a smooth
paste; cool slightly. Cream
shortening, sugar and vanilla in
large mixer bowl; blend in eggs.
Combine flour, baking soda and
salt; add alternately with
buttermilk or sour milk to creamed
mixture. Blend in cocoa paste.

Pour batter into two greased and
floured 9-inch or three 8-inch layer
pans; bake at 350°F. for 35 to 40
minutes for 9-inch or 25 to 30
minutes for 8-inch layers or until
cake tester inserted in center
comes out clean. Cool 10 minutes;
remove from pans. Cool
completely; frost with 2 cups
Butter Cream Chocolate Frosting,
Light Flavor (recipe follows).

*To Sour Milk: Use 1 tablespoon
  plus 1 teaspoon vinegar plus milk
  to equal 1⅓ cups.

BUTTER CREAM CHOCOLATE FROSTINGS

	To Make:	
	1 Cup	2 Cups
HERSHEY'S® Cocoa		
Light flavor	2 Tbsp.	¼ cup
Medium flavor	¼ cup	½ cup
Dark flavor	⅓ cup	¾ cup
Confectioners' sugar	1 cup	2⅔ cups
Butter or margarine	3 Tbsp.	6 Tbsp.
Milk or water	2 Tbsp.	4-5 Tbsp.
Vanilla	½ tsp.	1 tsp.

Combine amount of cocoa for
flavor you prefer with
confectioners' sugar. Cream butter
with ½ cup of cocoa mixture in a
small bowl; add remaining cocoa
mixture alternately with milk,
beating to spreading consistency.
Blend in vanilla. For a glossier
frosting, add 1 tablespoon corn
syrup to the mixture.

PINEAPPLE WEDDING CAKE

Small Layer:
1½ cups finely chopped
  DIAMOND® Walnuts
¾ cup finely chopped candied
  pineapple
2½ cups sifted all-purpose flour
1½ tsp. baking powder
½ tsp. salt
1 cup butter
½ cup granulated sugar
½ cup honey
5 eggs
½ cup (well-stirred) canned
  sweetened crushed pineapple
  with juice
3 Tbsp. brandy

Combine chopped walnuts and
candied pineapple. Sift flour,

baking powder and salt over
walnuts and pineapple; set aside.
Cream butter; slowly beat in sugar
and honey; continue beating until
well mixed and light in color. Add
eggs, one at a time, beating well
after each addition. Add the
canned crushed pineapple along
with the brandy to creamed
mixture. Stir in flour and walnut
mixture; blend thoroughly. Pour
into lightly greased round cake
pan, eight inches in diameter by
three inches deep. Bake at 275° for
about two hours. Let cool on rack
for 10 minutes and remove from
pan. Cool completely before
slicing.
   *Makes one 8-inch layer, three
     inches deep*

Large Layer: Double all ingredients
for cake to fill pan 12 inches in
diameter by three inches deep.
Bake this large layer at 275° for
about 2½ hours. Assemble cake by
using approximately four cups of a
stiff butter frosting or a white
decorator's frosting.
   *Makes one 12-inch layer, three
     inches deep*

BARBARA UHLMANN'S POUND CAKE

4 cups CERESOTA or HECKER'S
  Unbleached Flour, sifted
2 teaspoons baking powder
2 cups butter (or margarine)
2 cups sugar
12 large eggs, separated
2 teaspoons vanilla
1 teaspoon lemon flavoring

Sift flour and baking powder
together. Beat the egg yolks
lightly, and add the flavorings.
Cream the butter and sugar until
light, then add the egg yolks
alternately with flour, beating after
each addition. Beat the egg whites
until stiff but not dry, then fold
them into the other mixture, and
mix only until well blended. Pour
into a well-greased and floured 10″
tube pan. Bake in a preheated 350°
oven for 1¼ hours. Leave in pan
about 5 minutes, then remove and
cool on rack.

FRESH APPLE CAKE

1½ cups all-purpose flour
2 teaspoons baking soda
½ teaspoon salt
1 teaspoon ground cinnamon
1 teaspoon ground nutmeg
½ cup margarine or butter,
  softened
1 cup granulated sugar
2 eggs
4 cups finely chopped, pared
  apples
1 cup KELLOGG'S® ALL-BRAN®
  Cereal or KELLOGG'S® BRAN
  BUDS® Cereal

1 package (3 oz.) cream cheese,
  softened
1 tablespoon margarine or butter,
  softened
1 teaspoon vanilla flavoring
1½ cups sifted confectioners'
  sugar

Stir together flour, soda, salt,
cinnamon, and nutmeg. Beat the
½ cup margarine and the
granulated sugar. Beat in eggs. Stir
in apples, cereal and flour mixture.
Spread in greased 9 × 9 × 2-inch
baking pan. Bake at 350°F. about
45 minutes or until done.

To make frosting: beat cream
cheese, the 1 tablespoon
margarine and vanilla. Gradually
add confectioners' sugar, beating
until smooth. If frosting is too
thick, add 1 to 2 teaspoons milk.
Spread on cooled cake.
Yield: 12 servings

® Kellogg Company

GRANDMA'S UPSIDE DOWN CAKE

1 can (1 lb. 4 oz.) DOLE® Sliced
  Pineapple
¼ cup butter
⅔ cup brown sugar, firmly packed
Maraschino cherries
1 cup flour
¾ cup sugar
1½ teaspoons baking powder
½ teaspoon salt
½ cup milk
¼ cup shortening
1 egg
1 teaspoon lemon juice
1 teaspoon vanilla
¼ teaspoon grated lemon peel

Drain pineapple reserving 2
tablespoons syrup. Melt butter in a
10-inch cast iron skillet.* Stir in
brown sugar until blended. Remove
from heat. Arrange pineapple
slices in sugar mixture. Place a
maraschino cherry in center of
each slice. Combine flour, sugar,
baking powder and salt. Add milk
and shortening; beat 2 minutes.
Add egg, reserved syrup, lemon
juice, vanilla and lemon peel. Beat
2 minutes. Pour over pineapple in
skillet, spreading evenly. Bake in a
350°F. oven 40 minutes. Cool on
wire rack 5 minutes. Invert onto
serving plate. Serve warm.
Makes 8 servings
*If using a skillet with wooden
  handle, wrap well with foil.

FRESH COCONUT CAKE

1 fresh DOLE® Coconut
Seven Minute Coconut Frosting*
1½ cups sugar
¾ cup shortening
1 teaspoon lemon extract
2¼ cups cake flour
1 tablespoon baking powder
1 teaspoon salt
1 cup milk
5 egg whites

Puncture eyes of coconut. Drain
liquid and reserve. Place coconut
in 350°F. oven 20 minutes. Hit
warm coconut with a hammer to
remove shells. Remove any
remaining shell with a blunt knife.
Pare and chunk coconut. In a
blender jar, whir ½ cup coconut
with 1 tablespoon reserved
coconut liquid about 30 seconds
until grated. Remove grated
coconut; repeat with remaining
coconut. Should have 3 cups
grated coconut. (Reserve 1 cup for
Seven Minute Coconut Frosting.)

Grease and lightly flour two 8-inch
round cake pans. Cream ¾ cup
sugar, shortening and lemon
extract until light and fluffy.
Combine flour, baking powder and
salt. Beat ⅓ dry ingredients into
creamed mixture. Beat in ½ cup
milk. Repeat ending with dry
ingredients. Fold in 1 cup coconut.
Beat egg whites to foamy stage.
Gradually add remaining sugar,
beating until stiff peaks form.
Gently fold into batter. Pour into
prepared cake pans. Bake in a
350°F. oven 30 minutes until
toothpick inserted comes out
clean. Cool 5 minutes; turn onto

wire rack to complete cooling.
Frost one layer with Seven Minute
Coconut Frosting; sprinkle top with
¼ cup coconut. Add second layer.
Frost entire cake. Sprinkle top and
sides with ¾ cup remaining
coconut.   *Makes 8-10 servings*

*SEVEN MINUTE COCONUT FROSTING

2 egg whites
1½ cups sugar
¼ teaspoon cream of tartar
⅓ cup cold water
¼ teaspoon lemon extract
1 cup reserved freshly grated
  coconut

Combine egg whites, sugar, cream
of tartar, cold water and lemon
extract in top of double boiler; beat
1 minute. Set top of double boiler
over boiling water; cook 7 minutes,
beating constantly at high speed
until stiff peaks form. Remove from
heat. Fold in reserved grated
coconut.

A BANANA CAKE FOR ANY SIZE PAN

2¾ cups all purpose flour sifted
3½ teaspoons baking powder
¾ cup shortening
1 teaspoon salt
1½ cups sugar
3 eggs
1 teaspoon vanilla extract
2 cups mashed ripe CHIQUITA®
  Brand Bananas (5 to 6)

Preheat oven to 350°. Grease well
and flour 2 9-inch round layer pans
1½ inches deep or 1 13 × 9 × 2-inch
oblong pan or 2½ (dozen) medium
cup cake pans. Sift flour, baking
powder and salt together. Cream
shortening until soft. Gradually
add sugar, beating until light and
fluffy after each addition. Add eggs
and vanilla and beat until thick and
lemon colored. Add dry ingredients
alternately with bananas. Blend
well after each addition.

Bake 9-inch round layers 30 to 35
minutes
Bake 13 × 9 × 2-inch oblong 40 to
  45 minutes*
Bake cup cakes 15 to 20 minutes

Cake is done if center springs back
when touched lightly with finger.
Cool cakes in pan on rack 10
minutes before removing from pan.

*If using glass pan, reduce
  temperature to 325°.

BANANA PUDDING CAKE

1 double layer size banana cake
   mix*
1 can (17.5 oz) THANK YOU®
   Brand Banana Pudding
¾ cup milk

Preheat oven to 350°F. (325°F. for
glass pan). Prepare cake mix
according to package directions.
Spread batter into well-oiled
9 × 13-inch cake pan. Combine
pudding and milk. Carefully pour
pudding on top of batter. Do not
mix pudding and batter! Bake for
40-45 minutes or until cake tests
done. Serve warm from the oven.
Or refrigerate and serve chilled
cake with whipped topping and
garnish with banana slices.

*Other flavors of cake mix and
 pudding can be substituted.

BANANA SQUARES
(Low Cholesterol)

2 cups unsifted flour
1 cup sugar
1 tsp. baking soda
½ tsp. salt
1 cup mashed ripe banana
⅔ cup HELLMANN'S® or BEST
   FOODS® Real Mayonnaise
¼ cup water
1½ tsp. vanilla
½ cup finely chopped nuts

Grease 8 × 8 × 2-inch baking pan. In
large bowl stir together first 4
ingredients. Add next 4
ingredients. With mixer at medium
speed beat 2 minutes or until
smooth. Stir in nuts. Pour into
prepared pan. Bake in 350°F oven
35 to 40 minutes or until cake
tester inserted in center comes out
clean. Cool in pan. Cut into
squares.   *Makes 9 servings*

10 mg cholesterol per serving

CARROT CAKE

2 cups DOMINO® Liquid Brown
   Sugar
2 cups sliced carrots
¼ cup nonfat dry milk
2 tablespoons butter or margarine
½ cup butter or margarine
1½ teaspoons vanilla
2 eggs
2½ cups sifted all-purpose flour
2 teaspoons baking powder
1 teaspoon salt
½ teaspoon cinnamon

Preheat oven to 350°F. Grease and
flour two 8-inch round cake pans.
In medium saucepan combine
DOMINO® Liquid Brown Sugar,
carrots, dry milk and 2 tablespoons
butter. Cook over medium heat
until carrots are tender, about 20
minutes, stirring occasionally.
Strain carrots, reserving syrup. Let
syrup cool. Puree carrots and set
aside. Cream ½ cup butter with
vanilla. Slowly add 1 cup of
reserved syrup, beating until well
combined. Add eggs, 1 at a time,
beating thoroughly after each
addition. Beat in pureed carrots.
Sift together flour, baking powder,
salt and cinnamon. Beat dry
ingredients into carrot mixture in
four additions alternating with
remaining Liquid Brown Sugar
syrup. Pour batter into prepared
pans. Bake 35 minutes or until
done. Let cool. Frost and fill with
cream cheese frosting or frosting
of your choice.
        Makes two 8-inch cake layers

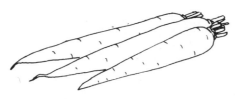

SUNLITE CARROT CAKE

1½ cups SUNLITE Oil
2 cups sugar
3 eggs
2 tsp. vanilla
2 cups all-purpose flour
2 tsp. cinnamon
2 tsp. baking soda
1 tsp. salt
1 (7-oz.) pkg. flake coconut
2 cups shredded carrots
1 (13½-oz.) can crushed
   pineapple, drained
1 cup chopped nuts

In a large bowl, thoroughly
combine SUNLITE Oil, sugar, eggs
and vanilla. Sift together flour,
cinnamon, baking soda, and salt;
add to first mixture and mix well.
Stir in coconut, shredded carrots,
pineapple and nuts. Pour into
greased and floured 13 × 9 × 2-inch
pan. Bake at 350° 50 to 60 minutes
until center of cake is firm to the
touch. Cool in pan. Frost as
desired.   *Makes 15 servings*

PEACHES 'N CREAM
PUDDING CAKE

1 can (17½ oz.) THANK YOU®
   Brand Vanilla Pudding
1 can (16 oz.) peach slices
1 package (9 oz.) single layer
   yellow cake mix

Drain peaches, reserving juice.
Arrange peaches in oiled 9 × 9-inch
(or 7 × 11-inch) baking dish.
Peaches may be cut into thinner
slices if necessary. Spread
pudding over peaches. Prepare
cake batter according to package
directions, substituting peach juice
for water. Spread batter over
pudding and peaches. Bake at
350°F. (325°F. if using glass pan)
for 45-55 minutes or until cake
tests done. Serve warm.
        Makes 7-8 servings

***Peaches 'n Cream Pudding
Cheesecake:*** Combine 3 oz.
package softened cream cheese
with pudding before spreading over
peaches in above recipe.

FROSTY DATE CAKE

2 tablespoons SWIFT'NING/
   JEWEL Shortening
1 cup chopped dates
1 cup boiling water
½ teaspoon salt
1 cup sugar
1 egg, beaten
1¼ cups sifted all-purpose flour
1 teaspoon soda
1 teaspoon vanilla
½ cup chopped nuts

Topping:
2 tablespoons SWIFT'NING/
   JEWEL Shortening
¼ cup flour
¼ cup sugar
½ cup chopped nuts

Mix SWIFT'NING/JEWEL
Shortening, dates, and boiling
water. Add salt, sugar, and egg.
Sift flour and soda together. Add
to date mixture. Mix well. Add
vanilla and nuts. Pour into an 8 by 8
by 2-inch loaf pan (bottom rubbed
with SWIFT'NING/JEWEL).

Cover batter with topping, made by
blending SWIFT'NING/JEWEL with
flour, sugar, and nuts. Bake in
moderate oven (350°F.) 1 hour.
        Yield: 8 by 8 by 2-inch loaf

TASTE OF TEXAS MOCHA CAKE

1 cup sifted cake flour
¼ cup cocoa
½ teaspoon baking soda
½ teaspoon ground cinnamon
¼ teaspoon baking powder
¼ teaspoon salt
¼ cup shortening
¾ cup sugar
1 egg, unbeaten
⅓ cup buttermilk
⅓ cup brewed MARYLAND CLUB®
  Coffee
½ teaspoon vanilla
Mocha Cream Frosting (recipe
  follows)

Sift flour with cocoa, soda, cinnamon, baking powder, and salt. Cream shortening; add sugar gradually, creaming together until light and fluffy. Add egg, beating thoroughly. Combine buttermilk, coffee, and vanilla. Add flour mixture to egg mixture, alternately with liquid, beating after each addition until smooth. Pour batter into well-greased and floured 9-inch square pan or Texas-shaped pan. Bake in moderate oven (350°F.) 35 minutes or until cake springs back when pressed lightly. Cool; frost with Mocha Cream Frosting.

MOCHA CREAM FROSTING

1¼ to 1½ cups sifted
  confectioners' sugar
2 tablespoons cocoa
⅛ teaspoon salt
¼ cup butter or margarine
2-3 tablespoons brewed
  MARYLAND CLUB® Coffee
¼ teaspoon vanilla

Sift sugar, cocoa, and salt together. Cream butter and gradually add part of sugar mixture, blending after each addition, until light and fluffy. Add remaining sugar alternately with coffee, until of right consistency to spread, beating after each addition until smooth. Blend in vanilla.
Makes about 1½ cups frosting, or enough to frost top and sides of one 9-inch square or Texas-shaped cake.

ELEGANT ORANGE CAKE

3½ cups sifted cake flour
2 teaspoons baking soda
½ teaspoon salt
½ cup butter or margarine
½ cup shortening
1½ cups sugar
4 eggs
1½ cups buttermilk
2 teaspoons orange extract
1 cup raisins, finely chopped
1 cup walnuts, finely chopped
Orange Frosting (recipe follows)
Grated orange peel (optional)

Grease and flour two 9-inch round cake pans. Sift together cake flour, soda and salt; set aside. Cream butter, shortening and sugar. Gradually beat in eggs and buttermilk alternately with the sifted dry ingredients. Add orange extract. Blend until smooth. Add raisins and walnuts to the mixture. Divide batter into prepared pans. Bake at 350 degrees for 30 to 35 minutes or until toothpick inserted in center comes out clean. Remove from oven and cool 5 minutes in pans. Turn out on wire racks to finish cooling. Frost tops and sides with Orange Frosting. Garnish with grated orange peel, if desired.

ORANGE FROSTING

⅓ cup butter or margarine,
  softened
4 cups (1 pound) powdered sugar
¼ cup orange juice

Beat all ingredients together until smooth and creamy. Add additional orange juice, if necessary.

California Raisin Advisory Board's favorite recipe

Mazola®

NO-CHOLESTEROL ORANGE CAKE

1½ cups sifted flour
1 cup sugar
2 teaspoons baking powder
¼ teaspoon salt
½ cup MAZOLA® Corn Oil
2 teaspoons grated orange rind
½ cup orange juice
4 egg whites

Grease and flour bottom of 8½ × 4½ × 2½-inch loaf pan. In large bowl stir together flour, sugar, baking powder and salt. Add corn oil and orange juice. With mixer at medium speed, beat until smooth. Add rind. In small bowl with mixer at high speed beat egg whites until stiff peaks form. Fold egg whites into flour mixture. Turn into prepared pan. Bake in 350°F oven 50 minutes or until cake springs back when lightly touched. Cool 10 minutes in pan. Remove from pan and cool completely on wire rack.   *Makes 8 servings*

AMARETTO RAISIN BUNDT® CAKE

Cake:
1 pkg. PILLSBURY Pound Cake
  Supreme BUNDT® Cake Mix
½ cup dairy sour cream
¼ cup margarine or butter,
  softened
½ cup water
⅓ cup HIRAM WALKER Amaretto
3 eggs
2 cups (1 lb.) candied fruit
  mixture
1 cup SUN-MAID® Raisins
1 cup chopped nuts

Sauce:
1½ cups sugar
4 tablespoons cornstarch
1½ cups water
4 tablespoons margarine or butter
¼ cup HIRAM WALKER Amaretto
2 tablespoons lemon juice
½ cup SUN-MAID® Raisins

Heat oven to 325°F. Grease 12-cup Bundt® pan. In large bowl, combine two clear packets of cake mix and remaining cake ingredients except fruit, raisins and nuts. Blend until moistened; beat 2 minutes at medium speed. Fold in fruit, raisins and nuts. Pour into pan. Bake at 325°F. for 70 to 80 minutes until toothpick inserted in center comes out clean. Cool upright in pan on rack 25 minutes; invert onto plate. Cool completely. Sprinkle or sift topping packet over top of cake.

To prepare sauce, mix sugar and cornstarch in saucepan. Gradually stir in water. Over medium heat, stirring constantly, heat to boiling; boil 1 minute. Remove from heat; stir in margarine, Amaretto, juice and raisins. Serve warm over cooled cake.   *16 servings*

HIGH ALTITUDE—Above 3500 feet: Bake at 325°F. for 55 to 60 minutes.

HELLMANN'S Best Foods

AMAZIN' RAISIN CAKE

3 cups unsifted flour
2 cups sugar
1 cup HELLMANN'S® or BEST FOODS® Real Mayonnaise
⅓ cup milk
2 eggs
2 teaspoons baking soda
1½ teaspoons ground cinnamon
½ teaspoon ground nutmeg
½ teaspoon salt
¼ teaspoon ground cloves
3 cups chopped peeled apples
1 cup seedless raisins
1 cup coarsely chopped walnuts
2 cups whipped cream

Grease and flour 2 (9-inch) round baking pans. In large bowl with mixer at low speed scraping bowl frequently, beat together flour, sugar, real mayonnaise, milk, eggs, baking soda, cinnamon, nutmeg, salt and cloves 2 minutes or beat vigorously 300 strokes by hand. (Batter will be thick.) With spoon stir in apples, raisins and nuts. Spoon into prepared pans. Bake in 350°F oven 45 minutes or until cake tester inserted in center comes out clean. Cool in pans on wire racks 10 minutes. Remove and cool on wire racks. Fill and frost with whipped cream.

Makes 8 servings

BLUEBERRY CRUNCH CAKE

½ cup butter (or margarine)
¾ cup sugar
2 eggs
⅓ cup milk
1 tsp. vanilla
2 cups flour
2 tsp. baking powder
½ tsp. salt
1 can LUCKY LEAF® Blueberry Pie Filling

Crumb Mixture:
½ cup sugar
½ cup flour
2 Tbsp. butter

Cream butter or margarine and sugar; beat in eggs. Blend in milk

and vanilla. Sift together dry ingredients and add to creamed mixture. Spread half the batter in a greased 9" x 9" x 2" pan; cover with ½ can blueberry pie filling; spread remaining batter over pie filling; top with remaining pie filling.

Mix ½ cup sugar, ½ cup flour and cut in 2 tablespoons butter and sprinkle this mixture over the surface of the dessert. Bake at 350° for 45 to 50 minutes.

TONY'S OLD-FASHIONED WALNUT CAKE

1½ cups coarsely chopped raisins
½ cup water
¼ cup bourbon
½ cup butter or margarine
¾ cup granulated sugar
1 egg
1½ cups sifted all-purpose flour
1 teaspoon baking powder
1 teaspoon baking soda
¾ teaspoon salt
1 cup medium fine chopped DIAMOND® Walnuts

Combine raisins, water and bourbon in saucepan; cover and bring to a boil. Remove from heat and let stand, covered, 10 minutes. Cream butter; gradually add sugar, continuing to beat until light and fluffy. Beat in egg. Resift flour with baking powder, baking soda and salt. Add to creamed mixture alternately with raisin mixture. Stir in walnuts. Turn into greased, wax paper-lined 9-inch square pan. Bake at 350°F. for about 30 minutes or until cake tests done. Cool in pan 10 minutes; turn out onto wire rack to complete cooling. Serve plain or topped with your favorite icing.

Makes one 9-inch square cake

BOURBON CAKE

2 cups red candied cherries, chopped
1½ cups light seedless raisins
2 cups OLD FORESTER Bourbon
1½ cups butter or margarine
2⅓ cups granulated sugar
2⅓ cups firmly packed brown sugar
6 eggs, separated
5 cups sifted cake flour
4 cups pecans (about 1 pound)
2 teaspoons nutmeg
1 teaspoon baking powder

Combine cherries, raisins and Bourbon. Cover and let stand overnight. Drain fruits; reserve Bourbon. Cream butter or margarine and sugar together until light. Add egg yolks and beat well. Combine ½ cup flour and pecans. Sift remaining 4½ cups flour, nutmeg and baking powder together. Add flour mixture and Bourbon alternately to butter or margarine mixture, beating well after each addition. Beat egg whites until stiff, but not dry. Fold egg whites into flour mixture. Fold soaked fruits and pecan-flour mixture into batter. Turn into greased 10-inch tube pan lined with greased waxed paper. Bake in slow oven (275°) 4½ hours. Cool. Remove from pan. Fill center with cheesecloth saturated with OLD FORESTER.

HOLIDAY GIFT CAKE

1 8-oz. pkg. PHILADELPHIA BRAND Cream Cheese
1 cup PARKAY Margarine
1½ cups sugar
1½ teaspoons vanilla
4 eggs
2¼ cups sifted cake flour
1½ teaspoons baking powder
¾ cup well-drained chopped maraschino cherries
½ cup chopped pecans

Glaze:
½ cup finely chopped pecans
1½ cups sifted confectioners' sugar
2 tablespoons milk

Combine softened cream cheese, margarine, sugar and vanilla, mixing until well blended. Add eggs, one at a time, mixing well after each addition. Gradually add 2 cups flour sifted with baking powder, mixing well after each addition. Toss remaining flour with cherries and chopped nuts; fold into batter. Grease a 10-inch Bundt® or tube pan; sprinkle with finely chopped nuts. Pour batter into pan; bake at 325°, 1 hour and 20 minutes. Cool 5 minutes; remove from pan. Cool thoroughly.

Glaze with mixture of confectioners' sugar and milk. Garnish with cherries and nuts, if desired.

EVER-SO-EASY FRUITCAKE

2½ cups unsifted flour
1 teaspoon baking soda
2 eggs, slightly beaten
1 (28-ounce) jar NONE SUCH®
 Ready-to-Use Mince Meat
1 (14-ounce) can EAGLE® Brand
 Sweetened Condensed Milk
 (NOT evaporated milk)
2 cups (1 pound) mixed candied
 fruit
1 cup coarsely chopped nuts

Preheat oven to 350°F. Grease a
9-inch tube pan; line with wax
paper and grease again (or use
generously greased and floured
10-inch fluted tube pan). Sift
together flour and baking soda; set
aside. In large bowl, combine
remaining ingredients; blend in dry
ingredients. Pour into prepared
pan. Bake 1 hour and 50 minutes
or until toothpick inserted near
center comes out clean. Cool 15
minutes. Turn out of pan; remove
wax paper. Garnish as desired.
Makes one 9-inch cake

NO-BAKE FRUIT CAKE

4 cups graham cracker crumbs
 (about 4 dozen 2½-inch graham
 crackers)
1 cup mixed candied fruit
1 cup golden raisins
1 cup chopped dates
1 cup chopped nuts
1 cup miniature marshmallows
1 can (14 oz.) sweetened
 condensed milk

Line a 9 x 5-inch loaf pan with
waxed paper. Mix all the
ingredients together, first with a
spoon and then with hands, until
the crumbs are thoroughly
moistened. Pack securely into pan.
Cover tightly. Chill at least two
days before slicing. To serve: slice
thinly or cut into small cookie
squares.
Makes one 2¼ pound loaf

California Raisin Advisory Board's favorite
recipe

GINGERBREAD

½ cup shortening
½ cup sugar
1 cup GRANDMA'S® Molasses
 (Unsulphured)
2 eggs
2½ cups sifted all-purpose flour
1 teaspoon salt
2 teaspoons baking powder
½ teaspoon baking soda
1 teaspoon ginger
2 teaspoons cinnamon
½ teaspoon ground cloves
1 cup hot water

Cream shortening with sugar.
Blend in molasses. Beat in eggs,
one at a time. Sift together flour,
salt, baking powder, baking soda
and spices. Add to creamed
mixture alternately with hot water.
Turn into a greased 9 x 9 x 2-inch
baking pan. Bake in 350°F. oven 40
minutes. Cool.
Yield: 9 to 12 servings

Buttermilk variation: Substitute 1
cup buttermilk for 1 cup hot water.
Omit baking powder and increase
baking soda to 1½ teaspoons.

MALTEX® DATE-NUT CAKE

1 cup hot water
1¼ cups finely chopped dates
⅓ cup MALTEX®
¼ cup shortening
1 cup sugar
1 egg
1 teaspoon lemon flavoring
1⅓ cups sifted flour
1 teaspoon soda
½ teaspoon salt
⅓ cup walnuts, finely chopped

Pour hot water over dates and
MALTEX®; let stand until cool.
Cream shortening, sugar, egg and
flavoring until light. Beat 5 minutes
with electric mixer at high speed.
Sift flour, soda and salt together.
Add to creamed mixture alternately
with dates/MALTEX® mixture. Do
not over-mix. Stir in nuts. Pour into
lightly greased and floured
9 x 9 x 1¾-inch square baking pan.
Bake in preheated 350°F. oven 40
to 45 minutes, or until tests done.
Serve with whipped cream, if
desired.
Makes one 9-inch square

JACK FROST CAKE

Combine and set aside:
1 18.5 oz. box regular spice cake
 mix
1 3¼ oz. box JELL-O® Brand
 AMERICANA® Tapioca Pudding
 (vanilla flavor)
Beat together:
2 eggs
1½ cups FARLEY'S Hard Cider

Add liquid ingredients to dry and
beat at medium speed for two
minutes or by hand for 200 strokes.
Pour into Bundt® pan (10-12 cup
size) and bake at 350° for 45-55
minutes, until cake springs to the
touch. Make your favorite white
frosting, and pour over cake while
warm. Garnish with chopped nuts
and CRACKER JACK® Candied
Popcorn.

TOMATO SPICE CAKE

2¼ cups cake flour or 2 cups
 all-purpose flour
1⅓ cups sugar
4 teaspoons baking powder
1 teaspoon baking soda
1½ teaspoons allspice
1 teaspoon cinnamon
½ teaspoon ground cloves
1 can (10¾ ounces) CAMPBELL'S
 Condensed Tomato Soup
½ cup shortening
2 eggs
¼ cup water

Preheat oven to 350°F. Generously
grease and flour 2 round layer
pans, 8 or 9″, or an oblong pan,
13 x 9 x 2″. Measure dry
ingredients into large bowl. Add
soup and shortening. Beat at low
to medium speed for 2 minutes
(300 strokes with a spoon),
scraping sides and bottom of bowl
constantly. Add eggs and water.
Beat 2 minutes more, scraping
bowl frequently. Pour into pans.
Bake 35 to 40 minutes. Let stand in
pans 10 minutes; remove. Cool.
Frost with a cream cheese
frosting.

Bundt® Pan: Proceed as above.
Bake in well-greased and lightly
floured 2½-quart Bundt® pan at
350°F. for 50 to 60 minutes or until
done. Cool right-side-up in pan 15
minutes; remove from pan. Cool. If
desired, sprinkle with
confectioners' sugar.

PISTACHIO PUDDING CAKE

1 package (2-layer size) yellow cake mix*
1 package (4-serving size) JELL-O® Brand Pistachio Flavor Instant Pudding & Pie Filling
4 eggs
1¼ cups water*
¼ cup oil
½ teaspoon almond extract
7 drops green food coloring (optional)

Combine all ingredients in large mixer bowl. Blend; then beat at medium speed of electric mixer for 4 minutes. Pour into greased and floured 10-inch fluted tube or tube pan. Bake at 350° for 50 to 55 minutes or until cake tester inserted in center comes out clean and cake begins to pull away from sides of pan. *Do not underbake.* Cool in pan 15 minutes. Remove from pan and finish cooling on rack.

In high altitude areas, use large eggs, add ¼ cup all-purpose flour and increase water to 1½ cups. (With pudding-included cake mix, use ⅓ cup flour, 1⅓ cups water and bake 40 to 45 minutes.)

*Or use pudding-included cake mix and 1 cup water.

SUNSHINE LOAF

2 3-oz. packages cream cheese
4 eggs
1 jar (7¾ oz.) GERBER® Junior Pears and Pineapple
1 package yellow cake mix
1 cup flour
1 tablespoon chopped candied lemon peel

Preheat oven to 350°F. Grease well and flour a 9 × 5 × 3 inch loaf pan. Blend cream cheese in a bowl. Add eggs, one at a time, beating after each addition. Mix in pears and pineapple. Add cake mix, flour, and candied lemon peel and mix just until dry ingredients are moistened. Turn into pan and bake at 350°F for 60 minutes or until loaf is done. Remove from oven and let stand 10 minutes before removing from pan.

KIWIFRUIT WINE CAKE

1 Plain yellow cake mix
1 Small package instant vanilla pudding
4 Eggs
¾ Cup CRISCO Oil
1 Teaspoon nutmeg
1 Cup GIBSON Kiwifruit Wine
Powdered Sugar

Combine all ingredients, except powdered sugar, and mix for two minutes at medium speed. Bake in a well greased, lightly floured Bundt® (or tube) pan for 45 minutes at 350 degrees. Cool in the pan for 25 minutes, and then turn out on serving plate. Allow to cool completely, and lightly sift powdered sugar over top of cake.

PRALINE® PECAN CAKE

1 package yellow cake mix
1 package (4 serving size) instant pudding and pie filling mix (vanilla)
4 large eggs (at room temperature)
½ cup cooking oil
¼ cup DOMINO® Liquid Brown Sugar
¾ cup PRALINE® Liqueur
½ cup HEATH® BITS 'O BRICKLE®
½ cup chopped pecans

In large bowl, blend cake mix and instant pudding mix. Add eggs, oil, DOMINO® Liquid Brown Sugar and PRALINE® Liqueur. Beat with electric mixer at low speed until thoroughly mixed, then at medium speed 3-4 minutes. Stir in HEATH® BITS 'O BRICKLE® and pecans. Bake in well greased 10-inch tube or Bundt® pan in a preheated 350° oven for 45-50 minutes, or until a cake tester comes out clean. Cool in pan, on rack, 10 minutes. Remove cake from pan, cool, then glaze* and garnish.

*GLAZE

1¼ cups sifted confectioners' sugar
2 tablespoons butter, melted
3-6 tablespoons PRALINE® Liqueur

In small bowl, combine sugar and butter. Beat with mixer, adding PRALINE® Liqueur gradually to achieve desired consistency. Pour over cake. Garnish with a few chopped pecans and brickle.

CLOWN CAKE

1 frozen SARA LEE Fresh Orange Cake
1 orange, cut into quarters
1 apple wedge
2 pieces orange peel, each about ¼ × 1 inch
1 strawberry, cut in half horizontally
2 chewy fruit flavored candies
10-15 carrot curls, about 2-3 carrots

Remove frozen Orange Cake from pan. Round off 2 corners to form bottom of oval face; place on serving plate. Decorate clown face using orange for ears, apple for mouth, orange peel for eyes, bottom half of strawberry for nose, candy for eyes and carrot curls for hair, using toothpicks to attach to cake.   *Makes 6 servings*

VARIATION:

Substitute orange peel for apple, red cherry for strawberry, gumdrops for chewy candies and bananas cut in half lengthwise (dipped in lemon-water mixture) for carrot curls.

COMFORT® CAKE

1 18½ oz. DUNCAN HINES® Yellow Cake Mix
1 3¾ oz. pkg. instant vanilla pudding mix
4 eggs
½ cup cold water
½ cup oil
1 cup chopped pecans or walnuts
½ cup SOUTHERN COMFORT®

Combine all ingredients; pour into greased and floured 10-inch tube or 12-cup Bundt® pan. Bake at 325° for 1 hour. Set on rack to cool. Invert on serving plate. Prick top. Immediately drizzle and brush half of glaze* evenly over top and sides. Reserve half of glaze. After cake has cooled, reheat glaze and brush it evenly over cake.

*GLAZE

⅛ lb. butter or margarine
⅛ cup water
½ cup granulated sugar
¼ cup SOUTHERN COMFORT®

Melt butter in saucepan. Stir in water and sugar. Boil 3 minutes, stirring constantly. Remove from heat and stir in SOUTHERN COMFORT®.

THE CHRISTIAN BROTHERS® SHERRY CAKE

1 package yellow cake mix
4 eggs
1 package (3 to 4 ounce) instant vanilla pudding mix
¾ cup THE CHRISTIAN BROTHERS® Cream Sherry
¾ cup cooking oil
1 teaspoon nutmeg

Preheat oven to 350°. Grease and lightly flour a fluted tube pan. Place all ingredients in large bowl. Beat together with electric mixer for five minutes. Pour into cake pan and bake 50 minutes. Cool one half hour. Dust with confectioner's sugar or glaze with a mixture of confectioner's sugar and sherry.

MARDI GRAS CAKE

1 can (30 oz.) DEL MONTE Fruit Cocktail
½ cup margarine or butter
1 cup firmly packed brown sugar
1 pkg. (18½ oz.) lemon cake mix
1 cup water

Drain fruit cocktail, reserving ⅓ cup syrup. Melt margarine in 13 × 9-inch pan or 12-inch skillet. Add sugar. Arrange fruit in sugar mixture. Prepare cake mix as package directs, using 1 cup water and reserved syrup. Spread over fruit. Bake at 350°F., 45 to 50 minutes or until tests done. Cool 5 minutes; invert onto large serving dish. Serve warm or cold with ice cream, if desired.   *16 servings*

CHERRY WALNUT CAKE

1 cup DIAMOND® Walnuts
1 1 lb. 2½-oz. package white cake mix
½ tsp. vanilla
1 3½-oz. package strawberry flavor whipped dessert mix
1 1 lb.-5 oz. can cherry pie filling

Chop ¼ cup walnuts coarsely and set aside to decorate top of cake. Chop remaining walnuts medium fine. Prepare batter from cake mix

as package directs, adding vanilla. Fold in ¾ cup walnuts. Bake in 2 greased and floured 9-in. layer cake pans, about 25 to 28 min., just until cake tests done. Cool in pan 5 min. Invert layers onto wire racks to cool. Prepare dessert mix according to package directions. Spread a rim of the mixture about 1 in. wide around top edge of each layer. Spread cherry pie filling in center of each layer. Stack the 2 layers together on serving plate, and spread remaining dessert mix around sides of cake. Chill until serving time. Sprinkle top of cake with reserved ¼ cup walnuts.
          Makes about 12 servings

CHEESECAKE

Graham cracker crumbs
1 pound small curd creamed cottage cheese
2 packages (8 oz. each) cream cheese, softened
1½ cups sugar
4 eggs
⅓ cup ARGO®/KINGSFORD'S® Corn Starch
2 tablespoons lemon juice
1 teaspoon vanilla
½ cup margarine, melted
1 pint dairy sour cream
Strawberry Glaze (recipe follows)

Grease 9-inch spring form pan; sprinkle with graham cracker crumbs. Sieve cottage cheese into large bowl; add cream cheese. Beat on high speed of mixer until well blended. Beat in sugar, then eggs. Reduce speed to low. Beat in corn starch, lemon juice and vanilla, then margarine and sour cream until smooth. Pour into prepared pan. Bake in 325°F oven 70 minutes or until firm around edge. Turn off oven. Let cake stand in oven 2 hours. Remove and chill. Remove side of pan. Cover with Strawberry Glaze. Chill.
          Makes 12 servings

STRAWBERRY GLAZE

Mix 1 tablespoon corn starch, ¼ cup water and ⅓ cup light corn syrup until smooth. Add ¼ cup crushed fresh strawberries. Bring to boil, stirring constantly, and boil 1 minute. Strain. Stir in 1 teaspoon lemon juice and red food coloring. Cool slightly. Arrange whole strawberries on Cheese Cake; cover with glaze.

SOLO® BLUEBERRY MINI-CHEESECAKES

8 oz. cream cheese
1 egg
½ C. sugar
½ tsp. vanilla extract
Vanilla wafers
1 can (12 oz.) SOLO® Blueberry Filling

Beat together cream cheese, egg, sugar and vanilla until light and fluffy. Line miniature muffin pans (1¾″ diameter) with paper baking cups. Place vanilla wafer in bottom of each cup. Fill cups with rounded teaspoon of cream cheese mixture. Bake in 375° oven for 10 minutes. Cool. Top with teaspoon of SOLO® Blueberry Filling.

CHEESECAKE SIBELIUS

3 cups dairy sour cream
1 pound FINLANDIA Swiss Cheese, grated
1½ cups sugar
¼ cup flour
1 tablespoon grated orange peel
1 teaspoon grated lemon peel
6 eggs
1½ cups graham cracker crumbs
½ cup finely chopped almonds
2 tablespoons sugar
¼ cup (½ stick) butter or margarine
3 cups fresh strawberries or blueberries
½ cup currant jelly, melted

In saucepan combine sour cream and cheese. Cook over low heat, stirring constantly until cheese is melted. Remove from heat and cool. Gradually stir in sugar, flour, orange and lemon peel. Beat in eggs, one at a time. Combine crumbs, almonds, 2 tablespoons sugar and butter. Press onto bottom and sides of 9 inch spring-form pan. Pour in cheese mixture. Bake at 350°F. for 40 minutes. Turn off oven, open door and let cool. Just before serving arrange fruit on top of cake in pattern. Spoon jelly over. Let stand at room temperature until jelly is set.
          Makes 8 servings

FRUIT CHEESECAKE
(Low Calorie)

½ cup evaporated skimmed milk
4 tablespoons lemon juice
6 tablespoons water
2 teaspoons SWEET 'N LOW®
   (8 pkts.)
1 envelope unflavored gelatin
1 cup cottage cheese
½ teaspoon vanilla extract
1 cup well-drained dietetic fruit
   cocktail
Crust optional

Place milk in freezer. Mix lemon juice with water, SWEET 'N LOW® and gelatin. Cook and stir until gelatin dissolves, then cool. Put cheese through sieve or blender and beat until smooth. Stir in gelatin mixture and vanilla, blending well. Chill until partially set. Whip frozen milk until it peaks. Fold fruit into partially set cheese, then fold in whipped milk. Spoon into springform pan or square cake pan and refrigerate overnight. If you like, you can make a crust of vanilla wafers.   *Serves 6*

55 calories per serving without crust; with crust add another 25 calories per serving.

MARBLE CHEESECAKE

Graham Crust (recipe below)
3 packages (8 ounces each) cream
   cheese, softened
¾ cup sugar
½ cup sour cream
2 teaspoons vanilla
3 tablespoons flour
3 eggs
¼ cup HERSHEY'S® Cocoa
¼ cup sugar
1 tablespoon oil
½ teaspoon vanilla

Prepare Graham Crust; cool. Combine cream cheese, sugar, sour cream and 2 teaspoons vanilla in large mixer bowl; beat on medium speed until smooth. Add flour, a tablespoon at a time, blending well. Add eggs, one at a time, beating well after each addition. Reserve 1½ cups batter; set aside. Combine cocoa and sugar in small bowl. Add oil, ½ teaspoon vanilla and reserved 1½

cups batter; mix until well blended. Spoon plain and chocolate batters alternately over crust, ending with dollops of chocolate on top; gently swirl with spatula or knife for marbled effect. Bake at 450° for 10 minutes; without opening oven, reduce heat to 250° and continue baking 30 minutes. Turn off oven; cool cheesecake 30 minutes without opening door. Loosen cake from rim of pan; cool completely before removing rim. Chill thoroughly.   *12 servings*

GRAHAM CRUST

1 cup graham cracker crumbs
   (about 7 crackers)
2 tablespoons sugar
¼ cup butter or margarine, melted

Combine crumbs, sugar and butter; press mixture into bottom and ½-inch up side of a 9-inch springform pan. Bake at 350° for 10 minutes.

NO BAKE CHOCOLATE MINT CHEESECAKE

¼ cup butter or margarine, melted
1 cup chocolate wafer crumbs
   (10 wafers)
20 miniature or 5 large YORK
   Peppermint Patties
2 Tbsp. butter
Two 8-oz. packages cream cheese
14-oz. can sweetened condensed
   milk
1 Tbsp. unflavored gelatin
2 Tbsp. lemon juice
1 tsp. vanilla
1 cup whipping cream
1 cup sour cream
8 miniature or 2 large YORK
   Peppermint Patties, grated

Mix melted butter and chocolate wafer crumbs. Firmly pat over bottom of 9-inch springform pan. Chill. Melt 20 miniature YORK Peppermint Patties and 2 Tbsp. butter. Drizzle over crumb crust. Chill. Beat cream cheese until light and fluffy. Gradually add sweetened condensed milk while beating until smooth. Soften gelatin in lemon juice and warm to dissolve. Add to cheese mixture with vanilla. Whip cream until stiff peaks form. Fold into cream cheese mixture. Pour into prepared pan. Chill. Cover with whipped sour cream. Garnish with grated YORK Peppermint Patties. Chill several hours.   *Serves 8 to 10*

NO-BAKE APRICOT CHEESECAKE

NO-BAKE CRUST:
½ cup butter or margarine
⅓ cup sugar
1½ cups KELLOGG'S® CORN
   FLAKE CRUMBS

Cook butter and sugar in small saucepan until mixture boils; remove from heat. Mix in Corn Flake Crumbs. Reserve 2 tablespoons mixture for garnish; press remainder in bottom of 9-inch springform pan. Chill.

VELVETY CREAM CHEESE FILLING:
1 can (30 oz.) apricot halves,
   drained (reserve syrup)
1 envelope unflavored gelatin
2 pkg. (8 oz. each) cream cheese,
   softened
1 can (14 oz.) EAGLE® Brand
   Sweetened Condensed Milk
2 tablespoons lemon juice
1 container (4½ oz.) frozen non-
   dairy whipped topping, thawed

Combine ½ cup reserved syrup and gelatin; stir over low heat until gelatin dissolves. Reserve 4 or 5 apricot halves for garnish; blend remaining apricots on high speed in blender until smooth. Combine apricot and gelatin mixtures; set aside. In large bowl, beat cheese until smooth. Add sweetened condensed milk and lemon juice; mix well. Stir in apricot-gelatin mixture. Fold in whipped topping. Turn into prepared pan. To garnish: slice reserved apricot halves into pieces; arrange in two-piece clusters around top of cheesecake. Spoon apricot glaze* over top of cake. Add mint leaves to clusters. Sprinkle crumbs around outer edge of cake. Chill 3 hours.   *Makes one 9-inch cake*

*EASY APRICOT GLAZE: (optional)
½ cup reserved syrup
1 teaspoon cornstarch

Cook and stir cornstarch and ½ cup reserved syrup until thick and clear. Cool. Spoon glaze evenly over top of cake.

California Apricot Advisory Board favorite recipe

267

IT'S A SNAP CHEESECAKE

1 envelope KNOX® Unflavored Gelatine
½ cup sugar
1 cup boiling water
2 packages (8 oz. ea.) cream cheese, softened
1 teaspoon vanilla extract (optional)
9-inch graham cracker crust

In large bowl, mix unflavored gelatine with sugar; add boiling water and stir until gelatine is completely dissolved. With electric mixer, beat in cream cheese and vanilla until smooth. Pour into prepared crust; chill until firm. Garnish, if desired, with fresh or canned fruit.

Makes about 8 servings

VARIATIONS:

Marbled Cheesecake: Before chilling, marble in ⅓ cup chocolate fudge, butterscotch, or your favorite flavor ice cream topping.

Lemon or Almond Cheesecake: Substitute ½ to ¾ teaspoon lemon or almond extract for vanilla extract.

Fruit'n Creamy Cheesecake: Chill cheesecake 10 minutes, then swirl in ⅓ cup strawberry or raspberry preserves.

Sunshine Cheesecake: Substitute ½ teaspoon orange extract for vanilla extract and add 1 teaspoon grated orange rind.

PEACHES 'N CREAM CHEESECAKE

Crust:
2 c. 3-MINUTE BRAND® Quick Oats
⅔ c. brown sugar
½ c. butter, melted

Filling:
11 oz. cream cheese, softened
¾ c. creamed cottage cheese
¾ c. sugar
3 eggs
1 tsp. vanilla

Glaze:
1 c. orange juice
2 tsp. cornstarch
¼ c. sugar
2 c. drained peach slices (canned or frozen)
Nutmeg

Combine oats, brown sugar and butter. Mix well and press into the bottom and about 1½ inches up the side of an ungreased 9 inch springform pan. Bake at 350°F. for 10 minutes. Cool.

For the filling, combine cream cheese and cottage cheese and beat at high speed of mixer for 7 minutes or until very smooth. Gradually add the sugar, beating constantly. Add eggs, one at a time, beating well after each addition. Mix in vanilla. Pour into the crust and bake at 350°F. for 35 to 40 minutes or until firm.

To prepare the glaze, combine orange juice, cornstarch, and sugar in a saucepan. Bring to a boil and cook until mixture is thick and clear. Cool to room temperature. Arrange sliced peaches on the cheesecake. Pour the cooked glaze over the peaches. Sprinkle lightly with nutmeg. Chill several hours before serving.

CINNAMON SPARKLED CHEESECAKE

3 cups coarse KEEBLER Cinnamon Crisp Cracker crumbs
½ cup butter or margarine, melted
1 carton (15 ounces) Ricotta cheese
1 package (8 ounces) cream cheese
4 eggs, lightly beaten
1 cup sugar
1 tablespoon vanilla extract
¼ teaspoon salt
2 tablespoons KEEBLER Cinnamon Crisp Cracker crumbs to sprinkle on top

In medium mixing bowl, combine crumbs and butter. Stir with a fork to blend. Press mixture over bottom and up sides of greased 9-inch spring form pan. In large mixing bowl, beat Ricotta and cream cheese together until smooth. Add eggs, sugar, vanilla and salt; beat until thick and smooth. Pour cheese mixture over crumbs in spring form pan. Bake in preheated 325°F oven 1 hour and 15 minutes or until knife inserted near center comes out clean. Cool 20 minutes in pan before removing sides. Cool completely and refrigerate until ready to serve.

One 9-inch Cheesecake

Serving Suggestion: Sprinkle top with KEEBLER Cinnamon Crisp Cracker crumbs.

SOUR CREAM CHEESECAKE

1½ cups zwieback crumbs
1 cup sugar, divided
6 tablespoons butter, melted
½ cup cream cheese
2 cups SEALTEST® Cottage Cheese
3 eggs, separated
2 tablespoons cornstarch
1 cup SEALTEST® Sour Cream
1½ teaspoons grated lemon peel
1 tablespoon lemon juice

Preheat oven to 325°. Mix zwieback crumbs, ¼ cup sugar, and butter. Press evenly on bottom and sides of greased 8-inch springform pan. Beat cream cheese and cottage cheese together with rotary beater until almost smooth. Add egg yolks and ¾ cup sugar; beat until blended. Add cornstarch, sour cream, lemon peel, and juice; mix well. Beat egg whites until stiff but not dry. Gently fold into cheese mixture. Pour into crumb-lined pan. Bake 1¼ hours or until set. Turn off heat. Partially prop open oven door and let cake cook 30 minutes before removing from oven.

BLENDER AVOCADO CHEESECAKE

1 California avocado, halved and peeled
8 oz. package cream cheese
½ cup sour cream
3-4 strips lemon peel
1 package instant vanilla pudding mix
Graham Cracker Crust*

Blend together avocado, cream cheese, sour cream and lemon peel in an electric blender till smooth. Add pudding mix and blend just until it's mixed in. Pour into the crust and chill several hours before serving.

*GRAHAM CRACKER CRUST

1¼ cups (about 15 crackers) graham cracker crumbs
2 tablespoons sugar
3 tablespoons butter or margarine, melted

Mix together crumbs, sugar and butter. Press mixture evenly in bottom of a 9″ springform pan. Bake at 350°F. for 7-10 minutes.

Favorite recipe from California Avocado Commission

GLAZED CHEESE CAKE

1 frozen SARA LEE Original Cream
   Cheese Cake (17 oz.)
¼ cup apricot preserves
6 walnut halves

Remove Cheese Cake from pan.
Spread apricot preserves over
frozen cheese cake; cut into 6
pieces. Place walnut half on each
piece. Thaw about 1 hour.
Makes 6 servings

VARIATION:

Stir 1 tablespoon brandy into
preserves, proceed as above.

HOLLYWOOD CHEESECAKE

Crust:
1 cup graham cracker crumbs
3 tablespoons sugar
3 tablespoons PARKAY Margarine,
   melted

Filling:
2 8-oz. pkgs. PHILADELPHIA
   BRAND Cream Cheese
½ cup sugar
1 tablespoon lemon juice
1 teaspoon grated lemon rind
½ teaspoon vanilla
2 eggs, separated

Topping:
1 cup dairy sour cream
2 tablespoons sugar
1 teaspoon vanilla

Heat oven to 325°. Combine
crumbs, sugar and margarine;
press onto bottom of 9-inch
springform pan. Bake at 325°, 10
minutes. Reduce oven temperature
to 300°.

Combine softened cream cheese,
sugar, lemon juice, rind and
vanilla, mixing at medium speed on
electric mixer until well blended.
Add egg yolks, one at a time,
mixing well after each addition.
Fold in stiffly beaten egg whites;
pour mixture over crust. Bake at
300°, 45 minutes.

Combine sour cream, sugar and
vanilla. Carefully spread over
cheesecake. Continue baking 10
minutes. Loosen cake from rim of
pan; cool before removing rim of
pan. Chill.

FATHER'S DAY DATE CHEESECAKE

¼ cup butter or margarine
1⅓ graham crackers, crushed
1 egg
2 Tbsp. honey
1 cup small curd cottage cheese
8 oz. pkg. cream cheese, softened
Grated peel and juice of one lemon
½ cup SUN WORLD® Dates, pitted
   and chopped

Topping:
1 cup sour cream
10 SUN WORLD® Pitted Dates,
   halved
6 SUN WORLD® Red Flame
   Seedless Grapes, halved

Melt the butter, add the cracker
crumbs and mix well. Turn into a
greased 8 inch springform pan and
press evenly over the bottom and
up about an inch on the sides. Mix
the egg, honey, cottage and cream
cheeses together, then add the
lemon juice and peel and the
chopped dates. Turn the mixture
onto the crumb crust and bake in a
moderate oven, 350°F, for 30
minutes. Turn the heat off, but
leave cake in the oven for another
30 minutes to prevent it from
sinking.

When cool, remove the tin and
place the cake on a serving dish.
Spread sour cream on the
cheesecake, then decorate with the
dates and grapes.

Frostings

BANANA BUTTER CREAM FROSTING

½ cup mashed CHIQUITA® Brand
   Banana
½ teaspoon lemon juice
⅛ teaspoon salt
¼ cup butter
3½ cups sifted confectioners'
   sugar

Cream butter with salt. Combine
banana and lemon juice. Add
alternately to butter with
confectioners' sugar. Beat until
fluffy.

BUTTER CREAM FROSTING

1 lb. DOMINO® Confectioners'
   10-X Sugar
¼ lb. (½ cup) soft butter or
   margarine
⅛ teaspoon salt
1 teaspoon vanilla extract
3 to 4 tablespoons milk

Cream one-third of sugar with
butter or margarine and salt in
large bowl. Blend extract, 2
tablespoons milk and remaining
sugar into mixture. Gradually stir
remaining milk into frosting until
desired spreading consistency is
reached.

*Yield: frosting for two
8" round layers*

CHOCOLATE FUDGE FROSTINGS

	1 Cup	2 Cups
Butter or margarine	3 Tbsp.	⅓ cup
HERSHEY'S® Cocoa		
Light flavor	2 Tbsp.	3 Tbsp.
Medium flavor	¼ cup	⅓ cup
Dark flavor	½ cup	⅔ cup
Confectioners' sugar	1⅓ cup	2⅔ cups
Milk	2-3 Tbsp.	⅓ cup
Vanilla	½ tsp.	1 tsp.

Melt butter in saucepan over
medium heat. Add amount of
cocoa for flavor you prefer. Heat
just until mixture begins to boil,
stirring constantly until smooth.
Pour into small mixer bowl. Cool
completely. Alternately add
confectioners' sugar and milk,
beating to spreading consistency.
Blend in vanilla.

CHOCOLATE "PHILLY" FROSTING

1 8-oz. pkg. PHILADELPHIA
   BRAND Cream Cheese
1 tablespoon milk
1 teaspoon vanilla
Dash of salt
5 cups sifted confectioners'
   sugar
3 1-oz. squares unsweetened
   chocolate, melted

Combine softened cream cheese,
milk, vanilla and salt, mixing until
well blended. Gradually add sugar,
mixing well after each addition.
Stir in chocolate.

*Fills and frosts two 8 or 9-inch
cake layers*

Pies and Pastries

GREEN APPLE PIE

6 tart green apples
⅔ cup sugar
⅛ teaspoon nutmeg
⅛ teaspoon salt
2 tablespoons dried currants
¼ teaspoon cinnamon
¼ teaspoon ginger
1 tablespoon corn flakes
1½ tablespoons butter
Never-Fail Pie Crust (recipe
    follows)

Peel, core and cut the apples into
thin slices. Combine and spread all
the dry ingredients over the apples,
and let stand 15 minutes. Place
this filling in the Never-Fail Pie
Crust. Dot with butter. Dampen
edge; put the top crust on; seal
and flute. Slash the top crust to let
out steam during baking. Bake in a
preheated oven at 450° for 10
minutes, then reduce heat to 350°
and bake for about 45 minutes.

NEVER-FAIL PIE CRUST

4-4¼ cups CERESOTA/HECKER'S
    Unbleached Flour, sifted
1 tablespoon sugar
3 teaspoons salt
1 egg
1 tablespoon vinegar
½ cup water
1¾ cups shortening

Sift the flour, sugar and salt into a
large bowl. Beat the egg and
combine with vinegar and water.
Cut the shortening into the flour,
sprinkle with the egg mixture, and
mix all together. Gather the dough
into a ball, wrap in wax paper and
chill for about 30 minutes before
using. This dough can be kept in
the refrigerator up to 1 week. Or,
you can divide it into 4 parts (1 pie

shell each), wrap each securely,
and freeze until ready to use.
Makes four 9" pie shells

To make the shell: Turn ¼ of the
dough on a floured board and roll
to fit a 9" pie pan. (Remember to
allow for the sides and leave a
little over besides.) Fold it in half,
gently lift into the pan, and with
your fingers fit it to the pan
without stretching it. Trim the edge
slightly larger than the outer rim of
the pan, and flute.

If the recipe calls for a baked shell:
Prick the bottom and sides of the
shell with a fork and bake for 12 to
15 minutes in a preheated 450°
oven, or until golden. Cool before
adding the filling.

Or a partially baked shell: Bake the
shell in a preheated 450° oven for
5 minutes; then cool.

*And if you want to prevent a soggy
bottom in a juicy pie:* Chill the
unbaked pie shell for 15 minutes
before making the filling; add the
filling just before baking. OR, bake
the bottom crust for 10 minutes in
a preheated 450° oven before
adding the filling.

DEEP-DISH APPLE PIE

2 (1-lb. 4-oz.) cans apple pie
    filling
2 Tbsp. grated orange rind
1 tsp. grated lemon rind
1 (10-oz.) pkg. PEPPERIDGE
    FARM® Frozen Patty Shells,
    thawed
1 egg yolk
1 Tbsp. water

Combine apple pie filling, orange
rind and grated lemon rind. Pour
into 1½-quart deep pie plate. Press
the patty shells together. Roll out
to make a circle ½ inch larger

than top of pie plate. Trim off a
½-inch margin and fit this onto
edge of pie crust on top of pastry
rim on dish. Press lightly to seal.
Trim off any surplus pastry. Crimp
edges. Brush top with egg yolk
mixed with water. Fashion shapes
from pastry trimmings and use to
decorate the crust. Brush the
trimmings with the egg yolk and
water mixture. Bake at 450° for 20
to 25 minutes.

CRANBERRY-APPLE PIE

Crust:
1½ cups flour
Dash of salt
½ cup shortening
1½ cups (6 ozs.) shredded
    CRACKER BARREL Brand
    Sharp Natural Cheddar Cheese
4 to 6 tablespoons water

Filling:
1½ cups sugar
3 tablespoons quick-cooking
    tapioca
½ teaspoon cinnamon
2 cups cranberries
⅓ cup water
6 cups peeled apple slices
1 tablespoon PARKAY Margarine

Combine flour and salt; cut in
shortening until mixture resembles
coarse crumbs. Stir in cheese.
Sprinkle with water while mixing
lightly with a fork; form into a ball.
Divide dough in half. Roll one part
to 11-inch circle on lightly floured
surface. Place in 9-inch pie plate.

Combine sugar, tapioca and
cinnamon. Stir in cranberries and
water. Cook, stirring constantly,
until mixture boils. Remove from
heat; stir in apples. Cool slightly.
Spoon into pastry shell; dot with
margarine. Roll out remaining
dough to 11-inch circle; place over
fruit mixture. Seal edges of crusts
and flute. Cut slits in top of pastry.
Bake at 400°, 45 to 50 minutes or
until apples are tender.

SWEDISH APPLE PIE

1 can (30 oz.) THANK YOU® Brand
  Apple Pie Filling
1 cup flour (all purpose OR whole
  wheat OR half of each)
⅔ cup sugar
1 tsp. baking powder
¼ tsp. salt
½ cup (1 stick) butter or margarine
1 egg, slightly beaten
½ cup chopped walnuts

Spread pie filling smoothly into
oiled pan(s). In mixing bowl, stir
together flour, sugar, baking
powder, and salt. Blend in softened
butter and egg, stirring to make a
thick batter. Drop batter from
spoon to cover pie filling. Sprinkle
with nuts. Bake at 350°F. for 45
minutes or until apples are bubbly
and topping is nicely browned.
Serve warm with dollop of whipped
topping or ice cream. Other canned
pie filling (cherry, blueberry) can be
substituted for apple.
*This can make 2 8-inch "pies"; 1
deep-dish 10-inch pie; or 1
9 × 9 × 2-inch dessert.*

APPLE PIE
(Low Calorie)

5 cups sliced apples (5 medium
  size)
2 teaspoons tapioca
2 teaspoons SWEET 'N LOW®
  (8 pkts.)
Cinnamon
2 recipes Dieter's Pie Crust
  (see below)

Roll ⅔ of pie crust recipe to fit an
8-inch or 9-inch pie pan. Arrange
apple slices in crust and sprinkle
tapioca, SWEET 'N LOW®, and a
little cinnamon over the top. Roll
out remaining pie crust, perforating
the top and arrange over apples.
Crimp edges securely, moistening
with a little water, if necessary.
Bake at 400 degrees for 30
minutes, or until apples are tender.

Total calories of pie 1360; ⅙ of pie
227 calories. (Prepared with sugar,
one serving 303 calories.)

DIETER'S PIE CRUST

⅓ cup sifted all-purpose flour
2 tablespoons shortening
⅛ teaspoon salt
½ cup cottage cheese

Use a cloth to squeeze cottage
cheese dry, then sieve. Discard
liquid. Cut shortening into dry
ingredients as for regular pie crust,
then add the cottage cheese,
mixing lightly with a fork until a
ball of dough is formed. Turn out
on very lightly floured pastry cloth
and roll to fit 8-inch or 9-inch pie
pan. For a baked pie shell, bake at
400 degrees for 20 minutes.

Total calories of crust 460. (Usual
recipe, for 9-inch single crust 657.)

HEARTLAND®

APPLE CREAM PIE
HEARTLAND® CRUMB CRUSTS

½ cup soft butter or margarine
¼ cup firmly packed brown sugar
1 cup all-purpose flour
1½ cups HEARTLAND® Natural
  Cereal, Plain Variety

Combine all ingredients with hand
until butter melts and ingredients
stick together to form a ball.
Spread half of mixture in each
9-inch pie plate. Bake in 400°F.
oven for 10 minutes. Remove from
oven. Immediately stir with spoon
to crumble. Press crumbs evenly
along sides and bottom of pie
plate with back of spoon. Return to
oven for 5 minutes more or until
lightly browned. Cool thoroughly
before filling.
Makes 2, 9-inch pie crusts

Note: The extra pie crust may be
  frozen until ready to use. Fill
  with a chiffon-type filling or
  a pudding.

APPLE CREAM FILLING

1 package (3¼ oz.) vanilla pudding
  and pie filling mix
2 cups milk
1 can (20 oz.) MUSSELMAN'S® Pie
  Sliced Apples, drained
1 teaspoon cinnamon
¼ cup HEARTLAND® Natural
  Cereal, Plain Variety

Combine mix and milk in
saucepan. Cook according to
package directions for pie filling.
Cool slightly. Add apples and
cinnamon. Pour into baked pie
crust. Sprinkle cereal over pie.
Refrigerate until set. Serve chilled.
Makes 1, 9-inch Apple Cream Pie

BANANA CREAM PIE

1 package pudding or pie filling
  mix (4 serving size)
Milk
1 baked 8-inch pastry shell
3 ripe CHIQUITA® Brand
  Bananas

Prepare your favorite mix
according to package directions
for pie filling; cool 5 to 10 minutes.
Fill pie shell with alternate layers
of filling and sliced bananas,
starting and ending with cream
mixture. Refrigerate. Garnish with
additional banana slices and
sweetened whipped cream.

VARIATIONS

Banana Tarts—Fill tart shells with
cooled filling. Place diagonal
banana slices on top. Top with
whipped cream.

Glazed Tarts—Divide cooled filling
among 6 baked tart shells. Top
each with a layer of sliced
bananas. Complete by spooning
melted apricot preserves over the
bananas.

BANANA CHOCOLATE
PIE

1¼ cups crushed KEEBLER Honey
  Grahams
½ cup KEEBLER Chocolate Fudge
  Sandwich Cookies
1 package (3⅝ oz.) Chocolate
  Pudding and Pie Filling Mix
1 package (3⅛ oz.) Vanilla Pudding
  and Pie Filling Mix
1½ teaspoon gelatin (to be added
  to each filling)
1 large banana

Crush Honey Grahams and
Chocolate Fudge Sandwich
Cookies to a fine consistency. In a
medium mixing bowl combine
crumbs and melted butter. Stir with
a fork. Press in bottom and up
sides of a 9-inch pie pan. Combine
gelatin with dry pudding mix.
Prepare pudding according to
package directions. Cool to room
temperature. Place one layer of
sliced bananas on bottom of pie
crust. Pour chocolate filling over
bananas. Next, pour the vanilla
filling over the chocolate. Top with
remaining bananas just before
serving. Refrigerate until ready to
serve.

HIRAM WALKER CREME DE BANANA/CHOCOLATE CHERRY CORDIAL PIE

½ cup cold water
1 envelope unflavored gelatin
⅔ cup sugar
⅛ teaspoon salt
3 eggs, separated
½ cup HIRAM WALKER Creme de Banana
2 oz. HIRAM WALKER Chocolate Cherry
1 cup Whipping Cream

Put water in saucepan. Sprinkle gelatin over it. Add ⅓ cup sugar, salt and egg yolks. Stir to blend. Place over low heat. Stir until gelatin dissolves and mixture thickens. Do not boil. Remove from heat and stir in the Creme de Banana and Chocolate Cherry. Chill until mixture starts to thicken. Beat egg whites until stiff. Add remaining ⅓ cup sugar and beat until peaks are firm. Fold meringue into mixture. Whip cream. Fold into mixture. Add food coloring, if desired. Turn mixture into chocolate wafer or graham cracker crust. Chill several hours or overnight. Just before serving, garnish with freshly sliced bananas.

GLAZED APRICOT CHEESE PIE

1 can (17 ounces) apricot halves
1 baked 9-inch pie shell or graham cracker crumb crust, cooled
1 package (8 oz.) cream cheese, softened
2 cups *cold* milk
1 package (6-serving size) JELL-O® Brand Vanilla Flavor Instant Pudding & Pie Filling
3 maraschino cherry halves
2 tablespoons corn syrup

Drain apricots, reserving ⅓ cup of the syrup. Set aside 6 apricot halves for garnish. Arrange remaining apricots in pie shell. Beat cream cheese until soft. Gradually add 1 cup of the milk and blend until smooth. Add remaining milk, measured syrup and pie filling mix. Beat at low speed of electric mixer until blended, about 1 minute. Pour at

once into pie shell over apricots. Chill 5 minutes. Meanwhile, cut reserved apricots into thirds and arrange on pie filling to resemble 3 flowers, with half cherry in center of each. Brush fruit with corn syrup. Chill at least 3 hours.

Favorite recipe from California Apricot Advisory Board

SOLO® APRICOT PARFAIT PIE

Crust:
½ C. butter or margarine
2 Tbsp. sugar
1 C. flour

Filling:
⅔ C. sugar
½ C. water
1 egg white, unbeaten
1½ tsp. vanilla extract
1 tsp. lemon juice
1 can (12 oz.) SOLO® Apricot Filling
1 C. whipping cream, whipped

Crust: Combine butter and sugar. Add flour and mix just until dough forms. Press mixture evenly over bottom and sides of 9″ pie pan. Bake at 375° for 12-15 minutes, or until light golden brown. Cool.

Filling: In small bowl of electric mixer, combine sugar, water, egg white, vanilla and lemon juice. Beat at high speed with mixer until soft peaks form, about 3-5 minutes. Fold whipped cream and SOLO® Apricot Filling into egg white mixture. Spoon into baked pie shell. Freeze until firm. Wrap well and store in freezer.

SUNRISE CHERRY PIE

Crust:
1 cup crushed graham crackers
¼ cup butter
¼ cup sugar

Blend together crushed crackers, sugar and butter. Line 9″ pie pan. Bake at 375° for 8 minutes. Cool.

Filling:
1 8-oz. pkg. cream cheese, softened
½ teaspoon vanilla
1 21-oz. cherry pie filling
1 20-oz. can crushed pineapple, well drained
1 cup heavy cream
¼ cup confectioners' sugar

Combine cheese, vanilla and 2 tablespoons pie filling, mixing until

well blended. Stir in ¼ cup well drained pineapple and ½ cup pie filling. Beat cream and gradually add sugar until soft peaks form. Fold into cream cheese mixture. Pour into crust. Top with remaining pineapple and pie filling. Chill until firm.

Favorite recipe from Western New York Cherry Growers Association

WHOLE GRAIN CHERRY CRISP

1 can (21-oz. or 30-oz.) THANK YOU® Brand Cherry Pie Filling
½ cup whole wheat flour
½ cup old-fashioned rolled oats
2 Tablespoons toasted wheat germ
2 Tablespoons miller's bran (optional)
¼ cup sugar
⅓ cup margarine

Pour pie filling into a 9-inch round pan. Combine remaining ingredients in food processor or by hand until mixture is crumbly. Pat topping evenly and lightly over cherries. Bake in conventional oven at 350°F. for 34-40 minutes or place microwave on High power 8 minutes, rotating once after 4 minutes. Serve warm or cold just plain or with vanilla ice cream or whipped topping.
Makes 6 generous servings

VARIATION:

Blueberry or Apple Pie Filling can be substituted for cherries in this recipe.

LIGHT 'N FRUITY PIE

1 package (3 oz.) JELL-O® Brand Gelatin, any flavor
⅔ cup boiling water
2 cups ice cubes
1 container (8 oz.) BIRDS EYE® COOL WHIP® Non-Dairy Whipped Topping, thawed
1 baked 9-inch graham cracker crumb crust, cooled

Dissolve gelatin completely in boiling water, stirring 3 minutes. Add ice cubes and stir constantly until gelatin is thickened, about 2 to 3 minutes. Remove any unmelted ice. Using wire whip, blend in whipped topping; then whip until smooth. Chill, if necessary, until mixture will mound. Spoon into pie crust. Chill 2 hours or freeze until firm.

"BEAU CATCHING" LEMON MERINGUE PIE

1½ cups sugar
¼ cup plus *2 teaspoons* cornstarch
¼ teaspoon salt
½ cup plus 1 tablespoon fresh squeezed SUNKIST® Lemon juice
½ cup cold water
5 egg yolks, well beaten
2 tablespoons butter or margarine
1¼ cups boiling water
1 to 3 teaspoons fresh grated SUNKIST® Lemon peel
Few drops yellow food coloring
1 baked 9 inch pastry shell*

Meringue:
5 egg whites
½ teaspoon cream of tartar
½ cup plus 2 tablespoons sugar

Filling Directions: In a 2 to 3 quart saucepan mix sugar, cornstarch and salt together, using a wire whisk. Still using whisk, gradually blend in cold water, then SUNKIST® Lemon juice until smooth. Add beaten egg yolks, blending very thoroughly. Add butter or margarine. Add boiling water gradually, stirring constantly with rubber spatula. Gradually bring mixture to full boil, stirring gently and constantly with spatula over medium to high heat. Reduce heat slightly as mixture begins to thicken. Boil slowly for *1 minute.* Remove from heat and stir in grated peel and food coloring. Pour hot filling into baked pastry shell. Let stand, allowing a thin film to form while preparing meringue.

Meringue Directions: Have egg whites at room temperature. Use a small, deep bowl when beating 4 egg whites or less. Beat with electric mixer several seconds until frothy (some fairly large air cells still remain). Add cream of tartar. Beat on high speed until whites have just lost their foamy appearance and bend over slightly when beaters are withdrawn, forming "soft peaks." Reduce speed to medium while adding sugar gradually, about a tablespoon at a time. Return to high speed and beat until whites are fairly stiff but still glossy and *soft peaks* are again formed when beaters are withdrawn.

Place meringue on the hot filling in several mounds around edge of pie. Using narrow spatula, push meringue gently against inner edge of pie crust, sealing well. Cover the rest of the filling by swirling meringue from edge of pie to center, forming decorative peaks with spatula. Bake at 350°F. for 12-15 minutes, until golden brown. Cool on wire rack at room temperature away from drafts for 2 hours before cutting and serving. Use sharp knife and dip into hot water after each cut for a perfect "clean cut" serving.   *9 inch pie*

*Use your favorite pastry recipe or mix. Remember "store bought" frozen pie shells hold less pie filling.

LEMON SPONGE PIE

1 can LUCKY LEAF® Lemon Pie Filling
¾ cup milk
2 Tbsp. melted butter
2 egg yolks, beaten
2 egg whites
¼ cup sugar
Graham cracker crumbs
1 9″ unbaked pastry shell

Mix pie filling, milk, butter and beaten egg yolks. Beat egg whites, gradually add sugar and beat until stiff but not dry. Fold into pie filling mixture. Pour into 9″ unbaked pastry shell. Cover with graham cracker crumbs. Bake at 350° for 30-35 minutes.

TANGY BUTTERSCOTCH LEMON PIE

1 cup boiling water
1 3-oz. pkg. lemon flavor gelatin
¼ measuring teaspoon salt
3 eggs
1 6-oz. pkg. (1 cup) NESTLÉ Butterscotch Morsels
1 9″ prepared graham cracker pie shell
Whipped cream

In small bowl, combine boiling water, gelatin and salt; stir until gelatin is dissolved; set aside. In blender container, process eggs at medium speed for 2 minutes. Add NESTLÉ Butterscotch Morsels and lemon gelatin mixture; blend until smooth. Set aside about 5 minutes; pour into prepared pie shell. Chill about 2 hours or until firm. Garnish with whipped cream.

Makes one 9″ pie

FRESH LEMON MERINGUE PIE

1½ cups sugar
¼ cup plus 2 Tbsp. cornstarch
¼ tsp. salt
½ cup cold water
½ cup fresh squeezed SUNKIST® Lemon juice
3 egg yolks, well beaten
2 Tbsp. butter or margarine
1½ cups boiling water
1 tsp. fresh grated SUNKIST® Lemon peel
Few drops yellow food coloring (optional)
1 (9-inch) baked pie shell
Meringue (recipe follows)

In saucepan, thoroughly combine sugar, cornstarch and salt. Gradually stir in cold water and lemon juice. Blend in egg yolks. Add butter and boiling water. Bring to boil over medium-high heat, stirring constantly. Reduce heat to medium and boil *1 minute.* Remove from heat; stir in lemon peel and food coloring. Pour into pie shell. Top with meringue, sealing well at edges. Bake at 350 degrees F. for 12 to 15 minutes. Cool 2 hours before serving.

Makes 6 to 8 servings

MERINGUE

3 egg whites
¼ tsp. cream of tartar
6 Tbsp. sugar

Beat egg whites until foamy; add cream of tartar and continue beating to soft peak stage. Gradually add sugar, beating until egg whites are stiff, but not dry.

VARIATION:

For higher meringue use 4 egg whites, ¼ teaspoon cream of tartar and ½ cup sugar. Follow Meringue directions.

FOOLPROOF MERINGUE

3 egg whites
Dash of salt
1 cup (one-half 7-oz. jar) KRAFT Marshmallow Creme

Beat egg whites and salt until soft peaks form. Gradually add marshmallow creme, beating until stiff peaks form. Spread over pie filling, sealing to edge of crust. Bake at 350°, 12 to 15 minutes or until lightly browned. Cool.

GRAPEFRUIT CHIFFON PIE

1 envelope unflavored gelatine
1 cup fresh squeezed SUNKIST® Grapefruit juice
4 eggs, separated
¾ cup sugar
¼ teaspoon salt
1 tablespoon fresh grated SUNKIST® Grapefruit peel
1 cup whipping cream, whipped
Toasted Coconut Pie Shell (recipe follows)

Soften gelatine in grapefruit juice. In top of double boiler, with electric mixer or rotary beater, beat egg yolks well with ½ cup sugar and salt. Gradually beat in gelatine mixture. Cook over boiling water until mixture *starts* to thicken (about 7 minutes), stirring constantly. Add grapefruit peel. Chill until mixture begins to thicken (about 1 hour), stirring occasionally. Beat egg whites until foamy; gradually add remaining ¼ cup sugar, beating until soft peaks form. Fold beaten egg whites and whipped cream into grapefruit-gelatine mixture. Spoon into Toasted Coconut Pie Shell. Chill 2 hours or until firm. Garnish with grapefruit sections if desired.
Makes 8 servings

TOASTED COCONUT PIE SHELL

2 cups flaked or shredded coconut, toasted
¼ cup firmly packed brown sugar
6 tablespoons butter or margarine, melted
1 tablespoon fresh grated grapefruit peel

Combine all ingredients. Press firmly into 9-inch pie plate; chill.

COOKIE CRUST FRUIT PIE

Cookie Crust Pastry (recipe follows)
½ cup sugar
3 tablespoons ARGO® / KINGSFORD'S® Corn Starch
1½ cups apple juice
1 teaspoon grated lemon rind
¼ cup lemon juice
6 cups assorted sliced or cut-up fresh fruit such as apples, pears, strawberries, grapes, bananas, drained orange sections

In saucepan mix sugar and corn starch. Gradually stir in apple juice until smooth. Bring to boil over medium heat, stirring constantly, and boil 1 minute. Remove from heat; stir in lemon juice and rind. Cool completely. Gently fold into fruit. Turn into baked pastry shell; chill 4 hours or until set.

COOKIE CRUST PASTRY

Stir ¼ cup margarine to soften; mix in ¼ cup sugar and 1 egg yolk. With pastry blender gradually mix in 1 cup flour until crumbs form. Press firmly into bottom and sides of 9-inch pie plate. Bake in 400°F. oven about 10 minutes or until edge is browned. Cool.

LUSCIOUS PEACH PIE

1 9" unbaked pie shell
Crumb topping (recipe follows)
¾ cup sugar
1 tablespoon cornstarch
2 tablespoons MINUTE® Tapioca
¼ teaspoon salt
1 quart fresh peeled, sliced peaches
¼ cup TAYLOR New York State Lake Country White
¼ teaspoon grated nutmeg

Combine sugar, cornstarch, tapioca and salt. Mix thoroughly with peaches and Lake Country White. Spoon peach mixture into prepared pie shell; sprinkle with nutmeg. Cover with crumb topping. Bake in a preheated 425°F. oven, lowest rack position, 40 to 50 minutes, or until bubbly and lightly browned.

CRUMB TOPPING

⅓ cup firmly packed light brown sugar
¼ cup all purpose flour
½ teaspoon cinnamon
3 tablespoons slightly softened butter

Combine brown sugar, flour and cinnamon. Blend in butter with pastry blender, fork or fingers until mixture is crumbly.

FROZEN PEACH MELBA PIE

1 lb. ripe fresh peaches, pitted, peeled, sliced
¾ cup KARO® Light Corn Syrup
1 Tbsp. lemon juice
2 drops red food color (optional)
1 pint raspberry sherbet, softened
2 drops yellow food color (optional)
1 cup vanilla ice cream, softened
1 (9") graham cracker crust

Place peaches, corn syrup and lemon juice in blender container; cover. Blend 30 seconds or until pureed. Fold 1 cup of the pureed peaches and red food color into raspberry sherbet. Pour into crust. Freeze 1 hour or until firm. Fold remaining 1 cup pureed peaches and yellow food color into vanilla ice cream. Pour over raspberry layer. Cover; freeze until firm. If desired, garnish with peach slices.
Makes 8 servings

EASY PLUM CREAM PIE

1 pkg. (8 oz.) cream cheese, slightly softened
½ cup KARO® Light Corn Syrup
1 cup cold milk
1 pkg. (3¾ oz.) instant vanilla pudding mix
1 (9") ready-made graham cracker crust
1 cup pitted, sliced ripe fresh plums
¼ cup red currant jelly, melted

With mixer at high speed beat cream cheese until smooth. Gradually beat in corn syrup until light and fluffy; set aside. With mixer at the lowest speed beat milk and pudding mix 2 minutes; fold in cheese mixture. Immediately spoon into crust. Refrigerate 2 hours or until set. Arrange plums on top of pie. Brush fruit with jelly.
Makes 6 servings

COCONUT PEAR TART SUPREME

1 fully baked 8″ or 9″ pie shell
1 container (15 ozs.) whole milk Ricotta cheese
¾ cup COCO CASA™ Cream of Coconut
1 Tbsp. candied fruit
1 Tbsp. mini chocolate bits
6 to 8 pear halves, stewed or canned
Apricot glaze, warmed
Garnish: bitter chocolate curls or rounds

Whip Ricotta cheese until smooth and glossy. Add cream of coconut and mix well. Fold in candied fruit and chocolate bits. Refrigerate for 3 hours or overnight. Spread Ricotta filling evenly into pie shell. Place drained pears in an attractive pattern over filling and brush with apricot glaze. Decorate with curls or rounds of chocolate.

PEAR CRUNCH PIE

¼ cup sugar
2 Tablespoons cornstarch
⅛ teaspoon salt
⅛ teaspoon nutmeg
1 can (1 lb. 13 oz.) STOKELY'S FINEST® Pear Halves
1 Tablespoon lemon juice
1 Tablespoon butter
1 9-inch pie shell, unbaked

Topping:
1 cup oatmeal
⅓ cup brown sugar
⅓ cup butter or margarine, melted
⅓ cup chopped pecans
¼ teaspoon nutmeg
¼ teaspoon cinnamon

In saucepan, combine first 4 ingredients. Drain Pears, reserving liquid. Add water to reserved liquid to make 1½ cups; stir liquid into saucepan. Cook over medium heat, stirring constantly until mixture is thick and clear. Remove from heat and stir in lemon juice and butter. Slice Pears and arrange in unbaked pie shell. Pour sauce mixture over Pears.

Combine topping ingredients and sprinkle over pie. Bake at 425°F. for 20 minutes.

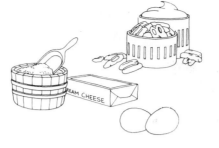

MYSTERY PECAN PIE

Pastry for 9-inch one crust pie
8-oz. pkg. cream cheese, softened
⅓ cup sugar
¼ teaspoon salt
1 teaspoon vanilla
1 egg
1¼ cups chopped pecans

Topping:
3 eggs
¼ cup sugar
1 cup light or dark corn syrup
1 teaspoon vanilla

Heat oven to 375°F. Prepare pastry. In small bowl, combine cream cheese, ⅓ cup sugar, salt, 1 teaspoon vanilla and 1 egg; beat at medium speed until well blended. Spread in bottom of pastry-lined pan. Sprinkle with pecans. In small bowl, combine all topping ingredients; beat on medium speed just until blended. Gently pour topping over pecans. Bake at 375°F. for 35 to 40 minutes or until center is firm to touch. Refrigerate leftovers.

8 servings

PILLSBURY BAKE-OFF® recipe

PASTRY SHELL

1 cup PILLSBURY All Purpose Flour
½ teaspoon salt
¼ cup cooking oil
3 tablespoons hot water

In large mixing bowl, combine flour with salt. In measuring cup, combine oil and water; beat rapidly with fork until combined. Pour over flour all at one time. Toss lightly with fork just until blended. Form into a ball. Roll out on floured surface to a circle 1-inch larger than inverted 8 or 9-inch pie pan. Fit loosely into pan. Flute or trim edge. Pour in filling and bake as directed in recipe.

THE DEVIL'S TEMPTING PECAN PIE

Dough for single-crusted pie pastry
4 eggs
1 lb. DOMINO® Light Brown Sugar
Pecan halves
¾ cup water
¼ cup soft butter or margarine
1 teaspoon vanilla extract

Line 9″ oven-proof glass pie plate with pastry. Beat eggs in small mixing bowl until frothy; set aside. Combine sugar and water in 2-qt. thick saucepan. Place over moderate heat, stirring until sugar dissolves. Bring to a full boil and cook for 3 minutes. Gradually stir hot syrup into eggs. Blend butter and extract into mixture. Turn filling into pastry-lined plate. Arrange pecans on filling in desired pattern. Bake in moderate oven 350°F. about 1 hour or until set. Remove to cooling rack.

Yield: one 9″ pie

Walnut Pie: Substitute walnut halves for pecans.

Toasted Almond Pie: Substitute toasted almond halves for pecans.

DELUXE PECAN PIE

3 eggs
1 cup KARO® Light or Dark Corn Syrup
1 cup sugar
2 tablespoons NUCOA® or MAZOLA® Margarine, melted
1 teaspoon vanilla
⅛ teaspoon salt
1 cup pecans
1 unbaked (9-inch) pastry shell

In medium bowl with mixer at medium speed beat eggs slightly. Beat in corn syrup, sugar, margarine, vanilla and salt. Stir in pecans. Pour filling into pastry shell. Bake in 350°F. oven 55 to 65 minutes or until knife inserted halfway between center and edge comes out clean. Cool. If desired, serve with whipped cream.

Makes 1 (9-inch) pie

SOUTHERN PECAN PIE

1 (9-inch) unbaked pastry shell
3 eggs
1 cup firmly-packed COLONIAL®
  Light Golden Brown Sugar
1 cup broken pecans
½ cup light corn syrup
1 teaspoon vinegar
½ teaspoon vanilla extract
¼ teaspoon salt
Whipped cream, optional

Preheat oven to 450°. In medium bowl, beat eggs. Stir in sugar, pecans, corn syrup, vinegar, vanilla and salt; mix well. Pour into pastry shell. Bake 10 minutes. Reduce oven temperature to 325°; continue baking 35 to 40 minutes. Cool. If desired, garnish with whipped cream.   *Makes one 9-inch pie*

PILGRIM PUMPKIN PIE

2 eggs, slightly beaten
1 16-oz. can of pumpkin or 2
  cups of cooked, mashed
  pumpkin
¾ cup SUE BEE® Honey
½ teaspoon salt
1 teaspoon cinnamon
½ teaspoon ginger
⅛ teaspoon cloves
1⅔ cups (1 13-oz. can) evaporated
  or whole milk or light cream
1 9-inch unbaked pastry shell

Prepare single pastry for 9-inch pie pan. In a bowl, beat eggs slightly, and then mix in the remaining ingredients. Pour into pastry-lined pie pan, and bake at 425° for 15 minutes. Reduce oven temperature to 350°, and bake 45 minutes longer or until pie is set or silver knife inserted in center comes out clean. Top with Honey Ginger Cream (recipe follows).

HONEY GINGER CREAM

Whip 2 cups whipping cream until stiff. Gradually add ¼ cup SUE BEE® Honey and ½ teaspoon ginger. Chill one or two hours before serving.

Makes 4 cups of topping

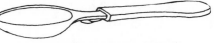

LIBBY'S FAMOUS PUMPKIN PIE

2 eggs, slightly beaten
1 can (16-oz.) LIBBY'S Solid Pack
  Pumpkin
¾ cup sugar
½ teaspoon salt
1 teaspoon cinnamon
½ teaspoon ginger
¼ teaspoon cloves
1⅔ cups (13 fl. oz.) evaporated
  milk or light cream
1 9-inch unbaked pie shell with
  high fluted edge
Crunchy Pecan Topping (recipe
  follows)

Preheat oven to 425°. Mix filling ingredients in order given. Pour into pie shell. Bake at 425° for 15 minutes. Reduce heat to 350° and continue baking for 45 minutes or until knife inserted near center of pie filling comes out clean. Cool completely on wire rack. Before serving, add Crunchy Pecan Topping as follows.

CRUNCHY PECAN TOPPING

1 cup coarsely chopped pecans
⅔ cup firmly packed light brown
  sugar
3 tablespoons butter or margarine,
  melted
Whipped cream or dessert topping
  and pecan halves, for garnish

Mix pecans and brown sugar in a small bowl. Drizzle with butter; stir until mixture is uniformly moistened. Sprinkle mixture over cooled pumpkin pie. Broil about 5 inches from heat for 1 to 2 minutes or until topping is bubbly. Serve while warm. Or let cool, then garnish with whipped cream or topping and extra pecan halves, if desired.

FAVORITE PUMPKIN PIE

Mix together 3 slightly beaten eggs, ¾ cup sugar, 2 to 3 teaspoons FRENCH'S® Pumpkin Pie Spice, ½ teaspoon salt, 1½ cups cooked or canned pumpkin, and 1 cup milk. Pour into 9-inch unbaked pie shell. Bake in 400°F. oven 45 to 50 minutes or until set.

CARNATION® PUMPKIN PIE

2 slightly beaten eggs
1½ cups canned pumpkin
1 cup sugar
½ teaspoon salt
1 teaspoon cinnamon
¼ teaspoon ginger
¼ teaspoon cloves
¼ teaspoon nutmeg
1⅔ cups *undiluted* CARNATION®
  Evaporated Milk
9-inch single-crust unbaked pie
  shell

Combine eggs, pumpkin, sugar, salt, and spices. Gradually add evaporated milk. Mix well. Pour into unbaked pie shell. Bake in hot oven (425°F.) 15 minutes; reduce to moderate oven (375°F.) and continue baking about 40 minutes, or until knife inserted near center of pie comes out clean. Cool before serving. Garnish, if desired.

Makes 9-inch pie

PUMPKIN PIE

1 9-inch unbaked pastry shell
1 cup brown sugar
2 tablespoons flour
½ teaspoon salt
¼ teaspoon cinnamon
¼ teaspoon nutmeg
1 cup cooked pumpkin
2 cups MILNOT®
2 eggs beaten
½ cup nut meats (optional)

Mix sugar, flour, salt and spices together and stir into pumpkin. Add MILNOT® and eggs. (Add nuts at this point, if used.) Pour into pie shell and bake at 450 degrees for 10 minutes; reduce heat to 350 degrees and continue baking for another 25 to 30 minutes, or until filling is firm (when knife inserted in pie comes out clean). Garnish with whipped MILNOT® Topping.

Whipping hints: To whip MILNOT® use clean, dry utensils. MILNOT® cannot be over-whipped. MILNOT® expands at least four times in volume when whipped.

NO-BAKE PUMPKIN PIE

1 can THANK YOU® Brand Egg
  Custard
1 cup canned pumpkin
⅓ cup sugar
1 tsp. nutmeg
¼ tsp. cloves
1 baked 9-inch pie shell, cooled

"Melt" Egg Custard according to
directions on label. Blend in
pumpkin, sugar, and spices. Pour
into pie shell. Chill 3 hours or until
set. Garnish with pecans and/or
whipped cream.

BEST-EVER RAISIN SOUR CREAM PIE

¾ cup sugar
2 tablespoons cornstarch
¼ teaspoon salt
2 eggs, beaten
2 cups sour cream
1 cup raisins
2 tablespoons lemon juice
1 *baked* 9-inch pie shell or
  crumb crust

In top of double boiler, blend
together sugar, cornstarch and
salt. Combine with beaten eggs,
1½ cups sour cream, raisins and
lemon juice. Cook and stir over hot
water until thick. Pour into baked
pie shell. When cool top with
remaining ½ cup sour cream. Chill
several hours.

*Favorite recipe from California Raisin
Advisory Board*

ALL AMERICAN RAISIN PIE

¾ cup sugar
2 tablespoons cornstarch
¼ teaspoon nutmeg
½ teaspoon cinnamon
Dash salt
2 cups cranberry apple juice
2 cups raisins
½ teaspoon almond extract
Pastry for 2 crust 9-inch pie

In large saucepan, combine sugar,
cornstarch, nutmeg, cinnamon and
salt. Blend in cranberry apple juice.
Add raisins and cook over low
heat, stirring constantly, until thick
and clear. Add almond extract.
Cool slightly. Pour mixture into
pastry-lined pie pan and cover with
top crust. Bake in preheated 450
degree oven for 10 minutes; reduce

heat to 350 degrees and continue
to bake 20 minutes longer, or until
pastry is golden brown.

*Favorite recipe from California Raisin
Advisory Board*

FRESH BERRY PIE

2½ tablespoons ARGO® /
  KINGSFORD'S® Corn Starch
1 cup sugar
4 cups fresh blueberries or
  strawberries, cut in half
Double crust pastry for 9-inch pie

Mix corn starch and sugar; toss
with berries. Turn into pastry lined
pie plate. Cut several slits in top
crust to permit escape of steam.
Cover pie with pastry; seal and
flute edge. Bake in 425°F. oven 35
to 45 minutes or until browned.

Makes 1 (9-inch) pie

MRS. KNOTT'S BOYSENBERRY PIE

7½ ounces water
6½ ounces sugar
Dash of salt
1 tablespoon corn syrup
1 teaspoon lemon juice
3 tablespoons cornstarch
2 ounces water
1 16-ounce bag KNOTT'S BERRY
  FARM™ Frozen Boysenberries
  (do not thaw)
2 crust pie shell

In a saucepan, combine water,
sugar, salt, corn syrup and lemon
juice and bring to a boil. Combine
cornstarch and water and blend
thoroughly. Add to saucepan and
mix well. Heat thoroughly. Add
frozen boysenberries. Pour into
unbaked 9-inch pie crust. Cover
with second top crust and seal
well around the edges. Make
several slashes in the top to
release steam. Bake in a preheated
400°F. oven for 40 minutes or until
top is golden brown. Cool on a
rack.

FRESH STRAWBERRY PIE

8 oz. CONTINENTAL Strawberry
  Glaze
1½ pints fresh Strawberries
1 9 inch pre-baked pie shell
Whipped topping

Wash berries, remove stems and
drain well. Pour glaze over berries
in mixing bowl and tumble gently
until berries are coated. Pour
glazed berries into pie shell and
smooth out to the edges.
Refrigerate one hour before serving
and decorate with whipped topping
before slicing.

FRESH STRAWBERRY YOGURT PIE

2 cups DANNON® Strawberry
  Yogurt
½ cup crushed strawberries
1 container (8 oz. or 9 oz.) thawed
  BIRDS EYE® COOL WHIP®
  Non-Dairy Whipped Topping
1 graham cracker pie crust

Thoroughly combine crushed fruit
and yogurt in bowl. Fold in COOL
WHIP®, blending well. Spoon into
crust and freeze about 4 hours.
Remove from freezer and place in
refrigerator 30 minutes (or longer
for softer texture) before serving.
Store any leftover pie in freezer.

STRAWBERRIES AND CREAM PIE

1 can THANK YOU® Brand
  Vanilla Pudding
1 (3 oz.) package Strawberry
  Gelatin
1 package Whipped Topping mix
  or 2 cups prepared topping mix
1 pint of fresh Strawberries
1 baked Pie Shell

Dissolve gelatin in 1 cup boiling
water. Combine gelatin and vanilla
pudding, mixing thoroughly. Chill
until slightly thickened. Whip
topping mix as directed on
package. Slice 1 heaping cup of
strawberries; fold berries and
topping into gelatin mixture;
reserve some topping for
decorating top. Spread in pie shell
and chill until set. Decorate with
whipped topping and remaining
strawberries.

STRAWBERRY BLACK BOTTOM PIE

⅔ cup half and half
1 package (6 ounces) semi-sweet chocolate morsels
3 eggs, separated
1 baked 9-inch pie shell
2 pints fresh California strawberries, washed and stemmed
2 teaspoons lemon juice
¼ cup sugar
1 package unflavored gelatin
¼ cup cold water

Heat half and half in saucepan over medium heat. Stir in chocolate morsels; beat smooth with wire whisk. Remove from heat; whisk in egg yolks one at a time, mixing until well blended. Return to heat. Cook, stirring, 1 to 2 minutes longer. Cool; pour into pie shell. Chill until set, 2 to 3 hours. Puree 1 pint of the berries with lemon juice (there should be about 1⅔ cups puree). Soften gelatin in water; warm over low heat to dissolve, then stir into berry puree. Chill until mixture begins to set. Meanwhile, beat egg whites, gradually adding sugar, until soft peaks form. Fold in thickened berry mixture. Pour over chocolate layer; chill until set. To serve, slice remaining pint berries; sweeten if desired. Spoon over wedges of pie.

Makes 6 to 8 servings

Favorite recipe from California Strawberry Advisory Board

WELCH'S® STRAWBERRY ANGEL PIE

4 egg whites
¼ teaspoon cream of tartar
1 cup granulated sugar
½ cup finely chopped almonds

2 cups heavy cream
1 tablespoon lemon juice
1 cup WELCH'S® Strawberry Preserves
Sliced almonds or candied violets

Beat egg whites and cream of tartar until foamy. Gradually beat in sugar and continue beating until meringue forms stiff, glossy peaks. Fold in chopped almonds. Spread over bottom and sides of a greased 9-inch pie plate; use a spatula or

back of spoon to spread meringue to about ¼-inch thickness on bottom and 1-inch on sides. Bake at 275°F. for 1 hour. Turn off oven; leave meringue in oven until cool.

Whip heavy cream to soft peaks. Fold in lemon juice and strawberry preserves. Spoon into cooled meringue shell. Chill or freeze overnight. Garnish with almonds or violets.

Makes 8 servings

Mrs. Paul's
SWEET POTATO PIE

1 package (20 ounces) MRS. PAUL'S® Candied Sweet Potatoes, partially thawed and diced
1 10-inch pie crust, unbaked
¼ cup butter
½ cup sugar
3 eggs
Dash of salt
¼ teaspoon ground cloves
¼ teaspoon ginger
¼ teaspoon nutmeg
½ teaspoon cinnamon
1 cup milk

Preheat oven to 350°F. In a large bowl cream butter and sugar. Gradually add diced sweet potatoes and blend until smooth. Add eggs, spices and milk to mixture, mixing well. Pour into unbaked pie crust. Bake for approximately 1-1¼ hours or until knife inserted halfway between center and edge comes out clean.

Makes one 10-inch pie

VARIATION:

Sweet Potato-Pecan Pie: Sprinkle Pecan Topping* on top of pie during last 10 minutes of baking time.

*PECAN TOPPING

2 tablespoons butter, melted
⅓ cup brown sugar, firmly packed
1 cup chopped pecans

Combine ingredients until crumbly.

CALIFORNIA WALNUT PIE

Pie Crust for 9-inch pan:
1½ cups sifted all-purpose flour
½ teaspoon salt
½ cup shortening
4 tablespoons cold milk or water

Resift flour with salt into mixing bowl. Cut in shortening with pastry blender or 2 knives until size of large peas. Sprinkle milk or water, a tablespoon at a time, over dry ingredients, and gently toss with a fork. Mix lightly until all flour is moistened. If necessary, add 1 or 2 teaspoons extra liquid. Gather dough together and gently shape into a ball. Roll out on floured cloth covered board to 10-inch circle. Roll from center to outside evenly in all directions and lift rolling pin at edge of dough to keep edges from becoming too thin. Fold dough in half and lift into pie pan. Unfold and ease dough gently into place to fit pan. Build up a shallow fluted edge.

Walnut Filling:
½ cup brown sugar, packed
2 tablespoons all-purpose flour
1¼ cups light corn syrup
3 tablespoons butter
¼ teaspoon salt
3 eggs
1½ teaspoons vanilla
1 cup halves and large pieces DIAMOND® Walnuts

Mix brown sugar and flour in saucepan. Add corn syrup, butter and salt, and warm over low heat just until butter is melted. In large bowl, beat eggs with vanilla. Stir in sugar mixture. Turn into pie shell and sprinkle with walnuts. Bake on lower rack at 350°F. for 40 to 45 minutes, until filling is set in center. Cool before cutting.

Makes one 9-inch pie

Tips for making flaky pie crust.
1. Cut shortening into flour just until pieces are size of large peas. 2. Sprinkle liquid on, a tablespoon at a time, mixing in lightly with fork to distribute evenly. Avoid using extra liquid which can make crust tough. 3. Use canvas pastry cloth and stockingette cover for rolling pin (rub flour into both before using). Keeps pastry from sticking, and keeps you from using extra flour which makes tougher crust. 4. Shape dough with hands into flattened round on cloth before rolling. Roll about 1-inch wider than inverted pie pan to allow for fluted rim.

FANTASTIC FROZEN PEANUT BUTTER PIE

9-inch baked graham cracker
   crumb crust
1 pkg. (8 oz.) cream cheese,
   room temperature
1 cup unsifted powdered sugar
½ cup ADAMS Old Fashioned
   Peanut Butter, room temperature
½ cup milk
1 tsp. vanilla
3 cups whipped topping or 1½
   cups whipping cream, whipped
¼ cup chopped peanuts

Beat cheese until fluffy. Add sugar
gradually, beating until smooth.
Add peanut butter, mixing well. Stir
in milk gradually. Add vanilla. Fold
topping into creamed mixture with
rubber scraper or whisk. Pour into
cooled crumb crust. Sprinkle with
chopped peanuts. Freeze at least 4
hours. Let stand 5-10 minutes at
room temperature before cutting
and serving. (If frozen longer than 4
hours, allow about 20 minutes
before cutting.)
Yield: 6-8 servings

CREAMY CHEESE PIE

3 cups KELLOGG'S® RICE
   KRISPIES® Cereal, crushed to
   measure 1½ cups
¼ cup sugar
½ teaspoon ground cinnamon
½ cup margarine or butter, melted
4 packages (3 oz. each) cream
   cheese, softened
2 eggs
1 teaspoon vanilla flavoring
⅓ cup sugar
1 teaspoon lemon juice
1 carton (8 oz., 1 cup) dairy sour
   cream
2 tablespoons sugar
1 can (1 lb. 5 oz.) cherry pie
   filling
1 teaspoon lemon juice

Combine crushed RICE KRISPIES®
Cereal, the ¼ cup sugar and the
cinnamon with the margarine.
Press firmly in 9-inch pie pan to
form crust. Set aside. In large
mixing bowl, beat cream cheese
until smooth. Add eggs, vanilla, the
⅓ cup sugar and the 1 teaspoon
lemon juice, mixing until well
combined. Pour mixture into crust.
Bake in oven at 375°F. about 20
minutes, or until set. While pie is
baking, stir together sour cream
and the 2 tablespoons sugar.

Remove pie from oven. Spread sour
cream mixture over top. Return to
oven. Bake 5 minutes longer.
Remove from oven. Cool. Stir
together pie filling and the
remaining 1 teaspoon lemon juice.
Spread over top of cooled pie.
Chill.   *Yield: one 9-inch pie*

® Kellogg Company

THE YOGURT PIE

1 Tbsp. unflavored gelatin*
¼ cup cold water
2 egg yolks, slightly beaten
¼ cup milk
2 cups DANNON® Vanilla Yogurt
8 ounces** Neufchatel cheese,
   room temperature
8 ounces cream cheese, room
   temperature
1 tsp. molasses
1 Tbsp. clover honey
½ cup graham cracker crumbs
1 graham cracker crumb shell
   (recipe follows)

Soften gelatin in cold water and
dissolve over hot water. Add milk
to the slightly beaten egg yolks
and cook with the gelatin over
gently boiling water until it coats a
silver spoon. Set aside to cool.
Cream the cheese, molasses and
honey together (if mixing machine
used-cream on low speed only),
add ONE cup of DANNON® Yogurt
and continue to cream until
smooth. Pour the cold gelatin
mixture slowly over the cheese,
stirring constantly. Add the second
cup of DANNON® Yogurt. Mix
well. Pour into baked graham
cracker crumb shell and chill until
firm. When ready to serve, sprinkle
top with graham cracker crumbs.
Makes 1 10-inch pie

 *If a softer filling is desired—use
   less gelatin.
**If Neufchatel is not available,
   you may substitute an additional
   8 ounces cream cheese.

GRAHAM CRACKER CRUMB
SHELL

24 graham crackers, finely rolled
   (about 2 cups)
¼ cup softened butter or
   margarine
¼ cup sugar

Blend together crumbs, softened
butter and sugar. Set aside ½ cup
crumbs to garnish top of pie. Press
firmly against bottom and sides of
greased pie plate. Bake at 375°F.
8 to 10 minutes. Cool.

ASPEN® PIE

¼ cup margarine
2 cups crushed NABISCO® OREO
   Cookies
1 8-oz. pkg. cream cheese,
   softened
1 14-oz. can sweetened condensed
   milk
3 Tbsp. lemon juice
½ cup ASPEN® Liqueur
¼ cup white creme de cocoa
1 9-oz. container BIRDS EYE®
   COOL WHIP® Non-Dairy
   Whipped Topping

Stir cookie crumbs into melted
margarine. Pat crumb mixture
firmly on bottom and sides of
buttered 9″ pie plate and chill.
Beat cream cheese until fluffy.
Gradually beat in condensed milk.
Stir in lemon juice and liqueurs.
Fold in COOL WHIP®. Pour into
crust and garnish with cookie
crumbs. Chill 4 hours.

FROZEN PARFAIT RIPPLE
PIE

1 cup (6 oz.) semi-sweet chocolate
   bits
¼ cup water
1 teaspoon vanilla
1 cup heavy cream, whipped
½ cup ARROW Choclair
½ cup sugar
1 egg white
1 teaspoon lemon juice
1 baked 9 inch pie shell

In a small saucepan, melt together
Choclair and chocolate bits. Cool.
In a small mixing bowl combine
sugar, water, egg white, vanilla,
and lemon juice. Beat until soft
peaks form. Fold cream and one
half of chocolate mixture into the
egg mixture. Spoon one half of this
into the pie shell. Drizzle one half
remaining chocolate sauce over.
Repeat, using remaining cream
mixture and chocolate sauce.
Freeze. Garnish with whipped
cream and sliced almonds.
Serves 8

CLOUD 90 PIE

1 can (17½ oz.) THANK YOU®
  Brand Lemon Pudding
1½ cups (12 oz.) lemon yogurt
1 carton (8 or 9 oz.) frozen
  whipped topping, thawed
1 graham cracker pie crust*

Beat together pudding, yogurt and whipped topping until well mixed. Spoon into crust (either store-bought or homemade). Freeze until set (at least three hours). Remove from freezer 15-20 minutes before serving. Best when served icy cool without ice crystals.

Makes 6-8 servings

Make-Your-Own Crust: Combine 1¼ cups graham cracker crumbs (or 1 c. graham cracker crumbs and ¼ c. wheat germ), ¼ cup melted margarine, and 2 Tbsp. sugar. Press into 9-inch pan, reserving 2-3 Tbsp. crumbs for garnish.

NESSELRODE PIE

Crust:
2 cups fine KEEBLER Deluxe
  Graham Cracker Crumbs
¼ cup butter or margarine
  melted

Filling:
1½ teaspoons unflavored gelatin
  (½ packet)
1 package (3 ounces) vanilla
  pudding and pie filling mix
2 cups whipped topping
1 cup chopped, drained
  maraschino cherries
½ cup chopped nuts
6 maraschino cherries, halved

In medium mixing bowl, combine crumbs and butter. Stir with a fork to blend. Press in bottom and up side of 9-inch pie pan.

Combine gelatin with dry pudding mix; prepare pudding according to package directions. Cool to room temperature. Fold in whipped topping, chopped cherries and nuts. Spoon filling into pie crust and chill until firm, 3 to 4 hours. Decorate top with cherry halves. Refrigerate until ready to serve.

Makes one 9-inch pie

DREAM PIE

2 envelopes DREAM WHIP®
  Whipped Topping Mix
2¾ cups *cold* milk
2 packages (4-serving size)
  JELL-O® Brand Instant Pudding
  & Pie Filling, any flavor
1 baked 9-inch pie shell, cooled

Prepare whipped topping mix with 1 cup of the milk as directed on package, using large mixer bowl. Add remaining 1¾ cups milk and the pie filling mix. Blend; then beat at high speed for 2 minutes, scraping bowl occasionally. Spoon into pie shell. Chill at least 4 hours.

BUTTERCRUNCH CHOCLAIR PIE

Crust:
½ cup butter
¼ cup firmly packed brown sugar
1 cup sifted all purpose flour
½ cup chopped pecans

In large bowl, blend all ingredients with pastry blender. Spread evenly in ungreased 13 × 9 × 2 pan. Bake in preheated 400° oven 10-12 minutes or until lightly browned. Remove from oven and stir with spoon. Reserve ½ cup crumbs. Immediately press remaining crumb mixture against bottom and sides of 9″ pie pan. Cool before filling.

Filling:
1 package (3½ oz.) instant vanilla
  pudding
1 cup heavy cream
½ cup milk
⅓ cup ARROW Choclair

In large mixing bowl beat ingredients until smooth and thick (about 2 minutes). Spoon into buttercrunch shell. Garnish with crumbs and additional chopped pecans. Chill for 2 hours.

Serves 6-8

TOM'S® QUICKIE MAGNOLIA PIE

For the Peanut Pastry Shell, add ¼ cup finely ground TOM'S® Toasted Peanuts to the flour of a one-crust pastry shell. Bake and cool.

Meanwhile, make up a family-size package of chocolate pudding and pie mix according to directions, but add ⅓ cup peanut butter to the hot mixture. Now let it cool while you prepare a package of dessert topping mix, spicing it with ¼ teaspoon each of cinnamon and nutmeg. Fold the cool chocolate pudding ever so lightly into the spicey whip, leaving lovely contrasting swirls of light and dark. Pile into the Peanut Pastry Shell. Scatter with chopped TOM'S® Toasted Peanuts. Chill well.

Ralston Purina
Company

GRASSHOPPER PIE

Crust:
4 cups RICE CHEX® Cereal
  crushed to 1¼ cups
¼ cup packed brown sugar
⅓ cup semi-sweet chocolate
  pieces, chopped
⅓ cup butter or margarine,
  melted

Filling:
⅔ cup milk
25 large OR 2½ cups miniature
  marshmallows
3 tablespoons green creme de
  menthe
3 tablespoons white creme de
  cacao
2 cups thawed frozen whipped
  topping

To prepare *Crust,* preheat oven to 300°. Butter 9-inch pie plate. Combine CHEX® crumbs, brown sugar and chocolate pieces. Add butter. Mix thoroughly. Press evenly onto bottom and sides of pie plate. Bake 10 minutes. Cool.

Meanwhile, prepare *Filling.* Cook and stir milk and marshmallows over low heat until marshmallows are melted. Remove from heat. Pour into large bowl. Cool 5 minutes. Stir in liqueurs. Chill until thick and syrupy (about 30 minutes). When filling is thickened, beat 2-3 minutes until fluffy (high speed electric mixer). Beat in topping. Spoon into pie shell. Chill 2-3 hours. Garnish with additional whipped topping and chocolate pieces.

Makes 6-8 servings

THANK YOU® GRASSHOPPER PIE

Crust:
1½ cups filled chocolate cookie crumbs (18 or 20 cookies) crush filling and all
¼ cup butter or margarine, melted

Filling:
1 envelope unflavored gelatin
⅓ cup cold water
1 cup chilled whipping cream or 1 envelope whipped topping mix
1 cup THANK YOU® Brand Vanilla Pudding
¼ cup white creme de cocoa
¼ cup green creme de menthe

Crush cookies. Add melted butter and mix thoroughly. May reserve 2 or 3 tablespoons for garnish. Press firmly to bottom and sides of 9″ pie pan. Chill.

In small saucepan, sprinkle gelatin on water to soften. Stir over low heat until gelatin is dissolved or pour gelatin over water in glass bowl, stir, heat in microwave oven approx. 40 seconds on full power, stirring after 20 seconds till gelatin dissolves. Whip cream or whip topping according to directions on package. Blend pudding, cream and liqueurs; fold in gelatin. Pour into crumb crust. Chill several hours.

DUBOUCHETT GRASSHOPPER PIE

2 Tbsp. butter
14 HYDROX® Cookies
32 large marshmallows
½ cup milk
4 Tbsp. DUBOUCHETT Creme de Menthe
2 Tbsp. DUBOUCHETT White Creme de Cacao
1 cup whipped cream

Melt 2 Tbsp. butter, stir into 14 crushed HYDROX® Cookies, use for crust (press into 8-inch pie plate). Melt 32 marshmallows in ½ cup milk over hot water; remove from water, let cool. Stir in 4 Tbsp. DUBOUCHETT Green Creme de Menthe, and 2 Tbsp. DUBOUCHETT White Creme de Cacao. Fold in 1 cup whipped cream, pour into pie shell. Freeze, serve frozen; save few crumbs of crust mixture to sprinkle over top.

HEUBLEIN®
FROZEN GRASSHOPPER PIE

3 tablespoons butter (or margarine), melted
24 chocolate wafers, finely crushed
20 marshmallows
1 cup HEUBLEIN Grasshopper
1 cup heavy cream, whipped

Combine butter and wafers. Press into 9-inch pie plate. Set aside. In medium saucepan, melt marshmallows in Grasshopper over very low heat. Cool. Mix until smooth. Fold thoroughly into whipped cream. Pour into pie shell. Freeze several hours or overnight.

Serves 6-8

HERSHEY® BAR PIE

Chocolate Petal Crust (recipe follows)
1 HERSHEY'S® Milk Chocolate Bar or Milk Chocolate with Almonds Bar (½ pound)
⅓ cup milk
1½ cups miniature or 15 regular marshmallows
1 cup heavy cream

Prepare pie shell; set aside. Break bar, chopping almonds into small pieces; melt with milk in top of double boiler over hot water. Add marshmallows, stirring until melted; cool completely. Whip cream until stiff; fold into chocolate mixture. Pour into crust; chill several hours until firm. Garnish with whipped topping or chilled cherry pie filling.

8 servings

CHOCOLATE PETAL CRUST

½ cup butter or margarine
1 cup sugar
1 egg
1 teaspoon vanilla
1¼ cups unsifted all-purpose flour
½ cup HERSHEY'S® Cocoa
¾ teaspoon baking soda
¼ teaspoon salt

Cream butter or margarine, sugar, egg and vanilla until light and fluffy. Combine flour, cocoa, baking soda and salt; add to creamed mixture. Shape soft dough into two 1½-inch rolls. Wrap in wax paper; chill until firm. Cut one roll into ⅛-inch slices; arrange, edges touching, on bottom and sides of greased 9-inch pie pan. (Small spaces in crust will not affect pie.) Bake at 375° for 8 to 10 minutes. Cool.

Note: Freeze leftover dough; use for pie crust or cookies.

NESTLÉ BLACK BOTTOM PIE

Chocolate layer:
1 9″ baked pie shell
1 cup sugar, divided
¼ cup corn starch
2 cups milk, scalded
3 eggs, separated
1 6-oz. pkg. (1 cup) NESTLÉ Semi-Sweet Real Chocolate Morsels
2½ measuring tablespoons vanilla extract, divided

Light layer:
¼ cup cold water
1 measuring tablespoon (one envelope) unflavored gelatin
¼ measuring teaspoon cream of tartar
½ cup heavy cream, whipped

Chocolate Layer: In large saucepan, combine ½ cup sugar and corn starch; mix well. Gradually stir in scalded milk. Add some of the hot milk mixture to the egg yolks; mix well. Return to remaining milk mixture. Cook over moderate heat, stirring constantly until mixture thickens (about 5 minutes). Remove 1 cup hot milk mixture to a small bowl; add NESTLÉ Semi-Sweet Real Chocolate Morsels and 1½ measuring teaspoons vanilla extract; stir until morsels melt and mixture is smooth. Pour into prepared pie shell; set aside.

Light Layer: In large bowl, combine cold water, unflavored gelatin and 2 measuring tablespoons vanilla extract; let stand 5 minutes. Add remaining hot milk mixture from saucepan; stir until gelatin dissolves. Cool 15 minutes at room temperature. Cover surface with plastic wrap or waxed paper. In small bowl, combine egg whites and cream of tartar; beat until foamy. Gradually add ½ cup sugar; beat until stiff peaks form. Fold into cooled gelatin mixture along with whipped cream. Pour over chocolate layer. Chill in refrigerator until set (about 2 hours).

Makes one 9″ pie

BLACK BOTTOM PIE

1½ envelopes unflavored gelatin
250 mL or 1 cup sugar, divided
10 mL or 1¼ tablespoons
  cornstarch
4 eggs, separated
500 mL or 2 cups scalded milk
2 squares unsweetened chocolate,
  melted
5 mL or 1 teaspoon vanilla
1 9-inch pie shell
75 mL or ⅓ cup TIA MARIA®
1.25 mL or ¼ teaspoon cream of
  tartar
Grated semi-sweet chocolate

Prepare the pie crust and cook until done but not browned. Mix gelatin, 125 mL or ½ cup of the sugar, and cornstarch in the top of a double boiler. Beat egg yolks and milk; add to gelatin mixture and cook over boiling water, stirring constantly until mixture coats spoon. Divide custard in half. To one part add melted chocolate and vanilla; mix well and turn into pie shell. Chill until firm. To second part add TIA MARIA® and chill until it starts to thicken. Beat egg whites with cream of tartar until frothy. Gradually add remaining sugar and continue beating until egg whites hold their shape. Fold in chilled custard and turn onto chocolate layer. Garnish with whipped cream, top with grated chocolate and chill.

GEORGIA BLACK BOTTOM PIE

Crust:
1¼ cups chocolate Sandwich
  Cookies
4 Tbsp. melted Butter

Press into pie pan. Set in refrigerator to chill.

Filling:
1 can THANK YOU® Brand
  Chocolate Pudding
1 can THANK YOU® Brand
  Vanilla Pudding
2 Tbsp. unflavored Gelatin
½ cup Water
2 Egg Whites
4 teaspoons Rum or ½ teaspoon
  rum flavor (optional)
Whipping Cream or Whipped
  Topping mix

Soften gelatin in cold water, stir over low heat until gelatin is dissolved or pour gelatin over water in glass bowl; stir, heat in microwave oven on high until dissolved, stirring after 20 seconds—approx. 50 seconds. Divide gelatin evenly between chocolate and vanilla pudding. Add rum to vanilla pudding; blend and chill. Whip egg whites until stiff; fold into vanilla pudding. Spread chocolate pudding in bottom of crumb crust. Top with vanilla pudding. Chill thoroughly. Top with whipped cream or whipped topping and decorate with shaved chocolate.

TRADITIONAL MINCE PIE

1 (9-ounce) package JIFFY® Pie
  Crust Mix
1 (28-ounce) jar NONE SUCH®
  Ready-to-Use Mince Meat
1 egg yolk plus 2 tablespoons
  water, optional

Preheat oven to 425°; place rack in lower half of oven. Prepare pastry for 2-crust pie. Turn mince meat into pastry-lined 9-inch pie plate. Cover with top crust; cut slits near center. Seal and flute. For a more golden crust, mix egg yolk and water; brush over entire surface of pie. Bake 30 to 35 minutes or until golden brown. *Makes one 9-inch pie*

VARIATIONS:

Peachy Mince Pie: Drain 1 (16-ounce) can sliced peaches. Turn mince meat into pastry shell; top with peaches. Proceed as above.

Mince Nut Pie: Stir together mince meat and 1 cup coarsely chopped nuts. Proceed as above.

Mince Apple Streusel Pie: Prepare pastry for 1-crust pie. Combine remaining pie crust mix, ¼ cup firmly packed brown sugar and 2 teaspoons ground cinnamon; cut in 2 tablespoons softened margarine or butter until crumbly. Stir in ¼ cup chopped nuts. Pare and slice 2 cooking apples; toss with 2 tablespoons flour. Arrange in pastry shell; top with mince meat, then streusel topping. Bake 25 to 30 minutes.

Cranberry Mince Pie: Stir together mince meat, 1 (14-ounce) jar cranberry-orange relish and 2 tablespoons flour. Proceed as above.

SHERRY EGG NOG PIE

Crust:
4 egg whites
½ tsp. cream of tartar
½ tsp. vanilla
Dash salt
1 cup sugar

Filling:
1 envelope (1 Tbsp.) unflavored
  gelatin
¼ cup cold water
4 egg yolks
⅔ cup sugar
½ cup THE CHRISTIAN
  BROTHERS® Cream Sherry
½ cup whipping cream, whipped

Topping:
1 cup whipping cream
2 Tbsp. sugar
½ tsp. vanilla

Prepare crust: in large mixing bowl beat egg whites, cream of tartar, vanilla and salt until frothy. Gradually beat in sugar; beat stiff. Spread on bottom and up sides of buttered 9″ pie plate. Bake in 275° oven about 1 hour, until creamy tan. Set aside.

Prepare filling: soften gelatin in cold water; warm over low heat to dissolve. In mixing bowl beat yolks until thick and pale, gradually adding sugar. Mix in dissolved gelatin and sherry; fold in whipped cream. Place in cooled crust. Chill 4 hours or overnight.

Whip topping ingredients to soften peaks; spread over filling. Top with chocolate curls, if desired. Chill.
Makes 1 9″ pie

1st Prize Winner THE CHRISTIAN BROTHERS® Contest

EGGNOG CUSTARD PIE

In saucepan, stir 1 envelope unflavored gelatin into 1½ cups commercial eggnog; heat to scalding. (OR **micro-cook** on High 3½-4 minutes to 160°F.) "Melt" 1 can THANK YOU® Brand Egg Custard according to directions on label. Combine Egg Custard and eggnog.* Pour into a cool 9-inch crumb crust (either chocolate or graham cracker). Chill 3 hours or until set. Decorate with whipped cream, chocolate curls, and red cherries. Or simply sprinkle with nutmeg.

*For a "spirited" dessert, add 2-3 tsp. rum at this point.

COFFEE YOGURT CHIFFON PIE

Crumb crust:
1⅓ cups chocolate wafer crumbs
3 tablespoons butter or margarine melted

Combine cookie crumbs and butter. Reserve 3 tablespoons of crumbs for top of pie and press remaining crumbs on bottom and sides of 9-inch pie plate.

Filling:
1 envelope KNOX® Unflavored Gelatine
⅔ cup sugar, divided
3 eggs, separated
¾ cup milk
1 container (8 ounces) DANNON® Coffee Yogurt

Mix gelatine and ⅓ cup sugar in saucepan. Beat egg yolks and milk together and stir into gelatine mixture. Cook, stirring constantly over low heat for 4 or 5 minutes, until gelatine dissolves and mixture thickens slightly. Cool slightly and blend in yogurt. Chill, stirring occasionally, until mixture mounds slightly when dropped from a spoon. Beat egg whites until soft peaks form. Gradually beat in remaining ⅓ cup sugar, beat until stiff. Fold into gelatine mixture. Turn into prepared pie shell and chill until firm. Garnish with reserved cookie crumbs.

RASPBERRY-CHOCOLATE ICE CREAM PIE

1 package (10 oz.) frozen red raspberries
2 teaspoons cornstarch
25 vanilla wafers (approximate)
1 pint chocolate ice cream

Thaw and drain raspberries, reserving syrup. In small saucepan, combine reserved syrup and cornstarch. Cook and stir over medium heat until thickened and clear. Stir in raspberries; chill. Line bottom and sides of a 9-inch pie plate with vanilla wafers, filling in spaces with broken pieces. Soften ice cream slightly. Spoon half of ice cream into vanilla wafer shell. Top with half of raspberry sauce. Freeze until firm, about 30 minutes. Top with remaining ice cream, then remaining raspberry sauce. Freeze

until very firm, about 1 hour, or cover and freeze overnight. Remove from freezer 10 minutes before serving. *Makes 1 (9-inch) pie*

Favorite recipe from Washington Red Raspberry Growers Association, Inc.

BITS 'O BRICKLE® ICE CREAM PIE & SAUCE

Pie:
Prepared 9″ graham cracker pie shell
½ gal. vanilla ice cream, softened to spoon easily but not melted
One-half 7.8 oz. bag HEATH® BITS 'O BRICKLE®

Spoon half of softened ice cream into prepared pie shell. Sprinkle ½ bag HEATH® BITS 'O BRICKLE® on top. Heap with remaining ice cream. Freeze.

Sauce:
1½ cups sugar
1 cup evaporated milk
Remaining ½ bag HEATH® BITS 'O BRICKLE®
¼ cup butter or margarine
¼ cup light corn syrup
Dash salt

Combine sugar, milk, butter or margarine, syrup and salt. Bring to boil over low heat; boil 1 min. Remove from heat and stir in remaining HEATH® BITS 'O BRICKLE.® Cool, stirring occasionally. Chill. **To Serve:** Stir sauce well, then spoon over individual pie wedges. Remaining sauce may be refrigerated in a tightly covered container for use as a topping. *Serves eight*

MILE-HI PIE

3 pts. vanilla ice cream
2½ oz. HIRAM WALKER Swiss Chocolate Almond
2½ oz. HIRAM WALKER Green Creme de Menthe
8 egg whites
12 chocolate wafers, crushed
Heavy cream, whipped
2 oz. sugar

Press the crushed chocolate wafers on bottom of a 10-inch spring-form pan, setting aside enough of the crumbs for the sides. Divide the ice cream in half, keeping second portion in freezer. Put first amount of ice cream into blender, add Swiss Chocolate Almond and blend until color is uniform. Pour into spring-form pan and freeze until set. Remove second portion of ice cream from freezer and blend with Green Creme de Menthe. Pour over first layer. Refreeze until set.

Beat egg whites until foamy. Gradually add sugar and beat until soft peaks form. Spoon meringue evenly over top of pie. Bake in an extremely hot oven (450°) about three minutes or until meringue is lightly browned. Freeze until set. When set, take from freezer and remove from pan. Spread a thin layer of whipped cream around sides of pie and gently pat on reserved wafer crumbs. Return to freezer. When ready to serve, cut the frozen pie with a hot knife.

FUDGE SUNDAE PIE

¼ cup corn syrup
2 tablespoons firmly packed brown sugar
3 tablespoons margarine or butter
2½ cups KELLOGG'S® RICE KRISPIES® Cereal
¼ cup peanut butter
¼ cup fudge sauce for ice cream
3 tablespoons corn syrup
1 quart vanilla ice cream

Combine the ¼ cup corn syrup, the brown sugar and margarine in medium-size saucepan. Cook over low heat, stirring occasionally, until mixture begins to boil. Remove from heat. Add RICE KRISPIES® Cereal, stirring until well coated. Press evenly in 9-inch pie pan to form crust. Stir together peanut butter, fudge sauce and the 3 tablespoons corn syrup. Spread half the peanut butter mixture over crust. Freeze until firm. Allow ice cream to soften slightly. Spoon into frozen piecrust, spreading evenly. Freeze until firm. Let pie stand at room temperature about 10 minutes before cutting. Warm remaining peanut butter mixture and drizzle over top.

Yield: 8 servings

® Kellogg Company

HOMEMADE PASTRY MIX

7 cups flour
4 teaspoons salt
1¾ cups lard for soft wheat
 flour or 2 cups lard for hard
 wheat flour

Mix flour and salt well. Cut lard
into flour mixture with a fork or
pastry blender until crumbs are
about the size of small peas. Cover
and store in refrigerator until ready
to use. This mixture will keep at
least a month in refrigerator.
 Yield: 10 cups pastry mix

SINGLE CRUST PIE

Use: **1¼ cups mix for 8-inch**
 1½ cups mix for 9-inch
 1¾ cups mix for 10-inch
 2 to 4 tablespoons ice water

Add water to mix, a small amount
at a time, mixing quickly and
evenly until dough just holds in a
ball. Roll to about ⅛ inch thickness
and line pie pan, allowing 1 inch
pastry to extend over edge. Fold
overhanging pastry under crust and
crimp edge. Prick pastry with a
fork. To make baked pie shell, bake
in very hot oven (450°F.) 8 to 10
minutes.

DOUBLE CRUST PIE

Use: **2¼ cups mix for 8-inch**
 2½ cups mix for 9-inch
 2¾ cups mix for 10-inch
 4 to 6 tablespoons ice water

Add water to mix, a small amount
at a time, mixing quickly and
evenly until dough just holds in a
ball. Divide pastry and roll half to
about ⅛ inch thickness and line pie
pan, allowing ½ inch pastry to
extend over edge. Roll other half,
making several gashes to allow for
escape of steam. Place over filling
and cut ½ inch smaller than lower
crust. Fold lower crust over top
crust and crimp edge. Bake
according to pie recipe.

Favorite recipe from Pork Industry Group
National Live Stock & Meat Board

WHOLE WHEAT PASTRY SHELL

1 cup ELAM'S 100% Whole Wheat
 Pastry Flour
½ teaspoon salt
⅓ cup soft shortening
¼ to ⅓ cup cold water

Combine flour and salt in bowl;
mix. Add shortening and cut into
dry ingredients with pastry blender
or knives until mixture resembles
coarse crumbs. Add water a few
drops at a time; stir quickly with
fork during addition. Add water as
needed to hold mixture together in
a ball. Shape into a flat patty;
cover and chill slightly. Roll on
lightly floured pastry cloth or bread
board into a round ⅛-inch thick and
1 inch larger than outside rim of
pan. Fit pastry into a 9-inch pie
pan. Trim pastry leaving ½ inch of
crust hanging over edge. Fold
edges under; flute edge. Prick
generously on bottom and sides
with fork. Bake in very hot oven
(450°F.) until done and golden
brown, 10 to 12 minutes. Cool. Fill
as desired.
 Yield: One 9-inch pastry shell

STIR-N-ROLL PASTRY

1⅓ cups sifted all-purpose flour
1 tsp. salt
⅓ cup SUNLITE Oil
¼ cup cold milk

Combine flour and salt in a bowl.
Add SUNLITE Oil and milk all at
once; stir with a fork until well
mixed. Press into smooth ball. Roll
out between wax paper. Peel off
top paper. Ease paper side up into
9-inch pie pan; peel off paper. Trim
and flute edge. **For baked shell:**
Prick thoroughly with fork. Bake at
475° 8 to 10 minutes or until
golden brown. Cool. **For unbaked
shell:** Do not prick. Bake as
directed in filling recipe.
 Makes 1 (9-inch) pie shell

Pastries

DELICIOUS DROP SCONES

½ cup SUNSWEET® Pitted Prunes
2 cups sifted all-purpose flour
¼ cup granulated sugar
2½ tsp. baking powder
¾ tsp. salt
½ tsp. baking soda
½ tsp. nutmeg
½ cup butter or margarine
1 large egg, beaten
⅔ cup buttermilk

Snip prunes into small pieces.
Resift flour with sugar, baking
powder, salt, soda and nutmeg.
Melt 1 Tbsp. butter for tops of
scones. Cut remainder into flour
mixture until particles are size of
peas. Stir in prunes. Add egg and
buttermilk; stir just until mixed.
Drop by heaping tablespoonfuls
onto lightly greased baking sheet
2″ apart to allow for spreading,
making 10 mounds. Brush tops
with melted butter. If desired,
spread a tsp. marmalade over each
or sprinkle with sugar. Bake in
oven center at 425°F. about 15
min. until browned. Serve hot with
butter and marmalade or jam.
 Makes 10 large scones

CHOCLAIR PARTY PUFFS

Cream Puffs:
¼ teaspoon salt
1 cup flour
1 cup water
½ cup butter
4 eggs

In a 2 quart saucepan, bring water
to a boil. Add butter and melt. Add
flour and salt all at once and stir
until mixture leaves sides of pan.
Remove from heat. Add eggs, one
at a time, beating thoroughly after
each addition. Drop dough by
scant ¼ cupfuls on baking sheet.
Bake in preheated 400°F. oven for
40-45 minutes. *Makes 12*

Filling:
2 packages (3½ oz.) instant vanilla
 pudding
2 cups heavy cream
1 cup milk
⅔ cup ARROW Choclair

In large mixing bowl, beat
ingredients until smooth and thick
(about 2 minutes). Slice top off
cream puffs. Spoon filling into
puffs. Replace top, and drizzle with
warm chocolate sauce (recipe
below).

RICH CHOCOLATE SAUCE

4 squares unsweetened chocolate,
 coarsely chopped
⅔ cup hot milk
½ cup sugar
½ cup ARROW Choclair
1 teaspoon vanilla
2 tablespoons soft butter

Place all ingredients in blender.
Blend until smooth (about 2
minutes). *Makes 1½ cups*

BAKLAVA

**2 pkgs. PEPPERIDGE FARM®
Frozen Patty Shells, thawed
overnight in refrigerator**
**3 cups finely chopped walnuts or
pecans**
1 cup honey, warmed
Whipped cream, optional

Line an 8 × 8 × 2-inch cake pan with
foil. Grease lightly. Stack 3 thawed
patty shells, one atop the other. On
lightly floured surface roll out into
a 9-inch square. With a sharp knife,
trim down to an 8½-inch square.
Place in bottom of cake pan.
Sprinkle with 1 cup chopped
walnuts and dribble with ¼ cup
honey. Repeat process three times,
making the top layer plain pastry.
Mark pastry into diamond pattern
with tip of sharp knife. Bake in
425° oven for 20-25 minutes. Let
cool slightly in pan. Brush surface
with last of warm honey. Remove
from pan and peel away foil. Cut
into diamonds. Serve with more
honey or whipped cream if desired.
Serves 12 easily

GINGER GLAZED PEAR RING

**1½ cups diced fresh Anjou, Bosc
or Comice pears**
½ cup raisins
⅓ cup chopped walnuts
½ teaspoon grated lemon peel
1 envelope dry yeast
¼ cup warm water
1 egg
2¼ cups buttermilk biscuit mix
6 tablespoons sugar, divided
1 tablespoon butter, softened
Ginger Glaze (below)

Combine pears, raisins, nuts and
lemon peel; set aside. Dissolve
yeast in warm water. Beat in egg,
biscuit mix, and 2 tablespoons
sugar. Turn out on floured board.
Knead about 20 times. Roll 16 × 9
inch rectangle. Spread evenly with
butter, pear mix, and remaining 4
tablespoons sugar. Roll up, from
long end. Pinch seam to seal.
Place roll, seam side down, on
greased baking sheet. Shape into
ring overlapping ends. Make cuts
⅔ way into ring at 1 inch spaces,

turning each on its side. Cover, let
rise for 1 hour. Bake at 375° for
15-20 minutes. Glaze while warm.
8-10 servings

GINGER GLAZE

Combine ¼ cup water, ¼ cup
sugar, 4 teaspoons corn syrup, ½
teaspoon powdered ginger in
saucepan. Bring to boil, simmer 5
minutes, stirring. Spoon hot over
ring.

*Favorite recipe from Oregon-
Washington Pear Bureau*

DANISH PRUNE CAKE

**1½ cups cooked SUNSWEET®
Prunes**
½ cup butter or margarine
⅔ cup granulated sugar
2 large eggs
1 cup sifted all-purpose flour
½ teaspoon salt
½ teaspoon baking powder
¼ teaspoon nutmeg
½ teaspoon grated lemon peel
3 teaspoons lemon juice
**2 tablespoons granulated sugar
for topping**
Lemon Glaze (recipe follows)

Cut prunes from pits into halves to
measure about 1¼ cups.
Thoroughly cream butter with
sugar. Beat in eggs, one at a time.
(Mixture may look slightly curdled.)
Resift flour with salt, baking
powder and nutmeg; blend into
creamed mixture. Stir in lemon
peel and 1 teaspoon of the lemon
juice. Turn into well greased 9-inch
spring form layer cake pan; place
prune halves close together over
top. Sprinkle with remaining 2
teaspoons lemon juice and 2
tablespoons sugar. Bake at 350°F.,
50 to 60 minutes, until cake tests
done. Cool. When cold, spread with
Lemon Glaze. (If preferred, top with
whipped cream or ice cream—or
sprinkle with powdered sugar.)
Makes 6 to 8 servings

LEMON GLAZE

Combine 1 cup sifted powdered
sugar, 1 teaspoon melted butter, 1
teaspoon lemon juice and 2
teaspoons water; blend together
until mixture is smooth.

PLUM KUCHEN

**½ cup butter or margarine,
softened**
1 cup sugar
1¼ cups flour
½ teaspoon salt
½ teaspoon cinnamon
¼ teaspoon baking powder
**1 can (1 lb. 14 oz.) STOKELY'S
FINEST® Purple Plums,
drained and pitted**
1 egg, slightly beaten
1 cup whipping cream

Cream butter and sugar. Sift
together next 4 ingredients. Blend
flour and butter mixtures together
until crumbly. Reserving ⅓ cup,
press remaining crumbs into
bottom and up sides (about 1 inch)
of an ungreased 8 × 8 × 2-inch pan.
Arrange Plums on crust; sprinkle
with remaining crumbs. Bake at
375°F. for 15 minutes. Blend egg
and cream; pour over Plums. Bake
20-25 minutes longer or until
custard is set. Cool completely.
Makes 9 servings

BRANDIED FRUIT BABA

**1 (13½ ounce) package hot-roll
mix**
½ cup sugar
6 tablespoons butter, softened
2 eggs
**1 (18 ounce) jar Brandied Fruit for
Salad or 1 (18 ounce) jar
RAFFETTO Brandied Peaches**

Prepare hot-roll mix according to
package directions. Stir in sugar
and butter. Beat in eggs,
thoroughly, 1 at a time. Place in a
well-oiled 6½ cup gugelhupf
(Bundt®) mold. Cover and let rise in
warm place, free from draft until
almost double in bulk, 30 to 45
minutes. Bake in preheated 400°
oven 30 minutes. (If necessary,
cover with aluminum foil the last
10 minutes of cooking to keep
from browning too much.) Drain
brandied sauce from peaches or
fruit into a saucepan. Heat lightly
but do not boil. Turn baba out of
mold into shallow pan. Spoon
brandied sauce over top of baba.
Keep basting with syrup until baba
has absorbed all of it. Serve warm,
topped with either brandied
peaches or fruit, with a topping of
whipped cream, if desired.
6-9 servings

POLISH DOUGHNUTS

1 cake yeast
2 cups milk, scalded
7 cups E-Z-BAKE Flour
4 egg yolks
1 egg
½ cup sugar
½ teaspoon vanilla
Rind of lemon grated
1 teaspoon salt
½ cup butter, melted

Dissolve yeast in lukewarm milk; add 2 cups flour. Let stand in warm place about ½ hour. Beat egg yolks, egg, sugar, vanilla, lemon rind and salt together until light; add to first mixture. Add butter. Add remaining flour; beat well. Cover and let rise until double in bulk. Place on floured board, pat until dough is ½ inch thick. Cut with doughnut cutter and let rise. Fry in deep, hot fat (365° to 375°F.) about 3 minutes.

First prize winner E-Z-BAKE Flour contest

SPICY BAKED RAISED DOUGHNUTS

1 cup milk
1½ cups sugar
1 teaspoon salt
⅓ cup FLEISCHMANN'S® Margarine
½ cup warm water (105°F.-115°F.)
2 packages FLEISCHMANN'S® Active Dry Yeast
2 eggs, beaten (at room temperature)
4½-5 cups unsifted flour
½ teaspoon ground cinnamon
½ teaspoon ground nutmeg
1 cup (2 sticks) FLEISCHMANN'S® Margarine, melted
1 tablespoon ground cinnamon

Scald milk; stir in ½ cup sugar, salt and ⅓ cup FLEISCHMANN'S® Margarine. Cool to lukewarm. Measure warm water into large warm bowl. Sprinkle in FLEISCHMANN'S® Active Dry Yeast; stir until dissolved. Add lukewarm milk mixture, eggs, 2 cups flour, ½ teaspoon cinnamon and nutmeg; beat 2 minutes on medium speed of electric mixer, scraping bowl occasionally. Stir in enough of the remaining flour to make a soft dough. Cover; let rise in warm place, free from draft, until doubled in bulk, about 50-60 minutes.

Punch dough down; turn out onto lightly floured board. Roll out to ½-inch thickness; cut into doughnut shapes with floured doughnut cutter. Place on greased baking sheet. Cover; let rise in warm place, free from draft, until doubled in bulk, about 30 minutes.

Brush doughnuts with melted FLEISCHMANN'S® Margarine. Bake at 425°F. for 8-10 minutes or until golden brown. Remove from sheets and cool slightly on wire rack. Dip in remaining melted margarine. Combine remaining 1 cup sugar and 1 tablespoon cinnamon; coat doughnuts with sugar mixture and serve warm.

Makes about 2 dozen

OLD-FASHIONED APPLE CRESCENTS

¾ cup sugar
1 tablespoon ARGO®/ KINGSFORD'S® Corn Starch
1 teaspoon ground cinnamon
6 apples, pared, cored and sliced
1 tablespoon lemon juice
2 recipes double crust pastry

Mix together first 3 ingredients. Toss with apples and lemon juice. Roll dough ⅛-inch thick and cut into 12 (7-inch) circles. Place ½ cup filling on one-half of each circle. Fold dough over filling to form crescent. Seal edge with fork; cut slits in top. Bake on cookie sheets in 425°F oven 15 minutes or until browned.

Makes 12

For Apple Pie: Use 1 recipe double crust pastry. Dot filling with 1 tablespoon margarine; bake 50 minutes.

Makes 1 (9-inch) pie

MAYPO® CHERRY SQUARES

½ cup sifted flour
½ teaspoon soda
½ teaspoon salt
1½ cups MAYPO® 30-Second Oatmeal
1 cup brown sugar, firmly packed
¾ cup melted butter or margarine
1 can (1 lb. 5 oz.) Cherry Pie Filling

Sift flour, soda and salt together. Mix MAYPO® brown sugar and melted butter with dry ingredients until well blended. Press ½ of the mixture into the bottom of buttered 11 × 7 × 1½-inch baking pan. Spread with Pie Filling. Sprinkle remaining mixture over filling; press in lightly. Bake in preheated 350°F. oven for 30 to 35 minutes, or until tests done. Cool in pan; cut into squares to serve.

SOLO® RASPBERRY PECAN TORTE

Torte:
½ C. butter or margarine
1 C. sugar
1 egg
¼ C. milk
1 tsp. vanilla extract
½ tsp. salt
1¼ C. flour
¼ C. chopped pecans

Filling:
½ C. butter or margarine
1½ C. sifted confectioners' sugar
1 egg
1 can (12 oz.) SOLO® Raspberry Filling
¾ C. whipping cream
3 Tbsp. sugar
½ C. chopped pecans

Torte: Cream butter or margarine. Add sugar gradually and cream well. Add egg, milk, vanilla, and salt, blending well. Stir in flour and pecans. Spread batter in 8" square pan, greased waxed paper on bottom. Bake at 350° for 30-35 minutes. Cool in pan 5 minutes. Remove from pan. Cool thoroughly. Cut in half horizontally with sharp knife to make two thin layers.

Filling: Cream butter or margarine; add sugar and cream well. Add egg and beat until fluffy. In a separate bowl, beat whipping cream until thick. Add sugar and beat until stiff. Fold in nuts. To assemble torte: Place one layer on serving plate; spread with butter filling and then with SOLO® Raspberry Filling. Top with second layer and spread whipped cream filling on top. Chill at least four hours before serving.

Serves 9

PETER PAN® TEA RING

¼ cup PETER PAN® Peanut
  Butter
½ cup cold water
2 cups packaged biscuit mix
1 teaspoon cinnamon
½ cup chopped dates
¼ cup honey

Add water to biscuit mix. Stir until
a soft dough forms. Turn onto a
lightly floured surface. Knead 6
times. Roll or pat into a rectangle
approximately 8 by 15 inches.
Spread peanut butter evenly to
edges of dough. Sprinkle with
cinnamon and dates. Roll from
long side, jelly roll fashion. Place
on cooky sheet, seam edge down.
Form a ring. With scissors cut
from outside edge of ring almost
to the center at 1 inch intervals.
Turn each slice cut side up. Bake
in a 400°F. oven about 20 minutes.
Brush surface with honey while
still warm. Serve warm or cold.
Yield: 6 to 8 servings or 1 ring

CHOCOLATE BUTTER
STREUSEL DESSERT

1 frozen SARA LEE Butter Streusel
  All Butter Coffee Cake
⅓ cup dairy sour cream
¼ cup semi-sweet miniature or
  regular chocolate pieces

Slice frozen Butter Streusel Coffee
Cake in half lengthwise to form 2
layers. Place bottom layer on
baking sheet or microwaveable
surface; spread with sour cream.
Sprinkle on 3 tablespoons
chocolate pieces. Replace top of
coffee cake; sprinkle on remaining
chocolate pieces. Cut into 6
servings. Heat in preheated 350°F.
oven 5-7 minutes. Transfer to
serving plate; serve warm.

Microwave instructions: place on
microwaveable surface and heat
on high power about 2 minutes;
serve warm.

Makes 6 servings

FEUILLETAGE PETER
PAUL

Crust:
Two 10-oz. packages frozen puff
  pastry, thawed

Peter Paul Filling:
¾ cup sugar
⅓ cup flour
4 eggs
3 cups milk, heated
1 Tbsp. butter
1 tsp. vanilla
2 Tbsp. lime juice
8 miniature or 2 large YORK
  Peppermint Patties, finely
  chopped

Roll one package pastry out on
lightly floured board to measure
10 × 13-inches. Place on greased
cookie sheet. Prick all over with a
fork. Place second greased cookie
sheet on top and weight down.
Bake in 400° oven 12 to 15 minutes
or until golden brown. Remove top
cookie sheet and brown pastry
slightly. Repeat for second
package. Cool on cake racks. Set
aside.

Mix sugar and flour in medium
saucepan. Beat in eggs. Add
heated milk while beating. Cook
and stir over low heat until mixture
thickens and coats spoon. Add
butter and vanilla. Cool. Stir in lime
juice and chopped YORK
Peppermint Patties. To serve, place
pastry sheets on cutting board and
cut into 24 pieces measuring
2 × 4 inches. Place one piece on
plate, spoon on cream-candy
filling. Add second pastry layer,
top with cream filling. Top with
third pastry piece. Dust top with
powdered sugar.   *Serves 8*

DORMAN'S CHEESE
PUFF-PASTRY

Prepare half the recipe for a 9-inch
double crust pie and roll dough
into an 8-inch × 10-inch oblong. Top
with 2 slices DORMAN'S Natural
Muenster Cheese and enclose by
folding dough over. Roll as for jelly
roll and press into a ball.
Refrigerate 30 minutes and roll
dough about ¼-inch thick. If
baking a shell, fit into 8-inch or
9-inch pie pan, flute pastry rim, and
prick dough all over. Bake in
preheated moderate 375°F. oven
about 3 minutes. Remove and prick

dough bubbles and, if necessary,
reshape flutes. Check in 5 minutes
to see if dough needs pricking
again. Bake until delicately
browned, about 10 minutes. Cool
before filling.

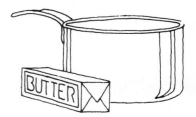

POPPY ROLL (STRUDEL)

3 to 3½ cups all-purpose flour
1½ tablespoons sugar
½ teaspoon salt
1 package active dry yeast
½ cup dairy sour cream
¼ cup water
½ cup butter or margarine
2 eggs, at room temperature
1 (12-ounce) can SOLO® Poppy
  Filling

In large bowl of electric mixer,
combine 1 cup flour, sugar, salt,
and dry yeast. In a saucepan,
combine sour cream, water, and
butter or margarine. Heat over low
heat until liquids are very warm
(120-130°F.). (Butter or margarine
need not melt entirely.) Gradually
add to dry ingredients; beat
mixture 2 minutes at medium
speed of electric mixer, scraping
bowl occasionally. Add eggs and
½ cup flour. Beat at high speed 2
minutes, scraping bowl
occasionally. Stir in enough
additional flour to make a soft
dough. Turn out onto a lightly
floured board; knead a few times
to form a ball. Cover and let stand
10 minutes. Divide dough in half.
Roll each half out into a 14 × 12
inch rectangle. Spread each with
½ can of filling. Roll each up from
one side, jelly-roll fashion. Seal
edges. Place on greased baking
sheet, sealed edges down. Cover
and let rise in a warm place, free
from draft, until doubled in bulk,
about 1 hour. Preheat oven to
350°F. Bake about 35 minutes, or
until lightly browned. Remove from
baking sheet and cool on wire
rack. When cool, drizzle with
confectioners' sugar icing, if
desired.

Cookies, Candy and Snacks

COOKIE MIX SPECIALS
(Basic Cookie Mix)

1½ c. flour
1 tsp. soda
1 tsp. salt
1 c. sugar
1 c. brown sugar
1 c. shortening
3 c. 3-MINUTE BRAND® Oats

Sift flour, soda, salt, and sugars. Cut in shortening until mixture is crumbly. Stir in oats. Store in tightly covered container at room temperature. When ready to bake, combine 1 egg, 1 Tbsp. water, and ½ tsp. vanilla with 4 cups of the cookie mix. If desired, 1 cup of raisins, chocolate chips or chopped nuts may also be added at this time. Mix well and drop by spoonful onto a greased cookie sheet. Bake at 350°F. for 12 to 14 minutes.

Yield: 3½ dozen cookies

To make into bars: Press above mixture into a greased 9 × 9 inch pan. Bake at 350°F. for 20 minutes.
Yield: 2 dozen 1½ × 2 inch bars

TOLL HOUSE® COOKIES

2¼ cups *unsifted* flour
1 measuring teaspoon baking soda
1 measuring teaspoon salt
1 cup butter, softened
¾ cup sugar
¾ cup firmly packed brown sugar
1 measuring teaspoon vanilla extract
2 eggs
One 12-oz. pkg. (2 cups) NESTLÉ Semi-Sweet Real Chocolate Morsels
1 cup chopped nuts

Preheat oven to 375°F. In small bowl, combine flour, baking soda and salt; set aside. In large bowl, combine butter, sugar, brown sugar and vanilla extract; beat until creamy. Beat in eggs. Gradually add flour mixture; mix well. Stir in NESTLÉ Semi-Sweet Real Chocolate Morsels and nuts. Drop by rounded measuring teaspoonfuls onto ungreased cookie sheets. Bake at 375°F. 8-10 minutes
Makes: One hundred 2" cookies

Toll House® Pan Cookie: To make quick Toll House® Pan Cookie, spread the original Toll House® Cookie dough into a greased 15″ × 10″ × 1″ baking pan. Bake at 375°F for just 20 minutes. Cool; cut into thirty-five 2″ squares.

CHOCOLATETOWN COOKIES

1 cup shortening or ¾ cup butter or margarine
1 cup packed light brown sugar
½ cup sugar
1 teaspoon vanilla
2 eggs
2¼ cups unsifted all-purpose flour
1 teaspoon baking soda
1 teaspoon salt
2 cups (12-ounce package) HERSHEY'S® Semi-Sweet Chocolate Chips or Mini Chips
1 cup chopped nuts (optional)

Cream shortening or butter or margarine, brown sugar, sugar and vanilla until light and fluffy. Add eggs; beat well. Combine flour, baking soda and salt; add to creamed mixture. Stir in chips and nuts. Drop by teaspoonful onto ungreased cookie sheet; bake at 375°F. for 8 to 10 minutes or until light brown. Cool slightly before removing from cookie sheet.
About 6 dozen 2½-inch cookies

JUMBO OATMEAL CHIP COOKIES

1 c. shortening
¾ c. sugar
¾ c. brown sugar
2 eggs
1 tsp. vanilla
1½ c. sifted flour
1 tsp. salt
1 tsp. soda
1 Tbsp. hot water
2 c. 3-MINUTE BRAND® Oats
1 c. chopped pecans
1 c. (6 oz.) chocolate chips

Cream shortening and sugars. Add eggs and vanilla and mix well. Blend in remaining ingredients. Spoon dough into a ⅓ c. measuring cup and turn out onto a greased cookie sheet, spacing cookies at least 6 inches apart and 2½ inches from edge of pan. Lightly grease the bottom of a pie pan, dip into sugar and use to flatten each cookie into a 4-inch circle. Bake at 350°F. for 12 minutes. Cool before removing from baking sheet.
Yield: 15 jumbo cookies

Note: To make "regular" sized cookies, drop by teaspoonful onto a greased cookie sheet. Bake at 350°F. for 12 minutes.

CHOCOLATEY CHOCOLATE CHIP COOKIES

1 cup soft butter or margarine
1 cup firmly packed brown sugar
½ cup granulated sugar
1½ cups sifted all purpose flour
½ teaspoon baking soda
1 teaspoon salt
2 tablespoons cocoa
2 eggs
1 tablespoon milk
1 teaspoon vanilla
3 cups HEARTLAND® Natural Cereal
1 cup (6 oz.) semi-sweet chocolate pieces

Beat together until fluffy, butter and sugars. Sift together flour, baking soda, salt and cocoa. Add to sugar mixture. Beat in eggs, milk and vanilla. Stir in cereal and chocolate pieces. Drop from teaspoonfuls onto greased cookie sheets. Bake in 375°F. oven for 10 minutes. Remove immediately to cooling racks. Cool completely before storing.

Makes 6 dozen cookies

POLKA DOT PEANUT BUTTER JUMBOS

1 cup margarine
1 cup peanut butter
1 cup granulated sugar
1 cup firmly packed brown sugar
2 eggs
2 cups flour
1 teaspoon soda
1½ cups M & M'S® Plain or Peanut Chocolate Candies

Beat together margarine, peanut butter and sugars until light and fluffy; blend in eggs. Add combined flour and soda; mix well. Stir in candies. Drop dough by level ¼ cup measure onto greased cookie sheet about 3 inches apart. Bake at 350°F. for 14 to 15 minutes or until edges are golden brown. Cool on cookie sheet 3 minutes; remove to wire rack to cool thoroughly.

Makes about 2 dozen 4-inch cookies

VARIATION:

For 2½-inch cookies, drop dough by rounded tablespoonfuls onto greased cookie sheet. Bake at 350°F. for 12 to 13 minutes.

Makes about 4 dozen cookies

PEANUT BUTTER & JELLY THUMBPRINTS

1 cup butter or margarine, softened
1¾ cups packed brown sugar
2 eggs
2 teaspoons vanilla
3 cups unsifted all-purpose flour
1 teaspoon baking powder
1 teaspoon salt
1½ cups quick-cooking oatmeal
2 cups (12-ounce package) REESE'S® Peanut Butter Flavored Chips
¾ cup jelly or preserves (apple, grape, peach, etc.)

Cream butter or margarine and brown sugar in large mixer bowl. Add eggs and vanilla; beat until light and fluffy. Combine flour, baking powder and salt in small bowl; add to creamed mixture. Reserve ½ cup peanut butter chips; stir in oatmeal and 1½ cups peanut butter chips. Shape small amounts of dough into 1-inch balls. Place balls on ungreased cookie sheet; press with thumb into center making deep depression about 1-inch wide. Bake at 400°F. for 7 to 9 minutes or until lightly browned. Remove from cookie sheet; cool on wire rack. Fill center of each cookie with ½ teaspoon jelly or preserves; top with several peanut butter chips.

About 5 dozen 2½-inch cookies

COWBOY PEANUT BUTTER COOKIES

½ cup butter or margarine, softened
½ cup peanut butter
1 cup COLONIAL® Granulated Sugar
1 cup firmly-packed COLONIAL® Light Golden Brown Sugar
2 eggs
2 cups unsifted flour
1 teaspoon baking soda
½ teaspoon baking powder
½ teaspoon salt
1½ cups quick-cooking oats
1 (6-ounce) package semi-sweet chocolate morsels

Preheat oven to 350°. In large mixer bowl, cream together butter, peanut butter and sugars; beat in eggs. Combine flour, baking powder, baking soda and salt; stir into creamed mixture. Mix in oats and morsels. (Mixture will be crumbly.) Roll into 1-inch balls; place on lightly greased baking sheets. Flatten with fork. Bake 7 to 9 minutes or until lightly browned.

Makes 6 dozen cookies

PEANUT BUTTER CRUNCHIES

1 cup (2 sticks) MEADOW GOLD Butter
1 cup granulated sugar
1 cup packed dark brown sugar
1 cup chunky peanut butter
2 eggs
1 teaspoon vanilla
2¾ cups sifted all-purpose flour
½ teaspoon soda
⅛ teaspoon salt
Granulated sugar

Beat butter, sugars and peanut butter until light and fluffy. Beat in eggs and vanilla. Sift together dry ingredients. Add gradually to butter mixture, mixing well. Shape into 1-inch balls. Dip half of ball into sugar; place on ungreased cookie sheet with sugar-side up. Flatten with fork. Bake at 350° for 10 minutes or until lightly browned.

8 dozen

CRISPIE TREATS

4 cups miniature marshmallows
¼ cup margarine
½ cup peanut butter
⅛ teaspoon salt
4 cups crisp rice cereal
1½ cups M & M'S® Plain or Peanut Chocolate Candies

Melt together marshmallows, margarine, peanut butter and salt in heavy saucepan over low heat, stirring occasionally, until smooth. Pour over combined cereal and candies, tossing lightly until thoroughly coated. With greased fingers, gently shape into 1½-inch balls. Place on waxed paper; cool at room temperature until set.

Makes about 3 dozen cookies

VARIATION:

After cereal mixture is thoroughly coated, press lightly into greased 13 x 9-inch baking pan. Cool thoroughly; cut into bars.

Makes one 13 x 9-inch pan of bars

GRANDMA'S® MOLASSES BUTTONS

¾ cup butter or margarine
2 cups sugar
2 eggs
½ cup GRANDMA'S® Molasses
  (Unsulphured)
2 teaspoons vinegar
3¾ cups sifted all-purpose flour
1 tablespoon ground ginger
1½ teaspoons baking soda
1 teaspoon ground cinnamon
½ teaspoon salt

In large bowl cream together butter, sugar, eggs, molasses and vinegar. Sift together flour, ginger, baking soda, cinnamon and salt; stir into creamed mixture. Shape into balls using 1 level teaspoonful for each. Place on greased cookie sheets. Bake in a 325°F. oven 8 to 10 minutes or until lightly browned.
Yield: 12 dozen 1-inch cookies

CHERRY WINKS

2¼ cups all-purpose flour
2 teaspoons baking powder
½ teaspoon salt
¾ cup margarine or butter,
  softened
1 cup sugar
2 eggs
2 tablespoons milk
1 teaspoon vanilla flavoring
1 cup chopped nuts
1 cup finely cut, pitted dates
⅓ cup finely chopped maraschino
  cherries
2⅔ cups KELLOGG'S® CORN
  FLAKES® Cereal, crushed to
  measure 1⅓ cups
15 maraschino cherries, cut into
  quarters

Stir together flour, baking powder and salt. Set aside. In large mixing bowl, beat margarine and sugar until light and fluffy. Add eggs. Beat well. Stir in milk and vanilla. Add flour mixture. Mix until well combined. Stir in nuts, dates and chopped cherries. Portion dough using level measuring tablespoon. Shape into balls. Roll in crushed cereal. Place about 2 inches apart on greased baking sheets. Top each with cherry quarter. Bake at 375°F. about 10 minutes or until lightly browned. Remove immediately from baking sheets. Cool on wire racks.
Yield: about 5 dozen
® Kellogg Company

SECRET KISS COOKIE

1 cup butter or margarine, softened
½ cup sugar
1 teaspoon vanilla
1¾ cups unsifted all-purpose flour
1 cup finely chopped walnuts
1 6-ounce package HERSHEY'S®
  Kisses, about 36
Confectioners' sugar

Cream butter or margarine, sugar and vanilla in large mixer bowl. Gradually add flour and nuts; beat on low speed until well blended. Chill dough about 1 hour or until firm enough to handle. Heat oven to 375°F. Mold approximately 1 tablespoon of dough around an unwrapped chocolate kiss and roll to make a ball. Be sure to cover kiss completely. Place on ungreased cookie sheet. Bake 12 minutes or until cookies are set, but not brown. Cool slightly; remove to wire rack. While still warm, roll in confectioners' sugar. Cool. Store in tightly covered container. Roll in sugar again before serving, if desired.
36 cookies

PEANUT BLOSSOMS

½ cup shortening
¾ cup peanut butter
⅓ cup sugar
⅓ cup packed brown sugar
1 egg
2 tablespoons milk
1 teaspoon vanilla
1½ cups unsifted all-purpose flour
1 teaspoon baking soda
½ teaspoon salt
Granulated sugar
9-ounce package HERSHEY'S®
  Kisses, about 48

Cream shortening and peanut butter; add sugar and brown sugar. Add egg, milk and vanilla; beat well. Combine flour, baking soda and salt; gradually add to creamed mixture, blending thoroughly. Shape dough into 1-inch balls; roll in granulated sugar. Place on ungreased cookie sheet; bake at 375°F. for 10 to 12 minutes. Remove from oven; immediately place unwrapped Kiss on top of each cookie, pressing down so that cookie cracks around the edge. Remove from cookie sheet; cool.
About 4 dozen cookies

CRUNCHY PEANUT BUTTER COOKIES

½ cup DOMINO® Granulated
  Sugar
½ cup firmly packed DOMINO®
  Light Brown Sugar
½ teaspoon salt
½ cup butter or margarine
½ cup crunchy peanut butter
1 egg
½ teaspoon vanilla extract
1 cup sifted all-purpose flour
½ teaspoon baking soda

Cream sugars, salt, butter and peanut butter thoroughly in large mixing bowl. Beat egg and extract into creamed mixture until light and fluffy. Sift together flour and soda. Blend into creamed ingredients gradually. Form into 1″ balls and place 2″ apart on ungreased cookie sheets. With floured fork, make a criss-cross design to flatten cookies. Bake in hot oven 400°F. 6-7 minutes or until light brown around edges. Store in airtight container.
Yield: 6 dozen cookies

Gerber®

OATMEAL CRUNCHIES

1 cup soft shortening
2 cups granulated sugar
2 eggs, unbeaten
4 tablespoons grated orange rind
3 tablespoons GERBER® Orange-
  Apricot Juice
1 teaspoon nutmeg
1 teaspoon salt
4 teaspoons baking powder
2 cups sifted flour
2 cups GERBER® Oatmeal Cereal

Preheat oven to 375°F. Cream shortening and sugar together. Add eggs, and beat well. Stir in grated orange rind. Sift together nutmeg, salt, baking powder and flour. Add alternately with juice. Mix in cereal until well blended. Drop dough from teaspoon onto greased cookie sheet. Bake 12-15 minutes.
Yield: approximately 5 dozen cookies

VARIATION:

Substitute lemon rind for orange rind and lemon juice for orange-apricot juice.

SHAKESPEARE OATMEAL COOKIES

1½ cups CERESOTA or HECKER'S
Unbleached Flour, sifted
1 teaspoon salt
1 teaspoon baking soda
1 teaspoon cinnamon
¼ teaspoon cloves
⅛ teaspoon nutmeg
1 cup shortening
1 cup brown sugar, firmly packed
1 cup granulated sugar
2 eggs
3 cups oatmeal*
1 cup raisins

Sift flour, salt, soda, and spices together. Cream shortening, add sugars, and cream thoroughly. Beat in the eggs. Add sifted dry ingredients and blend well. Stir in oatmeal and raisins. Form into balls about the size of walnuts. Place on lightly greased cookie sheets, and flatten. Bake in a preheated 350° oven for 12-15 minutes.

Makes about 4½ to 5 dozen

*For the sweet taste of maple, use MAYPO® Oatmeal.

SUN·MAID® RAISINS

RAISIN OATMEAL COOKIES

⅔ cup shortening
1 cup brown sugar (packed)
1 egg
1 cup sifted all-purpose flour
1 teaspoon salt
1 teaspoon baking powder
1 teaspoon vanilla extract
2 cups rolled oats
1 cup SUN-MAID® Seedless Raisins

Melt shortening and stir in sugar. Add unbeaten egg and beat until well blended. Sift together flour, salt and baking powder and stir into first mixture. Blend in vanilla, oats and SUN-MAID® raisins. Drop by teaspoonfuls onto greased baking sheet. Bake in moderate oven (350 degrees F.) 15 to 20 minutes. Remove to wire rack to cool. *Makes about 5 dozen*

PEANUT RAISIN JUMBOS

2¼ cups Ground Oat Flour*
1 cup raisins
1½ teaspoons soda
1 teaspoon cinnamon
¼ teaspoon salt
¾ cup margarine
1 cup chunk style peanut butter
1½ cups firmly packed brown sugar
2 eggs
1 teaspoon vanilla

Heat oven to 350°F. Lightly grease cookie sheet. In medium bowl, combine oat flour, raisins, soda, cinnamon and salt. In large bowl, beat together margarine, peanut butter and sugar; blend in eggs and vanilla. Add dry ingredients; mix well. Drop by rounded tablespoonfuls onto prepared cookie sheet. Bake about 12 to 14 minutes.

Makes about 3 dozen cookies

*GROUND OAT FLOUR

Place 1¼ cups QUAKER® Oats (Quick or Old Fashioned, uncooked) in blender or food processor; cover. Blend about 60 seconds. Store in tightly covered container in cool dry place up to 6 months. Use for baking, breading, thickening or dredging and browning. (When used in baking, substitute up to but not more than ⅓ of the all-purpose flour called for with oat flour.)

Makes about 1 cup

Note: To prepare larger quantities of Ground Oat Flour, repeat above directions to produce amount needed.

FAMOUS OATMEAL COOKIES

3 cups QUAKER® Oats (Quick or Old Fashioned, uncooked)
1 cup all-purpose flour
1 teaspoon salt
½ teaspoon soda
¾ cup vegetable shortening
1 cup firmly packed brown sugar
½ cup granulated sugar
1 egg
¼ cup water
1 teaspoon vanilla

Heat oven to 350°F. Grease cookie sheet. In medium bowl, combine oats, flour, salt and soda. In large bowl, beat together shortening,

sugars, egg, water and vanilla until creamy. Add dry ingredients; mix well. Drop by rounded teaspoonfuls onto prepared cookie sheet. Bake for 12 to 15 minutes. (For variety, add chopped nuts, raisins, chocolate chips or coconut.)

Makes about 5 dozen cookies

OATMEAL FRUIT DROPS

1 cup (2 sticks) butter
½ cup packed light brown sugar
½ cup granulated sugar
1 teaspoon vanilla
2 eggs
2 cups quick or old-fashioned oats, uncooked
2 cups all-purpose flour
1 teaspoon each: soda, salt
1¼ cups chopped LIBERTY Diced Fruit & Peel
1 cup coarsely chopped pecans

Beat butter, sugars and vanilla until light and fluffy. Beat in eggs. Stir together oats, flour, soda and salt. Gradually add to butter mixture, mixing well after each addition. Fold in fruit and nuts. Drop by teaspoonfuls onto lightly greased cookie sheet. Bake at 375° for 10 minutes. *7 dozen*

OATMEAL SCOTCHIES

2 cups *unsifted* flour
2 measuring teaspoons baking powder
1 measuring teaspoon baking soda
1 measuring teaspoon salt
1 cup butter, softened
1½ cups firmly packed brown sugar
2 eggs
1 measuring tablespoon water
1½ cups quick oats, uncooked
One 12-oz. pkg. (2 cups) NESTLÉ Butterscotch Morsels
½ measuring teaspoon orange extract

Preheat oven to 375°F. In small bowl, combine flour, baking powder, baking soda and salt; set aside. In large bowl, combine butter, brown sugar, eggs and water; beat until creamy. Gradually add flour mixture. Stir in oats, NESTLÉ Butterscotch Morsels and orange extract. Drop by slightly rounded measuring tablespoonfuls onto greased cookie sheets. Bake at 375°F. 10-12 minutes

Makes: 4 dozen 3″ cookies

WALNUT OAT CRISPS

1¼ cups DIAMOND® Walnuts
½ cup butter
1 cup brown sugar, packed
1 egg
1½ teaspoons grated orange peel
⅔ cup whole wheat flour
½ teaspoon salt
½ teaspoon soda
¼ teaspoon cinnamon
1⅓ cups uncooked quick cooking
　oats

Chop walnuts; set aside. Cream butter, sugar, egg and orange peel together. Stir whole wheat flour, salt, soda and cinnamon together; blend into creamed mixture. Stir in oats and ¾ cup walnuts. Shape into 1-inch balls, and place on lightly greased baking sheets. Flatten with bottom of glass dipped into sugar, and sprinkle with remaining ½ cup walnuts. Bake at 350°F. about 10 minutes. Cool slightly, then remove to wire racks to cool completely before storing.
Makes about 5 dozen 2-inch rounds

OATMEAL COCONUT CRISPIES

1 c. shortening
1 c. brown sugar
1 c. white sugar
2 eggs
1 tsp. vanilla
1½ c. sifted flour
1 tsp. salt
1 tsp. soda
1 tsp. cinnamon
½ tsp. nutmeg
1½ c. 3-MINUTE BRAND® Oats
1½ c. flaked coconut
¾ c. chopped nuts

Cream shortening and sugars. Add eggs and vanilla and mix well. Sift together the flour, salt, soda, cinnamon and nutmeg. Fold into the creamed mixture. Blend in oats, coconut and nuts. Drop by spoonful onto a greased baking sheet. Bake at 350°F. for 8 to 10 minutes.

SUGAR COOKIES

3½ cups sifted all-purpose flour
2½ teaspoons baking powder
½ teaspoon salt
⅔ cup butter or margarine
1½ cups DOMINO® Granulated
　Sugar
1½ teaspoons vanilla
2 eggs
1 tablespoon milk

Sift together flour, baking powder and salt. Cream butter; add sugar gradually and cream until light and fluffy. Add extract. Add eggs, one at a time, beating well after each addition. Alternately add flour mixture and milk, beating until blended after each addition. Wrap dough in foil or plastic wrap and chill several hours or overnight. Roll out part of the dough at a time about ⅛ inch thick on lightly floured board. Cut with floured 2½ inch cookie cutters. Sprinkle with granulated sugar and bake on ungreased baking sheets at 400°F. 8 to 9 minutes until edges are lightly browned. Cool on racks.
Makes 6 dozen cookies

WHEATENA® COCONUT COOKIES

3 cups sifted flour
1 teaspoon salt
2 teaspoons baking powder
⅔ cup shortening
1¼ cups sugar
2 eggs
2 tablespoons milk
1 teaspoon vanilla
½ cup WHEATENA®
½ cup shredded coconut
½ cup chopped nuts

Sift flour, salt and baking powder together. Blend shortening, sugar, eggs, milk and vanilla together. Stir WHEATENA® into sifted dry ingredients; add, with coconut and nuts, to creamed mixture. Mix until well blended. Roll dough out on floured board to about ⅛-inch thickness. Cut with cookie cutter. Place on ungreased cookie sheets; bake in preheated 375°F. oven about 10 minutes or until lightly browned. Remove from pan immediately and place on wire rack. If desired, sprinkle tops with sugar.　*Makes about 6 dozen*

WALNUT CHEESECAKE COOKIES

½ cup butter or margarine,
　softened
1 package (3 oz.) cream cheese,
　softened
1 large egg, separated
1 tsp. vanilla
1 tsp. grated lemon peel
¼ tsp. salt
1 cup sifted powdered sugar
1 cup sifted all-purpose flour
1 cup finely chopped DIAMOND®
　Walnuts
Apricot or cherry jam

Cream together butter, cream cheese, egg yolk, vanilla, peel and salt until well blended. Gradually mix in powdered sugar, then flour to make a stiff dough. Chill dough for easier handling. When dough is chilled, shape into 30 small balls, about 1 in. diameter. Beat egg white until foamy. Dip balls one at a time into the egg white, allowing excess to drip back, then roll in finely chopped walnuts. Arrange about 2 in. apart on ungreased cookie sheets and make a depression in the center of each with handle of knife. Bake at 325°F. for about 15 minutes, until cookies begin to brown on the bottom. Carefully remove to wire racks and, while hot, fill each center with about ½ tsp. jam. Cool thoroughly.　*Makes 30 cookies*

CRISS-CROSS PETER PAN®-NUTTY COOKIES

1 cup PETER PAN® Peanut Butter
½ cup margarine
½ cup granulated sugar
½ cup packed brown sugar
½ teaspoon vanilla
1 egg
1½ cups sifted flour
¾ teaspoon soda
½ teaspoon baking powder
¼ teaspoon salt

Cream together peanut butter, margarine and sugars until light and fluffy. Add vanilla and egg and beat well. Sift together flour, soda, baking powder and salt and add, mixing thoroughly. Chill dough. Shape into 1 inch balls and place about 2 inches apart on cookie sheet. Flatten with fork in crisscross pattern. Bake in 350°F. oven for 10 to 12 minutes.
Yield: 5 dozen

MELTING MOMENTS

1 cup unsifted flour
½ cup ARGO®/
   KINGSFORD'S® Corn Starch
½ cup confectioners sugar
¾ cup NUCOA® or
   MAZOLA® Margarine
1 teaspoon vanilla

In medium bowl stir flour, corn starch and confectioners sugar. In large bowl with mixer at medium speed beat margarine until smooth. Add flour mixture and vanilla and beat until combined. Refrigerate 1 hour. Shape into 1-inch balls. Place about 1½ inches apart on ungreased cookie sheet; flatten with lightly floured fork. Bake in 375°F oven 10 to 12 minutes or until edges are lightly browned.

Makes about 3 dozen cookies

VARIATIONS:

Anise: Follow recipe for Melting Moments. Add 2 teaspoons ground anise seeds to flour mixture or 1 teaspoon anise extract with vanilla.

Rich Chocolate: Follow recipe for Melting Moments. Stir 1 square (1 oz) semisweet chocolate, melted and cooled into margarine.

Orange-Clove: Follow recipe for Melting Moments. Add 1 tablespoon grated orange rind and ½ teaspoon ground cloves to flour mixture.

Food Processor Method: Follow recipe for Melting Moments. In work bowl of food processor with metal blade stir together flour, corn starch and confectioners sugar. Cut cold margarine into 1-inch chunks. Add to flour mixture. Process, adding vanilla through feed tube 15 seconds or until mixture forms a ball around blade. Continue as in basic recipe.

LEMON CARAWAY COOKIES

2 cups CERESOTA or HECKER'S
   Unbleached Flour, sifted
½ teaspoon baking soda
½ teaspoon salt
1 egg
1 cup sugar
2 tablespoons lemon juice
½ cup shortening, softened
1 tablespoon caraway seeds

Sift flour, soda and salt together. Beat the egg, add sugar and lemon juice and beat well. Add shortening and caraway seeds, and cream thoroughly. Add flour mixture and blend thoroughly. Chill for several hours. Shape dough into balls about the size of a walnut, place on lightly greased cookie sheet, and flatten. Bake in a preheated 400° oven about 10-12 minutes, or until lightly browned.

Makes about 2½ dozen

PEANUTTY CHOCOLATE SURPRISES

1 cup PETER PAN® Peanut Butter,
   Creamy or Crunchy
1 stick (½ cup) butter or margarine
1 cup packed brown sugar
2 eggs
1 cup flour
1 teaspoon baking powder
1 teaspoon cinnamon
2 milk chocolate candy bars
   (8 ounces each) Or 1 pound bag
   chocolate kisses or stars
Powdered sugar, optional

Cream peanut butter, butter and sugar. Beat in eggs. Combine flour, baking powder and cinnamon. Add gradually until well blended. Chill dough. Break chocolate bars, if used, into pieces. Wrap about 1 teaspoon of dough around each chocolate piece. Place on cooky sheet and bake in 350°F. oven 10 to 12 minutes. Remove and cool slightly. Roll in powdered sugar if desired and let cool completely.

Yield: About 72 cookies

PEANUT BRAN COOKIES

1 cup butter or margarine, softened
1 cup light brown sugar, firmly
   packed
1 egg
1 teaspoon vanilla extract
1½ cups all-purpose flour
1 cup NABISCO® 100% Bran Cereal
1 teaspoon baking powder
½ teaspoon baking soda
½ cup chopped salted peanuts

Preheat oven to 350°F. With electric mixer at high speed, beat together butter or margarine and sugar until creamy. Beat in egg and vanilla. In small bowl, mix together flour, NABISCO® 100% Bran Cereal, baking powder and baking soda. Add to sugar mixture, using mixer at low speed; blend

well. Stir in peanuts. Drop mixture by teaspoonfuls on lightly greased cookie sheets. Bake 10 minutes or until lightly browned. Remove from cookie sheets and cool on wire rack.

Makes about 3-dozen cookies

GINGERBREAD BOY COOKIES

½ cup shortening
½ cup sugar
½ cup GRANDMA'S® Molasses
   (Unsulphured)
1 egg yolk
2 cups sifted all-purpose flour
½ teaspoon salt
1 teaspoon baking powder
½ teaspoon baking soda
1½ teaspoons cinnamon
1 teaspoon ground cloves
1 teaspoon ginger
½ teaspoon nutmeg

Cream together shortening, sugar and molasses. Add egg yolk; mix well. Sift together flour, salt, baking powder, baking soda and spices. Stir flour mixture into shortening mixture; mix well. Chill. To make gingerbread boys, roll out a portion of the dough ¼ inch thick on lightly floured board or pastry cloth. (Keep remaining dough chilled.) Cut with 5-inch gingerbread boy cookie cutter; place on ungreased baking sheets and decorate with raisins or nuts, if desired. Bake in 350°F. oven 8 to 10 minutes. Cool. Decorate with Ornamental Frosting.* To make stars, or other shapes, roll dough ⅛ inch thick and cut with desired 3-inch cookie cutters. Bake in 350°F. oven 8 to 10 minutes.

Yield: 2 dozen 5-inch gingerbread boys or 4 dozen 3-inch cookies

*ORNAMENTAL FROSTING

1¼ cups sifted confectioners'
   sugar
⅛ teaspoon cream of tartar
1 egg white
¼ teaspoon vanilla

Mix confectioners' sugar and cream of tartar in small bowl. Add egg white and vanilla. Beat at high speed of electric mixer or with rotary beater until frosting holds its shape. Cover with damp cloth until ready to use. Spoon into cake decorator with plain tip. If frosting is not stiff enough to go through a cake decorator, add a little more confectioners' sugar.

MALT-O-MEAL® REFRIGERATOR COOKIES

½ cup butter or margarine
   (1 stick)
½ cup shortening
1 cup confectioner's sugar
½ to 1 tsp. Almond Flavoring
   (or 2 tsp. vanilla extract)
1 cup flour
1 cup MALT-O-MEAL®
½ tsp. salt
1 tsp. cream of tartar
1 cup chopped nuts (almonds are
   suggested)
1 to 1¼ cups coconut

In mixer bowl thoroughly cream butter, shortening, confectioner's sugar and almond flavoring. Blend in remaining ingredients except coconut. Shape cookie dough into a roll on waxed paper 1½ inches in diameter. Sprinkle coconut on paper and roll cookie dough until coated. Wrap wax paper to hold roll in shape, twist ends. Chill until firm. Cut ¼ inch slices and place on ungreased cookie sheet. Bake at 375° for 8 to 10 minutes. Cookies will be very light—do not overbrown. Let baked cookies cool slightly before removing from cookie sheet.   *4 dozen cookies*

WHEAT GERM SOUR CREAM COOKIES

2 cups ELAM'S® Unbleached White
   Flour with Wheat Germ
1 teaspoon baking soda
½ teaspoon salt
¾ teaspoon nutmeg
1 cup ELAM'S® Natural Wheat
   Germ
¾ cup butter
1½ cups (packed) brown sugar
2 teaspoons vanilla
1 teaspoon finely shredded lemon
   rind
2 eggs
½ cup thick sour cream
½ cup chopped pecans or walnuts

Combine and sift first 4 ingredients into bowl. Stir in wheat germ; reserve. Beat butter until creamy. Add brown sugar, vanilla and lemon rind; beat until fluffy. Add eggs, one at a time; beat well

after each addition. Add dry ingredients and sour cream alternately to creamed mixture; blend well after each addition. Stir in chopped nuts. Drop rounded tablespoonfuls of dough onto lightly greased baking sheets. Bake in moderate oven (350°F.) until done and lightly browned, 12 to 14 minutes.
   *Yield: 4 dozen cookies, about
      2½ inches in diameter*

MOLASSES SUGAR COOKIES
(Homemade Gingersnaps)

¾ cup shortening
1 cup sugar
¼ cup BRER RABBIT Light *or*
   Dark Molasses
1 egg
2 cups sifted all-purpose flour
2 teaspoons baking soda
1 teaspoon cinnamon
½ teaspoon ground cloves
½ teaspoon ground ginger
½ teaspoon salt
Granulated sugar

In large bowl, cream together shortening and the 1 cup sugar. Add molasses and egg; beat well. Sift together flour, soda, cinnamon, cloves, ginger and salt; add to first mixture. Mix well; cover; chill. Form into 1-inch balls, roll each in granulated sugar and place on greased cookie sheets about two inches apart. Bake in a preheated moderate oven (375°F.) for 8 to 10 minutes or until golden brown. Let stand one minute, then remove cookies to wire rack; cool.
   Makes 48 cookies

NUT COOKIES
(Low Calorie)

½ cup sifted cake flour
¼ tsp. baking powder
⅛ tsp. salt
½ tsp. SWEET 'N LOW®
   (2 pkts.)
2 Tbsp. orange juice
½ tsp. vanilla extract
2 Tbsp. shortening
2 Tbsp. finely chopped walnuts
2 tsp. grated orange rind

Grease cookie sheet lightly. Sift together flour, baking powder and salt. Blend SWEET 'N LOW® with combined orange juice and vanilla. Work shortening with spoon until fluffy and creamy. Add the liquid ingredients and mix well. Add the

sifted dry ingredients and work until light. Add walnuts and orange rind. Shape dough into roll and wrap in wax paper. Chill well. Cut into 12 even slices. Arrange 2½" apart on cookie sheet. Bake in 400°F. oven 12 min. or until brown around edges.   *Makes 12*

1 cookie equals 41 calories.

HUNGARIAN PRINCESS KIPFELS

1 cup butter
1 cup cream cheese
Pinch of salt
1 Tbsp. thick sour cream
2 cups flour
1 jar SIMON FISCHER Apricot or
   Prune Butter (Lekvar)

Combine butter, cream cheese and sour cream with pinch of salt—sift in flour and knead mixture until it has smooth texture. Make a ball of this and chill for at least 3 hours. When ready to bake, roll the dough very thin and cut into 3-inch squares. Spread each square with Apricot or Prune Butter. Roll the squares from the corners to form crescents—bake at 375 degrees for 20 minutes. Serve cool.

KASHA COOKIES
(Buckwheat Groats)

1 cup shortening
1 cup sugar
1 cup brown sugar
3 eggs
4 cups all-purpose flour
½ tsp. salt
2 tsp. baking powder
1 tsp. soda
1 Tbsp. cinnamon
¾ cup uncooked WOLFF'S®
   Kasha (buckwheat groats)

Cream shortening and sugars until fluffy; add eggs and beat well. Sift together dry ingredients, except kasha, and add to creamed mixture. Stir in kasha. Form into 2-inch diameter rolls; wrap in waxed paper or plastic wrap. Chill. When firm, slice and bake at 350°F for 10-15 minutes or until slightly browned.   *Makes about 6 dozen*

Coarse or *whole* kasha makes cookies with nut-like texture and flavor. *Fine* or *medium* kasha makes cookies with flavor and texture of oatmeal cookies.

ROCKY ROAD WALNUT DROPS

½ cup butter
⅔ cup brown sugar, packed
1 teaspoon vanilla
1 egg, beaten
½ cup (3 ounces) semi-sweet real chocolate pieces, melted
½ cup chopped DIAMOND® Walnuts
1½ cups sifted all-purpose flour
½ teaspoon soda
¾ teaspoon salt
1 teaspoon instant coffee powder
⅓ cup milk
12 to 14 marshmallows
36 to 40 DIAMOND® Walnut halves or large pieces
Chocolate Frosting (recipe follows)

Cream butter, sugar and vanilla until light and fluffy. Beat in egg. Add melted chocolate and walnuts, mixing well. Resift flour with soda, salt and coffee powder. Add to creamed mixture along with milk; stir until well blended. Drop by rounded teaspoonfuls onto greased cookie sheets. Bake at 350°F., 10 minutes or just until cookies test done. (Be careful not to overbake as cookies should be moist.)

Cut marshmallows crosswise into thirds. As soon as cookies are baked, top each one with a marshmallow slice and return to oven a minute to set marshmallows. Remove cookies to wire racks; top each marshmallow with a walnut half or piece, pressing down lightly to make it stick. When cookies are nearly cool, place racks over waxed paper and carefully spoon or ladle warm Chocolate Frosting over each top. Let stand until set. Frosting that drips on waxed paper may be scraped up and reheated to use again.
Makes 3 to 3¼ dozen cookies

CHOCOLATE FROSTING

¼ cup butter or margarine
⅓ cup milk or light cream
½ cup (3 ounces) semi-sweet real chocolate pieces
¼ teaspoon salt
1 teaspoon vanilla
2½ cups sifted powdered sugar

Combine butter, milk and chocolate in top of double boiler. Place over hot (not boiling) water until melted and smooth, stirring occasionally. Add vanilla and salt; beat in powdered sugar until smooth. Spoon warm frosting over baked cookies.

Note: If a doubly-thick frosting is desired, just double the frosting recipe. This heavy coating will make an almost candy-like cookie.

"BEACON HILL" COOKIES

2 egg whites
⅛ teaspoon salt
½ cup sugar
½ teaspoon vinegar
½ teaspoon vanilla or almond extract
½ cup BAKER'S® ANGEL FLAKE® Coconut
¼ cup chopped walnuts or toasted almonds
1 cup BAKER'S® Semi-Sweet Chocolate Flavored Chips, melted*

Beat egg whites with salt until foamy throughout. Add sugar very gradually and continue beating until mixture will form stiff shiny peaks. Beat in vinegar and vanilla. Fold in coconut, nuts and melted chips. Drop from teaspoon onto greased baking sheets. Bake at 350° for 10 minutes.
Makes 2½ to 3 dozen

*Or use 4 squares BAKER'S® Semi-Sweet Chocolate, melted

Note: Total beating time—10 minutes.

NO-BAKE BREAKFAST COOKIES

½ cup honey
½ cup creamy peanut butter
½ cup instant nonfat dry milk
2½ cups coarsely crushed TEAM Flakes Cereal
½ cup DROMEDARY Chopped Dates

Heat honey and peanut butter in medium saucepan over low heat, stirring until blended. Remove from heat; blend in dry milk. Fold in cereal and dates. Drop by heaping tablespoonfuls onto wax paper to form mounds. Cool to room temperature. Store in refrigerator.
Makes 2 dozen (about 2-inch) cookies

MALTEX® GINGER COOKIES

3½ cups sifted flour
1 teaspoon salt
2 teaspoons soda
4 teaspoons ginger
1 teaspoon cinnamon
½ cup shortening
½ cup butter or margarine
1 cup sugar
1 cup molasses
1 cup MALTEX®*
2 eggs
1 teaspoon vinegar
2 tablespoons water

Sift flour, salt, soda and spices together. Cream shortening, butter, sugar and molasses together. Add MALTEX® and eggs to creamed mixture. Combine vinegar and water; add to MALTEX® mixture and blend in. Add sifted dry ingredients; mix thoroughly. Drop by teaspoonsful onto lightly greased cookie sheets. Bake in preheated 350°F. oven 8 to 10 minutes, or until tests done. Remove from pan; cool on rack.
Makes about 7 dozen

*1 cup WHEATENA® can be used in place of MALTEX®. Omit water.

RALSTON® CRACKLE COOKIES

½ cup vegetable shortening
½ cup packed brown sugar
½ cup sugar
1 egg
1 tablespoon milk
1 teaspoon vanilla
1 cup all-purpose flour*
1 teaspoon baking powder
½ teaspoon salt
½ teaspoon cinnamon
1 cup Instant or Regular RALSTON®

Preheat oven to 350°. Grease baking sheet. Cream shortening with sugars. Add egg, milk and vanilla. Beat until fluffy. Stir together flour, baking powder, salt and cinnamon. Add to creamed mixture. Blend thoroughly. Stir in RALSTON®. Drop by level tablespoons onto baking sheet. Bake 9-12 minutes or until lightly browned. Let stand on baking sheet 1 minute before removing. Cool.
Makes 3 dozen

*Stir flour; then spoon into measuring cup.

TOFFEE CRUNCH COOKIES

1½ cups sifted flour
½ teaspoon baking soda
½ teaspoon salt
½ cup butter or margarine
¾ cup packed brown sugar
1 egg
1 teaspoon vanilla
1 cup finely chopped HEATH® Bars
   (6 ounces in bar form) or 1
   bag HEATH® BITS 'O
   BRICKLE®
⅓ cup coarsely chopped pecans

Combine and sift flour, soda and salt. Cream butter with sugar, add egg and vanilla; mix until smooth and creamy. Stir in dry ingredients; blend in candy bits and pecans. Drop tablespoonfuls 2″ apart onto well greased and lightly floured baking sheets. Bake in 350° oven 10 to 12 minutes. Remove from baking sheets immediately; cool.

Yield: about 3 dozen cookies

Note: Best way to use HEATH® Bars for baking is to freeze the bars first. Unwrap and put in heavy plastic bag. Strike with mallet until broken into small bits. Six ounces candy in bar form equals 1 cup chopped candy.

SHREDDED WHEAT COOKIES

1 cup shortening
1 cup light brown sugar, firmly
   packed
1 cup granulated sugar
2 eggs, well beaten
1 teaspoon vanilla extract
1½ cups all-purpose flour
1 teaspoon baking soda
1 teaspoon salt
12 NABISCO® Shredded Wheat
   Biscuits, finely rolled (about 3
   cups crumbs)
½ cup chopped walnuts

Thoroughly cream shortening and sugars. Beat in eggs and vanilla, blending well. Sift together flour, baking soda and salt; stir into batter. Stir in shredded wheat crumbs and nuts. Drop by teaspoonfuls onto greased cookie sheets. Bake in preheated moderate oven (350°F.) 10 to 12 minutes. Remove to wire racks to cool. *Makes 5 dozen (about 2-inch) cookies*

ALMOND MERINGUE COOKIES
(Low Calorie)

4 egg whites
8 tablespoons powdered skim milk
1 teaspoon vanilla extract
1 teaspoon almond extract
1 teaspoon SWEET 'N LOW®
   (4 pkts.)
Cinnamon

Beat egg whites until stiff. Add skim milk powder. Mix well. Add extracts and SWEET 'N LOW®. Spoondrop onto cookie sheet. Bake at 275 degrees for 45 minutes. Remove from sheet and dust with cinnamon.

1 cookie equals 32 calories.

PEANUT MERINGUES
(Low Sodium/Low Calorie)

2 egg whites
⅔ cup sugar
½ teaspoon vanilla extract
1½ cups low-sodium cornflakes
½ cup chopped PLANTERS® Dry
   Roasted Unsalted Peanuts

In a mixing bowl beat egg whites until soft peaks form. Gradually add sugar, a tablespoon at a time, beating until stiff peaks form. Beat in vanilla. Fold in cornflakes and PLANTERS® Dry Roasted Unsalted Peanuts. Drop mixture by teaspoonfuls, 1 inch apart, onto greased baking sheets. Bake at 275°F. for 25 minutes, or until done. Remove from baking sheets and cool on wire racks.

Makes 4 dozen

Per meringue: 25 calories, 2 mg. sodium

GEORGIA MERINGUES

2 egg whites
⅛ teaspoon cream of tartar
⅔ cup sugar
½ cup SKIPPY® Creamy or Super
   Chunk Peanut Butter

Beat egg whites and cream of tartar until stiff peaks form. Add sugar, 1 tablespoon at a time, beating well after each addition. Continue beating until very stiff peaks form. Lightly fold in peanut butter just until mixed. Drop by

teaspoonfuls onto greased cookie sheet. Bake in 300°F oven 25 minutes or until lightly browned. Remove from cookie sheet immediately.

Makes about 3 dozen cookies

HERMITS

2 cups flour
2 teaspoons baking powder
¼ teaspoon salt
½ teaspoon nutmeg
1 teaspoon cinnamon
½ teaspoon mace
¼ cup shortening
½ cup sugar
½ cup firmly packed brown sugar
2 eggs, well beaten
1 cup raisins
¾ cup chopped walnuts

Sift together flour, baking powder, salt and spices. Cream shortening, sugar and brown sugar until light and fluffy. Add eggs and beat well. Add sifted dry ingredients, blending well. Add raisins and walnuts; mix well. Drop by teaspoonfuls onto greased baking sheets. Bake at 350 degrees about 15 minutes or until lightly browned.

Makes about 3 dozen

California Raisin Advisory Board's favorite recipe

COCONUT CASHEW COOKIES
(Low Sodium)

½ cup FLEISCHMANN'S®
   Unsalted Margarine, softened
½ cup firmly-packed light brown
   sugar
1¼ cups unsifted flour
1 cup old-fashioned oats,
   uncooked
¾ cup PLANTERS® Dry Roasted
   Unsalted Cashews
½ cup shredded coconut
¼ cup milk
1 teaspoon vanilla extract

Cream FLEISCHMANN'S® Unsalted Margarine with brown sugar. Stir in flour, oats, PLANTERS® Dry Roasted Unsalted Cashews, coconut, milk and vanilla. Drop mixture by rounded teaspoonfuls onto ungreased baking sheets. Bake at 350°F. for 12 to 14 minutes. Remove from sheets and cool on wire racks. *Makes 2½ dozen*

Per cookie: 100 calories, 3 mg. sodium

OLD FASHIONED LEMON SUGAR COOKIES

1 cup butter or margarine, softened
1½ cups sugar
1 egg
⅓ cup frozen MINUTE MAID®
   Lemonade Concentrate, thawed
   and undiluted
4 cups flour
1 teaspoon baking powder
1 teaspoon soda
¼ teaspoon salt
½ cup buttermilk
2 tablespoons sugar
½ teaspoon nutmeg

In large mixer bowl, beat butter and 1½ cups sugar until creamy. Add egg and lemonade concentrate; beat at medium speed until fluffy. Combine flour, baking powder, soda and salt; mix well. Add to lemonade mixture, alternately with the buttermilk; blend at low speed until moistened. Drop by teaspoons onto ungreased cookie sheets. Combine 2 tablespoons sugar and nutmeg. Wet the bottom of a glass in water; dip in sugar-nutmeg mixture. Flatten cookies slightly with sugar-coated glass. Bake at 375°F. for 10 to 12 minutes until light golden brown.
Makes 60 to 72 cookies

FLORENTINES

1 cup slivered BLUE RIBBON®
   Almonds
¾ cup candied orange peel
5 tablespoons flour
½ cup whipping cream
½ cup sugar
Pinch salt
¼ teaspoon almond extract
3 squares (1 oz. each) semi-sweet
   chocolate

Coarsely chop almonds. Mix orange peel with 1 tablespoon flour so it isn't sticky; chop fine. Mix all ingredients except chocolate; drop by teaspoonfuls about 4 inches apart on well-greased cookie sheets. Flatten slightly with wet knife blade. Bake at 350 degrees 9 or 10 minutes. Allow to cool on pan 1½ to 2 minutes, then loosen with spatula and invert on wire

racks to cool. (Keep spatula clean to prevent tearing the cookies.) Melt chocolate in saucepan over hot water; spread onto flat sides of cookies. *Makes 2½ dozen*

ORANGE FLAVOR COCONUT CHEWS

1 cup unsifted all-purpose flour
1 teaspoon CALUMET® Baking
   Powder
½ teaspoon salt
¼ cup butter or margarine
1 cup sugar
2 tablespoons TANG™ Orange
   Flavor Instant Breakfast Drink
1 egg
2 tablespoons water
1⅓ cups (about) BAKER'S®
   ANGEL FLAKE® Coconut
1 square BAKER'S® Semi-Sweet
   Chocolate, melted (optional)

Mix flour wth baking powder and salt. Cream butter. Combine sugar and instant breakfast drink; gradually blend into butter. Add egg and water and beat until smooth. Fold in flour mixture; stir in coconut. Spread batter in greased 8-inch square pan. Bake at 350° for 35 to 40 minutes, or until cake begins to pull away from sides of pan. Cool in pan. Drizzle with melted chocolate. Let stand until firm; then cut into squares or bars. *Makes about 20 cookies*

COCO WHEATS COOKIES

½ cup butter
¾ cup sugar
2 eggs
1½ cups flour
3 teaspoons baking powder
½ cup COCO WHEATS
¼ teaspoon salt
½ cup chopped raisins
1 teaspoon cinnamon

Cream butter and sugar together. Add eggs. Add dry ingredients and raisins. Mix until all ingredients are moist. Drop by spoonfuls on buttered cookie sheet. Bake in moderately hot oven at 375°F. for about 15 minutes.
Makes 36 cookies

PEANUT BUTTER CANDY COOKIES

½ cup PETER PAN® Peanut
   Butter, Creamy
½ cup sugar
¼ cup evaporated milk
2½ cups cornflakes

Mix peanut butter, sugar and milk to a smooth cream. Stir in cornflakes until thoroughly blended with peanut butter mixture. Drop by teaspoonsful onto an ungreased baking sheet. Bake in a 375°F. oven for 6 minutes, or until evenly browned. *Yield: 32 cookies*

PEANUT BUTTER CHIP CHOCOLATE COOKIES

1 cup butter or margarine
1½ cups sugar
2 eggs
2 teaspoons vanilla
2 cups unsifted all-purpose flour
⅔ cup HERSHEY'S® Cocoa
¾ teaspoon baking soda
½ teaspoon salt
2 cups (12-ounce package)
   REESE'S® Peanut Butter
   Flavored Chips

Cream butter or margarine, sugar, eggs and vanilla until light and fluffy. Combine flour, cocoa, baking soda and salt; add to creamed mixture. Stir in peanut butter chips. Drop by teaspoonsful onto ungreased cookie sheet, or chill until firm enough to handle and shape small amounts of dough into 1-inch balls. Place on ungreased cookie sheet and flatten slightly with fork. Bake at 350°F. for 8 to 10 minutes. Cool 1 minute before removing from cookie sheet onto wire rack.
About 5 dozen 2½-inch cookies

CRUNCHY DROP COOKIES

1¼ cups all-purpose flour
½ teaspoon soda
¼ teaspoon salt
½ cup shortening
1 cup firmly packed brown sugar
1 egg
3 tablespoons milk
1 teaspoon vanilla
2 cups QUAKER® 100%
 NATURAL Cereal

Heat oven to 350°F. Grease cookie sheet. In small bowl, combine flour, soda and salt. In large bowl, beat together shortening, sugar, egg, milk and vanilla until creamy. Add flour mixture; mix well. Stir in cereal. Drop by teaspoonfuls onto prepared cookie sheet. Bake for 10 to 12 minutes.

Makes 3 dozen cookies

CORN FLAKES® MACAROONS

4 egg whites
¼ teaspoon cream of tartar
1 teaspoon vanilla flavoring
1⅓ cups sugar
1 cup chopped pecans
1 cup shredded coconut
3 cups KELLOGG'S® CORN
 FLAKES® Cereal

In large mixing bowl, beat egg whites until foamy. Stir in cream of tartar and vanilla. Gradually add sugar, beating until stiff and glossy. Fold in pecans, coconut and cereal. Drop by rounded measuring tablespoon onto well-greased baking sheets. Bake at 325°F. about 20 minutes or until lightly browned. Remove immediately from baking sheets. Cool on wire racks.

Yield: about 3 dozen

VARIATION:

Merry Macaroons: Fold in ½ cup crushed peppermint candy with pecans and coconut.

® Kellogg Company

CHOCOLATE "JETS"

1 6-ounce package semi-sweet
 chocolate pieces
1½ cups lightly crushed FRITOS®
 Brand Corn Chips

Melt chocolate in double boiler. Stir in FRITOS® Brand Corn Chips until thoroughly covered with chocolate. Drop by spoonsful onto waxed paper. Chill and serve.

Makes 24 cookies

COCONUT MACAROONS

2 (7-ounce) packages flaked
 coconut (5⅓ cups)
1 (14-ounce) can EAGLE® Brand
 Sweetened Condensed Milk
 (not evaporated milk)
2 teaspoons vanilla extract
1½ teaspoons almond extract
Candied fruit or nuts for garnish,
 optional

Preheat oven to 350°F. In large bowl, combine coconut, sweetened condensed milk and extracts; mix well. Drop by rounded teaspoonfuls onto generously greased baking sheets; garnish as desired. Bake 8 to 10 minutes or until lightly browned. Immediately remove from baking sheets (macaroons will stick if allowed to cool on baking sheets). Store loosely covered at room temperature.

Makes about 4 dozen

VARIATIONS:

Chocolate Macaroons: In large heavy saucepan, melt 1 (6-ounce) package semi-sweet chocolate morsels; remove from heat. Stir in 1 (7-ounce) package flaked coconut, 2 cups graham cracker crumbs and sweetened condensed milk. Proceed as above; bake 6 to 8 minutes.

Makes about 6 dozen

Nutty Oat Macaroons: In large bowl, combine sweetened condensed milk, 2 cups fresh bread crumbs, 1 cup oats, 1 cup chopped nuts, 1 cup raisins and 1 teaspoon vanilla extract. Proceed as above; bake 8 to 10 minutes.

Makes about 4 dozen

TIGER COOKIES

1¾ cups all-purpose flour
½ teaspoon baking soda
½ teaspoon salt
1 cup margarine or butter, softened
1 cup sugar
2 eggs
1 teaspoon vanilla flavoring
3 cups KELLOGG'S® SUGAR
 FROSTED FLAKES® OF CORN
 Cereal, crushed to measure 1½
 cups
1 package (6 oz., 1 cup) semi-sweet
 chocolate morsels, melted

Stir together flour, soda and salt. Set aside. In large mixing bowl, beat margarine and sugar until light and fluffy. Add eggs and vanilla. Beat well. Add flour mixture, mixing until well combined. Stir in crushed cereal. Drizzle melted chocolate over dough. With knife, swirl melted chocolate gently through dough to achieve marbled appearance. Drop by rounded measuring tablespoon onto ungreased baking sheets. Bake at 350°F. about 12 minutes or until lightly browned. Remove immediately from baking sheets. Cool on wire racks.

Yield: about 5 dozen

® Kellogg Company

Bars

BROWNIES
(Low Calorie)

2 cups fine graham cracker crumbs
 (about 24 crackers)
½ cup chopped walnuts
3 oz. semisweet chocolate pieces
1½ teaspoons SWEET 'N LOW®
 (6 pkts.)
¼ tsp. salt
1 cup skim milk

Start heating oven to 350°F. Place all ingredients in bowl; stir until blended. Turn into greased 8″×8″×2″ pan; bake 30 mins. Cut into 2″ squares while warm.

Makes 16

1 brownie equals 95 calories.

COCOA BROWNIES
(Microwave Recipe)

⅓ cup butter or margarine
2 tablespoons shortening
6 tablespoons HERSHEY'S® Cocoa
1 cup sugar
2 eggs
½ teaspoon vanilla
1 cup unsifted all-purpose flour
¼ teaspoon baking powder
¼ teaspoon salt
½ cup chopped nuts

Microwave butter or margarine and shortening in medium glass mixing bowl on high (full power), about 1 minute. Stir in cocoa until smooth; blend in sugar. Add eggs and vanilla; beat well. Stir in remaining ingredients. Spread batter into lightly greased 8-inch round glass baking dish. Microwave on medium (½ power) for 7 minutes, turning ¼ turn every 3 minutes. Microwave on high (full power) for 3 to 4 minutes, or until puffed and dry on top. Cool until set. Cut into wedges. Serve brownie wedges topped with a scoop of ice cream and chocolate syrup, if desired.

SUPER OATMEAL BROWNIE

2½ cups rolled oats
1 cup DURKEE Flaked Coconut
¾ cup packed light brown sugar
¾ cup flour
½ teaspoon baking soda
¼ teaspoon salt
¾ cup butter or margarine, melted
1 package (22 oz.) brownie mix

Mix oats, coconut, sugar, flour, soda, and salt in bowl; stir in butter. Reserve ¾ cup mixture. Pat oatmeal mixture in bottom of greased 13 x 9 x 2-inch baking pan. Bake at 350°F. for 10 minutes. Cool 5 minutes. Prepare brownie mix according to package directions for fudgy brownies. Spread batter evenly over baked crust. Sprinkle with reserved oatmeal mixture. Bake according to brownie mix package directions; cool. Cut into squares.

Makes 36

PRINCESS BROWNIES

1 pkg. family size brownie mix
1 8-oz. pkg. PHILADELPHIA BRAND Cream Cheese
⅓ cup sugar
1 egg
½ teaspoon vanilla

Prepare brownie mix as directed on package. Combine softened cream cheese and sugar; mix until well blended. Stir in egg and vanilla. Spread half of brownie batter onto bottom of greased 13 x 9-inch baking pan. Cover with cream cheese mixture; spoon on remaining brownie batter. Cut through batter with knife several times for marble effect. Bake at 350°, 35 to 40 minutes or until wooden pick inserted in center comes out clean. Cool; cut into squares.

CHOCOLATE SCOTCHEROOS

1 cup corn syrup
1 cup sugar
1 cup peanut butter
6 cups KELLOGG'S® RICE KRISPIES® Cereal
1 package (6 oz., 1 cup) semi-sweet chocolate morsels
1 package (6 oz., 1 cup) butterscotch morsels

In large saucepan, cook corn syrup and sugar over medium heat, stirring frequently, until mixture begins to boil. Remove from heat. Stir in peanut butter. Mix in cereal. Press in buttered 13 x 9 x 2-inch pan. Melt chocolate morsels and butterscotch morsels over hot (not boiling) water, stirring constantly until smooth. spread over cereal mixture. Chill until firm, about 15 minutes.

Yield: 48 bars, 1 x 2 inches

® Kellogg Company

BROWN SUGAR BROWNIES

½ cup butter or margarine, softened
2 cups firmly-packed COLONIAL® Light Golden Brown Sugar
2 eggs
1½ cups unsifted flour
½ teaspoon vanilla extract
1 cup chopped nuts

Preheat oven to 375° (350° for glass dish). In medium mixer bowl, cream together butter and sugar; beat in eggs. Stir in flour, vanilla and nuts. Spread into lightly greased 8- or 9-inch square baking pan. Bake 30 to 35 minutes or until toothpick inserted near center comes out clean. Cool. Cut into squares.

Makes 2 dozen brownies

FESTIVE FUDGE-FILLED BARS

2 cups quick oats, uncooked
1½ cups flour
1 cup chopped nuts
1 cup firmly packed brown sugar
1 teaspoon soda
1 teaspoon salt
1 cup margarine, melted
2 tablespoons vegetable shortening
2¼ cups (1 pkg. 16 oz.) M & M's® Plain Chocolate Candies
1 can (14 oz.) sweetened condensed milk
½ cup flaked or shredded coconut, if desired

Combine oats, flour, nuts, sugar, soda and salt; mix well. Add margarine; mix until dry ingredients are thoroughly moistened and mixture resembles coarse crumbs. Reserve 1½ cups; press remaining crumb mixture onto bottom of greased 15½ x 10½-inch jelly roll pan. Bake at 375°F. for 10 minutes. Melt shortening in heavy saucepan until warm. Add 1½ cups candies; continue cooking over very low heat, stirring constantly with metal spoon and pressing candies with back of spoon to break up. (Chocolate mixture will be almost melted and pieces of color coating will remain.) Remove from heat; stir in condensed milk, mixing well. Spread over partially baked crust to within ½-inch of edge. Combine reserved crumb mixture, coconut and remaining candies. Sprinkle over chocolate mixture; press in lightly. Continue baking 20 to 25 minutes or until light golden brown. Cool thoroughly; cut into bars.

Makes one 15½ x 10½-inch pan of bars

CHOCOLATE-ALMOND HONEYS

1 ¾ cups finely crushed graham cracker crumbs (about ¼ lb.)
1 can (14 oz.) sweetened condensed milk
2 tablespoons honey
2 tablespoons orange or apple juice
1 teaspoon grated orange rind
1 package (6 oz.) semi-sweet chocolate chips
½ cup chopped blanched BLUE RIBBON® Almonds

Combine graham cracker crumbs with sweetened condensed milk, honey, orange juice and rind; mix thoroughly. Stir in chocolate and almonds. Spread in a well-oiled, 9-inch square pan. Bake at 350 degrees 30 minutes; remove from oven and let cool a few minutes. While still warm, cut into 16 squares or bars; remove from pan with a spatula. Cool thoroughly on rack, then cut into smaller pieces, if you wish.

Makes 16 to 32 cookies

Nestlé

TWO-TONE BITES

1 12-oz. pkg. (2 cups) NESTLÉ Butterscotch Morsels
1 measuring tablespoon butter
1 measuring tablespoon water
1 cup chopped nuts
1 6-oz. pkg. (1 cup) NESTLÉ Semi-Sweet Real Chocolate Morsels
3 measuring tablespoons corn syrup
1 measuring tablespoon water

Combine over hot (not boiling) water, NESTLÉ Butterscotch Morsels, butter and water. Stir until morsels melt and mixture is smooth. Add nuts; mix well. Press into foil-lined 8″ square pan. Combine over hot (not boiling) water, NESTLÉ Semi-Sweet Real Chocolate Morsels, corn syrup and water; stir until morsels melt and mixture is smooth. Pour chocolate mixture evenly over butterscotch layer. Chill in refrigerator until firm (about 2 hours). Cut into 1″ squares.

Makes: sixty-four 1″ squares

CHEWY APRICOT SQUARES

1 package (8 ounces) semi-sweet chocolate squares
½ cup chopped dried California apricots
2 cups dry cereal (KELLOGG'S® RICE KRISPIES® Cereal, CHEERIOS, WHEAT CHEX® Cereal, etc.)
½ cup dark raisins
2 cups miniature marshmallows

Melt chocolate squares over low heat and transfer to large bowl. Gently fold in remaining ingredients until all particles are coated. Pour mixture evenly into a foil-lined 8-inch square pan. Chill. With a sharp knife, cut into 2-inch squares. Chill until ready to serve.

Makes 16 two-inch squares

California Apricot Advisory Board Favorite Recipe

CRUNCHY FUDGE SANDWICHES

1 6-oz. pkg. (1 cup) NESTLÉ Butterscotch Morsels
½ cup crunchy-style peanut butter
4 cups oven toasted rice cereal
1 6-oz. pkg. (1 cup) NESTLÉ Semi-Sweet Real Chocolate Morsels
½ cup sifted confectioners' sugar
2 measuring tablespoons butter
1 measuring tablespoon water

In large saucepan, combine NESTLÉ Butterscotch Morsels and peanut butter; heat until morsels melt and mixture is smooth. Add rice cereal; stir until well coated with butterscotch mixture. Press half cereal mixture into buttered 8″ square baking pan. Chill in refrigerator while preparing fudge mixture. Set remaining butterscotch mixture aside. Combine over hot (not boiling) water, NESTLÉ Semi-Sweet Real Chocolate Morsels, confectioners' sugar, butter and water; stir until morsels melt and mixture is smooth. Spread over refrigerated butterscotch mixture. Spread remaining butterscotch mixture evenly over top. Press gently. Chill in refrigerator until firm (about 1 hr.). Cut into 1½″ squares.

Makes: twenty five 1½″ squares

OATMEAL FUDGE BARS

Crust:
½ c. soft shortening
1 c. brown sugar
1 egg
½ tsp. vanilla
¾ c. sifted flour
½ tsp. soda
½ tsp. salt
2 c. 3-MINUTE BRAND® Oats
½ c. chopped nuts

Fudge layer:
1 c. (6 oz.) semi-sweet chocolate chips
1 Tbsp. butter
⅓ c. milk
¼ tsp. salt
½ c. chopped nuts
1 tsp. vanilla

Cream shortening and brown sugar. Add egg and vanilla and beat well. Sift flour, soda and salt and add to creamed mixture. Finally stir in oats and nuts. Reserve one cup of this mixture to use for topping. Press remaining mixture into a greased 9 × 9 inch baking pan.

Meanwhile, combine chocolate chips, butter, milk and salt in saucepan. Place over low heat until the chocolate chips are melted. Stir in nuts and vanilla. Spread this mixture over the bottom crust. Sprinkle reserved crust mixture on top. Bake at 350°F. for 25 minutes or until lightly browned. Cool. Cut into bars.

HONEY DATE SNACKS

3 cups QUAKER® Puffed Wheat or Puffed Rice
½ cup chopped dates
⅓ cup firmly packed brown sugar
¼ cup butter or margarine
¼ cup honey

Grease 8-inch square baking pan. In large bowl, combine cereal and dates; set aside. In medium saucepan, combine sugar, butter and honey. Bring mixture to a boil over medium heat, stirring occasionally until smooth. Pour over cereal mixture; mix until well coated. Press firmly into prepared pan. Chill; cut into bars. Store in refrigerator.

Makes 8-inch square pan of bars

SOLO® PRUNE BARS

2 C. all-purpose flour
1 tsp. salt
½ tsp. baking soda
1 C. sugar
¾ C. butter or margarine
1½ C. coconut
1 C. chopped nuts
1 can (12 oz.) SOLO® Prune
Filling

Combine flour, salt, baking soda and sugar. Cut in butter or margarine as for pie crust until mixture is crumbly. Stir in coconut and nuts. Reserve 2 cups of mixture for topping. Press remainder into a 9″ x 13″ pan. Bake in a 400° oven for 10 minutes. Remove from oven and spread with SOLO® Prune Filling. Top with reserved crumb mixture and bake for 15 minutes or until lightly brown. Cut into bars when cool.

TANGY LEMON SQUARES

1 cup (½ lb.) butter or margarine,
    softened
½ cup powdered sugar (unsifted)
2⅓ cups all-purpose flour
    (unsifted)
4 eggs
2 cups granulated sugar
⅓ cup MINUTE MAID® 100% Pure
    Lemon Juice
1 teaspoon baking powder
About 2 tablespoons powdered
    sugar

In a large bowl, cream together butter and the ½ cup powdered sugar until fluffy. Add 2 cups of the flour, beating until blended. Spread evenly over the bottom of a well-greased 9 by 13-inch baking pan. Bake in a preheated 350°F. oven for 20 minutes.

Meanwhile, in a small mixing bowl beat the eggs until light and foamy. Gradually add granulated sugar, beating until thick and blended. Add lemon juice, remaining ⅓ cup flour, and baking powder; beat until thoroughly blended. Pour lemon mixture over baked crust and return to oven; bake 25 to 30 minutes until golden and custard is set. Remove from oven and sprinkle evenly with powdered sugar; let cool. To serve, cut in small squares or bars.
            Makes about 20 pieces

RICH TWO-LAYER APRICOT SQUARES

1 stick (½ cup) ALLSWEET®
    Margarine
¾ cup dried apricots
1 cup sifted flour
¼ cup granulated sugar
1 cup packed light brown sugar
2 SWIFT'S BROOKFIELD® Eggs,
    well beaten
⅓ cup sifted flour
½ teaspoon baking powder
¼ teaspoon salt
½ teaspoon vanilla
½ cup chopped pecans
Powdered sugar

Cover apricots with water. Boil 10 minutes. Drain, cool, and chop apricots.

Lower Layer: Sift into a bowl 1 cup flour and the granulated sugar. Cut in margarine, using a pastry blender or fork, until the mixture is the consistency of corn meal and small peas. Pack into a pan. Bake in a slow oven (325°F.) 25 minutes.

Top Layer: Add brown sugar to the eggs. Stir in ⅓ cup flour sifted with baking powder and salt. Add vanilla, nuts, and chopped apricots. Mix thoroughly. Spread over the baked layer. Return to the slow oven (325°F.) and bake 35 minutes. (The top will be soft.) Cool several hours. Cut into squares. Sprinkle with powdered sugar.   *Yield: 16 squares
      (9 by 9 by 1¾-inch pan)*

LAND O' LAKES® LEMON-BUTTER SNOWBARS

Crust:
½ c. LAND O LAKES® Sweet
    Cream Butter, softened
1⅓ c. all-purpose flour
¼ c. sugar

Filling:
2 eggs
¾ c. sugar
2 Tbsp. all-purpose flour
¼ tsp. baking powder
3 Tbsp. lemon juice
Confectioners' sugar

Preheat Oven: 350°. In 1½-qt. mixer bowl combine crust ingredients; mix at low speed until blended (1 min.). Pat into ungreased 8″ sq. baking pan. Bake near center of 350° oven for 15 to 20 min. or until brown on edges. Meanwhile, prepare filling; pour filling over partially baked crust. Return to oven for 18 to 20 min. or until set. Sprinkle with confectioners' sugar. Cool. *Filling:* In 1½-qt. mixing bowl combine all filling ingredients; blend well.
            Yield: 16 bars

LAND O' LAKES® MERRY CHERRY CHEESECAKE BARS

Crust:
⅓ c. cold LAND O LAKES®
    Sweet Cream Butter
⅓ c. firmly packed brown sugar
1 c. all-purpose flour

Filling:
8-oz. pkg. cream cheese, softened
¼ c. sugar
1 egg
1 Tbsp. lemon juice
½ c. chopped glazed red and
    green cherries

Preheat Oven: 350°. In 1-qt. mixer bowl cut butter in chunks; add brown sugar and flour; mix at low speed. Beat at med. speed, scraping sides of bowl often, until well mixed (1 min.). Reserve ½ c. crumb mixture for topping; press remaining crumb mixture into 8″ sq. baking pan. Bake near center of 350° oven for 10 to 12 min. Prepare filling. Spread filling over crust; sprinkle with remaining crumb mixture. Continue baking for 18 to 20 min. or until filling is set and lightly browned. Cool. Cut into bars. Store bars in refrigerator. *Filling:* In 1-qt. mixer bowl beat cream cheese, sugar, egg and lemon juice at med. speed until fluffy (1 to 2 min.). Stir in chopped cherries.   *Yield: 36 bars*

SPICED MOLASSES BARS

¾ cup SUNSWEET® Pitted Prunes
1¾ cups sifted all-purpose flour
1 tsp. ground ginger
½ tsp. allspice
¼ tsp. cardamom
½ tsp. salt
½ tsp. baking soda
½ cup shortening
½ cup granulated sugar
1 large egg
⅓ cup light molasses
½ cup flaked coconut
Granulated sugar for tops of
  cookies

Snip prunes into small pieces. Resift flour with spices, salt and soda. Cream shortening with sugar, egg and molasses. Add dry mixture, blending until well mixed. Stir in prunes and coconut. Chill dough about 30 min. Spread dough into 2 strips 3½″ wide and 14″ long, on lightly greased baking sheet. Mark diagonally into 2″ slices. Sprinkle lightly with sugar. Bake above oven center at 350°F. 15 to 18 min., until cookies spring back when touched in center. Remove from oven; let stand 5 min. Cut at markings into diagonal slices. Cool on wire racks.

Makes 14 large cookies

PEANUT BUTTER NOUGAT BARS

1 (6-oz.) pkg. butterscotch pieces
⅓ cup peanut butter
2 Tbsp. butter or margarine
3 cups miniature marshmallows
¼ tsp. salt
2½ qts. popped ORVILLE
  REDENBACHER'S Gourmet
  Popping Corn
1 cup granola
1 (6-oz.) pkg. semi-sweet
  chocolate pieces

Melt butterscotch pieces, peanut butter, butter, marshmallows and salt in top part of double boiler over hot water. Stir constantly until melted and smooth. Combine with popped corn and granola in buttered 9 × 13 × 2-inch pan. Toss until well mixed; press smooth in pan. Melt chocolate over hot, not boiling, water; spread over nougat mixture to form lacy pattern. Cool until firm; cut in 1 × 2-inch bars.

Makes 4½ dozen

MARSHMALLOW TREATS

¼ cup margarine or butter
1 package (10 oz., about 40)
  regular marshmallows or 4 cups
  miniature marshmallows
5 cups KELLOGG'S® RICE
  KRISPIES® Cereal

Melt margarine in large saucepan over low heat. Add marshmallows and stir until completely melted. Cook over low heat 3 minutes longer, stirring constantly. Remove from heat. Add cereal. Stir until well coated. Using buttered spatula or waxed paper, press mixture evenly into buttered 13 × 9 × 2-inch pan. Cut into 2-inch squares when cool.

Yield: 24 squares, 2 × 2 inches

Note: Best results are obtained when using fresh marshmallows.

VARIATIONS:

To make thicker squares: Press warm mixture into buttered 9 × 9 × 2-inch pan.

Marshmallow Creme Treats: About 2 cups marshmallow creme may be substituted for marshmallows. Add to melted margarine and stir until well blended. Cook over low heat about 5 minutes longer, stirring constantly. Remove from heat. Proceed as directed above.

Peanut Treats: Add 1 cup salted cocktail peanuts with the cereal.

Peanut Butter Treats: Stir ¼ cup peanut butter into marshmallow mixture just before adding the cereal.

Raisin Treats: Add 1 cup seedless raisins with the cereal.

COCOA KRISPIES® Cereal Treats: 6 cups KELLOGG'S COCOA KRISPIES® Cereal may be substituted for the 5 cups KELLOGG'S® RICE KRISPIES® Cereal.

® Kellogg Company

HIKER'S BRAN SNACK SQUARES

½ cup honey
½ cup creamy peanut butter
3 tablespoons butter or margarine
½ cup nonfat dry milk
2½ cups NABISCO® 100% Bran
  Cereal
3 tablespoons sesame seeds,
  toasted

Combine first three ingredients until well blended. Stir in next two ingredients. Press firmly in bottom of 8 × 8 × 2-inch baking pan. Sprinkle with sesame seeds pressing into surface. Chill for 1 hour. Cut into squares. Wrap individually to carry on hikes.

Makes 16 (about 2-inch) squares

CHEESE CRUNCHERS

1 12-oz. pkg. (2 cups) NESTLÉ
  Butterscotch Morsels
6 measuring tablespoons butter
2 cups graham cracker crumbs
2 cups chopped nuts
2 8-oz. pkgs. cream cheese,
  softened
½ cup sugar
4 eggs
¼ cup unsifted flour
2 measuring tablespoons lemon
  juice

Preheat oven to 350°F. Combine over hot (not boiling) water, NESTLÉ Butterscotch Morsels and butter; heat until melted and smooth. Transfer to large bowl; stir in graham cracker crumbs and nuts with a fork until mixture forms a small crumb. Reserve 2 cups crumb mixture for topping. Press remaining mixture into 15″ × 10″ × 1″ baking pan. Bake at 350°F. 12 minutes. In large bowl, combine cream cheese and sugar; beat until creamy. Add eggs, one at a time, beating well after each addition. Blend in flour and lemon juice. Pour evenly over hot baked crust. Sprinkle top with reserved crumb mixture. Bake at 350°F. 25 minutes. Cool completely; cut into 2″ × 1″ bars. Chill in refrigerator before serving.

Makes: seventy-five 2″ × 1″ bars

AUSTRALIAN SQUARES

½ cup butter, softened
½ cup firmly packed brown sugar, divided
1 measuring tablespoon grated lemon rind
1 measuring teaspoon vanilla extract
1 egg, separated
1 cup unsifted flour
¼ cup water
1 6-oz. pkg. (1 cup) NESTLÉ Semi-Sweet Real Chocolate Morsels

Preheat oven to 375°F. In large bowl, combine butter, ¼ cup brown sugar, lemon rind and vanilla extract; beat until creamy. Add egg yolk; mix well. Alternately add flour with water. Stir in NESTLÉ Semi-Sweet Real Chocolate Morsels; set aside. In small bowl, beat egg white until stiff (not dry) peaks form. Gradually add remaining ¼ cup brown sugar and beat until stiff and glossy. Fold into batter. Pour into lightly greased foil-lined 8″ square pan. Bake at 375°F. 25-30 minutes. Cool. Cut into 2″ squares.

Makes sixteen 2″ squares

CHOCO-PEANUT BUTTER CHEWS

1 cup sugar
1 cup light corn syrup
1½ cups peanut butter
6 cups POPEYE Puffed Wheat or Puffed Rice
1 package (6 ounces) semi-sweet real chocolate morsels
1 package (6 ounces) artificial butterscotch flavored morsels

Butter a 13 × 9 × 2-inch pan. Combine sugar and corn syrup; bring to a boil. Remove from heat; add peanut butter; mix until smooth. Pour over Puffed Wheat; blend well. Press into prepared pan. Melt chocolate and butterscotch over low heat or in microwave oven. Stir to blend and spread evenly over cereal mixture. Allow to stand at room temperature until set; cut into squares. *48 small squares*

BANANA CHOCOLATE CHIP BARS

½ cup butter or margarine, softened
¾ cup packed brown sugar
1 cup mashed banana (about 2 medium)
½ teaspoon vanilla extract
1¼ cups all-purpose flour
½ cup untoasted wheat germ
½ teaspoon baking soda
¼ teaspoon salt
1 package (6 ounces) semi-sweet real chocolate pieces
¾ cup BLUE DIAMOND® Chopped Natural Almonds, toasted

Cream butter and sugar; add banana and vanilla. Combine flour, wheat germ, baking soda and salt; stir into banana mixture. Fold in chocolate pieces and ½ cup of the almonds. Spread in bottom of greased 13 × 9 × 2-inch baking pan; sprinkle with remaining almonds. Bake in 350 degree F. oven for 18 to 20 minutes or until toothpick inserted in center comes out clean.

Makes about 30 bars

MAGIC COOKIE BARS

½ cup margarine or butter
1½ cups graham cracker crumbs
1 (14-ounce) can EAGLE® Brand Sweetened Condensed Milk (not evaporated milk)
1 (6-ounce) package semi-sweet chocolate morsels
1 (3½-ounce) can flaked coconut (1⅓ cups)
1 cup chopped nuts

Preheat oven to 350°F. (325°F. for glass dish). In 13 × 9-inch baking pan, melt margarine in oven. Sprinkle crumbs over margarine; pour EAGLE® Brand evenly over crumbs. Top evenly with remaining ingredients; press down firmly. Bake 25 to 30 minutes or until lightly browned. Cool thoroughly before cutting. Store loosely covered at room temperature.

Makes 24 bars

VARIATIONS:

Apricot Bars: Substitute 1 (6-ounce) package dried apricots, chopped, (1 cup) for chocolate morsels. Proceed as directed.

Butterscotch Bars: Substitute 1 (6-ounce) package butterscotch-flavored morsels for chocolate morsels. Proceed as directed.

Confetti Bars: Substitute 1 cup plain multi-colored candy-coated chocolate pieces for chocolate morsels. Proceed as directed.

Raisin Bars: Substitute wheat germ for graham cracker crumbs. Substitute 1 cup seedless raisins for chocolate morsels. Proceed as directed.

CHEWY CHOCOLATE CHIP BARS

¾ cup butter or margarine, melted
1 pound COLONIAL® Dark Brown Sugar
3 eggs
2¾ cups unsifted flour
2½ teaspoons baking powder
½ teaspoon salt
1 (6-ounce) package semi-sweet chocolate morsels or 1 cup raisins

Preheat oven to 350°. In large mixer bowl, cream together butter and sugar. Beat in eggs, 1 at a time, beating well after each addition. Combine dry ingredients; beat into sugar mixture. Stir in morsels. Spread evenly into lightly greased 15 × 10-inch jellyroll pan. Bake 25 minutes or until toothpick inserted near center comes out clean. Cool. Cut into bars.

Makes 40 bars

PRETZEL BARS

1½ cups ROLD GOLD® Brand Pretzels, measured after crushing very fine in blender or between waxed paper
3 egg whites
1 cup sugar
1 teaspoon baking powder
1 cup chopped nuts

Beat egg whites until stiff. Fold in remaining ingredients. Pour into well-greased 8″ square pan. Bake at 350°F. for 25 to 30 minutes. Cut into bars while hot.

GOLD'N HONEY NUT CRUNCH BARS

PAM® Vegetable Cooking Spray
⅓ cup SUE BEE® Honey
⅓ cup margarine or butter
1 cup packed brown sugar
½ teaspoon ground cinnamon, if desired
1 teaspoon vanilla
5 cups GOLDEN GRAHAMS® Cereal
1 cup FISHER® Mixed Nuts or Peanuts

Spray square pan, 9 × 9 × 2 inches, with PAM® Vegetable Cooking Spray. Heat honey, margarine, brown sugar and cinnamon to boiling in 3-quart saucepan; boil 2 minutes. Remove from heat; stir in vanilla. Gradually fold in cereal until completely coated. Fold in nuts. Press cereal mixture in pan with a piece of waxed paper. Let stand at least 1 hour. Cut into bars, about 2¼ × 1½ inches.

24 bars

WALNUT LINZER BARS

1 cup DIAMOND® Walnuts
¾ cup butter
½ cup granulated sugar
1 egg
½ teaspoon grated lemon peel
½ teaspoon salt
½ teaspoon cinnamon
⅛ teaspoon cloves
2 cups sifted all-purpose flour
1 cup raspberry or apricot jam

Chop or grind walnuts very fine; set aside. Cream butter with sugar, egg, lemon peel, salt and spices. Blend in flour and walnuts. Set aside about ¼ of dough for lattice top. Pat remaining dough into bottom and about ½-inch up sides of greased 9-inch square pan. Spread with jam. Make pencil-shaped strips of remaining dough, rolling against floured board with palms of hands. Arrange in lattice over top, ends pressed against dough on sides. Bake at 325°F. about 45 minutes, until lightly browned. Cool in pan, then cut into bars.

Makes 2 dozen small bars

SALTED PEANUT CHEWS

Crust:
1½ cups PILLSBURY'S BEST® All Purpose, Unbleached or Self-Rising Flour*
⅔ cup firmly packed brown sugar
½ teaspoon baking powder
½ teaspoon salt
¼ teaspoon soda
½ cup margarine or butter, softened
1 teaspoon vanilla
2 egg yolks
3 cups miniature marshmallows

Topping:
⅔ cup corn syrup
¼ cup margarine or butter
2 teaspoons vanilla
12-oz. pkg. (2 cups) peanut butter chips
2 cups crisp rice cereal
2 cups salted peanuts

Heat oven to 350°F. Lightly spoon flour into measuring cup; level off. In large bowl, combine all crust ingredients except marshmallows until crumb mixture forms. Press in bottom of ungreased 13 × 9-inch pan.

Bake at 350°F. for 12 to 15 minutes or until light golden brown. Immediately sprinkle with marshmallows. Return to oven for 1 to 2 minutes or until marshmallows just begin to puff. Cool while preparing topping. In large saucepan, heat corn syrup, margarine, vanilla and peanut butter chips just until chips are melted and mixture is smooth, stirring constantly. Remove from heat; stir in cereal and nuts. Immediately spoon warm topping over marshmallows and spread to cover. Chill; cut into bars.

36 bars

TIP: *If using PILLSBURY'S BEST® Self-Rising Flour, omit baking powder, soda and salt.

High Altitude—Above 3500 Feet: No change.

NUTRITIONAL INFORMATION PER SERVING

SERVING SIZE: 2 BARS/SERVING		PERCENT U.S. RDA PER SERVING	
Calories	420	Protein	10
Protein	7 g	Vitamin A	10
Carbohydrate	48 g	Vitamin C	*
Fat	23 g	Thiamine	10
Sodium	305 mg	Riboflavin	8
Potassium	215 mg	Niacin	20
		Calcium	4
		Iron	10

*Contains less than 2% of the U.S. RDA of this nutrient.

PILLSBURY BAKE-OFF® recipe

Candy

FIESTA FUDGE

2½ cups sugar
¾ cup margarine
⅔ cup (5⅓ oz. can) evaporated milk
½ teaspoon salt
1½ cups creamy peanut butter
1 jar (7 oz.) marshmallow cream
1 teaspoon vanilla
1½ cups M & M'S® Plain or Peanut Chocolate Candies

Combine sugar, margarine, milk and salt in heavy 3-qt. saucepan; bring to full rolling boil over high heat, stirring constantly. Continue boiling over medium heat 5 minutes, stirring constantly. Remove from heat; stir in peanut butter until melted. Add marshmallow cream and vanilla; beat until well blended. Fold in candies; immediately spread into greased 13 × 9-inch baking pan. Cool at room temperature; cut into squares.
Makes one 13 × 9-inch pan of fudge (about 3 lbs.)

MILNOT® FUDGE

1 cup MILNOT®
3 cups sugar
⅓ cup butter or margarine
1 jar marshmallow creme (approx. 7 oz.)
1 12-ounce package (2 cups) chocolate chips
1 cup chopped nuts, optional
1 teaspoon vanilla, optional

Combine sugar, MILNOT®, marshmallow creme and butter in a heavy saucepan (3½ quart or larger). Heat slowly to boiling, stirring frequently. When mixture boils vigorously (so that boiling cannot be slowed by stirring) start timing, continue boiling for 4 minutes, stirring constantly. Remove from heat, stir in chocolate chips until melted, add nuts and vanilla. Pour into buttered pan (9 × 9-inch or larger). Cool at room temperature.
Yield: almost 3 pounds

VARIATIONS:

Substitute butterscotch or peanut butter chips for chocolate.

304

DIAMOND® WHITE FUDGE

2 cups granulated sugar
½ cup dairy sour cream
⅓ cup white corn syrup
2 tablespoons butter
¼ teaspoon salt
2 teaspoons vanilla, rum or brandy flavoring
¼ cup quartered candied cherries
1 cup coarsely-chopped DIAMOND® Walnuts

Combine first five ingredients in saucepan; bring to a boil slowly, stirring until sugar dissolves. Boil, without stirring, over medium heat, to 236 degrees on candy thermometer, or until a little mixture dropped in cold water forms a soft ball. Remove from heat and let stand 15 minutes; do not stir. Add flavoring; beat until mixture starts to lose its gloss (about eight minutes). Stir in the candied cherries and walnuts, and quickly pour into a greased shallow pan. Cool completely and cut into squares.

Makes about 1½ pounds of candy

VARIATIONS:

You can do interesting, pretty things with this fudge, and they're easy. Just form the candy in your hands, handling it lightly, and taking care that it should not be worked too much.

Walnut Sandwiches: Shape fudge into tiny round balls, then press between two walnut halves.

Bon Bons: Roll fudge into round balls, and coat with chopped walnuts.

Squares: Cut fudge into squares. Place on fork and dip in melted chocolate to coat sides. Cool on waxed paper.

Log Roll: Form fudge into a log shape, and roll in chopped walnuts.

NOTE: *Three methods to prevent sugary fudge.* Use a heavy 2-quart saucepan with straight sides. Stir while mixture heats so candy will not stick and burn. For creamy fudge, remove sugar crystals from pan above the boiling level. To do this: 1. Wipe sides of pan with wet pastry brush, or 2. Use part of butter in the recipe to grease pan, or 3. When candy boils, cover pan for one minute to allow steam to wash down the crystals.

CHOCOLATE FUDGE

2 squares BAKER'S® Unsweetened Chocolate
¾ cup milk
2 cups sugar
Dash of salt
2 tablespoons butter or margarine
1 teaspoon vanilla

Place chocolate and milk in heavy saucepan. Cook and stir over very low heat until mixture is smooth, well blended and slightly thickened. Add sugar and salt; stir over medium heat until sugar is dissolved and mixture boils. Continue boiling over medium heat, without stirring, until small amount of mixture forms a soft ball which can be rolled with the fingers into a definite shape in cold water (or to a temperature of 234°). Remove from heat; add butter and vanilla. *Do not stir.* Cool to lukewarm (110°). Beat until mixture begins to lose its gloss and holds its shape. Pour at once into buttered 8 x 4-inch loaf pan. Cool until set; then cut into squares. Let stand in pan until firm. Store in covered container.

Makes about 1 pound or about 1½ dozen pieces

DOUBLE DECKER FUDGE

1 cup REESE'S® Peanut Butter Flavored Chips
1 cup HERSHEY'S® Semi-Sweet Chocolate Chips or Mini Chips
¾ cup evaporated milk
¼ cup butter or margarine
2¼ cups sugar
1¾ cups (7-ounce jar) marshmallow creme
1 teaspoon vanilla

Measure Peanut Butter Chips into one mixing bowl, and Mini Chips or Chocolate Chips into second bowl; set aside. Butter an 8-inch square pan. Combine evaporated milk, butter or margarine, sugar and marshmallow creme in a heavy 2¾-quart saucepan. Cook over medium heat until mixture begins to boil, stirring constantly; continue cooking and stirring 5 minutes. Remove from heat; stir in vanilla. Immediately add about one-half of hot mixture to Peanut Butter Chips, stirring until completely melted; pour into prepared pan. Add remaining hot mixture to Mini Chips or Chocolate Chips, stirring until completely melted. Spread over top of peanut butter layer in pan; cool.

About 4 dozen squares

Peanut Butter Fudge: Omit 1 cup HERSHEY'S® Mini Chips or Chocolate Chips and place 2 cups (12-ounce package) REESE'S® Peanut Butter Flavored Chips in one bowl. Cook fudge mixture as directed above; add to peanut butter chips, stirring until melted. Pour into prepared pan; cool.

Nestlé

MARSHMALLOW CREAM FUDGE

1 jar marshmallow cream*
1½ cups sugar
⅔ cup evaporated milk
¼ cup butter or margarine
¼ measuring teaspoon salt
One 12-oz. pkg. (2 cups) NESTLÉ Semi-Sweet Real Chocolate Morsels
½ cup chopped nuts
1 measuring teaspoon vanilla extract

In medium saucepan, combine marshmallow cream, sugar, evaporated milk, butter or margarine, and salt; bring to *full boil*, stirring constantly over moderate heat. *Boil 5 minutes*, stirring constantly over moderate heat. Remove from heat. Add NESTLÉ Semi-Sweet Real Chocolate Morsels; stir until morsels melt and mixture is smooth. Stir in nuts and vanilla extract. Pour into aluminum foil-lined 8" square pan. Chill in refrigerator until firm (about 2 hours). *Makes: 2¼ lbs.*

*5-oz.—10-oz. jar Marshmallow Cream

QUICK NUT FUDGE

1 lb. DOMINO® Confectioners' 10-X Powdered Sugar
½ cup cocoa
¼ teaspoon salt
6 tablespoons butter or margarine
4 tablespoons milk
1 tablespoon vanilla extract
1 cup chopped pecans or walnuts

Combine all ingredients except nuts in top of double boiler. Place over simmering water and stir until smooth. Add nuts and mix. Spread candy quickly in buttered 9″ × 5″ loaf pan. Cool; cut in squares.
Yields 2 dozen pieces

FIVE-MINUTE FUDGE

2 tablespoons butter
⅔ cup undiluted CARNATION® Evaporated Milk
1⅔ cups sugar
½ teaspoon salt
2 cups (4 ounces) miniature marshmallows
1½ cups (1½ 6-ounce packages) semi-sweet chocolate pieces
1 teaspoon vanilla
½ cup chopped nuts

Combine butter, evaporated milk, sugar, and salt in saucepan over medium heat, stirring occasionally. Bring to full boil. Cook 4 to 5 minutes, stirring constantly. Remove from heat. Stir in marshmallows, chocolate pieces, vanilla, and nuts. Stir vigorously for 1 minute (until marshmallows melt and blend). Pour into 8-inch square buttered pan. Cool. Cut in squares.
Makes 2 pounds

NEVER-FAIL CHOCOLATE FUDGE

2½ cups sugar
½ stick butter or margarine
1 small can (¾ cup) evaporated milk
1 7½ oz. jar MARSHMALLOW FLUFF
¾ teaspoon salt
¾ teaspoon vanilla extract
1 large (12 ounce) package semi-sweet chocolate pieces
½ cup chopped walnuts, if desired

Combine first 5 ingredients. Stir over low heat until blended. Bring to a *boil* over moderate heat, being careful not to mistake air bubbles for boiling. *Then boil slowly, stirring constantly, for 5 minutes.* Remove from heat. Stir in vanilla and chocolate until chocolate is melted. Add nuts. Turn into a buttered 9 × 9-inch pan and cool.
Makes about 2½ pounds

FANTASY FUDGE

3 cups sugar
¾ cup PARKAY Margarine
⅔ cup (5⅓-fl. oz. can) evaporated milk
1 12-oz. pkg. semi-sweet chocolate pieces
1 7-oz. jar KRAFT Marshmallow Creme
1 cup chopped nuts
1 teaspoon vanilla

Combine sugar, margarine and milk in heavy saucepan; bring to full rolling boil, stirring constantly. Continue boiling 5 minutes over medium heat, stirring constantly to prevent scorching. Remove from heat; stir in chocolate until melted. Add marshmallow creme, nuts and vanilla; beat until well blended. Pour into greased 13 × 9-inch baking pan. Cool at room temperature; cut into squares.
3 pounds

THE JUDGE'S PRALINE® FUDGE

1⅓ cups sugar
1 small can evaporated milk (⅔ cup)
3 tablespoons butter or margarine
3 packages (6 oz. each) semisweet chocolate pieces
3 cups miniature marshmallows
½ cup chopped pecans
⅓ cup PRALINE® Liqueur

Combine the sugar, evaporated milk and butter in a medium size, heavy saucepan. Bring to a boil over medium heat, stirring constantly. Cook for 6 minutes or until candy thermometer reaches 227 degrees. Remove from heat. Add chocolate pieces and marshmallows; stir until melted and mixture is smooth. Quickly stir in pecans. Add PRALINE®. Spoon into buttered 8 × 8 × 2-inch pan. Chill until set.
Makes 64 one-inch squares

CHOCOLATE "PHILLY" FUDGE

4 cups sifted confectioners' sugar
1 8-oz. pkg. PHILADELPHIA BRAND Cream Cheese
4 1-oz. squares unsweetened chocolate, melted
1 teaspoon vanilla
Dash of salt
½ cup chopped nuts

Gradually add sugar to softened cream cheese, mixing until well blended. Stir in remaining ingredients. Spread into greased 8-inch square pan. Chill several hours or overnight; cut into squares. Garnish with additional nuts, if desired.
1¾ pounds

VARIATIONS:

Peppermint "Philly" Fudge: Omit nuts and vanilla; add a few drops peppermint extract and ¼ cup crushed peppermint candy. Sprinkle with ¼ cup crushed peppermint candy before chilling.

Coconut "Philly" Fudge: Omit nuts; add 1 cup shredded coconut. Garnish with additional coconut, if desired.

Cherry "Philly" Fudge: Omit nuts; add ½ cup chopped maraschino cherries. Garnish with whole cherries, if desired.

NO COOK CREAM CHEESE FUDGE

1 package (3 ounces) cream cheese, softened
1 teaspoon milk
2 cups sifted powdered sugar
2 envelopes (1 ounce *each*) no-melt unsweetened chocolate
½ teaspoon vanilla extract
⅓ cup BLUE DIAMOND® Chopped Natural Almonds, toasted

Blend cream cheese with milk until smooth. Gradually beat in sugar, chocolate and vanilla; stir in almonds. Press into buttered 9 × 5 × 3-inch loaf pan. Chill until firm.
Makes 1 pound

BITTER-CHOCOLATE ALMOND BALLS

2 cups BLUE DIAMOND® Whole
  Natural Almonds
½ cup unsweetened cocoa
1 teaspoon grated orange peel
⅓ to ½ cup honey
Sifted powdered sugar

Lightly toast 20 almonds; reserve.
Whirl remaining almonds in
blender until finely ground. In
medium-size bowl thoroughly mix
ground almonds, cocoa and orange
peel; blend in enough honey to
form very stiff mixture. Cover and
chill one hour. Wrap about one
tablespoon dough around each
toasted almond, covering
completely. Roll in powdered
sugar. Store in air tight container.

Makes 20 almond balls

Food Processor Directions: Lightly
toast 20 almonds; reserve. Process
remaining almonds with metal
blade until finely ground; add
cocoa and orange peel and blend.
With machine running add enough
honey through tube and mix until
mixture is stiff. Remove dough
from bowl, wrap in waxed paper;
chill one hour. Proceed as directed
above.

BUTTER-ALMOND CRUNCH

1½ cups HERSHEY'S® Mini Chips
1¾ cups chopped almonds
1½ cups butter or margarine
1¾ cups sugar
3 tablespoons light corn syrup
3 tablespoons water

Lightly butter a 13 × 9 × 2-inch pan.
Spread 1 cup Mini Chips evenly
over bottom; set aside. Spread
almonds in shallow pan or on
baking sheet; toast at 350°F.
stirring occasionally, for 7 to 8
minutes or until golden brown. Set
aside. Melt butter or margarine in a
2½-quart saucepan; blend in
sugar, corn syrup and water. Cook
over medium heat, stirring
constantly, to hard-crack stage
(300°F.). Remove from heat; stir in
1½ cups of the toasted almonds.
Immediately spread mixture evenly
over Mini Chips in pan, being
careful not to disturb chips.
Quickly sprinkle with remaining ¼
cup almonds and ½ cup Mini
Chips; score into 1½-inch squares,
if desired. Cool; cover pan and

store overnight. Remove from pan;
break into pieces. Store in tightly
covered container.

About 2¼ pounds candy

CHOCOLATE ALMOND DATES

1 package (8 ounces) whole pitted
  dates
6 squares (1 ounce *each*) semi-
  sweet real chocolate
¼ to ⅓ cup BLUE DIAMOND®
  Whole Blanched Almonds,
  toasted

Stuff dates with almonds. Melt
chocolate in top of double boiler
over hot, not boiling, water. One at
a time, drop stuffed dates into the
chocolate, turning to coat. Remove
to waxed paper-lined cookie sheet.
Allow chocolate to harden.
(Refrigeration will speed the
process.)

Makes about 30 to 35 candies

SUN WORLD®

VALENTINE STUFFED DATES

1 8 oz. package cream cheese,
  softened
1-2 Tbsp. milk or cream
1 lb. SUN WORLD® Pitted Dates
Assorted nuts; pecans, walnuts,
  almonds OR shredded coconut

Mix cream cheese with milk or
cream. Stuff the dates with
mixture. Garnish with nut meats or
roll in coconut.

QUICK PRALINES

¼ cup water
2 tablespoons butter or margarine
1 cup firmly-packed COLONIAL®
  Light Golden Brown Sugar
1 cup COLONIAL® Confectioners'
  Sugar
½ teaspoon vanilla extract
¾ cup chopped pecans

In medium saucepan, bring water
and butter to a boil; stir in sugars.
Return to boiling; boil and stir 1
minute. Remove from heat; stir in

vanilla and pecans. Beat until
mixture begins to thicken slightly.
Immediately drop from teaspoon
onto wax paper. Cool. Store in
covered container.

Makes about 1½ dozen pralines

TRADITIONAL PRALINES

3 cups firmly-packed COLONIAL®
  Light Golden Brown Sugar
1 cup COLONIAL® Granulated
  Sugar
¾ cup water
2 cups pecan halves

In large saucepan, combine sugars
and water. Cook and stir over
medium heat until mixture boils
and sugar is dissolved. Continue
cooking, without stirring, to 238°
on candy thermometer or until
small amount dropped in cold
water forms a firm ball. Remove
from heat; stir in pecans. Return to
heat and bring to a boil. Remove
from heat. Stir until creamy and
slightly thickened (about 10
minutes). Immediately drop from
teaspoon onto greased baking
sheets. Cool. Store in covered
container.

Makes about 2½ dozen pralines

PRALINES

2 cups IMPERIAL Granulated
  Sugar
1 teaspoon soda
1 cup buttermilk
⅛ teaspoon salt
2 tablespoons butter or margarine
2½ cups pecan halves

In large (3½ quart) heavy saucepan
combine IMPERIAL Granulated
Sugar, soda, buttermilk and salt.
Cook over high heat about 5
minutes (or to 210°F. on candy
thermometer); stir often and scrape
bottom of pan. Mixture will foam
up. Add butter or margarine and
pecans. Over medium heat,
continue cooking, stirring
constantly and scraping bottom
and sides of pan until candy
reaches soft ball stage (234°F. on
candy thermometer). Remove from
heat and cool slightly, about 2
minutes. Beat with spoon until
thick and creamy. Drop from
tablespoon onto sheet of
aluminum foil or waxed paper. Let
cool.

*Makes about 20 pralines, 2" in
diameter*

FLUFF CORNFLAKE KISSES

2 egg whites
¼ teaspoon salt
2 cups MARSHMALLOW FLUFF
½ teaspoon vanilla extract
2½ cups cornflakes
2 cups flaked coconut

Beat egg whites and salt until stiff. Beat in MARSHMALLOW FLUFF and vanilla until mixture forms very stiff peaks. Fold in cornflakes and coconut. Drop by teaspoonfuls on lightly greased baking sheet. Bake in a 300°F. oven 30 minutes. Cool 5 minutes on pan. Remove from pan and cool on cake rack.

Makes 4 dozen

VARIATIONS:

1. Add ¾ cup chopped pecans. 2. Add ¾ cup chopped walnuts and ¾ cup chopped dates.

Karo.
Mazola.

SESAME CRUNCH

2 cups sesame seeds
1 cup sugar
1 cup KARO® Light Corn Syrup
⅓ cup water
2 tablespoons NUCOA® or MAZOLA® Margarine

Grease cookie sheet. In 3-quart saucepan stir together sesame seeds, sugar, corn syrup, water and margarine. Bring to boil over medium heat, stirring constantly. Continue cooking, without stirring, until temperature reaches 270°F on candy thermometer or until small amount of mixture dropped into very cold water forms a ball which is hard enough to hold its shape, yet plastic. Turn onto prepared cookie sheet and spread with greased metal spatula or greased wooden spoon to ¼-inch thickness. Score with sharp knife into pieces 1½ × ½ inch. Let cool completely. Break apart by placing knife in scores and tapping gently with spoon.

Makes 1¾ pounds or about 175 (1½ × ½ × ¼-inch) pieces

PEANUT BUTTER KISSES

2 egg whites
⅛ teaspoon cream of tartar
⅔ cup sugar
½ cup SKIPPY® Creamy or Super Chunk Peanut Butter

In small bowl with mixer at high speed beat egg whites and cream of tartar until mixture holds stiff peaks when beater is raised. Add sugar, 1 tablespoon at a time, beating well after each addition. Continue beating until mixture holds very stiff peaks when beater is raised. Lightly fold in peanut butter just until mixed. Drop by teaspoonfuls onto greased cookie sheet. Bake in 300°F oven 25 minutes or until lightly browned. Remove from cookie sheet immediately.

Makes about 3 dozen cookies

BANANA COCONUT "LEATHER"

6 medium DOLE® Bananas
¼ cup lemon juice
2 tablespoons sugar
½ cup flaked coconut

Peel and slice bananas to measure about 1 quart. Combine with lemon juice and sugar in blender jar, and blend until smooth. Stir in coconut. Line 2 pans (10 × 5 × 1-inch) with plastic wrap or heavy plastic bag cut open. Turn half the mixture into each pan. Spread evenly. Place in gas oven with pilot light, and let stand 24 hours. Remove from oven and check drying. If leather is dry enough to form a sheet that can be lifted, gently peel leather off plastic, and turn over. Return to oven until no moist spots remain, about a half day. Peel off when dry, and roll up. Wrap in plastic wrap to store.

Makes 2 (10-inch) rolls leather

To dry in electric oven: Heat oven to 200°F. Place prepared pans in oven 5 minutes. Turn oven off and let stand without opening oven door for several hours. Remove from oven, reheat to 200°F. and turn oven off. Return pans to oven and let stand as before. After third period, the leather should be dry enough to turn. Heat oven again to 200°F., turn off, and place pans in again. Leather should be dry in about 24 hours.

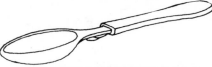

APRICOT SNOWBALLS

2 cups uncrushed cornflakes (or bran or wheat flakes)
⅓ cup diced pitted dates
⅔ cup diced dried California apricots
½ cup chopped pecans
¼ cup honey
3 tablespoons butter or margarine
1 teaspoon vanilla
Granulated sugar (optional)
Strips of dried California apricots, red glace cherry halves, for garnish

Using a rolling pin, crush cornflakes between 2 sheets of waxed paper. Stir crushed cornflakes, dates, apricots and pecans until well mixed in large bowl. Melt honey and butter in small pan; blend in vanilla. Pour over cornflake mixture; mix thoroughly. Chill 30 minutes. Use one tablespoon of mixture to form each ball. Roll balls in sugar, if desired. Garnish each with a strip of apricot or a cherry half. Serve immediately or cover and chill until needed.

Makes about 30 balls

California Apricot Advisory Board Favorite recipe

Snacks

CARAMEL APPLES

49 (14-oz. bag) KRAFT Caramels
2 tablespoons water
4 or 5 medium size apples, washed, dried
Wooden sticks

Melt caramels with water in covered double boiler or in saucepan over low heat. Stir occasionally until sauce is smooth. Insert a wooden stick into stem end of each apple. Dip into hot caramel sauce; turn until coated. Scrape off excess sauce from bottom of apples. Place on greased waxed paper; chill until firm. Keep in cool place.

ORIENTAL ALMONDS

1½ tablespoons butter or
  margarine
1½ tablespoons Worcestershire
  sauce
1 teaspoon salt
¼ teaspoon cinnamon
⅛ teaspoon chili powder
Dash hot pepper sauce
1 package (10 ounces) BLUE
  DIAMOND® Blanched Whole
  Almonds (2 cups)

Melt butter in two-quart baking
dish in a 300 degree F. oven. Stir in
Worcestershire sauce, salt,
cinnamon, chili powder and hot
pepper sauce. Add almonds; stir
until completely coated. Bake,
stirring occasionally, 15 minutes or
until almonds are crisp.

Makes 2 cups

COFFEE GLAZED
PECANS

1½ cups pecans
¼ cup sugar
2 measuring tablespoons water
2 measuring teaspoons TASTER'S
  CHOICE Instant Freeze-Dried
  Coffee
¼ measuring teaspoon cinnamon

In large skillet or electric skillet*,
combine pecans, sugar, water,
TASTER'S CHOICE and cinnamon;
bring to a boil over medium heat,
stirring constantly. Boil 3 minutes,
stirring constantly until pecans are
well glazed. Spread on waxed
paper to cool.

Makes: 1½ cups glazed pecans

*NOTE: In electric skillet, heat all
    ingredients approximately
    4 minutes at 225°F.
    stirring constantly.

ROASTED PARTY
PECANS

Toss 1 cup unsalted pecan halves
in 1 tablespoon olive or salad oil
mixed with 1 tablespoon
Worcestershire sauce. Roast in
shallow baking pan in slow oven
(275°) for 30 minutes, stirring often.
Drain on paper towel; sprinkle with
salt.

VARIATION:

For a less spicy taste, place 1
pound of pecan halves in baking
pan with ½ stick of butter or
margarine. Bake at 225° for 30 to
45 minutes, stirring frequently.
Spread on wax paper and salt to
taste.

*Favorite recipe from National Pecan
Marketing Council*

PEANUT BUTTER PARTY
MIX

2 tablespoons MAZOLA®/NUCOA®
  Margarine
⅓ cup SKIPPY® Creamy Peanut
  Butter
2 cups bite-size toasted wheat
  biscuits
2 cups bite-size toasted rice
  biscuits
¼ cup dry-roasted peanuts

In large skillet melt margarine over
low heat. Stir in peanut butter until
thoroughly mixed. Toss cereal and
nuts in mixture until coated.
Remove from heat. Spread on
ungreased cookie sheet. Bake in
375°F oven 8 minutes or until
golden brown. Drain on paper
towels. *Makes about 4 cups*

BARBECUE RANCHO
SNACKS
(Low Calorie)

¼ cup butter or margarine
3 tablespoons barbecue sauce
¾ teaspoon garlic salt
¼ teaspoon barbecue spice
4 cups NABISCO® SPOON SIZE
  Shredded Wheat

Melt butter or margarine in a
13 × 9 × 2-inch baking pan. Blend in
next three ingredients. Add SPOON
SIZE Shredded Wheat. Cook and
stir gently until cereal is well
coated. Bake in a preheated
moderate oven (350°F.) 15 to 18
minutes or until lightly browned
and crisp. Cool. *Makes 4 cups*

About 6 calories per Barbecue
Rancho Snack

SCRIMMAGE

½ cup butter or margarine
4 cups NABISCO® SPOON SIZE
  Shredded Wheat
1 cup mixed nuts
¼ cup granulated sugar
1½ teaspoons ground cinnamon
½ cup DROMEDARY Chopped
  Dates

In large skillet melt butter or
margarine. Stir in next two
ingredients; sauté over medium
heat until toasted, shaking skillet
occasionally. Combine sugar and
cinnamon. Toss with cereal
mixture and dates; let cool.

Makes about 5½ cups

MAYPO® GRANOLA MIX

1 box 14 oz. MAYPO® 30-Second
  Oatmeal
1 cup WHEATENA®
¾ cup brown sugar, firmly packed
1 teaspoon salt
⅓ cup instant non-fat dry milk
  (optional)
½ cup oil
½ cup water
½ cup *each:* sesame seeds, small
  sunflower seeds, finely chopped
  nuts
¾ cup shredded coconut
½ cup raisins or dates, finely
  chopped

In a large bowl, mix MAYPO®
WHEATENA®, brown sugar, salt and
dry milk. Combine oil and water;
add to cereal mixture and stir only
until mixed. Add the sesame
seeds, sunflower seeds, nuts,
coconut and fruit; stir only until
mixed. Spread mixture on large
cookie sheet (or use four 9-inch pie
pans). Bake in preheated 250°F.
oven for 1 hour, stirring mixture
about every 15 minutes to brown
evenly. Remove from oven; cool;
store in air-tight container.

*Makes about 2¼ pounds
(eight 1 cup servings)*

TRADITIONAL CHEX®
PARTY MIX

½ cup butter or margarine
1¼ teaspoons seasoned salt
4½ teaspoons Worcestershire
  sauce
2 cups CORN CHEX® Cereal
2 cups RICE CHEX® Cereal
2 cups BRAN CHEX® Cereal
2 cups WHEAT CHEX® Cereal
1 cup salted mixed nuts

Preheat oven to 250°. Heat butter
in large shallow roasting pan
(about 15 × 10 × 2-inches) in oven
until melted. Remove. Stir in
seasoned salt and Worcestershire
sauce. Add CHEX® and nuts. Mix
until all pieces are coated. Heat in
oven 1 hour. Stir every 15 minutes.
Spread on absorbent paper to cool.

Makes about 9 cups

HOMEMADE TORTILLA CHIPS

3 cups flour
1 cup yellow cornmeal .
4 teaspoons baking powder
1 tablespoon shortening
1 egg, beaten
1 cup water
Oil
MORTON Popcorn Salt

**Up to 1 Week or Day Before
Serving:** In large bowl, mix flour,
cornmeal, and baking powder. Mix
in shortening with fork. Stir in egg
and water to form a stiff dough.
Knead 5 minutes. Divide into 4
parts. Roll each into a 10-inch
square, about ⅛-inch thick; cut into
2-inch squares. Divide each square
into 2 triangles. Fry in 1-inch hot
oil (about 360°F.) about 2 minutes,
or until golden on both sides. Drain
on paper towels. Sprinkle with
popcorn salt. Cool. Store in airtight
containers or plastic bags.

Just Before Serving: Place tortilla
chips in lined basket or on
decorative plate.
*Makes about 1½ pounds or
200 chips*

NATURAL MUNCH

2½ quarts popped POPEYE
Popcorn (about ⅓ cup
unpopped)
1 cup salted peanuts
1 cup wheat germ
1 cup sugar
⅓ cup honey
⅓ cup water
¼ cup butter or margarine, melted
½ teaspoon salt

Preheat oven to 250°F. Grease two
15 × 10 × 1-inch jelly-roll pans. In a
large greased bowl toss together
popcorn, peanuts, and wheat germ.
Set aside. Combine remaining
ingredients in 2-quart saucepan.
Cook over medium heat, stirring
constantly until sugar is dissolved
and mixture begins to boil.
Continue cooking until mixture
reaches 250°F. on candy
thermometer (hard ball stage). Pour
over popcorn mixture slowly,
stirring to coat. Spread in prepared
jelly-roll pans. Bake 45 minutes,
stirring every 10 or 15 minutes.
Remove from oven; stir to
distribute flavor. When cool, store
in tightly covered containers.
3 quarts

SUPER SNACK CRUNCH

½ cup butter or margarine
⅓ cup sugar
⅓ cup strawberry or apricot
preserves
2 cups QUAKER® Oats (Quick or
Old Fashioned, uncooked)
¾ cup coarsely chopped nuts
1 cup raisins or chopped dates

Heat oven to 325°F. In large
saucepan, combine butter, sugar
and preserves. Cook over low heat,
stirring constantly, until well
blended and smooth; remove from
heat. Add oats and nuts; mix until
dry ingredients are thoroughly
coated. Spread mixture evenly into
ungreased 13 × 9-inch baking pan.
Bake for 35 to 40 minutes or until
golden brown, stirring
occasionally. Add raisins; mix well.
Spread mixture onto ungreased
cookie sheet or aluminum foil;
cool. Store in tightly covered
container in cool dry place or
refrigerator.
Makes about 6 cups

VARIATION:

Omit raisins or chopped dates.

GOLD'N NUT CRUNCH!

1 can (12 ounces) FISHER®
Mixed Nuts or 1 jar (12 ounces)
FISHER® Dry Roasted Peanuts
¼ cup LAND O LAKES® Sweet
Cream Butter, melted
¼ cup grated parmesan cheese
¼ teaspoon garlic powder
¼ teaspoon ground oregano
¼ teaspoon celery salt
4 cups GOLDEN GRAHAMS®
Cereal

Heat oven to 300°. Mix nuts and
butter in medium bowl until well
coated. Add cheese, garlic powder,
oregano and celery salt; toss until
well coated. Spread in ungreased
jelly roll pan, 15½ × 10½ × 1 inch.
Bake, stirring occasionally, 15
minutes. Stir in cereal; cool. Store
in airtight container.
About 6½ cups snack

Skillet Method: Heat butter in
heavy 10-inch skillet until melted.
Add remaining ingredients; stir
until well coated. Heat over low
heat, stirring occasionally, 5
minutes; cool.

CEREAL SCRAMBLE

¼ cup butter or margarine
2 tablespoons light brown sugar,
firmly packed
¾ teaspoon ground cinnamon
2 cups NABISCO® SPOON SIZE
Shredded Wheat
2 cups coarsely crushed TEAM
Flakes Cereal
1 cup DROMEDARY Chopped
Dates
¼ cup chopped salted peanuts
Milk, optional

Melt butter or margarine in large
skillet; blend in brown sugar and
cinnamon. Add next four
ingredients and toss over low heat
until well coated. Cool to room
temperature. Store in airtight
container in refrigerator. Serve with
milk, if desired.
Makes about 5½ cups

DRIED FRUIT TRAIL MIX

½ cup coarsely chopped
DIAMOND® Walnuts
½ cup flaked or shredded coconut
⅓ cup sunflower seeds
1 cup SUNSWEET® Pitted Prunes
½ cup SUNSWEET® Dried Apricots
½ cup SUNSWEET® Dried Apples

Combine walnuts, coconut and
sunflower seeds in shallow baking
pan. Bake at 350°F. about 10 min.
until lightly toasted, stirring once
or twice. Cool. Snip prunes,
apricots and apples into small
pieces. Combine with toasted
mixture. Store in covered
container.
Makes 3 cups

QUICK PEANUTTY POPCORN BALLS

½ cup light corn syrup
¼ cup sugar
¾ cup SKIPPY® Creamy or Super
Chunk Peanut Butter
2 quarts plain popped corn

In 1-quart saucepan mix corn syrup
and sugar. Cook over medium heat,
stirring constantly, until mixture
comes to boil and sugar is
completely dissolved. Remove from
heat. Stir in peanut butter until
smooth. Immediately pour mixture
over popped corn in large bowl.
Stir until evenly coated. Grease
hands and shape into 8 (2½-inch)
balls.
Makes 8

CRISPY CARAMEL CORN

3½ quarts popped POPEYE
  Popcorn (about ½ cup
  unpopped)
½ cup cocktail peanuts (optional)
½ cup butter or margarine
1 cup firmly packed light brown
  sugar
¼ cup light corn syrup
½ teaspoon salt
½ teaspoon vanilla extract
¼ teaspoon baking soda

Preheat oven to 250°F. Grease well
a 15 × 10 × 1-inch jelly-roll pan.
Place popped popcorn and peanuts
in large well greased bowl. Melt
butter in large heavy saucepan; stir
in brown sugar, corn syrup, and
salt and bring to a boil. Reduce
heat and boil 5 minutes. Remove
from heat and stir in vanilla and
baking soda. Pour syrup over
popcorn mixture and mix well.
Spread on greased jelly-roll pan.
Bake 1 hour, stirring every 15
minutes. Remove from oven and
separate kernels when cool enough
to handle. Store in tightly covered
containers. *3½ quarts*

SUGAR AND SPICE
POPCORN

¼ cup vegetable oil
3 Tablespoons sugar
¼ teaspoon cinnamon
¼ teaspoon nutmeg
1 Tablespoon light corn syrup
⅓ cup unpopped POPEYE Popcorn

Generously grease cookie sheet.
Use only a hand-turned popcorn
popper for this recipe because all
ingredients must be agitated
constantly. Combine all ingredients
in popper, except popcorn. Stir well
and heat until bubbling. Add
popcorn; cover and shake constantly
over medium heat until all corn is
popped. Immediately pour onto
greased cookie sheet to cool.
About 2 quarts

BAKED POPCORN
CRUNCH

½ cup butter or margarine
½ cup firmly packed brown sugar
3 quarts popped POPEYE Popcorn
  (about ½ cup unpopped)
1 cup pecan halves

Preheat oven to 350°F. Cream
butter and brown sugar together in
large bowl. Mix warm popcorn with
creamed mixture. Add nuts. Spread
in 15 × 10 × 1-inch jelly-roll pan.
Bake 8 minutes. Cool in pan.
3 quarts

BAKED CARAMEL CORN

1 c. (2 sticks) butter or
  margarine
2 c. firmly packed brown sugar
½ c. light or dark corn syrup
1 tsp. salt
½ tsp. baking soda
1 tsp. vanilla
6 quarts popped JOLLY TIME®
  Pop Corn

Melt butter; stir in brown sugar,
corn syrup and salt. Bring to a boil
stirring constantly. Boil without
stirring 5 minutes. Remove from
heat; stir in soda and vanilla.
Gradually pour over popped corn,
mixing well. Turn into 2 large
shallow baking pans. Bake in 250
degree F. oven 1 hour, stirring
every 15 minutes. Remove from
oven, cool completely. Break apart.
Makes about 5 quarts
Caramel Corn

PRALINE® POPCORN
CRUNCH

10 cups popped corn
1½ cups whole pecans
½ cup slivered almonds
1⅓ cups sugar
1 cup butter
¼ cup PRALINE® Liqueur
¼ cup light corn syrup
1 tablespoon PRALINE® Liqueur
¼ teaspoon salt

Heat oven to 325°F. Butter baking
sheet and large bowl. Toast
pecans and almonds until light
brown, about 12-15 minutes. Mix
popped corn and nuts in large
bowl. Combine sugar, butter, ¼
cup PRALINE® Liqueur and corn
syrup in heavy 2-quart saucepan.
Cook over medium-high heat,
stirring occasionally to 275°F., or
until small amount dropped into

very cold water reaches soft crack
stage (separates into hard, but not
brittle, threads). Remove from heat,
quickly stir in 1 tablespoon
PRALINE® Liqueur and salt. Pour
over popped corn and nuts, mixing
until evenly coated. Immediately
spread mixture on baking sheet.
Let stand about one hour. Break
into bite-size pieces.
Makes about 14 cups

SPUN PINK-CINNAMON
POPCORN

2 quarts popped POPEYE Popcorn
  (about ⅓ cup unpopped)
¾ cup sugar
¼ cup light corn syrup
3 Tablespoons water
1 Tablespoon red cinnamon candy

Preheat oven to 325°F. Place 2
quarts popped corn in large
buttered bowl and set aside.
Combine remaining ingredients in
small saucepan. Heat slowly to
boiling point, stirring constantly.
Cook without stirring to 285°F.
(soft crack stage on candy
thermometer). Remove from heat at
once and drizzle over popcorn,
stirring to coat evenly. When well
mixed, pour onto buttered cookie
sheet and place in oven for about
10 minutes to crisp corn. Separate
kernels when cool enough to
handle. *2 quarts*

POPCORN BASKETS

1 pan (5 oz.) JIFFY POP® Popcorn
1 cup granulated sugar
½ cup corn syrup
½ cup water
¼ cup butter

Prepare popcorn carefully
following package directions. Pour
into a large pot kettle. Combine
sugar, corn syrup and water. Boil
mixture until it reaches 240°F. on a
candy thermometer (or until a little
mixture dropped in cold water
forms a soft ball). Remove from
heat; stir in butter. Pour mixture
over popcorn and mix well with
wooden spoon. With greased
hands press popcorn around inside
of medium sized bowl. Reserve a
generous handful for handle. Roll
popcorn into rope between palm.
Make a semicircle, attach to top to
form handle. Remove from bowl.

Desserts

BAKED APPLES ENCORE

1 can LUCKY LEAF® Whole Baked
  Apples (3 apples)
2 Tbsp. raisins
2 Tbsp. chopped walnuts
1 Tbsp. brown sugar

Combine syrup from apples with
raisins, walnuts and brown sugar.
Boil 10 minutes. Place apples in
baking dish. Fill them with raisins
and walnuts from syrup. Pour
remaining syrup over apples. Heat
at 400° for 10 minutes or until
syrup becomes bubbly.

DOUBLE TEMPTATION DESSERT

6 apples
2 tablespoons sugar
1 teaspoon cinnamon
⅛ teaspoon nutmeg
1 can (21 oz.) cherry pie filling
Chocolate syrup
Chopped nuts

Wash and core apples. Leave an
opening large enough to fill with
pie filling. Place apples in glass
casserole. Combine sugar with
spices. Place one teaspoon of
sugar mixture in the center of each
apple. Fill with cherry pie filling.
Cover and bake in hot oven 400°F.
for 20 minutes or until apples are
tender but still slightly firm. Let
stand 10 minutes. (FOR
MICROWAVE: Cook on HIGH for
8-10 minutes or until tender; let
stand 5 minutes.) Pour warmed
chocolate syrup over each apple.
Top with chopped nuts.

VARIATION:

To glaze, follow same procedure as
above, but before cooking sprinkle
lightly with sugar or spread with
maple syrup.

*Western New York Apple Growers Assn., Inc.
favorite recipe*

BAKED APPLES
(Low Calorie/Low Cholesterol)

12 packets SWEET 'N LOW,® or
  equivalent sugar substitute
2 packets BUTTER BUDS®
1 teaspoon cinnamon
8 apples, cored
1 tablespoon flour
1 tablespoon cinnamon
1 tablespoon cocoa (or carob
  powder)
1 tablespoon oil
½ cup chopped nuts
½ cup brown sugar (or equivalent
  in brown sugar substitute)

Combine the first three ingredients
and sprinkle inside the apple
cavities. Then, combine the last
six ingredients, stir until
blended and place on top of apples
as "Streusel" topping. Bake in
350°F. oven, 40-50 minutes or until
done.   *Makes 8 servings*

Calories: 224 w/brown sugar;
174 w/brown sugar substitute;
Cholesterol: 0

BAKED APPLES DELICE

¼ cup raisins
½ cup MANDARINE NAPOLEON
6 large baking apples
¼ cup chopped walnuts or pecans
½ cup brown sugar, packed

Sprinkle raisins with 2 tablespoons
MANDARINE NAPOLEON; let
stand. Core apples to within ½
inch of bottom; remove an inch of
peel around top. Combine raisins,
nuts and brown sugar. Fill centers
of apples with mixture. Place
apples in shallow baking pan; add
about 1 cup boiling water to pan.
Pour 1 tablespoon MANDARINE
NAPOLEON into each apple. Bake
in preheated 375°F. oven until
tender (about an hour) basting
occasionally with liquid in pan. As
apples cool, baste with pan juices.
Good topped with MANDARINE

NAPOLEON-flavored whipped
cream.

HONEY BAKED APPLES

6 medium baking apples
1½ tablespoons melted butter
¼ cup SUE BEE® Honey
¾ cup nut-like cereal
  (POST® GRAPE-NUTS® Brand
  Cereal, for instance)
¼ cup raisins

Wash and core apples. Peel top
half or slit peel horizontally around
each apple, about an inch from the
top, to allow steam to escape.
Place in baking dish lined with
aluminum foil. Bake at 400° for 40
minutes. Combine butter, honey,
cereal, and raisins. Fill apples with
mixture and bake 10 additional
minutes.   *Makes six servings*

APPLE BETTY

4 cups cored and thinly sliced
  cooking apples
1 tablespoon lemon juice
⅔ cup packed brown sugar
⅓ cup all-purpose flour
½ teaspoon cinnamon
¼ teaspoon nutmeg
1½ cups BRAN CHEX® Cereal
  crushed to ¾ cup
⅓ cup butter or margarine, melted

Preheat oven to 375°. Butter 9-inch
pie plate. Place apples in pie plate.
Sprinkle with lemon juice.
Thoroughly combine sugar, flour,
cinnamon and nutmeg. Stir in
BRAN CHEX® crumbs. Add butter.
Mix until crumbly. Stir ¾ cup
CHEX® mixture into apples.
Arrange evenly in pie plate.
Sprinkle remaining mixture over
apples. Bake 25-30 minutes or until
apples are tender and topping is
browned. Serve warm.
          Makes 6 servings

Note: Raisins make a nice
  addition. Stir into apples.

PEANUTTY APPLE SLICES

1 large, unpeeled apple, cored, quartered
¾ cup SKIPPY® Creamy or Super Chunk Peanut Butter
1½ cups slightly crushed corn flakes

Cut each apple quarter into 3 slices. Spread cut sides of apple slices with peanut butter. Roll in corn flakes. *Makes 12 slices*

SUNSHINE® APPLE BETTY

1½ cups SUNSHINE® Sugar Honey Graham Crackers, crumbled
¾ cup sugar
½ cup melted butter or margarine
1 teaspoon cinnamon
4 medium-size apples, pared and diced

Preheat oven to 350°F. (moderate oven). Mix Sugar Honey Graham Cracker crumbs with ½ cup of sugar. Stir into melted butter or margarine. Mix remaining sugar with cinnamon. Place ⅓ of crumb mixture in a shallow 8- or 9-inch square pan; alternate layers of apples, cinnamon-sugar mixture and crumbs. Cover, and bake at 350°F. for 30 minutes. Uncover, and continue to bake for 15 minutes. *Yield: 6 servings*

EASY APPLE CRISP

⅔ cup brown sugar, firmly packed
½ cup sifted flour
1 cup MAYPO® 30-Second Oatmeal
½ cup melted butter or margarine
1 can (1 lb. 4 oz.) Apple Pie Filling

Mix dry ingredients together; blend in melted butter. Press ⅔'s of mixture into a lightly buttered 8-inch square cake pan. Cover with Pie Filling. Sprinkle with remaining MAYPO® mixture. Bake in preheated 350°F. oven 30 to 35 minutes, or until lightly browned. Cool; cut into squares and serve topped with ice cream or whipped cream. *Makes one 8-inch square*

APPLE/GRAPE COBBLER

4 cups sliced pared tart apples
1 can (6 ounces) Frozen WELCHADE Grape Drink Concentrate
2 tablespoons quick cooking tapioca
1½ cups unsifted flour
2 teaspoons baking powder
½ teaspoon salt
½ cup sugar
1 egg, well beaten
½ cup milk
½ cup butter, melted

Arrange apples in buttered 9-inch square baking dish. Combine Frozen WELCHADE Grape Drink Concentrate and tapioca. Pour over apples. Sift together flour, baking powder and salt. Add sugar. Combine egg, milk and butter. Stir into flour mixture gently. Spread over apples. Bake at 425°F. for 30 minutes. Serve dessert with vanilla ice cream or vanilla sauce. *Makes 9 servings*

APPLE CRISP

1 cup Quick Oats
½ cup Brown Sugar
¼ cup Flour
¼ teaspoon Salt
4 Tbsp. Butter
½ teaspoon Cinnamon
⅛ teaspoon Nutmeg
1 can (21 ounce) THANK YOU® Brand Apple Pie Filling

Cut butter into oats, sugar, flour, salt and spices until crumbly. Spread pie filling in pie pan or square baking dish. Sprinkle crisp topping over top and bake in 350° oven for approx. 35 to 40 minutes. Serve topped with Vanilla Ice Cream.

FRESH APPLE CRISP

3 pounds apples, pared, cored and sliced to make 8 cups slices
½ cup soft butter or margarine
½ cup all-purpose flour
½ cup PET® Instant Nonfat Dry Milk, dry form
½ cup firmly packed brown sugar
1 teaspoon cinnamon
½ teaspoon nutmeg
2 cups HEARTLAND® Natural Cereal, Plain or Coconut Variety

Generously butter a 13 × 9 × 2-inch baking pan. Arrange apple slices in pan. Combine butter, flour, nonfat dry milk, brown sugar, cinnamon and nutmeg until crumbly. Stir in cereal. Sprinkle evenly over apples. Bake in 375°F. oven for 25 minutes or until browned on top. Serve warm with ice cream. *Makes 12 servings, ½ cup each*

OATMEAL APPLE CRISP

16 SUNSHINE® Oatmeal Cookies, coarsely crumbled
6 cups apples, cored and sliced
½ cup chopped dates
¼ cup sugar
½ cup orange juice
¼ cup (½ stick) butter or margarine, melted
½ cup chopped pecans or walnuts
Ice cream or whipped cream

In ungreased 1½-quart baking dish, combine ½ crumbled cookies, apples, dates, sugar, orange juice, and butter. Blend remaining cookies with nuts. Sprinkle over apple mixture. Bake at 350°F. for 45 minutes or until apples are tender. Serve warm with ice cream or sweetened whipped cream. *Yield: 6 servings*

BANANA CRUNCH

⅓ cup light brown sugar, firmly packed
¼ cup chopped walnuts
½ teaspoon ground cinnamon
4 all-yellow bananas
⅓ cup honey
4 NABISCO® Shredded Wheat Biscuits, finely rolled (about 1 cup crumbs)
Milk or cream

Combine first three ingredients. Cut bananas in half crosswise and lengthwise. Brush generously with honey. Roll in NABISCO® Shredded Wheat Biscuits crumbs, coating heavily. Place in a greased baking dish. Sprinkle with nut mixture. Bake in a preheated hot oven (425°F.) about 10 minutes. Serve warm with milk or cream. *Makes 4 (about 3½-ounce) servings*

APPLE PECAN DESSERT

1 can LUCKY LEAF® Apple Pie
  Filling
¾ cup water
1 pkg. refrigerated biscuits
¼ tsp. nutmeg
¼ cup chopped pecans

Mix pie filling, water and nutmeg.
Pour into greased 10″ × 6″ × 2″
baking pan. Sprinkle with pecans.
Top with biscuits. Bake at 375° for
35 minutes.

BLUEBERRY SURPRISE

3 cups toasted angel food cake
  cubes (½ inch)
3 cups fresh or frozen blueberries
1 can (6 oz.) frozen orange juice
  concentrate, thawed
1 cup water
¼ cup sugar
¼ teaspoon each: cinnamon,
  cloves, nutmeg
½ cup chopped FISHER®
  Pecans
1 tablespoon flour

Oven: 350°. Combine ingredients;
mix well. Spoon into buttered
8-inch square pan. Bake at 350° for
40 minutes. Serve warm with sour
cream, ice cream or whipped
cream.   4 to 6 servings

SOLO® BLUEBERRY CRISP

½ C. butter or margarine
1 C. flour
1 tsp. cinnamon
⅛ tsp. nutmeg
½ C. sugar
2 C. fresh blueberries or whole
  frozen blueberries, thawed and
  drained
1 jar (16 oz.) SOLO® Blueberry
  Glaze

Using pastry blender, cut butter
into flour, sugar, cinnamon and
nutmeg until crumbly. Combine
blueberries and SOLO® Blueberry
glaze. Pour into 8″ or 9″ square
pan. Sprinkle crumb topping over
blueberries. Bake in 400° oven
30-40 minutes or until topping is
golden. Serve warm with cream or
milk if desired.

CHAMBORD

FLAMBÉED CHERRIES CHAMBORD

2 oz. CHAMBORD
1 can cherries, pitted and drained
1 cup of the cherry juice
1 oz. Brandy or Kirschwasser
½ cup sugar
Juice of 1 lemon
Juice of 1 orange
1 oz. butter

Place the butter and sugar in a
saucepan and heat until golden.
Add the lemon, orange and cherry
juices and cook until smooth. Add
the cherries and CHAMBORD and
simmer for a few more minutes.
Then add the Brandy or
Kirschwasser and ignite—be sure
not to burn yourself! Serve over
crepes or vanilla ice cream.
                        Serves 8

NO-MIX CHERRY SUPREME

¼ cup butter (or margarine)
½ cup flour
½ cup sugar
1 tsp. baking powder
¼ tsp. salt
½ cup milk
1 can LUCKY LEAF® Cherry Pie
  Filling

Melt butter in a 1½ qt. casserole.
Blend flour, sugar, baking powder,
salt and milk. Pour mixture over
melted butter. Do not stir. Pour pie
filling evenly over the mixture but
do not stir. Bake at 350 degrees for
45-50 minutes.

CHERRIES JUBILEE

1 16-oz. can pitted black Bing
  cherries in heavy syrup
1 tsp. cornstarch
1 cup SOUTHERN COMFORT®
1 quart vanilla ice cream

Pour cherry juice from can into
bowl. Add cornstarch, mix
thoroughly, and pour into chafing
dish. Stir continuously over
medium heat until mixture has
thickened (3-4 minutes). Add
cherries and stir 1-2 minutes. Add

in SOUTHERN COMFORT® ignite
and stir thoroughly. Ladle, while
flaming, over individual servings of
ice cream.   Serves 6-8

FRUIT KABOBS

1 (8-ounce) can DROMEDARY Date
  Nut Roll
4 large fresh or canned peach
  halves, each cut into 3 pieces
2 all-yellow bananas, cut into 12
  (1-inch) slices
2 tablespoons butter or margarine,
  melted
2 tablespoons lemon juice
2 tablespoons granulated sugar
Ground cinnamon
½ cup dairy sour cream
2 tablespoons orange juice
1 teaspoon grated orange rind

Cut DROMEDARY Date Nut Roll
crosswise into 3 pieces; then cut
each piece into quarters. Thread
alternately with fruit on 6 (about
7-inch) skewers. Brush nut roll
pieces on all sides with butter or
margarine. Brush fruit with lemon
juice; then sprinkle with 1
tablespoon sugar and cinnamon.
Grill or broil about 10 minutes, or
until lightly browned, turning
occasionally. Meanwhile, stir
together next three ingredients and
remaining sugar. Serve with
kabobs.
  Makes 6 (about 7-inch) kabobs and
                    ⅔ cup sauce

FRUIT SALAD
(Macedonia Di Frutta)

1 ripe pineapple, cut in spears
2 grapefruit, sectioned
4 oranges, sectioned
2 red apples, cored and cut in
  eighths
2 ripe pears, cored and sliced
Black and white grapes
1 cup LIQUORE GALLIANO®
1 cup red currant jelly

In large shallow bowl, combine
fruit, stir in 1 cup LIQUORE
GALLIANO®. Chill 4 hours or
overnight. Drain, reserving liquid. In
saucepan, melt jelly. Stir in
reserved liquid. Brush mixture
thickly on fruit.

NOTE: Red grapes, persimmons,
    pomegranates, tangerines,
    or kumquats may be
    substituted.

FRUIT 'N HONEY CELEBRATION

2 envelopes KNOX® Unflavored
  Gelatine
2 cups DANNON® Plain, Vanilla,
  or Lemon Yogurt
1½ cups orange juice
1 can (11 oz.) mandarin oranges,
  drained (reserve syrup)
2 Tbsp. honey
½ cup raisins
½ cup chopped walnuts
2 bananas, cut into ½ inch slices

In medium saucepan, sprinkle
unflavored gelatine over 1 cup
orange juice. Stir over low heat
until gelatine dissolves, about 3
minutes. With wire whisk or rotary
beater, blend in yogurt, remaining
orange juice, reserved syrup and
honey; chill, stirring constantly,
until mixture is consistency of
unbeaten egg whites. Fold in
oranges, raisins, walnuts, and
bananas. Turn into 6-cup mold or
individual dessert dishes and chill
until firm, about 3 hours.

Makes about 6 servings

FRUIT SHORTCAKE

1 cup all-purpose flour
¾ cup NABISCO® 100% Bran
  Cereal
1 teaspoon baking powder
¼ teaspoon salt
⅔ cup butter or margarine,
  softened
1 (3-ounce) package cream cheese,
  softened
½ cup granulated sugar
1 egg
1 tablespoon lemon juice
1 teaspoon grated lemon rind
1 (29-ounce) can sliced peaches,
  chilled, drained
1 medium banana
2 cups sweetened whipped cream
  or whipped topping

Preheat oven to 350°F. Grease and
flour two 8-inch layer-cake pans. In
small bowl, combine flour,
NABISCO® 100% Bran Cereal,
baking powder and salt. In large
bowl of electric mixer, beat butter
or margarine, cream cheese and
sugar until fluffy. Blend in egg,

lemon juice and rind. Beat in flour
mixture. Divide batter evenly
between two pans. Bake 20 to 25
minutes until edge of cake pulls
away slightly from side of pan.
Cool in pan on wire rack 10
minutes. Loosen edges and turn
out to cool completely. Cut banana
into 14 slices and reserve 10 peach
slices for top layer of cake. Thinly
slice remaining peaches. Spread 1
cup whipped cream or whipped
topping on one layer; arrange
thinly sliced peaches over whipped
cream. Top with second layer;
spread remaining whipped cream
and top with reserved fruit slices.

Makes 8 (3-inch) wedges

FRUITED SHORTCAKE SUPREME

1½ cups sifted all-purpose flour
2 teaspoons baking powder
¾ teaspoon salt
4 tablespoons sugar, divided
⅓ cup vegetable shortening
1 egg
⅓ cup milk
1 tablespoon melted butter
1 can (17 oz.) LIBBY'S Chunky
  Mixed Fruits
Whipped cream or dessert topping,
  garnish

Preheat oven to 450°F. Sift flour,
baking powder, salt and 3
tablespoons of the sugar together
into a medium bowl. Cut in
shortening until mixture resembles
coarse cornmeal. Beat egg in small
bowl; stir in milk; add all at once to
flour mixture. Stir just until mixed.
(Dough will be stiff.) Spread dough
in well-greased 8-inch round cake
pan. Brush top with melted butter;
sprinkle with remaining tablespoon
sugar. Bake at 450° for 15 minutes
or until center is firm and top is
golden brown. Loosen edge from
pan with a knife. Remove
shortcake from pan; place on
serving plate. Drain Chunky Mixed
Fruits, reserving syrup. Spoon
fruits on top of warm cake; drizzle
with 2 tablespoons of the syrup.
Garnish with a ring of whipped
topping. Serve shortcake with extra
syrup and whipped topping if
desired.   *Yields 6 servings*

PEACH COBBLER
(Low Cholesterol)

3 cups peaches, peeled, sliced
  (1½ lb.)
½ cup sugar
1 tablespoon ARGO® or
  KINGSFORD'S® Corn Starch
2 teaspoons lemon juice
¼ teaspoon ground cinnamon
¼ teaspoon ground nutmeg
1 tablespoon NUCOA® or
  MAZOLA® Margarine
1 cup unsifted flour
1 tablespoon sugar
2 teaspoons baking powder
¼ teaspoon salt
¼ teaspoon ground nutmeg
¼ cup MAZOLA® Corn Oil
⅓ cup skim milk

Mix together first 6 ingredients.
Turn into 10 × 6 × 1¾-inch baking
dish. Dot with margarine. In bowl
stir together next 5 ingredients.
Add corn oil and milk; stir until
moistened. Drop by teaspoonfuls
onto peach mixture. Bake in 400°F
oven 30 minutes or until lightly
browned.

Makes 6 servings

0 mg cholesterol per serving

PEACH MELBA CAKE

1 envelope KNOX® Unflavored
  Gelatine
2 tablespoons sugar
1 cup boiling water
1 package (10 oz.) frozen
  raspberries, slightly thawed
1 can (16 oz.) sliced peaches,
  drained and chopped (reserve
  syrup)
1 container (4½ oz.) frozen
  whipped topping, thawed
8 or 9-inch angel food cake, cut
  into 1-inch cubes (about 2 qts.)

In large bowl, mix unflavored
gelatine with sugar; add boiling
water and stir until gelatine is
completely dissolved. Stir in
raspberries until melted and
reserved syrup. Chill, stirring
occasionally, until mixture is
consistency of unbeaten egg
whites. Fold in peaches, whipped
topping and cake. Turn into 9-inch
spring-form pan or 8-cup mold or
bowl and chill until set.

Makes 8 to 10 servings

PEACHES MELBA

1 pint LOUIS SHERRY® Vanilla Ice Cream
4 fresh peach halves
Melba Sauce (recipe follows)

On a dessert plate or in a stemmed dessert glass, place a slice or scoop of ice cream. Top with a peach half, cut side down. Spoon Melba Sauce over peaches. Top with whipped cream if desired.
Makes 4 servings

MELBA SAUCE

1 package (10 ounces) frozen raspberries, thawed
½ cup currant jelly
1½ teaspoons corn starch
1 tablespoon water

Combine raspberries and jelly in a saucepan and bring to a boil over medium flame. Mix corn starch and water. Add to raspberry mixture and stir constantly until thickened. Strain and chill. *Makes 1 cup*

PEACHES WITH MELBA SAUCE

1 pkg. (10 oz.) frozen raspberries, thawed
1 can (16 oz.) DEL MONTE Yellow Cling Peach Halves, drained
Vanilla ice cream

Place raspberries in blender container. Cover and run on high. Strain out seeds. Place peach halves in chilled dessert dishes. Top with scoop of ice cream. Serve with raspberry sauce. Serve immediately or freeze ahead. Serve with additional raspberry sauce.
4 servings

DRAMBUIE® PEACH BLUEBERRY SHORTCAKE

2 10-ounce packages frozen sliced peaches, thawed
1 pint fresh blueberries
   or 1 16-oz. bag frozen blueberries
⅔ cup DRAMBUIE®
1 pound cake
Whipped cream or ice cream, optional

Thirty minutes before serving, add DRAMBUIE® to undrained peaches.

Add fresh blueberries. If using frozen blueberries, drain thoroughly and add just before serving. To serve, spoon fruit over slices of pound cake, top with whipped cream or ice cream, if desired.
Six to eight servings

FRUIT COMPOTE

2 cups SUNSWEET® Dried Apples
2½ cups water
1 stick cinnamon
1 can (12 oz.) pineapple juice
   (1½ cups)
1 cup SUNSWEET® Pitted Prunes
1 cup SUNSWEET® Dried Apricots
2 slices lemon
2 whole cloves
½ cup granulated sugar

Combine apples, water and cinnamon in 2-qt. saucepan and heat to boiling. Turn heat low and simmer 15 min., frequently pressing apples down into liquid with back of spoon. Add pineapple juice, prunes, apricots and lemon slices stuck with cloves. Bring back to a boil; simmer 5 min. Remove from heat, add sugar and mix lightly. Let stand several hours or overnight before serving.
Makes about 5½ cups

DRIED FRUIT COMPOTE

1 package (11 oz.) mixed dried fruit
1 cup raisins
3 cups water
⅓ cup sugar
3 tablespoons lemon juice
1 orange, thinly sliced

Combine mixed dried fruits and raisins together in a 2-quart casserole. Add water. Cover and bake at 325 degrees for 1 hour. Add sugar and lemon juice, stirring until sugar is dissolved. Add orange slices. Serve warm or chill and serve topped with a mound of sour cream.
Makes 6 to 8 servings

California Raisin Advisory Board's favorite recipe

CITRUS BAKED PEARS

6 fresh Pacific Mountain Bartlett pears
½ cup packed brown sugar
⅓ cup chopped walnuts
2 tablespoons butter
2 cups orange juice
1 tablespoon *each* slivered lemon peel and orange peel

Core pears and remove skin halfway down. Combine brown sugar, walnuts and butter. Fill center of each pear with mixture. Place pears in 8 or 9-inch baking dish. Pour orange juice over pears. Sprinkle with grated lemon and orange peel. Bake at 350°F. 1 hour; baste occasionally.
Makes 6 servings

A favorite recipe from Pacific Bartlett Growers, Inc.

POACHED PEARS WITH RASPBERRY SAUCE

2 cups WELCH'S® White Grape Juice
1 cup sugar
Juice of one lemon
6 firm pears
10-ounce package frozen raspberries, partially thawed

In a large saucepan, combine white grape juice, sugar and lemon juice. Bring to a boil. Peel pears leaving stems on but removing end cores. Put into boiling syrup. Cover, reduce heat and simmer until tender. Remove from syrup and chill. When ready to serve, whirl raspberries in blender. Serve on pears. *Makes 6 servings*

PEARS WITH RASPBERRY SAUCE

1 cup fresh or frozen raspberries
5 Tablespoons of CANADA DRY® Club Soda
1 teaspoon granulated sugar
1 17 ounce can pear halves, chilled and drained

Put raspberries, Club Soda and sugar into a blender. Cover and blend for 30-60 seconds at high speed until pureed. Serve over pear halves. *Makes 4-6 servings*

POACHED RUBY PEARS

2 cups cranberry juice cocktail
1 cup SMUCKER'S Strawberry Preserves
2 cinnamon sticks (each 4 inches long)
12 whole cloves
6 firm, large Bartlett pears

In large saucepan or small kettle, combine cranberry juice, Strawberry Preserves, cinnamon and cloves. Bring to a boil. Cover; simmer over low heat 15 minutes. Meanwhile, peel pears, leaving stems intact. Cut thin slice off bottom of each pear so that it will stand up. Remove cinnamon sticks and cloves from liquid. Add pears; cook over low heat 35 to 45 minutes or just until tender, occasionally turning and basting pears. Remove from heat; cool on rack. Cover; refrigerate pears in liquid, turning occasionally to color pears evenly. With slotted spoon, transfer pears to serving dish.

6 servings

Tip: Use leftover poaching liquid as a marinade for chopped fresh fruit.

LAND O' LAKES® BUTTER CRUST FRUIT PIZZA

Crust:
¾ c. LAND O LAKES® Sweet Cream Butter, softened
⅔ c. sugar
2 c. all-purpose flour
¼ c. milk

Glacé:
¼ c. sugar
1 Tbsp. cornstarch
¾ c. reserved pineapple juice

Topping:
20-oz. can pineapple chunks, drained (reserve juice)
11-oz. can Mandarin oranges, drained
⅔ c. flaked coconut
⅔ c. pecan halves
10-oz. pkg. frozen strawberries, thawed and drained

Heat oven to 400°. In 1½-qt. mixer bowl beat butter and sugar at med. speed until light and fluffy (1 to 2 min.). Gradually add flour and milk; mix until thoroughly combined.

Press dough out onto 12″ round pizza pan to form crust. Bake for 13 to 18 min. or until light and golden brown. Cool on wire rack.

Meanwhile, prepare glacé. In 1-qt. saucepan combine sugar and cornstarch; blend well. Add juice; cook over med. heat, stirring constantly, until mixture comes to a boil. Boil 1 min. Cool 10 min.

Arrange pineapple chunks and oranges on cooled crust; sprinkle with coconut and nuts. Top with strawberries. Drizzle glacé over fruit. Cut into wedges to serve.

MENEHUNE PINEAPPLE BREAD

4 eggs, slightly beaten
1 cup sugar
¼ cup butter, melted
2 Tbsp. flour
1 can (15¼ oz.) DEL MONTE Crushed Pineapple In Its Own Juice
4 slices white bread, cubed*

Combine eggs, sugar, butter, flour and pineapple. Mix in bread. Pour into a greased 1½ quart casserole. Bake 1 hour at 350°F.

6-8 servings

*Whole wheat bread may also be used.

PINEAPPLE CHEESE DESSERT
(Low Calorie)

15 oz. part-skimmed ricotta cheese
Juice of ½ lemon
1 can DOLE® Crushed Pineapple (yellow can)
3 packages of SWEET 'N LOW® (1 gram pkts.) or ¾ teaspoon SWEET 'N LOW® (regular teaspoon)
1 teaspoon vanilla
1 egg
1 package of KNOX® Unflavored Gelatine
Cinnamon

Mix together egg, vanilla, SWEET 'N LOW,® lemon juice—until smooth. Add cheese, mix until smooth. Drain pineapple juice into glass and add crushed pineapple to mixture and mix until smooth. Mix gelatine to pineapple juice and

add to mixture and mix until smooth. Put into pie plate and sprinkle with cinnamon and bake in 350° oven for 45 to 50 minutes. Cool for 4 hours and then refrigerate.

Makes 10 servings

85 calories per serving

STRAWBERRIES IN CASSIS

1 pint fresh strawberries
1 pkg. frozen red raspberries (thawed)
2 oz. HIRAM WALKER Creme de Cassis

Reserve 6 strawberries for garnish. Halve the remaining strawberries. Puree the raspberries and combine with Creme de Cassis and strawberries. Pour into goblets. Garnish and chill. *Serves 6*

STRAWBERRY FESTIVAL SHORTCAKE

¾ cup shortening
1½ cups IMPERIAL Granulated Sugar
3 beaten egg yolks
2¼ cups sifted flour
½ teaspoon salt
3½ teaspoons baking powder
¾ cup cold water
¼ cup crushed strawberries
1 teaspoon almond extract
3 egg whites, stiffly beaten
1 cup whipping cream, sweetened with 2 tablespoons IMPERIAL 10X Powdered Sugar
2 pints fresh strawberries sweetened with ½ cup IMPERIAL 10X Powdered Sugar

Cream shortening and IMPERIAL Granulated Sugar; add egg yolks, beat well. Add sifted dry ingredients alternately with water, crushed strawberries and almond extract (and few drops red food coloring, if desired). Fold in stiffly beaten egg whites. Bake in 2 waxed-paper-lined 9″ round cake pans at 350°F. for about 20 minutes, or until cakes test done. Cool and put together with a layer of whipped, sweetened cream and a layer of sliced, sugared strawberries. Top with more cream and garnish top and sides with whole berries. *Serves 8 to 10*

ELEGANT STRAWBERRIES ROMANOFF

Marinate 2 baskets of whole strawberries in ⅓ cup of orange flavored liqueur for about an hour. Puree half of them. Whip 1 cup whipping cream with ⅓ cup sugar; fold in puree. Spoon over whole berries.   *Serves 6*

Favorite recipe from the California Strawberry Advisory Board

NEW ORLEANS STRAWBERRIES

Flavor Variations*
1 cup (8 ounces) sour cream
1 quart fresh strawberries, cleaned and hulled
COLONIAL® Dark Brown Sugar

Stir desired Flavor Variation into sour cream. To serve, place sour cream, sugar and strawberries in individual serving bowls. With fork or toothpick, dip strawberries into sour cream, then brown sugar.
                    Makes 6 to 8 servings

*FLAVOR VARIATIONS

½ teaspoon vanilla extract OR
½ teaspoon rum extract OR
½ teaspoon ground cinnamon OR
½ teaspoon ground nutmeg

STRAWBERRY PINEAPPLE BOAT

Use one fresh CALAVO® Pineapple, ½ cup fresh strawberries and 2 ozs. Kirsch (optional). Lay pineapple on side. Cutting lengthwise, cut ¼ of the pineapple off. Remove fruit from shell by first removing core down the center. The fruit may be easily removed from shell by using a grapefruit knife and cutting all around pineapple about ¾ inch from shell. Wash and hull strawberries. Cut in pieces. Cut pineapple into chunks. Pour ¼ of the Kirsch over strawberries and remainder over the pineapple. Chill. Just before serving mix strawberries and pineapple. Put into chilled pineapple shell. Serve with picks.

CREAMY PRUNE AMBROSIA

1 package (3¼ ounces) vanilla pudding mix
1½ cups milk
½ cup whipping cream
½ teaspoon vanilla
1 cup cooked spiced or plain SUNSWEET® Pitted Prunes
1 cup orange sections
¼ cup flaked coconut

Prepare pudding mix as package directs, reducing milk to 1½ cups. Cover and cool. Beat cream with vanilla to soft peaks; fold into cooled pudding. Cut prunes into halves or large pieces. Layer pudding, prunes, oranges and coconut into serving dishes.
                    Makes 6 to 8 servings

HEAVENLY AMBROSIA

2 firm medium DOLE® Bananas, peeled and sliced
1 can (8¼ oz.) DOLE® Crushed Pineapple in Syrup, well drained
1 cup miniature marshmallows
1 cup toasted coconut
1 cup seedless grapes
½ cup broken walnuts
½ cup whipping cream
1 tablespoon lime juice
2 teaspoons sugar
½ teaspoon grated lime peel
1 can (11 oz.) mandarin oranges, drained

Combine bananas, pineapple, marshmallows, ½ cup coconut, grapes and walnuts in a bowl. Beat together whipping cream, lime juice, sugar and lime peel until stiff peaks form. Fold into banana mixture. Fold in oranges. Spoon onto dessert plates or into tall glasses. Sprinkle each serving with remaining coconut.
                    Makes 4 to 6 servings

SOUSED WATERMELON

Cut plug out of watermelon. Pour in DUBOUCHETT Triple Sec. Replace and chill thoroughly.

AMBROSIA PACIFICA

6 SUNKIST® Oranges, peeled, sliced in cartwheels
1 cup pitted dates, cut in half lengthwise
½ cup shredded coconut
1 cup dairy sour cream
2 Tbsp. brown sugar
2 tsp. fresh grated SUNKIST® Orange peel

In glass compote or serving dish, arrange alternate layers of orange cartwheels, dates and coconut; chill. Combine sour cream, brown sugar and 1 teaspoon orange peel; chill. Serve over fruit; sprinkle with remaining orange peel.
                    Makes 6 to 8 servings

DESSERT FONDUE

1 package (12 oz.) chocolate chips
½ cup water
1 teaspoon vanilla extract
½ teaspoon ground cinnamon
1 small (or ½ medium) DOLE® Fresh Pineapple
2 firm medium DOLE® Bananas, peeled
1 cup whole strawberries

Melt chocolate chips with water, vanilla and cinnamon in fondue pot, using manufacturer's directions. Cut pineapple in half lengthwise. Remove fruit; core and cut into wedges. Slice bananas in diagonal chunks. Arrange pineapple, bananas and strawberries on a plate. Dip fruits in chocolate to serve.
                    Makes 4 to 6 servings

CARAMEL APPLE FONDUE
(Microwave)

1 (12 oz.) jar Caramel Ice Cream Topping
1 #303 can THANK YOU® Brand Butterscotch Pudding
⅓ cup Rum
Apple Wedges or Chunks

In ceramic fondue pot or mixing bowl, combine topping, pudding and rum. Cover, heat at high power 6 minutes, stirring every 2 minutes. Transfer to fondue burner or turn into fondue pot. Spear apple pieces with fondue fork; dip in mixture.

DESSERT CHEESE FONDUE WITH FRUIT

1 pound California seedless grapes
1 large apple, sliced
1 small pineapple, sliced
1 package (8 ounces) cream
　cheese
8 ounces Port Salut or other mild
　cheese, grated
½ cup white wine
Dash of nutmeg
Pound cake cubes

Wash grapes and chill with other fruit. Melt cheeses and wine over low heat, stirring until smooth and bubbly. Add nutmeg and use as a dip for fruit and cake.

Makes 6 servings

Favorite recipe from California Table Grape Commission

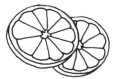

ELEGANT ESPRESSO CUSTARDS

2 cups half-and-half
¼ cup instant MEDAGLIA D'ORO®
　Espresso Coffee
2 teaspoons grated orange peel
3 eggs
1 egg yolk
½ cup sugar
1 teaspoon vanilla extract
½ teaspoon salt

Scald half-and-half. Stir in espresso and orange peel; cool 10 minutes. Meanwhile, with wire whisk, beat eggs, yolk and sugar until blended. Gradually add espresso mixture, vanilla and salt. Strain; fill 6 six-ounce custard cups. Place in large shallow baking pan partly filled with hot water. Bake at 350°F. about 40 minutes or until knife inserted in center comes out clean. Serve warm or cold, in the cup or unmolded. Top with Orange Whipped Cream.

Makes 6 espresso custards

ORANGE WHIPPED CREAM

Just before serving, beat ½ cup heavy cream with ½ teaspoon sugar until soft peaks form. Then beat in ½ teaspoon orange extract and ½ teaspoon grated orange peel. Optional: a drift of grated Brazil nuts.

BAKED CUSTARD
(Low Cholesterol)

Egg substitute to equal 3 eggs
⅓ cup sugar
¼ tsp. salt
3 cups POLY PERX® Frozen
　Polyunsaturated Non-Dairy
　Creamer
1 Tbsp. vanilla

Beat eggs slightly. Stir in remaining ingredients. Mix well. Pour into slightly greased custard cups. Place cups in large baking pan and fill with boiling water to the height of custard. Bake at 350° for 30 to 35 minutes or until knife comes out clean. Remove cups and cool on rack. Chill. Serve in cup or loosen at edges with knife and invert on plate. Serve plain or with fruit topping.

Makes 6 to 8 servings

PUMPKIN RUMKINS

1 can (16 ounces) STOKELY'S
　FINEST® Pumpkin
1 cup firmly packed brown sugar
½ teaspoon salt
1 teaspoon cinnamon
½ teaspoon nutmeg
¼ teaspoon ginger
4 eggs, lightly beaten
1 cup evaporated milk
1 teaspoon grated orange peel
¾ cup orange juice
1 teaspoon rum extract

Sweetened Sour Cream:
2 tablespoons sugar
¼ teaspoon vanilla extract
1 cup commercial sour cream

Preheat oven to 350°F. Grease ten 6-ounce custard cups. Combine pumpkin, sugar, salt, cinnamon, nutmeg, ginger, and eggs; mix well. Stir in evaporated milk, orange peel, orange juice, and rum extract. Pour into prepared custard cups, filling each cup to about ½ inch from top. Set in shallow baking pan. Fill pan with hot water to depth of half the custard cups. Bake about 50 minutes, or until set. Cool. Serve with Sweetened Sour Cream.

To make Sweetened Sour Cream: combine sugar, vanilla, and sour cream. Mix well and serve with Pumpkin Rumkins. Garnish with shredded orange peel if desired.

10 servings

OLD-FASHIONED RICE PUDDING

1¾ cups water
½ cup UNCLE BEN'S®
　CONVERTED® Brand Rice
½ teaspoon salt
2 cups milk
2 eggs, beaten
⅓ cup sugar
1 teaspoon vanilla
¼ cup raisins, steamed in water
　and drained (optional)
Nutmeg or cinnamon (optional)

Heat oven to 350°F. Bring water to boil. Stir in rice and salt. Cover and simmer until all water is absorbed, about 30 minutes. Add milk and boil gently, stirring occasionally, until mixture thickens slightly, about 5 minutes. Combine eggs, sugar and vanilla in bowl. Gradually stir in rice mixture; mix well. Pour into a greased 1½-quart casserole. If desired, stir in raisins and sprinkle nutmeg or cinnamon over top. Place casserole in a pan containing about 1 inch hot water. Bake, uncovered, in 350°F. oven for 45 to 50 minutes or until knife inserted near center comes out clean. Serve warm or chilled.

Makes 5 to 6 servings

COCONUT RICE PUDDING

1 bag SUCCESS® Rice
2 cups milk
½ cup sugar
2 tablespoons butter or margarine
2 eggs, slightly beaten
1 teaspoon rum flavoring
¼ teaspoon cinnamon
½ cup toasted coconut

Cook bag of rice according to package directions. Drain. While rice is cooking, heat milk, sugar, and butter in a 2-quart saucepan to scalding point. Add the cooked rice; cook and stir over moderate heat for 10 minutes, or until slightly thickened. Remove from heat. Combine the eggs, rum flavoring, and cinnamon. Slowly pour egg mixture into the hot rice, stirring constantly. Pour into individual serving dishes. Sprinkle with the toasted coconut.

Makes 6 servings (about ½ cup each)

RICE FESTIVAL PUDDING

½ cup long grain rice
1 cup water
½ teaspoon salt
1 quart milk
½ stick butter or margarine
3 eggs, beaten
½ cup IMPERIAL Granulated
   Sugar
1 cup seedless raisins
½ teaspoon vanilla

Add rice and salt to boiling water in a large saucepan. Cover and cook over low heat 7 to 10 minutes, or until water is absorbed. Add milk and butter or margarine, stir and bring to boil. Turn heat to very low and when milk has ceased boiling (to prevent boiling over), cover and cook for about 1 hour, or until milk is almost absorbed. Add IMPERIAL Granulated Sugar, raisins and vanilla to beaten eggs. Pour into the rice, stirring slowly until rice begins to thicken. May be served hot, warm or cold.

Serves 4 to 6

PEACH COTTAGE PUDDING

1 can (29 oz.) sliced peaches
¼ cup chopped nuts
½ cup LOG CABIN® Syrup
2 tablespoons MINUTE® Tapioca
¼ cup butter or margarine
½ cup sugar
1 egg
1 teaspoon vanilla
½ teaspoon ginger
¼ teaspoon nutmeg
1½ cups LOG CABIN® Regular
   Pancake and Waffle Mix
½ cup milk

Drain peaches, reserving ¾ cup of the syrup. Place peaches in well-greased 9-inch square baking dish and sprinkle with nuts. Combine measured peach syrup with ½ cup syrup and the tapioca. Pour over peaches; set aside. Cream butter. Gradually beat in sugar. Add egg, vanilla and spices, beating until well blended. Add pancake mix alternately with milk, beating after each addition until smooth. Carefully spread over peach mixture. Bake at 350° for 45 to 55 minutes or until cake tester inserted into center of cake comes out clean. Serve warm with additional pancake and waffle syrup, if desired.

ALL-TIME FAVORITE PUFF PUDDING

¼ cup butter or margarine
½ cup sugar
1 teaspoon grated lemon rind
2 egg yolks
3 tablespoons lemon juice
2 tablespoons all-purpose flour
¼ cup POST® GRAPE-NUTS®
   Brand Cereal
1 cup milk
2 egg whites, stiffly beaten

Thoroughly cream butter with sugar and lemon rind. Add egg yolks; beat until light and fluffy. Blend in lemon juice, flour, cereal and milk. (Mixture will look curdled, but this will not affect finished product.) Fold in beaten egg whites. Pour into greased 1-quart baking dish; place the dish in pan of hot water. Bake at 325° for 1 hour and 15 minutes or until top springs back when lightly touched. When done, pudding has a cakelike layer on top with custard below. Serve warm or cold with cream or prepared whipped topping, if desired.

Makes 6 servings

PISTACHIO PUDDING ROYALE

2 egg whites (at room temperature)
2 tablespoons sugar
1½ cups cold skim milk
2 teaspoons light rum
1 package ROYAL Instant
   Pistachio Pudding
Flaked coconut

Beat egg whites until foamy. Gradually beat in sugar; continue beating until soft peaks form. Set aside. Pour cold skim milk and rum into mixing bowl. Add ROYAL Instant Pistachio Pudding and slowly beat with egg beater 1 minute. Let set 3 minutes. Fold into prepared meringue. Spoon into serving dishes. Chill until ready to serve. (Serve on day prepared.) Garnish with flaked coconut.

Makes 4 to 6 servings

BUTTERSCOTCH FARINA PUDDING

2 cups milk
⅓ cup Quick CREAM OF WHEAT®
   Cereal
⅓ cup light brown sugar, firmly
   packed
2 eggs, beaten
¼ teaspoon salt
2 tablespoons butter or margarine
Milk, optional

Place first five ingredients in a medium saucepan and mix well. Bring to a rapid boil over medium heat, stirring constantly. Reduce heat and cook 5 minutes, stirring frequently. Add butter or margarine; cover and remove from heat. Let stand a few minutes, then stir to blend in butter or margarine. Serve hot with milk, if desired.

Makes 4 (about ⅔ cup) servings

SUGARPLUM PUDDING

1 cup SUNSWEET® Pitted Prunes
2 tablespoons orange juice
1 teaspoon grated orange peel
¾ cup sifted all-purpose flour
½ teaspoon baking powder
¼ teaspoon salt
¼ teaspoon cinnamon
¼ cup butter or margarine
¾ cup brown sugar, packed
1 large egg
½ cup chopped DIAMOND®
   Walnuts
Brown Butter Cream (recipe
   follows)

Snip prunes in small pieces; mix with orange juice and peel. Resift flour with baking powder, salt and cinnamon. Thoroughly cream butter with sugar and egg (batter looks slightly curdled). Add dry mixture; blend smooth. Stir in prunes and walnuts. Turn into greased and floured 8-inch round layer cake pan. Bake at 350°F. for 30 to 35 minutes. Serve warm or cold, spooning into dessert dishes. Top with Brown Butter Cream.

Makes about 6 servings

BROWN BUTTER CREAM

Beat ½ cup whipping cream stiff. Heat 2 tablespoons butter in small saucepan until foamy and lightly browned. Combine with ¾ cup sifted powdered sugar, 1 large egg and ½ teaspoon vanilla. Beat smooth. Fold in whipped cream.

Makes 1⅔ cups

Nesselrode Pie **(Keebler)**

Traditional Mince Pie
(None Such®/Jiffy®)

"Beau Catching" Lemon Meringue Pie
(Sunkist®)

Bits 'O Brickle® Ice Cream Pie & Sauce

Old-Fashioned Apple Crescents
(Argo®/Kingsford's®)

Eggnog Custard Pie **(Thank You® Brand)**

Pumpkin Pie **(Milnot®)**

Aspen® Pie

Frozen Grasshopper Pie **(Heublein)**

Whole Grain Cherry Crisp
(Thank You® Brand)

Libby's Famous Pumpkin Pie

Luscious Peach Pie **(Taylor Wine)**

Grasshopper Pie **(Rice Chex®)**

Deluxe Pecan Pie **(Karo®/Mazola®/Nucoa®)**

Pear Crunch Pie **(Stokely's Finest®)**

Black Bottom Pie **(Tia Maria®)**

Fresh Berry Pie **(Argo®/Kingsford's®)**

Frozen Parfait Ripple Pie
(Arrow Choclair)

Toll House® Cookies **(Nestlé)**

Magic Cookie Bars **(Eagle® Brand)**

Double Decker Fudge, Chocolatetown
Special Cake, Chocolate Chip Party
Muffins, Peanut Blossoms, Marble
Cheesecake, Bar Pie **(Hershey's®)**

Famous Oatmeal Cookies **(Quaker®)**

Milnot® Fudge

Land O'Lakes® Merry Cherry Cheesecake Bars

Tangy Lemon Squares (Minute Maid®)

Cocoa Brownies (Hershey's®)

Praline® Popcorn Crunch

Peanut Butter Nougat Bars
(Orville Redenbacher's)

Natural Munch (Popeye Popcorn),
Gatorade® Popsicles

Secret Kiss Cookies, Peanut Blossoms,
Peanut Butter & Jelly Thumbprints
(Hershey's®/Reese's®)

Wheat Germ Sour Cream Cookies
(Elam's®)

Brown Sugar Brownies (**Colonial®**)

Crispie Treats (**M&M's®**)

Toffee Crunch Cookies (**Heath®**)

Coconut Macaroons (**Eagle® Brand**)

Valentine Stuffed Dates (**Sun World®**)

Oatmeal Scotchies, Two-Tone Bites
(**Nestlé**)

New Orleans Strawberries (**Colonial®**)

Grape-Glazed Steamed Pudding
(**Smucker's**)

Drambuie® Peach Blueberry Shortcake

Easy Homemade Chocolate Ice Cream **(Eagle® Brand)**

Peach Melba Cake **(Knox®)**

Lemon Ice **(Bertolli®)**

Strawberry Pineapple Boat **(Calavo®)**

Mocha Mousse **(Hiram Walker)**

Frangelico® Velvet

"Just a Trifle" **(Thank You® Brand)**

Poached Ruby Pears **(Smucker's)**

Apple Betty **(Bran Chex®)**

Amaretto Strawberries **(Hiram Walker)**

Easy Sodas **(Kool-Aid®)**

Strawberry Limeade **(ReaLime®)**

Strawberry-Orange Frosty **(Sunkist®)**

Lemonade **(ReaLemon®)**

Hot Spiced Cider **(Tree Top)**

Fruit Medley Punch (**ReaLemon**®)

Black Russian, White Russian (**Tia Maria**®)

Home Run Refresher (**Lipton**®)

South of the Berry (**Gibson**)

Jamaican Coffee (**Tia Maria**®)

Tonic Water Classics, Cranberry Shrub, Bristol Bracer, Canterbury Cooler, Dustcutter (**Schweppes**®/**Rose's**®)

The Roaring '20's Bloody Mary (**Tabasco**®)

Bardolino Punch (**Bertolli**®)

GRAPE-GLAZED STEAMED PUDDING

½ cup butter or margarine
1½ cups SMUCKER'S Grape Jelly
2 large eggs
1 cup whole-wheat flour, stirred
    before measuring
¾ cup all-purpose flour, stirred
    before measuring
¼ cup wheat germ
2½ teaspoons baking powder
1 teaspoon pumpkin or apple pie
    spice*
½ teaspoon salt
½ cup milk
½ cup chopped walnuts
½ cup seedless raisins

Generously grease and lightly flour 1½-quart brioche pan or steamed pudding mold. In large bowl, beat butter until fluffy. Beat in 1¼ cups Grape Jelly. Add eggs and beat until well mixed. Add whole-wheat and all-purpose flours, wheat germ, baking powder, spice, salt and milk. Beat on low speed just until mixed. Beat on medium speed until fluffy. Fold in walnuts and raisins. Spoon into prepared pan. Cover tightly with greased foil.

Meanwhile, in large saucepan, place rack in about 3 inches water. Cover and bring to a boil. Place pan on rack. Add more boiling water, if necessary, to come halfway up side of pan. Cover, reduce heat and steam about 1½ hours or until skewer inserted in center comes out clean. Remove pudding from saucepan. Let pudding stand in pan on rack 5 minutes. Loosen pudding around edge of pan. Invert onto serving plate; remove pan. In small saucepan, heat remaining ¼ cup Grape Jelly until melted. Brush over pudding to glaze. Garnish top with walnut halves, if desired.

8 servings

*Or your own blend of ground cinnamon, nutmeg, cloves and allspice.

CHERRY PUDDING

1 cup E-Z-BAKE Flour
½ cup sugar
1 teaspoon baking powder
⅛ teaspoon salt
1 teaspoon melted butter or
    margarine
½ cup milk

Mix ingredients thoroughly and place in well-greased, deep bread pan, 4 × 8 inches. Then mix together:

1 cup drained, canned cherries
1 cup sugar
½ cup hot cherry juice
1 teaspoon melted butter

Place cherry mixture on top of batter. Bake in hot oven (400°F.) 40 to 45 minutes. Dough rises up through cherries.

First Prize Winner E-Z-BAKE Flour Contest

FRANGELICO® VELVET

4 eggs, separated
1 tablespoon sugar
6 oz. package semisweet
    chocolate pieces (1 cup)
¼ cup boiling water
¼ cup FRANGELICO® Liqueur

Beat egg whites until foamy gradually adding sugar until stiff. Whirl chocolate pieces in blender until very finely grated. Add boiling water and blend until chocolate melts. Add egg yolks, FRANGELICO® blend until very smooth. Gently fold chocolate mixture into whites. Spoon into dessert dishes. Chill until set. Garnish with hazelnuts if desired.

6 to 8 servings

PUDDING IN A CLOUD

2 cups *or* 1 container (4 oz.)
    BIRDS EYE® COOL WHIP®
    Non-Dairy Whipped Topping,
    thawed
1 package (4-serving size) JELL-O®
    Brand Instant Pudding and Pie
    Filling, any flavor
2 cups *cold* milk

Divide whipped topping among 6 dessert glasses, using about ⅓ cup in each. With the back of a spoon, make a depression in the center and spread topping up the sides of the glasses. Prepare pudding mix with milk as directed on package for pudding. Spoon pudding mixture into glasses. Chill. Garnish as desired.

Makes about 3½ cups or
6 servings

LAYER DESSERT

1 cup Flour
1 stick Margarine
½ cup Nuts, chopped
1 8 ounce package Cream Cheese
2 cans THANK YOU® Brand
    Chocolate Pudding
1 cup Powdered Sugar
1 10 ounce Package Frozen
    Whipped Topping

Mix flour, margarine, and nuts together. Spread on bottom of 13 × 9 inch baking pan. Bake for 15 minutes at 350°. Let cool. Mix cream cheese, powdered sugar and 1 cup of whipped topping. Spread over crust. Spoon pudding on top of cream cheese mixture. Top with remaining whipped topping. Chill.

QUICK LEMON ANGEL DESSERT

1 small angel food cake
1 can THANK YOU® Brand Lemon
    Pudding
1 pkg. dessert topping mix
½ cup slivered blanched almonds

Break angel food cake into pieces—about 1". Spread in bottom of 8½ × 11 glass dish. Mix dessert topping according to directions. Combine with pudding and nuts and pour over cake. Stir enough to cover cake pieces and refrigerate at least 6 hours.

ORANGE RICE DESSERT
(Low Calorie)

1 bag SUCCESS® Rice
1 cup vanilla flavored yogurt
¼ cup honey
1 tablespoon lemon juice
1 tablespoon grated orange rind
1 orange, peeled, sectioned and
    chopped
1 banana, peeled and sliced

Cook bag of rice according to package directions. Drain and cool slightly. In mixing bowl, combine the yogurt, honey, lemon juice, and orange rind. Stir in the rice, orange, and banana. Mix gently. Spoon into dessert dishes and chill.

Makes 6 servings (about ½ cup
each)

157 calories

PRUNE BREAD AND MERINGUE PUDDING

2 Tbsp. butter
2 cups milk, scalded
3 eggs
¼ cup sugar
¼ teaspoon salt
1 Tbsp. lemon juice
1 tsp. grated lemon rind
1 cup stale bread cubes
⅓ cup SIMON FISCHER Prune Butter (Lekvar)

Melt butter in hot milk. Break eggs into a bowl, but save one egg white for meringue. Beat eggs lightly and then add sugar and salt, lemon juice and lemon rind. Add milk mixture gradually to egg mixture, stirring vigorously. Then pour over bread cubes in a buttered baking dish and let stand for 15 minutes. Bake in a moderate oven (350 degrees F.) for 35 minutes. Beat egg white slightly, then beat in Prune Butter and continue beating until mixture is stiff. Pile on pudding and bake 15 minutes longer.

This makes approximately 6 servings

BAKED PUMPKIN PUDDING

⅓ cup SWIFT'NING/JEWEL Shortening
1⅔ cups sifted flour
1⅓ cups sugar
1 teaspoon soda
½ teaspoon salt
¼ teaspoon baking powder
½ teaspoon cinnamon
¼ teaspoon cloves
⅓ cup water
1 cup cooked or canned pumpkin
½ cup chopped nuts
1 egg, unbeaten
1 cup chopped dates

Sift flour, sugar, soda, salt, baking powder, and spices together into mixing bowl. Add shortening, water, pumpkin, and nuts. Beat 2 minutes at medium speed in an electric mixer (or 300 strokes by hand). Scrape bowl constantly. Add egg and dates. Beat 2 minutes longer. Pour into two well-greased

1 quart ring molds or one 6½ cup ring mold, or a 9 by 9 by 1¾ inch square cake pan. Bake in a moderate oven (350°F.) about 35 minutes for 1 quart ring molds, or 45 minutes for a 1½ cup ring mold, or a 9 inch square pan. Serve warm with Creamy Sauce.

CREAMY SAUCE

1 small egg
1 tablespoon melted butter or margarine, cooled
1¼ cups powdered sugar
1 cup whipping cream, whipped stiff
½ teaspoon vanilla

Beat egg until foamy. Stir in melted butter. Add powdered sugar and beat until smooth. Blend in whipped cream and vanilla.

Yield: about 2 cups

VARIATION:

Omit vanilla. Add ½ teaspoon brandy flavoring and ¼ teaspoon rum extract.

CHOCOLATE PECAN PUFF

1 package (regular size) ROYAL Chocolate Pudding
1 tablespoon sugar
2 cups milk
1 package (3-ounce) ROYAL Cherry Gelatin
1 cup boiling water
½ cup cold water
1 cup heavy cream, whipped
½ cup finely chopped PLANTERS® or SOUTHERN BELLE Pecans

Empty ROYAL Chocolate Pudding into saucepan. Add sugar; gradually blend in milk, stirring to keep mixture smooth. Cook over medium high heat, stirring steadily, until mixture just starts to boil. Place wax paper or plastic wrap directly on pudding; chill at least 1 hour. Dissolve ROYAL Cherry Gelatin in boiling water. Add cold water. Chill until slightly thickened. Fold in cooled pudding, whipped cream and PLANTERS® or SOUTHERN BELLE Pecans. Pour into 6-cup mold. Chill until firm. Unmold; if desired, garnish with additional whipped cream.

Makes 6 to 8 servings

HEAVENLY HASH

1 package (3 ounces) vanilla pudding
1½ cups milk
½ cup WELCH'S® Grape or Strawberry Preserves
1 cup heavy cream, whipped
¾ cup pineapple tidbits
½ cup miniature marshmallows
¼ cup coarsely chopped toasted almonds
¼ cup diced maraschino cherries, well drained

Prepare pudding according to package directions using 1½ cups milk. Pour into a bowl; place plastic wrap directly on pudding. Chill. Blend strawberry or grape preserves into chilled pudding. Gently fold in remaining ingredients. Spoon into dessert dishes. Chill until ready to serve. If desired, garnish with additional whipped cream and a whole maraschino cherry.

Makes 6 servings

"JUST A TRIFLE"

1 frozen pound cake (10¾ oz.), thawed
½ cup sherry, brandy, rum or orange juice
2 cans (17½ oz.) THANK YOU® Brand Vanilla Pudding
1 can (21 oz.) THANK YOU® Brand Cherry Pie Filling
1 carton (4 oz.) frozen whipped topping, thawed

Cut cake into ½-inch cubes. In pretty glass bowl, place a layer of cake cubes. Sprinkle with sherry (or liquid of your choice). Spread about 1 cup pudding over cake, forming a thin layer. Top with a few spoonfuls of cherry pie filling (doesn't need to make a complete layer). Continue layering until ingredients are used (except whipped topping). Make final layer of whipped topping. Refrigerate at least two hours before serving.

Makes 6-8 servings

MERRIE OLDE BRANDIED MINCEMEAT

1 small navel orange
1 small lemon
8 cups finely diced unpeeled
   apples
1½ cups golden raisins
1½ cups seedless raisins
1 cup mixed diced candied fruits
1 cup orange juice
4 cups packed brown sugar
1 tablespoon cinnamon
1½ teaspoons each ground
   nutmeg, cloves and allspice
1½ teaspoons salt
1¼ cups THE CHRISTIAN
   BROTHERS® Brandy

Quarter and seed orange and lemon. Grind in food grinder or food processor fitted with steel blade. In Dutch oven combine ground orange and lemon, apples, raisins, candied fruits and orange juice. Bring to boil, reduce heat and simmer 15 minutes, stirring occasionally. Add sugar, spices and salt. Simmer 15 minutes, stirring occasionally. Add 1 cup of the brandy. Simmer, stirring occasionally, until mixture is thick like jam, about 1 hour. Remove from heat. Stir in remaining brandy. Store covered in refrigerator up to 2 months.

Makes about 2½ quarts

BROKEN WINDOW GLASS CAKE

1 package (3 oz.) JELL-O® Brand
   Orange Flavor Gelatin
1 package (3 oz.) JELL-O® Brand
   Cherry Flavor Gelatin
1 package (3 oz.) JELL-O® Brand
   Lime Flavor Gelatin
3 cups boiling water
1½ cups cold water
1½ cups graham cracker crumbs
⅓ cup butter or margarine, melted
1 package (3 oz.) JELL-O® Brand
   Lemon Flavor Gelatin
¼ cup sugar
1 cup boiling water
½ cup canned pineapple juice
1 container (8 oz.) BIRDS EYE®
   COOL WHIP® Non-Dairy
   Whipped Topping, thawed

Prepare the orange, cherry and lime gelatins separately, dissolving each in 1 cup of the boiling water and adding ½ cup of the cold water. Pour each flavor into separate 8-inch square pan. Chill until firm, at least 3 hours or overnight. Cut into ½-inch cubes.

Mix crumbs with butter. Set aside about ¼ cup for garnish, if desired, and press remaining crumb mixture evenly over bottom and up sides to within 1 inch from top of 9-inch springform or tube pan. Chill. Dissolve lemon gelatin and sugar in 1 cup boiling water; add pineapple juice. Chill until slightly thickened. Blend in whipped topping. Fold in gelatin cubes. Spoon into crumb-lined pan. Chill overnight or until firm. Just before serving, run a spatula around sides of pan; then gently remove sides. Garnish with reserved crumbs or with additional whipped topping and flaked coconut, tinted, if desired.

Makes 12 or 16 servings

SHERRIED DOME DELIGHT

1 pound semi-sweet chocolate
⅓ cup strong coffee
10 egg yolks
⅓ cup THE CHRISTIAN
   BROTHERS® Meloso Cream
   Sherry
1 pound butter, *slightly* softened
1¼ cups powdered sugar
6 egg whites
Genoise Layer (recipe follows)

Filling:
2 cups whipping cream
¼ cup THE CHRISTIAN
   BROTHERS® Meloso Cream
   Sherry
2 tablespoons granulated sugar
½ cup *each* chopped blanched
   almonds and crushed vanilla
   wafers
⅓ cup grated semi-sweet
   chocolate
Chocolate curls
Strawberries, halved

In 1-quart saucepan melt chocolate in coffee over low heat. Thoroughly beat egg yolks; whisk yolks into melted chocolate mixture. Remove from heat; whisk in ⅓ cup sherry; cool to room temperature. In large bowl beat butter and powdered sugar just until fluffy. Gradually beat in *cooled* chocolate mixture just until smooth and thoroughly blended. In another bowl beat egg whites until stiff but not dry; fold into chocolate mixture, one fourth at a time, just until white streaks disappear. Line an 8-inch mixing bowl with plastic wrap. Fill with chocolate mixture; pack down and smooth top. Cover and chill until firm, 4 to 6 hours. Meanwhile, prepare Genoise Layer; cool.

Prepare filling: In large bowl whip cream to form soft peaks; gradually beat in ¼ cup sherry and granulated sugar. Remove half of cream mixture; cover and chill. Into remaining cream mixture fold almonds, vanilla wafers and grated chocolate.

Place Genoise Layer on serving plate; top with almond mixture, spread to within ½ inch of edge. Carefully remove chocolate dome from bowl; invert on Genoise Layer and peel off plastic wrap. Fit pastry bag with large star tip. Fill with reserved cream mixture. Garnish dessert with piped cream, chocolate curls and strawberries. Chill. To serve, cut in wedges.

Makes 14 to 16 servings

GENOISE LAYER

4 eggs
⅔ cup sugar
½ teaspoon vanilla
⅔ cup sifted flour
¼ cup clarified butter, cooled*
⅓ cup THE CHRISTIAN
   BROTHERS® Meloso Cream
   Sherry

In large bowl set over simmering water mix eggs, sugar and vanilla until lukewarm and syrupy. Remove from heat; beat at high speed for 10 to 15 minutes until mixture is pale and tripled in volume. Sprinkle flour over egg mixture, ⅓ cup at a time, folding in gently after each addition. Gradually fold in the butter just until thoroughly blended. Turn into buttered and floured 8 × 2½-inch cake pan or springform pan. Bake in 350 degree oven about 30 minutes until cake is golden and begins to shrink from pan. Remove side of pan; cool. Brush side and top of cake with sherry.

*To clarify butter: Place in small deep pan; melt over low heat. (Be careful not to brown.) Skim foam from top and gently pour off clear portion. Discard sediment.

Note: Genoise Layer may be prepared in advance, wrapped and frozen. Brush with sherry after defrosting.

1st Prize Winner THE CHRISTIAN BROTHERS® contest

STRAWBERRY MARSHMALLOW WHIP

1 package (3-ounce) ROYAL
  Strawberry Gelatin
1 cup boiling water
1 cup cold water
2 cups prepared whipped topping
1½ cups CURTISS ROYAL
  Miniature Marshmallows
1 can (13½-ounce) crushed
  pineapple, drained

Dissolve ROYAL Strawberry
Gelatin in boiling water. Add cold
water. Chill until slightly thickened.
Set bowl of gelatin firmly in bowl
of ice. Whip until very light and
fluffy. Blend into whipped topping.
Fold in CURTISS ROYAL Miniature
Marshmallows and pineapple. Pour
into 8-cup mold and chill until firm.
Unmold to serve. Garnish with
fresh strawberries, if desired.

Makes 8 to 10 servings

CALIFORNIA CREME

1½ cups THE CHRISTIAN
  BROTHERS® Chateau La Salle
  Light Wine
1 cup sugar
1 orange
1 lemon
1 Tbsp. cornstarch
6 egg yolks, beaten
2 egg whites

Combine sugar, 1 cup wine and
juice and grated rinds of orange
and lemon; bring to boil. Stir in
cornstarch dissolved in remaining
wine. Cook 1 minute, stirring
constantly. Stir a little sauce into
egg yolks; return to pan. Cook over
low heat, stirring, 5 minutes; chill.
At serving time, fold in stiffly
beaten egg whites. *Serves 6*

QUICK CHOCOLATE-LEMON BAVARIAN CREAM

10 HYDROX® Cookies
1 (3 ounce) package lemon flavor
  gelatin dessert
1 cup boiling water
1 cup heavy cream, whipped
Additional HYDROX® Cookies

Crush HYDROX® Cookies into very
fine crumbs between two sheets of
waxed paper and set aside. Pour
boiling water over the gelatin and
stir until dissolved. Chill until the
gelatin reaches the consistency of
unbeaten egg white. Gently fold in
whipped cream and cookie crumbs.
Pour into oiled 4-cup mold or bowl.
Refrigerate until set. When ready
to serve, unmold on a plate and
frame with whole cookies.

Yield: 6 servings

Note: Chilling can be hurried by
  placing in a bowl of ice
  cubes and water. Stir almost
  constantly to prevent
  lumping.

CHOCOBERRY MOUSSE

Whip together with electric mixer
until soft peaks form:
1 4⅛ oz. package JELL-O® Brand
  Chocolate Fudge Instant
  Pudding & Pie Filling
1 cup GIBSON Raspberry Wine (or
  Loganberry Wine)
1 cup heavy cream (well chilled)

Cover mixture and cool in
refrigerator 1 hour.

Whip with electric mixer until well
thickened (before peaks form):
2 cups heavy cream

Into cream, spoon chilled
chocolate mixture and whip
together until stiff peaks form.
Spoon into parfait glasses, chill
until ready to serve. Garnish with
chocolate shavings. *Serves 8*

CHOCOLATE MOUSSE

8 ounces semi-sweet chocolate
½ cup water
6 eggs, separated
½ cup DOMINO® Super Fine
  Sugar
2 teaspoons vanilla extract
1 cup heavy cream, whipped
Dash of salt
¼ cup DOMINO® Super Fine Sugar

Melt chocolate and water over low
heat in a small saucepan; cool a
few minutes. In a medium bowl
beat egg yolks with ½ cup sugar
until thick and pale. Blend
chocolate and vanilla into egg
yolks. Fold in whipped cream. Beat
egg whites with salt and sugar
until stiff peaks form. Fold into
chocolate mixture. Chill at least 6
hours before serving. Serve with
sweetened whipped cream.

Serves 8 to 10

DANNON® YOGURT

RED RASPBERRY YOGURT MOUSSE

2 cups DANNON® Red Raspberry
  Yogurt (or any fruited yogurt
  desired)
2 egg whites stiffly beaten
½ cup whipped cream
2 Tbsp. rum
1 cup toasted coconut
2 Tbsp. grated orange rind

Stiffly beat egg whites, whip cream
and fold together. Stir in rum and
add red raspberry yogurt. Blend in
coconut and orange rind. Spoon
into serving bowl and freeze until
firm, but not solid.

Makes approximately 4 servings

RASPBERRY ROSÉ MOUSSE

1 12 oz. pkg. frozen raspberries
1 3 oz. pkg. raspberry gelatin
1 Tbsp. sugar
THE CHRISTIAN BROTHERS®
  La Salle Rosé Wine
½ cup whipping cream, stiffly
  beaten

Thaw berries; drain juice into
measuring cup. Add enough La
Salle Rosé to measure 1½ cups;
heat to boiling. Add gelatin and
sugar; stir to dissolve. Cool until
slightly thickened; beat until fluffy.
Fold in whipped cream and
raspberries. Spoon into serving
dishes; chill. *Serves 6*

MOCHA MOUSSE

2 envelopes whipped topping mix
3 cups cold milk
1 pkg. instant chocolate pudding
  mix
2 oz. HIRAM WALKER Coffee
  Flavored Brandy

In mixer bowl prepare whipped
topping with 1 cup of cold milk.
Add remaining milk and pudding
mix. Blend well and beat at high
speed for 2 minutes. Blend in
Coffee Flavored Brandy. Pour or
spoon into glasses or serving
dishes. Top with chocolate sauce,
if desired. *Serves 6-8*

BOYSENBERRY MOUSSE

2 envelopes KNOX® Unflavored
   Gelatine
½ cup sugar, divided
⅛ teaspoon salt
3 eggs, separated
1 cup milk
2 cups DANNON® Boysenberry
   Yogurt
1 cup heavy cream

Combine gelatine, ¼ cup sugar and salt in medium saucepan. Mix together yolks and milk in medium bowl and stir into gelatine. Place over low heat; stir constantly until gelatine dissolves, about 6 minutes. Cool slightly and add yogurt. Chill, stirring occasionally, until mixture mounds slightly when dropped from a spoon. Beat egg whites until soft peaks form, beat in remaining ¼ cup sugar and beat until stiff. Whip heavy cream until still. Mold egg whites and whipped cream into boysenberry mixture. Turn into 9-cup mold and chill several hours or overnight.

Yield: 10 servings

EZ FRESH LEMON ICE CREAM

2 cups whipping cream or half &
   half
1 cup sugar
1 Tbsp. fresh grated SUNKIST®
   Lemon peel
⅓ cup fresh squeezed lemon juice
7 to 10 lemon shells or boats*
   (optional)

In large bowl, combine cream and sugar; stir to dissolve sugar. Blend in lemon peel and juice. Pour into shallow pan. Freeze until firm, about 4 hours. Serve in dessert glasses, lemon shells or boats. Garnish with fresh mint leaves and strawberries if desired.

Makes about 3 cups

To make Lemon Shell: Cut ⅓ off end of large lemon. Carefully ream out juice; reserve. Scrape shell "clean" with spoon.

To make Lemon Boat: Cut large lemon in half lengthwise and with a shallow "V" shape cut, remove white center core. Carefully ream out juice; reserve. Scrape shell "clean" with spoon.

Note: Citrus shells may be made ahead and frozen until ready to use.

ICE CREAM SANDWICHES

½ cup corn syrup
½ cup peanut butter
4 cups KELLOGG'S® RICE
   KRISPIES® Cereal
1 pint ice cream, cut into 6 slices

In medium-size mixing bowl, stir together corn syrup and peanut butter. Add RICE KRISPIES® Cereal. Stir until well coated. Press in buttered 13 × 9 × 2-inch pan. Place in freezer or coldest part of refrigerator until firm. Cut cereal mixture into twelve 3-inch squares. Sandwich each slice of ice cream between 2 squares. Freeze until firm. Cut each large sandwich in half and wrap individually in foil. Store in freezer until needed.

Yield: 12 sandwiches

® Kellogg Company

BAKED ALASKA

Sponge angel food or pound loaf
   cake
1 quart LOUIS SHERRY® Ice
   Cream (your favorite flavor)
4 egg whites
⅛ teaspoon cream of tartar
⅛ teaspoon salt
½ cup sugar
½ teaspoon vanilla

Cover two thicknesses of corrugated cardboard, 8 × 6 inches, with aluminum foil. Cut enough ½" thick slices of cake to construct a rectangle 7 × 5 inches. Place cake on foil and freeze.

Let egg whites stand at room temperature for 1 hour. Beat egg whites until frothy. Add cream of tartar and salt; continue beating until soft peaks form when beater is slowly raised. Gradually beat in sugar, 2 tablespoons at a time, beating well after each addition. Add vanilla and continue beating for about 3 minutes.

Place ice cream on cake base. Quickly spread ice cream and cake with meringue, spreading down onto foil all around to seal completely. Make swirls on top and sides. Place the Alaska on a cookie sheet and bake at 500° for about 3 minutes or until meringue is light brown. Remove to chilled platter. Serve at once.

Serves 12 to 16

STINGER PARFAIT

1 pt. vanilla ice cream
4 oz. DUBOUCHETT Green Creme
   de Menthe
4 oz. DUBOUCHETT Dark Creme
   de Cacao

Pour ½ oz. Creme de Menthe in bottom of parfait glass, spoon in some ice cream. Add ½ oz. of Creme de Cacao, more ice cream, etc. until glass is full. Put in freezer until serving time—Cordials will keep ice cream at spooning consistency.

CHOCOLATE ICE CREAM ROLL

3 eggs, separated
½ cup sugar
½ cup unsifted all-purpose flour
⅓ cup HERSHEY'S® Cocoa
¼ cup sugar
½ teaspoon baking soda
¼ teaspoon salt
⅓ cup water
1 teaspoon vanilla
1 tablespoon sugar
1 quart FRIENDLY® Peppermint
   Stick Ice Cream, softened
HERSHEY'S® Chocolate Fudge
   Topping

Line a 15½ × 10½ × 1-inch jelly roll pan with aluminum foil; generously grease foil. Beat egg yolks 3 minutes on medium speed. Gradually add ½ cup sugar; continue beating 2 minutes. Combine flour, cocoa, ¼ cup sugar, baking soda and salt; add alternately with water on low speed just until batter is smooth. Add vanilla. Set aside. Beat egg whites until foamy; add 1 tablespoon sugar and beat until stiff peaks form. Carefully fold into chocolate mixture. Spread batter evenly into prepared pan. Bake at 375°F. for 14 to 16 minutes, or until top springs back when touched lightly. Invert onto slightly dampened towel; carefully remove foil. Immediately roll cake and towel together from narrow end. Let stand 1 minute. Unroll; reroll without towel. Cool completely on wire rack. Unroll cake and spread with softened ice cream; reroll. Cover with aluminum foil and freeze immediately. Serve warmed chocolate fudge topping over slices of ice cream roll.

EASY HOMEMADE CHOCOLATE ICE CREAM

1 (14-ounce) can EAGLE® Brand Sweetened Condensed Milk (not evaporated milk)
⅔ cup chocolate flavored syrup
2 cups (1 pint) whipping cream, whipped

In large bowl, stir together sweetened condensed milk and syrup. Fold in whipped cream. Pour into aluminum foil-lined 9 × 5-inch loaf pan; cover. Freeze 6 hours or until firm. Scoop ice cream from pan or remove from pan, peel off foil and slice. Return leftovers to freezer.

Makes about 1½ quarts

VARIATIONS:

Coconut Almond: Omit chocolate syrup. In large bowl, combine sweetened condensed milk, 2 tablespoons water, 2 egg yolks and 4 teaspoons vanilla extract. Fold in whipped cream with ½ cup toasted flaked coconut and ½ cup toasted slivered almonds.

Coffee: Omit chocolate syrup. In large bowl, combine sweetened condensed milk, 1 tablespoon instant coffee dissolved in 2 tablespoons water, 2 beaten egg yolks and 4 teaspoons vanilla extract. Fold in whipped cream.

French Vanilla: Omit chocolate syrup. In large bowl, combine sweetened condensed milk, 2 tablespoons water, 2 beaten egg yolks and 4 teaspoons vanilla extract. Fold in whipped cream.

Lemon: Omit chocolate syrup. In large bowl, combine sweetened condensed milk, 2 tablespoons REALEMON® Reconstituted Lemon Juice, 1 tablespoon grated lemon rind and few drops yellow food coloring. Fold in whipped cream.

Mint Chocolate Chip: Omit chocolate syrup. In large bowl, combine sweetened condensed milk, 2 teaspoons peppermint extract, 3 to 4 drops green food coloring and 2 tablespoons water. Fold in whipped cream and ½ cup small dark chocolate-flavored baking chips.

Mocha: Dissolve 1 tablespoon instant coffee in 1 teaspoon hot water; combine with sweetened condensed milk and chocolate syrup. Fold in whipped cream.

Raspberry: Omit chocolate syrup. Thaw 1 (10-ounce) package frozen raspberries in syrup. With blender, blend until smooth. In large bowl, combine raspberries and sweetened condensed milk. Fold in whipped cream.

Strawberry: Omit chocolate syrup. Thaw 1 (10-ounce) package frozen strawberries in syrup. With blender, blend strawberries until smooth. In large bowl, combine strawberries and sweetened condensed milk. Fold in whipped cream.

Peanut Butter: Omit chocolate syrup. In large bowl, combine sweetened condensed milk, 2 tablespoons water, 2 beaten egg yolks and ½ cup peanut butter. Fold in whipped cream.

Peppermint Candy: Omit chocolate syrup. In large bowl, combine 2 beaten egg yolks, 2 tablespoons water, sweetened condensed milk and 4 teaspoons vanilla extract. Fold in whipped cream and ¼ cup crushed hard peppermint candy.

Peach: Omit chocolate syrup. Drain 1 (16-ounce) can peaches. With blender, blend until smooth. In large bowl, combine peaches, sweetened condensed milk, 3 beaten egg yolks and ½ teaspoon almond extract. Fold in whipped cream.

Butter Pecan: Omit chocolate syrup. In small saucepan, melt 2 tablespoons butter; stir in ¼ cup chopped pecans. In large bowl, combine sweetened condensed milk, 2 beaten egg yolks, 1 teaspoon maple flavoring and buttered pecans. Fold in whipped cream.

ICE CREAM ECLAIRS

1 cup water
½ cup butter or margarine
¼ teaspoon salt
1 cup unsifted all-purpose flour
4 eggs
½ gallon FRIENDLY® Butter Pecan Ice Cream
HERSHEY'S® Chocolate Fudge Topping

Heat water, butter and salt to a rolling boil in medium saucepan.

Add flour all at once; stir vigorously over low heat about 1 minute or until mixture leaves side of pan and forms a ball. Remove from heat; cool slightly. Add eggs, one at a time, beating after each addition until smooth and velvety. Shape scant ¼ cupfuls of batter into fingers 4 inches long and 1 inch wide about 2 inches apart on ungreased baking sheet. Bake at 400°F. for 35 to 40 minutes or until puffed and golden brown. Remove from oven. Cool on wire rack. Slice top from each eclair; fill with scoops of ice cream. Replace tops; glaze with fudge topping. Freeze.

12 eclairs

SUNSHINE® ICE CREAM CAKE

1½ cups crushed SUNSHINE® Vanilla Wafers (45 wafers)
¼ cup butter or margarine, melted
12 whole SUNSHINE® Vanilla Wafers
1 quart strawberry ice cream, softened

Combine 1 cup crushed SUNSHINE® Vanilla Wafers with butter or margarine. Press into bottom of 8-inch springform pan. Stand whole Vanilla Wafers around sides of pan, pressing gently into crumb mixture. Freeze at least ½ hour. Remove from freezer. Spoon in half of softened ice cream, pressing down firmly. Sprinkle with remaining crushed vanilla wafers. Top with remaining ice cream. Freeze at least 4 hours. Remove rim of pan 15-20 minutes before serving. If desired, garnish with whipped cream and fresh strawberries.

Yield: 6-8 servings

AMARETTO STRAWBERRIES

2 oz. HIRAM WALKER Amaretto
1 pint fresh strawberries
Vanilla ice cream

Marinate strawberries overnight in Amaretto. Serve over ice cream, sprinkled with slivered almonds.

Serves 4

QUICK 'N EASY ICE CREAM IDEAS FOR GROWN-UPS

Combine orange liqueur with mincemeat. Serve warm over LOUIS SHERRY® Butter Pecan Ice Cream.

Combine cherry liqueur with frozen mixed fruit (thawed). Serve over LOUIS SHERRY® Strawberry Ice Cream.

Combine banana slices with coffee liqueur. Refrigerate 30 minutes. Alternate layers of bananas with LOUIS SHERRY® Chocolate Ice Cream in parfait glasses.

Pour white creme de menthe over mandarin orange sections. Top with a scoop of LOUIS SHERRY® Vanilla Ice Cream.

Combine peach slices, frozen red raspberries (thawed), brown sugar and pink champagne. Serve over LOUIS SHERRY® Pineapple or Orange Fruit Ice.

Flavor butterscotch sauce with rum. Serve warm or cold over LOUIS SHERRY® Vanilla Ice Cream.

Pour green creme de menthe over LOUIS SHERRY® Lemon Fruit Ice.

FROZEN AMARETTO CREAM
(Gelato Di Crema Amaretto)

1 cup heavy cream
¼ cup AMARETTO DI GALLIANO™
1 pint vanilla ice cream, softened
⅓ cup finely chopped, toasted almonds

Whip cream until stiff peaks form. Combine cream, softened ice cream and AMARETTO DI GALLIANO™. Pour into cupcake papers which you have set in muffin tins. Sprinkle with almonds and freeze until firm.

Serves 6

ALMOND SIERRA DESSERT

Dissolve 1 Tbsp. instant coffee in 2 Tbsp. hot water. Stir into a 16 oz. can chocolate fudge topping. Spoon warm or cold over vanilla, chocolate or coffee ice cream. Splash on a little brandy. Top with lots of BLUE RIBBON® Blanched Slivered Almonds, plain or toasted. To Toast: Place almonds in 350° oven about 8 minutes; stir once or twice.

QUICK 'N EASY ICE CREAM IDEAS FOR KIDS

Pour chilled apricot nectar over mandarin orange sections. Top with a scoop of LOUIS SHERRY® Vanilla Ice Cream.

Combine ½ cup honey with ½ cup chunky peanut butter. Alternate mixture with LOUIS SHERRY® Chocolate Ice Cream in parfait glass.

Spoon banana slices, fresh strawberries and green grapes into dessert dish. Top with LOUIS SHERRY® Orange Fruit Ice.

PEANUTTY VALENTINE TREAT

½ cup PETER PAN® Peanut Butter, Creamy or Crunchy
1 quart vanilla ice cream, softened

Meringue Valentines:
3 egg whites
½ teaspoon vinegar
¼ teaspoon vanilla
⅛ teaspoon salt
1 cup sugar
Honey

Place peanut butter and ice cream in a blender or mixing bowl. Blend well, being careful not to over mix. Pour mixture into ice cream carton and return to freezer.

Meringue Valentines: Combine egg whites, vinegar, vanilla and salt in a deep narrow bowl. Beat on high speed until soft peaks form. Gradually add sugar and beat until peaks are very stiff. Cover cooky sheet with brown paper. Draw 8 hearts approximately 3½ to 4 inches in diameter. Using back of spoon or a spatula, shape meringue into shells by forming a hollow in the center of each. Bake in a 300°F. oven for 45 minutes. Remove from paper immediately. Cool. To serve, spoon peanut butter ice cream into meringue hearts and drizzle with honey.

Yield: 8 servings

Featherweight®
STRAWBERRY LAYERED PARFAIT
(Low Calorie)

2 envelopes FEATHERWEIGHT Strawberry Gelatin Dessert
1½ cups boiling water
1½ cups cold water
1 pint fresh strawberries (cleaned and sliced)
1 envelope FEATHERWEIGHT Whipped Topping

Directions: Dissolve gelatin in boiling water; add cold water. Add fruit to gelatin stirring carefully. Chill until partially set. Spoon into bottom of parfait glasses and chill. ***Prepare:*** FEATHERWEIGHT Whipped Topping as directed. Layer in Whipped Topping alternately with strawberry gelatin, chilling until set. After each layer top with whipped topping and garnish with sliced strawberries.

Makes approximately 6 servings

GRAPE ICE

1½ cups SMUCKER'S Grape Jelly
2 cups ice cold water
1 teaspoon grated lemon peel
1 tablespoon lemon juice

Place Grape Jelly in saucepan. Cook over low heat, stirring constantly, until melted. Remove from heat. Stir in water, lemon peel and juice. Refrigerate until chilled.

If you have an ice cream maker, pour into freezer can; adjust dasher; set cover in place. Process according to directions accompanying your ice cream freezer. After ice is soft-frozen, remove dasher. Repack ice in small container; freeze several hours or until firm.

To make ice without ice cream freezer, pour mixture into 9 × 9-inch shallow baking pan. Cover with foil. Freeze until firm, about 3 hours. Place large bowl of electric mixer or food processor container and beaters or blade in refrigerator or freezer to chill. Scoop grape ice into bowl or container and beat or process until fluffy. Return to pan. Cover; freeze until firm. Beat and freeze again. *About 1 quart*

Karo®

CANTALOUPE SHERBET

1 envelope unflavored gelatin
½ cup milk
3 cups cubed cantaloupe
1 cup KARO® Light Corn Syrup

In small saucepan sprinkle gelatin over milk. Stir over low heat until dissolved. Place in blender container with cantaloupe and corn syrup; cover. Blend on high speed 30 seconds. Pour into 9 x 9 x 2-inch baking pan. Cover; freeze overnight. Soften slightly at room temperature, about 10 to 15 minutes. Spoon into large bowl; with mixer at low speed, beat until smooth, but not melted. Pour into 4-cup mold or freezer container. Cover; freeze about 4 hours or until firm. Unmold or soften at room temperature for easier scooping.
Makes about 4 cups

VARIATIONS:

Blueberry Sherbet: Follow basic recipe. Use 3 cups whole blueberries; omit cantaloupe.
Makes about 3½ cups

Honeydew Sherbet: Follow basic recipe. Use 3 cups cubed honeydew melon; omit cantaloupe.
Makes about 4 cups

Nectarine or Peach Sherbet: Follow basic recipe. Use 3 cups cubed nectarines or peaches and 1 tablespoon lemon juice; omit cantaloupe.
Makes about 4 cups

Papaya Sherbet: Follow basic recipe. Use 3 cups cubed papaya and 1 tablespoon lemon juice; omit cantaloupe.
Makes about 4 cups

Pineapple Sherbet: Follow basic recipe. Use 3 cups cubed pineapple; omit cantaloupe.
Makes about 4 cups

Strawberry Sherbet: Follow basic recipe. Use 3 cups whole strawberries; omit cantaloupe.
Makes about 3½ cups

Watermelon Sherbet: Follow basic recipe. Use 3 cups cubed watermelon; omit cantaloupe.
Makes about 4 cups

LEMON ICE

1½ cups water
1 cup sugar
½ cup BERTOLLI® Soave Classico Wine
Grated rind of 4 lemons
¾ to 1 cup lemon juice

Heat water and sugar to boiling in saucepan; boil 3 minutes. Cool. Mix all ingredients. Freeze in 9-inch pan until firm, about 3 hours.

FRESH GRAPE SORBET*

2 cups freshly frozen green grapes
½ cup CANADA DRY® Club Soda
2 teaspoons sugar or honey

Crush the grapes in a blender or food processor, adding club soda and sugar slowly. Mixture is ready when mixture begins to thicken. Serve in champagne glasses and garnish with coconut.
Makes 4-6 servings

*Cantaloupe can be substituted for grapes and decorated with a fresh strawberry; or, strawberries and bananas may be substituted and decorated with fresh mint.

BASIC DANNON® YOGURT DESSERT

2 cups DANNON® Plain Yogurt
½ cup sugar
2 Tbsp. lemon juice
3 Tbsp. orange liqueur
1 pint softened vanilla ice cream

Mix sugar, lemon juice, orange liqueur and DANNON® Plain Yogurt. Stir softened vanilla ice cream and fold into other ingredients.
Serves about 4 people

VARIATIONS:

1. Mold in salad mold and freeze. Unmold on serving plate and surround with fresh strawberries, peaches, blueberries, raspberries, grapes, etc.

2. Alternate layers in a glass bowl: grapes, raspberries, blueberries, melon balls and Basic DANNON® Yogurt Dessert.

3. Mix any type of fruit and Basic DANNON® Yogurt Dessert and use as a filling for crepes.

4. Mix any type of fruit and Basic DANNON® Yogurt Dessert and spoon into pie crust and freeze until set.

FRUIT 'N' NUT FREEZE
(Low Sodium/Low Calorie)

2 cups water
1 cup sugar
1 can (8 oz.) crushed pineapple in unsweetened juice
⅓ cup freshly squeezed orange juice
2 tablespoons freshly squeezed lemon juice
½ cup mashed banana
⅛ teaspoon ground ginger
¼ cup chopped PLANTERS® Dry Roasted Unsalted Cashews

In a saucepan combine water and sugar; bring to a boil. Reduce heat and simmer 5 minutes. Remove from heat and stir in pineapple, orange juice, lemon juice, banana, and ginger. Pour into a 9 x 5 x 3-inch loaf pan. Cool. Freeze until ice crystals begin to form, about 2 hours. Stir thoroughly. Repeat freezing and stirring procedure again, mixing in PLANTERS® Dry Roasted Unsalted Cashews. Freeze until firm. Remove from freezer 15 minutes before serving. Spoon into individual portions to serve.
Makes (4½ cups) 9 servings

Per ½ cup serving: 150 calories, 1 mg. sodium

COCONUT FROZEN YOGURT

1½ cups COCO CASA™ Cream of Coconut
4 cups (4 containers) plain yogurt or any other flavored yogurt— orange, lemon, raspberry, coffee, vanilla, etc.
4 egg yolks
4 egg whites, stiffly beaten

In a bowl, mix cream of coconut and yogurt. Stir in egg yolks. Fold in beaten egg whites. Pour mixture into a 1½ quart freezer container. Cover and freeze until hard.
Makes 1½ quarts

CHOCO-ALMOND CARROT TORTE

1 cup whole natural (unblanched) BLUE RIBBON® Almonds
Butter or margarine
2 squares (1 oz. each) semi-sweet chocolate
6 large eggs, separated
1 cup sugar
1 tablespoon grated orange rind
¾ teaspoon cinnamon
¼ teaspoon salt
⅓ cup dry fine bread crumbs
1 cup grated carrot, lightly packed
Chocolate Glaze (recipe follows)

Grate almonds in Mouli grater or process about ¼ cup at a time in electric blender until finely ground. Heavily butter a 7½-inch tube pan 2¾-inches deep. Line bottom with a circle of baking parchment or heavy wax paper and butter it. Sprinkle pan with 2 tablespoons of the grated almonds. Grate chocolate; set aside.

In mixing bowl, beat egg yolks until thick and lemon-colored; add ¾ cup of the sugar, the orange rind, cinnamon and salt. Beat at medium speed 3 minutes; turn speed low, and gradually mix in remaining almonds and bread crumbs. Press any excess liquid from carrots and stir in by hand.

In a large mixing bowl, using clean beaters, beat egg whites until stiff. Gradually beat in remaining ¼ cup sugar until stiff peaks form. Fold about ¼ of the meringue into batter until thoroughly mixed. Gently fold in remaining meringue and chocolate. Turn batter into prepared pan. Bake at 350 degrees 45 to 50 minutes or until cake springs back when touched lightly. Cool thoroughly before removing from pan. Turn out onto serving plate. Spread top with Chocolate Glaze, allowing some to drizzle down sides. If you wish, grate additional almonds to sprinkle over top.

Makes 1 cake (7-inch)

CHOCOLATE GLAZE

Over hot water, melt 1 tablespoon butter with ½ of a 1-oz. square semi-sweet chocolate. Stir in ½ cup sifted powdered sugar and 1 tablespoon boiling water; stir until smooth.

Makes about ¼ cup Glaze

GRASSHOPPER TORTE

2 cups (24) crushed cream-filled chocolate cookies
¼ cup PARKAY Margarine, melted
1 7-oz. jar KRAFT Marshmallow Creme
¼ cup creme de menthe
2 cups heavy cream, whipped

Combine crumbs and margarine; reserve ½ cup. Press remaining crumbs onto bottom of 9-inch springform pan. Chill. Combine marshmallow creme and creme de menthe; mix until well blended. Fold in whipped cream. Pour into pan; sprinkle with reserved crumbs. Freeze.

VARIATION:

Prepare the torte in a 9-inch pie plate.

VIENNESE TORTE

1 frozen SARA LEE Original All Butter Pound Cake, thawed
3 tablespoons rum or orange juice
2 tablespoons strawberry preserves
2 tablespoons apricot or pineapple preserves
1 cup frozen whipped topping, thawed
¼ cup toasted sliced almonds

Cut Pound Cake lengthwise into 3 layers. Sprinkle 1 cut side of each layer with 1 tablespoon rum. Place bottom cake layer on serving plate; spread with strawberry preserves. Top with middle cake layer; spread with apricot preserves. Replace top layer of cake. Frost top, sides and ends of cake with whipped topping; garnish with almonds.

Makes 10-12 servings

GATORADE® POPSICLES

1 bottle (32 ounces) GATORADE® Thirst Quencher

Fill each popsicle mold ¾ full with GATORADE.® Insert popsicle holder into each mold and freeze until solid. Or, freeze in small pointed paper cups (add the holder when GATORADE® begins to harden). Snap mold to release popsicles and serve immediately.

16 popsicles

FROSTY FREEZER TREATS

2 medium DOLE® Bananas
½ cup peanut butter
¼ cup milk
2 tablespoons honey
½ cup chopped toasted almonds

Peel bananas. Wrap each closely in plastic wrap and place in freezer until frozen. Blend peanut butter with milk and honey until smooth. Unwrap bananas and spread with the mixture. Roll each in almonds. Wrap again and freeze. To serve, cut into ¼-inch slices.

Makes 2 frozen bananas or 4 servings

LEMON MINT DESSERT MOLD

1 package (3 ounces) lemon flavored gelatin
½ cup RICHARDSON Butter Mints
1¾ cups boiling water
1 can (1 pound) sliced peaches, drained
¼ cup sliced maraschino cherries

Place gelatin and mints in mixing bowl. Add boiling water, stirring until gelatin and mints are dissolved. Chill until partially set. Fold in fruit. Turn into 1-quart mold. Chill until firm.

4 to 6 servings

DESSERT TOPPING

1 cup NABISCO® 100% Bran Cereal
½ cup coarsely chopped walnuts
¼ cup light brown sugar, firmly packed
¼ cup butter or margarine, melted

Combine NABISCO® 100% Bran Cereal, walnuts and sugar. Toss with melted butter or margarine. Serve as a topping over any fruit-ice cream combination. Refrigerate surplus in airtight container.

Makes 1½ cups

Beverages

Nonalcoholic

SUNKIST®'S LEMONADE SYRUP BASE

1½ cups sugar
½ cup boiling water
1 tablespoon fresh grated
  SUNKIST® Lemon peel
1½ cups fresh squeezed
  SUNKIST® Lemon juice

Dissolve sugar in boiling water. Add lemon peel and juice. Store in covered container in refrigerator.
Makes about 2⅔ cups base

Lemonade by the glass:

¼ to ⅓ cup lemonade syrup base
¾ cup cold water
Ice cubes

In large glass, combine all ingredients; stir well.
Makes about 1 cup

Lemonade by the pitcher:

2⅔ cups lemonade syrup base
5 cups cold water
Ice cubes

In large pitcher, combine all ingredients; stir well.
Makes about 8 cups

LOWER-CAL LEMONADE SYRUP BASE
(Low Calorie)

1 cup plus 3 tablespoons
  granulated sugar replacement
¼ cup sugar
½ cup boiling water
2 teaspoons fresh grated
  SUNKIST® Lemon peel
1½ cups fresh squeezed
  SUNKIST® Lemon juice*

Dissolve sugar replacement and sugar in boiling water. Add remaining ingredients. Store in covered container in refrigerator.
Makes about 2¼ cups base

Lower-Cal Lemonade by the glass:
In large glass, combine ¼ cup lemonade syrup base, ⅔ cup cold water and ice cubes; stir well.
Makes about 1¼ cups

1 serving = 45 calories

VARIATION:

For "pink" lemonade add a few drops red food coloring.

*To yield more juice, have lemons at room temperature before squeezing.

LEMONADE

Sugar
REALEMON® Reconstituted Lemon
  Juice
Cold water

Dissolve sugar in REALEMON® add cold water. Serve over ice. Garnish as desired.

To Make:

1 serving (8 ounces)	2 tablespoons sugar 2 tablespoons REALEMON® ¾ cup cold water
1 quart	½ cup sugar ½ cup REALEMON® 3¼ cups cold water
1 gallon	2 cups sugar 2 cups REALEMON® 3 quarts plus 1 cup cold water
2 gallons	4 cups sugar 1 (32-ounce) bottle REALEMON® 6½ quarts cold water

VARIATIONS:

Sparkling Lemonade: Substitute club soda for cold water.

Slushy Lemonade: In blender container, combine ½ cup REALEMON® and ½ cup sugar with 1 cup water; add ice to make 1 quart. Blend until smooth. Serve immediately.
Makes about 1 quart

Pink Lemonade: Stir in 1 to 2 teaspoons grenadine syrup or 1 or 2 drops red food coloring to 1 quart lemonade.

Minted Lemonade: Stir in 2 or 3 drops peppermint extract to 1 quart lemonade.

REAL OLD FASHIONED LEMONADE

Juice of 6 SUNKIST® Lemons
  (1 cup)
¾ cup sugar or to taste
4 cups cold water
1 SUNKIST® Lemon, unpeeled,
  sliced in cartwheels
Ice cubes

In large pitcher, combine lemon juice and sugar; stir to dissolve sugar. Add remaining ingredients; blend well.
*Makes about 6 cups
(six 8-ounce servings)*

VARIATION:

Substitute honey to taste for sugar.

For "pink" lemonade add a few drops red food coloring.

LEMON ORANGE BEVERAGE

1 can (6 fl. oz.) BIRDS EYE®
   ORANGE PLUS® Frozen
   Concentrate for Orange
   Breakfast Beverage
1 envelope KOOL-AID® Lemonade
   Flavor Soft Drink Mix
1 cup sugar
1 quart water and ice

Reconstitute beverage as directed
on can. Combine soft drink mix,
sugar, orange beverage and water
in a glass pitcher. Stir until sugar
and soft drink mix are dissolved.
Serve with additional ice, if
desired.

Makes 2 quarts or 8 servings

MIAMI LIME LIFT

2 fresh Florida limes
½ cup sugar
1 quart boiling water
Lime slices for garnish

Slice limes thinly. Put in bowl with
sugar. Let stand 1 hour. Pour
boiling water into bowl. Cool; then
chill. To serve: pour limeade and
several lime slices over ice in tall
glasses. Hang a lime slice over
edge of glass. Serve with long
straws.   *Makes 1 quart*

VARIATION:

Fill glasses only ¾ full. Add a
splash of soda water.

*Favorite recipe from Florida Lime
Administrative Committee*

STRAWBERRY LIMEADE

2 (10-ounce) packages frozen
   strawberries in syrup, thawed
3 cups cold water
1 (8-ounce) bottle REALIME®
   Reconstituted Lime Juice
½ to ¾ cup sugar
Ice
Whole strawberries or mint leaves
   for garnish, optional

In blender container, blend
strawberries well. In pitcher,
combine pureed strawberries,
water, REALIME® and sugar; stir
until sugar dissolves. Serve over
ice. Garnish as desired.

Makes about 1¾ quarts

FLORIDA LIME COOLER

Combine equal parts frozen
limeade concentrate and soda
water in tall glass, filling about ⅔
full. Top with scoops of lime
sherbet. Hang a lime slice over
edge of glass. Serve with straw
and iced tea spoon.

*Favorite recipe from Florida Lime
Administrative Committee*

DUSTCUTTER

1½ oz. ROSE'S® Lime Juice

Fill tall glass with ice; add lime
juice; top off with SCHWEPPES®
Tonic Water.

ICED APPLE TEA

6 tea bags
3 cups boiling water
3 cups TREE TOP Apple Juice
¼ teaspoon ground allspice
⅓ cup honey
Lemon slices, optional

Remove boiling water from heat,
let tea bags brew for 5 minutes.
Remove. Add allspice, honey and
apple juice, simmer over low heat
until honey is blended, about 1
minute. Chill. Serve over ice with
lemon slices to garnish.

Serves 6

ROSE'S SUMMERTIME COOLER

Open 1 qt. unfiltered apple juice.
Add 4 CELESTIAL SEASONINGS®
CINNAMON ROSE™ Tea Bags.
Close and shake. Refrigerate 24
hours. Remove Tea Bags.

SPICED TEA REFRESHER

2 cups boiling water
2 tea bags
2 cinnamon sticks
2 tablespoons lemon juice
1 bottle (24 ounces) or 3 cups
   WELCH'S® White Grape Juice

Pour water over tea bags. Add
cinnamon sticks and steep for 5
minutes. Remove tea bags and
cinnamon. Add lemon juice and
white grape juice. Pour over ice in
tall glasses. Serve with twist of
lemon rind.   *Makes 4 servings*

THE ZINGER TWIST

1 small bottle CANADA DRY® Club
   Soda
Dash of Grenadine syrup

Serve in a martini glass with ice.
Garnish with twist of lemon.

PURPLE QUENCHER COOLER

1 Quart WELCH'S® Grape Juice
3 Cups Apple Juice
1 Can (6 ounces) Frozen
   Concentrated Pineapple-Orange
   Juice, thawed
Crushed Ice
Lemon or Lime Slices (Optional)

Combine WELCH'S® Grape Juice,
apple juice and pineapple-orange
juice. Fill pitcher with crushed ice.
Pour into thermos jugs. Add lemon
and lime slices.

Makes about 2 quarts

STRAWBERRY SQUIRT

6 fresh ripe strawberries
1 cup DANNON® Vanilla Yogurt
6½ oz. chilled PERRIER®

Blend berries and yogurt at high
speed until smooth. Stir in chilled
PERRIER®.

To make Strawberry Squirtsicle:
Pour the Strawberry Squirt drink
into a 4 oz. paper cup. Insert a
wooden stick in center and freeze.
When frozen, peel off paper cup
and eat as a frozen pop.

STRAWBERRY-ORANGE FROSTY

2 scoops crushed ice
10 fresh or frozen strawberries
4 oz. fresh squeezed SUNKIST®
   Orange juice
1 oz. simple syrup (recipe follows)

Combine in blender; blend until
smooth. Serve in 16 oz. glass.
Garnish with orange twist and
strawberry.

SIMPLE SYRUP

In saucepan, combine 2 cups sugar
and 1 cup water. Bring to boil,
stirring until sugar dissolves. Boil
gently for 5 minutes. Will keep 6
months in refrigerator.

Makes about 2 cups

ORANGE OASIS

½ cup crushed ice
1 small SUNKIST® Orange, peeled,
    cut into chunks
Juice of ½ fresh SUNKIST® Lemon
2 to 3 teaspoons sugar
Splash of club soda
1 SUNKIST® Orange and Lemon
    cartwheel
Fresh mint (optional)

In blender, combine ice, orange
chunks, lemon juice and sugar;
blend until smooth. Pour into
10-ounce glass. Fill with soda.
Garnish with orange and lemon
cartwheel slices and mint.
Makes one 8-ounce serving

FRESH ORANGE NOG

Juice of 3 SUNKIST® Oranges
    (1 cup)
1 Tbsp. honey or sugar
1 egg
2 or 3 ice cubes

In blender, combine all ingredients;
blend until smooth.
Makes 1 to 2 servings
(about 1½ cups)

ORANGE "SHAKE"

Peel 1 SUNKIST® Orange; cut in
bite-size pieces. In blender,
combine orange pieces, ¼ cup
instant non-fat dry milk powder, 2
teaspoons brown sugar and 6 to 8
ice cubes; blend until smooth.
Makes 1 to 2 servings
(about 1½ cups)

"CALORIE CONSCIOUS" FRUIT NOG
(Low Calorie)

Peel 1 SUNKIST® Orange; cut in
bite-size pieces. In blender,
combine orange pieces, ½ banana,
chunked, ¼ cup non-fat milk, 1
egg white, 1 teaspoon granulated
sugar replacement and 2 to 3 ice
cubes; blend until smooth.
Makes 2 servings

About 85 calories each

CITRUS YOGURT DELIGHT

1 cup DANNON® Lemon Yogurt
¼ cup frozen orange juice
    concentrate
1 fresh peach, sliced, or 1 large
    canned peach
3 ice cubes

Combine lemon yogurt, orange
juice concentrate, peach and ice
cubes in a blender. Blend until
frothy. Pour into glass and serve
immediately.   *Makes 1 serving*

PEACH FROST

3 ripe fresh peaches, pitted,
    peeled, quartered
½ cup KARO® Light Corn Syrup
¼ tsp. ground ginger
1 cup lemon sherbet
½ cup ginger ale
2 scoops vanilla ice cream

Place peaches, corn syrup and
ginger in blender container; cover.
Blend until smooth. Add sherbet
and ginger ale; cover. Blend until
smooth. Serve in large glasses
with vanilla ice cream.
Makes 2 servings

BANANA MILK SHAKES

Peel and mash one CHIQUITA®
Brand Banana. Add a cup of cold
milk and shake or beat until
smooth and creamy.

To Vary Flavor: Add a tablespoon
of chocolate syrup, a few
teaspoons of honey, some
prepared coffee, or one packet of
flavored instant breakfast.

VARIATIONS:

BANANA FROSTED
Add a scoop of ice cream or
sherbet before shaking.

RICH EGG NOG
Follow banana milk shake
directions and add one egg and a
pinch of salt.

BANANA FRUIT SHAKES
Mash one ripe banana and beat or
shake with 1 cup of cold fruit juice,
any flavor—orange, apple,
pineapple—all of them are good.

SPECIAL-T MILK SHAKE

4 scoops vanilla ice-cream
¼ cup milk
¼ cup MR. & MRS. "T"®
    Grenadine Syrup

Place all ingredients in blender and
blend until smooth. Serve in a tall
glass.   *Serves 1*

FROSTY APPLE SHAKE

1 quart apple juice (chilled)
1 pint vanilla ice cream (softened)
1 can (8¾ oz.) crushed pineapple
    (optional)
½ tsp. cinnamon or sprinkle with
    nutmeg

Combine all ingredients in blender
or with mixer until frothy.

*Favorite recipe from Michigan Apple
Committee*

PINK COW
(Low Calorie)

1 c. SUGARLO® Diet Raspberry
    Yogurt
1 c. skim milk
1 fresh peach, peeled and sliced
1 packet SUGARLO® Sweetener

Blend together thoroughly and
serve chilled.

Calories: 106/8 oz.

REFRESHING RASPBERRY FROST

1 can (46 oz.) DOLE® Pineapple
    Juice, chilled
1 quart raspberry sherbet
1 bottle (28 oz.) ginger ale, chilled
1 package (10 oz.) frozen
    raspberries

Combine half of pineapple juice,
sherbet and ginger ale in blender.
Whir until light and frothy, about 1
minute. Pour into large punch
bowl. Repeat with remaining
amounts of these three
ingredients. Stir in undrained,
thawed raspberries.
Makes about 3 quarts

VARIATION:

Substitute orange sherbet for
raspberry sherbet and 1 thinly
sliced orange for frozen
raspberries.

COFFEE FROST

1 cup milk
½ cup water
1 tablespoon thawed BIRDS EYE™ AWAKE® Frozen Concentrate for Imitation Orange Juice*
1 tablespoon MAXWELL HOUSE® or YUBAN® Instant Coffee or SANKA® Brand Instant 97% Caffein Free Coffee
Ice cream or ice cubes

Combine milk, water, concentrate and instant coffee in bowl. Beat with rotary beater or blend in electric blender until frothy. Serve as a punch topped with ice cream, or serve over ice. Sprinkle with cinnamon sugar, if desired.
Makes about 2 cups or 4 servings

*Or use TANG™ Orange Flavor Instant Breakfast Drink.

STRAWBERRY CLOUD
(Low Calorie)

1 c. (8 oz. container) SUGARLO® Diet Strawberry Yogurt
1 c. skim milk
1 tsp. fresh grated orange peel

Combine ingredients in blender, run at medium speed for 20 seconds. Serve chilled.

Calories: 105/8 oz.

CRANBERRY COOLER
(Low Calorie)

1 c. (8 oz. container) SUGARLO® Diet Raspberry Yogurt
1 c. low calorie cranberry juice

Combine two ingredients in blender. Run at medium speed for 15 seconds. Serve chilled.

Calories: 89/8 oz.

THE LIFESAVER

¼ cup LIPTON® Lemon Flavored Iced Tea Mix
2 cups milk
1 can (6 oz.) frozen orange juice concentrate, slightly thawed
1 teaspoon vanilla extract
10 to 12 ice cubes

In blender, combine all ingredients except ice cubes. Process at high speed, adding ice cubes one at a time, until blended.
Makes about 5 servings

HOME RUN REFRESHER

6 bananas
½ cup LIPTON® Lemon Flavored Iced Tea Mix
2 cups milk
1 bottle (28 oz.) ginger ale, chilled

In blender, puree bananas. Add LIPTON® Lemon Flavored Iced Tea Mix and milk; process at high speed until smooth. Pour into pitcher; chill. Just before serving, add ginger ale.
Makes about 8 servings

EASY SODAS

1 envelope KOOL-AID® Unsweetened Soft Drink Mix, any flavor
1 cup sugar
1 cup cold water
1 bottle (28 fl. oz.) club soda, chilled
1 pint vanilla ice cream or fruit-flavored sherbet

Dissolve soft drink mix and sugar in water in nonmetal bowl or pitcher. Stir in soda. Place a small scoop of ice cream in each of 6 tall glasses. Stir in soda mixture; top with a second scoop of ice cream.
Makes about 2 quarts or 6 large servings

ORANGE NOG

2 cups milk
1 packet Mix 'n Eat CREAM OF WHEAT® Cereal
¼ cup frozen orange juice concentrate, thawed
¼ cup granulated sugar
2 eggs

Scald milk; pour into blender container. Cover and turn to low speed. Gradually add cereal through small opening in lid or move lid slightly to the side. Blend at medium speed 1 minute. Reduce to low speed and add orange juice concentrate and sugar. Add eggs, one at a time. Continue to blend a few more seconds until thoroughly mixed. Chill overnight. Blend or stir and serve.
Makes 2 (about 1⅓ cup) servings

BANANA EGGNOG

3 cups whole milk, chilled
1 cup mashed bananas
2 eggs
4 ice cubes
1 Tablespoon honey
1 cup CANADA DRY® Club Soda

Mix milk, banana, eggs, ice cubes and honey in electric blender for 30 seconds at medium speed. Pour in CANADA DRY® Club Soda just before serving and stir to blend. Garnish with banana slices.

VARIATIONS:

Lime Eggnog
Substitute ½ cup freshly squeezed lime juice for the cup of mashed bananas in above recipe, and garnish with lime wheel.

Tomato Eggnog
Substitute ½ cup tomato juice, chilled, for 1 cup mashed bananas in above recipe; add ¼ teaspoon grated lemon or lime rind. Garnish with cherry tomato.

Low Cholesterol Hint: The above three eggnogs can be made without the eggs for those who are cholesterol conscious.

KIDDIE COCKTAIL

Mix one part MR. & MRS. "T"® Margarita Mix with three parts orange juice. Pour over ice in a tall glass. Garnish with orange or lemon slice.   *Serves 1*

CURIOUS CARIBBEAN PUNCH

2 cans (46 oz. each) DOLE® Pineapple Juice
2 quarts lemonade
1½ quarts orange juice
1 quart cranberry juice cocktail
2 cups apple juice
Ice cubes
1 lemon, thinly sliced

In a large punch bowl, mix together pineapple juice, lemonade, orange juice, cranberry juice and apple juice. Add ice cubes. Float lemon slices on top for garnish.
Makes about 2 gallons

SPARKLING PUNCH

1 gallon TREE TOP Pear-Apple
  Juice
2 teaspoons lemon juice
4 cups ginger ale
Ice cubes

Combine all ingredients. Pour over
ice in tall glasses.   *Serves 15*

ROSY APPLE PUNCH

1 pkg. cherry flavored gelatin
1 cup hot LUCKY LEAF® Apple
  Juice
3 cups cold LUCKY LEAF® Apple
  Juice
2 Tbsps. lemon juice
1 10-oz. bottle ginger ale

Dissolve gelatin in 1 cup hot apple
juice. Add cold apple juice and
lemon juice. Mix well. Stir in ginger
ale just before serving.

FRUIT MEDLEY PUNCH

Della Robbia Ice Ring, optional*
2 (10-ounce) packages frozen
  strawberries in syrup, thawed
3 cups apricot nectar, chilled
3 cups cold water
1 cup REALEMON® Reconstituted
  Lemon Juice
1 (6-ounce) can frozen unsweetened
  orange juice concentrate, thawed
1 cup sugar
1 (32-ounce) bottle ginger ale,
  chilled

Prepare ice ring in advance. In
blender container, blend
strawberries well (about 30
seconds). In large punch bowl,
combine strawberries, apricot
nectar, water, REALEMON® juice
concentrate and sugar; stir until
sugar dissolves. Slowly pour in
ginger ale; add Della Robbia Ice
Ring if desired.
           Makes about 3½ quarts

*DELLA ROBBIA ICE RING

2½ cups ginger ale, chilled
½ cup REALEMON® Reconstituted
  Lemon Juice
Any of the following:
  Canned apricot halves, drained
  Seedless white grapes
  Strips of orange peel, curled
  Whole strawberries
  Mint leaves
  Maraschino cherries, drained

In 1-quart measure or container,
combine ginger ale and

REALEMON® Pour ½ the mixture
into 1-quart ring mold; arrange
fruits, peel and mint leaves in
mold. Freeze. Pour remaining liquid
over fruit in mold. Freeze.

WELCOME PUNCH

2 cans (46 oz. each) DOLE®
  Pineapple Pink Grapefruit Juice
  Drink, chilled
1 can (46 oz.) DOLE® Pineapple
  Juice, chilled
1 can (46 oz.) apricot nectar,
  chilled
1 bottle (28 oz.) club soda, chilled
Ice cubes
Fresh mint sprigs

In a large punch bowl, mix together
pineapple pink grapefruit juice
drink, pineapple juice, apricot
nectar and club soda. Add ice
cubes. Garnish with mint sprigs.
        Makes 1½ generous gallons

FROTHY ORANGE-PINEAPPLE PUNCH

48 ounces pineapple juice, chilled
1 quart pineapple or orange
  sherbet
4 12-ounce cans WELCH'S®
  Sparkling Orange Soda, chilled
Mint

Pour pineapple juice into chilled
punch bowl. Add half of sherbet
and mix until frothy. Pour in soda.
Float remaining sherbet in punch.
Garnish each serving with sprigs of
mint, if desired.
          Makes 24 ½-cup servings

Morton Salt
NATURE'S COCKTAIL

1½ teaspoons MORTON NATURE'S
  SEASONS® Seasoning Blend
1 jar or can (1½ quarts) tomato
  juice
1 large carrot, peeled and cut
  into 8 sticks
4 celery ribs with leaves, cut in
  half lengthwise
1 lime, cut in 8 wedges

Day Before Serving:
Add seasoning blend to tomato
juice; mix or shake well.
Refrigerate until serving time.

Just Before Serving:
Pour chilled cocktail into eight
6-ounce glasses. Place a celery
and a carrot stick in each glass;
anchor a lime wedge on the edge.
                 Makes 8 servings

If desired, use larger glasses filled
with ice and serve immediately.

BREAKFAST-IN-A-GLASS

1 medium DOLE® Banana
1 large egg
⅓ cup water
1½ tablespoons frozen orange
  juice concentrate
1 teaspoon wheat germ
1 teaspoon honey
Dash salt

Slice banana into blender jar. Add
all remaining ingredients and blend
at high speed 1 minute.
                 Makes 1⅓ cups

PERFECT ESPRESSO—EASILY

The New Idea: make espresso at
home in any coffeemaker which
makes good regular coffee!
For the Coffee: Use only
MEDAGLIA D'ORO® Espresso
Coffee. After opening, keep it
sealed in the refrigerator. The
water should be drawn from the
cold water tap for best flavor. If the
coffeemaker calls for boiling water,
make sure it's really boiling. The
coffeemaker should be cleaned
daily following manufacturer's
directions. Never brew at less than
minimum capacity.
Proportions: a "coffee measure"
holds 2 measuring tablespoons of
coffee. For a rich brew, use 2
coffee measures to every ¾ cup (6
oz.) water—enough for 2 demitasse
cups. For a lighter brew, use 1
coffee measure to make 2
demitasse cups. Serve with sugar
and a twist of lemon peel, if
desired.

ESPRESSO IN A 30-CUP ELECTRIC PERCOLATOR

Fill the percolator to the 30-cup
line with cold water. Fill the basket
with 3 measuring cups ground
MEDAGLIA D'ORO® Espresso
Coffee (that's a bit less than a
12-oz. can). Perk as usual.
            Makes 60 demitasse cups

FIRESIDE BUTTERED "RUM"

1 cup butter or margarine, softened
½ cup confectioners' sugar
½ cup packed brown sugar
1 teaspoon DURKEE Ground Cinnamon
1 teaspoon DURKEE Ground Nutmeg
1 pint vanilla ice cream, softened
1 bottle (1 fl. oz.) DURKEE Imitation Rum Flavor
Boiling water

Cream together butter or margarine, confectioners' sugar, brown sugar, and spices. Beat in softened ice cream and rum flavor until smooth. Pour into a 4-cup freezer container and freeze (mixture will not freeze solid). To serve, place ¼ cup mixture in each mug. Add ½ cup boiling water to each mug. Stir well. Garnish with cinnamon stick and a sprinkling of nutmeg, if desired.
Makes 12-14 eight ounce servings

HOT MULLED CIDER

1 quart apple cider
½ cup SUE BEE® Honey
6 lemon slices
12 whole cloves
⅛ teaspoon nutmeg
6 cinnamon sticks

Combine all ingredients except cinnamon sticks in pan. Simmer 8-10 minutes. Pour into six mugs, removing lemon slices if desired. Add cinnamon stick to each mug for stirring.

HOT SPICED CIDER

2 qts. TREE TOP Cider
2 Tbsp. brown sugar
1 tsp. whole allspice
1 tsp. whole cloves
¼ tsp. salt
Dash of ground nutmeg

Combine cider and spice ingredients. Bring to slow boil, cover, simmer 20 minutes. Remove from heat and pour through strainer. Add cinnamon stick to each mug. *Makes 8 servings*

NO-FUSS SPICED CIDER, NATURALLY

Heat 2 quarts of cider to boiling. Remove from heat. Add 12 CELESTIAL SEASONINGS® CINNAMON ROSE™ Tea Bags. Steep for 10 minutes. Remove tea bags. Stir in ½ cup honey, if desired. Mix hot flavored cider with 2 quarts plain cider. Serve warm.
1 gallon recipe

Alcoholic

SUNSHINE SPRITZERS

Over ice in a tall glass pour equal parts of ALMADÉN Mountain Rhine Wine or Sauterne, or Mountain Nectar Vin Rosé, and chilled club soda. Stir gently. If you wish, add a fruit garnish such as a lemon, orange or lime slice, a strawberry or maraschino cherry, a stick of fresh pineapple, a tiny cluster of grapes or a slice of peach.

WINE SPRITZER

1 small bottle CANADA DRY® Club Soda (chilled)
⅓ cup white wine (chilled)

Serve in a 10 ounce glass with ice, if desired, and garnish with twist of lemon.

KIR NAPOLEON

1 oz. MANDARINE NAPOLEON
2 oz. dry white wine, chilled
Club soda, chilled
Orange slice

Pour MANDARINE NAPOLEON and wine over ice, in an 8-oz. wine glass. Stir quickly. Add a light splash of club soda and orange slice. Stir once.

KIR

For each drink fill a 7 or 8-ounce wine glass about two-thirds full with well chilled ALMADÉN Mountain White Chablis. Stir in 2 to 3 teaspoons Creme de Cassis liqueur. *Makes 1 drink*

BLONDIE

Stir in ice 8 oz. DUBONNET Blonde, juice of 1 large orange, juice of 1 lime, 4 oz. pineapple juice. Serve in tall glasses.
Serves 2

SOUTH OF THE BERRY

Shake together:
1 cup GIBSON Currant Wine
1 oz. orange curaçao
¼ cup orange juice
1 oz. Tequila Gold (or Dark Rum)

Pour over ice; garnish with squeeze of lime. (If you prefer, with Tequila, salt the rim!) *Serves 2*

SUNSHINE SANGRIA

2 oranges
1 lemon
¼ cup sugar
1 bottle THE CHRISTIAN BROTHERS® Chateau La Salle Light Wine
1 small bottle (7 oz.) club soda

Cut 1 orange into thin slices; reserve. Squeeze remaining orange and lemon into pitcher. Add sugar and wine; mix well. Stir in club soda, sliced fruit and ice. *Serves 4*

SASSY SANGRIA

1 gallon (4 liters) dry red wine, chilled
½ cup sugar
1 can (46 oz.) DOLE® Pineapple Juice, chilled
1 can (8 oz.) DOLE® Chunk Pineapple in Juice
1 orange, thinly sliced
1 lime, thinly sliced
Ice cubes

In a large punch bowl, mix together wine and sugar. Stir in pineapple juice and undrained pineapple chunks. Float orange and lime slices on top for garnish. Add ice cubes, if desired.
Makes about 1½ gallons

BLONDE SANGRIA

Place ⅓ to ½ cup sugar in punch bowl or large pitcher. Cut 2 or 3 thin slices from the centers of each of 2 lemons and 2 oranges; set slices aside. Squeeze juice and pulp from end pieces of fruit into bowl and mix well to dissolve sugar. Add 1 half-gallon ALMADÉN Mountain Rhine Wine (or Chablis). Add ice and 1 pint club soda. (Do not stir after adding soda.) Garnish with slices of fruit.
Serves 6 to 8 (about 20 4-ounce servings)

CHAMPAGNE CUP

1 ounce Triple Sec
2 ounces brandy
4 teaspoons superfine sugar
6 ounces CANADA DRY® Club Soda
1 pint champagne, chilled

Fill a large glass pitcher with ice cubes and add first 4 ingredients. Add champagne. Stir well and decorate with as many fruits as available. Garnish with rind of cucumber inserted on each side of pitcher. Top with small bunch of mint sprigs. Serve as soon as possible in punch glasses.
Serves 3 to 4

CLASSIC CHAMPAGNE COCKTAIL

½ tsp. sugar
Dash of bitters
Twist of lemon peel
THE CHRISTIAN BROTHERS® Champagne, chilled

Place sugar in bottom of stemmed glass; add bitters and lemon twist. Fill with champagne and stir lightly.

TWO FINGERS® MIMOSA

2 ounces TWO FINGERS® Tequila
4 ounces champagne
4 ounces orange juice

Fill a glass with cracked ice, and add the tequila, bubbling cold champagne and orange juice. Serve with an orange wedge on the side or an orange twist in the glass. *Makes 2 drinks*

THE ROARING '20'S BLOODY MARY

1 quart tomato juice
¼ teaspoon TABASCO® Sauce
4 teaspoons lime juice
3 teaspoons LEA & PERRINS Worcestershire Sauce
1 teaspoon salt
Vodka

Combine all ingredients, except vodka, in pitcher; stir well. Pour over ice in glasses. Garnish with lime or celery stalk. Use 1 to 1½ ounces vodka per serving.
Yield: 6-8

Or, you may use TABASCO® Bloody Mary Mix.

MINT JULEP

3 oz. ANCIENT AGE Bourbon
Mint sprigs
Sugar to taste

Trim stems from fresh sprigs of mint. Muddle with 1 teaspoon each sugar and water, in a tall glass or mug. Pack glass with chipped ice. Stir. Add ANCIENT AGE, stir briskly. Add more sugar and ice, if required.

PERFECT MANHATTAN

2 oz. OLD CHARTER Bourbon
¼ oz. STOCK Dry Vermouth
¼ oz. STOCK Sweet Vermouth
2 dashes bitters

Stir briskly with ice in an Old Fashioned glass. Add twist of lemon peel.

FRESH PINEAPPLE DAIQUIRI

½ large DOLE® Fresh Pineapple
1 can (6 oz.) DOLE® Pineapple Juice
½ cup light rum
½ can (6 oz.) frozen limeade concentrate
1 cup crushed ice

Remove pineapple from shell; core and cut fruit into chunks. Freeze until firm. Mix half of pineapple chunks, pineapple juice, rum and limeade in blender. Whir at high speed until blended. Add remaining pineapple and ice. Blend until frothy. *Makes 1 quart*

CHAMBORD DAIQUIRI

¾ oz. CHAMBORD
¾ oz. light rum
Juice of ½ lime
1 teaspoon powdered sugar

Add 1 cup crushed ice and put in a blender for 30 to 60 seconds; strain into a champagne glass.

BANANA DAIQUIRI

1 lime slice
1 medium DOLE® Banana
6 tablespoons lime juice
¼ cup crème de banana
2 tablespoons bar or powdered sugar
9 ounces light rum
3 cups finely crushed ice
Banana slices, mint sprigs for decoration

Rub rim of serving glasses with lime; chill. Measure all ingredients into blender jar. Cover and blend at high speed a few seconds until smooth and snowy. Pour or strain into chilled glasses. Decorate each with a banana slice and mint sprig.
Makes 3 to 4 servings

BITTER SCOT

2 oz. DEWAR'S Scotch
Bitter lemon

Pour DEWAR'S over ice in a tall glass. Add bitter lemon and stir quickly. Garnish with lemon slice.

MARGARITA

Moisten the rim of a cocktail glass with lemon or lime peel. Gently coat the entire rim with salt. Stir with ice one jigger of OLÉ Tequila, ½ oz. STOCK Triple Sec, and the juice of ½ lemon or lime. Strain and serve.

CHAMBORD
ROYAL MARGARITA

1 oz. CHAMBORD
1 oz. tequila
½ oz. fresh lime juice

Shake with ice and strain into a cocktail glass that has been rimmed with salt.

ALEXANDER

Shake well with cracked ice: one ounce DUBOUCHETT Creme de Cacao Dark, one ounce CORONET VSQ Brandy and one ounce heavy cream. Strain into cocktail glass.

BRANDY ALEXANDER

Use one oz. of STOCK Creme de Cacao, one oz. STOCK Brandy and one oz. sweet cream. Shake well with cracked ice, strain and serve.

FINLANDIA® MARTINI

Pour several drops of dry vermouth into a cocktail glass, swirl, empty out vermouth. Add lemon twist. Fill with ice cold FINLANDIA® Vodka from the freezer.

STINGER

One jigger DUBOUCHETT White Creme de Menthe, one jigger CORONET VSQ Brandy. Shake vigorously with cracked ice. Strain into chilled cocktail glass. Or pour over cubes in old-fashioned glass.

GREEN MINT FRAPPÉ

Into cocktail glass filled with crushed ice, pour two ounces of DUBOUCHETT Creme de Menthe. Add teaspoon lime juice and sip through short straw.

WHISKEY SOUR

2 oz. SCHENLEY RESERVE
1 scant ounce lemon juice
½ teaspoon sugar, or to taste

Shake all ingredients vigorously with cracked ice. Strain into Sour glass or large cocktail glass. Garnish with cherry and orange slice.

TENNESSEE MULE

3 oz. GEO. DICKEL Sour Mash
½ oz. lemon juice
Ginger beer, chilled

Stir GEO. DICKEL Sour Mash and juice with ice in a large glass or mug. Add ginger beer. Stir quickly. A dash of DUBOUCHETT Peach Cordial is a nice addition.

CRUZAN® GIMLET

2 oz. CRUZAN® White Rum
1 tablespoon sweetened lime juice
Lime or lemon slice

Shake CRUZAN® and lime juice briskly with ice. Strain into cocktail glass. Garnish with fruit slice.

OLD FASHIONED

2 oz. I.W. HARPER Bourbon
Small sugar cube
2-3 dashes bitters
Fruit garnish

Muddle sugar, bitters and a light splash of water in an Old Fashioned glass to dissolve sugar. Add ice cubes and I.W. HARPER. Stir to chill; garnish with cherry, orange or fresh fruit in season.

BLACK RUSSIAN

½ TIA MARIA®
½ vodka

Serve over ice and stir gently in a glass of your choice (6 oz.)

WHITE RUSSIAN

⅓ TIA MARIA®
⅓ vodka
⅓ milk

Shake with ice and pour into frosted glass, if desired.

THE GIMLET

Stir together: one part ROSE'S® Lime Juice, 4 or 5 parts vodka. Serve straight up or on the rocks.

Or you can use gin, light rum, or tequila.

Schweppes®

LIME RICKEY

1½ oz. gin
¾ oz. ROSE'S® Lime Juice

Fill tall glass with ice; add ingredients; top off with SCHWEPPES® Club Soda.

JOHN COLLINS

2 oz. blended whiskey

Fill Collins glass with ice; add whiskey; top off with SCHWEPPES® Collins Mixer; add slices of orange and lemon; serve with straws.

SLOE GIN COLLINS

2 oz. sloe gin

Fill Collins glass with ice; add sloe gin; top off with SCHWEPPES® Collins Mixer; add slices of lemon, orange and a cherry; serve with a straw.

CRANBERRY SHRUB

1 oz. gin
1 oz. cranberry juice

Fill 8 oz. glass with ice; add ingredients; top off with SCHWEPPES® Tonic Water.

CANTERBURY COOLER

1 oz. ROSE'S® Lime Juice
1 oz. light rum
1 oz. dry gin

Fill 12 oz. chimney glass with ice; add ingredients; top off with SCHWEPPES® Tonic Water; add twist of lime peel and 2 straws.

BRISTOL BRACER

1½ Tbsp. unsweetened grapefruit concentrate (undiluted)
2 oz. vodka

Fill tall glass with ice; add ingredients; top off with SCHWEPPES® Tonic Water; add cherry.

TONIC WATER CLASSICS

1½ oz. of either gin, vodka, rum or tequila

Squeeze wedge of lime into tall glass filled with ice; add liquor; top off with SCHWEPPES® Tonic Water.

PINK VELVET

1 oz. HIRAM WALKER Chocolate
   Cherry
½ oz. HIRAM WALKER Creme de
   Cassis
3 ounces vanilla ice cream

Combine in blender until smooth.
Pour into champagne glass.
Garnish with chocolate shavings.

PINK SQUIRREL

1 oz. HIRAM WALKER Creme de
   Cacao (White)
1 oz. HIRAM WALKER Creme de
   Noyaux
4 oz. strawberry ice cream

Mix in blender until smooth. Pour
into on-the-rocks glass. Float a
fresh strawberry on top.

ROMAN CANDLE

1 oz. SAMBUCA di GALLIANO™
½ oz. AMARETTO di GALLIANO™
½ oz. grenadine
1 oz. orange juice

Shake and pour into highball glass
with ice. Add club soda to taste.

GENEROUS OLD
FASHIONED

½ teaspoon superfine sugar
1 teaspoon water
2-3 dashes Angostura bitters
1½ oz. JOHNNIE WALKER Red
Orange slice
Cherry
Unpeeled apple wedge

Muddle sugar with water and
bitters in an old fashioned glass,
until sugar dissolves. Add ice and
JOHNNIE WALKER Red. Stir to
chill. Garnish with fruit.

ROB ROY

1½ oz. JOHNNIE WALKER Red
½ oz. sweet vermouth
Dash of Angostura bitters
Maraschino cherry
   or lemon slice

Stir JOHNNIE WALKER Red, sweet
vermouth and bitters with ice.
Strain into chilled cocktail glass or

over fresh ice in an old fashioned
glass. Garnish with cherry or
lemon slice.

Dry Rob Roy: Simply substitute dry
vermouth for half or all of the
sweet vermouth.

FROSTY PIÑA COLADA

1 fresh DOLE® Coconut
1 cup milk, scalded
1 cup crushed ice
¼ cup pineapple juice
3 ounces light rum
2 tablespoons powdered sugar

Puncture eyes of coconut. Drain
liquid and reserve. Place coconut
in a 350°F. oven 20 minutes. Hit
warm coconut with a hammer to
remove shells. Remove any
remaining shell with a blunt knife.
Cut unpared coconut into chunks.
In a blender jar, whir coconut
chunks, warmed milk and coconut
liquid until just blended. Drain
coconut milk and cool. Combine
coconut milk, crushed ice,
pineapple juice, light rum and
powdered sugar in blender jar and
whir 1 to 2 minutes until smooth.
Makes 3 cups

STRAWBERRY FROST

¾ cup strawberry preserves or
   fresh strawberries crushed
¼ cup instant non-fat dry milk
4 ice cubes, crushed
1 jigger vodka
¼ teaspoon vanilla
2 cups CANADA DRY® Club
   Soda

Mix strawberries in blender with
dry milk, ice cubes, vodka, and
vanilla. Whirl about 30 seconds at
medium speed. Pour in CANADA
DRY® Club Soda just before
serving. Stir to blend. Garnish with
fresh whole strawberry.
Makes 4 servings

STAR SPANGLED BERRY

Frappé together in blender:
¾ cup GIBSON Loganberry Wine
⅓ cup orange juice
⅓ cup half & half
1 cup cracked ice
4 teaspoons sugar
1 egg
Juice of ½ lemon

Serve immediately.   *Serves 2*

ALEXANDER THE GREAT

Blend in blender until creamy 1 oz.
WILD TURKEY Liqueur, 1 oz.
brandy, 3 oz. vanilla ice cream.
Pour into wine goblets and garnish
with chocolate sprinkles if desired.

FROSTY FRIAR

1½ oz. FRANGELICO® Liqueur
¾ oz. white rum
Scoop strawberry ice cream
½ cup finely crushed ice
Whole strawberry

Chill blender container. Pour in
FRANGELICO® Liqueur, rum, ice
cream and ice. Blend until just
smooth. Pour into a chilled glass.
Garnish with strawberries.

ASPEN® SKI LIFT

Combine 1 jigger of ASPEN®
Liqueur, 1 jigger of creme de
banana, and 2 scoops pineapple
sherbet with crushed ice in a
shaker or blender.

VIA VENETO

1 oz. LEMONIER™ Liqueur
2 oz. CAMPARI® (or other beverage
   bitters)
4 oz. grapefruit juice (fresh or
   frozen)

Pour LEMONIER™ Liqueur and
CAMPARI® over ice in goblet.
Stir. Squeeze in a lemon wedge,
add rind. Add grapefruit juice. Stir
and serve.

LEMONIER™ CAESAR

1½ oz. LEMONIER™ Liqueur
½ oz. brandy
¼ oz. anisette

Pack a small Old Fashioned glass
with finely crushed ice. Twist an
orange peel, and poke under ice.
Combine LEMONIER™ Liqueur,
brandy and anisette. Pour into
glass. Let chill for a moment.

THE MERRY MARCO

1 oz. FRANGELICO® Liqueur
1 oz. white rum
Strip of orange peel

Pack a small Old Fashioned glass with finely crushed ice. Twist orange peel over, and sink peel in ice. Combine FRANGELICO® Liqueur and rum well; pour into prepared glass.

Note: This works equally well with GRANT'S Scotch.

FRANGELICO® FIZZ

2 Jiggers FRANGELICO® Liqueur
½ Jigger KAHLUA®
Juice of ¼ lime
Club Soda

In a cocktail shaker half filled with cracked ice, pour FRANGELICO® KAHLUA® and lime juice. Shake and strain into a highball glass filled with ice. Add club soda and garnish with a slice of lime.

Yield: 1 serving

FARLEY'S LEMON QUENCHER

Frappé together in blender:
1 cup FARLEY'S Hard Cider
¼ cup vodka
2 tablespoons ROSE'S® Lime Juice
3 tablespoons frozen lemonade concentrate
1 cup small ice cubes

Pour frothy liquid over ice cubes in large glass. Garnish with sprig of mint. *Serves 1*

ROSY LEMONADE PUNCH

1 bottle MATEUS Rosé, chilled
1 pint lemonade, chilled
1 tablespoon grenadine
1 lemon, sliced

Pour MATEUS Rosé, lemonade, and grenadine over ice in a bowl, and stir. Float lemon slices on. Serve in cups or glasses. Decorate each portion with a cherry if you like. *10-12 servings*

BARDOLINO PUNCH

1⅔ cups cranberry juice
½ cup sugar
¼ teaspoon ground cloves
¼ teaspoon ground cinnamon
1 bottle (fifth) BERTOLLI® Bardolino Wine, chilled
1 bottle (32 ounces) sparkling water, chilled
1 tablespoon lemon juice
Ice cubes
1 lemon, sliced

Heat cranberry juice, sugar, cloves and cinnamon to boiling in saucepan; boil 5 minutes. Cool; refrigerate. Mix cranberry syrup, wine, water and lemon juice in punch bowl; add ice. Garnish with lemon slices.

Makes 18 servings (¼ cup each)

SANGRIA PUNCH

2 cups red wine
½ cup water
2 scoops COUNTRY TIME® Lemonade Flavor Drink Mix
4 lemon slices
4 lime slices
4 orange slices
1 bottle (12 fl. oz.) ginger ale, chilled

Combine wine, water and drink mix in a pitcher; stir until drink mix is dissolved. Add fruit and chill well. Just before serving, add ginger ale. Serve over ice, if desired.

Makes 4 cups or 8 servings

BUBBLY BIRTHDAY PUNCH

Mix 1 can (6 oz.) pink lemonade concentrate, thawed, and ¼ to ⅓ cup sugar in a punch bowl or large pitcher, stirring to dissolve sugar. Pour in 1 half-gallon chilled ALMADÉN Grenache Rosé. Add ice, then 1 quart chilled club soda. Decorate with 1 lemon, thinly sliced, and maraschino cherries.

Serves 8 to 10 (about 25 4-ounce servings)

BRIDE'S BOWL

Peel, core, slice and wedge 1 whole pineapple. In a large container combine pineapple, ¼ cup maple syrup, 1 cup lemon juice, 2 cups unsweetened

pineapple juice and 1½ fifths dark rum. Chill for 2 hours. Pour mixture over ice in a bowl. Add 2 large bottles chilled CANADA DRY® Club Soda and 1 quart sliced strawberries. Stir gently.

Serves 20 people twice

TROPICAL WINE PUNCH

1½ cups COCO CASA™ Cream of Coconut
2 bottles (4/5 quart each) white wine, chilled
4 cups pineapple juice, chilled
1 cup orange liqueur
Orange slices
Strawberries

In a bowl, mix cream of coconut and wine. Stir in pineapple juice and orange liqueur. Serve well chilled in a punch bowl, garnished with orange slices and hulled halved strawberries.

Serves 12 to 14

EGG NOG FRANGELICO®

8 egg yolks
1¼ cups granulated sugar
8 egg whites
¼ tsp. salt
1½ pts. heavy cream
8 oz. FRANGELICO® Liqueur
3½ oz. semi-sweet chocolate

Combine egg yolks and ½ cup of the sugar in mixing bowl. Beat the mixture until light and the color of lemon. The mixture will thicken. In a second mixing bowl, combine egg whites and salt and whip to a soft peak. (Egg whites whip best at room temp.) When a soft peak is reached, slowly add the remaining sugar—¾ cup—a Tbsp. at a time. In a third mixing bowl, whip heavy cream to a soft peak. Add FRANGELICO® to whipped egg yolk and sugar mixture. Blend well. Fold in whipped cream. When cream is incorporated, fold in stiff egg whites. Pour into glass punch bowl* and top with grated semisweet chocolate.

Yield: 12-15 servings

*Do not serve in silver.

COMFORT® EGGNOG

Serving for 1
1 part SOUTHERN COMFORT®
4 parts Dairy Eggnog

Pre-chill ingredients. Pour SOUTHERN COMFORT® into a short glass, and add eggnog. Stir with spoon to blend. Dust with nutmeg.

Serving for 10
1 cup (8 oz.) SOUTHERN COMFORT®
1 qt. Dairy Eggnog

Pre-chill ingredients. Blend together in punch bowl by beating, dust with nutmeg.

COCONUT HOLIDAY EGGNOG

6 eggs
1½ cups COCO CASA™ Cream of Coconut
1 quart milk
2 cups (1 pint) heavy cream
1 Tbsp. vanilla
1 cup dark rum
Ground nutmeg or coconut flakes

In a large bowl, beat eggs until fluffy. Beat in cream of coconut. Gradually beat in milk and cream. Stir in vanilla and rum. Chill for several hours. Serve in punch cups. Sprinkle each serving with nutmeg or coconut flakes. For a thicker eggnog, beat heavy cream until stiff and fold into egg mixture.
Serves 10 to 12

DEWAR'S BOWL

1¾ litre bottle DEWAR'S Scotch
1 can (6 oz.) frozen orange juice concentrate
1 can (6 oz.) frozen lemonade concentrate
2 pints club soda, chilled

Mix half-thawed juices with DEWAR'S in a large bowl. Stir in club soda and serve immediately. Decorate bowl with thinly sliced lemon or orange, if you wish.

HOT CHOCOLATE WITH RUM
(Low Calorie/Low Cholesterol)

For each cup of Hot Chocolate (made with skim milk and sugar substitute) add 1 tsp. of BUTTER BUDS.® Spike this rich mixture with rum (add to taste) and then spear it with a fresh stick of cinnamon.

Calories: 100; Cholesterol: 7 mg.

GLÖGG

3 bottles THE CHRISTIAN BROTHERS® Burgundy
1 cup raisins
½ cup THE CHRISTIAN BROTHERS® Sweet Vermouth
6 whole cardamom pods, crushed slightly
5 whole cloves
2 sticks cinnamon
Peel from 1 orange
1 cup sugar
1 cup whole blanched almonds

In saucepan, mix 1 bottle wine, raisins and vermouth. Place cardamom, cloves, and cinnamon in cheesecloth bag; add to wine. Simmer, covered, 15 minutes; remove spices. Stir in remaining wine, orange peel and sugar; bring to boil, stirring to dissolve sugar. Add almonds. Serve hot with spoons to scoop up raisins and almonds.
12 8 oz. servings

TOBOGGANER'S TODDY

3 cups boiling water
8 LIPTON® FLO-THRU® Tea Bags
3 cups apple juice
¼ cup brown sugar
8 whole cloves
1 cinnamon stick, broken
½ cup burgundy wine

In large saucepan, pour boiling water over LIPTON® FLO-THRU® Tea Bags; cover and brew 5 minutes. Remove tea bags. Stir in apple juice, sugar, cloves and cinnamon stick. Simmer 10 minutes; remove spices. Add wine and heat through.
Makes about 10 servings

JAMAICAN COFFEE

1 oz. TIA MARIA®
1 oz. rum

Fill with hot coffee topped with whipped cream.

For an added touch of elegance, prior to mixing, moisten the coffee cup rim with lemon juice and then dip rim in sugar.

CAFE OLÉ

6 tsp. chocolate syrup
6 oz. heavy cream
1 tsp. cinnamon
¼ tsp. nutmeg
1½ Tbsp. granulated sugar
2 cups strong, hot coffee
8 oz. FRANGELICO® Liqueur
4 cinnamon sticks

Place 1½ tsp. chocolate syrup in each coffee cup. Combine ½ tsp. cinnamon, nutmeg and sugar. Mix with heavy cream and whip to stiff peak. Stir remaining ground cinnamon into hot coffee. Pour hot coffee into coffee cups and add 2 oz. FRANGELICO® per serving. Stir to blend well. Top each with spiced whipped cream. Serve each with a cinnamon stick.
Yield: 4 servings

CAFE CHAMBORD

¾ oz. CHAMBORD

Pour into a cup of hot coffee; stir. Top with whipped cream.

VIENNESE COFFEE

1 jigger California brandy
1 cup hot coffee
Sugar (optional)
Whipped cream
Semi-sweet chocolate shavings

Add brandy to coffee. Sweeten to taste. Top with a float of whipped cream and sprinkle with chocolate shavings. *Serves 1*

California Brandy Advisory Board favorite recipe

RED WINE WARM-UP

In a large kettle combine 1 quart water, 1⅔ cups sugar, 1 lemon, thinly sliced, 1 cinnamon stick, 1 tablespoon whole cloves, 1 tablespoon whole cardamom and 1 cup raisins. Bring to boiling, stirring to dissolve sugar, simmer for 10 minutes, then cool to room temperature. Mix in 1 half-gallon ALMADÉN Mountain Red Burgundy and 1 fifth ALMADÉN Brandy. Heat until the mixture just simmers. Keep punch warm while serving.
Serves 10 to 12 (about 20 6-ounce servings)

Acknowledgements

The Editors of CONSUMER GUIDE® wish to thank the companies and organizations listed for use of their recipes and artwork. For further information contact the following:

Adams Peanut Butter, see International Multifoods

Adolph's, see Chesebrough-Pond's

Alaska Crab Institute, see Pacific Kitchen

Allsweet® Margarine, see Swift & Co.

Almadén Vineyards
Sub. National Distillers &
Chemical Corp.
P.O. Box 5010
San Jose, CA 95150

Amaretto di Galliano™, see "21" Brands

American Beauty Macaroni Co., see Pillsbury

American Egg Board
1460 Renaissance
Park Ridge, IL 60068

American Home Foods
Div. American Home Products Corp.
685 Third Ave.
New York, NY 10017

American Lamb Council
200 Clayton St.
Denver, CO 80206

American Soybean Association
P.O. Box 27300
St. Louis, MO 63141

Ancient Age, see Schenley Affiliated Brands

Argo®/Kingsford's®, see Best Foods

Armour and Co.
111 W. Clarendon
Phoenix, AZ 85077

Arnold Sorensin, Inc.
401 Hackensack Ave.
Hackensack, NJ 07601

Arrow Choclair, see Heublein/Spirits Group

Aspen® Liqueur
Spar, Inc.
P.O. Box 52831
New Orleans, LA 70152

Atalanta Corp.
17 Varick St.
New York, NY 10013

Aunt Jemima®, see Quaker Oats

Austin, Nichols & Co., Inc.
1290 Ave. of the Americas
New York, NY 10019

B&M® Baked Beans, see Underwood, Wm.

Baker's® Chocolate, see General Foods

Baltimore Spice Co., The
P.O. Box 5858
Baltimore, MD 21208

Banquet Foods Corp.
100 N. Broadway
St. Louis, MO 63102

Bays English Muffin Corp.
500 N. Michigan Ave.
Chicago, IL 60611

Beatrice Foods Co.
1526 S. State St.
Chicago, IL 60605

Bell, William G., Co., The
Div. Brady Enterprises, Inc.
P.O. Box 99
East Weymouth, MA 02189

Bertolli USA
P.O. Box 931
So. San Francisco, CA 94080

Best Foods
A Unit of CPC North America
Englewood Cliffs, NJ 07632

Birds Eye®, see General Foods

Bison Foods Co.
196 Scott St.
Buffalo, NY 14204

Blue Bonnet®, see Standard Brands

Blue Diamond®
California Almond Growers
Exchange
P.O. Box 1768
Sacramento, CA 95808

Blue Ribbon®
Continental Nut Co.
P.O. Box 400
Chico, CA 95927

Bob Evans Farms®
P.O. Box 07863 Station G
Columbus, OH 43207

Booth Fisheries Corp.
2 N. Riverside Plaza
Chicago, IL 60606

Borden Inc.
180 E. Broad St.
Columbus, OH 43215

Brer Rabbit Molasses, see Del Monte

Breyers® Yogurt, see Kraft, Inc.
Dairy Group

Bronte Champagne & Wines Co., Inc.
930 W. Eight Mile Rd.
Detroit, MI 48220

Brownberry®
Div. of Peavey Co.
P.O. Box 388
Oconomowoc, WI 53066

Bud of California®, see Castle & Cooke

Buddig, Carl, & Co.
11914 S. Peoria St.
Chicago, IL 60643

Bumble Bee®, see Castle & Cooke

Butter Buds®, see Cumberland Packing

Butterball® Turkey, see Swift & Co.

Calavo Growers of California
Box 3486 Terminal Annex
Los Angeles, CA 90051

California Apricot Advisory Board
1280 Boulevard Way
Walnut Creek, CA 94595

California Avocado Commission
4533-B MacArthur Blvd.
Newport Beach, CA 92660

California Brandy Advisory Board
426 Pacific Ave.
San Francisco, CA 94133

California Iceberg Lettuce
Commission
P.O. Box 3354
Monterey, CA 93940

California Raisin Advisory Board
P.O. Box 5335
Fresno, CA 93755

California Strawberry Advisory
Board
P.O. Box 269
Watsonville, CA 95076

California Table Grape Commission, see Pacific Kitchen

Calumet® Baking Powder, see General Foods

Campbell Soup Co.
Campbell Place
Camden, NJ 08101

Canada Dry Corp.
A Norton Simon Inc. Co.
100 Park Ave.
New York, NY 10017

Carmel Kosher Food Products
Div. of Douglas Food Corp.
4840 S. Kedzie Ave.
Chicago, IL 60632

Carnation
5045 Wilshire Blvd.
Los Angeles, CA 90036

Castle & Cooke Foods
P.O. Box 3928
San Francisco, CA 94119

Catalina French Dressing, see Kraft, Inc.

Celestial Seasonings, Inc.
1780 55th St.
Boulder, CO 80301

Ceresota/Hecker's, see Standard Milling

Chambord, see Jacquin, Charles

Cheez-It®, see Sunshine Biscuits

Cheez-Ola®, see Fisher Cheese

Chef Boy-Ar-Dee®, see American Home Foods

Chef's Delight®, see Fisher Cheese

Chesebrough-Pond's Inc.
Trumbull Industrial Park
Trumbull, CT 06611

Chex® Cereals, see Ralston Purina

Chiquita Brands, Inc.
1271 Ave. of the Americas
New York, NY 10020

The Christian Brothers®
Fromm and Sichel, Inc.
655 Beach St.
San Francisco, CA 94109

Claussen, see Oscar Mayer

Coca-Cola Co., The
Foods Division
P.O. Box 2079
Houston, TX 77001

Coco Casa™, see Holland House Brands

Coco Wheats
Little Crow Foods
Warsaw, IN 46580

Colonial Club Liqueurs
Paramount Distillers Inc.
3116 Berea Rd.
Cleveland, OH 44111

Colonial Sugars, Inc.
P.O. Box 1646
Mobile, AL 36633

Continental Strawberry Glaze, see Globe Products

Cookin' Good® Chicken
Showell Farms, Inc.
P.O. Box 58
Showell, MD 21862

Corn Diggers Snack, see Nabisco

Coronet V.S.Q. Brandy, see Schenley Affiliated Brands

Country Pride Foods Ltd.
P.O. Box 1997
El Dorado, AR 71730

Country Time®, see General Foods

Cracker Barrel, see Kraft, Inc.

Cracker Jack Div.
Borden Inc.
4800 W. 66th
Chicago, IL 60638

Cream of Wheat®, see Nabisco

Creamette Co., The
428 N. First St.
Minneapolis, MN 55401

Cruse Beaujolais, see Garneau, Jos.

Cruzan® Rum, see Schenley Affiliated Brands

Cumberland Packing Corp.
2 Cumberland St.
Brooklyn, NY 11205

Curtiss Royal Miniature
Marshmallows, see Standard Brands

Dannon Co., Inc., The
22-11 38th Ave.
Long Island City, NY 11101

Darigold
Consolidated Dairy Products Co.
Box C 19099
Seattle, WA 98109

Del Monte Corp.
P.O. Box 3575
San Francisco, CA 94119

Delft Blue-Provimi, Inc.
Provimi Rd.
Watertown, WI 53094

Denmark Cheese Association
4415 W. Harrison St.
Hillside, IL 60162

Dewar's, see Schenley Affiliated Brands

Diamond® Walnuts, see Sun-Diamond

Dole®, see Castle & Cooke

Domino® Sugars
Amstar Corp.
American Sugar Div.
1251 Ave. of the Americas
New York, NY 10020

Doritos®, see Frito-Lay

Dorman, N., & Co.
125 Michael Dr.
Syosset, NY 11791

Drambuie®, see Taylor, W.A.

Dream Whip®, see General Foods

Dromedary, see Nabisco

Dubonnet, see Schenley Affiliated Brands

DuBouchett, see Schenley Affiliated Brands

Durkee Foods-Div. of SCM Corp.
16651 Sprague Rd.
Strongsville, OH 44136

E-Z-Bake Flour
Acme-Evans Co.
Div. of General Grain Inc.
902 W. Washington Ave.
Indianapolis, IN 46204

Eagle® Brand, see Borden Inc.

Eckrich, Peter, & Sons, Inc.
P.O. Box 388
Ft. Wayne, IN 46801

Elam's®
2625 Gardner Rd.
Broadview, IL 60153

Enrico's Spaghetti Sauce
Ventre Packing Co., Inc.
373 Spencer
Syracuse, NY 13204

Farley's Hard Cider, see Gibson Wine

Featherweight®
Chicago Dietetic Supply, Inc.
P.O. Box 40
La Grange, IL 60525

Figaro Co., The
P.O. Box 10875
Dallas, TX 75207

Finlandia Swiss Cheese, see Atalanta

Finlandia® Vodka
Buckingham Corp.
620 5th Ave.
New York, NY 10020

Fisher Cheese Co.
P.O. Box 409
Wapakoneta, OH 45895

Fisher Nut Co.
Sub. of Beatrice Foods Co.
P.O. Box 43434
St. Paul, MN 55164

Fleischmann's,® see Standard
Brands

Florida Lime Administrative
Committee
18710 S.W. 288 St.
Homestead, FL 33030

Franco-American, see Campbell
Soup

Frangelico® Liqueur, see Grant,
William

French, R.T., Co., The
P.O. Box 23450
Rochester, NY 14692

Friendly Ice Cream Corp.
1855 Boston Rd.
Wilbraham, MA 01095

Frito-Lay, Inc.
P.O. Box 35034
Dallas, TX 75235

G. Washington's,® see American
Home Foods

Gallo Salame
250 Brannan St.
San Francisco, CA 94107

Garneau, Jos., Co., Inc., The
Div. of Brown-Forman Distillers
Corp.
P.O. Box 1080
Louisville, KY 40201

Gatorade,® see Stokely-Van Camp

Gebhardt Mexican Foods
Div. of Beatrice Foods Co.
P.O. Box 7130, Station A
San Antonio, TX 78285

General Foods Corp.
250 North St.
White Plains, NY 10625

Geo. Dickel, see Schenley Affiliated
Brands

Gerber Products Co.
445 State St.
Fremont, MI 49412

Gibson Wine Co.
P.O. Drawer E
Elk Grove, CA 95624

Globe Products Co., Inc.
P.O. Box 1927
Clifton, NJ 07015

Golden Grain
1111-139th Ave.
San Leandro, CA 94578

Good Seasons,® see General Foods

Grandma's® Molasses
Duffy-Mott Co., Inc.
370 Lexington Ave.
New York, NY 10017

Grant, William, & Sons, Inc.
130 Fieldcrest Ave.
Edison, NJ 08817

Green Giant,® see Pillsbury

Gulden's® Mustard, see American
Home Foods

Heartland® Cereals, see Pet

Heath, L.S., & Sons, Inc.
Box 679
Robinson, IL 62454

Heinz U.S.A.
P.O. Box 57
Pittsburgh, PA 15230

Hellmann's,® see Best Foods

Herb-Ox®
The Pure Food Co.
P.O. Box N
Mamaroneck, NY 10543

Hereford's Amaretto Cows,
see Heublein/Spirits Group

Hershey Foods Corp.
19 E. Chocolate Ave.
Hershey, PA 17033

Heublein/Spirits Group
330 New Park Ave.
Hartford, CT 06101

Hi Ho® Crackers, see Sunshine
Biscuits

High Sea, see Robinson Canning

Hillshire Farm®
Div. Kahn's and Co.
Route 4, Box 227
New London, WI 54961

Hiram Walker, Inc.
P.O. Box 14100
Detroit, MI 48232

Holland House Brands Co.
A Div. of National Distillers
P.O. Box 336
Ridgefield, NJ 07657

Homemade Soup Starter™, see
Swift & Co.

Honey Maid Graham Crackers,
see Nabisco

Hungry Jack,® see Pillsbury

Hunt-Wesson Kitchens
1645 W. Valencia Dr.
Fullerton, CA 92634

Hydrox® Cookies, see Sunshine
Biscuits

I.W. Harper, see Schenley Affiliated
Brands

Ideal Macaroni Co.
26001 Richmond Rd.
Bedford Heights, OH 44146

Idaho-Washington Dry Pea &
Lentil Comms., see Pacific
Kitchen

Imperial Sugar Co.
P.O. Box 9
Sugar Land, TX 77478

International Multifoods
1200 Multifoods Bldg.
Eighth & Marquette
Minneapolis, MN 55402

International Sausage Council
400 W. Madison Ave.
Chicago, IL 60606

Irish Mist,® see Heublein/Spirits
Group

Iroquois Grocery Products, Inc.
111 High Ridge Rd.
Stamford, CT 06905

Jacquin, Charles, et Cie, Inc.
2633 Trenton Ave.
Philadelphia, PA 19125

James River Smithfield,
see Smithfield Ham & Products

Jays Foods, Inc.
825 E. 99th St.
Chicago, IL 60628

Jell-O® Brand, see General Foods

Jennie-O Foods, Inc.
P.O. Box 778
Willmar, MN 56201

Jenos®
525 Lake Ave., S.
Duluth, MN 55802

Jiffy® Pie Crust Mix, see Borden Inc.

Jiffy Pop,® see American Home
Foods

Jimmy Dean® Companies
1341 W. Mockingbird Ln.
Suite 1100 E
Dallas, TX 75247

John Morrell & Co.
208 S. LaSalle St.
Chicago, IL 60604

Johnnie Walker Red, see Somerset
Importers

Jolly Time® Pop Corn
American Pop Corn Co.
Box 178
Sioux City, IA 51102

Karo® Corn Syrup, see Best Foods

Keebler Co.
One Hollow Tree Ln.
Elmhurst, IL 60126

Kellogg Co.
Battle Creek, MI 49016

Kikkoman International Inc.
P.O. Box 784
San Francisco, CA 94111

King Arthur Flour
Sands, Taylor & Wood Co.
155 N. Beacon St.
Brighton, MA 02135

King Oscar Fine Foods
Div. of Chr. Bjelland & Co., Inc.
89 Millburn Ave.
Millburn, NJ 07041

Kitchens of Sara Lee
A Consolidated Foods Co.
500 Waukegan Rd.
Deerfield, IL 60015

Knotts Berry Farm™
8039 Beach Blvd.
Buena Park, CA 90620

Knox® Gelatine, see Lipton,
Thomas J.

Kool-Aid,® see General Foods

Kraft, Inc.
Kraft Court
Glenview, IL 60025

Kraft, Inc. Dairy Group
P.O. Box 7830
Philadelphia, PA 19101

Krakus/Atalanta/Polka Polish Ham,
see Atalanta

Kretschmer Wheat Germ, see
International Multifoods

La Choy® Food Products Div.
Beatrice Foods Co.
Stryker St.
Archbold, OH 43502

Land O'Lakes, Inc.
P.O. Box 116
Minneapolis, MN 55440

Lawry's Foods, Inc.
568 San Fernando Rd.
Los Angeles, CA 90065

Le Sueur® Peas, see Pillsbury

Lea & Perrins, Inc.
Pollitt Dr.
Fair Lawn, NJ 07410

Leafy Greens Council
2 N. Riverside Plaza
Chicago, IL 60606

Lemonier™ Liqueur, see Grant,
William

Lender's Bagel Bakery Inc.
Post Rd.
West Haven, CT 06516

Libby, McNeill & Libby, Inc.
200 S. Michigan Ave.
Chicago, IL 60604

Liberty Diced Fruit & Peel, see
Beatrice Foods

Li'l Butterball™ Turkey, see
Swift & Co.

Lindsay International Inc.
5327 W. Hillsdale Dr.
Visalia, CA 93277

Lipton, Thomas J., Inc.
800 Sylvan Ave.
Englewood Cliffs, NJ 07632

Liquore Galliano,® see "21" Brands

Log Cabin,® see General Foods

Louis Rich, Inc.
P.O. Box 288
Liberty, IA 52776

Louis Sherry Ice Cream Co., Inc.
40 Franklin Ave.
Brooklyn, NY 11205

Louisiana Brand, see Robinson
Canning

Lucky Leaf® Products
Knouse Foods Cooperative Inc.
Peach Glen, PA 17306

M&M/MARS
High St.
Hackettstown, NJ 07840

Maine Dept. of Marine Resources
Augusta, ME 04333

Maine Sardine Council, The
P.O. Box 337
Brewer, ME 04412

Malt-O-Meal Co.
1520 TCF Towers
Minneapolis, MN 55402

Maltex,® see Standard Milling

Mandarine Napoleon, see Somerset
Importers

Marshmallow Fluff
Durkee-Mower, Inc.
2 Empire St.
Lynn, MA 01903

Martell Cognac, see Garneau, Jos.

Maryland Club® Coffee, see
Coca-Cola

Mateus, see Schenley Affiliated
Brands

Maxwell House,® see General Foods

Maypo,® see Standard Milling

Mazola®/Nucoa,® see Best Foods

McCormick & Co., Inc.
Grocery Products Div.
414 Light St.
Baltimore, MD 21202

Meadow Gold Butter, see Beatrice
Foods

Medaglia D'Oro® Espresso Coffee
S.A. Schonbrunn & Co., Inc.
Sub. American Maize-Products Co.
21 Grand Ave.
Palisades Park, NJ 07650

Michigan Apple Committee
2726 E. Michigan Ave.
Lansing, MI 48912

Milky Way® Bars, see M&M/MARS

Milnot Co.
P.O. Box 190
Litchfield, IL 62056

Minute Maid,® see Coca-Cola

Minute® Rice/Tapioca, see General
Foods

Miracle Whip, see Kraft, Inc.

Morton Salt
Div. of MortonNorwich
110 N. Wacker Dr.
Chicago, IL 60606

Mr. and Mrs. "T"® Products
Div. of Taylor Food Products, Inc.
P.O. Box 1280
Long Beach, CA 90801

Mrs. Paul's® Kitchens, Inc.
5830 Henry Ave.
Philadelphia, PA 19128

Mueller, C.F., Co.
180 Baldwin Ave.
Jersey City, NJ 07306

Musselman's,® see Pet

Nabisco
East Hanover, NJ 07936

Nalley's Fine Foods Div.
Curtice-Burns Inc.
3303 S. 35th
Tacoma, WA 98411

National Capon Council
National Duckling Council
2 N. Riverside Plaza
Chicago, IL 60606

National Live Stock & Meat Board
444 N. Michigan Ave.
Chicago, IL 60611

National Marine Fisheries Services
NOAA
Washington, DC 20235

National Pecan Marketing Council
1800 Peachtree Rd., N.W., Suite 516
Atlanta, GA 30309

National Red Cherry Institute
678 Front St., N.W., Suite 140
Grand Rapids, MI 49504

Nestlé Co., Inc., The
100 Bloomingdale Rd.
White Plains, NY 10605

New Bedford Seafood Council, Inc.
60 N. Water St.
New Bedford, MA 02740

Recipe Title Index

For ease of use, the Index is divided into two sections. The Recipe Title Index provides quick page reference when the title of a specific recipe is known. The General Index (beginning on page 356) is arranged according to names of products and types of foods, with applicable recipes listed under each entry.

General Index

For ease of use, the Index is divided into two sections. The General Index is arranged according to names of products and types of foods, with applicable recipes listed under each entry. The Recipe Title Index (beginning on page 344) provides quick page reference when the title of a specific recipe is known.

(Recipe Title Index begins on page 344.)